Applied Human Behavior in the Social Environment

Brad W. Lundahl
University of Utah

Grafton H. Hull, Jr.
University of Utah

PEARSON

Boston Columbus Indianapolis New York San Francisco Upper Saddle River
Amsterdam Cape Town Dubai London Madrid Milan Munich Paris Montréal Toronto
Delhi Mexico City São Paulo Sydney Hong Kong Seoul Singapore Taipei Tokyo

Editor in Chief: Ashley Dodge
Editorial Assistant: Amandria Guadalupe
Managing Editor: Denise Forlow
Program Manager: Carly Czech
Project Manager: Doug Bell, PreMediaGlobal
Executive Marketing Manager: Kelly May
Marketing Coordinator: Jessica Warren
Senior Operations Supervisor: Mary Fischer
Operations Specialist: Eileen Collaro
Senior Art Director: Jayne Conte

Cover Designer: Karen Noferi
Interior Designer: Joyce Weston Design
Cover Art: dpaint
Digital Media Director: Brian Hyland
Digital Media Project Manager: Tina Gagliostro
Full-Service Project Management: Murugesh Rajkumar Namasivayam, PreMediaGlobal
Printer/Binder: RR Donnelley BAR/Harrisonburg
Cover Printer: RR Donnelley BAR/Harrisonburg

Credits and acknowledgments borrowed from other sources and reproduced, with permission, in this textbook appear on appropriate page within text.

Many of the designations by manufacturers and seller to distinguish their products are claimed as trademarks. Where those designations appear in this book, and the publisher was aware of a trademark claim, the designations have been printed in initial caps or all caps.

Library of Congress Cataloging-in-Publication Data

Lundahl, Brad W.
  Applied human behavior in the social environment / Brad W. Lundahl, University of Utah, Grafton H. Hull, Jr., University of Utah.—1 Edition.
     pages cm
  Includes bibliographical references and index.
  1. Human behavior.   2. Social psychology.   I. Hull, Grafton H.   II. Title.
  HM1033.L86 2013
  302—dc23
                                                                                    2013038172

ISBN-10:   0-205-70636-3
ISBN-13: 978-0-205-70636-5

Contents

PART TWO: HUMAN BEHAVIOR IN THE SOCIAL ENVIRONMENT

Preface

To Susan, Emma, Sara, and Laura
— Brad Lundahl

To Jannah
— Grafton H. Hull, Jr.

Understanding is the foundation to progress. Understanding allows engineers to build bridges that span miles. Understanding allows physicians to heal broken bones. And, understanding the human condition helps social workers enhance human well-being. The human condition is complex and multifaceted, and some aspects of humanity are beyond understanding. Despite these limitations, much is known about the human condition and such knowledge promotes our ability to improve the lives of individuals, families, and groups as well as the functioning of larger systems. This text attempts to provide a foundation of understanding that will help you help others. It provides theories and attending research on the many influences on human well-being and human suffering. True to our social work roots, this text examines micro-level influences such as biological, social, and psychological influences as well as macro-level influences such as culture and policy. Given that most graduating social workers will launch into careers where you are expected to help individuals, families, or groups, we have attempted to write this book with application in mind.

We organized this text into three major sections:

1. **Methods for Understanding the Human Condition**—how scientists and others produce knowledge about the human condition
2. **Human Behavior in the Social Environment (HBSE)**—including biological, psychological, and social influences on human behavior
3. **Theories of Intervention for HBSE**—covering theories of interventions commonly used in direct practice at the micro level

Together, the material within the three sections should equip students with an appreciation for how knowledge about the human condition is produced, a broad understanding of human functioning, and strategies for helping individuals, families, and groups who need such help.

Features

There are many features of this text to enhance your experience; however, they are only as useful as you make them. By engaging with this text and its resources, you'll learn about human behavior through:

- **An applied focus**—bridging knowledge about influences on human behavior and decision-making in varied social work practice settings
- **A topical approach**—providing a focus on issues while noting the influence of developmental considerations, allowing for easy identification of information

- **A multidimensional framework**—providing an in-depth examination of biological, psychological, social, cultural, and systemic influences
- **Well-test theories and current evidence**—including helpful diagrams, figures, graphs, and tables to promote students ability to grasp concepts
- **Current topics**—including immigration, trauma and abuse, and discrimination, school violence, sexual orientation, poverty, and health care
- **Multimedia resources**—including videos, case examples, and narratives

Learning Outcomes

Students will be able to achieve a variety of learning outcomes by using this text and its resources, including:

- **Critical thinking skills.** Students can develop their critical thinking skills by reviewing the competency boxes (indicated by the CSWE's core competencies series icon) and engaging with the multimedia resources highlighted in blue boxes throughout the chapter.
- **Oral communication skills.** Students can develop their oral communication skills by engaging with others in and out of class to discuss their comprehension of the chapter based on the chapter's learning objectives.
- **Assessment and writing skills.** Students can develop their assessment and writing skills in preparation for future licensing exams by completing topic-based and chapter review assessments for each chapter.
- **CSWE's core competencies.** Students can develop their comprehension and application of CSWE's core competencies and practice behaviors by discussing the competency box critical thinking questions.

Acknowledgments

We gratefully acknowledge the efforts and support of many who have contributed directly or indirectly to this text. We acknowledge the support of Dr. Jannah Mather, Dean of the University of Utah's College of Social Work, who provided emotional and instrumental support for this project. Several research assistants contributed meaningfully to this project, including Brian Droubay, Kwangyeop Lee, Doug Crews, and Tian Tian. We also thank Dr. Rosemarie Hunter, Director of University Neighborhood Partners, for her assistance with examples for the chapter on immigration. We are grateful to Patricia Quinlin who provided encouragement and helped us formulate the initial vision and structure of the book and to Ashley Dodge who succeeded Patricia. At Pearson, we thank Carly Czech who organized many efforts to obtain feedback on our book and patiently clarified next steps. Similarly, we are deeply indebted to Doug Bell for his patience, keen eye, and support—even while sick or on vacation. Crystal Parenteau, Barbara Smith, and Audra Gorgiev also assisted at various stages of the book's development. We are appreciative of the colleagues who reviewed drafts of the manuscript and provided cogent suggestions for improvement. We are also indebted to the many students and working social workers who have helped us learn what is important and how to present such information. Most importantly, we acknowledge our family members who patiently allowed us time to work on this book and cheered us on through discouraging moments.

Brad Lundahl and Grafton H. Hull, Jr.

This text is available in a variety of formats—digital and print. To learn more about our programs, pricing options, and customization, visit www.pearsonhighered.com.

This listing of Theories of Interventions readings are integrated throughout the Pearson eText and are offered in printed format through Pearson Custom Library. For more information, please contact your local Pearson representative. http://www.pearsonhighered.com/replocator

THEORIES OF INTERVENTION

Systemic Theory

Multicultural Feminist and Gender-Sensitive Theories

This listing of Theories of Interventions readings are integrated throughout the Pearson eText and are offered in printed format through Pearson Custom Library. For more information, please contact your local Pearson representative. http://www.pearsonhighered.com/replocator

1

Social Work and Human Behavior

Social workers seek to understand how best to enhance the emotional, psychological, physical, and social well-being of all people—especially vulnerable people. The first sentence of the National Association of Social Workers (NASW) Code of Ethics reads,

> The primary mission of the social work profession is to enhance human well-being and help meet the basic human needs of all people, with particular attention to the needs and empowerment of people who are vulnerable, oppressed, and living in poverty.

How can social workers enhance human well-being and meet the basic needs of all people, especially vulnerable populations? To answer this question, we must ask many other questions such as What is human well-being? Does a specific tool exist for measuring and assessing human well-being? Does a common definition exist for the term *basic human needs*? And, what is the meaning of vulnerable, oppressed, and poverty? Also, how can social work accomplish this lofty mission of empowering people and enhancing well-being? These questions reflect a need to define terms and consider the available methods to accomplish the profession's goals.

The statement, "enhance human well-being," implies human well-being is not always maximized—that is, people struggle. Scan the news on any given day and you will certainly view stories illustrating human pain and suffering. Social work is interested in identifying aspects of human functioning that need to be changed and working to improve the human condition.

Solving a problem generally requires a rudimentary understanding of the problem. If you want to fill a flat tire, it's good to know whether the tire went flat because it has a hole or someone let the air out. Filling air into a ruptured tire, without repairing the hole, will not result in a permanent solution.

1

We humans are always looking to solve problems.

But, knowing how to solve a problem is not enough. Before putting effort and resources into an activity, it's good to know *why* we should expend energy. Questions of *what* problems exist, *how* to solve them, and *why* they should be solved are important in social work. The second and third sentences of the NASW Code of Ethics provide answers to the *how* and *why* questions. They read,

A historic and defining feature of social work is the profession's focus on individual well-being in a social context and the well-being of society. Fundamental to social work is attention to the environmental forces that create, contribute to, and address problems in living.

Historically, social work exists to enhance the well-being of individuals and society. Have you known people who struggled with a mental illness such as depression, post-traumatic stress disorder (PTSD), anxiety, drug addiction, or marital problems? Can you name a person who has taken his or her life through either suicide or an addiction? Have you witnessed or experienced the devastating effects of poverty, illiteracy, or discrimination? Certainly you are aware of social injustices, such as slavery, discrimination, war, poverty, hunger, and other phenomena that undermine human well-being, that adversely affected millions of people. The suffering resulting from such maladies motivates social workers to improve the human condition and to identify the causes of maladies and the methods to prevent and alleviate suffering.

USING A MULTIDIMENSIONAL FRAME FOR UNDERSTANDING THE HUMAN CONDITION

Social contexts and environmental forces are implicated in the creation and maintenance of well-being or problems in living. Consider how a child's primary social network, the family, can influence the child's well-being across his or her life span. Have you ever heard a strong, tough-looking athlete say, with tears in his eyes, something like, "My mother is my hero. I owe everything good in my life to her." This athlete is attributing success to his early social environment. Social influences can be positive and, unfortunately, negative. Physical abuse perpetrated by parents early in a child's life can have a strong negative impact on the child (Arata, Langhinrichsen-Rohling, Bowers, & O'Farrill-Swails, 2005; Griffin & Amodeo, 2010; Stith et al., 2009; Thompson, Kingree, & Desai, 2004). Prior to entering kindergarten, a severely abused child may inhibit exploring her environment out of fear, have difficulty concentrating on lessons because of worry about future abuse, and develop poor self-esteem. During elementary school, physical abuse may lead a child to isolate from friends out of insecurity; she may not perform well in school because threats of abuse command more attention than the joys of learning to read. Memories of abuse may interfere with learning, undermine trust in the social fabric, and contribute to painful mental health symptoms. In middle school and high school, a child who has suffered abuse may feel insecure in pursuing her interests, experience social difficulties because of expectations surrounding intimacy, and possibly begin to experiment with risky behaviors such as drug use or sexual promiscuity. The effects of child physical or sexual abuse can haunt young and middle-aged adults through nagging insecurity and self-doubt, difficulties in trusting others, or fear of conflict. While most parents who were abused as children do not abuse their own children, the risk is high as we shall see later. Research reveals that parents who were neglected as children are 260% more likely to neglect their children and 200% more likely to physically abuse their children compared to parents who did not recall being neglected as children. Similarly, parents who recall being physically abused as children are 500% more likely to abuse their children compared to parents who do not report being abused as children (Kim, 2009). These numbers are staggering. Consider the following statistics gathered by the U.S. Department of Health and Human Services (2012): During 2011, an estimated 3.4 million referrals, including well roughly 6.2 million children, were made to Child Protective Services (CPS) agencies. The national rate was 27.4 referrals per 1,000 children, which is, fortunately, lower than the rate of 35.9 referrals per 1,000 children in 2003.

Using some of these statistics, let's do some basic calculations to show the importance of the social environment. If the national rate of referrals for child abuse is about 43 per 1,000, what would be the rate for a parent who was physically abused as a child? Kim (2009) suggests that the rate would be about 500% higher, so it would be about 215 per 1,000. This translates into about a 20% likelihood of perpetuating abuse. The good news: 20% is not 100%, so not all victims of abuse perpetuate the cycle. The bad news: 20% is far higher than the 4% for the national average. (Note that these rudimentary calculations did not control for statistical assumptions.)

Social work recognizes that problems in living arise from many sources—all of which interact with each other. So, the profession endorses a multidimensional perspective toward understanding the human condition. That is, the human condition and human behavior are so complex that they require us to look through multiple lenses. Such a commonly used multidimensional perspective is called a *biopsychosocial framework*, which we'll look at within the context of schizophrenia—a mental health disorder targeted by many social workers.

Biological Influences

The *bio* stands for biological influences, which include genetics, the nervous system, physical health, neurological functioning, and disease. Schizophrenia can be understood from at least two biological perspectives. First, evidence reveals a genetic link. Review Figure 1.1 that lists the risk of developing schizophrenia based on genetic factors: just over 10% for fraternal twins of the same sex, nearly 60% for identical twins, and only about 1% for the general population. Clearly, genetics matter.

Second, the brain structure of individuals with schizophrenia tends to be different than those without the condition (see Figure 1.2); specifically, those with schizophrenia have larger ventricles and likely have more of a neurotransmitter called *dopamine* than their counterparts (Copolov & Crook, 2000; Meltzer, Tong, & Luchins, 1984).

Understanding that biological factors influence schizophrenia is important and could relieve, or could have relieved, the guilt levels of many parents. Past explanations of schizophrenia squarely blamed families, particularly mothers. The term *schizophrenogenic mother* was used to describe the mother who "caused" schizophrenia by placing her child in a series of "damned if you do and damned if you don't" situations known as *double binds*. An example of a double bind is of a parent who buys her child two shirts; when he wears one shirt, the mothers says, "Why didn't you wear the other shirt I gave you. Don't you love me?" The son cannot win—a situation that was believed to instill "craziness" into the child. Equipped with the knowledge that schizophrenia is strongly influenced by genetic factors could have saved many mothers the guilt that they somehow failed their child.

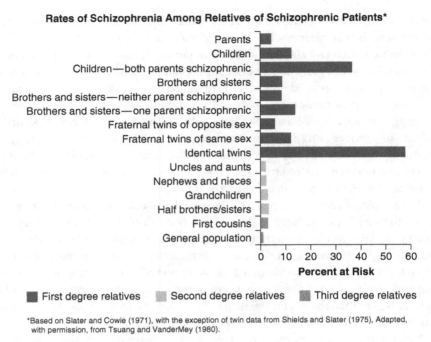

Figure 1.1
Evidence of Biological Influences on Human Functioning
Source: Retrieved from http://www.schizophrenia.com/research/hereditygen.htm on June 10, 2013.

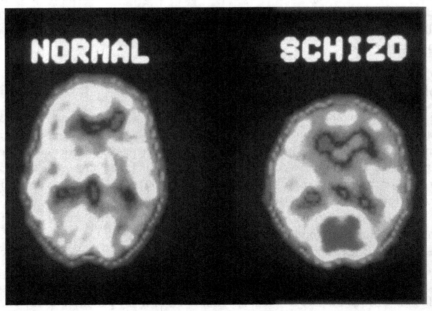

Figure 1.2
Difference in Brain Structure of an Individual With and Without Schizophrenia
Source: Retrieved from http://www.schizophrenia.com/research/hereditygen.htm on June 10, 2013.

Psychological Influences

Psychological factors also strongly influence human functioning. Again, we turn to schizophrenia to illustrate the role of psychological factors. Psychological influences include states of mind, intelligence, emotionality, and, among others, how humans process information. In schizophrenia, stress is critically important as research has shown that higher levels of stress predict higher expression of symptoms. Social workers often teach stress management skills to help individuals manage the symptoms of schizophrenia. Similarly, compliance with medications targeting schizophrenia symptoms can improve outcomes. An individual's willingness or ability to adhere to medication recommendations is partly a function of memory, motivation, organizing skills, and other psychological processes. For example, higher levels of intelligence and executive functioning skills are related to increased treatment adherence (Maeda et al., 2006).

An example of schizophrenia reveals that human functioning cannot simply be explained by a singular focus on biological or social or psychological factors. Rather, the complex interactions among the factors need to be considered. Other important factors influencing the human condition include spiritual, cultural, age, geographic location, political environment, gender, sexual orientation, political party, privilege, education, and socioeconomics.

Social and Other Influences

Before we blame schizophrenia totally on biological and psychological factors, you should know that social factors also contribute. Families, it turns out, do matter. Among individuals with similar genetic predispositions for schizophrenia, those who grow up in families with high levels of expressed conflict are more likely to develop schizophrenia than those in families without high levels of conflict. The hospitalization relapse rate for individuals who return to families with high levels of expressed emotion, conflict, criticism, or hostility is roughly 200% higher than for individuals who return to families with low levels of expressed emotion (Kymalainen & Weisman de Mamani, 2008). Examples of expressed emotion are yelling, loud arguing, and high levels of conflict to trigger relapses into active schizophrenia symptoms.

Social work textbooks often reinforce the multidimensional influences on human functioning. Why is this? Isn't it intuitive? You might think, "Sure back in the day, funny scientists attributed cause to a single factor … but nowadays we know better!" Has science evolved enough to clearly reveal the multiple contributions to the human condition? Of course it would be nice if society, scientists, or even social workers were sufficiently evolved to always consider multidimensional perspectives to understanding human behavior. Sadly, we have not yet arrived.

A best-selling book in 1994, *The Bell Curve* by Herrnstein and Murray, was criticized for promoting racism by suggesting intellectual functioning (or IQ) was largely determined by racial factors. That is, the authors argued that genes—based on race— are responsible for IQ. They also claimed that because minorities tend to perform less well on IQ-type performance tests, it stands to reason that their genetics are somehow "less" than the dominant culture. Who were these "crackpot" authors who suggested such a thing? One was the late Harvard psychologist Richard J. Herrnstein; the other was Charles Murray who was a political scientist at the American Enterprise Institute. True, Herrnstein and Murray did note that both genetics and environmental factors contribute to IQ scores, but the popular media had a heyday emphasizing that genetics are responsible for IQ, and therefore, if certain groups tend to score lower, they must have inferior genes. This message was pushed throughout much of the popular media despite volumes of research showing that IQ tests have a cultural bias that artificially depresses scores for minorities (Reynolds, 2000). That is, the tests work against minority groups because they use phrases and language that is common to the majority group. Further, research by Claude Steele (1997) has clearly shown that certain groups are likely to score lower on standardized tests because of anxiety, not the lack of ability, through a mechanism called *stereotyped threat*, which is explained in the following "Did You Know?" box.

Did You Know?

Stereotyped Threat

Who Is More Intelligent?

Who are more intelligent, Blacks or Whites? Who are better at math, males or females? These questions are frequently asked and many people believe they have answers. Some research has suggested, for example, that Blacks do less well on tests than Whites. What can one conclude from this? Cecil Reynolds (2000) suggests that four explanations are often advanced to explain such differences:

a. Genetics
b. Environment (economic challenges, social stigma, educational deprivation)
c. Interaction between genetics and environment
d. Faulty testing: knowledge from minorities is not adequately assessed or tests use language/concepts that would be familiar in one cultural group but not another

Another scientist, Claude Steele (1997, 2012) designed experiments to test why differences are often found between African Americans and Whites on cognitive tests. In brief, here is what Steele did.

First, he identified African American and White students who performed equally on cognitive tests. Second, he would tell each group that they were going to take a test that was important for their academic careers: do well and they were likely to succeed; do poorly and their success would be in doubt.

Third, he would attempt to activate a stereotype in each group by saying to the African American students something like, "African Americans tend to do poorly on this test," and to the Whites something like, "Whites tend to do poorly on this test." In this example, the only group to really be faced with a stereotype would be African Americans because Whites would not naturally think, "I'm less capable than an African American on testing," because society has directly and indirectly broadcast this message for generations. (The same was true when Steele tested math ability across men and women.)

Fourth, Steele and his associates would administer a valid test that measured cognitive ability.

What were the results? As mentioned, prior to the stereotype threat, results on measures of cognitive ability were statistically equal. However, the performance of African Americans plummeted after the stereotyped threat was evoked. Why is this case? It appears that the stereotyped threat over-arouses people's anxiety system, which directly interferes with performance. Remember, the students were the same prior to the testing—thus, the stereotyped threat caused lower performance, not genetics or a genetic x environment interaction.

What are the implications of this research? Importantly, it is devastating for those who carry stereotype threats because their true abilities are artificially muted, and the consequences are real in terms of mental health, earning potential, and access to opportunities. Lower scores on such tests will close doors, and higher scores will open doors.

What can be done about this? Steele offers several suggestions. First, strengthen the relationship between students and teachers as a means of discrediting the stereotype. A strong relationship between a professional and a person for whom the stereotype should apply discredits or neutralizes the stereotype because the message is that the professional does not believe the stereotype and neither should the individual. Second, provide challenging material to students at risk of believing the stereotype threat. The symbolic meaning is, "you have the capacity; the stereotype does not apply." Third, emphasize that intelligence and ability are malleable, and work and effort can expand one's ability and performance. Individuals, not racial status, determine their outcomes. Fourth, highlight the impact of role models in their area of interest. Revealing the many "exceptions" to the stereotype should work to erode the power of the stereotype in a particular student's mind.

Diversity in Practice

Practice Behavior Example: Appreciate that, as a consequence of difference, a person's life experiences may include oppression, poverty, marginalization, and alienation as well as privilege, power, and acclaim.

Critical Thinking Question: Considering the research on stereotype threat, how might belonging to a minority or marginalized group influence key elements of the human experience such as personal identity and approach to life?

If you have read the news lately, you likely have heard there is a gene that causes drinking, depression, propensity to have an affair, criminality, risk taking, anxiety, or political party affiliation. Many of these reports suggest a single gene, or combination of genes, causes a specific behavior and neglect social, cultural, environmental, and psychological contributions to the behavior. Even though most texts will indicate that human behavior is a mix of nature and nurture, many scientists, public figures, reporters, and the public may come to believe that human behavior is mostly caused by only one force, such as genetics or the environment. However, the human condition is much, much more complex.

The notion that human behavior is "simple" to understand is danger-ous because if our understanding of a problem is simple, our solutions will tend to be simple. Given the complexity of the problems social workers are called upon to address—such as poverty and racism or mental illness and child abuse, we must remember and be open to the reality that the human condition is complex.

Assess your comprehension of Social Work and the Human Behavior by completing this quiz.

VALUE OF UNDERSTANDING THE HUMAN CONDITION

Understanding that humans are influenced by biological, psychological, social, and other forces provides great hope that positive changes can be made (see Figure 1.3). When an airplane crashes, teams of experts are dispensed to investigate what went wrong to guide how to improve flight safety. Similarly, if the causes and influences of problems in living and healthy living can be identified, social workers and other professionals can make recommendations on how to enhance human well-being.

Watch the video on Working Mothers. What are the multiple influences on work and mother-hood? From the video, what are some factors that will influence you as a social worker?

Knowledge about human behavior can guide decisions about how to improve human functioning. Throughout your career as a social worker, you will make thousands and thousands of decisions. For example, consider how many decisions need to be made in a first appointment for a rather "straightfor-ward" counseling session with Keon, a 21-year-old, African American male majoring in chemistry who requests help for depression. Imagine you are placed in the college's counseling center for an internship. The following are a few of the decisions that need to be made during the first counseling session:

1. Should you shake Keon's hand?
2. How do you address Keon? How should he address you?
3. How will you begin the session?
4. When do you discuss confidentiality?
5. How deeply do you explore Keon's family history?
6. How might you go about assessing Keon's concerns about feeling depressed?

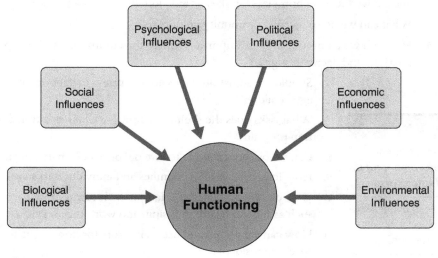

Figure 1.3
Influences on Human Behavior

7. Do you assess for major depression, bipolar disorder, dysthymia, or some combination or none of the above?

8. Do you investigate protective factors?

9. Do you investigate risk factors?

10. Do you assess substance use patterns?

11. Would you consider Keon's age and how that might influence depression?

12. How will your age and sex influence how you interact with Keon?

13. What might you do to strengthen the therapeutic alliance?

14. If you are (or are not) African American, how would you approach Keon?

15. Would you refer Keon to a physician for a medical examination?

16. Would you recommend he investigate receiving medications?

17. Is there a particular "brand" of counseling (e.g., behavioral therapy, cognitive therapy, interpersonal therapy) you would recommend?

18. How much self-disclosure would you use?

19. Are you aware of any stereotypes that you might hold about Black men? If so, how do these beliefs influence your decision-making?

20. During the interview, would you take a directive or collaborative role?

21. Would you look him in the eye?

22. Would you discuss how his race and cultural background may influence his current concern?

23. Would you begin with a formal assessment or "small talk"?

24. How would you explain counseling to Keon?

25. Would you take notes during your session?

These questions represent only a brief sample of the questions and decisions you face in working with clients. In a single job, some social workers act as clinician, executive director, grant writer, advocate, human relations specialist, and manager. Imagine the questions that Linda, a director of a small homeless shelter, would need to ask to fulfill her role:

1. How will I secure funding for the after-school children's program?

2. Should we adjust our admission policy to favor displaced workers?

3. Should we focus on homeless families or individuals?

4. What can we do to recruit community volunteers?

5. How can we communicate our important role to the community to build public relations and decrease stigma?

6. Should we adjust our rules about curfew to support school-aged children?

7. What risks does the shelter assume if we launch a transportation program?

8. Can we obtain resources to hire or "borrow" a part-time nurse?

9. How long can we allow families and individuals to stay?

10. How can we build better relations with community partners such as mental health, housing, and workforce service?

11. How can we obtain and use translators for non-English-speaking residents?

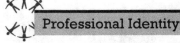

Professional Identity

Practice Behavior Example: Commit themselves to the profession's enhancement and to their own professional conduct and growth.

Critical Thinking Question: How can understanding the human condition promote social worker's ability to advance the profession's mission?

12. Should we have a policy on visitors—and, if so, how do we decide?

13. In reporting to our funders, what information should be included or excluded?

14. What type of training should our case managers receive?

15. How should I prioritize repair and maintenance projects?

Understanding Guides Decision-Making

Effective helping requires effective answers to these and many other questions, which have neither easy answers nor absolutely "correct" responses. Approaching such questions is a process made up of several "ingredients." Several models related to decision-making have been advanced. Some deal with how an individual processes information. For example, Milner (2000) and associates have examined the social information processing (decision-making) of parents, and Crick and Dodge (1994) have examined decisions made by adolescents. Other researchers have examined decision-making in contexts similar to those in which social workers are employed (Lutz et al., 2006; Seidenstücker & Roth, 1998).

A composite of these models is depicted in Figure 1.4. In this model, the first step is a need for social work intervention. Next, this need must be perceived or recognized. For example, if poverty, racism, or sexism are ignored or not seen, no possible change actions can take place. In direct clinical situations, the social worker needs to perceive a problem—such as depression or anxiety. Once a problem has been perceived and appears to be worthy of intervention, social workers can begin to conceptualize the problem. What factors promote the problem? What factors maintain the problem? What does research say about the nature of the problem? What interventions does research or experience suggest will be effective?

After conceptualizing the problem, social work as a profession is committed to trying to help solve the problem. The next step is to select a response. Choosing a course of action requires more complex thinking. What resources are available? Will the response have a good chance of success? What risks might arise from intervening? How does the intervention fit within the clients' value system? Is the intervention feasible?

At this point in the model, most of the work has been "mind-work." You have applied reason to a problem. With a response or intervention selected, it's time to act and then to evaluate the consequences of the action in relation to the original need or problem. Did the problem diminish? Did the problem grow? In either case, did additional positive or negative consequences arise? Notice that in this problem-solving model, there are a number of factors positioned at the center of the circle. These factors inform how we conceptualize, understand, consider interventions, and evaluate our decisions. Our fund of knowledge as individuals and professionals guides this process as do professional values, personal experiences and beliefs, ethical considerations, and, very importantly, the client's needs/wants.

Watch the video on Critical Thinking and consider how complexity influences decision-making in social work settings.

Human Behavior

Practice Behavior Example: Critique and apply knowledge to understand person and environment.

Critical Thinking Question: How can understanding the multiple influences on human functioning positively influence social workers' decision-making?

Assess your comprehension of Decision-Making in Social Work by completing this quiz.

Social workers seek to understand problems before applying interventions.

Andrew Hobbs/Thinkstock

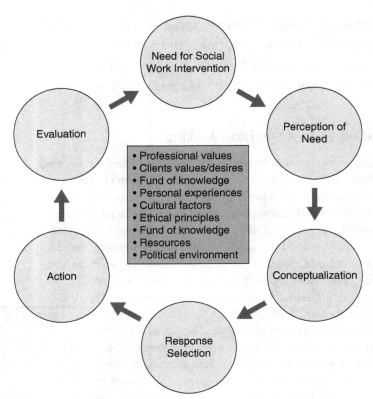

Figure 1.4
Information Processing Model Applied to Social Work

This textbook provides you with an overview of knowledge that often informs decision-making in social work settings and provides tools for evaluating the relevancy of such knowledge. No text can provide you with enough knowledge to make perfect decisions for your clients because their needs are nuanced, idiosyncratic, and highly individual. However, increased knowledge and a commitment to be a lifelong learner will help you better meet your clients' needs.

WHAT SOCIAL WORKERS DO: COMMON ACTIVITIES

Part of the reason no textbook can offer all the knowledge needed to make good decisions for every client is that social workers engage in a very wide range of activities. Each area and activity requires unique knowledge and skills. The NASW Code of Ethics sums up what social workers do:

> Social workers seek to enhance the capacity of people to address their own needs. Social workers also seek to promote the responsiveness of organizations, communities, and other social institutions to individuals' needs and social problems.

Based on these sentences, social work activities can be grouped into two broad categories: (1) direct activities with clients and (2) activities designed to benefit clients indirectly. Notice that a multipronged approach to enhance people's quality of life is advanced: work with individuals to strengthen their ability to meet their needs *and* work to change the context in which people live and operate. This two-pronged approach might seem familiar. When a child is sick, we might give her medicine and encourage her to sleep (i.e., efforts directed at the individual level) *and* ensure that environmental disturbances are minimized and that her resting conditions are comfortable (i.e., efforts at the environmental level). Similarly, in sporting events, such as a swim meet, coaches both provide specific training to athletes (e.g., how to kick to promote power) and ensure that the playing conditions are agreeable (e.g., swimming pool is clean and at the right temperature).

The NASW Code of Ethics provides more details about what social workers do, and the levels on which such activities occur:

> These activities may be in the form of direct practice, community organizing, supervision, consultation, administration, advocacy, social and political action, policy development and implementation, education, and research and evaluation.

If you are new to social work, some of these terms may be unfamiliar. If you are a social work veteran, you'll realize that it is not easy to precisely define each term. The activities (e.g., direct practice, community organizing) are verbs that describe actions. Following is a brief introduction to each of these activities; as you read them, consider the question, "How might an understanding of human behavior influence this activity?"

Note that many of these ideas came from *The Social Work Dictionary* by Robert Barker (1999). Let's take a look at each of them.

Ethical Practice

Practice Behavior Example: Know about the value base of the profession, its ethical standards, and relevant law.

Critical Thinking Question: How might understanding the profession's value base influence your approach to understanding influences on the human condition?

Key Social Work Activities

Direct practice

Many activities fall under the direct practice term, such as case management, counseling, child and adult protective services, therapy, triage, discharge planning, assessment, family counseling, parent training, casework, outreach, and child protective service work. What ties most of these activities together is that a specific social worker interacts directly with a specific client, generally in a face-to-face meeting. The broad goal of direct practice is to help individuals realize their goals and successfully adapt to their environment. How might an understanding of human functioning in the social environment influence direct practice efforts?

Community organizing

Community organization entails activities such as mobilizing groups of people, recruiting both material and intellectual resources, and promoting collaboration to address social problems. It differs from direct practice in that the goal is a broad response to a social problem rather than working with a specific individual or group. For examples of community organizing efforts, see reports from the U.S. Department of Housing and Urban Development's list of success stories at http://archives.hud.gov/offices/cpd/communitydevelopment/cdbg30/successstories.cfm (retrieved on July 10, 2012). How might an understanding of human functioning in the social environment influence community organizing efforts?

Advocacy

A central value of social work is to champion the rights of individuals and groups who are subjected to discrimination, suffering, or disenfranchised. Advocacy efforts include drawing public attention to issues, lobbying policy makers, launching grassroots campaigns, or supporting causes that promote empowerment and justice. Within an organizational body (e.g., a workplace), social workers may work to establish policies that will protect all employees. At the individual level, a social worker may advocate for a particular client by interfacing with community organizations or institutions. For example, a social worker may attend a court hearing and speak on behalf of the client or write a letter to a public housing commission to support a client's application for rent assistance. How might an understanding of human functioning in the social environment influence advocacy efforts?

Social policy

Social work realizes that laws and policies strongly influence the human condition. Some laws promote human well-being while others work against it. During the 20th century, some laws and policies that social workers believed needed to be changed included the right for all adults to vote, race relations, affirmative action, women's right to choose, parity in pay for women and minorities, and legalization of same-sex marriage. What are the policies of interest in the 21st century? There are many, and at the time of this writing, immigration, same-sex marriage, parity in coverage for mental health services from insurance companies, access to health care for all citizens, human rights, continued debates over parity for women and minorities, and so on. Changes in social policies can have sweeping effects. For example, a Harvard study (Wilper et al., 2009) suggests that as many as 44,000 U.S. deaths could be prevented annually if all citizens had health care. How might an understanding of human functioning in the social environment influence policy-making efforts?

Political action

How do social workers influence social policy? One method is through political action efforts such as organizing campaigns to support candidates or issues, serving as elected officials, mobilizing voters, lobbying, monitoring and reporting on the work of elected officials, and testifying on behalf of an issue. Political action work can also involve work as advisors to elected officials in which social workers draft policies, comment on policies, and make suggestions about why and how to frame certain policies.

Consultation

Social workers may engage in a variety of consulting activities. They frequently provide expert opinions to physicians, nurses, psychologists, educators, law enforcement, the court system, policy makers, corrections, business, and religious leaders. Consultations can occur in a number of settings, such as hospitals, mental health clinics, correction facilities, local and state social service divisions, public and private schools, government agencies, political action groups, administrative teams, private individuals and families, religious settings, and think tanks. How might an understanding of human functioning in the social environment influence consulting efforts?

Administration

Social workers frequently become administrators and leaders in social service organizations, such as philanthropic organizations, charities, mental health clinics, hospitals, and correctional facilities. Training in social work provides administrators with an understanding of the human condition and how to interact with individuals, families, and groups. Importantly, social workers who rise to positions of leadership within agencies can advance social work's values because they can exercise the leverage that comes with positions of leadership. How might an understanding of human functioning in the social environment influence administrative efforts?

Education

Social work is firmly integrated into many aspects of education. At the front end of education, social workers may work in preschools that service children facing risks, such as those in Head Start programs. From kindergarten to high school, social workers often provide counseling services to children with emotional and behavioral difficulties, and support teachers with ideas on how to best help students with special needs. Support activities may include one-on-one counseling, initiating and leading groups for special concerns/risks (e.g., bereavement, divorcing parents, tragedy), or implementing large-scale prevention programs (e.g., anti-bullying, drug education). Social workers are also found on many college campuses where they provide services toward helping students with mental health concerns, adjusting to school, making life transitions, and promoting environments that support all students.

Supervision

Social workers often supervise direct practice activities—an activity that is often regulated by state statute. A licensed master-level social worker, for example, can supervise bachelor-level social workers and social workers who are working toward licensure. The role of a supervisor is first and foremost to ensure that the services being delivered by supervisees are not harming clients. Other roles include helping future social workers develop the competencies to deliver high-quality, effective services. How might an understanding of human functioning in the social environment influence supervisory efforts?

Research and evaluation

A key value of social work is to provide services that actually help clients and society. The simple assumption that good intentions will lead to positive outcomes cannot be supported. Section 5.02 of NASW Code of Ethics states,

a. Social workers should monitor and evaluate policies, the implementation of programs, and practice interventions.

b. Social workers should promote and facilitate evaluation and research to contribute to the development of knowledge.

c. Social workers should critically examine and keep current with emerging knowledge relevant to social work and fully use evaluation and research evidence in their professional practice.

Monitoring and evaluating practice behaviors provides feedback about the effectiveness of interventions and allows others to judge the benefits of our services. A powerful way to be relevant and valued by society is to show that our efforts matter. If we can demonstrate that our efforts reduce problems or enhance the quality of life, society will demand that social work is supported.

What ties together these varied social work activities? We believe the verbs *empower* and *strengthen* capture the essence of social work activities. Social workers strive to empower individuals and strengthen the environment in which people live. Exactly *how* social workers go about empowering and strengthening is not the focus of this book. Rather, this book will provide foundations of knowledge about the human condition that will allow for informed, rational decision-making about enhancing people's well-being.

Assess your comprehension of What Social Workers Do by completing this quiz.

STRUCTURE OF THE TEXT

This text is written with applied social workers in mind, whether you work at a micro or macro level, so the information can guide practical decision-making whether you are advocating for a policy on housing or trying to help an older adult work through a depressive episode. Thus, this textbook favors presenting information that can be of use in everyday decision-making.

We have adopted a topical focus over a developmental focus for two reasons: (1) the developmental approach, which is often followed in developmental psychology courses, places what seems to be an inordinate amount of emphasis on the biological unfolding of human experiences; and (2) a topical approach seems to better fit the needs of social workers because a broader array of material can be covered with more attention to depth and applied knowledge. The topical approach is used in other disciplines, such as psychology (Santrock, 2008).

True to social work's history, this text will cover topics using micro, mezzo, and macro analysis. Further, we will present both normal and abnormal human functioning with an emphasis on how to incorporate strengths.

Assess your analysis and evaluation of this chapter's content by completing the Chapter Review.

2

Examining the Human Experience

Attempting to examine and capture the whole of human experience is at least daunting and more likely impossible. Consider the difficulty in capturing the "whole" of one aspect of the human experience: love. Poets, philosophers, scientists, children, adults, and you and I have thought and experienced some form of love. Yet, despite having experienced love, it is impossible to define the whole of love in words, art, or science. Although we cannot capture the whole of human experience, we can try to understand some aspects of it.

UNDERSTANDING HUMAN FUNCTIONING

Many methods exist for trying to understand aspects of life, and each method has advantages and disadvantages. Consider the following sentence as an example: Maria is smart because she went to college. If we examine this statement, one might assume that people are either smart or not smart. Further, we may wonder if going to college makes people smart and, therefore, people who don't go will not be smart. Of course, you should fully disagree with this reasoning because it is false. "Smartness" is not an "either–or" dichotomous category; intelligence lies on a continuum. Some people are really smart, others are really not smart, and most of us are somewhere in the middle. Further, some people who are really smart in classical literature are illiterate in jungle survival. With regard to college, some smart people go to college and some smart people do not. And attending college may not increase a particular person's intelligence.

What is the point? The point of this example is that looking at the world in either–or categories does not adequately capture the human experience. The following are some commonly used frames for understanding the human experience:

- Normal and abnormal functioning
- Basic and applied knowledge
- Level of analysis: micro, mezzo, macro, temporal
- Lifespan development and topical approach
- One-way and systemic or bidirectional causal inferences
- Dichotomous/categorical and continuous frameworks

What Is Normal?

Normal versus abnormal; health versus pathology; typical versus deviate; strengths versus deficits

The words *normal* and *healthy* and *typical* are loaded terms as are *abnormal* and *pathology* and *deviate*. Universal agreement does not exist about what is normal or healthy about most aspects of the human condition. What is the normal family? Is there a normal response to trauma? Is it normal to spank children? What is the normal age at which someone reaches puberty? What types of relationships are normal? Social workers normally work with people who are struggling with some form of a problem—using the term *problem* suggests that something is outside of normal functioning. So, what is normal functioning? Well, that depends. Many adolescents think smoking marijuana is normal. Many parents of these same adolescents may believe it is normal to experiment with marijuana while also being very uncomfortable with their children using illicit drugs. Then again, there are parents who both condone and support their children's use of drugs. So, how does one sort out concepts of what is normal? To answer this question, we need to realize that many of these terms possess at least two types of meanings: statistical and value based.

Normal from a statistical or value-based perspective

From a statistical perspective, the term *normal* has a very precise, technical meaning. Statisticians have discovered that most natural-occurring phenomena, such as human height, weight, or intelligence, have a "normal distribution." A distribution refers to the spread or number of incidents for a particular phenomenon. For example, all humans are not 5′10″ tall with a weight of 190 pounds. If one were to plot the incidents of height, one would see very few U.S.-born adults shorter than five feet tall. Similarly, one would see very few adults over seven feet tall. There would be, however, many people within the range of five and six feet. Thus, one could say it is typical for U.S.-born people to be between five and seven feet tall.

Statistically speaking, it is more likely or normal for a person to be about 5′8″ and yet some people "deviate" from this typical or likely height. Is the deviation "good" or "bad"? From a statistician's point of view, the terms *normal* and *deviation* are value free; there is no morality or value about whether someone is tall, short, or average—it is neither good nor bad.

We humans are richly diverse.

Andresr/Shutterstock

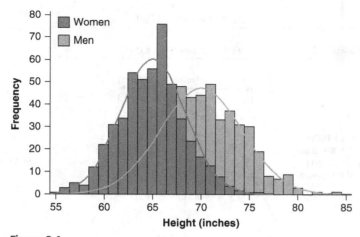

Figure 2.1
Height: Men and Women
Source: Retrieved from http://www.usablestats.com/images/men_women_height_
histogram.jpg on October 19, 2012.

Figure 2.1 illustrates a normal distribution of height of men and women.

The normal distribution is very important in statistics and is characterized by a symmetric bell-shaped distribution. People's heights, weights, and IQ scores are all roughly bell shaped and symmetrical around a mean. Many other aspects of the human condition also have a distribution that resembles this bell-shaped pattern. Referring to Figure 2.1, notice that at the peak of the curved lines is the "mean" or the arithmetic average. For women, the mean height is approximately 65 inches (5′5″), whereas men are about 5 inches taller (5′10″) on average. The average or normal height, however, is only part of the story. Notice that some men were over 85 inches tall while others were shorter than 55 inches. Variance exists.

Figure 2.2 is another graph that represents the bell curve with bars indicating "standard deviations." Notice 6 standard deviations are listed: 3 are above and 3 are below the mean (middle line). Also listed are the percentages or likelihood of having a particular score. Approximately 68% of the population will be within 1 standard deviation of the mean. For the example of height, males had a standard deviation of 4 inches and females had a standard deviation of 3.5 inches. For the males, then, 68% of the population is expected to be between 66 and 74 inches.

The frequency of incidents becomes much smaller as one moves away from the mean. A full 95% of the population is captured within 2 standard deviations of the mean. Using the height example for men, 95% of the population will be between 62 inches (5′2″) and 78 inches (6′6″). Finding people beyond 3 standard deviations away from the mean is very unlikely. If you see 1,000 men at random (e.g., not at a professional basketball game), only 3 would be either above 82 inches (6′10″) or below 58 inches (4′10″).

When statisticians use the term *normal*, they refer to the likelihood of a particular event (e.g., depression, height, age at entering puberty, age at death). They may express surprise when finding someone who is 3 or more standard deviations beyond (above or below) the mean because it is such a rare event. You and most of the people you know, however, are probably not statisticians (note: joke intended!).

When many people use the term *normal*, it takes on a value or a morality position. Normal is good and deviation is bad. Who, after all, wants to be a deviate? The term *deviate* likely conjures images of thugs, drug users, thieves, and others who have not conformed to society's expectations. Would you want your child to date a deviate? Here, the term *deviate* connotes undesirability.

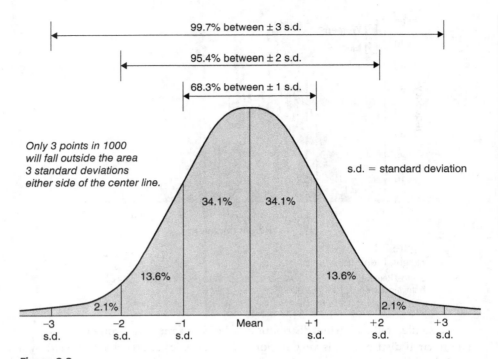

Figure 2.2
Bell Curve and Distribution
Source: Retrieved from http://syque.com/quality_tools/toolbook/Variation/Image375.gif on October 19, 2012.

Let's use an example of depression. Imagine that 100 people completed a question-naire assessing depression. Statistically speaking, about 68% would be within 1 standard deviation and 95% would be about 2 standard deviations from the mean. What about those people who score really high? Their scores significantly deviate from the normal, which means they agreed with more items suggesting depression than most people who took the test. They have deviated from the norm and are unfortunately suffering from many symptoms of depression.

And yet, deviation can also be good. True confession: the authors would love to be deviates—financial deviates. If only we could be billionaires! The median (i.e., middle point) household income in the United States in 2011 was approximately $49,500 (U.S. Census Bureau, 2012). So, if we made a billion dollars a year, we would be way above the average—we would be deviates.

Is being a deviate bad? Society has labeled some forms of deviation as "bad" and others as "good." Einstein's intelligence certainly represents a deviation from the aver-age, and he is generally revered. By contrast, an individual with an IQ score in the 40 to 50 range, where 100 is average, would be considered by many as "less than." The term for someone who scores low on IQ tests is *mentally retarded*. In today's language, calling someone a *retard* is unambiguous criticism.

While most of us probably hold respect and compassion for individuals with mental challenges, we may cringe at other types of deviance. How do you feel about people who are "sexually deviate"? What is your opinion on open relationships, gay marriage, mas-ochism, bondage, voyeurism, or pedophilia? Statistically speaking, these types of sexual behavior are rare—or deviations from the typical. Are they wrong? What about homo-sexuality? From a statistical point of view, homosexuality is uncommon. In Table 2.1, we adapted research conducted by Savin-Williams (2006, p. 41) that shows relatively few adults in the United States, only 1% to 2%, identify as being gay. This number is higher

Table 2.1   Percent of Population Identifying as Gay in 2006

Country	Female (%)	Male (%)
United States—youth	8	3
United States—young adult	4	3
United States—adults	1	2
Australia—adults	4	7
Turkey—young adults	2	2
Norway—adolescents	5	5

Source: Adapted from Savin-Williams (2006).

among adults in Australia, between 4% and 7%. Does "uncommon" translate to the wrong kind of deviate? Social work unequivocally says "NO!" Ideas about homosexuality have changed overtime, as can be seen in the "Did You Know?" box.

How does this discussion of normality and health relate to social workers? Social workers interface with both the statistical definition of normal and the value-based meanings of normal. From a statistical perspective, social workers need to know the percentage of people within a certain group who struggle with depression, live below the poverty line, use drugs, get better with a certain brand of treatment, identify as gay, or successfully transition from foster care to adult living. It is also good to know the average age at which children move into puberty or begin to experiment with sex, drugs, or rock and roll. Knowing the statistical average can inform decision-making. Should programs designed to prevent drug use be directed toward school-aged children or middle-school-aged children or high-school-aged children and so on, or not at all?

In addition to an understanding of the statistical use of terms such as *normal, average*, or *deviate*, social workers will interact with the value-based usage of these terms. Many of our clients struggle with feeling "deviate" because they suffer from postpartum depression, anxiety, posttraumatic stress disorder (PTSD), or schizophrenia. And,

Human Rights and Justice

Understand the forms and mechanisms of oppression and discrimination.

Critical Thinking Question: How can something as simple as a belief about "right" and "wrong" become a mechanism of oppression?

Did You Know?

Identifying as Gay

In 1973, the American Psychiatric Association's Board of Trustees passed a resolution that removed homosexuality from the *Diagnostic and Statistical Manual of Mental Disorders (DSM;* Spitzer, 1981). Prior to 1973, the American Psychiatric Association, which was largely considered to be the authority on mental illness, openly declared homosexuality to be a form of mental illness along with schizophrenia, depression, anxiety, and so on. So, what happened after 1973? Did the field evolve quickly? No, rather the term *sexual orientation disturbance* replaced homosexuality as a form of mental illness. Not until 1986 was some reference to sexual

orientation completely removed as a class of mental illness from the *DSM*. What is the current belief about the "deviance" or morality of homosexuality? In 2009, the American Psychological Association (note: different from the American Psychiatric Association that publishes the *DSM* series) made a clear and landmark statement on therapies designed to change people's sexual orientation. In short, the press release notes that mental health practitioners should not encourage therapies designed to change a person's sexual orientation and mental health professionals should not judge homosexuality as being mental illness (see American Psychological Association, 2009).

Human Behavior

Critique and apply knowledge to understand person and environment.

Critical Thinking Question: How might ideas about "normal" and "abnormal" influence individual's experience of self and how social workers approach their work?

even though homosexuality was removed from the *DSM* series in 1986, society often stigmatizes and harshly judges gay, lesbian, and transgendered individuals. The process of coming out and embracing a nondominant sexuality is not easy as evidenced by high rates of suicidality among gay individuals. Specifically, the suicide rate within the gay population is approximately 300% higher than the rate for heterosexual population (Plöderl & Fartacek, 2009). Here, the suicide rate among LGBTQ individuals strongly deviates from the average suicide rate revealing a need to support this group.

Stigmas can dramatically lower one's quality of life, promote shame and doubt, and even lead to dangerous behaviors such as suicide. Consider the diagnostic label *borderline personality disorder*. Focus on the last two words—personality disorder! This term is certainly demeaning. Imagine the conversation when you say to an emotional, sensitive, and fragile person, "Oh, you're suffering because you have a defective personality—or a personality disorder." Certainly, the symptom cluster that corresponds to borderline personality disorder can be difficult on others—but let's not forget that the person with this symptom cluster is suffering considerably.

Social workers need an understanding of both normal and abnormal human functioning. While there are valuable movements afoot in social work and allied disciplines to strengthen normal human functioning, notice that the goal is logically linked to avoiding pathology. Social work has championed the *strengths-based approach*, which is a commendable reaction to a focus on only pathology or illness. The strengths-based approach is an approach that focuses on clients' abilities, resources, skills, values, and abilities to respond to life's challenges and frustrations (see Barker, 1999). Focusing on client's strengths is believed to help clients recognize that they have the ability to respond to difficult situations and, therefore, feel more confident. Further, a focus on strengths can help clients design plans of actions that emphasize positives rather than a focus on "deficits" that can be discouraging.

Just as you will be exposed to normal and abnormal human experiences in your social work career, this text will focus on both normal and abnormal human functioning.

What is the value in separating out the statistical from the moral or value-based usage of terms such as normal? How might you shift your language by knowing there is both a

Watch the video on Assessment and connect it to ideas on normality and abnormality. What material do you believe is important to assess?

statistical and a common usage of such terms? Our hope is that as a new social worker, you will realize that statistical deviation in no way dehumanizes or diminishes the value and worth of a person. Further, people who find themselves at the margins of the bell curve often have unique needs. Consider weight as an example. At one end of the curve are individuals suffering from anorexia, and at the other end are those suffering from obesity. Both need the help of social workers.

Basic and Applied Knowledge

This book often presents research designed to better understand the human condition and ultimately to help social workers make a positive difference. The purpose of research can often be grouped into two different categories: basic and applied research.

Basic research often does not have a clear application at the time the research is conducted. For example, knowing the human brain has lateralized functioning (i.e., the left and right sides of the brain tend to perform unique functions) is not likely to influence your professional decisions.

Applied research, on the other hand, is clearly oriented toward decision-making. For example, determining which interventions best treat childhood separation disorders can lead to an increasing number of children being effectively helped. Similarly, understanding the implications of tax policies on the poor can lead to advocacy for tax laws that help the poor.

Before reading further, answer this question: Is group-delivered or individually delivered parent training better for low-income populations? What is your rationale for your answer? People who think group-delivered parent training is superior often suggest inclusion of additional parents will provide support and comfort and allow parents to learn from each other. By contrast, those who think individually delivered parent training is superior often suggest individual sessions allow for a customized strategy and may allow parents to explore issues at a deeper level. In a meta-analysis of parent training programs that targeted low-income families, individually delivered parent training was approximately 300% better than group-delivered parent training (Lundahl, Risser, & Lovejoy, 2006). This knowledge is applied because someone weighing a decision whether to offer group or individually delivered parent training to low-income families should clearly suggest individual parent training.

Assess your comprehension of Understanding Human Functioning by completing this quiz.

Level of Analysis and Intervention

Understanding the human condition requires more than a simple examination of "visible" influences. If we only look at a person's physical characteristics, family of origin, or peer influences, for example, we miss the influence of community, culture, and political factors. As a crude example, it is widely known that many Western societies tend to be individualistic, whereas many Eastern societies tend to be more community oriented. How might these differences influence an emerging adult's decision-making about taking a certain job, going away to school, or marrying? In individualistic cultures, the emerging adult and her family would expect her to make choices that would make her happiest or best advancer of her opportunities. This may entail marrying a person whom the family does not approve or moving long distances to pursue work or school. By contrast, in a community-oriented culture one would expect the emerging adult to strongly value how her decisions reflect upon her family. To please her family, she may forgo taking a "better" job or moving far to pursue educational opportunities. Explaining human behavior requires more than a look at cultural differences, however. Within Western and Eastern cultures, individual differences exist that defy tendencies. Some individuals do not follow cultural expectations.

As social workers, we strive to understand the complexities of life to provide effective solutions to our clients.

Social work has embraced perspectives that consider multiple levels of influence. Read Box 2.1 and search for the levels of influence that social work deems important.

In support of the view that the human condition is impacted by multiple levels of influence, social work adopted an ecological systems theory. This theory, advanced by developmental psychologist Urie Bronfenbrenner, highlights the importance of four nested systems: microsystems, mesosystems,

Box 2.1   Preamble to the Code of Ethics of the National Association of Social Workers

Task: Search for terms that speak to levels of influence on the human condition.

The primary mission of the social work profession is to enhance human well-being and help meet the basic human needs of all people, with particular attention to the needs and empowerment of people who are vulnerable, oppressed, and living in poverty. A historic and defining feature of social work is the profession's focus on individual well-being in a social context and the well-being of society. Fundamental to social work is attention to the environmental forces that create, contribute to, and address problems in living.

Social workers promote social justice and social change with and on behalf of clients. "Clients" is used inclusively to refer to individuals, families, groups, organizations, and communities. Social workers are sensitive to cultural and ethnic diversity and strive to end discrimination, oppression, poverty, and other forms of social injustice. These activities may be in the form of direct practice, community organizing, supervision, consultation administration, advocacy, social and political action, policy development and implementation, education, and research and evaluation. Social workers seek to enhance the capacity of people to address their own needs. Social workers also seek to promote the responsiveness of organizations, communities, and other social institutions to individuals' needs and social problems.

Source: Retrieved from http://www.socialworkers.org/pubs/Code/code.asp on July 11, 2012.

---

exosystems, and macrosystems (see Figure 2.3). In addition to these systems, the function of time or developmental level was included. As a developmental psychologist, Bronfenbrenner focused much of his work on young children; yet, the ecological model can be applied to adults of all ages. Let's look at how the systems influence a child and interact.

Microsystem

The microsystem refers to the direct influences on a person and his or her immediate environment. For a child, the microsystem would include parents, siblings, neighborhood children, schoolmates, teachers, babysitters, grandparents, aunts and uncles, and other people with whom the child routinely interacts. Consider the impact a supportive and patient teacher may have on a student struggling to learn compared to an impatient and critical teacher. The supportive teacher may inspire interest and commitment to learning while the critical teacher may extinguish a desire to learn. For an adult, the microsystem may include partners, spouses, friends, work colleagues, neighbors, children, in-laws, ex-laws, and other people with whom the adult typically interacts. A woman who faces verbal and physical assaults from her spouse or partner will have a different experience than her counterpart who enjoys support. An elderly widower may remain in his home and keep his independence longer if his children help with home maintenance and supports.

Mesosystem

The mesosystem refers to the interactions among separate microsystem influences. Consider a few examples of mesosystem influences for children. Parents' involvement with their child's schoolteachers may ultimately influence the child. Imagine two polar examples to illustrate this point. The parents of Rosa, an 11-year-old female, are heavily involved in her school. They go to parent–teacher conferences, volunteer in the classroom, and understand what the school expects. Further, Rosa's parents know her friends and their parents. Rosa's parents plan excursions and barbeques with her friends strengthening Rosa's bonds with her friends. Further, her friends' parents help monitor Rosa's well-being when she visits them. Lastly, Rosa's parents get along with each other and with

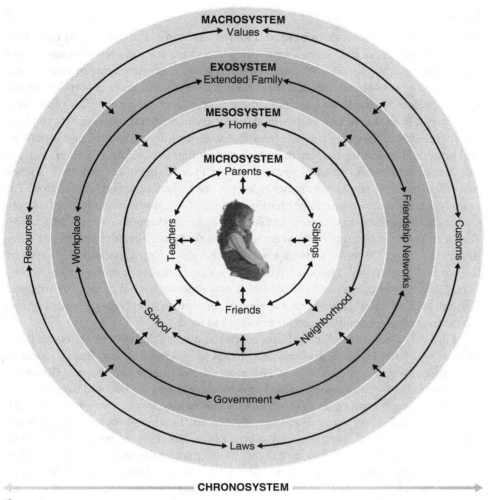

Figure 2.3
Bronfenbrenner's Ecological Model
Source: Pearson Education.

their respective in-laws, as evidenced by a general sense of harmony and cooperation within the family.

In contrast to Rosa's mesosystem, Stephan is not so lucky. His parents divorced and continue to fight bitterly. They often place Stephan in the middle of their arguments. Relations among his parents' respective families are highly conflicted. His father's side of the family openly speaks negatively of his mother. Stephan's parents have limited involvement in his school. They know he is in the fourth grade but cannot name his teacher and are unaware of school expectations. With regard to neighborhood functioning, Stephan lives between two homes and is, therefore, somewhat limited in developing strong peer associations. When at his father's house, Stephan hangs out with older peers who introduced Stephan to ideas and experiences (e.g., drugs, sexual material) beyond what one would expect for a child of his age. Stephan's parents have little understanding of his peer activities.

These examples show how the mesosystem—the interactions among individual microsystems—strongly impacts a person's functioning. Consider how the mesosystem affects a teenager, young adult, middle-aged person, or older adult? What would be different or the same?

Exosystem

Exosystem influences result from local traditions, customs, and policies. At first blush, exosystem influences may seem absent compared to micro- and mesosystems because they are indirect. We consider the case of a child, Rosa, to examine exosystem influences. Rosa's mother could be employed in two vastly different environments—work is an exosystem to Rosa. In the first place, her mother's employer allows her "flex time" to be home when Rosa is sick. This employer also has on-site childcare. Further, this employer is structured and disciplined; sexual harassment is not tolerated, equal pay is ensured, and retirement planning and health insurance are offered. Imagine a counter example. Rosa's mother works for an employer who creates a very different environment. The second employer demands Rosa's mother to keep a strict schedule or face termination. This employer is not sympathetic to her mother's desires to be home when Rosa gets home. Getting permission to take time off to take Rosa to medical appointments is difficult and Rosa's mother is accused of lying to get out of work. Neither health benefits nor retirement are offered. To make matters worse, this employer considers sexual harassment laws to be "overblown." There is a culture of sexual harassment that goes unchecked. While Rosa's mother has not been physically assaulted, the verbal comments are upsetting and abusive. She feels powerless against such comments yet feels she must keep her job or risk losing her ability to pay for housing and food.

How might Rosa be indirectly impacted by her mother's work? The effects on Rosa's mother will "trickle down" to Rosa. In the first work environment, Rosa's mother is likely to feel secure, content, valued, and more confident about the future. Compared to the second job, Rosa's mother is likely to come home less stressed and happier. In the second work environment, Rosa's mother experiences high levels of stress that may thin her patience and ability to meet Rosa's needs. She may develop physical or mental health problems as a result of work that may subtract from her ability to support Rosa, which could place Rosa at risk of neglect or abuse. Now, consider the impact of the two different work environments if Rosa has special needs, such as a chronic medical illness (e.g., diabetes) or a learning disability. What are some other exosystem influences? For children, the school district indirectly influences the child by determining the expectations and resources given for a particular school. Community and neighborhood leaders also influence the child. Does the community have a program to quickly clean gang-related graffiti? Do communities set up parks and recreation centers that offer opportunities for healthy interactions (e.g., basketball nights, swimming pools, outdoor parks)? For adults, indirect exosystem influences include local government, neighborhood associations, religious centers, or the appearance of the neighborhood. What other exosystems can you think of for children, adolescents, adults, and older adults?

Macrosystems

Culture, political systems, laws, and market conditions are examples of macrosystems. Social cultures include dominate spiritual or religious beliefs. Some countries or regions are known to be primarily Hindu, Buddhist, Christian, Jewish, Muslim, secular, and so on. These belief systems influence how individuals see the world and how the world treats them. The caste system of India provides a powerful example as it stratified people into several different categories. At the "top" were the Brahmins who held occupations such as priests, scholars, and teachers. The Kshatriyas are next to the top and could be warriors and rulers. In the middle were the Vaishyas, who could be traders and businessmen. At the bottom of the social ladder are the Sudras, who are manual laborers and servants. Outside of the class system are the Dalits, also known as the untouchables. While this represents a simple overview of the caste system, imagine how it controlled the lives of

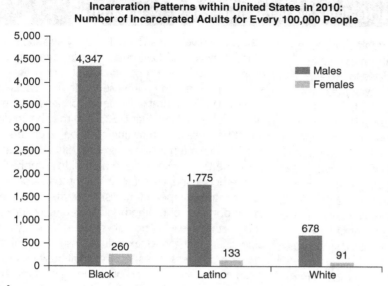

Figure 2.4
Disproportionate Rates of Incarceration

Source: Adapted from Lauren Glaze. (2011). Table 3. Correctional Populations in the United States, 2010. Retrieved from http://www.bjs.gov/content/pub/pdf/cpus10.pdf on June 20, 2013.

individuals and families across generations. Some compare India's caste system to America's early laws that allowed slavery. Even though slavery has been outlawed in the United States for nearly 150 years, its effects have not disappeared.

In addition to social culture, political forces influence behavior. In the United States, the government establishes laws that dictate who can and cannot marry. Government choices about taxes and war also influence the human condition. Consider the residual effects of government choices about going to war in Vietnam, Korea, Iraq, and Afghanistan. Macro-level influences include the economy, health care, and government involvement in industry (e.g., banking). Laws surrounding incarceration also influence communities and individuals. The United States has the highest incarceration rate in the world, with Blacks being disproportionately jailed compared to Hispanics and Whites. See Figure 2.4 for an overview.

With regard to incarceration rates, the United Nations (2003) published results showing that the U.S. incarceration rate is approximately 500% higher than the overall world rate. What factors of macrosystems might explain this rate? How might this rate affect individuals, families, communities, and the country?

Macrosystem influences have direct and indirect effects. The Vietnam War certainly impacted the deployed individuals and their families. Thousands were killed while others suffered emotional problems and such effects trickled down to service members' families. The previous examples reveal how policies can powerfully influence the human experience. In Box 2.2, we present another example of how policies influence basic aspects of human functioning.

Watch the video on Participating in Policy Changes and provide some ideas on the importance of policies in relation to human well-being and how individuals might influence such policies.

Lifespan Versus Topical Analysis

Understanding the human experience demands an understanding of development across the life span. Consider this: A client indicates that something is wrong with his brother. The problem is that he cannot solve a simple mathematical problem "2 + 2." What do

---

Box 2.2   Postpartum Maternal Health Leave in the United States: A Departure

The United States and Australia stand alone among industrialized nations in postpartum maternity leave policies. Neither country has laws to provide paid leave for mothers to stay home with their newborns (Vahratian & Johnson, 2009). Australia at least provides new parents with a substantial bonus (Ray, Gornick, & Schmitt, 2009). In the United States, the Family Leave and Medical Act (FMLA) of 1993 mandates that new parents be granted job security for 12 weeks of *nonpaid* leave. To be eligible, persons must have worked for the employer for at least 12 months; furthermore, the employer falls under law only if it has 50 or more employees (U.S. Department of Labor, 2009). Thus, roughly 40% of employees don't qualify for FMLA leave (Ray et al., 2009).

This policy stands in sharp contrast to most other industrialized nations. In an analysis of 21 financially well-off countries, Ray et al. (2009) state that the United States ranks 20th in terms of time given off. The U.S. private sector is not nearly compensating for the tremendous gap between the United States and other prosperous countries. Less than one-fourth of U.S. employers offer any period of full-time paid maternity leave. So, why the difference in U.S. policy? That is a tough question to answer. While some might argue that maternal health leave should be left to the

states, only five states (New Jersey, New York, Rhode Island, Hawaii, and California) have laws requiring employers to have temporary disability programs that support mothers. In an interview with the Associated Press (2005), Columbia University professor Jane Waldfogel postulates that U.S. policy may be so different because of contrasting goals between the U.S. and European feminist movements. She says that while the U.S. feminist movement didn't emphasize motherhood, and, in fact, didn't want to talk or hear about it, the European feminist movement stressed the importance of motherhood, including childcare and postnatal leave. Another reason U.S. policy may differ is an aversion to taxes. It seems highly unlikely that U.S. businesses (especially small businesses) could alone carry the load of providing paid maternal leave. Most of the European countries accumulate money to pay for leaves through a payroll tax (Ray et al., 2009).

How might these differences in policy affect the mother, the child, the family, or the workplace? If policy affects the experience of individuals and groups, what variables seem to influence policy?

Sources: Associated Press (2005); Ray et al. (2009); U.S. Department of Labor (2009); and Vahratian and Johnson (2009).

---

you make of this? What problem might underlie the inability to complete a simple equation? A stroke? Extreme stress? Amnesia? Dementia? Each of these conditions could explain the inability to complete the equation; it could also be that the brother in question is only two years old.

Time and developmental stage also influence social relationships. Newlywed couples tend to enjoy higher levels of marital satisfaction than couples who have several young children. Later, marital satisfaction tends to climb again. This pattern of higher satisfaction when first married followed by a dip in satisfaction that ultimately climbs after about 20 years of marriage is referred to as the U-curve (Vaillant & Vaillant, 1993). A visual depiction of the U-curve can be found in Figure 2.5.

Critical Thinking

Requires the synthesis and communication of relevant information.

Critical Thinking Question What value comes from understanding that the human experience is influenced by multiple, interacting influences, as advanced by Bronfenbrenner, versus viewing the human experience as determined by single causes?

How much difference does a year make in a person's life? If you were to take a year off from school right now, what would be the impact? What about taking a year off from school when you were five years old? Consider the ability level of a 35-year-old person relative to a 36-year-old. Do you expect a large difference in abilities such as walking, talking, feeding oneself, or solving problems at 35 years of age? Now consider the ability level of a 2-month-old child versus a 14-month-old child, still a one-year difference. The older child can rollover, climb stairs, walk, call for help with words, and hold her head up for long periods of time. How much more can a 26-month-old do than a 14-month-old child? A lot! She can use many words, possibly urinate in the toilet versus in

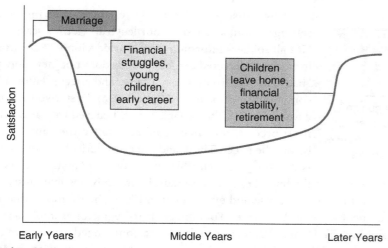

Figure 2.5
Marital Satisfaction Is Influenced by Lifespan Milestones

her pants, comb her hair, say "NO" clearly, and begin to write letters. Clearly 12 months at the front end of life makes a huge difference. How about at the end of life? Toward the end of the life span, say 95 years, the impact of 12 months can seriously affect functioning. Abilities that were once secure—such as walking, bathing or feeding oneself—may begin to deteriorate.

Assess your comprehension of Levels of Influence by completing this quiz.

Thus, age or developmental level influences the human condition—though the influence is not uniform across time. Some approaches to teaching about the human experience organize topics around age. For example, how does cognitive functioning occur in infancy, toddlerhood, adolescence, young adulthood, and through the end of life? This approach is often called a *lifespan* or *developmental* approach. Other approaches take on a specific topic, such as attachment, and discuss it while emphasizing the role of developmental stage. This method is called a *topical* approach. In this text, we chose a topical approach because we believe it allows broader coverage of topics of interest to the human experience while still allowing for developmental considerations.

ASSOCIATIONS, CAUSATION, AND BIDIRECTIONAL EFFECTS

Understanding the human condition requires an examination of associations or linkages. For example, the ability to problem solve is associated with age. Infants cannot solve complex problems, such as algebra, but many adults can. Note that a difference exists between the terms *association* and *causation* and this difference is important.

Association means two or more variables tend to co-occur. For example, effective preparation for an exam is associated with performance. The longer one prepares, the more likely one will do well on a test. With associations, one must use terms such as *tends, is likely to, probably, is correlated with,* or is *associated with* rather than terms such as *caused* or *determined.* A pattern may be fairly stable, but the pattern does not universally hold in associations. An intellectually gifted person may not study at all and do very well on the test. Conversely, another person may diligently study only to perform at an average level. Thus, we learn preparation is associated with but does not guarantee or cause test outcomes.

Ethical Practice

Tolerate ambiguity in resolving ethical conflicts.

Critical Thinking Question: Given that human behavior is rarely "caused" in an absolute sense, what language might social workers use to express tentativeness or ambiguity in discussing human functioning?

Few cause-and-effect relationships exist in social work settings. Child abuse does not leave all victims scarred for life. Not all soldiers returning from war develop PTSD. Growing up in resource-depleted neighborhoods does not inevitably produce "bad" citizens. To establish a cause-and-effect relationship, three conditions must be met (Whitley, 1996). First, two variables must covary. Second, the variable that is believed to "cause" the effect must precede the effect. Said differently, the cause must come before the effect. Third, and the most difficult condition to fulfill, is that no other plausible alternative explanation exists. That is, the hypothesized cause must be the only possible cause.

Can you think of any cause-and-effect relationships? The examples that come to mind for us involve physical processes. For human life to begin, for example, a zygote has to be established. To form a zygote, two cells have to come together: a sperm cell from a male has to join with a female's egg. No other plausible explanation can be found for humans. What are the implications of knowing that true cause-and-effect relationships are rare in human functioning? We can think of several. First, this knowledge should promote flexible, open-minded thinking. Rather than trying to find the "one answer" that definitively explains some aspect of life, we should recognize that many influences contribute to outcomes. Second, in line with our first implication, impulses to blame people should be tempered. Recall from Chapter 1 that professionals historically blamed mothers for causing schizophrenia in their children. The development of schizophrenia is complex and children with schizophrenia place a tremendous strain on parents, which may have promoted the behaviors blamed for causing schizophrenia. Thus, the classic question of "which came first: the chicken or the egg" also applies to the relationship between schizophrenia development and parenting (King, 2000). Third, because most problems social workers address do not have a singular cause, a singular, simple solution is unlikely to exist. Rather than feeling pressure to produce the one right answer, which doesn't exist, we can choose from a variety of interventions to positively influence our clients.

In addition to examining association and causation, it is important to look at "direction of effect" questions or what influences what. For years, researchers often assumed that associations went one way. For example, most early research on child development looked only at how parenting actions influenced children—not how children influenced their parents (Bell, 1979). This simple relationship is shown in Figure 2.6.

In these one-directional models, a child's behavior would be attributed to parenting. If a child misbehaved, parents would be blamed. If a child was well behaved, parents would be credited. Certainly, parenting practices influence child behavior—volumes of research has demonstrated that parenting practices do influence children (Forehand & Long, 2010; Lundahl et al., 2006). However, children also influence parents. Children with medical problems, attention deficit/hyperactivity disorder, or difficult temperaments are more difficult to parent compared to easy-going, healthy children (Flaherty, 2006; Jaudes & Diamond, 1985). Bell (1979) and others reinforced the idea that researchers and

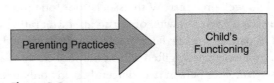

Figure 2.6
Example of a One-Way Effect

clinicians should consider the reciprocal or bidirectional influences in relationships, as shown in Figure 2.7.

Consider a pattern common in family relationships. A teenage son withdraws from his mother. The mother scolds him for withdrawing because she wants to be closer. The child does not appreciate the scolding and decides to withdraw more, which encourages what? You got it, more scolding from mom. How do you think the son responds to more scolding? More withdrawal is likely. Here, the son's behavior strongly influences the mother and the mother's behavior strongly influences the son's behavior. They operate on each other in a bidirectional manner.

What implications arise from considering human functioning from a bidirectional or reciprocal perspective? One notable advantage is that a measure of hope is gained through client empowerment. If clients can accept their contribution to situations, they have some capacity to create desired change. Another advantage is that a more accurate understanding is gained of what is really happening. From the previous example about the mother and son, neither the mother nor the child is simply at fault—both contribute to the problem. A more clear understanding of "reality" promotes empathy and effective problem solving.

Figure 2.7
Example of a Bidirectional Effect

Categorical or Continuous?

Investigating the human experience assumes the ability to measure human phenomena. So, how do we measure human phenomena? Two measurement types are most common: categorical or continuous approaches.

Categorical

Some aspects of the human experience can be measured with "categorical" or "nominal" classifications. Nominal classifications suggest discrete groupings such as sex (male, female, transgender), marital status (single, married, divorced, widowed), or work status (employed, unemployed). In a nominal classification, a person can belong to only one subgroup. Nominal classifications do explain some aspects of human functioning, though exceptions are often present, and often provide only a shallow view of human behavior. Marital status is an example. We can validly say someone is either "married" or "not married," but this does not tell us a lot about the person. Is the person in a committed relationship that does not involve marriage? Is the person married but desperately unhappy in the relationship? Is the person engaged to marry or on the verge of divorce? Marital status tells a piece of the story, but clearly, more detail is needed to better understand a particular person.

Knowing that a person "belongs" to a certain category is a good place to start, but it is not enough to fully understand the uniqueness of a person. An example from one of the author's clinical experience demonstrates this point. BL worked with Regina who was categorized into these boxes at the point of referral: female, refugee of well-known vicious ethnic war, mother, and widow. With this amount of information, what inferences might we draw about her? How confident should we be in these inferences? Some of us might think Regina is likely to suffer from depression or PTSD because she witnessed and lost friends to an ethnic cleansing campaign and lost her husband in the war. Further, we might hypothesize that she is disoriented because of culture shock and experiencing adjustment problems secondary to losing her husband. These inferences seem reasonable. However, they would have been completely wrong. Regina was highly stressed due to the many changes in her life, but she also had a very strong resilient response and was looking for ways to cope and progress. She wanted to go to college, get a job, and adjust to her new environment. While she held some lingering pain about her past, she had resolved many of these issues prior to our meeting and was looking for ways to grow.

Categorical variables are, however, useful for examining some aspects of the human condition from a broad view. Answering the following questions will help you understand this point. First, who tends to make more money, men or women? Second, in the United States, who has a longer life span, African Americans or Caucasians? The answer to the first question is that men consistently make more money than women for doing the same job (see http://www.nytimes.com/2006/12/24/business/24gap.html, retrieved on September 19, 2009). Said differently, women are underpaid for doing equal work—underpaid to the tune of earning only about 75 cents for every dollar a man earns. With regard to the second question, African American men die about six years earlier than Caucasian men and African American women die about six years earlier than Caucasian women (see Figure 2.8).

What is the bottom line? Categorical variables tell us some things about the human condition, but should not be relied upon to understand the intricacies of a particular person's life.

Continuous

Many aspects of the human condition exist in degrees rather than in discrete categories. Height and weight serve as good examples. The terms *heavy, heavier, heaviest* or *skinny, skinnier,* and *skinniest* demonstrate weight. Similarly, think of Olympic medal winners. We know that all medal winners are excellent athletes and we can further rank them by saying one earned a gold medal, another silver medal, and another bronze medal. These examples describe rankings or "ordinal" measurement systems. They provide more information than categorical language, such as "tall" or "skinny" or "medal winner." Yet, we can even get more information by precisely measuring height, weight, or running

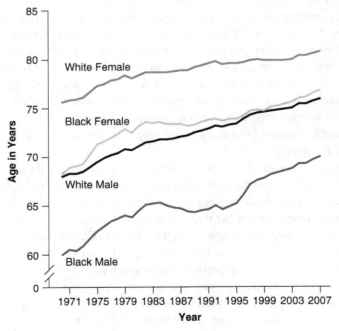

Figure 2.8
Life Expectancy by Race, Sex, and Birth Across Time
Source: Retrieved from http://www.cdc.gov/nchs/data/nvsr/nvsr59/nvsr59_09.pdf on September 16, 2013.

speed, which provides even more objective information. For example, the "tallest" person may be 82.00 inches, the "taller" person may be 81.95 inches, and the "tall" person may be 75 .00 inches. Notice that providing specific data (interval or ratio) gives a more accurate picture of height. In this example, the average person probably could not discern between the "taller" and "tallest" people because they only differed by 00.05 of an inch, yet it would be easy to distinguish these two from the 75.00-inch individual.

Assess your comprehension of Relationship Types by completing this quiz.

Social workers often confront situations in which descriptions of people that should be framed in terms of a continuous scale are actually reduced to a categorical description. Rather than saying "My client's level of depression is moderately high," we say things such as "My client is depressed." Notice the difference? What images does one statement conjure relative to the other? Here is another example. A caseworker might say, "John is incompetent. He is not able to get a job" as opposed to "At this time, John's competency is on the low end which will make job seeking more difficult." Although the language differences are subtle, they do matter. In the first two examples, the statements have an air of finality. There seems to be little room to consider alternatives. Further, our guess is that the statements that define people using discrete categories (e.g., client is depressed; John is incompetent) are not factual. There may be times when a person who is struggling with depression enjoys relief or even joy. Also, John may not have many employable skills, but he likely has some skills that would allow him to work somewhere. Many corporations hire individuals with some form of challenge as a means of promoting their confidence and self-determination.

Assess your analysis and evaluation of this chapter's content by completing the Chapter Review.

Purestock/Getty Images

3

Methods for Understanding Influences on Human Behavior

KNOWLEDGE HAS VALUE

What is the value of knowledge? What would be the value of knowing a cure for cancer, alcoholism, poverty, hate, or social injustice? Consider the amount of money that has been spent in trying to understand and treat each of these conditions.

Knowledge is what allows engineers to build cars that work, film directors to create movies that touch us, and so on. It is fundamental to social work. Reducing drug abuse, creating safe living environments, overcoming depression, increasing motivation to change, and minimizing child abuse all rest on the hope of understanding the factors that cause and maintain social and individual problems.

Consider efforts to reduce drug use among teenagers. In the 1980s, the Partnership for a Drug-Free America ran television commercials focused on scare tactics. Viewers were shown a picture of a raw egg. An announcer would say, "This is your brain." Later, the egg was cracked and dropped into a hot skillet. The announcer would then say, "This is your brain on drugs," and the egg would fry and sizzle. The purpose of this commercial was to inform teenagers that using drugs could damage the brain and to scare them to such a degree that they would not use drugs. Unfortunately, these commercials didn't work (Hanson, 2007). Teenagers would go to parties where they saw their friends using drugs, and contrary to what the commercial showed, their friends' brains did not immediately fry when they used drugs. Indeed, their friends may have appeared to have fun while receiving positive reinforcement for drug use. For instance, one student at the University of California at Berkley stated the following in recalling the advertisement in a CNN interview: "When I saw people that were on the high school honor roll smoking pot, I realized that the commercial's message was false…. I remember thinking, 'When are their brains going to fry?' " (Alexander, 2000).

The failure of these strategies led the U.S. government to try different tactics to discourage teenage drug use. Based on the research of Gerald Patterson and colleagues, the government developed commercials that emphasized the role of parents in preventing drug use. Specifically, commercials indicated that parents were the "antidrug." These commercials informed parents that they should monitor their children's whereabouts and told children that their parents could support them in making decisions. The message that parental involvement is an antidrug is based on research that shows a negative correlation between parental involvement and the likelihood that their teenager uses drugs: Higher involvement is linked with lower drug use.

All Knowledge Is Not Equal

In your career as a social worker, you will daily rely on knowledge to make decisions. Given the critical role knowledge plays in guiding practice decisions, it's good to understand some properties about knowledge. To begin, all knowledge is not equal. Some knowledge can reliably predict the future. For example, meteorologists are good at predicting tomorrow's weather by using knowledge of variables such as humidity, temperature, air pressure, and wind velocity. They make predictions based on physical and mathematical relationships and use satellites, weather balloons, radars, and other complex equipment to inform predictions. But as we all know, meteorologists aren't 100% correct in their predictions. And, as described in the next two Did You Know? boxes, being incorrect can have dramatic consequences.

Some knowledge is simply better than other knowledge. In social work settings, differentiating valid knowledge from poor knowledge is crucial to making good decisions because people's well-being is at stake. If we can agree that knowledge is valuable in decision-making and that all knowledge is not equally valid, we can discuss the properties of knowledge, what kind of knowledge is better, how knowledge is created, and the uses and limitations of knowledge. We begin by exploring a basic definition of knowledge.

Did You Know?

Could Valid Knowledge Have Saved 20 "Witches" From Death?

An example of the importance of examining one's foundation of knowledge occurred in the 1600s in Salem, Massachusetts. In 1692, a local minister reported two of his children were displaying strange symptoms and complaining of pain. The minister and his wife prayed for their children but did not see improvement. The minister called a physician who examined the children and charged they were not sick physically but possessed by witchcraft. This was not an unusual charge among the Puritans in New England at the time (Adams, 2008). Witchcraft was considered a grievous crime, which, between 1692 and 1693, resulted in 20 deaths and imprisonment of about 200. In short, cultural zeitgeist, authority, oppression, and social pressure all supported the famously misguided witch hunt.

How did "knowledge" fuel this tragic example of injustice? What guidelines about knowledge would have protected the Salem community from making such tragic mistakes?

Knowledge Defined

What is knowledge? This question has had been debated for thousands of years and defies a simple answer. Knowledge is often considered to be "facts" or beliefs about facts. What are facts and beliefs? Facts and beliefs can be thought of as learned associations (some of which are more valid than others). Take the following sentence as an example of a fact: "Most U.S. readers know that a significant historical event in U.S. presidential history occurred on November 22, 1963, in Texas." What happened on November 22, 1963? If you said, "President John F. Kennedy was assassinated," you'd be right. How did you come up with that answer? You probably made associations among the following words: significant historical event, U.S. presidential history, Texas, and 1963.

Knowledge is the associations between two or more facts, concepts, ideas, or events. Associations imply a relationship. If you know that your best friend eats ice cream when he's sad, you have observed a pattern or relationship among three variables: best friend, emotional upset, and ice cream consumption.

Social work, like all professions, seeks to uncover knowledge to promote our ability to realize our mission.

Knowledge can be thought of as a proposed *inference* between two or more variables. To "infer" is to draw a conclusion, to assume a certain connection, or to propose a relationship (Dewey, 2011). Consider the word *proposition*. I can make a proposition that you buy my car because I am selling it at a great value. I have suggested a relationship or inference: Buying my car is a great opportunity because I am selling it below market value. Will you automatically buy my car? Of course not. You have to agree or disagree with my proposition before you act on it. In this same manner, social scientists propose many relationships or inferences about the human experience. Some propositions will make sense to you, others will not. Whether or not you agree with a proposition, some propositions enjoy considerable support from research studies while others do not. Anybody can make propositions. You likely have been the recipient of propositions to buy diet supplements, exercise equipment, phone services, and automobiles. You may hear propositions that child abuse is bad for children, that taking LSD is dangerous, that psychotropic medications are more effective than behavioral therapies for treating anxiety disorders, that diagnosing people is oppressive, that the strength of the therapeutic alliance is critical to change, or that a certain agency successfully serves the needs of older adults.

AP/Fotolia

If anybody can make propositions and certain propositions have been proven to be patently false, how do we judge knowledge? This question relates to the degree of confidence we place in a certain piece of knowledge. Because confidence in propositions is so crucial in making decisions,

Good Intentions, Bad Outcomes

The American Iatrogenic Association's (2002a, 2002b) mission is to research and report medical ideas that, despite good intentions, lead to disease and death. Iatrogenic refers to a problem caused by a person who is expected to "heal" it. An example of an iatrogenic outcome from social work comes from a study on efforts to help adolescents in trouble with the law. Gatti, Tremblay, and Vitaro (2009) reported that economically challenged youth, who are involved with deviant friends, are poorly supervised by their parents, and display impulsivity and hyperactivity, are more likely to have juvenile justice involvement than their counterparts. They went on to find that involvement with juvenile justice services *increases* the chances these youth will enter the criminal justice system as adults (when other variables are controlled for). Furthermore, the more intense the intervention provided by juvenile justice services, the more harmful the results.

considerable effort has been applied to understand how to systematically assess confidence in propositions. It is important to realize that different sources of knowledge exist and all have limitations and strengths.

SOURCES OF KNOWLEDGE

Next, we explore six sources of knowledge along with their strengths and weaknesses: tradition, authority, intuition, common sense, science, and personal experience.

Tradition

Much of what we "know" is based on tradition, custom, or repetition. Such knowledge is generally accepted as absolute truth because it passes from generation to generation in stories, customs, and rituals. Consider the case of Greek or Roman mythology. Stories about gods and their wars and interactions with humans were told, written, and distributed. Surely, the Greek and Roman people of the time did not say, "This story about Zeus and Hades sure is interesting, even though it is just a myth." Rather, they likely believed the stories about Zeus and Hades, and it is only the future generations who debunked or changed the stories call them "myths."

Many traditions are not questioned by the masses, such as the view of U.S. history advanced within the United States (see the following Did You Know? box). Also, consider the case of Santa Claus. Ask just about any Christian child younger than five years old in the United States if he or she believes in Santa Claus and how to identify Santa Claus. Most of these children would give a hearty, "Yes, I believe in Santa," and then describe Santa Clause as an older jolly elf who dons red clothing, sports a white beard, has rosy red cheeks, and has a rather large belly that jiggles when he laughs. They would further indicate that Santa delivers toys to all the girls and boys in the world—in one night! Logic alone will not convince many of these children that this tradition is false.

Sources of traditional knowledge include religious and spiritual sources, governments, families, and organizations. For example, do you think democracy is the best form of government? If you were raised in the United States, you probably do because you have been told so repeatedly. As is evident in the news, other cultures do not accept democracy above other systems. Another source of traditional knowledge is familial religious beliefs. Myers (1996) found adult religiosity among offspring is strongly related to parental religiosity such that as children move through adolescence, grow into adults, and start their own families, "parental influences [on religiosity] have considerable staying power" (p. 864). Thus, children born into Christian families and societies often adopt Christian beliefs, those born into Muslim families and cultures tend to adopt Islam, and those born into Hindu families and cultures tend to identify themselves with Hinduism.

In social work settings, traditions are also passed on. For example, most readers probably have heard of Sigmund Freud's concept of the id, ego, and superego. These concepts have been repeatedly taught, yet what evidence exists that an id or ego or superegos exist? None. Another example is that a social worker may defend his method of working with people as, "I've always done it this way," or a policy maker might say, "This is how the funding has been distributed and we are going to repeat what we did last year."

Did You Know?

History Is Shaped by Tradition

In the United States, traditions such as "How the West Was Won" suggest European's descendants legitimately obtained this land. Natives to this land have a different tradition or knowledge of how Europeans secured possession of America. Indeed, you might spot a T-shirt that emphasizes this point through a picture of a Native American with the slogan: "Homeland Security: Fighting Terrorism Since 1492." This example illustrates that knowledge derived from traditions varies across groups.

Did You Know?

Official Apology for Slavery Comes Too Late

There is a strong reticence in U.S. government culture to apologize for past mistakes. The first state to officially apologize (or, more accurately express "regret") for slavery was Virginia—in what year? 2007! A full 142 years after the Civil War ended (Koch, 2007).

What are the strengths and limitations of traditionally derived knowledge? Tradition often speaks to questions of morality and values. From a social evolutionary perspective, traditions arise to help groups survive. Take the Judeo-Christian belief in several of the Ten Commandments as an example: *Thou shall not kill* and *Thou shall not steal* (Exodus 20:13–15, King James Version). Murder and stealing disrupt societies by undermining trust, fostering malicious feelings, and encouraging revenge. Thus, traditions can stabilize a society. This point is made in the musical *Fiddler on the Roof*, which examines the role of tradition in changing times through the eyes of a Jewish husband and father named Tevye. When confronted with geographical and social change, Tevye states:

> Because of our traditions, we've kept our balance for many, many years. Here in Anatevka, we have traditions for everything: how to eat, how to sleep, how to wear clothes … you may ask, how did this tradition start? I'll tell you, I don't know! But it is a tradition because of our traditions, everyone knows who he is and what God expects him to do. Tradition. Without our traditions, our lives would be as shaky as—as a fiddler on the roof! (Stein, 1964, pp. 1, 6; cited in Monette, Sullivan, & DeJong, 2005)

A disadvantage of knowledge derived from tradition is that it's difficult to change or acknowledge that it is sometimes wrong (see the following Did You Know? box). Consider the price that was paid to change slavery, women's right to vote, and civil rights for all people in America. Another disadvantage is that traditional knowledge is rarely questioned or challenged—a condition that can lead to misguided decisions. For example, slavery in the time of Christopher Columbus was generally accepted as long as the slave was not Christian.

Another problem with knowledge derived from tradition is that it can mask or camouflage "reality." If tradition indicates, for example, that mothers are responsible for causing schizophrenia, evidence to the contrary can be ignored, dismissed, or simply not heard. Albert Einstein is attributed with the following definition of insanity: Insanity is doing the same thing and expecting different results. Relying solely on traditional sources of knowledge will likely produce similar outcomes, which may be desirable or undesirable. If social problems continue, traditional approaches to addressing them are, to say the obvious, not working.

Authority

Authority figures provide data that influence human behavior. An authority is credited with having deep, expert-level knowledge. Physicians are considered authorities in medical arenas, electricians with specialized knowledge in electricity, and so on. To a large degree, we accept knowledge from authorities who are often able to provide helpful knowledge.

By being in a social work program in a college, you are preparing to be an authority and people will look to you for advice on how to solve problems. Knowledge from authorities, however, is fallible and can even be manipulated to persuade. Many authority figures have risen and fallen in social work–related professions. Sigmund Freud's ideas shaped much of what clinical social workers did for many years and continue to influence our practice efforts, yet few follow his advice to a tee. In her book, *Raising America*, Ann Hulbert (2003) details how parenting advice delivered by authorities has changed dramatically over time—often in diametrically opposite fashion. For example, parents have been told to not pick up their children when they cry because it may spoil them, whereas other advice has encouraged parents to reassure their children when they cry. Advice on spanking and corporal punishment has gone back and forth across time, as has advice on breast feeding, day care, and how to promote learning.

Some references to authority-based knowledge are meant to persuade and may be motivated by values other than clients' best interests. For example, a social worker may claim to have specialized knowledge in treating addictions as a means of recruiting clients despite evidence to support the proposition. Or, a professor may refute challenges to his way of believing because he has received an advanced degree.

Intuition

Have you ever felt like you've known something without experiencing or reasoning through it? Which *Star Trek* character do you better relate with, Spock, who uses rationalism and calculates everything logically, or Captain Kirk, who goes with his gut and acts intuitively? Probably, you fall somewhere between the two extremes. While strict empiricists and rationalists might suggest that acting strictly on intuition is foolhardy and even, at times, dangerous, research suggests that we often do act without consciously thinking through all possibilities (see Myers, 2009). Take this example: Have you ever been driving some distance and been deep in thought or singing to your radio and later realize you've arrived at your destination without realizing exactly how you got there? This example suggests that we do many things outside of our conscious, rational minds. The subject of intuitive knowledge is often a central theme relating to religion and spirituality: faith. Believers may not directly see God, but report intuitively knowing that God exists. Thus, intuition may affect not only how we drive home at night, but also how we lead our lives and come to conclusions about existential matters.

We often pride ourselves on intuition and have confidence in its ability to help us navigate decisions. In social work, *clinical judgment* is a term often used interchangeably with intuition. Relying solely on intuition can lead to errors. Our purpose here is not to demerit the influence of intuition related to the human experience. After all, feelings such as love, empathy, and spirituality are difficult to look at solely by means of hard-and-fast facts derived from empiricism. As Myers (2009) states, "Our subjective experiences are the stuff of our humanity—our art and our music, our enjoyment of friendship and love, our mystical and religious experiences" (p. 126). That said, intuition has its limits and can lead to unfounded assumptions and beliefs.

Common Sense

Common sense knowledge is similar to traditional knowledge in that certain notions are simply accepted as "true." Often, common sense is very helpful. Benjamin Franklin's book series *Poor Richard's Almanac* was replete with good advice based on common sense. Going to bed early and saving money do seem like good ideas that are without refute. Individuals use common sense in a variety of ways. Take, for example, President Obama's State of the Union address in 2010. He called for Congress to stop the "tired battles" and try common sense (Office of the Press Secretary, 2010). Certainly, common sense is used daily by persons from all walks of life. We make judgments and come to conclusions without empirical evidence and often without complete rationality. This is not to say that common sense is not useful or even necessary at times. As college students, you are likely very busy with your studies and social lives (in that order, hopefully). Even with vast sources of information around you, it is impossible for you to empirically test or logically think through every facet of what it means to be human. It is even impossible to Google everything that you might have questions about; there simply isn't enough time in the day. Common sense, then, is often necessary for each of us to help fill in the gaps of the unknowns.

What are the possible downsides of relying on common knowledge? At times, common sense provides contradictory ideas. Which piece of common sense prevails when speaking of separation from a loved one: "absence makes the heart grow fonder" or "out of sight out of mind." Common sense is often unreliable, contradictory, and not applicable to all people. It can often lead us to false conclusions and abhorrent judgments and actions. Racism, sexism, and heterosexism all seem to be "common sense" propositions to their advocates while gross miscarriages of justice to their targets. Study political positions on issues such as taxes, human rights, guns, drugs, and education and you will certainly notice that singular issues produce monumentally different claims of what is "common sense."

Drew, Hardman, and Hart (1996) delineate how common sense differs from science as a way of knowing. Science is more systematic than common sense in the way theories are developed and ideas are formulated and tested, and in comparisons of relationships among variables and in controlling for variables. These authors state that common sense operates in a more loose fashion and relies on more individual perception, feeling, and judgment. Finally, like intuition, common sense wisdom can delve into the metaphysical. Science, for the most part, requires that phenomena be observable and empirically verifiable (pp. 13–15).

> **Read Research-Based Practice and provide a summary of the main arguments and key ideas in relation to different types of knowledge.**

Science

As briefly mentioned earlier, one thing that separates science from other ways of knowing is that the process to arrive at "knowledge" is systematic (Kuhn, 1996). Another distinguishing feature of science is that it is "based on experience external to the knower, in that the primary source of information is observation that is designed to be objective" (Drew et al., 1996, p. 12). Science prizes knowledge obtained through observation or "empiricism." Some of the basic steps of the scientific process include:

- Observation
- Formulating a question or hypothesis based on the observation
- Designing a test of the hypothesis
- Testing the hypothesis in a manner that minimizes confounds
- Gathering and analyzing data from the test
- Analyzing the results to assess degree of fit with the hypotheses
- Making new observations and hypotheses depending on the results
- Allowing others to replicate by publicly communicating results

The systematic nature of science is designed to manage bias and control potential confounding variables (i.e., variables that might undermine confidence in the findings). Another key component to the scientific process is replicability, or repeated observations by independent researchers to assess consistency in outcomes. Science is expected to be a public process in that tests, analyses, and results are transparently communicated.

Personal Experience

Significant amounts of knowledge are derived from our personal interactions with the world. Indeed, experience is one of the greatest instructors in social work and other professions. Medical schools often employ the "see one, do one, teach one" method where students observe a procedure, execute the procedure, and lastly discuss what they did as a means of solidifying their understanding. In social work, interactions with people of different backgrounds help us understand that others hold different, valid worldviews and, at the same time, most people cherish universal principles of self-determination, encourage respect for life, and value interpersonal connection. Another positive result from personal experience is emotional knowledge; that is, directly interacting with clients promotes perspective taking—a precursor to empathy (Marton, Wiener, Rogers, Moore, & Tannock, 2009).

Our experiences with clients can help us determine which interventions tend to work and which do not work. For example, observing that a particular middle-aged client begins to cry or become tense every time he speaks of his father can help the social worker learn that this client may have unresolved concerns about father. The social worker can investigate whether the client is aware of this pattern (i.e., strong emotional reaction when speaking of his father) and propose to focus time in this area (Peebles, 2012).

While clear advantages from personal experience exist, such knowledge can be misguided. Several factors can promote misguided or invalid knowledge. Peer pressure can, for example, influence knowledge derived from personal experiences. The classic research of Asch (1956) revealed that a person looking at several lines of different lengths would conform to saying that an obviously shorter line was equal to an obviously longer line because of peer pressure.

> **Critical Thinking**
>
> *Practice Behavior Example: Know about the principles of logic, scientific inquiry, and reasoned discernment.*
>
> **Critical Thinking Question:** How might different forms of knowing advance or retard social work's primary mission?

GENERALIZATION VERSUS CASE SPECIFIC

Let's get back to the purpose of knowledge. Knowledge is useful because it guides decision-making. Some forms of knowledge are universal. The Law of Gravity, articulated by Sir Isaac Newton, revealed that objects with mass attract one another with larger objects having more pull. On earth, the effects of gravity are universal, and there are no exceptions. Every time an object is dropped, and no other forces are at work on the object, it falls to earth. As complicated as the Law of Gravity may seem, it pales in comparison to trying to understand human behavior. Indeed, we do not come close to predicting 100% of human behavior. Such a realization was not always held. John Watson, an early behaviorist, wrote:

> Give me a dozen healthy infants, well-formed, and my own specified world to bring them up in and I'll guarantee to take any one at random and train him to become any type of specialist I might select—doctor, lawyer, artist—regardless of his talents, penchants, tendencies, abilities, vocations and race of his ancestors. (Watson, 1930, p. 104)

This statement, while acknowledged by Watson to "go beyond [his] facts," exemplifies the hopes of early social scientists. Understanding the human condition was expected to help eliminate social problems such as poverty, mental illness, discrimination, and crime. Unlike the Law of Gravity, there are no universals in social sciences, and this realization has led to differing perspectives on the reach of scientific knowledge—often known as generalization. Two terms speak to the goals or nature of knowledge with regard to generalization: nomothetic and idiographic research. *Nomothetic research* expects that findings will generalize to a population of people, whereas *idiographic research* focuses on individuals and does not expect to be generalized.

We generalize when we expect the divorce rate in the United States to match the divorce rate in countries across the world. Of course, the divorce rate in the United States, Saudi Arabia, and India differ. A more accurate generalization is that the divorce rate in Pennsylvania is similar to the divorce rate in Ohio. Social workers often make generalizations. You have likely heard of a study that indicated psychotropic medications help people with depression. Or, maybe you have heard of a study that suggested cognitive therapies are better than nondirective therapies in helping people overcome depression. These findings were derived from studies with people you have never met. The people in the studies may or may not resemble the people you are trying to help. If the sample of people in the study resembles those whom you are trying to help, your confidence in the results should rise. However, if the study sample is vastly different from those you are attempting to help, caution is warranted about whether the results from the study will be replicated in your work.

Case studies, or idiographic research, by contrast, purport no ability to generalize. In part, the goal of idiographic research is to develop a thorough, subjective understanding of an individual. To develop a thorough understanding of the individual, questions might include What is Paul's narrative about working late into life? How did Rosie work her way into independence from foster care? How did Robert and Cindie respond to the death of their son in the Afghanistan war? Case studies paint a full and rich picture of people, policies, or interventions providing readers with a deep understanding of the topic despite their inability to be generalized to wider populations.

Assess your comprehension of Properties of Knowledge by completing this quiz.

Theories

Theories are statements that explain observed phenomena and lead to testable hypotheses (Prochaska & Norcross, 2010). They also serve to organize observations. Theories hold both advantages and disadvantages. One advantage of theories is that they include a structure that can help organize thoughts and data pertaining to human behavior. Another advantage is that theories can be compared allowing for a "test" of which theory better explains the aspects of the human condition. Further, theories can act as shortcuts—allowing for quick processing of data.

One disadvantage of theories is that they can be misleading yet passionately held because of tradition. For centuries, people believed the world was flat, which influenced exploration patterns and heightened fears. For decades following Freud's theory of the personality, it was believed that females reporting sexual exploitation by men represented women's fantasies about sex or their desire to have a penis that undermined social justice and promoted violence and sexist behavior against women (see Peebles, 2012). Another disadvantage of theories is that they may stifle creativity and restrict thorough exploration of a phenomenon. Take behaviorism as an example. A social worker who fully ascribes to the theory that all human behavior can be explained by stimuli and response will struggle in helping clients facing existential or spiritual crises. At a macro level, ascribing strongly to one theory about policies related to self-determination (e.g., abortion, right to marry, right to bear arms) tends to produce an inflexible worldview that interferes with effective problem solving by dampening motivation. Lastly, theories can lead to biased assessments and biased decision-making that obscures the "true" nature of things.

Humans have argued about the nature of knowledge for centuries, allowing for a rich understanding of the world in which we live.

Purestock/Getty Images

Social workers will become familiar with many theories about the human experience. Some provide a detailed explanation for most of human behavior while others offer more limited views. At this point, we provide very brief reviews of selected theories as a means of illustrating the breadth of theories available to consider.

- **Nature/evolution.** Evolutionary theory proposes that human behavior resulted because it has survival value. Biological processes explain cognition, emotion, motivations, and behavioral patterns. Genes that control biological processes that offer a survival advantage are more likely to pass to future generations.

- **Nurture/environment.** In contrast to "nature" theories, those holding a "nurture" theory argue human behavior is a function of learning. Younger members of a species learn how to act through direct teaching from older members of the species or through indirect means such as observation and modeling. Nurture may also include shaping forces such as culture, political systems, and traditions.

- **Nature/nurture.** Research has clearly demonstrated that holding a singular "nature" or "nurture" position is flawed (Sternberg & Grigorenko, 1999). Most aspects of human behavior targeted by social workers are influenced by a combination of nature and nurture.

- **Psychological theories (e.g., psychodynamic, psychoanalytic, attachment, cognitive theories).** Sigmund Freud proposed human behavior is understood by competing forces within the mind (i.e., id, ego, and superego) and that humans progress through certain stages of development. Later, psychological theories (e.g., Kernberg, Ainsworth, Bowlby) proposed human connection and attachment are central to understanding much of human functioning. Other psychological theories (e.g., Beck, Ellis) proposed that thinking patterns are related to emotional well-being and behavioral patterns.

- **Learning theories (e.g., behaviorism, social learning theories).** Several theorists proposed that behavior is learned from conditioning, modeling, or the consequences following particular behaviors (e.g., Bandura, Skinner, Watson, Pavlov).

- **Systems theories (e.g., communications, family systems theories).** Derived from cybernetics, theorists began to view human functioning in terms of interrelated systems that strive for homeostasis, the formation of alliances, and can be understood by the structure of interaction patterns and power (e.g., Haley, Jackson, Satire, Minuchin, Bowen).

- **Strengths-based approach.** In social work and allied professions, attention has historically focused on human deficits or pathology, which makes sense given that most people who seek social workers are looking for relief from problems. Interventions are developed and geared toward problematic conditions or psychopathology such as alcoholism, depression, anxiety, and antisocial personality. More recently, social workers from the University of Kansas launched a perspective or theory, which held that focusing on individuals' strengths and capabilities has more promise than a singular focus on pathology (McMillen, Morris, & Sherraden, 2004). Similarly, the "positive psychology" movement has gained ground as a method of promoting human well-being by emphasizing growth, health, and happiness rather than by only studying problems (Seligman & Csikszentmihalyi, 2000).

- **Multidimensional.** Each theory proposed to understand the human condition possesses strengths and weaknesses. A multidimensional approach rejects fidelity to any one theory in favor of taking the strengths of many different theories to provide a more balanced, holistic approach to understanding. Most social workers in micro clinical practice identify themselves as being "eclectic" or "integrative," which is a form of multidimensionalism (Prochaska & Norcross, 2010).

- **Person in environment.** Another form of multidimensionalism endorsed by social work is the person-in-environment approach. This theory recognizes that the human condition is influenced by an interaction of personal and environmental factors. Examples of personal factors include biological forces, psychological forces, relational forces, personality, and among others, disposition. Examples of environmental forces include opportunities, culture, war, politics, discrimination, support, religion, geography, weather, and many others.

Read Blending and Integrating for more information.

At some point, you will likely be asked to identify to which theory you ascribe. At this point, you cannot be expected to know because you have only a brief introduction to theories. As you consider theories, however, it will be good to use critical thinking to guide your decision-making.

CRITICAL THINKING

Rarely do social workers encounter simple problems. Simple problems tend to be resolved rather quickly with simple solutions. And, if problems were simple to solve, they would have been solved. Understanding complex problems and devising effective responses to problems require good thinking—that is, critical thinking. Indeed, a social worker's ability to think critically is probably the most important tool he or she has. Critical thinking allows social workers to ask the right questions to develop knowledge that will promote understanding of problems, solutions to problems, and opportunities to prevent problems and enhance the quality of life. Further, critical thinking allows social workers to continually monitor the degree to which their actions are making the desired impact.

Before discussing some models of critical thinking, let's review some hypothetical situations that require critical thought.

- You work in a community center dedicated to helping former inmates reintegrate into their community. Community support for your center decreased after several of your clients were caught engaging in obnoxious and suspicious behavior. Though no charges have been levied at your clients, evidence suggests they are causing trouble that jeopardizes their freedom, community well-being, and the health of your center. How will you respond? Who is your client? What steps may be most beneficial, and at what cost?

- You read a book that suggests a new treatment for children with reactive attachment problems. The treatment suggests that children with reactive attachment failed to have a secure attachment directly after their birth. The new treatment is titled "Rebirth Them and Re-Love Them." The treatment involves wrapping the children into sleeping bags and blankets that represent the birth canal and having the children fight their way out that represent the birth process, after which parents and therapists are suppose to hold the children and feed them with a prosthetic breast. Will you try this new treatment with a child you are working with who struggles with reactive attachment? What might be right or wrong with this treatment? (WARNING: Do not try this treatment as it has been found to be unethical and dangerous; Chaffin et al., 2006.)

- A social worker in child protection services interviews a young mother who reports she slapped her young son after a night of no sleep, mounting financial pressure, and a lack of support from her extended family. The mother promises it will never happen again. What should you do?

Note that in each of these examples ambiguity exists. You do not have enough data to make a clear, obvious decision. Because social work usually involves ambiguity, we need tools, such as critical thinking skills, to make decisions (Pica, 1998).

We wager that almost every decision you make as a social worker should involve critical thinking, regardless if you practice at micro, mezzo, or macro levels. Critical thinking is needed in the data collection aspect of social work, the assessment phase, the conceptualization phase, the intervention phase, and the evaluation and reformulation phase. Lee (2007) argues that "the development of critical thinking and a commitment to lifelong learning requires a student to reason on the basis of the best available evidence, while remaining cognizant of the fact that knowledge is constantly evolving" (p. 216). This sentence exemplifies why critical thinking is so important—because knowledge is ever changing and no client is exactly the same.

Critical thinking involves (1) systematically searching for evidence, (2) weighing and judging the quality and validity of the evidence, and (3) applying and integrating the evidence to better understand. Understanding may include assessment activities, designing interventions, and monitoring or evaluating outcomes. Critical thinking is an approach to data, evidence, and decisions. Some ingredients of critical thinking include the following (derived in part from Bassham, Irwin, Nardone, & Wallace, 2011; Orchowski, Evangelista, & Probst, 2010; Overholser, 1995).

- **Clarity over confusion.** In social work settings, confusion can seriously undermine our efforts. For example, confusing "normal adjustment" and "abnormal adjustment" can lead to misguided social work activities. For example, a political refugee who is wary of authority figures may be showing normal adjustment based on her history of persecution. Grieving the loss of a loved one is also normal. By contrast, a political refugee who refuses to leave her home and staunchly rejects any effort to understand a new culture may be viewed as unhealthy. Similarly, grieving the loss of a loved one to the point of functional incapacity for years has stretched into an unhealthy region. In medicine, there is a common phrase that supports the need for clarity: "Diagnosis is half the cure."

- **Precision over vagueness.** When a person says that he is not sleeping, what exactly does that mean? Is not sleeping equated with 0, 2, 4, 6, or 10 hours of sleep? Does thinking about suicide mean your client is considering existential issues, wondering about death because her friend committed suicide, or has she recently given away all of her possessions and bought a high-powered gun with the intent of killing herself today?

- **Relevance over extraneous.** In attempting to discover factors linked to an elderly woman's depression, would you ask her about her id, her superego, her own childbirth, the loss of her spouse, financial pressures, the year she graduated from high school, the age at which she began dating, her thoughts, or her level of support? In attempting to motivate community action to stop discriminatory practices against migrant workers, would you highlight the accomplishments of immigrants, discuss problems in the home country of immigrants, cite the Bible's and Koran's position on supporting other human beings, recount the U.S. history of immigration, legal arguments, and social justice? In both these examples, you see that some information is likely to be more relevant than other information.

- **Consistency over randomness.** Critical thinking involves assessing the degree to which knowledge or positions hang together. Inconsistency often reduces confidence in knowledge. You may work with a domestic violence survivor who says she will not return to her abusive partner but then indicates she needs the abuser or actually returns to her abuser despite having other options. A teenager may swear that the marijuana in his pocket belongs to a friend, yet this is the fifth time he has been caught with an illegal drug.

- **Completeness over partiality.** Critical thinking involves looking at most or all of the factors related to an issue rather than only looking at a "slice." Take the case of poverty. Some may argue poverty is simply a function of laziness, rebellion, or other undesirable personal attributes. A deeper look at poverty often reveals a lack of opportunity, heavy demands for basic survival needs (e.g., shelter, food), limited engagement in activities that are a luxury to others (e.g., college), or challenges such as mental illness, physical illness, or generational deprivation (Mistry, Brown, Chow, & Collins, 2012; Sharkey, 2009). On a micro level, critical thinking involves taking a multidimensional view of the human condition. Depression, for example, is seen as having a biological component (e.g., hormones, neurotransmitters), a social component (e.g., social support, social rejection, abuse, loss, fear), an environmental element (e.g., opportunities, war, context), and, among others, personal components (e.g., behaviors, habits, thinking patterns).
- **Fairness versus bias.** Critical thinking puts a premium on an open-minded approach that is as impartial and free from bias as possible. Bias is a powerful force. Bias often arises out of an ego-centric mind-set. Examples of ego-centric thinking include that one group is special and superior to others, such as American values are superior to all others, Christianity is superior to other forms of spiritual thought, light-skin color is superior to dark skin, or men are better than women.

Several barriers exist to critical thinking, such as prejudice, superstition, pressure to conform, lack of time, pressure to decide quickly, failing to gather relevant information, wishful thinking, emotional decision-making, and an unwillingness to be self-reflective. Fortunately, barriers to critical thinking can be overcome because critical thinking is a skill that can be learned. Essentially, critical thinking involves several processes that can be routinely and systematically applied:

- Clarify which information is needed
- Clarify the problem
- Clarify your purpose in engagement
- Identify what you already know
- Explore the issue
- Assemble what is known
- Test your thinking for bias, logical errors, blind spots
- Integrate information into a working theory or hypothesis
- Draw connections among the data you have
- Review what is not known
- Honor multiple perspectives
- Strive to obtain a broad understanding
- Seek to find the best explanation rather than being motivated to be correct
- Favor rationality over emotionality—although emotions are data
- Be reflective and self-aware: examine your motives, biases, assumptions

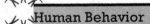

Human Behavior

Practice Behavior Example: Critique and apply knowledge to understand person and environment.

Critical Thinking Question: How can critical thinking improve our ability to accurately understand and promote healthy living?

- Commit to careful thought: avoid quick judgment and manipulation appeals from others
- Actively seek data and try to make connections

Antithesis to Critical Thinking

We now examine several types of biased thinking. Biased thinking is dangerous because it can distort "reality."

Ethnocentric thinking

Ethnocentrism often takes two forms: (1) the tendency for groups to ascribe special value or a sense of superiority to their own group, often at the expense of those who are outside of the group; and (2) the tendency of members within a group to believe that other groups think and feel similar to the "in group." Ethnocentric thinking can affect both social workers and their clients.

To begin, ethnocentric thinking can have devastating effects upon individuals, families, and groups with whom social workers often engage. Ethnocentric thinking of the first type, the perceived superiority of the in group, is associated with both direct and indirect harm to outside groups. Poignant examples of direct harm coming from ethnocentric superiority thinking are "ethnic cleansing" campaigns and persecution of out groups. Many groups have been the target of such campaigns, including Jews in the Holocaust, Native American Indians in the effort to "Win the West," Bosnian Muslims, Tutsis in Rwanda, Armenians in Turkey, Blacks in the United States, and many others. Millions upon millions of individuals have been killed or displaced in such campaigns. Direct effects of ethnocentric thinking need not result in massive death tolls and can be found in your own town or city. Other direct effects include disenfranchising individuals from power, such as not allowing groups to vote (e.g., women, minorities) and discriminatory practices based on group membership (e.g., unequal access to marry and to resources such as drinking fountains, loans, school admission, and housing). Another example of direct effects of ethnocentric thinking involves hate crimes. Individuals may be the target of violence simply because of group membership. Mathew Shepard was brutally murdered in 2011 only because he was a gay (Brooke, 1998).

Indirect effects also arise from when a group has significant power over other groups, which breed ethnocentric thinking. Individuals in the minority group often begin to identify themselves as inferior—essentially internalizing perspectives from the majority group. Groundbreaking research by Claude Steele (1997, 2012) reveals that internalized stereotypes have the power to undermine individual performance, thus limiting opportunities for success. Other research conducted by Kenneth Clark revealed that young female African American children preferred White dolls over Black dolls suggesting they internalized a sense that White children were better than they were (see Freeman, 2008; Jackson, 2006). Lowered self-confidence and self-rejection certainly undermine quality of life—an unfortunate and even tragic residue from ethnocentric thinking. Consider the recent case of Tyler Clementi, a college student at prestigious Rutgers University, who committed suicide by jumping off a bridge after having aspects of his personal sexual life secretly filmed and posted on the Internet (http://topics.nytimes.com/top/reference/timestopics/people/c/tyler_clementi/index.html, retrieved on September 14, 2013). Although it is not known if Tyler's sexual orientation was directly connected to his suicide, it may have been. That is, if Tyler's sexual activities had been heterosexual and secretly aired, he likely would not have felt a need to take his life. Why? Because of the stigma attached to sexual orientation with the majority group projecting messages that homosexual activity is wrong.

Lastly, ethnocentric thinking is corrosive to those who hold such positions. The psychological and emotional cost of perpetrating hate crimes is high (Scurfield & Mackey,

2001; Sun, 2006). Hate and a sense of superiority freeze the ability to connect with people who are different from us.

Social workers are not immune from biased or ethnocentric thinking. Social workers who believe, for example, that delinquent child behavior is fully the responsibility of parents may tend to seek evidence consistent with their view. Social workers who believe that unemployment reveals a character flaw, such as laziness, may ignore evidence to the contrary. Social workers who strongly identify with one political party, say the Democrats, may fail to identify the strengths espoused by Republican's philosophy on governing or neglect to see troubles within the Democratic party.

Two common biases that may influence social workers include confirmation bias and the halo effect. In brief, confirmation bias is the tendency to unknowingly or unintentionally favor evidence that supports one's beliefs at the same time as discounting evidence that runs counter to one's belief (Nickerson, 1998; Rassin, Eerland, & Kuijpers, 2010). Confirmation bias differs from consciously building a case that favors evidence supportive of one's position while rejecting contrary evidence. Because confirmation bias occurs below the level of consciousness, it is particularly dangerous because it is difficult to detect. Claims that "unconscious" biases are less damaging do not hold because the effects of the bias, whether conscious or not, may be the same. In a similar vein, social workers may engage in biased thinking when overemphasis is given to a particular trait, such as attractiveness, agreeability, or intelligence (Kaplan, 1974). This is known as the halo effect. In essence, a general positive bias is given to an individual because he or she ranks high on a particular trait. For example, social workers may feel "star struck" and underestimate the struggles of a physically attractive individual. A physically attractive client may express legitimate concerns of depression or loneliness, yet the social worker may think the client is exaggerating because the client is, after all, beautiful and being beautiful is associated with success and healthy functioning. The halo effect can influence many aspects of social work, as illustrated by the work of Bricklin (1995) who discusses custody evaluations. Imagine the following decision: making a recommendation on custody for two young children. The father is handsome, successful, confident, intelligent, and seemingly secure. The mother appears to be tired, stressed, and depressed. Here, the tendency may be to favor the father. However, digging deeper may reveal that the father is controlling, detached, abusive, and negligent in his parenting. His motives in seeking the children are to punish/control his ex-wife with no genuine interest in raising the children, whereas the mother is feeling the full weight of her children's emotional pain during a difficult period of life. The halo effect may prevent a deeper look into the father's psychology.

Confirmation bias and the halo effect produce biased, albeit unintentional, thinking, and biased thinking likely results in biased decision-making, which can hurt individuals and groups at a scale that may be mild or dramatic. Overcoming biased thinking requires a lifetime of reflective work. All people hold prejudices and biases. It is not a question of IF we hold biases, it is a question of WHAT our biases are and IF we are willing to manage or contain the effects. While overcoming biases is not the focus of this text, considerable research has examined how professionals, such as social workers, can manage biases (Boysen, 2010; Helmes & Gee, 2003; Lidderdale, 2002).

Assess your comprehension of Critical Thinking by completing this quiz.

VARIABILITY AND SOCIAL WORK

If everything "depends" and nothing is 100% certain in the human condition, what is the use of knowledge? Maybe we should just follow intuition because nothing is really known. However, knowledge cannot simply be reduced to an argument of "we know nothing" or "we know everything." Somewhere between "I am certain of …" and "I have no idea about …" lies "probable." It is possible to accurately predict aspects of human behavior and higher levels of probability can effectively influence decision-making. An example from sports demonstrates this point. In baseball, decisions about who bats and pitches are largely governed by probability. All things being equal, a player with a batting average of 0.205 will not play when his replacement bats 0.385. Put yourself in the coach's shoes. If your salary and reputation are influenced by the number of wins you rack up, who would you have bat? A guy who gets a hit 20 out of 100 bats or a guy who gets 38 hits out of 100 bats? All other things being equal, the coach will play the higher probability player every time. On any given batting opportunity, the coach *does not* know which player will get a hit, yet the averages favor the player with a higher batting average.

Knowledge about the human condition is founded on probabilities. Before reading further, complete the activity in Box 3.1 and then return to this point.

How well did you predict height based on names? Scientists who indicate that one group of people is somehow different from another group of people are talking about probability, not certainty. People in large, urban cities tend to vote for democrats and people in rural areas tend to vote for republicans. That is, it is *relatively safe* to say that rural groups will vote for republicans and urban groups will vote for democrats. However, if you sample 100 rural and 100 urban dwellers at random, you will have a very difficult time being 100% certain of the voting persuasion of any given individual. Uncertainty exists alongside trends. The key question, then, is how certain—or uncertain—are we in a particular finding? To answer this question, we need to look at the goals of research that examines the human condition from a nomothetic perspective.

Box 3.1   Prediction, Prediction, Make Your Prediction

Question #1. Make a prediction about which group is, on average, taller?

Group A	Group B
1. Maria	1. Jacob
2. Beth	2. Juan
3. Carla	3. Matthew
4. Rachel	4. Ethan
5. Sophia	5. Terrance
6. Isabella	6. Antonio
7. Ava	7. Michael

Question #2. Look at the following pairs of names and circle who is taller. Just so you know, in two of the name pairs, the female is taller.

1. Maria	or	Jacob	5. Sophia	or	Terrance
2. Beth	or	Juan	6. Isabella	or	Antonio
3. Carla	or	Matthew	7. Ava	or	Michael
4. Rachel	or	Ethan			

Answer #1: The average height for Group A is 5'4" and 5'7" for Group B. So if you predicted Group B, based on names, you would be correct because males, on average, tend to be taller than females.

Answer #2: How confident are you in your choices? See Box 2.2 for answers.

Box 3.2

The bolded names are taller. Out of the seven pairs, how many did you correctly pick? Was your accuracy based on luck or skill?

1. Maria (5'1")   or   **Jacob** (5'10")
2. Beth (5'2")   or   **Juan** (5'9")
3. Carla (5'3")   or   **Matthew** (5'8")
4. Rachel (5'4")   or   **Ethan** (5'7")

5. Sophia (5'5")   or   **Terrance** (5'6")
6. **Isabella** (5'6")   or   Antonio (5'5")
7. **Ava** (5'7")   or   Michael (5'4")

FIVE GOALS OF SCIENCE

Read the Engage, Assess, Intervene, Evaluate document and compare and contrast the main ideas to the five goals of science.

Social work is in the fortunate place of not being isolated in trying to improve the human condition through generating knowledge. Many professions and disciplines seek to understand the human condition such as nursing, medicine, sociology, psychology, political sciences, philosophy, religion, health and nutrition, economics, anthropology, and others. Social workers can use the knowledge generated by other fields to enhance our knowledge and to promote our goals. What do these varied professions have in common? Most attempt to answer some of the following five basic goals of science (Monette et al., 2005; Whitley, 1996):

1. **Describing.** For example, 69% of students graduate high school, but only 56% of Hispanic, 54% of African American, and 51% of American Indian and Alaskan Native students graduate (http://www.all4ed.org/about_the_crisis/students/grad_rates, retrieved on February 12, 2013). In this example, the reader simply cites or describes what is known.

Engage, Assess, Intervene, Evaluate

Practice Behavior Example: Assess client strengths and limitations.

Critical Thinking Question: How might the five goals of science be used to engage clients into social work practices, understand clients' strengths and struggles, inform interventions, and ultimately evaluate social work practices?

2. **Understanding.** For example, high school students are more likely to succeed if they are involved in school activities and have a belief that school will help them in life.

3. **Predicting.** For example, high school students who drop out are more likely to suffer mental health problems and legal problems.

4. **Influencing or controlling.** For example, early detection and intervention programs can increase the graduation rates among at-risk students.

5. **Evaluating.** For example, evaluating how successful an intervention is, such as Head Start or the school breakfast programs.

These goals are interdependent and complement each other. Consider the case of height, growth, and puberty. Research has *described* growth patterns of infants, children, and adults. Ages when most males and females reach puberty are readily described from growth charts. Research also *understands* that growth patterns are influenced by an interaction between genetics and environmental forces. For example, nutrition influences growth patterns, as revealed by the tendency of overweight girls developing into puberty earlier than their normal weight counterparts (Currie et al., 2012). Research can *predict* that in the human family, males tend to be taller than females. Research has also detected a trend where girls in the United States are reaching puberty at an earlier age as evidenced by a groundbreaking study (McDowell, Brody, & Hughes, 2007). Given an understanding of factors related to growth patterns, researchers or consumers of research can effectively *influence* and *control* growth patterns. Girls who reach puberty at a very early age, say at age six or seven, face increased risk of emotional and behavioral problems (Belsky, Steinberg, Houts, & Halpern-Felsher, 2010; Deng et al., 2011), which have led to medications being used to slow down or delay puberty in these girls (Kaplowitz, 2009; Kaplowitz & Oberfield, 1999). Logic might applaud the finding that medications can delay puberty in these at-risk girls, yet the outcomes of such programs need to be thoroughly *evaluated* before we can definitively claim an advance. Logic, as we have seen, can be wrong. Prescribing medications to slow down the onset of puberty may lead to intended outcomes, may result in unintended outcomes, and may result in undesirable outcomes.

Assess your comprehension of Five Goals of Science by completing this quiz.

Assess your analysis and evaluation of this chapter's contents by completing the Chapter Review.

Biological Influences on Human Behavior

Physical Development

Did you know that your birth month can predict whether you become a professional soccer player, and it has nothing to do with your horoscope? Becoming a professional athlete generally entails moving up the ranks of competitive divisions within a particular sport. For example, athletes who have excelled in town or city leagues are more likely to play at the high school level, and excelling athletes at the high school level are more likely to play at the college level, and star college athletes have the best chance at reaching a professional level. In Germany, birth month predicts this progression (Ashworth & Heyndels, 2007). Here's how it works: Young children interested in soccer are grouped by age so that the playing field will be "level" with regard to age. The problem is that the age-playing field is not level. Imagine what happens if the cutoff date to join a beginner soccer league is January 1. Children born from January 2 through December 31 need to wait until the following year to join. Now imagine that Javier turns six years old on January 15 and Eric turns six years old on December 15 of the same year. Both Javier and Eric will play on the same team because their birthdays fall within the same cutoff period—but Javier has an 11-month age advantage over Eric.

Why does this matter? At a very young age, an 11-month age advantage will predict greater physical strength, size, coordination, and ability to think strategically about the game. Coaches also favor children who show increased talent. Favoring from a coach may include increased playing time and instruction, both of which will prepare Javier, relative to Eric, for more competitive play and more positive attention. Ashworth and Heyndels (2007) reported that of the young children (ages six to eight) who were "promoted" to a more competitive division, 46% were born within three months after the cutoff date in comparison to only 7% who were born in the three months just prior to the cutoff date—this represents a 700% advantage. Even though birth date is not the sole determinant of progression, it can be a major contributor.

What do age and soccer selection have to do with social work? Directly, not a lot unless you are counseling discouraged soccer players who did not progress as far as they wished. Indirectly, this information provides a glimpse into how physical development influences the human condition.

BIOLOGY AND THE HUMAN CONDITION

Humans are physical beings, and physical aspects play a dramatic role in explaining the human condition. Consider an example closer to social work. Age of puberty onset influences behavior in a manner that directly concerns social workers. Girls maturing early are at higher risk for using alcohol and cigarettes. One study found that girls who enter puberty early were 200% more likely to try cigarettes and 350% more likely to try alcohol compared to those who enter puberty later (Westling, Andrews, Hampson, & Peterson, 2008). Other studies, across many cultures, show that early entry into puberty for girls is associated with depression, anxiety, and early introduction to sexual behavior linked to pregnancy (Belsky, Steinberg, Houts, & Halpern-Felsher, 2010; Boden, Fergusson, & Horwood, 2011; Joinson, Heron, Lewis, Croudace, & Araya, 2011). Does this risk hold for boys? Boys who enter puberty early are also at increased risk for illegal substance use, though the risk is lower compared to girls. In fact, early maturing boys may have a social advantage because their peers rate them as more physically adept and socially poised, whereas early maturing girls are at risk for being teased and as targets of sexual advances from older boys. This example shows how two aspects of physical development, age and puberty onset, contribute to the human experience.

Biology and Environment Factors Interact

As social workers, we might treat this information in a fatalistic manner. After all, how can social workers slow puberty onset or control an individual's gender? Medical doctors, by contrast, have found methods to influence both the rate at which children enter puberty and an individual's sex (Kaplowitz, 2009; Nield, Cakan, & Kamat, 2007). Medications have been developed to slow a child's entry to puberty and medical technology can be employed to reassign the outward sexual characteristics of an adult or promote the conception of either a boy or a girl (Harden, Cowan, Velasquez-Mieyer, & Patton, 2007; Sutcliffe et al., 2009). Clearly, such interventions have ethical implications that may involve social workers as shown in the example in Box 4.1.

Biological factors, such as age, exert a strong influence on the human experience.

Manipulating puberty onset and the risks associated with early puberty are not beyond the reach of typical social work interventions. That is, social work interventions could influence age of puberty onset without the use of medications. Yes, you read that correctly. Puberty can be influenced by the things social workers do because environmental factors are also linked to maturation rates. For example, not all early maturing children develop problematic behaviors.

Box 4.1   Ethics Corner Playing God

Social workers often participate in debates about morals, ethics, and political decisions that arise from advances in medical knowledge and technological practices.

One controversial new medical practice is preimplantation genetic diagnosis (PGD). PGD allows prospective parents to choose their baby's sex. The Fertility Institutes (located in New York, Los Angeles, etc.) has been at the center of attention regarding this procedure. From its website, PGD takes place in the following way:

- Several eggs are extracted from the mother by our doctors; sperm is supplied by the father.
- The father's sperm is used to fertilize the mother's eggs in our lab.
- After 3 days, several 8-cell embryos will have developed.
- Our doctor-scientist specialists examine the genetic makeup of the embryos, screening for both genetic diseases and desired gender.

- Healthy embryos of the gender you desire are implanted in the mother.
- Any additional healthy embryos may be cryo-frozen for future use.
- Gestation and birth take place as normal. (The Fertility Institutes, 2012)

These procedures have been banned in some countries (Guy, 2009). Why the controversy? The procedure raises many ethical issues. Could PGD sponsor a new form of sexism, especially in regions where females or males are seen as less valuable (Kalb & Springen, 2004)? Is choosing your child's gender playing god (Hobson, 2009)? Does such practice lead down the slippery slope of eugenics? Is PGD human engineering? What is next? Blue eye color? Auburn hair? Olive skin (Kalb & Springen, 2004)?

The relationship between early maturation and problematic behaviors is influenced by variables such as parental monitoring (Stattin, Kerr, & Skoog, 2011) and peer relations (Simons-Morton, 2004). When parents are more aware of their children's activities and closely monitor their children's whereabouts, the likelihood for engagement in risk behaviors decreases dramatically for early maturing children (Dishion, Andrews, & Crosby, 1995). The U.S. government's advertising campaign that suggests "parents are the antidrug" is born out of research in this area. Consider Figure 4.1 from the research of Westling et al. (2008). This graph shows the dramatic influence that parental monitoring has on children's alcohol use. In effect, the risk of early maturing was negated by high

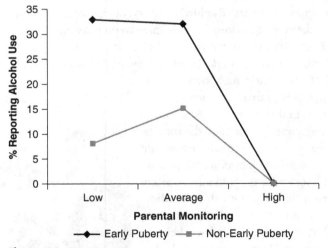

Figure 4.1
Biology and Environment Interact
Source: Westling et al. (2008).

parental involvement. Interestingly, moderate levels of parent involvement did not dramatically reduce risk of drinking alcohol. The bottom line is that high monitoring tends to negate the risk of early puberty onset.

Can social workers influence rates of parental monitoring? Yes. In one longitudinal study among low-income African American adolescents and their caregivers, an intervention was delivered to encourage parental monitoring named ImPACT (Informed Parents and Children Together; Stanton et al., 2000). The program included education and discussion about the need to monitor their children and strategies for doing so. The program increased parental supervision and reduced adolescent risk behaviors.

In addition to parental monitoring, peer associations influence the trajectory in early maturing adolescents. In males, early maturation often leads to improvements in peer status, whereas in females, early maturation can be devastating. Early maturing females are more likely to be sought out by older deviant males. Older deviant males may seek early maturing girls because they have lacked "success" with girls their age while early maturing girls may have been ostracized by girls their own age or developed heightened interest in romantic themes because of early development (Westling et al., 2008). Unfortunately, early physical maturation does not equate to advanced social and emotional development. Psychologically young children who mature early begin to interact with themes such as sex and drugs for which they are unprepared—placing them at risk for making unhealthy decisions.

Human Behavior

Practice Behavior Example: Critique and apply knowledge to understand person and environment.

Critical Thinking Question: How might knowledge about differences in maturation timing and sex influence your understanding of, and approach to, working with adolescents in a clinical setting?

The consequences of poor decision-making are especially difficult for young girls. If a young girl becomes pregnant, her life will take a major turn and may result in leaving school, becoming a young parent, having an abortion, and possibly rejection from her family—all of which can be psychologically and emotionally taxing for years to come (Rowe, 2000, 2002).

At this point, we hope that you're gaining a sense that biological development is *not* independent of social, environmental, or psychological influences. Rather, biological, psychological, environmental, and psychological forces interact to influence the human condition. Such an interaction is made clear in the research described next.

Influencing Biology Through Social Work an Example

Can social work interventions prevent early puberty maturation? Yes. Two factors linked to early puberty onset can be influenced by social workers: body fat and presence of a male figure. Overweight children are more likely to begin puberty early (Lanza & Collins, 2002; Tremblay & Frigon, 2005). Children's level of exercise predicts early onset into puberty, given that weight and exercise are related (Malina, Bouchard, & Bar-Or, 2004; Rogol, Clark, & Roemmich, 2000). Thus, the notion that "moving more and eating better" applies to readers of this text and to children at risk of entering puberty early. Social workers can encourage better exercise and eating habits among children. For example, social workers in school settings may influence policies about the availability of junk food in schools and lobby for breakfast and lunch programs intentionally promoting healthy food.

Family structure and functioning also influence puberty onset (Tither & Ellis, 2008). Females who experience high family conflict, or have fathers who exhibit high levels of aggression or antisocial behavior, are more likely to enter puberty early. Divorce also promotes early menarche compared to

Assess your comprehension of Biology and Environment by completing this quiz.

biologically intact families (Tither & Ellis, 2008). Researchers are not certain why father absence and/or dysfunction promote daughter's early entry into menarche, but a pattern has been noted.

PHYSICAL DEVELOPMENT DURING STAGES OF LIFE

In the remaining chapter sections, we cover prominent physical development forces that influence the human experience. To be sure, one chapter cannot adequately describe how physical development influences human behavior and social work activities. Indeed, entire professions (e.g., medicine, physiology, anatomy, genetics, evolution) research such relationships.

Humans and all things living change physically across time. The Giant Sequoia Redwood trees start as a small seed, and can grow inch by inch to about 250 feet tall. In a parallel manner, humans begin as two microscopic cells that join, grow cell by cell into a fetus, a newborn, a toddler, a teenager, an adult, and, if all goes well, an older adult with up to 50 trillion cells.

Biology and the Beginnings of Life

When does life begin? The answer depends on one's definition of life and a shared definition does not exist. However, notions of the basic biological definition of life are more certain. Specifically, life is said to exist when the following are in place in an organism:

1. The organism is organized with one or more cells.
2. The organism consumes energy through some form of metabolism, resulting in some form of growth.
3. The organism responds or adapts to the environment to promote survival.
4. The organism is able to reproduce or germinate.

In considering these agreed-upon characteristics of life, humans pass the test. For many reasons, you may have been drawn to the last criterion: reproduction. Human reproduction results in children who can (hopefully) eventually live independent of their parents. An interesting relationship exists between human children and their parents: Children are both similar to and different from their parents and children possess some, but not all, characteristics of their parents. Transmitting characteristics from one generation to the next is explained through genetics.

Genetics

How does social work interact with genetics? To this point in your education, you likely have studied genetics. However, most social workers are probably not comfortable with knowing the differences between DNA and RNA. We also rarely use the information that DNA is made up of four chemical bases: adenine, guanine, cytosine, and thymine. Further, social workers rarely make statements such as this one found on the National Institutes of Health's (2012) website:

> DNA bases pair up with each other, A with T and C with G, to form units called base pairs. Each base is also attached to a sugar molecule and a phosphate molecule. Together, a base, sugar, and phosphate are called a nucleotide. Nucleotides are arranged in two long strands that form a spiral called a double helix. The structure of the double helix is somewhat like a ladder, with the base pairs forming the ladder's rungs and the sugar and phosphate molecules forming the vertical sidepieces of the ladder.

What should social workers know about genetics? To begin, much of human behavior is attributed to genetic influences. Read any news outlet for more than a month and you will likely read that a study has linked some aspect of the human condition to genetics. Our intelligence, tolerance for pain, willingness to take risks, response to rejection, interests, taste preferences, and propensity to get cancer are all linked to genetics. Your clients will also likely have a basic understanding that genetics influence the human condition.

Watch the video How the Human Genome Map Affects You. Consider how a deeper knowledge of genetics directly and indirectly influences social work practice.

Parents worried about their children's misbehavior may attribute it to genetics, an anxious person may claim that she has no control over her anxiety because of genetics, or a client may be considering how he will deal with Alzheimer's or cancer because his parents experienced these illnesses. Because our clients often know that genetics influence the human condition, we should have a basic understanding of some aspects of genetics and inheritance.

All human characteristics are influenced by genetics. Physical characteristics such as height, eye color, skin color, body size, handedness, speed, and nose shape are just a few influenced by genes. Similarly, personality characteristics such as intelligence, openness to new experience, propensity to use alcohol, and style of interacting with others are influenced by genes. Note that we use the word *influence* over *cause*, because genes are only part of the story of the human experience as was seen earlier. So, what exactly are genes?

Genes

Humans are made up of trillions of cells. Among other structures, each cell (except for red blood cells) contains 46 microscopic structures called chromosomes. Chromosomes are strands of an organic substance called deoxyribonucleic acid (DNA). Genes are found on chromosomes and are their functional unit. Genes determine the production of proteins and enzymes, which serve as the building blocks of human tissue and facilitate chemical reactions (e.g., digestion and neural transmissions).

The process by which proteins and enzymes work to influence cells and cells work to influence physical characteristics and personality traits is beyond what most social workers need to know. It's enough to know that each of our 46 chromosomes has approximately 25,000 genes (International Human Genome Sequencing Consortium, 2001) and the turning on and off of these genes ultimately influences us.

Some genes influence outcomes independently, whereas others work in concert. Many characteristics that are passed on from parent to child require the interaction of multiple rather than a single gene, such as a person's propensity to abuse alcohol or other substances is known to be influenced by an estimated 700 different genes working together (Doweiko, 2009).

How do genes function? Genes are transmitted across generations such that each child inherits 50% of her father's genes and 50% of her mother's genes in processes you have learned earlier in your education (e.g., mitosis, meiosis, germ cells). In short, genetic transmission occurs when an ovum (egg from female) and a sperm (cell from male) unite and create a new cell called a zygote. The zygote immediately begins to divide through mitosis (normal cell division). Soon the zygote becomes two cells, then four, then eight, then 16, and so on until they take the shape of a human with millions of cells.

Human offspring vary from their parents because the building blocks of the 23 matched chromosome pairs combine in different sequences. Genes on the same location of the chromosomes are called alleles. The combination of an allele from the father and an allele from the mother constitutes a person's genotype. The alleles send messages to the cell that, as discussed earlier, shape who we are and become. Genes influence physical, emotional, and psychological characteristics. Take eye color as an example. Let's say that Sarah inherits an allele from her mother that would usually produce brown eyes and an allele from her father that would usually produce green eyes. Both alleles provide a blueprint for melatonin production that results in eye color; however, the brown allele is such that higher quantities are produced. The two alleles represent Sarah's genotype—she carries both the brown and green-eyed alleles. However, her eyes are brown that represents her phenotype, or outward expression of a trait. If Sarah has children, she will pass on both alleles to her children: the brown-eyed allele, "B," and the green-eyed allele, "g."

Of interest, alleles of the same gene often have a dominant–recessive relationship. If a dominant and a recessive allele are combined, the dominant allele will be expressed and the recessive gene will be suppressed with regard to phenotype. In the previous example, Sarah carries both a dominant and a recessive allele for eye color. Even though she is brown-eyed, she is a carrier of the green-eyed allele. Thus, simply observing what a person looks like does not fully explain what is happening at the genetic level. The dominant–recessive relationship is important in understanding some genetically driven disorders, as we shall see momentarily.

To be sure, most human traits are not caused by single genes. How does it help to know that most "issues" with which social work interacts, say depression or addiction, are not caused by a single gene? Ascribing responsibility for complex problems to a single "thing"— whether genetic or environmental factors—ultimately misses the mark and can mislead social work efforts. That said, some traits are linked to single genes such as blood type, dimpled cheeks, ability to roll one's tongue, and reactivity to poison ivy. Notice that traits linked to a single gene are rather simplistic and will not likely bear on social work practice.

Sex Determination

Chromosomes determine sex: male or female. How does this work? The 23rd chromosome pair on the ovum and sperm is known as the sex chromosomes. In females, the 23rd pair of chromosomes is stretched and looks like an "X," whereas in males, one side of the 23rd chromosome is shorter making the pair look like a "Y." When a female's germ cells divide, the result is two equal "stretched" chromosomes that look like 50% of an "X." By contrast, when a male's germ cells divide, one sperm takes the longer chromosome and the other sperm takes the shorter chromosome. If the sperm that fertilizes an egg contains the longer chromosome, the child will be a female because the resulting 23rd chromosome pair will be an "XX." However, if the sperm that fertilizes an egg contains the shorter chromosome, the child will be a male because the resulting 23rd chromosome pair will be an "XY." The XY zygote will eventually lead to the development of testes that produce relatively more testosterone, which, through a series of very complicated processes known as sex differentiation, leads to male development.

As a bridge to the next section, the XY chromosome pair differs from the XX chromosome pair in such a manner that social workers may become involved. Why? The male genotype does not carry as much genetic material on the 23rd chromosome, and a shorter chromosome is a risk factor to survival and for genetically based problems. The sperm carrying the Y chromosome is more likely to fertilize an egg at a ratio that may be as high as 105 to 100 (Yashon & Cummings, 2011). Yet, the number of male births is only slightly higher than female births. Thus, male zygotes are spontaneously aborted at a higher rate than female zygotes.

Why do social workers care about X and Y chromosomes? It is doubtful that we will spend much time explaining the transmission of eye color or why some people go bald. Yet, the joining of chromosomes does affect our work because the process does not always go well. We now turn to some problems that are chromosomal in origin.

Chromosomal Abnormalities

Many chromosome abnormalities exist, though some are more common than others. Four well-known chromosomal abnormalities derive from a deviation on the 23rd chromosome pair. A brief introduction is listed in Table 4.1.

Genetically based abnormalities also result from the 22 autosomes that are similar in males and females. Down syndrome, also known as trisomy-21, is the most common autosomal abnormality. In this syndrome, a child inherits an extra 21st chromosome—meaning that three chromosomes are in place rather than two. Individuals with Down syndrome have lower levels of intellectual functioning, often in the mild to moderate range of mental retardation. Besides lower intellectual functioning, individuals with Down syndrome often have congenital problems with hearing, eyesight, and cardiovascular problems.

Assess your comprehension of Genetics by completing this quiz.

Table 4.1 Commonly Known Chromosomal Abnormalities

Chromosomal Abnormality	Rate	Sex/Genetic	Developmental Presentation	Treatment
Turner's syndrome	1 in 2,500	Female only; X only or XO. That is, one X chromosome is missing.	Sexual underdevelopment; mental retardation is likely. Small in stature with small fingers and toes; webbed neck and broad chest.	Hormone therapy in childhood and puberty.
Poly-X or "super female" syndrome	1 in 1,000	Female only; XXX or XXXX.	Possible menstrual irregularities; possible increased risk of learning problems; generally few problems.	None, unless learning problems arise.
Klinefelter's syndrome	1 in 750	Male only; XXY or XXXY.	Males have secondary sex characteristics (e.g., breasts, larger hips) and may be taller than usual. Underdeveloped testes and they are sterile. Possible lower intellectual functioning.	Hormone therapies are often used. If emotional or educational problems arise, counseling and education can be provided.
Super male syndrome	1 in 1,000	Male only; XYY or XYYY.	Appear taller than most males; often lack coordination. Increased risk for learning disabilities, acne, and infertility.	No special treatment required except if emotional or behavioral problems arise from learning or emotional difficulties.
Fragile X syndrome	More common in males than females.	Abnormality in X chromosome.	Mental retardation, attention difficulties, speech problems; physical characteristics such as large, protruding ears, flat feet.	Speech therapy; special education interventions.
Down syndrome	Risk increases as age of mother increases; 1 in 1,900 births at age 20; 1 in 30 births at age 45.	Extra 21st chromosome.	Mental retardation, learning difficulties, physical complications (hearing, sight, ability to reproduce), and unique facial features.	Depending on level of cognitive ability, supportive, employment training, independent living.

Source: Adapted from Ashford, LeCroy, & Lortie (2006); Santrock (2008); and Shaffer & Kipp (2009).

Clinical Corner

Imagine you are a social worker employed at a community mental health center. The school refers a 16-year-old boy because of his aggressiveness toward his peers and frequent temper tantrums. You learn that the adolescent is developmentally delayed in all areas; in fact, he has always done poorly in school. In reviewing his history, you read that he underwent intelligence testing at eight years of age. The results showed that he was at borderline intellectual functioning with a score of 76. He especially struggled with language tasks. Shortly after intelligence testing, he was placed in a class for emotionally disturbed children. He is further described as withdrawn and impulsive.

Being a thoughtful and compassionate social worker, you try to imagine what life has been like for this boy and his family. You know you'll never *really* know what it's been like, but you imagine anyway. Imagine how frustrated and tired his mother has been at different points, loving her son so much, and knowing something was "different" about him from early on—but never receiving any concrete answers. She has coped with his sometimes poor behaviors and parented him to the best of her knowledge. Imagine what life has been like for the boy. He has most likely received bullying from his peers because of his developmental deficiencies and behaviors. As a result, he's never had any friends, hates school, feels like a failure because of his slow progress, and always gets into trouble at home.

Now, how would you proceed? Would you immediately go through the *Diagnostic and Statistical Manual of Mental Disorders (DSM)* and look for the best diagnostic fit? Surely, he would be a good candidate for oppositional defiant disorder or attention deficit/hyperactivity disorder (ADHD). How would you proceed in assessment? Then, you remember back to this day when you were basking in the glory of reading *Human Behavior in the Social Environment*. You think, "Hmm … there could be a biological component to what is going on here. I remember reading something about chromosomal abnormalities."

Based on your insight, you suggest that the boy be examined by his physician. The physician discovers that the boy, in addition to the earlier findings, is starting to develop breasts and has underdeveloped testicles. He referred the boy for further testing, and true to his suspicions, the boy came back with a diagnosis of Klinefelter's syndrome. Instead of having an XY sex chromosome, he has an extra X chromosome. This diagnosis of the primary cause of the difficulties will lead to specific interventions such as the physician administering testosterone to assist in normal male physical development.

This example is loosely taken from a case study done by Mandoki and Sumner (1991). It describes some of the things a boy might experience in having Klinefelter's syndrome. Mandoki and Sumner encourage a multidisciplinary approach to treatment of Klinefelter's syndrome. Just think how differently this boy's life might have been had he been diagnosed and treated earlier in life.

Social Work and Genetics

Human behavior is clearly influenced by genetic and chromosomal forces. How can a typical social worker use this knowledge about genetics and transmission of genetic traits in a practical manner? We admit it is rather difficult to directly apply this type of knowledge in most social work settings. Mitosis and meiosis unfold quite naturally, with no need for social work intervention. So, why present the information at all? After all, once a genetic abnormality is present, there is no way to reverse course—technology does not permit professionals to splice out the genetic abnormality.

Nevertheless, several reasons make knowledge of genetic abnormalities important. First, knowledge of genetic transmission definitely proves that the human condition is influenced by factors outside our direct control. At the genotype level, we cannot control if our skin is lighter or darker, or if we are likely to go bald. Knowing that much of the human experience is influenced by factors outside of our direct control should give social workers a deep respect that some of the "problems" we confront are not the fault of our clients. That is, compassion and respect are warranted rather than a condescending or judgmental perspective.

A second reason to know about genetic abnormalities is that such awareness can promote good practice. In your career, you may well work with individuals who have special needs and challenges that are driven by genetics. One of the authors, for example, worked with parents in a state's Child Protective Services (CPS) who refused to allow their child to receive legally mandated screening for phenylketonuria (PKU; American Academy of Pediatrics, 2001). PKU is a disease caused by an autosomal recessive genetic trait characterized by the lack of a liver enzyme that breaks down an amino acid, phenylalanine, found in foods containing protein such as meat, cow's milk, and baby formula. PKU can be treated by eliminating phenylalanine through dietary restrictions. If such dietary restrictions are not followed, the presence of phenylalanine leads to irreversible brain damage—functional mental retardation. While only 1 in every 17,000 live births is expected to have PKU, if it goes undetected, the consequences are significant. Our role as CPS workers was to help the parents understand the risks associated with not testing their child and helping them decide whether or not to follow state law. Even though we eventually referred them to a registered nurse and physician to discuss the details, our basic knowledge about PKU allowed us to more effectively consult with the family—who eventually pursued testing.

A third reason that awareness of genetic-related issues is important is that the advice we give does matter. At the time we were writing this section, an interesting situation was happening in Minnesota as reported by the Associated Press (2009). A woman reportedly refused to accept conventional medical treatment for her 13-year-old son who suffers from Hodgkin's lymphoma—a highly curable form of cancer when treated with chemo and radiation therapies. The woman reportedly found information on the Internet suggesting a treatment that included vitamins, ionized water, and herbal supplements. Rather than accepting standard treatment, she fled with her son to avoid court orders to receive the medical care advised by physicians. While we do not wish to begin an argument about different positions on Western medicine, religion, existential questions, or parents' rights, we can learn from this story that people do take information seriously—even sketchy information found on the Internet. Among those who have Hodgkin's lymphoma, survival rates are reported to be above 90% for patients who receive chemo and radiation therapies (Stein & Morgan, 2003), whereas there is little or no research on rates for those relying on vitamins, herbs, and ionized water. Social workers should be careful to about giving advice and about the advice they give.

PREGNANCY

We now turn to pregnancy as it relates to social work. (Well, this certainly is an interesting position: two male authors writing on pregnancy). What do social workers need to know about pregnancy? To begin, pregnancy is many things. Pregnancy is a biological event: the joining of two cells that ultimately divide and replicate to produce a human. For the woman, pregnancy brings about dramatic changes in how her body functions: the temporary suspension of menses, nausea, spreading of the hips, and weight gain. For the child to be, pregnancy is the time of development from a single cell organism to a life form with billions of cells. Pregnancy is a social event because, in many cases, the expectant mother and her family share in decisions and emotions about the pregnancy. Further, society has expectations surrounding pregnancy. In many cultures, pregnancy is a time for giving gifts, talking about delivery, and discussing future plans. Pregnancy is a legal event because certain laws govern when and how conception should occur and when and how a pregnancy may end. A 30-year-old man cannot, for example, legally impregnate a female under the age of 16 in the United States. For many people, pregnancy is a spiritual or religious event that gives a sense of meaning and purpose in life. Pregnancy is also a very personal event that influences a parent's emotions, self-esteem, and life plans. Of course, pregnancy can be a stressful event because it represents massive change on the part of the expectant parents.

Pregnancy clearly influences the human condition and it is likely that social workers will work with individuals who are pregnant, wanting to become pregnant, or wanting to end a pregnancy. Pregnancy carries certain risks and social workers are often called upon to mitigate these risks for both the woman and the fetus. Let's now explore some basic physiological facts about pregnancy, after which we will discuss areas where social workers may intervene in relation to pregnancy.

Biological Facts of Pregnancy

Pregnancy lasts approximately 266 days (Santrock, 2011). Pregnancy begins at the time of conception, which occurs when a sperm cell unites with a female's egg (ovum) within the female's fallopian tube. Statistically speaking, most conceptions occur through sexual intercourse with the male depositing sperm into the female's reproductive tract. This process includes several steps: (1) ovulation—a woman must release an egg from one of her ovaries; (2) next, the unfertilized egg must travel through the woman's fallopian tube toward the uterus; (3) fertilization—the man's sperm must be released within the woman's reproductive tract and unite with the egg within the fallopian tube; (4) implantation—the fertilized egg must attach to the inside of the uterus wall. It is estimated that one in seven couples struggle with infertility (Bhattacharya et al., 2008), and many single women and lesbian couples utilize artificial insemination methods to conceive, which differ from the process just mentioned.

Smoking, obesity, drug use, body weight, medications, exposure to environmental toxins, and many other somewhat controllable factors are linked to infertility (see Fact Sheet on infertility mentioned earlier for more information and proposed interventions). How might a social worker use knowledge about the causes and interventions associated with infertility? First, there is hope that couples who want to conceive can succeed. Second, knowledge that conceiving can be difficult, even leading to clinical depression, may lead you to feel empathy and compassion for those in this situation. Third, it would be wise to make referrals to appropriately trained professionals if you are working with individuals struggling to conceive.

Did You Know?

Infertility is an emotional issue affecting women, men, and family members. When efforts to conceive a child fail, many people seek medical advice. Investigations into the causes of infertility include semen analysis, tubal patency tests, and ovulation assessment (Bhattacharya et al., 2008). It is estimated that 10% of women have difficulty conceiving for reasons that can be attributed to biological and behavioral factors in women and men (see Fact Sheet on infertility developed by the Office of Women's Health, http://www.womenshealth.gov/publications/our-publications/fact-sheet/infertility.pdf, retrieved on October 6, 2013).

Prenatal Care

Social work can play an important role in promoting healthy pregnancy through supporting prenatal care. Prenatal care interventions are designed to promote the health and well-being of the woman and fetus during pregnancy and prior to birth. Though evidence clearly indicates that prenatal care reduces some pregnancy-associated risks, perhaps 20% of mothers receive late or no prenatal care (Friedman, Heneghan, & Rosenthal, 2009; Taylor, Alexander, & Hepworth, 2005). Children of women who receive prenatal care enjoy better outcomes on all infant health indicators compared to children of mothers who do not (Taylor et al., 2005). As an example, a preterm child was born to roughly 10% of mothers who received preterm care and to 27% of mothers who did not receive such care.

To show the richness of the human experience, think about how age influences denial of pregnancy. Would you expect younger or older women to deny pregnancy more often? In a sample of 61 women who did not seek prenatal care because they denied being pregnant, 23% were younger than 18 years of age, 59% were between 18 and 29, and 18% were older than 30 (Friedman et al., 2009). These statistics reveal that denial of pregnancy is not just an "age thing" or a function of education. The majority of those denying pregnancy were between 18 and 30 years of age and "should" have had sufficient knowledge about pregnancy to not deny it. Why do you think a woman may deny a pregnancy? Some mothers in this study simply did not recognize the typical signs of pregnancy, others suffered from some form of mental illness such as schizophrenia, and others confused pregnancy symptoms with side effects from other medical interventions (e.g., chemotherapy). Why do you think a woman would try to conceal or hide a pregnancy? Of those who tried to hide a pregnancy, roughly 50% were younger than 18 years of age. This statistic seems intuitive. Pregnant teenagers may fear judgment from friends, family, and possible rejection from important systems such as school or church. Others reported fear that they would be pressured to give the child up for adoption or to terminate the pregnancy. Note that a full 50% of the women who concealed a pregnancy were over 18 years of age—many were older than 30, were married, and had other children. Why do you suppose someone in this situation would conceal a pregnancy? Some of these women reported concerns that they would be judged for having too many children or were concerned that their spouse or partner would not approve. Variance in the reasons mothers denied or attempted to conceal a pregnancy is evidence that the human experience cannot be reduced to a single type and that social workers should be curious about what motivates people rather than making assumptions or accepting stereotypes.

Sociodemographic variables also are linked to seeking prenatal care. In a study of over 125,000 mothers giving birth to a single child, six clusters of variables predicted not securing prenatal care (Taylor et al., 2005). The predictors were unmarried, young age, low education, being foreign born, and living in an urban location. The highest risk group was young, unmarried Black women. The study's authors suggested that interventions should be tailored to groups least likely to benefit from existing programs, targeting public health messages to high-risk groups, and providing outreach and educational campaigns to support high-risk women.

Pregnancy and Mental Illness

Certainly many women enjoy pregnancy. They look forward to expanding their family, feeling the baby move, and planning for their new little one. From a strengths-based position, social workers can appreciate the excitement and joy associated with pregnancy. Eighty to 90% of pregnant women do not struggle with

Did You Know?

Women not seeking prenatal care on their own are frequently referred to social workers for an evaluation. In a study examining patterns of seeking prenatal care in an urban medical center, Friedman et al. (2009) found that 92% of the women who did not seek prenatal care were referred for a social work evaluation. Various factors predict whether a particular mother will seek prenatal care. Friedman et al. (2009) found that of the women who did not receive prenatal care, 30% struggled with substance abuse, 29% denied the pregnancy altogether, 18% cited financial barriers to care, 9% concealed the pregnancy, and 6% indicated no need for prenatal care.

Diversity in Practice

Practice Behavior Example: Understand the dimensions of diversity as the intersectionality of multiple factors including age, class, color, culture, disability, ethnicity, gender, gender identity and expression, immigration status, political ideology, race, religion, sex, and sexual orientation.

Critical Thinking Question: Using pregnancy as an example, what are some of the intersecting influences on the human experience?

elevated depression symptoms (Marcus, 2009). Said differently, a minority of pregnant women suffer from depressive symptoms despite rapidly fluctuating hormone levels, shifts in a woman's body, social and personal changes, and environmental changes that accompany pregnancy. While social workers certainly should celebrate the tendency for health during this stage, we are often called upon to help those who struggle.

Depression during pregnancy has significance for both the mother and the child to be. Pregnant women who suffer from depression are more likely to have poor nutrition during pregnancy, fail to gain adequate weight, not utilize prenatal care, and use alcohol or illicit drugs (Talge, Neal, & Glover, 2007). Importantly, pregnant women struggling with depression may also experience more stigma than is common for depression. Society expects pregnant women to experience "pregnancy bliss," yet pregnant and depressed women feel anything but bliss including sadness, a sense of worthlessness, self-doubt, and a loss of pleasure. Many women underreport depression symptoms during pregnancy because of stigma that can interfere with receiving helpful interventions. Another reason depression is often missed during pregnancy is because many of the physical symptoms of depression, such as poor sleep quality or a sense of tiredness or problems with weight gain, are common in pregnancy (Marcus, 2009).

Before discussing how social workers can work with pregnant women who may be struggling with depression, stress, and/or anxiety, we must recognize that children are also affected. Maternal reports of depression and stress during pregnancy are associated with early delivery, lower birth weight, smaller head circumference, lower scores on measure of infant health (e.g., APGAR, Brazelton, or Bayley scales), poorer cognitive functioning, and a more difficult temperament (Talge et al., 2007). One study found that scores on depression and anxiety inventories during a woman's third trimester of pregnancy accounted for about 25% of the variance associated with an infant's negative emotions and motor activity that in turn are linked to shyness and anxiety disorders in later childhood (see Talge et al., 2007). Other possible links between maternal depression and problems for children include ADHD and conduct-related problems. Of course, depression and stress during pregnancy do not determine untoward outcomes in children—they only increase the risk. This risk is important, however. Raising children is both a beautiful and a stressful time of life. Parents have remarked that raising young children is the springtime of life full of wonder, joy, and renewal. It is also difficult and, like spring, has its storms.

Did You Know?

Stress During Pregnancy Can Have Long-Lasting Consequences

Interestingly, toddlers of mothers who were pregnant during the Quebec 1988 Ice Storm, which resulted in lost electricity and water for up to five weeks, displayed lowered language development scores. Further, infants born in New York City shortly after the September 11, 2001, World Trade Center attacks were twice as likely to have birth weights below the 10th percentile (Talge et al., 2007). These findings show how stress during pregnancy can affect both the quality of the pregnancy and the child's first few years of life.

Imagine being depressed and trying to raise a child with a difficult temperament. Research suggests that the combination of maternal mental health problems and a difficult child increase the potential for child abuse or neglect (Flaherty, 2006; Jaudes & Diamond, 1985). Women with depressive symptoms tend to have infants who sleep less and enjoy lower quality sleep than infants of nondepressed women. Infants who do not receive enough higher quality sleep are less content and, therefore, place more demand on already stressed parents.

How might depression, anxiety, or stress during pregnancy connect to childhood functioning directly after birth and years down the road? These questions are still being investigated, though it seems that some of the hormone changes linked to depression (e.g., adrenocorticotropic hormone and cortisol levels; Marcus, 2009; Talge et al., 2007) are passed on to the fetus in the uterus. Also, certain regions of the developing human's brain may be more susceptible to neonatal insults. For example, healthy development of the hippocampus (connected to memory functioning) may be particularly susceptible to neonatal insults. Low birth weight may also predict long-term functioning with studies showing links to adult cardiovascular disease and metabolic disorders such as diabetes (Talge et al., 2007).

How Can Social Workers Respond?

Clearly, depression, stress, and anxiety during pregnancy influence the woman and fetus in a negative manner. Social work takes interest in such problems. What can be done? One strategy is to effectively screen for depression in pregnant mothers. A variety of screening measures such as the Center for Epidemiologic Studies Depression Scale (CES-D), the Edinburgh Postnatal Depression Scale (EPDS), the Beck Depression Inventory (BDI), and the Structured Clinical Interview for Depression (SCID) exist (Marcus, 2009). It is also important to advocate screening for depression among pregnant women. Campaigns to make health care providers aware of the reasons to screen for depression among pregnant women can help. Further, social workers might engage in training health care providers to recognize the specific symptoms of depression and stress overload in pregnant women.

One social work research project focused on prenatal attachment to understand which factors strengthen pregnant adolescents' ability to form healthy attachments once their children were born (Feldman, 2007). Pregnant adolescents are at risk of having both mental health struggles and poor pregnancy outcomes. Feldman cites the importance of five factors that can be influenced to help adolescent mothers improve their attachment with their infants both before and after birth: (1) social support expectations, (2) lowered stress levels, (3) improved self-esteem, (4) gestational age, and (5) planning the pregnancy. What implications might this knowledge have on social work practice? Social workers can design interventions to enhance social support and lessen a sense of social isolation, manage or limit stress, improve self-esteem, and educate pregnant adolescents about prenatal and postnatal development.

Teenage Pregnancy: Risks to Mom

The Centers for Disease Control and Prevention (CDC) estimates that approximately 370,000 adolescent-aged females in the United States gave birth in 2010—a 64% decrease from 1957 but still the highest rate in the industrialized world despite similar sexual activity (Hamilton & Ventura, 2012). What might account for these differences across countries?

Within the United States, rates of adolescent pregnancy differ significantly by geographic region as can be seen in Figure 4.2. Within the 50 states, the birth rate per 1,000 adolescents between 15 and 19 years of age ranges from a low of 15.7 in New Hampshire to a high of 55.5 in Mississippi. This difference approaches an increase of 400%. Why might such differences exist? What is the social work implication?

As mentioned, the birth rate among adolescents has decreased dramatically over the past 50 years. The National Campaign to Prevent Teen and Unplanned Pregnancy fact sheets report a 33% decrease in the teen birth rate between 1991 and 2002, translating into 1.2 million fewer children born to teen mothers. Had the rate not gone down, another 460,000 children would be at risk for living in poverty and a full 700,000 would likely live in single-mother households. The chances that a child born to a teen mother will grow up in poverty is 64% if the mother was unmarried at the time of birth and did not receive a high school diploma (see http://www.thenationalcampaign.org/why-it-matters/pdf/introduction.pdf, retrieved on April 29, 2013). Another way of

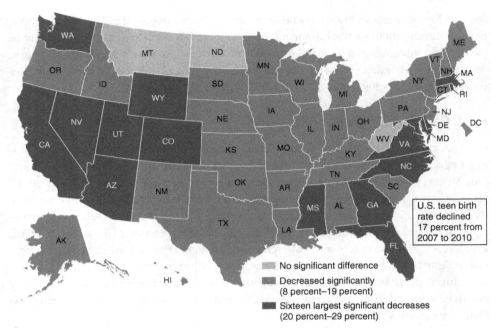

Figure 4.2
Birth Rates Among U.S. Teens Over Past 70 Years
Source: Hamilton & Ventura (2012).

saying this is that if a child is born to a parent with these three risk factors (teen, no high school diploma, and unmarried), the child is 900% more likely to grow up in poverty compared to children without these risk factors. The risk of growing up in poverty decreases to 42% if only two of the three variables are present and to 27% if only one of the three variables is present (see also http://www.childtrendsdatabank.org/?q=node/312, retrieved on April 29, 2013).

Poverty is a cruel risk factor negatively impacting families across generations. Children born to teen mothers are 300% more likely than their counterparts to become teen mothers themselves. If the cycle of poverty is not bad enough, the National Campaign to Prevent Teen and Unplanned Pregnancy suggests that children born to teen mothers are more likely to be born prematurely, with low birth weight, and are 200% more likely to suffer neglect or abuse (Hoffman, 2006).

Clearly, social workers are interested in preventing poverty, which makes preventing adolescent childbearing a target for social work interventions. Moreover, the estimated annual public cost of adolescent childbearing is $9 billion (Hoffman, 2006). The need for interventions with adolescent populations in the foster care system is especially great because these vulnerable adolescents are more likely to become pregnant, to drop out of school, and to have substance abuse problems. One research group (Kerr, Leve, & Chamberlain, 2009) found that nearly 50% of girls in the foster care system reported a pregnancy by 19 years of age, compared to only 20% of their counterparts. This increased rate of pregnancy is likely associated with adverse advents in childhood. That is, adolescents who experience problems such as academic failure, delinquency, poor family support, economic challenges, abuse, and/or substance abuse are more likely to engage in risky sexual behavior that often leads to pregnancy. The same risk factors that increase the likelihood of engaging in risky adolescent sexual practices are likely to interfere with these women's ability to take care of themselves and their children.

Interventions to reduce teenage pregnancy

Kerr and colleagues (2009) examined an intervention, Multidimensional Treatment Foster Care (MTFC; Chamberlain, 2003), designed to reduce pregnancy rates in adolescent girls in foster care. MTFC is designed to work with adolescents in the juvenile justice system, foster care, or adolescents with multiple mental health problems. The MTFC goals are to decrease problem behavior and increase adolescent's ability to succeed in normative arenas (e.g., school, work, and independent living). These goals are accomplished through focusing on the multiple settings where adolescents in out-of-home care settings typically interact, such as school, home, and mental health centers. Interventions include supervision, development of fair and consistent limits and associated consequences, reduced exposure to peers with problems, and attempts at engineering a supportive relationship with a mentoring adult. Kerr et al. (2009) evaluated the effectiveness of MTFC through two randomized control trials, the gold standard of research designs, and found that 26.9% of adolescents who received MTFC reported pregnancy compared to 46.9% among their counterparts who received standard group care.

Interventions other than MTFC exist. Leah Robin and colleagues (2004) review other behavioral interventions designed to reduce risky sexual behavior and pregnancy. The interventions ranged in their population of focus: community groups, YMCA attendees, and so on. Some names of the programs that were judged to be successful were Be Proud, Be Responsible; Making Proud Choices: A Safer-Sex Approach; Focus on Kids; Reach for Health; Reducing the Risk; Safer Choices; and the Teen Outreach Project. These programs focused on areas such as motivation to engage in safe-sex practices, providing information, the Health Belief Model, social factors of importance to teens, cognitive strategies to deal with decision-making, and others.

Of interest, Robin et al. (2004) noted that several of the programs had null effects, meaning they offered no measureable benefit. The names of some of these programs were Working on the Right Direction; Facts and Feelings; and SNAPP. The review authors also found that some programs, such as the Postponing Sexual Involvement and Teen Talk, consistently had negative effects—that is, program participants tended to do worse than those in the comparison groups. Stated differently, these programs seemed to do more harm than good. Evidence of mixed results supports the importance of being thoughtful and evidence based in how we practice. Despite being well intended, our interventions can do more harm than good—and the stakes are high.

Pregnancy: What Is Good for the Fetus

So far, most of the focus has been on pregnancy in relation to the woman who carries and bears the child. We will now turn to some biological issues for the fetus. At conception, the fetus (actually a zygote) is made up of two cells, and upon birth, the child has billions of cells (including the neurons). One can safely state that pregnancy is a time of remarkable change for the fetus. Pregnancy is often divided into three stages: the first, second, and third trimesters. Fetal development is also often divided into three periods: germinal (lasting two weeks), embryonic (between two weeks and about two months), and fetal (from month two until birth).

Physiologists, physicians, and developmental psychologists are among the professions that investigate the specific biological processes unfolding during development. These professions have amassed a rich and interesting knowledge base, yet, much of this

Research-Based Practice

Practice Behavior Example: Use research evidence to inform practice.

Critical Thinking Question: What implications can be drawn from the fact that some programs designed to reduce teenage pregnancy do not work?

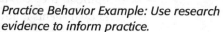

information is not directly useful for most social workers. For example, social workers will rarely, if ever, apply knowledge that an embryo's endoderm ultimately develops into the respiratory and digestive systems. However, some knowledge on the biological development from sex cell to zygote to blastocyst to embryo to fetus to child does relate to social work.

An example is spina bifida, which results when the neural tube fails to fully close within the first month after conception resulting in some degree of lower limb paralysis (Santrock, 2011). The paralysis often requires assistive devices such as wheelchairs, crutches, and/or braces. Researchers have found that adequate amounts of *B vitamin folic acid* can prevent spina bifida—highlighting the need for prenatal care, education, and dedication of resources. Thus, social workers can encourage adequate consumption of B vitamin folic acid.

As with spina bifida, other influences on the developing fetus can be impacted. While you may not routinely work with pregnant women or suggest they take vitamin B, social work routinely works with other situations known to adversely affect developing fetuses. When an infant is born with physical problems, it is termed a *congenital malformation* or *defect*. Wendy Chung (2004), a physician at Columbia University, indicates that the causes of congenital malformations are roughly distributed in the following manner:

- 20 to 25% genetic factors
- 3% from intrauterine infections
- 4% due to maternal metabolic disorders
- 4% from environmental chemicals
- <1% from drugs and medication
- 1 to 2 % from ionizing radiation
- 65 to 75% multifactorial or unknown

Notice that the most common causes of genetic defects either are unknown or involve multiple factors not easily teased apart. We will now consider three influences that threaten normal fetal development over which social work can have some influence: (1) environmental/chemical teratogens, (2) domestic violence, and (3) malnutrition.

Environmental/chemical teratogens

Teratogens are agents that cause physical or mental defects in a developing embryo or fetus and include nicotine, lead, mercury, alcohol, lithium, pollution, and prescription drugs. Teratogen agents are most damaging when embryos are experiencing rapid differentiation, which is during the earliest months of pregnancy. When the structures of an embryo's organs, limbs, and brain are making massive changes, they are more susceptible to a teratogen. At the same time, the introduction of a teratogen prior to the zygote's implantation can easily result in a spontaneous miscarriage. Figure 4.3 shows that teratogens have a different impact at different stages of fetal development.

Even though teratogen agents are most damaging during early embryonic development, they can damage a fetus throughout pregnancy. A review of these commonly known agents follows.

Nicotine

Women who smoke increase the risk of giving birth to an underweight and premature baby. Further, the risk of spontaneous abortion is approximately 1.7 times higher than for nonsmoking women (Chung, 2004; Ratey, 2002). Ratey (2002) cites research indicating the incidence of mental retardation is roughly 50% higher among women who smoke

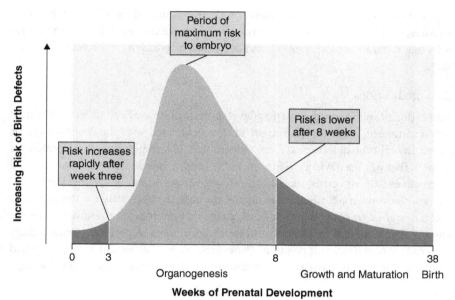

Figure 4.3
Effects of Teratogens on Fetus at Various Time Points
Source: Pearson Education.

during pregnancy. Nicotine reduces blood flow to the embryo, which decreases the supply of oxygen and nutrients that may adversely affect mental development. Research also suggests that women who smoked during pregnancy are more likely to lose a child to sudden infant death syndrome (SIDS) than those who did not smoke. Ratey (2002) notes that research is still tentative in this area, though it is thought that nicotine interferes with how neurons connect, prune, and migrate during development and nicotine may deregulate the dopamine system.

Alcohol

Normal embryonic and fetal development is severely compromised by alcohol. Even moderate alcohol consumption (two to three ounces of hard liquor) can cause problems, such as prenatal and postnatal growth deficiency, mental retardation, and other malformations such as fetal alcohol syndrome (FAS). FAS is associated with lower IQ scores, learning disabilities in reading and math, and problematic behaviors such as hyperactivity, acting out, and depression. While treatments exist for individuals with FAS, many of the effects (including growth deficiency and lowered IQ scores) are permanent, which argues the need for prevention rather than corrective efforts. Alcohol consumption is most damaging during the first six weeks of pregnancy, when many pregnant women do not realize they are pregnant (Ratey, 2002).

Cocaine

Beliefs about the effects of prenatal exposure to cocaine have changed over time. During the 1980s, reports in the media suggested that society would be fully unprepared to deal with the wave of children and adults whose mothers had used cocaine during pregnancy (Lewis et al., 2009). Popular press stories suggested that cocaine would interfere with the central or core nature of being human and that infants would neither bond to caretakers nor respect social mores. Researchers have since concluded that cocaine-related deficits are not as severe as once thought. Indeed, alcohol is believed to be more toxic to embryos than cocaine. Cocaine exposure is associated with prematurity, low birth weight, poor APGAR scores, difficulties in maintaining arousal and emotional regulation, some cognitive deficits that last into early childhood, and decreased responsivity to caretakers (Lewis et al., 2009).

Prescribed medications

Many medications can disrupt the normal development of an embryo or fetus. Retinoic acid, used in some oral medications to treat acne, is associated with the development of a cleft palate, neural tube defects, and facial deformities. The tranquilizer thalidomide is a hypnotic agent that was used widely in Europe in 1959 and caused a syndrome that included limb abnormalities (legs and arms) such that limbs were either absent or severely shortened. Thalidomide also caused malformations in organs, the ears, the heart, and the urinary tract. Medications designed to control convulsions, such as phenytoin, can retard embryonic growth and promote mental retardation and facial deformities. A pregnant woman diagnosed with cancer is in a difficult position. Cancer treatments, especially before the third trimester, can interfere with normal cell differentiation and thus impact a fetal functioning.

Disease

A mother who contracts congenital rubella or German measles is more likely to have a child who has seeing and hearing difficulties, with an increased risk for heart defects. Interestingly, the timing of the rubella matters. Maternal rubella during the first four to five weeks of pregnancy is associated with poor vision (cataracts), while exposure in the second and third trimesters is associated with hearing loss and mental retardation (Chung, 2004).

Environmental toxins

Consistent with the person-in-environment approach, social workers are aware that environmental factors can influence an embryo or fetus. At the "mild" end, owning a cat may become a teratogen to an embryo. Cats can spread a parasite, known as toxoplasmosis, through their feces. Cats can become infected with toxoplasmosis by eating infected mice, birds, or other small animals. The parasite can be passed to humans through exposure to the cat's feces—such as changing the litter box. An embryo exposed to the parasite can develop serious symptoms in later life, such as mental disabilities, serious eye problems, and blindness. The CDC (http://www.cdc.gov/print.do?url=http%3A//www.cdc.gov/toxoplasmosis/pregnant.html, retrieved on July 21, 2012) suggests that medications are available if a woman is infected with such a parasite. However, the clear recommendation is to prevent the transmission of the parasite by avoiding cat litter when pregnant, changing the litter box daily because the toxoplasma parasite does not become infectious until one to five days after it is shed in a cat's feces, feeding your cat commercial food, keeping your cat indoors to prevent it from eating infected animals, not getting a new cat during pregnancy, and wearing gloves when gardening because the soil may be infected.

Why would this topic arise in a social work text? Because many social workers, especially child welfare workers, interact with families in their homes and commonly find several that range from untidy to disastrously messy. In fact, a family can be referred to protective services if their house is not neat enough and if people are routinely exposed to animal feces. Social workers may be one of the few professionals who see the home environment of a pregnant woman and, therefore, may have an opportunity to prevent the spread of this parasite.

On a macro level, children are likely to suffer from our "fossil-fuel addiction" (Perera, 2008). An environmental health scientist, Frederica P. Perera, notes that the by-products of fossil-fuel consumption and production place both the fetus and children at risk. She notes that the public health burden is significant and rising. Rates of childhood asthma, cancer, learning disabilities, and other problems have increased over time. Asthma, for example, may be on the rise because pollutants find their way to the fetus in uterus, leading to increased respiratory problems throughout the life span. Further, Perera (2008) notes that these problems are exacerbated by poverty and states:

> Poverty and racism compound the susceptibility of the fetus and child. Poor children, especially those in urban areas and developing countries, are most at risk, because the effects of toxic exposures are magnified by inadequate nutrition and psychosocial stress due to poverty or racism.

Social workers are frequently called upon to work with pregnant women, many of whom use substances, such as nicotine, alcohol, or illegal drugs, that could negatively affect the embryo. Because a teratogen may affect a person across his or her life span, we often help pregnant women limit exposure to the toxin (Topley, Windsor, & Williams, 2008).

Domestic Violence During Pregnancy

Another threat to the pregnant woman and fetus is domestic violence. Statistics from the CDC (http://www.cdc.gov/reproductivehealth/violence/IntimatePartnerViolence/sld011.htm, retrieved on October 19, 2012) suggest that between 4% and 8% of women report violence during pregnancy—making it more common than gestational diabetes, preeclampsia, and neural tube defects. While any woman may become the victim of domestic violence, the rates are highest when the pregnant woman is young (adolescent aged), lacking social support, smoking, using alcohol and drugs, and having an unplanned pregnancy. Within the United States, pregnant women are more likely to be murdered than to die from any other cause—with many pregnant homicide victims being killed by their intimate partners (Horon & Cheng, 2001).

The possible effects of domestic violence to the fetus are categorized into direct and indirect effects. Direct effects might include spontaneous abortion as a result of fetal injury. Indirect effects include increased stress, depression, and possible suicide attempts by the mother that expose the fetus/embryo to high levels of stress hormones. Further, to cope with the stress, some pregnant women use cigarettes, alcohol, or drugs—agents that negatively influence embryonic and fetal development.

While focusing on the effects of domestic violence on an embryo or fetus, another perspective needs to be considered. The Abortion Rights Coalition of Canada—in a position paper titled "Talking Points Against the Unborn Victims of Crime Act"—cautions that a singular focus on the fetus may, deliberately or inadvertently, lead to restricted rights for women. Concern is raised that focusing on the fetus' needs detracts focus from the woman. Further, the coalition expresses concern that if legislation is enacted recognizing a fetus as a person or protecting the fetus from domestic violence, women's ability to make health care and other choices is limited because the fetus' rights must be considered. The coalition notes that situations may arise where the fetus' and the woman's interests conflict. For example, a pregnant woman with cancer may elect to receive chemotherapy, yet a physician concerned with the impact of chemotherapy on the fetus may refuse treatment to the woman. Many of these issues of fetal health and rights play into the debate over abortion.

Engage, Assess, Intervene, Evaluate

Practice Behavior Example: Develop a mutually agreed-upon focus of work and desired outcomes.

Critical Thinking Question: How might social workers partner with both health care practitioners and clients to use RADAR to promote assessment of domestic violence during pregnancy?

Did You Know?

What can social workers do with regard to domestic violence and pregnancy? To start, we can engage in efforts that would improve effective screening. One of the authors recently worked with Rosa, a 30-year-old woman from Central America who was living in the United States. She had some college education, was successfully employed, and had a supportive family. The client appeared confident and capable in all regards. She sought counseling because her boyfriend "lost it" after learning of the pregnancy. The Caucasian boyfriend had serious misgivings about becoming a father and pressured the client to have an abortion. Rosa indicated that she was committed to having the baby, yet the stress between her boyfriend and her led to Rosa feeling depressed. At first glance, the author privately doubted that Rosa would be a victim of domestic violence because she appeared so capable and strong. When asked a simple question about whether she was being physically threatened or hurt, Rosa revealed that her boyfriend had done both. Knowing that domestic violence was occurring allowed for both a more complete understanding of Rosa's needs and the opportunity to make more helpful interventions.

Research suggests most pregnant women are not asked about domestic violence by health care providers because of time constraints, discomfort with the topic, and fear of offending the woman or partner. Other health care providers may feel powerless in the face of domestic violence by thinking, "What can I do if she says yes?" What do you think of these four barriers? How might you overcome the barriers? If you were an administrator, what training or policies could you implement to overcome these barriers?

The Massachusetts Medical Society is credited with devising an acronym to promote screening for domestic violence. The acronym is RADAR, which stands for:

- **R**outinely screen every patient
- **A**sk directly, kindly, without judgment
- **D**ocument your findings
- **A**ssess the patient's safety
- **R**eview options and provide referrals

What are your impressions of this acronym? How do you think clients would receive such questions? Would cultural variables influence *whether* you would screen? What cultural variables may influence *how* you would screen? What cultural variables may influence *how* the client would respond to such a screening?

Malnutrition During Pregnancy

Pregnant women's physical health impacts the fetus, the newborn, the child, and ultimately the adult (Budge, Stephenson, & Symonds, 2007). Pregnant women who are malnourished and anemic tend to deliver underweight babies because of intrauterine growth retardation (IUGR). Specifically, the fetus adapts to a nutritionally deprived environment in uterus by reducing its growth. IUGR is associated with increased mortality for the fetus, the child, and adults (Budge et al., 2007; Mahajan, Singh, Shah, Gupta, & Kochupillai, 2004). Infants born with IUGR are 500% to 1,000% more likely to die in their first year of life than infants with average gestational growth. Research has further revealed that IUGR is a significant risk factor for chronic degenerative cardiovascular disease, diabetes, and obesity throughout the life span (Budge et al., 2007; Mahajan et al., 2004).

Mahajan et al. (2004) explains this connection in the following manner, "Malnutrition which is due in part to an insufficient amount of iron, folic acid and dietary protein, leads to anemia, a condition that inhibits the ability of the blood to carry oxygen which decreases a person's immunity towards infectious diseases, causes fatigue, and hinders physical and mental productivity" (p. 198). Children's ability to learn is also associated with maternal malnutrition. To further complicate matters, women who are malnourished likely face other risk factors, such as poverty or mental illness (e.g., an eating disorder). Notice in Figure 4.4 from the World Health Organization the flow of problems that promote maternal malnutrition and eventual consequences to mothers and children (Black et al., 2008).

Assess your comprehension of Pregnancy by completing this quiz.

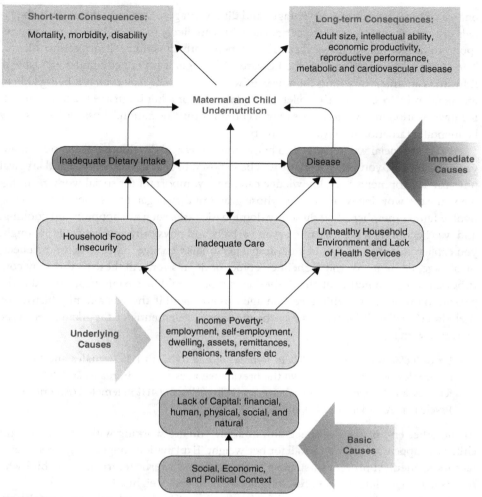

Figure 4.4
Malnutrition: Correlates and Causes

Source: World Health Organization. Retrieved from http://www.who.int/nutrition/topics/Lancetseries_Undernutrition1.pdf on July 26, 2012.

BIOLOGICAL INFLUENCES BEYOND PREGNANCY AND BIRTH

We have covered some of the biological factors that take place at the front end of life: from conception to birth. We now consider other biological factors influencing the human experience.

The physical body changes dramatically across the life span. In Greek mythology, the classic riddle the Sphinx at Thebes posed to travelers was, "What walks on four legs in the morning, two legs in the noon, and three legs at night?" The answer: man. At the beginning of life, man crawls on four limbs, during the middle of life man walks on two legs, and toward the end of life man uses a cane plus his two legs. This ancient riddle reveals a very basic understanding that the human life span can be divided into segments or phases.

Our life span is often divided into well-known categories such as infancy, childhood, adolescence, young adulthood, adulthood, middle age, senior, and old age. Labeling the phases of life offers certain advantages and disadvantages. One key advantage is the labels distinguish phases in which certain activities are likely to occur. How would you respond to the statement: Edward cannot independently dress himself or use the toilette? The answer depends in part on the Edward's life stage. It is perfectly understandable if Edward is an infant or young child or if Edward is very old. However, not being able to independently dress or use the toilet as an adolescent or adult is outside the norm, meriting investigation into what factors may account for this "deviation." Possible causes may be mental retardation or physical disability.

What do social workers need to know about physical development? In your undergraduate classes, you likely were or will be exposed to research on typical and atypical physical development. Such knowledge can be very important for social workers. Imagine you were working with a family whose grandmother began to lose her ability to recognize family members, had difficulty doing basic tasks such as shopping and cooking, and was becoming less pleasant or even verbally and physically aggressive. How might you explain this change? Could it be simple personality change, bereavement, the effects of old age, dementia of the Alzheimer's type, or depression? All these factors may contribute, though dementia of the Alzheimer's type should be strongly considered if the person in question is within a certain age category and if there is a family history of Alzheimer's. *DSM-IV-TR* reports that the incidence of dementia of the Alzheimer's type increases with age:

> From 0.6% in males and 0.8% in females at age 65 ... to 11% in males and 14% in females by age 85. At age 90 the prevalence rises to 21% in males and 25% in females, and by age 95 the prevalence is 36% in males and 41% in females. (American Psychiatric Association, 2000, p. 156)

At the other end of the age spectrum, imagine you are working with a preschool-age child who appears to be very small for her weight. Explanations might range from being factors to medical problems, such as *failure to thrive*, a term referring to a child who suffers from a feeding disorder resulting in failure to gain weight.

These examples show our need for knowledge of biological influences on the human experience and how physical development changes across time. Several professions and disciplines, such as medicine and developmental psychology, are primarily geared to understanding physical development across the life span.

Social workers who interact with young families often confront questions such as, "Is my child developing at the right pace?" and concerns such as, "I do not think my child is developing at the right pace." While we may ultimately refer such questions to a medical professional (e.g., a nurse or physician), it is good to know that information exists that can provide guidelines.

Gross Motor Skills

Table 4.2 shows some norms for gross motor skills development among infants and young children.

In reviewing Table 4.2, you get a sense of where a particular child may be relative to other children. Consider the skill of crawling. Only 50% of children crawl by seven months of age. If a parent of a seven-month-old expressed concern that her child is not crawling, she might be reassured that this is perfectly normal because only 50% of children of this age are crawling. On the other hand, a child not crawling by 9 or 10 months may begin to raise concern as less than 10% of children fail to crawl by this age. Delayed mastery of skills may signal a reason for concern and further investigation.

Table 4.2　Milestones for Developing Gross Motor Skills

Motor Skill	Range (in months) When Motor Skills Develop	Month When 50% Achieve Mastery	Month When 90% Achieve Mastery
Prone, lifts head while lying on stomach	2.0–4.0	2.2	3.2
Rolls over	2.0–5.0	2.8	4.7
Sits propped up		2.9	4.2
Sits without support	4.5–7.8	5.5	7.8
Stands holding on	4.9–10.0	5.8	10.0
Crawls		7.0	9.0
Walks with support (using others, furniture for support)	7.2–13.0	9.2	12.7
Stands alone momentarily		9.8	13.0
Walks well	11.0	12.1	14.3

Source: Adapted from Shaffer & Kipp (2009) and Santrock (2008).

Interestingly, cultural differences influence motor development. For example, African children (Santrock, 2011; Super, 1976) often reach motor skill milestones before children in the United States and other industrial countries. What might explain such variation is up for debate. Mothers in developing countries may stimulate their children more by stretching or massaging their children's limbs. By contrast, infants in the Algonquin culture in Quebec, Canada, are often strapped to a cradle board for much of their infancy—yet they develop motor milestones within a range similar to most children. These examples reveal that variation may be driven by culturally typical practices and most children eventually develop skills regardless of cultural practices.

Motor development across early life should be marked by increased skill and ability. At the age of three years, children run, jump, hop, and chase with relative ease and do so because it is fun. By age four, children will be more adept at climbing and scrambling over objects such as rocks and jungle gym obstacles. By age five, children's gross motor skills allow them to play sports such as soccer, kickball, and even golf and tennis. If you follow tennis, or even if you are remotely aware of tennis, you probably have seen video footage or pictures of Serena and Venus Williams hitting a tennis ball at an early age.

Unless a significant problem exists, children's gross motor skills will continue to develop through adolescence and into adulthood. At some point, however, motor skills begin to decline with age. At what age do you think adults begin to slow down? Research suggests that most of us reach our physical peak around 30 years of age (Schultz & Curnow, 1988). For most adults, this means that they will lose some gross motor coordination—though not all. Professional sports are replete with "older" athletes who compete with young rookies. For example, Dara Torres won three silver medals at the age of 41 years (see http://www.cnn.com/2009/HEALTH/07/16/athletes.comeback .endurance/index.html#cnnSTCText, retrieved on September 27, 2009).

Research clearly demonstrates that regular exercise and attention to physical functioning delay loss of motor skills while improving gross motor skill ability (Hindin & Zelinski, 2012; Stolee, Zaza, & Schuehlein, 2012). The adage "use it or lose it" applies. Older adults with regular exercise patterns enjoy greater physical and cognitive abilities than inactive older adults.

Fine Motor Skills

Gross motor skills include large muscle activity, whereas fine motor skills involve finger dexterity to do things such as write, type, tie a knot, or button one's shirt. As you might expect, the general pattern of development follows that of gross motor skills. Compared to young adults, infants' fine motor skills are significantly underdeveloped. For infants, fine motor skill milestones include the ability to grasp objects with their entire hand—known as the *Palmar grasp*. Later infants will pick up small objects through coordination of their thumb and index finger using the *pincer grip*. The Palmar grasp may allow a child to manipulate a bottle or a rattle, whereas the pincer grip can be used to help a child use a pencil or a spoon.

Across time children develop the ability to dress, tie their own shoes, button shirts, and pull up zippers. While many of us may take these skills for granted, they are liberating to parents because such skills allow children to get ready by themselves and, very importantly, go to the bathroom by themselves.

In middle age and later adulthood, fine motor skills may decrease making writing and dressing more difficult. Many adults compensate for declines by taking more time to do such activities or by developing other compensating behaviors. For example, rather than using a shirt with small buttons an older adult may use shirts with larger buttons or no buttons at all. Or, rather than using a pencil to write notes, an older adult may type or use a voice recorder.

Body Weight

Body weight also changes across the life span—with the most pronounced changes (hopefully) early in life. The CDC has published average body mass index (BMI) charts as a means of identifying whether a particular person is underweight or overweight. The BMI is a number calculated from an individual's height and weight and is a reliable indicator of body fat. In Table 4.3 and Figure 4.5 that follow, you will notice that the range for "normal" or healthy weight is considered to be between the 5th and 85th percentile. Individuals below the 5th percentile are considered to be underweight, whereas those between the 85th and 95th percentile are considered to be overweight. Obesity is defined as being equal or greater than the 95th percentile (see http://www.cdc.gov/healthyweight/assessing/bmi/childrens_BMI/about_childrens_BMI.html, retrieved on July 26, 2012).

Interpretation of BMI for Adults

For adults 20 years old and older, BMI is interpreted using standard weight status categories that are the same for all ages and for both men and women. For children and teens, on the other hand, the interpretation of BMI is both age and sex specific. The standard weight status categories associated with BMI ranges for adults are shown in Table 4.4.

Table 4.3   Classifying Weight: Too Little, Too Much

Weight Status Category	Percentile Range
Underweight	Less than the 5th percentile
Healthy weight	5th percentile to less than the 85th percentile
Overweight	85th to less than the 95th percentile

Source: Retrieved from http://www.cdc.gov/healthyweight/assessing/bmi/childrens_BMI/about_childrens_BMI.html on July 26, 2012.

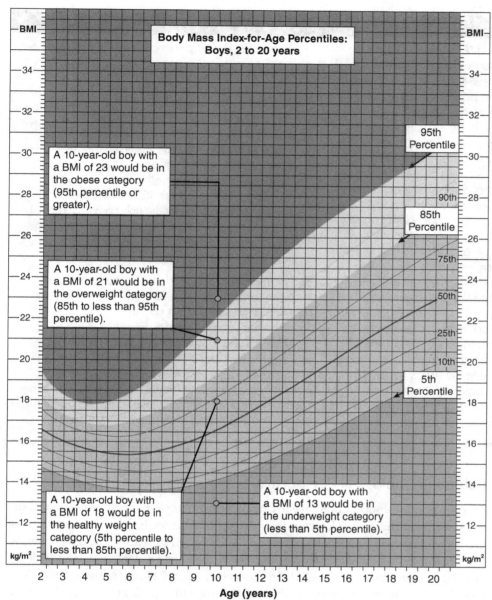

Figure 4.5
Expected Body Mass Index for Boys Ages 2 to 20
Source: Retrieved from http://www.cdc.gov/healthyweight/assessing/bmi/childrens_BMI/about_childrens_BMI.html on July 26, 2012.

Table 4.4   BMI for Adults

BMI	Weight Status
Below 18.5	Underweight
18.5–24.9	Normal
25.0–29.9	Overweight
30.0 and above	Obese

Source: Retrieved from http://www.cdc.gov/healthyweight/assessing/bmi/adult_bmi/index.html on October 19, 2012.

Did You Know?

In an interesting article titled "Eating Disorders and Obesity as Social Justice Issues: Implications for Research and Practice" Russell-Mayhew (2007) argues that the dual effect of health problems arising from obesity and its growing prevalence suggest a need for intervention at many levels. He also argues that obesity is often portrayed from a simplistic point of view—individuals are responsible for their weight, which neglects other forces such as advertising and policy influences. Further, the author notes that gross disparity exists: While the death rate is lowered in some countries because of excess (consequences of obesity causing death), the mortality rate in other countries is low because of want (lack of resources leading to death by starvation). Does such an irony have social work implications? Social justice efforts, the author argues, should both empower individuals and ensure equal opportunity to all.

How might social workers engage in issues of obesity or starvation at micro, mezzo, or macro levels?

Another interesting perspective on social work roles and obesities came from the Social Issues Research Center's website (http://www.sirc.org/articles/poverty_and_obesity.shtml, retrieved on September 29, 2009), which is based on England.

A local GP, Dr Gerry Spence, for example, comments:

"A lot of people are on benefits, living from week to week, relying on convenience foods and eating out of the chippy. Give people jobs and the ability to be masters of their own destinies and they will make healthy decisions about their lives. You bring employment into here and I guarantee the pubs will empty, the kids will stay at school and the place will flourish. You can't blame the people when they are victims of circumstances. It's not really a medical problem, it's something for the politicians to sort out. I hope the drop in life expectancy is a turning point and the politicians are called to account. They should hang their heads in shame."

Bob Holman, who quit academia to work on projects in socially deprived areas, is similarly unimpressed with current initiatives to combat obesity.

"This is not rocket science. Poor health is a well-known feature of deprivation. Mothers are not daft and they do know fat and crisps are bad for children but they can't afford the alternative. The Government has to give them the means. Initiatives are not going to change anything unless you've got the cash in your pocket. If you buy a salad at Sainsbury's, it's still very expensive."

Puberty: A Biological Perspective

Another primary contribution on early human experience is puberty, which marks the transition from child to adolescence (see Chapter 10 for more information). Around the time of adolescence, individuals go through both a significant growth spurt and puberty. The growth spurt is characterized by increases in height and weight, with boys typically growing between 28 and 31 cm and girls between 27.5 and 29 cm (Abbassi, 1998). Girls typically enter the growth spurt at about 10.5 years with a peak growth rate by age 12 (Pinyerd & Zipf, 2005). Boys lag behind girls by two to three years typically starting their growth spurt at age 13 and peaking at about 14 or 15 years.

After the growth spurt, the adolescent looks much more like an adult. Noticeable changes include the appearance of breasts and a widening of the hips in females and a broadening of the shoulders in boys (Shaffer & Kipp. 2009). Adolescents' facial features also resemble adults by changes in the nose and jaw and enlarging of the lips.

Puberty is the process by which individuals reach sexual maturation—meaning the reproductive system becomes functional. Puberty is driven by hormones controlled by the pituitary gland (Pinyerd & Zipf, 2005). What do social workers need to know about puberty? Social workers may interface with puberty on a number of levels. We may, for example, teach some of the basics of human development, such as the average age at which girls and boys enter puberty and the typical changes associated with its onset.

The physical changes associated with puberty for girls include breast development, beginning with "breast buds," the accumulation of fatty tissue around the nipple. Full breast development takes roughly three to four years and often finishes at about age 14

(Pinyerd & Zipf, 2005). The presence of pubic hair often develops after the breast buds—but not always. Later in puberty, girls experience increased hair growth on the arms, legs, and face (though to a lesser degree than males). In addition to these visible changes, internal changes occur (Shaffer & Kipp. 2009). Specifically, the sex organs mature. The vagina becomes larger and the uterus walls develop the muscles that can one day accommodate a fetus during pregnancy and push it through the birth canal during labor. At about age 12, in Western societies, girls often have their first menstruation or "menarche." Menstruation is the body's process of discharging blood from the uterus of non-pregnant women. The blood flows from the uterus through the vagina and typically occurs once a month from puberty throughout a woman's reproductive age.

The physical changes for boys include growth of body hair in the pubic area, under arms, and on the face. Further, hair growth becomes thicker on both the arms and legs. A boy's testes and scrotum also grow during this period, which is accompanied by changes in color and shape. During puberty, a boy's penis will grow in length and width until about age 14 (Pinyerd & Zipf, 2005). Ejaculation is the process by which semen is carried from the testes to the outside of the body through the penis. The semen carries sperm that, as was mentioned earlier, has the potential to fertilize a female's egg. Sperm production begins roughly at age 13 to 14, at which point a boy can father a child. Puberty also results in a change in a boy's vocal cords, resulting in a deeper voice.

This summary of some of the changes that accompany puberty is brief and basic. To fully and competently teach about puberty, a social worker would need additional training or research. In addition to knowing some of the basic physiological changes associated with puberty, social workers should be aware of the social implications arising from puberty.

MIDLIFE FROM A BIOLOGICAL PERSPECTIVE

Remember, Schultz and Curnow (1988) noted that most of us reach our physical peak at about 30 years of age. Of course, this does not mean that our bodies are in a constant state of decline. Even a brief search for physical fitness in the years beyond 30 will reveal that there is still plenty of "kick" in our bodies to work, play, and have sex. This is not to say that our bodies have unlimited energy. Gaining weight seems easier as we age, and losing it seems harder. Also, our bodies are not as forgiving when staying up all night to cram for a test or take care of a sick child. And, it takes longer for our bodies to heal from physical accidents.

One interesting article titled "Triple Whammy: Women's Perceptions of Midlife Mothering" (Morgan, Merrell, Rentschler, & Chadderton, 2012) notes that many women who have children near the age of 40 experience three relatively new events during the middle part of their biological clock: parenting, menopause, and a sense of being out of sync with their bodies. Further, many such women (and men) are asked to take care of their aging parents while trying to keep up with their own children—a dynamic known as the *sandwich generation* at a time when our own bodies are beginning to decline.

Menopause

At about age 45 to 55, women's bodies begin to change such that they can no longer conceive a child. These changes are caused by lower production levels of two hormones: estrogen and progesterone. Lower levels of these hormones result in the eventual stop of menstruation and the release of ovum (eggs). Once a woman has not had a period in approximately one year, she is considered to be in a "postmenopausal" stage though this does not mean without symptoms. While the body naturally moves into menopause, surgical procedures and some treatments for cancer remove the ovaries that cause a drop in estrogen, which then triggers menopause.

For many women, menopause is accompanied by unwanted symptoms that can last for up to 10 years with an average of about five years. Symptoms include hot flashes, racing heart, night sweats, disrupted sleeping, vaginal dryness, decreased interest and pleasure from sex, headaches, emotional struggles (depression, anxiety, irritability), aches and pains, and urine leakage. Understandably, relief from such symptoms is desired and biological, dietary, exercise, and other interventions have been explored. Controversy, however, exists on the efficacy of such interventions and concern that treatments such as hormonal therapies may cause more problems. Thus, a social worker helping an individual struggling with menopausal symptoms should strongly consider making a referral to a medical provider. (Information gathered from http://www.menopause.org.)

BIOLOGICAL FACTORS INFLUENCING LATE LIFE

Menopause is only one of several physical indicators that our bodies continue to change well into later life. Recall the riddle that the Sphinx at Thebes posed to travelers. As we approach the "night" of our life, physical functioning begins to deteriorate in a manner that can be both frustrating and embarrassing.

Watch the video Successful Aging: Thelma. What beliefs about aging does this video challenge? How does this video shape your ideas about successful aging?

Control over basic bodily functions and skills is often lost or minimized. The fine motor dexterity needed to zip a zipper, button one's pants, write checks, diminish with age, and ultimately become compromised. Gross motor skills and muscle mass also diminish with age, which can result in problems with doing tasks needed for independence such as walking, lifting, and doing household chores. Similarly, the ability to control one's bowels can be lost because of loss of control over muscles associated with automatic bodily functions. Further, many older adults experience diminished vision and hearing, which may jeopardize travel options, limit driving privileges, undermine communication, and reduce participation in meaningful hobbies or pursuits. While certainly not even across people, the gradual degradation of physical functioning is inevitable for all of us eventually ending in death. Further, as we age, the risk of contracting serious and frightening diseases, such as cancer, rises, which carries emotional, psychological, social, and existential issues.

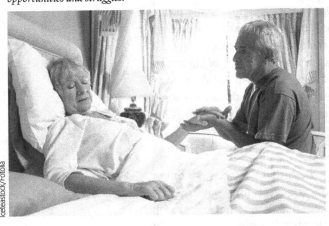
Aging brings both opportunities and struggles.

The decline of physical functioning has inspired a variety of human responses. Ancient Egyptians supplied their deceased with material resources to help them in the afterlife. Other people have sought to find a mythical elixir that would curb the aging process such as the fountain of youth. Modern super-popular story, Harry Potter, includes the "Philosopher's Stone," which produces the elixir of life to prevent death. And, a host of modern commercial products, procedures (read surgery), and "secrets" are available that claim to have "antiaging" properties. While some of the products designed to slow aging sound hokey, science is very much involved in looking at the "cellular" causes of aging and in identifying the processes of aging. In May 2013, a Google search with the term *antiaging* produced nearly 80 million results. Thus, we humans continue to think about aging and our mortality.

Aging brings both opportunities and struggles.

Social work is interested in human aging as evidenced by having a scientific journal focused on aging, *Journal of Gerontological Social Work* (Taylor & Francis), and both the National Association of Social Workers (NASW) and the Council on Social Work Education (CSWE) have major sections dedicated to social work and aging. The following are a few beginning links to such resources:

- NASW: http://www.naswdc.org/aging.asp
- CSWE: http://www.cswe.org/CentersInitiatives/GeroEdCenter.aspx/

LIFE EXPECTANCY

As we have mentioned, the body reaches its physical peak some time near the age of 30, and at some point, physical functioning declines. Of course, variability exists with regard to how long a person lives. A few years back, the oldest British veteran from World War I, Harry Patch, died at the age of 111. The story carried by the Associated Press on July 25, 2009, stated:

Patch had been the last surviving soldier from the British army to have served in the 1914-18 war. The only other surviving U.K.-based British veteran of the war, former airman Henry Allingham, died a week ago at age 113.

The Ministry of Defense called Patch "the last British survivor of the First World War," although 108-year-old Claude Choules of Australia is believed to have served in the Royal Navy during the conflict.

These brief accounts of Harry Patch, Henry Allingham, and Claude Choules suggest that the downside of the human body's physical peak in the thirties can be a rather long, enjoyable, and meaningful journey.

Life expectancy refers to the age one can expect to reach before dying. Interestingly, life expectancy varies greatly across country of origin. Examine Table 4.5 for a moment. You will notice a variety of countries listed with the life expectancy of males and females. In Afghanistan, the average male and female will only live up to 44 years of age. By contrast, the average male in Australia will live up to 79 years and the average female will live up to 84 years. The country with the lowest age expectancy is Sierra Leone where the life expectancy is just about half of what it is in countries such as Japan, China, France, and Italy. Countries within the African continent have very low life expectancy rates, which likely result from the long-standing political upheaval, war, and inability of governments to meet people's basic needs such as food, shelter, medical care, and protection. Also, the high infant mortality rate in Africa tends to suppress the overall life expectancy.

Notice that the life expectancy of U.S. citizens is 75 for males and 81 for females. However, these numbers do not tell the complete story of life expectancy in the United States, as is shown in Table 4.6. Within the United States, life expectancy is also related to race (Arias, 2011) such that Blacks do not live as long as Whites and males do not live as long as females.

To conclude this chapter, we include a list of the top causes of death in the United States. Among children between the ages of 10 and 18, the leading cause of death

Table 4.5   Life Expectancy by Country and Sex

Country	Male	Female
Afghanistan	44.0	44.4
Australia	79.16	84.02
Bahamas	62.5	69.0
Botswana	51.3	49.0
Chad	46.4	48.5
Chile	73.9	80.6
China	71.4	75.2
Cuba	75.0	79.6
European Union	74.0	80.8
France	77.7	84.2
Gaza Strip	71.6	74.8
Germany	76.1	82.3
Hong Kong	79.1	84.7
Israel	78.5	82.8
Japan	78.7	85.6
Lesotho (South Africa)	40.1	39.3
Macau (China)	81.4	87.5
Malawi (Africa)	43.8	43.2
Mozambique (Africa)	41.6	40.4
Pakistan	63.1	65.3
Russia	59.2	73.1
Rwanda (Africa)	48.6	51.0
San Mario (within Italy)	78.43	85.6
Sierra Leone (Africa)	38.6	43.3
United States of America	75.3	81.1

Source: Adapted from CIA website. Retrieved from https://www.cia.gov/library/publications
/the-world-factbook/rankorder/2102rank.html on June 10, 2013.

Table 4.6   Life Expectancy in the United States by Race and Sex

	Male	Female
Black	69.5	76.3
White	75.7	80.1

Source: Adapted from Arias (2011).

was unintentional injury (45%) and included motor vehicle and other accidents. Homicide was the third leading cause of death and accounted for about 14% of deaths. Suicide accounted for approximately 10% of deaths among children in this age group. Other causes, such as illness and disease, were grouped and accounted for approximately 30% of deaths among children (see National Center for Injury Prevention and Control, CDC, 2006).

Among adults, the top 10 causes of death in the United States in 2008 can be found in Table 4.7.

Assess your comprehension of Biological Development by completing this quiz.

Assess your analysis and evaluation of this chapter's contents by completing the Chapter Review.

Table 4.7   Top Causes of Death in the United States Among Adults

1. 25.4% Heart disease
2. 23.2% Malignant neoplasms (often cancer)
3. 5.6% Cerebrovascular diseases (e.g., stroke)
4. 5.3% Chronic lower respiratory diseases
5. 5.1% Accidents
6. 3.1% Alzheimer's disease
7. 2.9% Diabetes mellitus
8. 2.1% Influence and pneumonia
9. 1.9% Kidney problems (nephritis)
10. 1.4% Suicide

Source: Retrieved from http://www.cdc.gov/nchs/data/nvsr/nvsr60/nvsr60_06.pdf on July 26, 2012.

Kumar Sriskandan/Alamy

5

Biological Influences on Human Behavior

Central Nervous System

Optical illusions are both fun and revealing. Before reading further, search for some optical illusions on the Internet. For example, look for an optical illusion that shows a "face" and the word "liar" or an optical illusion that shows the face of both an older and a young woman.

Optical illusions reveal that it is possible to see two or more valid things from one image, which may give some clues to the human experience. In optical illusions, some people are more likely to initially see one image while others are more likely to see another image. Further, some people really struggle to see the "hidden" image once they see the dominant image. Why do we see different objects and why do people vary in what they see in the exact same picture? What mechanisms are responsible for this variation? And, what can we learn about the human condition and social work from this optical illusion?

Variation in how an optical illusion is viewed reveals that "interpretation" has occurred. Interpretation is the act of assigning meaning to data or an experience. How are interpretations produced? The simple answer is that the brain interprets data and makes inferences. While the next sentence may seem ridiculously obvious, an important point is made. Not all brains interpret data the same way. Cats, dogs, fish, and monkeys all possess brains but they probably do not see what people see in optical illusions. In this chapter, we review the brain and the context in which it functions. We will examine the human nervous system including the structure and function of the brain, neurotransmitters, and the autonomic nervous system. This chapter also examines brain disorders and how medications influence human functioning. Before getting into brain specifics, we review *information processing models*, which provide a method for understanding how data is interpreted and used such that social work interventions can be devised.

INFORMATION PROCESSING MODELS

Great interest exists in understanding how humans process information. Indeed, it is human's ability to process information at a high level that distinguishes us from other animals, such as fish, turtles, or monkeys. Ancient philosophers and modern scientists have questioned the nature of knowledge and how humans process it. We present a few of these models as an introduction to this chapter on the central nervous system. In general, two types of information processing models exist: (1) multi-store (staged information) and (2) connectivist (parallel) processing models.

Human's ability to process complex information differentiates us from other living organisms.

Multi-Store Information Processing

Multi-store models presume information processing involves several discrete mental actions that occur in a sequence. An example is depicted in Figure 5.1.

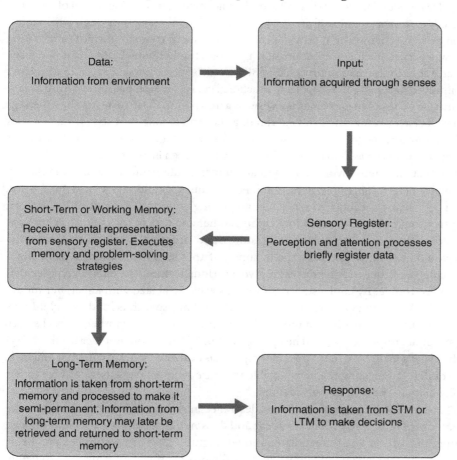

Figure 5.1
Information Processing Model
Source: Based on Atkinson & Shiffrin (1968).

Atkinson and Shiffrin (1968) proposed a model, whereby information is first perceived through the senses and moved to a sensory register. Information in the sensory register is believed to be stored very close to its original form—such that sounds are captured in a type of echo and images are stored visually. Information stays in the sensory register for a short amount of time—possibly less than 1 second. Next, some information is moved to a short-term memory or a working memory stage in which information is either lost to decay or rehearsed, which will move it to long-term memory. Information not rehearsed in short-term memory is believed to be active for about 15 to 30 seconds before it is lost. Long-term memories may stay with us indefinitely as there is no compelling evidence that such information is lost (Surprenant & Neath, 2009).

Several types of rehearsal can promote transfer of information from the working memory to long-term memory stage, such as verbal repetition that involves repeating a concept to solidify information. When learning to spell, young children are taught to say the letters over and over. On the way to the grocery story, adults may repeat a shopping list several times to remember. Rehearsal can also involve the visual system—a person may study an image to transfer it from short-term to long-term memory. In a similar manner, rehearsal can involve motor actions. When learning to spell words, children are asked to write the words over and over, as well as repeating the letters aloud, and looking at them.

Another stage-based information processing model was advanced by Crick and Dodge (1994) titled the "Social Information-Processing Model of Children's Social Adjustment." This model (Figure 5.2) is similar to the information processing model of memory advanced by Atkinson and Shiffrin (1968) in that it identifies stages through which information processes. However, it provides more on the social context in which information processing occurs, including emotions and a person's fund of knowledge and experience.

Early social information processing (SIP) models were simple and straightforward. They involved four steps: (1) recognizing situational cues—for example, a smile from a classmate may be a cue or bid for friendship, whereas a frown from a classmate may be a message that one's behavior is unwanted, (2) interpreting and representing the cues, (3) searching for possible responses, and (4) selecting a response (Crick & Dodge, 1994). A visual depiction of the early model may have looked something like what is seen in Figure 5.3.

The first two steps involve taking in and understanding information while the last two involve determining how to respond. For example, a child says a "naughty" word, such as _____ (just checking to see if you are paying attention) in front of his mother. In the first stage, the child would look at his mother and take in the cues from her face, eyes, mouth, body posture, hand/arm gestures, and language. In the second stage, the child would attempt to decipher the meaning of the data. If the mother has a slight smile, laughs a little, and then tries to give a serious lecture, the child may infer that he is not in trouble. By contrast, if the mother's eyes are ablaze with anger, her mouth is curled back, her finger waves back and forth, and her speech is loud, the child may interpret trouble. Depending on the child's interpretation of his mother, he will search for appropriate responses. Should he apologize? Run? Blame it on his older brother? Cry? Laugh? Make a joke? Next, each possible response is evaluated in terms of what will be in his best interest. Selecting the best possible response requires knowledge of his mother and his ability to respond to the situation.

This early model is simple and provides a nice introduction into how decisions are made. However, the early model is linear and does not include factors such as culture, emotion, or history. The reformulated model (Figure 5.2) is more complex and likely comes closer to understanding how people really process social information. To begin, the reformulated model includes six steps with arrows that go in both directions (e.g., nonlinear) and a database that interacts with each of the six stages. The database is a type of personal history that has been created from the child's past experiences.

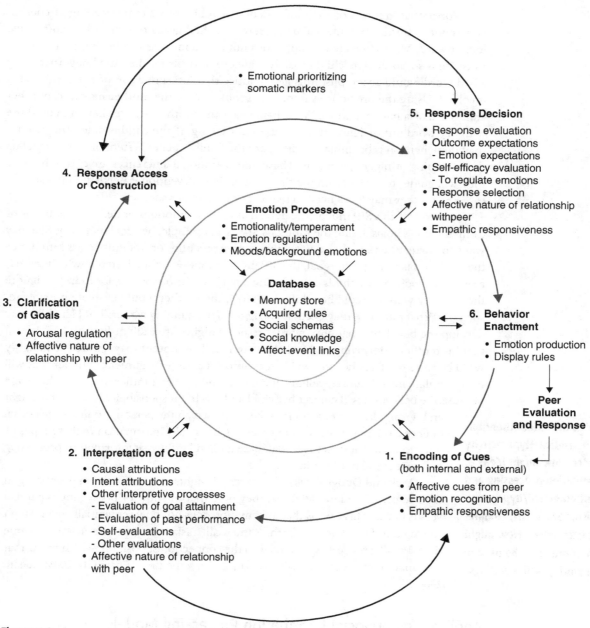

Figure 5.2
Crick and Dodge's (1994) Social Information Processing Model
Source: From Arsenio & Lemerise (2004).

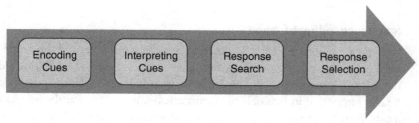

Figure 5.3
Early Social Information Processing Models
Source: Based on Crick & Dodge (1994).

Notice that in Step 1 of the model depicted in Figure 5.2 that encoding of cues involves both external and internal data. Here, the child needs to look at his mother *and* look inward. Maybe the child simply does not care about his mother's interaction because he is so upset. The child possibly wants to hurt his mother and knew that using a bad word would accomplish this goal. Notice that interpretation of meaning is very involved. Using the previous example, let's look at how the mother may interpret her child's use of a naughty word. What happens if the mother believes her child used the naughty word out of ignorance because he is young. If the child is older, the mother may think her son is beginning to disregard the family's belief system or rules, signaling the beginning of bigger problems. These interpretational differences are critical because they will guide future steps. In the first case, little intervention is needed. In the second case, the mother may feel a need to redirect or correct her son.

In Step 3 of this SIP model, the person attends to emotions or desires as a means of clarifying one's goals. Using the mother's SIP as an example, her goal may vary. She may want to correct her son, bond with him, embarrass him, or not embarrass him. Once the mother has clarified her goal, the SIP model proposes a fourth step in which there is a search for possible methods of achieving a goal. The mother may, for example, ignore the naughty word or scold her child. In Step 5, the mother would evaluate possible responses. What outcome may occur if she ignores the naughty expression? Her child may develop the belief that naughty words are not naughty after all, or he may be grateful that his mother is forgiving and feel closer to her. The mother may ignore the naughty word because she fears her son will launch into yet another argument with her that will likely escalate into shouting, yelling, and name-calling. The mother may scold her child because she believes it will correct her child and it is her responsibility to teach him right and wrong. In Step 6, action is taken after which the person monitors the consequences. Is ignoring or scolding meeting her goals? Information to these types of questions contributes to the database and will influence information processing in future social interactions.

Crick and Dodge (1994) offer several insights into information processing in their reformulated model. First, they note that the flow of processing is parallel versus linear. This means that information does not flow sequentially from Step 1 to Step 2 to Step 3 and so forth. Rather, all "tasks" or steps interact at the same time. Parallel processing is similar to the connectionist position, which posits that information processing activities occur at the same time (Eliasmith, 2005; Logan, 2000).

Watch the video Attention-Deficit/Hyperactivity Disorder. How might ideas of information processing and attention deficit/hyperactivity disorder (ADHD) complement each other? How might such information be used in social work practice settings?

Applications of Social Information Processing Models

Social workers may use the SIP model (see Figure 5.2) proposed by Crick and Dodge (1994) to guide decisions. The following is a few possibilities for social workers engaging in micro-level practice.

Step 1—encoding of cues

Influencing a person's ability to take in sensory cues is beyond the scope of most social workers. Other professions, however, are working in this area. Hearing aids and cochlear devices can improve people's ability to hear. Teaching sign language provides a means for hearing-impaired individuals to communicate. Eye glasses and contacts improve visual input. Further, biomedical engineers and scientists are developing methods for regenerating damaged sensory nerves, which may provide cures to sensory input deficits. For example, biomedical engineers have developed prostheses that hold promise for helping visually impaired individuals see by connecting a camera to the optic nerve (Li et al., 2008).

While social workers are not developing technologies to advance sensory input, we can appreciate the impact sensory deficits have on individuals. An example illustrates this point. One author (BL) worked with a 4-year-old male, Javier, who had been referred because he had been expelled from three preschools for misbehavior. Javier had difficulty understanding and producing speech because he had a partial hearing impairment, which was connected to his behavioral problems. He tried to join several play groups at the preschool; however, he did not fit in well because he had difficulty hearing and communicating. Javier made several "social errors" because he did not understand the rules by which the other children were playing. The other children became upset with Javier and asked him to leave. Further, the preschool teachers heard the complaints of the other children and assumed Javier had done something wrong, so they scolded him. This left Javier feeling sad and frustrated. Although his hearing impairment was not fully responsible for Javier's difficulties, it did play an important role because it compromised his ability to understand his peers and to effectively learn the social rules his peers had established.

Step 2—interpretation of cues

Social workers can positively intervene at the interpretation stage of information processing. Research has demonstrated that some children tend to perceive neutral social cues as hostile, which leads them to act aggressively. For example, a child may cross paths with another child who is laughing with his friends. Children with aggressive tendencies may perceive the laughing to be directed at them or as being a lack of respect and use aggression in retaliation. Such interpretations can be adjusted. Van Manen, Prins, and Emmelkamp (2004) used an 11-session treatment designed to help children with tendencies toward aggression soften their negative, hostile interpretations of other people's behavior. Compared to children in the no-intervention group, those who received the intervention increased in appropriate social behavior, self-control, and decreased aggressive behaviors.

Research has also demonstrated that adults' perceptions of child behavior are linked to parenting behaviors, including child abuse. When parents perceive their children to be compliant rather than disobedient, they are more likely to act with softer, child-centered parenting strategies (Dopke, Lundahl, Dunsterville, & Lovejoy, 2003). In an unpublished research conducted by the first author (BL), mothers who were at risk to abuse children were taught what constitutes child compliance and noncompliance. After learning about these definitions, participants were less likely to perceive compliant behavior as noncompliant.

Step 3—clarification of goals

People can change their goals and, therefore, influence the actions they take. Motivational interviewing has been shown to help people change goals around substance abuse patterns (see Lundahl & Burke, 2009; Lundahl, Kunz, Brownell, Tollefson, & Burke, 2010). Another study conducted by one of the authors (Lundahl, 2005) manipulated one of two qualitatively different parenting goals in mothers of young children. One parenting goal was child centered; the other parenting goal was to look good to an evaluation team. Specifically, one group of mothers was told that while interacting with their children they should focus on their children's well-being, whereas the other group of mothers was told that they would be evaluated and compared to other mothers. Mothers who were told they would be evaluated tended to act with less patience and more harshness toward their children compared to the mothers in the other group. In another study, re-searchers (MacLeod, Coates, & Hetherton, 2008) found that an intervention focused on goal setting increased their sense of well-being.

Step 4—response access

Successful interventions have been applied to Step 4 that involves identifying possible social responses. Individuals can be taught to consider more response options and to weigh responses in light of consequences (Crick & Dodge, 1994). Further, people can be taught new response skills to promote functioning such as stress manage-ment, assertiveness training, cognitive restructuring, emotional regulation, forgive-ness, relaxation, domestic violence prevention, parent training, relapse prevention, and many other interventions that are designed to improve people's repertoire of responses.

Step 5—response decision

Social workers often help people consider advantages and disadvantages of decisions they may take through cognitive therapy or problem-solving therapies. A meta-analysis of problem-solving therapy (Bell & D'Zurilla, 2009) revealed it to be as effective as other psychosocial therapies and more effective than no-treatment or supportive therapies. This therapy helped people make good decisions by teaching them to (1) define prob-lems, (2) develop alternative solutions to problems, (3) make clear decisions, and ulti-mately (4) implement solutions and observe outcomes.

Step 6—behavioral enactment

The last step in SIP models is implementing the selected response. Behavioral thera-pies are often applied to anxiety disorders, such as obsessive compulsive disorder (OCD). Many behavioral therapies encourage clients to take actions to overcome the anxiety such as confronting the situation or events that trigger anxiety. A person who obsesses about germs and compulsively washes her hands, for example, may be asked to handle objects she believes to have germs (e.g., a hotel remote control de-vice) without washing her hands. This technique is known as exposure and response prevention and has considerable research support (Rosa-Alcázar, Sánchez-Meca, Gómez-Conesa, & Marín-Martínez, 2008; Verdellen, van de Griendt, Hartmann, & Murphy, 2011).

Connection Models

In contrast to the stage-based models of information processing, connectionist per-spectives argue that the human brain processes information through the millions of neural networks in parallel (i.e., nonlinear) manner. That is, information and decision-making occur simultaneously. Research on how the brain actu-ally functions favors a connectionist approach over the linear, stage-based models (de Zubicaray, 2006; Foorman, 1994). For the purposes of social work, however, the stage-based mod-els may be superior because they delineate specific cognitive processes, such as interpretation or response formation, which can be the targets of interventions.

We now turn to the structure of the nervous system where information is actually processed.

Engage, Assess, Intervene, Evaluate

Practice Behavior Example: Assess client strengths and limitations.

Critical Thinking Question: How might the dif-ferent information processing models be used to assess a client's both strengths and limitations?

Theory to Practice

Information Processing as Strategic Macro Practice

Understanding SIP can also influence macro-level social work activities such as influencing policy makers. Consider the first step of the SIP model: encoding data. When policy makers are considering a social problem, they receive information (data) from constituents, family, colleagues, lobbyists, and so on. Social workers engaged in macro practice might consider how to best get the attention of lawmakers, so the latter will recognize and encode desired data. What are some methods to get the attention of policy makers amid a crowd of other voices? How might the social media grab the attention of decision-makers?

In addition to securing the attention of macro-level decision-makers, social workers might consider the second step of the SIP model: interpretation of the message. The idea is to stage messages in such a way that interpretation by policy makers will be consistent with what the social worker desires. How might this be done effectively?

CENTRAL NERVOUS SYSTEM

Our nervous system controls nearly all human activities, including emotions and basic bodily functions such as breathing, sleeping, and digestion. The nervous system also controls complex mental activities such as reasoning, practicing faith, memory formation, and making meaning out of experience.

Prior to discussing the specifics of our nervous system, we provide some examples of the many tasks our nervous system manages in everyday activities. Imagine two activities: running alongside Florida's beautiful ocean and shoveling Wisconsin's beautiful snow. The nervous system coordinates the following activities needed to run along the beach: gauges the length of your stride, determines the pace at which you run, prevents you from falling over, helps you avoid danger, monitors and controls body temperature, regulates energy output, and evaluates if you need to add or reduce clothing. At the same time, the nervous system takes in information about Florida's beautiful coastline and allows you to have a complex conversation about the meaning of life with a running companion. The same is true when shoveling Wisconsin's snow. The nervous system tells you whether the snow needs to be shoveled, helps you estimate the amount of time needed to shovel the snow, provides information about how warmly you should dress, and controls the actions needed to shovel the snow. Lastly, the nervous system of a Wisconsin snow-shoveling person may produce fantasies about moving to Florida where one could run on a snow-free beach.

Science has provided an explosion of knowledge about how our brains function.

Building Blocks of the Nervous System

Like the rest of the human body, the nervous system is made up of cells. Two main types of cells make up the nervous system: neuron (which transmit information) and glial (which support neuron cells). Glial cells keep neuron cells in place, supply oxygen and nutrients to the neurons, insulate the neurons from each other, facilitate the transmission of messages between neurons, and protect against pathogens. A well-known type of glial cell

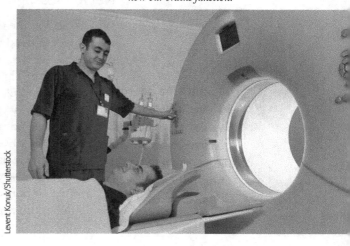

Levent Konuk/Shutterstock

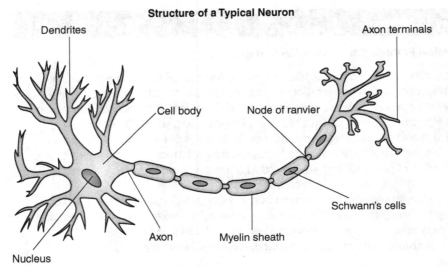

Figure 5.4
Basic Anatomy of a Nerve Cell
Source: Retrieved from http://training.seer.cancer.gov/anatomy/nervous/tissue.html on February 8, 2013.

makes up the *myelin sheath*, which speeds the transmission of signals between neurons (Kalat, 2009). Neurons are messenger cells and their work produces the human experience. That is, all that humans experience is a function of what happens between neural connections. To accomplish this remarkable function, neuron cells have four basic structures: dendrites, cell body, the axon, and synaptic terminals (see Figure 5.4).

Dendrites receive information from other neurons and ultimately transmit that message to the cell body. The *cell body* of a neuron is similar to other cells in that it contains a nucleus, mitochondria, and other functional units necessary for cell life. After a message is received in the dendrites and is transmitted to the cell body, a message maybe sent along the long shaft of the cell known as the *axon*. The message travels along the axon and is "communicated" to other cells through the *synaptic terminals*.

Three types of neurons exist: sensory, motor, and interneurons. Sensory neurons carry messages from the body to the nervous system. Motor neurons transmit messages from the nervous system to the body (e.g., muscles, glands). Interneurons are found only within the nervous system and communicate neuron to neuron.

Nerve Message

What exactly is the message that nerve cells communicate or transmit? The simple answer is an electrical charge that is converted to a chemical message that is then transformed back into an electrical charge that is then converted to a chemical message, and so forth. Thus, messages are a combination of electrical charges and chemical messages. Electrical charge? Yes, our brains are centers for electrical activity. You probably have heard of an EEG (electroencephalography) test. This test measures electrical activity from the scalp (Snyder & Nussbaum, 1999). Among other uses, the EEG is useful for diagnosing seizure disorders and sleep problems.

Where does the electric charge come from? Harkening back to basic biology and chemistry, you will remember that atoms have differing electrical properties. For our purpose, it is enough to know that electrical charges in the nervous system result primarily from the balance of sodium and potassium ions within and

Watch the video Brain Building. What ideas from this video might be applied to micro-level social work practice? What information from this video might be applied to social policy?

outside of a particular cell (Kalat, 2009). The electrical charge, also referred to as an *action potential*, travels down the axon to the synaptic terminals that then stimulates the release of *neurotransmitters* (a chemical) into the space between neurons, which is known as the *synaptic cleft*. If neurotransmitters are released from the synaptic terminals into the synaptic cleft, they may be picked up or temporarily bound to the dendrites of another neuron. What happens once a neurotransmitter binds to or is picked up by a receiving neuron? Neurotransmitters change the chemical nature of the cell membrane of the receiving neuron. By changing the cell membrane, we mean that neurotransmitters make the cell more or less open to the passing of sodium and potassium ions (and others), which subsequently influences the electrical charge within the cell. If the balance of positively and negatively charged ions reaches a certain threshold, an electric impulse (action potential) is released restarting the message transmission. If the threshold is not reached, the message is stopped. Thus, some neurotransmitters promote action potentials, others inhibit them.

The last paragraph is a very simple rendition of many very complex processes. Of these information, what sounds familiar to you? What information do you predict is most relevant to social work? Our strong guess is you have heard more about *neurotransmitters* and *synaptic cleft* and *binding* and *receptors* and considerably less about *sodium ions*, *potassium ions*, and *action potentials*.

> **Assess your comprehension of Central Nervous System by completing this quiz.**

Neurotransmitters

You are likely familiar with neurotransmitters because they are associated with mood, impulse control, decision-making, energy level, and many aspects of human functioning (Gatchel & Kishino, 2011; Kalat, 2009). Beyond being associated with aspects of human functioning, neurotransmitters and receptor sites can be influenced through human interventions such as drugs or electroconvulsive shock therapy. That is, targeting neurotransmitters and how they function influences how we function. Table 5.1 provides a partial list of well-known neurotransmitters and hormones.

Efforts to change behavior through changing neurotransmitters are big business. Consider how many pharmacological company advertisements you have seen within the last month. Advertisements for medications targeting depression, anxiety, sexual

Table 5.1   Common Neurotransmitters

Amines	Pituitary peptides
• Serotonin	• Growth hormone
• Dopamine	• Oxytocin
• Norepinephrine	
• Epinephrine	
• Acetylcholine	
Amino acids	Circulating hormones
• Gamma-aminobutyric acid	• Insulin
• Glycine	• Calcitonin
Opioid peptides	Gut hormones
• β-Endorphin	• Pancreatic polypeptide
	• Secretin

Source: Adapted from Stahl (1997, 2008).

functioning, sleep, and many others are commonly found on the Internet, radio, and television.

It is important to have a basic understanding of how messages are communicated between the millions of neurons that are bundled together and run throughout the body. Why? Because, at least in the direct practice realm, you will be confronted with questions about how psychotropic medications function. Further, some problems commonly targeted by social workers, such as ADHD and anxiety disorders, are linked to processes at the neural level. In the following box, we discuss the prevalence of medications targeting depression.

Theory to Practice

Are We Dependent on Antidepressants?

Medications that influence neurotransmitters are big business. Pratt, Brody, and Gu (2011) from the Centers for Disease Control and Prevention reported that antidepressants were the third most common prescription drug taken by Americans of all ages from 2005 through 2008 and the most frequently used by persons aged 18 to 44. From 1988–1994 through 2005–2008, the rate of antidepressant use in the United States among all ages increased nearly 400%. They further reported that 11% of the U.S. population over the age of 12 takes antidepressant medications.

The most commonly prescribed antidepressants are selective serotonin reuptake inhibitors (SSRIs). SSRIs take action when the presynaptic neuron releases its chemical message to the postsynaptic neuron through the synaptic cleft (the gap between the neurons). If neurotransmitters remain in the synaptic cleft for too long (because the postsynaptic neuron does not receive it and, thus, does not start an action potential), the presynaptic neuron essentially "gobbles up" the neurotransmitter and the message is never relayed properly. Individuals with depression are thought to have problems with neurons receiving chemical messages from serotonin. SSRIs are thought to inhibit this "gobbling" (aka reuptake) of the presynaptic neuron, so the serotonin stays in the synaptic cleft for longer and allows more time for the postsynaptic neuron to receive the message and for a successful transmission to occur.

While many practitioners, researchers, and consumers have hailed antidepressants as a godsend for depressed persons, their efficacy is hotly debated. Researchers have no consensus on if or how well antidepressants actually work. For instance, Kirsch et al. (2008) conducted a meta-analysis on all clinical trials submitted to the U.S. Food and Drug Administration (FDA) for licensing on four antidepressants. They found virtually no differences between placebo and treatment group outcomes for individuals with mild to moderate depression. Positive outcomes for severely depressed persons taking antidepressants versus placebo were relatively small—and these effects were due to not an increased effectiveness of the medications but a decreased effect in the placebo. This study is controversial and significant in the sense that these authors drew from the actual data used by the FDA to approve the four drugs. The authors conclude that new generation antidepressants should be used for mild to moderately depressed individuals only after alternative options have been tried. On the other hand, Arroll et al. (2005) and Liu et al. (2011) also conducted a meta-analysis comparing SSRIs and tricyclic antidepressants to placebo in primary care settings. They conclude that both types of antidepressants are effective and show more positive outcomes than placebo. Further, Marks, Abramowitz, and Spielmans (2012) contest research suggesting antidepressants do not work. Thus, the jury is still out.

Are You Unknowingly on Antidepressants?

Some of you who are reading this book are currently on a psychotropic medication of some kind without realizing it. Associated Press writers Donn, Mendoza, and Pritchard (2008) recently reported that pharmaceuticals, including drugs used to treat mental illness, are finding their way into many Americans' drinking water. They posit that this includes at least 41 million Americans. Just how do these particulates of medication get into the water? Some of it likely gets in through people dumping old pills down the toilet. On the sketchier side, when individuals take medication some of it is absorbed in the body but some is excreted and then flushed down the toilet. Ultimately, humans recycle their own waste water—though treatment facilities do not necessarily filter out all of the remaining pharmaceutical particulates (we sincerely hope you can block these ideas out of your mind). Experts are now trying to decipher what types of consequences these drugs might have on the general population. By the time persons consume water containing another person's pharmaceutical particulates (after it has been treated), the amount of drug residue remaining in the water is miniscule at most and nowhere near a prescription dosage. Still, some are concerned about what kind of long-term effects drinking others' drugs might have.

How neurotransmitters function

Under the direction of mRNA, a structure within the cell body of neuron cells, neurotransmitters are manufactured by enzymes. Once manufactured, neurotransmitters target receptors on the receiving dendrite that are specific to it. That is, for a message to be transmitted across neurons, the neurotransmitters being released must be picked up by a certain receptor. One might think of this like a key and a lock. The neurotransmitter is the key and the receptor site is the lock; a match will promote the message, whereas a mismatch does not transmit the message. Scientists have capitalized on this knowledge by developing medications that either increase or decrease receptor site sensitivity or increase or decrease neurotransmitter availability. If medications that alter the availability of neurotransmitters and/or the sensitivity of receptors influence a person's emotions and cognitions, it stands to reason that neurotransmitters and their receptors are important contributors to psychological and emotional well-being. Stahl (1997) states, "If a drug with a well-understood mechanism of action on a receptor or enzyme causes reproducible effects upon the symptoms of a patient with a brain disorder, it is likely that the symptom is also linked to the same receptor or enzyme that the drug is targeting" (p. 73). Why is this important? We can learn which neurotransmitters or receptors are linked to certain mental and emotional processes by observing how medications work. Given that most antidepressants block the reuptake of norepinephrine or serotonin, they are strongly implicated in the presence of depression.

MEDICATIONS INFLUENCING THE HUMAN CONDITION

Although controversy over the use of medications to treat concerns of living exists, they are routinely used and successfully treat problems frequently targeted by social workers such as anxiety, depression, psychoses, and behavioral problems. Thus, it is good to have a basic understanding of medications typically used to address psychological, emotional, and behavioral difficulties. Let's look at three common examples where medications targeting the nervous system are used to influence the human condition: depression, psychoses, and anxiety (see Stahl, 1997, 2008).

Assess your comprehension of Psychotropic Medications by completing this quiz.

Medications and Depression

If you watch television, listen to radio, or read magazines, we confidently predict you have seen or heard advertisements for medications targeting depression. When we ask our students if they know someone who is taking medications for depression, nearly all reply "yes." In U.S. culture, there seems to be a high degree of comfort for taking medications to treat feelings of sadness, discouragement, and depression. As a social worker, you will likely be asked about your opinion regarding the use of antidepressants. Questions may range from how antidepressants work, what can be expected from taking antidepressants, and whether you recommend taking them. Most of these questions should be directed to medical professionals licensed to dispense medications such as physicians and certain types of nurses.

How do antidepressants work? The simple answer is that they increase the supply or potency of neurotransmitters such as serotonin and norepinephrine. Exactly how increased levels of serotonin and norepinephrine influence people's subjective sense of self, mood, and energy levels is not well understood. However, several hypotheses have emerged. One was that situational stressors or environmental insults (e.g., loss of a loved one, changes in living situations, trauma, drugs/alcohol) depleted monoamine neurotransmitters, which then led to depressive symptoms. This hypothesis arose from observations that medications which functioned to increase neurotransmitters decreased depressive symptoms.

At this point in time, several classes of antidepressants exist: tricyclics, SSRIs, monoamine oxidase inhibitors (MAOIs), and nontraditional antidepressants. Each class of medication serves to increase the availability of serotonin or norepinephrine through different mechanisms. SSRIs block the update and subsequent demise of serotonin, thereby allowing them to continue to function. MAOIs inhibit the activities of monoamine oxidase that eliminate neurotransmitters. The different classes of antidepressants are not equal, as evidenced by differing levels of effectiveness and side-effect profiles. Thus, as social workers, we strongly recommend that patients receive care and explanation from professionals trained in medical fields.

Medications and Psychoses

Social workers often work with individuals who suffer from psychosis because such mental difficulties often lead to difficulty maintaining employment and relationships, which in turn can promote the likelihood of poverty and homelessness. Commonly known disorders involving psychoses include schizophrenia, delusional disorders, brief psychotic disorders, and schizophreniform (*DSM-IV*). At the core of these disorders are hallucinations or delusions. Hallucinations can include perceptual distortions such as hearing voices, seeing images, and (less frequently) experiencing smells or tastes that are not physically present. Some hallucinations involve feeling sensations such as having a spider walking on one's arm. Delusions are defined as firmly fixed false beliefs. They may drive paranoia such as beliefs that the government or others are spying on or interfering with a person's life. They can also include beliefs that one is inhabited by demons, worms, or other odd ideas such as a God-like figure. Psychoses can involve severe disturbances in motor functioning, such as going into a rigid posture, inappropriate grins, talking to oneself, mumbling, muttering, and other behaviors that suggest a person is interacting with another person when no one is present.

Many people with schizophrenia cannot orient themselves to time (month, date, day of the week, night/day), place (location within a country, state, region), situation (on the street, in a hospital), or person (name of self or others) in part because of delusions or hallucinations. Lastly, psychosis can take on the form of "negative symptoms" that include symptoms such as low to no motivation, a dulling of emotions and thinking, lack of pleasure, and extreme passivity.

The specific biological basis of psychoses is not known, though dopamine is strongly implicated. Basically, higher levels of dopamine are linked to "positive symptoms" of psychoses such as hallucinations, paranoia, and agitation. By contrast, "negative psychotic symptoms"—such as dulled emotions and amotivation—are associated with lower levels of dopamine. Stahl (1997) states, "For more than 20 years, it has been observed that diseases or drugs that increase dopamine will enhance or produce positive psychotic symptoms, whereas drugs that decrease dopamine will decrease or stop positive symptoms" (p. 254). Further evidence for the role dopamine plays in psychotic symptoms comes from how people act when on certain drugs. Stahl suggests that "stimulant drugs such as amphetamine and cocaine release dopamine and, if given repetitively, can cause a paranoid psychosis virtually indistinguishable from schizophrenia.... All known antipsychotic drugs capable of treating positive psychotic symptoms are blockers of dopamine receptors, particularly D2 dopamine receptors" (p. 254).

Neurotransmitters, then, are linked to schizophrenia and explain this disorder better than theories that attributed the causes of schizophrenia to unhealthy or undesirable mothering practices (recall Chapter 1). How do antipsychotic medications work? All antipsychotic medications basically work to lower the effect of dopamine by blocking postsynaptic dopamine receptors.

Without doubt, antipsychotic medications can dramatically improve people's ability to function through managing hallucinations and delusions. However, antipsychotic medications frequently have a rather heavy side-effect profile such as sedation, constipation, dry eyes and mouth, blurred vision, memory problems, and confusion. Other side effects include dizziness, muscle spasms, and "pseudoparkinsonism" that include symptoms associated with Parkinson's disease. Specifically, antipsychotic medications can produce drooling, a shuffling gait, facial muscle problems, and muscle rigidity. Individuals taking antipsychotic medications are also at risk for "akathisia" that includes an internal sense of agitation or restlessness and outward symptoms of fidgeting with one's hands, tapping one's feet, and shifting weight when standing or rocking back and forth.

Another well-known side effect from antipsychotic medications is Tardive dyskinesia that involves abnormal movements of the mouth, tongue, and jaw (e.g., smacking one's lips, pronounced blinking, rolling of tongue) along with abnormal movements of the legs and arms (e.g., knee tapping, purposeless movements, tremors) and trunk (e.g., rocking, twisting one's hips). Certainly, the side-effect profile from antipsychotic medications can be impressive. Would you trade the benefits of managing hallucinations for the untoward side effects? Many patients have difficulty staying on these medications because the side effects are so severe. Fortunately, some side effects can be managed with other medications and some classes of antipsychotics have less-severe side-effect profiles.

Medications and Anxiety Disorders

Have you ever noticed that certain foods, such as mashed potatoes and gravy, have a calming effect? We may eat copious amounts of ice cream or chocolate after having a bad day. And, after eating a turkey dinner, we may want to take a nap. What is the point of this obvious connection between mood and what we eat? Food can either calm or excite us. In the morning, many of us reach for coffee to supply us with increased brain activity. How does the consumption of food regulate mood? Well, mostly at the neurotransmitter level. Let's consider the sleepiness that we may feel after eating a turkey dinner. Part of the reason we may feel sleepy after eating turkey is that turkey contains relatively high amounts of tryptophan, which is an amino acid that increases the level of serotonin and melatonin in the brain—both of which increase a sense of tiredness (Wurtman, Hefti, & Melamed, 1980).

While all can relate to how food can either calm or excite us, certain people struggle with intense feelings of anxiety that can cripple their ability to function in a normal manner. Individuals with OCD, for example, often spend several hours a day engaging in anxiety-related behavior. People with phobias will avoid activities such as flying in planes, traveling to certain areas, or working because of an unrealistic fear. A client of one of the authors struggled with a spider phobia, which became devastating when her company changed to an older building where many spiders resided. She avoided going to work, which, understandably, resulted in poor performance reviews, lowered income, and embarrassment.

Human Behavior

Practice Behavior Example: Critique and apply knowledge to understand person and environment.

Critical Thinking Question: Social workers are often asked about the role of medications to promote the human experience. What are some potential risks and rewards of using medications to treat "problems in living" versus mental illness?

Assess your comprehension of Mental Illness and the Central Nervous System by completing this quiz.

Neurotransmitters contribute to feelings of anxiety and relaxation. This realization came in part from observations that benzodiazepines, such as Valium and Xanax, reduced many symptoms of anxiety. Three neurotransmitters are primarily implicated in the biological basis of anxiety: GABA (benzodiazepine receptor complex), serotonin, and norepinephrine (Stahl, 1997, 2008).

How do antianxiety medications work? Benzodiazepines facilitate GABA's ability to bind to its receptor site that enhances the effects of this neurotransmitter. Increased effectives of GABA results in reduced anxiety, muscle relaxation, reductions in seizure activities, and increased sedation (Kalueff & Nutt, 2007). Interestingly, the opposite effect is suspected with serotonin; enhanced levels of serotonin are associated with increased anxiety. This finding is interesting because increased levels of serotonin are associated with decreased levels of depression. Thus, an oversimplified explanation is that anxiety may involve serotonin excess, whereas depression involves serotonin deficiency (Stahl, 1997, 2008). The oversimplification of this statement is supported by emerging evidence that medications that increase the presence of serotonin can reduce symptoms of OCD, which is in the anxiety disorder family. Medications targeting anxiety are typically grouped into two classes: anxiolytics and sedatives. Anxiolytics reduce anxiety and sedatives induce sedation or sleepiness.

BRAIN STRUCTURE AND FUNCTION

To this point, we have looked at the primary functional building block of the nervous system, neurons and neurotransmitters, and how medications may influence human well-being. We now turn to the major functioning systems within the central nervous system.

Structure of the Nervous System

The nervous system has two main divisions: (1) the central nervous system (CNS) and (2) the peripheral nervous system (PNS). The CNS consists of the brain and spinal cord, whereas the PNS consists of the nerves that go to and from the CNS. Table 5.2 provides an organizational outline of the nervous system.

Table 5.2 Structural Organization of the Nervous System

Nervous system

    A. Central nervous system

      1. Spinal cord

      2. Brain

        a. Cerebrum

          1. Cerebral cortex

          2. Subcortical brain areas

        b. Cerebellum

        c. Brain stem

    B. Peripheral nervous system

      1. Somatic nervous system

      2. Autonomic nervous system

        a. Sympathetic nervous system

        b. Parasympathetic nervous system

Source: Adapted from Baars & Gage (2010); Carlson (2009); Stahl (2008); Strominger, Demarest, & Laemle (2012).

Central Nervous System

The CNS is awe inspiring. It is estimated that there are approximately 1 trillion points of communication from the 100 billion neurons each of which may communicate directly with 2,000 other neurons (see Lent, Azevedo, Andrade-Moraes, & Pinto, 2012). These neurons and neural connections are primarily responsible for processing information. Kindness, appreciation, hate, revenge, decision-making, creativity, depression, happiness, and all other human actions and experiences are directly linked to the CNS. Given its crucial role in human functioning, what do social workers need to know about the CNS? The answer clearly depends on your role in social work.

If you work in a medical setting serving individuals with brain injury or spinal cord damage, you may need more intimate knowledge of the CNS. If you are advocating policy on the effects of lead or other toxins on infants developing brain, you will need to have some specific knowledge of the brain. If you work with individuals who are addicted to alcohol or drugs, an understanding of their effects on the CNS is also important. Further, if you work with clients who have learning disabilities, mental retardation, depression, ADHD, and a host of other mental health challenges, you will be able to better serve them if you have some knowledge of the CNS.

While knowledge of the CNS is helpful in many areas of social work, research on the structure and function of the CNS primarily comes from allied professions with whom social workers often collaborate such as neuropsychologists, physiologists, physicians, speech and language professionals, nurses, and neuroscientists. One implication of our profession not dedicating resources to the study of the CNS is that we do not have deep technical expertise in this area. Specific questions about CNS functioning are likely to be directed to the allied professions previously mentioned. Thus, in this text, we will not go into the vast amount of knowledge on the CNS. We do, however, introduce you to some of the basic functioning elements of the CNS and introduce issues that you may face as a practicing social worker.

Our nervous system is a communication machine. It sends and receives messages throughout the body. Within the nervous system are several divisions, the first is between the CNS and the PNS. The CNS includes the brain and the spinal cord (see Figure 5.5). Think of these two as central because they are the "hub" of communication.

The spinal cord is a set of nerves that run from the lower brain to roughly the tail bone region. Most of the nerves within the spinal cord are protected by the backbone. Spinal cord nerves are continuous with the brain and serve as an integration center where messages are sent and received from the brain to the entire body. For the most part, the spinal cord is simply a relay pathway for messages between the body and the brain. The exception is that some nerves within the spinal cord act without the brain's influence—these nerves make up our reflexes that do not require the brain to function.

Considering that the spinal cord is continuous with the brain and the relay center for the brain, it stands to reason that injuries to the spinal cord are serious. The impact of spinal cord injuries is partly influenced by the injury location. In general, injuries to the upper spinal cord region are more severe. Injuries in the cervical region often result in paralysis to the arms and legs or quadriplegia with injuries above C-4 region requires a ventilator for the person to breathe. Injuries in the thoracic region typically affect the legs and the chest. Injuries to the lumbar nerves often result in functioning loss in the legs and hips. Injuries to the nerves in the spinal cord are not equal. Severe injuries can result in complete loss of functioning below the injury as evidenced by the absence of sensation and voluntary movement on both sides of the body. Other injuries are incomplete, meaning the nerve pathways were not completely destroyed. In these cases, a person may have sensation and some voluntary movement below the injured area. The range of problems resulting from a spinal injury is broad, including bowel and bladder control, sexual functioning, dexterity, balance, and breathing.

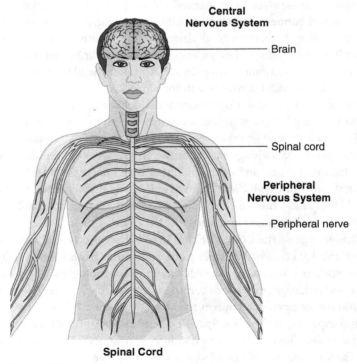

Figure 5.5
The Nervous System: Central and Peripheral
Source: Retrieved from http://www.nlm.nih.gov/medlineplus/ency/images/ency /fullsize/8679.jpg on February 8, 2013.

Understanding the range of problems arising from a spinal cord injury can promote an accepting mind-set for social workers because, in such cases, biology overcomes psychology. Imagine that you are called to work with a war veteran who sustained a spinal injury. The individual often smells like urine and is disheveled. Rather than attributing the individual's poor hygiene to character flaws, you can realize that bladder control was impacted by the injury.

THE BRAIN

The adult brain weighs approximately three pounds and is made up of neurons that can be organized into three major divisions: hindbrain, midbrain, and forebrain.

The hindbrain connects to the upper spinal cord and is responsible for controlling many automatic bodily processes, such as digestion, breathing, and heart rate. It also contains the pons and the cerebellum, which are structures that coordinate balance, equilibrium, sensory conduction, and movement. Damage to the hindbrain is very dangerous given its role in sustaining basic life functions, such as breathing, heart rate, and body movement.

The midbrain connects the hindbrain and the forebrain and is the smallest brain region. Functions in this region influence sensations such as hearing, vision, and some motor function. The substantia nigra is involved in body movement and the degeneration of neurons in this region is associated with Parkinson's disease.

The forebrain is responsible for many functions, including thinking, producing and understanding language, processing sensory information, and controlling motor function. Damage to the forebrain can result in a wide variety of dysfunction. For example, damage to the Broca's area does not undermine ability to understand language but is linked to an inability, or severe difficulty, in producing language due to impaired motor functioning associated with speech production. Individuals with Broca's aphasia can read, write, and take in information but labor to produce understandable speech. By contrast, damage to the Wernicke's area produces an effect opposite that of Broca's aphasia. Individuals with Wernicke's aphasia can produce speech that is clearly understood, yet they struggle in understanding the meaning of spoken language, which results in communication that is often rambling and meaningless despite being clearly articulated. Damage to both areas can leave individuals unable to understand language through spoken or written mediums or produce meaningful language verbally or in written format. Strokes commonly cause these types of aphasias.

Did You Know?

The Brain and Macro-Level Practice: Taking Lessons from Superman on Advocacy for Our Brains and Backs

Social workers interested in macro-level practice may advocate for policy change around spinal cord injuries (SCI). Consider the work accomplished by the late actor Christopher Reeve (aka "Superman"), who became paralyzed after falling from his horse and breaking his neck. He and his wife, Dana Reeve, brought increased attention to the problem of SCI, championed enhanced rights for people with disabilities, advocated for research (including stem cell research) to treat SCI, and developed a foundation to support the understanding and treatment of paralysis (see http://www.christopherreeve.org). While Christopher and Dana were not trained social workers, their efforts clearly fit into the mission and vision of how to promote human well-being by developing awareness, changing policy, and identifying methods to prevent and ameliorate the effects of SCI.

Beyond the three major divisions of the brain is the cerebellum, which almost appears to be a small brain near the hindbrain. The cerebellum coordinates many functions, many of which are related to movement and motor control. It is also associated with attention, language, and emotional regulations, including fear and pleasure.

In addition to dividing the brain into regions, it is often described in terms of hemispheres and regions or lobes. The brain has two hemispheres often referred to as the "left brain" and the "right brain." The two hemispheres are not in fact independent and are connected through several systems, including the corpus callosum that is found near the top of the brain. Nevertheless, people often describe certain functions to either the left or the right brain because the two sides do have certain dominant functions or specializations. That said, simple pronouncements of "I'm left-brained so I am logical" underestimate the connections across the two hemispheres and do not capture the entirety of the human experience. A simplified overview of tasks predominately associated with brain hemisphere follows.

Right Hemisphere

- Spatial abilities such as drawing, understanding maps, completing tactile puzzles
- Facial recognition
- Artistic processes including music, drawing, painting, poetry
- Visual imagery

Left Hemisphere

- Math
- Language
- Logic

Interestingly, the left side of the brain controls the right side of the body and the right side of the brain controls the left side of the body. Handedness, left or right, is said to reveal which side of the brain may be more dominant. Again, while there is some truth to such statements, social workers cannot make determinations or assessments based on handedness. Being left-handed does not guarantee that someone will be strong in spatial abilities and weak in logic. That said, social workers may work with individuals who have undergone surgeries on the corpus callosum, the connecting system. Such surgeries may target severe seizure disorders or other medical problems. The severing of the corpus callosum can produce subtle cognitive deficits.

Understanding that the brain has two hemispheres produced a better understanding of brain functioning, as does studying the function of specific areas. The brain is often divided into five primary "lobes," which are shown in Table 5.3.

Research-Based Practice

Practice Behavior Example: Use research evidence to inform practice.

Critical Thinking Question: How might knowledge that TBIs are frequently associated with increased anger and impulsivity be used when working with individuals who have suffered a TBI and their family?

As can be seen from Table 5.3, certain brain regions perform specific functions. For example, visual processing is primarily centered in the occipital lobe and an injury to this area will affect vision but not motor or critical thinking functions. How might social workers use knowledge of what functions certain brain regions perform? Most of the time, understanding that the occipital lobe is responsible for visual processing is irrelevant to how we work with people because most people have fully functioning brains. However, if you are working with an individual with a brain injury, often known as TBI for traumatic brain injury, knowing the profile of deficits that come with a TBI will help you

Table 5.3   Brain Lobes, Functions, and Problems

Lobe	Function	Effects of Damage
Frontal lobe	Cognition, reasoning, expressive language, motor skills, personality, intellect, executive functioning (problem solving)	Reduced mental abilities, problem solving, paying attention, emotional regulation
Parietal lobe	Processing tactile sensation such as touch, physical pain, pressure; processing senses such as smell, speech, and hearing; memory	Difficulty navigating space, recognizing familiar locations, understanding visual information, understanding written and/or spoken language
Temporal lobe	Sensory integration, limb movement, planning, reading, object recognition	Deafness, inability to process verbal language, memory problems, facial recognition
Occipital lobe	Visual abilities	Blindness, inability to interpret visual objects
Cerebellum	Movement coordination, balance	Difficulty eating, talking, walking, balance

Source: Adapted from Baars & Gage (2010); Carlson (2009); Stahl (2008); Strominger et al. (2012).

better understand the individual and his or her environment that can promote your ability to develop effective interventions. For example, TBI in the frontal lobe is often associated with increased levels of anger and impulsivity because this region of the brain is primarily responsible for thought and impulse control (Kolb & Whishaw, 2009).

Several other brain regions often come to the attention of social workers in direct practice. Table 5.4 shows some of these regions and their major functions.

Table 5.4   Brain Regions and Functions

Region	Function
Thalamus	Sensory relay center; signals senses and motor functioning; regulation of consciousness, awareness, alertness, sleep
Hypothalamus	Links the nervous system to the endocrine system through the pituitary gland; control of body temperature, thirst, hunger, circadian cycles, sleep, heart rate, blood pressure, perspiration, feeding, and memory
Pituitary gland	Human's "master gland" that regulates homeostasis through the hypothalamus. Synthesizes and secretes hormones and endorphins. Hormones and endorphins, in turn, regulate breast milk production, growth, blood pressure, sex organ development, temperature regulation, and the conversion of food into energy.
Hippocampus	Memory for experiences, spatial, orientation, inhibition
Amygdala	Memory for emotional events, processing emotional events such as fear, memory consolidation
Broca's area	Language processing, speech production, language comprehension
Wernicke's area	Language development, comprehension of spoken and written language
Reticular activating system	Mental alertness, sleep cycle, attentiveness

Source: Adapted from Baars & Gage (2010); Carlson (2009); Stahl (2008); Strominger et al. (2012).

Use the images of the brain's lobes and regions depicted in Figures 5.6 and 5.7 as you study more about the brain. Note how much has been learned about how the brain functions.

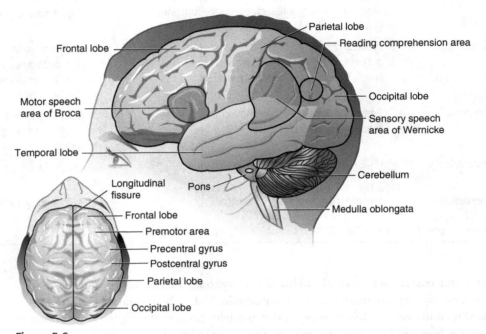

Figure 5.6
Structure of the Brain
Source: Retrieved from http://www.nlm.nih.gov/medlineplus/ency/images/ency/fullsize/1074.jpg on February 8, 2013.

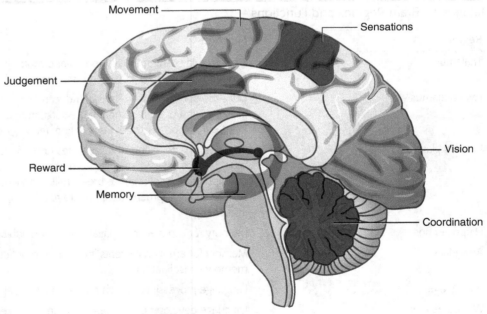

Figure 5.7
Research Has Identified Specific Areas of the Brain That Tend to Be Responsible for Specific Functions
Source: Retrieved from http://www.drugabuse.gov/sites/default/files/uslide-3.gif on February 8, 2013.

Peripheral Nervous System

The CNS, which we just reviewed, includes the brain and the spinal cord. Whereas the CNS can be considered to be "smart," the PNS could be considered to be the relay center between the CNS and the rest of the body. Nerves from the PNS connect bodily systems to the brain and the spinal cord. The PNS is divided into two different systems, the somatic nervous system (SNS) and the autonomic nervous system (ANS).

The SNS controls voluntary body movements such as the neck, shoulders, arms, legs, fingers, toes, and other bodily parts by stimulating muscles. If you think "I am going to move this part of my body" and it moves, it is very likely controlled through the SNS. Unlike nerves in the CNS, those in the PNS are not protected by bone—either the backbone system or the skull.

Social workers need to know about the ANS relative to the SNS because the ANS is connected to several forms of psychopathology, such as anxiety. The ANS is further divided into two separate divisions: sympathetic and parasympathetic nervous systems. In general, the ANS regulates aspects of human functioning that cannot be controlled voluntarily. Heart rate, digestion, perspiration, breathing, pupil dilation, and salivation are examples of functioning largely controlled by the ANS.

The two divisions of the ANS are often referred to as the "fight-or-flight response" for the sympathetic nervous system and the "rest and digest" for the parasympathetic system. The sympathetic nervous system can protect us from harm. When it is activated, a host of neural and hormonal signals are rapidly sent throughout the body to prepare it for fighting or fleeing. The digestive system shuts down and redirects energy to the large muscle groups (e.g., legs, arms); breathing and heart rate increase to distribute oxygen to the muscles and remove carbon dioxide so that the muscles can work more effectively; blood is moved away from the skin so that if an injury occurs, blood loss will be minimal; and pupils dilate to allow more light to enter to increase the field of vision. Activation of the sympathetic nervous system occurs without much conscious thought. Think of a time when you were faced with a dangerous situation such as getting hit by a car or faced a person you interpreted to be a threat. Your sympathetic nervous system jump-started your body in a significant manner. You had energy because there is an adrenaline uplift. This energy is good for staying alive, but it can create mental health problems if triggered *without* a genuine threat.

Sympathetic nervous system activation in the absence of a real threat could be called a *panic attack*. Look at the symptom profile for panic attack and you will see some of the following: racing heart, feeling faint or dizzy, tingling or numbing in the extremities (fingers, hands, feet), sweaty or chills, breathing difficulties, a sense of lost control. Activation of the sympathetic nervous system without actually fighting or fleeing creates an interesting physiological situation. Your heart rate is elevated and you are breathing fast—yet your large muscle groups are not working. Hyperventilation ensues which creates an atypical balance of oxygen and carbon dioxide in your system and respiratory alkalosis (shift in blood pH), which accounts for the feelings of numbness, dizziness, and tingling in their fingers. When this occurs, most people feel as though death is impending through a heart attack.

Emotions felt during a panic attack or significant sympathetic nervous system arousal are noted by individuals and, through conditioning, can lead to a number of debilitating anxiety disorders such as OCD, generalized anxiety disorder, social phobia, separation anxiety, panic disorder, specific phobias (e.g., heights, spiders), and agoraphobia. Anxiety disorders can be cruel in that they interfere with daily functioning, restrict enjoyment in basic activities, and can cause people to live in an almost constant state of fear. It is not

Read Behavioral Theories to learn more about emotions felt by individuals and through conditioning.

uncommon for individuals struggling with anxiety disorders to lose their jobs, restrict or severely limit their interactions with loved ones, and can lead to death from a lack of self care in some cases.

Fortunately, anxiety disorders are readily treated—often by social workers (Middleton & Craig, 2012; Salloum, Sulkowski, Sirrine, & Storch, 2009; Tolman et al., 2009). For example, Gail Stekettee is a social worker at Boston University and a leading expert in the treatment of anxiety disorders ranging from OCD to hoarding.

Assess your comprehension of Brain Structure and Function by completing this quiz.

Understanding physiology contributes to the treatment of anxiety disorders. Remember, the ANS is also made up of the parasympathetic nervous system that acts like a brake on the sympathetic nervous system. After the extreme arousal generated by the sympathetic nervous system, the parasympathetic nervous system releases hormones that reverse the arousal bringing one back to a state of relaxation. Understanding the interplay between these two systems has allowed the development of interventions that successfully treat anxiety disorders. Interventions such as "exposure and response prevention behavioral therapy" and "systematic desensitization" are effective and use knowledge of the ANS.

The CNS and Social Work

Many social workers direct their time and energies toward helping individuals with mental illnesses. Ultimately, all human psychopathology is connected to the nervous system. Certainly, the environment influences our neural functioning. War, poverty, crime, trauma, and stress strain our nerves system and increase the probability of mental illness—possibly by changing the functioning of neurotransmitters. In future chapters, we will discuss mental illness in greater depth with increased appreciation for the role the CNS plays.

Neural plasticity

It was once believed that neurons were fixed and could not be shaped. Now, we know that the brain changes and morphs across life. This changing of the brain and neurons is referred to as *neural plasticity*. In essence, the synapses and dendrites of a neuron can grow, be maintained, or be removed. Some theorists have drawn an analogy between the brain and a tree. Pruning is needed to remove neurons and neural circuits that do not promote information processing while other pathways or "branches" are developed as learning takes place. Of course, like maintaining a tree, it is possible to either over-prune a tree (cut it too much) or let it go overly wild (see Baars & Gage, 2010; Carlson, 2009; Stahl, 2008; Strominger et al., 2012).

Some of the well-known diseases resulting from neural cell death (possible over-pruning) include diseases such as Huntington's disease, Alzheimer's disease, and Parkinson's disease. Each of these diseases severely undermines the health of the individual and can lead to death. Further, family and friends of those affected by these diseases experience collateral challenges and difficulties. Social workers are often called upon to help those affected by health-related CNS diseases.

Assess your analysis and evaluation of this chapter's contents by completing the Chapter Review.

On a positive note, nerves within the CNS have some ability to regenerate or replenish themselves—even into adulthood (Rakic, 2002). Indeed, learning and experience are believed to change the CNS structure and research may show that stem cells can provide some hope to those suffering from disorders arising from the CNS.

6

Biological Influences on Human Behavior

Health and Sickness

Friedrich Stark/Alamy

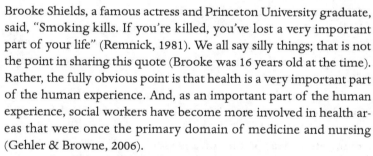

Brooke Shields, a famous actress and Princeton University graduate, said, "Smoking kills. If you're killed, you've lost a very important part of your life" (Remnick, 1981). We all say silly things; that is not the point in sharing this quote (Brooke was 16 years old at the time). Rather, the fully obvious point is that health is a very important part of the human experience. And, as an important part of the human experience, social workers have become more involved in health areas that were once the primary domain of medicine and nursing (Gehler & Browne, 2006).

You have heard that death and taxes are the only two certainties in life; however, another certainty is that people confront health and sickness. Health can be like a gas pedal that allows individuals to enjoy peak experiences such as traveling, playing, socializing, creating, inventing, loving, and relaxing. Good health also promotes one's ability to work and meet life's demands. Health, of course, is not a guarantee. Its opposites include injury, disease, and sickness. If health is the gas to peak experiences and meeting life's demands, disease can be thought of as the brake. Disease, injury, and sickness can disrupt life from mild levels all the way to death. Just as fish always swims in water, social workers always need to consider how health influences their clients.

HEALTH DEFINED

Defining health is not easy. If asked to define health, we recommend you to adopt our favorite phrase: *it depends*. At a basic level, health involves physical systems that function well enough to meet

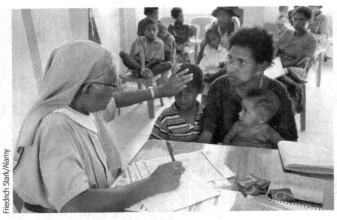
Health is critical to the human experience.

age-appropriate life demands. What exactly has to be functioning well enough before one can be considered healthy? Our body is composed of 11 major systems that help organize how we think about health, so health might be defined as adequate functioning in each system. For example, the respiratory system brings air in and out of our body. The muscular system allows mobility. The skeletal system provides the structure upon which other systems depend and protects vital organs. The immune system protects the body against disease. Of course, the term *functioning* is broad. If an 18-year-old claims he or she ran a mile between four and eight minutes, nobody will likely get very excited. By contrast, if a three-year-old or a 95-year-old claims he or she ran a mile between four and eight minutes, lots of people would get very excited. This simple example reveals physical performance expectations are relative. In Chapter 2, we noted that some aspects of the human condition can be measured using nominal categories (e.g., nationality, employment status) while other aspects should be measured using continuous scales (e.g., ability to run, degree of anxiety). Health can also be measured on nominal categories (e.g., HIV positive or negative; pregnant or not) and on continuous scales (e.g., visual acuity, weight).

Like health, disease can also be considered on a continuum. Two people struggling with cancer can be in very different stages. One may be in a terminal stage where quality of life is very poor including intense pain, difficulty with breathing, and loss of ability to engage in simple activities. Another person may feel 100% healthy, look in the mirror and see no sign of illness, yet through diagnostic testing know cancer is present.

Body weight can also be considered from both continuous and discrete perspectives. We could say people are "underweight" or "normal" or "obese." Of course, these categories do not communicate a clear picture of a person's health. The label *obese* can be applied to a person weighing 200 pounds and to a person weighing 450 pounds.

Diversity in Practice

Practice Behavior Example: Appreciate that, as a consequence of difference, a person's life experiences may include oppression, poverty, marginalization, and alienation as well as privilege, power, and acclaim.

Critical Thinking Question: How might difference in a person's body type and degree of health at an early age shape a person's approach to life's struggles and identity formation?

MAJOR SYSTEMS OF THE HUMAN BODY

Let's turn to a brief introduction to the body's 11 major systems. While a vast amount of knowledge exists on the functioning and malfunctioning of each system, our review only introduces you to these systems. As a social worker, you will collaborate with allied professions in nutrition, medicine, nursing, physical therapy, and others to provide optimal interventions. For example, a social worker in micro practice may use motivational interviewing to help his client lose weight and consult a dietician to provide specific information on the physiology of weight loss. At a mezzo level, a social worker may advocate for improved work conditions for employees and draw upon the expertise of a physician who can provide data about the impact of a stressful work environment on physical functioning. Social workers advocating for policy changes to support children exposed to high levels of abuse and domestic violence will likely team with neurologists and psychologists who research the impact of trauma on the brain and other systems.

The 11 Major Body Systems

Nervous system

Chapter 4 reviewed the nervous system in detail. This system controls the entire body and is responsible for complex thought and emotion. A healthy nervous system involves the ability to process information and control bodily functions. Unhealthy nervous system functioning may include mental retardation, learning disorders, brain damage, spinal cord damage, dementia, Alzheimer's, schizophrenia, memory problems, visual disorders, mental illness, and other challenges. On the micro level, social workers might directly help people overcome or manage symptoms originating from the nervous system or refer them to medically based professionals specializing in this area. On the mezzo level, social workers might advocate for healthy systems, say at work, to both prevent and respond to problems such as mental illness. On the macro level, social workers may work to modify or establish policies that prevent problems associated with nervous system functioning or change policies that are unhelpful. The range of policies affecting the nervous system is enormous. Policies that influence stress (e.g., market policies), civil rights (e.g., affirmative action, right to marry), health (e.g., access to health care), foreign affairs (e.g., war), and so on are but a few policy areas of interest to social workers.

Skeletal system

The human skeletal system is made up of about 206 bones along with cartilage, tendons, and ligaments that hold the skeletal system together and help it to function. This system provides structure and frame to the human body, as well as protect vital organs, store minerals such as calcium, and house bone marrow that makes blood cells. The skeletal system is vulnerable to a vast number of environmental insults or injuries such as car accidents, war, and on-the-job injuries such as carpal tunnel or worse (e.g., loss of a limb). In fact, the number of injuries to factor workers early in the Industrial Revolution led workers to organize into unions to protect workers from unsafe conditions—a form of social justice advocacy. The skeletal system is also vulnerable to developmental and genetic problems, such as arthritis and spina bifida. Social workers do not fix broken bones or perform surgery on tendons, yet they may be asked to help people with skeletal problems. For example, returning military personnel who suffered skeletal injuries (e.g., amputation of a limb) may need social work services such as case management or counseling. Can you think of how social workers might work to prevent problems with the skeletal system for children, adults, and older adults?

Muscular system

We have hundreds of unique muscle groups that provide many important functions, such as facilitating movement of the skeletal system and moving blood through the body. Some muscles are under voluntary control, whereas others expand and contract without conscious awareness. The heart, for example, is a muscle that beats without requiring conscious thought. Moving arms, legs, and the mouth by contrast are voluntary actions. Strong muscles allow us to carry out daily living tasks and pursue work and recreation. Problems with the muscular system include genetic-based conditions where muscle wastes away, a form of muscular dystrophy, which is debilitating. The Centers for Disease Control and Prevention (CDC, 2011b) reports that heart disease is the leading cause of death in the United States. Heart disease is influenced by genetic, individual (e.g., smoking, obesity), and environmental (e.g., pollution) factors. Social workers may promote heart functioning through efforts to improve everyone's health, such as with advertisement campaigns or advocacy. First Lady Michelle Obama, for example, has championed the Let's Move effort designed to decrease childhood obesity. Social workers may also work to help individuals stop smoking through behavioral and cognitive interventions.

Circulatory system

The circulatory system moves blood through the body through veins and arteries. Smooth muscles partly control the flow of blood through veins and arteries by contracting or relaxing—all of which is done automatically. Problems with the circulatory system include heart diseases, high blood pressure, blood clots, rupturing of veins or arteries, and restriction of blood to the body that causes tissue death. Heart attacks and strokes are directly linked to our circulatory systems. Like other human systems, our circulatory system is influenced by genetic, individual, and environmental factors. For example, plaque buildup in the circulatory system is linked to diet (e.g., cholesterol), exercise, smoking, genetics, and environmental toxins. How might social workers promote healthy circulatory functioning at micro, mezzo, and macro levels?

Immune system

The immune system provides defenses against infectious organisms, such as bacteria and viruses that cause disease. This system has two primary components. First, the skin and mucous membranes form an external barrier to infectious organisms. Second, if a foreign substance penetrates these external barriers, the body produces white blood cells, antibodies, T cells, and other cellular responses to the foreign organisms.

Many problems can arise within the immune system that undermine life quality and cause havoc. Roughly 33% of Europe's population was killed by the bubonic or "black plague" in the 14th century as the result of germs spread by rats and fleas. Smallpox, measles, diphtheria, scarlet fever, and other diseases have been and could still be threats to human functioning. Consider, for example, the threat of the "bird flu" and cholera, which can potentially kill large numbers of people in a very short amount of time. We are all familiar with HIV (human immunodeficiency virus) and AIDS (acquired immunodeficiency syndrome), which destroy the immune system by rendering it unable to defend the body against common infections. Cancer treatment can also undermine the functioning of the immune system. Other problems in this system include *autoimmune disorders* that involve the immune system attacking the body's healthy systems. For example, lupus and juvenile rheumatoid arthritis involve the immune system attacking muscles and joints causing inflammation and pain. Allergies are another immune system disorder caused by an overreaction to foreign organism, which range from discomfort similar to the common cold to asthma.

How do social workers interact with the immune system? Again, our favorite response: it depends. One common focus is on HIV/AIDS. Social workers engage in efforts to halt the spread of HIV through efforts such as policy changes related to sexual education, distributing clean needles to drug-using populations, and promoting safe sex practices among those likely to contract or spread HIV. Social work is also involved in helping those with HIV/AIDS obtain care that will extend life and promote life quality. Finally, social work is often involved in hospice activities that are designed to support individuals who are dying.

Digestive system

The digestive system is made up of the digestive track, which includes bodily systems that process food including the mouth, esophagus, intestines, stomach, colon, liver, pancreas, and gallbladder. This system is responsible for processing food into smaller molecules and nutrients that can be used by the body for energy and nourishment. Transforming bread, fruit, meat, and gyros into molecules small enough for cells to absorb is a complex process that utilizes physical (e.g., chewing) and chemical (e.g., production of enzymes) actions. Problems of the digestive system range from common uncomfortable and inconvenient challenges such as heartburn, nausea, diarrhea, and stomach cramps to problems where the digestive system does not process certain types of food (e.g., lactose intolerance) or problems with digestion in general. Crohn's disease, for example, is an inflammatory bowel disease that can lead to malnutrition. Irritable bowel syndrome is a disease of the intestine system that causes constipation, diarrhea, and abdominal pain. Think back to a time when you suffered from diarrhea, bloating, or cramps—not much fun. Now imagine living with such symptoms on a regular basis. Problems such as these can undermine individual's mental health and motivation to engage in life activities such as work, school, and socializing.

Endocrine system

The endocrine system is responsible, in part, for metabolism, tissue functioning and growth, mood regulation, and reproductive processes including sexual functioning. These functions are carried out through hormones that influence nearly every biological aspect of the human body. Hormones are produced by the hypothalamus, pituitary glands, pineal glands, the thyroid and parathyroid, pancreas, and adrenal glands. Hormones act as chemical messengers that deliver and transfer information across cellular structures.

Many hormones exist. Endorphins are a commonly known hormone that reduces pain sensitivity by acting on cells in the central nervous system. Growth hormones regulate the growth of bodily tissue and bone. Other hormones control the balance of water in the body, milk production for breast feeding, uterus contractions during labor, and, among many other functions, cellular functioning such as burning fuel to produce energy and controlling tissue development. The level of control exerted by the endocrine system on human functioning is truly amazing, and therefore, it comes as no surprise that problems in this system can result in dramatic problems. Commonly known problems include diabetes, Graves' disease, hypothyroidism, and early entry into puberty. Problems with endocrine functioning, such as thyroid disease, are strongly connected to depression; in fact, clinical social workers may apply considerable efforts to help someone misdiagnosed with a primary depression when in reality thyroid disease is primary and depression is secondary.

Lymphatic system

The lymphatic system protects the body from dangerous microorganisms such as viruses, fungi, and bacteria. A well-known component of this system is white blood cells that seek and destroy possible dangerous invaders, such as bacteria. Other components of the lymphatic system include the tonsils, the appendix, and the spleen. In addition to providing a protecting role, the lymph system influences the circulation and regulation of bodily fluid and metabolism. Cancers that develop within the lymphatic system, such as Hodgkin's disease, are dangerous because they can easily spread through major bodily areas such as the tonsils, the spleen, the liver, and the bone marrow. Individuals with HIV/AIDS are at risk of developing such cancers known as lymphoma.

Reproductive system

The reproductive system was covered in Chapter 4. For a brief review, this system includes the sex organs such as the ovaries, the uterus, the fallopian tube, the vagina, the testes, the prostate, and the penis. At a global level, dysfunction in this system would result in the elimination of the human race. At a micro level, dysfunction in the reproductive system can lead to sexual problems, which may result in emotional pain, relational problems, and even identity crises (Weeks, 2002). Dysfunction in sexual functioning affects both the individual with the problem and his or her sexual partner(s) (Grellet & Faix, 2011; McCarthy, 2002).

Respiratory system

The respiratory system delivers oxygen to cells and removes carbon dioxide. Cellular metabolism produces energy to run all systems of the human body and requires oxygen. If the body is robbed of oxygen, cells cease to function and die. The production of energy produces a toxic by-product that needs to be expelled from the body, carbon dioxide. The respiratory system is made up of the lungs, the trachea, the bronchi, and the diaphragm. Many well-known and dangerous diseases are found within this system, such as asthma, chronic obstructive pulmonary disease, pneumonia, croup, bronchitis, respiratory infection, cystic fibrosis, emphysema, whooping cough, embolisms, and even the common cold or flu. A common thread to these diseases is difficulty with breathing, which impacts the distribution of oxygen and removal of carbon dioxide.

Like other systems, social workers do not perform direct interventions on the respiratory system. However, many respiratory diseases are influenced by activities that draw social work's attention, such as smoking, secondhand smoke, and access to health care to prevent the progression of minor respiratory problems into significant problems.

Integumentary system

The integumentary system is the largest organ in the body as it includes our skin, hair, finger and toe nails, and some glands. This system provides several impotent functions such as protection from outside contaminants (e.g., bacteria, viruses), temperature regulation, and sensory reception. The skin also plays a role in vitamin D synthesis and protects against harmful ultraviolet rays. Disorders of the integumentary system probably do not reach direct social work intervention very often. Rashes, athlete's foot, skin cancer, some sexually transmitted diseases (STDs; e.g., genital herpes), and acne are examples of disorders of this system. Direct intervention for problems of this system are the domain of medicine, though social workers may be involved with secondary care such as working with individuals who have skin cancer, advocating for the prevention of STDs, or supporting the self-esteem of a teenager with acne.

Assess your comprehension of Health Systems by completing this quiz.

THE IMPACT OF HEALTH AS AN INDEPENDENT AND DEPENDENT VARIABLE

Critical Thinking

Practice Behavior Example: Use critical thinking augmented by creativity and curiosity.

Critical Thinking Question: How might you explain to a client of moderate to low intellectual functioning that health is both an independent and a dependent variable?

In research, dependent variables are influenced by independent variables. For example, a professor may investigate whether giving pop quizzes (yes, no) influences students' rate of keeping up with readings (high, low). The independent variable, choosing to give pop quizzes, is something that can be directly controlled by the professor and is expected to impact reading rate, the dependent variable that cannot be directly controlled. Health is both an independent and a dependent variable.

Health as an Independent Variable

As an independent variable, health has a dramatic impact on quality of life—just as Brooke Shields mentioned. Let's look at how health problems influence the quality of life through three brief case studies.

Case Example 1: Adolescent With Diabetes

Jane is a 14-year-old girl diagnosed with type 1 diabetes, a disease which destroys the cells that produce insulin. Insulin is important because it helps move glucose (sugar) out of cells to give the body energy. If glucose is not moved out of cells, it can seriously damage blood cells, the nervous system, and other organs. Specifically, type 1 diabetes can damage the kidneys, cause blindness, and cause nerve damage to the point that amputation of extremities (e.g., feet, hands) may be required. No cure for type 1 diabetes exists, though its symptoms can be managed by insulin injections and controlling one's blood sugar levels through diet and exercise. Managing diabetes requires consistent monitoring and high degrees of self-control and motivation. Further, considerable resources are needed to effectively manage diabetes such as regular visits to physicians and medical professionals, equipment to test and deliver insulin, and access to healthy food and exercise opportunities.

Typically, 14-year-old adolescents do not have to worry about the many issues facing Jane due to diabetes. In fact, research suggests that many adolescents dismiss the seriousness of type 1 diabetes (Chen et al., 2012). How will diabetes influence the life of an adolescent like Jane? Thanks to science, Jane has a solid chance of living a rather normal life. She can go to school, play sports, and engage in the activities her friends pursue. However, Jane's quality of life will be affected. She will need to eat more carefully than her friends and monitor her blood sugar levels. Travel will be more difficult as she will need constant access to insulin and sophisticated equipment.

The time and energy required to monitor diabetes may subtract from Jane's willingness or ability to engage in normal activities. The cost of managing diabetes may strain her family's budget causing stress to her parents. Jane's diabetes may also strain relationships. Her parents may need to be more controlling to get her to manage her diabetes, possibly leading to parent–child conflict. If Jane's medical problems become an issue with securing health insurance, it is conceivable that her parents may lose job mobility given the preexisting condition.

Jane may have friends who exclude her from activities knowing diabetes could be problematic. Pursuing a long-term, committed romantic relationship may also be influenced by diabetes. Jane may feel self-conscious leading her to be more reserved; the interested partner may not want to "deal" with diabetes or be fearful of committing to a person with a life-long disease. Jane may also face workplace discrimination. An employer may worry that diabetes will impact Jane's work ability or the costs of taking on an employee with a life-long medical condition.

These potential implications could influence Jane's mental health. She may feel guilty, embarrassed, confused, angry, and discouraged about the prospects of living with diabetes. Of course, none of these problems may materialize. This example shows how health influences many other aspects of life in a rather dramatic fashion. See Figure 6.1 for an overview of how diabetes can affect different systems of a person's life.

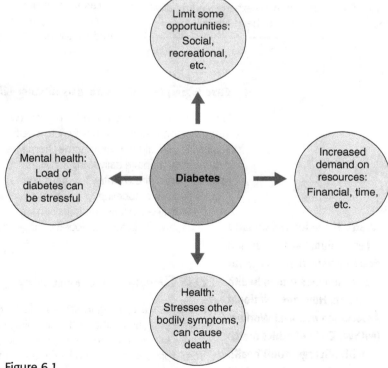

Figure 6.1
Physical Health/Illness Influences Other Systems

Case Example 2: Stroke at Middle Age

Let's look at another example of how health influences the human condition. Benjamin recently had a stroke. He is a 43-year-old married man with two children. Two kinds of strokes occur in the brain, and both cause brain tissue to die. A hemorrhagic stroke results when blood crosses the blood-brain barrier, reaches the brain, and damages brain tissue. Ischemic strokes occur when a blood vessel is blocked, often from a blood clot, reducing blood supply and causing brain damage. Some strokes result in death, whereas others are so small that symptoms abate within hours (see National Institutes of Health, 2007).

Common problems from a stroke include vision loss; paralysis; body weakness; numbing; change in personality and emotionality; difficulty with cognitive functions such as memory, judgment, and reasoning; and difficulty with speech reception and production. The location of the stroke predicts which losses may occur (see Chapter 5 for discussion of regional specialization of the brain). A stroke in the occipital lobe, for example, affects vision, whereas a stroke in the frontal lobe may influence personality, reasoning, and motor functioning.

Benjamin's stroke resulted in memory impairments, loss of cognitive functioning, and physical paralysis on one side of his body. Considering the person-in-environment model, how might this health event influence him? Benjamin's personality changed following the stroke because he could not understand the world around him as before the stroke. After the stroke, simple tasks became difficult or impossible because his problem-solving skills and memory diminished greatly. Benjamin also became less patient and often lost his temper. The stroke left Benjamin unable to work in construction despite his employer's attempts to accommodate the changes. His stroke undermined his marriage and family relations. Benjamin became self-conscious of his physical and mental impairments and distanced himself from his wife. Further, Benjamin and his wife did not solve common marital problems following the stroke because he would anger easily. Benjamin's partner faced a new, difficult reality of sole financial provider and house manager and caretaker to her former partner. This stress was felt by her children and friends. Benjamin isolated himself from social systems and struggled with depression, furthering the challenges initiated by the stroke.

Engage, Assess Intervene, Evaluate

Practice Behavior Example: Promote social and economic justice.

Critical Thinking Question What role might a social worker take in promoting social and economic justice for clients who have experienced medical insults such as a stroke or heart attack?

Case Example 3: Osteoporosis in Later Life

Now imagine the impact of osteoporosis (weak bones) on 75-year-old Fran who lived alone in a rural community. On her way to check the mail, Fran fell and broke her hip. Following surgery, Fran could not return to her home because of the many stairs and could no longer independently manage daily living activities. Her daughter agreed to have Fran live with her in a different part of the country. The transition to her daughter's home was challenging because it required some remodeling to accommodate her wheel chair and challenged typical operating patterns. Fortunately, the transition was mostly successful because Fran and her daughter and granddaughter developed stronger relationships.

Watch the video Health Care Legislation: Early Ideas and describe your thoughts about government's role in health care. How does National Association of Social Workers (NASW) Code of Ethics match with (diverge from) health care legislation?

Case Example 4: Healthy at Thirty

In this last case, imagine 30-year-old Jennifer who enjoys good health that allows her to assist her aging mother with gardening, participate in camping trips with her friends and family, take care of her home, volunteer at her child's preschool, and easily get to and from work. Jennifer's good health also promotes confidence, allowing her to comfortably date and take on challenging tasks at work.

These four case studies reveal that individual health influences micro and mezzo systems. Individual health also has macro-level effects. Consider the impact of smoking and obesity on U.S. policy and spending revealing that a healthier population is less expensive and more productive. Illness and disease, as was shown through the four case descriptions, can have wide and significant impacts. The following are some dimensions to consider in assessing how a person's illness influences his or her environment.

Duration of illness:	Short	——————	Chronic
Impact of illness:	Circumscribed	——————	Broad
Onset of illness:	Abrupt	——————	Gradual
Phase of illness:	Early	——————	Late stage
Visibility of illness:	Not obvious	——————	Obvious
Social impact of illness:	Low	——————	High
Treatment availability:	Low	——————	High
Manageability of illness:	Low	——————	High
Social acceptance:	Low	——————	High
Return to previous activities:	Low	——————	High
Recovery potential:	Low	——————	High

Where might the following physical illnesses fall on these dimensions? Heart attack, lung cancer from smoking, stroke, obesity, HIV/AIDS, dementia, Alzheimer's, balding, osteoporosis, breast cancer, brain tumor, hip replacement, diabetes, emphysema, dwarfism, hearing loss, leukemia, arthritis, asthma, cancer, chicken pox, STDs, encephalitis, hepatitis, muscular dystrophy, Parkinson's disease, sickle-cell anemia, or syphilis. What about mental health conditions, such as depression, alcohol abuse, schizophrenia, anxiety, mental retardation, and autism?

Health as a Dependent Variable

Our health can also be considered a *dependent variable* because many factors impact it. For example, living in a rural or urban area will affect people's health, as will access to resources such as medical care, food, and safe environments. Some of the common influences on physical health are seen in Figure 6.2 and include the environment, biological factors, individual factors, and psychosocial factors.

Given the importance of human health, it is not surprising that monumental efforts have been applied to understanding the causes and correlates of health. In the United States, the National Institutes of Health (NIH) coordinates 27 separate institutes that conduct a broad array of research on the causes and correlates of health (http://www.nih.gov/icd/index.html, retrieved on August 1, 2012). Some well-known health targets of these institutes include cancer, the heart, the lungs, blood, infectious diseases, allergies, teeth, mental health, diabetes, the digestive system, kidney disease, neurological disorders and strokes, human development, vision, alcoholism and drug abuse, aging, skin diseases, hearing and communicative disorders, genetics, and health and health disparities among minority groups.

Given the massive effort to study the causes and correlates of health and illness, a lot is known. Much of the research generated from NIH is now well-known fact. For

Watch the video AIDS in Black America. What are some causes of disproportionality of AIDS in African Americans relative to other Americans? What are some of the implications of the disproportionality of AIDS in Black citizens?

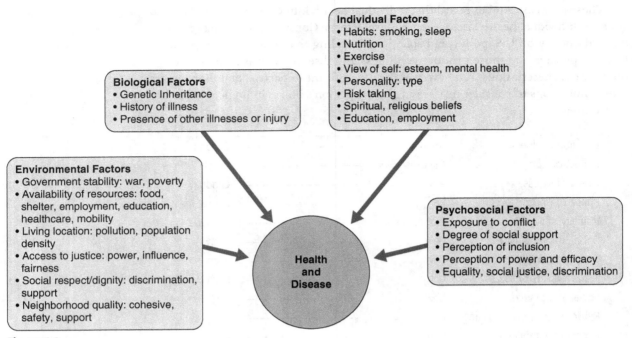

Figure 6.2
Health as a Dependent Variable: The Many Influences on Our Health

example, Americans know for certainty that smoking is dangerous. NIH research states that smoking is linked to heart attacks, lung cancer and damage, strokes, blood clots, asthma, and adverse pregnancy outcomes and undermines the body's ability to respond to other illnesses. Roughly 33% of all cancers in the United States are attributed to cigarette use (http://www.surgeongeneral.gov/library/tobaccosmoke/factsheet.html, retrieved on January 1, 2011).

Physical well-being is multi-determined and no single book can review all of the many influences on our health discovered by NIH's 27 institutes and other research groups. For the purpose of social work, we review three broad factors that impact physical health:

- Individual factors: behavior and psychology
- Social factors: culture
- Environmental factors: neighborhood, work, culture, and political

Prior to examining a particular group of factors, it is important to realize that the factors interact with each other. Consider how two seemingly individual factors, diet and exercise, are influenced by environmental factors. Healthy eating and regular exercise are linked to health. If we limit ourselves to this amount of knowledge, we can grossly oversimplify judgments and decisions on health. Imagine what solutions a social worker may propose if he or she believes that the only two influences on health are diet and exercise. For the rise in obesity in the public high schools, this social worker would suggest more exercise and better diet. To reduce the risk of heart attack among homeless veterans, again diet and exercise. What is missing from this social worker's knowledge base is how other factors interact with people's ability to access healthy food and exercise. Eating healthy is easier for middle- and upper-income individuals who can afford healthier food options. Further, financially secure individuals likely have the disposable time needed to prepare healthy food and exercise because less time is dedicated to basic survival. Environmental factors, such as policy and neighborhood factors, influence the availability and accessibility of diet and exercise opportunities.

Health is influenced by a myriad of factors.

Imagine a low-income, inner-city neighborhood that has experienced high levels of crime. Businesses such as fully stocked grocery stores and exercise gyms may leave because of the threat of crime. Lowered tax base in such a neighborhood may discourage the city from investing in public exercise options, such as parks and community recreation centers. A lowered tax base may also result in the degradation of existing facilities. Even motivated individuals living in such a neighborhood will struggle to access healthy food choices or exercise options. In this example, the environment serves a moderating role by influencing accessibility and availability of diet and exercise options. Other obvious environmental influences on diet and exercise include war, population density, and living region. Environmental influences that are less visible include racism, economic health, and policies supporting community development and individual development (e.g., block grants, government support to obtain advanced education; Benjamin, 2008; Veugelers, Sithole, Zhang, & Muhajarine, 2008).

In sum, multiple factors and their interaction must be considered to gain a realistic perspective of biological well-being and functioning.

Assess your comprehension of Health as Independent and Dependent Variables by completing this quiz.

Individual Factors on Health: Behavior

Health is strongly shaped by individual behaviors and habits. Health-promoting behaviors include routine exercise, healthy eating, sleep, balancing work and leisure activities, and preventative dental and health care. Physical health is also undermined by smoking, drug abuse, poor eating habits, lack of exercise, and engagement in high-risk lifestyle choices.

Most people probably have a good idea of what constitutes healthy and unhealthy habits. If most people have fairly sound ideas on behaviors that promote and undermine health, why does variance exist? Clearly, if people followed well-known healthy behaviors, disease would lower dramatically. Consider the following assumption regarding healthy behavior.

Knowing = Doing

Many health care workers rely heavily on this assumption. Physicians say: eat less and move more to lose weight. Dentists say: floss to keep your teeth healthy. Researchers say: get more calcium to avoid osteoporosis. Antidrug campaigns say: drugs are bad, don't do them. Does knowledge alone cause people to change unhealthy behaviors? Obviously, not.

Several models have been developed to extend our understanding of health care–related behavior that go beyond the notion that information alone guides health care choices. Using motivational interviewing as a guide (Lundahl, Kunz, Brownell,

Figure 6.3
Factors Influencing
Health Behaviors
Source: Brad Lundahl

$$\text{Performing Health Behavior} = \frac{\text{Knowledge} \times \text{Motivation} \times \text{Confidence} \times \text{Resources} \times \text{Values}}{\text{Resistance}}$$

Tollefson, & Burke, 2010; Miller & Rollnick, 2013; Rollnick, Miller, & Butler, 2008), for example, would add several key elements to the previous formula such as (1) motivation, (2) confidence and self-efficacy, (3) resources, (4) values/vision, and (5) resistance. The resulting formula may look something like Figure 6.3.

The variables beyond "knowledge" provide a richer picture of why people may or may not engage in healthy living behaviors. Even if a woman knows she should follow through with a routine health screening for breast cancer, and if motivation is low because she believes breast cancer only happens to "older women," she will likely not seek the screening. Similarly, a person who knows that he should stop smoking and is somewhat motivated to stop but does not feel confident that he can stop will probably not try saying, "I'll try, but it won't work. So why try at all." Resources also matter. If a person wants a health screening (motivation), knows screenings are important (knowledge), and is confident screenings work (confidence), but does not have health insurance or money (resources), she will not get the screening. A person's values are critical as they influence motivation and vision for what one wants in life. Resistance is also a key to health-linked behaviors. Resistance may include not believing one has a problem or may arise when one is fearful or does not believe change will help. One author (BL) worked with a 78-year-old woman who refused to get routine screenings for cancer based on a fear she may have cancer—and knowing she had cancer would force her to confront mortality and loss.

Several other variables could be added to the formula found in Figure 6.3. What variables or ingredients would you include? We think ownership, vision, goals, and many resources (support, access) are necessary to fully understand a client's behavior.

Beyond our ideas on why people chose to engage in health-related behaviors, many well-tested models have been developed. For example, the Health Belief Model (HBM; Carpenter, 2010; Rosenstock, Strecher, & Becker, 1988; Tanner-Smith & Brown, 2010) identifies the following factors believed to be important to people's decisions to engage in health-related behaviors:

- **Perceived susceptibility of risk.** People must believe their health is at risk before they will change. Consider the case of the tobacco industry that fought to discredit research revealing that smoking is harmful (Brandt, 2007). Once science established that smoking is harmful, public health efforts could combat smoking by emphasizing its dangers. Consider the role of perceptions of susceptibility and HIV. Efforts to curb the spread of HIV in the United States and abroad lead with information that people who engage in certain behaviors (e.g., unprotected sex, needle sharing) are susceptible to contracting HIV regardless of age, ethnicity, gender, or sexual orientation (see Fraze et al., 2009; Orel, Stelle, Watson, & Bunner, 2010; Wringe et al., 2009). However, beliefs that deny the existence of HIV or advance a belief that one can avoid the disease because of being special increase the risk of engaging in unsafe sexual practices and, therefore, the risk of acquiring and spreading HIV (Kalichman, Eaton, & Cherry, 2010; Riley & Baah-Odoom, 2012).

The perceived risks associated with distracted driving are frequently discussed (Ship, 2010). Driving while under the influence of alcohol or drugs, sending and reading text messages, and talking on cellular phones is clearly dangerous (see Wang et al., 2009; Young, Salmon, & Cornelissen, 2012). Adolescents and young adults seem to be especially at risk for engaging in this type of risk behavior (Atchley, Hadlock, & Lane, 2012; Lerner, 2011). Efforts to reduce the risk of distracted or impaired driving include education and legal sanctions. Watch television and you will likely notice commercials put out by automobile insurance companies, law enforcement agencies, and other interested groups that send the message: drive distracted and you are susceptible to risk—risk of an accident and risk of legal action. Of interest, efforts that led to widespread support for laws against drunk driving in the 1980s may not be as effective in today's culture to combat distracted driving from technology such as texting (Atchley et al., 2012; Lerner, 2011).

- **Perceived severity of health-related behaviors.** In the HBM, simple exposure to risk is not sufficient to alter behavior. Risk severity also matters. For example, the severity of contracting HIV is vastly different than the risk of contracting a common cold. Further, the severity of a speeding ticket is vastly different than getting arrested for driving under the influence.

  You have probably seen campaigns designed to prevent health problems by highlighting the severity of health-related behaviors. To prevent car accidents, universities have placed a wrecked automobile on campus prior to holiday breaks (Thanksgiving, Spring Break) to command attention of students who likely will be traveling. In our community, a popular local news anchor died from colon cancer; shortly after his death, a billboard showed his face with a caption that indicated that a routine screening may have saved his life.

- **Perceived benefits of health-related behaviors.** The HBM notes people are motivated to engage in healthy behaviors if desired benefits are likely. The adage, "An apple a day keeps the doctor away," is an example. People engage in many health-oriented behaviors for the promise of enhanced life quality. Flossing will help teeth last, exercise should stave off obesity and heart disease, driving the speed limit should reduce the risk of an accident, not drinking while pregnant should prevent complications for the child, consuming calcium should prevent osteoporosis, and quitting smoking reduces the risk of cancer and increases pulmonary functioning.

- **Perceived barriers to health-related behavior.** The HBM realizes that factors beyond perceived benefits and consequences influence engagement in health behaviors. Exercising and healthy eating is resource intensive in both time and cost. Further, many health-related behaviors are difficult. Getting up early in the morning to exercise can be daunting—even without kids, a job, and cold weather. Safe sex practices can also be perceived as difficult or awkward.

  Changing habits is also difficult on numerous levels. Imagine an individual who smokes and attempts to quit. He is physiologically addicted to nicotine and behaviorally and socially reinforced for smoking in many circles. Behaviorally, the smoker is able to take a break and relax by smoking. Socially, the individual finds smoke breaks with his friends to be the best moments of the work shift. Other barriers include the hassle of accessing health care, such as taking time off or arranging for transportation or childcare.

- **Perceived self-efficacy.** Confidence in one's ability (self-efficacy) to engage in health-related behaviors is another component of the HBM. The higher the sense of efficacy, the greater the likelihood people will participate in healthy behaviors. Many individuals addicted to substances have a saying that goes something like this: I know I can quit; I've already quit 50 times—the problem is I've started 51 times. People who are overweight often say they've tried every diet imaginable. Discouragement and lack of confidence undermine change efforts. If you do not believe you can succeed, why try?

  Fortunately, self-efficacy can be strengthened through practice and education. Self-efficacy is posited as an important factor for older individuals who are on rather complex medication regimes (Buchmann, 1997; Cholowski & Cantwell, 2007). Taking medications as prescribed is important for several reasons, including getting the targeted benefit and not introducing "interaction effects," wherein taking two or more medications may enhance, diminish, or completely alter the original intent of a medication. Researchers from Connecticut tested a technology-assisted education program designed to teach older individuals about proper medication use. The program was delivered via a computer and the results indicate that those in the intervention group enjoyed higher confidence in their ability to manage their medication regimes as a result of the program (Neafsey, Strickler, Shellman, & Chartier, 2002). Such results have been replicated and show promise (Ruppar, 2010).

- **Cues to action.** The HBM also emphasizes the role of "reminders" or "nudges" to engage in health-related behaviors. Cues come from numerous sources, from public service announcements and commercials to posters in a health care setting and reminders from one's family or friends. Some cues target the entire population while others are targeted. Getting the flu shot serves as an example. Most individuals in the United States are encouraged to get a flu shot through the mass media and interaction with health care providers. However, certain groups, such as older people, may receive more cues with a stronger thrust. Similarly, parents of newborns are encouraged to seek immunization shots for their child. Cues come from the mass media, physicians, and nurses. If parents do not get their children immunized, the cues get much, much stronger. One author (BL) worked with a family referred to Child Protective Services because they had not immunized their child within a certain time window—with the potential of having their child temporarily removed from their home (the legality and morality of such a decision is not being questioned here—just noting that cues do get stronger).

  The strength and availability of cues varies. For example, communities differ on their comfort level with school-based sex education programs resulting in some children receiving more information than others. Even though some mixed data exist on the efficacy of school-based sex education (Milhausen et al., 2008; Poobalan et al., 2009), decisions to provide such education and the nature of the education are strongly linked to politics, emotions, and cultural beliefs surrounding sexuality (see Fields, 2008; Luker, 2006; Milhausen et al., 2008).

  The strength and availability of cues can also differ based on resources. Impoverished clinics may simply not have the resources to secure cues that will effectively capture the attention of targeted populations. Further, individuals who cannot read or access media outlets may not benefit from public service announcements or other cues.

  An example of the HBM is shown in Figure 6.4. Notice how the word *perceive* is in all but two elements of the model. Perceptions are, of course, individual beliefs and vary for many reasons. In the HBM, perceptions are believed to vary based on factors such as cultural beliefs and demographic variables.

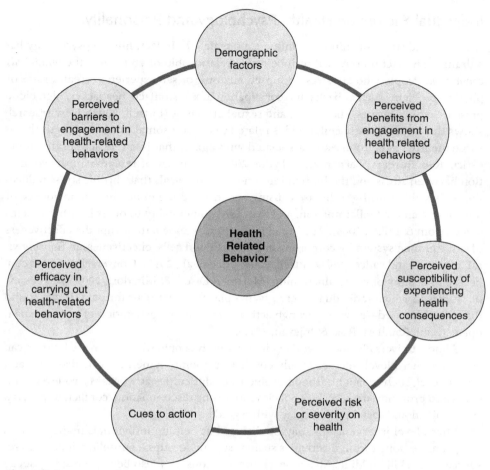

Figure 6.4
Health Belief Model (HBM)

• **Demographic/sociological variables.** In the HBM, demographic variables impact each component. At the risk of insulting your intelligence, here is an oversimplified example. Females are more likely than males to perceive that they are susceptible to breast cancer. Here the demographic of gender moderates perception of susceptibility. Both men and women do get breast cancer, though less than 1% of breast cancers occur in men (Korde et al., 2010).

Age also influences perceptions of susceptibility and severity of risk. Younger people worry less about diseases such as cancer or osteoporosis compared to older people. Race and culture also influence elements of the HBM. Some minority groups perceive more barriers to accessing health care resources compared to majority populations. One research group found Hispanic, Vietnamese, and Cambodian American women perceived more barriers to obtaining a mammogram compared to nonminority women (McGarvey et al., 2003). Further, the Vietnamese and Cambodian women differed in their perceptions of barriers indicating a need to understand the unique culture beliefs within minority groups rather than lumping all groups together.

Many demographic variables may influence HBM elements such as religion, sexual orientation, gender, race, immigration status, socioeconomic status, and education level. What role might these variables have on aspects of the HBM?

Assess your comprehension of Influencing Client Health by completing this quiz.

Individual Factors on Health: Psychology and Personality

Attitudes and states of mind also influence our health. In fact, human psychology has a dramatic impact on physical well-being—a relationship often termed the *mind–body connection*. People who are stressed, upset, anxious, or sad experience greater rates of physical problems such as back pain, constipation, upset stomach, headaches, high blood pressure, colds, herpes, chest pain, and sexual problems (Littrell, 2008). New research shows that stress in early childhood is related to chromosomal telomere length that is subsequently linked to diseases associated with aging; that is, stress accelerates aging (Price, Kao, Burgers, Carpenter, & Tyrka, 2012). A century of research on the connection between stress and the human immune system reveals that chronic stress reduces the body's ability to fight disease-causing agents resulting in heightened incidence of infection, increased inflammation, and increased vulnerability to other health problems (Segerstrom & Miller, 2004). At a broad level, stress is known to disrupt the effectiveness of our immune system by compromising white blood cells' effectiveness in fighting viral infections and cancer cells (Littrell, 2008; Price et al., 2012). Conversely, hope is connected to healthy physical functioning (Meissner, Distel, & Mitzdorf, 2007). In a review of studies in which individuals were given a placebo treatment for pain, it was found that pain decreased—possibly through activating the body's generation of a natural pain opiate (Puhl, Reinhart, Rok, & Injeyan, 2011).

Almost universally, social workers interact with people who are stressed. Stress can arise at a micro level, such as family conflict or unemployment. It can also arise at a mezzo level, such as neighborhood problems or difficulties at work. Macro-level influences also promote stress, such as policies supporting discrimination, conflict, or poverty. What role should social workers play with regard to stress?

Micro-level interventions may be directed at helping individuals manage stress and promote hope through activities such as support groups, counseling, linking to resources, and skill building. Mezzo-level interventions may also be influenced by social workers, such as advocating for the availability of childcare, health insurance, and flexible work hours. Macro-level interventions can also impact stress. Poverty, neighborhood quality (e.g., access to parks and recreation), discrimination-related policies, and economic factors are linked to the stress individuals experience (Littrell, 2008).

Indeed, social work's mission to support those in greatest need is an argument to consider the role of stress. Chronic stress is most damaging to individuals whose immune systems are already compromised. For example, individuals carrying the HIV who experience more stressful events without social support and who do not adequately manage stress tend to develop AIDS more rapidly and have a more rapid decline in CD4+ cell count, enter treatment with higher levels of the virus, and respond less well to antiretroviral therapy (Littrell, 2008). Science has even begun to understand the mechanisms by which stress compromises the functioning of individuals with HIV. Littrell states "Norepinephrine and Substance P, a stress hormone released by the sympathetic neurons enervating major organs and blood vessels, will increase the replication of HIV and increase the expression of receptors to which HIV can attach to gain entry into cells" (p. 23). That is, the sick may get sicker because a compromised immune system translates into a less adaptive system for fighting illness, which can result in even more stress.

Along with stress, "personality type" influences health. Cardiovascular disease is linked to "type D personality," which is characterized by high experience of negative emotion with low social connection (Grande, Romppel, & Barth, 2012). It appears that individuals with type D personality have higher levels of the stress hormone cortisol, which is linked to heart disease (Whitehead, Perkins-Porras, Strike, Magid, & Steptoe, 2007).

Anger is also associated with cardiovascular disease (Haukkala, Konttinen, Laatikainen, Kawachi, & Uutela, 2010; Shivpuri et al., 2011) across a variety of cultures. Persons who tend to be anxious and depressed are also prone to increased health problems. A review of studies examining the link between personality types that tend toward depression, anxiety, and anger suggests that a general disposition toward negative emotion is predictive of cardiovascular disease (Suls & Bunde, 2005).

Social Factors Related to Health

As can be seen earlier, individual personality and behaviors influence physical health and disease. Human health is also influenced by other people. For example, marriage increases life expectancy for males and reduces it for females. Specifically, men who marry tend to live about one year longer than those who don't. By contrast, women who marry tend to live about one year less than those who don't (Felder & Zhang, 2006). Will this research change your mind about marrying or staying married?

Social support is believed to promote health by increasing our ability to cope with stress (O'Donovan & Hughes, 2008). For example, among women affected with HIV, those who have higher levels of social support had a greater percentage of T cytotoxic/suppressor cells that serve to support the body's immune system (Danielson, 2003) and experience less stress (Lopez, Antoni, Fekete, & Penedo, 2012; Peterson, 2011). Of interest to social work, Danielson's study suggests that interventions can modify people's perceptions of social support, which then may rally the body's immune system. Other research suggests that having a strong social network may promote health through influencing healthy behavioral patterns (Jorm, 2005). Imagine a person, Regina, who participates in several friendships characterized by openly sharing emotions, concerns, and hopes. Regina reveals to her friends that she does not feel well; her friends strongly encourage Regina to seek medical attention and then follow up by asking if she has sought medical care. Further, her friends may provide material (e.g., babysitting, providing meals, transportation), financial, or emotional support and encouragement.

Social involvement may also provide salutary benefits through other pathways. Socially connected people may be more optimistic and generative, which is subsequently linked to improved health (Lu, 1997). Being socially connected affords opportunities to help others, which leads one to have positive feelings about the self and a sense of purpose (Schwartz, Keyl, Marcum, & Bode, 2009).

Interestingly, the benefits of social connection are not limited to humans. Research on nonhuman primates has consistently shown that good social skills are linked to positive health. Further, humans benefit from social interactions with nonhumans. Human involvement with animals, such as dogs, is linked to improved mental and physical health (Cutt, Giles-Corti, Knuiman, & Burke, 2007; Knight & Edwards, 2008; Owen et al., 2010; Salmon, Timperio, Chu, & Veitch, 2010). The reasons for improved health among pet owners are not fully known, though having certain pets, such as a dog, is linked to more exercise. Of course, owning a dog is not causally linked to improved health as people who like to exercise may be more likely to own a dog. Whatever the reason, pet ownership tends to benefit adults and children alike. Further, some therapies utilize animals to improve health (Nimer & Lundahl, 2007). Despite the beneficial tendencies of pet ownership, people with certain health problems, such as asthma, often fare more poorly if they own certain pets due to increased exposure to allergens (McConnell et al., 2006). However, there is also evidence that early exposure to furred animals protects against allergy development (Gern et al., 2004). In thinking about the impact of animals on health, the phrase *it depends* applies again.

Other evidence linking social relations to physical health comes from research on abuse, discrimination, and other negative social influences. A review of the impact of domestic violence, including physical and psychological and sexual abuse, showed a strong link between exposure to violence and mental health problems such as depression, substance abuse, and physical problems such as chronic pain and gastrointestinal problems (Macy, Ferron, & Crosby, 2009). A study conducted in association with the World Health Organization that sampled women from multiple countries found domestic violence was strongly linked to self-reported poor health, pain, memory loss, emotional distress, and suicidal thoughts and attempts (Ellsberg, Jansen, Heise, Watts, & Garcia-Moreno, 2008; Wu, Chen, & Xu, 2012). The associations between domestic violence and physical problems were strong and multicultural, meaning culture is not a safeguard against violence perpetrated against women. Further, research suggests that the untoward physical effects of domestic violence on women continue for years if the women survive. Indeed, domestic violence often results in significant trauma or death to women; police reports indicate that nearly 33% of murdered women were killed by intimate partner (Fox & Zawitz, 2007).

Researchers on the health effects of domestic violence conclude that in addition to being a violation of human rights, domestic violence is a public health issue (Humphreys, 2007; Macy et al., 2009). That is, the emotional and physical damage to survivors of domestic violence and abuse is costly. Imagine that a woman, Dianna, is severely attacked by her partner resulting in a black eye and a broken arm. Dianna's injury will likely prevent her from going to work—undermining her financial stability and costing the company money. Dianna will also need treatment for the broken arm and head injury, which, if she does not have health insurance, could cost hospital money and taxpayer monies. It is also possible that Dianna will receive money through a "victim's reparation fund," which may also be supported by taxpayer funds. Certainly, Dianna deserves the care needed and protection despite any costs—this example just goes to show how interpersonal relations are a public health issue as money that could possibly be spent elsewhere is directed to a preventable source—domestic violence. Further, the costs of responding to Dianna's attacker would need to be considered, including police costs, possible court-related costs, and possibly the broad costs associated with incarceration (e.g., actual security costs, loss of income from incarceration). This example shows how social phenomena of interest to social work, such as domestic violence, are a public health issue directly and indirectly. Cost estimates of domestic violence stretch to over 42 billion in the United States each year revealing the multiple tragedies of domestic violence (National Coalition Against Domestic Violence, 2007).

Human Behavior

Practice Behavior Example: Know about human behavior across the life course; the range of social systems in which people live; and the ways social systems promote or deter people in maintaining or achieving health and well-being.

Critical Thinking Question In your experience, what are the major social systems that promote and detract from physical health? What might be done to improve social systems to improve physical health?

Another example of how social relations impact health comes from child abuse. Child abuse can result in permanent physical problems (e.g., brain damage) and even death. Not all effects from child abuse are readily visible. One meta-analysis showed that health problems arising from child abuse last for many years and include problems such as general health complaints, gastrointestinal problems, pain, and obesity (Irish, Kobayashi, & Delahanty, 2010). Other studies have shown the physical effects of child abuse can easily last into midlife (Springer, 2009). For example, adults who were abused as children are more likely to smoke, which is linked to cancer and pulmonary and cardiac disease. Child abuse is also linked to obesity, which is associated with diabetes and other gastrointestinal problems.

Environmental Influences on Physical Health

Environmental factors also impact health. Both subtle and extreme examples provide support for this linkage. Well-known and obvious examples include the impact of war. Living in a country that has experienced chronic war dramatically reduces life expectancy through pathways such as poverty, combat, disease, and stress. Recall from Chapter 4 that life expectancy differs dramatically from those living in war-torn Sierra Leone (males = 38.6 years, females = 43.3 years) to those living in the United States (males = 75.3, females = 81.1). War also maims soldiers and impairs their ability to function due to head injuries, loss of limb, and posttraumatic stress disorder (Zinzow, Grubaugh, Monnier, Suffoletta-Maierle, & Frueh, 2007).

Other dramatic examples of environmental influences on physical health come from living in toxic areas or experiencing a disaster. The Chernobyl nuclear disaster in Russia is linked to thyroid cancer, genetic abnormality, death, mental health problems, and possible birth defects with long-term consequences that are still unfolding (Baverstock & Williams, 2006; Bromet, 2012; Jargin, 2011). Within the United States, Mexico, and other developing countries, physical health problems have resulted from exposure to mercury, lead, and other environmental toxins (Acosta-Saavedra et al., 2011; Goldman, 2005; Lee et al., 2009).

Many environmental influences on physical functioning are not dramatic, such as the impact of living near a busy motorway (Brugge, Durant, & Rioux, 2007; Karadžinska-Bislimovska et al., 2010). Communities living near major highways are exposed to high levels of ultrafine particulates, carbon monoxide, and other toxins linked to asthma, pulmonary stress, and cardiac problems. Quality of neighborhood is also linked to physical health. A study examining the impact of neighborhood quality in the Baltimore found that people living in "disadvantaged neighborhoods" were 400% more likely to experience heart attacks, 350% more likely to have a stroke, and about 400% more likely to have vascular problems compared to people living in "nondisadvantaged neighborhoods" (Augustin, Glass, James, & Schwartz, 2008). Neighborhoods were characterized using a scale that assessed disadvantage by looking at characteristics such as acts of violent crime, abandoned buildings, and signs of incivility such as graffiti—all of which promote a state of threat and stress among residents.

In another study, a relationship was established between living in a socioeconomically distressed neighborhood and perceptions of pain and physical dysfunction among children living with sickle-cell disease; this relationship was independent of a family's individual socioeconomic status (Palermo, Riley, & Mitchell, 2008). That is, regardless of a family's particular economic situation, neighborhood factors influenced how children with sickle-cell disease experience the disease. While research cannot tease out cause-and-effect relationships in these examples, evidence does link neighborhood quality to physical health and it is unlikely that children's perception of living with sickle-cell disorders cause neighborhood decline.

HEALTH DISPARITY

Some groups suffer poor health because of factors unrelated to personal choice or individual psychology. In the previous examples, what can a child living with asthma possibly do to improve his situation if he lives in an economically deprived neighborhood that just happens to be located near a major motorway? While asthma can strike any child, those living in poverty will suffer more. Health disparities based on group membership is a significant concern for social work as it speaks to issues of social and economic justice.

Unfortunately, many health disparities exist—too many to document in this textbook. Infant mortality is one such unfortunate example. Research from the CDC in 2000 and 2008 show that non-Hispanic Black and Puerto Rican families are much more likely to lose their infant children to death compared to other demographics (CDC, 2012). In fact, the infant mortality rate of non-Hispanic Blacks is more than double most other demographics as is shown in Figure 6.5.

Other examples of health disparity arise from statistics on cardiovascular disease and strokes among non-Hispanic White and Black populations. Data from the CDC suggest that the percentage of Black males who die before the age of 75 as a result of a stroke or coronary heart disease is about 60% compared to only about 35% of non-Hispanic White men. The same pattern held for women. About 38% of Black women died before the age of 75 due to coronary heart disease or stroke compared to only about 18% of White women (CDC, 2011a).

What explains such striking differences? What can be done to overcome such disparities? Considerable efforts are being made to both understand such discrepancies and close the gaps. For example, the work of Warnecke et al. (2008) reveals concerted efforts to improve the health of all individuals with an express goal of reducing discrepancies. The authors state:

> When the National Center on Minority Health and Health Disparities was established as part of the Minority Health and health Disparities Research and Education Act of 2000, all National Institutes of Health (NIH) institutes and centers were required to develop strategic plans for modifying and eliminating health disparities. (p. 1608)

From this work, a model has been developed to explain health disparities that can then guide efforts to reduce these disparities (a detailed overview of a health disparity model and related work can be found in the Centers for Population Health and Health Disparities, 2007). The model of health disparities includes factors that can be grouped

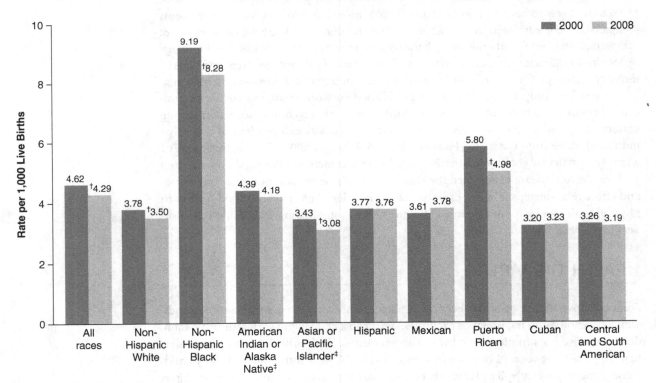

† Significant decline.
‡ Includes persons of Hispanic and non-Hispanic origin.

Figure 6.5
Infant Neonatal Mortality Rates by Race and Ethnicity of Mother in the United States
Source: CDC, 2012.

into three categories: proximal, intermediate, and distal. Proximal factors include biological influences such as genetics, disease, and other bodily systems. Intermediate factors include a mixture of factors that can be directly and indirectly influenced. Factors that can be directly influenced include individual risk/protective behaviors such as exercise, food consumption patterns, drug use, safety behaviors (e.g., sex practices), social engagement, and spiritual/religious practices. Other factors are rather indirect, though of interest to social work, such as one's physical context, neighborhood quality, access to health care, and social support. Distal factors include contexts that are influenced by policy (availability of health care, maternal leave policies) and social/cultural mores (stability of government, poverty). The health disparity model also considers factors such as developmental stage of life, and interactions among biological and environmental factors—much like Bronfenbrenner's model that was discussed in Chapter 2.

SOCIAL WORK AND BIOLOGICAL HEALTH

Social work is actively involved in efforts to preserve and improve physical health and limit the impact of poor health and disease. To get a sense of the breadth of social work's influence in areas of health, we conducted a brief search on an academic search engine. Three terms were used: *social work* AND *health* NOT *mental*. The search engine was PsychInfo via EBSCOhost in the fall of 2012. A total of 8,588 journal articles were identified. We highlight a fraction of topics that cross social work and some aspect of health care among the first 50 articles.

- Child development
- Child safety from physical abuse
- Health promotion
- Health disparity
- Coordinating health care activities
- Health care referrals surrounding childbirth
- Stigma related to disease, poor health
- Reducing incidents and impact of diseases such as
  - Cancer
  - HIV, AIDS
  - Diabetes
  - Fibromyalgia
  - Obesity
- Reducing risk behaviors
  - Smoking
  - Illegal drug consumption
  - Unsafe sex practices
  - Overeating
  - Poor exercise
- End of life care
- Stress management and prevention
- Genetic testing and counseling
- Ethical decision-making
- Vaccinations

- Health care policy (costs, disparity, ethics, social justice)
- Training health care workers about discrimination, social justice
- Human papillomavirus (HPV)—STD lined to cervical cancer
- Healthy eating/nutrition
- Management of health care teams
- Sleep hygiene
- Pregnancy: promoting healthy pregnancies, women's right to choose abortion
- Developing access to health care

Quite a list! Social work has become very involved in health care activities on all levels.

To be sure, social workers cannot perform many tasks related to biological functioning that are the domain of medical professionals such as nurses, doctors, and dentists. Social work does work collaboratively with allied professions, however. In fact, one aspect of the NASW Code of Ethics requires us to do so. Specifically, 2.03a states:

Assess your comprehension of Factors Influencing Health by completing this quiz.

> Social workers who are members of an interdisciplinary team should participate in and contribute to decisions that affect the wellbeing of clients by drawing on the perspectives, values, and experiences of the social work profession. Professional and ethical obligations of the interdisciplinary team as a whole and of its individual members should be clearly established.

ORGANIZATION OF HEALTH CARE INTERVENTIONS

Many health care interventions are organized into three broad types: primary, secondary, and tertiary prevention.

Primary prevention efforts are designed to avoid disease or injury. Interventions in this category are consistent with what most people recognize as prevention—avoiding problems before they begin. Population-wide efforts are common here, such as laws requiring citizens to wear seat belts, putting fluoride in the water, immunizations, and information campaigns aimed at preventing problems such as obesity or drug use. *Secondary prevention* efforts may not actually seem like prevention. Interventions in this class are designed to identify and treat existing problems in early stages as a means to limit the impact of the disease on individuals and communities. Secondary prevention may include activities such as depression screenings or prenatal assessments and care. Social workers routinely work in secondary prevention efforts. A school social worker may help a student who is struggling in class, and a social worker in a mental health clinic may be asked to help a person who recently lost a loved one to death and is beginning to show signs of depression.

Tertiary prevention efforts target people with an identified disease or health care problem. Efforts in this category are designed to either restore functioning to previously enjoyed levels or limit problems associated with a disease. A person struggling with a chemical addiction can be helped to overcome the addiction and to return to a consistently sober life. By contrast, a person who lost a limb, say a leg, will not be able to regenerate a leg, so efforts are designed to help the person function as well as possible. A fourth type of "prevention" involves ensuring that health-care interventions do not overreach or cause harm. This may involve efforts to not overprescribe medications, to ensure that a person is free to choose the least restrictive intervention, and to not deliver unnecessary treatments.

Assess your analysis and evaluation of this chapter's contents by completing the Chapter Review.

Juptierimages/BananaStock/Getty Images/Thinkstock

Cognitive Influences on Human Behavior

The degree to which humans think differentiates us from all other living things. Lions are not concerned about the morality of killing; humans are. Trees weep no tears as children starve under their leaves; humans do. Apes do not use their brains to develop technologies that, at the same time, produce tremendous good and evil; humans have and continue to do so. Yes, the degree to which we think differentiates us from all other living things on the planet and, therefore, has a remarkable impact on the human experience.

In Chapter 5, we introduced you to the biological structure and functioning of the human brain and models for how we take in, process, and utilize information. In this chapter, we cover other key tasks of the brain, such as learning and memory, which shape the human experience.

LEARNING

What do you already know about learning? As a student, you likely have heard many ideas about learning, such as "experience is the best teacher" or "tell me and I forget, show me and I learn," or, from medical school, "see one, do one, teach one." Multiple theories on learning exist, suggesting it is important. Prior to reviewing aspects of learning in depth, we provide examples that reveal why social work is concerned with learning:

- **Human development.** Many early childhood tasks are geared toward learning. Children learn language, social and behavioral rules, facts, and about what is safe and dangerous. Learning is the focus of elementary school, middle school, vocational and high schools, and college. Throughout the life span, learning is key to surviving and thriving. Success in the workplace, family, and recreation all requires learning to navigate unique demands.

- **Prosperity.** Learning can promote life quality by decreasing mistakes and promoting rewarding experiences. With regard to decreasing mistakes, remember Einstein's famous adage, which essentially states that "insanity is doing the same thing over and expecting a different result." Learning can change patterns leading to mistakes. Learning not only averts mistakes, it is associated with happiness and stability (Rego & Pina E Cunha, 2009). One micro-level practice theorist asserts counseling is fundamentally about helping individuals learn to live healthier (Peebles, 2012).

- **Pain.** Learning is not always healthy. Humans learn bad habits ranging from how to manipulate to how to participate in genocide. Machiavelli, the Italian author and political consultant, wrote an instructional manual on methods to gain and maintain control, often through violent means. Social workers in micro practice often see individuals who have "learned" maladaptive behaviors. For example, strong evidence indicates oppositional defiance during childhood is partially caused by positive and negative reinforcement—a form of learning (Webster-Stratton & Reid, 2010). In brief, children who do not get their way throw tantrums that are noxious to parents. Parents often give into the child's tantrums, which positively reinforces the child's tantrum throwing. Once the child gets his way, he stops throwing the tantrum that removes the noxious experience for the parent, a form of negative reinforcement (Forehand & Long, 2010). Many anxiety disorders are also a function of learning. For example, obsessive compulsive disorder (OCD) and posttraumatic stress disorder (PTSD) are partially explained by maladaptive learning. In short, people begin avoiding stimuli that make them uncomfortable. Short-term avoidance helps to manage anxiety in the short term, though it strengthens anxiety over the long term (Abramowitz, Deacon, & Whiteside, 2011). These two broad examples, disruptive child behavior and anxiety, reveal that learning can undermine life quality and is thus of interest to social work.

Humans are naturally curious.

Poonsap/Shutterstock

- **Inability to learn.** Some conditions, such as anterograde amnesia and mental retardation, interfere with learning. The inability to learn leaves individuals in an incredibly vulnerable position. Imagine not being able to learn how to use money, navigate a bus line, or prepare food. Social work obligates itself to supporting vulnerable populations, such as those who cannot learn effectively.

- **Learning is power.** Social work prizes learning that can promote the human condition. For example, we learned that individual parent training is more effective than group-delivered parent training for families facing economic and social disadvantage (Lundahl, Risser, & Lovejoy, 2006), and such information can guide treatment choices.

Having discussed the importance of learning, we now turn to some biological, psychological, and social explanations of learning.

Biological Explanations of Learning and Memory

At the most basic level, learning occurs when brain neurons change their configuration. A common phrase among neuroscientists studying learning and memory is, "neurons that fire together, wire together." Scientists have been able to watch neural pathways change during learning trials in the Aplysia sea snail (Vaughan, 1997). In humans, learning and memory are associated with brain structures, such as the hippocampus, the cerebellum, the amygdala, the caudate nucleus, the basal ganglia, and, among other regions, the frontal lobes. The amygdala and the hippocampus seem to be primarily responsible for the consolidation of memory, however. These brain areas control aspects of memory such as recognition, rehearsal of facts (working memory) that promotes their transfer to long-term memory, emotional memory such as fear, procedural memory, declarative memory, episodic memory, and semantic memory.

- **Working memory.** The temporary storage of information that can be manipulated for processing information or long-term memory development. For example, learning that one needs to buy milk at the store and rehearsing this information on the way to the store.

- **Procedural memory.** Unconscious memories about how to do things such as ride a bike, walk, or type.

- **Declarative or explicit memory.** Knowledge of facts such as "In 1492 Columbus sailed the ocean blue."

- **Episodic memory.** Autobiographical memories related to events such as when, where, and how one got to school.

- **Semantic memory.** Memories related to meaning, such as cheating is wrong.

- **Short-term memory.** The capacity to hold information in the mind for a short period of time (roughly 20 to 30 seconds) such that the information can be manipulated or rehearsed. For example, trying to recall people's names or numbers.

- **Long-term memory.** The capacity to recall information after a prolonged time, such as knowing the name of your first-grade teacher and remembering information related to your final examinations.

> **Human Behavior**
>
> *Practice Behavior Example: Utilize conceptual frameworks to guide the processes of assessment, intervention, and evaluation.*
>
> **Critical Thinking Question** How might the different types of memory promote a deeper understanding of the human experience among young children, adults, older adults, and individuals exposed to trauma?

> **Assess your comprehension of Memory by completing this quiz.**

While most social workers will not be involved in the neurobiological aspects of learning, we often engage in psychological and social forms of learning. Next, we provide a very brief overview of several major psychological theories of learning.

PSYCHOLOGICAL AND BEHAVIORAL THEORIES OF LEARNING

Near the beginning of the modern age of psychology and social work, circa 1900, two prominent theories of human behavior existed: Freud's psychodynamic model and Watson's and Pavlov's behavioral model. The behavioral models assumed human

> **Did You Know?**
>
> Do you know how neuroscientists learn which brain regions are associated with which memory or learning task? One method utilizes information from brain traumas. Scientists identify which aspect of memory is not functioning and then identify which brain region was damaged. Another method is to study brain activity during learning trials: Those regions that are "working harder" are linked to learning and memory.

Read Psychoanalytic-Based Approaches and Behavioral Theories to learn more about these approaches.

behavior is learned, whereas Freud assumed human behavior is impacted by drives. Next, we review some of the major forms of learning that originated from behavioral theories.

Classical Conditioning

Ivan Pavlov, an early pioneer in behaviorism, "stumbled" upon and developed a theory of learning while studying the digestive system. Of interest, he won the Nobel Prize in physiology/medicine in 1904 for his contribution to understanding the digestive system. Pavlov's work on learning launched a theory that rivaled Freud's and continues to guide effective psychotherapies in modern times. While studying the digestive system, Pavlov observed that his research subjects, dogs, would salivate to sounds and objects that were not food related. In brief, here is how the discovery came about. Pavlov would provide food for his dogs in a controlled laboratory setting and study their digestive patterns (see Figure 7.1 for an overview). He noticed that whenever he did certain tasks, such as opening a door, the dogs would begin to salivate even if he did not have food to present. This is extremely interesting as opening doors does not naturally generate a salivating response. To understand his work, we must first identify several elements in the learning process:

- **Unconditioned stimulus (UCS).** An UCS is an external phenomenon that naturally produces an internal result. For example, rich odors from cooking food (UCS) will produce the salivating response (unconditioned response) every time just as a loud and unexpected sound (UCS) will produce a startle response (unconditioned response) every time. Reactions to these stimuli do not need to be taught, they just happen likely due to instinct.

- **Unconditioned response (UCR).** UCRs are the naturally occurring responses to UCS. In the previous example, the startle reflex (UCR) and salivation (UCR) are not taught—they just happen. In classical conditioning, responses mostly arise from the autonomic nervous system, such as startle, salivation, increased heart rate, or blinking.

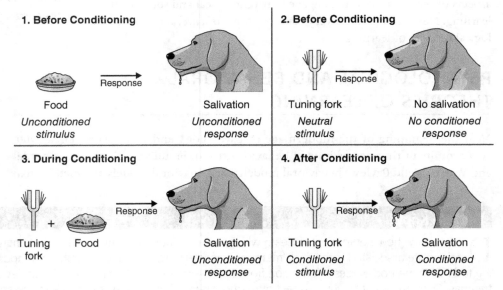

1. Before Conditioning

Food → Response → Salivation
Unconditioned stimulus   *Unconditioned response*

2. Before Conditioning

Tuning fork → Response → No salivation
Neutral stimulus   *No conditioned response*

3. During Conditioning

Tuning fork + Food → Response → Salivation
Unconditioned response

4. After Conditioning

Tuning fork → Response → Salivation
Conditioned stimulus   *Conditioned response*

Figure 7.1
Pavlovian Response

- **Neutral stimulus (NS).** A NS is a phenomenon that does not naturally elicit any response. For humans, many NS exist. Carpet, trees, clouds, pencils, shoes, money, and the like do not naturally produce autonomic physiological responses such as startle, salivation, or increased heart rate. For example, consider a check written for $1,000,000. If someone gave that to you, it is very likely your sympathetic nervous system would get very excited. Give the same check to a caveman of old and he would look at it and probably remain calm other than a slight curiosity of seeing paper with markings. There would be no extreme emotional reaction. Why the difference? Because a piece of paper with writing on it is a NS and will only evoke a strong response if we have been trained to think money is a good.

- **Pairing.** Learning occurs by pairing NS to UCS. If enough pairings happen, with the NS preceding the UCS, the person will begin to respond to the NS as if it were an UCS. Two things happen at this point. First, the NS is now a conditioned stimulus and the response is now a conditioned response even though it is the exact same response (i.e., salivation is still salivation). In Pavlov's case, opening the door or hearing a bell (conditioned stimulus) came before the dogs were fed (UCS). When the dogs heard the bell, they began to expect food because the bell often signaled the presentation of food and they would salivate even when no food was present (conditioned response). The bell began to act like an UCS—and yet it should be a NS. So the NS was transformed into a conditioned stimulus and the response, salivation, can now be a conditioned response.

- **Conditioned response (CR).** A CR is an autonomic nervous system response that occurs when presented with a stimulus that previously was a NS that has been transformed into a conditioned stimulus.

- **Conditioned stimulus (CS).** A CS is a stimulus that used to evoke no response from the autonomic nervous system that now does because it was repeatedly paired with an UCS.

Social workers in direct practice frequently interact with clients struggling with symptoms that arise from maladaptive learning understood through classical conditioning. Consider the case of a man in his early eighties who began a round of chemotherapy to treat cancer. After several rounds, the man becomes nauseous at the sight of any room that resembles the room where he receives chemotherapy. What has happened? To begin, there is an UCS and an UCR: chemotherapy (UCS) produces an involuntary bodily reaction of nausea (UCR). There is also a NS, the treatment room, which becomes—through associative learning—a CS as evidenced by the fact that rooms appearing similar to the treatment room automatically elicit feelings of sickness—and the feelings of sickness to treatment rooms now become a CR.

Research on classical conditioning has revealed several factors that influence the strength of and rate at which associated learning occurs. The following are terms and findings related to classical conditioning:

- **Generalization.** CS can generalize to stimuli that are similar, though not exact, to the original stimuli (UCS). For example, imagine that a mail carrier is rather comfortable (UCR) interacting with dogs (NS) until one day when he approaches a large, long-haired brown dog that barks very loudly at him and nearly bites him (UCS), which results in the man becoming very fearful (UCR). The mail carrier may begin to fear all large, long-haired dogs—not just the dog that almost bit him. Generalization does have limits. The more similar a NS is to the CS, the greater the likelihood of a similar CR. In this example, a large, long-haired brown cat or a miniature dog would not likely produce the same CR as the larger, long-haired dog.

- **Higher-order conditioning.** Similar to the concept of generalization, associations can be made between NS and CS, which will result in the NS producing a CR similar to the original CS. We will use Pavlov's dog experiment as an example. Once the bell has been established as a CS, the experimenter can get another NS, say turning on music, to produce the salivating response even if food is not delivered. That is, if the experimenter routinely turns on music and then opens the door that rings the bell and then provides food to the dog, the dog will begin to salivate at the turning on of the music. This tendency to broaden the range of stimuli that produce an UCR increases the likelihood that a response will occur.

- **Extinction.** A CS does not necessarily produce a CR in perpetuity, meaning that associative learning can fade or become extinct. *Extinction* is the term used for breaking the association between the CS and the CR. Extinction occurs when the CS is routinely presented without the original UCS, which will, over time, return the CS to a NS. For example, if the bell to Pavlov's dog kennel is routinely rung and no food is provided, then the bell will cease eliciting the salivation response and has returned to a NS over time.

- **Spontaneous recovery.** After a CS has reverted to a NS because of extinction, a phenomenon often occurs where the CR returns for a brief time. Thus, it appears that the CS is actually dormant but can return either with or without the presence of the UCS. Of interest, a repeated pairing of the UCS and the NS often returns the NS to a CS very quickly.

Application of classical conditioning

Assess your comprehension of Classical Conditioning as Learning by completing this quiz.

Social workers in direct practice utilize many principles of classical conditioning. Interventions guided by classical conditioning target aspects of the human condition linked to the autonomic nervous system such as emotions (e.g., fear, anxiety), arousal, and other reflexive conditions. Commonly treated problems include anxiety disorders, phobias, sexual disorders, and addictions (e.g., smoking, drugs). For example, systematic desensitization and exposure with response prevention are used to help people suffering from OCD and PTSD.

Operant Conditioning

Operant conditioning is the learning that occurs from the consequences that follow actions. Operant conditioning differs from classical conditioning on two primary factors. First, operant conditioning is linked to voluntary behaviors, such as jogging in the morning or hitting the snooze button, whereas classical conditioning is linked to involuntary experiences, such as hunger or fear that arise primarily from the autonomic nervous system. Second, operant conditioning focuses on what occurs after a person acts, whereas classical conditioning focuses on the pairings of stimuli before the body responds.

Consider two examples of operant conditioning. First, imagine a middle-school-aged child, Lara, on a diving board for the first time. The youngster stands fearfully at the end of the board while her friends chant "Jump! Jump! Jump!" Finally, Lara jumps and to her pleasant surprise neither drowns or is injured. After she gets out of the water, nobody is yelling at her. Would you expect the chances that Lara will go off the diving board again will increase or decrease? From an operant learning perspective, chances are that Lara is more likely to jump. Why? Because something uncomfortable has been removed after she jumped—the jeers of her peers. If an action brings relief, we are more to repeat that action. If you have a headache (an uncomfortable experience) and take medicine (an action) and the headache leaves (removal of an uncomfortable experience), you will be more likely to take the headache medicine in the future. This is called *negative reinforcement*.

Here is another example of operant conditioning. Benjamin is a 78-year-old widower who moved into a community of older individuals several years ago. Benjamin finds himself feeling rather lonely and decides it is time to take action by hosting a party. The party is a big success. Benjamin begins several new friendships, receives many compliments on his party-throwing skills, and secures a date. Would you expect the chances that Benjamin will throw another party will increase or decrease? From an operant learning perspective, the chances will increase. Why? Because Benjamin was positively reinforced. People who act and receive desirable outcomes are more likely to repeat the action that brought rewards. This is termed *positive reinforcement*.

From these examples, you probably have a good sense of many principles of operant conditioning. We now turn to some of the specifics. To begin, there are four technical terms that are critical to understanding operant conditioning.

- **Positive.** Positive means a consequence is present or added. In operant conditioning, positive has nothing to do with desirability, worth, or goodness. It simply means "present" or "added to" similar to how the term is used in pregnancy tests. If the woman is pregnant, the test is said to be "positive," regardless of whether the woman wants to be pregnant.

- **Negative.** Similarly, *negative* in operant conditioning simply means "removal" of a consequence or experience rather than some valuation of an experience. That is, negative does not refer to desirability, worth, or value.

- **Reinforcement.** The technical meaning of "reinforcement" in operant conditioning speaks to the probability that a behavior will occur in the future. If the probability is higher following a consequence, the consequence is said to have "reinforcing" value. Again, reinforcement in operational conditioning says nothing about desirability, kindness, or supportiveness.

- **Punishment.** The technical meaning of "punishment" is the exact opposite of reinforcement, a consequence that reduces the likelihood that a behavior will occur in the future is said to be a punishment. Thus, punishment is neither good nor bad, rather a consequence is said to be "punishment" if it suppresses the likelihood of future occurrence.

From these terms, four types of learning exist:

- Positive Reinforcement: Reward

  Something is added, the behavior is more likely to occur

- Negative Reinforcement: Relief

  Something is removed, the behavior is more likely to occur

- Positive Punishment: Pain

  Something is added, the behavior is less likely to occur

- Negative Punishment: Loss

  Something is removed, the behavior is less likely to occur

In teaching these terms, we find some students have difficulty letting go of their long-held meaning of each term. The best advice we have is, "don't think about the terms from a moral perspective." Rather, consider the terms from a technical point of view. If something is "added," use the word *positive*. If something is "removed," use the term *negative*. If the chance of a behavior increases, use the term *reinforcement*. If the chance of a behavior decreases, use the term *punishment*.

Box 7.1 illustrates a few examples that are often found on licensing tests. Try this strategy in figuring out which type of operant conditioning is at play. First, ask yourself—is the character more or less likely to repeat the behavior. If more likely, it is reinforcing; if less likely, it is punishment. Next, ask whether something was added or subtracted.

Box 7.1   Licensure Preparation: Know Your Operant Conditioning Terms

- Quiz 1. Rolando bullies a smaller student during class. Rolando's teacher yells at him to stop. Rolando teases the smaller student even more.
  - Is this an example of
    - a. Positive punishment
    - b. Negative punishment
    - c. Positive reinforcement
    - d. Negative reinforcement

  The correct answer is "C." Why? First, reinforced because Rolando bullies even more—the likelihood of bullying went up regardless of his teacher's intent. Second, it is positive because something was added—the teacher's "yell." Like you, we do not find bullying desirable nor do we find yelling at children positive. But, in this scenario, the operant conditioning theorists would unequivocally state that Rolando's bullying was positively reinforced by the teacher's action.

- Quiz 2. Regina bullies a smaller student during class. Regina's teacher yells at her to stop. Regina teases the smaller student less in the future.
  - Is this an example of
    - a. Positive punishment
    - b. Negative punishment
    - c. Positive reinforcement
    - d. Negative reinforcement

  The correct answer is "A." Why? Punished because Regina bullied less in the future. Positive because something was added—the teacher's "yell." Notice that the teacher's behavior (yelling) is the same in the first example. What matters is Regina's behavior, not the teacher's intent. Like you, we are glad that Regina bullies less in the future. However, we disagree with the teacher's method of yelling.

- Quiz 3. Hannah chooses to drive while drunk. She is pulled over, arrested, and taken to jail. The judge takes away her driving privileges for one year in addition to giving her a large fine. Hannah learns her lesson and never drives intoxicated again.
  - Is this an example of
    - a. Positive punishment

    - b. Negative punishment
    - c. Positive reinforcement
    - d. Negative reinforcement

  This one is a little tricky because of semantics. However, we say it is an example of "B." We know it is punishment because Hannah never drives intoxicated again. Negative because several things were removed from Hannah: her money via the fine, her freedom via going to jail, and her driving privileges. One could argue that this is an example of positive punishment because someone issued her a fine, sentenced her to jail, and ordered her to surrender her driver's license. Semantics may be at play here, though the real consequence is loss—items dear to Hannah were removed.

- Quiz 4. A social work professor, Dr. Flimsy, is excitedly talking about the assignments on the first day of class. Dr. Flimsy is sure the many assignments will help the students develop into effective social workers. The class, however, feels differently. They think Dr. Flimsy has asked too much of them. In collective fashion, the class complains there are simply too many assignments. They beg for a reduced workload and Dr. Flimsy gives in and cuts the assignments by half. In their next class, with Dr. No-nonsense, the class again makes bids for a reduced workload.
  - Is this an example of
    - a. Positive punishment
    - b. Negative punishment
    - c. Positive reinforcement
    - d. Negative reinforcement

  The correct answer is "D." The students continue to make bids for a reduced course work, which means their behavior has been reinforced. It is negative because something has been removed—the threat of a large workload. The students experience relief, and this relief encourages them to try the same strategy again. (*Note*: Do not try this in your home department.)

If something was added, it is positive; if something was subtracted or removed, it is negative.

Operant conditioning has a substantial theoretical and evidence base beyond the four types of learning. The schedule by which consequences occur following a behavior influences the degree to which "learning" occurs. There are five reinforcement schedules, which are described next. Note that these schedules are often used by teachers, human resource departments, employers, businesses, parents, policy makers, and social workers who are trying to shape or influence other people's behavior.

Reinforcement schedules

1. **Continuous ratio.** On a continuous ratio, a response is given each time a behavior occurs. If interested in punishing a behavior, such as selling illegal drugs, a strategy may be to assign a consequence to every person who sells or buys drugs regardless of circumstances. Further, each and every instance of buying or selling drugs would be met with a consequence—no exceptions. In reality, this is very hard to do.

   Presenting continuous feedback is beneficial in immediately shaping a behavior. However, the continuous presentation of a response often "habituates," meaning that the response no longer influences behavior. Give a child enough smiley faces and pretty soon she doesn't care about getting more. Lock a man up in prison for life and you might find he doesn't care if he uses drugs in prison.

2. **Fixed interval.** This schedule of reinforcement provides feedback, usually something designed to be desirable, after a fixed time period. Most people who work for an employer are paid on this pattern—a check comes (feedback) every 15 days (interval), regardless of job performance. The two primary aspects of this schedule are that it is fixed and that it is a function of the passing of time, not performance. Imagine a program designed to help people overcome addictions that relies on drug testing on a fixed interval: every 60 days a person will be tested for drugs. What do you imagine would happen about five days before the drug testing? What about the day after the drug testing?

3. **Variable interval.** In this schedule, the passing of time (interval) continues to be one key element. Thus, what a person actually does—does *not* determine the presentation of a consequence. The second aspect is variability. Here a response to behavior can occur after any amount of time, such as 1 day, 1 minute, 1 month, or 56 minutes; variability means there is no predicting when the response will come. Compared to the fixed interval schedule, the variable interval schedule is a stronger schedule in shaping human behavior or influence learning. Imagine the drug testing scenario using a variable interval schedule. The person is told, "You will be tested for drugs randomly for 60 days. It may be once, twice, or 60 times. Further, we may test you on consecutive days or not at all." This message is more likely to produce clean drug tests compared to the fixed interval schedule.

4. **Fixed ratio.** In this schedule, we again see the term *fixed*, meaning that consequences are applied consistently. A new term, *ratio*, emerges. Ratio refers to a behavior, such as chewing gum, swearing, driving while distracted, saying please, or calling your mother. Putting fixed and ratio together means that every time a target behavior is observed, a consequence will occur. For example, every time a child gets on the honor roll, the child's parents throw a party. Or, if every

Diversity in Practice

Practice Behavior Example: Appreciate that, as a consequence of difference, a person's life experiences may include oppression, poverty, marginalization, and alienation as well as privilege, power, and acclaim.

Critical Thinking Question How might living in an economically depressed and high-crime area influence patterns of operant conditioning and, therefore, learning?

Assess your comprehension of Operant Conditioning as Learning by completing this quiz.

time a person drinks alcohol while taking certain medication, she feels nauseous and wants to vomit. The fixed ratio pattern provides a stronger learning experience than the preceding three types (i.e., continuous, fixed interval, and variable interval) because a specific behavior must originate from the person, not the passage of time.

5. **Variable ratio.** Of the five interval schedules, the strongest "teacher" is the variable ratio. In fact, most of the money brought in through gambling is predicated on this reinforcement schedule. Variable means that a consequence happens on some but not all occasions and it is difficult to predict when the consequence will occur. Ratio, again, indicates a performed behavior. Put your dollar in the slot machine (ratio = action) and sometimes you win and sometimes you lose (variable). Many teenagers who develop patterns of illegal behavior (e.g., theft, drug abuse) will readily tell you that they are only occasionally caught (variable) for their illegal behaviors (ratio). On the positive side, if you intermittently (variable) praise a child who is working hard (ratio), you will likely see increased efforts at work.

Like classical conditioning, operant conditioning principles are widely used by social workers to influence the human experience. We now review two theories that provide slightly different takes on human learning: social learning theory and education.

SOCIAL LEARNING THEORY

To understand social learning theory, one simply needs to observe changing fashions. In the 1970s and 1980s, a popular hair style among men was the mullet—a distinctive style where the hair nearest the face was short while being worn long in the back. Some referred this hair cut as "business in the front and party in the back." Many women during this same time period, relying on copious amounts of ozone-depleting hair spray, wore their hair very high and very puffy. Now, why in the world would these two hair styles be popular? Instincts, classical conditioning, and operant conditioning clearly fail to explain style fads. You might think that operant conditioning can explain fads; however, why do certain styles take off all at once? It is unlikely that each individual practiced wearing his or her hair in such a manner and was reinforced. Social learning theory, by contrast, does explain fashion trends and other phenomena.

Social learning theory, advanced by Bandura (1977), posits that people learn by observing other people. The idea is simple. People (1) observe the behaviors of others, (2) notice the consequences that follow such behaviors, and (3) if interested in realizing similar consequences and (4) if able to remember what the other people did to elicit the consequences, and (5) will repeat such behaviors. Thus, if we observe in others a hairstyle that seems to bring considerable success, we are likely to try the style ourselves even though we personally did not experience the reinforcing consequence. Or, if a person notices that a particular haircut brings ridicule from important referent groups (e.g., peers, superiors), the person will likely avoid that haircut.

Social work generally does not get very interested in haircuts or fashion. We do, however, care about many behaviors connected to social learning theory. Aggression and prosocial behaviors have been shown to be, in part, a function of social learning. Kaiser,

Snyder, and Rogers (1995) found that children introduced to "antisocial toys" or "prosocial toys" by adult models tended to act consistent with the toys. That is, young children modeled aggression or prosocial behaviors based on what they observed. If the adult modeled aggression, the child would tend to emit aggression. Other behaviors that may be learned through modeling include belonging to a gang, using drugs, joining a sporting team, going to college, and choosing to engage in social demonstrations, altruism, and so on. How might social workers leverage social learning theory to promote the human experience?

The following are five basic ingredients to social learning:

1. Attention is paid to a model who demonstrates a behavior (e.g., smoking, helping, asking for a job).

2. Attention is paid to the consequences the model experiences. If smoking brings about a perceived sense of social attraction, the observer is "learning" that smoking is desirable. By contrast, if smoking brings about ridicule and punishment, the observer learns smoking is undesirable.

3. Retention of the modeled behavior. The observer must retain a mental representation of the modeled behavior and mentally rehearse the behavior.

4. Enactment capacity. The observer must be capable of repeating the behavior. That is, even though we social workers might (1) watch (attend) a gymnast do a fantastic routine on the parallel bars and (2) receive hearty applause (attend to positive consequences) and (3) think about doing the parallel bars ourselves, we will likely not do what the gymnast did because (4) we cannot enact such a complicated behavior. Closer to social work, it may be very difficult for some individuals to enact behaviors such as asking for a job, assertively responding to a violent partner, or engaging in mindfulness because these behaviors are complex.

5. Motivation. Motivation from social learning comes from expected consequences from the behavior, depending on what was observed from modeling and from a sense of efficacy.

Once an observer has "acted," the forces of learning from classical and operant conditioning will come into play as will other cognitive forms of learning. For example, imagine that a young adolescent, Ronnie, observes his peer, Johnny, being socially rewarded for disrupting a school class through sarcastic and aggressive remarks. Specifically, other kids laugh at Johnny's remarks, saddle up to Johnny in an attempt to befriend him, and give him compliments. Further, they talk "war stories" about how

Much of our learning comes from modeling others.

"cool" Johnny is because he is disruptive. Ronnie notices that disruptive behavior brings about social rewards and tries mimicking Johnny's behavior. Once he has acted, the world will either reward or punish the action.

Social learning theory guides interventions targeting a wide range of unhealthy behaviors such as poor diet, aggression, depression, unprotected sex, and criminal behavior. Other applications of social learning theory aim to increase adoption of healthy behaviors. Learning environments often encourage the adoption of socially desirable behaviors by drawing attention to desired behaviors (e.g., staying on task) while providing rewards (e.g., verbal praise) as a method to help other children attempt similar behaviors.

EDUCATION

Education is a major force on human behavior. On a national level, a strong education system is positively associated with life satisfaction, effective government, and economic development (Advisory Committee on Student Financial Assistance, 2012; Jones, 1998). Countries with better education systems provide a better opportunity for their populations to thrive. Further, when individuals do not go to school, they tend to suffer in many aspects, such as increased experimentation with drugs, alcohol, higher rates of crime, increased teen pregnancy, and higher rates of poverty—plenty of reasons why politicians often campaign on the need to improve education systems (Clark et al., 2010; Coalition for Evidence-Based Practice, 2008).

That you are studying in college means there is no need to preach to you about the benefits of education. However, what is social work's role in education and how do we collaborate with educators? After all, education is a well-established profession and trains teachers to educate individuals at all levels. That said, going to school is not all about the learning to read, write, and do arithmetic—a fact that rarely escapes college students around spring break. The following are some areas in which social workers align with educators to promote learning.

Many students do not benefit from education because personal issues interfere with their ability to attend school. A child from an economically challenged family may not routinely attend school because, despite being "free," public school costs money. Bus passes, gasoline, registration fees, and school supplies all cost money. Further, economically challenged families may limit school attendance because of work conflicts or health care issues. A family without insurance may not be able to respond to their children's illnesses, which may prolong an illness and prohibit the child from attending school.

Attendance is not the only area where the interest of social workers and educators cross. Once a child is in school, several factors may undermine performance such as a child's homelife. Imagine a child who is fearful that her mother will be physically attacked by the mother's boyfriend—this child will have difficulty thinking about basic math or reading when her mother's safety is at risk. Hunger is another issue. A persistently hungry child cannot be expected to perform as well as a child with similar mental abilities who is not hungry. For these reasons, school breakfast and lunch programs have been developed. Other children struggle to focus in school because of mental health issues, such as learning disabilities, low intelligence, or mental illness. A 16-year-old girl who is experiencing positive symptoms of schizophrenia, such as hallucinations, will have a difficult time focusing. Similarly, a child with attention deficit/hyperactivity disorder will struggle to attend to information needed to succeed or follow through with routine tasks. Severe depression will impede a student's motivation to work, undermine focus, and decrease the mental capacities needed to complete work.

School is also an environment—an environment where students both thrive and struggle. On the thriving side, students can participate in extracurricular activities, such as musical experiences and sports, and develop deep and lasting relationships. On the negative side, students can be bullied and experience deep rejection. The recent spate of school shootings by students reveals the deep feelings students experience within the walls of school.

The preceding examples reveal areas of interest to social workers that go beyond learning the facts. Social workers hired on school campuses work with students individually and in groups to promote success in school. They also advocate for policies and programs that support students.

INTELLIGENCE

Not all humans have equal capacity to learn, remember, solve problems, appreciate complexity, do math, create music, play sports, or survive in urban or wilderness conditions. Such variation in capacity is often understood broadly through the concept of "intelligence." Awareness of variation in mental capacity has been around for centuries, as evidenced by the value placed on great thinkers such as philosophers and classic writers. However, only within the last 100 or so years have attempts been made to formerly assess intelligence. The history of intelligence assessment is interesting because attempts to understand intelligence initially advanced narrow ideas on intelligence only to give way to expanded views on intelligence (Murdoch, 2007).

A narrow view of intelligence initially arose because of a problem. Specifically, in about 1900, the French government enacted a policy requiring all children attend formal school. However, not all children were prepared to enter and succeed in school. To identify which students would need extra support, the government commissioned psychologists to develop tests of mental ability. This effort gave birth to the "intelligence test," which rather narrowly examined individual ability to perform on problems found in formal education settings. Alfred Binet and other French psychologists developed tests of mental ability that rather accurately predicted which students would do well and which would need support. To organize their findings, Binet and colleagues developed the concept of "mental ability." It was noticed that students of a certain age tended to know and be able to solve problems of a certain sort. An example in modern U.S. culture is that most children under four years of age cannot read nor do multiplication while most children over age nine can read and multiply. Thus, an early definition of intelligence was the ability to perform certain school-related tasks—such as reading, understanding concepts, performing math, solving problems, focusing, and remembering material. Binet and colleagues developed batteries of questions that assessed performance in such tasks and reported on the average ability of certain age groups. Two concepts were important to this type of intelligence testing: mental age (mental ability) and chronological age. Mental ability represents performance within a certain area, regardless of age. Thus, some precocious four-year-old children can read and do multiplication, while some adults do not read and cannot multiply. Combining these two concepts, mental age and chronological age produced the term *intelligence quotient* (IQ). Indeed, the term *IQ* has become synonymous with mental capacity. For years, however, the term *IQ* was viewed from the perspective of education—in part because the first efforts at formally assessing mental ability were in the schools. More recently, the term *IQ* is applied to a variety of tasks such as emotional reasoning or emotional IQ. Thus, you may well hear terms such as *football IQ, dating IQ,* or *music IQ.*

Of interest, the rather narrow view of intelligence and the method of understanding mental ability ultimately caused problems for certain groups. Specifically, Binet applied his standardized questions to large groups of children to determine the average ability (mental age) of children within certain age groups (chronological age). However, Binet's original test questions and iterations of other intelligence tests used language and problem solving that were simpler for some groups of children because of familiarity. For example, language used by most White communities differs from language used by Black or Latino communities. One can understand, then, that the children of White families will have greater familiarity with terms used on the tests than children from diverse backgrounds translating into better scores on IQ tests, which also translates into greater opportunities and access to resources. While Binet reportedly warned against this problem, clear evidence exists that standardized testing of abilities disproportionately favors certain groups based on test construction rather than actual ability (Murdoch, 2007). More on racial bias follows.

Another historical factor played an important role in measuring intelligence. Similar to the French's effort to identify the unique needs of students, the U.S. government was keenly interested in assessing the mental abilities of large numbers of men during the buildup to World War 1. The army literally needed to process hundreds of thousands of men into military divisions, such as frontline soldiers, leadership positions, and logistic experts. Further, the military wanted to identify recruits not suited to war because of low mental ability. To support this effort of processing potential recruits, tests of ability or intelligence were developed.

Efforts to identify and help school-aged children in France, and the U.S. government's attempt to process soldiers in a sensible manner, spawned many debates on the nature of intelligence and how to assess it. As we have mentioned, these debates have morphed over time—moving from rather narrow views of intelligence, which required doing well in traditional school settings, to broader views of intelligence. We now turn to some common frames for understanding intelligence, though we fully expect they will give way to new frames across time. Further, we do not try to identify any one "winning theory," as each theory has both support and criticism (see Boake, 2002; Gardner, 1999; Reynolds & Kamphaus, 2003; Santrock, 2008; Sternberg, 2000).

Two-Factor Theory on Intelligence

Some theorists argued that intelligence can be divided into two broad factors: a general intelligence and discrete intelligences. The *s-factor* was the term assigned to performance on *specific* or discrete abilities, such as memory, attention, verbal comprehension, abstract reasoning, spatial reasoning, vocabulary knowledge, and fund of knowledge. The second factor was considered the general ability or *g-factor*. The g-factor assumes that performance in specific mental abilities is determined by an overall intelligence. Ability to perform well in one area, such as math, should predict the ability to perform in other areas, such as verbal reasoning. A popular test of mental ability in current use, the Wechsler Adult Intelligence Scale (WAIS; Wechsler, 2003; see also Boake, 2002), is roughly based on this two-factor model where there are 14 subtests (s-factors) that test two broad areas (verbal IQ and performance IQ) and an overall composite IQ score.

Three-Factor Theory of Intelligence

Another framework for understanding mental ability is termed the *triarchic* theory of intelligence, proposed by cognitive psychologist Robert Sternberg (2000). This theory proposes that intelligence is much more than being able to take a test that will predict how well someone does in school. Rather, intelligence is about how well humans do in adapting to life demands through problem-solving performance. Those with better adaptive intelligence are more likely to survive and thrive in life. Much like information processing and problem-solving models, Sternberg's theory notes that the mind needs to (1) recognize problems, (2) propose potential responses, (3) evaluate responses to problems, (4) enact responses, and ultimately (5) learn from the effectives of tried solutions. This more pragmatic notion of intelligence has three subdivisions.

1. **Component/analytical intelligence.** This strain of intelligence is the ability to recognize conventional problems and break them down into component parts. Strengths in this area are evident by having good "book smarts"; that is,

an ability to apply conventional knowledge to solving problems. Interestingly, Albert Einstein may not have been viewed to have high levels of component intelligence as he performed very poorly in traditional classes.

2. **Experiential/creative intelligence.** Another strain of intelligence is the ability to deal with routine versus novel problems. Being adept at solving routine problems, such as how to negotiate the bus and subway system, may not be linked to the ability to solve novel problems, such as global warming and immigration challenges. Creativity is not easily measured by standardized tests of intelligence that focus on performance in conventional settings. Thus, individuals high in creativity may score poorly on traditional IQ tests, but go on to develop theories on relativity and energy like Einstein did.

3. **Practical/contextual intelligence.** Another strain of intelligence is the ability to adapt to one's environment—also known as *street smarts*. Fitting into one's environment is critical to surviving and thriving. Imagine the many tasks involved in moving to a new environment, such as a new school or a new job. Practical or adaptive intelligence describes how individuals may successfully make a healthy fit between their environment and themselves, using three possible strategies: adaptation, shaping, and selection.

   - Adaptation refers to when an individual changes to adjust to the surroundings. For example, imagine an individual who is making a career shift—possibly from the role of a student to that of an employee. If the student had a very loose dress code during school but now works in a formal environment, the adaptive response would be to change her dress. Or imagine the demands of a teenager who moves to a neighborhood dominated by a certain gang. Although the individual may not want to join the gang, survival may hinge on adopting gang-like behaviors or joining the gang.

   - Shaping refers to efforts to change one's environment to suit one's preferences. An example of shaping is to request a night shift so that one can go to school during the day. In another case, after discovering that a child has been drinking alcohol in the house with a particular friend, parents may institute a rule that friends are only invited when parental supervision is present. At macro levels, laws are instituted to prevent underaged individuals from buying tobacco and alcohol products.

   - Selection refers to identifying an environment that matches one's needs. Choosing to pursue a degree in social work, for example, represents an effort to select a career that matches one's personality. Individuals routinely select an environment that fits their life goals—whether it involves leaving one's homeland or choosing a job—we humans attempt to select environments that promote adaptation. Of course, true selection requires resources.

Multiple Intelligences

Similar to concepts proposed by the "s-factor" of intelligence, mental ability or intelligence has been viewed to go beyond tasks associated with school-like performance. Howard Gardner (1999) proposed a variety of cognitive abilities within the "multiple intelligences" that humans exhibit such as musical, mathematical, spatial reasoning, physical, linguistic, social or interpersonal, knowledge of self (intrapersonal), and existential.

Similar to the Gardner's theory of multiple intelligences, Cattell, Horn, and Carroll (McGrew, 2005) advanced a concept of intelligence that included 10 broad areas of intelligence that have up to 70 narrow or discrete intelligences. The 10 broad areas include the following:

1. Crystallized intelligence—fund of acquired knowledge/facts and the ability to communicate such knowledge; what we know

2. Fluid intelligence—ability to reason, problem solve, and form concepts using unfamiliar information and procedures; ability to interact with new concepts

3. Quantitative reasoning—ability to interact with numbers and reason about symbols and numbers

4. Reading and writing—basic skills in reading and writing

5. Short-term memory—ability to hold and use information for a few seconds

6. Long-term memory and retrieval—ability to move information from short-term memory to a long-term storage and the attendant ability to retrieve it upon will

7. Visual processing—ability to perceive, analyze, manipulate, and synthesize visual patterns

8. Auditory processing—ability to perceive, discriminate, analyze, and synthesize auditory stimuli

9. Processing speed—ability to speedily perform tasks

10. Reaction time—ability to speedily react to a stimulus or demand

The multiple theories of intelligence reveal that no one concept captures human's mental capacity. Indeed, it seems "unintelligent" to seek a single explanation to describe the mind's ability to recognize, process, analyze, synthesize, and use experience.

Intelligence: A Dependent and an Independent Variable

If defining intelligence seems difficult or contentious, you are in for a surprise when asked to consider what intelligence does for humans and what factors influence intelligence. What are the benefits of intelligence? In general, science can comfortably state that having higher levels of intelligence is good. Intelligence, in all its many forms, is positively associated with socioeconomic status, performance in work and education, income, wealth, health, and staying out of trouble (Austin et al., 2002; Furnham & Christoforou, 2007; Sjöberg, 2008). Correlations between measured intelligence and benefits are certainly not 100%. That is, at some point, higher levels of intelligence do not continue to be helpful. Given that intelligence is positively correlated to desirable outcomes, it would be good to know how to promote it. Intelligence is multiply determined—meaning that no factor is solely responsible for intelligence. Fortunately, several key factors have been identified, though the nature and degree of their contribution is still being explored and debated. The following ingredients are linked to intelligence: genetics (heritability, chromosomal disorders), brain health (injury, stroke, disease, nutrition, fetal development, drugs), age (dementia, Alzheimer's), experience (educational opportunities, socioeconomic status), trauma (abuse, war), and general health.

Watch the video Mainstreaming Children With Special Needs. How might social workers promote cognitive development among special needs children? What controversies might surround mainstreaming special needs children within educational settings?

Many of the factors linked to intelligence cannot be modified because they are related to biological processes that either cannot be influenced or, depending on ethics, should not be modified. However, some influences on intelligence certainly can be impacted. Nutrition can be influenced through policies that promote access to healthy food and education about the benefits of healthy eating. The fetal environment can be influenced through policies about substance use, such as the impact of smoking or drinking while pregnant, and support for prenatal care. Living environments can be enriched, especially for those who have historically not enjoyed exposure to varied experiences, to promote learning.

A remarkable theory and strategy for enhancing people's mental abilities derives from Russian psychologist Lev Vygotsky who proposed that individuals tend to have two performance abilities: (1) the capability to perform independently or without guidance and (2) the capability to perform with guidance or support. The combination of these two capacity levels is termed the *zone of proximal development*. The lower end of the zone is what individuals can accomplish without guidance or support and the upper end of the zone is what individuals can accomplish with support that gently stretches performance. Considerable research reveals that learning is accelerated when support is given. For example, children with Down syndrome acquire task proficiency more quickly if given tailored feedback and support that stretches their learning (Nilholm, 1999; Poehner, 2010). The term for providing support is *scaffolding*, with the image that scaffolding near a building is dynamic and changes as needed. Once a task is mastered, scaffolding or support in that particular area is no longer needed and can be directed to other areas. The zone of proximal development does not espouse a belief that all people can achieve equal cognitive capabilities—just that most individuals' capabilities can be stretched with proper guidance. Application of ideas derived from the zone of proximal development have been applied to many areas of cognitive ability, such as learning material typically taught in schools and developing vocational skills.

> **Engage, Assess, Intervene, Evaluate**
>
> *Practice Behavior Example: Implement prevention interventions that enhance client capacities.*
>
> **Critical Thinking Question** How might knowledge of the different theories of intelligence influence prevention and intervention approaches in a manner consistent with National Association of Social Workers Code of Ethics?

CULTURAL BIAS IN ASSESSING MENTAL ABILITY

As was briefly mentioned earlier, tests of mental ability carry biases that produce invalid pictures of actual ability. In general, test bias produces higher scores for the majority race, White populations in the United States, compared to minority populations (Elliott, 1988; Reynolds & Suzuki, 2013). The implications arising from potential bias are staggering—both immediately and in the future. Imagine this scenario: two students of equal mental ability but of different cultural backgrounds have aspirations of attending college. They take a test that purportedly assesses mental ability, but the test is racially biased such that despite being equal in ability, the White student scores better than the minority student. The White student is admitted while the minority student is not. At the individual level, the White student now has access to resources, a college education, and connections to professionals who can open many career doors and the potential for higher income. These opportunities will likely translate into a life of greater potential for the individual and his or her family. Conversely, the minority student will encounter greater challenges to upward mobility and could easily experience greater pressure and stress. The combination of missed opportunities and increased stress could also easily impact this individual's future family in a negative manner.

> **Watch the video Drapetomania, which shows that, during slave times, runaway slaves were given a diagnosis. If this is the case, how might IQ tests also be invalid?**

Other examples of test bias do not rely on the hypotheticals offered in the previous example. Employers have required tests of ability that were proved to discriminate against racial minorities, meaning that doors of opportunity were shut based on unfair testing. In response to this practice, laws were established prohibiting such practices (Elliott, 1988). Further, companies designing tests of mental abilities are required to

{ Assess your comprehension
of Intelligence by completing
this quiz. }

design their tests in a manner believed to minimize the potential for racial bias and to investigate the degree to which their assessment tools carry bias.

A review of the literature reveals that many questions exist about the degree to which many standardized ability tests are culturally loaded or biased. Further, the degree to which culturally sensitive tests are valid or helpful is also debated. For example, developing two separate IQ tests, one for White individuals and one for Black individuals, may ultimately cause more damage than good by establishing two baselines.

STAGE MODELS OF COGNITIVE DEVELOPMENT BY AGE

You do not need to be told that thinking ability depends, in part, upon age. Three-year-old children cannot be expected to know or perform mental operations of the same complexity as college students. A pioneer in examining children's cognitive development was Jean Piaget (1896–1980) who, as a scientist and father, noticed that his children's thinking involved qualitatively different operations, rather than simply more of a particular ability (Santrock, 2008; Shaffer & Kipp, 2009). That is, Piaget noticed that cognitive development progresses in stages. By studying his children's reasoning about certain problems, Piaget produced a theory of cognitive development that continues to spark interest and research after nearly 60 years. Certainly, many of his ideas have been challenged—though his primary work continues to be influential. The stages and abilities can be found in Table 7.1. Note that ages at which the stages tend to develop are also presented—though in practice you may find great variation to abilities based on age.

Piaget also developed other terms that significantly help us understand cognitive development, namely the notion of *assimilation* and *accommodation*. Assimilation refers to bringing in new information and accommodation refers to integrating new information into existing models of understanding. A metaphor may help with understanding these terms. Imagine you buy a new house and you have no furniture. Assimilation would involve bringing new things into the house. The first items you bring in are likely to require very little initial "decorating coordination" because the house is empty—there is no decoration scheme or model. However, once you start bringing things into the house, you need to accommodate. How will one piece of furniture interact with other decorations or furniture items? Accommodation is the process of either modifying established beliefs or forcing new information into existing beliefs.

Assimilation is at work when young children learn that four-legged creatures with long tails are called *dogs*. However, a young child is very likely to see other four-legged creatures with long tails that are actually cats. Because of lack of experience, the child will call the cat a dog—because that is the child's scheme. Parents and siblings will say, "No, that's a cat," and the child must now accommodate an existing belief: moving from thinking that all four-legged creatures are dogs to understanding that some four-legged creatures are cats.

Piaget believed that a central task in learning to interact with the world is to assimilate information and accommodate it in such a way that represents "reality." This task is a lifelong activity that involves areas such as interacting with people who differ from you in terms of gender, age, religion, race, socioeconomic status, and ability. Other examples involve learning about human behavior in the social environment (shameless plug intended), assimilating information about different types of intelligence, and accommodating this new information into an understanding.

Table 7.1   Piaget's Stages of Cognitive Ability

Stage	Age	Ability
Sensorimotor	Birth to 2 years	Infant develops an understanding of the world through interactions with the environment. The child can track objects by coordinating eyes and neck muscles, develop repeated actions to accomplish goals (e.g., suck thumb to calm self), experiment with objects (e.g., banging a dish and spoon to make a sound), and begin to use symbols, revealing a step toward insightful thinking and more complex reasoning. Toward the end of this stage, children notice that they are different from their environment and can hold mental pictures of objects, producing a sense of object permanence. Prior to object permanence, an infant's mother may leave the room and the child will not become distressed presumably because the infant does not have a permanent memory of the mother. Once the child begins to experience distress when the mother leaves, it is hypothesized that the child knows the mother should be present but is not. Similarly, prior to object permanence, an object, such as a toy, can be taken away from the baby and the baby will not become distressed because the toy no longer exists in memory. After object permanence, however, taking a toy away from a baby will be upsetting.
Preoperational Symbolic	2 to 4 years	Increases in the symbolic substage reveal increased mastery over language. In this stage, children still have difficulty with abstract reasoning and rely on magical beliefs to explain the world. Thinking tends to be egocentric, with little ability to perspective taking despite increasing ability to engage in pretend play.
Intuitive	4 to 7 years	Emerging reasoning develops that does not rely on magical thinking or egocentric perspectives. Children display high levels of curiosity, often asking "why" questions. Children at this stage, however, have difficulty with many formal mental operations. For example, they have difficulty with "conservation," which involves transforming substances or objects. When presented with two beakers of the same size and the same amount of liquid, children in this stage of cognitive development show the ability to logic that there is an equal amount of liquid; however, if one of the liquid containers is poured into a beaker of a different shape (shorter but wider), the child will likely say the taller beaker has more liquid. This failure to realize that liquid volume across the beakers are equal reveals that children focus too much on one property, beaker height, rather than logically indicating that no liquid was removed so it must be the same. This error arises from children's overreliance on one aspect or characteristic—a term known as *centration*, or focusing all attention on one central aspect.
Concrete operational	7 to 11 years	In this stage, reasoning becomes more logical, though still reliant on concrete, observable properties of materials. Conceptualization about nonphysical aspects of the world is difficult. That said, children at this age can do basic logical operations, such as classify objects more effectively, sort objects on a variety of characteristics, and consider the perspective of others that leads to decreased egocentric thinking.
Formal operational	11+ years	From puberty and beyond, children tend to think in complex and abstract terms. They can reason logically and consider problems that do not rely on concrete facts. This stage is marked by the ability to engage in inductive and deductive reasoning, as well as to develop and refute hypotheses. While individuals in this stage may think about only themselves, they have the capacity to consider other people's perspectives.

Source: Adapted from Santrock (2008); Shaffer & Kipp (2009).

Clinical Corner

How can social workers apply ideas from Piaget's cognitive development model? To begin, appreciation should be given to the fact that mental abilities seem to develop in stages and it is unreasonable to expect performance beyond one's stage. For example, a social worker who really likes cognitive therapy will bump into frustration when attempting to get a five-year-old child to engage in the abstract reasoning needed to evaluate and dispute distorted, automatic beliefs.

Assess your analysis and evaluation of this chapter's contents by completing the Chapter Review.

Another application of Piaget's theory is that accommodation can be hard. Imagine, for example, an individual who developed a belief or scheme (through repeated iterations of assimilation and accommodation) that a certain religion is true over the course of her early life. Accommodating information contrary to the existing scheme, a model of deity and a plan for life and death, will likely result in confusion and anxiety for some amount of time. Similarly, a new parent who has a scheme that his newly born son will gleefully go hunting, fishing, and camping may have a difficult time accommodating to new information that his child is not interested in such activities and actually prefers radically different pursuits.

8

Mat Hayward/Fotolia

Social Influences on Human Behavior

The debate about origins of human behavior and the relative impact of the social environment and biology on individual behavior has been ongoing for years. While some scientists argue that biology or genetics is the major factor in how people develop, others believe that the social environment plays a key role in almost all areas of human life. Guerin (2001) argues, for example, "the contexts for acting are almost all provided by other people, even when one is alone" (p. 411). He also suggests that "all of the most important verbal or cognitive functional activities of adults have . . . their control in social origins" (p. 412). From this perspective, it is easy to see how powerful the social environment can be in shaping human behaviors.

The interaction of an individual with the social environment can influence human behavior in at least two ways. First, the social environment can impact the individual's genetic or inherited makeup that predisposes him or her in a particular way. However, genetic predisposition does not guarantee or predetermine how the person will actually behave. It is the combined influence of the environment and one's genetic makeup that better explains individual behavior than genetics alone. For example, take a multi-generational family history of substance abuse, which would suggest that genetics plays a role in predisposing a family member to potential addiction. But, whether children or grandchildren from this family develop substance abuse problems may be influenced by factors in the social environment. Parental behavior that discourages alcohol consumption, membership in groups that frown on drug use (e.g., churches), and association with peers who do not use drugs can counter a genetic predisposition toward substance abuse.

A second way that the social environment can influence human behavior involves areas in which there is no biological predisposition.

Mat Hayward/Fotolia

Social influences occur in all phases of our lives.

That is, the individual is more or less a blank slate and the social environment can exert enormous influence on development. Using the example of substance abuse again, it is clear that the social environment can have a major influence on things such as drinking behavior. Rose (1999), found that use of alcohol by peers significantly predicted alcohol use by the individual. Similarly, Borsari and Carey (2001) concluded that peers were a major influence on college student's abuse of alcohol.

In this chapter, we'll look at several social influences on human behavior covering areas such as personality, identity formation, socializing forces, peer relations, social support, relationships, and moral development.

PERSONALITY

We often encounter the word *personality* in everyday use. Examples include "Mary has a great personality" (blind dates beware?), "Juan has an outgoing personality" (talks incessantly?), and "Arthur has a laid-back personality (doesn't care about anything?). When used this way, the term *personality* can have different connotations. Here, it is used to identify traits or characteristics, such as ways of thinking, feeling, or behaving that establish us as unique individuals. We tend to think of these traits as consistent across time and situations and that they cause us to act in certain ways. Personality influences not only how we interpret experiences but also what we should do in a variety of social interactions.

Review Examining the Human Experience, Integrative Framework, Psychoanalytic-Based Approaches, Behavioral Theories, Cognitive Behavioral Theories, Person-Centered and Motivational Interviewing Approaches, and Systemic Theory to learn more about theories of personality.

Personality does influence one's behavior in these and other interactions, particularly when the individual encounters new contexts in which old response patterns no longer apply. In these instances, one's dispositions can prove either helpful or problematic. Personality traits such as lack of planning, lack of perseverance, acting rashly when in distress or when experiencing positive affect (feeling high), and sensation seeking can interfere with prudent decision-making. So, when students encounter the relative freedom and new setting associated with the first year of college, new experiences may elicit behaviors guided by one or more of these basic personality traits. These traits, in turn, can play a major role in decisions in predicting drinking behavior and drinking-related problems.

Typically, personality is measured or assessed using a variety of instruments such as the Minnesota Multiphasic Personality Inventory (MMPI) or the California Psychological Inventory (CPI).

Personality Change

Historically, we have thought of personality as relatively stable over time and highly influenced by our genetic makeup. However, a significant amount of research has shown that personality does change over time and that those changes tend to be similar regardless of gender, age grouping, and culture (Helson, Jones, & Kwan, 2002). However, the potential for personality change is highest during childhood and much less so over adulthood (Ferguson, 2010). Other researchers have also noted that some personality change is related to age. For example, McCrae et al. (1999) noted that "Older adults differed from late adolescents and younger adults chiefly in being better at controlling impulses, lower in thrill seeking and cheerfulness, more morally responsible, and . . . generally less open to new experience" (p. 472). Other researchers have identified similar findings about personality change and aging (Specht, Egloff, & Schmukle, 2011). This suggests that while personality influences our interactions with others and our environment, there is a reciprocal relationship at work. In other words, personality change can be influenced by aspects of the social environment. Interestingly, there is little evidence that a person's basic personality changes as a result of therapy, although some patients and therapists still adopt this as a goal of intervention. This lack of change appears to be consistent for both normal and abnormal personalities. It is also true across Western and most other cultures that have been studied (Ferguson, 2010).

Personality and Behavior

Personality influences human behavior in a variety of ways, but the relationship is not simple. Personality factors cannot reliably predict a specific act of behavior, but rather are used to identify a constellation of behaviors. For example, individuals with an aggressive personality are more likely to lose their temper, hit others or inanimate objects, or get into a fight. Similarly, a personality with exhibitionistic traits is more likely to engage in public displays designed to draw attention, such as showing off, seeking to be the center of attention, or trying to stand out from the crowd. Impulsive personality types may behave in ways that show a disregard for deadlines, fail to obey generally accepted laws and rules, and pursue risky behaviors (Javdani, Sadeh, & Verona, 2011; Wu & Clark, 2003).

Personality Differences and Creativity

Personality differences have been documented between creative people in different lines of work. For example, in an orchestra, string players differed from brass players on some aspects of their personality. Visual art students in general score differently than psychology students in terms of thinking style, and there is some evidence that in this particular area of creative endeavor, people are more likely to be emotionally unstable (Haller & Courvoisier, 2010). Art students describe themselves as "antagonistic, egocentric, and as behaving less cooperatively" (p. 155). Artists tend to be more open to new experiences and unconventional than do individuals in other fields. Similarly, they are less open to working with others or valuing their suggestions. By contrast, people in fields such as engineering are readily committed to accepting input from others. These characteristics associated with artistic creativity may be positive attributes in fields where creativity is highly regarded but much less so where agreeableness and cooperation are valued, such as in social work and psychology. In other words, fields where one works alone give the individual freedom to be less cooperative than in work environments where getting alone with peers is essential.

Assess your comprehension of Personality Development by completing this quiz.

IDENTITY FORMATION

According to Erik Erikson (1968), developing one's identity is a process that involves figuring out one's social and personal world, identifying options or choices, making decisions, and coming to see oneself within the larger world. It is most often during adolescence that the individual begins to struggle with identity issues such as "Who am I?" "What do I want to become?" and "Where do I fit in society?" (Forthun, Montgomery, & Bell, 2006, p. 142). The goal is a positive or mature identity "that is self-selected, unified, competent, and, in a civil society, prosocial" (Ferrer-Wreder, Palchuk, Poyrazli, Small, & Domitrovich, 2008). Positive identities are associated with higher academic achievement, lower rates of substance abuse and premature sexual activity, and low levels of antisocial behavior.

Family, Parenting, and Peer Influences

An individual's identity or sense of self is influenced by more than one factor, but it is generally agreed that parents and family relationships play a major role in the process. Several studies have demonstrated the importance of parents in the development of identity. For example, Forthun et al. (2006) noted that "a healthy sense of individuation from parents and family is important for individual identity development" (p. 143). Parents who allow children to explore various social roles with a minimum of intervention and exhibit lower family conflict are more likely to foster a positive identity in their offspring. On the other hand, family conflict is not necessarily detrimental to the individual's development, especially when the conflict is seen as an expression of individualization (Papini, Micka, & Barnett, 1989). Strong family bonds encourage exploration while too much cohesion (enmeshment) strains the adolescent and undermines exploration of identity-relevant issues.

Likewise, adolescents with a secure attachment to parents are better able to engage in identity-related behaviors. "Other characteristics of the family environment that have been found to be related to the formation of an identity during adolescence include . . . parent–adolescent conflict, and parenting style" (Forthun et al., 2006, p. 143). Authoritarian parenting, in particular, was related to poorer identity formation.

Peers also play a role in healthy identity formation. Adolescents who felt social support from their friends were more likely to engage in exploration in the relational, school, and occupational domains. Undermining identity formation are issues such as high dependency on peers, inability to resist peer pressure, and an asocial orientation (Flum, 1994; Forthun et al., 2006).

Race and Identity

One aspect of identity development that has received more recent attention is racial identity. It is generally recognized that individuals from multiracial backgrounds experience unique challenges that do not characterize their monoracial peers. These challenges include obstacles such as being pressured to adopt one particular group with which to identify, dealing with biracial issues, being viewed or defined inconsistently by others in society, and justifying their racial identity to themselves and others. An example of the latter situation occurs when an individual of dual or multiple heritages self-identifies as a member of a particular group but encounters rejection because others of that group do not accept the person as part of the group. Mark, whose mother is Latina and father is African American, chooses to identity with his father's culture and race. However, when he entered high school, he was not accepted by other African American students because he did not share their attitudes, beliefs, and values. To them, he was a Latino and not Black. It is not uncommon for people of mixed racial backgrounds to be viewed by others as members of one group only. One example is President Barack Obama, who is often referred to as African American despite being biracial.

Mixed racial individuals may also face the problem of a lack of role models to help them navigate society (Lou, Lalonde, & Wilson, 2011; Shih & Sanchez, 2005). This is

much less of a challenge for monoracial individuals who routinely see themselves portrayed or represented in the media. It is
also problematic because multiracial individuals may lack support
groups or others to help them adopt a sense of self. To complicate
matters a bit more, the parents of mixed race children may not be
in agreement about which groups, if any, their child should identify with. Such children may receive confusing messages from parents and other family members about who they are. Finally, they
may experience rejection by both the dominant society and the
minority groups with which they might seek to identify. This is a
common phenomenon in mixed race and religion families where
double rejection may occur.

Diversity in Practice

*Practice Behavior Example: Gain sufficient
self-awareness to eliminate the influence of
personal biases and values in working with
diverse groups.*

Critical Thinking Question: Recognizing that
people who select different professions or
fields of endeavor often have similar personality
characteristics, how does a social worker avoid
stereotyping all members of that field?

From these challenges, one might conclude that children of
mixed backgrounds are destined to experience problems in iden-
tity and adapting to life's challenges. Shih and Sanchez (2005), however, in a meta-analysis
of existing studies, found evidence that these challenges do not necessarily result in
difficulty in the realms of academic performance, behavior, mental health problems, or
identity formation. In fact, they concluded that multiracial individuals do not generally
suffer negatively in terms of identity development.

Identity and International Adoptees

Developing an identity can be particularly difficult for adopted children, including
those from other countries. Many potential international adoptees have experienced
tremendous challenges including pre- and perinatal and post-birth trauma. Mothers
of many of these children have suffered from "stress, malnutrition, or disease during
pregnancy and may receive inadequate medical care, any of which can affect the developing fetus. After birth, many children experience (continuing) malnutrition, discon-
tinuous caretaking, poor adult-child relationships, abuse, and lack of both affection and
adequate stimulation, as well as poor medical care" (Bimmel, Juffer, van Ijzendoorn, &
Bakermans-Kranenburg, 2003, p. 65). The traumas can be especially acute when a child
comes from countries with a recent history of war, significant poverty, disease, and/or
hunger.

Striving for identity as an adolescent is difficult for many children and this is even truer
for international adoptees. These children typically come from different racial backgrounds
than their new parents and must struggle with the reality that a part of their background
is missing. They may feel divided loyalties toward their adopted parents while coping with
the realization that their birth parents gave them up. Feelings of anger and confusion are
not uncommon responses to such situations. To the extent that they were adopted relatively late in their childhood, these children may not have a good sense of who their adoptive parents are, generally a given for most children developing their own identity. Peers
may also present a dilemma because many adopted children are different from their friends
by virtue of experiences, race, or other factors. Developing a positive identity under these
circumstances is difficult and has implications for social workers working in the adoption
field. A meta-analysis by Bimmel et al. (2003) of past studies of international adoptions
concluded that adopted adolescents had higher numbers of behavior problems
than non-adopted adolescents. However, despite the number of international
adopted children who display difficulties in adolescence, the authors conclude
that most such children are well adjusted and exhibit no more serious challenges than non-adopted peers. Developing a healthy and positive identity is

**Assess your comprehension of
Identity Formation by completing
this quiz.**

not only possible, but likely for international adoptees though the process will not be without difficulty.

SOCIALIZING FORCES

Several forces contribute to the process of socialization, including parents, attachments, culture, and learning theories. By socialization we mean the transmission of things such as the customs, norms, and beliefs needed to participate in a society. Socialization is a process by which individuals learn what is expected of them, how others will behave, and the roles that one will be expected to play to fit in. It occurs through direction and instruction from adults, the influence of peers, and institutions of society such as schools or churches.

Parenting

We would expect that parents act as a major socializing force on children and adolescents. They represent the first contact most children have with other human beings and children are dependent upon parents for food, shelter, and companionship. How well the parents perform the socializing function can be affected by a variety of factors. For example, parents who believe that cheating and stealing are acceptable will probably not help their children learn honesty and respect for others. Parents who accept the social norms relative to appropriate behavior are much more likely to transmit these norms to their offspring. However, not all parents are equally effective as socializing influences on their children. Parents without social support may experience parenthood as a stressful event and be unable to help children learn what is expected of them. Parents experiencing financial struggles may be struggling so hard for physical resources that they have little time or energy left to engage their role as socializers. Single parents without friends or family to provide social supports such as love, empathy, and care may lack the emotional resources to perform other parental roles appropriately. Stressors that interfere with mother–child attachment (to be discussed shortly) can lead to toddler behavior problems. Inadequate or expensive childcare resources may also force parents to rely on substandard resources to care for children. Likewise, parents with children who have disabilities may also experience higher levels of stress that overwhelm their parenting capabilities. Mothers who receive emotional or material support are more likely to interact with their children suggesting that programs providing such help may have direct benefits for the children involved (Andresen & Telleen, 1992; Schechtman & Gilat, 2005). Parents should be helped to access programs such as the Special Supplemental Nutrition Program for Women, Infants, and Children (WIC) and subsidized childcare whenever such assistance is needed.

Kazdin (1987), Patterson, Reid, & Dishion (1992), Piotrowski (2011), and Li (2008) have helped us understand how parental behavior can play a role in the behavior problem of their children. Fortis and Bigram (1997) have identified three categories of factors—child based, family centered, and contextual—that place children at risk for future behavioral difficulties. Other researchers have documented similar findings (Murray, Farrington, & Sekol, 2012; Rohrer, Cicchetti, Rogosch, Toth, & Maughan, 2011).

Risk Factors

Child-based factors include things such as neonatal complications (premature birth and low birth weight), gender, temperament, cognitive abilities, and social abilities. Neonatal complications seem to be a risk factor only when combined with other risk factors, such as low socioeconomic status, traumatic life events, parents with low intelligence, problematic mother–child relationships, and family chaos.

Gender seems to play a role in that boys are several times more likely to engage in problematic behavior than girls. While both genders experience similar levels of emotional problems, it is the males whose behavior becomes an issue. This may be partly attributable to the fact that males appear more vulnerable to stress and are more likely to react to a stressful environment.

Temperament of a child plays a role in that it influences things such as activity level and mood, emotions, and socialization. For example, children whose mood is basically negative or angry are more likely to react similarly to environmental stressors.

Cognitive abilities play a role to the extent that they affect verbal skill, the ability to interact appropriately with peers, or interfere with learning and make the school environment an unpleasant experience. Typical behaviors include failing to follow rules and aggressiveness toward others.

Social abilities involve a child's ability to interact and maintain healthy relationships with their peers. Children with low social ability often do not perceive the reactions of others accurately, don't recognize when their actions hurt others, and fail to perceive accurately the level of peer acceptance. Their ability to process social information is different from their peers. Consequently, these children may experience more rejection from other children, which leads in turn to more hostility and anxiety, both of which undermine the child's ability to function.

Family-centered factors include marital relationship, parent–child attachment, quality of parenting, parental substance abuse, and the presence of parental depression. The marital relationship is important for modeling how to handle conflict, as are parental roles for modeling caretaking and problem-solving strategies. Parents who employ abusive or negative approaches to solving problems, engage in violence, or avoid conflict entirely are likely to have children who display aggression and refuse to follow adult rules.

Parent–child attachment will be discussed later in this chapter, but poor quality of parent–child attachment clearly tends to be associated with various psychological and social difficulties. This appears to be especially true for mother–son relationships, which seem to be more vulnerable to familial stress, conflict, and lack of resources.

Quality of parenting can be measured by the extent to which parents engage in consistent use of positive reinforcement and punishment in raising children. When parents respond inconsistently to a child's behavior, it may reinforce antisocial actions, which tend to generate the most parent–child interaction. Moreover, it leaves the child without a sense of which behaviors the parent seeks and values in the child. Conversely, some children respond to stress in their relationship with the parent by withdrawing. Other parent behaviors that are likely to generate problems in the children are poor parental supervision, punitive methods of child rearing, emotional instability of the parent, failure to provide structure and discipline, and low or nonexistent parental competence (Kazdin, 1987; Rohrer et al., 2011).

Parental substance abuse is often associated with higher incidence of referral to protective services, reports of attention deficits in girls, and behaviors such as hyperactivity and acting out. Interestingly, these problems are often the same experienced by the parents in their own development.

Depression among parents is often associated with children who fail to involve themselves in school activities and passivity, particularly among children under age five. These differences, however, seem to disappear after the child enters kindergarten.

Contextual factors include environmental stressors, such as insufficient economic resources, as well as interpersonal stressors, such as a lack of affective resources (the capacity to recognize feelings and emotions in others and respond appropriately). A variety of emotional and mental health problems appear to be influenced by poverty and financial insecurity. These include substance abuse, depression, and family conflict. Each stressor alone may be sufficient to contribute to individual behavior, but the combination of two or more tends to be even more troublesome. Poverty, for instance, becomes more of a stressor when the family is also experiencing marital discord or isolation (Fortis & Bigram, 1997; Grant et al., 2006).

It is important to recognize that the categories of factors just described do not necessarily mean that their presence causes observed behavior problems in children. It is clear, however, that they are risk factors and are associated with various problems. Because individuals are different, a given risk factor may influence the development of one child but not another, even in the same family. In addition, we cannot quantify the level of risk in a meaningful way so that we could say that a particular risk is twice as high as another stressor. The individual strengths that each person demonstrates as he or she copes with a risk factor play a signification role in how the stressor will be perceived, reacted to, and experienced. A child may be capable of dealing with a given risk factor but become overwhelmed when confronted by multiple factors. However, parental support and influence can ameliorate many of the risk factors. Conversely, a lack of parenting skill can exacerbate the ways in which a given risk factor influences the individual child.

Assess your comprehension of Socialization by completing this quiz.

Attachment

We have discussed briefly the role that attachment can play in parenting and as a risk factor for problem behavior in children. The quality of attachment (affectional bond) that develops between caregiver and infant is a significant factor in the biopsychosocial functioning of the child. "Children with secure attachments in childhood develop more positive social-emotional competence, cognitive functioning, physical health and mental health" (Ranson & Urichuk, 2008, p. 129). Satisfactory attachment allows children a "home base" from which they can explore their environment (Rice, 1990). It is to this home base that children return when they are frightened or confronted with experiences they are not prepared to handle (Aunt Sadie's first visit?). Attached children feel that they can retreat to the protection of the caregiver and want to be physically close to the caregiver in times of stress. A typical attachment behavior among infants and toddlers is clinging to the caregiver. For an adolescent away from home for the first time, it may entail emails or phone calls to the parents.

Indicators of secure attachment between caregiver and child might include actions such as easily separating from the caregiver and exploring his or her environment, as long as stressors are absent from the situation. If stress occurs, the child will reconnect with the parent but will return to exploring the environment after the situation improves. Conversely, problematic indicators would be a child who does not explore the environment, avoids contact with the caregiver, seeks the caregiver in times of minimal stress, or resists when the caregiver tries to comfort the child.

Successful attachment for a child requires responsive caregivers who are sensitive to the child's needs and reliable in meeting those needs (Bernier & Meins, 2008; Rice, 1990). Sensitive caregivers pick up on the cues provided by the infant, correctly identify the problem, and respond accordingly (Goldsmith & Alansky, 1987). This process helps the child come to see the parent as someone who can be trusted to meet his or her needs. A successful attachment helps produce children with a healthy degree of autonomy and willingness to explore or undertake new experiences. Conversely, a weak or insecure attachment is reflected in a lack of trust of the caregiver or others on whom the child would normally rely. The attachment period generally is perceived as beginning at birth and culminating at about two years of age.

Typical behaviors of the caregiver that support secure attachment include "responsiveness to crying, timing of feeding, sensitivity, psychological accessibility, cooperation, and acceptance" (Goldsmith & Alansky, 1987, pp. 807–808). Caregivers who demonstrated these characteristics were gentler in their interactions, talked more to the child, encouraged the child, and recognized when the child needed physical contact or proximity. As the child develops, the caregiver allows a great degree of autonomy that encourages exploring the environment and pursuing areas of interest, such as riding a motorcycle (just kidding!).

While much focus has been placed on the role of an infant's caregiver, attachment is important at other times in an individual's development. For example, Allison and Sabatelli (1988) are among many researchers who have established a link between the attachment relations of adolescents, their development, and life adjustments. Areas where the attachment relationship between parent and adolescent appear to influence the latter include "ego identity development, and social and emotional adjustment to different situations" (Rice, 1990, p. 517). Rice notes that one may predict an adolescent's future adaptive functioning based on the quality of the attachment to parents. He also summarizes prior research by pointing out other areas where healthy attachment is predictive of things such as high self-esteem, satisfaction with life, positive self-concept, and a satisfactory family environment. Also influenced positively were lower scores on depression and anxiety, irritability and anger. Rice concludes by stating: "Adolescents and young adults who report secure, trusting attachment relationships with their parents also report high levels of social competence, general life satisfaction, and somewhat higher levels of self-esteem" (p. 525).

Attachment theory has also been employed to help explain problematic behavior observed in children and adults. Bowlby (1969, 1989) believed that disruptive experiences in the child–parent relationship—resulting from abuse or neglect by the parent, parental conflicts, and disorganization—and that occur in the child's first year of life could affect later development. Bronfman, Parsons, & Lyons-Ruth (1999) attempted to measure disruptive caregiving by looking at several parental behaviors, including errors in communicating parental feelings, disorientation, confusion over parental roles and boundaries, intrusive or negative interactions, and parental withdrawal. Other researchers have found similar effects of disorganized parenting behaviors (Bernier & Meins, 2008). De Wolff and van Ijzendoorn's (1997) meta-analysis of past research identified parental factors—such as positive attitude, emotional support, sensitivity, and stimulation—as helping to lead to secure attachments. Secure attachments, in turn, allow the infant to explore the environment and to be confident that the caregiver will be available. Fraley (2002) and others have found that the attachment developed in infancy can continue to affect individuals throughout their life span. Behaviors associated with a positive attachment include sharing with others, reciprocity and cooperation with peers, compliance with parental instructions, development of a conscience, and greater interpersonal competence. Other characteristics demonstrated by these children included social activity, popularity with peers, and higher self-esteem.

Bowlby and others have suggested that attachment disruptions are risk factors rather than directly causative (Madigan, Moran, Schuengel, Pederson, & Otten, 2007). That is, they can, when combined with later experiences, produce deviant and maladaptive behavior. Problematic behaviors related to poor quality of attachment include increased dependence on caregivers, aggressiveness, social anxiety, social withdrawal, noncompliance with adults, impulsivity, hostility, conduct disorders, academic failure, and failure to complete school. One example of this is the adolescent mother–child dyad, in which children of adolescent mothers show more emotional problems and other risk factors such as violence and dropping out of school. As further evidence of the importance of parents in the child's development, subsequent research has demonstrated that helping parents improve their effectiveness reduces the number of child behavior problems (NICHD Early Child Care Research Network, 2006). Infants experiencing attachment problems may display anger and anxiety in the absence of the caregiver and be resistant to caregiver's attempts to comfort them (Ranson & Urichuk, 2008).

The behavioral correlates of poor attachment can appear at any stage of development. Thus, behaviors such as noncompliance and aggression may manifest in kindergarten or poor interpersonal relationships in adolescence. These children are often disliked by both their teachers and their peers and are more likely to engage in fights with others (Ranson & Urichuk, 2008). In adulthood, poor attachment experiences can lead to higher rates of drug and alcohol use, increased sexual acting out, higher medical service usage, and greater complaints about health issues such as fatigue, heart problems, and other nonspecific medical concerns.

Mental health is also influenced by attachment. Reactive attachment disorder is often associated with insecure attachment and manifests in social misbehavior such as sexual acting out, "sadism, violence, disordered eating, counterfeit emotionality, kleptomania, compulsive lying, sexual obsessions or compulsions, passive-aggression and defective conscience" (Ranson & Urichuk, 2008, p. 142). Likewise, antisocial personality disorders and substance abuse are associated with insecure attachments early in life. Some adults may experience depression, anxiety, borderline personality disorder, and other mental health problems.

Another area where attachment becomes important is with respect to cognition. More secure attachment seems to engender brain growth, improved problem-solving skills, higher levels of intelligence, earlier development of reading and language skills, increased attention spans, positive career goals in later adolescence, and higher grades in schools (Ranson & Urichuk, 2008). While mothers are more likely to be key to development of attachment, fathers also play a role although their impact on the child's later development has been less researched. For example, research has shown that daughters with positive attachments to their fathers are less likely to engage in sexual activity by age 16 than daughters without a positive attachment to their fathers (Freeman & Almond, 2010). Daughters with secure attachments to either parent are also less likely to develop eating (Howard, 1997; McCarthy, 1998). Clearly, the importance of positive attachment between child and caretakers underscores the value of parent education programs and support for new parents.

Culture

Another critical social influence on human behavior is the cultural context in which an individual is born and raised. Culture can be defined in many ways but for our purposes it refers to the beliefs, values, attitudes, shared meanings, and knowledge acquired by groups over an extended period of time. It is transmitted in a social context and incorporates things such as communication patterns, symbols, and behavioral expectations that help set one group apart from others. In effect, it is learned and passed down from one generation to another. While it is customary to think about Native American or Latino culture, many people do not recognize that everyone has a culture. Those composing the dominant society often see themselves as the norm and don't recognize that they are operating from a worldview that affects all aspects of their lives. For example, individuals from a European background (e.g., English, French, German) often are blind to the fact that they too are the product of their culture.

Our culture tends to be seen as "typical," and we use it to judge other cultures with which we come in contact. Too often, we view the "other" culture as strange or different

Rejection of Own Culture   Acceptance of Own Culture
Figure 8.1
Continuum of Acceptance of Own Culture

because the behaviors of its members do not make sense to us because we have different beliefs, attitudes, knowledge, and shared meaning that we use in navigating through life. The traditional Native American value of sharing with others is seen at odds with a Eurocentric value of acquiring. Even when Hindis are starving, beliefs about life before and after death help explain their decision to avoid slaughtering cows. Likewise, it is cultural experiences that make many African Americans perceive law enforcement as an actual or potential enemy.

Of course, not all members of any cultural group think the same, share the same values, or see experiences from the same perspective. It is more realistic to view members of most groups as somewhere along a continuum in terms of how close they come to one extreme or the other. Figure 8.1 suggests how this might look.

Some people will adopt nearly all the features associated with their culture while others will reject most, if not all, aspects of their culture. Most of us would locate ourselves somewhere along the continuum, holding to some beliefs and attitudes but rejecting others. The following example may help demonstrate this perspective.

Case Example: The Hennessey Family

The Hennesseys were an Irish American family with strong cultural ties to the Catholic Church that were reflected in a variety of ways. These ties had been carried over when the first members of the family immigrated to the United States and persisted through several generations. However, when the family patriarch died after an alcoholic binge, the family's attempts to have him buried in a Catholic cemetery were rejected by the local priest. The family's cultural connection to the church was immediately broken and family members began to express negative attitudes toward the Catholic Church and its members. Other connections to Irish culture such as foods, celebrations, and attitudes were maintained but the religious component was completely absent. Children were socialized to think badly about the Catholic Church and carry on the family grudge.

Many individuals must operate from a bicultural perspective; that is, they must navigate within at least two cultures: the larger one in which they live and the other into which they were born. Some people must navigate multiple cultures to survive. For example, an Hispanic American who is deaf will be influenced not only by the larger society, but also by the Hispanic culture, and finally the deaf society. A gay African American adolescent similarly must operate within multiple cultures. In practice, this means that the way one views the world, the attitudes and beliefs one holds, and the meaning that one gives to events can be influenced by more than one culture. Regardless of whether the individual is influenced by one or more cultures, his or her attitudes, beliefs, and values will continue to operate throughout the person's life, often without conscious awareness. Some will remain unchanged over time while others will be reevaluated, modified, or discarded based on subsequent learning and introspection. Racist views that have been passed from one generation to another, for example, may give way to respect, acceptance, and comfort following new learning experiences. At the same time, some problematic beliefs and attitudes will become hardened if the individual associates with groups holding extremist viewpoints such as nativist, racist organizations, and hate groups.

Likewise, many individuals have multiple cultural or racial identities and claim membership in multiple groups. The proportion of individuals who fall in this category has risen dramatically and the change is reflected in census choices afforded. Previously, each person was required to select one racial category and designate oneself as a member of that group. Now, listing multiple groups is possible and the results more accurately show national makeup.

Learning Theories

Learning involves the acquisition of knowledge, skills, and values. By definition, much of what is learned is cognitive in nature, focused on acquiring facts, information, ways of thinking, and rules. In the academic setting, testing whether cognitive information is learned involves assessment tools such as examinations, papers, and assignments. The assumption is that learning is reflected in the student's behavior on the assessment instrument—if you answered 90% of the test questions correctly, you learned well.

But much learning is affective; that is, learning reflects beliefs, values, and attitudes that are harder to assess. These beliefs, values, and attitudes can predispose us to respond in a certain way to specific situations and imply both positive and negative reactions to specific stimuli, such as people, ideas, or situations. Attitudes can be viewed as having "behavioral, affective and cognitive facets" (Heimlich & Ardoin, 2008, p. 221). That is, attitudes involve our thoughts, feelings, and behaviors.

Both cognitive and affective learning occurs throughout life and in multiple venues. We learn from observing parents, peers, teachers, and just about anyone to whom we pay attention. We learn both the things that others want us to learn and behaviors, beliefs, and attitudes they prefer we didn't learn. We also learn through direct experiences, such as touching a hot stove, falling down, spinning in a circle until we are dizzy, and skateboarding down the stairs. Learning is not passive: We don't just wait for an experience to teach us something. Human beings reach out for experiences and acquire knowledge, skills, and values in the process.

How we utilize the information we acquire differs greatly from person to person and situation to situation. For example, most of us have learned to drive with the help of others, whether driving instructors and/or parents. We learn by reading laws and rules required for procuring a license. We also learn by listening to the wisdom (and outbursts) of our instructors and modeling their behaviors. Once learned, the information and behaviors involved in driving occur without much conscious thought. For example, we don't have to think about signaling every time we make a turn or pressing the brake pedal when the car ahead brakes. This automating of our responses is very important as Heimlich and Ardoin (2008) observe, "If every behavioral choice required an individual's undivided attention, we would become immobilized by the overwhelming number of decisions" (p. 219). The process of routinizing learned behaviors is essential in a complex world.

Formal learning theories, which we discussed in Chapter 7, indicate that learning is a social influence on human behavior. It helps us develop social skills, acquire both general and specific knowledge, and adopt the attitudes, beliefs, and values of society and its members. How one learns is individual: Some hear information and remember it for different lengths of time; others learn best when presented with both visual and aural information. Still others benefit from engaging in the behavior or action being learned. Just as learning to ride a bike requires actual practice on the bike, social workers learning how to interview clients typically must do more than read about it or listen to a lecture. Actual experience—in which we pose questions or observations in response to a client or simulated client—tends to be more useful. For social workers, this process becomes somewhat routinized as we learn which information to seek and how best to respond to a client's statements.

Social Learning Theory

At the heart of social learning theory is the proposition that our behaviors are a consequence of learning from others, such as primary groups and peers. Thus, deviant behavior is learned in the same fashion as more socially acceptable behaviors. Research shows that social learning theory explains academic cheating, substance abuse, cigarette smoking, steroid use by bodybuilders, and using forged identification to obtain alcohol. Learning from peers has been shown repeatedly to be associated with student drinking (Ichiyama & Kruse, 1998). Durkin, Wolfe, and Clark (2005) demonstrated the importance of social learning theory in explaining binge drinking among about 40% of college students who drink (Johnston, O'Malley, & Bachman, 2002). These findings have been supported by Scott-Sheldon, Terry, Carey, Garey, and Carey (2012). Binge drinking consists of the consumption of significant quantities of alcohol during a single event and can lead to fighting, being assaulted, missing class, blacking out, and breaking the law. Other consequences include death from alcohol-related injuries, alcohol-related health problems, and unwanted sexual intercourse. An increase in risky behaviors often accompanies binge drinking (Cyders, Flory, Rainer, & Smith, 2008).

In discussing affective and cognitive learning, one might assume that they are separate entities operating independently. However, most behavior involves a "complex intermingling of affective and cognitive processes that guide decisions in the short- and long-term" (Heimlich & Ardoin, 2008, p. 220).

Changing Learned Behavior

Once learning has occurred, changing learned behavior is often a challenging process but possible. For example, attitudes may be changed through direct experience with the attitude object (i.e., the individual or situation about which one has an attitude). Attitudes can also be changed through communication designed to persuade the person to hold a different attitude, such as how marketing tries to convince us to replace a favored product with another. Another means of changing attitudes is through inducements, such as companies rewarding employees who quit smoking or engage in pro-health activities by giving them a bonus or reducing the cost of health insurance. Or, one partner in a relationship may agree to stay if the other partner agrees to seek counseling.

In general, we tend to behave in a way consistent with our attitudes. The interrelationship between attitudes and behavior, however, is not always consistently clear. Some argue that the attitudes drive behaviors, which might explain why an individual with negative attitudes toward immigrants makes derogatory comments about fellow employees who are not native-born residents of the United States. Others point out that changing a person's learned behavior can subsequently result in a change in their attitude, such as when antidiscrimination laws make it illegal for employers to discriminate against someone because of their race or gender. An employer with negative attitudes toward women, for example, is now faced with behaving in a way that does not match his negative attitudes. When one's behavior is at odds with one's attitude, it is usually the attitude that changes—according to cognitive dissonance theory, which posits that we seek consistency in our attitudes and

Read Cognitive Behavioral Theories for a more detailed discussion of how learning theory is used in practice to help clients change their behavior. Evaluate the credence you place in this model of understanding and changing behavior.

Along with parents, peers are a significant social influence on adolescents.

behaviors. Having to reconcile the dissonance between conflicting attitudes and behaviors is uncomfortable and leads to changing one's attitudes.

Peer Relations

We have mentioned previously the potential influence of peers and peer groups on the development of an individual. Peer groups are a major social influence on children, adolescents, and to a lesser degree, adults. Several studies have demonstrated that peers are a potent influence on health behavior (La Greca & Prinstein, 1999; Wilson & Evans, 2003). One example from a study by Mackey and La Greca (2008) found that adolescent girls were heavily influenced about their weight by their peer group's attitudes. Not only were the peer groups influential in the girls deciding they were overweight, but they also shaped the weight control behaviors chosen by the girls. The authors conclude that this information would be useful when developing prevention programs aimed at teen obesity. This research supports the theory of reasoned action (TRA; Fishbein & Ajzen, 1975), which states that before a behavior occurs, one considers his or her attitudes toward the behavior, as well as the subjective norms of significant others regarding the behavior. Other researchers have found evidence that the TRA is applicable to a wide variety of decision-making situations (Fazekas, Senn, & Ledgerwood, 2001; White, Charles, & Nelson, 2008).

Coie (1990) argued that a child who has unsuccessful experiences in a peer group is often subject to stress, which can, in turn, precipitate or exacerbate mental health problems. This is particularly true for kids treated for aggression and exclusion and those who are lonely and anxious. Rejection by peers limits the availability of social supports and curtails the chance to develop coping skills and competencies. Because of the significance of peer influence on mental health, Dishion, Ha, and Véronneau (2012) recommended that peer relationships should be included in the life history of adolescents with behavioral problems. A meta-analysis on children's peer relations conducted by Newcomb, Bukowski, and Pattee (1993) found that children who were popular with their peers displayed an array of competencies that helped engender positive reactions from others. These competencies included things such as "being helpful and considerate, following rules, and demonstrating athletic and academic" ability (p. 101). These children demonstrated "greater social problem-solving skills, positive social actions, positive so-cial traits, and friendship relations than average children" (p. 118). Peers seek out children who are fun to be with, who share their interests, and whose behavior is trustworthy. Popular children demonstrate the capacity for empathy, self-disclosure, and loyalty—all behaviors that are consistent with their peers' goals. Interestingly, Schwartz, Gorman, Nakamoto, and McKay (2006) found that being popular could be a double-edged sword for students who had displayed higher levels of aggression. These popular students were more likely to have lower grade point averages in school and increased unexplained ab-sence from school.

On the other hand, less popular children who were more likely to be rejected by their peers exhibit more aggressive behavior, were disruptive, and failed to follow the rules. Newcomb et al. (1993) found that less popular children showed lower degrees of sociability and fewer cognitive abilities. Peers routinely rejected children they deemed as lacking in positive social skills and whose levels of aggressiveness were not balanced by other positive traits. These rejected children were more likely to be ostracized from their peers and to experience stress, depression, and anxiety as a result. Rejected children who experience anxiety are more likely to engage in unpredictable behavior and "are at risk in their social development" (p. 121).

A third group of children were viewed by the peers as controversial in that they were very aggressive, made their peers angry, and engaged in disruptive behavior that "both amused the peer group and attracted teacher reprimand" (p. 101). These contro-versial children have a variety of social skills that help balance their aggressiveness and keep them from being rejected by their peers. In practice, they shared characteristics with both their popular and their rejected peers.

A final group of peers were kids who were less social, tended to engage in solitary play, withdrew from others, and exhibited below-average levels of aggression. This group had fewer friends and engaged in infrequent peer interactions.

While it is clear that peer influence can be a major factor in how children develop, peers are also engaged in a reciprocal relationship with the individual child. The behav-iors and competencies demonstrated by the child are a significant factor in how their peers treat them. This again shows the mutual influence of the individual and his or her social environment: Both are affected by behaviors and the characteristics of the other.

Peers influence biology

The influence of peers and other environmental factors has also been shown to affect the biological realm of human development. For example, high levels of adolescent stress and aggression can impact the onset of puberty, while positive social interactions dur-ing adolescence can have the opposite effect (Susman, Worrall, Murowchick, Frobose, & Schwab, 1996). The idea of social experiences influencing hormonal levels may sound odd, but repeated studies have demonstrated the connection. The influence of such so-cial experiences has been identified in studies conducted on conduct problems of boys (Lahey, McBurnett, Raine, Stouthamer-Loeber, & Loeber, 2002), oppositional defiant disorder (van Goozen, Matthys, Cohen-Kettenis, Thijssen, & van Engeland, 1998), and anxiety and depression (McBurnett, Lahey, Frick, & Risch, 1991). One's susceptibility to social stressors appears to be idiosyncratic with some individuals having a greater bio-logical predisposition to environmental challenges (Ramirez, 2002).

The connection between social environmental stressors and hormonal levels is important for another reason. As Ramirez (2002) points out, "Children of both sexes showed consistent relations between aggression and other negative attributes [anger, antisocial behavior, delinquency, rebelliousness, conduct disorder (CD) with higher levels of hormones of adrenal origin" (p. 634). To put it succinctly, individuals exposed to certain social and environmental experiences can end up with hormonal changes that lead them to display behavior, such as aggression, conduct disorders, and delinquency. The reciprocal and interactive nature of experiences and hormones is evident in other ways as well. Ramirez points out that "one's own aggression creates stress which in turn can cause changes in adrenal steroids" (p. 637). To be sure, the relationship between hormones and aggression is not one of cause and effect but of a factor that can predispose the individual to certain responses in the face of psychosocial stimuli. Like much of our understanding of human behavior, there is still a great deal to be learned about the interaction of biology and environment (van Goozen, Fairchild, Snoek, & Harold, 2007).

Social Support

Studies show that social support can successfully shape behavior and that it has been identified as a factor in helping people cope with stresses and life traumas. This has led to the creation of support programs for parents, families, and clients with mental health or substance abuse challenges, among others. One of the most researched areas is the connection between social supports and the behavior and attitudes of mothers. When Andresen and Telleen (1992) conducted a meta-analysis of studies exploring the relationship between social supports and mother's maternal behavior, they found that mothers with social support networks experienced two advantages. First, they were less likely to perceive their parenting roles as stressful and more likely to believe they can successfully manage their parental roles and, second, the availability of support made stressors appear more manageable.

According to the authors, support can occur in many forms—including emotional, material, or informational. Important maternal behaviors include things such as responding to a child's needs, communicating and playing with the child, and stimulating infants. Equally important was the influence of social support for the mother and its impact on the child. Higher levels of social support are associated with greater responsiveness and adaptability of the parent to the child, more compliance with parental instructions, and lower incidence of child behavior problems. However, Andresen and Telleen concluded that insufficient studies exist to demonstrate a relationship between social supports and child outcomes. They concluded that a significant relationship exists between social supports and material behaviors, further underscoring the importance of community-based family support programs.

Assess your comprehension of Peer Influence by completing this quiz.

Relationships

So far, we have discussed the importance of relationships between parent and child and between the individual and peers. It is clear that the existence and quality of relationships factors into the development of the individual, as well as that individual's capacity to withstand stressors associated with living. As the individual matures, the number and types of relationships increase and peers become of great importance while parental oversight typically lessens. One of the most important relationships is classified as friendships. Dow and Wood (2006) point out the importance of friendships throughout an individual's life span. They provide enjoyment, trust, acceptance, respect, mutual assistance, understanding, and someone to confide in (Santrock, 2008). Relationships can help us deal with stressful situations and boost our self-image and often involve closer, more supportive assistance than families can provide.

Friendships

Friendships tend to occur among individuals in the same age bracket and many extend throughout one's lifetime. However, what we seek from friendship is apt to change at different times. Preschool children seek playmates but those friends may not endure long. Later in grade school, children's friendships are more complex and involve emotional connections between the individuals. As children become adolescents and then adults, their friendship needs focus on those who demonstrate mutual understanding, shared loyalty, and a higher degree of intimacy (Berk, 2009). These relationship qualities continue to be important throughout life.

A large factor in relationships is related directly to proximity. Obviously, friendships are much easier to develop when each party shares a common space. As children recognize the qualities of their associates, factors such as self-disclosure, generosity, and mutual affirmation become hallmarks of close relationships. While disagreements occur, a secure sense of liking between friends tends to prevent breakups. Friends tend to share more than just a relationship, however. It is common for adolescent friends to have similar identities, educational goals, belief systems, and behavior. Later on, late adolescents and adults will begin to form friendships with others who are different from themselves. Status, physical prowess, and/or beauty may well be the attractant with superficial characteristics becoming more important (Berk, 2009). This attraction may be aspirational as the individual seeks others with qualities he or she does not possess. However developed, once created, relationships are capable of enduring through many years and even sustain infrequent contact between friends.

Gender seems to play a role in friendships. For example, men do not have as many close friendships as women and are less likely to seek or get sympathy from their male friends. Male friends often engage in competition or a degree of one-upmanship in ways that are foreign to women. When friends share problems, men tend to offer solutions, regardless of the friend's gender, and typically expect this kind of response. Women, however, often expect a sympathetic response and may be put off when a male friend focuses on pragmatic solutions. The male's response can be seen as uncaring or unfeeling. Men, on the other hand, may be frustrated when a woman friend does not enthusiastically endorse the proposed solution.

Among their numerous benefits, relationships:

- Lead to improved attitudes toward academics
- Provide opportunities to explore one's interests and attitudes
- Offer opportunities to deepen relationships with others
- Create the foundation for future intimate relationships
- Help reduce everyday stressors
- Provide mutual assistance
- Promote acceptance by others (Berk, 2009; Bowker, Rubin, Burgess, Booth-La-Force, & Rose-Krasnor, 2006; Santrock, 2008; Wentzel, Barry, & Caldwell, 2004).

Case Example: Joan's Surgery

Joan, recovering from surgery for stomach cancer, looked at herself in the mirror. The surgery had left several scars on her body and she cried as she looked at them. "I look horrible," she said to her partner, Derek. "It looks like I have several navels instead of just one." Derek looked over at Joan and said, "The scars aren't that bad, besides, you can just have a plastic surgeon do a little nip and tuck and you'll be good as new." Derek's comment, meant to be encouraging, suggested a solution that involved additional surgery for someone who was still recovering from the previous one. Joan threw herself on the bed and buried her head in a pillow. She was both hurt and angry at her partner's response. Joan needed Derek to just listen and understand her bad feelings and not suggest a solution, particularly one that involved more surgery. Derek thought he was identifying a practical solution and could not understand Joan's reaction to his suggestion.

Love relationships

While both love and friendship share many characteristics and involve similar benefits to the individual, love tends to be a much more exclusive relationship. Santrock (2008) divides love into three types: romantic, affection, and consummate. Romantic love is often what we think of when we talk of a heterosexual or homosexual relationship. It is viewed as passionate and typically involves sexuality in some form. It can also involve things such as joy and jealousy, fear and anger, and a myriad of other emotions. Romantic love is what drives us to marriage and what often produces depression when it ends.

Human Behavior

Practice Behavior Example: Critique and apply knowledge to understand person and environment.

Critical Thinking Question: What might explain Joan's reaction to Derek's suggestion? What role might gender differences in socialization play in Derek's suggestion and Joan's reaction?

Affectionate love involves the need to have someone near, to spend time with the other, and to enjoy the other's company. It reduces loneliness and, sometimes, romantic love evolves into affectionate love as sexuality becomes less crucial in a relationship. To the extent that both partners are comfortable with this type of relationship, it can last until death. It becomes more problematic, however, when one partner still seeks the attributes of romantic love and the other does not reciprocate. Many long-term marriages dissolve when one partner no longer finds affection alone as sufficient to maintain the relationship.

Consummate love involves both the passionate aspects of romantic love and the intimacy and closeness of affectionate love. However, it also includes one other element—namely an enduring commitment to the other person. This commitment is characterized by a determination to continue a relationship, come hell or high water. Couples who share this kind of love can weather many hardships and never lose the belief that they are in this to the end. Examples of this include partners who provide end-of-life care for their significant other despite the difficulties involved and refuse to turn over care responsibilities to others. The commitment inherent in consummate love does not consider any other outcome.

Interestingly, when a romantic relationship ends, it is generally thought to produce negative developmental and emotional outcomes. There is some evidence, however, that such breakups can lead to positive growth. This may include things such as better mental health, greater independence, strengthening or repair of relationships with others, and a sense that one has learned something from the experience.

Love relationships that evolve into marriage have a variety of benefits for the individuals involved. These include a longer life span, lowered stress levels, and reduced incidence of health-related ailments, such as high blood pressure (Gallo, Trowel, Matthews, & Kuller, 2003). At the same time, unhappy marriages have the potential of damaging one's immune system and reducing one's life span by as much as four years (Gove, Style, & Hughes, 1990). Of course, ending a dysfunctional marriage is not a panacea for erasing unhappiness. Following divorce, feelings of loneliness, anxiety, and diminished self-worth are common for both genders. Higher rates of mental health problems have been shown for men and women, and chronic physical health difficulties are evident for many. While both men and women experience

Did You Know?

One of the earliest books concerned about adolescent love was published in 1939 (Butterfield, 1939). It argued that more education was needed to help adolescents deal with matters of sex and love. Some things don't change.

difficulty following a divorce, women tend to end up with lower income and a decline in other resources. This financial disparity is less of a problem for women who have previously worked outside the home.

The relatively high remarriage rate following divorce suggests, in part, that the value of relationships remains a strong pull on the psyche of individuals. While some subsequent marriages will occur for other reasons, reestablishment of a relationship with another human being represents a powerful incentive for remarriage.

We have noted that unhappy marriages often produce emotional and physical problems for the adults involved. Children raised in homes with high levels of parental conflict also experience negative outcomes including problems at school entry (Sturge-Apple, Daview, Winter, Cummings, & Schermerhorn, 2008). These include anxiety, fear, anger, and aggression toward others. Some children blame themselves for the conflict and seek to remedy the parental discord. Problems in development are common, a phenomenon that seems to be applicable across many cultures (Bradford et al., 2003).

> While we might not think of love relationships as socialization activities, we are deeply influenced by those with whom we fall in love. Love's Young Dream speaks to the influence that both parties in a love relationship have on the other person. After reading this case, identify the ways in which Sharon and Stewart engaged in socializing each other about relationships.

Mentor relationships

We have identified both friendships and love relationships as important to individuals at different stages of their lives. Other relationships may exist that have significant meaning for men and women. One of these is the mentor relationship in which a more experienced individual provides modeling, guidance, counsel, and encouragement to a less experienced colleague. The individual serving as a mentor may be a teacher, youth group leader (e.g., in scouting or big brother/big sister programs), coach, supervisor, or other adult. Mentors serve as positive role models and teachers for both men and women. However, men seem to be more likely to have such a helper than are women (Hannon, 2011; Noe, 1988; Williams-Nickelson, 2009).

Case Example: Edgar and Gregg—A Mentor–Mentee Relationship

Edgar Goodwill was the new vice president for academic affairs at a small private college. One of his first challenges was how to deal with a dysfunctional academic department that contained the disciplines of social work, criminal justice, and sociology. For a year, Edgar served as acting head of the department while conducting a national search for a new chairperson. At the end of the year, Edgar asked Gregg, a junior social work faculty member, if he would be willing to accept the position as department chair. Gregg agreed and that decision began a mentoring relationship that lasted for more than three decades. Edgar took the young department head under his wing, giving him opportunities to serve on key college committees and to attend multiple social work conferences. Gregg took advantage of the opportunities by learning as much as possible about being a department chair, supervising others, working with task groups, and organizational theory.

Several times a week Gregg would come to Edgar's office and the two would just talk about issues in higher education, challenges facing the college, Gregg's plans for the department, and his career goals. They shared their individual discomfort about having to talk to the parents of prospective students and the difficulty Edgar encountered making friends in his new community. From Edgar, Gregg learned how to conduct a national search that adhered to affirmative action guidelines, strategies in reviewing candidate qualifications, scheduling of interviews, and other aspects of recruitment. It was a first-rate educational experience for Gregg.

Edgar and Gregg went their separate ways after three years of working together, each leaving for new challenges. After more than 30 years, they continue to keep in touch via email, Christmas cards, and an occasional visit.

This differential access to mentors for women is problematic for a number of reasons. First, mentoring has been shown to have clear benefits for adults including better first jobs and career experiences, enhanced preparation for work, more promotions, higher salaries, and faster achievement of licensing and credentialing (Williams-Nickelson, 2009). Second, women often face the need to balance both home and work obligations and guidance in how to do this is needed and sought.

Mentors typically see their mentee's potential and share this information with them, thereby providing encouragement. The mentor also shares personal experiences relevant to the mentee's needs and facilitates access to resources and other opportunities. Mentors can serve as coach, sponsor, role model, friend, counselor, colleague, and protector for their mentee (Williams-Nickelson, 2009). They provide constructive feedback and help the mentee identify goals and the steps to achieve them. They can also encourage balance in the life of the mentee, an increasingly important quality for adults who are pulled in different directions by multiple demands on their time. Mentors may be encountered in one's both personal and professional life. The benefits of having a mentor–mentee relationship appear to be positive in most instances.

MORAL DEVELOPMENT

Moral development concerns the evolution of moral reasoning that allows us to recognize whether a behavior is right or wrong. Why do we view some behaviors as wrong and others as right? How do we arrive at this decision?

Moral development is also focused on things such as learning prosocial behaviors; that is, actions (e.g., helping others) that are considered supportive of one's fellow human beings. The development of moral judgment has been explored exhaustively in the context of understanding human beings. The acquisition and demonstration of the attitudes, values, and concomitant prosocial behaviors is a common goal in most cultures (Eisenberg, Cumberland, Guthrie, Murphy, & Shepard, 2005). Helping others, empathy, and caring are important in maintaining positive human relationships and play a large role in most civilizations. Developing higher levels of moral reasoning often occurs with age as the individual becomes less focused on himself or herself and more attuned to others. Typically, higher-order moral orientations develop as a consequence of age and are often paired with a diminution in self-orientation. Such maturation is generally seen as a positive indicator of adulthood and allows one to see someone else's perspective. Motivation for more prosocial behaviors derives from a variety of factors but it can be inhibited by experiencing personal distress. In other words, it is more difficult to experience empathy toward others when your situation is dire or when another's situation is so bad that it overwhelms your capacity to be caring.

Ethical Practice

Practice Behavior Example: Make ethical decisions by applying standards of the National Association of Social Workers Code of Ethics and, as applicable, of the International Federation of Social Workers/International Association of Schools of Social Work Ethics in Social Work, Statement of Principles.

Critical Thinking Question: Under what, if any, circumstance is it right to punish a child for engaging in bad behavior? If the citizens of a state vote overwhelmingly for a particular law, is that law inherently right? If a specific behavior is legal, is it automatically moral? Is taking a person who no longer has any brain function off life support the right thing to do?

Moral Reasoning

Kohlberg (1984) and others found that the capacity to engage in moral reasoning increases during the individual's life into late adolescence and adulthood. The quality of moral reasoning varies considerably across developmental periods. Children, for example, often use hedonistic reasoning: first, focusing on "what's best for me," and then, considering how their actions will be seen by others. Children are more concerned with winning the approval of adults, behaving in accordance with norms, and strengthening their relationships with peers. As they develop further, their capacity to verbalize the reasoning behind their decisions increases and may allow them to express more abstract principles, as well as describing things such as "guilt or positive affect about the consequences of one's behavior for others" (Eisenberg et al., 2005, p. 240). The process of moral development, however, is not consistent from individual to individual nor from one age to another. For example, some kinds of prosocial functioning increases across maturity levels but others do not. Feeling sympathetic or empathic toward others seems to follow an irregular trend, with early adolescents experiencing these emotions, but dropping off in late adolescence, and returning again in early adulthood (Eisenberg et al., 2005).

Gender Differences

In addition to age differences in moral development, gender differences are evident. Women tend to be more focused on the needs of others, act less on their wants, and score above men on care-related moral reasoning (Eisenberg et al., 2005; Gilligan & Attanucci, 1988; Jaffee & Hyde, 2000). They tend to be less involved in hedonistic reasoning for moral decision-making and are more aware of the internal states and needs of others. This may be partly because parents are more likely to discuss certain emotions with girls, but not with boys, and encourage girls more than boys to engage in prosocial behaviors (Kuebli, Butler, & Fivush, 1995; Power & Shanks, 1989). Other researchers have speculated that girls are more likely than boys to have experienced relational aggression in childhood and, therefore, are more sensitive to the negative consequences of hurting others (Horn, 2003).

Murray-Close, Crick, and Galotti (2006) found other gender-specific differences in the reasoning of elementary schoolchildren regarding physical and relational aggression. Physical aggression included things such as hitting or kicking others, while relational aggression included behaviors that harm relationships such as ignoring friends or gossiping about them in ways designed to hurt.

Girls rated physical and relational aggression as more wrong than boys. In addition, they viewed relational aggression as more harmful than boys did. Girls tended to rely on a moral orientation in their judgments. Likewise, women are more likely than men to recognize that those victimized by aggression experience suffering and sadness. At the same time, women are more likely to be both perpetrator and victim of relational aggression, which may help explain why they more readily define it as harmful. This topic will be explored further in Chapter 9.

Moral Orientation

We should stop for a minute to identify what we mean by a morel orientation and compare it to other systems of judgment. A moral orientation focuses on how a behavior affects the welfare of others. If an action is likely to hurt another individual, the person operating from a moral orientation will define the behavior as wrong or bad. However, a moral orientation is not the only orientation that may be used in evaluating a given behavior. For example, children with a social convention orientation tend to use societal norms when deciding whether a behavior is good or bad. If a behavior breaks a rule, such as "no running in the hallway," then it is considered wrong simply because it is contrary to an established guideline. The fact that the "no running" rule was adopted to prevent injury to others is not really taken into account by those with a social convention orientation. It's wrong simply because it broke a rule.

Another system for making judgments is the "personal domain" method in which a behavior is considered within a narrow context. Behaviors in this area have to do with issues that are considered private or personal in nature. Those operating within this system will look at another person's dress (Goth or preppy) without making any judgments about whether it is appropriate or not. As dress is one of those things that is innately personal, others have no right to make such judgments (Nucci, 1996). Those who adhere to this orientation will defend the rights of others to behave differently and reject attempts to categorize their behavior as wrong.

A final orientation to judging behavior is prudential. A prudential approach to decision-making looks at certain behaviors as personal decisions that can be harmful to the individual. The fact that a person uses drugs may be defined as wrong—not because it is unlawful or harms others, but because it is an unwise behavior. Even when judged wrong, however, the person using the prudential approach will still recognize the behavior as a personal decision that the drug user is free to make. Interestingly, those who engage in specific behaviors (e.g., aggressiveness or substance abuse) are more likely to view it not as a moral issue but as a personal choice that they are free to make. They do not define the behavior as harmful or wrong. Interventions aimed at reducing problem behaviors in adolescents, such as aggressiveness, have focused with success on helping them redefine aggressive behavior as hurtful (Guerra & Slaby, 1990). Changing the thinking process of these adolescents results in behavior modification, an observation consistent with rational behavior theory.

It is important to note that children who are aggressive do recognize that their behavior causes harm to others. In fact, they may view aggression as an effective behavior to get what they want from others. Knowing that it hurts others makes it a powerful tool in interpersonal relationships (Murray-Close et al., 2006). This is particularly true for the relatively few girls who view aggressive behavior from a social convention or personal domain orientation. As these girls do not operate from a moral orientation, they are more likely to engage in aggressive conduct with their peers. Interestingly, girls who operate from a prudential perspective are not as likely to use aggression as a relationship tool. For these girls, avoiding aggression may simply be a protective mechanism to reduce the chances of being hurt by others' actions.

As you might expect, the orientation that one takes to judging behavior is clearly a function of socialization and culture. Boys, for example, tend toward more aggressive physical play, which may help inculcate the belief that aggressiveness is acceptable. Girls are more likely to be socialized into seeing aggressiveness as harmful or wrong. In some cultures, violence and aggression against others is justifiable under certain circumstances, while in others, any form of violence is considered wrong. An example of the former can be seen in the behavior of some terrorist groups who believe the killing of innocent noncombatants is justified by either religion or political ends. In direct contrast are groups such as Quakers, who object to violence as an inherently unjustified act under almost any circumstances. It is important to understand the orientation of the individual making judgments. The rationale for a decision clearly differs from person to person. For example, children who are aggressive seem to have different patterns of processing information. For example, they appear to "interpret social cues hostilely, to generate aggressive responses, to adopt instrumental rather than relational goals and to evaluate aggressive responses in a relatively positive manner" (Murray-Close et al., 2006, p. 346). In other words, they seem to view the actions of others as potentially hostile and are more likely to respond with aggression. An aggressive response is considered acceptable by these children. By contrast, nonaggressive children will interpret the same situation as nonthreatening and, therefore, see no need to adopt a hostile response.

Assess your analysis and evaluation of this chapter's contents by completing the Chapter Review.

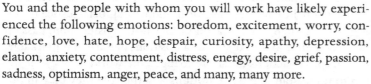

9

Emotional Influences on Human Behavior

You and the people with whom you will work have likely experienced the following emotions: boredom, excitement, worry, confidence, love, hate, hope, despair, curiosity, apathy, depression, elation, anxiety, contentment, distress, energy, desire, grief, passion, sadness, optimism, anger, peace, and many, many more.

Emotions connect every aspect of the human experience. Whether the person is employed or not, is married or not, is young or old, is from this country or another, belongs to organized religion or not, comes from the city or country, hails from a large or small family, is male or female, or is wealthy or poor, emotions play a central role. Whether a person is active or inactive, sitting on a beach or looking for a job, celebrating the birth of a child or grieving the loss of a parent, or wondering about engaging in a social activity, emotions play a role. Given the central role emotions play in human functioning, social workers need to both appreciate and understand emotional functioning.

SOCIAL WORK AND EMOTIONS

What do social workers need to know about emotions? A lot! First, we need to understand our emotions to clarify how we go about our work. Consider the role emotion plays in decision-making: A social worker who labors under a strong emotion, maybe a strong discomfort with diversity, will behave differently toward immigrants compared to a social worker who is comfortable with diversity. In the former case, the social worker may apply less effort to help clients of diverse backgrounds or, worse yet, actively

Monkey Business/Fotolia

Emotions, such as love, are powerful and ubiquitous.

work against such clients. Research by Rivaux and colleagues (2008) revealed that children from African American families are placed in foster care at higher rates and are provided fewer services that could strengthen families relative to families of other races. How might emotions explain such a disturbing practice tendency? Consider emotional words associated with decision-making about children's out-of-home placement: caseworker's *motivation*, caseworker's *trust* in biological parents or extended family, and caseworker's *comfort* with ambiguity. Harris and Skyles (2011) note that African American children going into the foster care system are more likely to suffer than their White peers as supported by research showing that only 29% of African American children leave foster care compared to 46% of White children. To the degree that emotions influence our decisions, we need to develop emotional awareness.

While our emotions can lead to unhealthy or unethical practice, emotions are also the driving force that has led most of us to social work as a profession. Social workers are often known for their strong desire (an emotion) to improve the human condition—which often trumps the desire for personal wealth. Leaders of monumental social justice movements, such as Dr. Martin Luther King, possess high passion (an emotional state) about a position that drives remarkable, inspiring actions that have changed the world.

Second, in addition to understanding our emotions and the role they play in our work, social workers need to understand clients' emotions as a means of promoting well-being. After returning from war, soldiers can become paralyzed by emotions such as fear and guilt. Young children may refuse to attend school because of anxiety. Sadly, thousands of individuals choose to kill themselves when in the grips of despair. The National Institute of Mental Health reported that in 2007 approximately 35,000 U.S. citizens took their lives, making suicide as the 10th leading cause of death (http://www.nimh .nih.gov/health/publications/suicide-in-the-us-statistics-and-prevention/index.shtml, retrieved on September 14, 2011). These examples reveal emotions play a central role in many of situations for which social work is involved.

At a macro level, social workers can benefit from understanding the role emotions play in policy-making activities. Emotions influence decisions to declare war, send peace envoys to war-torn regions, and share resources with groups ravished by natural disasters. Similarly, emotions influence policies related to education, helping vulnerable populations, and responding to criminal behavior. Efforts associated with the War on Poverty (circa 1964)—which included policy and legislation such as the Economic Opportunity Act (1964), Volunteers in Service to America (VISTA), the Food Stamps Act (1964), and the creation of Medicare and Medicaid (1965)—had connections to President John F. Kennedy's emotional reaction to poverty he encountered in West Virginia mining towns.

At this point, we hope you have a healthy respect for the importance of emotion in social work activities. Assuming so, we turn to understanding emotions.

Ethical Practice

Practice Behavior Example: Recognize and manage personal values in a way that allows professional values to guide practice.

Critical Thinking Question How might your emotions surrounding common elements of the human experience (e.g., sexual orientation, poverty, drug use, immigration, religion) influence the decisions you make as a social worker?

EMOTIONS AS INDEPENDENT AND DEPENDENT VARIABLES

Emotions, like health, can be viewed as both an independent and a dependent variable. Emotions can act as independent variables. You are better able to apply your knowledge if you feel confident about taking a test than if you feel anxious (Brown et al., 2011; Cohen, Ben-Zur, & Rosenfeld, 2008). Here, emotions influence test performance. Confidence, or at least the lack of anxiety, allows people to perform better on problem-solving tasks. Emotions can also act as dependent variables; that is, emotions are influenced by other phenomena. Imagine you complete a school assignment and feel very proud of your efforts. Your instructor doesn't return it for several months, and when you do get it, there's a big "D" written on it—the worst grade you have ever received. This combination of events (initial pride at completing an assignment, then excessive waiting for the assignment to be returned, and then receiving a poor grade) will influence your emotions. You are likely to feel some combination of despondency, anger, anxiety, confusion, and fear. Next, you talk with your instructor and discover the grade was mistakenly given and you actually earned an "A." This change in events leads you to a mixture of feelings including relief, pride, and frustration. These two examples show emotions influence and are influenced by contextual factors.

EMOTIONS DEFINED

Certainly, you know the names of many emotions: joy, anger, peace, rage, excitement, and (hopefully not from this text) boredom. But, what exactly is an emotion? A founding father of psychology, William James (1884), posited emotion to be a physiological reaction to a subjective experience. Said differently, emotions are believed to reside within the "bodily" rather than the "cognitive" or thinking system.

Although volumes of research have explored emotions since James's definition, much is not known. Not too long ago an expert on emotions boldly stated that the question of "what is an emotion" has not been satisfactorily answered (Russell, 2003). While scientists and philosophers have debated over and enumerated certain core emotions, cartoonists have confidently developed long lists of emotions that are easily recognized and widely accepted, as shown in Figure 9.1.

While we appreciate what cartoonists have done to help people identify emotions, we also think it is wise to examine what science has to offer on emotions.

Scientific Perspectives of Emotions

We now turn to how science considers emotion. A review of how neuroscientists think about emotions reveals two broad approaches. First, there is a school of thought that emotions can be divided into basic categories such as anger, sadness, fear, or happiness (Barrett & Wager, 2006). While not exactly the same, categorizing emotions is similar to how chemists categorized the basic elements in the Periodic Table of Elements. The second school of thought suggests that emotions can be best understood by considering dimensions of emotion. We first look at categories of emotions.

Categorical view of emotions

In Table 9.1, we overview four relatively modern categories of basic emotions proposed by different research groups. The table is organized from left to right based on the date the categories were proposed. Notice that the research groups differ in both how many basic emotions are believed to exist and what the emotions are.

Figure 9.1
Emotions From a Cartoonist's Perspective

Note: Some emotions are well recognized and have been characterized in commonly seen cartoons.

Source: Retrieved from http://teens.drugabuse.gov/sites/default/files /WOD-Limbic-System-300x300.jpg on October 5, 2013.

Table 9.1   Overview of Four Models of Emotional Categories

Johnson-Laird & Oatley (1989) 5 Basic Emotions	Ekman (1992) 11 Basic Emotions	Parrott (2001) 6 Basic Emotions	Plutchik (2005) 8 Basic Emotions
Happiness	Enjoyment	Joy	Joy
Fear	Fear	Fear	Fear
Sadness	Sadness	Sadness	Sadness
Anger	Anger	Anger	Anger
Disgust	Disgust		Disgust
	Surprise	Surprise	Surprise
			Trust
		Love	
			Anticipation
	Contempt		
	Shame		
	Guilt		
	Embarrassment		
	Awe		

Source: Based on work of Johnson-Laird & Oatley (1989); Ekman (1992); Parrott (2001); and Plutchik (2005).

An argument against the listing of basic emotions is that the range of human emotions certainly extends beyond five or even 11 emotional states. In Table 9.2, for example, we list other emotions and their "synonyms." Notice the rich range and nuances of emotions that are very common to the human experience.

Before agreeing to throw out categorical models of emotions, consider some arguments in support of this approach. In a seminal article, Ekman (1992) defended categorizing "basic emotions" from an evolutionary perspective. In brief, Ekman's research on facial expressions found that certain discrete facial expressions are universal across different world regions and cultures. Ekman suggests that specific facial expressions reflect particular emotions and, therefore, infers that particular emotions are also universal. The universality of these emotions is taken as proof that they provided an evolutionary advantage by helping humans deal with fundamental life tasks, such as goal realization (reproduction, collecting food), protection, or responding to loss. Ekman states that "the primary function of emotion is to mobilize the organism to deal quickly with important interpersonal encounters" (p. 171).

Basic emotions, like those proposed by Ekman, are believed to be innate rather than learned. If basic emotions exist, then there must also be complex emotions. It is believed that complex or mixed emotions are learned through experience—they are not innate—and they're more likely to differ from culture to culture. Pride, gloom, and morose are examples of complex emotions that are not believed to be universal.

Table 9.2 Emotions and Synonym Emotions

Emotion Category	Synonym Emotions
Happiness	Thrilled, joy, euphoric, cheer, hopeful, pleased, jolly, awesome, ecstatic, elated, superb, terrific, exhilarated, jubilant, content, peaceful
Offended	Betrayed, dismissed, hurt, abused, crushed, wounded, discredited, belittled, exploited, mistreated, neglected, mocked, devalued, discounted, unappreciated
Anger	Cross, irritated, annoyed, bothered, vengeful, furry, irked, enraged, impatient, bitter, hateful
Caring	Respect, prize, trust, value, accepting, tenderness, enamored, madly in love, worship, adore, like, admiration
Confusion	Lost, flustered, floored, troubled, conflicted, uncertain, torn, befuddled, puzzled, trapped, lost, ambivalent, frustrated
Strong	Confident, powerful, brave, prepared, trusting, capable, firm, conviction, motivation, secure, motivated, inspired, full of purpose, successful, daring
Anxious	Frantic, fearful, vulnerable, panicky, terrified, jumpy, nervous, uneasy, doubtful, hesitant, rattled, nervous, timid, frightened, intimidated, shy
Sad	Depressed, grim, blue, deflated, pessimistic, unhappy, disappointed, gloomy, dejected, hopeless, brokenhearted, betrayed, demoralized

Source: Adapted from Ekman (1992); Hepworth, Rooney, Rooney, Strom-Gottfried, & Larsen (2010); Johnson-Laird & Oatley (1989); Parrott (2001); and Plutchik (2005).

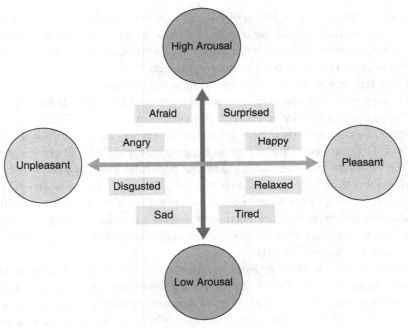

Figure 9.2
Russell's Circumplex Model of Emotions

Note: Emotions arising from two dimensions: feeling valence and arousal level.

Source: Adapted from Russell (2003).

Dimensional view of emotions

In contrast to the approach of grouping emotions, the dimensional model of emotions proposes all emotions can be best understood along two dimensions (Russell, 2003):

- Feeling valence   Positive (pleasant)   Negative (unpleasant)
- Arousal level   Aroused (active)   Not aroused (sleepy)

Previously, we stated that the 11 emotions advanced by Ekman could not capture the entire range of emotions we experience. Thus, how could all emotions be understood along two dimensions? Russell (2003) crosses the two dimensions, feeling valence and arousal level, to obtain "core emotions" that seem remarkably similar to the basic emotions presented earlier. In Figure 9.2, we present Russell's circumplex model of emotions.

Notice in Figure 9.2 that by using both dimensions, many emotional states can be understood. For example, high activation crossed with high pleasure is associated with emotions such as "excitement" or "happiness." Conversely, high activation crossed with high displeasure is associated with emotions such as "tenseness," "distress," or "anger." Low activation crossed with pleasure is described as emotions such as "serene" or "calm." And, low activation crossed with displeasure may include emotions such as "gloom" or "lethargy." Like most dimensional phenomena, the extremes are more easily defined than are center points.

Clinical Corner

Emotions do not exist in a vacuum—they are directed at some object. Consider the sentences in which you use an emotion, such as "I'm disappointed in myself," "I love her," or "I hate him." In each case, there is an object to the emotion. If you say while reading this book, "This is boring!" the object of the emotion is this book. How might this knowledge influence your social work practice?

DETERMINANTS OF EMOTIONS

There is no simple answer to the question, "What determines emotions?" What is known is that emotions vary and this variability allows for greater understanding of the determinants of emotions. We now review several well-established influences on our emotions.

Watch the video Cultural Depression. How might the information in the video help you in your profession? How might the information help the clients with whom you will work? What did you think of the video's message about mood and its determinants?

Biological Influences on Emotions

Genetics influence emotions. In a classic study using identical and fraternal twins to isolate the contribution of genetic and environmental influences, Emde and Plomin (1992) showed that children's emotions (also known as *temperament*, which will be discussed later in this chapter) were strongly influenced by genetics. In addition to genetics, other biological factors influence emotions. Hunger, fatigue, and illness certainly influence our emotions. Spend extended time with a toddler and you will quickly see just how powerful an effect hunger, fatigue, and illness can have on a child's emotions. What we consume also influences our emotions. Sugar and caffeine can provide temporary emotional highs, whereas carbohydrates and alcohol have a calming effect. Drugs, both prescribed and illegal, act to elevate, depress, or temper emotions. Exercise also influences emotions by releasing hormones such as endorphins. The rhythms of life, such as women's menstrual cycle, also influence our emotions. Further, baseline hormonal levels have a strong influence on emotions. Adolescence and puberty are known for wide mood swings that are driven by dramatic changes in hormone levels. These examples reveal that biological factors play a strong role in emotions. What strategies could be taken to "temper" some of the biological influences on mood listed earlier? Of course, medications target mood and so do behavioral strategies such as exercise and diet.

Psychological and Contextual Influences on Emotions

Biological influences are not solely responsible for our emotions; otherwise, the mythical drug *soma* that always produced pleasure in Aldous Huxley's classic *Brave New World* would be the answer to all of humanity's problems. Psychological factors also influence our emotions. For example, what we think in certain situations will influence our emotions. A few examples demonstrate this point. Imagine the following story. On a Saturday morning in Small Town USA, a tremendous rainstorm hits the area much to the despair (an emotion) of Sarah and delight (an emotion) of Emma. How is it that the same rainstorm causes two radically different emotions? Well, for Sarah the softball player, her championship game was cancelled and she felt despair. On the other hand, Emma the farmer had worried that her crops would not grow without rain and she felt delight because the storm brought much-needed rain. This story reveals that emotions are influenced by our perceptions of certain contexts, not contexts themselves.

Imagine another story. You are sitting in a room with a few close friends when three masked gunmen rush through the door and demand money while making threatening remarks. What emotions might you experience? Our guess is fear, anxiety, worry, anger, and disgust. After a minute, the three gunmen point their guns directly at you and pull the trigger at which point water squirts you in the face. The masked gunmen pull of their masks revealing some pranksters you know. Now what will you feel? Probably, your emotions will immediately shift from fear and anxiety to rage and anger. Why? Because the nature of the prank is not funny as it suggested a serious threat.

Emotions are clearly influenced by how we perceive events.

The rainstorm and hostage examples reveal that psychological appraisal of situations influences emotion. Note that it is not simply the situation but also one's appraisal or perception of the situation that influences emotions (discussed at greater length later in this chapter).

Clinical Corner

Change in people's typical emotional experience is often a precursor for seeking help from social workers as is shown in the following example. The Hernandez family sought counseling for their second child, Ernie (nine years old), following the death of his older sister. The family reported that a full year after his sister's death, Ernie continued to be sad, irritable, and unmotivated in school and social settings. Prior to his sister's death, Ernie was described as being outgoing, happy, social, and positive. Interestingly, Ernie's younger brother, Javier (seven years old) did not show dramatic changes in his emotions following his sister's death. While Javier had been sad shortly after his sister's death, he returned to his typical emotional functioning within a month. This example reveals two basic points. First, social work services are often sought following a change in a person's typical emotion pattern. Second, individuals differ in their emotional responses to environmental events.

Neurological Influences on Emotions

As mentioned in Chapter 5, human functioning—including the production of emotions—ultimately occurs between the brain's neurons. Neurotransmitters such as dopamine, acetylcholine, norepinephrine, and serotonin are strongly linked to emotions such as anxiety, aggression, happiness, and depression. Further, certain brain regions or structures are linked to emotional processing. The question of which neurotransmitter or brain region influences a particular emotion is not fully answered and neuroscientists continue to explore how the brain originates and regulates emotions. What is known is that many brain regions, neurotransmitters, and hormones interact to influence emotionally functioning. That is, no single gene, neurotransmitter, or brain structure is fully responsible for a particular emotion or our general emotional functioning. Therefore, if you hear someone say that they have the "depression gene," take the information with a large grain of salt because it simply is not true (El Hage, Powell, & Surguladze, 2009). When discussing where emotions reside in the brain, Barrett and Wager (2006) indicate that "emotion category-location correspondences are neither consistent nor specific ... indicating that is it's currently not possible to characterize each emotional category by a biological signature" (p. 82). That said, science has revealed that certain structures and elements within the brain are strongly connected to emotional functioning. For example, anger appears to be closely connected to the lateral orbitofrontal cortex, whereas discuss is closely connected to the basal ganglia and fear is mostly centered in the amygdala (see Barrett & Wager, 2006).

Social Influences on Emotions

Social factors also strongly influence emotions. One classic study revealing the power of social influences on emotions involved separating baby rhesus monkeys from their mothers (see Blum, 2002). Psychologist Harry Harlow developed a laboratory where two groups of baby rhesus monkeys were removed from their mothers and both groups were introduced to two "surrogate" mothers: a terrycloth mother and a wire mother,

Did You Know?

Does today's modern, technology-rich world promote social isolation? Does high-Internet use restrict or promote social interaction? At least one study suggests that adolescents who spend a lot of time on the Internet are, in fact, less likely to engage socially with friends and family. However, levels of depression among high- and low-Internet users did not differ (Sanders, Field, Diego, & Kaplan, 2000). By contrast, some studies show that social isolation in adolescents is linked to increased risk for drug use, feelings of alienation, depression, and anger (Tani, Chavez, & Deffenbacher, 2001).

which either did or did not provide nourishment. In both groups, the baby monkeys would cling to the soft, comforting "social" monkey, regardless of whether it provided nourishment. This study provided evidence that the emotional need to connect is just that "a need." In referencing the importance of social contact, a colleague of ours stated, "we humans need people like we need water."

Closer to our species, research has shown that when people are isolated from others, they tend to experience increased emotions of threat and anxiousness (Lau, Moulds, & Richardson, 2009). Remember back to when you were a child and how being picked (or not) to join a team, to attend a birthday party, or to go on a date influenced your emotions.

Research on adolescents and adults who tend to socially withdraw found that these individuals generally perceive greater threat in the environment than do their peers. They experience increased stress in the autonomic nervous system, which triggers the "fight-or-flight" response system, and, by definition, choose flight—that is, removing themselves from social situations. The impact of social withdrawal is, unfortunately, linked to outcomes such as anxiety, insecurity, and depression (Pérez-Edgar et al., 2010).

At this point, a case has been made that unfavorable social situations can promote emotional problems. What about the opposite? Mason (2010) found that strong social networks protect urban adolescents from mental illness and drug-related problems. It could be that strong social ties among adolescents promote their identification and success in school, which is associated with a strong goal direction. Social support is not just good for the very young, older adults also benefit emotionally from social connection. A study of older African American women found that high levels of social support enhanced their emotional and physical well-being and protected against the harmful effects of family violence (Paranjape & Kaslow, 2010). In this study, social support was defined as the availability of people to provide assistance with physical, psychological, and material needs in times of distress. In general, older adults who have high social support are able to remain independent longer, which leads to an increased sense of independence and esteem.

Clinical Corner

It stands to reason that if social support promotes emotional health, efforts would be taken to improve social connections—especially among vulnerable individuals. Winningham and Pike (2007) introduced a program to increase social support for institutionalized older adults because this group is particularly at risk for emotional problems, given their likely loss of independence and loss of previous social support networks (from death of friends or family, or moving from their previous community). These researchers introduced a group-based intervention in which residents in the assisted living centers met three times a week for 45 minutes. Group leaders led discussions about issues related to aging while also facilitating social interactions. Specifically, participants were engaged in structured activities that encouraged social connection, such as learning each other's names, learning about their history, and talking about their current and past experiences. Compared to residents not placed in these programs, participants in these friendship groups experienced less loneliness and sadness, which was predicted to increase general and cognitive well-being. Just providing an activity to increase social connection does not, however, guarantee that the intended results will happen. For example, another research group provided a course on Tai Chi with the expectation that participants would experience greater social support and, therefore, mental health; however, their hoped expectation was not realized (Lee, Lee, & Woo, 2010). In comparing the results and interventions of these two studies, it might be that simply having people assembled together and doing an activity is not enough to meet our emotional needs—as was the case with the Tai Chi group. Rather, it may be that for social interactions to have salutary benefits, real connection and sharing need to occur.

Many other social factors influence emotional functioning. When you witness someone cry, for example, you may feel sad, which may promote bonding (Hendriks & Vingerhoets, 2006). Anticipating what others think of us also produces emotions, such as pride or shame (Svensson, Müssener, & Alexanderson, 2006). When we believe others accept and value us, we tend to feel a sense of social pride, which is linked to increased social interaction and a willingness to perform without hesitation. By contrast, when we believe others view us negatively, we may experience a sense of shame that causes withdrawal and risk avoidance.

Social interactions can also influence emotions that ultimately influence economic decisions. A group of researchers experimentally demonstrated that emotions arising from social interactions play a strong role in economic decision-making. Classical economics theory espouses a "rationalist" perspective, which hypothesizes that decisions are made primarily on one variable: the advancement of one's self-interest. The rationalist perspective strongly emphasizes logic over emotions. Yet, research has shown that feelings of "unfairness" lead to decisions that go fully against self-interest. One variation of this research is to allow two parties to negotiate a settlement in a controlled experiment called the *ultimatum game*. In this game, there are two players: one is given money and each party can take home the amount of money they agree upon. In this experiment/ game, person A proposes a split of money to person B, who must either accept the split and take whatever amount is offered or reject the split, in which case neither party receives any money. Regardless of the split arrangement proposed by person A, the rationalist perspective would hold that person B will accept because something is better than nothing. However, when the split becomes increasingly "unfair," person B often refuses the split on the emotion of unfairness. That is, person B will reject free money because the deal felt unfair. This simple experiment illustrates the strong role emotions play in many decisions that we make (Moretti & di Pellegrino, 2010).

A last example of the relationship between social factors and emotions is relevant to macro-level social change. Consider the following concept: Groups, like individuals, possess emotions. In 2011, group-based emotion was prevalent in what was called the Arab Spring, in which a variety of pro-democracy uprisings occurred in the Arab world. Tunisia, Egypt, Libya, Syria, and Yemen, for example, witnessed mass protests fueled by anger and frustration against seated governments. Interestingly, these civil uprisings rippled through different countries in a very concentrated time frame—suggesting that some form of group emotion across country boarders both fueled and maintained this unique period of uprising. Intergroup emotion theory proposes that people define themselves in relation to a group and that individuals experience feelings based on events that happen to the group even if the particular event does not directly impact them as individuals. In the Arab Spring, collective anger against political abuse united individuals to the cause of democracy even though they did not directly experience political abuse (Livingstone, Spears, Manstead, Bruder, & Shepherd, 2011).

Historically, group emotion has played a significant role in change within the United States. For example, Harriet Beecher Stowe's classic *Uncle Tom's Cabin* is credited with unifying support in the Northern states against the South's slavery by provoking collective anger about the injustices of slavery, which provided support for a harrowing civil war during a very tenuous time in U.S. history. How has group-level emotion influenced the direction and energy of social change in areas such as Occupy Wall Street, the Tea Party, the Right to Marry, and the Civil Rights. Might the December 14, 2012, shooting at Sandy Hook Elementary school promote group emotion that influences policies surrounding guns?

Policy Practice

Practice Behavior Example: Analyze, formulate, and advocate for policies that advance social well-being.

Critical Thinking Question How do emotions influence policy formation and implementation? What efforts might be used to leverage emotions to promote policies consistent with National Association of Social Workers (NASW) Code of Ethics?

Environmental Influences on Emotion

Environmental factors also influence emotions. Not surprisingly, living in a neighborhood marked by considerable disadvantage (e.g., boarded-up homes, graffiti, closed businesses) is linked to increased emotional problems, such as stress and discouragement. Why? One hypothesis is that individuals with poor and mental health cluster together and produce disadvantaged neighborhoods. This hypothesis, known as the *compositional effect*, lays "responsibility" of poorer and mental health on characteristics of residents, not of the environment, which is a type of "blaming the victim." An alternative hypothesis, known as the *contextual effect*, is that there is something about disadvantaged neighborhoods that challenges residents' health regardless of the residents' characteristics. Of interest, the quality of the neighborhood in which one lives has been found to influence emotions independent of personality characteristics (Kwag, Jang, Rhew, & Chiriboga, 2011). That is, living in a neighborhood characterized by poverty is likely to cause stress and unhealthy emotions.

Unfortunately, there is evidence to suggest that once a neighborhood begins to decay, the decay accelerates, which is known as the *broken window effect*. Essentially, once a neighborhood begins to decline (evidenced by broken windows, graffiti, crime), many residents engage in behaviors that further the deterioration of the environment, by breaking more windows for example, which can lead to businesses and services leaving the area (Keize, Lindenberg, & Steg, 2008). Under these conditions, pessimism tends to rise, as do rates of depression. A particularly disturbing finding reported by Yen, Yelin, Katz, Eisner, and Blanc (2006) found that adults with asthma who reported high levels of neighborhood problems were far more likely to report a lower quality of life, poorer health, and a five-fold increase in depression. The adage, "the rich get richer and the poor get poorer," aptly applies to quality of life in dilapidated neighborhoods. Those living in economically disadvantaged neighborhoods are more likely to suffer, and this suffering may lower hope and increase pessimism—two emotions critical for overcoming challenge.

In considering the quality of a neighborhood, it is impossible to separate the physical space from the social context. If you go to a very exclusive neighborhood, for example, you are more likely to interface with people who appear safe, compared to going into a neighborhood characterized by blight and disorder. In fact, individuals living in troubled neighborhoods often report high levels of concern about their safety (Kruger, 2008). Concerns about safety drain a person's emotional reserves and are linked to increased rates of mental and emotional problems. Further, witnessing violence within one's neighborhood is strongly linked to increases in depressive symptoms (Mendelson, Turner, & Tandon, 2010).

Children and adolescents are particularly affected by neighborhood quality. In a study of Hispanic adolescents, it was found that reports of neighborhood quality were associated with the adolescents' sense of self. Adolescents who reported that their neighborhood was characterized by lower education, lower wealth, more families on welfare and unemployed adults, and more individuals who could not speak English were more likely to have lower self-esteem, self-confidence, grades, and academic aspirations. Notice the words that speak to emotions in the previous sentence: self-esteem, self-confidence, aspirations. Interestingly, the adolescents' perceptions of neighborhood distress were confirmed by reports from census data and police reports. That is, the youth accurately gauged the quality of their neighborhood in relation to more objective indicators (Plunkett, Abarca-Mortensen, Behnke, & Sands, 2007).

What can be done to support neighborhoods that are in decay? What can be done to support families living in challenged neighborhoods? Fortunately, research shows that many of the untoward effects of neighborhoods are mediated through social and psychological factors, such as social support and family resilience. That is, individuals who have supportive social systems tend not to suffer emotionally despite living in distressed neighborhoods (Wickrama & Noh, 2010). The ability to support others is clearly linked to resources. Individuals and families who struggle to make ends meet are hard-pressed to reach out and support others. This reality speaks to the need to support legislation aimed at lowering poverty and helping families find and maintain employment and health care, in addition to improving neighborhood quality (Brooks-Gunn, 2010; Brooks-Gunn, Duncan, & Aber, 1997).

We leave the discussion of environmental influences on emotions with an interesting finding about the amount of sunshine and the New York Stock Exchange. Considerable evidence (Akhtari, 2011) suggests that highly logical stock brokers tend to be more optimistic (an emotion) on bright, sunny days compared to cloudy days as evidenced by greater than expected returns on sunny days. In essence, sunshine positively affects the mood of stock brokers who then positively influence market returns. Good, old-fashioned "light therapy"?

Psychological Influences on Emotions

Emotions are also influenced by our thoughts. Previously, we talked about several influences on emotions. A simplistic view can be depicted by saying that a stimulus causes a response: "stimulus → emotional response." The stimulus might be neighborhood quality or social interactions. Thus, we could say, "poor neighborhood quality → individual depression." However, this clearly is not the case as many people living in poor-quality neighborhoods do not suffer from depression. In fact, from poor-quality neighborhoods arise many great leaders—think Abraham Lincoln.

To explain the variability in responses to other influences, the "stimulus → response" model has been revised to the following:

Stimulus → Organism's interpretation of stimulus → Emotional response

Cognitive theories on emotion suggest that factors such as values, goals, worldviews, and intentions influence which emotions derive from particular experiences (Lazarus, 1991). That is, emotions are linked to what is important to an individual. Remember the example about the rainstorm and the varied responses of Sarah the softball player and Emma the farmer. It was not the rainstorm that caused the different emotions but their interpretation of the rainstorm.

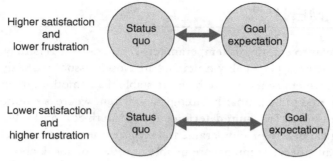

Figure 9.3
Emotions, Goals, and Progress
Note: Degree of personal satisfaction is related to goals and progress toward such goals.

One important psychological factor influencing emotion is goals. The degree to which a person is accomplishing his or her goals shapes emotional responses. For example, a "driven" person who is asked to vacation by sitting on a beach and smelling the roses will likely be unhappy. He or she would be much happier climbing a mountain or going on a bike tour. By contrast, a "laid back" personality would prefer the relaxed beach vacation. Figure 9.3 illustrates the amount of distance between the status quo and a person's goal or expectation predicts the degree of satisfaction or dissatisfaction.

In addition to motivation, another psychological process critical to emotions is appraisal. Consider Figure 9.3 to reveal that without appraisal, a clear sense of emotion could not be predicted. If people are unaware of the relationship between their status quo (progress) and their goal or expectation, then the distance between the two shouldn't matter. In his model of cognitive influences on emotions, Lazarus (1991) argues that the type of emotion a person experiences is predictable. Emotions resulting from situations perceived to involve harm, loss, or threat are expected to produce emotions such as anger, anxiety, fear, shame, jealousy, disgust, envy, or guilt. Getting hurt generally produces an emotion of anxiety or anger, whereas if a person harms another, she or he is likely to feel shame or guilt. By contrast, emotions resulting from situations perceived to benefit a person include joy, happiness, pride, love, and gratitude. Notice the role of perception over truth. Little Red Riding Hood was excited by the untrue perception that the wolf was her grandmother. If during a walk in the woods you misperceive a stump to be a bear, you will feel inappropriately threatened. Lazarus advances the following "basic emotional categories," which are founded on the relationship between appraisal and motivation:

Human Behavior

Practice Behavior Example: Utilize conceptual frameworks to guide the processes of assessment, intervention, and evaluation.

Critical Thinking Question How might biological, social, psychological, and environmental models of emotion be integrated to understand a client's emotional functioning?

Assess your comprehension of Emotions by completing this quiz.

1. **Anger.** When a person believes his or her goal is at stake (see Figure 9.3), the person will probably get angry. Anger usually involves appraisal of rejection, betrayal, unfairness, or a lost opportunity.

2. **Anxiety.** When one's existence is threatened or the meaning of his or her existence is threatened, a person is likely to become anxious because success is unlikely.

3. **Sadness.** When one loses a commitment of importance—such as one's social role (e.g., a job, public reputation, family role) or loss of a relationship (e.g., the death of a loved one, loss of a friendship).

4. **Pride.** The positive emotion of pride is likely to occur when one realizes a goal of importance.

TEMPERAMENT

A concept similar to emotion is temperament. Temperament generally refers to behavioral tendencies or personality traits that are closely associated with emotions. A person's temperament is believed to be more stable than emotions because temperament is considered to be primarily biologically driven, whereas emotions are more transient because they are multi-determined (Goldsmith & Alansky, 1987). Evidence for the biological nature of temperamental styles comes from research on infants' personality traits. Because infants are unable to reflect or speak about themselves, the data supporting temperamental styles come from behavioral observations. One research team, Thomas and Chess (1991), found three basic types of childhood temperament:

1. Easy child temperament (40%): positive mood, quickly establishes regular routines, adapts easily
2. Difficult child temperament (10%): tendency to react negatively, cry frequently, irregular in daily routines, slow to adapt to, or accept, new experiences
3. Slow-to-warm-up child temperament (15%): low activity level, mildly negative mood, low adaptability

Twin adoption studies reveal that heritability of temperament is high, with up to 50% to 60% of the variance in temperament due to genetics (Plomin, Reiss, Hetherington, & Howe, 1994). What goes into temperament? Thomas and Chess (1991) and others have assessed temperament on the following nine dimensions:

1. **Activity.** The amount of movement, physical energy, the ability to relax, and the ability to participate in a structured environment.
2. **Reactivity to novelty.** An individual's reaction to novelty can be categorized by a tendency toward approach or avoidance. Does the person hesitate in a novel situation or boldly move forward?
3. **Regularity.** An individual's rhythm in biological functions such as approaching sleep, waking, and eating is known as regularity.
4. **Adaptability.** The ease and rate at which an individual adjusts to change is called adaptability.
5. **Distractibility.** An individual's tendency to focus and concentrate when confronted with distraction is a measure of distractibility.
6. **Attention and persistence.** The degree to which an individual can persist with a task and stay focused versus losing interest.
7. **Mood.** An individual's baseline or tendency toward being happy, positive, negative, unhappy, critical, cheerful, or upset.
8. **Sensitivity.** The degree to which an individual is bothered by environmental stimuli. Some individuals need their environment to be "just right" while others tolerate significant environmental stimuli such as noise, texture, light, and chaos.
9. **Intensity.** The degree of energy put into an activity describes intensity. For example, some individuals celebrate quietly, while others are boisterous and raucous.

Watch the video Temperament. How do you think temperament will influence a person across his or her lifetime? How will a person's temperament influence the person's family and friends?

Children's Temperament and Parenting Style: Goodness of Fit

While we do not intend to be insensitive, this classification system begs a question. What temperament would you want your child to be? Our guess is that most would say the easy temperament. Indeed, parents of children with an easier temperament tend to enjoy greater parental satisfaction (McMahon, Barnett, Kowalenko, Tennant, & Don, 2001) and higher marital satisfaction (Mehall, Spinrad, Eisenberg, & Gaertner, 2009). Note that the word *satisfaction* is a form of emotion. Further, some research suggests that children with difficult temperaments tend to engage in more parent–child conflict as adolescents and use alcohol more than their peers—both of which are risk factors for children and parents (Neighbors, Clark, Donovan, & Brody, 2000).

If temperament is stable and primarily biologically driven, can anything be done to help children and parents who are "mismatched"? With or without external help, a key factor in predicting successful child development is the degree to which parents are sensitive to their child's temperamental needs (Healey, Flory, Miller, & Halperin, 2011; Kiff, Lengua, & Bush, 2011). Consider these examples.

- John is a four-year-old who lives with a single parent in a low-income, high-density apartment. On the temperament dimensions, John is highly active, very intense, and highly distractible. What kind of parenting style would work best with John? A good fit would be a parent who can help John to be active by finding outlets such as visits to the park, finding a play group, or finding sports teams or other activities that allow him to be active. With regard to John's intensity, his parent will need patience to allow John to express himself and, at the same time, maintain regularity and boundaries. As a rather distractible child, John's parent will provide a good fit by having a variety of activities that John likes and can transition between. By contrast, a poor fit would be a parent who does not have the energy or creativity to allow John to be active with a variety of options. Further, a poor fit would be a parent who is bothered by John's intensity and scolds him for being intense, active, and distractible.

- Laura is an eight-year-old who lives with her parents and older sister. The family attempts to move Laura to a new school. However, Laura's temperament is such that she shies away from novel experiences and is very cautious about reaching out to new friends. Laura struggles to adapt to the new school and expresses concern that she does not like school and would like to quit. Her school performance worsens and she isolates herself from social opportunities at the new school and with her old friends. For Laura, which type of parent would be a good fit? Parents who are understanding and supportive of Laura's emotions would be helpful. They would need to be patient and allow Laura to develop and adjust at her pace. Further, it may be that her parents will need to be adaptive and try to move Laura back to her original school. A poor fit for Laura would be parents who criticize and judge her for not adapting. Pressuring Laura to "just make everything okay" would be inconsistent with her sensitivity and slowness to adapt.

The term *goodness of fit* describes the need for parents to try to adapt to their child's temperamental style. Parents who can be child oriented and match their parenting style to their child can thwart some of the potential challenges that "difficult" and "slow-to-warm-up" children have. Fortunately, research on efforts to educate parents about their children's temperament and how to adapt seems promising (Healey et al., 2011; Kiff et al., 2011; Lavigne et al., 2008; Sheeber & Johnson, 1994). In a study conducted by Sheeber

}
**Assess your comprehension
of Temperament by completing this quiz.**
}

and Johnson (1994), some parents were educated on temperament and provided with advice on how they could match parenting strategies to their children, while other parents were put on a waitlist. Parents receiving the intervention showed significant and meaningful improvement in their comfort with parenting, in addition to reporting improvements in their children's behaviors. Thus, there is hope for parents of children who seem to have "difficult" temperaments.

EMOTIONAL REGULATION

At the beginning of this chapter, you read a wide variety of adjectives describing emotions. You certainly noticed that not all emotions are on the "desirable" side. So, what do you do with negative or "bad" emotions? One argument is to do nothing. The human condition cannot simply be positive all the time and accepting this reality might actually lessen the discomfort of untoward emotions (Hayes, Strosahl, & Wilson, 2003). In U.S. culture, it is fully appropriate, even expected, for individuals to feel grief and sadness following the death of loved ones, the loss of friendships, and other disappointments. Further, U.S. culture is fairly tolerant of intense emotions. Consider the role anger plays in society. We see how anger is tolerated by watching professional sports; coaches and players get angry and can still be involved in the game. There also seems to be a strong appetite in U.S. culture for revenge as evidenced by the many movies with this theme put out by Hollywood.

Although U.S. culture tolerates negative emotions, there are limits. Employers, educators, and families become uncomfortable when employees, students, and members of our families exhibit negative emotions that seem to leave a "normal zone." Further, as individuals we prefer positive compared to negative emotions. When individuals are so radically sad or depressed that they cannot get out of bed and function, society becomes concerned. When an employee gets so angry that he verbally or physically assaults fellow employees, society becomes concerned. When a student is so anxious that she cannot function in school, society becomes concerned. While "society's concern" is certainly important, individuals who harbor strong negative emotions are unhappy and deserve to be happy. After all, the U.S. Constitution says that "Life, Liberty, and the pursuit of Happiness" is central.

Emotional regulation is a commonly used phrase to describe the action of moving from one emotion state to another. In many contexts, it is expected that a person shift from a negative to a positive mood (Koole, 2009). A family example reveals how important emotional regulation is. One of the authors witnessed his sibling state, "The $1.00 I spent on a binky is the best money I've ever spent." A binky is a plastic nipple-like pacifier devise given to infants to help them stop crying. Ask almost any parent how they helped their crying infant stop crying (a form of emotional regulation) and you'll hear some very innovative strategies, such as vacuuming, going on long drives, walking up and down stairs, cooing, acting like clowns, and feeding them non-infant friendly foods such as soda, chocolate, and other sweets. Thus, parents are expected to help children regulate their emotions and do so by providing routines, consoling, cheerleading, and many other creative endeavors (Bariola, Gullone, & Hughes, 2011). Further, by managing young children's emotions, adults regulate their emotions. Moving a child from a crying to a content state is reinforcing because it makes us feel confident and provides relief from distraught babies.

As we become older, we are expected to regulate our emotions. Being called *a baby* when one does not get his way, after outgrowing the infant/toddler stage, is not a compliment. Adults referred to as *babies* generally receive such an insult when emotional regulation is expected but not present. Emotional regulation involves more than just moving from a negative to a positive mood. When we are in a formal setting, we are expected to regulate our emotions to match the setting. For example, laughing or raging during a funeral is judged inappropriate. Also, when you have a romantic inclination toward a client, you are expected (read: legally and ethically expected) to regulate this emotion. Thus, emotion regulation is about increasing, changing, or decreasing either positive or negative emotions (Koole, 2009). So, how do we regulate our emotions? In a review of emotion regulation, Koole provides many strategies used to regulate emotions, such as:

- **Divert or manage attention.** If you are very angry at a police officer for giving you a speeding ticket, you might think about your summer vacation rather than rage at the police officer—because raging at a police officer may get you arrested.

- **Avoidance.** People routinely avoid activities or stressors to manage their emotions. Feeling bored? Read, watch television, call friends, or go to a movie.

- **Focus on the emotion.** Interestingly, meditation and many exposure therapies try to regulate emotions by helping people become comfortable with the negative emotion. In trauma, for example, avoidance of the stimuli that caused the trauma often results in prolonging and intensifying unwanted emotions (Abramowitz, Deacon, & Whiteside, 2011; Hayes et al., 2003; Koole, 2009).

- **Use a substance.** Chemicals (glass of wine, comfort food) certainly shift emotional states. Of course, regulating emotions through substances can cause more damage than good.

- **Exercise.** Unless we are injured, exercise generally makes us feel better.

- **Changing one's environment.** To change emotions, a person may move, change jobs, get a job, or even quit a job. Vacations also seem to help, until we have to return to the grind. Calling friends and family and pursuing hobbies also change emotions.

- **Changing one's thoughts.** Talk therapies, from Sigmund Freud to David Burns, all provide strategies to change how we think so we can shift emotional states.

Clinical Corner

A pioneer in studying emotional functioning, Lazarus (1991) proposed two types of emotional coping: problem- and emotion-focused coping. In the *problem-focused coping* method, the person attempts to resolve the problem driving the unwanted emotion, thereby producing relief from untoward emotions. If a person is unhappy with a romantic relationship—she can break up with her partner, work to improve the relationship, change herself, or suggest the partner change. If a person is unhappy with her job, she can find a new one or make bids for an improved work situation. If a person is displeased with a personal characteristic, say being anxious about tests in school, he can find strategies to perform better. The *emotion-focused coping* method is utilized when the problem cannot be directly changed, which means the unwanted emotion will continue. Emotion-focused coping attempts to minimize emotional distress rather than change the problem driving the emotional distress. Hospice care is an example. There comes a point when medical efforts to save a dying person are discontinued and efforts at promoting comfort are emphasized. Emotion-focused coping might also be used in the case of loss. The death of a loved one and past traumas are examples of events that cannot be directly changed despite lingering emotional baggage. Thus, emotion-focused efforts will attempt to bring about relief of the emotional baggage through activities such as distraction, avoidance, forgiveness, and radical acceptance.

EMOTIONAL INTELLIGENCE

You likely have heard the term *emotional intelligence* as popularized by Daniel Goleman's (1995) book. The central thesis of Goleman's book is that emotional intelligence is every bit as important to success as cognitive intelligence. Emotional intelligence is characterized as the ability to monitor one's emotions as well as other people's emotions in an effort to guide decisions. Thus, the emotionally intelligent professor who tends to give hard tests to anxious students will not gloat about the test's rigor or tell horror stories about students who have failed. Goleman argues that emotional intelligence comprises four "tasks":

1. Developing awareness of one's emotions and intentions
2. Developing emotional management skills (see earlier)
3. Reading other people's emotions—generally through perspective taking
4. Handling relationships by using these three skills to solve and prevent relationship-related problems

MENTAL ILLNESS

Regulating emotions is easier said than done for most of us. At times, emotions can become troubling and even life-threatening. As mentioned at the beginning of this chapter, suicide is the 10th leading cause of death in the United States. Taking one's life is strongly linked to feelings of sadness, depression, despair, and hopelessness (Clark et al., 2011). An estimated 5% of the U.S. population struggles with persistent depression and anxiety at any one point in time—and roughly 51% of these individuals consider suicide (Young, Klap, Shoai, & Wells, 2008). The National Institute of Mental Health puts the rate of depression at around 7% at any given time, with as many as 16% having experienced depression at some point in their life, as illustrated in Figure 9.4.

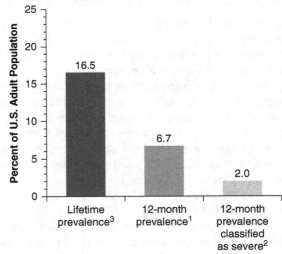

Prevalence
- 12-month prevalence: 6.7% of U.S. adult population[1]
- Severe: 30.4% of these cases (e.g., 2.0% of U.S. adult population) are classified as "severe"[2]

Figure 9.4
Rate of Major Depression in the United States
Source: Retrieved from http://www.nimh.nih.gov/statistics/1MDD_ADULT.shtml on August 11, 2012.

Depression and anxiety are just a few "mental health disorders" that can devastate individuals, families, and groups. In your studies, you will likely be exposed to the *Diagnostic and Statistical Manual of Mental Disorders (DSM)*, which overviews common mental illnesses. While we do not go into these conditions at this point, it is important to know that a common thread that links all of these emotional disorders is that they disrupt and interfere with basic tasks of living. Any social worker who has worked in the field for a few years knows that mental illness can cause individuals and families massive pain and suffering. For example, bipolar disorder can lead to loss of employment, severe relationship stress, and financial ruin. Posttraumatic stress disorder can cripple former military men and women even though their physical body looks strong and capable. Anxiety disorders can ruin relationships and retard growth in life's major tasks such as education, social relations, and occupational pursuits. And, as was mentioned, mental illness claims lives through suicide or engagement in other high-risk behaviors such as alcohol and illicit drug use. Individuals struggling with anorexia nervosa are between 5 and 12 times more likely to die early compared to the general population (Arcelus, Mitchell, Wales, & Nielsen, 2011).

NASW Code of Ethics clearly indicates that the profession is dedicated to improving the quality of life. Many populations targeted by social work suffer from emotionally based mental illnesses—in part because they face high levels of stress. Homelessness, domestic violence, child abuse, war, and poverty increase the likelihood of mental illness and are areas targeted by social work research and practice.

HAPPINESS AND POSITIVE PSYCHOLOGY

Since the late 1800s and early 1900s, social work and like-minded professions (e.g., psychology, psychiatry) have been interested in understanding, preventing, and treating mental illness. Indeed, volumes of researchers and direct practice professionals have focused on mental illness. More recently, a movement has begun that emphasizes happiness and positive psychology. (Note that Chapter 20 provides significantly more information on positive psychology.)

In 2000, the president of the American Psychological Association officially launched efforts to study and promote positive psychology. The lead proponents of this movement, Martin Seligman and Mihaly Csikszentmihalyi (2000), argued that psychology and like-minded professions have focused too much on problems in living that undermined research and intervention efforts that can promote optimal living. They proposed more be done to understand and promote human experiences or states such as happiness, thriving, peace, perseverance, responsibility, altruism, moderation, virtue, improved citizenship, wisdom, talent development, work ethic, tolerance, acceptance, nurturance, creativity, interpersonal skills, purpose, meaning, optimism, hope, the capacity to love, success in vocational pursuits, and forgiveness. Just reading the proposed topics makes us feel better, how about you? Understanding why some people thrive can propel social work's goal of improving the human condition.

Assess your comprehension of Emotional Regulation and Positive Psychology by completing this quiz.

Of course, an emphasis on positive living was not simply born in 2000. A main focus of Socrates was finding and living "the good life." In 1943, Abraham Maslow noted that humans have great potential and can develop into positive, generative beings, meaning that they give to the world more than they take. At about the same time, the humanism movement began, which also emphasized quality of living. In fact, social work owns the distinction of launching a strengths-based approach to understanding and helping individuals (Saleebey, 2012). Regardless of its particular birth point, a focus on the positive aspects of the human condition will help you succeed in social work.

Assess your analysis and evaluation of this chapter's contents by completing the Chapter Review.

Gender and Sexuality Influences on Human Behavior

As noted in throughout this book, human behavior is influenced by multiple factors, including biology and social interactions, among others. Often, these factors intertwine in such a way that teasing out what is biological based and what results from social influences becomes nearly impossible. In this chapter, we'll look at ways in which gender and sexuality impact human behavior, recognizing that both nature and nurture play a role in shaping behavior. In particular, we'll look at the influence of sex differentiation, sexual maturation, puberty, gender identity, and coping behavior, and how gender intersects with aggression, leadership, and helping behavior. We'll also look at sexual orientation, and finally at sexual dysfunction and sexual disorders.

SEX DIFFERENTIATION

The single most important variable in differentiating males from females appears to be biological. This is not to suggest that other influences (e.g., social and cognitive) do not play a role. However, the role of biology is paramount—primarily through the impact of chromosomes and hormones. Differentiation occurs early in the gestational period when the influence of the X chromosome appears. Genes on the X chromosome start the development of testes, which in turn produces the hormones known as *androgens* that lead to male sexual organs (Santrock, 2008). *Estrogens*, another group of hormones, play a significant role in the development of physical characteristics in women. Sexual differentiation has been identified as occurring in the early developmental period (11 to 21 weeks of gestation) of humans (Auyeung et al., 2009). Gonadal hormones (in particular, androgens) appear to play a significant role in changing both the brain and the behavior. Children as young as one year show differences in toy preferences, and these differences increase with age (Golombok & Hines, 2002; Servin, Bohlin, & Berlin, 1999). In addition, choices of playmates and the activities pursued show differences that have been traced back to fetal testosterone levels and appear independent of other variables, such as maternal age or education. Thus, the two most important predictors of a child's choice of friends, toys, and play activities are the sex of the child and the amount of testosterone to which the child was exposed during prenatal development.

Interactions with other adolescents influence gender relationships.

Fetal testosterone has also been linked to the differences in social cognition, particularly the capacity for empathy (Geary, 2002; Knickmeyer, Baron-Cohen, Raggatt, Taylor, & Hackett, 2006). Generally speaking, individuals who experienced lower levels of fetal testosterone in early development exhibit greater empathy. Higher levels of the hormone correlate negatively with certain developmental milestones, including vocabulary size and amount of eye contact at one year and social relationship quality at age four. Testosterone also influences the brain's anatomy for one's level of aggressive behavior and spatial navigation ability. Overall, a higher level of the hormone is considered detrimental to important social abilities.

While biology's influence is well recognized in sexual differentiation, there are other explanations for gender differences. Social theories about gender suggest that many of the men–woman differences also result from the different roles they play, power differentials between the sexes, and modeling to which children are exposed. Parents often treat male and female children differently, praising or otherwise favoring gender-specific behaviors and activities. Children in families where discussions about feelings are commonplace demonstrated greater awareness of the feelings of others (Dunn, Brown, Slomkowski, Tesla, & Youngblade, 1991). It is also likely that mothers spend more time talking with daughters about feelings than with sons, helping produce different capacities for empathy. Even autism may be influenced by higher levels of fetal testosterone, a finding that may explain the greater incidence of autism in males (Baron-Cohen, 2002).

Boys and girls are often given different toys that reflect cultural influences. Each gender is subjected to different media influences. Advertising often targets one gender or the other with specific messages about the desirability of toys that are gender specific. Princess dresses and American Girl dolls are not peddled to young boys.

Social institutions also help differentiate females and males. Schools and churches also encourage and reinforce gender-specific behaviors and attitudes for both males and females. Peers play a role that is evident as early as age three. At some point, children begin to see themselves as either boys or girls and the types of activities they pursue become more consistent with that self-view. This self-view influences choices that they make with regard to playmates and recreational activities. Most play activity after that point occurs in same-sex groups and the nature of the play is often different. Boys are more likely to engage in wrestling and competitive activities that involve some level of dominance, while girls tend to pursue collaborative play involving conversation and reciprocity.

Some believe that evolution plays a role in shaping sex differences. Traits such as aggressiveness and risk taking had more value as early survival strategies for men (though not necessarily as helpful today). Traits that involved nurturing and caring for the young were more valuable as strategies for women. Today, these survival traits can be seen in gender differences regarding attitudes toward sexuality and sexual behaviors. For example, men are more likely to engage in sexually risky behavior with more partners than is generally true for women, a fact some psychologists attribute to the influence of evolution.

Assess your comprehension of Sex Differentiation by completing this quiz.

SEXUAL MATURATION

Sexual maturation is a process that has biological, social, emotional, and psychological components and affects. Most of us mark the onset of sexual maturity by physical changes, such as the enlargement of genitalia for boys and burgeoning breasts for girls. The appearance of pubic hair usually follows, although some children develop this before puberty. Sexual maturity is also marked by increased height and weight. Other indicators associated with sexual maturation in children and adolescents include menarche, development of acne, changes in voice, facial hair, and nocturnal emissions. Perhaps more importantly, sexual maturation is closely connected to brain development. This occurs through increases in the number of brain cells, development of connections between areas of the brain, elimination of some previous connections, and organization or reorganization of brain circuitry (Neufang et al., 2009). These developments typically occur in puberty, discussed at length later in this chapter.

Not all children and adolescents achieve sexual maturity at the same time. Significant delays in the development of secondary sex characteristics—such as breasts, genitalia enlargement, and pubic hair—can be an indicator of health problems ranging from hyperandrogenism, which can cause infertility, to hypogonadotropism, which is associated with anorexia nervosa (Schubert et al., 2005). Such delays indicate the need for a medical evaluation. In addition, there is evidence that maturation may be affected by socioeconomic factors, standard of living, and childhood living conditions (Wronka & Pawlinska-Chmara, 2005). Girls from higher socioeconomic classes mature at an earlier age than their economically disadvantaged peers. Girls from urban areas mature faster than girls from rural environments. These and related differences have been observed in many different countries, although the exact cause of the association is unclear.

Nutritional differences also play a role in sexual maturation. For example, Elias (2012) notes that a hormone, leptin, helps explain early sexual maturation. Leptin is produced by body fat and can trigger the brain to begin puberty. Higher body weight children and adolescents are more likely to consume foods low in fiber and protein and high in fat and calcium, all factors associated with the early onset of sexual maturation (Talpade, 2004). African American girls, in particular, tend to have diets that are potentially problematic with respect to nutrition (Pratt & Pratt, 1996). Similar observations were reported by Kim, Bursac, DiLillo, White, and West (2009). Explanations for these finding include both higher levels of stress and lower socioeconomic status.

Some observers suggest that sexual maturity is occurring earlier in children living in the United States (Herman-Giddens et al., 1997). The evidence for such a trend, however, is very weak. Sun and colleagues (2005), studying changes from 1966 to 1994, found a mixed trend in which neither White girls nor African American children showed any such result. They did find some evidence that seemed to show a trend toward earlier sexual maturation among non-Hispanic White boys and Mexican American boys and girls.

Their findings suggest modest changes in timing of sexual maturation among some ethnic groups, but not others.

PUBERTY

Puberty is a period in which individuals experience significant physical and emotional change. These changes include sexual and reproductive maturity, both of which are preparation for moving into adult status in society. Successful completion of puberty often influences how successful an individual will be later in life. Among the factors for which puberty is credited are social and cognitive development, mental health, decision-making ability, and, of course, physical development (Shirtcliff, Dahl, & Pollak, 2009). Unfortunately, much research on male puberty has been drawn from studies on rats, hamsters, and other nonhuman species, providing little guidance in understanding humans (Romeo, Richardson, & Sisk, 2002). What evidence there is shows the importance of steroidal hormones on behavioral maturation. Naturally occurring steroids in the male body are associated with healthy development. Experiences or events that can impact steroid levels in puberty include anorexia nervosa, extreme exercise, and the introduction of anabolic steroids. The first two have the potential to delay pubescent brain development, while the latter is associated with higher levels of aggression in adulthood.

Reactions to Puberty

In turn, puberty produces a variety of outcomes for both genders. Depression rates, for example, increase during puberty especially for females. Challenges to coping with assorted physical, emotional, and social changes are dramatic. Puberty tends to be one of the most stressful developmental periods with elevated rates of anxiety and/or panic, particularly for early maturers. About 20% of adolescent women welcome the onset of menarche as a positive sign in their lives. They relish the idea of becoming a woman and the benefits of adulthood. Typically, these adolescents have been prepared for the event by their mothers. Another 30% considered it as just a part of growing up and simply took it in stride. However, about 12% of female adolescents find it a source of humiliation and shame, and experience fear at their first period (Lee, 2009). Others report feeling guilty, dirty, embarrassed, a loss of their innocence. Others had no memory of the entire event. Those most troubled by menses tended to come from conservative families less open to discussing bodily functions (Bornstein, 2002). Many were taunted by brothers about being gross and dirty after finding out about their sisters' menses. It is somewhat common for girls to hide the onset of menses from their parents (Lee, 2009). Some resent the sense that their childhood has ended without their consent and some are outright terrified. Others found that menses interfered with their father–daughter relationships and missed the prior closeness they had maintained with their fathers.

Puberty and Ethnicity

Much research about puberty's onset and its effects on the individual has not considered ethnicity. Consequently, there may be differences in experiences across racial and ethnic groups (Reardon, Leen-Feldner, & Hayward, 2009). For example, research suggests that sexual maturation occurs earlier in African Americans (Talpade, 2010) and Mexican American girls (Jean, Bondy, Wilkinson, & Forman, 2009). African American boys are more than one-half year ahead of White boys in beginning their genital development and growth of public hair (Susman et al., 2010). Explanations for the early sexual maturation reflect specific theories. Some scientists believe early maturation occurs because of poor health and nutrition of the individual adolescent, others view it as caused by growth hormones found in milk and meat (Talpade, 2010). Poor nutrition has also been linked to the amount of fast foods consumed by adolescents (p. 25).

Puberty as a Phase

Fortunately, puberty is a phase rather than a specific point in time. The mean onset of puberty is between 10 and 13 years of age, although this can vary by individual. Girls usually begin puberty at about 10.5 years with menarche delayed for another two or more years. Because individuals maturate at different rates, puberty periods can be relatively circumscribed or lengthy depending upon a variety of factors, including nutrition. Nutrition has been shown to be a significant factor in several health risk behaviors. Obesity, for example, is more of a health risk for African Americans than Caucasian Americans (Kumanyika et al., 2007).

Environmental Influences on Puberty

Environmental chemicals also affect sexual maturity. Den Hond et al. (2002) compared groups of adolescents residing in polluted suburbs in Flanders, Belgium, with another group living in a rural control area. They found that adolescents in the polluted suburbs exposed to polychlorinated biphenyl (PCB) had delayed breast development in females and genital development in males. Disruption in endocrines was hypothesized as the catalyst for these outcomes. Factors that impact sexual maturation have implications for social policy and public health. For example, obesity is a contributor to a number of serious medical conditions, ranging from stroke to heart attacks to diabetes. Likewise, the impact of environmental pollutants underscores why social workers must be concerned about conditions in the social environment that can adversely affect human reproduction.

Body Image and Puberty

Childhood obesity has been linked to psychological problems, largely because of the importance of body image to teenagers. Adolescents become more aware of and concerned about their bodies, which can lead to worries about weight, can lead to dissatisfaction about their bodies, and can precipitate eating disorders (Lindberg, Grabe, & Hyde, 2007). Knowing which adolescents are likely to be dissatisfied with their body image becomes important in prevention. Body image appears related to three factors: (1) one's sense of one's body as viewed by others, (2) whether that view conforms to cultural standards, and (3) the degree to which a person thinks he or she can control the way he or she looks. Adolescents with a negative view of their body are likelier to experience depression, eating disorders, sexual dysfunction, and low emotional well-being (Lindberg et al., 2007). Self-awareness of one's body is often triggered by pubertal changes, sexual comments, looks, sexual harassment by others, and choice of clothes. Clothes that emphasize one's weight and size tend to increase self-awareness about one's body, while loose fitting clothes do not. Other factors that increase the objectification of the body are media messages about attaining ideal body size and weight. These factors increase the risk that adolescents will adopt a body image that is negative (American Psychological Association, 2007). Children and teens who see their bodies as objects to be viewed and assessed by others tend to objectify themselves. This self-objectification appears to be much more common for females than for males, and it can occur as young as age 11. Males, however, can also develop poor body images as a result of increased body mass index (BMI) and peer sexual harassment (Lindberg et al., 2007).

Body image perceptions vary between different groups, however. African American girls tend to feel greater satisfaction with their bodies than is true of Caucasian girls (Flynn & Fitzgibbon, 1996; Lawrence & Thelen, 1995). Adolescent males tend to focus less on their body image despite the physical changes accompanying puberty. They are less likely to be secretive about or attempt to conceal the physical changes, while female adolescents may try to hide the fact that they are in menses, especially around males (Lee, 2009).

Puberty and Hormonal Changes

As suggested earlier, some of the most important changes occurring during puberty result from biological processes, particularly hormones, the levels of which may fluctuate wildly. Much of the control over hormones is the responsibility of the pituitary, a tiny gland in the brain. These hormones produce the secondary sexual characteristics that characterize men and women. For example, puberty causes the pituitary to release hormones that produce growth and directs the production of testosterone in the testes of males and estrogen and progesterone in females. Puberty also causes the female's ovaries to begin their monthly ovulation or secretion of eggs that were initially produced during the adolescent female's fetal development. Males, on the other hand, continually produce a fresh set of sperm. Hormones also contribute to changes in various intellectual or cognitive capabilities, resulting in faster processing and better impulse control (Peper et al., 2009).

Assess your comprehension of Puberty by completing this quiz.

Risk Factors in Puberty

Forbes and Dahl (2010) argue that puberty brings about affective changes that have both emotional and motivational implications. One of the most important of these changes is the way in which behavior changes during puberty. Puberty is a time when fluctuating hormone levels can stress both family and child; for example, female adolescents become moody or withdrawn and males become aggressive and challenging. It is also a time of greater interest in sensation seeking, more attraction to peers, and increased sexual interest. Impulsivity is also high during puberty, beginning as early as age 10 and lasting until the late twenties (Steinberg et al., 2008). This period of adolescence is one in which overall health of the individual is high but mortality and morbidity rates are also high (Centers for Disease Control and Prevention [CDC], 2009). Rates of suicide, accidents, homicides, and substance abuse are higher during this period, as are eating disorders, depression, and unwanted pregnancies (Cleveland, Feinberg, & Jones, 2012; Jackson & Chen, 2011; Ozer, Macdonald, & Irwin, 2002).

Early puberty and risks

Entering puberty early can be problematic through increased risk of breast cancer, cardiovascular disease, and multiple sclerosis for women; testicular cancer for men; and delinquent and aggressive behaviors for both (Ramagopalan et al., 2009).

Human Behavior

Practice Behavior Example: Know about human behavior across the life course, the range of social systems in which people live, and the ways social systems promote or deter people in maintaining or achieving health and well-being.

Critical Thinking Question: What might explain the paradox between adolescence as both a time of great health and a high risk period for death and disease? Why might suicides be a higher risk during adolescence?

Early maturing adolescents are at increased risk for poor health, obesity, and some forms of cancer (Adair & Gordon-Larsen, 2001). Early puberty can also contribute to babies being born underweight (Coall & Chisholm, 2003). It also poses risks for a variety of emotional challenges, including anxiety, lower self-esteem, depression, and schizophrenia (Cohen, Seeman, Gotowiec, & Kopala, 1999). Early puberty is associated with several behavioral issues, including delinquent behaviors, smoking, substance abuse, early sexual intimacy, and teenage pregnancy (Hayatbakhsh, Najman, McGee, Bor, & O'Callaghan, 2008; Jaffee, 2002; Talpade, 2010).

Early maturation is a factor in teen pregnancy, which in turn increases the chance of both mother and child being poor. Likewise, adolescent girls who were sexually abused are more likely to have experienced early sexual maturation. Clearly, early maturation has implications that suggest the importance of identifying and assisting at-risk adolescents.

Late maturing adolescents also experience difficulties. Late maturing boys may experience depression and related symptoms (Graber, Lewinsohn, Seeley, & Brooks-Gunn, 1997) while late maturing girls experienced much lower rates of depression. Conley and Rudolph (2009) found early maturing girls had higher levels of stress. By contrast, early maturing boys experienced very low stress. While boys appear to enjoy early maturation, girls do not.

Reasons for the associations between early maturation and health and social problems experienced by these adolescents are unclear. Potential explanations may involve the inability of early maturers to manage the challenges they face, weaker relationships between these adolescents and their parents that eliminate emotional resources, or increased associations with older peers driven by these adolescents' earlier physical maturity (Graber et al., 1997, p. 60). The loss of parental emotional resources leaves the adolescent without an adult with whom they can share their feelings, receive feedback, and learn to deal with stressful emotions.

Early maturing adolescents also elicit different reactions from peers. For example, the degree to which depression and stress characterize those whose puberty comes early or late may be moderated by the level of support from peers. Adolescents facing profound physical changes that put them out of sync with their peers, accompanied by negative interaction with peers, are more likely to experience stress and depression (Conley & Rudolph, 2009).

Puberty and sexual harassment

Peer responses to being developmentally out of sync can include relational aggression, sexual harassment, and violence from same gender and cross-gender peers (Haynie & Piquero, 2006). About 50% to 60% of boys and girls report sexual harassment in their middle school years. Boys appear to be the victims of same-gender harassment more often than girls. The most typical peer actions experienced by both boys and girls were jokes, hand gestures, comments of a sexual nature, and stares (Petersen & Hyde, 2009). Other unwanted treatment from boys toward girls included grabbing, pinching, touching in a sexual manner, and brushing up against the other person. Boys were more likely to encounter sexual pictures, messages, and being flashed or mooned by girls. From their male counterparts, boys were more likely to be called *gay*, while girls were the victims of sexual rumors spread by other girls.

Some variables increase the likelihood of being sexually harassed in adolescence. As noted earlier, early maturing adolescents were more likely to be harassed. Boys perceived as powerful were more likely to be harassed by their female peers. Interestingly, this was not the case with powerful girls. The pattern of sexual harassment begins as early as fifth grade and increases into high school. Overall, boys tend to experience more sexual harassment because they are the target of both genders (Petersen & Hyde, 2009).

Not all sexual harassment in this age group is intended to be harmful. A study by the American Association of University Women (AAUW, 2001) found that more than one-half of sexual harassment by peers was an attempt to show affection for or attraction toward the victim. Much of the problematic behavior exhibited by adolescents in the area of cross-gender relationships reflects sexual curiosity and increased interest in other gender peers. Girls are attracted to boys who are perceived as more powerful while boys engage in aggressive behaviors intended to dominate their peers. This can lead to attempts to attract the attention of the boys through the use of sexual messages. In turn, boys can respond by behaviors that, while designed to demonstrate romantic interest, are easily defined as sexual harassment. This back and forth interaction is consistent with studies that suggest perpetrators of sexual harassment are also often the victims of this same behavior (McMasters, Connolly, Pepler, & Craig, 2002).

Regardless of the intent, receiving unwanted sexual behaviors from one's peers is associated with multiple outcomes including higher levels of depression and a lower sense of self-worth (Xie et al., 2005). For overweight adolescent girls, the risk may be even greater (Compian, Gowen, & Hayward, 2009). The consequences of sexual harassment for school age victims strongly suggest the importance of reducing this behavior to the extent possible.

> **Assess your comprehension of sexual harassment by completing this quiz.**

Puberty, Parents, and Peers

Social factors, such as relationships with parents and peers, have significant impact on the development of the pubertal adolescent. These relationships can mediate (reconcile or resolve) a variety of events ranging from the onset of menarche to decisions about when and if to have intercourse (Quinlan, 2003). Puberty is a time when both peers and parents begin to see adolescents, particularly girls, differently. It is also a period where children spend less time with parents and experience a higher degree of conflict with parents (Hombeck & Hill, 1991). Positive affect (feeling good) is also often a casualty during this period. Parents may regret the loss of closeness and growing independence in decision-making by their children. Relationships with parents can be affected by the quality of their marital situation. Parents struggling with their issues and unable to provide consistent and sensitive communications with children can contribute to various forms of adolescent antisocial behavior. Conflict with siblings can also contribute to this outcome.

Despite the changes taxing parent–child relationships during puberty, it is both possible and desirable for parents to provide appropriate supervision and pay attention to their children's choice of friends. Parents can help mediate the emotional and social problems occurring during puberty and lessen the potential for teenage delinquent behavior and substance abuse (Richards, Viegas-Miller, O'Donnell, Wasserman, & Colder, 2004; Vander Zanden, Crandell, & Crandell, 2007).

Parents who encourage independence, expression of ideas, and decision-making help lessen the tumult associated with puberty. Adolescents do value their parents' input in some areas and see them as resources. Parents, particularly mothers, frequently provide information to the child about puberty. Ellis and Essex (2007) found that the most important factor in predicting the onset of early puberty was the quality of parental investment in the child. Adolescents whose parents demonstrated a high-quality involvement tended to enter puberty later than those for whom the parent–child relationship was weaker or problematic. Parental investment was evident from the level of supportiveness provided to their children and stability within the family. This is consistent with other research demonstrating that many biological and social factors can influence the onset of puberty. Jean and colleagues (2009) note that 55% of adolescents talk with their parents about a variety of problems and more than three-quarters talk to their peers. The importance of communication for ameliorating some of the problems adolescents face cannot be ignored. Cultural attitudes and norms can also play a role. Hispanic women generally have a more positive attitude toward heavier body weight in themselves and their children, but those who are most assimilated into American culture adopt the preference for smaller body size (Olvera, Suminski, & Power, 2005).

Adolescents also form close attachments to peers during this period, relationships that assume great importance, particularly regarding dress, entertainment choices, and personal issues such as dating (Gardner & Steinberg, 2012; Lau, Quadrel, & Hartman, 1990;). Adolescents' choice of friends is often directly impacted by the neighborhoods in which they reside, similarity in values, and educational plans. In short, youth usually select as pals those who are most like themselves in key areas. Peers provide an opportunity to try out new behaviors (not always wisely) and to pursue activities that are more risk taking. This has both positive and negative aspects because the heightened focus on oneself make teens especially sensitive to criticism or hurtful responses from peers, especially when it comes to talking with peers about puberty and accompanying bodily changes. However, without positive peer relationships, pubescent adolescents are more likely to make negative self-evaluations. The importance of peers in moderating or influencing adolescents is further evidence that the social environment plays a major role in individual development.

GENDER IDENTITY

It is clear that gender differentiation is a function of multiple influences—biological, social, and cognitive. As we have seen, different combinations of these influences can produce different outcomes. Some people perceive themselves as masculine or feminine, describing themselves accordingly. Others have a gender identity that does not fall clearly into one group or the other. Such androgynous individuals have both feminine and masculine personality characteristics (Berk, 2009). It is interesting that one's gender identity often serves as a predictor of emotional adjustment. Androgynous and masculine identities are associated with higher levels of self-esteem than is true for those whose gender identity is feminine (Harter, 2006).

Forming a sexual identity is much more complicated for gay, lesbian, bisexual, or transgender (GLBT) adolescents who comprise at least 2% to 3% of adolescents (Savin-Williams & Diamond, 2004). Childhood is often characterized by feelings of differentness for these individuals. This may show up in the choices of play activities. Girls may become more involved in physical activities and sports while boys may prefer more sedentary activities. Most GLBT children become consciously aware of their feelings and wonder why they are different from others. Being aware of these differences, however, does not mean that they can articulate it, limiting their ability to share their feelings with others (McAndrew & Warne, 2010). Feelings of anxiety and unhappiness with their assigned gender are common (Carver, Egan, & Perry, 2004). These feelings become more pronounced in one's teen years, typically in early adolescence for boys and mid-adolescence for girls. The absence of role models and lack of support from parents and peers makes this a very difficult period.

For these adolescents, managing this period may take the form of adopting more gender-expected behaviors and activities, dating, and leading a double life. The strains of this effort too often lead to substance abuse (both illicit drugs and misuse of prescription medication) and/or suicide. For example, bisexual adolescent girls appear to engage in greater

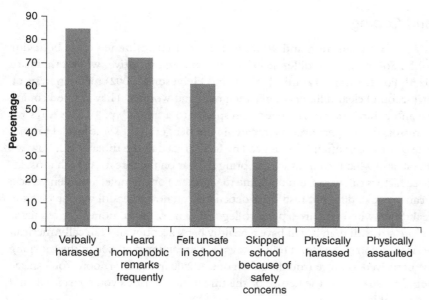

Figure 10.1
School Experiences of Sexual Minorities Within Previous Month
Source: Based on National School Climate Survey (2011).

use of drugs than other sexual minorities (Corliss et al., 2010). In addition, GLBT adolescents have more difficulty accessing substance abuse services, and such services often don't address their needs (Corliss, Grella, Mays, & Cochran, 2006). Homosexual youth also are frequently bullied and taunted by peers and often experience depression. Figure 10.1, based on data from the National School Climate Survey (2011), shows some of the difficulties that sexual minority adolescents reported experiencing in the previous 30 days. It is clear that many adolescents regularly face a variety of unpleasant peer interactions.

Lacking others to talk to and no role models with whom to identify, adolescent sexual minorities struggle at a level not understood by most peers or adults. Stresses associated with adolescence and sexual orientation likely contribute to suicide rates that are higher than for heterosexual youth (Savin-Williams, 2001). Grade point averages are also lower for students who experience substantial harassment.

By late adolescence, most sexual minority teenagers have acknowledged their identity to themselves. Many feel like outsiders, a theme that may continue throughout their lives. Equally problematic is that some sexual minorities internalize society's homophobia, which can contribute to depression, denial, and self-hatred (McAndrew & Warne, 2010). Coming out or sharing their feelings with significant others is difficult, particularly with respect to parents. Many choose not to come out because of the stigma, negative reactions, and hostility they fear. Interestingly, Savin-Williams and Ream (2003) found that most parental reactions are not rejecting, although some parents refuse to believe the news. Parental acceptance and support are critical for the emotional and social adjustment of gay and lesbian adolescents. Positive parental reactions can help youngsters become more accepting of themselves. Engaging with other sexual minorities is also common in late adolescence and is helpful in reaching a settled sense of self. Later in this chapter, we will delve further into the topic of sexual orientation.

Engage, Assess, Intervene, Evaluate

Practice Behavior Example: Collect, organize, and interpret client data.

Critical Thinking Question: You are a school social worker asked to consult with a teacher concerned about one of her female students. Lately, the girl has been having academic problems, has recently attracted the interest of boys, feels self-conscious about herself, has relatively few friends among the other girls in her class, and is feeling stressed and depressed. What kinds of questions might you ask the teacher to get a better idea of what is causing the recent changes in her student?

Gender and Coping

Differences exist between men and women in areas that influence their behavior throughout life. Some of these differences are obvious and intuitive, while others are less recognized. For example, Tamres, Janicki, and Helgeson's (2002) meta-analysis of coping behavior found clear differences between men and women. They defined coping as "cognitive and behavioral efforts made in response to a threat" (p. 3). The ways we respond to stressors can be perceived as threatening or dangerous at some level. How we respond in these situations often is influenced by factors such as the threat itself, how we assess the threat, and what resources we can bring to bear on the threat. As with most individuals, these factors can vary from one time to another. For example, a sudden vehicle breakdown can provoke different responses depending on how stressful we perceive the event. A breakdown when you are a poor college student with no money for repairs is likely to be more stressful than if you have a healthy bank account and can call American Automobile Association (AAA) for a tow. Likewise, a breakdown at 2:00 in the morning is likely to be perceived as more troubling than one at 2:00 in the afternoon. You can see how your coping is shaped by the nature of the threat, how serious you consider it, and the resources available.

Coping mechanisms can usually be classified as either problem or emotion focused. Problem-focused coping is designed to eliminate or change the stressor, while emotion-focused behaviors deal with our response to a threat. Tamres et al. (2002) found that women use a greater variety of coping strategies than men. In particular, women are more likely to use active coping that attempts to change or remove the stressor and to seek social support in times of threat. They also engage in planning to deal with the threat. Women are more likely to use avoidance, to reevaluate the threat, and to worry about and engage in wishful thinking when stressed. Finally, women were more likely to use religion to cope with a threat.

The nature of the stressor typically influences the way we respond to a threat. Problems with one's personal health, and that of others who are close, tend to elicit emotion-focused coping from women more so than from men. Such responses include venting, wishful thinking, and relying on religion. Men are more likely to use venting, avoidance, and withdrawal to cope with relationship problems, while women use more isolation in such situations. Contrary to conventional wisdom, there is no evidence that men use more problem-focused approaches to coping. In fact, women tended to use more general, problem-focused coping mechanisms than do men. This difference in the number of coping strategies employed may be related to how seriously women view a given threat because a more stressful situation may be perceived as needing more coping efforts. If a given threat is very serious, then one is more likely to call upon a variety of approaches to deal with it.

What explains the different choices of coping strategies for men and women? There is some evidence that seeking support from others, as women do more frequently, is related to higher levels of oxytocin (a hormone in the pituitary), which can lead to more "tend-and-befriend" responses to stressors (Tamres et al., 2002, p.22). Men do not have the same levels of oxytocin, and this may better explain their fight-or-flight responses to threats.

Gender and Aggression

Historically, men have been perceived as more likely to fight or show aggression than women. Earlier research by Frodi, Macaulay, and Thome (1977), however, raised doubts about this perception, at least in some circumstances. Their review of the experimental literature suggested that when individuals feel that aggression is either justified or pro-social (viewed positively by others), women can act as aggressively as their male coun-terparts. The tendency for men to choose aggression may reflect a higher propensity to interpret a situation as anger provoking, while women respond to the same stimuli by becoming anxious. At the same time, men who believe strongly in traditional male gender role norms are more likely to engage in aggression than men with more relaxed gender role ideas (Moore & Stuart, 2004). The fact that men are socialized to avoid ex-pressions of vulnerable emotions is thought to be one of the reasons why they do not share feelings of fear, guilt, or sadness (O'Neil, 2008). Men tend not to feel guilty about behaving aggressively and aggression becomes a coping strategy in response to perceived provocations. By contrast, women experience greater inhibition and discomfort toward their aggressive impulses. Some researchers have described emotional dysregulation as the factor that explains men's aggressiveness (Cohn et al., 2010).

Emotional dysregulation involves several components: a lack of awareness, under-standing, or acceptance of emotions; few strategies for controlling emotional responses that do occur; unwillingness to endure emotional feelings; and an inability to control behavior when in emotional distress. In summary, many men are afraid of experiencing their emotions and use aggression when facing difficult emotional challenges.

Women typically show greater degrees of empathy then do men in similar situations. The capacity to deal with one's emotions may be related to the findings of Vishnevsky and her colleagues that women who have experienced major traumas in their lives (e.g., sexual assault, cancer, natural disasters) exhibit more posttraumatic growth than their male counterparts. In addition, women think more about their experiences in ways that are both productive and contemplative (Treynor, Gonzalez, & Nolen-Hoeksema, 2003).

While men are typically seen as more physically aggressive than women, women are more likely to engage in *relational aggression*. Relational aggression is a deliberate attempt to harm others through a social relationship (Bowie, 2007). This difference likely reflects the relatively higher importance females place on social relationships. Relational aggres-sion can take many forms: excluding others from participation in one's group, shunning, withholding friendship, lying, and gossiping about others. Interestingly, female relational aggression appears to be a common behavior observed in large international studies with varied ethnic groups. If overt (typically noted in males) and relational aggression are measured and compared, the results show that levels of aggression are not vastly dif-ferent between the genders.

It is likely that different types of aggression are the result of social experiences, rather than only biological in origin. When boys engage in physical aggression, the be-havior is more likely to be either praised or ignored (Zahn-Waxler & Polanichka, 2004). Girls, on the other hand, receive more direct negative messages about aggressiveness and are socialized to avoid overt aggression. The media plays a role in this process since al-most two-thirds of television programs include violence and most protagonists are male (Roberts, Henriksen, & Foehr, 2004). Likewise, Coyne and Archer (2005) found a sig-nificant relationship between the amount of indirect aggression viewed by girls and the amount of such aggression they directed toward their peers.

Other factors influencing the use of indirect or relational aggression include associ-ating with aggressive peers and feedback from teachers and other adults. Another influ-ence may be the fact that boys and girls differ with respect to the development task of achieving autonomy and independence. Women place more emphasis on interpersonal relationships than do men and are likely to measure themselves in terms of the number and quality of such relationships. Males tend to focus more on their achievements and less on peer relationships.

Language also plays a role, in part, because girls develop language skills earlier than boys. This capacity to use language skills is more useful in relational aggression while less verbally adept males resort to physical aggression. Less-developed or poor social skills, including verbal ability, can also influence the way in which social cues are interpreted. This increases the risk of pursuing unacceptable behaviors such as physical aggression (Estrem, 2005). Finally, we don't know as much as we need to about the role played by emotions in interpreting and responding to social cues. Children who cannot control their emotional responses to an event may interpret a situation as threatening and resort to overt aggression in response. The failure to adequately regulate one's emotional responses has been associated with higher levels of overt aggression and oppositional disorders in boys, while girls are more likely to react with anxiety and depression in the same situation (Baucom et al., 2012; Dodge, 1991; Eisenberg, Cumberland, & Spinrad, 1998).

As was mentioned in Chapter 8, moral reasoning is also seen as playing a role in both physical and relational aggression. Murray-Close, Crick, and Galotti (2006) found that girls see physical and relational aggression as wrong more often than boys. Perhaps because of an increased sense of empathy, girls also rated the latter as more harmful than their male peers. This supports the contention that among boys, one's social group tends to see physical aggression as a normal and an appropriate response to a provocation. As mentioned, this finding does not suggest that aggressive children are unaware of the harm they cause to others. To the contrary, aggressive children, whether overt or relational, are more likely to recognize the hurt they cause for others. However, they tend to view the hurt as an effective means of power, therefore reinforcing its use to control and manage their environment (Xie et al., 2005).

It has been repeatedly argued that the patriarchal way in which society is structured is a significant contributor to violence against women (Brownmiller, 1975; Hall & Barongan, 1997; Wood & Eagly, 2002). A variety of theories have been posited to explain why, for example, the United States has one of the highest rates of rape in the world. Murnen, Wright, and Kaluzny (2002) conducted a meta-analytic literature review and were able to identify the specific aspects of individual males that tended to predict violent behavior. These included adversarial sexual beliefs, attitudes toward women, acceptance of the rape myth, acceptance of interpersonal violence, hostility toward women, hostile masculinity, and hypermasculinity. Each is addressed as follows:

- **Adversarial sexual beliefs** are male beliefs that male–female relationships are inherently exploitive. It includes the belief that both genders employ manipulation to get what they want in relationships.
- **Attitudes toward women** are associated with sexual aggression and include beliefs that men are better able to handle difficult situations, women do not possess the same rights as men, and women are inferior to men in important attributes needed for success in the world.
- **Acceptance of the rape myth** means that men have an inaccurate perception about rape, its victims, and its perpetrators. Such beliefs suggest that women who are raped are seeking it by their behavior and that rape is justified by the circumstances. Myth believers develop intellectual and emotional justifications for sexual aggression.
- **Acceptance of interpersonal violence** entails a belief that physical violence and the threat of it are appropriate means to achieve one's ends. Within this belief, the use of coercion in male–female interactions is portrayed as sexually exciting to the female and, therefore, justified.

- **Hostility toward women** suggests that sexual aggression occurs when men are insecure and distrustful of women. Such men adopt a defensive orientation toward women. Hostility toward women is accompanied by hostile masculinity, in which men feel a need to control and dominate women in sexual and other relationships. It may also lead to sexual promiscuity.

- Finally, hypermasculinity is perhaps best identified by macho attitudes held by some men. These men adhere to traditional stereotyped male roles where men are supposed to be tough, fearless, and rejecting of any form of weakness. They view themselves as powerful and others, particularly women, less so.

These characteristics are not necessarily the only ones associated with sexual aggression toward women, but they are the most influential. Carried to their logical extreme, these combinations of characteristics help explain high rates of sexual assault occurring in the United States (Murnen et al., 2002). However, it is important to note that these characteristics are not inherent in males across all cultures. Many societies are not rape-prone and men in those societies do not hold negative attitudes toward women that contribute to sexual aggression. This fact undercuts biological explanations for sexual aggression and suggests that cultural factors create and sustain sexually aggressive behavior in men. These factors may include parents who (1) discourage males from displaying fear or other emotions and (2) encourage sexual activity among male children. Hostile relationships between sons and parents are another factor, with father–son negativity especially problematic. Delinquent behavior as a child or adolescent may also play a role. Other factors that are thought to influence men include media portrayals of men dominating and exploiting women, and the degree to which women in a society accept the aggressiveness of men as "normal." A society that maintains a high degree of differentiation between men and women, values men over women, and supports male aggressiveness is most likely to experience higher acceptance and incidence of sexual aggression.

Gender and Leadership

The 2008 presidential election saw several relatively new gender-related firsts emerge. First, Senator Hillary Clinton mounted a serious challenge to Senator Barack Obama in the Democratic primary and came closer to winning that party's nomination than any other woman candidate in history. Second, the Republican Party nominee for president, Senator John McCain, chose a woman to be his vice presidential running mate. The choice was Sarah Palin, then governor of Alaska. While a woman had previously run on the Democratic slate several years prior, no woman had ever been in a similar situation in the Republican Party.

For some, these milestones announced that women had reached the pinnacle of political success, despite the fact that neither Senator Clinton nor Governor Palin won their respective political campaigns. To have women attain these heights was still a major accomplishment. For others, the possibility of a woman as president or vice president was frightening. In addition to the usual questions about prior experience or competence, the candidate's gender was raised as an issue in various ways. Historically, many women had encountered a "glass ceiling" that kept them from rising to the highest levels of their professions. This has been a problem for both women in general and women of color in particular (Sanchez-Hucles & Davis, 2010).

Did You Know?

Women hold over 40% of management positions in the United States but only 6% of positions with titles such as chairman, president, chief executive officer (CEO), or chief operating officer. Only 2% of those with the title of CEO are women. Corporation boards of directors are comprised of 15% females (Eagly & Carli, 2007).

Reasons for the glass ceiling are many and varied, although perhaps the most often cited is outright gender discrimination. Women have been denied promotions and higher pay on the grounds that a male counterpart had a family to support and, therefore, needed the promotion and higher pay more. They have also encountered sexual harassment in the workplace that grew out of cultural values about men and women. Complaining about the unwelcome and hostile behavior often labeled the woman as a troublemaker, which then precluded her from future promotions and raises.

Other reasons grew out of realities that women encounter more than men. Women are more likely to take time away from a career to perform child-rearing functions, which often negatively impacts their career success. Despite recent gains in sharing of household duties, most married women still do the dominant share of housework and child rearing.

Another reason cited for the discrepancies in women's rise in an organization or success in political arenas is based on perceptions about women and leadership. The same leadership behavior in a woman can be interpreted differently when displayed by a man. Assertiveness displayed by women can be defined in negative terms based on stereotyping, which would not have occurred with male colleagues. Eagly, Makhijani, and Klonsky (1992) noted that an autocratic style of leadership resulted in favorable evaluation when employed by men and unfavorably when adopted by women leaders. This was especially true when women occupied roles traditionally filled by men.

Most revealing, the devaluing of women leaders was more likely to be done by women subordinates, not their male counterparts. At the same time, men in general are much more likely than women to devalue women leaders. While the strength of this difference in preference for a male leader over a female leader is small, it is consistent with other studies showing women face discrimination in hiring. Interestingly, both men and women who engaged in leadership styles that might be stereotyped as feminine, such as "democratic and interpersonally oriented," produced similar evaluations, suggesting that men who adopt such leadership styles do not face the same challenges as women who adopt more masculine styles of leading (p. 16). The authors conclude that women have less freedom in adopting a leadership style than is true for men. These findings are consistent in various fields of employment, including business, athletics, and manufacturing. Despite both successful and competent leadership by women, the possibility of negative evaluations by supervisors, subordinates, and peers remain risks, especially when women leaders engage in supposed gender-incongruent leadership styles.

Cheung and Halpern (2010) acknowledge the difficulties women encounter as they pursue the level of CEO, CFO (chief financial officer), and CIO (chief information officer), and argue that women do rise to the top of their professions through a combination of skills that overcome traditional barriers. They introduce a model that includes the following three characteristics of successful women who maintained significant family responsibilities (i.e., children, disabled sibling, aging parent) while rising to the top of their professions:

1. Leadership traits that are relationship oriented

2. A belief in teamwork and consensus building as important methods of making decisions

3. Effective work–family interfaces

One of the most useful things that characterized these women was strong family and spousal support. In addition, they engaged in several behaviors that allowed them to avoid the usual problems experienced by women with families. These included things such as:

- multitasking,
- bringing children to work and on business trips,
- working from home part of the time,
- selecting times to work that did not interfere with important home responsibilities such as dinner times,
- outsourcing household tasks when possible,
- accepting that they could not do everything,
- redefining their norms for being a good mother and leader

At work, women employed flatter organizational structures while promoting communication to ensure that everyone felt included. Their leadership styles were characteristic of what Burns (1978) and Eagly and Johannesen-Schmidt (2003) referred to as transformational. This style of leadership engages with others, inspires others, and challenges them to new ways of thinking and doing. It also acknowledges the help of mentors who assisted them to achieve and encourage the development of mentors for their employees. Interestingly, while the term *glass ceiling* is still used frequently to portray the barriers that women encounter in achieving success, Eagly and Carli (2007) suggest that a more apt description for the barriers is that of labyrinth. Using the experiences of women who have achieved success, they believe that rather than an unbreakable barrier, women must navigate their way through a variety of confusing and complex paths leading to their goal.

Gender and Helping Behavior

Gender also plays a role in the kind and degree of helping behavior exhibited by men and women. Eagly and Crowley (1986) found that men engaged in more helping behavior than did women under specific circumstances. In situations where helping might be perceived as dangerous, men were more likely to help others. Men were more likely to help if an audience witnessed the assistance being provided or if other helpers were available. In each of these three situations, women were less likely to intervene. This is not to say that women do not engage in helping behavior. Rather, they are more likely to help if there is no one else available to assist another person regardless of whether the situation is considered dangerous. Men were also more likely to give help to a woman than to another male. Women, on the other hand, are more likely to help other women than to offer assistance to a male. One factor in whether a person helps another is the extent to which the helper perceived themselves as competent and comfortable in that role. Men tend to offer help more readily than women whether the helpee requests assistance or not. However, the differences between men and women tend to diminish in the case of direct appeals for help.

Studies such as the one reported earlier, however, are less likely to include helping behaviors that occur in everyday life as might be the case within a family, for instance. It is pretty clear that women engage in substantial helping behavior in situations involving close relationships while most studies report only on helping that involves strangers. It is also unclear why these observed differences between men and women occur. Potential explanations involve things such as norms that require chivalrous behavior and the fact that men tend to be more assertive/aggressive in their behavior.

SEXUAL ORIENTATION

Sexual orientation may be defined as a continuum of one's sexual attraction to other people. Individuals can be sexually oriented to those of a different sex, the same sex, or both. We often use the term *heterosexual* to refer to men attracted to women and women attracted to men. The term *homosexual* is commonly applied to men (gay men) and women (lesbians) whose sexual attraction is to members of their own sex. Bisexual connotes those with sexual attractions to both sexes, although the degree of attraction may favor one gender more than the other. These labels do not, however, capture the richness of individual differences. As Tolman and Diamond (2001) note, some women and men feel constrained by such labels that do not accurately describe their sexual and romantic attractions to other people.

As noted earlier, 2% to 3% of the U.S. population self-identifies as homosexual with actual population estimates rising as high as 10%. These figures do not include those who have previously had a same-sex partner, who are merely attracted to individuals of the same sex, or who are unsure about their orientation. While the vast majority of people consider and identify themselves as heterosexual, getting accurate information on those who are homosexual or bisexual is much more difficult. The stigma and discrimination experienced by many gay men and lesbian women tend to deter self-identification.

One's identity as a gay man or lesbian woman evokes a variety of reactions from others. Those who see homosexuality as a choice often use the term *sexual preference* to refer to gays and lesbians. They presume that one's identity is simply a matter of selecting one option over another. It places the emphasis on individual free will, similar to "I prefer prime rib to filet mignon." This point of view is typically held by those with strong religious values who simply attribute sexual orientation to a choice made by the individual (Whitehead, 2010). In questioning this choice perspective, one might reasonably ask why a person would deliberately decide to identify with a group in society that faces ongoing discrimination in employment, housing, and other areas while denied rights routinely available to heterosexuals.

Others argue that choice does not truly enter into whether one is homosexual or heterosexual—that it is a matter of biology. They use the term *sexual orientation* to denote that one is likely born with a particular orientation toward either men or women, or both. Many, but not all, gay or lesbian adults have experienced attractions to the same sex throughout their lives. This pattern is more common for gay men, but lesbian women report their growing orientation toward the same sex waxed and waned over the years (Baumeister, 2000). Similar patterns have been noted with bisexual men and women (Worthington & Reynolds, 2009).

The Role of Biology

There is some evidence that biology is the major, if not sole, determinant of sexual orientation. For example, Savic and Lindstrom (2008) found significant differences in the brains of homosexual and heterosexual men and women. The brains of gay men were more similar to the brains of heterosexual women and the brains of lesbian women were more similar to those of straight men. Their research followed many other studies showing brain differences, most of which are connected to in utero development (Cahill, 2006; Ponseti et al., 2007; Rahman, Cockburn, & Govier, 2007; Shaywitz et al., 1995). Scientists have found differences in areas of the brain dealing with endocrine, genes, and anatomy

Did You Know?

While legislators debate whether new laws prohibiting employment discrimination on the basis of sexual orientation are needed, past research has shown that such laws are effective in reducing discriminatory acts against, gay, lesbian, and other similar groups (Barron & Hebl, 2012).

(Johnson, 2003). While these studies do not definitively identify biology as the only factor in the development of gay men and lesbian women, they reflect the best data available at this time. Other explanations such as parent–child interactions, relationships with a particular parent, and other sociobehavioral theories have been either discredited or lack empirical research. This is not to say that the behaviors of parents and peers do not influence children's behavior. It is parents who identify the child as one particular gender, select clothes and toys appropriate to that gender, and reinforce the child's sex-congruent activities and actions. Their influence, however, does not appear to change the underlying sexual orientation of a child. Parental behavior can make it difficult or impossible for a gay or lesbian child to discuss sexual orientation. Often, one parent (often the mother) will be perceived as sensitive and trustworthy enough with whom to share one's orientation.

The general public's knowledge and understanding of sexual minorities is limited and often viewed through a prism of social, religious, or other bias. Much of the general public does not know about some of the clear differences within the brain structure and function for sexual minorities and heterosexuals. These differences are important for understanding the genesis of sexual orientation. Other differences between straight and sexual minorities do exist, but their importance is relatively small. For example, although stereotypes about lesbian women suggest that they are both heavier and taller than their peers, Bogaert (2010), using data from one of the largest samples ever employed to study sexual orientation, found no evidence to support this belief. However, gay and bisexual men were, on average, lighter in weight and shorter in stature than their heterosexual counterparts. Potential explanations for this difference include prenatal exposure to androgens and maternal stress during pregnancy. A genetic cause may also explain the height/weight anomaly.

Sexual minorities typically experience discrimination in multiple areas of their lives. Bishop, Caraway, and Stader (2010) note that it is not illegal to discriminate against sexual minorities in most U.S. school districts. Coming out can mean the loss of one's teaching job and/or being harassed, consequences of an attitude that not only permits but tolerates this treatment. While the courts have helped protect some teachers who were terminated because of their sexual orientation, the climate for sexual minority teachers remains problematic.

A critical Supreme Court case Lawrence et al. v. Texas was a major legal decision rejecting the efforts by many states to make homosexual behavior a crime. Review the case record and evaluate the key reasoning used by the justices. Why do you think this took this approach to resolve the case?

As mentioned earlier in this chapter, there is also evidence that sexual minorities are more likely to experience some forms of mental health disorders (Bostwick, Boyd, Hughes, & McCabe, 2010). Meyer (2003) found that lesbians, gays, and bisexuals were twice as likely as heterosexuals to suffer from mood and anxiety disorders. Bostwick et al. found, however, there are major within-group differences with respect to mental health issues. For example, bisexual women tended to experience a much higher level of lifetime disorders than was true for heterosexual or bisexual women. On the other hand, exclusively lesbian women had the lowest rates of these disorders among sexual minorities. Figure 10.2 shows the relative frequency of mental health disorders.

Explanations for the higher frequency of reported mental health problems often focus on the higher levels of stress, stigma, discrimination, and victimization faced by sexual minorities.

Sexual minority youth have been shown to engage in higher levels of health risk behaviors and to have worse outcomes compared to their heterosexual peers (Coker, Austin, & Schuster, 2010). We previously discussed some of these risks: substance abuse, eating disorders, suicide, sexually transmitted diseases (STDs), victimization and

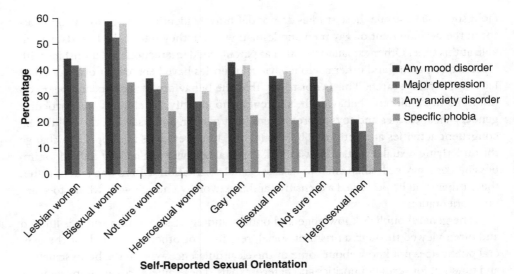

Figure 10.2
Self-Reported Lifetime Prevalence of Selected *DSM-IV* Disorders
Source: Adapted from U.S. Census Bureau (2005).

violence, and homelessness. Such risks increase the need for competent and effective interventions with sexual minority adolescents. Unfortunately, many health care professionals, including social workers, have negative attitudes toward this population. Even those who have appropriate professional attitudes often fail to inquire about the adolescent sexual orientation, despite most LGBT youth being open to the question. Some general suggestions for assisting sexual minority adolescents and adults are listed in the Clinical Corner that follows.

Clinical Corner

Guidelines to Assist Social Workers in Assessing and Addressing Needs of Sexual Minorities

- Increase one's knowledge about sexual minorities
- Recognize one's prejudices and homophobia
- Provide services that are nonjudgmental and sensitive to the client's experiences
- Use gender-neutral language in interviews
- Do not assume that any client is heterosexual—be open to difference
- Ask questions about past and present attraction to girls, boys, or both
- Inquire about any current significant other
- Remind client of confidentiality
- Remind adolescents that they have a right to be seen without their parents
- Ensure that reading materials given to adolescents uses gender-neutral language
- Reduce power imbalances between worker and client
- Remember practitioners have no right to challenge or change one's sexual identity

Source: Adapted from Coker et al. (2010).

Developing a sexual identity as a gay man, lesbian woman, or bisexual individual is a challenging complex task for most sexual minorities. Since this identity is at odds with the dominant culture, it takes courage to move in this direction. Pretending to be heterosexual or "passing" leads to internal contradictions and potential conflicts with others. Coming out to others does not necessarily mean the individual is comfortable with his or her orientation, but it does help deal with the inner conflict (McAndrew & Warne, 2010). Some sexual minorities manage their orientation carefully, deciding with whom they can safely share and identifying individuals and situations where disclosure is unwise (Lasser, Ryser, & Price, 2010).

Relationships between gay couples share many of the characteristics and challenges noted in heterosexual couples with a few exceptions identified in the literature. One of those is in regard to the tangible investments in the male–male partnership. Gay male couples, for example, tend to invest less in their relationship than is true for heterosexual couples. This concept of investment refers to both tangible and intangible resources that individuals put into a relationship. Lowered investment also coincides with a lowered commitment to one another, compared to that of heterosexual males (Lehmiller, 2010). Those with higher levels of commitment are more satisfied with their relationships and aware that alternatives to the partner and relationship are lacking. They also see themselves as having a high investment in the relationship because too much would be lost were it to end (Agnew, Hoffman, Lehmiller, & Duncan, 2007). This is consistent with previous research covering marginalized relationships, including interracial or those with large age differences between partners. The lack of commitment may reflect the absence of legal recognition of the union and, thus, fewer barriers to ending the relationship. It may suggest that homosexual partners have fewer opportunities to make the mutual tangible investments typically seen in heterosexual relationships and marriages.

This is not to say that homosexual partners do not make commitments to one another. The couple's emotional ties and intimacy can be as strong as those of straight couples. These intangible investments represent barriers to leaving a relationship and apply in both gay/lesbian and straight unions. Tangible investments include things such as being legally married, possessing joint financial resources, having children, and having shared possessions (Lehmiller, 2010).

We talked earlier about some of the challenges faced by GLBT individuals in society. Currently, the mixing of supposed biologic urges with social construction helps explain some of the homophobia that exists in American society. If, for example, gay men and lesbian women are seen as people with high levels of sexual desire, then it follows that vulnerable populations must be protected from those who are seen as primarily driven by biological urges. States that have adopted laws and constitutional amendments restricting marriage to a man and a woman often justify these actions by suggesting that a homosexual "agenda"—with a goal of attacking the heterosexual norm—is at work. This argument is then used to justify other laws that allow school districts to fire homosexual teachers and to prevent gay and lesbian individuals and families from adopting children and serving as foster parents or as camp counselors. Discrimination against homosexuals is socially sanctioned based on beliefs about biology that are simply wrong. Despite the fact that the vast majority of child sexual abuse is done by heterosexual men, gay men are the ones perceived as prone to attacking children.

As Bishop et al. (2010) note, logic does not enter into the thinking of those fearful of having gay and lesbian teachers. The fact that homosexual parents end up with the same percentage of homosexual children as heterosexual parents underscores the fact that parental sexual orientation does not affect children's sexual orientation. While this fact refutes the argument that sexual minority teachers will convert a student's sexual orientation, too many people's reality is based on social definitions of good and

Diversity in Practice

Practice Behavior Example: Understand the dimensions of diversity as the intersectionality of multiple factors including age, class, color, culture, color, culture, disability, ethnicity, gender, gender identity and expression, immigration status, political ideology, race, religion, sex, and sexual orientation.

Critical Thinking Question If most sexual abuse of children is done by heterosexual men, what explains the belief of many people that gay men are a threat to children? How could you address this misconception when talking to a public group?

bad, or normal and abnormal, and not informed by research or science. This social construction of reality allows discrimination against people based on information and opinions not grounded in reality.

Sexual Orientation and Race

Race does not appear to be a factor in whether one becomes gay or lesbian, but it does seem to impact where different groups reside. Using Census Bureau statistics, Baumle (2010) found that a high concentration of unmarried, same-sex partners lived in the border areas between the United States and Mexico. Referring to it as an ethnic enclave, the author went on to study whether this was a measurement error or evidence of a group that chose to live in this particular area. Previous studies have shown that gay and lesbian racial minorities face double discrimination impacting where they could live and work. Minority women who are lesbians face triple discrimination, as the intersection of their characteristics provides multiple opportunities for adverse experiences. Baumle concluded that the border areas identified in the census represented a unique population of gay and lesbian individuals and families. Attraction to the area included a combination of acceptance by existing residents and prevalence of Hispanic language speakers. The region has a critical mass of gay and lesbian bars, further suggesting a supportive community with sufficient clientele to support such establishments. In other words, this rural region possessed the kinds of resources meeting the needs of gay and lesbian families often found in cities with sizeable populations of sexual minorities.

Our understanding about the sexuality of adolescents is hampered by the unwillingness to support such research. Some fear asking teenagers about sexual topics will trigger inappropriate sexual behavior. Others fear funding sources will not pay for such research and avoid applying. The reactions from those fearful of researchers studying sexual behavior are also seen in school systems where parents and others protest providing students with birth control information or resources such as condoms. Those who espouse abstinence as the only acceptable prophylactic often do not want their children learning anything that conflicts with their religious or personal views, regardless of the risks associated with unprotected sex.

Assess your comprehension of Sexual Orientation by completing this quiz.

EXPRESSION OF SEX ACROSS THE LIFE SPAN

It is common to view sexuality and the expression of sex as behaviors that begin in adolescence and continue throughout adult life, tapering off in the later stages of life. In fact, sexuality is expressed throughout the life span, beginning with infancy and childhood. Children engage in sexual play and express interest in their own body but those of others. It is not uncommon for children to take their clothes off in front of family and friends, and an occasional stranger. Typically, it is only after parent admonitions that this behavior changes. A good example of this is a recent letter from a personal help counselor who reported that her children often ran around the house nude. This worked fine until the kids had friends over for a play date with children whose parents did not allow them the same degree of freedom.

Infants manipulate their own genitalia and show curiosity about their bodies. Thigpen (2009), for example, studied the sexual behaviors of children in the age of 2 to12 and found a vast array of activities of a sexual nature. Most frequent behaviors included touching or attempting to touch the breasts of their mothers or others, touching their own private parts at home and in public, and trying to look at others who are nude or undressing. This sort of behavior can be surprising to parents who do not recognize that such behavior is normal. The behaviors children display with others can be categorized as boundary violations, exhibitionism, sexual aggression or intrusiveness, sexual anxiety, sexual interest, sexual knowledge, self-stimulation, and voyeurism. Boys are more likely to show greater interest in the opposite gender and to touch their private parts at home or in public than is true for girls. Boys display a slightly higher overall level of sexual behavior than girls, but the differences generally are not significant. The incidence of most sexual behaviors declines as children moved from preschool age to about 10 to12 years old. Areas where sexual behavior increased with age included interest in the opposite gender, talking flirtatiously, pretending that stuffed animals or dolls were having sex, attempting to look at nude or partially dressed people, and talking about sexual acts.

Knowing the extent and commonness of specific behaviors is important for practitioners working with children whose sexual actions are deemed unacceptable. Because adult reactions to sexual behaviors noted earlier are often negative, it is difficult for parents to know which behaviors are normal and which are not. However, this is an important distinction for the practitioner because of the risk of defining normal sexual curiosity as pathological.

Curiosity and interest in sex carries through into adolescent and adult years. One-quarter of adolescents have had sexual intercourse by the time they are age 15 and about one-half of American adolescents report having had sex by high school graduation (CDC, 2004; Mosher, Chandra, & Jones, 2005). The average age of first intercourse is 16.9 years for males and 17.4 years for women (Alan Guttmacher Institute [AGI], 2002). These facts, of course, raise concerns on both health and moral grounds for some groups. Health concerns include risk of pregnancy and STDs, as well as psychological issues (Meier, 2007). Age at first sex varies across different groups in society. For example, non-Hispanic White, Hispanic, and Asian adolescents have first sex later than African Americans. Adolescents from middle- and high-income families typically have sex later than their low-income peers.

Early sex increases the potential for depressive symptoms for girls who had sex before their peers, for young girls whose relationship ended soon after first sex, and for those whose relationships were either expected within one's social group or characterized by a lack of commitment.

As might be expected, self-esteem suffers the most in girls who had first sex early in adolescence, particularly if they were not romantically attached to their partner (Meier, 2007). Ultimately, having sex as an adolescent does not increase mental health problems for most girls except as noted earlier. Only this subset of girls appears to be negatively affected. Conversely, male adolescent sex does not produce similar symptoms.

Culture, Biology, and Sexuality

A great deal of the research about sexuality and sexual expression has focused on two different dimensions, biology and culture (Tolman & Diamond, 2001). Because of gender bias and other social and political forces, there has been relatively little research that looks at the intersection of these two dimensions. For example, the issue of sexual desire has been relegated to the realm of males, with emphasis given to the role of testosterone. Yet it is clear that the expression of sexuality encompasses more than just desire. While biology plays a role in sexuality, few would argue that mediators such as social and cultural factors are not influential. Even strong sexual desires are controlled by cultural norms and values that circumscribe when and where the desires can be met. Religious, legal,

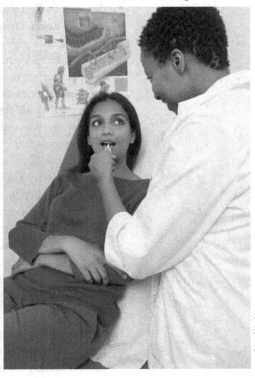

Some women prefer to seek health care services from female providers as this woman is doing.

Moodboard/Corbis

and cultural expectations play a significant role in most behaviors, including sexual ones. The fact that men report higher levels of sexual urges is likely not the result of biology alone, but rather the interplay of cultural norms and biology. In cultures where women are expected to be less interested in sex than men, it would be logical that the former would report lower interest when this information is solicited. In other words, sexuality is at least as much a social construction (cultural invention) as a biological phenomenon.

Cultural influences on the expression of sexuality can be seen in how different societies and religious groups view male and female needs for sex. Islam, for example, puts greater emphasis on the husband pleasuring and satisfying the wife, while many other religions see sexual intercourse as primarily a means of procreation (Mernissi, 1987). However, this recognition of female sexuality and desire is tempered by values that condone things such as genital mutilation, whipping of women who have been raped under the guise of controlling women, and forgiving the rapist if he marries the survivor. Similar observations can be made about the views that saw African American men and women as people with heightened sexuality different from that of Whites. Again, controlling people whose desire might get out of hand was used as justification for both laws and customs that discriminated against this group.

Managing sexual behavior is also part of the rationale for the many cultural cues and other messages provided to adolescents during puberty. These cues cover topics such as appropriate sexual behavior (e.g., non-provocative clothing, no boys/girls in your bedroom), expectations about the behavior of the opposite sex, and a built-in predilection toward heterosexuality. Girls may come to see boys as potential predators and boys may similarly buy into this image. These are just a few of the messages that adolescents are given from their culture. Some of the ways these messages are different for male and female adolescents show up in decisions around sexual intercourse. Males tend to receive a consistent message about their maleness and it supports their biological disposition to initiate sexual intercourse. Females receive conflicting messages about their sexuality that affects their decisions about having intercourse. For example, they are influenced by behaviors of their peers, particularly whether or not their peers engaged in coitus. Their degree of adherence to religious dictates can also influence the decision along with the individual's popularity. Teens are influenced by media portrayals, advertisements, and other material that give mixed messages about premarital sex (Halpern, 2003; Udry & Billy, 1987). Interestingly, there were clear differences between White and Black adolescents in the decision to have sex. Female African American adolescents were not influenced by the same factors as other groups. Rather, the only variable that predicted whether these teenagers would have sex is whether they looked sexually mature to their peers. Having intercourse was much more probable for sexually mature Black adolescents.

All too often, adolescents have not received clear, accurate, or timely information about sexuality (Lear, 1995). This is especially true for adolescents with intellectual disabilities (Isler, Tas, Beytut, & Conk, 2009). Neither professionals nor parents had talked about sexuality to about 50% of those included in Isler et al.'s study. Much of this reluctance seems to come from the belief that those with intellectual disabilities are somehow asexual. Needed information for this group that totals about 6.5 million in the United States includes instruction about their own bodies, sexuality in general, and relationships (National Dissemination Center for Children With Disabilities, 2011).

Sexuality in Adults

Sexual activity among adults is a common activity regardless of marital state. Males report an average of six to eight female partners during the ages 30 to 44 while women in those age bracket report an average of four male partners (Mosher et al., 2005). Only a small percentage of adults indicate no sexual partners after age 18 (Laumann, Gagnon, Michael, & Michaels, 1994). About a fifth of men and about a third of women have had only one sex partner during their lives, while over one-half of men and almost a third of women have had five or more partners.

The frequency with which adults have vaginal sex varies by age group and gender. Table 10.1 show percentages by gender and age (National Survey of Sexual Health and Behavior [NSSHB], 2010).

Table 10.1   Percentage of Men and Women Reporting Frequency of Vaginal Sex, N = 2,396

Age Group		18–24	25–29	30–39	40–49	50–59	60–69	70+
Single								
Not in past year	Men	56.9	46.6	39.6	48.9	67.7	86.4	81.6
	Women	50.8	43.0	72.3	71.1	85.4	84.5	100
A few times per year to monthly	Men	13.9	21.9	24.2	18.4	14.9	8.6	5.3
	Women	16.4	21.5	10.7	16.9	5.4	6.5	0.0
A few times per month to weekly	Men	19.0	27.1	23.1	22.4	11.6	3.7	13.2
	Women	19.7	24.1	12.5	9.9	7.0	6.5	0.0
2–3 times per week	Men	8.0	4.1	1.7	8.0	5.3	1.2	0.0
	Women	8.2	1.3	4.5	2.1	2.2	2.6	0.0
4 or more times per week	Men	2.2	0.0	5.5	2.3	0.5	0.0	0.0
	Women	4.9	10.1	0.0	0.0	0.0	0.0	0.0
Partnered								
Not in past year	Men	26.0	20.8	15.6	29.9	34.1	27.3	26.3
	Women	12.9	10.6	14.8	20.6	21.1	14.8	30.8
A few times per year to monthly	Men	8.0	10.4	6.5	9.2	10.6	11.4	10.5
	Women	16.1	11.7	13.6	13.7	18.3	11.1	15.4
A few times per month to weekly	Men	30.0	36.4	32.5	24.1	31.8	20.5	63.2
	Women	31.2	36.2	43.2	24.5	36.6	48.4	23.1
2–3 times per week	Men	26.0	27.1	39.0	25.3	18.8	38.6	0.0
	Women	32.3	28.7	18.2	31.4	18.3	18.5	7.7
4 or more times per week	Men	10.0	6.3	6.5	11.5	4.7	2.3	0.0
	Women	7.5	12.8	10.2	9.8	5.6	7.4	23.1
Married								
Not in past year	Men	4.2	1.6	4.5	9.1	20.6	33.9	54.2
	Women	11.8	3.5	6.5	8.1	22.0	37.9	53.5
A few times per year to monthly	Men	12.5	9.3	15.6	16.2	25.0	21.2	24.2
	Women	14.7	11.6	16.3	21.7	23.7	20.0	25.4
A few times per month to weekly	Men	16.7	46.3	47.3	51.0	38.3	35.4	15.0
	Women	14.7	47.7	50.2	46.6	36.2	35.9	18.3
2–3 times per week	Men	45.8	37.1	26.8	19.9	15.0	9.5	5.8
	Women	35.3	35.2	21.9	20.8	16.9	6.2	1.4
4 or more times per week	Men	20.8	5.9	5.8	3.7	1.1	0.0	0.8
	Women	23.5	2.0	5.1	2.7	1.1	0.0	1.4

Source: NSSHB (2010).

Adults engage in a variety of sexual activities, including masturbation alone, masturbation with a partner, purchasing x-rated movies, and vaginal, oral, and anal sex. About 60% of men reported engaging in masturbation during the past month and this percentage remains relatively unchanged to about age 49, at which point it begins to decline to less than 30% at age 70 and beyond. Women's use of masturbation in the previous month begins at 26% for those under age 20 and increases to about 50% by age 29. It drops to about 38% for those between ages 30 and 50, and then declines slowly, dropping to about 12% after age 70. Masturbating with a partner increases in frequency between the ages of 18 and 50 and declines after that. It reaches a high of almost 50% during the 25 to 29 age range (NSSHB, 2010).

About 27% of men and 19% of women had oral sex in the year prior to the survey and about 9% to 10% of women had engaged in anal sex over that time period. The buying of pornographic movies was still more of a male attraction (23%) than a female attraction (11%) (Laumann et al., 1994).

Among adults, sexuality is a form of communication that involves negotiation between all parties. Issues to be communicated include things such as safe sex, along with preferences. It requires a degree of assertiveness and, to the extent that one has multiple partners across time, continuous efforts to ensure that one's needs are fulfilled. The decision to become sexual with another person requires some degree of trust depending upon the sexual activity being undertaken. Unfortunately, sexual encounters that occur early in a relationship often involve little verbal communication. Instead of clarity, there is ambiguity that allows both partners to interpret and reinterpret what actually occurred (Lear, 1995). Moreover, there is relatively little discussion about past sexual partners, whether one has been tested for HIV or STDs, or other risk factors. Many adults just assume that their partner is "ok" by the way they look or smell. This can and does lead to the transmission of STDs at all ages.

Sexuality, regardless of the age of the participants, involves risk. The risks include health concerns such as HIV or other STDs and psychological concerns associated with emotional attachments involving a high degree of intimacy (Lear, 1995). Within American culture, there is a long-standing expectation that it is the male who initiates greater degrees of intimacy and the role of the female to establish her limits while also taking responsibility for the use of contraception. Such cultural norms place inordinate responsibility on the woman and leave men off the hook. This can be problematic when dealing with risk because the cultural power and privilege differentials accorded males in many societies makes true negotiation difficult. Negotiation about things such as condom use, for example, presumes two parties of equal power and influence. It can also communicate messages that are unwanted. A woman who is responsible about her sexuality and carries condoms to protect herself may feel embarrassed and self-conscious, afraid that being prepared conveys a message of easy availability (Lear, 1995). At the same time, many women are culturally trained to deny their sexual desires. This helps reinforce male efforts to push ahead because more than one-third of women who said no initially eventually had intercourse with that partner (Muehlenhard & McCoy, 1991). In about 50% of these cases, women simply gave in to men's entreaties without explicitly agreeing to intercourse.

Another factor that increases sexual risk among young adults is the use of alcohol. Alcohol (and other drug use) interferes with the ability to think clearly about what one is doing or agreeing to. Too often, incidents of rape and unwanted intercourse occur when one or both partners are drunk or high. While women peers will talk about and encourage their friends to use protection, men appear to have no such compunction. Typically, we choose friends based on shared values and these values can either encourage or discourage risk taking in sexual relationships (Lear, 1995).

There are some clear differences in the way that men and women interpret and report their level of satisfaction from intercourse. While 85% of men say their most recent partner had an orgasm, only about 64% of women say they attained an orgasm with their most recent partner (Whole lot of faking going on?). Just over 60% of women in a relationship with a partner report satisfaction with the frequency and consistency of orgasms (Davis, Blank, Hung-Yu, & Bonillas, 1996). The likelihood of having an orgasm decreases for men age 18 to 59 and increases for women as they get older (NSSHB, 2010). Beginning at age 25, most sexual behaviors occur in the context of a relationship (*Two and a Half Men* notwithstanding). Men involved in relationships reported greater satisfaction (arousal, pleasure, and orgasms) and fewer problems (erectile dysfunction and pain) than with their most recent nonrelationship partner (NSSHB, 2010).

Sexuality and Aging

Not unlike those with intellectually disabilities, older adults in our society are seen as somehow asexual despite the fact that sexual activity and interest remain important in most men and women. Decreases in libido (sexual interest) and activity are common in older adults, sometimes attributed to things such as disease, boredom, biological and psychological factors, and declining mental states (Kontula & Haavio-Mannila, 2009). Yet, sexual interest and activity in this group is clearly associated with improved mental health and greater enjoyment of later years. Sexuality is inherently connected to identity, self-esteem, and emotions and these continue to be salient for older adults. Of course, availability of a partner is a benefit and often the loss of one's partner signals the end of sexual interest for some women.

As might be expected, a regular partner is perhaps the best predictor of sexual activity for older adults. About 80% of men have a sexual partner after age 70 while the percent of women with a partner is less than 50 (Kontula & Haavio-Mannila, 2009). At age 70, about 25% of men had intercourse at least once a week. The percentage of women was about 10. As a counterpoint, however, another 25% of men and 50% of women had not had intercourse in the past 12 months. At this age, multiple sex partners are rare.

By age 60, lack of sexual desire was common for about 50% of women and about 15% of men. The best predictor for frequency of sexual intercourse for older men was good health, their sense of sexual self-esteem, overall satisfaction with sex life, and a history of multiple sex partners. At the same time, about 30% of men between the ages of 60 and 69 report using erectile medication during their most recent sexual activity. The percentage of use drops to about 23 between 70 and 79 years of age and to around 19 for men over 80 years of age. For women, the best predictors for frequency of sexual intercourse were overall satisfaction with their sex life, valuing of sex in the relationship, a higher level of desire, and a partner in good health (Kontula & Haavio-Mannila, 2009).

We have talked earlier about risk in sexual relationships among adults. Older adults are not immune from acquiring STDs. Some retirement communities have experienced high incidents of STDs as women who long ago stopped using birth control engage in unprotected sex with new partners. After age 50, both men and women use condoms less frequently and about two-thirds report no use of a condom during their last sexual intercourse (NSSHB, 2010). Those individuals who are sexually active but fail to use protection increase the risk for themselves as well as for future partners. Failure to be tested regularly, weakened immune systems, and age-related changes in vaginal wall thickness and lubricity all increase this risk.

SEXUAL DYSFUNCTION

Sexual dysfunction refers to a problem that occurs in one of the four phases of the sexual response cycle. The cycle consists of the excitement stage, the plateau phase, orgasm, and resolution. In the excitement stage, an individual becomes aroused by sexual thoughts or stimuli leading to changes in sensitivity in both genital and nipple area. Heart rate increases and blood pressure and breathing rate rise. The plateau phase occurs between the excitement stage and orgasm as the physical changes continue leading to orgasm. The third stage, climax or orgasm, involves additional constriction and contraction of the pelvic muscles leading to a wave of pleasurable feelings and tension release. The last stage, resolution, is one in which the body relaxes, returns to its original stage, and engorgement ends.

Sexual dysfunction is perhaps the most common problem cited by both men and women at some point in their lives. Over 40% of men and 30% of women experience these difficulties (Laumann, Paik, & Rosen,, 1999). Despite its commonness, it is often not openly discussed, sometimes even between the partners. This can interfere with the quality of a relationship and contribute to other difficulties. The following discussion is not intended to make the reader an expert on sexual dysfunction, but to identify some of the more common problems that may be discovered when working with clients around sexual or other relationship issues.

Hypoactive Sexual Desire Disorder

The most common reported sexual problem among women between the ages of 18 and 59 is a lack of sexual desire, also known as *hypoactive sexual desire disorder* (HSDD; Laumann et al., 1994). Low sex drive or libido was identified as problematic for just over one-third of women. A lack of a physical or emotional reaction to sexual stimulation is typically associated with this sexual dysfunction (Kontula & Haavio-Mannila, 2009). It can present as a lack of desire or excitement or inability to have an orgasm, as well as a diminution in one's sexual fantasies. HSDD is a persistent condition that can't be attributed to some other disorder, such as depression (Zakhari, 2009).

Sexual Aversion Disorder

Sexual aversion disorder is, as the name implies, characterized by one's aversion to genital sexual contact. The aversion may take the form of a lack of desire, disgust, or revulsion and is not the normal loss of interest that occurs with age. It can also involve sensory issues such as negative reactions to a partner's genitalia or bodily secretions. Some individuals avoid all sexual encounters while others' aversions relate only to sexual intercourse. To be a true disorder, the aversion must cause personal distress and be persistent over time (Basson et al., 2000).

Female Sexual Arousal Disorder

Women with sexual arousal disorder are simply not aroused by sexual stimuli. They typically report that sexual stimuli do not produce lubrication generally associated with arousal nor is there swelling of vaginal tissue needed until intercourse is complete (Feldhaus-Dahir, 2009). The absence of lubrication is painful and affects anywhere from 11% to 19% of women under age 30 and perhaps as much as a quarter of women over age 50 (Fugl-Meyer & Fugl-Meyer, 1999; Laumann et al., 1999). An equally important criterion is that the disorder causes distress or interpersonal difficulty (Graham, 2010). Most explanations for this dysfunction involve a lack of estrogen, blood flow problems, loss of vaginal nerve sensations, and conflict with one's partner.

Male Erectile Disorder

Male erectile disorder occurs when either no erection develops in response to sexual stimuli or an erection cannot be maintained. This is oftentimes referred to as male impotence or erectile dysfunction (ED). On a positive note, invention of the class of drugs that includes Viagra, Levitra, and Cialis has produced favorable results among men and encouraged more open discussion about ED. On a negative note, men using ED drugs are two to three times as likely to acquire an STD as a result of having unprotected sex (Jena, Goldman, Kamdar, Lakdawalla, & Lu, 2010).

Female Orgasmic Disorder

Women who experience this disorder usually complain that they have either a greatly delayed orgasm or none at all, despite being satisfactorily aroused/excited. About one-quarter of women exhibit this disorder (Laumann et al., 1999). Causative factors may be either physiological or psychological in origin.

Male Orgasmic Disorder

This disorder in many ways mirrors the one above in that an orgasm is inordinately delayed or fails to occur in spite of arousal. It is a relatively rare and usually involves a medical condition or is drug related. In some cases, it may be the result of performance anxiety.

Premature, Retarded, and Retrograde Ejaculation

Premature ejaculation, as the phrase implies, occurs before the client wanted. It can occur before penetration or shortly after, and often with only minimal stimulation. Other common complaints from men are retarded, slow, and retrograde ejaculations. Both premature and slow ejaculations are often related to one not being attracted to a partner, problematic past events that traumatized the individual, and sometimes religious beliefs that paint sex as sinful. Nervousness can play a role in premature ejaculation and some antidepressant medications contribute to slow ejaculations. Retrograde ejaculation occurs when the ejaculate is forced back into the bladder and is more often associated with damage to nerves following prostate surgery.

Dyspareunia

Dyspareunia is genital pain that interferes with sexual intercourse (Binik, 2010). It is considered a sexual dysfunction under the category of sexual pain disorders similar to vaginismus and can occur with both men and women. The diagnosis usually is defined as medically based, psychologically based, or some combination of the two.

Vaginismus

Vaginismus occurs when women experienced muscle spasms in the vagina that are persistent and involuntary (Zakhari, 2009). It may occur with all partners or just some partners and can be both recent and long-standing in occurrence. About 14% of women experience pain during intercourse with vaginismus. It is often associated with relationship difficulties and sometimes depression and anxiety disorders (Dunn, Croft, & Hackett, 1999).

Secondary Sexual Dysfunction

This category of sexual dysfunction is employed when other illnesses or disorders are believed to have caused one of the problems identified earlier. Disorders of the thyroid, depression, and the influence of various drugs can all contribute to or cause the secondary sexual dysfunction (Laurent & Simons, 2009). Likewise, physical problems such as prostate disease, high blood pressure, arthritis, heart disease, and diabetes can play a role. As noted earlier, some medications, most notably antidepressants, can also impact sexual performance.

If, during assessment, it becomes clear that a client is experiencing one or more of the sexual dysfunctions described earlier, it is wise to refer the individual to his or her primary physician. As noted, many sexual dysfunctions are affected directly or indirectly by chronic diseases (Verschuren, Enzlin, Dijkstra, Geertzen, & Dekker, 2010). Treatment for many dysfunctions involves blood and other tests, and sometimes prescription medications. Individuals and couples may still require and/or benefit from therapeutic assistance from the social worker as an adjunct to medical treatment.

SEXUAL DISORDERS

Sexual disorders include a multitude of behaviors that run the gamut from fetishes to sexual abuse and from homoeroticism to sexual addiction. Some sexual disorders involve individual behaviors that cause little or no harm to others, such as cross-dressing, while others profoundly hurt the victim, such as child sexual abuse. Some of the more common types encountered by social workers include paraphilias and gender identity disorder.

Paraphilias

Paraphilias include things such as sexual sadism and masochism, fetishes, transvestism, exhibitionism, voyeurism, frotteurism, and pedophilia. Each will be briefly described as follows.

Sexual Sadism

Sadism involves infliction of humiliation or pain on another to achieve sexual gratification. Sadists tend to have fantasies that involve hurting others. Victims can be either consenting or nonconsenting. In practice, sadism takes place most often with the consent of another person. There is sometimes a fine line between what is enjoyable to the other person and what constitutes abuse. Sadism is sometimes lumped together with rape, but rapists are motivated by other factors including power.

Masochism

Masochism is the enjoyment of pain being inflicted upon oneself, also as a means of sexual gratification. The harm can be physical or psychological and, like sexual sadism, masochism usually occurs between consenting adults. Activities may involve bondage, simulated rape, spanking, blindfolding, and others. Some masochists do not have partners and inflict pain or discomfort upon themselves. Media reports of adolescents and adults who asphyxiate themselves to achieve a higher perceived state of sexual excitement may fall into this category.

Fetishes

Fetishism is the deriving of sexual pleasure from inanimate objects. Examples include women's underwear, shoes, and leather items but can include anything that the individual finds erotic. A fetish can also be focused on a part of an individual's body such as feet, ears, or breasts. Sometimes the fetish becomes part of the sexual interaction with a willing partner and at other times becomes so overwhelming that it interferes with one's functioning in partner relationships or other aspects of their life.

Transvestism

Transvestism is cross-dressing or wearing the clothes of the opposite sex. The clothing is worn for the purposes of sexual gratification, which distinguishes it from things such as wearing unisex clothes or putting on a garment normally worn by someone of the opposite sex. Transvestism becomes problematic when it causes difficulties in other realms of the individual's life. The social worker is more likely to encounter a transvestite in a clinical setting when others (often spouses, employers or courts) insist they get help. The goal usually is not to terminate the behavior but to help the client control and accept their urges without producing other problems in their lives.

Exhibitionism

Exhibitionists are individuals who expose their genitals to others for their sexual pleasure. The target of this exposure may be children or any adult (typically, female). The reaction of the target is an important part of the gratification and exhibitionists may simultaneously engage in masturbation to engender additional shock in the victim. Like pedophiles, they have a chronic disorder that will cause them to repeat the behavior throughout their lives. Most exhibitionists are men. Both men and women exhibitionists may elect to pursue careers where their impulses are rewarded, such as in the porn and related industries.

Voyeurism

Voyeurs achieve sexual enjoyment from watching other people undressed or engaging in sexual activities without the person's knowledge or consent. Peeping Toms fall into this category. Most of these individuals do not want to actually engage in sexual activity with their victims, but may masturbate or have fantasies about the victim. Voyeurism is sometimes used to describe individuals who frequent strip clubs, but because consent is given in these situations, such actions do not fall into the clinical category of voyeurism.

Frotteurism

Frotteurs gain their sexual gratification from rubbing up against people usually without those persons' consent or sometimes knowledge. This can occur in crowded situations such as buses, subways, or any other place where people are in proximity to one another. By definition, it is an ongoing activity lasting at least six months and interferes with the person's emotional, social, or occupational lives. Men are the most frequent frotteurs with most victims being female.

Pedophilia

Pedophiles receive their sexual enjoyment by preying on children, usually those who have not reached puberty. Social workers may encounter pedophilia when working with sexually abused children and adults. Most often, the individual offender is a male.

While there have been multiple recent instances in the media of older women engaging in sexual activity with teens, this is less common. Pedophiles may be attracted to either boys or girls or have no preference. Within the past 10 years, the extent of pedophilia within various churches has become clear as clergy took advantage of their position to engage in inappropriate and harmful sexual activities (often looking and touching) with children. The harm done to child and adolescent survivors is great and many require or seek out professional counseling and other clinical services. Common symptoms include depression, posttraumatic distress, eating disorders, anxiety, personality disorders (e.g., borderline personality disorder), substance abuse, and sexual dysfunction, including involvement in high-risk sexual behavior (Maniglio, 2009).

The typical pedophile is someone known to the child, often a parent, stepparent, or close relative. It can also be anyone in a position of authority, such as a priest or teacher. Often the pedophile will use coercion to enforce silence about the events, which may entail threats against the child, family members, or pets. Because pedophilia tends to be a chronic disorder, many believe that it cannot be overcome through treatment or incarceration. These individuals commonly have other problems, such as drug abuse, depression, or both. Pedophiles usually come to the attention of authorities through complaints made by the survivors or adult relatives. In a recent case, the sexual abuse went unreported by the survivors until the perpetrator announced plans to begin associating with children again. At that point, the three adult sisters who had been sexually abused by their father reported him to the police. As in this case, oftentimes the abuse comes to light years after its occurrence.

Gender Identity Disorder, Transgender, and Transsexualism

The transgendered are those individuals who have sought or undergone sex reassignment from a man to a woman or a woman to a man. A *DSM* diagnosis of transsexualism is used to describe someone who has an ongoing and powerful cross-gender identification and discomfort with their sex and who feel they do not belong in the assigned gender role. In their minds, they are in the wrong body. Through surgery or hormonal treatments, transsexuals seek to rid themselves of those things that assign them to their

> **Lisa Dazols, in her vignette entitled Culturally Competent Social Work Practice with Transgender People, provides a look at the consequences of defining transgender as a mental disorder and the challenges transgender individuals face. What is your view on whether a transgendered individual should be considered as having a mental disorder?**

current sex. Like other sexual minorities, those who are transgendered have the same basic needs as heterosexual clients. A number of studies have identified that transgendered adolescents suffer from self-mutilation, depression, HIV infection, homelessness, high-risk sexual behaviors, and suicide ideation (thoughts) and attempts, among others (Coker et al., 2010).

The *DSM-IV-TR* also identifies gender identity disorder (GID) as a diagnosis that describes a divergence between one's assigned sex (physical sex) and one's psychological sex (Cohen-Kettenis & Pfäfflin, 2010). It is described as a disorder that likely began in the person's childhood or adolescence. This is different from the experience of transgendered individuals whose development is believed to start only in childhood. The utility and value of this diagnosis is a source of contention within the mental health community. Some argue that its effect is to create a mental illness that is no more appropriate than were the long-since discarded view of homosexuality as a mental disorder. It is also criticized for subjectivity and vagueness.

Other Common Sexual-Related Problems

Mitchell et al. (2005) identified the most common sexual-related problems encountered by mental health professionals as overuse, pornography, and risky behaviors connected to use of the Internet. The use of Internet pornography sites is largely a male behavior:

Men are more than four times as likely to use these sites as women (Buzzell, 2005). Males comprise about two-thirds of the users of pornographic Internet sites (Cooper, Scherer, Boies, & Gordon, 1999).

Causes of Sexual Disorders

Many explanations for sexual disorders have been postulated, ranging from biological influences to the role of one's parents. Traumatic events occurring during childhood or adolescence have been suggested, along with exposure to sexual experiences that the individual was too young to understand. For example, being a survivor of sexual abuse as a child may lead to the individual developing one or more of the sexual disorders described earlier.

Others look at the role of biology in predicting abnormal sexual behavior. A recent study examined the role of dopamine, a brain chemical, in risky sexual behaviors such as promiscuity and infidelity. While neither may be viewed as a disorder, the authors found that those with a particular genetic disposition influencing dopamine levels were significantly more likely to engage in these problematic behaviors (Garcia et al., 2010). At the same time, some with the same genetic anomaly did not engage in risky behaviors, suggesting that while the risk is higher in these individuals, the existence of the anomaly does not guarantee that such behavior will occur.

Assess your analysis and evaluation of this chapter's content by completing the Chapter Review.

11

Major Life Phases Influencing Human Behavior

Childhood

Childhood is an exciting and important time in life. From a child's perspective, early life is a time to bond with family, learn a language, understand the world, develop social relations, and begin to develop preferences. From a perspective outside of the child, this time represents a critical developmental period that has lifelong implications. Childhood is often seen as a trajectory that will influence most aspects of an individual's future: health, learning, socializing, and producing. While analogies are inadequate representations of human functioning, one might draw a parallel between the growth of a tree and a child. The developmental path of a young tree will certainly influence its later life. If a young tree leans to the south, it will probably lean to the south throughout its life. Again, this analogy is limited as research on plasticity has shown that positive and negative changes occur in response to life experiences. However, there are some parallels between the two. Failure to learn how to read in childhood is associated with higher rates of delinquency and poorer health in adolescence and adulthood (DeWalt & Hink, 2009; Vacca, 2008). With regard to criminality, some estimate that 50% to 75% of U.S. correctional inmates have not achieved sixth grade reading skills (Tewksbury & Vito, 1994). Thus, patterns in early life are often similar to patterns in later life.

CHILDHOOD DEFINED

When does childhood begin and end? In the United States, there is some consensus that childhood begins at about three years of age

Table 11.1   Major Stages of Life in the United States

Life Stage	Age
Prenatal period	Conception to birth
Infancy	Birth to about 12 months of age
Toddler	Roughly 12 to about 36 months of age
Childhood: preschool	Roughly 3 to 5 years of age
Middle childhood	Roughly 5 years of age to onset of puberty (~12 years)
Adolescence	Roughly 12 to 20 or so years of age
Young adulthood	Roughly 20 to 40 years of age
Middle age	Roughly 40 to 65 years of age
Old age	Roughly 65 years of age and beyond

Source: Adapted from Centers for Disease Control and Prevention (http://www.cdc.gov/lifestages/, retrieved on August 12, 2012).

and ends at around 12 years of age. Table 11.1 presents a chronological overview of human development.

Applying labels to different life stages helps organize thinking about the unique needs and experiences that occur across the human life span. However, it is important to note that the different labels for different stages are not empirically derived. That is, no study has proven these shift points and cross-cultural expectations differ for children at different ages. Thus, one can conclude that labels of human development are not a biological given but a social construct. Notions of childhood have varied and continue to vary over time and across cultures (Hedegaard, 2009).

Consider how expectations, and therefore perceptions, of children vary within the United States in current times. Parents who farm or run small family businesses likely have very different expectations about how children spend time compared to well-off families who have had wealth for generations. They would expect their children to contribute to the business by working during summers and after school due to the need to make the business functional. Such expectations may override a child's desire to be involved in activities such as sports or the arts. By contrast, parents who have generational wealth may have different expectations for their children, encouraging them to have many broad experiences, such as lessons in sports, the arts, and travel. Further, in families of generational wealth, work during childhood may be viewed as detracting from the child's ability to succeed long term, whereas the exact opposite may be expected among families of small businesses.

Policies That Protect or Expose Children

Ideas about childhood are reflected in laws and policies. Within the United States, policies have been made to protect children. For example, laws exist that restrict children's access to drugs, alcohol, and cigarettes and protect them from abuse or heavy work. However, these laws have not always been in place. Roose and Bouverne-De Bie (2007) reviewed periods when children had no *protection rights*, which left them vulnerable to victimization from business, the government, and parents who abused or neglected them. The content of many literary masterpieces set during the Industrial Revolution (think of Charles Dickens) highlights the plight of children who did not enjoy protection from laws or policies. While laws in modern-day United States are designed to protect children and offer them many rights, this is not the case throughout the world.

The news about war-torn countries in Africa and South America inevitably highlight stories about children being forcibly enlisted into military organizations. Children conscripted into military organizations both participate in and are victims to obscene attacks against humanity, such as being forced to observe or participate in the killing, raping, abusing, or plundering of other humans. Understandably, these children are at extraordinarily high risk for developing mental health problems, such as depression, anxiety, posttraumatic stress disorder, and relationship problems (Betancourt, Borisova, de la Soudière, & Williamson, 2011). The Human Rights Watch (2008) reported that hundreds of thousands of children under 18 years of age are believed to be child soldiers in current times.

The previous paragraphs introduce evidence that perceptions of what is appropriate and inappropriate for children varies across time and culture. At some time points within certain cultures, children's well-being was not strongly valued or prized. Rather, they were seen as commodities to be used for the advancement of some position suggesting that childhood is a social construct and not a biological reality (Roose & Bouverne-De Bie, 2007). However, biological realities do exist. Younger children are biologically immature compared to adults in all areas of physical development. A five-month-old child is not expected to talk, walk, or prepare food regardless of culture or time. Similarly, a 10-year-old child is expected to talk, walk, and maybe prepare some food, but he or she is not expected to understand meta-physics, do hard labor, or show advanced dexterity. Does the last sentence ring true across the globe? Not fully. While 10-year-old children are certainly not expected to do meta-physics, some cultures do expect them to work long days. Consider the report by the Human Rights Watch titled *The Small Hands of Slavery: Bonded Child Labor in India* (1996, p. 2):

> With credible estimates ranging from 60 to 115 million, India has the largest number of working children in the world. Whether they are sweating in the heat of stone quarries, working in the fields sixteen hours a day, picking rags in city streets, or hidden away as domestic servants, these children endure miserable and difficult lives. They earn little and are abused much. They struggle to make enough to eat and perhaps to help feed their families as well. They do not go to school; more than half of them will never learn the barest skills of literacy. Many of them have been working since the age of four or five, and by the time they reach adulthood they may be irrevocably sick or deformed—they will certainly be exhausted, old men and women by the age of forty, likely to be dead by fifty.
>
> Most or all of these children are working under some form of compulsion, whether from their parents, from the expectations attached to their caste, or from simple economic necessity. At least fifteen million of them, however, are working as virtual slaves.

Read the case study Impact of Childhood Trauma on Development. What are some of the problems that arise from childhood trauma? From the case study, what elements of the intervention and conceptualization did you find most helpful and why?

Clearly, children are impacted directly and indirectly by the views adults hold about children. At this time in the United States, adults generally see childhood as a time to support children's development by encouraging them to learn through school, enjoy peers, and dabble with exploring who they are—especially if a family has access to basic resources. Childhood has not always been so favorable in this country. Given that the United States was founded on Judeo-Christian beliefs, the Old Testament has had a significant influence on perceptions and actions toward children. Consider a popular scripture that continues to be used to support corporal punishment:

> He who spareth the rod hateth his son: but he that loveth him correcteth him betimes (Proverbs 13:24) and Withhold not correction from a child: for if thou strike him with the rod, he shall not die. Thou shalt beat him with the rod, and deliver his soul from hell (Proverbs 23:13–14).

In the United States, which do you think came first—a movement for protecting animals against abuse or a movement for protecting children against abuse? By virtue of asking the question, you can likely guess the answer. In 1866, Henry Bergh was founder and president of the Society for the Prevention of Cruelty to Animals (Williams, 1983). Eight years later, Bergh went on to find the Society for the Prevention of Cruelty to Children. Bergh launched a media campaign that highlighted the tragedies of child abuse in the United States that led to many societies taking interest in child protection. However, the first known legal protection for children did not come until 1930, with the passage of the Social Security Act of 1930, which required that child welfare services be developed for neglected children and for those at risk of becoming delinquent (Williams, 1983). This law, however, did not directly protect children from being abused. In 1962, a group of physicians (Kempe, Silverman, Steele, Droegemuller, & Silver, 1984) published an article that introduced the term *battered child syndrome* that caught the public's attention and once again drew public attention to child abuse. By 1967, all states in the nation had laws that required child abuse reporting by professionals (Williams, 1983). The fact that professionals were legally mandated to report child abuse reveals a resistance or disbelief of child abuse. Interest in preventing and responding to child abuse led to the Child Abuse Prevention and Treatment Act, which was signed in 1974—100 years from the founding of Bergh's society to protect children.

Today, debates continue about the value of corporal punishment, despite clear research showing that high levels of corporal punishment are strongly associated with untoward outcomes and are rarely associated with positive outcomes (Gershoff, 2002).

The Children's Liberation movement, which launched in the 1960s, due in part to scientific findings such as those mentioned by Kempe, has significantly changed both perceptions and laws relating to children. Laws are designed to protect children against abuse or neglect by requiring education and forbidding work and treatment from adults deemed to be harmful. Indeed, children are now viewed, legally and socially, as having rights *beyond protection*. Childhood actors, for example, have legal rights to their earnings and are not considered to simply be the property of their parents. Society and policies influence a number of activities of children, such as whether they can vote, join the military, use alcohol, drive, marry, smoke, and make medical decisions for themselves (Hedegaard, 2009).

Several points can be taken from reviewing the history of policies affecting children, such as the reality that societal forces and policies directly and indirectly impact child development. Further, notions of childhood continue to shift across time.

Policy Practice

Practice Behavior Example: Understand that policy affects service delivery and they actively engage in policy practice.

Critical Thinking Question: How might current policies surrounding child abuse and neglect both protect children and put them at risk?

Assess your comprehension of Childhood by completing this quiz.

MAJOR INFLUENCES ON CHILDHOOD

We now turn to several influences on child development, namely family, social, biological, and societal influences.

Attachment in Childhood

Humans are born into a social world. While not universally the case, consider the "typical" birthing scene in the United States. One expects the delivering mother to be supported by her partner, her parents, and possibly extended family and good friends.

Upon birth, the newborn is immediately attended to by nurses, doctors, and family members. Having a child is cause for celebration, birth notices, and special photos. These activities reveal the importance of having children in society.

While this chapter is on childhood and not infancy, notice that immediately upon birth infants are introduced to the social world. Newborns are spoken to as if they can understand language. Adults talk with an infant as if the infant could understand complex ideas, such as "Aren't you the cutest little girl in the world?" Clearly, the newborn is capable of understanding neither the words nor the meaning of the phrase. Further, when pressed, most adults will readily acknowledge that they do not expect newborns to understand such sentences—so why do parents talk with infants? For many reasons, including that speaking to human newborns begins to develop the relationship or bond between adult and child.

The term *attachment* is one of the key phrases used to describe the nature and quality of the parent–child relationship or bond. Research reveals that the quality of attachment between child and parent is absolutely critical as a predictor of children's emotional, behavioral, and social functioning during childhood and beyond (Cassidy & Shaver, 2008; Wallin, 2007).

For infants and children, attachment to others is necessary because they are fully dependent upon others for survival. Adults provide food, shelter, and protection for their young children. Attachment, however, involves much more than promoting survival. Attachment is a type of "teacher" or guide believed to exert a strong influence on a child's entire life. The history of research on attachment is very interesting and is briefly described next.

Sigmund Freud suggested that children are affected lifelong by how their parents behaved. However, it was John Bowlby who conducted initial research revealing the importance of the parent–child relationship or bond (Cassidy & Shaver, 2008). Using a variety of theoretical perspectives, Bowlby noted that children use their relationship with their parent as a type of "secure base" from which they explore and return when feeling threatened. Observations revealed that young children in novel situations tend to seek protection and comfort from their primary caregiver. Further, children take cues from their primary caregiver regarding issues of safety. For example, imagine a situation in which a parent and child find a harmless water snake. If the parent is calm while the child plays with the snake, the child will learn one message about snakes. By contrast, if the parent shows heightened fear, the child will learn another message about snakes.

Unfortunately, not all parents provide "safe bases" for their children. Indeed, some parents provide toxic and dangerous bases for their children. Like all aspects of human functioning, individual variation exists with regard to the nature of the parent–child attachment. One popular system for measuring children's attachment style comes from the work of Mary Ainsworth (1989; George & Solomon, 2008). Using the idea of a secure base, Ainsworth and colleagues devised the "strange situation task," wherein young children and their primary caretaker, usually the mother, would go to a laboratory setting and go through a series of short separations and reunions. In addition to separations and reunions, the children would interact with a researcher who was a stranger to them. This series of events, being separated from the primary caregiver, exposed to a novel person, and reuniting with the primary caregiver, tested children's approach to the parent as a secure base (see Table 11.2). The findings from this clever research design have been remarkable. What was found, in part, was that children tend to group into one of the following four attachment styles.

Table 11.2   Overview of the Strange Situation Task

Sequence	Duration	Activity
1	1 min	Introduction to room: parent, child
2	3 min	Explore time: child encouraged to explore room
3	3 min	Stranger 1: stranger (researcher) introduced by entering the room and attempting to play with the child during the last minute
4	3 min	Separation 1: parent leaves the room, child is left in the room with researcher
5	3 min	Reunion 1: parent returns, researcher leaves the room
6	3 min	Separation 2: parent leaves child in room alone
7	3 min	Stranger 2: researcher enters the room and stays with child only interacting with child if necessary
8	3 min	Reunion 2: parent returns, researcher leaves

Source: Based on George & Solomon (2008).

1. **Secure.** This child uses the mother as a secure base while in physical proximity. The child may examine and explore the environment and gradually stretch his range of exploration. When the mother separates, the child shows signs of missing the mother as evidenced by distress and scanning for her. Upon reunion, the child seeks the parent with a sense of relief and happiness; once comforted, the child is likely to continue exploring.

2. **Anxious-avoidant.** This child readily explores the environment taking little notice of her mother while in physical proximity. Upon separation, the child shows minimal distress. Upon reunion, the child avoids the parent, moves away, and focuses on environmental objects rather than her parent. If the mother attempts to pick the child up, the child is likely to lean away or go back to toys.

3. **Ambivalent or resistant.** This child is notably distressed and does not explore while in physical proximity of his mother. Rather, the child is clingy and dependent upon the parent for emotional regulation. Separation is marked by distress. The reunion is often confused, with some bids for contact with his mother and rejections of his mother. After separation, the child is not comforted by his mother's return.

4. **Disorganized.** This child is not easily classified in these three attachment classification types. Rather, the child seems to lack a goal with regard to her parent.

Where does "attachment" come from? Ainsworth and other researchers (George & Solomon, 2008) linked four highly intercorrelated parental behaviors to children' attachment classification. The parental behaviors were the following:

- **Sensitivity.** The parent is responsiveness to children's signals in a timely (prompt) and accurate manner. By accurate we mean that the parent tunes into children's real needs and provides an effective response. For example, a hungry child receives food and a sleepy child is encouraged to sleep.

- **Acceptance.** The child is accepted for who she is without much criticism or contempt.

- **Cooperation.** The parent and child enjoy a relationship characterized by getting along; however, the parent is child centered and meets the child's needs.
- **Psychological accessibility.** The parent is available to the child in a predictable manner.

Of interest, mothers who rated high on sensitivity, acceptance, cooperation, and psychological accessibility tended to have children with secure attachments. Mothers of avoidant children tended to provide their children with little positive experience and were often rejecting or critical of their child. Children with an ambivalent attachment pattern often had mothers who were inconsistent and unresponsive to their needs. Attachment classification is believed to have long-lasting implications for children. Indeed, some theories suggest that the quality of parenting is directly linked to a child's internal working model of the social world (Wallin, 2007).

Children's Internal Working Models

The quality of a child's attachment is believed to lay the foundation for how children view the world (Bretherton & Munholland, 2008). A child who is provided with a safe, consistent, and supportive relationship is expected to view the world in a similar manner. Essentially, because a child experienced a safe world, he or she will expect a safe world. By contrast, a child who does not feel supported, who is criticized, and who does not enjoy the support of his or her parent is likely to view the world as dangerous and unsafe (Wallin, 2007). In this regard, Lundahl, Bettmann, Hurtado, and Goldsmith (2013) recently published a report on a study examining children's internal working models. The study included two groups of children: an "at-risk" population and a "normal" population. The at-risk population had parents who struggled with finances and employment and who reported high amounts of stress in the parenting role. By contrast, the parents in the normal condition viewed parenting as manageable and enjoyable and tended to have access to adequate resources. Children in both groups were asked to view a series of pictures, which depicted rather ambiguous situations of a child interacting with other children or with adults. After viewing each picture, the child was asked to construct a story about

Assess your comprehension of Influences on Children by completing this quiz.

what they saw in the picture. Of note, the at-risk children tended to report themes that involved hostility and a lack of safety relative to the not-at-risk children. This finding is consistent with other research that suggests that the way children take in and process information is partly a function of the relationship foundation they were given during early childhood (Fonagy, Gergely, Jurist, & Target, 2005).

Parenting and Child Socialization

Child socialization refers to a dynamic process that prepares children to function adequately in the adult world. Adequate preparation includes the acquisition of "habits, skills, values, and motives that will enable them to (a) avoid deviant behavior ... (b) ... support self and family ... (c) ... form and sustain close relationships ... and (d) be able to rear children in their turn" (Maccoby, 1992, p. 1006). Others have defined effective socialization as "taking over the values and attitudes of society as one's own so that socially acceptable behavior is motivated not by anticipation of external consequences but by intrinsic or internal factors" (Grusec & Goodnow, 1994, p. 4).

There are many socializing forces in a child's life. For example, family, peers, neighborhood influences, and school are linked to child socialization (see Kochanska, 1995; Kuczynski, Marshall, & Schell, 1997; Maccoby, 2002; Patterson, Reid, & Dishion, 1992). During early childhood, parents are considered to be the most influential socializing agent because of children's intense reliance on parents (Maccoby, 1992). Although the mechanisms by which parenting behaviors influence child socialization are debated (Darling & Steinberg, 1993; Grolnick, Deci, & Ryan, 1997; Grusec & Goodnow, 1994; Grusec, Goodnow, & Kuczynski, 2000), the impact parents have on their children has been well documented (Maccoby, 1992).

Many components of parenting have been investigated in relation to child socialization. Reviews on key family characteristics associated with child socialization outlined five broad sources of influence, including (1) child socialization strategies or parenting behaviors, (2) the child-rearing environment, (3) parental characteristics, (4) the quality of the marital relationship, and (5) demographic factors (Lytton, 1990; Mason & Frick, 1994). Of these five characteristics, parenting behavior and the child-rearing environment are believed to be most important because they are what the child experiences most directly (Campbell, 1997; Darling & Steinberg, 1993; Deater-Deckard & Dodge, 1997; Grusec & Goodnow, 1994; Gutman & Eccles, 1999; Rutter et al., 1996; Wahler, 1997).

Parents are a strong influence on children's psychological and emotional development.

Parenting behavior and the child-rearing environment have generally been studied from either a molecular (parenting practices) or a molar (parenting styles) perspective (Darling & Steinberg, 1993). While both levels of analyses are helpful, parenting styles are generally used in research because they incorporate many parenting practices that likely have the same function and thus promote a certain child-socializing context. Furthermore, using parenting styles as the unit of analysis has generally proven more effective in predicting child outcomes (Darling, 1999). Parenting practices and styles, however, are not equivalent constructs and likely act in concert to influence child development. Parenting style is believed to provide an emotional climate that influences children's willingness to be socialized by specific parenting practices (Darling & Steinberg, 1993; Grusec & Goodnow, 1994).

Parenting style can be described along many dimensions (Grolnick & Ryan, 1989) in which the parent supports autonomy, offers support, provides warmth, and provides consistency, as well as providing expectations for their children, the style of relating and managing children's behaviors, and the intensity level of parental behavior (Barber, 1996; Grolnick & Ryan, 1989; Maccoby, 1992). Current depictions of parenting style generally refer to the seminal work of Diana Baumrind (for a review, see Maccoby, 1992) who examined how parents attempt to control or guide their children. She proposed that parental control is a function of parents' responsiveness to children's needs (acceptance, involvement, warmth) and demandingness/control (expectations, standards, consistency).

Based on Baumrind's work, Maccoby and Martin (1983) suggested four parenting styles that could be defined depending on whether parents are high and/or low in responsiveness and demandingness. Parents characterized as being high in responsiveness and demandingness were labeled as *authoritative*, while those low in both dimensions were labeled as *neglectful*. Parents high in responsiveness and low in demandingness were labeled as *indulgent*, while those low in responsiveness and high in demandingness were labeled as *authoritarian*. (See also Chapter 14 for more information on parenting styles.)

Research has consistently found that children raised in an authoritative-like environment fare at least as well as, or have an advantage over, children raised in environments characterized by the other three parenting styles. This advantage has been found in domains such as social competence, academic performance, internalization of societal rules, and mental health (Darling, 1999; Lamborn, Mounts, Steinberg, & Dornbusch, 1991; Shaw et al., 1998; Steinberg, Lamborn, Darling, Mounts, & Dornbusch, 1994). In contrast, children raised in an uninvolved or neglectfully permissive environment generally fare most poorly across the same domains (Glasgow, Dornbusch, Troyer, Steinberg, & Ritter, 1997; Lamborn et al., 1991). Parenting styles, however, do not influence all socialization outcomes in a similar manner. For example, adolescents raised in a predominately authoritarian environment tend not to have behavioral problems, such as drug abuse, while those raised in a predominately indulgent environment are likely to develop good social skills but have behavioral problems (Lamborn et al., 1991). Although considerable research has demonstrated that the benefits of an authoritative rearing style are partially culturally bound (Chao, 2001; Huntsinger, Jose, & Larson, 1998; Leung, Lau, & Lam, 1998), European American children exposed to an environment high in authoritative-like qualities are likely to be more self-regulated and better adjusted socially and behaviorally.

Given the general socialization advantage provided in an authoritative child-rearing environment, considerable research has examined the properties of this style. Authoritative parenting is characterized by "a constellation of parent attributes that includes emotional support, high standards, appropriate autonomy granting, and clear, bidirectional communications" (Darling & Steinberg, 1993, p. 487). Furthermore, although authoritativeness is characterized by high behavioral control (expressed expectations, demandingness), it is low in psychological control and power assertion (love withdrawal, guilt induction, threats, criticism, shaming; Barber, 1996; Grusec et al., 2000) and high in the use of reasoning and relationship building (Grusec et al., 2000; Kochanska, 1997). Thus, authoritativeness is characterized by a cooperative parent–child relationship, wherein parents clearly outline high expectations, value children's autonomy, and support their children emotionally (Crockenberg, Jackson, & Langrock, 1996). Although components of the authoritative parenting style have been associated with many child outcomes, we will review only two associations: the approach to academics and compliance with societal rules.

Parenting and Children's Academic Performance

Children are more likely to perform well in school and express a positive approach toward learning if their parents are authoritative (Cooper, Lindsay, & Nye, 2000; Hess, Halloway, Dickson, & Price, 1984; Pomerantz & Eaton, 2001). For example, in a series of studies examining adolescents' academic adjustment and parenting style, Steinberg and colleagues found that adolescents who perceived their parents to be authoritative enjoyed greater academic confidence, were more academically oriented, and were better behaved in school than children who perceived their parents to be authoritarian, indulgent, or neglectful (Steinberg, Elmen, & Mounts, 1989; Steinberg, Lamborn, Dornbusch, & Darling, 1992). Importantly, data from a longitudinal study conducted by Steinberg et al. (1994) suggest adolescents' perceptions of their parents' child-rearing style predict school performance across time. Compared to adolescents raised in an authoritative environment, those who reported a neglectful family environment, and to a lesser degree, those who reported authoritarian and indulgent environments, showed decreases in optimal school orientation and competence across a 12-month span. These studies show that parenting practices early in a child's life have an impact in school performance well into adolescence.

Others researchers have found similar results. Ginsburg and Bronstein (1993), for example, examined the influence parents' in-home behavior and attitudes toward managing their fifth grade children's learning activities had on the children's grade point average, achievement, and approach to learning (based on child and teacher reports). Children of parents who were authoritative in nature performed better in school and possessed more intrinsic motivation toward learning. In another study, children who were judged by their teachers to have high competence, high self-regulation, and good behavioral adjustment were more likely to have parents who both supported their autonomy and avoided using controlling techniques (Grolnick & Ryan, 1989). These same authors also found that maternal structure and involvement were associated with children's increased sense of self-efficacy, competence, behavioral adjustment, and school performance. Just as the positive qualities of the authoritative parenting style have been linked to desirable child outcomes, power assertion—which is associated with the authoritarian parenting style—undermines children's academic and social competence (Barth & Parke, 1993).

Parenting style may also be linked to children's development of intrinsic motivation toward learning. Although there is no direct test, Grolnick, Kurowski, and Gurland (1999) proposed that school-aged children's intrinsic motivation for learning is facilitated when parents support three basic needs children have, namely (1) a sense of competence, (2) a strong parent–child bond, and (3) a sense of autonomy. These authors provide preliminary evidence suggesting that children from families who are structured, consistent, emotionally supportive, and respectful of children's ability to choose are likely to be intrinsically motivated to learn. Of interest, some components of the authoritative parenting style match the basic needs and sociocontextual factors advanced by Grolnick et al. (1999). Specifically, authoritative child-rearing environments are also characterized by interpersonal warmth, responsiveness, autonomy support, and a sense of structure.

The relationship between parenting style and children's academic performance and approach to learning may not be direct. Rather, the authoritative parenting style is believed to increase children's sense of competence, self-efficacy, and ability to regulate their behaviors, all of which are associated with school success (Grolnick et al., 1999). Research by Steinberg et al. (1989) supported this proposition by demonstrating that the relationship between parenting style and adolescents' academic achievement was mediated through adolescents' self-reliance, work attitudes, and identity. Children's approach to learning is influenced by factors beyond the influence of parents; and the direction of influence between parenting style and children's academic performance cannot often be definitively established given the correlational nature of most studies (see Bell & Chapman, 1986; Grolnick & Ryan, 1989). Nevertheless, parenting behaviors do play an important role in children's academic performance and approach to learning (Ginsburg & Bronstein, 1993; Grolnick et al., 1999).

Diversity in Practice

Practice Behavior Example: Recognize the extent to which a culture's structures and values may oppress, marginalize, alienate, or create or enhance privilege and power.

Critical Thinking Question: How might parenting beliefs and practices be influenced by cultural factors such as immigration status, religion, political systems, or geography?

Parenting and Children's Behavior

Similar to research linking parenting practices to children's academic performance and approach to school-like tasks, children's conduct is influenced by parents' behavior. Multiple programs of research have clearly identified that certain parenting practices and child-rearing environments are related to children's behavior (Kuczynski & Kochanska, 1995; Patterson et al., 1992). For example, the work of Patterson and colleagues has demonstrated that children who are frequently exposed to coercive parent–child interactions are more likely to exhibit behavioral problems (Patterson, 1993; Patterson et al., 1992). These researchers have shown that "basic training" for antisocial behavior in the home is primarily a function of escape-avoidant conditioning, wherein the child is inadvertently negatively reinforced for coercive behavior (e.g., whining, aggressive acts). They have also demonstrated that punitive and aggressive parenting practices are associated with higher rates of disruptive child behaviors, including children's use of aggression (Frick et al., 1993; Stormshak, Bierman, McMahon, Lenguna, & CPPRG, 2000; Sutton, Cowen, Crean, & Wyman, 1999).

Clinical Corner

Young children are often referred to social workers because of the exhibit behaviors such as refusing to do what is asked of them, whining and complaining when they do not get what they want, and using verbal or physical aggression toward others to get their way. What is to be done? To begin, parents often accidently reinforce these very behaviors—even though such behaviors are annoying, bothersome, and embarrassing. While not always the case, the following pattern of interaction between child and parent is fairly typical among children who have behavioral problems. Figure 11.1 is adapted from the work of Patterson (1993) and his research lab.

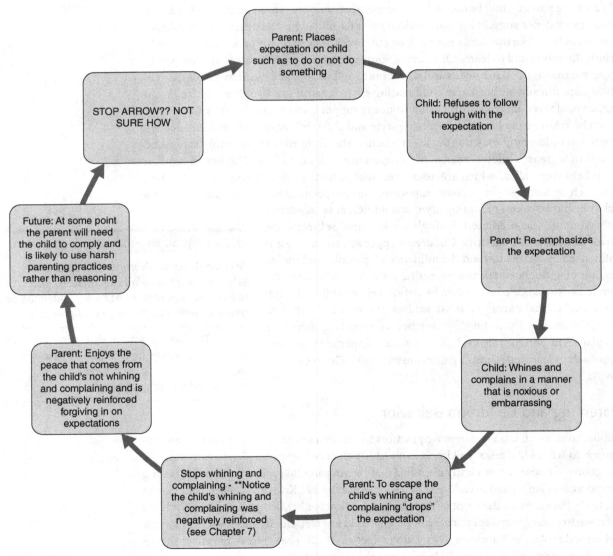

Figure 11.1
Reinforcing (Inadvertently) Child Misbehavior
Source: Adapted from Patterson (1993).

The matching of parenting practices to children's needs and wants, known as *synchrony*, is also an important influence on children's behavioral development. Wahler (1997), for example, proposed that the source of conduct problems is asynchronous or noncontingent parenting—that is, the failure to reinforce prosocial child behaviors while reinforcing, often unintentionally, aversive child behaviors. Noncontingent parenting is proposed to increase parent–child conflict, similar to Patterson's basic training model, which leaves children feeling confused and anxious (Westerman, 1990). To avoid anxious feelings, Wahler (1997) proposed that children engage in increasingly coercive and hostile behaviors that tend to evoke predictable, though harsh, behaviors from caretakers. Have you ever heard the following "folk wisdom" about children: "kids prefer negative attention to no attention"? Research supports this position. Essentially, children of parents who tend to be neglectful may push their parents' buttons to draw interaction time—even if it is negative. For example, a child may tease her sibling to the point of the sibling crying, which then draws attention from a parent.

In addition to child management practices or parenting behaviors, the child-rearing environment is linked to the development of conduct problems (Kochanska, 1997; Kuczynski & Kochanska, 1995; Parpal & Maccoby, 1985; Wakschlag & Hans, 1999). A landmark study conducted by Parpal and Maccoby (1985) demonstrated that high levels of parental attentiveness to children's behaviors increased children's prosocial behaviors. When children and parents enjoy a sense of mutual cooperation and shared positive emotion, children are more likely to adopt parental values and comply with parental requests (Kochanska, Aksan, & Koenig, 1995). Also, a positive parent–child relationship is theorized to keep children in proximity to the parent, allowing for more socializing opportunities (Grusec & Goodnow, 1994; Wahler, Castellani, Smith, & Keathley, 1996). The lack of parental warmth and involvement has also been shown to predict externalizing behaviors (Lindsay, Mize, & Pettit, 1997; Stormshak et al., 2000). For example, unresponsiveness and maternal rejection are related to conduct problems in boys (Mann & MacKenzie, 1996; Shaw, Keenan, & Vondra, 1994; Shaw et al., 1998). Although a responsive environment is generally associated with improved child behaviors, a responsive environment that is also characterized by permissiveness or noncontingent parenting may support conduct problem development in children (Chamberlain & Patterson, 1995). For example, inadequate parental supervision has been linked to conduct problems possibly because unsupervised children learn problematic behaviors from deviant peers (Patterson, 1986).

Remember, the term *socialization* refers to the degree to which children adopt or internalize widely held societal values. Societies universally value principles such as honesty, commitment, strong work ethic, kindness, and fairness. The degree to which children adopt or internalize such values is also related to parenting practices. Specifically, the degree to which children internalize such values is promoted by environments characterized by mutual responsiveness between parents and children, parents' reliance on reasoning to teach children versus a reliance on force or coercion, and parent–child synchrony as was previously mentioned (Grolnick et al., 1997; Grusec & Goodnow, 1994; Kochanska, 1997; Kuczynski et al., 1997). Such environments are believed to lead children to internalize such values because they can autonomously chose to integrate the values rather than acting out of fear of punishment or promise of a reward. Said differently, if a child adopts only society's expectations out of the hope of obtaining a reward or avoiding a punishment, the child may give up on the value when the "stick" or "carrot" is removed.

Assess your comprehension of Child Socialization by completing this quiz.

Cognitive and Emotional Influences of Parenting Behavior

Because parenting behavior has been shown to influence children's socialization, researchers are interested in understanding what determines (influences) parents' behavior. One influential model of the determinants of parenting behavior proposes three central influences on parental action: (1) environmental factors such as access to resources, stress, quality of a parent's social network, and primary relationships, (2) the parent's psychological characteristics such as patience, values, intelligence, and confidence, and (3) the child's characteristics such as temperament, likeability, and health (Belsky, 1984). However, not all influences on parenting behavior are equal. Belsky and others (Abidin, 1992; Bugental, Blue, & Lewis, 1990) argue parents' psychological makeup and resources are the most influential factors in determining parent behavior because they mediate contextual and child effects. For example, a very "evolved" parent who is patient, calm, and secure with herself will likely be less affected by a difficult child than a parent who is young, insecure, and emotionally unstable. In this example, the "evolved" parent would be expected to behavior in a more child-centered manner than the parent who has more struggles.

Many psychological constructs have been studied in relation to parenting behavior. Among others, parents' personality (Friedrich, Tyler, & Clark, 1985), developmental history (Belsky, 1993), and the presence of psychopathology (Kochanska, Kuczynski, & Maguire, 1989; Lovejoy, Graczyk, O'Hare, & Neuman, 2000) have been linked to parenting behavior. How parents' think about others and parents' emotional maturity are believed to contribute strongly to parental action because they can help parents be more child centered especially during difficult times (Bank, Forgatch, Patterson, & Fetrow, 1993; Bugental et al., 1990; Dix, 1991; Pinderhughes, Dodge, Bates, Pettit, & Zelli, 2000). Understandably, the relationship between parents' thoughts about children, their emotional maturity in general and particular emotional state (such as anger or pride) at the moment of parenting, and parenting behavior is complex and multifaceted.

Clinical Corner

Raising Special Needs Children

As a member of the human family and as a social worker, you will inevitably interact with parents raising a child with a physical, genetic, emotional, or mental disability or struggle. If you do so in your role as a social worker, it is good to keep several ideas in mind. To begin, parents of special needs children love and care for their children deeply. In fact, the amount of attention demanded by children with a special need or disability can create a strong bond between the parent and the child. At the same time, children with special needs place an extra "dose" of stress and demand on parents, which can be associated with mental health problems such as discouragement, guilt, frustration, and resentment in parents (Benzies et al., 2011; Vinayak & Sekhon, 2012). Such stress may be partially responsible for the higher than average divorce rate, as much as 100% higher among some groups, when there is a child with a disability (Hartley et al., 2010).

Parents of children with special needs often feel conflicted and guilty because while they want the best for their child, they often find themselves becoming frustrated with a child's disability—a factor that can fuel even more guilt as parents know they should not be frustrated by something their child cannot control. Further, parents of children with a disability often have to reconsider the dreams and hopes they have for their children. One highly educated parent (a physician) of a child with a serious form of mental retardation took no comfort when she was told that her mentally retarded daughter might be able to work at a fast-food chain.

Fortunately, there are many community supports for parents raising children with special needs. For example, a Google search with the following words "support group parents of autistic children" revealed many support opportunities. Further, effective clinical interventions and education are also available (see Sofronoff. Jahnel, & Sanders, 2011, as an example), which is a "win-win" situation because both parents and children benefit.

Social Information Processing Perspectives to Understand Parental Behavior

Several models have outlined the proposed relationships between parents' social cognitions, emotions, and behaviors. Dix and colleagues (Dix & Grusec, 1985; Dix & Lochman, 1990), for example, proposed a three-step cognitive-emotional model that maps parents' social cognitions during parent–child interactions. During these interactions, parents are believed to:

1. Perceive and interpret child-related information

2. Form beliefs about the child's responsibility, intentions, and disposition in any given interaction, which then influences parents' emotions toward their child

3. Consider parenting choices

In general, Dix and associates and others (Geller & Johnston, 1995) have found that when parents believe children's negative behaviors are intentional and under the children's control, they are likely to feel upset and respond with greater forcefulness.

In another model that examines the relationship between parents' attributions, emotions, and behavioral responses to children, Bugental and colleagues (Bugental, Blue, & Cruzcosa, 1989; Bugental et al., 1990) examine the intersection of parental beliefs along three dimensions: social locus (self, other), controllability (controllable, uncontrollable), and valence (good, bad). Parents are expected to be emotionally and behaviorally reactive to children's negative behaviors when they perceive they can do little to control their children's behavior and when they perceive children to be intentionally engaging in a negative manner. In a review of Bugental's empirical work, Miller (1995) generally found support for the model's main predictions, namely that parenting beliefs were related to parents' emotions, which was in turn were related to caregiving behavior.

In both of the previously discussed models, parents' social cognitions and emotions interact to influence parent action. When parents believe they have little control over a negative situation—or perceive their children to be deliberately engaging in an undesirable behavior—they are expected to experience negative emotion. Because negative emotion is aversive, parents attempt to quickly regain control through coercive or authoritarian methods. Negative emotion may also undermine optimal child-rearing behaviors because it can decrease parents' tolerance for unpleasant child behaviors, which, as parents know, is rather common (Abidin, 1992; Crnic & Acevedo, 1995; Ritchie & Holden, 1998).

Parenting Goal Perspectives

Parenting goals are linked to parents' thoughts, emotions, and child-rearing behaviors and theoretically play an "executive or organizational role in guiding parenting actions" (Hastings & Grusec, 1998, p. 465). That is, parenting goal perspectives recognize that parents are intentional when interacting with their children. Parents, for example, want their children to do well in school, to be fair and honest, and to be good citizens.

Researchers have conceptualized two forms of parenting goals: (1) parents have *global* socialization goals for their children, such as the desire that children develop and maintain friendships, internalize societal values, and become self-sufficient (Maccoby, 1992) and (2) parents have *discrete* goals during specific parent–child interactions. So, if two parents hope to accomplish different outcomes during interactions with their children, one would expect them to use different methods (Hastings & Grusec, 1998). After conducting a series of studies, these researchers asserted, "goals of parents are identifiable and quantifiable and function as important cognitive determinants of parenting behavior" (p. 476). To realize long-term socialization goals for their children, parents are believed to develop short-term goals during individual parent–child encounters. In this model, then, discrete parent–child goals help parents evaluate whether their child is "on track" with a given socialization goal and assess whether a particular parent behavior would advance or retard their child's progress toward a socialization goal. Rubin and Mills (1992) did not identify different qualities of discrete parental goals; rather, discrete goals function within a set of broader socialization goals.

Other parenting goal perspectives were advanced by Dix (1992) and Hastings and Grusec (1998). These perspectives fundamentally differ from that of Rubin and Mills (1992) in that they propose discrete parenting goals are characterized by the tension between parents' and children's needs. Whereas Rubin proposed discrete parenting goals serve as mileposts that provide information about children's trajectory toward (or away from) a global socialization goal, other goals may focus on immediate outcomes. That is, parents may be primarily interested in meeting either their children's needs *or* their own needs—possibly at the expense of the child's well-being. Conceptualizing parents' discrete goals as serving either the best interest of the parent or the child speaks to the parents' motivation.

Like other social information processing models of parenting, Dix's (1992) goal-regulation model of parenting identifies several stages of information processing. Parents are believed to (1) select goals, implicitly or explicitly, based on possible outcomes (emotional, behavioral) for the child and/or parent, (2) formulate plans and enact behaviors to achieve their selected goals, (3) evaluate the outcomes of their behavior based on situational and child characteristics (child well-being), and (4) experience an emotion after appraising the outcome of the behavior relative to the intended goal. The emotional experience then directs future regulation of parent behavior.

The distinctive contribution Dix made was that he proposed that parents' goals may not all be in the service of advancing a child's socialization process. That is, parents' goals during discrete parent–child interactions may be parent oriented rather than child oriented, which is expected to differentially influence parents' beliefs, emotions, and behaviors as they interact with their child.

Dix (1992) proposed discrete parenting goals can be understood along a dimension of concern. *Self-oriented* goals primarily benefit parents, while *child-oriented* goals primarily benefit children. Dix further organized child-centered goals into *empathic* and *socialization* goals. Empathic goals are "intended to achieve outcomes that children want" while socialization goals "benefit children, but will not necessarily please them" (p. 323). Despite a possible negative connotation associated with the phrase self-oriented goals, Dix notes that self-oriented goals are necessary for parents to function as individuals and as parents, and are a normal part of parental functioning. Self-oriented goals only become problematic when such goals are not balanced by child-oriented goals or when children's socialization needs call for parents to be child oriented yet they remain parent oriented. Dix's model, then, is consistent with current thinking that effective parenting entails the flexible use of a wide variety of child-rearing practices that come into play depending on situational demands, including cultural, child, and parent characteristics (Darling & Steinberg, 1993; Grusec & Goodnow, 1994; Grusec et al., 2000).

Dix (1992) proposed that the adoption of different discrete parental goals leads to differences in how parents feel and act. In general, parents operating from a child-centered orientation, relative to a self-centered orientation, are expected to interact more warmly with their children, to rely more on reason and open communication to solve problems, to be more appropriately involved in their children's activities, and to use fewer power-assertive or punitive disciplinary strategies. Consistent with the emphasis on emotion as a primary contributor to parent behavior, Dix (1991, 1992) proposed that parents' adoption of child-oriented goals is associated with empathy for the child while the adoption of self-oriented goals is related to stress—factors that connect to the perpetration of child abuse, which is discussed later in this chapter.

CHILDREN AND PLAY

Parents are not the only influence on children's development. Children's play, both solitary and social, is important in children's development, socialization, learning, and well-being. Indeed, aside from time spent in school, play is one of the top four activities in which children engage (Harkness et al., 2011). One of the reasons that children spend so much time in play is that it has evolutionary purposes. Specifically, children's play promotes language acquisition and development, strengthens intellectual functioning, builds both social skills and social relationships, decreases stress, and promotes physical aptitude and strength (Xu, 2010). Considering that play promotes children's development is fun—it almost sounds as if play is better than school, right? In all actuality, play is very purposeful and important in human development. Further, play is ubiquitous across cultures (Harkness et al., 2011) and is judged to be an "essential ingredient in early childhood programs" (Xu, 2010, p. 489).

How does play support children's development? According to Vygotsky's theory, development is believed to be like scaffolding such that previously learned material is a foundation for more advanced material (see Holzman, 2008). Through play, children are exposed to modeling and activities that lay a foundation for advanced learning. For example, a young child who is playing with peers may observe older peers state rules such as "It is not nice to hit." Play also forces children out of "ego-centric" thinking. In social play, children must learn to share, regulate impulses, communicate, and take others perspectives to successfully remain in the group or risk rejection. Other types of play give children opportunities to develop skills. For example, a child who uses markers to color learns increased hand-to-eye dexterity, as well as an increased understanding of shading, perspective, and patience.

Researchers (Xu, 2010) have identified several types of play, such as:

- Functional play: repetitive motor activities, such as bouncing a ball, jumping a rope
- Constructive play: building something, such as engaging with blocks, coloring material
- Dramatic play: make-believe activities, such as playing house, creating stories
- Games with rules: playing games that have preset rules, such as checkers, kickball, and soccer
- Social play: interacting with others, often in dramatic play or in games with rules

Children tend to go through stages of play that require less-to-more social interaction. That is, a play taxonomy has been developed

Human Behavior

Practice Behavior Example: Know about human behavior across the life course; the range of social systems in which people live; and the ways social systems promote or deter people in maintaining or achieving health and well-being.

Critical Thinking Question: How important are parenting behaviors in influencing human functioning and how can social workers influence parenting behaviors through micro- and macro-level interventions?

Play provides enjoyment and instruction at the same moment.

Golden Pixels LLC/Shutterstock

(we realize the "irony" of having a taxonomy for play). Specifically, in 1932, Mildred Parten (Dyer & Moneta, 2006) proposed children engage in six types of play—with three of them having strong social components:

1. Unoccupied play: child is not actually playing, may be observing others or sitting quietly

2. Solitary play: child is not socially engaged while playing on his or her own

3. Onlooker: child watches others play while not engaging directly in play

4. Parallel play: children play next to each other, but not with each other

5. Associative play: children interact with each other though not in an organized, themed manner; here, children share, borrow, lend but without a theme

6. Cooperative play: children coordinate play through direct engagement with others with a theme or organized activity (e.g., playing in a game with preestablished or developed rules)

Which variables may influence children's social play behavior? Research is mixed on the impact of both gender and socioeconomic status (SES). Some research suggests that children of a lower SES would engage in less "sociodramatic play," which includes sharing and lending (associative play) than children of higher SES. However, the results are mixed (Dyer & Moneta, 2006). Similarly, males and females tend to engage in parallel, associative, and cooperative play in rates similar to each other. Earlier hypotheses posited that children from disadvantaged backgrounds may not have the modeling or resources to engage in as much cooperative play—a factor that may further disadvantage them as play is seen as a method to learn how to cooperate in areas such as education and the workforce (Parten, 1933).

Watch the video Play in Early Childhood. What are some of the functions of play across a child's life? Make a case that social work should invest in children's play.

Of course, not all play is social play. Research has found that gender stereotypes are both demonstrated in children's play and influence children's play. That is, when children are roughly between 18 and 20 months of age, they begin selecting toys based on the "genderization" of the toy. Boys will prefer traditionally masculine toys (trucks, guns), whereas girls will prefer traditionally feminine toys (doll, dress ups). The impact of gender or sex-stereotyping toys can be dramatic, as children begin to associate certain life roles based on play. For example, girls should be caretakers and boys should be protectors (Cherney & Dempsey, 2010). The rigidity by which gender roles are assigned to certain play activities varies across age. There seems to be increased flexibility prior to 2 years of age, followed by increasing rigidity until about 5 to 7 years of age, increased flexibility again during middle childhood, and a return to rigidity during adolescence (Cherney & Dempsey, 2010). To put it another way, a teenage boy may be more worried than an early elementary school-aged student about engaging in ballet as a sport, rather than baseball.

How do toys and different play activities become stereotyped as belonging to one gender or another? Evidence suggests that prenatal levels of maternal testosterone and androgen influence children's engagement in types of play (Burton, Henninger, Hafetz, & Cofer, 2009). For example, higher levels of testosterone are associated with higher levels of rough-and-tumble play. Females with unusually high prenatal levels of androgen (specifically, congenital adrenal hyperplasia [CAH]) engage in more aggressive forms of play and social interaction. However, biological influences do not work alone to influence play preferences. Children are also "taught" to play along gender-stereotyped lines. Boys are criticized or discouraged from playing in traditionally female activities and females are discouraged from playing in traditionally male activities. Our strong guess is that you have been exposed to gender-stereotyped information about play and have also perpetuated such stereotypes at some point in your life. What color should the outfit be for a newborn? Pink is for girls and blue for boys, right? Well, this tradition is passed on by hospitals, family, friends, business, and the media.

Another determinant of play is the availability of play equipment. Farley, Meriwether, Baker, Rice, and Webber (2008) found that playground and schoolyard environments influence play behaviors of young school-aged children. Specifically, they found that children congregated in areas with "fixed play equipment" such as swings, slides, basketball standards, and monkey bars. Further, the proportion of such equipment tends to be linked to physical activity. That is, higher numbers of fixed play equipment promotes physical activity. Simple fields or asphalted areas were found to be poor in attracting children to play. What are some social work implications of this finding?

PHYSICAL HEALTH AND CHILDHOOD

Like so many of the subjects covered in this book, there is not enough space to cover all that needs to be said about childhood and physical health. As you think about these two factors, what comes to mind? To us, we think that young children are lucky—they don't have to think about physical health too much. The undesired processes of aging are not readily acting on children. That is, young children rarely think of physical problems such as wrinkles, gaining weight, losing strength, decreased stamina, lowered metabolism, problems with vision, and increased likelihood of physical illness such as strokes, cancer, or heart attacks. Indeed, most children enjoy good physical health. Unfortunately, children do struggle with issues related to physical health. Some of these issues are beyond our control, such as cancer or type 1 diabetes. Other physical health issues in childhood can be influenced, such as accidents and poor nutrition.

Like other phenomena discussed in this book, physical health acts as both an independent and a dependent variable. Let's first look at how physical health influences children's experiences as an independent variable. Consider the case of cancer. Surviving cancer is wonderful, but it is not the end of the story (Paxton et al., 2010). Child survivors of cancer report lowered levels of social, physical, mental, and emotional functioning compared to their peers. Paxton and colleagues report the following sobering statistics.

Children who survive cancers (e.g., leukemia, lymphoma) are:

- 1.7 times more likely than siblings to engage in antisocial behaviors
- 1.5 times more likely than siblings to suffer from depression and anxiety
- 3.0 times more likely than siblings to report other problems with physical functioning
- 2.0 times more likely than siblings to report disabilities
- Roughly 50% of childhood survivors of cancer report neurocognitive deficits

Fortunately, there is some evidence to suggest that these unwanted "side effects" of cancer can be minimized through long-term engagement in physical activity (Paxton et al., 2010).

Consider the impact of other physical problems on quality of life indicators found within National Child Development Study (NCDS) conducted in Great Britain that followed 17,634 babies from birth until 50 years of age (Goodman, Joyce, & Smith, 2011). Physical problems beginning in childhood such as epilepsy, speech and hearing deficits, visual problems, diabetes, and asthma influenced children throughout their lifetime. Certainly, the degree of physical problems in childhood was correlated with degree of problems later in life. For example, children born with a very low birth weight can reliably be expected to earn less money into adulthood. Further, children with hearing or visual problems were negatively affected by these conditions in terms of earning power and ability to function in the adult world.

Of interest, the greatest predictor of "trouble" into adulthood from childhood health comes from psychological problems (e.g., mood or behavioral problems). Children of parents who reported that their children had high levels of emotional or psychological problems earned 14% to 28% less money in adulthood compared to children without emotional problems (Goodman et al., 2011). While difficult to tease out the reasons, children with emotional and behavioral problems also had greater difficulty staying in stable, committed relationships and keeping a job. Further, children with emotional or behavioral difficulties were shown to have lower success in upward social and economic mobility.

If physical and emotional health in childhood casts a long shadow into adulthood, what factors predict childhood health? As can be expected, there are multiple influences on children's health. Genetics influences factors such as activity level, transmission of risk to develop health problems, and body weight. Child abuse is also directly linked to children's health. The *Journal of Pediatric Psychology* dedicated a special edition to the impact of child abuse on physical health (Noll & Shenk, 2010). Some of the key findings are as follows.

Child sexual abuse is significantly and reliably linked to increased problems in the following physical areas: general health, pain, gastrointestinal problems, gynecologic symptoms, obesity, and cardiopulmonary symptoms (Irish, Kobayashi, & Delahanty, 2010). Child sexual abuse was also linked to increased likelihood that children would engage in risky sexual behaviors, which can have dramatic and deadly health implications (Houck, Nugent, Lescano, Peters, & Brown, 2010). Child maltreatment is linked to a significantly increased risk of smoking cigarettes; specifically, a 58.3% increased risk of daily smoking (Topitzes, Mersky, & Reynolds, 2010). Clark, Thatcher, and Martin (2010) reported that the degree of child abuse was significantly related to multiple health problems measured into adulthood. They note that abuse is linked to stress, which is subsequently linked to health problems. Children exposed to higher levels of abuse were at greater risk for developing general health problems, sleeping and eating problems, neurological functioning, pain in muscles and joints, abdominal problems, urinary problems, problems with skin and bleeding, increased blood pressure, and higher body mass indices.

Further studies show that children who are abused or neglected are much more likely to be admitted to hospitals for problems such as asthma, infectious diseases, and cardiovascular and respiratory issues (Lanier, Jonson-Reid, Stahlschmidt, Drake, & Constantino, 2010). Another unfortunate finding is that neglected children are about two to three times more likely to be obese than their counterparts (Knutson, Taber, Murray, Valles, & Koeppl, 2010). Children in foster care, often resulting from some form of abuse, were reported to have greater problems with stress, developmental delays, and eating problems (Oswald, Heil, & Goldbeck, 2010).

In sum, child abuse is clearly linked to increased physical problems for children at the point of abuse or neglect and into adulthood. Child abuse appears to increase risk factors, such as increased stress (which suppresses immune system functioning and promotes other risky health behaviors such as smoking). The adage "the rich get richer and the poor get poorer" seems to also apply to children of abuse and neglect. They are more likely to experience physical problems, which are more likely to undermine well-being in psychological, social, economic, and familial areas. Clearly, these results show how a vulnerable population is made more and more vulnerable (MacMillan, 2010). What can be done about child abuse and neglect? Chapter 16 deals with ideas on how social work can work to prevent child abuse and neglect.

Assess your analysis and evaluation of this chapter's contents by completing the Chapter Review.

12

Colin Bennett/Alamy

Major Life Phases Influencing Human Behavior

Adolescence

Adolescence is a time for the exploration of encompassing domains such as attitudes and values and societal roles and norms, and gives teens opportunity to adopt new behaviors and definitions of oneself (Forthun, Montgomery, & Bell, 2006). The goal during adolescent development is to help teens become competent in various sectors of their lives: intellectually, physically, emotionally, socially, and morally. Fortunately, most adolescents survive this stage of life and go on to successful roles as spouses, parents, employee, or employer. Many give back much to their communities as adults and make a lasting contribution to society. Our goal in this chapter is to look more closely at the challenges that accompany adolescence and explore those that social workers will likely encounter in practice.

As most of us know, the adolescence life phase can be problematic as one begins a struggle for identity. In the process, many adolescents engage in behaviors at odds with parental and social expectations. Mostly, these aberrations carry no adverse consequences and may be just a normal part of growing up. In some cases, neither parents nor other societal institutions know of the problem behavior. Some instances are simply written off as youthful indiscretions with no serious sanctions. At other times, the behavior is identified as significantly out of the norm and adolescents may find themselves involved in the juvenile justice system, remedial services, or therapeutic interventions. Some adolescents experience all three

Adolescence is a risk period for beginning use of drugs.

systems. Whether one faces consequences often is a matter of luck as well as the reactions of others.

It is important to keep in mind that adolescence is a period of growth, development, experimentation, and exploration ultimately designed to create a healthy identity. It is also a time to prepare for adulthood through educational pursuits, building relationships, and overcoming the risks associated with adolescence. In the next section, we will look at the process of developing a healthy and positive identity.

IDENTITY

Erik Erikson (1972) argued that the formation of one's identity is the most significant developmental task experienced by adolescents. The development of a stable identity typically occurs after a period characterized by introspection and reconsideration during which adolescents evaluate themselves. The period is also associated with varying degrees of commitment to one's identity. Adolescents are trying to answer questions such as "Who am I?" "What do I want to become?" and "Where do I fit in society?" (Forthun et al., 2006, p. 142). These queries may be voiced or mulled over in one's conscience but they characterize the challenges youth face. The identity formation process is not necessarily one of progressive change; it is associated with brief periods of regression, progression, and stability that occur; it is debated, in early or later adolescence (Meeus, Iedema, Heisen, & Vollebergh, 1999; Waterman, 1982). A mature identity, according to Ferrer-Wreder, Palchuk, Poyrazli, Small, and Domitrovich (2008), exhibits the following characteristics:

- self-selected rather than imposed by parents or others
- unified
- competent
- prosocial

A healthy identity is most closely associated with lower levels of delinquent behavior, behavior problems, substance abuse and sexual behavior, and higher academic achievement levels.

In Chapter 8, we discussed the importance of attachment to individual development. Attachment to one's parents also plays a role during adolescent identity formation (Rice, 1990). A solid relationship with parents is associated with the capacity to adapt to new and unfamiliar challenges that face adolescents. Rice concluded that "adolescents and young adults who report secure, trusting attachment relationships with their parents also report high levels of social competence, general life satisfaction, and somewhat higher levels of self-esteem" (p. 525).

We previously indicated that boys and girls mature at different rates, with females having the edge through late adolescence (Klimstra, Hale, Raaijmakers, Branje, & Meeus, 2010). Girls are also more likely to engage in introspection regarding their identities, a self-reflective characteristic that also tends to be higher among women (Burwell & Shirk, 2007). At the same time, girls are much less likely to change their identities, largely because they are so intricately intertwined with their social networks.

Not all adolescents resolve this phase with a prosocial identity. Many develop identities alien to society or adopt antisocial behaviors that further estrange them from their environments. Both family members and peers play a role in an adolescent's identity development. To the extent that adolescents come to the attention of agencies of social control—such as law enforcement, social welfare institutions, or mental health services—they are likely to end up in settings designed to reorient their identities. Treatment programs for troubled adolescents, juvenile detention programs, and group homes exist, in part, to change the direction of a problematic identity and behaviors associated with it.

PREPARING FOR ADULTHOOD

Preparing for adulthood is the sine qua non of adolescence. Adolescence is a period where an individual completes a significant amount of education, often in preparation for more advanced educational achievement in college or in some specialized training program. This period offers adolescents an opportunity to test out behaviors, ways of interacting, and an opportunity to consider what the future holds for them. Perhaps the most important preparation for adulthood involves developing life skills that will aid in transitioning out of adolescence. Life skills include abilities such as managing money and developing a work ethic that supports success in academic and employment pursuits. Adolescents need to learn how to use a checkbook, balance it, develop a budget, and handle credit cards. The latter is critical for young adults who do not understand the ramifications of high credit card fees and make only the minimum monthly payments. Learning to save a portion of whatever income they receive is yet another important skill.

Those employed during adolescence learn responsibility to employers and interpersonal skills in dealing with other workers, supervisors, and the public. They also learn to handle disappointments, problem solve, and have the chance to make mistakes. Mistakes tend to be good teaching tools, though the learning process is sometimes painful. All these experiences prepare youth for adulthood as each foreshadows challenges associated with growing up.

Preparation for employment, or further training and education, is part of planning for adulthood. While a high school education is economically essential, additional preparation for future employment should be emphasized. Though adolescents may now consider a part-time job well paying, it will not look adequate when they begin adult life.

Another life skill involves caring for one's self and outgrowing dependence on parents by learning how to clean and maintain clothing, shop for groceries, prepare meals, and maintain a healthy and sanitary life space. This doesn't mean that adolescents should stop relying on parents completely. Knowing that parents and other adults can still be counted on when needed is part of learning when and how to use resources. Other resources that adolescents need to be familiar with are how to obtain a driver's license, register to vote, and locate and secure important documents and records, such as one's birth certificate, social security card, and immunization records (New York Administration for Children's Services [NYACS], 2006).

As a critical part of the adolescent's life, parents can facilitate or impede an adolescent's acquisition of life skills. Adolescents who are encouraged to help prepare meals, complete chores, and do the laundry also develop the self-esteem that comes with such skills. Parents assist by reinforcing the adolescent's accomplishments, providing information, teaching skills, and being supportive while setting appropriate expectations, guidance, and standards (Hunter College School of Social Work, 2007). On the other hand, parents who oversee every aspect of their adolescents' lives deprive them of great learning opportunities.

Did You Know?

Suicide is the third leading cause of death for 15- to 24-year-olds. It is also the sixth leading cause of death for those ages 5 to 14.

Overly close monitoring can undermine the adolescence's self-esteem and suggest parents do not think the youth competent.

Another life skill comes from understanding sexuality and taking responsibility for one's sexual behavior. Adolescent sexuality remains an area in which most teens frequently desire more information and many parents would prefer that someone else do the teaching (Kaiser Family Foundation/ABC Television, 1998). Despite the awkwardness that both teens and parents may feel about sex-related conversations, the fact is that most teens do get information about sexuality from their parents. Figures 12.1 and 12.2 identify the percentage of teenagers receiving formal sex education by topic, when the

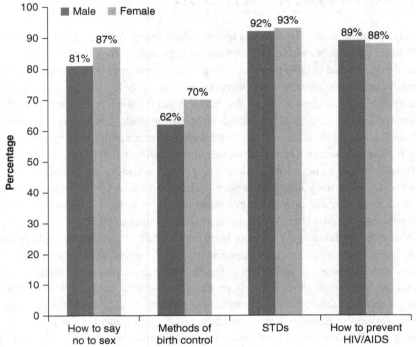

Figure 12.1
Teenagers 15 to 19 Who Received Formal Sex Education by Topic and Sex: United States, 2006–2008
Source: CDC/NCHS (2009).

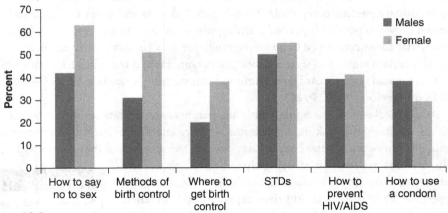

Figure 12.2
Teenagers 15 to 19 Who Talked With a Parent About Sex Education by Topic and Sex
Source: CDC/NCHS (2009).

formal education occurred, and the percentage of teens receiving various kinds of information from their parents.

In Figure 12.2, we see at what age teens learned about sexuality from their parents and the type of information provided (CDC/NCHS, 2009).

As we see, children can and should begin to learn about sexuality well before they become teenagers. A part of sexuality education should include information about STDs and HIV risks associated with various sexual activities, as well as the emotional consequences that frequently accompany sexual intimacy. Despite agreement between parents and teens about the value of sex education, 30% of teenage males do not receive any sexuality education before their first intercourse. For Black male teens, the rate of not receiving instruction is 45% (Kaiser Family Foundation/ABC Television, 1998). Discussions about relationships are also an important component in learning this life skill.

While we have been talking primarily about adolescents in general, the same life skills are needed by specialized populations, such as adolescents moving out of foster or group care, those with a physical disability, and those with challenges such as autism and mental disabilities.

EDUCATION

Education is both a process and a product for adolescents. It is a process that begins for some as early as the fifth or sixth grade and culminates for many at ages 17 to 18 with graduation from high school. For those who continue their education after high school, it a product in that a high school diploma or general education diploma/general equivalency diploma (GED) is often required for admission for further academic or skill-based education. The GED tests students in five subject areas and is designed for students who have not completed their high school diploma.

Dropping Out

Not all adolescents enjoy school. For some students, the educational milieu is problematic and, for others, it can be traumatic. Students who struggle with subject matter, or whose elementary school preparation was weaker, often find middle school and high school challenging. Other students may be dealing with learning deficits or disabilities that make their achievement in school onerous. Attention deficit disorder, dyslexia, and other impairments can affect not only the educational process, but also the outcome. Every year, about 8% of students nationwide drop out of high school—and the dropout rate for certain groups is even higher. For example, Black adolescents drop out at twice the rate of White students and the rates for Hispanic students was over 18% in 2008, with American Indians/Alaska Natives not far behind at 14.6% (U.S. Department of Education, 2010). By comparison, the dropout rates for Asian and Pacific Islanders are below that of White students (4.4% vs. 4.8%, respectively). Figure 12.3 shows the most current dropout rates and their historical trend lines.

While dropout rates have been steadily decreasing since 1972, they still show substantial disparities. Dropout rates tend to be higher in the Southern and Western United States and in cities, compared to other locales (Boostup.org, 2012; Orfield, Losen, Wald, & Swanson, 2004).

Dropping out of school has micro, mezzo, and macro consequences. At the micro level, students who do not finish school generally earn substantially less per year, are more likely to be poor, and are more likely to be unemployed at any point in time because they lack the skills needed in a complex workplace. Moreover, the typical high

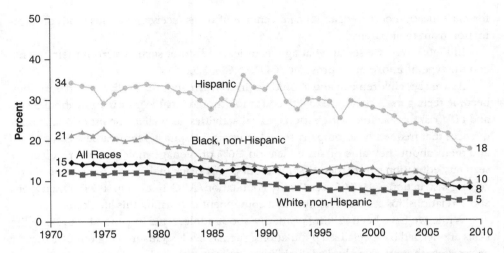

Note: This indicator uses the status dropout rate which measures the percentage of young adults aged 18 to 24 who were not enroled in a high school program and had not received a high school diploma or obtained an equivalency certificate. Due to changes in the race categories, estimates from 2003 are not strictly comparable to estimates from 2002 and before. Prior to 2001, the black race category included Hispanics.

Figure 12.3
Dropout Rates Among Youth Ages 16 to 24 by Race and Hispanic Origin, October 1972–2009
Source: U.S. Department of Education (2010).

school dropout earns $400,000 less between the ages of 18 and 64 compared to high school graduates. At the mezzo level, this affects families and other groups in which the dropout is a member. Lower income often means continued financial strain, less job mobility, and greater risk in bad economic times. Macro effects include a less productive workforce, lower tax receipts for all government levels, and the increased need for safety net programs in bad times. High school dropouts are also more likely to engage in criminal behavior, experience poorer physical and mental health, and place a higher economic burden on society (Child Trends, 2011).

Risk factors for dropping out of school include things such as:

- Frequent absenteeism

- Little or no school engagement

- Low parental education with concomitant low expectations for student

- Family or work responsibilities that conflict with school attendance

- Antisocial or deviant behavior in the school

- Changing schools in the ninth grade

- Foreign born

- Attending a school with a poor achievement record (Child Trends, 2011)

Students who were born outside the United States have a very high dropout rate, often exceeding 20%. Though they make up only 10% of all students, these students comprise 25% of those who have dropped out. Figure 12.4 shows this information more clearly.

As noted earlier, enrollment in a school with a poor achievement record is a significant contributor to the decision to drop out. Students who come from low income homes are also more likely to be served by heavily segregated, poor performing schools, with minority populations approaching 90% to 100%. Most exist in large urban school districts, are typically underfunded, have more inexperienced teachers, and have

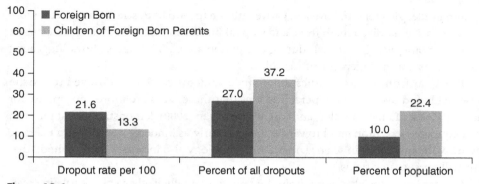

Figure 12.4
Dropout Rate (Percentage of All Dropouts) and Percent of Population of Youth, Aged 16 to 24, by Nativity, 2009
Source: Child Trends (2011).

educational environments that do not support learning (Kozol, 2005; Tozer, Senese, & Violas, 2006).

School Performance

Students who perform well in school generally come from higher socioeconomic classes as measured by factors such as income, occupation, and parental education. They usually complete more grades in school, receive academic honors, and participate in extracurricular activities (band, sports, or student government). Their higher academic performance will be reflected in standardized test scores on the ACT or other college admission tests. Conversely, they will have fewer behavioral problems in school, such as truancy or dropping out (Vander Zanden, Crandell, & Crandell, 2007). Explanations for these differences include school bias in favor of middle-class students, differing parental and family values and expectations regarding education, fewer economic resources (e.g., computers, Internet access), and greater risks for kids from lower socioeconomic classes (Ogbu, 2003; Tapia, 1998; Thernstrom & Thernstrom, 2003). Other factors include the fact that children from poorer homes move more often, each time resulting in a setback, and language difficulties make learning harder for some groups for whom English is not their first language.

> **Diversity in Practice**
>
> *Practice Behavior Example: Recognize the extent to which a culture's structures and values may oppress, marginalize, alienate, or create or enhance privilege and power.*
>
> **Critical Thinking Question:** What factors might explain the differences in school dropout rates for different groups of students such as Asians and Whites? What factors in your life worked to keep you in school?

Gender differences

Gender differences in education have been known for decades as girls outperform boys in many academic subjects. Typically, females are ahead of males in reading during elementary school and continue this lead into high school (LoGerfo, Nichols, & Chaplin, 2006). Moreover, their growth rates in reading are also higher than those for males. On the other hand, both males and females begin at about the same level in kindergarten with respect to their math scores. By the 10th grade and until graduation, boys outperform girls. The advantage boys enjoy in math has also been observed in the fields of science and technology. The gender difference that favors males in science, technology, and math appears to operate regardless of racial or ethnic identity. However, explanations for the differential interest of women in these fields vary. Some argue that female students do not like science and math as much as males, do not see it as useful for their future, and may lack confidence in their ability to perform well in these fields (Oakes, 1990). By the 10th grade, girls tend to have a negative attitude toward both science and math, score less well on standardized math tests, and stop taking courses in these areas. Interestingly, the grade point averages of girls during this period are higher than for boys suggesting that ability is not the independent variable.

It is clear from several studies that female students can be encouraged to pursue these fields and overcome the perceived bias that these areas are more appropriate for males. Patrick, Mantzicopoulos, and Samarapungayan (2009) demonstrated that girls can be encouraged and motivated toward science as early as kindergarten. Having peers or parents with an interest in science, math, or technology also increases the likelihood that girls will pursue such fields.

Gender-based socialization within the family is equally likely to play a role in creating and maintaining a gender gap (Entwisle, Alexander, & Olson, 1997) in these fields. Increased freedom enjoyed by boys versus greater social controls placed on girls can lead to vastly different experiences relative to the fields of math and science. (Based on the biological influences on behavior that you learned about in Chapter 11, which gender, if left unsupervised, do you think would be more likely to experiment with making bombs or sneaking into a military gun range to collect lead?)

Interestingly, the impact of gender differences appears to extend into college enrollments. The academic achievement females attain in elementary, middle, and high school is also seen in college. Not only are women attending college in numbers that rival men, but they are more likely to complete their college degree (Buchmann & DiPrete, 2006; Francis, 2012).

Gender differences have been found in the academic performance and learning of high school students. Some differences carry over from elementary school and others appear to emerge only at the middle or high school levels. This has been explained by the fact that girls develop fine motor skills before boys, sit still and pay attention better, and have greater verbal skills (Garbarino, 1999). Girls' social and behavioral skills help them achieve throughout school. Boys, on the other hand, tend to encounter more problems in development such as reading disabilities, dyslexia, speech problems, attention deficit disorders, intellectual disabilities, and antisocial behavior (Buchmann, DiPrete, & McDaniel, 2008), have greater need to move about (attributable to hormonal changes), and appear less able to pay attention (Vander Zanden et al., 2007). The physical and emotional manifestation of these differences can be seen in several ways. Males are about 2½ to 3 times more likely to be diagnosed with ADHD (attention deficit/hyperactivity disorder) and sent to special education classes (CDC, 2011). About 5.4 million children between 4 and 17 years of age have been diagnosed with ADHD. Surprisingly, the rate for new diagnoses of the disorder is now higher among older teens versus younger children. Figure 12.5 shows the state-by-state percentage of children diagnosed with ADHD (CDC, 2011).

Additional explanations for the boy–girl performance gap have been proposed and supported by research. One explanation involves teacher bias in giving higher grades to students whose behavior is better in the classroom, regardless of actual performance on exams and other assessment measures. A second explanation, mentioned earlier, derives from the fact that girls develop fine motor skills sooner than boys. This allows girls to neatly complete their work in a timely manner. In addition, girls are more likely to participate in class discussions, an ability that is highly dependent on interpersonal skills. Finally, it is argued that the learning environment rewards kids who fit into a rigid institutional system, which is truer of girls than boys (DiPrete & Jennings, 2009).

Racial differences

In addition to gender differences in academic performance, several racial differences have been identified. These racial differences may be significant by themselves or may

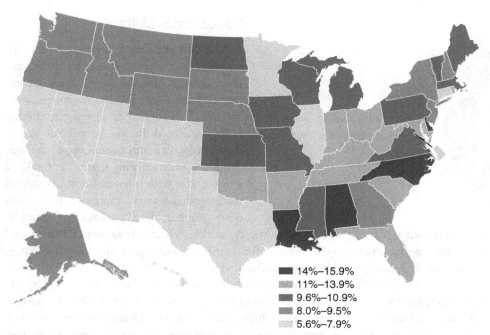

14%–15.9%
11%–13.9%
9.6%–10.9%
8.0%–9.5%
5.6%–7.9%

Figure 12.5
Percentage of Children Ages 4 to 17 Ever Diagnosed With ADHD by State
Source: CDC (2011).

intersect with gender. For example, LoGerfo et al. (2006) found that Black males start kindergarten behind White males in reading skills. This discrepancy continues into high school with Black males significantly behind their White counterparts by graduation. Black females do less well than White females, but they continually outperform Black males in reading.

In math, Black children begin kindergarten with lower skills, and by third grade, the differences are dramatic. The differences between Black males and females are not significant during elementary school, at least up to the third grade. After that point, Black females outperform Black males, a trend that continues throughout high school. However, it is unclear why the gap widens between third and eighth grades (LoGerfo et al., 2006).

Hispanic males also start with deficits in reading skills compared to White males, but gain ground by the time they reach high school. While they graduate behind White males in reading skills, Hispanic males do not differ significantly from Hispanic females.

Hispanic males also begin elementary school with fewer math skills than White males and this discrepancy grows as they go through the grades. Hispanic females begin ahead of Hispanic males at kindergarten, but lose this advantage over the new few years.

Asian males and females do not seem to show the same differences in reading skill as do the other groups. Partly, this may be the result of Asian females, like White females, learning more in the last two years of high school compared to grades 8 to 10. The reasons for this learning hiatus are unknown, but by the end of high school, both Asian males and females are at about the same place with respect to reading skills.

Math skills begin at a higher level for Asian children than for Whites and this difference remains during elementary school. By 12th grade, Asian males outscore Asian women although the differences are relatively small. Clearly, differences in academic performance do exist and many explanations have been put forth to account for the differences. Racial factors, gender, and economic explanations alone—or in interaction—help us understand why some differences exist.

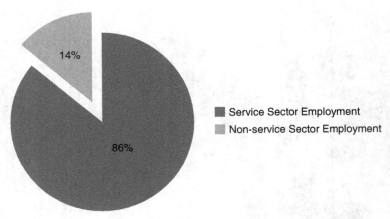

Figure 12.6
Sources of U.S.
Employment in 2008
Source: Apte et al. (2008).

Educational Skills

Educational skills needed for survival in society fall into two categories: hard and soft. Hard skills include the ability to use a computer, fluency in a foreign language, writing ability, and analytical or critical thinking skills. These skills are usually acquired through formal educational opportunities, beginning with learning that occurs in K–12 schools. Soft skills often result from external learning that occurs from employment and other group-involved pursuits. For example, soft skills such as learning to deal with conflict, working effectively as part of a team, and the ability to give and take criticism are often learned through part-time employment or can be acquired through involvement in athletics.

The need for adolescents to acquire both hard and soft skills is underscored by the U.S.' transition from a largely industrial economy to a service economy. This change emphasizes the importance of innovation, information, and knowledge over the more traditional skills. Areas such as telecommunications and financial services grew while areas such as manual labor and hands-on production skills shrunk. In the 10-year period ending in 2005, the United States lost over 3 million manufacturing jobs while gaining 17 million jobs in the service sector.

Apte, Karmarkar, and Nath (2008) break the U.S. employment picture down, as shown in Figure 12.6.

This change reflects realities in the macro environment. Among the new service jobs were positions at near minimum wage (Would you like fries with that?) and others in information services that were high paying. Fields such as medicine/health care, law, engineering, and marketing/sales are fast growing and generally high paying (Bureau of Labor Statistics, 2012; Council on Competitiveness, 2008). Employers have emphasized increasing productivity by having frontline workers learn computer skills, greater utilization of self-managed teams, and regular meetings of employees, among others (Black & Lynch, 2003). This reflects increased attention to information sharing decentralizing decision-making, communication skills, and flexibility (Partnership for 21st Century Skills, 2008). Jobs with the highest growth potential require a college degree or at least some college. This is consistent with current trends among U.S. workers over age 25, 64% of whom have some postsecondary education (Bureau of Labor Statistics, 2010). The globalization of the economy also places a premium on workers who are culturally sensitive, adaptable, and fluent in other languages.

Unfortunately, students in the United States lag behind their international counterparts in some significant ways. U.S. students, for example, ranked 29th out of 40 countries on a generic test of problem solving (Organization for Economic Cooperation and Development, 2004). Only about 40% of White students in the United States read at their grade level and the percentages are even lower for non-White and low-income children. A similar percentage are competent in mathematics, science, and writing (Grigg, Lauko, & Brockway, 2006; Lee, Grigg, & Dion, 2007a, 2007b; Salahu-Din, Persky, & Miller, 2008).

**Assess your comprehension
of Dropouts and Academic
Performance by completing
this quiz.**

Life Skills

UNICEF (2011) identifies a list of psychosocial and interpersonal life skills that are generally considered important for success across multiple countries. This life skills–based education

Box 12.1 Critical Life Skills

Communication and Interpersonal Skills
Interpersonal communication skills
- Verbal/nonverbal communication
- Active listening
- Expressing feelings, giving feedback, and receiving feedback

Negotiation/refusal skills
- Negotiation and conflict management
- Assertiveness skills
- Refusal skills

Empathy
- Ability to listen and understand another's needs and circumstances and express that understanding

Cooperation and teamwork
- Expressing respect for others' contributions and different styles
- Assessing one's abilities and contributing to the group

Advocacy skills
- Influencing skills and persuasion
- Networking and motivation skills

Decision-Making and Critical Thinking Skills
Decision-making/problem-solving skills
- Information gathering skills
- Evaluating future consequences of present actions for self and others
- Determining alternative solutions to problems

- Analysis skills regarding the influence of values and attitudes of self and others on motivation

Critical thinking skills
- Analyzing peer and media influences
- Analyzing attitudes, values, social norms and beliefs and factors affecting these
- Identifying relevant information and information sources

Coping and Self-Management Skills
Skills for increasing internal locus of control
- Self-esteem/confidence-building skills
- Self awareness skills including awareness of rights, influences, values, attitudes, rights, strengths, and weaknesses
- Goal setting skills
- Self-evaluation/self-assessment/self-monitoring skills

Skills for managing feelings
- Anger management
- Dealing with grief and anxiety
- Coping skills for dealing with loss, abuse, trauma

Skills for managing stress
- Time management
- Positive thinking
- Relaxation techniques

Source: UNICEF (2011).

is identified as a basic learning need for all children. Many skills listed in Box 12.1 can and often are acquired as students move through various educational settings. At the same time, students may need to seek out and augment skills, not taught in their academic settings. As a lifelong process, education involves both learning what is provided in one's academic settings and locating needed resources that are not.

Educational Transitions in Adolescence

One of the more challenging transitions within the educational experience of adolescents is that from elementary to middle school/junior high (Eccles & Roeser, 2003; Wigfield, Byrnes, & Eccles, 2006). The difficulties adolescents experience often present as criticism or dissatisfaction about various aspects of the new school. This can include a dislike of teachers, complaints about the quality of education, or other signs of unhappiness. It does not appear that academic achievement has any bearing on the negative perceptions—even students with good grades make the same complaints. Adolescents must adjust to a larger peer group, a different teaching format with multiple instructors instead of just one, and changes in their status. On the positive side, some students find subjects that interest them more than in elementary school. Others appreciate the greater independence from parents and availability of a larger pool of friends

(Santrock, 2008). (The sixth grader who dresses in Goth will now find others of similar interests.)

Another challenge faced during the transition to junior/middle school and later to high school is that of bullying. According to the U.S. Department of Education (2010), as many as 50% of high school students have either been bullied themselves or bullied others. Typically, bullying takes the form of verbal taunts or physical intimidation. Boys tend to experience more of the latter while girls are more likely to be verbally harassed.

The past decade has seen the rise of cyberbullying in which the internet is used to harass other students. The most recent data suggest that anywhere from 8% to 18% of middle school students have been cyberbullyied (Meredith, 2010). Girls are most likely to engage in cyberbullying but also most likely to be victimized by it. In some highly publicized cases, the victim has committed suicide in response to this form of bullying.

Because much bullying takes place outside of classes (to and from school, during the lunch hour, and in the school hallways), teachers and principals may have little knowledge of what is transpiring. Monitoring the problem is even more difficult with cyberbullying that often takes place outside of school. Bullying often comes to the attention of school personnel through reports by parents and sometimes peers of the victim. Development of interpersonal skills, such as assertiveness and friendship, appears to reduce the extent of being bullied (Rigby, 2002). School-wide programs aimed at curbing bullying have also had some success, but the school climate and the attitudes of teachers and administrators often become barriers. Perhaps the most extensive systematic review on the effectiveness of anti-bullying programs was completed in 2009 by Farrington and Ttofi, under the aegis of the Campbell Collaborative (an international network of re-

Assess your comprehension of Bullying by completing this quiz.

searchers dedicated to improving decision-making in education, social welfare, and crime and justice). The findings suggest that bullying decreased by 20% to 23% on average and victimization decreased by 17% to 20%. Children age 11 and above were most likely to benefit from anti-bullying programs. Box 12.2 is a summary of the effective bullying prevention approaches.

Box 12.2   Characteristics of Effective School-Based Anti-Bullying Programs

According to Farrington and Ttofi, the most effective bullying prevention programs were more likely to incorporate:

- Parent training and/or meetings
- Extensive and intensive training of teachers in handling bullying
- Playground supervision by adults
- Firm methods for dealing with bullying that included serious talks, referral to the principal, requiring victim to stay within close proximity to teacher during recess, and privilege deprivation for the abuser
- Punitive methods for younger children such as after-school detention and non-punitive methods for older children such as shared concern interviews
- Social learning theories that "encourage and reward pro-social behavior and discourage and punish bullying" (p. 72)
- Empathy and perspective-taking skills for older children

Source: Farrington & Ttofi (2009). Used with permission.

RELATIONSHIPS

A major phase in adolescence involves dating and other romantic relationships. Dating is a common experience and by age 18, more than 80% of adolescents have dated. A majority of adolescents describe their relationships as romantic (Carver, Joyner, & Udry, 2003), which children entering early teens and even those who have not dated report that they look forward to experiencing. Adolescent cross-gender relationships involve a confluence of components that include communication, sexuality, and emotionality. The meanings that adolescents ascribe to these relationships have significant import for individual well-being (Giordano, Longmore, & Manning, 2006).

We pointed out previously that boys and girls engage in different types of peer friendship differences that can have a major impact on cross-gender relationships. One would expect, for instance, that males would pursue cross-gender relationships with the same level of self-assurance, competitiveness, and lowered emotional engagement that they use in same-gender relationships (Gilligan, 1982). The evidence available, however, is mixed. Some researchers report male adolescents do carry their competitiveness and lowered emotionality into relationships with females while others question whether this pattern is true (Giordano et al., 2006). Because neither girls nor boys have engaged in romantic relationships in childhood, this marks new and unfamiliar territory for both genders. The unfamiliarity influences communication, emotions, and power. Typically, boys report a greater degree of awkwardness in their communications, a result that operates irrespective of family structure, self-esteem, race, ethnicity, or age. Boys who were sexually active with girls also reported the awkwardness and problems with communication. Interestingly, this awkwardness was reported less often by African American adolescents.

Male adolescents report lower levels of self-confidence within the context of cross-gender relationships than girls. This is especially true for males who do not see themselves as attractive, because of either physical features or other attributes. Factors that increase the adolescent's self-confidence include relationships of longer duration and engaging in sex with the partner.

Despite the belief that boys are more likely to be emotionally distant within romantic relationships, this does not seem to be the case. Giordano and colleagues (2006) found that boys were very likely to experience strong emotions within these relationships. In many ways, adolescent males were just as likely as females to report feelings of love, anxiety, and commitment within the relationship and emotional pain if the relationship ended. Perhaps equally surprising is that males reported their love interest as having great influence on them and their behavior. Generally, the more serious the relationship, the higher the degree of influence the female partner has on the male. As might be expected, boys with lower self-esteem experienced were influenced more by their female partner. Areas where girls positively influence boys include performance in school, relationship intimacy, degree of self-disclosure, and involvement in delinquency.

Sexuality

Engagement in sexual relationships is a common occurrence among adolescents—it is estimated that 62% have had sexual intercourse by 12th grade. The rate of teens having sexual intercourse is 33% for ninth graders (CDC, 2004). The mean age of first sexual intercourse occurs at about 17 years for boys and about 17½ years for girls, although sex before age 14 is reported by 6% of girls and 8% of boys. According to the CDC, 11% of 12th grade girls report having four or more partners while 18% of their male peers report four or more partners (Guys wouldn't exaggerate, would they?). Ninety-eight percent of teens who had sexual intercourse indicate that they used one or more methods of contraception. Condoms (94%) and birth control pills (61%) were most commonly employed. The percentage of sexually active teens using contraceptives has increased over the past decade (Abma, Martinez, Mosher, & Dawson, 2004).

About one-quarter of girls engaged in their first sexual intercourse with partners who were at least four years older, underscoring the observation that "the younger a girl is when she has sex for the first time, the greater the average age difference is likely to be between her and her partners" (Abma et al., 2004). This age disparity becomes important because these adolescents are less likely to use contraceptives and more likely to get pregnant.

Adolescents with more sexual partners tend to be characterized as having poor ability for self-regulation and a high need for excitement or sensation (Moilanen, Crockett, Raffaelli, & Jones, 2010). Their decision-making skills are weaker than those of their peers.

Despite media messages about teen sexuality, the rates of sexual intercourse for adolescence have been dropping over the past decade. This has led to fewer teenage pregnancies and abortions. About two-thirds of high school students report having been abstinent from intercourse for the previous three months (CDC, 2004). The most common reasons for abstinence were fear of pregnancy and getting HIV/AIDS or STDs. These reasons are sound in light of the fact that over one-third of sexually active teens became pregnant at least one time before they reach age 20, and about 25% contract a sexually transmitted disease every year (Hershaw, 2003). Moreover, about a quarter of sexually active teens engaged in sexual behavior that they really did not want to do with almost 30% feeling pressured to have sex. Another 9% to10% reported being forced to have sex (Abma et al., 2004).

Diversity in Practice

Practice Behavior Example: Critique and apply knowledge to understand person and environment.

Critical Thinking Question: What possible explanations can you think of that might explain the higher rate of HIV diagnoses among Blacks compared to other ethnic groups? What kinds of additional information might you need to help understand the differential HIV diagnoses?

One particular concern for sexually active adolescents is that about 40% of those who are sexually active never consult a doctor or other health care provider about their sexual health (Kaiser Family Foundation and Seventeen, 2001). This occurs despite the fact that almost 50% of teens express an interest in getting more information about their sexual health.

Peers

We have discussed in Chapter 8 how peers influence adolescent development. Adolescents who perceive social support from peers tend to more successfully achieve the goal of a positive identity formation. Adolescents who have at least one friend are more likely to demonstrate prosocial behavior, have better grades, and have less emotional concerns than those with no friends. They are more likely to be seen as cooperative, sharing, and willing to assist others (Wentzel, Barry, & Caldwell, 2004). On the other hand, conflict with peers can lead to problems in identity development (Reis & Youniss, 2004). Adolescents very dependent upon their peers and heavily influenced by them are more likely to develop diffuse identities, including adopting asocial attitudes (Flum, 1994). Those with diffuse identities often feel they lack control over events in their lives, have weaker relationships with parents, and are more likely to rely on their peers for help in decision-making. In the following Clinical Corner box, it's clear that this adolescent is developing an identity that relies on peers and rejects parental influence.

Clinical Corner

"I can't stand my parents. If they aren't ragging on each other, they're complaining that I disappoint them because I didn't turn out like my brother, the 'A' student. Well, I don't need them because I have friends who like and support me. While we may get into trouble together, they never scream at me for my mistakes or dis me. Besides, it's not my fault that my brother got all the brains in our family. S*** happens, but I'm learning how to make it without my parents. My friends help me and they don't give me a lot of s***!"

Some adolescents cultivate or adopt an identity that is deviant or negative in significant ways. Often, these are the individuals who will come to the attention of social workers through our roles in either the correctional or mental health systems. Changing problem identities may involve reducing the influence of peers, increasing the influence of parents, or both (Forthun et al., 2006). The goal is usually to restructure the identity largely through the medium of changing behaviors that support the negative identity.

Some teens have a great deal of trouble with peers. CDC (2011) reports that kids with ADHD have almost three times as many peer problems compared to students without the diagnosis. These difficulties often result in the ADHD-diagnosed teen being 10 times as likely to have difficulty making friends.

For a brief video on the breadth of influence peers have on each other, please review Peer Groups and consider the ways that your peers have influenced you over the past five years.

RISK FACTORS IN ADOLESCENCE

Most observers know that adolescence is a time of risk-taking and problematic behaviors. Risky behaviors include drug usage, delinquency, running away, early sexual relationships, antisocial behavior, and academic problems (Wilson & Widom, 2010). Some risk taking arises from the nature of adolescence, lack of maturity of boys and girls, peer and media influences, and some from the behaviors of others.

Child Abuse and Neglect

A major example of adolescent risks that arise from the behavior of others can be seen in the case of child abuse and neglect. For example, adults engaged in prostitution often came from backgrounds characterized by abuse and neglect (Nixon, Tutty, Downe, Gorkoff, & Ursel, 2002). Adult prostitutes are twice as likely to have come from homes with a history of child abuse and neglect (Wilson & Widom, 2010). Likewise, a history of being abused or neglected in childhood has been linked to premature sexual initiation, delinquency, and school difficulties (De Bellis, 2001). Early sexual initiation (before age 15) is of particular importance because of its association as a predictor of future prostitution.

Running away from home is often a reaction to an abusive or neglectful home environment and is more common in adolescents from this background (Yoder, Whitbeck, & Hoyt, 2001). Because adolescents usually lack marketable skills and financial resources, they may rely on other behaviors to obtain money, shelter, or survival needs. Trading sex for these resources is a common practice and can lead to emotionally distancing oneself from sex, lower self-esteem, and prostitution (Wilson & Widom, 2010).

Delinquency and criminal behavior by adolescents may be a peer-associated activity or occur as a means to surviving while running away. Often criminal behavior, such as burglary or theft, is connected to drug use as adolescents seek to pay for their drug of choice.

School problems are challenges for several reasons. First, adolescents who miss substantial amounts of schooling or who drop out risk a lifetime of poverty. They lack skills necessary for surviving in a heavily technological world and have less chance of obtaining satisfactory employment. Too frequently, truancy and academic difficulty is preceded by child abuse and neglect. The abuse/neglect experienced at home can interfere with cognition, emotions, and behaviors, all important for academic success (Veltman & Browne, 2001).

Drug use for some adolescence begins as early as age 13. In general, the earlier the use begins, the more serious the problem becomes in later adolescence and adulthood. Adolescents' use of drugs may be a response to depression, a coping mechanism for trauma at home, or the result of peer influence. It is a self-destructive behavior often seen in adolescents with poor self-esteem and self-worth (Wilson & Widom, 2010).

The association of child abuse and neglect with various risk-taking behaviors suggests that survivors of these traumas need assistance in navigating adolescence. While all adolescents face challenges in areas such as sexual expression, self-esteem, and academic performance, those who experienced child abuse or neglect are particularly at risk (Wilson & Widom, 2010).

Eating Disorders

Eating disorders include obesity, anorexia nervosa, binge eating, and bulimia nervosa (Heller, 2009). Almost all eating disorders pose major health risks, including premature death. Eating disorders can be found in males and females, in different age groupings, and in most racial or ethnic groups. The potential of developing eating disorders in adolescence is exacerbated by a variety of factors: media portrayals of attractive people as inherently thin, peer support for weight loss, parental influences, and the individual's inaccurate or unrealistic self-assessment of their body size, weight, and shape (American Psychiatric Association, 2000; Fallon, Katzman, & Wooley, 1996; Hick & Katzman, 1999). For example, Hick and Katzman found that adolescents with anorexia nervosa were unable to accurately ascertain and report their degree of sexual maturity. In the pages that follow, we will explore each of the eating disorders identified earlier.

Obesity

Among eating disorders, obesity is the most common, constituting a significant public health challenge. Obesity is defined as having a weight that is considered unhealthy for a given height. It is calculated using a body mass index (BMI) that relates weight to height and compares it to norms. An individual whose BMI ranks them in the 85th to 94th percentile is generally considered overweight with those above the 95th percentile defined as obese. The CDC provides a chart to show typical BMI ranges; let's now look at Figure 12.7, which illustrates a BMI chart for boys, ages 2 to 20 years old.

Obesity is caused by both behavioral and genetic factors, so interventions include changes to diet as well as counseling, exercise, and social support. In some instances, medication may be prescribed to assist with other efforts to reduce obesity. Untreated, obesity contributes to multiple health difficulties that include high blood pressure, stroke, gout, cancer, and diabetes, to name a few. It is also associated with sleep apnea, a disorder in which one's sleep is characterized by a failure to breathe normally, reducing oxygen in the blood and brain.

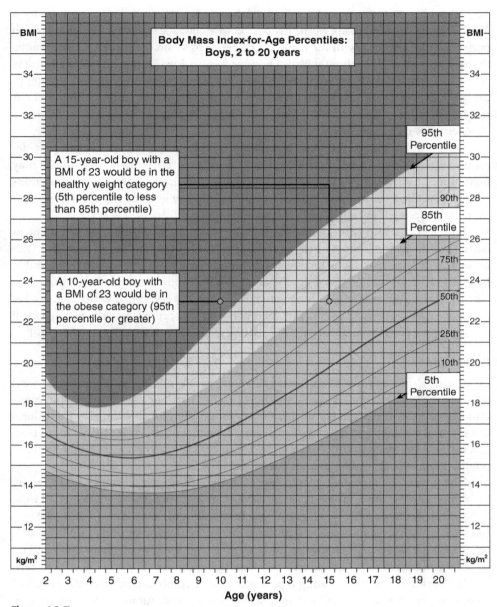

Figure 12.7
Body Mass Index-per-Age Percentiles: Boys, 2 to 20 Years (2012)
Source: From http://www.cdc.gov/healthyweight/images/growthchart_example2.gif.

Anorexia nervosa

Anorexia nervosa is a psychological disorder in which the individual deliberately refuses to maintain an appropriate body weight and displays an obsessive anxiety about weight gain. To become thinner, the client (almost 95% are women) diet, exercise, and often take medications that will further weight loss. Among other strategies to lose weight, those with anorexia are likely to use laxatives, enemas, and diuretics. The real purpose of these strategies is to gain perceived control over one's body. Anorexia is most often seen in adolescence and among Caucasians, although it can appear in other age and racial groups.

Anorexia's causes are mostly unknown although genetics may play a role. Attempts to identify the role of various brain elements have shown mixed results. A social history of an individual with anorexia is likely to turn up family factors such as maternal depression, eating problems in infancy, and self-image deficits. However, it is not uncommon for a client's family situation to appear nearly perfect to an outside observer. The emphasis on perfection can intersect with the adolescent's desire to attain the perfect weight. Sometimes, a history of child abuse will also present. Most adolescents with eating disorders refuse to admit it despite excessive weight loss and family pressure to get help. Failure to deal with the disorder often leads to a serious health crisis. Anorexia may also present as extreme thinness, distorted self-perceptions of one's weight, and amenorrhea (failure to experience menstrual periods).

Behavioral manifestations can include obsession about food and weight loss, decreased attention span, sleep disturbances, and irritability. Clients with anorexia may hoard food, cut their meals into smaller bites, and may show signs of other addictions such as gambling or substance abuse. Compulsive behaviors, such as seeking sex and overexerting oneself during exercise, are common.

Interventions with anorexic clients can occur on either an inpatient or an outpatient basis. Hospitalization is more often required when the anorexia has led to problems with other bodily systems such as kidney, heart, circulatory, gastrointestinal, or glandular. Likewise, adolescents can lose a significant amount of bone density rather quickly. Obviously, a focus on weight gain is needed but it is usually combined with cognitive behavioral, and may involve both family members and support groups. The therapist will work with the client around issues such as self-perception, perfectionism, and control.

Binge eating

Binge eating (or compulsive overeating) involves eating significant quantities of food over a short time interval. It appears to be a practice that one can't control and brings remorse after the binging is completed. Indications of binge eating are very short durations between meals (two hours or less), eating to reduce stress rather than control hunger, eating food very rapidly, and eating alone to avoid embarrassment. Binge eating is not the same as bulimia that involves purging of food.

The origin of binge eating is unclear. A social history may discover other family members with the same problem. Binge eating can develop if the client begins to treat depression, stress, or anxiety by consuming foods and this pattern gets out of the person's control. Binge eaters often have the same perfectionistic outlook on life as with other eating disorders. They are also likely to have a poor image of their bodies and reflect the attitudes of a culture where thinness is highly valued.

Interventions for binge eating typically involve a combination of medication and counseling, particularly behavioral approaches. Some medications, such as antidepressants, have proven effective with certain clients. At the same time, some of the other comorbid problems associated with binge eating may need attention, such as obesity and depression (Heller, 2009).

Bulimia nervosa

Bulimia is an eating disorder characterized by binge eating followed by purging of what was eaten. This involves laxatives or self-induced vomiting (Heller, 2009). Foods eaten often may be of high caloric value. Some bulimia associated with adolescence is peer related in that the process of bingeing and purging begins as a social activity. Both anorexia and bulimia may be found among various socioeconomic groups and is not limited to those with significant income.

Indications of this eating disorder are similar to the others already discussed—underweight, poor body image, and the overuse of exercise as a means of controlling one's weight. Comorbidity often includes substance abuse, obsessive-compulsive disorders, mood disorders, and impulse control issues (Heller, 2009). A history of sexual abuse is common.

Interventions for bulimia nervosa often include the antidepressant Prozac or other selective serotonin reuptake inhibitors (SSRIs). However, the usefulness of these medications is highest after the client has achieved normal weight (Kaye, Gendall, & Strober, 1998). The same appears to be true for cognitive-behavioral interventions.

Evidence of effective treatments for eating disorders is weak and clients should not be oversold on the efficacy of any particular intervention. Clients from families where sexual abuse occurred, or where substance abuse or other eating disorders are present, are most at risk. A family history of affective disorders should be included in assessment. In all cases, referral to a physician is indicated. It is common to have a client recover from an eating disorder only to begin to show signs of other problems, such as depression (Heller, 2009).

Drug Use and Abuse

Another risk factor in adolescence is drug use and abuse. Although many assume that this is primarily a problem for urban youth, Levine and Coupey (2003) found that there were no significant differences with respect to substance abuse in rural, urban, or suburban youth. The nature of adolescence as a time of testing—coupled with increased influence of peers—can explain some drug use among this age group. There appears to be a connection between drug use and sexuality for a portion of the teen population, with about 25% using drugs or alcohol in their latest sexual encounter. Male teens typically reported higher alcohol use than females. Over one-half of these teens were fearful that the alcohol or drug use might lead them to be more sexually involved than they intended to be.

Substance abuse often begins during adolescence and is associated with early maturation in both girls and boys (Kaltiala-Heino, Marttunen, Rantanen, & Rimpela, 2003; Reynolds et al., 2007). Early pubertal developmental status is a risk factor and early maturing females tend to engage in a variety of behaviors that compromise their health besides early sexual behaviors such as alcohol abuse, and smoking (Markey, Markey, & Tinsley, 2003). Markey and her colleagues also identified personality traits that increased the risk for adolescent girls. For example, girls who were identified by themselves and their parents as less conscientious and less agreeable were significantly more likely to engage in risk behaviors. These girls were frequently described as unkind, rebellious, and irresponsible. Girls who were more open to new experiences were also more likely to engage in risk behaviors. Conversely, girls who developed later than their peers were significantly less likely to engage in risky behavior or did show openness to new experiences.

Male adolescents show a similar pattern in that boys described as disagreeable engaged in more risky behaviors both in their teens and in adulthood. Reduced longevity, delinquency, and behavioral problems are also associated with this personality type (Hoyle, Fejfar, & Miller, 2000). At the same time, an elevated rate of testosterone among males is related to some types of alcoholism among adolescents. As might be expected, adolescents whose peers engage in deviant behavior are more likely to develop substance abuse problems. Serious social maladjustment that occurs between childhood and mid-adolescence is also a risk factor for later substance abuse (Kirisci, Vanyukov, & Tarter, 2005). The same appears to be true for teens popular with their peers. These adolescents are at risk for delinquency and other antisocial behavior (Allen, Porter, McFarland, Marsh, & McElhaney, 2005). Reynolds et al. (2007) concluded that a combination of early sexual maturation and a predisposition toward socially assertive and deviant behavior predicted substance abuse disorder with 68% accuracy.

For a short video on the role that alcohol plays in adolescence, view Adolescent Alcohol and Drug Use. How does this information differ from what you already believed about adolescent alcohol use?

School-based efforts to combat drug abuse among adolescents have not proven effective, perhaps because of the interactions of some of the factors just described. One of the best known drug prevention programs, DARE (Drug Abuse Resistance Education), uses specially trained police officers to teach an antidrug curriculum in elementary, middle, and high schools. Periodic reviews of the effectiveness of DARE have had disappointing results (Ennett, Tobler, Ringwalt, and Flewelling, 1994; Kanof, 2003). Not only did the program fail to prevent students from using drugs, but graduates of the program had increased rates of alcohol consumption and cigarette smoking compared to students who had not completed the DARE program (Sloboda et al., 2009). The program remains popular among parents, students, teachers, and police officers despite not achieving its goals.

Delinquency and Antisocial Behavior

Adolescent delinquency and antisocial behavior can take many forms that violate commonly accepted norms, hurt others, and damage property. Volz and Kerig (2010) report that rates of interpersonal violence and aggression among adolescents in a relationship may be as high as 32%. Thirteen percent of those who had been in multiple relationships encountered dating aggression in two or more of the relationships while 32% encountered dating aggression in one of their relationships. Both boys and girls admit to engaging in some degree of aggression within the context of a relationship. Those adolescents who have a neutral or accepting attitude toward dating aggression are at most risk for future episodes of violence. An approach to reducing relationship violence might focus on factors such as expressions of hostility and negative affect, both of which tend to rise to significant levels and lead to relationship aggression.

The classroom is another place where antisocial behavior is likely to show up. Not only does this behavior challenge the learning of other students, but it is also predictive of poorer grades, lower scores on standardized tests, and less time on task for the disruptive student (Stage & Quiroz, 1997).

Runaways and Throwaways

Running away from home is common. The Urban Institute reports that between ages 10 and 18 one out of every seven kids will run away at some point (Pergamit, 2010). The National Runaway Switchboard (2010) assists kids who have or are thinking of running away. They estimate that 1 to 3 million youth are living on the street because they either ran away or otherwise are homeless. Typically, absconding can be divided into two groups, runaways and throwaways. Runaways are children who left home willingly without parental knowledge. Throwaways have left against their will, usually as a result of an action by their parent/guardian.

Runaways

Reasons for running away are frequently related to anger and hurt that occurs within the runaway's family. Figure 12.8 identifies the most common causes as identified by youth contacting the National Runaway Switchboard during 2010. About one-quarter of the callers had run away previously.

Other reasons for absconding can be avoidance of criticism over some adolescent behavior such as delinquency and staying out past curfew. Many kids seek to leave their home because of child abuse or domestic violence. In other cases, it is a reaction to a parental separation, divorce, or emergence of a new partner for the caretaking parent. Other changes in the family constellation can trigger absconding, such as the birth of a

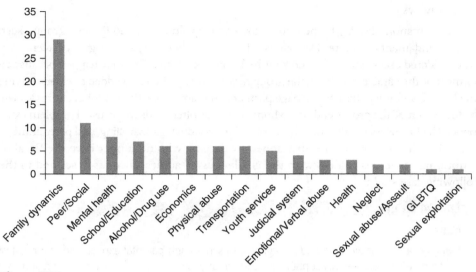

Figure 12.8
Caller-Identified Problems—National Runaway Switchboard, 2010
Source: National Runaway Switchboard (2010).

new baby or the death of a family member. Adolescents who are struggling academically may feel that their only option is to drop out of school and run away to avoid dealing with the pain and frustration that this will engender in the family. Those who have had behavior problems in school, or have been victimized by a bully, may see running away as the only recourse. Adolescents may also be faced with problems and have no one to help problem solve. For some adolescents, peer pressure plays a role, as in the situation in the following case.

Clinical Corner

Bill and Dwayne

Bill was a 15-year-old living in a residential group home for kids who had been unsuccessful in foster care and needed group-based care. He had no history of absconding and, despite a minor intellectual disability, was making good progress in school. Bill was also not particularly delinquent and his problems were more or less relational in nature.

Dwayne, a 16-year-old who had been involved in various delinquent activities, was infamous for running away from home. He frequently would be gone all night, stealing one car after another. He was placed in the group home after one such episode in which he stole a total of seven cars in a single evening.

Within a few weeks of placement in the group facility with four other boys, Dwayne decided to run away. In the process, he persuaded Bill to join him in his cross-country venture after which they planned to stay with Dwayne's distant relative. The boys made it across three states before a state trooper spotted the stolen car in which they were driving. The officer pulled the car over, and as he approached the vehicle, Dwayne shot the officer with a handgun the car's owner had left in the glove compartment. Although seriously wounded, the officer radioed the situation and both boys were apprehended in a matter of minutes. Both were waived from juvenile court and prosecuted as adults, each receiving several years in prison. The officer eventually recovered from his wounds.

While Dwayne's absconding was not surprising, Bill had given no indication of being unhappy at the group home. Dwayne's influence over his peer, however, provided the impetus for Bill's departure with terrible consequences for both of them.

Throwaways

In some situations, leaving home is more forced than voluntary. Among some groups, such as the Fundamentalist Latter Day Saints (FLDS) and other polygamous groups, teens may be considered excess inventory and banished from the group. This may happen because all or most of the eligible females in the group have been promised or wedded to elders, leaving the boys few if any potential marriage partners. In many cases, these adolescent males will be forced out of the group, ending up homeless. This often leads to the usual problem experienced by homeless youth: drug abuse, sexual misconduct, panhandling, and petty crime.

Still other youth may be abandoned by parents who no longer have the fiscal or emotional resources to deal with the challenges of adolescence, as described in the following case study.

Clinical Corner

Matt

Matt was a 17-year-old who had struggled with school and parental expectations for most of his teen years. Between his sophomore and junior years of high school, he found a summer job helping out at a small ranch. The job required a driver's license and involved hauling supplies and transporting people as needed. A visitor to the ranch owner stopped to talk to Matt and ask him where he was from. "I was from Pueblo, Colorado but now I'm not sure." Thinking that a bit odd, the visitor asked "How come you're not sure?" Matt responded "My mom and dad moved a couple of months ago and I don't know where they went." In Matt's case, the parents could no longer manage their difficult adolescent and simply left.

Running away, of course, rarely solves any important problem but it does create a series of other challenges. Absent resources, adolescents often have no place to stay and no money to support themselves. Life on the street can be extremely difficult and teens can turn to crime to survive. Those with substance abuse problems face even tougher times. It's hard enough to steal to feed yourself but it's much more difficult to steal enough to support a drug habit. Mental health problems, including depression, are common. Some adolescents turn to trading sex for money or drugs, and increase their risk of developing HIV or other STDs. Of those contacting the National Runaway Switchboard, the primary means of survival is shown in Figure 12.9.

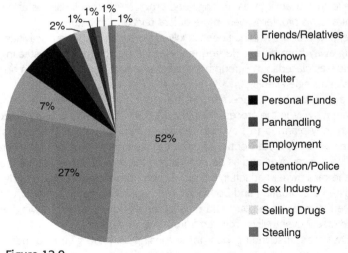

Figure 12.9
Method of Survival on the Street, 2010
Source: National Runaway Switchboard (2010).

It is important to keep in mind that this data show self-reports, and many runaways or throwaways may be reluctant to admit they are engaged in drug dealing, stealing, or prostitution during their calls to the switchboard. In addition, many runaways utilize multiple ways of supporting themselves rather than just one method.

Academic Problems

Adolescent academic problems are often related to the risks identified earlier. Family struggles, poverty, absconding, bullying, and poor educational preparation can all help explain students who perform poorly in school. Ultimately, anything that interferes with paying attention, thinking, and/or concentration can contribute to academic problems. Relationship problems, for example, can make it harder to focus or to concentrate on learning in the classroom. Homes where parents do not support academic achievement or who are involved in significant conflict with each other are likely to challenge even bright students. Turmoil within the home from any cause can sidetrack a good student. An example is the case of Ofa.

Many adolescents experience academic challenges that interfere with their success in school.

Clinical Corner

Ofa's Case

Ofa lived with his mother and younger sister on an economically depressed side of the city. Originally from Tonga, he had just enrolled in a BSW program at a nearby University. Although his grades in his general education courses were relatively low, he showed a great deal of promise. During his first year, Ofa seemed distracted and not truly engaged in his social work courses and faculty wondered if admitting him had been a mistake. Near the end of the first year, he told his advisor that he would have to drop out because of some stuff going on at home. Later, it became clear that he had become responsible for his sister because his mother was no longer able to provide for her care. In Ofa's case, it was a cultural obligation for the oldest male to assume responsibility for the care of younger siblings in the event of a family crisis.

Over the next two years, during which Ofa remained out of school, he worked and ensured that his sister got to school each day, had adequate housing and food, and did what was necessary to graduate from high school. Once his sister had graduated, Ofa returned to school, focused intently on his studies, and became one of the most valued members of the student body. He was appointed to leadership roles by his peers and demonstrated the promise that the admissions committee originally believed he possessed.

While Ofa's case did not include domestic violence, any violence in the home can make school work seem insignificant compared to the very real task of ensuring one's own safety and that of loved ones. Adolescents fearing for their lives or those of family members are carrying a burden that can threaten the best academic preparation and intentions.

Some students experience academic disruption due to pregnancy and are faced with deciding whether to abort the baby, give birth and raise the child, or give birth and place the child for adoption. Raising children requires personal and financial resources that tend to come more readily with additional education and experience. Whatever decision the adolescent makes has ramifications, as illustrated in Figure 12.10.

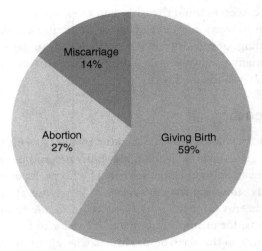

Figure 12.10
Outcomes of Teen Pregnancy, 2010
Source: Kost, Henshaw, & Carlin (2010).

Dropping out of school before or following the baby's birth has perhaps the most significant consequences. Suddenly, teens are responsible for someone else besides themselves. That someone has major needs that must take precedence over parents' needs for sleep, quiet, and time alone. Keeping the child and going back to school immediately may be an option for an adolescent with a strong support network of family and friends. But even with support, the teen's plate is just that much fuller and academics may be the thing that suffers the most. Adolescents most likely to keep a child are those already considered high risk. As can been seen in Figure 12.11, use of contraceptives helped reduce the frequency of U.S. teenage pregnancy.

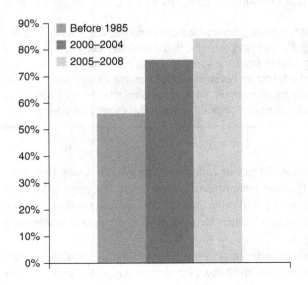

Figure 12.11
Teen Use of Contraceptives at First Intercourse
Source: Mosher & Jones (2010).

The increased frequency in use of contraceptives may indicate one or more of the following:

- Effectiveness of teen pregnancy programs
- Increased access to contraceptives by teens
- Increased awareness and fear of HIV/AIDS or another STD

Though contraceptives usage has increased, many adolescents do not use it every time they have intercourse. The most effective programs to combat adolescent pregnancy use a combination of encouraging teens to delay sexual intercourse and, when they decide to begin, to use contraceptives consistently. Programs that focus solely on abstinence have proven to be much less effective (Harris & Allgood, 2009; Moore et al., 2009). Trenholm et al. (2007), in a study for the U.S. Department of Health and Human Services, found that abstinence-only programs were no more effective than no sex education at all. Other approaches such as abstinence pledges were also proven ineffective. Those who had made a public pledge to remain abstinent were less likely to use birth control when they did have sexual intercourse and, therefore, placed themselves at greater risk of pregnancy and STDs (Rosenbaum, 2008).

As mentioned earlier in this chapter, some adolescents find the transition to middle and/or high school problematic. The student who is very accomplished in elementary school suddenly is immersed in a classroom where many students are equally accomplished. Going from being a big fish in a small bowl to just another inhabitant of the aquarium can be a letdown. A similar challenge can occur when the adolescent moves on to higher education and discovers that there are lots of very capable students against whom he or she must compete. Such transitions can undermine the adolescent's self-confidence. Students who proclaim "I've never had a grade below A before" may find it disheartening to learn that other grades can be assigned.

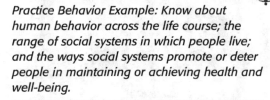

Human Behavior

Practice Behavior Example: Know about human behavior across the life course; the range of social systems in which people live; and the ways social systems promote or deter people in maintaining or achieving health and well-being.

Critical Thinking Question: The majority of pregnant teenagers choose to have the baby rather than pursue an abortion. What explanations would you give to someone who asked why these teens make such a decision despite the difficulties and risks involved?

Assess your comprehension of Risks in Adolescence by completing this quiz.

Assess your analysis and evaluation of this chapter's contents by completing the Chapter Review.

wavebreakmedia/Shutterstock

Major Life Phases Influence Human Behavior

Adulthood

Adulthood is typically identified as starting at the end of adolescence and culminating in death. Obviously, this is a very long period of time for most of us and in this chapter we will discuss many of the major influences on adulthood. This includes relationships, education, choosing a career, recreation, midlife crises, late life, retirement, preparing for death, and widowhood. In each case, we will explore how the topic informs and influences adulthood and identify challenges associated with each.

RELATIONSHIPS

Relationships in adulthood are often resources that provide love, support, and comfort to those involved. At the same time, creating and maintaining healthy relationships takes a lot of work. Tolerance of other's behaviors, the ability to forgive, and a willingness to compromise are important qualities that help in this process. As you are probably aware, adults engage in all kinds of relationships in different spheres of their lives. For example, adults have relationships with coworkers and friends, employees and employers, friends, romantic partners, and family members. We may even have relationships with people we come in contact with on a daily basis—mail carriers, store clerks, and others. (For those with a penchant toward road rage, a relationship with other drivers on the road may occur.) In this chapter, we have chosen to focus on two kinds of relationships: romantic and relationships with one's parents because these two tend to have the most

13

salience for our well-being. Chapter 14 will also look at parent–child relationships when we consider family influences on human behavior.

Romantic Relationships

Romantic relationships tend to be among the most significant experiences of adult life. Langer (2009, p. 752) argues that love is a "universal human emotion" that can be expressed throughout one's life. Indeed, romantic relationships are celebrated in songs, books, television, movies, and other media. The interest in romantic relationships typically begins in adolescence for both heterosexuals and homosexuals. In fact, much of adolescence revolves around the activities of dating and investment in these relationships. These relationships are seen as one way in which adolescents develop their identities and self-concept (Brown, et al, 1999; Hare, Miga, & Allen, 2009). Though adolescent romantic relationships may be of limited duration, in many ways the activity is practice for such connections in adulthood. Unfortunately, there is relatively little longitudinal research that evaluates how adolescent romantic relationships influence adult relationships.

Romantic relationships can be incredibly positive or amazingly negative, depending on a variety of factors. They are characterized as being voluntary associations in many, but not all, societies. Attraction to the other person is common, although the degree and type of attraction can vary. It can be extremely strong and passionate with a sexual component, although the latter may be impacted by one's community, spiritual, or religious values. Sometimes, the attraction is present but is less passionate and more focused on feelings of intimacy and caring for the other person. Companionship may be an important element in the relationships (Brown et al., 1999). Romantic relationships are typically exclusive in the sense that both members are committed to one another and the happiness of the other becomes an important goal. For our purposes, we believe that Karney et al. (2007) best captured the richness and depth of these relationships in this definition: "a romantic or intimate relationship is one in which the individual perceives an ongoing, reciprocated, emotional, erotically charged connection with a partner" (p. 8). They note that the relationship has an erotic component, but that it is not necessary for the individuals to engage in sexual activity for the definition to apply.

Brunell et al. (2010) found that positive relationships are more likely when individuals realistically and clearly see themselves and act in accordance with their own beliefs and values. Willingness to discuss emotions is an important component of healthy relationships. Being authentic, willing to self-disclose, and having the ability to trust one's partner tend to have positive impacts on romantic relationships.

Relationships and childhood experiences

The choices adults make in forming relationships often reflect the attachment qualities they experienced as children. For example, people often select partners who share their same beliefs and perspectives about relationships. Those whose early attachments were not characterized by trust and feelings of closeness are likely to select partners with a similar background. This becomes problematic for a couple of reasons. First, they are unable to rely on the partner when distressed, thus depriving themselves of a supportive environment. Second, crises in the relationship lead to greater insecurity as they question the partner's motives and care (Simpson, Rholes, & Phillips, 1996). A similar pattern was noted between the quality of childhood attachment and adolescent romantic relationships (Dinero, Conger, Shaver, Widaman, & Larsen-rife, 2011).

The kind and nature of adult relationships that individuals experience are influenced by factors that extend back into childhood (Hazan & Shaver, 1987; Zayas, Mischel, Shoda, & Aber, 2010). For example, the bonding and attachment that typically develop in infancy and early childhood play a role in adult relationships. Infant and caretaker engage in a great deal of nonverbal interaction in addition to the verbal communication that occurs in childhood. A healthy and positive bonding experience in early life helps predict similar adult interpersonal relationships. Conversely, less positive childhood bonding experiences can result in adults who have difficulty creating and sustaining successful relationships. Unable to understand their own emotions, they often have difficulty accurately perceiving those of others.

Other adulthood experiences can also be influenced by the attachments between infant and caretaker. One such area is the ability to respond to and manage crises and stressors and to rebound from disappointing or troubling events. Individuals with a history of attachment difficulties are less likely to be forgiving of others. A secure attachment history benefits adult relationships in several ways including (Hazan & Shaver, 1987; Segal, Jaffee, & Barston, 2010):

- Feeling secure and safe in our interactions with others
- Balancing our own emotions and emotional responses
- Connecting to other human beings
- Anticipating positive relationships with others
- Developing and maintaining good memories of past relationships
- Managing stressful events so that they do not become overwhelming
- Providing confidence to openly experience life and explore one's world

Conversely, adults with troubled attachment experiences demonstrate this through problematic relationships behaviors including (Fraley, 2010; Frazier, Byer, Fischer, Wright, & DeBord, 1996):

- Remaining emotionally distant from others
- Maintaining physical distance in relationships
- Alternating availability and rejection
- Being insensitive to the needs of others
- Becoming angry and aggressive in response to relationship challenges
- Developing rigidity and intolerance toward others
- Attempting to control the behaviors and feelings of others
- Lacking in trust even within close relationships

Healthy adult relationships typically share several characteristics. These include the ability to handle interpersonal conflict without feeling attacked or devalued. While some adults refuse to deal with conflict and avoid it at all costs, this does not allow relationships to grow and develop. Couples achieve an interdependence in which each partner is connected to the other person, relying on and trusting the other. To an extent, it involves giving to another person a measure of control over our lives. This carries an inherent risk that our partner can hurt us.

Another characteristic of healthy relationships is the maintenance of interests and relationships external to the couple's dyad. For example, attempting to rely on one person to have all your needs met is a recipe for problems. Couples cannot rely on each other for everything and interacting with others brings a degree of richness and stimulation to relationships. We all benefit from participation in social networks. At the same time, couples in healthy relationships remain continually involved with each other, communicating about issues, and engaging in activities that strengthen the relationship. Whether this includes hang gliding together, walking, talking, or bungee cord jumping doesn't matter, as long as the interaction is of mutual interest.

Communication and relationships

Communication in a relationship is crucial to its survival. Both partners need to feel safe in expressing needs and wants. They must trust that their partner will react positively to this process and not blame or dismiss the other's concerns. As in most areas of life, communication includes both verbal and nonverbal elements. The goal is to hear and understand the other person's perspective, not to "win" the discussion (Saisan, Smith, & Segal, 2010). Sometimes, the communication can provoke problems. Consider two people in a relationship who have enjoyed each other's company, shared many interests, and spent significant time together. One partner, seeking clarification in the relationship asks, "Where are we going?" At this point, the relationships can atrophy or grow, depending on the answer. If both partners are hoping to move the relationships to a new level, all is likely well. If they are at different points, however, the question can end the relationships or at least diminish its quality. A case in point is Yuri's and Alicia's relationship, as we'll now explore.

Clinical Corner

Yuri and Alice

Yuri and Alice dated for about six months before Yuri invited Alice to move in with him. The relationship had grown over this period as both shared multiple interests. Yuri, who had never been married, decided one day that it was time to propose to Alice. He reasoned that they had been together for about a year and were clearly living like a married couple. When he asked Alice to marry him, Yuri was not prepared for the answer.

Alice said no because she was not ready to get married. She explained that she was only about a year out of her first marriage, a breakup that she took quite hard. "I just think it's too soon for me to jump into another marriage," she told him. Shocked and hurt, Yuri took the message as a rejection. "I'm not like your ex-husband," he said, pointing out that he was not abusive, did not use drugs, or run around on her. "I love you and I want to be with you; but it just feels to soon," she responded. With that, the topic was dropped for the next two years. Finally, Alice told Yuri she was ready to get married. "Nope," said Yuri. "I asked you to marry me and you told me no," suggesting that despite all of the time that had passed, Yuri was still smarting and aggrieved by the previous rejection. Instead of letting the past go and joyfully marrying his partner, he elected to stay hurt and unmarried. Surprisingly, the relationship between Alice and Yuri is still ongoing despite the passage of many years.

Critical Thinking Questions

1. What might be Yuri's motivation for refusing to marry Alice but staying in the relationship?
2. Why might Alice have decided to remain in the relationship despite Yuri's response to her request to get married?

The choice of a relationship partner can be influenced by multiple factors. Parents are often one of the more influential sources of modeling for their adult children. For example, an individual who experienced sexual abuse as a child may find sex as an adult unappealing. Others from this kind of background may be challenged by the kind of intimacy inherent in adult relationships. They may be unable to develop closeness to others. Some adults seek to replay relationships from their childhood, hoping to change the previous outcome—a frequently unsuccessful goal (Rapp, 2004).

The role of parental modeling

Some adults reject the modeling they perceived from their own parents and seek out different experiences. One client, involved in a marriage that no longer was fulfilling, remained married because he did not choose to emulate the example of his thrice-divorced father. However, attempts to avoid repeating the mistakes of one's parents can lead to other problems.

Parental divorces also have the potential to influence the nature and types of relationships that adults maintain. Painful experiences associated with a parental divorce, for example, may create anxiety about marriage and foster distrust toward the whole idea of permanency in a relationship (Johnston & Thomas, 1996; Whitton et al., 2008). In addition, divorce often deprives children of at least one parental model normally present. Adult children from a divorced family may evidence a variety of reactions to this experience including lack of social skills, problems managing conflict in adult relationships, higher levels of distrust, and an increased tendency to divorce in their own marriages (Amato, 2000; Wallerstein & Lewis, 2004). Similar challenges face adults whose parents abused alcohol. Kearns-Bodkin and Leonard (2008) found that children raised in alcoholic homes experienced problems in their own relationships. Interestingly, it was the parent of the opposite gender whose alcoholism most influenced the adult child. Men whose mothers were alcoholics rated satisfaction with their own marriages lower and were more likely to engage in physical violence. Women with alcoholic fathers were likely to have lower degrees of intimacy in their own marriages but were less likely to engage in physical violence against their husbands. Other relationship patterns associated with having had an alcoholic parent include a tendency for women to live with their partners for longer lengths of time before marrying, suggesting hesitancy about committing. Couples are also less likely to have their own children if either had an alcoholic mother or if both parents suffered from alcoholism (Kearns-Bodkin & Leonard, 2008).

Cui, Fincham, and Durtschi (2010) found another way in which parental divorce influences the relationships of their children. Young adults from families where parents divorced maintained a more positive attitude toward divorce than is true of adults from intact families. This tends to lower their level of commitment within their own relationships with the result that fewer of these relationships lasted as long as those of offspring from intact families. Factors affecting attitudes toward the acceptability of divorce show some important patterns. For example, young adults who saw a divorce as a positive outcome to parental fighting were more inclined to see divorce as ok. For young adults who did not witness high levels of parental conflict, divorce was less acceptable. At the same time, many children from divorced families are determined to be successful in their own marriages and relationships. How much parental divorce influences adult children appears to depend on the context in which the divorce occurs.

Adult romantic relationships between same-sex couples have also been explored to some degree. Roisman, Clausell, Holland, Fortuna, and Elieff, (2008) found that those in committed same-sex relationships shared most of the characteristics as committed heterosexual partners. About the only difference noted is that lesbians in a romantic relationship were more effective at working together with their partner. The researchers' findings conclude that positive views of their relationships were typical for married men and women, gay males, and lesbian women in relationships. Those in committed relationships also had higher quality interactions, compared to partners who were just dating.

Endings of romantic relationships

The end of a romantic relationship, as one might expect, is often difficult for one or both partners. More than 85% of adults have gone through at least one breakup of a romantic relationship (Battaglia, Richard, Datteri, & Lord, 1998). As Perilloux and Buss (2008) point out, ending a romantic relation is neither a recent phenomenon nor one that is culture specific. In some cultures, breakups happen more frequently than in the United States, but the experience of breakup appears to be universal among humans. The degree to which breakups have significant consequences for the partners is often related to the investment that they have placed in the relationships. The more one is committed to a relationship and has invested heavily in it, the more one is likely to experience more negative consequences when a breakup occurs. Both men and women show both similarities and differences in such situations, engaging in similar behavior depending upon whether one is the rejector or the rejectee. For example, after a breakup, both men and women rejectees engage in intrusive contact at about the same rate. This may entail showing up at the ex-partners home, leaving phone or text messages, or otherwise inflicting one's self on the ex-partner. Women, however, are more likely to find this behavior as anxiety producing and experience fear at their ex's behavior (Duntley & Buss, 2002). Women are more likely to encounter male behaviors designed to prolong a relationships such as offering to get married, cohabit with the partner, or have children. Each of these behaviors is designed to signal increased emotional commitment to the relationships that the male perceives as more important to women. Not surprisingly, men reported that these attempts to show increased commitment were often successful in preventing a breakup (Perilloux & Buss, 2008).

Rejectees who see the relationship's termination as leading to a lower status or reputation among peers or who feel it will reflect on their attractiveness as a prospective mate are more likely to act negatively in such situations. Although breakups are typically painful to some degree, people respond differently based on a variety of factors. Those who are rejected tend to experience more depression, more rumination, and reduced self-esteem after the breakup compared to the rejector. Rejectees are also more likely to engage in pleading, crying, and threats of suicide in an attempt to hold on to the rejector. Rejectees were more likely to experience sadness, anger, shock, jealousy, and confusion following the breakup than was true of those who rejected them (Perilloux & Buss, 2008).

Rejector males are more likely than rejector women to engage in sex with others as a prelude to the breakup. They tend to fear being seen as cruel for insisting on the breakup but also experience both guilt and happiness afterward.

Interestingly, both rejectors and rejectees shared some similar emotional reactions to the breakup. These included remorse and regret, vengeful feelings, and fear or indifference. Both male and female rejectees experienced equal amounts of these emotions. Rejected women, on the other hand, were more likely to report feeling scared, confused, and sad. Figure 13.1 shows some of the differences between men and women who were the rejectors in ending the relationship (Perilloux & Buss, 2008).

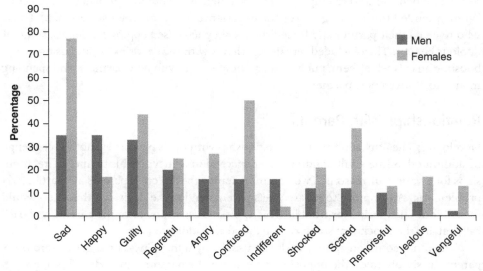

Figure 13.1
Emotions Experienced by Male and Female Rejectors
Source: Perilloux & Buss (2008).

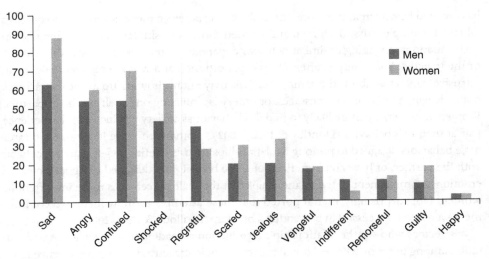

Figure 13.2
Emotions Experienced by Male and Female Rejectees
Source: Perilloux & Buss (2008).

Those who were rejected by a partner tend to experience stronger emotional responses to the breakup. Their reactions are shown in Figure 13.2 (Perilloux & Buss, 2008):

It is easy to conclude that ending a romantic relationship carries emotional costs. Regardless of whether you are the person seeking to leave or the person being rejected, feelings of sadness and regret are common. Based on the differences in reactions between men and women shown on the chart, it's easy to see that women's emotional reactions tend to be more serious and the emotional costs of breakup higher than is true for men.

Adapting to breakups typically involve a combination of behaviors designed to produce some degree of equilibrium. These include discussing the breakup with family or friends, pleading with, crying and threatening the ex-partner, and avoiding the ex-partner. These behaviors were employed by both men and women who had been rejected. Women tended to shop to get over the experience. (No, it's not a stereotype.) Those who rejected their partner and forced the breakup also used coping strategies, some of dubious benefit. They included remaining friends with the ex, drinking and using drugs, boosting an ex's self-esteem, public displays of affection with new partners, and spending money to attract a new partner.

Relationships With Parents

Developing a healthy adult-to-adult relationship with one's parents is another challenge of adulthood. Some adult children never succeed in achieving this quality of relationships for a variety of reasons. Two common approaches to one's parents are particularly problematic. Attempting to please one's parents and make decisions that they would make is one such recipe for trouble. This approach cedes power to the parents and basically retains the dependent status of childhood and adolescence.

The other common approach, driven usually by unhappiness or anger toward one's parents, is simply to do the opposite of whatever the parents would do. This approach also places the parents in control because it is their behavior to which the children are still responding. In reality, neither of these approaches can help adult children attain the independence that is the mark of adulthood.

A sensitive issue between parents and their adult children is the degree and type of sharing that occurs. One spouse or the other may see sharing certain information with a parent as a betrayal of intimacy. Sometimes the sharing pattern developed following a divorce in which the child became the parent's confidant. At other times, it is a response to a parent's prying into the new couple's relationship. Finding a healthy or mutually acceptable balance regarding sharing private information is one task of many associated with being in an intimate relationship.

Other causes of conflict include things such as making decisions that are different from what the parents would have made in the same circumstances. This is unavoidable in most cases because we are not carbon copies of our parents. Education and life experiences produce changes and no two individuals are likely to be identical in either education or experience. While parents often give lip service to wanting children to grow up and become independent, many still find it surprising when adult children begin to make up their own minds about the world.

Both parents and adult children are going through their own developmental processes and this can influence how and what kind of decisions they make. While the adult child is collecting antiques, the parents may be seeking to get rid of their old stuff. Young adults acquiring items and experiences that help them maintain their desired lifestyle may discover their parents seem more focused on saving money and consider some of their kids' actions wasteful.

Cultural changes can also play a role in the relationships between parents and their adult children. First–generation parents may still view things from the perspective of the old country, while their second–generation offspring tend to be influenced more by the dominant culture. These generational differences can be reflected in values, beliefs, and practices precipitating conflict between parent and child.

Arriving at a healthy relationship between parents and their adult children requires that both generations begin to view the other as adults. Adult children must respond to parental suggestions and admonitions in the same vein they would employ with their friends. Every parental suggestion is not a hidden criticism of the adult child's actions, although some adult children respond as if it were. At the same time, adult children's ideas about raising their own children may be better than the approach used by their parents. If such decisions are viewed by parents as a repudiation of their parenting style, this can lead to communication problems and hard feelings.

While it is natural for parents to worry about their children, even as adults, this can be a source of contention. Hay, Fingerman, and Lefkowitz (2008) found that while some adult children found their parents worrying a sign of affection and love, others found it irritating and annoying. This worrying, however, can be a two-way street. Adult children may be concerned about their parents' health, ability to live alone, or care for themselves. The greater the amount of worrying expressed by adult children or parents, the more likely that it will be seen as problematic. Worrying occurred in both men and women and in Black and White families, with Black families experiencing a greater level of concern than White families.

Intergeneration tension appears more pronounced in the case of mothers (Birditt, Miller, Fingerman, & Lefkowitz, 2009). Both male and female adult children experience greater degrees of tension with their mothers than with their fathers. Sources of irritation often were around issues such as money management, housekeeping, and the frequency of interactions. Of course, any issue can become a strain on the relationship—child-rearing practices, differences in communication styles, lifestyle choices of the adult children, and/or differences around religion or political views.

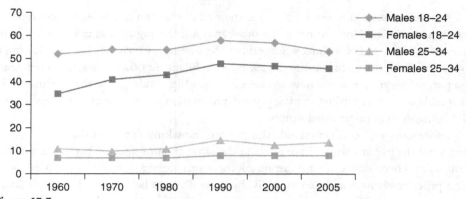

Figure 13.3
Percentage of Young Adults Living With Parents
Source: InfoPlease (2011).

Relationships can also be stressed if adult children are living with their parents. This happens most often when the child pursues an education and remains with the parents for financial and convenience reasons. It can also occur when adult children move back home after a period of being independent, which appears to occur in about 10% of families. Figure 13.3 shows the trends in these respective situations.

Loss of job, family breakup, and other factors can force adult children to consider moving back home. The recession of 2008–2009 is not reflected in the data shown in the chart, but it is highly likely that subsequent figures will show an increase in the number of adult children who lived with their parents.

As a stopgap measure, moving in with parents often proves successful allowing the displaced adult to become more financially stable with the support of caring parents. Many parents feel guilty if they do not offer the adult child a place to stay, despite the changes it will bring to their lives. At the same time, it can lead to strains when the lifestyles of parents and adult child are vastly different. The child who gives up looking for work can come to depend upon the parents to do everything from providing meals to making car payments. Even parents with the financial resources to assist can become resentful at the expectation and the seemingly interminable nature of this "temporary" situation. At the same time, most parents find the challenges of the new experience positive. Only in situations involving an adult child with substance abuse problems do parents report serious problems with the arrangement (Umberton, 2006).

Parent–adult child relationships can also be affected by the latter's problems (e.g., health, mental health, financial, substance abuse). Pillemer and Suitor (2002) found that these problems of adult children are associated with their parents' well-being. Children with more problems tend to have parents who are more depressed, less healthy emotionally, and more ambivalent toward the parent–child relationship. This is especially true for single parents (Greenfield & Marks, 2006). Apparently, if the adult child's parents are married and living together, it helps to act somewhat as a buffer to parents' negative reactions to their adult child's situation. Another possible explanation is that single parents are more susceptible to being influenced by their children's difficulty because, absent a partner, the parent–child relationships is more needed or valued.

As parents grow older, they often seek more contact with their adult children. However, this may occur at the point when the adult children are busy caring for children, establishing themselves in a career, and making their own friendships. In such instances, adult children are more likely to perceive the parents' needs as intrusive. Despite this possibility, Fingerman, et al., (2007) found that most adult children focused on the positive aspects of the situation, including getting to spend more time with their parents. They also felt that their parents really appreciated the care they were able to provide to them. This is consistent with Birditt, Miller, Fingerman, and Lefkowitz (2009) who found that parents and adult children usually find ways of adapting to or accommodating each other's needs. Those who cannot achieve this healthy level of interaction often end up avoiding each other or engaging in angry exchanges that worsen the relationship.

While most adult children grow up and move away from their parents, there are important exceptions. Umberton (2006) points out that many parents provide ongoing care for their children who are experiencing major mental illnesses, and those with serious intellectual or physical disabilities. This often reflects a continuity of care beginning with the child's birth and continuing as he or she enters young adulthood. In these situations, the dependency needs of the adult child drive the relationship.

Like romantic relationships, the parent–child connection has aspects of interdependence. It is not uncommon, for example, for parents to try to help their adult children financially. This may involve lending or giving money for a down payment on a home, passing along a vehicle at little or no cost, or serving as babysitters. At the same time, adult children may provide services to their parents such as mowing the lawn, fixing the plumbing, or in extreme cases, providing care for an aging parent. The latter situation even has its own name: the sandwich generation. Adult children are seen as sandwiched between caring for their aged parents and raising their own children. This can place enormous stress on adult children with multiple responsibilities. It can also be embarrassing and humiliating for parents who now must rely on their children for things such as meal preparation, laundry, and bathing.

The stress of this new relationship challenge can exacerbate long-dormant issues between parents and children. It can also produce resentment at being placed in the role of caretaker and provoke conflicts with siblings who are not perceived to be shouldering an equal share of responsibilities. These stressors are often lessened when the prior relationship between parent and adult children was solid. Such connections often serve as a supportive mechanism helping both parent and child adapt to their changed roles.

EDUCATION

For most individuals in the United States, education has been a critical part of their development. Parents have typically assumed that their children would complete K-12 and then acquire additional knowledge or skills through technical training or graduation from a college or university. As we have previously pointed out, this assumption has been challenged by the actual outcomes of education. Many students drop out without completing high school, although some will return and later earn a GED. Pursuing post–high school training or education is not necessarily a given for millions of late adolescents and young adults. Clearly, students who did not complete high school are much less likely to enroll in higher education or specialized training programs. For some, their experiences in high school were so unpleasant that further education is not even contemplated. Others who did not perform well in high school may lack the credentials and grade point average to be admitted to higher education. For still others, the poor quality of their educational preparation compromises their ability to be successful in college.

Despite the challenges faced by some students, enrollment in colleges and universities is at the highest level in history. This is particularly true for young adults between the ages of 16 and 24. Figure 13.4 shows the enrollment trend over the past 50 years.

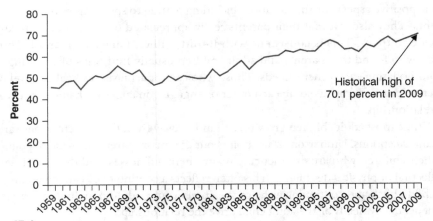

Figure 13.4
College Enrollment Rate of Recent High School Graduates Age 16 to 24, October 1959–2009
Source: U.S. Bureau of Labor Statistics (2011).

While Figure 13.4 covers only young adults, other individuals will pursue and succeed in higher education later in their adult years. The returning or nontraditional student is now a fixture on most campuses. While a portion of these students are earning additional degrees to bolster their earning potential, many others are either returning to college after raising a family or pursuing a different career. In addition, many adults are entering higher education for the very first time.

While it might have been expected that pursuing higher education would be an equal-opportunity endeavor, recent statistics tell a different story. According to the Bureau of Labor Statistics (2011), 23% of women had earned a bachelor's degree by the age of 23 compared to 14% of men of the same age. The gap in educational attainment also affects other groups in society. For example, non-Hispanic Whites are more than twice as likely to earn a bachelor's degree as Hispanics or non-Hispanic Blacks.

Enrollment in community colleges is outpacing other higher education institutions, which may reflect several trends. First, two-year schools often are less expensive and many of their courses are accepted at four-year colleges and universities. This makes them an economical choice for students during their first two years in college. Second, the relative smallness of community colleges often feels more comfortable to students, particularly those who are returning to school later in adult life. Third, students whose K-12 education was either substandard or who performed less well during high school can often get accepted to a two-year college and have the opportunity to demonstrate their ability to do college-level work and receive help in weaker areas of academic preparation. Finally, community colleges have been working directly with employers to develop training programs designed to meet specific employment needs. The technical training offered in such programs often leads directly to employment. These programs are particularly valuable for students not seeking a bachelor's degree or for those wishing to find suitable employment.

Education in the United States is also closely related to employment. Individuals who attain higher education receive employment benefits that clearly overshadow those without such preparation. Figure 13.5 demonstrates how the difference in education plays out with respect to employment. Overall, those with more educational attainment were more likely to have a job and be employed for longer periods.

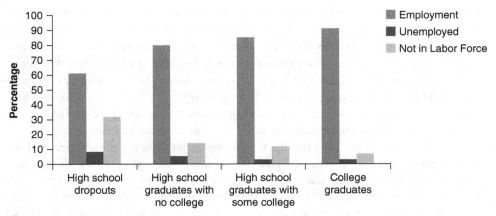

Figure 13.5
Percent of 23-Year-Olds Employed
Source: Bureau of Labor Statistics, 2011.

CHOOSING A CAREER

One marker of adulthood that is generally recognized in the United States is locating and maintaining full-time employment (Santrock, 2008). Typically, most young people have held part-time jobs, and by their early twenties have been employed in almost five positions. About 6% of those who had not earned a high school diploma or GED by age 24 had held no jobs since leaving high school (Bureau of Labor Statistics, 2011). High school dropouts were about 50% less likely to be employed than their peers who completed high school but no college.

While one might conclude that higher education leads to specific careers, this is often not the case. A college degree might initially be sought with a goal of preparing for employment in one area, but often other factors influence the careers we ultimately pursue. Most people have preferences that affect the careers they seek: some like working with people, some with data, and some with things, such as car repair or construction (Huckaby, 2008). In many cases, these preferences are related to skills we have developed over our lifetimes. Some skills are drawn from direct experience, such as jobs we have held or internships, while others are a product of formal education. Still others are things we simply picked up by watching others or through trial and error. These preferences and skills often influence our choice of career preparation and majors in college.

The choice of a career is sometimes a conscious decision. A nephew of mine decided in high school that he wanted to be an actuary. (Why is anybody's guess. No one in the family ever had this background.) He took college courses designed to prepare him for the field, did an internship with a firm, and accepted employment as an actuary upon graduation. Another family member wanted to be a dentist and pursued the training to achieve this goal. A third family member pursued college with the goal of getting married and succeeded. For each of them, his or her goals were clear and conscious. At the same time, not everybody knows what he or she wants to be when he or she grows up. College students often change majors as they struggle to identify a field that interests them and matches their skills. In fact, some students make multiple changes in majors in this pursuit.

The desire to change one's major may be necessitated by any number of factors. First, it is natural that a large percentage of college students would have no firm idea about a future career. Given the enormous array of options available within higher education—and the even more vast list of potential careers—it is perhaps surprising that anyone has made up his or her mind. Considering that most of us are exposed to only a tiny subset of career possibilities, uncertainty is normal. Second, some adolescents choose a college major based on parental wishes. When they get to college, they sometimes find the chosen field is not a good fit, find the chosen field isn't sufficiently interesting, or find another field more enticing. As an academic advisor, I've had students come to me nearly in tears because they were going to have to tell their parents that they no longer were pursuing a business degree and wanted to be a social worker.

Third, some students discover that the chosen major does not match their skill set. They begin to question whether the goal of becoming a dentist meshes with their lack of ability and interest in the sciences or if they still want to be an actuary despite poor mathematics and statistics skills. Finally, some students are simply unable to be admitted to the major they had planned on. Perhaps it is a very popular major with limited openings or one with academic requirements so high that the only students admitted are those with a 4.0 GPA.

Many career counselors advise the importance of learning about yourself—values, skills, interests, personality—to help you select an appropriate career. Factors such as your natural talents and work preferences would be considered. For example, if you are a social animal who loves being around and interacting with people, then a career as a geologist wandering the mountains in search of natural resources might not be your best choice. Do you like the outdoors, like being in the woods, and value nature? This might lend itself to geography, natural resources, or another science-related field. Do you enjoy sitting at your computer, accessing websites, and experimenting with various software programs? A field related to computer science might make more sense than becoming a psychologist.

Even those who take advantage of career planning assistance and see a career counselor may find themselves torn between different areas. A colleague of mine completed a series of interest inventory tests designed to show how his interests compared to people working in various career fields. The results suggested that his interests were very similar to professional social workers and to forest rangers, a seemingly dichotomous choice. Unless he wanted to provide social work services to bats, bears, and badgers, he did not see how he could connect these two seemingly disparate fields. A career counselor pointed out that it was common to have different interests like this. Often it meant that one of the areas would become a hobby or leisure time pursuit rather than a career. In my colleague's case, it made great sense. He loved the woods and rivers and enjoyed hunting with a bow and arrow, fishing, and boating. Clearly, his avocational interests could not easily merge with his social work career, but served as a welcome getaway from the challenges of his chosen field. How we spend our leisure time and balance our work and family lives—that is, what we do for recreation—has a great impact on our mental health and, consequently, our behavior.

RECREATION

Recreation refers to the kinds of activities we engage in when we are on our own time. We learn to engage in recreation from the earliest point in our lives: playing with our first toy. From childhood to adult status, we learn to play—with others or by ourselves. As adults, our leisure time is often spent pursuing activities that give us pleasure or enjoyment. For many people, even a portion of work time is spent recreating. According to a survey by Salary.com (2012) 64% of employees reported visiting nonwork related websites every day while on the job with some reporting as much as 5 hours per week.. The primary reason—relaxation—may prove to be beneficial to both the worker and the employer (McNamara, 2009).

Benefits of Recreation

Recreation becomes an important facet in adult lives for several reasons. First, recreation serves to rejuvenate and recharge our social and psychological batteries. It gives us an opportunity to consider what we think is important, to get away from the normal, and to help shed workweek worries. In many respects, recreation is considered fundamental to the well-being of society. For children, play is work—it is what they do as they learn to get along with others and it's essential for their physical and social development. For adults, it can also be a means of social inclusion—providing a sense of participation, acceptance, belonging, and being valued (Donnelly & Coakley, n.d.). Some types of recreation can also play a role in helping human beings deal with a variety of health problems. Challenges ranging from obesity to depression and diabetes to suicide can be ameliorated through physical activity (California State Parks, 2005). With estimates that most American adults engage in relative sedentary leisure time activities and almost 70% of Americans over the age of 20 are either overweight or obese, recreation that involves physical activity can have many benefits (CDC, 2010). While there is continued debate about the causes of obesity, it is clear that a lack of physical activity is a significant contributor (Apovian, 2010; Welk & Blair, 2000). Physical activity can reduce the risk of multiple serious diseases, including cardiovascular disease, heart attacks, hypertension, type II diabetes, colon and breast cancer, and osteoporosis (Haennel & Lemire, 2002; Health and Human Services, 1996; Slattery, 2004; Wannamethee, Shaper, & Alberta, 2000). There is also evidence that physical activity has benefits for the human immune system (MedlinePlus, 2012; Mooney, Stanten, & Yeager, 2002; Smith, Kennedy, & Fleshner, 2004) as shown in Table 13.1.

While physical activity can benefit one's mental health, high levels of activity are not required in all cases. Activities of a social nature, for example, provide benefits by helping to alleviate loneliness and giving individuals events to anticipate that do not

Table 13.1 Mental Health Benefits of Physical Activity

Mental Health Area	Level of Influence	Notes	Study
Anxiety	Moderate influence	Reduces short-term anxiety	Ahn & Fedewa, 2011; Fontaine, 2000; Larun et al., 2006
Self-esteem	Moderate influence	Increases self-esteem	Ahn & Fedewa, 2009; Ekeland, Heian, & Hagen, 2005
Energy level	Large influence	Increases energy level	Fontaine, 2000; Plante et al., 2006
Cognitive functioning	Small influence	Also strengthens executive functioning in adults and children	Keeley & Fox, 2009; Winneke et al., 2012
Depression	Moderate influence	Reduces symptoms with mild to moderate depression	Ahn & Fedewa, 2009; Fontaine, 2000; Larun et al., 2006
Panic disorder	Small influence	Reduces panic over time if continued regularly	Fontaine, 2000; Richardson et al., 2005
Positive affect/ well-being	Small to moderate influence	Best results if physical activity involves social interaction	Fontaine, 2000; Lampinen et al., 2006

necessarily require physical activity. Hobbies and spending time with friends can also produce mental health benefits. Stress relief can occur through almost any recreational activity that the individual finds enjoyable. Looking out one's window at nature has been shown to reduce stress (Tarrant, 1996). Activities that provide the individual a feeling of control over various aspects of his or her life can increase self-esteem.

For those who prefer more solitary time, recreation can provide ample opportunity to be by oneself. For social animals, recreation easily can include spending time with family, friends, or just colleagues. Recreational activities might be as sedate as quietly reading a book on the beach or as strenuous as rock climbing or spelunking in caves. For some individuals, high-risk behaviors that bring a jolt of adrenalin are considered recreation because they are so different from their day jobs. Compare downhill skiing and roller-coaster rides with cross-country skiing and relaxing on a slow-moving pontoon boat and you get a sense of how different people require different kinds of recreation. Clearly, people's ideas of recreation are vastly different. Yet, human beings can become quite passionate about their recreation and vociferously defend its virtues. The benefits to recreation apparently are best known and explained by those who select the activity rather than the casual observer.

Social benefits of recreation are also common. They include strengthening of communities by providing places for people to get together. Some communities have used recreational opportunities for their citizens as a means of reducing crime. By developing communal activities that draw in residents, they help move gangs and other undesirable groups out of parks. Offering after-school recreational activities helped reduce the incidence of crimes committed by and against children (FCIK, 2001; Groese, 2002; Mahatmya & Lohman, 2011). While most benefits of recreation accrue to the individual, it is clear that others may assist a community to improve its quality of life.

The importance of recreation is underscored by the ways in which a society provides opportunities to recreate. Parks, forests, camping spaces, off-road vehicle tracks, jogging and walking trails, and skateboard areas are often provided by various levels of government from federal to local. Communities offer opportunities for volleyball, softball, and bowling teams to compete in sanctioned events. Many communities maintain community centers with swimming pools, basketball and tennis courts, and similar recreational facilities. Community golf courses can be sponsored by the city, county, state governments, or private entrepreneurs. The availability of these community resources is directly correlated with the amount of physical activity engaged in by community members (Brownson, Baker, Housemann, Brennan, & Bacak, 2001).

In addition, most communities of any size support the arts, theatre, and music performances to enable residents with interests in these areas. Similarly, institutions and organizations in a community sponsor recreational activities for their members and sometimes the general public. The Catholic Church often offers bingo during the week while some churches encourage scrapbooking, quilt making, and other organized activities. Often, these activities are designed to be social events bringing people together to have fun. Sometimes, they can be employed on behalf of a civic purpose such as collecting items for the local food pantry. Even events with an ulterior purpose can be enjoyable and meet the definition of recreation.

THE MIDLIFE CRISIS AND MIDDLE ADULTHOOD ISSUES

The term *midlife crisis* has been used to describe a period in middle adulthood when an individual begins to reassess his or her life. Middle adulthood is variously described as occurring between the ages of 35 and 60, 40 and 60, and 30 and 70. For our purposes, we will use the middle age grouping, 40 and 60, although the boundaries on both ends appear fuzzy and vague (Freund & Ritter, 2009). Jaques (1965), who coined the term *midlife crisis*, believed that the principal task of midlife was coming to terms with one's own mortality. Since then, the term has been associated with comparing where one is in life to where one expected to be. For example, the quality of one's marriage may be evaluated as well as one's career with the result that a degree of dissatisfaction with one or both begins to set in. Some have suggested the crisis is related to changes of various sorts. One proposed argument is that environmental factors such as changes in expected societal roles and family changes produce pressures that affect the middle age adult (Helson & Soto, 2005). Another explanation is that changes in personality occur during this period as the individual becomes less motivated to reach the top of one's field and recognizes that it was not going to happen anyway (Ogilvie & Rose, 1995). Adult development experts have identified changes in psychological resources such as cognitive capacities, impulse control, and personality traits as possible factors that might contribute to one having a midlife crisis (Gough & Bradley, 1996; Helson & Soto, 2005).

> **Human Behavior**
>
> *Practice Behavior Example: Apply theories and knowledge from the liberal arts to understand biological, social, cultural, psychological, and spiritual development.*
>
> **Critical Thinking Questions:** Because these factors tend to be common phenomena in middle adulthood, we would expect that midlife crises may produce changes in most of us. What form might these changes take? Why might some people experience more profound changes than others?

One purported consequence of the midlife crisis is an aberrant change in behavior. The wife runs off with the milkman (Do they still deliver milk door-to-door?) leaving the children to be raised by a depressed husband. Or conversely, the husband raids his retirement savings, purchases a $200,000 Lamborghini Gallardo, and moves to Tahiti. The behavior is completely out of the norm for the individual and brings catastrophic results. You must know several people who have experienced a midlife crisis and behaved this way, right?

Ok, no. While a midlife crisis does occur in some individuals, the vast majority of evidence suggests that it affects no more than a quarter of U.S. adults (Wethington, Kessler, & Pixley, 2004). Most adult development researchers have concluded that the concept of midlife crises is not well founded (Santrock, 2008). Perhaps responding to societal or cultural influences, Americans tend to label any crisis that occurs during middle adulthood as a midlife crisis, while most researchers adopt a much narrower definition (Wethington, 2000).

Though middle adulthood is associated with many changes, they are not all potentially upsetting. In middle adulthood, for example, we typically become less anxious and more in control with respect to our careers. Financial stability often is associated with this phase as is a greater sense of mastery over various aspects of our lives. Emotional stability is relatively common in middle adulthood and we are much better able to manage our impulses (Siegler & Costa, 1999). Higher levels of both autonomy and self-determination typically exist during this period (Keyes & Ryff, 1999).

Middle adulthood is sometimes considered a transition period to the second half of one's life (Becker, 2006). Different theorists have viewed middle adulthood as a specific developmental period characterized by a number of changes (Erikson, 1972; Jung, 1971; McFadden & Swan, 2012). Changes that occur in middle adulthood can be unsettling. Changes in one's body and health are common, and researchers have noted that these changes can be particularly concerning to women (Banister, 2000). Physiological changes affecting sexuality and attractiveness and menopause are common examples. While a majority of women experience menopause with a minimum of difficulty, as many as 40% noted some symptoms of depression. Brown, Gallicchio, Flaws, and Tracy (2009) traced a large portion of perimenopausal symptoms to sleep disturbances brought on by hot flashes, muscle stiffness, and urinary incontinence. However, in even these situations, the vast majority of women did not develop clinical depression unless they had simultaneously or recently experienced negative life events or were in poor health to begin with. Degges-White (2001) notes that for most women, menopause represents a new era of emotional and creative fertility, motivation, and desire. A major factor associated with unpleasant menopausal symptoms, such as negative moods, included unhappiness in one's marriage (Kurpius, Maresh, & Nicpon, 2001). Women with happy marriages had lowered rates of symptomatology. This is consistent with other studies that link marital happiness with feelings of emotional well-being (Earle, Smith, Harris, & Longino, 1998).

In a culture where youth and attractiveness are prized, women in middle adulthood may experience a degree of uncertainty and ambivalence about their own bodies as well as undermined self-esteem. In some cultures, women who have obtained elderhood are revered and their wisdom sought. In many Western cultures, though, this is not the case. In the United States, media paints a picture of middle age for women that is decidedly unappetizing. Advertisements for everything from wrinkle removal to repairing sagging breasts appear regularly, suggesting that aging is a disorder that needs to be cured (Degges-White, 2001).

Even the prevalence of menopausal symptoms appears to be culturally influenced. Japanese women, for example, report fewer symptoms and saw transitioning through menopause as unremarkable (Lock, 1991). Similar results were noted in Australia with menopause not associated with depressed mood. Women who reported positive moods prior to menopause continued this outlook throughout menopause (Marcus-Newhall, Thomson, & Thomas 2001). Rural Mayan women look forward to menopause and the conclusion of their child-bearing responsibilities, and Swedish women experienced increased self-esteem and sense of identity from menopause (Mills, 2011; Oloffson & Collins, 2000). Once again, a positive attitude toward menopause seemed to play a large role in how the phase was experienced.

Cultural values regarding the ideal female body contribute to the difficulties experienced by some women in adulthood, just as they do in the case of younger women. Public media reinforces this ideal and helps perpetuate a cultural problem. However, many women reject those values that undermine their own sense of self. For example, several of the women whom Banister (2000) interviewed found a renewed interest in their own sexuality in middle adulthood, which challenged the stereotype that interest in sexuality declines during this period.

There is substantial evidence that women begin to report less sexual satisfaction in late midlife (Carpenter, Nathanson, & Kim, 2009). At the same time, most middle-aged adults say that sex is as good or better than it was at earlier points in their lives. Not surprisingly, men habitually report greater sexual satisfaction than do women of the same age. Research into the reasons for one's level of sexual satisfaction has identified individual-level differences. For example, permissive beliefs about sex tend to lead to increased satisfaction while the opposite is true for less-permissive individuals (Haavio-Mannila & Kontula, 1997). Other factors—such as socioeconomic level, religion, ethnicity, and race—do not seem related to sexual satisfaction level with a couple of exceptions. Higher-income Caucasian women tended to feel less satisfied than Black women (Christopher & Sprecher, 2000).

Other factors that influence sexual satisfaction include the relationship between the partners. Married couples are generally more satisfied than their single counterparts. As might be expected, the more people have invested in a relationship, the higher their level of satisfaction. Likewise, monogamous relationships have higher satisfaction levels than nonexclusive relationships. Not surprisingly, those who engage in sexual behavior more frequently tend to report higher satisfaction levels than those for whom sex was less frequent. In addition, more adventurous lovers using a variety of sexual techniques report higher satisfaction levels (Haavio-Mannila & Kontula, 1997).

A third category of influences on sexual satisfaction is culture. Cultural beliefs about sexuality can enhance or impair satisfaction. Younger members of societies tend to adopt more permissive attitudes toward sexuality compared to older members resulting in higher satisfaction levels. Similarly, older lovers may feel pressure to avoid sexual behavior after a certain point because a younger generation deems it unseemly. Langer (2009, p. 752) captures our confused views toward sexuality: "We think our parents are too old to; we think our kids are too young to; our kids think we are too old to; so, who in the heck is supposed to?" If older adults are considered incapable of having sex and lacking in sexual desire and are seen as weird if they do, this is an unhealthy view of human sexuality. Societal ideals of youth and beauty also play a role in discouraging sexuality. In this view, older adults are neither youthful nor beautiful and, therefore, not sexually desirable. Such ageist views serve to undermine an important characteristic of older adulthood—the pursuit of appropriate, positive, and ongoing sexuality. It is ironic that societal views paint older adults as somehow asexual beings, while the availability of drugs for erectile dysfunction have allowed many couples to increase the frequency of sexual intercourse.

Male Menopause

Several researchers have proposed the existence of male menopause (andropause) as a counterpart to female menopause (Jacobs, 2000; Watson, 2000). The fact that men do not menstruate, of course, makes the use of this analogy inappropriate. Attempts to discover changes in hormone levels in men and compare them with women also produce no discernable similarities (Boul, 2003). Unlike women, men's hormones do not stop but rather decline at a low rate into late adulthood. Although physiological and psychological changes occur in middle adulthood men, they are related more to lifestyles than hormonal changes. Physiological changes in men are often related to factors such as smoking, alcohol use, cholesterol level, obesity, poverty, and diseases (hypertension and heart disease), among others (Boul, 2003; Chew, Earle, Stuckey, Jamrozik, & Keogh, 2000). For some men, midlife stressors are associated with unhappiness with employment or problems at home. These factors can lead to irritability and outbursts. However, most of the changes reported by men in middle adulthood are neither gender nor age specific.

Personality changes have also been studied over time, and the results suggest that middle adulthood tends to move in predictable ways for both men and women (Helson, Jones, & Kwan, 2002). These directions include an increase in norm-adherence and a decrease in areas of social vitality. Scores on scales dealing with independence and dominance also increased at middle adulthood on the California Personality Inventory. These changes underscore the belief that personality change is an ongoing phenomenon that does not end at age 30.

As in other phases of life, it is clear that significant variations occur among individuals. While some may react to the realization that they are never going to be president of their company and find this disheartening, others use the realization to relax and enjoy their accomplishments. When a crisis does occur in midlife, it is often caused by some life event—such as losing one's job or contracting a serious illness. Illnesses that can precipitate a crisis include things such as loss of vision or others that impair functioning in employment or family environments (Boerner, Wang, & Cimarolli, 2006).

Social activity for older adults enhances mental health. Here a bingo game provides a venue for socializing

Sometimes, it is not a major event that precipitates challenges in middle adulthood. For some individuals, the daily grind of life, work, marriage, low income, and so on finally wears down the individual's resources to the point that a crisis is precipitated. While middle adulthood stressors can be enormous, they mostly occur in people capable of managing them. Middle adulthood brings with it the experience to weather events that would upset a younger person. As always, there are exceptions to this observation. For example, many adults in midlife who were victims of child abuse and neglect find that their risk for drug-use problems increases. Those who were victimized as children do not age out of this trauma as they enter middle adulthood (Widom, Marmostein, & White, 2006; Wilson & Widom, 2010).

Middle adulthood is the phase in which the postparental syndrome can occur as children grow up and move out, leaving parents suddenly alone. This can lead to some parents feeling less satisfied with their marriage, which, in turn, may provoke a crisis. On the other hand, the parents more often celebrate their new freedom and enjoy increased financial resources. The child's bedroom becomes an office or a hobby room; parents may rejoice that they now have time to take the cruise they always wanted. Overall, middle adulthood seems to be characterized as a period of greater sense of personal identity, self-efficacy, and awareness of one's mortality (Stewart & Ostrove, 1998). It is important to recognize that while change is a common occurrence in adulthood, the result is more often stability than instability. Midlife crises can occur, but it's best not to plan on getting that Lamborghini.

Keeping active in later life is easier if you have hobbies or other interests.

Assess your comprehension of the Influence of Education and Middle Adulthood by completing this quiz.

LATER LIFE

Defining the later life period is always open to interpretation and often overlaps with the last portion of middle adulthood. Baker and Gringart (2009) define the period from age 65 to 85, while Holland, Schutte, Brennan, and Moos (2010) use age 55 as the starting point. Although a bit arbitrary, we'll use age 60 as the starting point because that was the end point for middle adulthood used earlier in this chapter. The period of later life includes retirement, preparing for death, and widowhood, each of which will be examined separately although overlap is unavoidable.

Later Life and Self-Esteem

A major focus of later life research has been the issue of self-esteem. This is logical since self-esteem is clearly associated with maintaining a high quality of life. While much attention has been paid to negative aspects of old age, it is clear that many later life adults maintain or increase their levels of self-esteem. Although faced with a variety of physical, social, and psychological challenges, many refuse to allow these events to change their outlook (Shaw, Liang, & Krause, 2010). At the same time, the overall pattern of increased self-esteem in early and middle adulthood does not continue in later life. Some have argued that this lowered self-esteem is a reaction to the challenges associated with old age, while others suggest that it reflects a more realistic appraisal of oneself. Interestingly, older Blacks tended to experience loss of self-esteem at a rate up to three times higher than for Whites. This is in marked contrast to earlier life stages where Blacks maintain a high level of self-esteem, despite encountering a host of challenges. A major explanation for this drop in self-esteem is retirement.

Other researchers have focused on the role of body image in relation to self-esteem (Baker & Gringart, 2009). They observe that women have long been sensitive to societal stereotypes of the ideal body, but men have not been studied to the same degree. While it was thought that any relationship between one's self-image and an ideal body image is likely to operate more in young and middle adulthood, recent research questions this assumption. For example, whatever unhappiness women have about their bodies is more or less stable across the life span, with an increase in satisfaction noted in later life. Men, on the other hand, tend to see themselves as decreasingly attractive in later life. Much of this decline is related to feelings about lost coordination and diminished health. Though men in later life are more dissatisfied with their physical appearance, unlike women, they tend not to find ways to improve it.

Material Resources and Quality of Life

Other factors that influence the quality of later life include the availability of material resources (Alley et al., 2009). Material resources include the goods and services that our socioeconomic status allows us to purchase. More income tends to equal more goods and services. Health care, food, and housing are three key material resources in this period. Lack of health insurance and high out-of-pocket deductibles lead to lowered use of health care services and greater incidence of health problems. Required medications not purchased because of these same limitations contribute to poor health outcomes. Likewise, food insecurity contributes to poorer health outcomes in this population.

A significant percentage of adults age 65 and older have one or more disadvantages that affect their life quality. This is particularly true for non-Hispanic Blacks and Hispanics. Similar findings about the role of socioeconomic inequality have been noted in 10 European countries suggesting a degree of universality (Ladin, Daniels, & Kawachi, 2009).

Alley and colleagues (2009) concluded that food disadvantage "is as strong a predictor of later health declines as is heart disease, cancer, stroke, pulmonary disease, or diabetes" (p. 699). Their research underscores the need for better access to health care and health insurance, and illustrates how the macro environment impinges on the micro level.

Depression in Later Life

Later adulthood sometimes is characterized as a period of decline, with depression as a potential outcome. Blazer (2010) has looked at the biological risks associated with later life depression and concluded that vascular lesions in subcortical areas of the brain most often predict depression in this age group. The most common indicators of depression in this group are problems planning, organizing, extracting, and sequencing information. Later life adults with cardiovascular disease are at increased risk of developing depression, as are those experiencing chronic pain. Of course, depression is also associated with Alzheimer's disease and stroke, urinary incontinence, and shortness of breath.

Psychological factors are also blamed for some later life depression. Disturbed cognitive functioning may contribute to depression for those individuals who overact or overpersonalize events. Depression is a risk for those who overgeneralize from negative occurrences and have unrealistic expectations about their lives and others. The failure of a loved one to visit or the cancellation of a planned family event can lead to a downward spiral. Wisdom is an important protective factor that helps offset other psychological risks. As considered by Erikson and others, wisdom includes comfort in managing uncertainty, the ability to look beyond oneself, skill in reinterpreting past experience, and degree of acceptance of mortality (Blazer, 2010).

Social factors contributing to depression also exist. For example, Kraaij, Arensman, and Spinhoven (2002), studying the relationship between depression and negative life events, concluded that as the number of negative events and everyday stressors went up, so did the incidence of depressive symptoms. Impairment in one's social support network also contributes to development of depression. Loss of children and strained relationships with caregivers and friends can also contribute. Resistance to depression is influenced by spiritual and religious experiences. Depression rates are lower for those who regularly attend religious services irrespective of gender, race, social support, or physical health (Braam, Beekman, Deeg, Smith, & van Tilburg, 1997). Similarly, older adults often believe that the stressors they have experienced have resulted in a closer relationship with their God (Krause, 2007). This is consistent with social work's valuing of the influence of spirituality and religion in understanding human behavior and the wisdom of recognizing client strengths.

We have talked earlier about the potential influence of childhood experience on development later in middle adulthood. There is also some evidence that these experiences as a child can influence cognitions in later adulthood (Fors, Lennartsson, & Lundberg, 2009). Their study echoed previous research showing that early life socioeconomic conditions have a significant impact on late life cognitions. Factors such as the lower social class of the father and a pattern of family conflicts do influence cognitive ability later in one's life. These affects were moderated to an extent by educational level and adult social class of the child. Another mediating influence was moderate exercise, which in both midlife and later life reduce the chances of developing mild cognitive impairment after age 70 (Geda et al., 2010).

It is important to keep in perspective that while depression does strike many older adults, the overall incidence is likely no more than 5% of those individuals living in the community (Hinrichsen, 2009). Older adults demonstrate the same resilience in the last portion of their lives as they did in earlier years. Even among those in long-term residential care settings, only about 20% suffer major depressive disorders, although some researchers put the percentage higher (Walker & Steffens, 2010). Interestingly, those providing care to older adults are themselves at a certain amount of risk for depression. Overall, adults in later life experience much lower rates of depression than is true of younger people (Blazer & Hybels, 2005).

Later Life and Suicide

One problem in the population of older adults is suicide. While those age 65 and older represent about 12% of the U.S. population, they account for about 16% of deaths by suicide (CDC, 2005). The rates of suicide vary by ethnic group, as shown in Figure 13.6.

This population's suicide rate is related to several factors, depression, cognitive impairment, and decline in health. Many older adults struggling with depression benefit from the same interventions as younger individuals. A combination of medication and psychotherapy appear to benefit as many as 80% of those with depression. However,

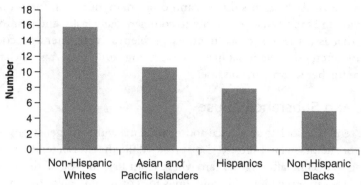

Figure 13.6
Suicide Rates per 100,000 People 65Years of Age and Older
Source: Centers for Disease Control and Prevention (2005).

those with severe physical health problems, coupled with memory and thinking impairment, do not appear to benefit from the addition of psychotherapy to a medicine regimen alone.

Later Life and Dementia

Another problem social workers are likely to encounter is dementias. Dementia rates range from 30% for those 85–89 to 50% for those 90–94. About 74% of people older than age 95 will develop dementias (Montine & Larson, 2010). The authors identify three common diseases that constitute the bulk of dementia: Alzheimer's disease, vascular brain injury, and Lewy body disease. Of these, the most common cause of dementia is Alzheimer's disease, affecting about 5.1 million Americans. According to the National Institute on Aging (2010), "Alzheimer's disease is an irreversible, progressive brain disease that slowly destroys memory and thinking skills, and eventually even the ability to carry out the simplest tasks. In most people with Alzheimer's, symptoms first appear after age 60" (p. 1). The disease interferes with communication skills, causes memory loss, and eventually affects most areas of life. A common characteristic is the reduced ability to accurately perceive the emotions of others. For example, the capacity to receive and decode facial expressions declines to some extent from normal aging and is exacerbated in those with dementia (Phillips, Scott, Henry, Mowat, & Bell, 2010). This can lead to problems in communicating with others.

Exact causes of this disease are hard to identity, but the brains of afflicted individuals often show abnormal clumps or plaques of tissue and tangles of brain fibers. Shrinkage of the brain regions associated with Alzheimer's is common. Multiple theories of causation have been suggested encompassing areas as diverse as environmental influences, genetics, and lifestyle choices. The disease can begin as early as 20 years before the behavior and thinking changes associated with Alzheimer's are noticeable.

Those in the early stages of Alzheimer's may show memory problems often associated with mild cognitive impairment. Slowly, other problems become more noticeable—"getting lost, trouble handling money and paying bills, repeating questions, taking longer to complete normal daily tasks, poor judgment, and small mood and personality changes" (National Institute on Aging, 2010, p. 1). Eventually, the degree of impairment worsens with problems in the areas of language, reasoning, and thinking. Tasks such as getting dressed may prove too difficult and new learning becomes impossible. Impulsive behavior, paranoia, delusions, and hallucinations may present. The final stage often sees the victim bedridden, unable to perform most routine tasks.

Assessment of Alzheimer's disease and other dementias can focus on questions about behavior and mood changes, ability to complete daily tasks, and past medical concerns. Tests that assess areas such as "memory, problem solving, attention, counting, and language" are often used (National Institute on Aging, 2010, p. 1). A physician can order other tests to further identify the disease.

Later Life and Substance Abuse

Though we tend to associate substance abuse problems with younger stages of life, there is evidence that adults in later life are also at risk. While the overall tendency is for excessive drinking to decline after age 55, anywhere from 10% to 50% of those over the age of 60 drink at a rate exceeding the guidelines for consuming alcohol. Episodic heavy drinking also occurs in as many as 20% to 25% of those over age 74 (Merrick et al., 2008; Moos et al., 2009). Older men who drink are likely to have problems when their drinking exceeds the guidelines. Drinking guidelines include no more than two drinks per day or seven per week. Consumption above that level is an assessment threshold for potential drinking problems (Moos, Schutte, Brennan, & Moos, 2009).

RETIREMENT

Retirement has multiple meanings within many societies and across different individuals within society. For some, it is a withdrawal from employment with more time for family, hobbies, travel, or new roles. For others, it is the equivalent of losing one's meaning in life (Schwingel, Niti, Tang, & Ng, 2009). Between these extremes, retirement often becomes a synonym for entry into old age, the meaning of which is highly individual. As might be expected, retirement for most people is a major life event. Most people invest a great deal in careers—economically, emotionally, and physically. We may define ourselves by our work. I can recall the first time I had to leave a voice message on my new office answering machine after retiring to part-time work. I started out saying, "This is Grafton Hull" and then silence. For more than 30 years I had described myself as "director" of this or that program; suddenly I no longer had a regular role. It took three tries before I could leave a satisfactory message. The importance of work is usually obvious when we ask people we've just met, "What do you do?" It is through work that we define who we are and our relationship to the larger community. For most people, employment has a relationship to self-esteem, how we view ourselves, and how others view us. It is a crucial piece of who we are because identities are often tied to our employment (Osborne, 2009).

Retirement can affect the individual in other ways. For example, it is common for coworkers to eat lunch together or spend recreational time together. These activities usually end for the retiring colleague. Work is also the place where most of us receive validation of our competence, intellectual and social stimulation, and perks such as clerical support (Osborne, 2009). Once retirement occurs, these benefits of employment end and we recognize the losses.

Coping with these losses is both possible and desirable. Competence in one's work can often be transferred to other activities, such as volunteering and participation in community organizations and projects. Of course, it can also lead to challenges. The story is told of the successful manager who retired and decided to put his organizational skills to work at home. However, his first venture proved problematic as he learned after putting all the food cans in his wife's pantry in alphabetical order. Sometimes it is best to avoid displaying one's skills in someone else's territory. Locating other sources of meaning in retirement is usually helpful when work has been our primary source of social legitimacy. Erikson's tasks of adulthood, intimacy versus isolation, generativity versus stagnation, and ego integrity versus despair are all played out to some degree in retirement. Retirees must cope with isolation associated with loss of employment by developing a new sense of intimacy with family members and friends. They must avoid stagnation by finding new interests and abilities that will bring satisfaction, such as spending more time with adult children and helping them in whatever ways are possible. Conversely, it may involve giving one's time to the community. In either case, it's important that the individual finds the activity gratifying and meaningful. Finally, retirees must become comfortable with the changes in who they are as identity is no longer provided by employment. This involves looking at oneself, increasing self-awareness, and coming to better understand the new person who is emerging (Osborne, 2009). The alternative is despair, a feeling that one's life is over and the future is bleak. Those who fail to confront the challenges outlined by Erikson are more likely to be among those older adults who become depressed following retirement.

Not surprisingly, what we do after retirement affects our mental health. Australian men who retired early, for example, tended to have poorer mental health (Butterworth et al., 2006) while retirees in Israel reported increased well-being (Nuttman-Shwartz, 2007). Banks, Breeze, Lessof, and Nazroo (2006) found that retirement was associated with a loss of satisfaction in life while Westerlund et al. (2009) found perceptions of one's health improved after retirement. One of the factors that helps explain these disparate outcomes may be the role played by social interaction and engagement with others. For example, retirees who volunteered or continued to work in some capacity were more likely to report enhanced mental well-being (Schwingel et al., 2009). While some retirees eventually return to part-time work in their previous area of expertise, others choose new activities that challenge and extend their competence.

Some retirees leave the environment in which they have worked and move to another location. This may be a retirement community, a community in which their children reside, or some other attractive place. Of course, the new environment comes with both advantages and disadvantages. For example, one's circle of friends is often geographically bound. We tend to hang out with people who live nearby and those we have worked with over the years. When we move, these associations are often lost or diminished. Without a shared history with these friends, the challenge is to make new friends. However, those living in the new location may already have their own friends, making the retirees development of new friends more difficult.

Retirement can also produce stresses when both members of a couple are retired. For example, it is likely that both partners will need to depend more on the other, a degree of dependency that may be difficult to accept. On the other hand, if only one member of a couple retires, it can lead to increased independence for the retired member and strain as one adapts to being at home while the other is still working.

The decision on when to retire has changed over the past decades resulting in more people retiring earlier. Overall, the drop in retirement age averaged about five to six years since 1950, with women experiencing the largest drop. However, the financial crisis and recession of the period 2007–2012 has likely changed this trend, at least for the time being. Many who previously planned to retire or retire early have extended their working years to cope with the uncertainty.

While retirement age has been dropping, life expectancies have increased dramatically over the same time period. Changes just over the past 60 years suggest that the time spent in retirement has ballooned. For example, the average man retiring in 1950 at 66.9 years only had a life expectancy of 65.47 years. In other words, he could look forward to zero years of retirement. Keep in mind, however, that these are medians and that 50% of men were expected to die before age 65.47 and 50% after that age. By 2005, the average man who retired at 61.7 years could anticipate spending more than 17 years in retirement as his life expectancy had increased to about 80 years. A woman retiring at 61.2 years could anticipate living at least four years longer than a man of the same age (CDC, 2007).

These statistics, however, do not provide a complete picture with respect to life expectancy. There are clear disparities in life expectancy for men and women and Blacks and Whites. For example, a Black man at age 60 has a life expectancy over two years shorter than a White male of that age. A similar differential exists between life expectancies of Black and White women (CDC, 2007). On a more positive note, with few exceptions, the differences between overall Black and White life expectancy rates have been decreasing over the past century from a high of 14.6 years in 1900 to a low of 5.2 years in 2004.

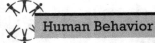

Human Behavior

Practice Behavior Example: Know about human behavior across the life course; the range of social systems in which people live; and the ways social systems promote or deter people in maintaining or achieving health and well-being.

Critical Thinking Questions: What might account for these differences in life expectancy among men and women? Would these same explanations apply to differences between Blacks and Whites? If not, what other reasons might explain different death rates for groups of people?

Living Location in Retirement

Where one spends retirement years appears to matter. Most older adults prefer to remain in their current home until death (AARP, 2003; National Association of Home Builders, 2005). Whether this is realistic depends upon factors such as health and mobility, availability of support systems, and finances. Those experiencing major health problems or mobility difficulties may find that staying in the same house or apartment is no longer feasible, especially when the structure does not facilitate those with a physical disability. The availability of support systems is important as maintaining a home, in particular, becomes more difficult. Chores such as mowing the lawn, shoveling snow, and maintaining a house can become overwhelming. If the older adult's children or friends can help with these responsibilities, remaining at home may be possible. Likewise, the availability of community organizations to assist in these areas is important.

Assisted Living Facilities

If informal or formal supports are not available, or not within the resources of the late life adult, looking at other housing options becomes necessary. Assisted living facilities and extended care facilities may be needed if the older adult can no longer remain at home. Assisted living facilities attempt to provide a home-like atmosphere with services provided to meet the needs of the residents (U.S. Department of Health and Human Services, 2002).

Generally, these facilities offer routine personal care in an institutional setting. This might include assisting with activities of daily living, including bathing, dressing, and meal preparation. Determining how many people reside in assisted living facilities is difficult. Typically, only estimates are available because of different definitions of long-term care. However, the best guess is perhaps 1 million individuals with a variety of health challenges and disabilities are in assisted living facilities. There is at least some evidence that assisted living is beginning to replace nursing home care. The change may be attributable to the lower cost of assisted living relative to nursing home care, state policy changes that favor the use of these facilities, better images of assisted living, and the composition of the older adult populations.

Nursing home care

Nursing home care generally focuses on residents with more severe physical disabilities and major health problems. About two-thirds of nursing home residents report they are in fair or poor health, compared to less than one-half of assisted living residents. Nursing facilities typically provide 24-hour supervision of the residents. About 7% to 8% of those on Medicare are residing in nursing homes, although the percentage varies from year to year. Nursing homes that provide the most care typically are larger facilities with 50 or more beds, although there are smaller homes with only a handful of residents. Over time, many of the services originally offered only in nursing homes have migrated to assisted living facilities as many residents did not need all of the services traditionally provided by the former.

The most common challenges in both assisted living and nursing facility residents are cognitive impairment or other mental disorders (U.S. Department of Health and Human Services, 2002). One-third of assisted living residents suffered from Alzheimer's disease and related dementia, compared to about one-half of nursing facility residents.

Not surprisingly, the housing segregation that exists in the United States continues to have an impact on residential living for those in later life. Howard et al. (2002) concluded that African Americans in assisted living and nursing homes were concentrated in a relatively few African American facilities, while Whites resided predominantly in White facilities. The quality of the African American facilities tended to be lower with respect to ratings covering lighting, cleanliness, and maintenance. Potential explanations may include resident choice, economic factors, or exclusionary actions on the part of facilities.

Assess your comprehension of Later Adult Life by completing this quiz.

PREPARING FOR DEATH

Preparing for one's death has cognitive, behavioral, and affective components. The same is true for those providing care for terminally ill friends and relatives (Hebert, Schulz, Copeland, & Arnold, 2009). By attending to these components, social workers are more likely to understand and correctly assess clients who are preparing for their own death.

Cognitive Components

Cognitive components of death preparation involve thinking about what needs to be accomplished in the time remaining, gathering information, making decisions, and communicating to others. It is also a time for reminiscing and thinking about the past (Cappeliez & O'Rourke, 2002). Reminiscing may help cope with one's emotions and assist the individual to discover meaning in the face of death. It may also be a means of simply escaping the reality for a time. Reminiscing may focus on remembering loved ones or happy past events. It can also focus on unresolved issues. Sometimes, reminiscing just becomes a means of communicating with family or friends about favorite times. Because time frames become compressed and long-term goals no longer hold as much attention, future-oriented thinking may decline. Instead, much of the remaining time will be spent on pursuits that are cognitively and emotionally rewarding. This might include reading, prayer, or simply withdrawing from the world. While not always the case, the cognitive work often provides the impetus for the behavioral component.

Behavioral Components

As one's forthcoming death becomes more real, many late life adults begin to plan for the event. This can include prepaying for a funeral or cremation, preparing a will and advanced health care directives, and explaining one's end-of-life desires to family. (Advanced Care Directives includes living wills and health care proxies identifying the individual's wishes in the event that he or she cannot make a decision.) Sometimes this involves a directive not to use life-prolonging procedures if it will only postpone death for a brief time. It may involve designating someone else to make decisions for you (also called durable power of attorney). Finally, it can include a do-not-resuscitate (DNR) order that identifies which medical and other procedures the individual wants in case of cardiac arrest and so on. In many cases, a DNR order specifies that in the event that the person's brain is no longer functioning, no efforts should be made to render additional treatment that would prolong life. Individuals can and should put their desires in writing, whether it be to live as long as possible or to avoid pain at all costs. In this way, they make the ultimate decision easier for those left behind (Harvard Medical School, 2005).

> **For an excellent review of the importance of individuals preparing advanced directions, review the case End-of-Life Decisions in an Intensive Care Unit and address the questions listed there.**

Historically, we have used the term *putting your things in order* to describe the process of preparing for one's death. As mentioned earlier, some people do this by preparing death-related documents or more informal methods of ensuring that their wishes are carried out following their death. Some will go throughout their house putting stickers on furniture items or other valuable items with the name of the intended recipient. Others invite friends and relatives to select items that they would like to have after the person's death. These methods might be considered an effort to control elements of a situation that is otherwise out of the person's hands. By deciding who will receive which items, the dying person asserts a measure of control over certain aspects of the future.

The process of preparing for one's death can be beneficial from a practical point of view, as well as an emotional one. It also can prevent confusion and mistakes from occurring. Of course, events may still not work out as planned. An example was a woman in her late fifties with a history of heart problems. She prepared her will, stipulating that upon her death she wanted to be cremated. Unfortunately, she did not provide a copy of the will to any relative but instead entrusted it to a bank trust officer. Her children arranged her funeral service and buried their mother the following week and then received a call from the trust officer. He wanted them to be present for the reading of the will the following day. Only then did they learn of their mother's wishes to be cremated.

Affective Components

Affective components of preparing for death involve coming to terms emotionally with one's mortality. This can have multiple dimensions. For example, Kotter-Gruhn, Kleinspehn-Ammerlahn, Gerstorf, and Smith (2009) report that as human beings approach their own death, they report feeling older and are less satisfied with how they are aging. Not surprising—few of us like to recognize the inevitability of our death. As we attain the furthest reaches of old age, it is often in conjunction with increased physical and psychological decline. Changes that were perhaps more mixed in middle adulthood are now seen as negative. Even a positive outlook on life is stressed as one's ailments mount and psychological and social resources decline.

Preparing for death also means dealing with loss of both the person you have become and those family and friends who will remain. Most people in late life have already experienced losses among those they held closest. They may have grieved the loss of their employment, good health, and pets. Parents, friends, and colleagues have died, and now it is their turn. One colleague phrased it like this, "Among the people I will miss most is me." While seemingly narcissistic, it reflected a general enjoyment of life and a recognition that this will be ending soon. The grief associated with these losses can be enormous and may be reflected in depression and despair. Carried to an extreme, or poorly dealt with, it can lead to suicide.

Some who are dying follow Kubler-Ross's (1969) five stages of dying—denial, anger, bargaining, depression, and acceptance. In denial, they may challenge a diagnosis and seek additional opinions and alternative explanations. When denial is no longer effective, they may turn to anger or rage at the disease or condition that is hastening death, with loved ones and caregivers experiencing the brunt of this anger. Those who are terminally ill may engage in a bit of bargaining with God, attempting either to prolong their life or to hasten the end of the discomfort or pain they are experiencing.

At some point, bargaining is not successful and the individual may experience depression. Depression may be a reaction to events associated with an illness or disease, as might be the case when a terminally ill diabetic patient loses a leg to amputation. It may also occur as we begin to think about all the things we will miss in the future—events, people, and places.

The dying individual may then come to acceptance of his or her own death. This is not giving up the fight necessarily, but recognizing that one's time is limited. Like all models, not every person will experience every stage and not all experts on the elderly accept Kubler-Ross's approach to death and dying. However, it is a readily understood and logical enough model to help in understanding those who are preparing for death.

Other theories about the tasks to be accomplished when a loss occurs or is pending have been put forth by Cohen, Mannarino, and Knudsen (2004). They "suggest that common tasks include (1) accepting the reality of the death; (2) fully experiencing the pain associated with the loss; (3) adjusting to life without the loved one; (4) integrating aspects of the loved one into one's own self-identity; (5) converting the relationship from one of ongoing interactions to one of memory; (6) finding meaning in the loved one's death; and (7) recommitting to new relationships with other adults" (Howarth, 2011, p. 5). Regardless of the specific theory that one uses, two things remain clear. First, the loss of someone close often provokes stages or tasks that should be attended to by the individual, and sometimes this requires the help of a social worker. Second, not all people will go through the same stages nor confront the same tasks and they will not always move from one stage to another in the order suggested by the writers.

Critical Thinking

Practice Behavior Example: Demonstrate effective oral and written communication in working with individuals, families, groups, organizations, communities, and colleagues.

Critical Thinking Question: You have been asked to talk to a group of adults who have lost their mother or father recently. One of the issues they want to talk about is why their surviving parent is not going through the expected steps associated with such losses. List the points you would want to share with them in your talk. Include two subtopics under each major point.

End of Life

How individuals and families cognitively prepare for death varies widely across societies. While churches may include references to death in sermons, it is not necessarily a common topic of conversation in other venues. Some cultures have traditional tasks that are to be completed before one dies, such as making amends for past behavior or addressing long time grievances to reach a state of peace. Some near death believe that loved ones who have already departed return to visit them in their sleep, providing a degree of comfort (Abrums, 2000). Caregivers may simply attribute such events to hallucinations. It is important to recognize that spiritual and religious beliefs, coupled with cultural values

For a sense of how sensitive the process of adapting to death or impending death of a loved one, read At a Loss: Helping to Let Go. How do you think you would handle this situation?

and attitudes, may play a role in how people respond to an upcoming death—their own or that of another.

While many helping professionals (including nurses and physicians) prefer not to address an impending death, the best evidence we have is that failing to do is counterproductive (Apatira et al., 2008). The urge to avoid the topic is understandable because it can diminish hope among the patient and caregivers. However, those who ultimately have to decide what limits to treatment should exist need the information to address practical concerns, as well as allowing time to access emotional and psychological resources.

Improving end-of-life care for those who are terminally ill has received a good deal of attention among medical personnel and institutions. While the historic goal of medicine is to prolong life, there is growing recognition that the quality of that life is of equal or greater importance. The Institute of Medicine (1998) provided a definition of a good death as "one that is free from avoidable distress and suffering for patients, families, and caregivers; in general accord with patients' and families' wishes; and reasonably consistent with clinical, cultural, and ethical standards" (p. 4).

Despite the goal of a good death, many patients at the end of life do not receive care consistent with their wishes (Vig & Pearlman, 2003). This can occur when medical personnel do not know the client's desires and priorities well enough to make appropriate decisions. It may occur because the client left no advanced directive or left an unclear or confusing one. Sometimes, an advanced directive was prepared but not shared with one's physician. Sitting in a file drawer at home, an advanced directive is of little use. Finally, physicians may be unwilling to strictly follow the dictates of an advanced directive. Practitioners working with terminally ill clients need to learn their priorities so that care provided maximizes quality of life.

Assess your comprehension of Preparing for Death by completing this quiz.

WIDOWHOOD

Widowhood is a fact of life for most individuals. Forty-six percent of women over age 65 are widowed, compared to 16% percent of men of that age. For men and women over the age of 75, 64% of women and 22% of men are widowed. Clearly, mortality rates differ significantly between men and women (Smith & Christakis, 2009) and most couples can expect that one partner or the other will spend a portion of their lives in widowhood.

Marriage has been repeatedly recognized as improving the quality of life of both women and men. Along with providing a sense of meaning in life, factors such as economic security, emotional support, and stability are considered the hallmarks contributing to this improvement (Ben-zur & Michael, 2009). Marriage can contribute to one's self-esteem, relieve stress, and improve overall health. These benefits appear to be present cross-culturally as well as within the United States. The benefits of marriage, of course, suggest some of the challenges facing those who have lost their husband, wife, or partner. In fact, much of the literature in the field of well-being identifies loss of a spouse as a significant stressor. As an example, those who have been widowed experience a higher level of suicide than those whose significant other has not died. Ben-Zur and Michael (2009) found that even after almost six years following widowhood, survivors experienced lower satisfaction with life and poorer psychosocial adjustment. Depression and a loss of motivation to improve one's situation were common reactions.

Similarly, several studies have highlighted the additional risk of death during the first 6 to 12 months of widowhood. The risk is highest for men, particularly in the first six months (Bowling, 2009). Dupre, Beck, and Meadows (2009) found that widowed women were 1.61 times more likely to die than their married counterparts during the same time frame. Interestingly, widowhood appeared to be more traumatic for those who had married between their 19th and 25th years as opposed to those who married later in life.

Bereavement is associated with increased cardiovascular risk for the survivor (Buckley et al., 2010). The risk is highest in the weeks immediately following the death of one's spouse, suggesting the importance of support from relatives and friends at this particular juncture. Research by Christakis and Iwashyna (2003) found that the actual cause of a spouse's death didn't seem to be a factor in the risk level, nor did it matter whether the death was expected or unexpected. However, Elwert and Christakis (2008) did find that the cause of death seemed to have some impact on risk for the surviving spouse. Their findings suggest, for example, that a wife's death from diabetes, lung cancer, infection, or heart disease increased the risk to her surviving husband while a wife's death from Alzheimer's or Parkinson's disease did not. Women whose husbands died of these two diseases also did not experience increases in their own mortality. Although there are no tested explanations for it, about a quarter of the deaths of surviving spouses were from the same diagnostic categories as the deceased spouse's death. Deaths among the spouses of deceased individuals occur from many causes, but suicide and accidents are common. As expected, the risk of death of the surviving spouse tends to diminish over time, although widowers whose wives experienced anxiety and pain during the last three months of their lives continued to report sleep disturbances four to five years after the fact (Jonasson et al., 2009).

Initial reactions to a spouse's death usually involve depression, anxiety, and anger. Sleep problems and appetite loss are common as are suicidal thoughts (Buckley et al., 2010). High anxiety can also act as triggering mechanisms for cardiac risk, as can high levels of anger. Carr and Boerner (2009) note that anger is particularly acute when the surviving spouse rated their marriage positively. Conversely, those who rated their marriages less highly or as conflicted tended to suffer fewer post-death symptoms of depression, anxiety, or anger. Spouses who were providing care to an ill spouse at the time of his or her death tend to rate the quality of their marriages as lower than is true for noncaregiving spouses. It appears that the strains of caregiving tend to lower the quality of the marital relationship in the caregiver's eyes. This can lead, in turn, to feelings of guilt and anger after the spouse dies. Perhaps as a means of coping with these symptoms, almost 20% of survivor spouses turn to alcohol use in the immediate aftermath of the death. Other potential symptoms during the post-death period include compromised immune systems and increased heart rate and blood pressure. Fortunately, most of the emotions and health impacts decline over the months following the death.

As mentioned, social support is an important means of reducing the mortality risk of the widowed individual. In situations where the deceased spouse was served by hospice care, there was also a decrease in mortality among surviving spouses. Surviving women with one to three children tend to have lower mortality rates than those with no children, while those with more than three children have a higher mortality risk. This suggests that some degree of social support mitigates mortality—but only to a point. After that, additional support may be seen as stressful (Manor & Eisenbach, 2003).

At some point in widowhood, most survivors begin to move on with their lives, such as through remarriage, involvement in other long-term relationships, and reintegration into the community. The quality of one's life during this period can vary dramatically. One individual will continue to mourn the lost spouse and gradually settle into a solitary life punctuated with periodic or sporadic contacts with family and friends. Another will become involved in group pursuits such as visiting a senior center, taking trips with friends or fellow church members, and engage again in activities enjoyed when the spouse was alive O'Rourke (2004) found that resilience in older widows was directly related to their overall satisfaction with life and the absence of psychiatric distress. Widows with these characteristics reported much high levels of well-being, regardless of factors such as duration of widowhood or length of marriage. A commitment to living was the most salient resiliency factor among this group of widows.

A portion of the recently widowed may experience what is known as *complicated grief*, a grief disorder that can be quite severe (Johnson et al., 2009). Those experiencing this disorder are likely to show a variety of symptoms including:

- Inability to accept the death of the spouse
- Believing that life no longer has any meaning
- Prolonged bitterness over the loss
- Unremitting yearning for the spouse
- Feeling distant and disconnected from other people
- Seemingly stuck in life with no chance of moving on

Although not included in the *DSM*, this symptom collection often requires clinical intervention. Johnson and colleagues gathered data on this group and found that most would have welcomed a diagnosis of complicated grief because it would help relieve the anxiety and fear associated with their symptoms. Moreover, they would welcome professional help to deal with the disorder.

Like other aspects of life, the period of widowhood has challenges. Smith and Christakis (2009) found that widowhood is also associated with increased sexual risk taking. We have addressed this issue in Chapter 10 but need to emphasize that unprotected sex in older adulthood carries many of the same risks as in younger years. Typical risk-taking behaviors included having multiple partners and failure to use a condom. The highest risk was borne by men and began about six months after a spouse's death and continued for three or more years. This was attributable to sexual desire levels, frequency of sexual intercourse, more sexual partners experienced by men, availability of drugs to treat erectile dysfunction, and the increased motivation of men to seek out new sexual partners.

Other challenges face elderly widows. For example, the median income for single older women was $12,600 in 2005. This is less than 80% of the income of single older men (Gillen & Kim, 2009). Widowed female-headed households age 65 and older also have significantly fewer assets. In 2005, one-half of these women were either in poverty or nearly so. Poverty rates for widows tend to be highest immediately after their spouses' death (Sevak et al., 2004). These outcomes are a combination of several factors, including the fact that women earn less than men in most jobs, are more likely to interrupt their careers for caretaking responsibilities, and engaged in more part-time work than men. These factors translate into lower social security and pension plan payments following retirement. In addition, women are more likely than men to lose a spouse through death, which further undermines financial resources.

Because social security benefits provide about half of the annual income for widows, it is the only thing keeping many out of poverty. Medical expenses of the late spouse can seriously diminish the assets in existence prior to death. Of course, being widowed does not require that one be above a given age. Younger widows actually have poverty rates that are higher than older widows (Sevak et al., 2004). Gillen and Kim (2009) looked at a group of women who were married in 2002 and widowed in 2004. This group saw a 41% drop in total income as a result of the death of the husband. Those women who did not lose a spouse during this period experienced only a minor income changes. A troubling aspect of this situation is the dramatic reduction in social security benefits that occurs after one's spouse dies. In most cases, the household income is cut in half because there is an immediate discontinuation of benefits for the deceased. Among policy suggestions put forth by those familiar with this practice is a more gradual reduction in benefits to the surviving spouse instead of a precipitous cut that both increases stress and anxiety and creates significant immediate financial trouble.

Assess your analysis and evaluation of this chapter's contents by completing the Chapter Review.

14

Family Influences on Human Behavior

"The family is a vital institution in American society. Families are often the first and frequently the last source of support for individuals" (U.S. Census Bureau, 2004, p. 6). However, the concept of "family" is evolving, with different meanings to different people. For many, a family is the basic nuclear unit involving a man, a woman, and 2.5 children. Others would argue that any of these elements could be missing and there would still be a family. Thus, a couple with no children might be viewed as a family, as would a gay or lesbian couple with or without children. How about a single parent raising one or more children? Is that not a family? What about the Joneses down the block with no children of their own, but who serve as foster parents for three adolescents? As is clear, the concept of family has diverse meanings. We can think of a family as a social system with its own characteristics, rules, roles, communication methods, problem-solving arrangements, and power structure (Goldenberg & Goldenberg, 2008). Viewing families from a social systems perspective is consistent with social work's emphasis on understanding human beings in their social environment. Like other social systems, families experience a life cycle and are affected by both external and internal environments. This chapter looks at the family from many different perspectives. In particular, we will look at the ways authors have described the family life cycle and what happens when members are separated from their family of origin. We will consider challenges, such as starting a family, dealing with romance and marriage, and the various diverse forms in which families exist. Equally important, we will discuss parenting and grandparenting, both of which are part of family life. Finally, we will describe and analyze some of the key transitions experienced by families, including divorce, empty nest, and death.

FAMILY LIFE CYCLES

Over many years, researchers have studied families with an eye to better understanding them. In the process, they have identified a variety of tasks (developmental, social, and emotional) that characterize most families (Trokan, 1998). Typically, a family life cycle is composed of five stages: (1) independence from one's family of origin, (2) coupling or marriage, (3) parenting, (4) launching a new generation of adults, and (5) retirement/senior years. In each of these stages, the individual acquires skills that will prove important for the next stage. For example, in the independence stage, young adults ideally acquire the skills to support themselves, develop experience in forming intimate relationships, and stabilize their identity as an individual. Pursuing a career is part of this stage.

Despite ongoing changes affecting the family, multigenerational families still flourish.

In the marriage or coupling stage, adults develop enduring relationships with a significant other, learn to adjust to a larger family network, and identify mutual goals. It is also a stage where sexuality becomes of greater importance as partners learn to meet each other's needs. Most families adopt ways of managing their finances, sharing recreational endeavors, and developing an interdependence that is the hallmark of a significant relationship.

The parenting stage involves everything from deciding to have a baby (although for many people, it still comes as a surprise), raising one or more children, and guiding them through the adolescent years. Having children creates multiple changes within most families and requires adjustment that may not have been foreseen. It often requires interacting with other systems in the community, particularly the educational sphere. Stress is a common occurrence in the process of raising children and not all parents handle this stage well. Instances of child abuse, neglect, incest, and filicide (killing of one's children) are common. Parenting requires the adoption of new roles and adapting those roles as children enter adolescence. The typical life of an adolescent is almost guaranteed to challenge even the most skilled parent. The goal of this period, besides trying to ensure that the adolescent survives, is to prepare them for independence while continuing to offer an emotionally safe and secure home environment.

The transition to the empty nest stage involves helping young adult children move on with their lives while simultaneously restructuring a marital relationship that, of necessity, changed after the arrival of children. This stage also offers a challenge to parents to develop a different kind of relationship with one's adult children, one characterized by greater equality. For most parents, this phase also involves transitioning into new roles as grandparents.

The last stage of the family life cycle is retirement and beyond. Like the other stages, it involves learning new skills or relearning old ones. Ideally, if the previous transition to the empty

Did You Know?

The Census Bureau reports births to unmarried women comprised over 42% of all births in 2008. The birth rate for women aged 40 to 44 was the highest in more than 40 years.

Human Behavior

Practice Behavior Example: Apply theories and knowledge from the liberal arts to understand biological, social, cultural, psychological, and spiritual development.

Critical Thinking Question: Using your own parent or caretaker as an example, identify the life cycle stages which you have seen him or her complete. Which, if any, of the stages seemed to be more difficult for him or her? What factors might explain this difficulty?

nest stage went satisfactorily, relationships with one's adult children become stronger. It is also a period associated with loss as one's friends and colleagues die or move away and we begin to prepare for our own eventual death.

The concept of a life cycle is used for a variety of reasons. First, it has its origins in the development of individuals as they proceed through a series of stages or steps that begin with birth and continue until death. In that sense, it is a familiar schema for looking at the family system. Second, it is based on the idea that various transformations occur over the life of a family and that each is related to prior and subsequent events. Third, life cycles are grounded in biological perspectives about the ways in which systems grow, mature, and evolve over time (O'Rand & Krecker, 1990).

Of course, like all schemas that help us understand human behavior, the concept of a family life cycle sometimes does not match reality. As noted earlier, the very idea of what constitutes a family is open to question. Perceptions of what is needed to comprise a family are imbedded within an ever-changing culture. Moreover, not every family goes through every stage, or at the same time, and certainly not in the same way. Also, most life cycle concepts are based on a normative model that operates as if there were some ideal or typical unit that exists. This family life cycle was based on the premise that a marriage occurred between a man and a woman, children arrived and subsequently left the nest, and the couple continued their existence until death.

In reality, we know this is not the case. Stresses of living sometimes interfere with the expected life cycle stage. Families face illnesses or other crises, each of which can prolong a stage or undermine the development of a set of life skills. Divorce is a common occurrence that ends marriages for about one-half of couples in the United States. Deaths occur at times and in ways that are at odds with the model. Roles of men and women have changed and challenged the traditional concept of a family life cycle.

Did You Know?

U.S. divorce rates are highest in the Southern states and lowest in Northeastern states.

Did You Know?

Utah had the highest proportion of households composed of husband and wife while New York and Louisiana had the lowest proportion.

Even the concept of a marriage as involving a man and a woman has changed. In several states and countries, marriages may occur between two men or two women and children may or may not be involved. As with most schemas, there have been many criticisms of the family life cycle model, including that it does not fit every family, particularly those who are different from the traditional definition of a family (Erickson, 1998).

Despite the inherent limitations in using a family life cycle model, it continues to provide a useful way of viewing the dynamics and processes that operate within families. There are several reasons for this. First, the vast majority of families do consist of a husband and wife with children. Second, despite the fact that most mothers work outside the home, they still remain as the primary caregivers to their children (Kapinus & Johnson, 2003). Third, even in the most egalitarian of homes, women continue to perform most of the chores and maintenance duties they have always assumed. Finally, the developmental life cycle of children has a profound influence on the life cycle of the marital couple and it's possible to predict a great deal about families by knowing whether they have children and the ages of those children. Thus, from our perspective, a family life cycle provides a valuable tool for understanding families.

We will now explore the first stage of the family life cycle—separation from one's family of origin and the beginning of a relationship with another—that leads to a long-term commitment.

SEPARATION FROM FAMILY OF ORIGIN

We anticipate that most young adults will separate from their families of origin at some point. After all, the idea of living with one's parents indefinitely is generally not among the goals of either parents or adult children. However, the decision to make this separation, despite it being expected, can be a challenge for both parties. For the parents, the prospect of an empty nest may be disconcerting as it simultaneously removes a major reason for one's existence (raising a child) while reestablishing the dyadic relationship that existed before the arrival of children. Both changes will upset the status quo—and not always in positive ways. In unhealthy families, those who separate may be seen as deserting the family despite the fact that this is a normal developmental process. Sichel and Cervini (n.d.) describe this situation well in an article titled, "The Ties That Bind, the Ties That Strangle," which highlights the struggles some families face in letting go of adult children. For many families, the changes associated with adult children leaving also precipitate other changes, including disillusionment with and divorce from one's spouse. By contrast, some parents may see children leaving as a chance to pursue dreams moved to the back burner years ago or to explore new vistas.

For adult children, leaving home can be both exciting and anxiety producing. While it ushers in new opportunities, it also means having to depend upon one's own resources, manage one's own affairs, and do those other things we associate with being a grown-up. Exhilaration and fear are the common emotional responses to going it alone. Fortunately, in most cases, the adult child's worries about leaving home are more than offset by the rewards of being on one's own or living with a significant other. As a result, most young adults are successful in separating from their families of origin and moving to the next stage of the family life cycle.

ROMANCE AND MARRIAGE

We discussed the topic of relationships in Chapters 12 and 13, underscoring both its importance in the lives of individuals and some requirements for maintaining healthy connections to others. Within dyadic relationships, we often use terms such as *romance* or *romantic love* to describe the connections between individuals. Romantic love is characterized as having high intensity, emotional engagement, sexual interest, and, in the initial stages, an almost obsessive quality. Romantic love is considered an important part of marriage in most Western societies and its absence, a reason for divorce. While some have argued that romantic love in marriage is often replaced by more sedate feelings over time, others believe that it can continue throughout a marriage, although usually without the obsessive element (Acevedo & Aron, 2009). Most researchers agree that romantic love is associated with high satisfaction levels and feelings of well-being in marriages and other long-term relationships.

While both men and women report the benefits of romantic relationships, there are differences in the way that both genders experience the intimacy in such relationships. Gilligan (1982) and others have described these differences in their own research. For example, compared to women, husbands are more reluctant to share feelings with their wives. Wives are also much more likely to have a broader array of emotions in their marriages and more likely to share them. Likewise, women and men experience sexual pleasure in different ways. For men, sexual intercourse tends to bring the highest degree of sexual pleasure while women are more focused on other forms of intimacy, such as touching and kissing (Larson, Peterson, Heath, & Birch, 2000). While men often find it difficult to express their feelings and emotions in words, women tend to be more attuned to and in synch with both their own feelings and those of others (Levant & Pollack, 1995; Levant, Hall, Williams, & Hasan, 2009). While such differences may be the product of gender socialization, they pose a challenge for both partners as they grapple with attitudes, beliefs, behaviors, and expectations with which they are unfamiliar. In turn, many of these differences can be traced directly back to the family of origin.

Assess your comprehension of the Family Life Cycle by completing this quiz.

Family of Origin Influences on Romance and Marriage

Families of origin can influence future romantic relationships and marriage in significant ways. This observation is consistent with Bowen's family systems theory (Bowen, 1978; Kerr & Bowen, 1987). In some cases, failure to accept the individuation of the adult child carries over into the adult child's post-marital relationships. Those familiar with the television show *Everybody Loves Raymond*, or some of the reigning soap operas, can get a flavor of the degree of intrusion that can result when parents do not accept the adult child's separation from the family of origin.

In addition, some families of origin have rules that impair the ability of their adult children to successfully separate and that interfere with forming significant relationships with others. Functional family rules encourage members to communicate with each other, be clear about their needs, and be sensitive to those of others. Dysfunctional rules have the opposite effect. For example, if a rule discourages talking about one's feelings, this is likely to be an impediment to relationship building with others. Rules that discourage getting too close to others undermine affectional displays and make it difficult to show the significant others how you really feel about them. Some rules may encourage family members to keep their needs to themselves, thereby preventing them from telling others what they want. Others may discourage members from displaying authenticity (Larson et al., 2000). Dysfunctional rules can influence romantic and other relationships long after the child has moved into adulthood. For example, adult children may experience anxiety about dating, difficulty moving from one stage of dating to another, lower satisfaction with their relationships, and lowered commitment to the dating relationship. Obviously, dysfunctional rules do not strengthen relationships.

Most studies agree that romantic and marriage partners typically demonstrate a high degree of commitment to one another and to their relationship (VanDenBerghe, 2000). Commitment indicates an intention to remain in a relationship indefinitely and is directly related to the stability of those relationships (Weigel, Bennett, & Ballard-Reisch, 2003). Usually commitment is based on an attraction between the partners that is seen as pleasurable or rewarding, although it may also be related to constraining factors such as religion, societal pressure, or other forces that preclude dissolution of the relationship. Much of the learning about issues of commitment occurs in one's family of origin, thereby making this an important influence in whether and how one demonstrates commitment to a partner. Children whose parents emphasized the importance of dedicating themselves to a partner, and communicated that marriages take work, were more likely to indicate greater happiness with their own marriages.

Adult children from divorced families tend to view commitments with a degree of caution compared to their peers whose parents did not divorce. At the same time, they were more likely to engage in sexual intercourse earlier, including with partners to whom they were not romantically attracted (Manning, Longmore, & Giordano, 2005; Weigel et al., 2003). Hooking up was not intended to deepen a relationship with one's partner, and most who engage in such actions view it with ambivalence or see it as a negative experience (Glenn & Marquardt, 2001).

Wildmon-White and Young (2002) found that women who married sexually addicted men often came from families where they experienced mistreatment, crisis, depression, abandonment, and chaos. In addition, members of their families of origin were more likely to be disengaged from one another. Marriages where one member is sexually addicted demonstrate lowered levels of intimacy and lowered sensitivity to the needs of the nonaddicted spouse. Nonaddicted spouses are likely to have poor psychological boundaries and need help validating their own needs, wants, and desires.

Similarly, the degree to which violence occurs in a marital relationship is often related to the amount of violence that occurred in the family of origin (Delsol & Margolin, 2004). The continuation of violent behavior from one generation to another is often explained using social learning theory (Bandura, 1977), although some have postulated that as much as 50% of the variance in aggression is accounted for by genetics (Miles & Carey, 1997). Other researchers have postulated that personal characteristics of the violent partner are a major factor. In other words, it is argued that psychopathology, personality disorders, and substance abuse play a role in whether a spouse is violent (Julian, McKenry, Gavazzi, & Law, 1999). Individuals whose families of origin were violent often display other symptoms in the marriage including impulsivity, hostility, feeling threatened, jealousy, high levels of anger, and emotional instability, among others (Dutton, 2003). Other studies suggest violence is more likely to occur in situations of high marital stress, where spouses lack conflict resolution skills, and where marital satisfaction levels are low (Cano & Vivian, 2003; Howell & Pugliesi, 1988; Taft et al., 2005).

Whether a spouse exposed to family of origin violence will engage in marital violence is likely to be mediated by a number of factors. Many men from violent families are not violent in their marriages. These men tend to have strong interpersonal connections with their spouses, friends, and relatives, and maintain psychological distance from their own parents. They are also more likely to fear the negative consequences of abuse, such as losing their partner, and view abuse as unacceptable (Delsol & Margolin, 2004).

Similar influences of the family of origin and the family of procreation have been noted among incest survivors. For example, levels of intimacy in one's family of origin and one's family of procreation are positively associated. Survivors describing their family of origin as disorganized often have similar opinions of their own marriages. Clearly, one's family of origin experiences affect the quality of relationships in the family of procreation (Carson, Gertz, Donaldson, & Wonderlich, 1991).

Other Factors Influencing Romance and Marriage

The process and nature of choosing a partner or spouse has changed dramatically over time. While parents or other institutions in the community often played a role in this process in the past, they are much less important today. With the exception of cultures in which marriages are still arranged by one's family, relationships today typically begin without significant parental input. Marriages are sought for economic, social, and interpersonal reasons. For some individuals, marriage is the logical progression along the path to happiness—getting married seems the logical thing to do. For others, reasons for marriage have less to do with the strength of a romantic relationship and more with escaping unhappy surroundings. Marriage becomes a means to escape the family of origin, avoid loneliness, or ensure a secure financial future. Sometimes, the relationship and marriage directly respond to parental disapproval and are a way of asserting independence.

While family of origin plays a large role, it is not the only factor in determining how successful individuals can be in forming romantic relationships and having satisfying marriages. For example, the choices couples make when trying to influence one another play a role. Where one or both members used indirect strategies to influence the other, both spouses were more likely to report lower marital satisfaction. The converse was true for partners who used direct strategies—suggesting that partners do not approve of covert efforts of the other to control them (Weigel, Bennett, & Ballard-Reisch, 2006). Control plays a major role in many romantic relationships and marriage. It has long been noted that marriages often are not a joining of equals but rather a union of individuals with different power, a fact that habitually works to the detriment of women. To be successful, marriages involve significant amounts of negotiation and give-and-take between the partners on issues from finances and when and where to vacation, to child-rearing practices, and to relationships with former friends and in-laws. Discussions are needed about family rituals, such as what happens at holidays, who prepares what kind of dinner for special events, and when to open holiday presents.

While marriage is often stereotyped as a positive experience for both men and women, the actual outcomes do not support this view. For women, marriage can be a health hazard with consequences for both physical and mental health (Bernard, 1982). It typically interferes to some degree with a woman's career, resulting in lower income and reduced chances for promotion. Women also tend to be less satisfied from a sexual perspective. For women especially, it is important to develop an identity independent from the union because historically they have been expected to fuse with their husbands. Men are under no such expectation.

Men, on the other hand, benefit greatly from marriage. Married men have better mental health, are financially more successful, use fewer drugs, and experience lower rates of depression than their single counterparts (Steinhauer, 1995). Men who are married have higher levels of sexual satisfaction and physical health than do single men.

Critical Thinking

Practice Behavior Example: Use critical thinking augmented by creativity and curiosity.

Critical Thinking Question: What reasons might explain why men find more benefits from marriage than is true of women? For example, why do men experience better mental health from marriage than is the case with women?

There are other observations about marriage that are important. For example, men with more education are more likely to marry, while the opposite is true for women. Gender differences also exist in the satisfaction level for single men and women. Single men do less well while single women tend to be quite successful outside of marriage.

The age at which one marries appears to have some impact on marital satisfaction. Those who are younger at the time of marriage often struggle adapting to the changes and tasks inherent in the relationship. Women marrying under age 20 are more likely to get divorced than those marrying after that age. If a women waits until she is at least age 30 to marry, the risk for divorce goes down.

The Influence of In-Laws

Many have stated that one does not simply marry another individual but rather the partner's entire family. This is often true because most spouses maintain some family of origin involvement. This can be a source of great satisfaction as well as a nearly constant irritant, depending on the quality of relationships with one's in-laws. In-laws may apply pressure for their child to behave in certain ways, which invariably affects the couple. Expectations of in-laws for grandchildren may be overt. Beliefs that certain traditions and rituals should be carried on by the new family can become oppressive.

Carter and McGoldrick (2005) point out that perhaps the most troubling triangle for a couple involves the wife, husband, and husband's mother. They point out the ease with which mothers-in-law and daughters-in-law can blame each other for all kinds of problems. This absolves the husband from any responsibility for the areas of conflict—child-rearing practices, financial decisions, and others. Boundary issues become problems as one or both women overstep the lines and the man takes no responsibility for setting clear guidelines.

At the same time, the tendency to blame women in a family for family problems is a consistent pattern of stereotyping.

Other family triangles can develop besides the one just described. These can involve sisters-in-law who clash over their respective roles, behaviors of the husband, or other issues. Carter and McGoldrick (2005) note that families with fewer of these challenges are often those whose parents tended to provide good role modeling in their own marriages. They also point out that couples who marry partners whose sibling positions are comparable to that in their families of origin tend to experience fewer instances of conflict. For example, a firstborn male with younger sisters would be more compatible with a female who had at least one older brother. This sibling positioning provides a couple of advantages to a wife–husband pairing. First, the woman has prior experiencing dealing with a male, and second, she is used to being more of a follower. On the other hand, more power conflicts might be expected when those marrying are both firstborn since each is used to being in leadership positions. Carter and McGoldrick are not recommending the former arrangement that places women in positions of less power in the marital relationship. Rather, they are simply commenting on the research related to sibling position and marriage.

On the other hand, many marital partners have found solace and a resource in their spouse's parents and siblings. The opportunity for shared interests can benefit some families, and in many families, the relationship with the in-laws survives a divorce of the original couple. This typically requires that the individuals involved have a healthy sense of who they are and the ability to see things objectively, rather than simply reacting emotionally to the divorce.

Achievement of a healthy marital relationship appears to be dependent upon a number of factors. In general, the more successful relationships tend to have several things in common (Carter & McGoldrick, 2005; Gottman, 1994; Green, 2003).

- Both partners believe in equality within the marital relationship
- Neither relies on criticism, defensiveness, contempt, or stonewalling in their interactions
- Partners share similar cultural, educational, and class backgrounds
- Engagement period lasted at least six months and less than three years
- Neither partner has experienced a significant loss just prior to marriage
- Both partners' parents are in stable relationships
- Partners have sufficient resources of their own so as not to be dependent upon parents
- Neither partner is marrying to escape an unhappy home environment
- Neither partner is economically dependent solely on the other
- Both partners have satisfactory relationships with their own parents

This list does not mean that couples who do not meet these criteria cannot have a satisfactory relationship and marriage. However, they most likely will have to make multiple adaptations to achieve this goal since previous research validates the importance of the bulleted items.

Cohabitation and Marriage

Not all couples fall in love, marry, and begin to live together as in the past. Today it is common to see the majority of couples living together prior to marriage. Cohabitation becomes a means of capturing "the economies of scale and the sexual access of marriage without a long-run commitment" (Brien, Lillard, & Waite, 1999, p. 535). The 2011 marriage of Prince William and Kate Middleton was a typical example of a marriage following a period of cohabitation. Cohabitation is relatively common prior to or following a first marriage. For some it is viewed as a substitute for marriage. Importantly, a large percent of cohabiting couples are still doing so at the time of the birth of their first child (Sigle-Rushton & McLanahan, 2002).

The trend in favor of cohabitation is influenced by several factors. First, adults from divorced families appear to be more likely to choose a period of cohabitation rather than getting married (Wolfinger, 2001). In addition, adults from families where the parental divorce was followed by remarriage have a similarly high rate of cohabitation, likely because the addition of a stepparent to the family of origin injected yet another traumatic change into an already difficult family environment. Growing up in divorced families may be engendering a degree of caution in young adults. In addition, cohabitation is seen more positively than in the past, making it appear as an acceptable alternative to marriage. A similar effect may occur with individuals whose prior marriage ended in divorce, leading them to hesitate before marrying again.

A second explanation for the increase in cohabitation may be related to changes in the median age of marriage for men and women. According to the U.S. Census Bureau (2004), the median age at first marriage has increased to 25.3 years for women and 27.1 for men, a dramatic change of five to seven years over the past four decades. In addition, more men and women are deciding not to marry. For example, the percentage of women ages 20 to 24 who had not married was 75% in 2003 compared to 36% in 1970. The comparable change for men in that age bracket went from 55% to 86%. Men who were between the ages of 30 and 34 were almost four times as likely to have never married as was true in 1970. Although many young adults are postponing marriage, they continue to be interested in forming relationships, with cohabitation a potential outcome. Figure 14.1 shows how these changes in marital age have played out between 1970 and 2003.

Most cohabitations are relatively short as befits a transitory union, with about 75% of cohabiters planning to marry the partner. While cohabitation leads to marriage in about 60% of cases involving Whites, Blacks are only about half as likely to marry their

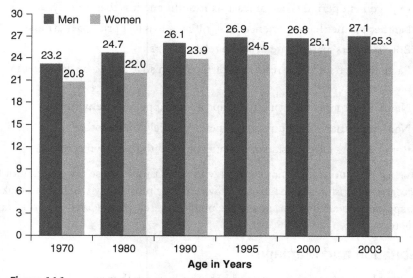

Figure 14.1
Median Age at First Marriage for the Population Aged 15 Years and Older, by Sex: 1970–2003
Source: U.S. Census Bureau (1970–2003).

partner, though the reasons for this difference are not clear. Brown (2000) notes that about one-half of cohabiting relationships last two years or longer. For both Blacks and Whites, the likelihood of getting married for cohabiting couples decreases the longer they are together. Wolfinger (2001) noted that unless cohabiting couples marry relatively quickly, the chances of getting married decline. It is also important to note that not all couples who are cohabiting plan to marry. Some with no plans to marry often had worse relationships than married couples, suggesting that their decision was appropriate (Brown & Booth, 1996).

Despite changes in the age at which one marries, the reality is that most individuals indicate their intention of marrying at some point in their lives. Though they show lower rates of marriage, most African Americans believe in the importance of marriage. Younger individuals anticipate marriage in the not-too-distant future, while older adults are much less likely to anticipate marriage at all. Gender and other differences do exist, however. African American women were less likely to expect to get married than were their male counterparts (Lincoln, Taylor, & Jackson, 2008). Higher-income African Americans were more likely to anticipate getting married than those with fewer financial resources.

Reasons for Marriage

The decision to marry is often based on multiple factors. For those who have cohabited, the most salient variable is often the satisfaction level each partner feels about the relationship. Some will view marriage as a way to share resources more efficiently, while others will see it as the first step to having children. Companionship and emotional support are also important motivators for most couples (Li & Wojtkiewicz, 1994). There is some evidence that for men, the decision to marry is related to their income potential. In other words, men are more interested in marriage if they judge they have sufficient income to support a family. Interestingly, economics does not appear to impact men's decisions to enter into cohabitation. For women, income potential is not a factor in their decision to marry or cohabit (Xie, Raymo, Goyette, & Thornton, 2003). Although the reasons for getting married are obvious, the factors that have led to adults postponing marriage remain constant and it is likely that we will continue to see couples cohabiting rather than entering directly into marriage (Cunningham & Thornton, 2005).

One factor in people's decision about whom and when to marry appears to be the role of risk aversion (Spivey, 2010). For example, men and women who are generally averse to risk taking in their lives are more likely to marry early compared to those who are less worried about risk. This is particularly true for male risk avoiders. Not only will strongly risk-avoidant men marry sooner, but they are more likely to be less selective in choosing a spouse. While risk-averse women are more likely to marry sooner, they appear to be more selective than their male counterparts. Interestingly, the risk-averse male may be seen more positively by women who view the aversion as indicative of someone who will be dependable and responsible both emotionally and financially.

There are also other factors that influence whether a person will marry (Raley, Crissey, & Muller, 2007; Spivey, 2010). For example:

- Urban living decreases the probability of marriage
- Living in the northeast United States decreases the probability of marriage
- Living in the southern United States increases the probability of marriage
- Living with one's parents while going to school decreases marriage probability
- Higher income levels increase the probability of marriage
- Late adolescent romantic relationships increase marriage probability

Constraining Beliefs About Romance and Marriage

Romance and marriage are also influenced by what are called *constraining beliefs*. These are belief systems that limit one's choice in mate selection, affect the amount of effort put into searching for a mate, result in ignoring one's own strengths and weaknesses as well as characteristics of others that are associated with successful relationships, and limit options for problem solving within the relationship (Cobb, Larson, & Watson, 2003; Larson, 1992; Larson & Holman, 1994; Waite & Gallagher, 2000). Each of these beliefs can impact one's success in mate selection.

The first constraining belief is that there is only one right person in the world for the individual. While the idea of searching for a soul mate is romantic, it is neither accurate nor beneficial. It often results in the searcher passing up good matches while somehow expecting to know when the right person appears. In many ways, it is a form of magical thinking.

The second belief is that there is a perfect person out there somewhere and one should wait to marry until that person arrives. The fallacy here is that there are no perfect people in the world. Everyone has some flaws or imperfections that become obvious with time. Searchers who begin to see these flaws then move on to look for another without such limitations.

The third belief is that one must postpone marriage until he or she feels completely confident about the decision. In fact, most who marry feel some insecurity or doubt about entering into a long-term commitment, a normal response to a serious life step.

The fourth belief is that individuals must prove that their relationship will work before getting married. There is no sure way to know beforehand whether the relationship will continue, improve, or deteriorate following marriage. The best approach is to look at the factors that one seeks in another, such as good communication skills, empathy, ability to solve problems, and comparable values and belief systems.

The fifth belief is that with hard work, any marriage or relationship can be successful. In reality, a romantic relationship is composed of two people, both of whom must be committed to making the marriage work. This makes it important to select a mate whose level of commitment to the relationship is similar to yours. Sometimes, nothing can save a doomed relationship.

The sixth constraint operates when the individual believes falling in love with someone is sufficient reason to marry. While being in love with another is an important requirement in Western societies, it is not an adequate reason for getting married. Overlooking other interpersonal and personal characteristics can doom a relationship.

The seventh belief is that by cohabiting before marriage a couple will be better prepared to live a happy married life. This "practice makes perfect" idea is inconsistent with research showing that married couples who cohabited first were often dissatisfied in marriage and more likely to divorce later on. This is not suggesting that cohabiting is the problem, but rather the characteristics of the people involved. These characteristics may include a lower opinion about the value of marriage, commitment issues, or a greater acceptance of divorce when marital problems occur.

The eighth constraint is based on the concept that opposites complement one another. "If I marry someone who is my opposite, his or her strengths and weaknesses will complement mine." Again, this is not consistent with research showing that those with similar characteristics are more likely to be successful in marriage. It is important to find someone whose beliefs, attitudes, values, and personality are consistent with one's own.

The final belief is that finding the right person will be easy and will happen by chance or accident. Finding a spouse requires thinking about what one wants in the other person, and behaving in ways that bring one into contact with potential mates. Sitting at home hoping that at any moment one's soul mate will ring the bell is a recipe for prolonged singlehood.

Acceptance of these beliefs occurs among both men and women. The latter, however, are more likely to accept the one and only perfect partner and complete assurance beliefs. Individuals from Asian backgrounds tend to score higher on scales measuring acceptance of constraining beliefs than is true for Whites or Hispanics.

Marital Survival

Some research has been done on the factors that influence whether marriages survive the normal stressors occurring in any relationship. Huston, Caughlin, Houts, Smith, and George (2001) found that couples who divorced within a few months of marriage tended to share certain characteristics. For example, the couple's romantic bonds were weaker than couples who persevered. Essentially, they were less in love with their counterparts. This difference showed up in various behaviors, including being less affectionate and responsive to each other. They also had relationships characterized by antagonism that may be related to the fact that they were more negative in their views about the partner. Frequently, their courtship period reflected this negativity, with conflict, turbulence, and emotional upset as common occurrences (Niehuis, Skogrand, & Huston, 2006).

Marriages lasting 13 years or longer tended to involve couples who had strong romantic bonds and viewed the partners as being responsive to their needs. Lower negativity and less ambivalence about the marriage were also common. However, predicting which couples will divorce after several years of marriage is more difficult. Often, divorcing couples grew disillusioned with their partner and the relationship over a period of time. They saw their partner as less affectionate and responsive, although in the early marital period these couples had higher than normal levels of affection toward each other. However, over time, these feelings tended to diminish and eventually one or both members lost faith that things will ever improve. Along with this loss of faith came criticism of and greater dislike for the spouse's shortcomings (Huston et al., 2001).

Typically, the first two years of a marriage seem to be the time frame in which couples begin to doubt the wisdom of the union and focus more on the other's faults. If couples are able to maintain their romantic feelings and responsiveness toward each other during this period, it increases the likelihood that the marriage will endure. Potential problems are more apt to surface during the first two years of marriage if any of the following is true:

- Short courtship with high levels of passion and a quick marriage
- Courtships lasting over 27 months with relatively little passion
- Couple engaged in high levels of premarital conflict
- Couple has unrealistic expectations of each other and the marriage.

Not all marriages that demonstrate these characteristics are doomed. Many marriages last because one or both parties elect to live with the other's perceived faults or lack of romance and responsiveness. Some marital partners hope things will change in the future. A portion of these partners will divorce when change is not forthcoming. As Niehuis et al. (2006) conclude, "moderate courtships, though they may seem mundane, may lead to longer lasting marriages" (p. 6).

Assess your comprehension of Family Conflict by completing this quiz.

STARTING A FAMILY

Parenthood is a major developmental milestone for most adults. It results in social, behavioral, and psychological changes that profoundly affect life. Among life events, it ranks along with employment and career as salient factors that define who we are and our respective roles in life. Traditionally, married couples had children at some interval following marriage. It was a rite of passage in the sense that the couple moved from just a dyad to the status of a family. For a variety of reasons, this traditional pattern is followed much less often than in the past. For example, the U.S. Census Bureau reports that the number of married couples with children has been decreasing for several years and is at the lowest rate in history. Today, only about 20% of families have children under 18 living at home, although some couples that had children are now empty nesters. The size of households was also decreasing at a steady rate until recently and now stands at 2.63 individuals (U.S. Census Bureau, 2009a, 2009b).

Deciding to Have Children

Adding children to the dyad is, in many cases, a carefully thought out process that reflects the adult desire to produce another generation. In other cases, the addition of children is an accident. For some couples, having children is a natural evolution from being a couple to becoming a family. At the same time, other couples have children for less desirable reasons, including the belief that having a child will somehow heal a dysfunctional dyadic relationship, as a response to pressure from in-laws and others to produce children, and concern about biological clocks and a fear that waiting until "the time is right" may preclude having children. It is interesting to note that about three-quarters of births to teens and those in their early twenties are nonmarital, indicating that marriage is not seen as a necessary precursor to having children. In fact, cohabitation increases the likelihood that nonmarital conception will occur since cohabiting couples have higher rates of sexual intercourse than is true for either married or single individuals (Rao & DeMaris, 1995).

The rates for nonmarital births vary by race and ethnicity with about 66% of Whites, 96% of Blacks, and 72% of Mexican Americans having their first child before marriage (Schoen, Landale, & Daniels, 2007). Deciding when to have children varies dramatically, but the arrival of a child does seem to precipitate marriage for many couples. Some couples plan to marry if the women becomes pregnant, while others get married although they had not originally intended to pursue this option (Brien et al., 1999). If a cohabiting couple does not marry soon after having a child, the likelihood of their ever marrying decreases. For White women who have a child but are not married or cohabiting, the chances of entering either union increases. Black women, on the other hand, are more likely to cohabit for the first few years of the child's life.

Both cohabitation and marriage appear to be acceptable choices in terms of becoming pregnant, but there is a definite trend for White cohabiting couples to marry before the child is born (Manning, 1993). This observation, however, is not true for Black women, for whom cohabitation remains an acceptable alternative to marriage. As noted earlier, all cohabiting couples are at greater risk for premarital pregnancy, with Puerto Rican women having the greatest risk (Manning & Landale, 1996).

Regardless of the rationale for having children, the consequences are similar. Having children requires additional learning, changes in parental roles, and negotiations among partners. It also increases financial obligations and introduces new stresses into the parents' lives. New parents often are woefully unprepared to understand the needs of a baby completely dependent on others for survival. They must learn to cope with reduced hours of sleep, new tasks, and learn to recognize the infant communications. Questions as basic as "Why is the baby hiccupping?" "Why is the baby crying?" and "Should we use cloth or disposable diapers?" arise early on.

Transitions to parenthood tend to follow similar patterns. For example, both men and women tend to become more traditional with respect to gender roles after the birth of a child. Women tend to change the most in both attitudes and behavior (Katz-Wise, Priess, & Hyde, 2010). Behavior changes affect division of labor among the parents and then extend to outside employment. Mothers are more likely to reduce the number of hours spent in outside employment, while undertaking more housework, than their partners. Societal factors often play a role in these changes because of (1) disparities in pay levels for men and women, (2) parental leave policies, and (3) social role expectations. In addition, many of these changes are a reaction to the needs and demands the first baby places on new parents. Subsequent children tend to elicit fewer changes in parents' attitudes and behaviors with respect to gender roles.

Parents must anticipate the needs of another who has limited means of communicating them. They also need to become more cautious and sensitive to the security needs of the child, while having to do so with diminished rest and little or no help from others. As the child grows, parents acquire new skills in recognizing and anticipating what is required and develop new knowledge about human development. In most cases, they develop child management skills and are able to foster their children's growth. Parents also relinquish a measure of control and responsibility for the child to teachers and other institutions (T-Ball team, religious organizations, youth organizations, and peers). They will also struggle when messages their children receive from these institutions challenge the parents' beliefs, values, and rules.

During adolescence, parents face still more daunting challenges. The development of the adolescent is marked by striving for independence, questioning rules, and looking to others for answers and guidance. This often produces conflict with one's parents. While children often view parents as all-knowing, adolescents tend to have a different impression. This impression can be summed up in the famous quote, "When I was a boy of fourteen, my father was so ignorant I could hardly stand to have the old man around. But when I got to be twenty-one, I was astonished at how much the old man had learned in seven years" (Anonymous, ND). While the quote appears to be quite old, it suggests that adolescence has long been a period of change and difficulty.

Coparenting

One area of parenting that has received more recent attention is that of coparenting (Morrill, Hines, Mahmood, & Cordova, 2010). Coparenting exists when both parents work together in child rearing or, in some cases, work against each other. Ideally, parents may be in an alliance with each other in regard to how best to raise their children and both take a role in managing the children's lives. They support each other's decisions and manage the children's attempts to triangulate parents. They share information about the children and both are invested in the child. In worst cases, parents may be antagonistic to each other's parenting styles, decisions, and child-rearing behaviors. While the more problematic examples of coparenting most often occur in divorced parents, they can also occur in intact families. When effective coparenting is employed, the marital relationship between partners is generally healthier. This mutually beneficial relationship is to be expected when teamwork, support, and collaboration exist within the marital dyad.

DIVERSITY IN FAMILIES

Stereotyped views of what constitutes a family often fail to take into account the many diverse forms in which families occur. We will now look at four particular family structures—blended, gay, single-parent, and foster families—which social workers are likely to encounter.

Blended Families

Blended families are those in which a parent has entered into a new spousal arrangement, resulting in the creation of a family that includes children of one or both parents. The new family may occur as a result of marriage or cohabitation. Blended or stepfamilies are a common pattern in the United States, directly related to the high rates of divorce and remarriage noted earlier in this chapter. Almost two-thirds of women and three-fourths of divorced men remarry (Dupuis, 2007). An estimated 17% of children under age 18 are living in blended families (U.S. Census Bureau, 2008). Some of these children live with stepsiblings from prior marriages of their stepparent. There are clear differences among various races with 18% of Blacks living in blended families compared to 4.5% of Asian children.

Despite their relative commonness, there are significant misconceptions about blended families, often nurtured by literature (e.g., *Hamlet*), children's tales (e.g., *Cinderella, Snow White*), movies (e.g., *Pan's Labyrinth*), and media reports of dysfunctional stepfamilies in which a child is abused or killed. There is some evidence that children who live with stepparents are at greater risk of filicide, with stepfathers more likely to harm the child than is true for genetic fathers (Harris, Hilton, Rice, & Eke, 2007). In addition, the risk to the stepchild is greater when the stepparent has his or her genetic children living in the home.

While there are some positive examples of stepfamilies (e.g., *Love Actually, The 40 Year-Old Virgin, Juno*), too often the term *stepmother* or *stepfather* is preceded by the adjective "wicked." In reality, most blended families struggle with the same kind of issues as genetic parents and the vast majority of stepfamilies are not abusive. At the same time, blended families face unique challenges including "feeling caught," managing boundaries, parental role ambiguity, "traumatic bonding," competing for resources, managing competing "conflict management" approaches, and creating a solid family unit (Golish, 2003). Each stepfamily develops its own system of communicating and problem solving with little guidance available about which approach is most effective. Perhaps the best indication of the challenges faced by blended families is that about 60% end in divorce, often more quickly than first marriages (Dupuis, 2007).

The divorce rate of subsequent marriages can be explained, in part, by the stresses and pressures such unions engender. For example, it is not unusual for one or

Blending children from two families can be a challenge but is often successful.

Angela Hampton Picture Library/Alamy

both partners to feel pressure to make this marriage work because their previous marriage had failed. This can lead to behaviors that actually hasten the demise of the relationship. Stressors that occur in any marriage may be seen as particularly problematic in subsequent marriages because they bring back memories of past unions. One or both spouses may have a déjà vu moment as they recognize that this problem occurred before and helped lead to the first divorce. Emotional baggage from previous marriages inevitably intrudes in subsequent relationships and can lead to misunderstandings and confusion. It can also contribute to spouses becoming self-protective and pushing the other spouse away in anticipation of being hurt (Faber, 2004).

In addition, some marriages involve situations where one spouse has been previously married and the other has not, with the spouses at different developmental points. These differences can affect communication styles, expectations, and opinions about what behavior is OK or not OK. Spouse age differences can also produce challenges related to life cycle phases, access to resources, and handling of finances (Bernstein, 2000). Other issues may also occur that involve the ability and desire of the new spouse to assume a parental role with the other spouse's children. Emotional connections between the stepparent and the stepchildren do not occur automatically and stresses associated with that issue can undermine the new marriage. To help weather the inevitable strains, the marital dyad system must be as strong as the parent–child system, despite the latter having developed over a longer period of time. As you can see, creating a blended family involves a number of challenges for both adults and children.

Blended family development

Typically, blended families develop in one of five ways: accelerated, prolonged, declining, stagnating, and high-amplitude turbulence (Baxter, Braithwaite, & Nicholson, 1999; Braithwaite, Olson, Golish, Soukup, & Turman, 2001). In the case of accelerated development, the most common pattern, the stepparent quickly assumed the role of parent while communicating that the children were not distinguished by their genetic or step status. This worked to create a single family entity with stepchildren referring to their stepsiblings as sister or brother. While some role strain occurred, it subsided as one or both parents adjusted to and became more comfortable with their new responsibilities.

By comparison, prolonged development often took significantly longer, was characterized by low solidarity levels, and an attempt to carry out typical family duties but without trying to create a single unit immediately. Getting to know one another and adapting to new roles required time, but after about four years, most members reported feeling like a family.

Declining blended families often started off perceiving themselves as one big happy family but later became distressed and disenchanted. The realization that they had failed to maintain their initial solidarity and perceptions was a reminder of how difficult it can be to establish a functional blended family. Family members recognized that feelings of solidarity felt initially were gone, replaced by conflict and tension. After four years together, members had disengaged from one another, either physically, emotionally, or both. Feelings ranged from jealousy to alienation, leaving family members without hope of ever feeling like a family.

Stagnating development typically occurs when roles never become clear and family expectations keep changing. This makes it hard for all family members to understand what is expected and where they stand. These families are like a car circling a giant parking lot and never venturing into traffic. No progress was achieved in creating a "we feeling" among members who ended up about where they started. Family members felt "thrown together" with too much to handle in terms of adaptation and boundaries.

Although individual family members will sometimes feel connected to another member, these experiences are typically transitory.

The final developmental trajectory is one of high-amplitude turbulence in which neither child nor parent accepts the family role changes. Conflict is a relatively common occurrence in such families. Family members feel like they are on a roller coaster with wide fluctuations in their sense of solidarity and connections with each other. Other reactions included instability, inconsistency, and attempts to periodically right the ship. Through repeated efforts, some families are successful in arriving at a successful conclusion; others found the task too difficult.

Several factors affect whether stepparents and stepchildren bond and the latter accepts the guidance and authority of the former. For example, the more contact the genetic father has with his child, the less likely the child is to accept the stepfather's role as a parent. High levels of conflict between biological parents have a similar impact (Portie & Hill, 2005). This shows the value of communicating and relationship-building between stepparent and stepchild.

An interesting difference noted by Manning and Lamb (2003) is that cohabiting stepfamilies had a higher incidence of adolescents with delinquent behavior, serious school academic and behavior issues. Married stepparents did not demonstrate any differences in these areas compared to married biological parents. This was attributed to married stepfamilies having more clearly defined roles than did cohabiting stepfamilies. Parental and neighborhood support appeared to protect stepchildren from more serious school and community problems and higher levels of parental monitoring helped reduce the incidence of acting out (Portrie & Hill, 2005).

Single-Parent Families

According to the U.S. Census Bureau (2012), about 21 million households comprised single parents raising children. Of this number, about 27% are single fathers and 73% are single mothers. While the proportion of single mothers rose in the past decade by about 10.6%, this mirrored the increase in total households. The proportion of single fathers, however, increased by over 27%, suggesting that more fathers are assuming child-rearing responsibilities than in the past. Moreover, the percentage of husband and wife family households fell to 48%, a drop from 52% in 2000 and 55% in 1990.

Single parents must assume an array of duties and responsibilities traditionally split between spouses or partners. The potential to be overwhelmed or stressed by these additional burdens is clear. To make the challenges more difficult, single families headed by women have a poverty rate of 31.6% while those headed by their male counterparts have a rate of 15.8%. This compares to a rate of 6.2% for married couple families (U.S. Census Bureau, 2011). This means that financial hardship is much more common among families headed by single men or single women, with the latter especially vulnerable.

The U.S. Census Bureau (2007) reports show about 60% of custodial mothers and 40% of custodial fathers receive some form of child support. However, custodial parents who received child support typically received less than two-thirds of what was owed, an amount that averaged $3,350 per year. For custodial families below the poverty line, child support equaled almost one-half of the average custodial parent's income. About 56% of mothers typically received noncash child support (gifts, payment of expenses, etc.) compared to about 67% of fathers. Of those parents with child support agreements, about 57% had some health insurance for their children. For parents without such agreements, only 17% had such coverage provided by the noncustodial parent. Households headed by mothers are at risk of both financial hardship and mental health challenges (Taylor, Larsen-Rife, Conger, Widaman, & Cutrona, 2010). The risk is higher for African

American families due to higher poverty rates and associated stress. Risks to single-parent families include a tendency to internalize problems, blaming oneself for negative life events, decreased energy needed for parental roles, and similar outcomes. High risk levels can lead to a failure in monitoring children adequately and in parenting characterized by anger, hostility, harshness, and inconsistency.

> The resilience level of the single parents often determines the success they achieve in managing risks. Resilience includes optimism about the future and life events, positive social networks, physical health, higher levels of self-efficacy, and self-esteem. Social support appears to be even more beneficial for single fathers than for single mothers (Wade, Veldhuizen, & Cairney, 2011). Research has shown that helping these parents reduce their stress levels, develop new coping skills, and become more optimistic leads to better outcomes (Taylor et al., 2010).

Single fathers are often at a disadvantage with respect to becoming the custodial parent. Dudley and Stone (2001) highlighted some of the reasons why males are much less likely to be given custody of their children. These include:

- Assuming that teen fathers and unmarried fathers are not interested in parenting
- Fear that fathers seeking custody are doing so to get back at the mother or for other inappropriate reasons
- Concern that fathers have neither the skills nor the aptitude to handle responsibilities of parenting
- Worry about father's ability to provide nurturance
- Tendency to see men as primarily financial providers, nothing more

Despite these stereotypes, the percentage of single fathers caring for their children is rising, making it imperative that custodial fathers receive the kinds of support and assistance traditionally provided to custodial mothers.

Single-parent families often must deal with multiple challenges and this is especially true for adolescents who bear children. The case of Stephanie and Rose Doer written by Rose Malinowski shows some of these challenges. After looking at the case, respond to the critical thinking questions raised by the author.

Same-Sex Families

A major challenge in gathering information about same-sex families is locating reliable and valid data about the number and experiences of such unions. On the one hand, research on gay and lesbian families has not been conducted to the same extent as with other family forms. On the other, the social stigma associated with same-sex relationships often makes individuals fear the reactions of others if they identify themselves as gay, lesbian, bisexual, or transgendered. In addition, even using the term *same-sex marriage* fails to acknowledge that not all gay men or lesbian women are homosexual. Indeed, some are bisexual as is the case with some nominally heterosexual marriages. Determining how to categorize dual-orientation families remains a work in progress. These and other factors complicate our discussion about this diverse family form (Allen & Demo, 1995). One place to start a discussion is around the number of same-sex families in the United States. According to the U.S. Census Bureau (2011), about 1% of families in the 2010 census were same-sex couples, split more or less evenly between gay and lesbian families. This represents about an 80% increase from the 2000 census. However, these data are complicated because of the issues of marriage, legal domestic partnerships, and simply living together. Allen and Demo (1995) highlight the diversity inherent in describing and counting same-sex families. These families may be composed of "one adult lesbian, one adult gay male, two adults (both gay males), two adults (both lesbians), two adults (one lesbian and one heterosexual or bisexual partner), two adults (one gay male and one heterosexual or bisexual partner), or some combination of more than two lesbian, gay, and/or heterosexual partners" (p. 114). This does not take into account families in which there are lesbian or gay children or gay, lesbian, or heterosexual stepchildren living with either same-sex or heterosexual parents.

Since 2000, more states have recognized and/or permitted marriages between same-sex couples, while others have created legal recognition for such families. Of course, many same-sex unions are created outside of legal recognition or marriages. While the U.S. Census has begun to gather information on family composition, persistent and well-documented homophobia in society continues to discourage adults from self-identifying as gay or lesbian, further complicating efforts to understand these families or even determine their numbers in the United States. For the most part, it means relying on estimates rather than exact figures. The 2006 American Community Survey estimated that there were almost 800,000 same-sex unmarried households in the United States, but this count is also affected by government policies that inhibit counts of married households composed of gay adults (U.S. Census Bureau, 2007).

Historically, legal and religious concerns about supposed risks to children being raised in same-sex unions dominated our understanding of these families. However, a great deal of research on the topic has concluded that children raised in these unions are as psychologically healthy as those raised in heterosexual families (Lambert, 2005). Studies comparing lesbian and heterosexual mothers found no differences in terms of psychological functioning, self-concept, overall adjustment, and happiness. There were no differences in parental sex role behavior, child management strategies, or parental warmth. Fears among some policy makers that children raised in same-sex families are more likely to turn out to be homosexual lack any research support and reflect a strong degree of heterosexism (Landau, 2009). It is worrisome that only in same-sex families do we judge the parents on the basis of how their children turned out, while no such assessment is routinely applied to heterosexual parents. For example, no one is particularly concerned about a girl being a tomboy in a heterosexual family, but this same behavior in a same-sex household is construed as evidence of the influence of homosexual parents.

Gay fathers were just as likely to be motivated to be parents as heterosexual fathers; and other similarities were noted on issues such as intimacy, warmth, and parenting patterns. There were also no differences between the gender identity, sexual orientation, or gender role behavior of children raised by gay men or lesbian compared to heterosexual couples. Peer relationships between the two groups of children revealed no difference with both having normal peer relations. As Chan, Raboy, and Patterson (1998) note, "qualities of relationships within families are more important than parental sexual orientation as predictors of children's adjustment" (p. 455). Moreover, Golombok et al. (2003) concluded that "the presence of two parents irrespective of their gender, rather than the presence of a parent of each sex, is associated with more positive outcomes for children's psychological well-being than is rearing by a single mother" (p. 31).

In addition, there is evidence that unlike most heterosexual couples, same-sex couples demonstrate greater equity in child care and household labor (Peel & Harding, 2004).

The positive research picture of same-sex families should not be taken to suggest that they do not have problems. In fact, they have many of the same problems that occur within any family. Partners may struggle with child-rearing approaches, values and attitudes, and finances related to their entire family, while also dealing with the typical challenges that occur in building and maintaining a dyadic relationship. Complicate this by adding in the likelihood that many families are composed of at least one parent who is divorced. Since lesbian women are much more likely than gay men to have custody of children from a previous relationship, this opens up the whole realm of dealing with at least one noncustodial parent. In this regard, same-sex families must manage the same dilemmas as different-sex marriages.

Children in same-sex families often grapple with the issue of sharing their parents' orientation with peers. Whether children keep this information secret or share it is often affected by the larger population's homophobia (Landau, 2009). Most available evidence suggests that many of the challenges faced by children raised in same-sex families is a response to heterosexual bias and actions of those subscribing to the bias (Robitaille & Saint-Jacques, 2009).

Strengthening same-sex families

Same-sex parents often developed ways to strengthen their sense of family within an unsupportive societal context (Oswald, 2002). One method was to create families from among their friends. By doing so, they produced a supportive and positive sense of family and helped avoid family members whose homophobia or disapproval would introduce negativity into the home environment. Sometimes, these friendships occur in support groups such as Parents and Friends of Lesbian and Gays (PFLAG) and may include both homosexual and heterosexual individuals. Same-sex parents are also likely to demonstrate significant care in how and when they disclose their orientation to others. The disclosure process is likely to be ongoing and not a single-time event of sharing to others who are most likely to be supportive. Often this means sharing one's orientation with sisters and mother before disclosing to male family members. Many gay and lesbian parents are careful not to engage in events or activities where their presence is likely to be problematic for the child.

Another useful tactic in same-sex families is to build a sense of community by participating in supportive events and services. This can include attending churches that support gay and lesbian members; using gay/lesbian community resources; and participating in local, state, and national organizations that respect and promote resilience. Rituals in the family may also be employed. This can include the nonbiological parent reading children bedtime stories to foster bonding or participating in community activities such as Pride Day celebrations. It may include attending gay and lesbian marriages and celebrations. Same-sex parents may engage in political activities designed to combat heterosexism and homophobia and celebrate affirming differences, such as also being a person of color or of a particular religion (Oswald, 2002).

Other same-sex parents have to deal with naming issues, such as what to call the co-parent and other fictive kin. Some change their names so that all family members share the same surname, a practice that helps with one's sense of identity and makes it easier when dealing with societal institutions. Finally, same-sex parents adopt a view of what it means to be a family that is not only broader than is true in most heterosexual families, but also more restrictive in that unsupportive relatives are excluded from the configuration. These efforts strengthen the same-sex family and reduce some of the stress inherent in a homophobic society.

Foster Families

Approximately 70% of U.S. children in out-of-home placements are living with foster parents (USDHHS, 2008). Serving as a foster parent is a tough role involving not only childcare and parental activities with one or more children, but also working with social workers and a child's genetic parent. The goal of foster care is providing permanency in living arrangements so foster children are not traumatized by living with multiple families (biologic and foster). In addition, the plan is to provide the child with an environment of loving and caring adults who will raise a child within the values of society and at least prepare him or her to move home or be adopted.

Although not always the case, foster parents are often sought from among families already having their own children. This appears to be based on the assumption that families with children have child-rearing experience and can employ those skills with the foster child. At the same time, single adults and gay/lesbian couples also serve as foster parents, sometimes for hard-to-place children and adolescents. In addition, perhaps as many as 45% of foster children are placed in families of relatives or close family friends who agree to care for them (Zinn, 2009). Foster parents are licensed by the state in which the child resides, receiving a stipend to help defray expenses of caring for a child who is a ward of the state. In addition to kin and nonrelative foster homes, some children enter specialized treatment foster homes designed to manage children or adolescents with particularly difficult health or mental health problems.

Children often enter foster care with a variety of concerns and problems (Heller, Smyke, & Boris, 2002). These include medical needs, mental health concerns, and educational challenges. Many have been physically abused or neglected. Developmental delays are not uncommon. These issues require intervention by specialists and a commitment of time and energy on the foster parents' part. At the same time, foster parents are faced with a dilemma. Do they take full responsibility for the foster child, integrating them fully into the family, loving and caring for them as they would for their own children? Or do they avoid that level of closeness because it comes with the very real risk that the child will be moved in the future, leaving the family with an emotional void? Of the two options, avoiding development of a close bond is more harmful to the foster child.

Foster parents must also share "ownership" of the child with others. This includes social workers, therapists, legal personnel, medical personnel, genetic parents, and others. The number of people involved with the foster child increases the potential for conflicts and disagreements. It can also be overwhelming, especially when more than one foster child is placed with a family (Heller et al., 2002). Unfortunately, foster parents have no prior history with the child and know little about what has transpired in his or her life. Sometimes the social worker knows nothing about the child's past. A good example is the case of Charlie, described next.

Clinical Corner

Charlie

The county foster care coordinator, Garrett, received a phone call at 8:00 p.m. stating that an 11-year-old boy needed immediate housing in a receiving home, a temporary or short-term emergency shelter for abused or neglected children in the custody of the local child welfare agency. When Garrett arrived at an address provided by his supervisor, he found Charlie with a babysitter. Piecing together information from the babysitter, Garrett learned that Charlie's mother had asked the babysitter if she could drop him off at the sitter's home and leave him for a couple of hours. Eight hours later, the mother had not returned for Charlie and the sitter became worried. With three younger children of her own, she was in no position to care for Charlie. Garrett helped Charlie gather up his things and drove him to the receiving home, which cared for the boy until a regular foster home could be found. Three weeks later, Charlie moved to the new foster home and lived there for the next two years. Attempts to locate Charlie's mom were futile and she never returned nor contacted the child. Garrett gathered what information he could about Charlie from his prior school but there was little to share with the foster parents. The foster family cared for him with essentially no medical information and only what details Charlie could share. After two years of efforts to locate his mom, her parental rights were terminated and the foster parents adopted him.

Selecting effective foster parents

In general, foster care is considered to be a temporary measure pending either reunification with parents or kin or adoption. Zinn (2009) found that in the five years following placement, just under 40% of foster children are reunified with parents while another 30% are adopted. The remaining children either remain in foster care permanently or until unification or adoption. This is particularly true of children placed in treatment foster homes.

For many years, studies have tried to identify the characteristics or attributes of foster parents and foster children that contribute to positive outcomes for the latter, leading to several conclusions. For example, having a positive outcome—that is, whether a foster child is reunified with a parent or adopted—does not seem influenced by such foster family characteristics as the foster parent's age or race, or the number of adults in the foster home. In situations where a single adult cares for a foster child, the outcome is likely to be the same as in two-parent foster homes. However, some factors do seem to be related to outcomes. For example, children placed with African American, non-kin foster parents are less likely to be adopted. The chances for reunification decrease and adoption increase when foster family income increases. This finding is particularly true for children in non-kinship families. The more experience a non-kin family has with fostering also seems to be positively related to the likelihood of a child being reunited with his or her parents and negatively related to being adopted. Neither of these outcomes appear affected in the case of kinship placements.

Zinn (2009) points out, however, that many factors may influence the outcomes in foster care but that behavior or characteristics of the foster parents may have little to do with them. Moreover, the causes of the various associations are unknown and can only be treated as hypotheses. Other studies have identified foster parent characteristics that do seem to be important to outcomes. The following list identifies some of the factors positively associated with foster care outcomes (Buehler, Cox, & Cuddeback, 2003; Chipungu & Bent-Goodley, 2004; Cole, 2005; Crum, 2010; Kirton, Beecham, & Ogilvie, 2006; Linares et al., 2006; Sinclair & Wilson, 2003; Orme et al., 2004):

- Foster parents with strong community service orientations
- Responsive and balanced parenting style
- More experience as foster parents
- Specialized training of foster parents
- Child-oriented caregivers
- Warm foster parents
- Effective child-rearing and problem-solving skills
- High level of satisfaction regarding relationship with spouse
- Positive relationship between foster parents and agency staff
- Support for foster parent role from friends and family
- Effective limit setting using a flexible and firm approach

Other factors influencing outcomes in foster care

As might be expected, there are also characteristics of children in foster care that lead to more positive outcomes. Those who were most well-adjusted behaviorally were more likely to have successful placements while those with physical disabilities or other serious health needs were more likely to have placements break down (Brown, 2008). Children whose prior placements had failed were more likely to have problems in succeeding placements. Successful placements included those in which the child felt supported and accepted. Placement breakdown was less likely if the foster child felt important in the family and felt the love of family members. At the same time, some experiences of foster children tended to lead to broken placements, including children who had been physically or sexually abused prior to placement.

Other factors influencing the levels of support and conflict experienced in foster families were interesting (Denuwelaere & Bracke, 2007). For example, when the foster parents have children of their own, foster children received more support from birth children if both were about the same age. If the foster child was a girl and the birth child a boy, it was the birth child who experienced the most conflicts with the foster father. The foster father's role is apparently of importance in other ways. For example, if the foster father gave support to the foster child, it translated into higher feelings of self-worth and self-efficacy for the latter. The foster mother's support had a distinct bearing on the child's sense of self-esteem. In general, the more support given by foster parents, the lower the incidence of emotional problems in foster children. Conflicts with the foster mother increased the rate of emotional problems of foster children.

When reunification is a possibility, it is not uncommon for foster parents who have been successful with a child to question the adequacy of the biological parent's environment. The foster parents are having trouble letting go of someone they care for, a normal reaction. Sometimes biological parents cannot improve their caregiving and parental rights are terminated. This can lead the biological parents to pressure one or more of their relatives to step forward and apply to adopt a child or seek a kinship placement. Rarely are these last minute arrangements helpful in providing a long-term resolution for the foster child (Heller et al., 2002).

Challenges with foster children

Foster parents frequently need help from social workers in dealing with the multiple issues that children bring to foster care (Heller et al., 2002). These may include problematic eating behaviors that can encompass eating a diet that is neither adequate nor appropriate, overeating, hiding or hoarding food, and eating inappropriate items (dog food, dirt, etc.). Foster children may have sleep disturbances, such as resisting going to sleep, trouble staying asleep, or nightmares. These may result from past sleep patterns that were not appropriate for growing children but permitted by biological parents.

Some foster children have problems related to toileting which can include enuresis or actively refusing to use the toilet, among others. This may be the result of a failure of the genetic parents or a reaction to the trauma associated with removal from one's home and placement in foster care. Another challenge faced by foster parents is a child who refuses to follow instructions and acts out. This may take the form of temper tantrums, risk-taking behavior, or other actions that make it hard for a parent to provide care.

It is common for children who have been abused in the past to engage in aggressive behavior with others, including both peers and foster parents. Children with language or speech deficits may also become aggressive when frustrated by their inability to communicate their needs. Still other problematic challenges fall into the category of regulatory disorders. Here we might encounter depressed or withdrawn behavior or a child hypersensitive to certain stimuli leading to aggression or acting out.

A final category of behavior that can occur is a foster child who engages in sexualized activities, such as playing with oneself, displaying sexual organs, or engaging in precocious sexuality. This behavior is generally not truly sexual in nature because the child is not sexually aroused, but more likely bored or anxious. At the same time, this unexpected behavior is likely to be upsetting to the foster parent (Heller et al., 2002).

Given the difficult backgrounds experienced by many foster children, some problematic behaviors are not unexpected. When birth parents provide inconsistent warmth and attention, these children learn not to trust foster parents who do because they fear that loving parental behavior could change quickly. Rejection by the foster child is often a major disappointment to the foster parent trying to be supportive and responsive. Trust issues arising from early childhood experiences can challenge even the well-motivated foster parent. Likewise, children who received little or no guidance in their birth home may have difficulty when foster parents attempt to set limits (Schofield & Beek, 2005). Issues of autonomy and boundaries are common problems. In many ways, successfully integrating a foster child into a family is similar to the process of linking children in blended families. The goal of both is helping a child feel a part of a whole, integrated, and valued as a member.

PARENTING STYLES

As you may recall, the issue of parenting styles was briefly introduced in Chapter 11 as a factor influencing children. Parenting styles have been of interest to researchers and practitioners for many decades. This interest derives from a belief that the parenting style may have an effect on a variety of outcomes. The breadth of studies on parenting styles is considerable—with everything from psychiatric illness to eating vegetables examined to determine what, if any, influence parenting style has on children's and adolescents' behavior. Typically, parenting styles are categorized as authoritative, authoritarian, indulgent, or uninvolved (Coplan, Hastings, Lagace, Seguin, & Moulton, 2002; Rothrauff, Cooney, & An, 2009). Each style has unique characteristics and there is research on the relative value of each. What is not known with assurance is whether these models accurately capture all parenting styles or whether they apply equally well to all ethnic or racial groups (Domenech Rodriguez, Donovick, & Crowley, 2009).

Authoritative Parenting Style

Authoritative parenting is usually characterized by high levels of support coupled with moderate to high levels of control over children and adolescents. Most of the research on authoritative parenting identifies a number of positive outcomes compared to the other styles. For example, this style is associated with lower rates of depression and substance abuse and higher levels of emotional well-being in children and adolescents. Strong support from parents is also associated with higher levels of self-worth and feelings of security. Adults who were raised by supportive parents engage in similar relationships as they mature, are physically healthier, and less likely to experience depression (Shaw et al., 2004). In addition, this style of parenting is negatively correlated with children's emotional eating (Topham et al., 2011).

Alegre (2011) also found that children's emotional intelligence was higher when parents were responsive to and positive in setting expectations for their children and when they coached their children in understanding emotions. Emotional coaching by parents involves allowing children to express emotions while helping them understand and act in ways that mediate and control the feelings. Emotional intelligence is typically defined as the capacity of an individual to recognize and understand one's own emotions and those of others, regulate his or her emotions, and respond appropriately. Each of these parental behaviors is associated with the authoritative style of parenting.

The importance of supportive parents can be seen in its absence, which can lead to feelings of inadequacy, hostility, anxiety, and insecurity (Rothrauff et al., 2009). Accompanying authoritative parenting are higher levels of control that help children learn to conform to expectations and norms, and develop self-control. Eventually, children learn which norms must be followed, which ignored, and consequences for circumventing expectations. At this point, they are more capable of making behavioral decisions and moral judgments.

In the absence of parental control, children struggle to learn the multiple rules and expectations imposed by society and its institutions. Although children complain about parental expectations, they ultimately find the combination of high demands and high support beneficial to their development. Authoritative parents demonstrate warmth and understanding of the child's needs and tailor their demands to the child's capability. Authoritative parenting tends to be used more frequently among White parents (Radziszewska, Richardson, Dent, & Flay, 1996).

Another area where an authoritative style parenting appears to have an influence is in the driving behavior of teens (Ginsburg et al., 2009). The authors compared adolescents raised by parents using the authoritative approach with those raised by uninvolved parents and found:

- One-half as many automobile crashes
- Reduced rates of driving while intoxicated (71%)
- Reduced rate of cell phone use while driving

Teens raised by either authoritative or authoritarian parents were twice as likely to use seat belts and half as likely to speed. No differences in seat belt use or crash risk between permissive and uninvolved parent styles was seen, suggesting the value of parents monitoring specific behaviors.

Authoritarian Parenting Style

Authoritarian parents are also high in their expectations for their children, but do not couple this with support and responsiveness to their needs. These parents tend to be perceived as cold because of their lack of sensitivity to the child. Adults raised with this parenting style report lower psychological well-being and higher depression rates (Rothrauff et al., 2009). This was especially true for White children raised by authoritarian parents. When parents belittle, punish, or otherwise devalue children's emotions, as often occurs in authoritarian style parenting, children are less likely to develop the same level of emotional intelligence as with authoritative parenting (Perlman, Camras, & Pelphrey, 2008). In addition, authoritarian parenting is often related to parent–child aggression and a potential for child abuse (Rodriguez, 2010).

Authoritarian parenting appears to be more common among African American and Hispanic families (Calzada, Huang, Anicama, Fernandez, & Brotman, 2012; Radziszewska et al., 1996). There is also some evidence that Asian American parents use this style as a child becomes older, while employing a more lenient style in infancy and early childhood (Garcia Coll & Pachter, 2002). Frequently, however, race is confounded by socioeconomic class variables, which may help explain some of the differences noted among various racial groups.

It is also important to point out that authoritarian parenting may be more appropriate in certain environments. For example, Baldwin, Baldwin, and Cole (1990) found that children in high-risk environments benefited by having strong, clear messages from parents about what they should and should not do. It also contributed to children's school performance. Authoritarian parenting styles may serve as a buffer to reduce the risk of self-destructive behavior in older adolescence among certain groups, as also for African American children suffering from depression. It had no such effect on depressed White children (Greening, Stoppelbein, & Luebbe, 2010).

Indulgent Parenting Style

Indulgent parents are very sensitive to their children's needs, but have few, if any, expectations for their behavior. They do not generally make demands on children, are more permissive, set far fewer rules, and believe that letting children make up their own minds is preferable to having to follow parental strictures. As adults, those raised by indulgent parents reported about the same overall level of well-being as children raised by authoritative parents. Indulgent parenting does raise the rehospitalization risk for children receiving psychiatric treatment, suggesting the value of parental limit setting on children's behavior (Fite, Stoppelbein, & Greening, 2009).

Uninvolved Parenting Style

Parents who are uninvolved tend to be low on both support and the setting of expectations. Neglectful, they place few demands on children and often appear emotionally distant or detached. As these children mature into adults, they report higher levels of depressive symptoms and substance abuse than those raised by authoritative parents. Unlike the other parenting styles, uninvolved parents do not choose this style out of a belief that it will benefit their children. More often than not, their parenting style is due to an underlying psychological or emotional problem. Frequently, they are struggling with their own demons and have neither the strength nor inclination to formulate a style of parenting that will benefit their children.

It is important to recognize that parents may have different parenting styles that present challenges for the family. The most positive outcome for adolescents is when both parents use an authoritative parenting style. However, even a single authoritative parent can benefit a child despite the other parent's style (Simons & Conger, 2007). When parents are in consort and not in conflict with regard to style, it affects sibling relationships in the family positively (Yu & Gamble, 2008). Greater warmth, support, and cooperation between siblings occur when parents are on the same page with respect to parenting style.

Despite much research on parenting styles and behavior of children and adolescents, even parents who did all the right things still have children with severe problems. Some children do not learn from their mistakes, engage in self-destructive behavior, and do not respond to parental guidance. DNA studies have shown that some children lack the means to become successful adults. It appears that while parenting styles and child-rearing behavior clearly affect outcomes for most children, genetic factors may have as much or more impact. While the debate over the relative importance of nature versus nurture in understanding human behavior will continue, it is clear that an interplay between both factors may account for certain outcomes.

Human Behavior

Practice Behavior Example: Critique and apply knowledge to understand person and environment.

Critical Thinking Question: Looking at the various parenting styles just described, consider which one or ones were employed by the person or persons who raised you. What did you see as the benefits and drawbacks to the parenting style?

Assess your comprehension of Parenting Styles by completing this quiz.

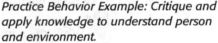

GRANDPARENTING

For many people, being a grandparent in an ideal world involves watching another generation come into being, grow, and mature under the care of one's children. Grandparents can serve as babysitters, mentors, friends, and in a variety of roles that complement a child's parents. They can also be a support and source of information for a young couple

Did You Know?

Almost 7 million children lived with a grand-parent in 2008, of which 4.4 million lived in the grandparents' home.

adjusting to the demands of parenthood. A part-time pursuit, being a grandparent to one's grandchildren can be a reward-ing and fulfilling activity. Unfortunately, not all grandparents are lucky enough to move into this role. Some spend their later years as surrogate parents when their own children are not able to adequately perform their responsibilities. We will now discuss both of these scenarios and some of the more common experiences of grandparents in each.

Surrogate Parenting

Serving as a surrogate parent for one's own child is not often identified as a desired or expected aspect of being a grandparent. Yet, almost 2.6 million grandparents are cur-rently playing this role for grandchildren under age 18 (U.S. Census Bureau, 2010). For some grandparents, this is a temporary activity while the children's parents are unable to provide care. However, almost a million grandparents have cared for their grandchildren for at least five years. Of those providing surrogate parenting, about 20% have incomes below the poverty line and 25% have a disability. The trend of grandparents caring for grandchildren has been increasing for decades, due largely to such factors as parental divorce or desertion, drug use by parents, or parental death (Glass & Huneycutt, 2002). In addition, some parents are absent because of military duty, jail or prison sentences, or diseases such as AIDS/HIV (Edwards, 2009).

The role of a surrogate can be taxing for many grandparents. For those with lim-ited financial resources, the addition of children can create a crisis. Some grandparents find the emotional burden difficult and could benefit from respite care. Others experi-ence stress and frustration dealing with the children's parents, custody rights, and related issues.

While the number of children raised by grandparents is significant, relatively little information is available about the children's functioning. Edwards (2009) found that teachers saw students raised by grandparents as having more behavior problems than other students. They also said that they noticed the children had "more somatic com-plaints," and were more "anxious/depressed" compared to other children (p. 140). These results suggest the importance of identifying and preventing problems in these children. Despite the challenges noted by Edwards and others, many children raised by grandpar-ents are successful in life and school and resilient enough to achieve their goals.

Besides those serving as surrogate parents, another 3.8 million grandparents live in households with their grandchildren, often with one or both of their grandchildren's parents. They may be residing in either the grandparents' home or that of the children's parents.

Grandparents Living Alone

Identifying the number of grandparents who do not live with their grandchildren and are not engaged in surrogate parenting is difficult, yet this is common for most grand-parents. Estimates as high as 54 million individuals have been made, but reliable numbers are not available.

Regardless of the living situation, grandparents often try to walk a fine line between being available to their adult children and not wanting to unduly intrude. Having raised their own children, grandparents can lay claim to experience in child rearing and have de-veloped clear opinions about what works and what does not. At the same time, they value the independence of their children and their right to make their own decisions. Balancing these two inclinations challenges even the most successful grandparents (Mason, May, & Clarke, 2007). A large percentage of grandparents have regular contact with their grandchildren. Common activities provided for grandchildren include the following:

- 65% provide money to grandchildren younger than age 15
- 61% care for grandchildren under age 15 during the day
- 55% provide babysitting services to their grandchildren in the evenings
- 53% have grandchildren under age 15 stay overnight at their home
- 52% take grandchildren to different kinds of activities
- 13% take grandchildren under age 15 on vacations

Grandparents must be simultaneously parents to their own children and grandparents to their children's children. The dual role can be stressful sometimes, but is generally considered a rewarding experience. However, grandparents who believe that their children see them as automatic babysitters to be called upon with short notice may resent that expectation (Mason et al., 2007). Being "on-call" limits grandparents' sense of self-determination. Others may object to grandchildren simply dropping in unannounced because it interferes with their freedom and control over their own lives.

The role of a grandparent can become more confusing than normal when the parents of grandchildren divorce, as divorce is often stressful and acrimony is common. Grandparents may find themselves at odds with the former spouse of their child, with potential consequences for their future interactions with the grandchildren. If they side with their own adult child, they risk a reduction or even a loss of contact with the grandchildren. Should they maintain a positive relationship with their former in-law, this can be uncomfortable for their own adult child.

The extent to which grandparents are able to maintain a relationship with grandchildren is affected by several factors (Mueller, Wilhelm, & Elder, 2002), with geographic proximity being perhaps the most influential. Typically, the closer that one lives to the other, the greater the potential for a significant relationship. A second factor is relational in nature. Most grandparents realize that the quality of the grandparent–grandchild relationship depends to a large degree on the quality of their relationship with the child's parents. Problems in this arena can preclude grandparents from forming much of a relationship with grandchildren. The gender of the grandparent appears also to be a factor, in that grandmothers tend to form closer relationships with grandchildren than is true for grandfathers.

The age of grandparents and grandchildren can also play a role in their relationship. The younger the grandparents, the more involved they tend to be with their grandchildren. As grandparents and grandchildren mature, the nature of their relationship is also likely to change. Having a large number of grandchildren limits, in some ways, the potential for a quality relationship between the generations. It is much easier to build and maintain a relationship with three grandchildren than it is with 20, as may occur in larger families (Coall, Meier, Hertwig, Wänke, & Höpflinger, 2009).

When parents divorce, this sometimes increases the opportunity for grandparents to be involved with their grandchildren, particularly if they are providing financial support to their children. This is especially true for maternal grandparents (Mueller et al., 2002). Other influencing factors can be such things as the existence of cross-generational family rituals, religious traditions encouraging interactions, and whether grandparents had positive experiences with their own grandparents. In general, grandparents who enjoy that role also feel younger and hope to live longer than those grandparents who do not. Interestingly, those who become grandparents at a relatively young age tend to feel older, although the quality of their relationship with their grandchildren reduces this sense of being ancient (Kaufman & Elder, 2003).

One topic not often addressed is how grandparent involvement with grandchildren affects the latter. As we noted in the section on grandparents as surrogate parents, children in these families tended to experience more problems in school than was true for children being raised by their parents. However, it is important to see if this negative influence extends to other grandparent–grandchild situations. Attar-Schwartz et al. (2009) studied how grandparenting affected adolescent adjustment among more than 1,500 students aged 11 to 16. Their research demonstrated several positive outcomes when grandparents were involved with their grandchildren. For example, the greater the level of involvement, the lower the number of emotional problems experienced by adolescents and the higher the amount of prosocial behaviors. The greatest benefit of grandparent interaction was in single-parent families and stepparent families. These results are consistent with other research that show that social support from outside the immediate family helps children and adolescents develop.

TRANSITIONS

Transitions are a fact of life for both individuals and families. Changes that occur include such things as divorce, death, and children leaving home. While some couples will never experience a divorce themselves, they will certainly have family and friends who go through this painful event. Death, of course, is a given for all living things and most families will experience the loss of a loved one. For couples, this typically involves the husband dying because the risk of a male dying before a female is well established. Less common is the death of a child in the family—either through disease, accident, or homicide. Many parents wish to protect their children from the risks in the outside world. However, while it may be theoretically possible to prevent children from leaving home, having a group of adult children locked in their bedrooms for life is unattractive and impractical. As a result, transitions are bound to occur and we will now highlight some of the more common responses that can be expected.

Divorce

In Chapter 13, we explored some of the immediate and long-term ramifications of divorce for adolescents. This section will focus more on how divorce affects the couple.

In the past, the death of a marital partner was the primary endpoint for a marriage, but this is no longer true (Pinsof, 2002). Divorce has become the most common reason for the end of a marriage and is no longer restricted to younger couples. It is common to see couples in their forties, fifties, and sixties divorcing. According to the Centers for Disease Control and Prevention (CDC, 2002), first marriages end in divorce within five years about 20% of the time and 33% end within 10 years. Figure 14.2 shows the disruption rates of marriages by length of marriage (CDC, 2001).

Of course, not all marriages that end lead to divorce. While White women who are separated from their husbands go on to divorce their mates 91% of the time, only 77% of Hispanic and 67% of Black women do so.

Remarriage of divorced women occurs in about 54% of cases within five years although the percentages are lower for Hispanic and Black women. The lower rates of remarriage for Black women has been attributed to fewer eligible Black males due to higher rates of incarceration, unemployment, and death among this group (CDC, 2001). Second marriages also have a high probability of divorce, with about 40% ending within

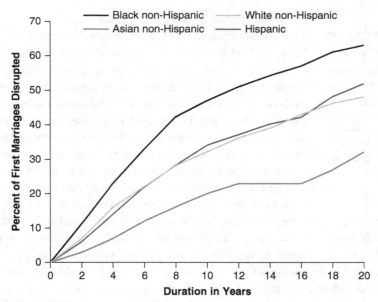

Figure 14.2
Marital Disruption by Group
Source: CDC (2001).

10 years. Interestingly, the percentage of divorced women who remarry has been drop-ping steadily since 1950. Compared to rates 40 years ago, marital dissolution is more likely now for both first and second marriages.

Figure 14.3 shows the probability of remarriage by length of divorce and race/ ethnicity of the women (CDC, 2001).

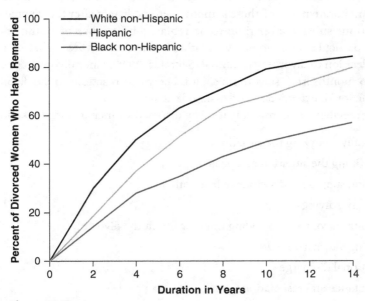

Figure 14.3
Remarriage Rates by Group
Source: CDC (2001)

Human Behavior

Practice Behavior Example: Apply theories and knowledge from the liberal arts to understand biological, social, cultural, psychological, and spiritual development.

Critical Thinking Question: What might explain the high probability of divorce for people entering second marriages?

While the statistics regarding divorce are disturbing, there are other problems associated with marriage dissolution. For example, "compared with married individuals, divorcees exhibit lower levels of psychological well-being, more health problems, more social isolation, less satisfying sex lives, more negative life events, greater levels of depression and alcohol use, and lower levels of happiness and self-acceptance. The economic consequences of divorce can be severe for women: most often, children remain with the mother after divorce and the loss of the ex-husband's income often results in a severe loss of income per capita. For men, the retention of income combined with decreased family size may actually result in an increase in his new household's income per capita" (CDC, 2001). Divorce appears to negatively impact the immune function and increase the rate of suicide, alcoholism, homicide, and car accidents (Amato, 2000; Sakraida, 2005). It is not unusual for the stress of divorce to aggravate existing illnesses and bring on acute episodes. Divorce appears to be particularly problematic for women in middle age compared to younger women. Some researchers have compared the consequences, including elements of chronic mourning, to that of a spouse dying (Sakraida, 2005). While these differences are initially lessened for those who sought the divorce, this benefit disappears in less than two years (Sakraida, 2005). One interesting finding is that depression appears to be less of a problem for African American women with sufficient financial resources (Varner & Mandara, 2009). Apparently, having adequate financial resources acts as a protective factor and helps ameliorate problematic mental health consequences.

For some divorcing couples, the termination of a conflictual relationship is a liberating and renewing experience, leading to feeling better about oneself and having a more positive outlook on life (Rice, 1994). Unfortunately, not all couples react in this way and enjoy a positive transition from marriage to divorce. Emotional reactions to divorce frequently include prolonged bouts of crying, persistent thinking about the divorce, trouble sleeping, loss of appetite, panic attacks, a sense of vulnerability, and fear (Rossiter, 1991; Sakraida, 2005). Social support (both formal and informal) and a spiritual belief system appear to ameliorate many of these symptoms immediately after the divorce. Typically, initial reactions subside after time to be replaced by a sense of optimism and self-confidence, particularly for women who either initiated the divorce or were in marriages where the decision to divorce was mutual (Sakraida, 2005). Since divorces appear to average about 15 months from start to finish, it is likely that reactions to the divorce process will continue for an extended period (Sakraida, 2008).

Coping mechanisms commonly used by divorced women include (Sakraida, 2008):

- Logically analyzing the situation
- Redefining the situation as a positive event
- Seeking support and assistance from others
- Problem solving
- Cognitive avoidance (avoiding thinking about the divorce)
- Seeking alternative rewards
- Emotional discharge
- Acceptance and resignation

The first few months after a divorce tend to be characterized as conflictual, reflecting both the challenge of creating a new family entity and dealing with the emotions inherent in the event (Stallman & Sanders, 2007). Some divorced spouses continue battling for years after the divorce. In most cases, one or both former spouses remain angry and employ aggressive communication styles reflecting this upset. Generally speaking, these responses are considered unhelpful and evidence of immaturity. Oftentimes, the former spouses use the court system to challenge or harass each other and are unable to resolve their anger (Kelly, 2003). Ultimately, it is the children who suffer from the parents' behavior.

As noted earlier, most divorced individuals end up getting married again. They will meet new potential partners and pursue dating and courtship rituals as in their previous marriage. However, this process is often more complicated when one or both individuals have children. In light of how divorce affects children it's appropriate to identify some of challenges divorced men and women encounter when they decide to date.

The decision to date is often related to divorced individuals' desire to connect in a romantic relationship. Research indicates that one key to divorced individuals' sense of well-being is forming such a relationship (Anderson & Greene, 2005). As many as 50% begin dating within a couple of months after filing for divorce and about 25% are already in a serious relationship. Within a year of filing, nearly 80% had begun dating again (Anderson et al., 2004). Dating, however, is often complicated by custody issues, cultural values, ethnicity, and gender. Men, for example, tend to date sooner than women. Women with custody responsibility often wait longer to date, although custody of children does not seem to affect divorced men. Women tend to have fewer options than men, largely due to demographic issues such as the availability of men of the same age, or older. In addition, women are less likely to date younger men while this option is readily available to divorced men. Black women may date less because of the demographic factors mentioned earlier, while Hispanic men are likely to date more than either Whites or Blacks.

The presence of children complicates dating and often leaves the parents feeling embarrassed or guilty. Many perceive their children as reacting badly when they begin to date (Anderson & Greene, 2005). The perception often becomes reality if the dating partner attempts to discipline the children or if the children feel they are in competition with the new individual for their parent's love and attention. In most cases, children are included in some activities by the dating couple during the first year of the relationship. Most children experience this as positive, or at least neutral, with only a small percentage reacting negatively. A complicating factor for children is the number of serious relationships the parent has with potential partners. This can lead to children feeling badly when a potential stepparent disappears from the scene. It can also teach them to avoid getting too close to a dating partner who may soon disappear.

Sleeping over and cohabiting are the next step for many divorced couples, although this is a sensitive issue for both parents and children. Most parents restrict sleepovers until they are certain the new partner is a serious one or make such arrangements only when children are not home. Once the relationship has become more serious, living together is a common practice for about two-thirds of parents who remarry (Dush, Cohan, & Amato, 2003). However, cohabitation may also increase the potential for conflict between children and the new partner.

If the divorced parent becomes pregnant as sometimes happens, it often precipitates marriage, especially among White and Hispanic parents. As might be expected, the pregnancy will affect both parents and existing children, but does not seem to be a long-term problem for either. If the relationship leads to engagement, about 75% of children see the new status as positive (Anderson & Greene, 2005). Remarriage is common for divorced individuals, with more than half being married within five years (Bramlett & Mosher, 2002).

Death

Chapter 13 covered the issue of death from the standpoint of preparing for one's own demise and discussed widowhood in some detail. Here we will explore other aspects of death that impact families.

Deaths in a family tend to fall into two categories: expected and unexpected. Expected deaths are those that accompany old age and poor health and, while the timing may be uncertain, the event's inevitability cannot be denied. Unexpected deaths are those that occur without warning and are nonnormative. Examples include premature death of a spouse because of health problems or an accident, as well as loss of other significant family members (child, grandparent, and close friend). In both cases, family members experience sadness, pain, and other emotions—and sometimes the consequences are long-term. For example, Bowser et al. (2003) found that unexpected deaths of family members occurring before age 15 and inadequate mourning of these losses were factors leading to contracting HIV and indulging in risk-taking behavior among intravenous drug users.

Death by suicide

Deaths by suicide often leave family members in grief and trying to fathom the reasons leading to the person's death. Surviving members often experience lowered levels of emotional bonding, and increased problems in adapting (Lohan, 2002). Parents may be too distraught dealing with their own grief to be available to other family members. In cases where a husband committed suicide, widows experienced higher levels of grief and blaming in their family compared to widows whose husbands died in accidents (McNiel, Hatcher, & Reubin, 1988). Parental suicide is often, but not always, preceded by stressors such as separations, legal trouble, or domestic violence (Cerel, Jordan, & Duberstein, 2008). The authors divided families that had experienced a suicide into three groups: chaotic, encapsulated, and functional. The *chaotic families* show higher rates of psychopathology and/or turmoil in multiple members prior to the suicide. *Encapsulated families* are those in which the suicide victim was the only member showing conflict or emotional problems. *Functional families* are those families where there was no evidence of family or psychological problems. In these families, the suicide most often occurred in someone suffering from a chronic illness.

Families in which a suicide has occurred are especially in need of social support. As Cerel and colleagues note, "Suicide is a confusing death. Its causes are complex, multidetermined, and poorly understood" (2008, p. 39). Blame is an often occurring theme in such deaths with survivors judged negatively. Observers may believe that the death was related to the survivor's behavior, especially in the cases involving suicide of a child. This can turn parents against each other, blaming the other for contributing to the death of a loved one. Other parents will blame themselves, regretting things they said to the deceased, or ruminating on how their own shortcomings may have contributed to the suicide.

Sometimes, parents attempt to conceal the actual cause of death from other family members or members of their support network. Parents' own shame and guilt may cause them to withdraw from their social networks just when these supports are needed. Other times, potential supporters do not know how to approach the subject and avoid the survivor, further isolating the individual in a time of grief.

Suicide survivors typically fall into two different categories (Cerel et al., 2008). The first are children, an estimated 60,000 of whom experience the suicide death of a family member each year. Of these, as many as 12,000 must deal with the suicide of a parent and another 8,000 experience the death of a sibling by suicide. These figures are from the United States and the rates are often higher in countries in which suicide is a culturally accepted means of death. Children are often affected by suicide in a variety of ways. One such outcome is mental health issues, including mood disorders, posttraumatic stress disorder, and suicidal behavior. Another outcome involves emotions such as guilt, anger, and sadness, which are generally expected in such situations. Functional problems are another possibility that may include doing poorly in school, engaging in drug use, and so on. Cerel and Roberts (2005) found that marijuana and alcohol use, suicidal thoughts and attempts, and other emotional problems are a common reaction to a family member's suicide. A final category is physical health, in which a surviving child develops a serious illness or an existing disease becomes worse.

A second category of survivors are those who lose an older adult to suicide. These individuals tend to grieve for longer periods than do those surviving a person who died from natural causes. They receive less social support and feel stigmatized by, ashamed of, and rejected by the deceased.

Death from any cause and the resulting bereavement is a major event in people's lives. Williams et al. (2007) found that more than 70% of a group of older adults, who were followed for 30 months, lost at least one loved one during that time. Further research shows the most common loss is of one's spouse, affecting about one-half of all women and 12% of men over age 65 (Arbuckle & de Vries, 1995). However, other death losses are very common: after age 60, over 40% of adults lose a sibling and about 10% face the death of an adult child (Moss & Moss, 1989; Moss, Lesher, & Moss, 1986–1987). In addition to direct family losses, the death of close friends is often experienced by older adults. For example, nearly 50% of adults older than age 70 had lost a close friend during a time span of 15 months (de Vries & Johnson, 2002). Deaths of family members and friends profoundly affect the survivors. These losses deplete social and instrumental supports, as well as eliminate individuals who might have provided care for an elderly parent. There is some evidence that losses of one's adult children may affect parents differently, depending on their gender.

Individuals who lose a spouse to death often report that their health is unsatisfactory and, in fact, experience negative health outcomes (Charlton et al., 2001). Depression, psychiatric disorders, and anxiety are common reactions to loss of a spouse. Physical symptoms are also quite common among older adults who experience bereavement.

Empty Nest

The term *empty nest* has been used to denote the period at which adult children leave home and strike out on their own. We briefly alluded to this concept in Chapter 13 as one influence in middle adulthood. For most parents, the empty nest period is a positive one—albeit with some tinge of sadness at the last child's departure. Mothers, in particular, seem to be more affected by the experience than is true for fathers (Mitchell & Lovegreen, 2009). Recent research highlights the fact that both marital and life satisfaction increase (Schmidt, Murphy, Haq, Rubinow, & Danaceau, 2004). For most women, at least, the empty nest period means a more positive outlook on life and fewer hassles (Dennerstein, Duley, & Guthrie, 2002).

Mitchell and Lovegreen (2009) found that the transition appears to be more difficult when a child leaves either too soon or too late. Parents who had been married for 30 years or more tend to find the empty nest experience more positive than those who have been married for 20 years, a likely concern being that the children are moving out too soon (Hiedemann, Suhomlinova, & O'Rand, 1998). A premature or unexpected departure is accompanied by sadness, while staying too long tends to generate frustration and sometimes conflict with the adult child. Parents who are older at the time their children leave seem to be less stressed by the event than younger parents. In cases where the parents are providing care for their own aging parents, the adult child's leaving often was a positive event.

Factors that explain the more positive view of an empty nest include changes in family structure and function. Most women now work outside the home and play many roles. As a consequence, their perceptions of self are influenced by more than just being a parent. In addition, launched children (boomerang kids) have started coming home again (which may explain why parents move and leave no forwarding address). This moving home phenomenon has lengthened the empty nest period for many families. Another factor that reduces the impact of the empty nest syndrome is the extent to which parents remain engaged in various activities (job, family, and community).

Assess your analysis and evaluation of this chapter's contents by completing the Chapter Review.

15

Miriam Reik/Alamy

Cultural Influences on Human Behavior

From a social work perspective, defining the word *culture* is a challenge. For some people, the term connotes beliefs, ideas, values, and knowledge that are passed from one generation to another. Typically, culture is transmitted within and across generations through a variety of means, including language, rituals and traditions, and institutions. Culture is reflected in art, music, and literature, all of which are shared within a given group. The Center for Advanced Research on Language Acquisition (2010) defines culture as "the shared patterns of behavior and interactions, cognitive constructs, and affective understanding that are learned through a process of socialization. These shared patterns identify the members of a culture group, while also distinguishing those of another group" (p. 1).

Culture includes symbolic features and both tangible and intangible representations. Artifacts, such as the automobiles we choose to drive and the products we purchase, are often culturally influenced. This is obvious when we compare the kinds of cars driven in other countries to those in the United States. While Americans tend to like large SUVs, Europeans drive small vehicles, less imposing, and more in keeping with other values. While U.S. supermarkets typically carry multiple brands of the same product (bread, toilet paper, canned vegetables, etc.), the array of products— even in close neighbors such as Canada—is much more limited.

Behavior is also influenced by culture. This can be seen when traveling internationally. Americans sometimes blanch when they see unrefrigerated eggs for sale in other countries because we tend to refrigerate everything but our socks. While men in the United States often carry a handkerchief to blow their nose, the Japanese have used tissues for this purpose for centuries. Somehow, putting a rag with nose refuse in your pocket like a treasure seemed anathema

Some cultures observe rites of passage such as this Bar Mitzvah.

to the Japanese who deposit their used tissues in trash bins. Behaviors such as shaking hands as a form of greeting tend to be employed cross-culturally, but even this action is culturally influenced. For example, shaking hands with a glove on is considered rude in many cultures, while customs often influence when a handshake is expected. Some cultures shake hands every time people meet and others only when meeting someone for the first time. In Islamic and some Judeo societies, men and women do not shake hands because it violates cultural norms about physical contact between the genders. Handshakes may be replaced with a kiss on the cheek in some cultures. It is these differences and a multitude of others that make us view culture as separating us from one another. However, it is important to recognize that culture influences us but does not eliminate the enormous similarities among human beings. While studying the role of culture, social workers should continue to see the ways we are all more alike than different.

CULTURE

The United States is a country settled largely through immigration, so exposure to the cultures of others was a common occurrence. Despite this history, the United States has always had a wary reaction to each new wave of immigrants. Cultural differences were frequently seen as problematic because newcomers often spoke different languages and maintained their own beliefs, practices, and attitudes. Each succeeding group of arrivals was viewed as a potential threat to the status quo, despite that within a generation or two, most immigrants and/or their children had adopted what we might consider American values. In addition, under various pressures, immigrants learned to speak English (Tran, 2008). At the same time, some immigrant families continued to celebrate holidays or other aspects of their country of origin. As time went by, others citizens came to accept these links to the homeland and sometimes joined in the celebrations. The New York and Boston parades on St. Patrick's Day owe their origin to these remnants of the past, as do Oktoberfests celebrated in both the United States and Canada. These and other cultural events—held everywhere from small towns to large urban areas—continue to represent ties to people's cultural past.

Although the idea that America is a melting pot—into which immigrant groups disappeared and later emerged as Americans—has been popular, the reality is much different. Immigrants did learn to speak English and adopt many traditional American values. At the same time, many retained aspects of their former culture and old values that they passed along to succeeding generations (Daniels, 1991). The immigration patterns that exist today are, however, of a different nature than those of the past, according to many observers. One difference is that assimilation into the mainstream culture is not occurring by the second or third generation as used to occur (Dicker, 2006). Recent immigrants continue to retain strong ties to their homeland and maintain more of their languages and culture than was previously true. Assimilation is made more difficult by the physical differences of newcomers (e.g., skin color) which are more obvious than was true with arrivals from Europe (Massey, 1995). Moreover, many immigrants return to their homelands regularly, a much less common practice in past immigrations. Economic conditions are also different today, with high unemployment and fewer avenues to middle-class status than was true for European immigrants. Because of continued ties to their homeland, many of the more recent immigrants have been referred to as *transnationals*. Included in this group are Dominican Americans, Mexican Americans, and others from Latin America. Both ties to their countries of origin and the number of Spanish-speaking immigrants make it unlikely that the language will disappear in the immediate generations to come.

The influence of culture on individuals and societies is inescapable. Not only does a culture provide tangible benefits to its members, but it helps regulate behaviors in ways that benefit the society itself. This chapter will focus on some dimensions of culture, as well as identify the ways in which culture influences us by considering topics such as rites of passage, individualism and collectivism, and ethnocentrism.

Rites of Passage

In many societies, the point at which a child is considered an adult is marked by one or more rituals and a ceremony by which the community acknowledges that transformation (Bell, 2003). The rituals that must be completed are often selected by the individual's community. This process is often referred to as *Rites of Passage* and originally was applied to any change in social status such as marriages, birth, or death (Van Gennep, 1960). For our purposes, we will look at the concept within the context of the transition from childhood to adulthood, also known as *coming of age*. One benefit of a rite of passage (ROP) is that it sends a clear message to individuals relative to their new status. For example, the message of an ROP is: "complete this ritual and we will consider you an adult." It often includes instruction from elders about what is expected from the individual, as well as organized events that are seen as steps in the process of becoming an adult (Groce, Mawar, & Macnamara, 2006). Instruction may include information about such things as interacting with the opposite sex, selecting a partner, sex, and expectations about marriage. The timing of this ROP is often associated with puberty, cognitive development, and mastery of a previous psychosocial task (Markstrom & Ibora, 2003).

In many cultures, the ROP involves three separate activities. In the first, the individual is physically or psychological separated from the community. Most commonly, the individual moves to another venue away from others. This is followed by a transition period of varying duration which may involve going into the wilderness, fasting, living off the land, or engaging in other actions that are expected during the transition period. It is often a period during which the person must overcome some individual challenges. However, some cultures employ group-based challenges rather than individually based ones. Depending on the culture, the transition period can last from as little as a day to months. The final stage is one of reintegration or reincorporation with the community.

One purpose of the discussed process is to separate the individual from his or her old identity and assist in the development of a new identity. In practice, the achievement of a new identity is considered a significant developmental milestone (Erikson, 1968). This means participants will be expected to play adult roles and abide by adult rules

Did You Know?

About 140 million girls and women across the globe have experienced female genital mutilation. This includes 92 million African girls 10 years of age or older.

Source: World Health Organization (2012).

Developing cultural competence in social work practice is a challenge that almost all practitioners will face at some point in their career. Cheryl Pascual's article "Culturally Competent Social Work Practice with Black Women" describes her experiences as a Filipina American woman trying to enhance her capacity to work with African American women in a mental health clinic. What do you see as the challenges you face in order to develop as a culturally competent practitioner?

after they are reintegrated with their community. (Personally, I always thought Peter Pan had the best idea—a permanent childhood with no adult responsibilities—oh well!) Because the person has not yet mastered the new roles, it is common to experience a degree of anxiety which will lessen with assistance from new mentors and role models (Markstrom & Ibora, 2003). Ultimately, the individual will be reincorporated into the community as an adult with the responsibilities and rights that this status confers. Markstrom and Ibora (2003) provide a description of an ROP for girls participating in the Navajo or Diné Kinaaldá ceremony. The process begins at menarche with a ceremony that includes such things as bathing, changing into adult clothes, traditional practices such as meal preparation, singing, physical exertion, mentoring, eating a meal, and a blessing. When completed, the adolescent female is recognized as an adult woman.

Each ROP has specific purposes associated with it. For example, the Diné Kinaaldá ceremony is intended to designate the girl as a woman, acknowledge her capacity as a reproductive being, teach appropriate roles for adult women in Diné society, build strength, endurance, teach good posture and beauty tips, enhance personality development, encourage generosity and giving to others, strengthen the girl for adult challenges, ensure future harmony and good luck, and solidify her identity as a changed woman.

Despite the value of rites of passage or coming of age rituals, they are becoming less common in urban societies, even among groups that have historically employed such rituals (Groce et al., 2006). While there are some rites of passage common to North American society, they are mostly limited to such religious ceremonies as Jewish Bar Mitzvahs and Bat Mitzvahs (for boys and girls, respectively), and Christian confirmations. For others, an ROP is acquiring a driver's license or a debutante's ball. These events tend to lack the emotional resonance associated with rites of passage in other cultures (Bell, 2003). Mostly, adolescents in North America are left to explore for themselves activities and behaviors that may convey adult status, which limits the opportunity to learn societal values. As Hill (1992) and Alford (2003) note, too often adolescents measure their level of adulthood by engaging in prohibited behaviors: promiscuity, drinking, and involvement in gangs.

Some groups have attempted to create rites of passage opportunities for various target populations. For example, Harvey and Hill (2004) discuss a program that targeted African American youth at risk of drug abuse by incorporating activities designed to build resilience within an Africentric perspective. It included an orientation phase, weekly meetings focusing on African and African American culture, skill-building activities, bonding experiences, and physical exercise and challenges. Finally, a ceremony was held at which the youth demonstrated to parents and others the knowledge, values, and skills they had acquired. The results showed that the youth who participated experienced higher self-esteem, and possessed accurate knowledge of the dangers associated with drug abuse.

Some rites have also been criticized on moral, ethical, and practical grounds. For example, the rite of female genital mutilation, practiced in several African cultures, has been actively opposed as a barbaric ritual designed to inhibit sexual responsiveness in the girls who undergo this surgery. The surgery is often performed by individuals with little or no medical training and involves partially or completely cutting away the external female genitalia. The practice exists among several religions including Christians, Muslims, animists, and one Jewish sect (Althaus, 1997). Young girls are either forced or pressured into undergoing female genital cutting or mutilation (FGC or FGM). Critics argue that it is a practice that oppresses women, is a violation of their rights, and should be universally banned (Prazak, 2007). Reasons for FGC include wishing to ensure that a young girl is a virgin, providing greater pleasure for the woman's future husband, and cleanliness. It is also argued that having had the procedure increases the power of women in patriarchal countries by increasing the respect men have for women. Most important, FGC is a social bonding phenomenon that helps promote closeness within some communities. In some societies, elders who usually take the lead in initiating the ritual also receive a share of the proceeds paid to the circumcisers, collect fines from those who do not participate, and participate in feasts celebrating the event (Prazak, 2007). The tradition of FGC has been likened to the cutting of an umbilical cord, symbolizing the infant's transition from an appendage of the mother to an independent being. Circumcision is viewed as transitioning the girl from childhood to a reproductive status. Interestingly, those opposed to the practice tend to be younger, better educated members of society. The practice has declined in popularity over the past two decades with over 70% of both boys and girls disapproving of the procedure. Despite its decreased popularity, many girls and their parents fear that not undergoing the procedure will leave the daughters unmarriageable and outcasts from society. Despite multiple attempts by governments, nongovernmental organizations (NGOs), and missionaries to end the practice of FGC, it has survived for centuries.

Whatever the supposed societal benefits of FGM, those who have endured the procedure often report unpleasant outcomes. These include infections, emotional trauma, less enjoyment from sex, and anger at family members who encouraged or demanded the procedure. Some females who underwent the procedure have experienced sterility, depression, hemorrhaging, and/or birth complications when they have their own children, while others die from FGM. While FGM can occur as early as two weeks of age, the most common age is just before puberty. The best estimate is that somewhere between 100 and 140 million girls and women have had the procedure (National Women's Health Information Center, 2009). A number of boys from these cultures also have undergone a circumcision as part of their own coming of age ritual. Social workers will most likely encounter clients who have experienced FGM when working with immigrant women from the northern part of Africa. It is also possible that social workers will work with families who want FGM performed on their daughters once the family arrives in the United States. This will raise questions of child and human rights abuse because, in the United States, the practice is not supported and is illegal to be performed on anyone under age 18.

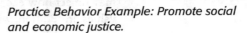

Engage, Assess, Intervene, Evaluate

Practice Behavior Example: Promote social and economic justice.

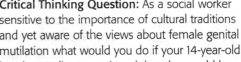

Critical Thinking Question: As a social worker sensitive to the importance of cultural traditions and yet aware of the views about female genital mutilation what would you do if your 14-year-old immigrant client mentioned that she would be undergoing this procedure within the week?

Individualism Versus Collectivism

Another way in which culture influences human behavior is through the concepts of individualism and collectivism. Cultures that value individualism emphasize individuals working alone in pursuit of their own goals. American culture is frequently cited as individualistic in orientation, while many other cultures—such as Chinese, Japanese, Native American, and Pacific Islanders—are viewed as collectivist in orientation. Individualist societies see the ties between people as loose with individuals largely responsible for taking care of themselves. Individualism is believed to foster greater creativity, independence, locating meaning in response to one's own feelings, thoughts, or behaviors rather than in those of others. Compared to many other societies, Americans tend to be more open to new experiences, nonconformist, self-confident, achievement motivated, and dominant. In addition, they tend to be more prone to hostility and impulsiveness (Zha, Walczyk, Griffith-Ross, Tobacyk, & Walczyk, 2006). The emphasis in individualistic cultures is on four key values: personal choice, intrinsic motivation, self-esteem, and self-maximization (Tamis-LeMonda et al., 2008). The value of personal choice maximizes individuals making their own decisions based on their own needs. Intrinsic motivation suggests that what we seek to achieve is based on inner goals and objectives, rather than being imposed by others. Individualistic cultures value self-esteem derived from achievement and accomplishments that reflect positively on the individual. In contrast, collectivist cultures emphasize the well-being of the family or unit over that of the individual member. Finally, self-maximization is captured in an old commercial for the U.S. Army that emphasized, "Be all that you can be." Maslow's hierarchy of needs identifies this goal as self-actualization or self-fulfillment, in which individuals achieve their potential.

By contrast, collectivist cultures value the group over the individual and expect people to work for the betterment of all members rather than pursue their own individual aims. The values of greatest importance in such cultures are connection to one's family, orientation to the larger community, respect for others, and obedience to authority (Tamis-LeMonda et al., 2008). Collectivist cultures see people as inherently part of a larger group that protects them while expecting unquestioned loyalty in return. Relationships between and among people tend to be viewed as having great importance (Triandis, 2002). Loyalty is owed to the group of which one is a part, and equality is valued more highly than personal achievement that sets one apart from others. Asian cultures are often cited as examples of collectivist societies in which success of the group is more important than success of the individual (Zha et al., 2006). The degree of interdependence is higher than in Western cultures as is accommodating one's behavior to the needs and wishes of others. The benefits of collectivist cultures are evident in such things as scores on standardized achievement tests and higher levels of problem-solving skills, as demonstrated in multiple studies (Stevenson, Lee, & Mu, 2000; Zha et al., 2006).

The differences in such things as creativity, problem solving, and mathematical ability may reflect how each culture organizes and focuses its educational systems to reflect its values. In addition, within any culture the degree to which individuals subscribe to an emphasis on individualism or collectivism is likely on a continuum (Leonard, Van Scotter, & Pakdil, 2009). The timing at which a particular value is displayed may also differ. For example, autonomy may be expected to be displayed earlier in one's life in some cultures, but is still important as a value in other cultures. There is also a tension between competing values within individual families. For example, while U.S. parents want their children to display independence and initiative, they don't find it nearly as attractive when children have tantrums in malls because they are denied a candy bar. Generally, at such times, parents would prefer children exhibit respect for authority and deference to the wishes of their elders. Likewise, the striving for independence associated with adolescence is often underappreciated by parents attempting to set boundaries and raise teens who respect societal and family values. No wonder kids get confused sometimes.

Other discrepancies can be seen within cultures emphasizing individualistic values. In the United States, for example, there are numerous examples of how belonging to—and allegiance to—a group is emphasized. Athletic teams, gangs, and military units often emphasize taking care of each other, working to further the goals of the group, and submerging individuality in a group effort. Moreover, individuals who were raised in collectivist cultures but live in individualistic societies may adopt the strategies for success that they see modeled in their peers and coworkers. One's behavior may be adapted to the work environment, but could be different at home where more traditional values prevail. There is also evidence that both Western and Asian cultures are adopting aspects of the other to achieve the benefits associated with each approach. This sharing or merging of divergent value sets is likely a consequence of the increased internationalization of world economies, travel, educational opportunities, and immigration.

Individualism and collectivism have a clear effect on communication. For example, the individual tends to be much more direct in his or her communications and less concerned about how others feel or think (Singelis & Brown, 1995). In work contexts, individualistic employees tend to restrict their communications with others because they believe that individual achievements receive the highest reward. By comparison, collectivist communication pays greater attention to the context in which a communication takes place. This makes it essential that those trying to understand this communication be familiar with contextual cues. Collectivists prefer greater face-to-face communication and seek more frequent discussions to make decisions and coordinate activities (Leonard et al., 2009). An example of communication differences is the tendency of Asians to email colleagues or others and copy everybody above them in the organizational hierarchy. This is confusing to Americans, who only copy their superiors in rare instances and certainly not in each individual email.

It is important to keep in mind that theories and approaches used in social work and other helping professions are often developed within the context of a particular cultural milieu. Thus, theories that value developmental themes emphasizing independence and self-esteem are likely to be out of synch with collectivist cultures. In addition, other variables—such as power and levels of equality—may confound efforts to understand the behavior of individuals within a cultural context (Oyserman, 2006).

On a macro level, the focus on individualism can be more problematic than in societies in which collectivism is a strong value. This can be seen in the current battles around the issue of immigration. In collectivist cultures, there is general agreement about what it means to be a member of that culture. However, in the United States, there is much less agreement or sense of what it means to be an American. A society created by immigrants from hundreds of countries has difficulty articulating the common elements that characterize its members. Is it a shared language, such as English? A certain set of values? A specific belief system? Efforts to make English the official language are an attempt to identify a commonality, but it conflicts with educational practices that include using bilingual teachers in classrooms with large non-English-speaking populations. The American tradition of welcoming newcomers as inscribed on the Statue of Liberty ("Give me your tired, your poor, your huddled masses, yearning to breathe free") clashes with ethnocentric values, a nativist movement that favors certain immigrant groups over others, and citizens who blame undocumented immigrants for a variety of social problems such as loss of job, criminal activity, and failure to acculturate. Nativist groups seeking to prevent these alleged and feared social problems have engaged in racism, violation of human and civil rights, and violation of other rights guaranteed by the U.S. Constitution (Bennett, 1990).

Assess your comprehension of the Cultural Differences by completing this quiz.

RACE AND ETHNICITY

Race and *ethnicity* are both cultural factors that influence human behavior. Separating the two terms, however, is often difficult. When talking about race, the topic of ethnicity is almost always brought up, largely because our commonsense understanding of these terms is intertwined. However, the concepts of race and ethnicity are neither synonymous nor clearly understood by many using these terms. When the term *race* is used to speak of Whites, Blacks, Native Americans, or Hispanics, it is a misnomer and biologically incorrect. For clarification, let's start with the concept of what it means to be a human being. Human beings are a single species of biological creatures which are extraordinarily homogeneous. The best estimates are that all human beings are 99.9%

identical from a genetic standpoint, which sets us apart from most other species (Collins, Green, Guttmacher, & Guyer, 2003).

By contrast, a race is a biological subspecies that possesses distinct anatomical differences from the others of its species. Characteristics, such as skin coloration, are evolutionary adaptations to ultraviolet radiation for populations in geographical areas where sun exposure is dangerously intense. They do not signify a different race. Likewise, we can categorize human beings in a variety of ways based on their differences, eye color, blood type, and height, but these characteristics do not constitute racial differences. On the contrary, they are simply part of what makes us different from one another, but all within the same species. The problem with using the concept of race to refer to humans with different color skin is that it supposes that there are other differences that make them unlike us. In addition, it allows groups to be discriminated against based on the supposed differences that make the other group less "human." Such was part of the reasoning behind Hitler's holocaust designed to exterminate the "Jewish Race."

The U.S. Census Bureau has recognized that race is not a biological or scientifically respected category. Although they gather data on race, they point out that the term is a social construct and is neither genetic nor biological in origin. In reality, few traits exist in only one group of humans and there is substantial cross-over between groups. However, some groups continue to self-identify as having a particular racial identity; hence, the Census Bureau allows individuals to identify themselves as belonging to one or more groups. At the very least, this recognizes the vast amalgam of groups that exist and with which we identify. It also underscores that race is a social construct used by individuals and groups to categorize themselves and others.

Critical Thinking

Practice Behavior Example: Use critical thinking augmented by creativity and curiosity.

Critical Thinking Question: If race is not a biological category and the term tends to be used arbitrarily, what would you replace it with, assuming that you were responsible for the U.S. Census?

Ethnicity, by contrast, refers to one's traditions, customs, and behaviors learned within a particular group or groups. It is a better term than race because it is more accurate, useful, and mutable. In other words, we can change our ethnicity. For example, if you were a Native American child raised by White parents, as an adult you can choose to identify with both groups, neither group, or to change from having a White identity by adopting the customs, beliefs, and practices of Native Americans. The term *ethnicity* is also helpful because it allows us to celebrate particular heritages. Thus, a White person can identify with the Irish side of his family or the English or Swedish sides. A Black person can choose to follow the customs and traditions of Africa from which his father came or those of Jamaica in which he was raised. From a social work standpoint, it is more useful to understand a person's ethnic values, beliefs, and behaviors than to know whether they are White or Black.

While the United States sees itself as a country in which opportunity, justice, and equality are available to all, the reality is much different. In fact, there is inequality evident in a number of areas, particular as it impacts those whose ethnicity is not European. For example, health outcomes are not equal from one group to another. Table 15.1 identifies just a few of these differences in the health realm (American Public Health Association, 2011; HealthReform.Gov, 2011; National Cancer Institute, 2008; U.S. Department of Health and Human Services, 2004).

There are many reasons for these disparities. For example, discrimination and blocked economic opportunities are stressors that can influence health, as well as access to health insurance (Brondolo, Gallo, & Myers, 2009). Influences on health outcomes include poverty and exposure to environmental threats; behavior and decisions of individuals; dropping out of school (rates of which are higher for some groups); overeating; smoking; sexual risk behaviors; and substance abuse. Other behaviors can contribute as

Table 15.1 Health Outcome Disparities in the United States (2004–2011)

Group	Problem Area
Blacks	Higher rates of hypertension and related complications, cancer, obesity, and AIDS
Puerto Ricans	High rates of premature death
White women	Highest rate of breast cancer
Native Americans	Highest rate of adult onset diabetes
Blacks and Native Americans	High rate of death before age one
Vietnamese women	Rate of cervical cancer five times rate for Caucasians
Hispanics	Less likely to receive optimal hospital care for myocardial infarction

Source: American Public Health Association (2011); HealthReform.Gov (2011); National Cancer Institute (2008); U.S. Department of Health and Human Services (2004).

well. Black students are more likely to have engaged in intercourse prior to age 13, had multiple sex partners, and to have participated in a physical fight than is true for White students. White students, on the other hand, are more likely to have used cigarettes, drunk alcohol, and sniffed glue or other toxic substances than either Black or Hispanic students (CDC/NCHS Centers for Disease Control/National Center for Health Statistics, 2009). At the same time, Black and Hispanic students were less likely to have used birth control measures than White students.

Ethnicity affects human behavior in many ways. For example, people from the Pacific Rim countries tend to report lower levels of happiness than people from the United States (Spiers & Walker, 2009). However, these differences may reflect the fact that North Americans tend to define happiness in terms of their personal achievement, while East Asians use interpersonal connectedness as their measure of happiness.

The influence of one's ethnicity depends to some degree on the social environment in which one is operating. For example, people behave differently depending on the social composition of their environment. When a person of color is in a group composed largely of individuals from other ethnicities, he or she is more likely to avoid behaviors that reinforce stereotypes associated with their ethnic background. This includes choices of foods when dining with others and the type of music selected for parties. When the composition of a group changes to include others of the same ethnic background, group members are likely to behave more naturally (Wooten, 1995).

Even in situations where one's ethnicity should not matter, it often does. For example, Pratt, Hauser, Urgray, and Patterson (2007) found that an individual's willingness to accept recommendations from an animated computer expert was dependent upon the ethnicity of the expert. Even the decision about how one defines oneself in terms of skin color and ethnicity is an interesting area of research. For example, Darity (2005) notes that recent censuses show an increase in those identifying themselves as American Indians that is inconsistent with the expected natural increase in this population. Likewise, even dark-skinned Latinos self-identify as White instead of Black or mixed. This is sometimes referred to as passing. Passing can be either a deliberate attempt to leave one's group history behind or a passive behavior that allows others to assume you belong to a less-stigmatized group. On the one hand, this behavior can be viewed as denigrating one's

Assess your comprehension of Race and Ethnicity by completing this quiz.

ethnic heritage, a criticism also leveled at governmental decisions to allow people to self-identify as belonging to several groups instead of just one. On the other hand, it may reflect the person's true sense of identity.

RELIGION AND SPIRITUALITY

Religion and spirituality are two other important aspects of how culture influences people. Although the concepts of religion and spirituality are often discussed together, they are not synonyms. Religion typically refers to one's adherence to the beliefs and values espoused by a particular organized group. Van Hook, Hugen, and Aguilar (2001) use the term *religious* to refer to a person who "belong to or identifies with a religious group; accepts and is committed to the beliefs, values, and doctrines of the group; and participates in the required practices, ceremonies, and rituals of the chosen group" (p. 13). Of course, not everyone who belongs to a religious group accepts all of the doctrines or participates in all the activities of the group. It is common to find large segments of any religious group who reject or question certain doctrines and who choose to participate in some, but not all, religion-sanctioned activities.

Spirituality, on the other hand, involves one's inner feelings and connections to a higher power. For some people, spirituality is directly connected to their religion, while for many others, there is little or no such relationship. Spirituality can lead to a higher sense of self-awareness, one's place in the universe, and the connectedness of all things. While spiritual individuals often feel happiness and satisfaction from engaging in prayer, by its breadth and very nature, spirituality is not necessarily connected to any specific religion. Thus, an individual can be religious but not spiritual, spiritual but not necessarily religious, or both spiritual and religious (Martinez, Smith, & Barlow, 2007). At the same time, spirituality is a component of many religions and certainly shares practices with some. For example, fasting can be a practice both within religions and with those who are spiritual. Likewise, prayer is a behavior that can occur in both. Meditation can also be found in both formal religious traditions and in those who are adherents of spirituality. About one-quarter of Americans define themselves as spiritual, though not religious, according to a poll conducted by *Newsweek* magazine (2005). About 57% of people rated spirituality as very important in their lives, with those over age 40 tending to rate it higher in importance. Like religion, spirituality can be found across the globe with different groups sharing fundamentally similar experiences (Piedmont & Leach, 2002).

The near universality of religion and spirituality as influences on human behavior are increasingly being recognized by social work practitioners. This is especially true for those from other cultures. Religiosity, for example, has a major influence on how soon adolescent females engage in sex. Those with higher degrees of religiosity are more likely to postpone sexual activity and avoid the associated risk factors. Adolescents whose friends also participate in religious activities are even more likely to delay their sexual debut, a finding which is consistent across gender and racial lines.

Spirituality has been recognized as an important component in the lives of most African Americans. It is a protective and coping factor in preventing and dealing with health concerns, as evident by numerous studies (Banks-Wallace & Parks, 2004; Lewis, 2008). African American adolescents are more likely to attend religious services and consider religion important in their lives than White adolescents (Rostosky, Wilcox, Wright, & Randall, 2004). Ironically, while church attendance declines in adolescence, the importance of religion and spirituality tends to remain stable.

Like other groups in which spirituality is a major dimension of their lives, African Americans tend to believe in the possibility of divine intervention, and trust in a transcendent force to help them through stressful times. The church becomes a source of social support by enhancing one's self-concept, encouraging existing coping efforts, inspiring more efficacious problem solving, providing concrete aid, and helping to buffer environmental stressors (Lewis, 2008). In areas as diverse as recovery from cancer and substance abuse, African American women identify their spirituality as helping them through their illness (Barg & Gullatte, 2001; Wright, 2003).

Joan Digges describes an example of how spirituality can be critical in the lives of clients and the challenges of working in these situations: "A Chronically Ill Patient Facing a Spiritual Crisis." Are there any aspects of this case that you would have handled differently? Why?

The influence of religion on individuals can come from many fronts. For example, participating in activities organized by one's religious group brings the person in contact with others who share the same beliefs, serving to reinforce them for the individual. This tends to encourage conformity and obedience to religious dictates. Religion also provides social support to participants while also creating a form of social control. The importance of religion and spirituality to individuals strongly suggests that this area should be explored in an assessment when trying to understand a client's life situation (Meyerstein, 2004). Hodge (2005) suggests that asking clients whether religion or spirituality plays a significant role in their lives is one way to learn what kinds of resources are used in time of need. Spiritual lifemaps have proven helpful in allowing clients to identify the important spiritual events in their lives. A lifemap is a pictorial representation of the path that the client has taken—where they were, what happened, and where they are now. In some ways, it is similar to a board game in which the player moves around and is affected by various events. At its simplest, it can be drawn by hand to show the client's spiritual biography or journey as you can see in the lifemap illustrated in Figure 15.1

In this lifemap, Deacon Mike's early life is marked by the death of his father which resulted in a downward trajectory that continued for several years before he recovered completely. This was followed by a love affair that ended badly and he sought solace in a church. Slowly Mike experienced a spiritual awakening during which time he fell in love again. From this point forward, Mike grew more self-confident in his ability to manage events in his life and he joined a church prayer group that further reinforced his sense of purpose and self-efficacy. Eventually, this led to his appointment as a deacon in his church, a high point in terms of Mike's spiritual life.

We have seen how religion can be a positive force in helping people cope with traumatic life events, manage health concerns, and serve as a resource for the well-being of individuals and families. Participation in religious activities at age 20 reduces one's odds of committing suicide and increases life expectancy (Gillum & Dupree, 2006). Religiosity has also been linked to improved mental health, and better outcomes following open-heart surgery (Dedert et al., 2004). Bierman (2006) points out that religion serves as a buffer to blunt the impact of discrimination within the African American community. Participation in religious activities appears to increase the willingness of the person to forgive others and improves his or her own mental health. In general, African American churches have been active in their emphasis on social justice and civil rights, which may strengthen their effectiveness in helping individual members confront and overcome discrimination, stress, and environmental traumas. Interestingly, the buffering effects of religiosity are significant for African American churches, but not for White churches (Bierman, 2006).

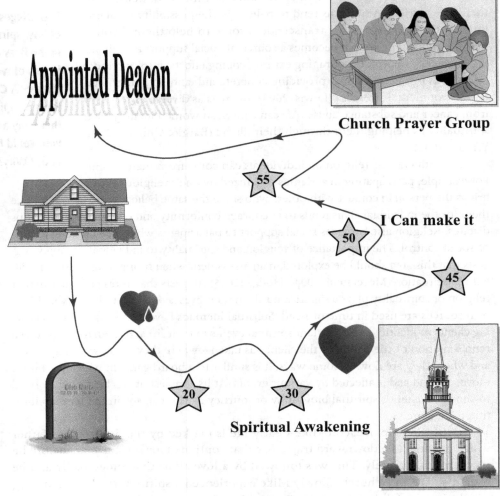

Figure 15.1
Life map of Deacon Mike

OTHER RELIGION-RELATED ISSUES

Despite the many benefits of organized religion, religion is not without some drawbacks. Across the globe, differences among religious groups have been a source of tension, hatred, discrimination, and sometimes killing. These differences can exist within a single religion, such as that which occurs between Sunni and Shia Muslims in the Middle East, and between religions such as with Jews and Muslims in Palestine, Hindus and Muslims in India and Pakistan, and Catholics and Protestants in Northern Ireland. Moreover, religion has a rich history of being the reason for war or persecution of those who were not seen as sufficiently religious. The crusades during the Middle Ages fall into the war category while the Catholic Inquisitions are examples of the persecution category. The animosities among different religious groups show up periodically in the political realm. John Kennedy's Catholicism was seen as a hurdle to be overcome during his 1960 campaign for the presidency and the Mormon faith of two Republican candidates for president in the 2012 election became an issue for groups of fundamentalist Christians. Stereotypes of other religious groups and their members are common and easily recognized.

The United States, all U.S. states, and many other countries have laws that restrict or forbid discrimination against certain groups of people. These laws usually identify certain groups as those characterized by race, color, ethnicity, national origin, religion, gender, disability, veteran status, and age. Recently, the list has been expanded in some states and communities to include sexual orientation. These restrictions are designed to protect group members in areas as diverse as housing, employment, financial services, and education. Despite the many protections that exist for certain groups or protected classes, discrimination is clearly evident in most societies (Fox, 2007). The attack on the World Trade Center in 2001 and the subsequent wars in the Middle East have helped provoke Islamophobia throughout the United States, Europe, and Australia (Bloul, 2008). Unfortunately, even in those locations which have laws protecting individuals from religious discrimination, the victims have relatively little recourse. It is important to point out that religious discrimination may occur for reasons that have nothing to do with religion. For example, groups that share the same religion may be discriminated against for political or economic reasons, such as control of resources in a country (Fox, 2007).

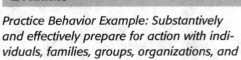

Engage, Assess, Intervene, Evaluate

Practice Behavior Example: Substantively and effectively prepare for action with individuals, families, groups, organizations, and communities.

Critical Thinking Question: If a new client is assigned about whom you know very little, how might you raise the question of religion or spirituality as aspects of his or her life?

On an international macro level, discrimination against minorities on the basis of religion or other factors has historically been viewed as an internal problem best left to the particular country experiencing the problem. Types of religious discrimination used include restricting or preventing people from participating in religious-related activities, preventing the building or rebuilding of churches and other places of worship, arresting or imprisoning religious leaders, forced religious conversions of individuals, and forcing people to participate in a particular religion, among others (Fox, 2007). More recently, this type of discrimination has been viewed as a human rights issue that may spur other countries to intervene. This is especially true if the discrimination results in the killing of minority members as witnessed in Bosnia-Herzegovina in the 1990s and the Darfur region of Sudan. In both cases, the genocide being carried out or supported by the country's government targeted people based on their religious or ethnic identity. Other recent examples include genocide in Rwanda and Somalia. In many of these examples, other countries and/or international organizations such as the United Nations or regional bodies such as the African Union intervened to stop the genocide.

Stereotyping of religion and religious people occurs in at least two dimensions. First, it is easy for those not associated with a religion to question the motives and actions of those who are active churchgoers. Fears that elected officials of a particular faith will impose their religious beliefs on the rest of society are common. In addition, devout religious individuals may view nonbelievers as immoral or amoral. How this plays out in actuality is implied in a question asked by a young mother during a church discussion: "How can I keep my kids from playing with non-xxx children?" Harper's (2007) study of stereotyping of nonreligious people by religious students identified other aspects of this issue. Nonreligious people were seen as "unbelieving, faithless, rebellious . . . nonspiritual, and anti-Christian" among others (p. 545). These stereotypes tend to have the greatest impact when the nonreligious individual is a minority in a highly religious community. This can lead to the nonreligious being seen as troublesome, evil, freaks, or worse. Clearly, religion and spirituality have both profoundly beneficial aspects, as well as more troubling ones as well.

MACIEJ NOSKOWSKI/Getty Images

*Discrimination by one's peers
is a challenge for adolescents.*

DISCRIMINATION AND ETHNOCENTRISM

Both discrimination and ethnocentrism are concepts that operate within a cultural context. *Discrimination*, as used in this text, is the act of treating another person in a prejudicial manner based solely on that person's membership in a group. The group may be categorized by ethnicity, age, gender, sexual orientation, religion, or any other characteristic. Typically, the judgment about the group is negative or undesirable. Discrimination may come in one or more of several forms. Interpersonal or individual discrimination occurs between individuals acting as private citizens or within institutional roles, such as employer and employee. Institutional discrimination exists when the policies, practices, laws, or rules of a nation or its entities discriminate against an individual or group. Finally, structural discrimination refers to how societies develop discrimination (Mohseni & Lindstrom, 2008). Structural discrimination is inherent in societal norms, behavior, attitudes, and routines that negatively affect segments of the population. This discrimination is passed from generation to generation and may be intentional or unintentional. Over time, structural discrimination contributes to institutional and individual discrimination. In the former case, norms and attitudes become rules or laws adopted by governments. In the latter, beliefs and attitudes are transmitted to the young through the normal socialization.

The fact that discrimination exists in societies should come as no surprise to most people. Devine, Plant, Amodio, Harmon-Jones, and Vance (2002) concluded that "White Americans, on average, possess some degree of implicit race bias toward Blacks" (p. 839). Prejudices and stereotypes may be explicit (conscious) or implicit (unconscious). Some are displayed openly while others are more subtle. Moreover, stereotypes learned in childhood remain in one's memory, even among those who consciously work to change them (Pratt et al., 2007). While a portion of our prejudices are the result of explicit learning, others are implicitly acquired (Chao & Willaby, 2007). Implicit learning occurs outside of human awareness as we come to regard certain ways of doing things as normal or certain situations as typical. If, for example, we often see minorities on news reports depicted as criminals, we slowly begin to interpret this view as the norm. If we do not encounter people of color in our everyday lives, we come to see this as the way it should be.

These learned stereotypes can be activated automatically by various stimuli and produce behaviors that are consistent with the stereotype. These reactions are applicable to both people with low prejudice as well as those with high degrees of prejudice. Those most able to control their prejudicial responses are those with strong internal motivation to be nonjudgmental and egalitarian. Those who are outwardly motivated (they don't want to *appear* biased) are much less successful in controlling their stereotyping (Amodio, Devine, & Harmon-Jones, 2008). For those whose learning occurred in an implicit fashion, the fact that they are unaware of their prejudices makes them resistant to change. If you don't see your worldview as reflecting the particular influences with which you grew up but see it as the norm, it becomes much more difficult to change one's perceptions.

Unconscious to their blind spots, people may espouse nondiscrimination while engaging in behaviors that reflect their bias (Chao & Willaby, 2007).

Discrimination operates in multiple spheres. For example, repeated studies have highlighted the high degree of residential segregation existing in the United States (Omer, 2005). A portion of this segregation is the result of institutional and individual discrimination. Other factors that influence housing patterns include such things as a preference to live within one's own group, income limitations, employment opportunities, housing types, and community attitudes. Residential segregation has implications for a person's quality of life. For example, non-Whites experience a higher rate of fear about crime, largely because they tend to live in areas with higher crime rates and low sense of community trust (Houts & Kassab, 1997). They are likely to believe that external forces in the community control their lives, while Whites are more likely to have an internal locus of control. Being a crime victim, as is likelier when in high crime areas, creates a sense of vulnerability that events are not under one's control. However, when Whites are crime victims, a similar fear of future victimization occurs. Those most fearful of becoming a crime victim include Whites who are older, have less education, or are female.

> **Did You Know?**
>
> Fear levels among minority groups are highest for African Americans (Houts & Kassab, 1997).

Underscoring the influences of the social environment, two factors tend to affect whether one is afraid of being a crime victim: trusting one's neighbors and prior experience as a victim of a crime.

Mental health is another sphere in which discrimination plays a role. Keith, Lincoln, Taylor, and Jackson (2010) found that discrimination had a significant effect on the mental health of African American women. One consequence of experiencing discrimination is the loss of one's sense of competence, mastery over life events, and overall resiliency. While discrimination can undermine both men and women, African American women are particularly vulnerable because of their dual status as both female and a minority. An interesting corollary to the impact of discrimination is that it tends to be more focused on darker skinned African Americans than their lighter complexioned peers, although there is some debate on this within the research (Herring, Keith, & Horton, 2004; Keith et al., 2010). Discrimination that undermines African American women's mastery includes such things as being treated badly, receiving substandard service, and persistent experiences with discourtesy. Continuing threats to one's sense of mastery contributes directly to depressive symptoms and emotional instability.

Overall, discrimination has a clear and robust impact on both symptoms and disorders (Williams, Neighbors, & Jackson, 2003). Feeling discriminated against can predict future depression and anxiety (Jasinskaja-Lahti, Liebkind, & Solheim, 2009). This is especially troubling in countries with large immigrant populations who feel discriminated against. In such situations, experiencing discrimination often results in the immigrants rejecting identification with the country and distancing themselves from mainstream society. This may result in increased discrimination against an immigrant population that is seen as refusing to adopt norms and values of the large society.

Not only does discrimination play a role in exacerbating mental health issues, there are also clear differences in the frequency with which various groups are given various diagnoses (Hays, Prosek, & McLeod, 2010).

Women are more likely than men to receive a diagnosis of personality disorder while those with a gay or lesbian sexual orientation are three to five times more likely to be labeled as depressed or having a panic disorder. Educational level also seems to play a role in that those with less education are diagnosed with schizophrenia rather than with mood disorders (Eriksen & Kress, 2005; Paniagua, 2005). Concerns

> **Did You Know?**
>
> Hispanics, as a group, are diagnosed with schizophrenia 50% more often than is true for Whites, while Blacks are more likely to be given diagnoses of dementia, substance abuse, and schizophrenia (Hays et al., 2010).

have been raised for years about whether those from oppressed groups are given more severe diagnoses than other groups. The findings of Hays, Prosek, and McLeod (2010) suggest this to be true. Clinicians with higher levels of cultural bias tended to see minority clients as having more serious mental health challenges. Practitioners with greater awareness of cultural bias seemed to assess clients from oppressed groups more positively than those exhibiting cultural blindness.

Much discrimination that occurs is related to ethnocentrism. *Ethnocentrism* is the practice of seeing the world largely from one's own cultural perspective. It appears to be a nearly universal tendency, existing in numerous cultures, and is sometimes considered an expression of group-level narcissism (Bizumic & Duckitt, 2008). Ethnocentrism is characterized by a strong belief in the importance of one's own group and a sense that other things in life revolve around the group. To an extent, being ethnocentric is expected in that we all tend to see our own values, beliefs, and practices as legitimate and reasonable. We take pride in our group and feel positive about it, which is generally OK (Raden, 2003). The problem arises when we not only view our culture as great but simultaneously see other cultures as inferior, a perception referred to as *classical ethnocentrism*. When we view other cultures as less valid than our own, it becomes easier to discriminate against them. We move from devaluing the other groups to exploiting them or denying their right to exist. The United States took this perspective to the extreme through governmental efforts to first control and then exterminate Native Americans. Similar motivation exists behind much of the anti-immigrant movement witnessed in the United States in the first decade of the 21st century.

Ethnocentrism becomes a stumbling block to success in a global economy saturated with multinational companies. Not only does it alienate other cultures with whom we must interact, but it blinds us to considering other ways of doing things. Within the United States, for example, the belief that our health care system is the best in the world helps prevent the development of universal health care for all citizens. Although the United States spends per capita more on health care than other countries, the outcomes achieved are below those of many countries. Furthermore, large portions of the population are without health care coverage when most other industrialized nations routinely provide this level of care to their citizens. When a nation's people come to perceive themselves as somehow exceptional and unique compared to all other human beings, the potential for problems is great. It leads to a sense of moral superiority over other nations, peoples, and cultures, which reinforces ethnocentric viewpoints.

We have previously identified religion as a basis for discrimination in the United States. However, religious discrimination is by no means a solely American practice. An international survey of religious discrimination between 1990 and 2002 identified an 11% increase in such actions in 55 out of 175 countries. A diverse set of countries, including China, France, India, Japan, and Venezuela, among others, experienced more religious discrimination. A decrease in religious discrimination was found in about 10% of the countries surveyed. All told, almost 75% of countries engaged in some form of religious discrimination in 2002 (Fox, 2007). Discrimination based on religion has been documented in Muslim-majority states and in Christian-majority states, with the highest overall levels occurring in Middle Eastern states. Even the existence of national constitutions prohibiting religious discrimination does not ensure that a country will behave accordingly. In fact, most states with constitutional clauses ensuring religious freedom engage in religious discrimination (Fox & Flores, 2009). Clearly, institutional protections embedded in law do not prevent, or address, the problem of discrimination.

Human Behavior

Practice Behavior Example: Apply theories and knowledge from the liberal arts to understand biological, social, cultural, psychological, and spiritual development.

Critical Thinking Question: In what ways do ethnocentrism and discrimination relate to one another? Is it possible to be ethnocentric but not engage in discrimination?

Assess your comprehension of Discrimination and Ethnocentrism by completing this quiz.

BILINGUALISM

Simply speaking, bilingualism is the capacity to speak two different languages. Throughout the world, there are many countries where children and adults are bilingual, having learned two languages simultaneously. Other individuals become bilingual by virtue of learning a second language after acquiring fluency in their native tongue. In the United States, immigrants often hear their native language spoken at home and learn English in school. In many countries, adults and children can speak multiple languages, sometimes referred to as multilingualism. The benefits of having skill in the use of more than one language have been repeatedly demonstrated in fields as diverse as business, health care, and education (NEA, 2007). This includes improved academic performance in other subjects, enhanced higher order and creative thinking, better career opportunities, and higher sense of achievement, among others. In addition, there is some evidence that bilingual individuals who have internalized two cultures can access cognitive structures or mental frames that are culturally specific (Bialystok & Viswanathan, 2009; Luna, Ringberg, & Peracchio, 2008). The ability to use multiple mental frames and cognitive flexibility are assets to understanding people within the context of their culture. Studying another language can result in positive attitudes toward the culture, people, and language (Dubiner, 2010). Given the need for increased international understanding, this benefit alone would be substantial.

In addition to those who come to the United States with bilingual skills, many more acquire these skills in school. For example, Spanish is taken by over a quarter of high school students with French studied by another 11% (Draper & Hicks, 1996). At the college and university level, over a million students are enrolled in foreign language courses with Spanish comprising about half that number (Welles, 2004). Interest in language education among students appears to have changed over the past decade with reduced enrollment in French and Russian and more students taking Chinese (Rhodes & Pufahl, 2009). Unfortunately, enrollments in upper-level language classes, including Spanish, are relatively low, indicating that students are not continuing to a level where they can be considered proficient in the language.

Another facet of bilingualism is the question of whether non-English-speaking students should be taught in their native language as they learn English and other subjects. While some forms of bilingual education have existed in the United States for more than 200 years, interest in this approach peaked in the 1960s and 1970s. More recently, challenges have been raised about the model. Some argue that bilingual education impairs the speed at which children learn English. Others argue that complete immersion in English is essential to becoming a full member of society. Those who support bilingual education believe that it builds upon a child's native language and enhances their learning of other topics. The extent of the debate can be seen in communities and states that have banned bilingual education, arguing that English should be the official language of the United States.

The tension that exists over bilingual education is not new. Schools were prohibited from teaching Native American languages in the middle of the 19th century and German bilingual classes were ended during World War I. Historically, many languages were considered to be inferior and immigrant students were forced to abandon their family of origin languages. The belief that bilingualism is somehow a deficit has been likened to colonist ideology, in which the colonizer is always perceived as superior (Brown & Souto-Manning, 2008). Not surprisingly, the impact of these prohibitions often shows itself through resistance to be assimilated, frustration, and undermined familial relationships. Some have argued that another consequence is the poor academic performance and high dropout rate of immigrant students (Crawford, 2004). Interestingly, the United Nations Convention on the Rights of a Child encourages respect for a child's cultural identity and supports the right of the child to use his or her native language. Only three countries (South Sudan, Somalia, and the United States) refused to ratify this agreement (Child Rights Portal, 2012; Rethinking Schools, 2003). Much of the current resistance to bilingual education is occurring during a period of heightened immigration and predictions of changes in population composition. For example, people of color will become the majority of U.S. citizens within the next 40 years. For some states, the shift will be even more dramatic, as in California where Whites will comprise only 30% of the population by 2040 (Byrd, 2010).

Other observers point out that English has remained the predominant language in the United States despite waves of immigrants who arrived speaking little or no English. Over time, English was adopted and, for the most part, the individual's native tongue ceased to be used. Hispanics, who make up the bulk of new arrivals, do not necessarily favor bilingual education, preferring that their children learn English as soon as possible. One indicator of this is the number of Hispanics who voted in favor of propositions in California and Arizona that ended bilingual education programs in schools. While there are differences within the Hispanic population on the wisdom of bilingual education, the majority appears to be indifferent or opposed. Attitudes toward bilingual education have waxed and waned across the decades and public policies along with them. While the Bilingual Education Act received reauthorization in 1994, the George W. Bush administration's No Child Left Behind Act dropped all references to bilingual education and made it more difficult for school districts to offer such programs. This occurred despite increasing evidence that bilingual education worked (Nieto, 2009). Students who had participated in such programs scored higher on standardized tests than similar students taught only in English. In addition, bilingual education improved learning of English, as well as content from other areas, such as history and science. Despite these findings, and as is often the case, science and research failed to trump prejudice and fear as grounds for public policy.

Another aspect of bilingualism is the policy decision to produce government documents in more languages than English. While many states and the national government have produced driver license booklets and other publications in various languages, other groups rail against these actions. Attempts to force governments to stop this practice and/or to make English the official language of the state and national government have been ongoing. For example, the State of Wisconsin publishes information in Spanish and Hmong, reflecting the needs of immigrant populations in the state. Florida operates a governmental website that is multilingual in English, Spanish, and Creole. Louisiana has governmental information available in English, French, and Spanish. Massachusetts state government has some documents and information available in German, French, Spanish, Japanese, Italian, Chinese, and Dutch, recognizing that not all visitors to the state will be fluent in English. The federal government has some publications in Russian, Polish, Arabic, Chinese, Tagalog, Portuguese, Korean, and Vietnamese, suggesting sensitivity to the needs of its citizens, despite the sentiments of some. Perhaps equally important, businesses have recognized the diversity of languages spoken in the United States and often post information in multiple languages.

MEDIA AND CULTURE

The relationship of media and culture has been clear at least since 1700 BC when Hammurabi published his law code. The code contained rules for a wide variety of behaviors, including contracts between individuals, the behavior of judges, and the duty of a husband to consummate any marriage he enters into with a woman. Previous sets of published laws may have been created, but they no longer appear to exist. The code was carved into a black monument about eight feet high so that any person could read and use it to guide his or her behavior. Some researchers have speculated that cave drawings dating even further back (30,000 BC) were designed to communicate with others, but this is largely speculation.

In the ensuing years, media has taken many forms: handwritten manuscripts, printed books, newspapers, radio, television, the Internet, and social media. While other inventions have spurred communication (e.g., the telegraph, telephone, and cell phone), their primary purpose was not to influence opinions or behavior of the general population. Most observers credit media with the capacity to shape cultural change, sway our perceptions, and influence the directions of our economic and political systems. Debrix (2001) provides an example of the power of the media in the Y2K frenzy that immediately preceded the year 2000. The media focused on the possibility that computers worldwide would cease to function properly as of January 1, 2000, because they were not programmed for a change to the millennium. Stories circulated throughout the media suggested that air traffic would be endangered, planes would be unable to fly, banks would cease to function, and telephones would no longer work. The doomsday scenarios associated with this event persuaded companies and governmental agencies to buy new computers, focus on retooling existing software, and provide public updates about their success in preparing for the event. The actual threat turned out to be much less significant than advertised, as evidenced by the fact that entire countries, large portions of U.S. school systems, and millions of businesses experienced no problems, and if at all, only minor glitches.

Today, some of the media have highlighted the threat of cyber terror, in which terrorists would use computers to sabotage worldwide services with a goal of preventing technologically dependent nations, such as the United States, from conducting business. The hype about such impending threats is overblown, as evident from the kinds of cyber attacks that usually occur. Often they are relatively harmless, intended to shut down a particular company or attack a particular program, such as Facebook or Windows Outlook. Others are greed-related as when a company's customers' credit card or social security card numbers are hacked. This is not said to denigrate the likelihood of future serious cyber attacks, but to underscore the media's tendency to elevate possibilities to probabilities and engender public anxiety.

McLuhan (1960) observed more than 50 years ago that the amount of information provided by the media—such as newspapers, television, radio, magazines, and films—was much greater than that conveyed by traditional books and classroom instruction. His comment that, "the medium shapes and controls the scale and form of human association and action" is perhaps truer now since the advent of social networking (1994, p. 9). Much of what we believe to be true is molded by media, whose primary activity is to reflect back to the consumer the "values, assumptions and stereotypes of the dominant culture" (Brookfield, 1986, p. 155). To the extent that this is true, media help maintain the status quo and ignore nondominant groups and perspectives. A more serious concern raised by Debrix (2001) is that the media has the ability to create their own version of social reality that may or may not coincide with that of others.

The potential influence of the media is particularly evident in totalitarian countries where government ownership and/or censorship is common. Such governments control the media because they fear unfettered reporting and seek to prevent coverage of antigovernment activities. This has been evident in the Middle East and other countries where the government has shut down television stations and blocked access to the Internet. However, when traditional television and radio media outlets are silenced as has happened in various countries recently, people find other means of communicating their ideas and points of view by using social media, cell phones, and old-fashioned landlines. The development of television stations in the Arab and Muslim world, such as Al-Jazeera, is partly the result of a belief that neither European nor American television is fair and balanced (Chouikha, 2007). Distrust of their own governments, which often control the news media, also plays a role.

Perspectives on the Influence of Media

How we view the media and its influence on culture often depends on the mindset or frame we already hold. Meyrowitz (2008), for example, points out various perspectives toward media. Some who operate from a power perspective see the media as both an arsenal for and the site of conflicts over power, resources, and information. In this view, the media is a means for the powerful to maintain their influence and discourage others from questioning or challenging it. The recent struggle over the influence of print media in England, allegations of illegal wiretapping and interception of phone messages, and the media's relationship with government leaders underscore this perspective. Media portrayals of individuals, groups, and ideas are often selected based upon the political or social frame of those reporting the news. Even the decision about what is considered newsworthy reflects a power dimension; for example, some stories do not get covered because they challenge the status quo. Decisions about topics such as race, ethnicity, gender, and class and how they will be represented inherently affect media consumers. As noted earlier, this tends to perpetuate hegemonic perspectives, ignores minority viewpoints, and fails to live up to the media's potential for teaching and introducing new information.

Did You Know?

It is estimated that almost 97% of U.S. households have a television set, totaling just under 115 million sets.

Source: Nielsenwire (2011).

A second perspective on media is that it serves to meet the needs of people for information about their societies and to provide pleasure. In this view, individual and group desires for social and cultural interaction, basic necessities (food and shelter), and fun are met through various media. The comics, news of road closures, movie listings and art shows, wedding and funeral notices, and other public events all serve this purpose. A newspaper can be used to receive discounts on food and other products, find a mate or a used car, locate garage sales, and hire a plumber. The media becomes a lookout tower allowing us to view the landscape or connect with friends and family (e.g., Facebook, Twitter). Television can be seen as a way for families to gather together to watch a representation of reality. Of course, this only works when there is a shared television. This perspective sees media as competing for the attention and interest of different audiences who actually control what is covered or displayed.

A third perspective on the media is that it is simply a part of the human environment and a reflection of who we are. Media represent a means to communicate and interact with others and provide a source of shared knowledge. Individual level of development influences access to some media; for example, using a news-paper requires learning to read, which need not be the case for television. Unlike verbal means of interacting and communicating, most media do not allow a back and forth interchange of information. Rather, it promotes being a listener rather than a questioner. Each media type allows different representations of culture. We can read about a cultural event in the newspaper but see it briefly represented on television. Movies and similar media allow us to see and understand even more of our environment.

Media Influences on Girls and Women

One area that has received a great deal of attention is the ways in which the media influence women and girls. For example, the media has been repeatedly criticized for the portrayal of women and the role it plays in eating disorders. Women often become dissatisfied when they compare their body image with those shown in the media. Dohnt and Tiggemann (2006) found clear evidence that appearance-focused television programs negatively impact the self-esteem and body image of adolescent and younger girls. Likewise, girls who perused women's magazines were more likely to be dissatisfied with their appearance. The concern is that low self-esteem and a poor body image are precursors to eating disorders and depression (Johnson & Wardle, 2005). These findings underscore the ways in which media representations of the typical woman as thin and physically fit influence body perceptions.

Media's influence on women is not restricted to the United States. Tsai (2009) has studied the influence of Western media on Chinese women in Taiwan. Exposure to Western culture through Taiwanese media has helped produce generations of women who have adopted views of "ideal weight" from American television shows and other media. On the one hand, this has led to an increase in physical exercise of all types to help produce this ideal body. On the other hand, it can and does lead to the same types of eating disorders now seen in the United States (Tsai, Chang, Lien, & Wong, 2011).

Of course, family and friends play a role in shaping how we see ourselves. Girls who are focused on becoming thinner influence their peers in the same direction (Dohnt & Tiggemann, 2005). In general, the more girls talked with their peers about body image, the unhappier they were with their own body. These and other studies suggest that a peer norm of thinness may well be developing among both young girls and adolescents. In addition, parental urging of a child to lose weight may interact with media messages emphasizing the "ideal woman" and contribute to both poor body image and eating disorders.

While repeated studies have demonstrated that viewing images of what is purported to be an ideal physique leads to dissatisfaction with one's body, the findings are not uniform across different groups (DeBraganza & Hausenblas, 2010). For example, this negative perspective on body image is not shared equally by Black and White women. Black women tend to be more comfortable with their bodies than White women.

A more critical view of the media's global influence on women is presented by Lazar (2006). She points out that the media have appropriated themes associated with feminism, such as empowerment, identity, and emancipation, to use as tools in advertising. For example, brands and products are presented as empowering women by helping them achieve their inner beauty. Products purport to give women the power to attract men by helping them lose weight in pursuit of an ideal body type. Advertisements suggest that participation in educational workshops and sessions will provide women with new skills in the application of makeup or other products. As advertised, certain household products are designed to emancipate women from housework or to free them from unpleasant chores. Likewise, getting in touch with your true identity will be made easier by purchasing certain products and services. The usurpation of these terms is problematic largely because they represent key elements of feminism but without the accompanying focus on challenging and changing institutions that hold women back in society.

Professional Identity

Practice Behavior Example: Practice personal reflection and self-correction to assure continual professional development.

Critical Thinking Question: Can you identify one way in which the media have influenced your own personal or professional behavior, beliefs, or attitudes?

Obviously it is not just women who are affected by the media. Males often learn what it means to be a man from the media. Unfortunately, this often involves depictions of traditional and rigidly defined gender roles, often associating violence with maleness. Frequently, these depictions reflect hegemonic masculinity which places males in dominant positions and women in positions of subordination (Kivel & Johnson, 2009). Sports and sporting contexts often reinforce ideals of maleness as do aspects of the media. The American Academy of Pediatrics (2009) identified media violence as one contributor to aggressive behavior among children under 18. Aggression in video games, coupled with the fact that the typical 18-year-old has viewed around 200,000 violent acts on television, helps explain some of the behaviors learned by males, who tend to be the primary consumers (Huston, Caughlin, Houts, Smith, & George, 2001).

On a more positive note, media treatment of gay, lesbian, bisexual, and transsexual (GLBT) individuals has evolved in a manner reflecting changes in society. From invisibility to a source of humor—and most recently to a recurrent theme in movies and television—GLBT people and their concerns are getting more attention. Stereotyping still occurs, but the challenges faced by GLBT individuals are beginning to be portrayed with a degree of sensitivity in some venues. The movie *Brokeback Mountain* and the television series *Modern Family* have been recent positive contributions to the genre. In addition, many public figures in the entertainment industry have come out publically as gay or lesbian, without much fear or concern about the consequences.

Racial issues are one area where less progress has been made The public tends to notice the incorporation of people of color in television and movies. Yet, with only a handful of exceptions, too few movies and television shows have main characters from these groups. People of color are often shown as sidekicks (*Mike and Molly, King of Queens*) or in peripheral roles (*NCIS*). As mentioned, there are exceptions in which a person of color becomes a major character or the focus of a particular movie or television role. Examples include *NCIS-Los Angeles, The Help, The Oprah Winfrey Show*, and some of the *Law and Order* series. Overall, people of color are more often included among the cast than was the case in the past, but they are nowhere as evident as their composition in the general population would justify.

The media also play a role in how individuals view the rest of the world. Despite the large number of people who travel to other countries, most of what we learn about nations comes through the media (Freeman, 2010; Lee, 2005). The coverage of foreign relations provided by the media shapes our views of other countries. Ideas about these countries can be formed from in-depth stories reported by news media or off-the-cuff comments from television shows. The impressions we have of foreign states, their leaders, and people are important within the context of globalization. Misunderstandings and insufficient knowledge about other nations have contributed to poor government policy decisions, business errors, and prejudice toward citizens of those countries. If, for example, the media focuses on the extent of drug-related violence in Mexico—and pays little or no attention to the thousands of international visitors to that country each year—it is easy to come to view Mexico as a dangerous place to be avoided at all costs. Likewise, if we see citizens of another country attempting to overthrow a dictatorial regime, it is easy to sympathize with them as freedom fighters and support them. Absent a strong familiarity about the history of the nation, we might be unaware of how the country's people have engaged in repeated civil wars, been torn by tribal loyalties, and have never achieved any semblance of a typical nation-state. Lack of understanding about other countries can have a profound effect on the decisions we make at the national level and the governmental policies we choose to support. In a recent example, Jackson (2010) found significant misrepresentation of Islam and Muslims in Western media since September 11, 2001. This intertwines with political and social issues. France and Belgium, for example, have elected to ban the public wearing of burkas, the head-to-toe clothes worn by Muslim women. Reasons for the prohibition range from fears about crime and terrorism to the ways in which wearing the burka contributes to women being treated as second-class citizens by their own religion. If media images of Islam and Muslims are associated with terrorism, public reactions are likely to reflect this. Disputes about locating mosques in several states highlight the ways in which the media play a role in the views of individuals, groups, and society in general.

Another area where media influences culture is in the area of suicide ideology. Since at least the time of Durkheim (1897), researchers have looked at how media portrayals of suicide have influenced the behavior of the living. A common conclusion from studies is that there is a positive relationship between media reports of suicide and subsequent suicide incidents (Stack, 2005). Not only can the report of a suicide influence suicidal ideation, but it also affects the means by which people choose to kill themselves (Stack, 2003). For example, Crabb (2005) found that the methods of suicide most often found in suicidal fantasies were "suggested by the mass media" (p. 211). In Crabb's study, 86% of the suicide materials and tools used in those with suicidal fantasies were provided by media, including movies, books, news stories, and television programming. The author concludes that this research is consistent with the results of other studies on the influence of media depiction of suicides on the methods employed in real suicides.

Similar research has been done on the influence of media violence on violent behavior in children and adolescents. The influence of media in these areas is often tied to social cognitive theory (Bandura, 2002), the role played by modeling, and the observation of others' actions. While most research in this area shows a positive correlation between media coverage and subsequent behavior, this has not allowed one to identify causation. However, a model developed and tested by Fu, Chan, and Yip (2009) did succeed in tightening the association and in operationalizing media influences on suicidal ideation.

The influence of the media must be seen within a larger context. For example, Morling and Lamoreaux (2008) point out that media messages do not necessarily cause specific reactions in those exposed to the message. Rather, the media message interacts with the individual's existing feelings, motivations, behavioral styles, and knowledge.

Assess your analysis and evaluation of this chapter's contents by completing the Chapter Review.

This again suggests the complex interplay between the individual and the environment. As is evident, culture plays a major role in influencing both the individual and the environment in multiple and interactive ways. The complex interplay among culture, the individual, and the environment is a challenge for social workers working with clients, regardless of their backgrounds.

16

Immigration Influences on Human Behavior

Immigration is a global phenomenon impacting economics, politics, social relationships, organizational behavior, and community affairs in most countries. Estimates suggest 2.3 million people migrate each year, leaving less economically developed regions and moving to more developed countries and regions. About 3% of Earth's population lives in a country other than their birth nation (United Nations Population Division, 2001, 2002). Several terms are commonly used in discussions on the topic: *migration, migrant, immigration,* and *emigration. Migration* is used simply to describe moving from one country or area to another. It is the same term used when describing bird migration. The *migrant* refers to individuals who make the move. In its most typical usage, *immigration* refers to those individuals who settle in another country on a rather permanent basis. We often refer to the United States as a nation of immigrants because only Native Americans and some Hispanics were here when the first White visitors arrived. Those who followed were immigrants from other countries.

Because of this history, U.S. residents tend to see moving from one's country of origin to the U.S. from the perspective of immigration. However, this is only part of the picture. The other part is emigration. *Emigration* is the term used to refer to people who leave their own country. We use the terms differentially because the impacts of each are different, depending on whether people are leaving your country or moving to it. For example, the emigration of lawyers, doctors, and other professionals from Iraq left that country with a shortage of people with special skills that were needed by its people. Clearly the process of leaving a country has consequences. As these émigrés settle in their new countries, they impact the new country as well. They may bring skills needed in

America has often shown ambivalent attitudes toward immigrants.

their new country or lose their professional credentials and have to start over. In some cases, immigrants bring only limited skills and end up providing services that existing workers are less willing to do because of low pay or the nature of the job. In other cases, immigrants bring skills not needed because they duplicate those already in excess. As you can see, the terms *emigration* and *immigration* depend on the perspective of the countries affected.

The following sections look at general global trends and within the United States, as well as how the issues related to immigration and emigration play out in the lives of individuals, families, and larger systems.

GLOBAL TRENDS

It is exceedingly rare for a nation not to be dealing with migration issues. Some countries are concerned about the numbers and characteristics of new arrivals, as well as the way they enter the country. Other nations are concerned because they are losing population. Countries as different as Ireland, Canada, Australia, Spain, France, Germany, South Korea, Israel, Mexico, and the United States are struggling with aspects of migration. Countries like Nigeria and others have experienced brain drains as well-educated professionals, in fields as diverse as health care and management, emigrate (Reynolds, 2009). About the only unaffected nations are those under totalitarian regimes who forbid their citizens to leave.

Immigration's impact on the economic system and labor markets is often debated. Most economists suggest the net result for developed countries is positive (Moses & Letnes, 2004). One major factor helps explain this phenomenon: demographics. In places like the United States, Europe, and Japan, an aging population is likely to experience a 10% to 23% drop in standard of living, absent an influx of younger immigrants (United Nations, 2009; United Nations Population Division, 2000). Other authors are more sanguine about the amount of standard of living decline but still predict a diminution as a result of aging populations (Bloom, Canning, & Fink, 2011). Some nations with robust economies like South Korea must import workers to deal with serious labor shortages and help maintain their standard of living (Lim, 2009).

Another reason for migration is to seek an environment providing common connections between the old and new residents. One example is Israel, a destination of choice for Jewish immigrants from many countries, including the former Soviet Union. As is common, most new arrivals spoke neither Hebrew nor English (languages common in Israel) and were from lower socioeconomic classes. Their acculturation struggles have contributed to higher rates of mental health problems, particularly for women, more secular Jews, those 50 years or older, divorced, better educated, and unemployed or underemployed individuals (Ponizovsky, Radomislensky, & Grinshpoon, 2009). Underemployment occurs when highly educated or skilled workers end up working at jobs that do not match their special skill sets. It is a pattern seen in many countries accepting immigrants. As might be expected, life changes that result from migration also contribute to psychological distress, including anxiety and depression, to be discussed later in this text.

Whether nations need migration to deal with an aging population, to make up for significant labor shortages, or for other reasons, it is common for new immigrants to be viewed with trepidation. Many nations fear the economic and social effects of immigrants and are taking actions to deal with the perceived threat. Australia, for example, has mobilized its armed forces to repel boatloads of asylum seekers considered a threat to national security. Sometimes efforts to discourage immigrants result from fear about what will happen if a predominantly White country accepts large numbers of immigrants of color (Devetak, 2004). Recent trends show that many seeking immigrant or refugee status are from Muslim countries, such as Iraq and Afghanistan, whose religion and nationality are not welcomed by nations that would otherwise accept White immigrants from Western countries. These latter nations—with legal, political, and social systems in which equality, liberty, and individual conscience are ideals—clash with the ideology of Muslim nations, some of which utilize religion as a guiding basis for law and individual behavior, with rigid rules governing all aspects of one's life (Siedentop, 2001).

In the second decade of the 21st century, multiple nations struggle with immigration issues. This includes the United States, England, France, Germany, Italy, Austria, Belgium, Denmark, and the Netherlands. Each nation struggles with maintaining its cultural identity amidst vast numbers of asylum-seeking immigrants and refugees. In addition, much of Europe maintains a social welfare safety net for its citizens, which creates fears that immigrants will overload those systems.

As many nations attempt to restrict immigration, discrimination against immigrants is common across the globe. Refugees from other countries report discrimination in countries such as Norway, Europe, Australia, North America, Georgia, Kazakhstan, Uzbekistan, Kyrgyzstan, Russia, Somalia, and the United States (Hadley & Patil, 2009). While not always the case, skin color, language, and cultural norms of the new country play major roles in discrimination against immigrants.

Because migration has such a profound effect on both the nation losing and the one gaining residents, most governments have established policies attempting to regulate or control the flow of people. This is true of the United States and scores of other nations that set macro-level policies in pursuit of a nation's goals. Often, the results or outcomes of those policies fall far short of the goals. It has been speculated that the gap between a country's immigration policy goal and its outcome is quite large and increasing in most developed countries. Several factors contribute to this gap, perhaps first among which are *migration networks*. Migration networks are social connections between those seeking to move to a new country and others already there (Elrick & Ciobanu, 2009). These networks provide material assistance and information that both assist movement into the new country and provide help adapting to it. Sometimes referred to as *social capital*, these connections between and among individuals is based on trust and reciprocity (Portes & Sensenbrenner, 1998). The longer a migration network has existed, the greater its ability to assist prospective migrants. It's also common sense that new arrivals would welcome contact with others who share their culture, language, or religion. However, the availability of such networks may reduce immigrants' integration in the host country. This strengthens the network's influence and reduces immigrants' connections to local people and organizations (Brüß, 2005). The network's help may ease the transition for new immigrants while undercutting the importance of adopting the new country's language, values, and norms.

In addition to migration networks, many immigrant groups in North and South America have formed associations (Moya, 2005). These can include mutual benefit associations, secret societies, political or religious groups, and financial societies. Joining various voluntary associations is a trait common to Americans, so it is perhaps natural that immigrants might create similar institutions. Sometimes, an association is simply an extension of existing groups in one's country of origin. Examples include the tongs and triad (China), and the Cosa Nostra (Italy). The frequency with which immigrant groups founded such associations varies from one ethnic group and one country to another. Also within the same group, participation and involvement varied with poorer, less-educated immigrants unlikely to participate.

With a few exceptions, newer immigrants appear less interested in establishing or participating in associations than was true in the 19th and 20th centuries (Bloemraad, 2005). One exception are the Igbo immigrants from Nigeria, who have actively formed hometown associations comprised of others from their same communities in Nigeria. These organizations serve as a means of socialization and discussing political events affecting their homeland (Reynolds, 2009). Organizations of Igbo speakers exist in Chicago, Houston, and other large cities. Typically, as immigrants become acculturated to their adopted country, they begin to access more traditional resources (such as banks, credit unions, mutual aid societies, religious organizations, and others), no longer relying on the voluntary associations that initially helped them (Moya, 2005).

Critical Thinking

Practice Behavior Example: Use critical thinking augmented by creativity and curiosity.

Critical Thinking Question: What do you think might explain the fact that more recent immigrants to the United States are less likely to participate in associations with others from their country of origin, a departure from immigration patterns in the past?

For some immigrants their country of origin was rife with corruption and inefficiency that made a mockery of laws and rules. Consequently, its citizens view such rules and laws as irrelevant, unjust, or to be ignored. This attitude may carry over to the new country's rules and laws which are seen as barriers to be overcome, or as guidelines, rather than laws. In addition, migration networks can play a role in reinforcing this perspective by downplaying the significance of immigration rules and laws. Sometimes, an industry has been created that assists undocumented workers to relocate to countries in violation of a country's immigration laws and policies. Often, those who work in this industry prey upon immigrants, taking their money, and subjecting them to conditions leading to injury or death. In the United States, for example, it is not unusual to see police reports of immigrants left to die in the desert between Mexico and the United States, suffocating in semi-trucks without food or water, drowning in unsafe boats, or being involved in serious vehicle accidents while being transported. Similar episodes have occurred in Great Britain, Greece, Thailand, Malta, and other popular migrant destinations. Even immigrants arriving safely face a variety of challenges.

The global immigration outlook is one of continued growth in numbers and increased attempts by nations to restrict or otherwise control the flow (National Intelligence Council [NIC], 2001). Spurring migration in the foreseeable future will be continued poverty and lack of upward mobility in some nations. Wars, ethnic conflicts, and political instability will also act as push factors as individuals seek safety and security for themselves and their families. Some nations will limit immigration to protect what they see as their national or cultural identities. Other countries like Japan are more likely to seriously restrict immigration unless labor-force needs overshadow the trend toward ethnic homogeneity. However, the greater the efforts of other countries to restrict immigration, the more the United States will experience both legal and illegal migration. At the same time, countries with significant labor shortages and stringent immigration controls are likely to suffer economically (NIC, 2001).

TRENDS IN THE UNITED STATES

The United States accepts more refugees and immigrants than any other nation (U.S. Department of State, 2008). Figure 16.1 shows which countries had the largest number of international migrants in 2010.

As is the case globally, migrants tend to be younger, generally in their twenties. In the United States, many arrive seeking to further their studies, although the number declined immediately after September 11, 2001, as the country pursued a more restrictive immigrant assessment process. More foreign students completing high school, more wealth in developing nations, and increased globalization of higher education all help account for the larger numbers of young people seeking to migrate. Most of the foreign students are from the developing countries with the majority coming from Asia. While many come to pursue education, a large proportion use their work experience to establish a permanent residence. This inclusion of a highly educated migrant workforce has provided great benefits to the United States.

Of course, other reasons contribute to the large proportion of younger migrants. Some are admitted to pursue seasonal work in the construction, tourism, agriculture, and service industries. Others are individuals seeking to reunite with family members already in the United States. Typically, these family reunification migrations account for

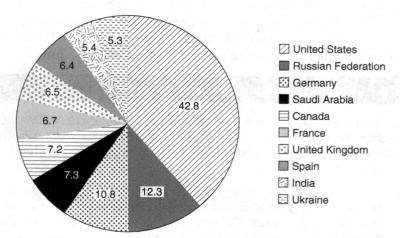

Figure 16.1

Countries with Most International Migrants 2010 (Millions)

Source: Adapted from United Nations, Department of Economic and Social Affairs, Population Division (2009).

over one-half of all admissions (United Nations Population Division, 2011). Some migration results from marriage between a U.S. citizen and an immigrant. This is particularly true for younger migrants. Adoption also occurs with high frequency as U.S. couples adopt children from other countries. Another category of immigrants to the United States are those seeking asylum, refugees, unaccompanied minors, and others needing assistance (United Nations Population Division, 2011).

The United States National Intelligence Council which reports to the Director of Central Intelligence issued a report discussing U.S. immigration trends (NIC, 2001). While acknowledging that immigration raises difficult issues for the United States, the Council suggested that the benefits include economic and demographic vitality for an aging population, reduced labor force shortages for both civilian and military needs, and an increased tax base.

One U.S. trend is a tendency for at least some immigrant groups to maintain their pre-immigration social class system. This appears to be true for immigrants from India, over half of whom arrived between 1990 and 2000 (Bhattacharya, 2008). We have previously mentioned the phenomenon known as transnationalism in which new immigrants create and maintain social relationships linking their country of origin with their adopted nation. This maintenance of regular contact with one's homeland is facilitated by the availability of phone service, air travel, the Internet, and country of origin policies that encourage maintaining ties to expatriated populations. Similar patterns have also been observed in Puerto Rican and Mexican immigrants, posing a challenge as to whether acculturation is likely to occur among these and other transnational groups. These groups tend to form cultural communities that maintain beliefs and practices from their home country (Cornfield & Arzubiaga, 2004). Compared to recent influxes of Indian immigrants, previous generations assimilated quickly, adopted American practices and lifestyles, and sought to increase their socioeconomic status. Most were professionals with both higher education and solid employment histories. More recent Indian immigrants tend to be less skilled and are more likely to find service industry employment (Bhattacharya, 2008). The exceptions tend to be software engineers working in the computer industry.

Like many immigrant groups, Indians have been mistaken as coming from the Middle East and attacked as "terrorists." Similar experiences have befallen both Arabs and Muslim Americans. Others are accused of taking American jobs away either by moving to the United States or by American firms outsourcing work to India. This contributes to the immigrants feeling unwanted, becoming a target of discrimination, and it reflects the hostility imbedded in recent U.S. immigration debates. Box 16.1 highlights one example of such hostility and hatred.

Assess your comprehension of Immigration Trends by completing this quiz.

Box 16.1   Hatred Toward Immigrants

In the immediate aftermath of the violence outside a Sikh Temple near Milwaukee, Wisconsin, the Southern Poverty Law Center quoted one of the most vicious of all the comments, by Alex Linder, who operates the racist website Vanguard News Network, as follows:

> You don't belong here in the country my ancestors fought to found, and deeded to me and mine, their posterity. Even if you came here legally, and even if you haven't done anything wrong personally. Go home, Sikhs. Go home to India where you belong. This is not your country. It belongs to white men.

Source: Vanguard News Network website: http://www.vanguardnewsnetwork.com/. (c) 2010 Alex Linder. A. Linder, POB 101, Kirksville MO 63501.

IMMIGRATION

There are many reasons for migration. Those who leave their homeland typically fall into four categories (Portes & Rumbaut, 1996). The first category constitutes labor migrants of many nationalities seeking employment in labor-intensive industries such as agriculture, construction, and service. Immigrants from Mexico have tended to be in this category. This often produces an overall increase in economic productivity as people move where their talents are better utilized. This produces an increase in the migrant's and international community's standard of living (Simon, 1999). Of course, economic downturns can have dramatic effects on new immigrants' incomes. Compared to nonimmigrants, immigrant incomes decreased during the recent recession, resulting in poverty or near poverty (Center for Immigration Studies, 2012). Moses and Letnes (2004) argue that allowing greater migration between countries would have an even more positive impact on economic productivity across the globe. At the same time, economic factors have produced significant hardships for some populations often because of restrictions on migration.

The chance to increase their standard of living, send money back to family members, and seek a better life are potent draws for millions of immigrants. To get a sense of the economic attraction, immigrants who work in the United States receive an average of $20,000 per year ($300,000 over a lifetime) above what they would have earned at home (Jasso, Massey, Rosenzweig, & Smith, 2000). Of course, the attraction of migrating can also encourage the young to forego education in their own country and pursue a better life in the new country.

The second category, migrant professionals have high levels of education and skills as engineers, physicians, scientists. Examples are the pre-1990 Indian immigrants mentioned earlier.

A third category includes entrepreneurial immigrants seeking the opportunity to develop successful businesses and industries. In some regions, such as New York City, the number of immigrants who are self-employed increased by 53% during the period of 1990–2000.

This pattern has existed since 1880 (Center for an Urban Future, 2007). Well-known examples of immigrant-founded businesses include El Pollo Loco, Panda Express, Liz Claiborne, Sun Microsystems, Google, Intel, Yahoo, eBay, YouTube, and Forever 21. Millions more exist, ranging from the local taco cart to flower shops to accounting and real estate (Forbes, 2007).

The final category includes refugees and asylum seekers composed of those leaving for the reasons described earlier: poverty, war, genocide, and other desperate situations. Refugees seek safety and security from repressive regimes or internecine warfare in their own land. This has been true of groups from Vietnam, Cambodia, Laos, Bosnia, Rwanda, Myanmar, Somalia, Iran, Russia, Burundi, Cuba, and other nations. Often refugees are minorities in their own country and migrate to escape marginalization, oppression, ethnic cleansing, discrimination, and other forms of mistreatment. Migrating, however, does not necessarily change their minority status unless they migrate to a country where they will be part of the majority.

Sometimes, a country's policies or international agreements promote migration. For example, the European Union's policies encourage and welcome migrants into areas

Did You Know?

In Mexico, the minimum wage is between $4.00 and $5.00 per day while in the United States the rate is $7.25 per hour.

Source: http://www.wageindicator.org/main/salary/minimum-wage/mexico/minimum-wage-faqs/minimum-wages-in-mexico-frequently-asked-questions.

Did You Know?

The Brookings Institution (2010, p. 11) reports that "immigrants are 30 percent more likely to form new businesses than U.S.-born citizens. Furthermore, evidence shows that foreign-born university graduates are important contributors to U.S. innovation—among people with advanced degrees, immigrants are three times more likely to file patents than U.S.-born citizens."

with significant labor needs. Despite this permeable border arrangement, however, new arrivals often experience discrimination and substandard working conditions (Dundon, Gonzalez-Perez, & McDonough, 2007). Often they perform domestic work, work in sweatshops, the construction industry, or as day laborers. Most often, they accept work in industries no longer attractive to others. In the agricultural arena, Mexican-born migrants comprise almost three-quarters of the U.S. labor force (Wise & Covarrubias, 2008). An estimated one-half of these workers are undocumented. Of the approximately 47 million Latinos living in the United States, about 25% or 11 to 12 million are undocumented (Davies, 2009).

In times of crisis, the United States and other countries have responded to ethnic cleansing and similar horrors around the world. They have opened their borders and facilitated the transition of these refugees on a short-term basis. Periodically, the United States has taken humanitarian action without a clear assessment of the ramifications of doing so. Sometimes, this helping effort allows other nations to divest themselves of citizens who are considered domestic problems—economic or social. It has been argued that U.S. foreign policy should be focused on changing the conditions in countries that are major suppliers of immigrants to the U.S. (Teitelbaum & Weiner, 1995).

Sometimes it is U.S. foreign policy that contributes to higher levels of immigration. For example, economic embargoes of and military action in other countries have frequently resulted in an influx of immigrants from these nations. In addition, encouraging countries to allow their citizens to freely move indirectly results in more immigration pressure for the United States. Ironically, some attempts to help others have unintended consequences.

In the United States, passage of the North American Free Trade Agreement (NAFTA) treaty contributed to an unprecedented level of migration from Mexico. These workers provide a cheap labor supply for U.S. businesses—about one-third of what U.S. workers receive—and, in some cases, have replaced higher paid unionized U.S. workers. The resultant lower production costs tend to make the United States more competitive in a global market. Employers, then, not only pay a lesser wage but also deny or limit benefits, and fail to meet obligations like paying overtime, giving reasonable notice of layoffs, and providing safety equipment. The trend then becomes one of replacing permanent workers with temporary ones who can be laid off or terminated easily and quickly. The consequences are serious: about 54% of Mexican immigrants have no health insurance at all (Wise & Covarrubias, 2008), they experience a very high poverty rate, live in substandard housing, and face regular discrimination. Overall, their household income averages 30% lower than that of native-born Americans (Pew Hispanic Center, 2009).

Lest one conclude that these Mexican immigration trends affect only the United States, another side of the coin is the impact on Mexico. That country has experienced population drops in about a third of its cities. Simultaneously, Mexico has become a transit route for immigrants from Central and South America seeking work in the United States. In a bit of irony, Mexico routinely imprisons or returns these immigrants to their own country.

As mentioned, not all countries actively seek or welcome new immigrants. One factor that influences opportunity for newcomers is the context of their reception (Portes & Rumbaut, 2006). Even nations that were welcoming in the past have undergone transformation. The past 30 years have seen a growing opposition to immigration in a variety of countries, including the United States, Germany, and France (Fetzer, 2000). This opposition has resulted in the creation of new political parties (France), nativist groups dedicated to stopping migration (United States), and a wide variety of political activities designed to achieve this end. These include California's Proposition 187, and a slew of new state and local laws purportedly designed to restrict illegal immigration. Explanations for these anti-immigrant efforts include: xenophobia, anomie, alienation, lack of experience with difference, poor education, immaturity, authoritarianism, cognitive rigidity, low political power, materialism, nationalism and isolationism, to name a few (Fetzer, 2000).

Whether the explanations are psychological, sociological, economic, political, or some combination, the result is often the same. Immigrants are treated badly, exploited, discriminated against, and sometimes harmed physically. At the same time, they are accused of using governmental resources without paying taxes, engaging in criminal behavior, depressing wages, and stealing jobs from the resident population (Davies, 2009). A major economic consideration arising from this effort to marginalize millions of undocumented immigrants is their potential contribution to a country's economy. Because of their undocumented status and threats of deportation should this be discovered, they comprise a large part of what is called an underground economy. This underground economy costs the United States an estimated 970 billion dollars per year in unpaid income taxes and may be growing at a rate above that of the regular economy, according to the *Wall Street Journal* (2005). Again, this is not just a U.S. problem, as evidenced by similar challenges facing Southern European nations (Reyneri, 2003).

Clinical Corner

Jacqueline

Thirty-two-year-old Jacqueline arrived at the refugee services office hysterical and crying. Both she and her husband Robert are undocumented, having arrived in the United States at ages 4 and 12, respectively. They met in high school, married, and had four children ages 3 to 12. One day as the family gathered on the front lawn, police arrived and asked for Robert's documentation. He was arrested and taken away. Twelve hours later, Jacqueline learned he was in a jail about an hour from their home and would be deported in four days. Despite the social worker's efforts, Robert was deported to a border town in a part of Mexico where he knew no one and had never been before. The social worker knew this was a dangerous situation because these deportees are often attacked and robbed by local criminals shortly after they are dropped off. In addition, some deportees do not speak Spanish because they arrived in the United States as children and are particularly vulnerable.

The social worker continued her efforts to help Robert by finding him a safe place to stay temporarily in the border town and connecting him with a program that would provide bus fare to Guadalajara where he had some extended family. After living apart for over a year, the wife and younger children moved to Mexico to be with Robert. The oldest child who is now in high school remained in the United States with relatives.

While acknowledging that economics and labor markets play a significant role in migration, some authors also note that migration itself is a vibrant social process (Castles, 2000; Miller, 2002). The migratory process is connected to the creation of social networks and often results in the formation of new relationships. Marriages and families occur and visitors become more involved in their communities, business, and other activities. Many send regular remittances to relatives remaining in their homeland, an amount that has grown by 30-fold to become Mexico's second largest source of foreign currency (Wise & Covarrubias, 2008). By 2009, remittances from immigrants worldwide exceeded $307 billion dollars, representing a sizeable addition to the Gross Domestic Product (GDP) of many nations (Ratha, Mohapatra, & Silwa, 2010). The impact of these remittances is not always positive, however. There is some evidence that while individual families benefit greatly via enhanced standards of living, remittances can also affect a country's economy, contributing to inflation and dependence. It is estimated that remittances in poor countries exceed the amounts provided through foreign aid and investment by foreign firms (Davies, 2009).

Typically, the longer immigrants (documented or not) remain in the United States benefitting from a higher standard of living, the more they see themselves as permanent members of a community and the more reluctant they are to return to their homeland. To maintain their status, many undocumented immigrants become invisible, avoiding any action that would make them stand out and increase risk of deportation. Others become vocal advocates for changes in immigration laws, appearing in demonstrations, such as those that have occurred in several U.S. cities over the past four to five years. Immigrant civic groups and organizations have forged relationships with local police departments and with others in their communities. One consequence is that numerous police departments refuse to enforce federal immigration laws or act as local agents of the Immigration and Customs Enforcement agency (ICE). The local agencies are focused on crime and want to know when it occurs within immigrant populations. They fear that immigrants will fail to report being victimized if they risk being deported for doing so. Other concerns include reduced cooperation of witnesses of crime, higher rates of immigrant exploitation and victimization, worries about police budgets and resources, potential errors and racial profiling leading to lawsuits, among others (Police Foundation, 2009).

Interestingly, the influx of Mexican migrants noted over the past decades appears to be diminishing. Several factors likely explain this change. First, the harsher state laws designed to penalize both illegal immigrants and businesses that hire them. Second, the U.S. recession that began in 2008 resulted in levels of unemployment not seen in decades. Third, Mexico's birth rate has declined, threatening the adequacy of the country's workforce to meet its own expanding businesses and industries.

Recent efforts to halt illegal immigration from Mexico often fail to take into account the size of the challenge. An estimated 11 to 12 million immigrants from Mexico and elsewhere are in the United States. They comprise about 20% of workers in the U.S. manufacturing industry and when all occupations are considered, foreign-born individuals comprise about 18% of the total. Foreign-born Hispanics tend to be clumped in occupations that involve cleaning and maintenance; construction and extraction; and installation, repair, and production (Pew Hispanic Center, 2009). Any effort to reduce the presence of foreign-born workers would likely have serious economic consequences for the United States. Figure 16.2 illustrates the overall size of the foreign-born population in the United States by region of origin.

Suggestions that all foreigners in the United States be deported does not take into account the financial cost of attempting such a massive undertaking—an estimated $94 billion in 2007, according to the chief of Immigrations and Customs Enforcement when asked at a U.S. Senate hearing. Annual costs of deporting the 300,000 to 400,000 people the United States currently sends home each year is roughly $9.2 billion, according to estimates from the Center for American Progress (2010).

One argument put forward in support of mass deportations is that it would save the United States a great deal of money, alleging that these individuals cost the United States over $300 billion annually in welfare and other expenses. These estimates have no basis in fact and are designed more to stir up immigration opponents than clarify the situation. FactCheck.org, an organization created to separate fact from fiction in political rhetoric and media reporting, has repeatedly pointed out the inaccuracies in such estimates. The Congressional Budget Office, a nonpartisan arm of the government, estimated that illegal immigrants do pose costs to state and local government but the amounts are

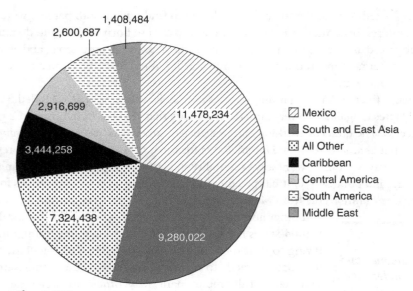

Figure 16.2
Foreign-Born Population of the United States, 2009

Source: Data from Pew Hispanic Center. (2009). Statistical Portrait of the Foreign-Born Population in the United States, 2009. Retrieved from http://pewhispanic.org/factsheets/factsheet.php?FactsheetID=69.

modest. They also concluded that there was no agreement on how to measure these costs on a national level (Congressional Budget Office, 2007).

At the same time, immigrants (documented or not) comprise a significant portion of the U.S. workforce and are, in some areas, the only source of labor (Davies, 2009).

Substantial disruptions would occur in industries heavily dependent upon immigrants. Moreover, it does not take into account the social consequences of deporting large numbers of undocumented immigrants. Recent raids on businesses by Immigration and Customs Enforcement officers have succeeded in arresting and deporting thousands of individuals with consequences for those left behind. For example, many of the children of

Did You Know?

"States with the largest proportion of unauthorized immigrants in the workforce include Nevada (10%), California (9.7%), Texas (9%) and New Jersey (8.6%)."

Source: Pew Research Center. (2011).

Many industries such as vegetable and fruit producers rely on immigrant labor to help gather the harvest.

those deported were in school and came home to find one or both parents were gone. These children become wards of the state as most were born in the United States and are recognized as citizens by the U.S. Constitution. The social, emotional, and economic costs of parental deportations are rarely considered in efforts to reduce the undocumented population.

Finally, the emphasis on immigrants as criminals who should be excluded from the United States is against the very American attitude that resulted in the country's growth and success. The ethos of working hard, reliance on the individual, and welcoming newcomers that characterized the United States for most of its existence is being replaced by a "go-away, we-don't- want-any" mentality infecting all aspects of American social, economic, and political life. It has produced efforts to deny access to resources for even legal resident immigrants from Mexico, restrictions on access to education for children, and other attempts to marginalize this population. Typically, the United States has vacillated between welcoming immigrants and trying to shut them out of American life. This vacillation is often related directly to economic conditions. When times are good with nearly full employment, newcomers are welcome—when times are bad with high unemployment, newcomers are rejected.

The United States has always had an ambivalent attitude toward at least some groups of immigrants, so the latest wave of anti-immigrant sentiment is not new (de Zoysa, 2006). Prior to the Civil War, the country worried about Irish Catholics and how they would fit into a primarily Protestant nation. Similar reservations were shown toward Germans in the same time frame; then followed by worries about immigrants from Eastern and Southern Europe between 1890 and 1920. In the past, quotas were established for various groups, such as restrictions placed on Chinese immigrants. Immigration became less restrictive after the 1960s when many quotas were eliminated. At the same time, though, other countries' immigration policies became more restrictive, leading some observers to argue that it was precisely American's openness that was responsible for its dynamic growth (Bhagwati, 2000).

Human Behavior

Practice Behavior Example: Apply theories and knowledge from the liberal arts to understand biological, social, cultural, psychological, and spiritual development.

Critical Thinking Question: The United States has historically feared the arrival of immigrants from such diverse places as Ireland, China, and Eastern and Southern Europe. These fears generally subsided over time with each batch of new immigrants becoming accepted. Would a similar process occur with more recent immigrants?

Assess your comprehension of Immigration Issues by completing this quiz.

ACCULTURATION

Most immigration scholars have identified three patterns among new immigrants; *assimilation or acculturation, multiculturalism,* and *transnationalism* (Nelson & Hiemstra, 2008). Assimilation or acculturation occurs when immigrants adopt the salient values, beliefs, attitudes, and behaviors of their new culture. By becoming part of the mainstream culture, they also willingly give up their previous cultural norms and homeland identities. This is the view inherent in the old melting pot concept often used to describe the United States. In practice, however, rarely was acculturation or assimilation an all or nothing proposition. More recent analyses have suggested that the process was only partial for many groups who maintained their identities and aspects of their native cultures. As might be expected, loss of one's culture of origin does not mean the end of its influence on the individual (Henry et al., 2009).

For others, the process of assimilation was not undertaken willingly. Rather, these individuals and groups felt forced or otherwise compelled to adopt the new set of values and norms without ever relinquishing their original beliefs. Instead, they utilized one set of norms within their own group and the dominant set of norms outside the group. Other groups of immigrants picked and chose the values, norms, and other aspects of the new culture they cared to adopt. This can help explain how an immigrant entrepreneur who builds a successful career employing current technologies and business strategies will still cling to values about women that are more in line with his country of origin. The values of one's country of origin are often connected to religious or cultural beliefs of long standing and seemingly compartmentalized from other elements of one's life.

Multiculturalism, by contrast, assumes that both the individual and the culture undergo a transformation in which each makes adjustments to the other. In a multicultural society, cultural differences are valued for the perspectives they bring and the contribution they make to the greater good. One shortcoming of this approach is that it is difficult to locate examples of a truly multicultural nation. Another is that it tends to overlook power differences between cultures or within the same culture, differences with significant import for the less powerful (Nelson & Heimstra, 2008). One of the first nations to officially self-identify as multicultural was Canada. The country has had an official federal policy of multiculturalism since 1971 that encouraged immigrants to maintain their original culture while simultaneously adopting the norms of Canada (Shariff, 2008). The policy also reflected recognition of the existing and forthcoming heterogeneity of the country as well as a commitment to equality among the many groups comprising the country.

A third approach, transnationalism, was mentioned earlier in this chapter. Transnationalism is not based on the assumptions of either assimilation or multiculturalism. Rather it acknowledges that immigrants often retain significant aspects of their origin identities as well as other associations and affiliations. Transnationals maintain contact with their homelands and live in both worlds more or less simultaneously (Rouse, 1995).

Acculturation is not a simple process and is affected by several factors (Berry, 1996). One factor is the history of any particular migration. In other words, the experience may be impacted by whether one is a refugee seeking asylum or a worker seeking better employment opportunities. If a migrant left a country to avoid ethnic cleansing, he or she would feel more favorable to acculturation. A second factor is the opportunities and supports available in the new country, including employment and social supports. Acculturation is less likely if one or both of these is absent.

A third factor is the resources the immigrant possesses—money, skills, personality, and other characteristics that make it more likely that one will have an easier time adjusting. The fourth factor is the prejudices and reactions of the host country. Will one face discrimination and violence or acceptance and fair treatment?

These factors cannot be considered in isolation from one another. Take, for example, immigrants to the United States from Muslim countries. Upon arrival they find a society focused on the rights of the individual and individual independence contrasted with that of their own country that values interdependence and community allegiance (Abdulahad, Delaney, & Brownlee, 2009). At the same time, there is enormous diversity within any Muslim group. Iraqi immigrants, for example, may be from a variety of ethnic groups including Turkman, Chaldean, Kurds, Arabs, Syriac, Armenians, Persians, Hebrews, and Assyrians. Some of these groups have longstanding grievances against U.S. policies and some have experienced U.S. military action. Moreover, some Americans will view them as potential terrorists given their history and events of September 11, 2001. Individuals may come to the United States as professionals in their own country, a potential resource, but find that their training and experience are not recognized here. If the immigrant has a sponsor or other connections in the United States, this is an important resource but again does not always guarantee a warm welcome.

Since acculturation involves changes in one's identity, behavior, and belief systems, it is easy to see how difficult such a transition might be. Gender may play a significant role in one's identity. If, for example, one's culture of origin views men as the top of the food chain, adjusting to a culture that sees the genders as equal poses a challenge. All of the factors identified by Berry (1996) are important variables affecting the likelihood that any individual will choose acculturation over other ways of adapting.

Generally speaking, in addition to gender, acculturation can also be affected by such things as age and ethnicity (Abdulahad et al., 2009; Akhtar & Choi, 2004). However, these factors may not have a great deal of impact on the acculturation rate among many Muslim groups who tend to maintain their identification with traditional religious and ethnic values. While not necessarily representing a rejection of the values of their new home, this tendency is important to understand.

Factors that help predict whether an immigrant will become acculturated have been identified among various groups. Choi and Thomas (2009) looked at Asian immigrants to the United States and found that Koreans were less positive about acculturation compared to Indian or Filipino immigrants. Two factors that correlate positively with acculturation are higher educational level and fluency in English. This may explain the differences among the two groups, as Korean's rated themselves less fluent in English. At the same time, immigrants favorable to acculturation were less likely to receive social support from their peers. This suggests that strong social support tended to reinforce the individual's retention of the culture of origin and negatively affect the likelihood of acculturation.

In some cases, acculturation has been strongly resisted by new arrivals, as evidenced by Israel which has struggled with two groups of immigrants, one from Ethiopia and the other from the former USSR (Mana, Orr, & Mana, 2009). The latter group tends to maintain its original social identity either by separating themselves from the rest of Israeli society or by attempting to somehow integrate cultural aspects from their past with those of Israel. Again, language and skin color appear to make significant differences. Immigrants from Ethiopia were persons of color and were treated differently by the Israeli government than was true for the Russians. Ethiopians were also seen by themselves and the host society as having a lower social status, a characteristic that also affects one's potential for acculturation. Unfortunately, newcomers who seek to maintain their differences are often perceived as threats by the host nation residents, resulting in the immigrants feeling the pressure to acculturate, a tactic that is rarely successful.

We often assume that most immigrant groups would look favorably on becoming part of their new country. However, sometimes there is a tension between the newcomers' desire to be included in their host country and a simultaneous wish to be distinctive (Gaertner & Dovidio, 2000). Some have characterized the process of adapting to a new life as similar to mourning the loss of a loved one (Murray, 2001). The wish and need to hold on to vestiges of the past culture can clash with the demands of the new culture. In many cases, the past becomes part of the individual even after acculturation has occurred. The relationship with the past provides support and emotional resources when adaptation to the new culture becomes challenging. Memories and cultural artifacts help link the new immigrants to their origins (Henry et al., 2009).

One's degree of acculturation does have several consequences. For example, Liu, Lau, Chen, Dinh, and Kim (2009) found that Chinese American mothers who were more acculturated tended to have adolescent children with lower levels of conduct problems. Reasons for this association seemed to relate to parenting styles (monitoring versus harsh discipline). Similar relationships have been found with respect to Mexican American families (Dumka, Roosa, & Jackson, 1997). Interestingly, the father's acculturation appeared to play no role in adolescents' conduct problems. The neighborhoods in which the Chinese American families lived appeared to impact maternal acculturation. For example, disadvantaged and stressful neighborhoods tended to result in mothers with less energy and more distress who then relied more on harsh discipline in dealing with their adolescents.

It is most likely that acculturation or assimilation occurs in something of a continuum, with some immigrants making wholesale adaptations to the new culture and others making few changes. As in other areas of human behavior, immigrants demonstrate various responses to challenges of adapting to a new culture and managing the loss of the old culture. There is no "normal" developmental process of acculturation that can be expected; only individual adaptations to new experiences, mourning of the past, and social and emotional adjustments.

LANGUAGE

Unless they are already bilingual, new immigrants often cite concern with language challenges (Carnegie Corporation of New York, 2010). However, even those with some fluency in their new country's language may not feel sufficiently confident in their communication ability. Inability to communicate readily in a new environment is another stressor that is common among immigrants. Lack of language fluency can result in the immigrant avoiding others, isolation, and dependence on one's children. It also reduces economic opportunities; for example, in the United States, a basic grasp of English is essential for most forms of employment and for participating fully in the political process. As Hou and Beiser (2006) point out, lack of language facility both increases service costs and reduces human capital.

One of the most important factors in immigrants developing language skills in their new country is the extent of exposure they have to it (van Tubergen & Kalmijn, 2009). In addition, economic factors play a role in whether and how quickly immigrants learn a new language.

Country of origin also plays a role as arrivals from more globalized nations often have better language skills. However, this enhanced language skill on arrival does not guarantee that the individual will learn the language once in the United States. Immigrants from countries that engage in high levels of political suppression often arrive with relatively low ability to speak English, but acquire the language more quickly once they are in. Finally, immigrants who locate in areas with high percentages of non-English speakers are less likely to acquire fluency. If more than 5% of an area's population speak the language of origin, the immigrant is 30% less likely to learn and speak English (van Tubergen & Kalmijn, 2009).

Thomas (2010) found that the ability of African immigrants to acquire English fluency is more often related to the proficiency of their mothers than their fathers. Mothers may be more likely to initiate conversations with children (Kalmijn, 1999). English language proficiency is typically higher among children when one parent speaks English fluently. The ability of older children in a family to speak English tends to support acquisition of English by younger children, as children learn from their siblings. The more siblings who speak English, the more likely the younger children will acquire the skill. In addition, the more conversations occurring in English within the family, the greater the exposure to the language.

Did You Know?

- Immigrants working outside the home are more likely to learn a new language
- Immigrants seeking jobs that require fluency in English are more likely to acquire it
- Younger immigrants are more likely than older immigrants to learn a new language
- Men tend to acquire language skills more quickly than women
- Immigrants with higher levels of education are more likely to acquire the new language

Source: van Tubergen & Kalmijn (2009).

Thomas (2010) also found that immigrants from Arabic-speaking countries are much less likely to develop English proficiency. This may be related to the vast differences between English and Arabic languages compared to smaller linguistic differences between most European languages and English.

A concern when migrating to a new country with an unfamiliar language is the reaction of teachers and school systems. Oftentimes, the student without English fluency, for example, is considered a blank slate. A student's native language should be recognized as a resource that teachers can use to benefit learning. Too often, children of immigrants lose their native tongue as they acquire their new language so that, in the end, they are monolingual rather than bilingual. This is frustrating for parents with lower language skills, who end up not being able to talk to their own children.

Another potential problem has to do with the name pronunciation. Some individuals have names that are difficult to pronounce. This is a concern because one's name is an important component of one's life. When teachers and others do not attempt to learn a person's name, it can be seen as a sign of rejection and become a barrier to meeting new people. It can also be embarrassing to immigrants who must continually say and spell their names, only to realize that the listener is not even attempting to remember the pronunciation. Others who make no attempt, may anglicize the name or give the newcomer a nickname that is easier to remember or pronounce. Sometimes, the newcomer will make this name change to better fit in. As a consequence, Mehitabel ends up as Mabel, Johannes becomes Jack, Nikhil becomes Nick, SeungJa becomes Sondra, Enrique becomes Henry, Hendrik changes to Hank, and Fientje evolves to Sophia. While these changes may appear minor to others, they may have greater significance to the immigrant. Among many cultures, names may have both familial and religious connotations. For example, one's name may be selected in honor of a revered relative or ancestor or it may have religious significance, such as Jesus, Yeshua, or Mohammed (Shariff, 2008).

Immigrants without good language skills are at risk for lower levels of medical care and a shortened length of life (Youdelman, 2008). If patients cannot acquire, understand, and consider health care information adequately, they are less likely to make informed decisions. The inability to process complicated health information also reduces the likelihood that one will engage in positive health behaviors, including self-management, use of preventive services, and appropriate care in the case of chronic illness. Absence of language skills makes it less likely that they will use available medical services, thereby increasing the risk of premature death.

Helping to offset the limitations of immigrants not fluent in English is a variety of federal and state laws. For example, the Civil Rights Act of 1964 (Title VI) requires health care providers receiving federal money to offer access to interpreters for non-English-speaking patients. This mandate and subsequent executive orders cover Medicaid, Medicare, and State Children's Health Insurance Program (SCHIP), as well as state health agencies, health care facilities of all kinds, medical care providers, and pharmacies (Youdelman, 2008). Likewise, the Emergency Medical Treatment and Active Labor Act requires facilities to develop means of communicating with non-English-speaking individuals. This typically means that interpreters must be available if the patient does not speak English. Notices of their obligation to provide services without discrimination must be posted in English and Spanish, as well as any other language spoken by at least 10% of the households in their catchment area (U.S. Department of Health and Human Services, 2011).

In addition, all states have laws or regulations that either clarify the intent of federal laws or go beyond them in ways designed to enhance patient health care. Some states exceed the federal requirements by covering all health care providers and health insurers whether or not federal funds are involved. Others mandate language services as a condition for licensure (Youdelman, 2008). While the broad array of federal and state laws and regulations should increase the effectiveness of health care services for non-English-speaking residents, this is not always the case. Provider's ignorance of requirements, lax enforcement, and immigrant fears often mean that these services are underutilized.

Clinical Corner

Jacob, a school social worker, is working with a new family of refugees arriving from Burma. Yusef and Leila have three children, 14, 11, and 2. For 12 years before they were resettled in the United States, the family lived in a refugee camp in Thailand. They can write in Burmese, but have no English language skills. They are living in a two bedroom apartment and both are working as hotel housekeepers. The two oldest children are in age-appropriate classes but both are having a great deal of academic trouble and are receiving social promotions to the next grade level without having mastered the content of their previous class. Both parents are stressed by high debt and their children's performance in school. The high debt exists because with their limited ability in English they cannot read their mail. Bills are either not getting paid on time or not paid at all. Their health care is primarily provided by emergency room visits, and medical bills are piling up.

Leila arrives at the social worker's office in a panic after learning that Yusef was arrested for driving with an expired registration and no insurance. After many calls, Jacob learns that getting Yusef out of jail and retrieving their impounded car will cost the family over $750. He is also beginning to worry about what else might be going on with the family. For example, given their language problems, has the family been filing tax returns, have they had an assessment of whether special education would be helpful for one or more children, will this arrest affect Yusef's ability to become a citizen?

As is evident from the case just mentioned, the overall importance of language acquisition for new immigrants should make this a key policy issue for lawmakers and others who work with newcomers. While agencies and organizations serving immigrants do provide language classes and encourage newcomers to learn English, it remains an area susceptible to cuts in tight budget times. It is perhaps ironic that those who argue that English should be the official language of the United States also support reducing funds for English as a Second Language (ESL) or English Language Learning (ELL) classes. As Hou and Beiser (2006) state, "Without language, one can never truly enter a culture" (p. 158).

Ensuring the availability of health care services to non-English speakers requires adequate funding for interpreters and setting minimum standards for those who seek to provide this service. Using the patient's relatives and children as interpreters often results in errors, violation of patient privacy rights, and failure of the interpreter to accurately provide medical information. Enforcement of existing state and federal laws and regulations is also needed along with training to inform providers about their legal obligations (Youdelman, 2008).

MENTAL HEALTH AND IMMIGRATION

Migration to any country is fraught with a variety of risks, and challenges. Stressors can be anything that can result in harm, loss, or threat to the individual (Lazarus & Folkman, 1984). New experiences can force change and adaptation, both of which are often perceived as stressful. Typical stressors include (Hovey, 2001; Lee, 2007):

- facing discrimination
- experiencing rejection
- feeling disconnected from one's past
- language difficulties
- loss of friends, family, and possessions
- adjustments to a new environment
- isolation
- feeling like a burden to one's family
- financial difficulties
- transportation problems
- loss of power and influence within one's own family
- economic-related dislocations.

Immigrants often have a sense of loss that includes such things as favorite foods, traditions, shared values, relationships, social status, and economic and social standing (Akhtar, 1999; Lee, 2007; Yaglom, 1993). Depression and disappointment are common reactions experienced by newcomers, and those who are refugees may be especially traumatized. Many refugees have lived in relocation camps and experienced torture and death of family members, mistreatment, deprivation, and discrimination prior to arriving in their new country. The individual's interpretation of the stressor tends to be affected by how serious the threat is and the resources that can be brought to bear to eliminate or ameliorate it.

Madianos, Gonidakis, Ploubidis, Papadopoulou, and Rogakou (2008) found that depression was less common among immigrants with greater degrees of acculturation, suggesting that the assimilation process may be a protective factor in helping deal with the obvious migration stresses. At the same time, Bui (2009) found that acculturation had negative effects on the family in that children from second and third generations were more likely to engage in delinquent acts than were first generation children. This is hypothesized to be the consequence of subsequent generations adopting values and behaviors of the dominant culture, diminished family bonds, and increased peer pressure. Bui's research is consistent with other studies that show a protective effect for first generation youth with regard to delinquency, substance abuse, and conflicts with parents, but a loss of this effect for future generations (Butcher & Piehl, 1997; Vega, 2001).

Another health/mental health risk among immigrant families is gender-based violence. Violence rates among intimate immigrant partners are higher than for other groups in society (Decker, Raj, & Silverman, 2007). This includes femicide in which the woman is killed by her partner. Immigrant status is also a risk factor for repeated instances of sexual assault, particularly for girls of age 15 or below. This may occur because the perpetrator considers the victim to be both legally and socially vulnerable.

Other mental health problems can arise from the clash of old and new values. For example, Lee (2007) notes that among Korean immigrants, taking care of one's aging parents is a moral expectation. Similar expectations are found in many Asian cultures. This value is not held as strongly in the United States where caring for an elderly person may involve an assisted living or nursing home placement rather than caring for parents in one's home. Both the elderly and their adult children may worry about how this responsibility will play out when the time comes.

Slonim-Nevo, Mirsky, Rubinstein, and Nauck (2009) have identified several familial and environmental factors that affect the adjustment of immigrants to their new surroundings. Transition to a new culture is facilitated by positive family relations and interactions among members. A major facet of this is the degree of immigrant self-esteem. This is consistent with other studies showing that healthy functioning families tend to have members who are themselves psychologically well adjusted (Jasinskaja-Lahti, Liebkind, & Solheim, 2001). A healthy functioning family environment can serve as a buffer against stress connected to immigration. Lowered stress, in turn, can help prevent immigration-associated problems such as grief, poor mental health, feeling alienated, psychosomatic symptoms, and other difficulties.

Another finding is that lower levels of perceived discrimination tend to increase the likelihood of positive adjustment to the new environment. Since experiencing discrimination and feeling alienated are both stressors, the absence of these factors predicts a more satisfactory adjustment. Feeling relatively accepted by one's new surroundings diminishes immigrant destructive behaviors and acting out.

One destructive behavior associated with some immigrants includes unprotected sex, resulting in HIV and other sexually transmitted diseases (STDs) (Rhodes et al., 2009). This problem is especially common in Hispanic/Latino immigrant populations and other socially vulnerable groups. According to the Centers for Disease Control and Prevention (CDC), the rate of contracting AIDS is twice as high for Hispanic/Latino men and four times as high for Hispanic/Latino women compared to their White counterparts (CDC, 2010). Another problem behavior experienced by some immigrant groups is alcoholism, a disease often associated with stress, depression, and aloneness (Rhodes et al., 2009). Latino immigrant men report difficulty in meeting traditional male cultural expectations, as well as having to take on roles such as cooking and cleaning not expected of men back home. Inability to meet traditional roles, such as income provider and social/political leader, may result in some displaying their masculine role through sexuality and sexually risky behavior. Similar trends have been seen in immigrant males from Jamaica and Africa (Whitehead, 1997). In addition, Jackson and Knight (2006) found that poor coping behaviors in response to stressors were associated with increased consumption of comfort food and substance abuse.

Immigrants who experience personal tragedies—family illness, divorce, or death of a loved one—are at greater risk of mental health problems and lowered functioning (Slonim-Nevo et al., 2009). The stress of these events can deplete the immigrant's emotional and other resources just as can occur with nonimmigrants.

Unfortunately, it is not just new immigrants who are at risk of experiencing mental health problems. Peña et al. (2008) in a study of Latinos found that subsequent generations also faced multiple challenges. These included higher rates for suicide, problematic use of alcohol, marijuana, and other drugs. Third generation Latino adolescents had higher rates for all of these risks compared to those in their second generation.

As is evident, risks of various mental health concerns continue into subsequent generations. Similar results were found in other migrating ethnic groups, including Blacks from the Caribbean, and immigrants from China and Africa (Breslau, Borges, Hagar, Tancredi, & Gilman, 2009). Immigrants from other areas—including Western Europe, Cuba, and Puerto Rico—do not appear to demonstrate the same patterns.

The U.S. Centers for Disease Control and Prevention (2012) provide a clear summary of why immigrant groups are likely to experience mental health issues:

> Long-distance journeys and resettlement entail a set of engulfing life events (losses, changes, conflicts, and demands) that, although varying widely in kind and degree, may severely test a refugee's emotional resilience. Resettlement in a new country

can produce profound psychological distress, even among the best prepared and most motivated. Given the nature of life-threatening experiences prior to and during flight from their home countries (or country of asylum/host country), as well as the difficult circumstances of existence in exile, refugees may be at particularly high risk for psychiatric symptoms.

Risk factors that predispose refugees and asylum seekers to psychiatric symptoms and disorders include: exposure to war, state-sponsored violence and oppression, including torture, internment in refugee camps, human trafficking, physical displacement outside one's home country, loss of family members and prolonged separation, the stress of adapting to a new culture, low socioeconomic status, and unemployment. Studies have shown a high prevalence of depression, posttraumatic stress disorder (PTSD), panic attacks, somatization, and traumatic brain injuries in refugees. Depression and PTSD are prevalent in refugees who are not in clinical care for mental health, in addition to those identified for mental health interventions. Major psychiatric symptoms may be present during the first months after arrival in the United States. Various factors including language, culture, religion, stigma, lack of transportation, work conflicts, and lack of child care may dissuade refugees from accepting mental health diagnosis and/or treatment.

This summary suggests why and how social workers play a vital role in services to immigrant populations. The challenges immigrants face mirror those of other vulnerable populations. Social work is the largest provider of mental health services in the United States (Substance Abuse and Mental Health Services Administration, 2010), which makes working with these challenges an important reason for our existence. It is our obligation to understand the experiences of the immigrant, provide competent assessment, and identify and implement salient interventions. However, assessing the demands of immigration on new or recent arrivals is not always easy. An instrument designed for this purpose is the Demands of Immigration Scale, which assesses an array of experiences of U.S. immigrants. The scale has been validated with immigrants from Taiwan, the former Soviet Union, Korea, Canada, Philippines, India, and Arabic women immigrants and may be helpful to social workers (Ma, Griffin, Capitulo, & Fitzpatrick, 2010).

Clinical Corner

Sonja, a social worker from Workforce Services, was meeting with her client, Ali, a 27-year-old physician from Iraq. Ali has been in the United States for two years and holds a day job as a case manager at a resettlement agency, drives a cab at night, and hopes to resume his medical career. This will require taking the two-part U.S. Medical Licensing Exam and having a clinical interview before he can apply for a residency position. Prior to applying for the residency program, he will likely need a letter of recommendation from a physician in his speciality area. This most likely entails completion of an observership. The licensing exam itself will require much preparation, including taking practice tests from past exams. He will also need to have his Iraq medical school transcripts notarized before he can take the exam. Each step in the process is lengthy and expensive. Despite being a hard worker and motivated, the process is discouraging, and Ali is feeling frustrated, anxious, depressed, and discouraged.

Sonja decides that Ali's best avenue is referral to a cooperative program involving a major university and a refugee settlement agency. This program has over 100 clients with professional degrees from foreign schools and works with them to help them make the transition to U.S. employment in their chosen field. They will also provide whatever counseling and support services Ali needs to make it through the challenges he faces.

HEALTH AND IMMIGRATION

Immigrants and their families often experience health challenges. Capps and Fortuny (2006) note that immigrant children are at least twice as likely to be in fair or poor health compared to nonimmigrant children. In addition, they are more likely to experience problems in development of cognitive and language skills, as well as in academic pursuits. In general, race, culture, and ethnicity are associated with less positive health outcomes and limited access to appropriate medical-related services. Lack of medical insurance is common among immigrants and their families because they are less likely to be employed full time in positions providing this coverage. Poverty also reduces the likelihood that they will be able to obtain health insurance through the private sector. Even a country like Canada, which provides universal health care, does not always provide quality care and ethnic minority groups there have experienced health disparities (Lai & Chau, 2007). Some disparities arise from language difficulty and knowledge about what services are available and how to use them. Others may distrust Western medical care and believe one's health is a matter of fate (Torsch & Ma, 2000).

Barriers to health care exist in many forms. In addition to language barriers, sometimes beliefs, personal values, and cultural practices interfere. Older immigrants may have cognitive limitations that interfere with understanding and communicating their health needs. Transportation needs have also been identified as barriers to health care access (Morgan & Sampsel, 1994; Tsai & Lopez, 1997). Lai and Chau (2007) identified other barriers for Chinese elders in Canada that included: (1) hearing negative experiences about medical care from other people, (2) dissatisfaction with services provided, (3) insufficient attention from service providers, (4) long waiting lists, (5) inconvenient office hours, and (6) services that were too expensive. A general distrust of the health care system also has been noted among some Latinos (Schwarzbaum, 2004).

SOCIAL WORK AND IMMIGRATION

The social work profession has been a leader in serving immigrant populations for over 100 years (Pine & Drachman, 2005).

Social workers provide help to immigrant populations in thousands of settings, including: immigrant settlement programs, hospitals, schools, correctional settings, child welfare services, substance abuse programs, and more. In these settings, practitioners can adopt the best available research on which interventions are most successful with various immigrant populations while extending their own cultural competence. They can also develop what Capitman (2002) calls cultural humility and the willingness to admit that their

Ethical Practice

Practice Behavior Example: Know about the value base of the profession, its ethical standards, and relevant law.

Critical Thinking Question: What values of the social work profession support the provision of services to immigrant populations, including those that are undocumented?

knowledge of a given culture is limited. This invites or permits clients to help educate the social worker about their respective cultures. This following section will identify some of those interventions and suggest those holding greatest promise for assisting immigrants make the transition to their new country.

We have used the term *immigrant* to cover several categories of individuals and families with whom social workers come into contact. These categories tend to fall into the following five groups (Capps, Passel, Periz-Lopez, & Fix, 2003; Pine & Drachman, 2005):

- Legal permanent resident—Individuals legally admitted through a formal application process, often via sponsorship from an employer or family member
- Undocumented immigrant—People lacking legal immigration documents. This includes those who have secretly entered the country and those who have overstayed a legal visa
- Refugee—Individuals admitted to the United States because they are in danger of persecution in their home countries
- Special immigration juvenile status—This applies to abused, abandoned, or neglected youth eligible for foster care who cannot be reunited with their parents
- Mixed-status families—These families contain individuals in more than one category, such as an undocumented parent, a legal U.S. resident, or a refugee.

Each category may have special needs based on several factors. For example, mixed-status families may come to the attention of child welfare services because they are more likely to be economically deprived, involve children who are U.S. citizens, and have one or more members who are always in danger of deportation. This can reduce a family's willingness to seek out medical or other care for children for fear of the consequences. This can also have differential impacts on various family members. Consider the case described next as an example of this.

Clinical Corner

Miguel

Miguel came to the United States with his then two-year-old son, Juan, following the death of Juan's mother. Juan is now 16 years old. Though undocumented himself, Miguel married Beth, an American citizen, and they had two children, Ned (age five) and Maria (age three). Recently, Miguel was detained during a raid by Immigration and Customs Enforcement officers at his job site and subsequently deported to Mexico. In his absence, Beth has been supporting the family. Now she has learned that Juan also will be deported because he is also undocumented. Juan has spent almost his entire life in the United States, helps care for his step-siblings while Beth works nights, and is doing well in school. Juan will be separated from the only mother he has known and the siblings he grew up with and loves. Beth will have to quit her job because she cannot afford child care and will likely go on welfare.

As this case illustrated, members of a mixed-status family can be affected differently and the possible consequences for each member may vary. This highlights one important aspect of cultural competence: namely, recognizing that the experiences of each immigrant or family member will be different to various degrees from those of others. This is true even if all family members are from the same country. In addition, differences from one ethnic group to another can be quite significant. Araújo (1996), for example, looked at the dynamics that influenced Portuguese immigrants and noted characteristics that differentiated them from other groups. One difference is the extent to which fatalism is a part of the culture, affecting how immigrants view their lives now and in the future. Hopelessness and unhappiness are often experienced by those for whom fatalism is a major life perspective. It often exists in groups that feel they have little or no control over life events. A second difference was ambivalence toward authority, a characteristic that is common among other ethnic groups.

Morrison and James (2009) provide a set of recommendations that will be helpful to practitioners working with many immigrant families. These include involving the immigrant's culture of origin, extended family, and support networks to the extent to which clients are comfortable. The family's current environment should also be considered an important factor in helping the immigrant adjust to a new life. The environment may be a source of support for immigrant families, as well as a potential stressor. Another useful approach is to recognize the strengths that the family and its members are acquiring as they adjust to the new environment. Sometimes, in the midst of chaos, families will not recognize which coping strategies they have developed and how those approaches are paying off. Resilience is likely to be one of those strengths (Walsh, 2006). Also keep in mind that some family members, who may not be in the country yet, still play an influential role in the family dynamics. Though not on site, they may be consulted by family members in the United States on topics such as health care or education (Pine & Drachman, 2005).

It is not uncommon to find different generations of a family in conflict over certain issues. There may be discord between first and second generation immigrants as the former works to retain aspects of the old culture while the latter moves more toward assimilation. One goal might be to help each generation understand the needs and values of the other and recognize how both have found it necessary to adopt a mixture of old and new ways of doing things.

A culturally competent practitioner will consider what role loss plays in the lives of immigrants and their families. Losses are likely, no matter how the immigrant came to the new country. Perhaps, the immigrant's native language becomes a casualty of education. For example, though millions of students speak Spanish as their native tongue, laws in California forbid teachers to use Spanish in their classrooms. This undercuts the benefits of bilingual education, as was discussed previously, and as shown by Ramirez, Perez, Valdez, and Hall (2009). Their findings demonstrate that long-term bilingual education programs contribute to long-term educational achievement, improved graduation rates for high school students, and cause no delay in the student becoming Americanized. Other studies have demonstrated the effectiveness of various interventions, and the next section will focus on two fields of practice, namely, delinquency prevention and child welfare services. The last section of the chapter will explore recommendations dealing with effective advocacy in the field of immigration.

Delinquency Prevention Interventions

One of the most effective tools for preventing delinquency among immigrant populations is maintaining quality family relationships and building close relationships among adolescents, their parents, and the school system (Bui, 2009). Immigrant families are more likely to fare best if their acculturation is selective and draws upon traditional means of parent–child interactions, and other methods that build family cohesion. Selective acculturation has been shown to produce better educational and financial success for both immigrant children and their families (Kibria, 1993; Zhou & Bankston, 1998).

Interventions to reduce ethnic bias in school systems can help promote school bonding for both students of color and immigrant children. Programs aimed at eliminating bullying may provide benefit for immigrant children who are frequently easy targets because of their differences.

Child Welfare Services

Access to and utilization of child welfare services are influenced by one's immigration status as well as other factors. Undocumented families and those who do not speak English are often unable to access services, making it difficult to meet court or agency mandates (Ayón, 2009). Recent policy changes have reduced access of these services even to immigrants who are here legally, especially those who are required to wait five years to access various programs. These policies increase the risk for unsuccessful outcomes, given the shortened time frame imposed by the Adoption and Safe Families Act (ASFA, 1997). One of the groups most affected by these changes are the Latinos, the fastest growing ethnic group in the various city, county, and state child welfare systems. Given the fact that child welfare social workers often experience large caseloads and limited resources, there is a tendency to work only with families where success is likely. It also can lead to limiting services provided to families and pursuing goals inconsistent with client needs (Smith & Donovan, 2003).

That many immigrant families require services available in their native language poses another challenge. English-speaking parents find it easier to access services but there are relatively limited resources for those lacking this ability (Ayón, 2009). Mental health services are often not readily available in different languages, and waiting lists tend to be long for clients needing assistance in their own language. Moreover, social workers must be very knowledgeable about the availability of such services and resources. Unfortunately, this capability varies widely from worker to worker.

Advocacy

Another role for social workers is intervention in the political arena to counter an increasingly strident anti-immigrant movement that demonizes newcomers and seeks to penalize both them and their children. This includes children of immigrants who were born in the United States and are American citizens under the U.S. Constitution. In this effort, it is important to recognize that criticism of immigrants is nothing new. Over 100 years ago, a well-respected U.S. educator wrote the following:

> everywhere these people settle in groups or settlements, and set up their national manners, customs, and observances. Our task is to break up these groups or settlements to assimilate and amalgamate these people as part of our American race, and to implant in their children, as far as can be done, the Anglo-Saxon conception of righteousness, law and order, and our popular government, and to awaken in them a reverence for our democratic institutions and for those things in our national life which we as a people hold to be of abiding worth. (Cubberly, 1909, pp. 15–16)

If this sounds vaguely familiar, it's because it reflects a current attitude toward immigrants, their putative harm to national identity, and an overall dissatisfaction with immigration policy. English-only movements, growing ethnocentrism, and laws designed to restrict opportunities for immigrants are rooted in some of the same concerns expressed by Cubberly in 1909. It should be no surprise that many of the immigration policies contribute to the risk factors we have discussed earlier in this chapter (Pine & Drachman, 2005).

Another venue for advocacy is the media. Martinez-Brawley and Gualda (2009) studied the influence of the media on public perceptions of immigrants and found that much of the information that social workers and other citizens have about immigration is derived from this source. When items appear in the news outlets, they often relate to dramatic events—such as efforts by Arizona and Alabama to prevent illegal immigration and political statements from those opposed to immigration. Their findings demonstrate that the preponderance of media articles is negative in tone. Social workers can influence this one-sided coverage by highlighting the other side of the picture. The United States has benefited from immigration and entire industries would be severely impacted if a significant portion of those in the country illegally were forced to leave. Attempts to associate immigrants with criminals can be counteracted by stories focusing on the more realistic portrait of the average immigrant: working hard, raising a family, and trying to achieve the same dream as others have before. Social workers can write letters to the editor addressing the benefits of immigration, challenging false and misleading information letters provided by others, and helping set a tone that is respectful of differences. We can also provide news stories that are fair and unbiased in their description of immigrants and their families.

Equally important, it is important to emphasize the role the larger macro-environment plays in many immigrant groups coming to the United States. For example, U.S. farm policy provides subsidies for corn growers in the United States that undercuts the price of Mexican corn. This makes it more economical for Mexico to import corn from the United States than to grow it at home. This, in turn, reduces the ability for Mexican farmers to make a living and forces rural dwellers to move to more urban environments (Relinger, 2010). Some U.S. policies have produced similar consequences throughout Latin America via economic treaties and support of repressive governments. For example, the assumption that changes in the market structure of other economies would produce significant economic gains for all parties has been challenged repeatedly (Furman, Sanchez, Langer, & Negi, 2007). Social workers must pay attention to the consequences of government policies, even in areas that appear outside our normal sphere of work.

The adoption of immigration laws reflecting social work values and ethics is another area where social workers can serve as advocates (Padilla, 1997). This involves communicating with elected officials, testifying about the experiences of immigrants, and emphasizing the importance of immigration to the nation and the economy. It also involves helping shape public opinion about immigration and speaking out against policies that dehumanize people.

The willingness of social workers to advocate for improved services to immigrant groups can produce clear benefits. New York City, for example, using information gleaned from talking with providers and immigrant groups, developed a series of steps designed to improve services to newcomers (Chahine & van Straaten, 2005). These changes included the following:

- Providing clients with a language identification card so that they could more easily explain the language with which they were most familiar (27 languages available)
- Ensuring that agency records reflected the client's language
- Ensuring that operators answering neglect or abuse calls had access to interpreters 24 hours per day (140 languages)
- Seeking relatives for kinship care when out-of-home placement of children is needed
- Developing a set of immigration and language guidelines for child welfare workers
- Providing automatic referrals to legal services for noncitizens and undocumented immigrants to help them access assistance
- Training agency staff about the needs of immigrants with limited fluency in English.

While no change can cover all of the unmet needs in child welfare or other service areas, workers advocating for improved services can produce positive outcomes. Social workers can also become more knowledgeable about resources that might help their agencies become more responsive to the needs of refugee populations. For example, Bridging Refugee Youth and Children's Services is an organization devoted to providing technical assistance to other organizations and agencies that serve immigrants and refugees (Morland, Duncan, Hoebing, Kirschke, & Schmidt, 2005). They maintain a database of other programs across the nation that can serve as models for effective assistance to these populations.

A major challenge facing the United States today is that the largest range of services available to immigrants are located in the most populous states while the immigrant population is growing fastest in a couple of dozen other states (Pine & Drachman, 2005). These states often lack the kinds of services needed by their growing immigrant populations and badly need practitioners with the requisite language skills. It is also some of these states, such as Arizona and Utah, that have enacted some of the most repressive laws aimed at immigrants.

One danger in discussing how social work can provide needed services to immigrant groups is the tendency to lump all immigrants into one category. As we have seen in the earlier section on mental health and immigration, there are clear differences in both the risk factors and the challenges faced by different groups. Treating immigrants from the same country as a monolithic group is bound to fail. In addition, the immigrant experience differs considerably from one newcomer to another. Values such as interdependence found in many cultures can clash with Western emphasis on independence. Variables—such as one's generation status, age, ethnicity, and gender—can influence the immigration experience. Social workers must consider a client's readiness to change, salient mental health issues, client needs, and one's own skill in working with immigrants.

Furman and his colleagues point out that within-group differences can dramatically affect how any given immigrant interprets his or her experience (2009). For example, the heterogeneity of the Latino population is enormous and it is important to understand the differences among various groups. Not all Latinos coming to the United States share the migrational experiences. For example, many from Mexico and Central America have experienced enormous hardship and risk in their migration to the United States while Puerto Ricans can move freely back and forth between the United States and their homeland. The degree of acculturation may also differ substantially from one group or individual to another. Social workers are urged to understand and value both traditional and nontraditional helping approaches and resources.

Cleaveland's (2010) study of male Mexican migrants illustrates why it is important to understand the client better. She notes that most of the men she interviewed were undocumented but refused to consider themselves *illegal*, a term they associated with criminality that injures others. Instead, they identified as migrant workers who supplied labor to assist the U.S. economy. For most Mexican immigrants, the decision to migrate to the United States was not a spur of the moment action, but rather a well-considered step reflecting the realities of trying to raise a family on the incredibly low wages available in Mexico. However, the act of being in the United States without documentation brings immigrants into contact with criminal elements that supply false documents and forged papers needed to find and maintain employment. This contradiction in self-definition is at least partly caused by immigration policies themselves.

As mentioned repeatedly, Mexican cultural values tend to differ in important ways from Western values. Mexican family and community cohesion are significant protective factors for this population. *La familia* and *familismo* are sources of support and resources during both normal and challenging times and social workers should pursue interventions that strengthen these connections (Hancock, 2005).

Social workers must also understand their own worldviews, biases, and values and how these may intersect with helping immigrant populations. This includes an awareness of the impact of race on one's experiences. Sharing of personal information may be more appropriate with many Latinos and does not represent a violation of professional boundaries (Furman et al., 2009). Social workers might also think carefully about how quickly we encourage immigrants to become acculturated and give up past behaviors. This may undercut family connections, force disruptions in intergenerational relationships, and diminish normally available community resources (Hancock, 2005).

A final possibility is that whenever possible social workers could ignore laws designed to oppress immigrant populations and adopt practices that recognize and reinforce human dignity. This is the position taken by Sakamoto (2007) and is consistent with social work values and ethics. It is an approach that decries the violence perpetrated on immigrants because of their documentation status and opposes attempts to criminalize behaviors taken to survive. The social work *Code of Ethics* stresses the need for social workers to pursue social justice and help those who are oppressed, vulnerable, or poor. It would be difficult to deny that this status aptly describes many of those who migrate to the United States (Cleaveland, 2010). As de Silva (2006) observes, punitive and oppressive immigration laws are a violation of social work ethics because they undermine the profession's commitment to social justice and human rights. Potential strategies include developing collaborations with agencies that do not discriminate based on immigration status, outreaching to immigrant organizations, and initiating political action to overturn and prevent harmful laws and regulations (Cleaveland, 2010; de Silva, 2006).

Assess your comprehension of Social Work and Immigration by completing this quiz.

If social workers fail to address the shortcomings of social policies and practices that demonize, deny service to, and criminalize immigrants, the profession will be marginalized as service providers and relegated to the role of enforcers of laws and regulations. We will be abdicating our role as change agents and supporting repressive and unjust treatment of fellow human beings.

Assess your analysis and evaluation of this chapter's contents by completing the Chapter Review.

Trauma and Abuse Influence Human Behavior

Most social workers know the first attempts to combat child abuse used laws designed to protect harm to animals. Almost 140 years ago, it was necessary to persuade a judge that a child was part of the animal kingdom and should be protected from abuse as were other creatures. Today, child abuse is illegal in all states and in most foreign countries, although what is defined as abuse varies from one jurisdiction to another.

CHILD ABUSE: DEFINITIONS AND IMPLICATIONS

The various definitions of child abuse pose a problem when it comes to intervention, as Corby (1997) and Krane and Davies (2000) point out. As the latter acknowledges, "With the exception of extreme or obvious cases of persistent physical assaults or sexual intrusions, consensus is lacking on the level of seriousness ... [warranting intervention]." Absent a uniform definition of child abuse applicable in all U.S. jurisdictions, social workers must rely on state-specific laws covering this topic. The definition used in federal law is contained in the Child Abuse Prevention and Treatment Act as amended (CAPTA, 2010) and states:

- Any recent act or failure to act on the part of a parent or caretaker which results in death, serious physical or emotional harm, sexual abuse or exploitation; or
- An act or failure to act which presents an imminent risk of serious harm.

soupstock/Fotolia

Child abuse is a significant challenge in the United States.

This definition covers both child abuse and neglect, so it is therefore broader than ideal. Separating abuse and neglect is often done in state law where courts generally rely on legislatures to provide specific wording. For example, as shown in Box 17.1, the State of Wisconsin laws specify different categories for abuse and neglect (U.S. Department of Health and Human Services, 2011).

As might be expected, careful definitions are critical to enforcement of laws prohibiting child abuse and neglect. Often, the more specific the easier it becomes for courts to uphold and validate decisions of child protection workers. Vague or unclear laws can be and are challenged in court and may be overturned by appeal courts. At the same time, the decision whether an incident of abuse is sufficient to warrant action by a child services

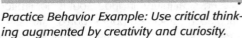
Critical Thinking

Practice Behavior Example: Use critical thinking augmented by creativity and curiosity.

Critical Thinking Question: What are the advantages (if any) of each state having its set of definitions of child abuse and neglect? What are the disadvantages (if any)?

worker or court often involves a degree of discretion by both worker and judge. Thus, professional judgment, experience, and training are requirements for workers in child protective services.

The Implications of Abuse

There is substantial evidence that survivors of neglect and physical and sexual abuse experience consequences that influence their behavior, often for the rest of their lives. About 20% of girls and 5% to 10% of boys report being sexually abused, although the actual rate is likely higher (World Health Organization, 2010). Sexually abused children are at higher risk for several challenges as adults (Leeners, Richter-Appelt, Imthurn, & Rath, 2006; Medrano, Hatch, Zule, & Desmond, 2003; Messman-Moore & Brown, 2004; Rodriguez, Ryan, Kemp, & Foy, 1997). These are reflected in Table 17.1.

Other risks associated with being a survivor of childhood sexual abuse include sexual dissatisfaction, sexually compulsive behavior, and aversion to certain sexual activities as an adult (Hall, 2005). This group is more prone to HIV infection and engaging in sexually risky behaviors (Walser & Kern, 1996). The risks are also higher when sexual abuse is

Box 17.1   Wisconsin Laws Specify Different Categories for Abuse and Neglect

Physical Abuse: Citation: Ann. Stat. §(4) 48.02; 48.981

"Abuse" means any of the following:

- Physical injury inflicted on a child by other than accidental means
- When used in referring to an unborn child, serious physical harm inflicted on the unborn child, and the risk of serious physical harm to the child when born, caused by a habitual lack of self-control of the expectant mother of the unborn child in the use of alcoholic beverages, controlled substances, or controlled substance analogs, exhibited to a severe degree
- Manufacturing methamphetamine in violation of § 961.41(1)(e) under any of the following circumstances:
  - With a child physically present during the manufacture
  - In a child's home, on the premises of a child's home, or in a motor vehicle located on the premises of a child's home
  - Under any circumstances in which a reasonable person should have known that the manufacture would be seen, smelled, or heard by a child

"Physical injury" includes, but is not limited to, lacerations, fractured bones, burns, internal injuries, severe or frequent bruising, or great bodily harm.

"Incident of death or serious injury" means an incident in which a child has died or been placed in serious or critical condition, as determined by a physician, as a result of any suspected abuse or neglect that has been reported, or in which a child who has been placed outside the home by a court order is suspected to have committed suicide.

"Incident of egregious abuse or neglect" means an incident of suspected abuse or neglect that has been reported under this section, other than an incident of death or serious injury, involving significant violence, torture, multiple victims, the use of inappropriate or cruel restraints, exposure of a child to a dangerous situation, or other similar, aggravated circumstances.

Sexual Abuse/Exploitation: Citation: Ann. Stat. § 48.02

The term "abuse" includes any of the following:

- Sexual intercourse or sexual contact
- Sexual exploitation of a child
- Permitting, allowing, or encouraging a child to engage in prostitution
- Causing a child to view or listen to sexual activity
- The exposure of one's genitals to a child

Emotional Abuse: Citation: Ann. Stat. § 48.02

The term "abuse" includes emotional damage for which the child's parent, guardian, or legal custodian has neglected, refused, or been unable for reasons other than poverty to obtain the necessary treatment or to take steps to ameliorate the symptoms.

"Emotional damage" means harm to a child's psychological or intellectual functioning. Emotional damage shall be evidenced by one or more of the following characteristics exhibited to a severe degree: anxiety, depression, withdrawal, outward aggressive behavior, or a substantial and observable change in behavior, emotional response, or cognition that is not within the normal range for the child's age and stage of development.

Neglect: Citation: Ann. Stat. § 48.02

"Neglect" means failure, refusal, or inability on the part of a caregiver, for reasons other than poverty, to provide necessary care, food, clothing, medical or dental care, or shelter so as to seriously endanger the physical health of the child.

The importance of knowing and understanding state definitions of child abuse is obvious. An action considered child abuse in Wisconsin may not be so construed in another state. For example, compare the breadth and specificity of the definition of physical abuse used in Wisconsin to the following definition used under Alabama law.

Physical Abuse: Citation: Ala. Code § 26-14-1(1)-(3)

Abuse means harm or threatened harm to the health or welfare of a child through:

- Nonaccidental physical injury
- Sexual abuse or attempted sexual abuse
- Sexual exploitation or attempted sexual exploitation

These differences become important when social workers must justify their actions in court.

Table 17.1 Adult Risks for Survivors of Child Sexual Abuse (CSA) Compared to Adults Without a History of CSA

Risk for Survivors of CSA to	Risk Level compared to Adults Without CSA History
Being raped as an adult	Twice as high
Engaging in substance abuse as an adult	42% higher
Engaging in prostitution as an adult	Twice as high
Experiencing death of a fetus during pregnancy	Twice as high
Suffering from PTSD	Four times as high

Source: Leeners et al. (2006); Medrano et al. (2003); Messman-Moore & Brown (2004); Rodriguez et al. (1997).

combined with other forms of neglect or abuse with outcomes that include delinquency and suicide (Hahm, Lee, Ozonoff, & Van Wert, 2010). Women who experienced child sexual abuse are more likely to have complaints and problems during pregnancy; suffer more stress, anxiety, and depression; experience more pain during labor than control groups; and report more postpartum difficulties (Leeners et al., 2006).

Frederick and Goddard (2008) and Howe (2005) found that children who suffered early attachment disruptions as a result of abuse are likely to experience later difficulties with adult relationships. This likely occurs because family members denied abuse occurred, minimized its severity, or blamed the child for its occurrence, none of which are supportive behaviors (Dunlap, Golub, & Johnson, 2003). These adults were more likely to be estranged from their families and received little of the support adult children typically get. Friendships tended to be less frequent among abuse survivors and they often find personal relationships stressful or difficult. Connections to others in the community are rare with very few organizational memberships, and many are only transient residents in their community.

CHILD PROTECTIVE SYSTEMS AND CHILD WELFARE SYSTEMS

Child welfare is a social work practice area focused on the safety and well-being of children. Although many private social service agencies offer child welfare services, primary responsibility for the protection of children and provision of child welfare services rests with various levels of government. When creating and implementing their laws and regulations, cities and states must abide by federal child welfare laws as a condition of receiving federal funds. Each state or city creates administrative structures needed to implement its laws and any applicable federal mandates. Several federal programs support child welfare services delivered at the state level. Initially, federal assistance to states began with the creation of the Social Security Act in 1935, which provided grants to states for things such as child abuse prevention, protective services, and foster care. Later laws and revisions to existing laws expanded the kinds of services provided and the funds to help support them. These include the previously mentioned Child Abuse Prevention and Treatment Act (CAPTA), title IV-B and IV-E of the Social Security Act, and Social Services Block Grants. CAPTA, passed in 1974 and revised several times since, was designed to improve state child abuse and neglect services.

Did You Know?

According to the Child Welfare Information Gateway (2012), in addition to the laws listed earlier, the federal government has several laws that deal with child protection and child welfare, including the Indian Child Welfare Act (1978), Adoption Assistance and Child Welfare Act (1980), Child Abuse Prevention, Adoption and Family Services Act (1988), Child Abuse, Domestic Violence, Adoption and Family Services Act (1992), Family Preservation and Support Services Program Act (1993), Foster Care Independence Act (1999), Fair Access Foster Care Act (2005), and Fostering Connections to Success and Increasing Adoptions Act (2008).

Each of these acts and related laws was designed to achieve improvements in services offered to children and adolescents involved in some aspect of state child welfare programs. Federal funds were allocated to help train social workers' public child welfare positions. Figure 17.1 illustrates the relationship between the federal and state government in the area of child welfare (Child Welfare Information Gateway, 2009).

As each jurisdiction decides how to implement its child welfare systems, differences among them arise. States such as Wisconsin operate a state-supervised system with services implemented by each county. Typically, child abuse and neglect allegations are reported to the respective county agency responsible for investigating the reports. Wisconsin state rules determine the steps to be taken by the county agency, as shown in Box 17.2.

Illinois, by comparison, operates state-wide agencies with all child protective workers being state employees. However, responsibilities of CPS workers are essentially the same, namely to investigate reports of child abuse or neglect, determine the validity

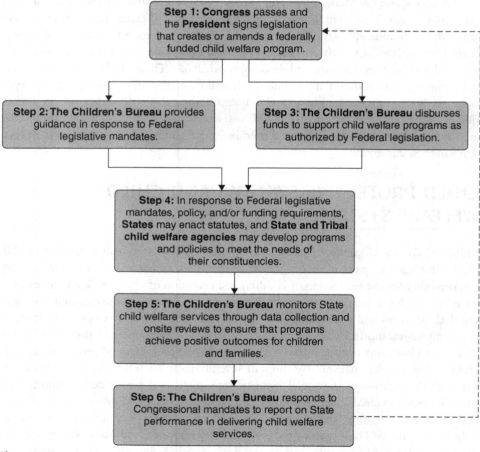

Figure 17.1
How Federal Legislation Impacts Child Welfare Service Delivery
Source: Child Welfare Information Gateway (2009).

Box 17.2   Example of Follow-Up Procedures Used by Child Protective Services Workers

Reports made to law enforcement agencies must be referred to the county Child Protective Services (CPS) agency within 12 hours of receipt. All cases of suspected sexual abuse of a child must be reported by the CPS agency to a law enforcement agency within 12 hours of receipt.

Upon receiving a report, the county agency first determines if the information constitutes an allegation of child maltreatment or threatened harm as defined by Wisconsin law. If the report is found to meet the definition of child maltreatment, the CPS worker in the agency must initiate an initial assessment within 24 hours after receipt of the report and complete it within 60 days. Reports that suggest a child is in current or imminent danger receive an immediate response.

The CPS assessment focus is on assuring child safety and working with the family to determine whether the child and family need services. The assessment must be conducted in accordance with state investigation standards (Wisconsin Department of Children and Families, 2010).

---

of the reports, assess the risk to children associated with various decisions, offer services to the family and child, and decide on the most appropriate disposition of the case. In time, the goal is to protect the child from harm through whatever services and interventions are needed. The type and extent of services and interventions are based on the realization that children who experience abuse and neglect suffer in multiple ways. Therefore, each child protective worker must consider the potential for the child to experience further trauma either by remaining in the home or by being placed out of the home. In other words, any decision made is likely to expose children to some degree of trauma. A child remaining in the home may suffer continued abuse or neglect but out-of-home placements also carry some degree of emotional trauma.

Risk Assessment

Most CPS agencies use a risk assessment system to determine how dangerous it is for children to remain in their homes. Risk assessment considers the seriousness of the injury or trauma suffered by the child and attempts to predict whether further abuse will occur. Some critics challenge the validity of risk assessment systems, questioning both the underlying assumptions and the weighting of various risk factors (Krane & Davies, 2000). They point out that while the factors used are associated with higher risk of abuse (e.g., caregiver unemployment, history of assaultive behavior, or age of child at time of abuse), they are not causative factors, just associations. They also argue that the risk assessment decisions made by practitioners are often guided by intuition rather than research.

In any case, most allegations of child maltreatment are not substantiated, regardless of the system of assessment used (McDaniel, 2005). This is especially true for allegations provided by the general public. Complaints made by mandated reporters—such as social workers, teachers, and health care professionals—are more likely to be substantiated. Possible reasons for this discrepancy may be related to the general public and mandated reporters seeing different aspects of a child's life. What they report often depends upon their view of the situation. Mandated reporters become aware of events that are evident outside of the home environment and, therefore, easier to substantiate, such as physical abuse of a child. Family members and neighbors, by contrast, are more likely to report events that are less obvious and harder to prove, such as sexual abuse. Another explanation offered by McDaniel is that the two groups of reporters are actually making allegations against different types of families. Mandated reporters tend

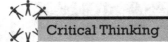

Critical Thinking

Practice Behavior Example: Demonstrate effective oral and written communication in working with individuals, families, groups, organizations, communities, and colleagues.

Critical Thinking Question: How would you explain to a group of lay people why most allegations of child maltreatment are not substantiated? What examples would you use?

to report families characterized by domestic violence or homelessness, or where the caregiver is learning disabled. Having a learning-disabled caregiver makes it four times as likely the family will be reported to CPS. Non-mandated reporters are more likely to report families experiencing domestic violence, with lower incomes, with large numbers of children, and with younger children.

The decision on what is best for the child, to remain in a home with the risk of future abuse or neglect or to be placed in an alternative care, is a difficult one. Attempts at family preservation that emphasized trying to maintain the child in his or her home while providing comprehensive services to the family have had mixed results (Lindsey & Schwartz, 2004). This lack of success helped usher in the 1997 Adoption and Safe Family Act that has the goal of placing children in adoptive homes if family rehabilitation is not likely to succeed. This act and efforts to improve the foster care system helped reduce the number of children in foster care while increasing the number of children placed in adoptive homes. Figure 17.2 shows the impact of these changes beginning in fiscal year (FY) 2002.

As is evident from the report, the number of children in foster care on a specific date dropped from 523,000 in 2002 to 406,000 in 2010, a 22% reduction. The number served (total number who spent time in foster care in a year) dropped from 800,000 to

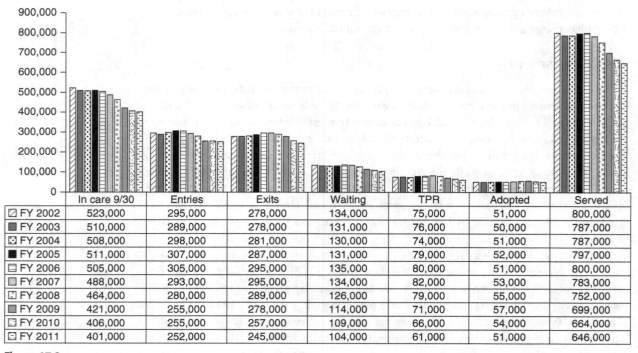

	In care 9/30	Entries	Exits	Waiting	TPR	Adopted	Served
▨ FY 2002	523,000	295,000	278,000	134,000	75,000	51,000	800,000
■ FY 2003	510,000	289,000	278,000	131,000	76,000	50,000	787,000
▩ FY 2004	508,000	298,000	281,000	130,000	74,000	51,000	787,000
■ FY 2005	511,000	307,000	287,000	131,000	79,000	52,000	797,000
▤ FY 2006	505,000	305,000	295,000	135,000	80,000	51,000	800,000
▢ FY 2007	488,000	293,000	295,000	134,000	82,000	53,000	783,000
▨ FY 2008	464,000	280,000	289,000	126,000	79,000	55,000	752,000
■ FY 2009	421,000	255,000	278,000	114,000	71,000	57,000	699,000
▨ FY 2010	406,000	255,000	257,000	109,000	66,000	54,000	664,000
▨ FY 2011	401,000	252,000	245,000	104,000	61,000	51,000	646,000

Figure 17.2

Trends in Foster Care and Adoption, 2002–2011

Notes:

1. Based on data submitted by the states as of June 2012.

2. TPR refers to termination of parental rights. This is done when there appears to be no hope of a child returning to his or her parents and must be approved by a judge.

Source: U.S. Children's Bureau (2012).

664,000, a 17% reduction. The number placed for adoption increased by a few percentage points. However, this small increase in adoptions is misleading. Prior to the law's enactment, only about 25,000 children per year were placed in adoptive homes by public agencies, a number that had almost doubled by 2010. In addition, the backlog of children waiting to be adopted dropped from 134,000 to 109,000 between 2002 and 2010. The number of children entering foster care also declined from a high of 307,000 in 2005 to 255,000 in 2010. These numbers suggest that positive changes are occurring in child welfare area dealing with out-of-home placements.

> Assess your comprehension of Child Abuse Risk Assessment by completing this quiz.

Racial Bias

Some debate exists regarding whether racial bias affects CPS decisions. The Casey Family Programs, a child advocacy organization, argues that racial bias does exist as is evident by the larger number of Black children removed from their homes and other differences in outcomes (Miller & Ward, 2008). Drake et al. (2011) and Bartholet (2009) in their studies argued that Black children are more often removed from their homes because they experience higher rates of serious parental maltreatment. Nam, Meezan, and Danziger (2006) found that after controlling for income and other factors, race was not a risk factor for the general population with whom CPS workers deal. However, among welfare clients, White families were more likely to be involved with CPS than was true for people of color. Lu and colleagues (2004) found that African Americans were the only overrepresented group among almost 4,000 children and adolescents placed in a San Diego County, California, receiving home (temporary care) for suspected maltreatment. Anglos, Asians, and Latinos were underrepresented not only in this group, but in length of stay in foster care and the amount of time before family reunion occurred. Because their examination did not look at socioeconomic background, it did not address whether this variable played a greater role than race. However, their review of prior studies found similar results in the areas of access to services, assessment, treatment, and outcomes.

Trauma in Protective Services

Almost everyone in the protective services system is at risk for a degree of trauma. This includes the abused or neglected child, the child's family, and in many cases the CPS workers themselves. In all three groups, the individuals who experience this trauma can develop posttraumatic stress disorder (PTSD) as well as other less serious reactions. The National Institute of Mental Health (NIMH, 2011) defines PTSD as "an anxiety disorder that some people get after seeing or living through a dangerous event. Anyone can get PTSD at any age. This includes war veterans and survivors of physical and sexual assault, abuse, accidents, disasters, and other serious events. Not everyone with PTSD has been through a dangerous event. Some people get PTSD after a friend or family member experiences danger or is harmed. The sudden, unexpected death of a loved one can also cause PTSD" (p. 1). Those who are traumatized may continue to exhibit PTSD symptoms long after the dangerous event has passed.

PTSD indications typically fall into three categories: reexperiencing symptoms of the event, avoidance symptoms, and

Did You Know?

PTSD is often assessed by mental health professionals when the individual has experienced all the following symptoms for at least a month:

- At least one reexperiencing symptom
- At least three avoidance symptoms
- At least two hyperarousal symptoms
- Symptoms that make it hard to go about daily life, go to school or work, be with friends, and take care of important tasks. (NIMH, 2011)

hyperarousal symptoms. Survivors may experience flashbacks in which they relive the traumatic events and exhibit physical reactions such as sweating, heart palpitations, sleep disturbances, and fear. They may avoid anything that reminds them of the traumatic event, feel despondent or guilty, or forget salient parts of the event. Other individuals startle easily, are quick to anger, and have trouble focusing on the present. In children, PTSD may be manifest by excessive clinging to a caregiver, enuresis, regression in speech, and disruptive or acting out behavior.

It's not clear why some individuals experience PTSD from certain events and others do not. Risk factors increasing the risk for PTSD "living through dangerous events and traumas, having a history of mental illness, getting hurt, seeing people get hurt or killed, feeling horror, helplessness or extreme fear, having little or no support after the event, and dealing with extra stress after the event" (NIMH, 2011, p. 4). Resilience factors that appear to protect against or limit the effects of PTSD include "seeking out support from other people, such as friends and family, finding a support group after a traumatic event, feeling good about one's own actions in the face of danger, having a coping strategy, or a way of getting through the bad event and learning from it, and being able to act and respond effectively despite feeling fear" (p. 4). For CPS personnel, the extent to which an event is perceived as traumatic can vary dramatically from one individual to another. The next section will look at how children, parents, and social workers may be affected by their participation in this area of practice.

Child trauma

Approximately 60% of reports to CPS involve allegations of neglect. Physical abuse is involved in more than 20% of cases and another 11% to 12% fall into the category of sexual abuse (Webb & Harden, 2003). The consequences of this maltreatment for the child can extend to developmental risks, major mental health problems, and substance abuse. In particular, studies of sexually abused children suggest that many of these children will experience the formal symptoms of PTSD (King, 2000).

About 10% to 20% of children are exposed to domestic violence in their homes (Carlson, 2000) and several studies have shown that about one-half of child maltreatment cases also involve cases of domestic violence (English, Edleson, & Herrick, 2005). These children are at risk for a variety of development challenges, whether they hear the violence occurring or see it firsthand. These problems include behavioral, social, and emotional challenges; cognitive and attitudinal problems; and others that can continue into adulthood (Child Welfare Information Gateway, 2009; Cohen, Brown, & Smailes, 2001). The children may exhibit high levels of aggression and hostility, oppositional behavior, and poor relationships with peers and others. Anxiety, fear, withdrawal, and depression are also possible. School performance often suffers and children may lack problem-solving skills. Many children display gender stereotypes and beliefs that emphasize male dominance. As adults, they tend to experience higher levels of depression and are more likely to tolerate and use violence in their relationships (Child Welfare Information Gateway, 2009).

Not all children experience the same degree of trauma from exposure to domestic violence. Protective factors appear to include the seriousness and frequency of the violence, coping skills of the children, older age of the child, and length of time since the abuse occurred. Intelligence and improved self-esteem and positive relationships with siblings, peers, or a supportive adult can also reduce the impact of domestic violence on children. Boys and girls tend to experience domestic violence differently with the former more likely to act out and the latter prone to withdrawal and depression (Child Welfare Information Gateway, 2009).

Parental substance abuse is also a trauma source for children. Children from such homes often engage in denial and secrecy to maintain the aura of a normal home, all the time knowing that things are not right. When a parent is both depressed and a substance abuser, the risk to the child increases (Kroll, 2004). A variety of negative consequences can arise in families where the caregiver is abusing one or more substances. This includes role reversal with the child having to be the caretaker for the parent, breakdowns in family functioning and resultant conflict, attachment losses, increased risk of violence, and distorted reality.

Another source of trauma for children of substance abusers occurs when parents engage in methamphetamine abuse and manufacture of the drug. Meth is a central nervous system stimulant that can be eaten, smoked, injected, or sniffed. Besides the high received from using the drug, it tends to last for hours. It also has a number of side effects including the capability to cause paranoia, hallucinations, and brain damage. Producing the drug (also known as crystal meth, speed, or crank) exposes children to toxic chemicals, fumes, and potential explosions (Hohman, Oliver, & Wright, 2004). Sometimes children come to the CPS's attention after law enforcement has raided the parents' home. Among parents, abuse of the drugs can lead to child neglect including malnutrition and hygiene problems. These parents are often charged with allowing the child to be placed in a dangerous environment (Stalcup, 2000; Wright, 2000).

Children exposed to the drug in utero are often characterized by premature birth and low birth weights. Congenital abnormalities and cerebral strokes may occur. Exposure to the drug during its manufacture can result in burning in the eyes, headaches, and dizziness. The drug's ingredients can lead to kidney and liver problems, some cancers, and neurologic damage. Meth ingested may cause seizures, heart arrhythmias, and death in children (Hohman et al., 2004).

From time to time, studies have been conducted to assess the impact of a child losing a social worker when under the care of protective services. Perhaps the best that can be said is that—at least for some children—the loss of that helper can be damaging. What is also evident is that a portion of the children in the CPS system should not be there while others who should be receiving help are not. Both are at risk (Waldfogel, 2000).

Of course, the ultimate trauma for children is death at the hands of their caregivers. On a regular basis, there are reports of a child being killed by his or her parents or other caregivers despite CPS involvement. Sometimes, foster parents murder the child. These events typically spark calls for investigation and attempts to blame CPS workers or the child welfare system (Lachman & Bernard, 2006). Sometimes all parties involved in the CPS system benefit from these investigations or from changes brought about as a result of court-ordered remediation. Several states have been placed under court order to improve the quality of the services they deliver and often results in increased resources for CPS. It is unclear whether these changes continue after the courts cease their involvement.

Parental trauma

There is also trauma for parents who are reported and investigated for alleged child abuse. Considering the large percentage of such cases found to be unsubstantiated, the potential harm to the family is obvious. Like people unfairly charged with a crime, parents who have not maltreated their child are likely to experience a host of emotions including fear, anger, sadness, and resentment. For those for whom a report is substantiated, there is also likely to be a mixture of anger and guilt about the situation. A parent might have survived domestic violence to which a child was exposed and still be held culpable for not protecting the child from this experience. Many parents struggling with substance abuse or mental health problems provide inadequate care for their children, resulting in their involvement with CPS. In both these types of cases, individuals already struggling with a serious condition may find increased trauma as a result of a CPS investigation. Ironically, it is parents or families with poor support networks that are more likely to experience problems in parenting and more likely to become involved with CPS (Nam et al., 2006).

Mothers are often traumatized in cases of domestic violence. When a mother is a survivor of domestic violence, it is assumed that the child is suffering as well. This often places an unfair burden on the woman who is accused of failing to protect the child from witnessing the violence. Even cases where the woman is single and trying to leave the home she shares with the batterer would have negative consequences. The woman may fear that leaving would place her and her children at greater danger because she may lack family and financial support. New immigrants may fear reporting abuse might result in being deported or losing custody of the children (Friend, Shlonsky, & Lambert, 2008). To the woman, this may seem like being victimized twice: once by the batterer and again by the system.

Critical Thinking

Practice Behavior Example: Demonstrate effective oral and written communication in working with individuals, families, groups, organizations, communities, and colleagues.

Critical Thinking Question: How would you explain to a friend who says she does not understand why battered women continue to remain in an abusive relationship? What reasons would you give her?

For women who have been battered and have their problems, such as drug abuse or other mental health concerns, an additional risk exists. Because of the time it takes to locate, be admitted to, and complete a substance abuse program, a woman risks losing her parental rights. The Adoptions and Safe Family Act of 1997 requires states to ask a court to terminate the parents' rights and locate an adoptive family for any child who has been in foster care for 15 out of the last 22 months. This relatively short period sometimes places unrealistic pressure on domestic violence survivors struggling with their challenges (Friend et al., 2008). The outcome in these situations can be to "disempower female victims and, at worst, tend to blame the victim" (p. 692).

Worker trauma

It is well documented that working in CPS is a stressful experience for many social workers (Institute for the Advancement of Social Work Research, 2005). The challenge of dealing with abused children, abusing parents, lack of resources, and bureaucratic policies often taxes practitioners' emotional strength producing "compassion fatigue" and potentially PTSD (Figley, 1995). For those who do the initial child abuse or neglect investigations, parental reactions are also likely to be hostile or defensive. Removing a child from a home, even a home where serious child abuse has occurred, is sometimes hard for the social worker. The need to separate children in the same family for placement in different foster homes can be difficult. The case of Guilliarmo, which follows, is an example of how this decision affected one social worker.

Guilliarmo's Remorse

Guilliarmo was a state social worker charged with finding foster home placements for children needing this resource. He was notified by a protective service worker that the Watkins boys, ages four and six, needed a foster home placement within a week. Their mother had been sentenced to prison for check fraud and their father was already in prison for a prior offense.

The family had no relatives that the agency could locate and placement with a foster family was indicated. For Guilliarmo, the timing could not be worse. The number of foster homes available was down as more families had both spouses working outside the home. Moreover, most families were willing to accept a single child, but not two. To make matters worse, Guilliarmo had two sons close in age to the Watkins boys. The thought of having to separate the Watkins boys was eating at him in a way that past placements had not. Despite trying to persuade several foster parents to take both boys, Guilliarmo was forced to place the Watkins boys in separate foster homes. Following the placement, he shared with his supervisor that this had been the hardest decision he had to make in all his years of placing children. It haunted him for months until the agency finally located relatives who agreed to have both boys placed with them.

Another source of stress for workers is created by high workloads and the difficulty of making decisions in the absence of certainty. Benbenishty, Osmo, and Gold (2003) note that in most cases "child welfare decisions are the result of case by case deliberations, based on vague definitions and the personal discretion of professionals who are entrusted with these decisions" (p. 138). A given event in the life of a child may be interpreted as a serious indication of abuse or a one-time aberration, and it is a decision that the social worker must make, often without an adequate history that might better inform. Information can be ambiguous and/or insufficient or too much information can overwhelm the decision-maker. Judgment calls by professionals must be made in grey areas and other professionals looking at the same situation may come to significantly different conclusions (Munro, 2005). When a child has been killed or seriously harmed, it is much easier for someone else to look at the same set of facts and conclude the practitioner missed some vital signs or just didn't put the facts together in arriving at a decision. These are stressful conditions that are too common to CPS workers and are exacerbated when the worker's decision results in harm to the child. In such cases, in addition to the emotional trauma experienced by the worker is the added risk of being found negligent in carrying out one's duties in a way that caused or contributed to the tragic outcome.

According to Munro (2005), 75% of child welfare deaths in England have been attributed to errors made by the professional handling the case. One of the possible reasons for these findings is that after a child dies, most investigations focus on the worker's actions and pay less attention to the role of the organization employing the worker. Questions that are not asked often include "Did the worker have adequate training for this kind of case?" "Was adequate supervision and support available to the worker handling a difficult case?" and "Were resources available that would have resulted in a different outcome had they been utilized?" Once a worker has been identified as having made a mistake, the tendency is to focus on this and end the inquiry. The consequences of these investigations can demoralize CPS staff and reduce the attractiveness of this line of work.

Several studies have looked at factors leading to burnout and trauma for child welfare workers (Brohl, 2004; Nissly, Mor Barak, & Levin, 2005). These include problems with supervision and agency management, safety concerns, lack of appropriate coping skills, absence of adequate training, and work schedules. Symptoms experienced by workers who are burning out include depression, headaches, anxiety, abuse of drugs or alcohol, and changes in interpersonal behaviors. The result is that turnover rates in many areas are as high as 90% (Child Welfare Information Gateway, 2011).

Sometimes there are critical differences of opinion among workers and supervisors in the same agency that make it difficult to do the job. For example, some staff may be what Testa, Cohen, and Smith (2003) called *adoption hawks*, who are dedicated to freeing children for adoption whenever possible, while *guardianship doves* do whatever is necessary to maintain family integrity. This clash in philosophy places workers in a position where others are continually questioning their decisions.

CHILD ABUSE: OUT-OF-HOME PLACEMENTS

Several hundred thousand children live in out-of-home placements at any given time as the result of abuse or neglect at home, parental incapacity, or other needs of the child. Although foster care is considered a short-term resource, almost half of the children who enter placement will be there for a year or more. According to Pecora et al. (2006), the average out-of-home stay is two years. While the goal is the protection of the child, out-of-home placements carry a variety of risks for children.

When out-of-home placements are needed, it is common for foster children to show emotional or behavioral challenges or both (Stone, 2007). They also experience behavior problems in school and higher suspension rates than children living in their homes. In addition, Aarons and colleagues (2008) found that children who had experienced multiple placements and entered the first placement at an older age were at risk for serious substance abuse problems. Jonson-Reid and Barth (2003) found similar findings with respect to future involvement in criminal and delinquent behavior. Silver et al. (1999) reported that even infants and preschool children placed in foster care had higher risks for language, cognitive, and motor development problems. Whether out-of-home placement is the cause of the academic problems experienced by these children has been debated. Fantuzzo and Perlman (2007) found that children in out-of-home placements were at risk for problems in both literacy and science even when birth risks and demographics were taken into account.

At the same time, there is evidence that some children's school difficulties may have existed at the time of placement in foster care (Blome, 1997; Evans, 2001). These challenges are often related both to child and family characteristics and to organizational and policy factors. Many of the factors that contribute to a child being abused or neglected are also associated with poor educational performance. This makes it more difficult to identify whether problems in academic performance are the result of prior maltreatment or the result of out-of-home placement in the child welfare system. However, multiple studies have shown that being maltreated, along with factors such as poverty and homelessness, tend to be reflected in lower math and reading scores, higher rates of absenteeism, and lower grades overall (Stone, 2007). An interesting distinction is that neglect tends to be more associated with poor academic performance while abuse tends to be associated with behavioral problems in the school environment. This does not mean that the abused child is not affected academically. In fact, being currently abused is associated with at least a one-point drop in grade point average. Likewise, children who are both abused and neglected tend to drop out of school more frequently. The younger children are at the time abuse or neglect begins, the more likely they will experience behavioral problems and fail a grade. Fantuzzo and Perlman (2007) conclude that out-of-home placement may not be the actual risk factor but rather the venue in which the effects of prior neglect, abuse, and homelessness are played out.

Children in foster care are more likely to be placed in special education classrooms than children not in care. Although a majority of foster kids are labeled learning disabled, they are more likely to be placed in special education classrooms because they are identified with mental retardation or emotional problems, rather than having learning or physical disabilities (Smithgall, Gladden, Howard, George, & Courtney, 2004). The more restrictive the out-of-home placement (kinship care versus foster care versus group home versus residential treatment center), the more likely the child will be deemed emotionally disturbed (Parrish et al., 2001). This suggests the importance of keeping children in less-restrictive venues such as kinship or foster care if at all possible.

A systemic aspect of out-of-home placements concerns the intersection between the school and the child protection agency. Common complaints involve clashes between the school's development of the child's Individualized Education Plan (IEP), which can raise issues of family privacy and confidentiality, and whether anyone is serving in the role of educational advocate for the child (Choice et al., 2001). A school may be reluctant to invest significant time with a foster child, realizing that such children are highly mobile. In addition, foster children in many cities tend to be located in some of the poorest school in the community, which does not bode well for their academic achievement (Smithgall et al., 2004).

Another systemic factor is related to the child welfare system itself. Because the emphasis of the system is on child protection, there is often less of a focus on the child's educational performance. About one-third of foster children experience more than one placement and this is also a factor contributing to academic difficulties (Smithgall et al., 2004; Wulczyn, Kogan, & Harden, 2003). Multiple placements in foster care usually mean new school and interference with attendance, a well-documented factor in school achievement (Burley & Halpern, 2001). Without a priority on education, these children are less likely to be referred by social workers or others for academic help.

Resilience

It is important not to overstate the potential negative consequences of out-of-home placements. Although the risks of dropping out of school are high for children in foster care, alumni of the foster care system tend to complete high school at about the same rate as other students (Pecora et al., 2006). This suggests a degree of resilience in the face of rather daunting life experiences. While former foster children are more likely to complete high school through a GED (General Educational Development) test, this is still a positive finding. However, relatively few go on to complete college or other postsecondary training despite having similar aspirations for future education (Blome, 1997). Unfortunately, the failure to complete additional training or education limits future economic prospects raising the risk of poverty, lack of health insurance, and homelessness. Foster care alumni are more likely to experience unemployment and to receive public assistance when compared to the general population (Pecora et al., 2006). When attempts are made to control for family background, however, some adult outcomes for foster children are quite positive (Buehler, Orme, Post, & Patterson, 2000). Improvements in physical and mental health have been noted by several researchers (Pecora et al., 2006). In addition, adolescents placed in foster homes appear four times less likely to engage in juvenile delinquency than children remaining in their home (Lemmon, 2006). This finding is consistent with Widom's (1991) and DeGue and Widom's (2009) studies results showing a salutary effect of foster care on future delinquency and criminal behavior, particularly for males.

In addition, many children display protective factors that allow them to overcome the negative experiences in their lives and succeed (Widom, 1991). For example, when compared with the nonsexually abused control group, girls who have been sexually abused were just as likely to have plans for post–high school education and be optimistic and future oriented. Further, they were no more likely to engage in substance abuse or delinquent behavior than their nonsexually abused counterparts (Edmond, Auslander, Elze, McMillen, & Thompson, 2002). This is remarkable given that the sexually abused

The risk that a foster child with serious problems will end up in multiple foster homes is increased by the following percentages:

Problem	Increased Likelihood of Multiple Placements
Major health problems	60%
Minor health problems	450%
Mental health problems	200%
History of delinquency	200%
History of being sexually abused	200%
Multiple caseworkers	150%

Source: Eggertsen (2008).

girls were more likely to experience mental health challenges and had encountered more physical abuse and neglect than the comparison group.

Multiple Placements

We have noted a significant portion of children end up being placed in more than one foster home. The reasons behind multiple placements for so many children have been explored by Eggertsen (2008) and others. One factor associated with multiple placements is the child's age. Older children are more likely than younger children to be placed in more than one home. Likewise, children with serious health challenges were much more likely to be placed multiple times. Even minor health difficulties often lead to replacement of the child, increasing four-fold the likelihood of three or more placements (p. 79). Those with mental health difficulties were twice as likely to be placed three or more times.

The consequences of repeated out-of-home placements are sometimes quite serious. This includes problems in brain growth and mental development, as well as emotional problems (American Academy of Pediatrics, 2000; Hochman, Hochman, & Miller, 2004). Other potential problems related to multiple placements include school difficulty and teen pregnancy, among others (Cook, 1994; Penzerro & Lein, 1995; Unrau, Fong, & Rawls, 2012). DeGue and Widom (2009) also found that youth who had four or more placements were significantly more likely to be arrested as adults. They also noted that 70% of those with four or more placements were arrested as adults and 60% were arrested both as a juvenile and as an adult. Forty percent were arrested for crimes of violence.

Kinship Placements

One alternative to out-of-home placement with strangers is placing children with relatives. One reason for the increasing use of such kinship placements is to lessen placement trauma for the child. Unfortunately, kinship placements often result in children receiving less-frequent services such as mental health or substance abuse counseling. Children placed with kin, however, experience fewer school transfers for behavioral problems, better school attendance, and fewer disciplinary events than children in foster or group care (Conger & Rebeck, 2001; Shore, Kelly, Le Prohn, & Keller, 2002). Children exposed to drugs in their original home and later placed in kinship foster homes performed less well in school than children without such exposure. Kinship placements also tend to have caregivers who are less emotionally involved with the children, more often unemployed, and experience higher levels of aggravation in their lives (Kortnenkamp & Ehrle, 2001).

CHILD ABUSE: TRANSITION TO ADULT LIVING PROGRAMS

Foster children who age out or move into independent living situations do not always enjoy the transition or subsequent new life. Instead, they have a higher risk of homelessness and other difficulties. Past studies have found that anywhere from 9% to 39% of the adult homeless population have previously been in out-of-home placements (Park, Metraux, & Culhane, 2005). The authors found that a prior history of out-of-home care is associated with an extra 25 days spent in homeless shelters. White et al. (2011) found about 20% of former foster kids had experienced homelessness after leaving foster care. These results are consistent with those of Pecora et al. (2006), suggesting that outcomes for foster care alumni are mixed at best.

Southerland, Casanueva, and Ringeisen (2009) found that young adults previously involved with the child welfare system face multiple risks at a time when they are challenged economically, raising children, sustaining a marriage, and dealing with criminal justice, substance abuse, and mental health issues. For example, these young adults are almost twice as likely to show risk of mental health problems as the general population (45.4% compared to 26.2%). The depression rate is about three times as high among those transitioning from child welfare services, and the rate of economic hardship is double. Transitioning youth are twice as likely to be married and four times as likely to be raising one or more children. In addition, this group is four times as likely to have been arrested in the year prior to the survey. Clearly, youth from the child welfare system are facing greater risks than is true for comparable youth without a history of out-of-home placement.

In addition, a portion of older teenagers in foster care end the placement by running away (Jonson-Reid & Barth, 2003). Unfortunately, it is not always possible to identify the factors that led the adolescent to abscond. In some cases, it may be to avoid a living situation that is viewed as negative, due to emotional problems, or some combination of these and other reasons.

Another factor affecting transition is the type of placement in which the adolescent resides just prior to emancipation. Mech, Ludy-Dobson, and Hulsemann (1994) found that adolescents in group home or residential treatment facilities were less ready to enter independent living than adolescents in foster care placements. A possible explanation is that the presence of supportive adults in foster homes helps ease the transition.

Posttraumatic stress symptoms have repeatedly been cited as common in survivors of child maltreatment (Clemmons, Walsh, DiLillo, & Messman-Moore, 2007). An estimated quarter of maltreated children suffers multiple kinds of maltreatment and tends to have even greater difficulties than those who experienced only one type (Higgins & McCabe, 2000). As an adult, these individuals are likely to suffer from a variety of psychiatric symptoms, lower self-esteem, sexual difficulties, and heightened anger. Victimization as an adult is also a risk factor for these children (Messman & Long, 1996). Children who were more frequently abused or on whom the perpetrator used physical force are at greatest risk. This suggests the importance of learning more about the actual experiences of an abuse/neglect survivor rather than simply noting that he or she has been maltreated. Assessment must take into account not only the occurrence but the type, severity, and frequency of maltreatment.

Many women survivors of childhood sexual abuse show signs of dissociation, whereby the feelings, memories, and thoughts associated with the abuse are compartmentalized. Unable to exert any sense of control over the traumatic event leads to an effort to at least control the associated emotions and perceptions. Unfortunately, this defense mechanism can result in further episodes of abuse as the individual shuts out the cues that might warn them of danger (Hetzel & McCanne, 2005). In addition, it can lead to PTSD symptomatology.

Survivors of child sexual abuse often experience difficulties in parenting—poor generational boundary setting, inconsistent or harsh discipline, and failure to adequately supervise and monitor (Martsolf & Draucker, 2008).

Many survivors view their lives as living out a legacy of family abuse and bad times that transcends their generation. The legacy includes abuse, substance abuse, family conflict, mental illness, and domestic violence, many of which the survivor perceives as normal. The behaviors of parents and other adults are often seen as reinforcing this dysfunctional perspective by denying, minimizing, or ignoring the abuse (Martsolf & Draucker, 2008). The result is that many feel like their adult lives are scripted from their past experiences. Even those who outwardly escape this scripting often have internal thoughts and feelings that perpetuate the legacy. Some survivors engage in the same problematic behaviors with their families, recreating the legacy for their children. One interesting finding by Wilson and Widom (2009) is that a legacy of child abuse is more predictive of adult substance abuse for women than for men, although men still experienced a range of problem behaviors, including delinquency, acting out in school, and adult criminal behavior.

Resilience

Some survivors are successful in escaping the influence of their past traumas. This may occur when individuals reject the behaviors, thoughts, and feelings associated with the legacy and are determined to create a new life free of mistreatment. Some are helped by professionals and others are assisted by friends or colleagues who challenge the family

A rape counselor works with a survivor.

legacy as abnormal and unacceptable (Martsolf & Draucker, 2008). Some of these adults decide that they will not saddle their children with the dysfunctions of the past and work hard to create a different, more positive life. Achieving this goal often involves some backsliding and cyclical behaviors as the survivor attempts to move in the desired direction, a pattern not uncommon among individuals seeking to adopt life changes.

ADULT SURVIVORS OF TRAUMA: RAPE, STALKING, AND ROBBERY

The U.S. Department of Justice (2002) reports that in an average year there are about 141,000 completed rapes, 109,000 attempted rapes, and over 152,000 attempted and completed sexual assaults (p. 1). Other statistics suggest that between 13% and 26% of individuals in the United States report being raped each year (Elliott, Mok, & Briere, 2004). Of this number, about 90% of the victims are female. Unfortunately, an estimated 60% of rapes and 75% of sexual assaults are never reported to the police. Failure to report occurs even though more than one-half of the survivors were physically injured in the course of an assault or rape.

Typical reasons for not reporting sexual assault or rape to the police include a belief that the incident is a personal matter, a fear of reprisal, concerns about police bias, or a wish to protect the offender. Close relationships between the offender and the victim also tend to be significantly underreported (U.S. Department of Justice, 2002). For example, some rape victims refuse to acknowledge their experience as rape because it occurred in the context of a relationship (date rape) and they may continue to have a relationship with the perpetrator following the event.

We have previously noted that being physically and sexually abused as children is a risk factor for similar subsequent abuse as an adult (Hetzel & McCanne, 2005). For at least some survivors, the subsequent rape in adulthood often lead to recalling earlier events long after they vanished from one's thoughts (Clancy & McNally, 2005/2006). Those who experience child abuse and adult sexual assault are doubly affected with significant disruption to their sex lives in areas related to sexual desire, emotional detachment, guilt and anxiety, pleasuring, intercourse, and orgasmic difficulties (Bartoi & Kinder, 1998; Mackey et al., 1991).

Adult rape survivors experience a range of consequences and outcomes that create problems in multiple areas of their lives (McMullin, Wirth, & White, 2007). Nadelson, Notman, Zackson, and Gornick (1982) found that more than 50% of rape survivors reported various sexual difficulties in their current relationships and 25% avoided sexual relationships completely. Other studies have identified common themes in the adult relationships of these survivors including communication difficulties, sexual fears, dissatisfaction, and dysfunction. A lack of commitment and emotional support in the relationship was also reported (Miller, Williams, & Bernstein, 1982). Similar negative outcomes have been observed in male victims of sexual assault (Turchik, 2012).

A common consequence of rape is loss of one's sense of control over aspects of life and feelings of powerlessness with respect to issues around reproduction, birth control, and related topics (Wyatt, Guthrie, & Notgrass, 1992). As in the case of child sexual assault, PTSD occurs in about 50% of rape victims. McCauley, Amstadter, Danielson, and Ruggiero (2009) found that being raped, or otherwise suffering from PTSD, increased the likelihood that the survivor would begin to use prescription drugs for nonmedical purposes. This was particularly true when the rape survivor had been intoxicated during the event, as a result of either his or her actions or through the agency of the perpetrator.

Sexual assault survivors appear to suffer more health problems and require greater health care resources than is true for the general public. The frequency of health concerns is positively correlated with the severity of the survivor's PTSD (Zoellner, Goodwin, & Foa, 2000). Women who refuse to acknowledge that rape occurred appear to experience a lower degree of health complaints than is true for those who reported the event (Conoscenti & McNally, 2005). Refusing to interpret an event as rape may be a protective factor that somewhat lessens the potential for developing PTSD. At the same time, this refusal may lead the survivor into future instances of sexual abuse and revictimization.

While most research on rape deals with female victims, about 3% to 5% of males are raped or sexually assaulted, although some studies report rates as high as 20% (Tewksbury, 2007). Like rapes of females, most male rape goes unreported, with even fewer men than women willing to report. There is some evidence that gay men are the most likely males to be sexually assaulted, with the perpetrator engaging in the equivalent of date rape (Keane, Young, Boyle, & Curry, 1995). Some studies have shown that being victimized as a child increases the likelihood that a male will be assaulted as an adult. Perhaps because male rape is so seldom reported, many rape crisis agencies are not set up to provide services to men (Washington, 1999).

When men are victimized, violence is often more severe than in the case of women (McLean, Balding, & White, 2005). However, unless seriously injured, most men do not seek medical treatment. Interestingly, it is men who are raped in their communities who suffer the most violence compared to men who are sexually assaulted in correctional settings. As with female rape survivors, men who have been raped experience a variety of symptoms—physical responses as well as substance abuse, depression, and anxiety disorders. They also show evidence of a sense of stigma and embarrassment. Other reactions include self-mutilation, anger, self-blame, sleep disturbances, and in some cases, suicide ideation (Tewksbury, 2007). In some cases, males may display an aura of composure and calm to cope with the traumatic event, while others withdraw from their social environment and contacts (Walker, Archer, & Davies, 2005). PTSD is also a common reaction to sexual assault, while the event causes some survivors to question their real sexual orientation. Still others will report disturbances in their subsequent sexual lives, including impotence (Tewksbury, 2007).

Community Reactions to Rape

If the challenges associated with surviving rape were not sufficiently traumatizing, community reactions may present an additional hurt for the survivor increasing the underreporting of rape. For example, Buddie and Miller (2001) studied the perceptions and beliefs of college students about rape victims, finding that stereotypical attitudes and myths about rape and its victims tend to fall into three categories: victim masochism, victim precipitation, and victim fabrication. With victim masochism, there is an attitude that the victim liked or wanted the experience of being raped. In victim precipitation, there is a belief that the victim somehow caused the attack by things such as dressing provocatively, getting drunk, or locating oneself in risky venues.

Victim fabrication suggests that the victim has exaggerated or is not telling the truth about the event (Koss et al., 1994). Past research suggests that males are more likely than women to accept the accuracy of rape myths and this may play a role in why so many rape cases never get to court (Buddie & Miller, 2001). While one would suspect that adolescent males who were raped would be viewed more sympathetically than adult male victims, this is not the case. Other males, in particular, are more likely to blame the male victim than they would a female victim (Davies, Rogers, & Whitelegg, 2009). Gay adolescents who are raped receive more blame than heterosexual males who are raped. Those who actively resist the rape are accorded more understanding.

The reactions of others to hearing details about a rape or sexual assault are often a mixture of adherence to rape myths, along with a degree of sensitivity to the harm that the victim has and will experience. The simultaneous holding of conflicting views about rape and its victims was one of the findings of Buddie and Miller (2001) and is consistent with other situations involving vulnerable or at-risk populations. It is also possible that an individual will hold one set of myths prior to the rape and a more supportive or empathic view after the fact. A similar set of mixed attitudes has often been seen with respect to sexism—in which the male may have coexisting beliefs that women are asking to be treated in some special manner while also feeling that women need to be protected (Glick, Diebold, Bailey-Werner, & Zhu, 1997).

A significant influence on how survivors deal with the trauma they have experienced is based on the behavior of various environmental institutions with which they interact. These include three key systems. The first is the legal system that comprises law enforcement, the prosecutor, and court and its officers and corrections. The second is the medical system, providing care and evaluation services needed by many sexual assault survivors. Included are paramedics, nursing and medical personnel, and hospitals or clinics. The final system includes the mental health institutions used by, or available to, the survivor. How survivors are treated by these different systems often shape how they adapt to the horrific event. If, for example, the victim is rendered powerless or perceived as at fault by the reactions of individuals or systems, this is a tremendous hurt inflicted on someone already feeling vulnerable and/or damaged. These contacts can increase one's guilt and shame, and result in revictimization. Similarly, a failure by any system to provide services needed by the survivor can exacerbate the situation. Campbell (1998) notes that even when the offender is caught and charged with rape, the ultimate outcome may appear negative to the survivor. For example, it is possible and often likely for a charge to be plea-bargained down to a less serious offense, with little or no serious consequences for the offender. This can seem like, and is, another form of victimization. In many states, even if the judge imposes a given sentence, the corrections system may free an offender early based on the person's good behavior or even prison overcrowding. Again, this feels like victimization for someone whose life was itself violated.

Medical services needed by the survivor can include treatment for the rape itself, injuries that occurred during the assault, and testing for pregnancy and sexually transmitted diseases (STDs). Inconsistent interventions can and do occur between different medical organizations, with some providing thorough treatment and accurate information while others neglect the survivor's fundamental needs.

Mental health services typically involve treatment to cope with the trauma associated with sexual assault, information and counseling for the survivor, friends, and relatives affected by the event, and interventions to help couples deal with the aftermath of rape. As with other community systems, some mental health providers neglect to provide information or offer counseling to those needing it. The quality and availability of services in a community may also impact directly on how well the survivor's needs are met (Campbell, 1998). In the worst of all worlds, some survivors felt betrayed or underserved by legal, medical, and mental health systems. In other situations, only survivors who fall into a narrow category receive services that fit their situations. The most promising scenario involves a victim who was raped by a stranger who using a weapon inflicted additional injury on the person. Such survivors must be suffering in some obvious way, receptive to help, and living in a community with an adequate array of services for rape victims. Of all the systems most likely to fail the survivor, it is the legal system that is most often cited (Campbell, 2005).

Resilience

Almost one-half of adult sexual abuse survivors appear to exhibit no psychopathology after the event (New et al., 2009). Their resiliency appears to be related to the capacity to regulate their emotional responses to negative events, a protective factor in their lives. In particular, they exhibit low depression rates, positive attitudes and emotions, and higher levels of optimism about the future. They also appear to have the capacity to focus deeply on negative emotional responses and use cognitive and other brain areas to deal with them.

Rape and Victim Advocates

Wasco and Campbell (2002) found that it is not only the rape survivors but also those who serve as victim advocates are traumatized. Sometimes referred to as *vicarious traumatization*, it encompasses intrapsychic reactions resulting from indirect exposure to rape. The reactions are often emotional in nature, reflecting anger and fear directed toward others. What is interesting is that while feeling anger is often nonproductive, it appears to be a positive characteristic for rape victim advocates. By expressing their anger about the rape and the shortcomings of community resources for the survivor, they simultaneously motivate themselves and others to improve service quality. An interesting side benefit is that the advocate's anger appears to help their clients translate their sadness into anger. On the negative side, fear engendered vicariously often interferes with other areas of the advocate's life. Both male and female advocates may become more fearful about their or their children's well-being. In addition, female advocates may develop a fear of men. For many advocates, this fear informs their self-protective behaviors and helps them avoid situations that pose unnecessary danger to themselves or others (Astin, 1997).

Stalking

In addition to rape, other forms of violence can produce trauma for the individual in the form of fear, anxiety, alarm, and distress. This includes being robbed, physically assaulted, or even stalked. In each situation, reporting the event to police is more likely than in cases of rape. In regard to stalking, there are also gender differences with about 50% of women who are stalked reporting it compared to 36% of men (Wigman, 2009). Men are also about half as likely as women to seek a restraining order against the stalker. Interestingly, men are likely to be victimized by stalkers who are convinced that the man loves them while women are stalked by men who are obsessed with them. Often, men who are stalked and report it are taken less seriously than women victims. This may be related to beliefs that a man should be able to manage such situations (especially if the stalker is a woman). However, both male and female stalkers are equally likely to threaten victims, use violence, and damage property (Purcell, Pathé, & Mullen, 2001). Regardless of the stalker's gender, it is not uncommon for the survivor to experience PTSD (Purcell, Pathé, & Mullen, 2005).

Determining the actual incidence of stalking is difficult due to several factors including questions of definition, underreporting, and the population being sampled. Some studies show that less than one-half percent of males and females in the general population are stalked while research among college students shows 31% of females and 17% of males have been stalked (Fremouw, Westrup, & Pennypacker, 1997).

It is stalkers who are former intimates constitute the greatest danger to the victim, although it is fear of stalking by strangers that engenders the most anxiety (Palarea, Zona, Lane, & Langhinrichsen-Rohling, 1999). The omnipresence of computers and smart phones has produced cyberstalking, which can have as serious consequences for the victim as being physically stalked or harassed.

Assess your comprehension of Sexual Assault Survivors by completing this quiz.

Robbery

Experiencing a robbery is a distressing event for most individuals, especially so if the perpetrator was armed. In these situations, survivors are more likely to suffer psychologically and report headaches, chronic anxiety, and sleep disturbances. Most also fear a repetition of the event, are less likely to trust other people, and may become both depressed and aggressive (Harrison & Kinner, 1998). Duration of these symptoms can be as long as six months for some victims. Those victims with a prior history of trauma, mental health challenges, or substance abuse issues tend to have the most difficulty after a robbery. In addition, the degree of severity of the incident and the degree of social support are both predictors of how the victim will react. As might be expected, severe incidents increase the level of the psychological reaction while post-event support has the opposite effect (Kaniasty & Norris, 1992). Feeling that one is especially vulnerable to victimhood is more troubling than viewing oneself objectively and recognizing that anyone can be victimized. Likewise, survivors who avoid thinking about the robbery are more likely to develop symptoms of PTSD and increased distress levels (Creamer, Burgess, Buckingham, & Pattison, 1990).

DOMESTIC VIOLENCE: FAMILIES, SURVIVORS, AND PERPETRATORS

We have talked earlier in this chapter about domestic violence, particularly as it affects children involved with CPS. As is obvious, it is not just children who are victimized by domestic violence. Every family member is affected in one way or another and we will now look at each component: family, victims, and perpetrators. There is substantial evidence that both men and women are victims of domestic violence, and sexual orientation, age, and socioeconomic level are not barriers to its consequences (Brown, 2007; Renzetti & Miley, 1996). Both men and women engage in violence against spouses, strangers, children, parents, partners, colleagues, siblings, and family members with a disability (Fitzroy, 2001). While the rate of fatal and nonfatal domestic violence incidents has been declining since 1993, there are still over 600,000 women and men who experience intimate partner violence each year (Bureau of Justice Statistics, 2012).

Families and Domestic Violence

Domestic violence is often separated into two types of abuse: severe and minor (Allen-Collinson, 2009). Minor abuse tends to include behaviors such as slapping, grabbing, shoving, or pushing another person. It is defined a minor because it is unlikely to cause victims serious physical harm. Severe abuse includes any behaviors that are likely to cause serious injury or pain. This would include obvious acts such as using a gun or knife, choking, using an object to inflict injury, kicking, and beating someone with fists. In reality, both types can be perceived as painful to the victim. Of course, this is only a small subset of actions that can cause pain to the individual and does not mention spousal or partner rape, which are examples of domestic violence.

Violence in the family is often thought to be a problem for younger families, occurring either prior to the arrival of children or during the child-raising years. This picture, however, ignores the amount of violence involving women 50 years and over. Domestic violence may occur long after children have departed. For example, the violence may be a continuation of long-standing abuse, evolve late in the relationship, or occur during the course of new relationships. Perpetrators may be spouses, partners, children, or others in a position to harm the survivor. The array of abusive tactics employed is similar to those for other age groups but may also include neglect. At the same time, the survivor may lack opportunities to leave being totally dependent on the abuser and/or lacking the social networks available to younger victims. Loss of family and friends through death can remove one effective resource for the older adult (Leisey, Kupstas, & Cooper, 2009).

Domestic violence tends to follow a predictable pattern beginning with a period of tension building, followed by outright abuse, and ending in expressions of sorrow for one's actions. This pattern can lull victims into thinking that things will improve and that the perpetrator really loves them. The incidence of domestic violence tends to vary from one group to another. For example, Field and Caetano (2004) found that the rate of interpersonal violence is 1.5 to 2.4 times higher for Latinos in the United States than for European Americans. Others have found a disproportionate incidence of domestic violence in urban dwellers, unmarried younger couples, and ethnic/racial minorities (Bureau of Justice Statistics, 2012; Field & Caetano, 2004). Figure 17.3 shows the relative rates of interpersonal violence from 2001 to 2005.

Survivors and Domestic Violence

The importance of listening to battered women's voices has been underscored by Goodman and Epstein (2007), who point out that too often professionals do not hear clearly the needs

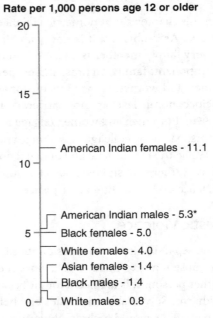

Figure 17.3
Average Annual Nonfatal Intimate Partner Victimization Rate, by Race and Gender, 2001–2005
Source: Bureau of Justice Statistics (2012).

of those who have survived domestic violence. Historically, too much emphasis has been placed on individual psychopathology at the expense of approaches that reflect awareness of how political, external, and systemic forces influence the life experiences of survivors of domestic violence. For example, domestic violence affects women from all socioeconomic strata but the needs of each may be different. Some women encounter significant external obstacles in their contacts with medical and legal systems and these are not ameliorated by mental health services designed to deal with only survivor's PTSD symptoms.

Another facet of domestic violence is the tendency for victims to accept that the violence directed against them is normal or typical of how couples interact. Repeated violence interspersed with expressions of loving and remorseful behavior sometimes convinces the victim to remain with the violent partner and try to work things out.

During the process of being abused, many victims engage in behaviors designed to stop the assault. For example, they may scream, try to evade the attacker, cry, attempt to talk their way out of the situation, and sometimes fight back. These strategies may not be effective and, in some situations, can exacerbate the violence (Migliaccio, 2002).

In addition, many victims refuse to report domestic violence for a variety of reasons. They include:

- stigma associated with victimhood
- embarrassment
- guilt about having contributed in some way to the violence
- fear of disbelief (primarily male victims)
- absence of available services (primarily male victims)
- fear of being seen as the abuser (primarily male victims)
- fear of ridicule from authorities (primarily male victims)
- fear of retribution or retaliation
- belief that perpetrator will change
- fear that a relationship breakup will occur with both social and economic consequences

The emotional and social consequences of abuse are traumatic for the survivor. Many experience a loss in self-confidence, depression, loss of self-esteem, sleep deprivation, anxiety, and fear. For some, it culminates in suicide or other psychological disturbances (Allen-Collinson, 2009). Blaming themselves is another consequence for many women who label themselves as *stupid* for remaining in abusive situations (Enander, 2010). Oftentimes, this is the same word used by the abuser to describe the victim and reflects the self-blame that is generated in many of these relationships. It also reflects the victims' perception that those outside the relationships do not understand the dynamics that hold it together and, therefore, conclude that women who refuse to leave a violent situation are not very smart. By using this self-epitaph, victims are blaming themselves for staying, allowing themselves to be abused, being blind to the abuse and the abuser's problems, allowing themselves to be fooled or manipulated by the abuser, and anticipating the reaction of others to they remaining in the violent situation (Enander, 2010).

Did You Know?

Many victims develop coping techniques designed to forestall violence in the home. These include:

- trying to anticipate what the batterer wants or needs
- avoiding violent partners so as not to rile them up
- blaming oneself for the abuse
- avoiding any show of anger or feeling of anger toward the abuser
- adopting strategies that help one remain calm in the face of threats

Domestic violence within families frequently comes to the attention of social workers indirectly. In the case written up by Rosalyn Baker, Dan and Ellen, the initial reason for meeting with the social worker was over marital discord following birth of their first child. Follow the case discussion and respond to the critical thinking questions the author provides.

Cultural and Environmental Factors

Relatively few studies have explored the extent to which cultural or environmental variables affect patterns of and reactions to domestic violence. One such study of Chinese college students in Taiwan found the trauma and negative outcomes of abuse are similar to those shown in the United States and Europe. One significant difference was that those survivors holding traditional Chinese cultural beliefs were more likely to experience trauma symptoms and behavioral problems as adults (Shen, 2009). Paranjape, Sprauve-Holmes, Gaughan, and Kaslow (2009) found that older African American women who had experienced high levels of family violence during their lifetimes also reported poorer health status compared to peers without such exposure. In addition, their health scores were significantly below those for both African Americans in general and women in particular.

Knickmeyer, Levitt, and Horne (2010) found that battered women within Christian faith communities are more likely to experience pressures to be silent and/or to blame themselves for abuse they received. Some of this is attributable to religious values that subordinate women to the authority of men and the institutional structure that supports and reinforces this hierarchy. Those reporting abuse identified three themes that allowed abuse and protected the abuser. The first theme arose when the perpetrator presented himself to his partner and others as a good Christian who would never be suspected of abuse. This made it more difficult for the victim to be believed in the event of reporting the abuse. It also increases the willingness of the victim to forgive the abuser. The second theme was the use of faith against the victim. Here, women were told they should be submissive to their spouses and adhere to the ideals of a Christian marriage. Abusers used biblical admonitions to silence the victim and demand that the man's right to lead not be challenged. The third theme was pressure to preserve the façade of a good Christian family by keeping abuse a secret. This was often encouraged by the church through denying or minimizing the existence of domestic violence, thus helping to trap the victim in an abusive relationship.

Stamm (2009) discussed the issue of partner violence in the military and the ways in which military culture tends to allow this abuse to continue. Whether the rate of domestic violence in the military is higher than in civilian life is difficult to determine as various studies have arrived at different conclusions. Some factors that increase the likelihood that abuse is higher in the military include recruits with high levels of prior exposure to domestic violence, younger age range of military families, frequent relocation of military families, and frequent deployments that require changes in spousal roles. The protocols put in place to handle domestic violence in the military affirm its existence. Unfortunately, one major criticism of the military's domestic violence evaluation system is that it fails to adequately protect victims and underestimates the seriousness of some abuse. Inadequate assessments to the severity of abuse prolong the victim's ordeal. Other factors in the military mitigate reporting incidents of domestic violence, such as limits on confidentiality and concerns about how the report will affect the perpetrator's career. When the victim is a member of the military, similar concerns about reporting exist.

Resilience and Domestic Abuse Survivors

Domestic abuse survivors may ameliorate the experience by a combination of support systems and individual characteristics, such as a sense of humor and hope, optimism, and spirituality (Davis, 2002). Social support has a positive impact on the well-being of women who have survived intimate partner violence (Beeble, Bybee, & Sullivan, 2009). Those survivors with strong social support networks report higher quality of life and lower rates of depression, particularly in cases in which the woman suffered lesser degrees of psychological abuse. Some who experience interpersonal violence cope by focusing on the present and avoiding thinking about what the future will be like if they remain with the abuser. Still others find mechanisms to strengthen their self-esteem and self-confidence, such as pursuing educational opportunities, networking with others, acquiring outside employment, reading, and participating in awareness-raising sessions that deal with domestic violence (Bostock, Plumpton, & Pratt, 2009).

Despite the importance of social support in helping domestic violence survivors, the initial reactions of others to learning a friend or family member are not always helpful (Trotter & Allen, 2009). Many women report that negative reactions or at least mixed reactions are common. These include blaming the victim, minimizing the harm experienced, or distancing by family and friends. Other reactions included refusing to help, telling victims what they should do, advising them to remain in an abusive relationship, and notifying the perpetrator about the survivor's location. The reactions tend to increase stress level and further traumatize the domestic violence survivor.

Human Behavior

Practice Behavior Example: Apply theories and knowledge from the liberal arts to understand biological, social, cultural, psychological, and spiritual development.

Critical Thinking Question: What factors might explain the lack of support many battered women experience from their friends and associates?

For women who eventually leave the violent situation, it typically follows a series of phases including (1) rationalizing prior incidents of violence to remain committed to the relationship, (2) becoming demoralized and immobilized by the situation, (3) coming to view the violence as unacceptable, and finally (4) leaving to start a new life (Bostock et al., 2009). To achieve the end result, many relied on family and friends, made concrete plans to leave, gathered evidence of the violence, and sought refuge where the perpetrator could not locate them. A few asked the violent partner to move out or did so themselves. Besides assistance from family and friends, others sought out formal agencies to help them relocate. Some sought temporary restraining orders or similar court-ordered injunctions. However, the effectiveness of these legal steps for controlling the abuser remains questionable.

The experiences of those who leave a violent relationship are sometimes quite negative. They may have inadequate resources to support themselves, lack housing options, experience isolation and loneliness from their social networks, and receive unsupportive treatment from police and others. Effective interventions tended to emphasize that no one deserves to be beaten, the perpetrator, not the victim, is responsible for the violence, and communications of interest in and belief about the person's experience. Providing both emotional and concrete assistance is often required. Unfortunately, in many circumstances, the survivor reconnects with the abuser and the cycle of violence continues unabated. For some, this process will be repeated until the survivor or the perpetrator finally leaves or one dies.

Domestic Violence Perpetrators

Those who engage in domestic violence appear to lack any sense of empathy toward their partner nor do they appreciate the pain, discomfort, anxiety, and stress that their behavior is causing (Browne & Herbert, 1997). They downplay the seriousness of the violence or explain it away as an accident. They also deny any intent to actually hurt the victim. The result is confusion about what is playful versus accidental versus deliberate violence. Perpetrators often, but not always, apologize and ask the victim to forgive their behavior only to repeat it in subsequent interactions. Motivations for perpetrators can include a desire to coercively control the partner or microregulate almost every aspect of the person's life (Stark, 2006). This can take the form of objecting and forbidding the partner to maintain associations with friends or family; holding control over family resources; and violence against others such as children, family members, and pets (Bostock et al., 2009). In addition, they may engage in sexual abuse, extramarital liaisons, and victim put-downs.

Many, but not all, perpetrators experienced violence in their families of origin. This can be violence directed at themselves, siblings, or other adults in the family. Wareham, Boots, and Chavez (2009) used social learning theory in their analysis of male domestic batterers to help explain factors contributing to becoming an abuser later in their lives. The research underscores the ways in which dysfunctional adults in one's family can model aggression and lead to its perpetuation in succeeding generations. Violence perpetrated by one's mother tended to increase the risk of engaging in serious interpersonal violence. This was especially true when combined with other friends and family who engaged in domestic abuse. Receiving corporal punishment from one's father also increased the risk of engaging in such behavior as an adult. Ireland and Smith (2009) found being exposed to severe domestic violence was significantly related to intimate partner violence in early adulthood. Other researchers have raised questions about whether social learning theory explains the use of violence by adults who grew up in violent homes. Some have argued that the process is more complex than social learning suggests, while others point to research that shows no higher incidence of dating violence among adolescent boys from violent homes (Øverlien, 2010; Wolf & Foshee, 2003).

Domestic Violence Perpetrators and Resilience

An important point to emphasize, however, is that both individual characteristics and aspects of the environment can act to mediate the effects of parental violence on children. How a child reacts cognitively to family violence can make a difference, as can both social and cultural factors (Chan & Yeung, 2009). A child's individual resilience and the availability and effectiveness of his or her support system tend to provide a degree of insulation from the impact of family violence. In addition, many children are exposed not just to violence against one or both parents but to violence against themselves. The presence of multiple sources of violence in a home may play a role in how often adult children later become abusers themselves. From a social learning standpoint, the more exposure to violence children have, the greater the likelihood they will themselves be violent. At the same time, there is evidence that the "a strong relationship with a competent, caring, positive adult, most often a parent" is perhaps the most important source of resilience among children who experienced violence in their homes (Osofsky, 2003, p. 38).

Before leaving the topic of domestic violence, it is appropriate to note that parents are not the only source of violence to which children are exposed. In many communities, violence is a common occurrence and children witness it on the way to and from school, at play, and sometimes in the school itself. According to Zinzow et al. (2009), over one-third of adolescents witnessed community violence of one type or another—ranging from murder, rape, and robbery to shooting, beating, and stabbing. Whether the child adopts this behavior as an adult is likely mediated by a similar set of factors to those already discussed. In particular, the role of parents in buffering these experiences

Assess your comprehension of Domestic Violence by completing this quiz.

is important (Ozer, 2005). Likewise, school programs on violence and adolescent students' sense of efficacy in school helped mediate the influence of violence. Neighborhoods with a strong sense of "mutual trust and a willingness to intervene for the common good" also helped moderate the influence of community and family violence (Foster & Brooks-Gunn, 2009, p. 86).

TRAUMA SURVIVORS: DISASTERS, TERRORISM, AND WAR

Disasters, terrorism, and war have become common experiences for people across the globe. Historical events—such as the destruction of the city of Pompeii by Mount Vesuvius in AD 79, the sacking of Rome in AD 410, and mass suicides at Masada in the first century AD as Jews fought against the Romans—are distant memories. Other events are more recent in occurrence and include the Chicago fire in 1871, San Francisco earthquake of 1906, sinking of the *Titanic* in 1912, Hurricane Katrina in 2005, and multiple wars culminating in those armed conflicts occurring in the first part of the 21st century. While terrorism is often considered a new edition to the traumas that afflict the world, this is erroneous. Examples of terrorism can be traced prior to the birth of Christ. In the past, both countries and individuals engaged in acts that we would describe as terrorism as means to achieve political or religious ends. Today, we tend to see terrorism as an act against the state and discount the actions of a country in pursuit of its goals. At the same time, multiple examples of terrorism perpetrated by non-states have flourished. These include hijacking and bombing of airlines, kidnappings and killings of civilians, and similar events. Ironically, terrorism often defies definition because how the term is used often depends on who is employing it. Thus, individuals who see themselves as freedom fighters or revolutionaries come to use many of the same actions and behaviors as those whom others would describe as terrorists. One person's freedom fighter is often another person's terrorist.

Terrorism has taken many forms in the United States over the past 200-plus years. More recent forms include the Weathermen during the 1960s, the 1995 bombing of the federal building in Oklahoma City, and the 2001 attacks that destroyed the World Trade Center in New York. Terrorism has been used as a rationale for multiple restrictions on personal freedom, including airport screenings and wiretapping without a warrant, and has led to the use of waterboarding, a torture technique, on suspected terrorists. Debates about what is justified to protect life and safety are often couched as either-or propositions. "If we don't take these actions, terrorists will harm us" versus "If we take these actions, we are giving up the freedoms we believe in and stand for."

Regardless of the debates, most would probably agree that terrorism, wars, and disasters have the potential to traumatize those caught up in the event. Because of the recency of several traumatic events, we will focus on how they affected the individuals most directly involved. These include Hurricane Katrina, the events of September 11, 2001, and recent armed conflicts. We will also look at how children and adults experience these events and the ways in which trauma is manifested.

Identifying common responses to disasters, wars, and terrorism is relatively easy. While various individuals will react in different fashion to these events, most members of the general public do not panic or become passive in the face of trauma. Rather, immediate responses following the initial fear or panic reactions are often rational and prosocial with relatively few individuals experiencing shock or prolonged panic (Perry & Lindell, 2003). People involved in disasters often terminate nonessential activities and focus on mutual support, helping others, and responding to immediate needs. Numerous examples of this type of response can be cited, ranging from the actions of the passengers on United Airlines flight 94 who elected to attack those who had hijacked their plane to the behavior of miners trapped underground who organize themselves, ration food and water, and remain calm while awaiting rescue.

Of course, some individuals will experience trauma under some conditions. For example, events that occur suddenly without warning and result in significant destruction of property, injury, or death are more likely to produce trauma. For the most part, whatever symptoms occur are likely to be mild, affect few people, and tend to last for shorter periods of time. The minority who do have long-lasting symptoms—and who may experience depression, grief reactions, and PTSD—have often endured unusually severe or extended periods of trauma (Norris et al., 2002). Young children and adolescents may be especially vulnerable to developing PTSD following exposure to a traumatic event. The young may show regressive behaviors such as incontinence, anxiety around separations, sleep disturbances, and dependence. Some react to the event by delinquency, temper outbursts, and aggression. Problematic reactions to disasters and terrorism tend to fall into several categories including nonspecific distress, health problems and concerns, chronic problems in living, specific psychological difficulties, and loss of psychosocial resources (Norris et al., 2002). Nonspecific distress includes general feelings of unease, feeling overwhelmed, and depressed affect. Health problems and concerns involve somatic distress, various medical maladies, and sleep disturbances. Some individuals with preexisting proclivities toward alcohol or drug use may increase their usage in response to an event.

Chronic problems in living include bouts of stress-induced anxiety, work or family conflicts, and other stressors that make life more difficult for the survivor. Specific psychological difficulties are likely to involve PTSD, anxiety, and depression. Psychosocial resource loss occurs when (1) an individual has lost the support of others through death, injury, or incapacity or (2) one's normative psychological strengths are weakened, lessening things such as a sense of optimism. Likewise, one's normal resources may be so impacted by the traumatic event that they are unavailable. One example of this is the loss of public and private services and facilities after Hurricane Katrina. The most troubled survivors were those who experienced mass violence, such as terroristic events. They were about twice as likely to be severely impaired as those who lived through a natural disaster, such as a hurricane (Norris et al., 2002). As in the case of Katrina, survivors of 9/11, including public safety officials, were left without the resources they might have previously relied upon.

Those directly affected by an event are most likely to experience mental health concerns. For example, individuals who lost loved ones or had their homes destroyed in an earthquake or flood are at greater risk of depression and PTSD than those who merely witnessed the event. Exposure to the temporal manifestations of disaster, terrorism, and war has a great potential for inducing severe mental health reactions. For example, the likelihood of psychological disability (Miller, 2004) increases when one sees, smells, and hears the sounds of death and witnesses the physical harming of friends, family members, and fellow soldiers. Likewise, human-initiated disasters such as terrorism tend to produce higher rates of trauma (Shariat, Mallonee, Kruger, Farmer, & North, 1999). For example, events such as the Oklahoma City and Boston Marathon bombing typically result in a significant percentage of survivors developing serious impairment including PTSD, auditory problems, anxiety, worsening of preexisting ailments, and depression. In the aftermath of the World Trade Center, a study of children and adolescents found depression rates and probable PTSD rates that were two to three times higher than before 9/11 (Hoven et al., 2005). Another factor increasing the impact of trauma occurs when the survivor suffers both a personal loss and a loss of community. Hurricane Katrina that destroyed much of New Orleans is an example of a combined personal loss compounded by loss of community.

Resilience

Resilience in the face of such events is often a matter of direct proximity to the event, being personally impacted by it, and the duration and intensity of exposure. Condly (2006) has identified three assumptions most individuals make that allow them to maintain a degree of composure and resistance to the normal vicissitudes of life. These include:

- the world is basically a good place
- my life and events of the world have meaning and purpose
- my person is both worthy and valuable

Traumatic events undermine some or all these assumptions and force people to re-think who they are. Resilient people respond to the trauma and then bounce back more quickly. Their reactions tend to be temporary and they more easily adapt to the new cir-cumstances. Those most likely to withstand trauma tend to have several factors in their favor (Garmezy, 1991). These include:

- Intelligence and temperament: These individuals are generally bright and get along well with others.
- Family relationships and family support: These elements tend to be stronger.
- External support from people and organizations: Social supports and resources available outside the family are present.

One fortunate outcome of traumatic events is that the impact on most participants is relatively short-lived. Most recover from the symptoms over a period of a month or two.

Other Factors

Studies of large-scale traumatic events have sometimes found interesting outcomes. For example, drinking problems among residents of New York City increased after 9/11 com-pared to rates prior to the event (Vlahov et al., 2006). Even New Yorkers watching events of 9/11 on television tended to report greater symptoms of PTSD and children appeared to be especially vulnerable (Ahern, Galea, Resnick, & Vlahov, 2004). Generally speaking, the more one watches such traumatic events, the higher the level of PTSD-related symptoms.

Service Providers

Those providing services to disaster survivors often encounter their trauma and become secondary victims to the event (Figley & Kleber, 1995). Typical feelings include guilt, an-ger, anxiety, and gratitude along with sleep disturbances and problems concentrating. Like other victims, providers often experience the same loss of community resources (e.g., phone service, referral sites, and physical access). Service disruptions are common in major disasters and the inability to communicate with family, friends, and clients can feel overwhelming. Providers may also be overwhelmed by the sheer numbers of people needing services and traumatized by the physical injuries suffered by victims. Moreover, professionals may be simultaneously coping with their reactions while trying to assist victims, raising issues of competence and ethics. Under these circumstances, overiden-tifying with the client is possible and maintaining one's professional distance is difficult (Schechter, 2008). The problems experienced by surviving first responders after 9/11 il-lustrate some of risks for professionals in such horrific situations. In addition to physical problems such as cancers, gastro-esophageal reflux, and respiratory illness, between 10% and 30% still struggle with PTSD and depression (Wisnivesky et al., 2011).

In the case of terrorism or certain types of disasters such as earthquakes, the poten-tial for subsequent traumatic events is unnerving to professionals as well as the general public. Attending to the mental health needs of survivors is complicated because some diagnoses cannot be made immediately. As assessment of PTSD, for example, requires that symptoms exist for at least a month (American Psychiatric Association, 2000). Use of rapid assessment instruments and self-report questionnaires may be more useful in the immediate aftermath of disasters.

War and Trauma

Warfare is another venue and experience that produces trauma for those caught up in its horror. Historically, wars were fought largely between military forces of one country against those of another. Civilian casualties occurred in most cases, but the effort to defeat the opposing military force was the primary goal. Wars of the late 20th and early 21st centuries have evolved in ways that seem to make civilians and the military equal targets. With the intertwining of terrorism with war, old rules no longer apply and the goal has evolved to wear down the will of a government or its people to prolong a conflict. Indiscriminate bombings, the fog of war, and sectarian conflicts take their toll on both innocent civilians and armed forces. Williams, Sawyer Baker, Allman, and Roseman (2007, p. 265) points out that the 10-year period between 1993 and 2003 resulted in the death of over 2 million children and the injury, or disabling, of 6 million more. One million children who survived the warfare were orphaned while another 20 million were displaced, often to refugee camps. Civilians constitute over 80% of the casualties during this period. In several situations, hundreds of thousands of children were conscripted into service as soldiers and directly participated in the carnage (Cohn, 2006).

The impact of war on military personnel and veterans has been recognized for decades but it's becoming more salient as a result of the recent multiple conflicts in which the United States and other nations have been involved. As mentioned earlier, exposure to injured and dying friends is a significant factor in the development of mental health problems. Almost two-thirds of U.S. combatants report seeing bodies of the deceased or other human remains and between 11% and 18% of veterans of the conflicts in Iraq and Afghanistan are at risk of PTSD (Hoge et al., 2004). In addition, almost 95% of soldiers in Iraq knew someone who had been killed or injured seriously. About one-half of the soldiers reported killing an enemy and almost 30% reported being responsible for death of a civilian. These characteristics are each predictive factors for PTSD. Constant vigilance and uncertainty are norms in wars that mix traditional combat with guerilla warfare and terrorism, and both contribute to mental health issues (Litz, 2006).

Clinical Corner

Armando

Armando had served three tours in Iraq and Afghanistan before an improvised explosive device (IED) cost him part of his right leg, beneath the knee. While recovering from his physical loss, Armando began to exhibit signs of PTSD and was supposed to see a veteran's counselor every week. After the third appointment, Armando stopped coming and dropped out of site. Despite efforts to contact him, Armando had disappeared. It was not until a year later that his whereabouts were located when police responded to a report of a fight under a local highway bridge. When they arrived, police found Armando with a self-inflicted gunshot wound. Despite the availability of effective and free care for his injuries, Armando was homeless. Eventually, his demons drove him to end his suffering.

A major concern is that military veterans who suffer PTSD appear to be less likely to recover than civilians with the same disorder (Hoge et al., 2004). This may be a combination of the normal consequences of war combined with the extended and repeated deployments experienced by most military personnel. Despite the fact that most veterans recognized the existence of their mental health issues, less than half were planning to seek treatment. Only about one-quarter actually received such care. Some of this reluctance to seek help may be related to the nature of an all-volunteer military where seeking treatment for mental health concerns is seen as a career risk (Litz, 2006).

Litz and colleagues (2009) have proposed the possibility that a portion of the challenge for veterans may be attributable to what they refer to as *moral injury* and the need to struggle with moral and ethical challenges. Situations that can induce moral injury include (1) seeing injured or sick families and children and not being able to help, (2) dealing with morally and ethically ambiguous events, and (3) continued uncertainty about who constitutes the enemy during insurgencies. Exposure to atrocities may also contribute to the PTSD found in so many veterans. Potentially, any act or omission that contradicts the individual's assumptions about himself or herself—and one's definition of right and wrong—can contribute to moral injury. The conflicts and internal dissonance created by these situations tend to produce shame, guilt, and anxiety.

Attempts to deal with the emotional distress can exacerbate it. For example, avoiding situations, thoughts, or experiences that trigger reminders of the distress prevent learning more functional ways of coping. Recurring memories of the trauma typically pass with time, but trying to avoid the memories undercuts this mechanism prolonging the distress. Other actions that delay recovery include hiding or withdrawing from others because of feeling ashamed of one's actions, and the inability to forgive oneself. The longer individuals fail to confront the guilt and the actions that elicited it, the more likely they will come to see their actions as inexcusable and themselves as unforgivable. Over time, these self-perceptions lead to continued memories, more avoidance, self-numbing, self-harming, self-handicapping, and demoralization (Litz et al., 2009).

Did You Know?

Military veterans suffer significantly from their experiences as follows:

- Deaths of soldiers and veterans from suicide have exceeded the number of personnel killed in action in the wars in Iraq and Afghanistan.
- Male veterans have a suicide rate twice as high as civilians.
- 5,000 veterans per year commit suicide. (Department of Veterans Affairs, 2012)

Resilience Among Trauma Survivors

As with the experiences of others exposed to traumatic events, it is difficult to know why some individuals suffer PTSD while others do not. Those who have higher levels of support and greater self-esteem appear to be better able to protect themselves from the experiences while those who are prone to shame and neurosis are less able.

Service Providers and Trauma

In addition to those who directly experienced the events that can lead to PTSD, there is recognition that those providing care for military trauma victims can suffer from secondary traumatization or compassion fatigue (Boscarino, Figley, and Adams, 2004; Tyson, 2007). Practitioners working with combat-related PTSD and related symptoms are exposed not only to details of the horror that the veteran experienced, but also to daily or periodic reminders that the world is no longer a safe place. Things such as terror warnings, attempted suicide bombings, and travel restrictions are constant reminders that one's safety is at risk (Tyson, 2007). Over time, the secondary trauma can affect the practitioner's identity, relationships with others, physical and/or mental health, and job morale. In turn,

Examples of compassion fatigue among helping professionals are provided in Joni Handran vignette entitled Trauma-Organized Versus Trauma-Informed Organizational Culture: An Organizational Case Study for Agencies That Provide Services to Survivors of Trauma. After reading the vignette, answer the critical thinking questions that the author has posed.

those who are in a relationship with a traumatized individual, client, or social worker may experience a degree of emotional contagion resulting in burnout in the caring family member (Figley, 1997). It is clear that almost anyone closely connected to veterans with PTSD and related symptoms is at some degree of risk of developing his or her set of psychological challenges.

As should be evident, trauma and abuse influence human behavior in multiple ways. From the child who is abused to the victims of crime and from domestic violence survivors to those who have experienced terrorism, disasters, and war, each endures a potential legacy of trauma. Equally troubling is the risk encountered by those who provide care for the traumatized. Learning to recognize the signs, symptoms, and challenges associated with trauma is an important task for social workers.

Assess your analysis and evaluation of this chapter's contents by completing the Chapter Review.

Paolese/Fotolia

Socially Deviant Behavior

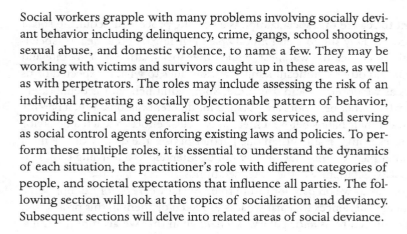

Social workers grapple with many problems involving socially deviant behavior including delinquency, crime, gangs, school shootings, sexual abuse, and domestic violence, to name a few. They may be working with victims and survivors caught up in these areas, as well as with perpetrators. The roles may include assessing the risk of an individual repeating a socially objectionable pattern of behavior, providing clinical and generalist social work services, and serving as social control agents enforcing existing laws and policies. To perform these multiple roles, it is essential to understand the dynamics of each situation, the practitioner's role with different categories of people, and societal expectations that influence all parties. The following section will look at the topics of socialization and deviancy. Subsequent sections will delve into related areas of social deviance.

SOCIALIZATION AND DEVIANCY

Socialization is a process by which societies teach and convey to their members the norms, mores, and cultural expectations that are shared by most of its members. The socialization process begins in infancy as parents and others help children learn what is expected of them. Along with their expectations, adults also teach children what to believe, which habits to acquire, and general knowledge considered critical to membership in a society. Socialization also helps the individual develop a sense of identity and the social skills needed to interact with others. Many societal institutions have a role in socialization. This includes the family, school systems, religious organizations, peer groups, and specialized groups, such as scouting, boys and girls clubs, community recreational programs, and others.

Paolese/Fotolia

Being victimized by the deviant behavior of others is a risk throughout one's life.

These systems help children learn cultural values and awareness of self and others. In addition, families play a prominent role in guiding children toward their gender identity.

Schools often reinforce family teaching while exposing children to individuals from different cultures. Like the family, schools also support gender identity. Often, schools represent the first external institution that children must learn to deal with, which is sometimes problematic because institutions often have rigid rules and bureaucracies that fail to account for individual differences. This may help explain instances in which a child is suspended from school for sexual harassment after calling a teacher *cute* or another when a seven-year-old child being choked by a bully kicked the offender in the groin and was investigated for engaging in sexual harassment. Children's encounters with institutional rules may help socialize them to the new values or simply convince them that schools are strange places.

It is important to realize that socialization is a lifelong process of acquiring social experiences that continually support and modify past learning. A great deal of socialization occurs without conscious awareness, while other socialization is deliberate and purposeful. Parents and other significant adults provide clues to what is expected of us by their behaviors as we observe them over time. Some adult behavior is deliberately intended to teach while other behaviors are pursued for different reasons. When parents send children to wash their hands before a meal, it is a clear effort to teach a behavior that the adult believes is important. When one partner praises the quality of the meal prepared by the other partner, this may or may not be intended as a learning tool. Humans learn of social expectations whether intended or not.

Socialization occurs as we prepare for future roles. Social workers, for example, take both classes and field experiences to learn what is expected of them in this profession. This is sometimes referred to as *anticipatory socialization* in that we acquire the skills, norms, and values we anticipate will guide us in our career. Of course, socialization is not simply a one-sided process but rather a mutual undertaking in which parents can also learn from their children. This learning may include what works with which child when shaping the youngster's behavior. For example, parents might learn that raising their voice is needed to get through to one child but will cause another child to burst into tears. As might be expected, a great deal of parental learning occurs after the birth of the first child as they try out different child-rearing approaches.

While the goal of socialization is to teach prosocial values, beliefs, and norms, this is not always what the child learns. For example, parents often teach behaviors that are not considered positive by society. Domestic violence, for instance, can be learned by watching this behavior displayed at home. Parents who abuse drugs or alcohol can easily model this behavior for their children. Poor communication skills can be taught by parents with limited ability to show or share their feelings in positive ways.

Professional Identity

Practice Behavior Example: Practice personal reflection and self-correction to assure continual professional development.

Critical Thinking Question: All of us are both receivers and providers of efforts to socialize other people. Looking at your behavior, in what instances have you deliberately attempted to socialize another person (adult or child) about societal, religious, or other norms?

A second way how antisocial norms can be learned is through associations with peers. Many children learn delinquent behavior from their friends including both specific antisocial actions and the values underlying this behavior.

A third influence on the socialization process comes from the mass media. Television, movies, Internet content, books, magazines, newspapers, and blogs all are in a position to teach children and adolescents. What is taught depends a great deal on (1) the extent to which the child is attentive to the media's content and (2) the relative significance to the child of the individual or character conveying the content. Models that are disliked or content of low interest are less likely to be successful in transmitting values or norms. Popular figures demonstrating interesting content are more likely to be noticed. (For more discussion on the media's influence, refer to Chapter 15.)

When socially deviant behavior occurs, it is usually focused on one segment of an individual's life. *Deviance* is any behavior that seriously offends established norms, although something as small as smoking in a no-smoking section can be considered as mildly socially deviant. Many minor social norm violations are simply annoying and are met with disdain, ridicule, and/or minimal consequences. In many cases, violations go unsanctioned unless the behavior has resulted in a more serious event. Failing to give another driver the right of way and entering the intersection first may be considered rude. If that failure results in a car accident, however, the rude behavior can escalate to a law violation and fine. Likewise, the school bully may be ignored for his or her behavior as long as it is does not cause obvious harm. Let it result in physical harm to the victim and it may become a crime.

It is easy to see that many socially deviant behaviors occur rather routinely and without substantial sanctions. When a behavior becomes so serious that it threatens harm to the perpetrator or others, societies may employ coercive power to remedy the situation. Both the adult and the juvenile justice systems are designed to coerce changes in antisocial and criminal behavior.

CRIMINAL JUSTICE SYSTEMS AND SOCIAL WORK

Within the criminal justice system, social workers are often considered agents of social control charged with increasing prosocial values and behaviors and decreasing antisocial values and behaviors. Various institutions have been established by societies to deal with those engaging in antisocial behavior. In the United States, these range from probation and parole services for juveniles and adults, juvenile and adult correctional settings (minimum, medium, and maximum security prisons), court systems, halfway houses, and similar creations. Social workers often work in these settings as part of efforts to resocialize the person whose actions violated societal norms. They also work directly with victims as advocates, as witness coordinators, and in other roles.

Laux et al. (2008) discussed how practitioners could assist women in the criminal justice system with substance abuse problems. Interventions these women need include gender-specific treatment approaches and family-oriented support for their dependent children. About 60% to 65% of women in prison and 70% of women in jail have minor children (p. 37). Most women have two children and will spend three years incarcerated and away from their families. About 10% of these children will be placed in the child welfare system (Dellaire, 2007).

Incarceration of the mother increases the potential for other problems for their children including heightened risk of

Did You Know?

At any given point in time, 1.3 million children are affected by a mother's incarceration (Poehlmann, 2005).

delinquency, poverty, recidivism, psychological dysfunctions, and victimization/violence (Simons, Simons, & Wallace, 2004).

In addition to the children of incarcerated parents, estimates are that six times as many individuals are on probation compared to the number in prison with corresponding risks to their children (Glaze & Palla, 2005). Because of the population' size, it is often inevitable that parents become involved with both the criminal justice and the child welfare services systems. This can occur in the following situations (Phillips, Dettlaff, & Baldwin, 2010).

Intersection of Criminal Justice and Child Protective Services Systems

- Arrest of one or both parents spurs Child Protective Services (CPS) involvement (12% of cases)
- CPS involvement leads to parent's arrest (6%)
- Both arrest and CPS involvement occur coincidentally (2%)
- Arrest histories of parents are a factor in decision to remove children (74%)
- Arrest histories of relatives are a factor in kinship placement decisions (25%)
- CPS involvement occurs while parent is incarcerated (12%)
- Incarcerated parent gives birth (4%)

Totals do not equal 100% because categories are not mutually exclusive.

While the involvement of more than one system in a given case may offer multiple opportunities to receive help, it is equally possible that involvement in one system will result in failure in the other. For example, a parent whose probation is revoked and sent to prison may be unable to meet the conditions imposed by the CPS system to allow family reunification. At the same time, loss of children to the CPS system often appears to lessen probationers' motivation for meeting requirements of the criminal justice system (Phillips, Leathers, & Erkanli, 2009). The child welfare and criminal justice interconnection can be seen from the following (Glaze & Maruschak, 2008; Phillips & Dettlaff, 2009; Phillips, Burns, Wagner, & Barth, 2004; Phillips, Erkanli, Costello, & Angold, 2007):

- One in eight children reported as mistreated have at least one parent who were recently arrested.
- One in three children not removed from parental caregiver live with a primary caregiver who has an arrest record.
- 11% of mothers and 2% of fathers in prison have children in foster care.
- 4.1% of children whose parents had arrest records had been in foster care, a rate double or triple that of children without such a parental record.

Engage, Assess, Intervene, Evaluate

Practice Behavior Example: Substantively and effectively prepare for action with individuals, families, groups, organizations, and communities.

Critical Thinking Question: What other alternatives (if any) should be explored before sending a sole caregiver with children to prison or jail?

Sometimes, action in one system simply spurs action in another. An example is the following discussion on Luann family.

Parents on probation often struggle with a variety of challenges including obtaining employment and avoiding substance abuse, and often this affects their parenting skills. Report of neglect—such as failure to supervise or provide for their children—is one of the most common reasons these families are reported to CPS agencies. Physical abuse was the basis for a report in about 25% of these cases (Phillips et al., 2009).

Alaggia, Lambert, and Regehr (2009) looked at the experience of parents in cases where allegations of child sexual abuse

Luann

Luann was on probation for assault and battery against a police officer while intoxicated and was subsequently arrested for mail theft. Following her trial, Luann was sentenced to prison for two years. Her husband was incarcerated at a minimum security prison following a previous conviction for theft from his employer. Luann's sentence resulted in both her son and her daughter being placed in foster care for a year until Luann's brother agreed to care for them until her release.

resulted in contact with the criminal justice system. They were able to identify six themes that affected how these parents viewed the justice system.

1. **Loss of parental control.** Once parents reported that their child had been sexually abused, they found themselves with little to no input on the steps that would be taken in the case. Decisions about which, if any, charges will be filed, the scheduling of court hearings, and other events are no longer influenced by parental wishes.

2. **Inconsistencies within the legal system.** Some parents found very positive experiences with police or court officers while others were exceedingly disappointed with different segments of the system. Some parents found the police unhelpful while court officers were viewed as inexperienced for their tasks.

3. **Treating children like adults within the criminal justice system.** Of particular concern for defense attorneys is the tendency for members of the criminal justice system to treat children as if they were adults, without regard for children's developmental states.

4. **Dissatisfaction with the outcomes and the consequences for the perpetrator.** This occurred in cases both where the accused person was found not guilty and when light sentences were imposed. These outcomes were especially disheartening given the emotional toll that the cases had taken on the child and parents.

5. **Participation in the justice system did more harm than good.** Parents felt a total lack of significant therapeutic benefit as a result of participating in the justice system. In fact, they actually believed that their participation—and that of their child—was a revictimization without any positive outcomes.

6. **Disenchantment with the legal system.** Parents are so seriously disenchanted with the legal system that they advise others to avoid it entirely. Expecting anything positive in terms of resolution is a mistake according to many parents. The only consistently positive experience parents shared was the helpfulness of the children's victim witness program in preparing the child to testify in court. Parents supported the value of such programs for both their children and themselves.

Human Rights and Justice

Practice Behavior Example: Recognize the global interconnections of oppression and are knowledgeable about theories of justice and strategies to promote human and civil rights.

Critical Thinking Question: In a recent case, a teenager was raped by two teenage boys who took pictures of the assault and circulated them on the Internet. The boys were later arrested and charged with the crime. Their lawyer arranged a plea deal that ended up with both boys being found guilty of felony sexual assault and a misdemeanor. Believing their prospective punishment was too light (at worst, one to five years), the girl revealed the boys' names on the Internet. Because the case had been handled in juvenile court where records are usually private, the girl was threatened with jail for doing so.

Taking into consideration the crime, the harm done to the girl, and the private nature of juvenile court records, what is your thinking about the following questions:

1. Did the girl have a first amendment right to publicize the name of her attackers despite the judge orders for no one to talk about the case?

2. Did the crimes in this case deserve more severe consequences than the maximum the boys would most likely receive?

3. If so, what would you consider a just sentence, and why?

Another role for social workers in the criminal justice system involves helping assure those systems operate humanely while recognizing and differentiating prisoners' needs. Many social workers have advocated the end of the death penalty because of the record of law enforcement and courts in prosecuting and sentencing individuals who are later declared innocent based on DNA testing. The National Association of Social Workers and American Psychological Association have filed numerous *amicus curiae* (friend of the court) briefs before the U.S. Supreme Court in cases where key professional values were at stake. In several cases, the court sided with the two organizations' position including the following:

- Challenge to life without parole for juveniles (Supreme Court finding: Violates Eighth Amendment ban on cruel and unusual punishment in nonhomicide cases)

- Challenge to death penalty in Louisiana for child rape (Supreme Court finding: Violates Eighth Amendment ban on cruel and unusual punishment, forces the child victim to testify repeatedly in capital cases, and gives perpetrator incentive to kill the victim)

- Challenge to Texas law on sodomy between consenting adults (Supreme Court finding: Violates due process clause of 14th Amendment)

- Challenge to Virginia law permitting execution of person with mental retardation (Supreme Court finding: Violates Eighth Amendment ban on cruel and unusual punishment)

The social work profession has actively sought to eliminate the death penalty. As noted earlier, multiple errors in the arrest, prosecution, and sentencing of offenders occur on a routine basis. Substantial evidence underscores the fact that capital punishment is used more often with African American men than with Whites for the same offense (Betancourt et al., 2006). Similar discrepant outcomes have also been reported in other countries (Duckett & Schinkel, 2008). One common reason given in support of the death penalty is that it operates as a deterrent. However, arguments that the death penalty deters criminal behavior are easily countered by the evidence. Likewise, the exorbitant costs of capital punishment compared to incarceration for life suggest that execution is also not an economical method for dealing with serious crimes.

Another area of the criminal justice system where social workers participate is in mitigation reviews. In capital punishment cases, courts ask for a review of mitigating circumstances that would inform the judge's decision about the most appropriate sentence to impose. This step is based on U.S. Supreme Court rulings that are designed to make the process in capital cases as fair as possible. It is common to have social workers contracted to perform these mitigation reviews, which take into account the individual's background, upbringing, nature of the crime, and similar factors that may place the offender's actions in context. For example, factors such as social disadvantage and deprived upbringing are often considered. In some cases, "acts of heroism by the offender, collateral pains suffered by the offender, [and] employment record of the offender" may be considered (Ashworth, 1994, p. 5).

An offender's age may be a mitigating factor. Adolescents tend to receive more lenient sentences based on their reduced decision-making capability, vulnerability to the influence of others, impulsivity, and relative incomplete state of psychological development that limit their culpability. This limitation in capacity also applies to cases in which the offender is considered to have mental retardation. Each of these factors can be effectively assessed and evaluated by social work practitioners with the necessary preparation.

Betancourt et al. (2006) argue that there is also a role for social workers providing services to the families of those who have been sentenced to death for their crimes. Empathy and help for family members preparing for the event are things social workers can provide, including preparation for the public circuses that often erupt in conjunction with an execution. A nonjudgmental attitude is essential in these situations and is consistent with professional values.

DELINQUENCY IN CHILDHOOD AND ADOLESCENCE

The challenges of dealing with socially deviant behavior in children and adolescents have been with us for centuries. Adults are often concerned about delinquent behavior in general and that exhibited by their children. A great deal of delinquent behavior, however, is simply a part of growing up. Neither alcohol use nor delinquency is automatically a sign of future adult criminality, mental illness, or problems in development. As Overbeek, Vollebergh, Meeus, Engels, and Luijpers (2001) note, "Previous research has clearly shown that a certain amount of norm-violating or delinquent behavior can be seen as a part of normal development and is not associated with severe emotional problems in adolescence" (p. 419). They also conclude that "testing personal boundaries and exploring values and beliefs are normative behaviors during adolescence and serve important developmental ends" (p. 419). Despite the normality of much antisocial behavior, it does not mean that serious delinquent acts should be ignored. It is important to understand why these behaviors occurred to decide how best to manage the situation.

> **Professional Identity**
>
> *Practice Behavior Example: Practice personal reflection and self-correction to assure continual professional development.*
>
> **Critical Thinking Question:** Consider your behavior as a child/adolescent. Were there actions you took that could be considered delinquent or antisocial? Estimate the number of times you engaged in that or similar behaviors. What percentage of the time was their punishment or consequences for these acts? What role did luck play in you not getting caught and/or punished?

Explanations for Antisocial Behavior

Explanations for delinquent or criminal behavior have ranged from possession by the devil and the biological "bad seed" to poor parenting and psychological problems. Social workers, however, are more likely to consider the influence of psychological factors, peers, parenting, and community influences than to attribute antisocial behavior to satanic causes. We have previously looked at the influence of peers and identified ways other children and adolescents transmit deviant values and behaviors to their comrades. Parents have also been cited as possible contributors to their children's delinquency through mechanisms such as modeling and reinforcing of deviance. Even professional drug dealers have helped provoke delinquent behavior by deliberately using minors to sell and deliver drugs, calculating that juveniles receive few serious consequences if caught.

Corff and Toupin (2009) looked at the role personality traits may play in producing delinquent behavior. They studied the association between traits of agreeableness and neuroticism and antisocial behavior in adolescents and young adults, finding delinquent adolescents scored lower on agreeableness and higher on neuroticism. This group also

Did You Know?

Gender Differences and Antisocial Behavior

Gender differences impact how childhood abuse plays out in adolescence. Abused males tend to become more aggressive toward others, display conduct problems, and engage in more sexually risky acts. Abused females (often victimized sexually) tend to turn the abuse inward to substance use as a means of self-medicating (Dembo, Schmeidler, & Childs, 2007). This, in turn, results in higher rates of self-blame, depression, eating problems, and suicidal actions and thoughts (Sullivan, Farrell, & Kliewer, 2006). While both males and females respond to abuse by becoming angry, the latter is also likely to couple this with guilt and anxiety (Bender, 2010).

scored higher on excitement seeking and lower on warmth compared to nondelinquent peers. Asendorpf, Denissen, and van Aken (2008) also found delinquency was highly associated with aggressiveness, has low levels of agreeableness and conscientiousness, and has higher levels of neuroticism. These delinquents were less likely to learn from their past experiences. The finding of an association between low scores on agreeableness and delinquency was also noted by Malouff, Thorsteinsson, and Schutte (2005). Other researchers identified low emotional self-control and high aggressiveness as personality factors in children predicting adolescent delinquency (Caspi, 2000; Tremblay, 2000). Aggressive children score lower on educational and occupational achievement (Asendorpf et al., 2008).

Some who have studied adolescent delinquency found associations between being maltreated as a youth and becoming a juvenile offender both in the United States and in other countries (Bender, 2010; Bergen, Martin, Richardson, Allison, & Roeger, 2004). Moreover, the influence of abuse may be cumulative in that more abuse increases the risk of violent delinquency in adolescence (Crooks, Scott, Wolfe, Chiodo, & Killip, 2007).

Another risk factor for at least some adolescent delinquency is parental suicide (Jennings, Maldonado-Molina, Piquero, & Canino, 2010). Studying Hispanic youth whose parents attempted suicide, researchers found them "engaged in more frequent and varied delinquency over time" (p. 315). They employed general strain theory (GST) to help explain this phenomenon. GST suggests that strains—such as the death of a parent or other significant losses—produces negative affect, such as anger and depression, and that the loss coupled with the negative emotions is a risk factor for delinquency (Agnew, 2006). The influence of anger on contributing to delinquent behavior has also been found in studies in other countries that focused on bullies and their victims (Sigfusdottir, Gudjonsson, & Sigurdsson, 2010).

Mediating influences between childhood maltreatment and adolescent delinquency can include running away from home. Unfortunately, this tends to increase the likelihood of engaging in delinquent behaviors for both males and females (Baron, 2003). Likewise, mental health problems may develop following maltreatment and these, too, predict delinquency. Children who develop posttraumatic stress disorder as a result of violence in their childhood are more likely to have impulse control problems in adolescence.

Childhood maltreatment is also predictive of substance abuse in adolescence. Adolescent substance abuse is another risk factor for delinquency, particularly acts involving violence (Bergen et al., 2004). Chabrol, Rodgers, Sobolewski, and van Leeuwen (2010, p. 263) found that cannabis use was "a significant independent predictor of delinquent behavior"—particularly for adolescents who scored high on depressive symptoms and psychopathic traits. Similar results were found by Chassin et al. (2010) when they studied alcohol and marijuana use among male offenders. Elevated use of both substances (particularly cannabis) in adolescents resulted in smaller increases in psychosocial maturity while those who reduced their use of the drugs experienced increased maturity. However, the authors cautioned these effects may be temporary and these adolescents may catch up to their peers' maturity level in adulthood.

Some researchers have focused on the fact that delinquent youth often anticipate an early death believing they have no future (Brezina, Tekin, & Topalli, 2008). Whether this belief in fatalism and an early death is the cause of delinquency is not known, however, the association between the two is relatively clear. Those who feel tomorrow might never come are more likely to engage in impulsive, high-risk, and criminal behaviors. Fatalism has often been noted in communities suffering economic distress and high crime rates (Anderson, 1999). According to this model, anticipating an early death may lead to other beliefs and actions that foster that outcome including:

- Discounting the risks and consequences of behavior
- Pursuing immediate gratification of need
- Maintaining a here and now orientation rather than being future oriented
- Engaging in high-risk behaviors

Community context is another factor that has been studied with respect to adolescent substance abuse and delinquency (Chilenski & Greenberg, 2009). Researchers looked at risk and resource factors in the community predictive of antisocial behavior. Factors included poverty, residential instability, crime rates, substance abuse environment, and school district risk. Resource factors in the community included the collective efficacy of the community to deal with problems, school leadership, youth activity opportunities, and the availability of youth-serving organizations. The authors conclude communities with higher levels of risk also had higher rates of adolescent antisocial behavior and substance use. Likewise, communities with greater resources for youth tended to have lower rates of adolescent antisocial behavior. These results suggest the potential wisdom of adopting community-level strategies in addition to clinical services as a means to deal with adolescent delinquency and substance use.

Providing services to juveniles accused of delinquent or criminal behavior is a common role for social workers. For a description of some of the issues and concerns facing the social worker, read Larry Botnick's case example, Travis: A Case on Working With Children in Juvenile Detention.

When children or adolescents have learned antisocial behaviors and values, often the goal is to resocialize them into prosocial norms. A great number of social programs exist with this purpose foremost in mind including foster and group homes, residential treatment facilities, juvenile corrections facilities and services, after-school programs, boys and girls clubs, and similar organizations.

The Role of Peers

While maltreatment as a child may constitute a risk factor for future delinquency, other intervening variables influence the outcome. For example, maltreated children and adolescents may also experience school difficulties and deviant peer groups, each of which increases the likelihood of engaging in antisocial behavior. However, while there appears to be a link between maltreatment, and mediating factors such as absconding, substance abuse, mental health problems, school disengagement, and deviant peers, the evidence is insufficient to ascribe causation or a direct connection across time.

Snyder, Wesley, Lin, and May (2008) summarizing research on peer influences on delinquency noted two ways they help create socially deviant behavior. The first is *coercive interaction* in which individuals, by their aggressive and disruptive behavior, alienate their peers. The peers, in turn, reject the aggressor, exclude them from social interactions, and use coercive treatment to show their displeasure. Without relationships with normative peer groups, these outcasts are more likely to be attracted to peers holding deviant attitudes.

A second mechanism for creating individuals with antisocial attitudes and behavior is through *peer deviancy training*. Once rejected by normative peers for whatever reason, the future deviants may choose to affiliate with and spend time with antisocial peers. In these associations, the outcast is exposed to conversation, rehearsal, and positive evaluations of deviant behavior. Involvement with deviant peers is associated with *overt conduct problems* such as aggression and *covert conduct problems* such as stealing, risky sexual behavior, and substance abuse (Snyder et al., 2008). The point at which these mechanisms begin to operate has been debated with more recent research suggesting that it may start as conduct problems appearing as early as kindergarten (Estell, Cairns, Farmer, & Cairns, 2002; Snyder et al., 2005).

Coercive interaction and deviance training are separate mechanisms, operating from different perspectives. From a behavioral standpoint, coercive interactions are decidedly aversive and punishing to the child while deviant peer training reflects modeling and reinforcement to change the child's thinking and actions. Some children with existing conduct disorders will experience peer coercion but not choose to affiliate with deviant peers. They may become loners with few, if any, friends. Other children will be drawn to deviant peer groups because of shared interests without necessarily facing peer coercion from normative groups. In many cases, these operate together and children who experience both are at greater risk for subsequent behavioral difficulties.

Clinical Corner

Rodney

Rodney is a 15-year-old male from a single-parent home. His parents are divorced and his mother works outside the home earning the only income for the family, which consists of Rodney, his mom, and his 12-year-old sister Rosalie. The children are often left alone while the mother works and basically take care of themselves. Rosalie is a bit shy but otherwise appears to be behaving appropriately. Rodney, on the other hand, has begun to get into some trouble. He spends time with Jake who has taught him how to make homemade bombs and rockets, which they shoot without any concern about what might happen or who might be hurt. Rodney also likes to stand on his front sidewalk and shoot arrows into the air to see how far they travel. However, the arrows often land on neighbors' property or in the city street. So far, no one has been injured by the boys' actions. In view of what you know so far, consider the following questions:

1. What would you predict will happen to Rodney if this behavior continues?
2. Given the absence of the mother, are Rodney and his sister candidates for foster care?
3. What do you think explains the apparent lack of concern of Jake and Rodney about the possible consequences of their actions?

Socially deviant behavior is often categorized into one of two groups: internalized and externalized syndromes. *Internalized syndromes* include common psychological disturbances such as depression, somatic problems, and anxiety while *externalized syndromes* typically cover things such as conduct and oppositional defiant disorders. Some children experience both syndromes and are at greater risk for involvement with deviant peer groups (Dishion, 2000). In these situations, the comorbidity of emotional problems and antisocial behavior represents a greater risk than either alone.

The influence of peers on problematic behavior has been addressed in Chapter 12. Research has shown peer influence plays a critical role in the early onset of substance use, sexual intercourse, and delinquency and violent behavior (Dishion & Patterson, 1999; Dishion, Andrews & Crosby, 1995). Moreover, substance abuse prevention programs for high-risk adolescents have shown little success if the adolescent belongs to a drug-using peer group

Family Influences

When young adolescents are also experiencing emotional problems, they appear to be more vulnerable to peer influence and deviance training. However, it is not only the influence of peers that impact the behavior of children and adolescents. A failure of parents to set expectations and adequately supervise their adolescent children's activities also plays a significant role (French & Dishion, 2003). Parenting behaviors—such as influencing the child's environment, deciding when and who a child is permitted to date, evaluating and managing children's friendships, setting clear expectations for appropriate behaviors, and discouraging premature sexual activity—are typically associated with lower rates of early sexual behavior by teens (Boislard, Poulin, Kiesner, & Dishion, 2009).

Research by Slomkowski, Rende, Novak, Richardson, and Niaura (2005) and Avenevoli and Merikangas (2003) looked at the influence of siblings and found sibling smoking is a more powerful risk factor for smoking than parental smoking. Smoking by older siblings influences both the level of smoking and the rate of use by their younger siblings. Similar sibling influence has been found with respect to adolescent deviancy including delinquency. Perhaps most interesting is that the influence of older siblings in these areas appears to be independent of genetic similarity. Other studies looking sibling relationship involving aggression relate problems such as delinquency, substance abuse, and antisocial behavior. Most findings found aggression by one sibling toward another increases tendencies toward antisocial behaviors during adolescence, academic failure, and problems with peer and adult relationships (Natsuaki, Ge, Reiss, & Neiderhiser, 2009). Gender differences have also been found with respect to adolescent deviance as is shown in Box 18.1.

Box 18.1 Gender Differences, Aggression, and Deviance

While most studies have focused on boys and conduct disorders, some have looked at gender differences. Keenan, Coyne, and Lahey (2008) found that girls employing relational aggression (behaviors designed to hurt another through a social relationship) were more likely to be assessed with oppositional defiant disorder or conduct disorders. They were also more likely to be socially isolated, which often leads to deviant behavior (Crick & Grotpeter, 1995). Compared to boys, girls tended to be more emotionally distressed when they were the victims of relational aggression and more likely to react in kind. Emotional distress appears to interfere with the cognitive processing and raise the likelihood of overt and relational aggression (Bowie, 2010). The link between depression and a lack of empathy and relational aggression has also been made, showing again the complex interplay between psychological challenges and deviant behavior (Zahn-Waxler, Park, Essex, Slattery, & Cole, 2005). Girls who engaged in relational aggression but also participated in prosocial activities were less likely to be involved in deviant social behavior (Bowie, 2010). Girls appear better able to regulate themselves and avoid problem behaviors than are boys from ages 10 to 12. However, this gender difference disappears by mid-adolescence (Kirisci, Mezzich, Aytaclar, Reynolds, & Tarter, 2009). Girls are also less likely to associate with deviant peers in late childhood and mid-adolescence and have lower drug involvement than boys. Once boys and girls reach their mid-adolescent years, there does not seem to be a significant difference between the genders with respect to involvement in antisocial behavior.

Juveniles engaging in delinquent behavior may find themselves incarcerated in youth detention facilities. An estimated 7,100,000 children under age 18 are living in such facilities with the number increasing annually (Hagner, Malloy, Mazzone, & Cormier, 2008). These juveniles may be incarcerated for actual criminal behavior or for what is known as *status offenses*, which are behaviors that are problematic because of the juvenile's age, such as violating curfew, being truant from school, and underage drinking.

GANGS

Short (1990, p. 148) defined a gang as "a group whose members meet together with some regularity, over time, on the basis of group-defined criteria of membership and group-defined organizational structure, and some sense of territoriality." Other definitions exist in the literature, but Short's description is both simply expressed and not pejorative in meaning. While the mass media report on the existence of gangs as a reality in both urban and some rural environments, relatively little is known about the topic. Political campaigns have used the fear of gangs as a talking point in past elections, and policy makers have identified gangs and gang violence as significant social problems (Lane & Meeker, 2000). The actual number and composition of gangs is not known. There are all male gangs, all female gangs, and gangs with both genders represented. The Federal Bureau of Investigation (FBI, 2012a) estimates there are 33,000 violent street gangs, motorcycle gangs, and prison gangs in the United States today with around 1.4 million members. Some are well organized and national or international in scope, while others are local in focus. Activities in which they engage include prostitution, drug trafficking, extortion, robbery, fraud, and gun trafficking. Dealing with gangs involves cooperation among national, state, and local law enforcement agencies in intelligence sharing, law enforcement, and investigation. In some cases, cooperation exists between the law enforcement communities in the United States and those in other countries such as El Salvador, Honduras, Canada, Guatemala, and Mexico.

Many gangs target middle and high school students for membership and make it difficult for adolescents to refuse to join. Some gangs are homegrown, composed of

Tattoos showing gang affiliations.

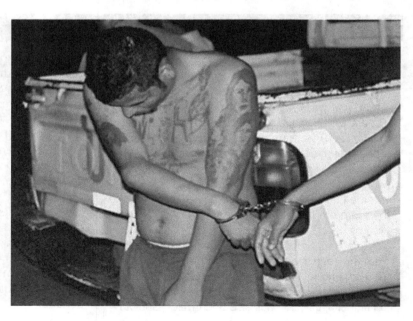

Source: Federal Bureau of Investigation (2012b).

neighborhood members, and operate in a relatively small geographical area. Other gangs such as Mara Salvatrucha (also known as MS-13) are largely composed of immigrants from El Salvador or first-generation Salvadoran Americans, although others from Central and South America do participate. The gang operates in the U.S. capitol and in at least 42 states. Their depredations include "drug distribution, murder, rape, prostitution, robbery, home invasions, immigration offenses, kidnapping, carjackings, auto theft, and vandalism" (FBI, 2008). Frequently, gang members bear tattoos marking their membership in a particular gang. Examples from the FBI files are shown in the following pictures.

The influence of MS-13 has been noted in the media. The Nightline television video, MS 13: Gang Life, provides a brief look at the origin, tactics, and criminal enterprises of this group. As you review the video, consider how a community might deal effectively with such groups.

Determining the actual amount of crime engaged in by gangs is difficult because reports submitted as part of the Uniform Crime Reports program do not separate out the kinds of crimes in which gangs were involved. However, other reports from law enforcement agencies do give a picture of the kinds of crimes in which gangs are involved, as is shown in Figure 18.1.

Reports from students about gang activity in their schools, as shown in Figure 18.2, also give a sense of the level of gang involvement in school settings as well as perceived changes over a 10-year period.

To be clear, gangs are not just a challenge for the United States; many nations experience gang activity (Spergel, 1990). For example, Zhang, Messner, Lu, and Deng (1997) described gang crime in China and how authorities respond to the problem. In many ways, Chinese gangs are similar to those in the United States with respect to member ages, tendency toward violence, focus on property crimes, and prior records of delinquency before joining a gang. Because gangs and gang crimes are considered especially

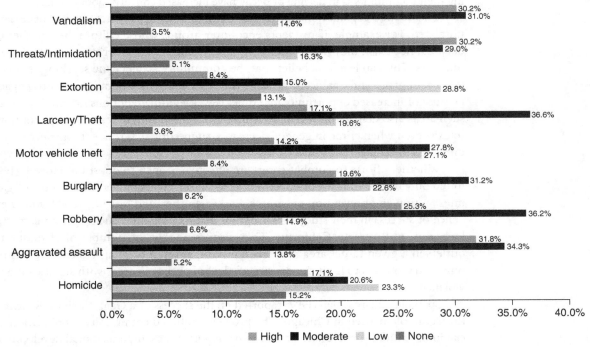

Figure 18.1

Percentage of Gang Involvement in Crime

Note: Responses of unknown rates of gang involvement are not visually represented in this chart.

Source: Federal Bureau of Investigation (2012a).

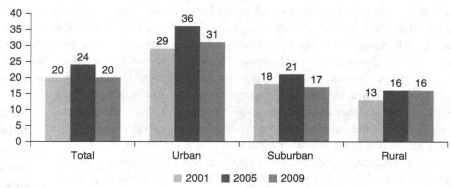

Figure 18.2
Percentage of Students Reporting Gang Activities at Schools for 2001, 2005, and 2009
Source: National Center for Educational Statistics (2012).

serious in China, official policy is severe on combating gangs. In China, engaging in crime as a gang member increases the severity of punishment meted out.

Fear of gangs tends to be more prevalent in areas where gang activity is most pronounced (Lane & Meeker, 2000). One important predictor of such fears is the community's or neighborhood's cultural diversity. This tends to stem from the fear of strangers and cultural misunderstandings. Older adults reacting to the changing or changed cultural diversity of their areas are most likely to be concerned about gang activity. Lower-income and minority individuals who live in gang areas also express greater fear of gangs. Lane and Meeker (2003) also point out the factors, trash, graffiti, deserted buildings, and a homeless population, making residents fear serious problems abound. Residents perceiving their community is in decline or decay have increased concerns about gangs.

These three explanations for fear of gangs and gang violence are not necessarily unrelated. For example, if residents encounter groups whose culture they neither understand nor trust, they may perceive negative changes are occurring within their communities. This can lead to a belief that the community is in decline sparking residents' fear about gangs and crime. At the same time, declining communities can attract gangs because of increased opportunity for crime. Fewer legitimate options for employment in such areas also help gangs recruit new members. Interestingly, fear of gangs continues to exist even when crime in general decreases, suggesting that residents' anxiety may be unrelated to actual crime rates.

Whether efforts to combat gangs are effective is open to question. Howell (1998) found only failure and lack of effectiveness when reviewing published accounts of gang intervention and prevention programs. Parker, Luther, and Murphy (2007) found evidence of success in their study of a program that focused on reducing gang-related violent crime in Riverside, California. They also found that the number of alcohol retail outlets in a given target area was related to the amount of gang violence. Their recommendation was to limit the density of alcohol outlets in areas with significant gang violence.

Spergel and Grossman (1997) reported on the success of a Gang Violence Reduction Project implemented in Chicago. The project combined community mobilization, social intervention, suppression, provision of opportunities, organizational development, and targeting. Interventions involved police officers, community youth workers, officers from adult probation, and neighborhood organization representative.

Gangs serve several purposes for members. Membership may be a means of economic survival in areas with limited or nonexistent work opportunities. Gang activity might be seen as an adaptation to poor economic options—gang membership means money for many members.

Others join gangs because it provides a degree of protection. Gangs actively seek to recruit new members and refusing to join after such invitations leaves one vulnerable to harassment, injury, or death. Gangs also provide refuge from dangers posed by other gangs, at least up to a point. Gang members always risk injury or death in disputes with other gangs over turf or even because one gang objects to colors of the clothes worn by the other.

In some neighborhoods, gangs are a means of becoming part of a popular group or being with friends with whom one has grown up. Gang membership may be a tradition handed down from one family generation to another.

Once adolescents become gang members, they often face initiations or other demands that put them at risk. These activities can include fighting, criminal behavior, or in the case of females, having sex with multiple gang members. Getting out of the gang is often problematic. Attempts to quit the gang may be met with violence or death. Even those who end up in prison are often expected to remain a member while incarcerated and after release. Those successful in quitting the gang, other difficulties await them, including the existence of gang tattoos, substance abuse problems, and/or a criminal record that reduces employment opportunities.

SCHOOL SHOOTINGS

Perhaps one of the most frightening events faced by society is violence in the school setting. School shootings are often appear random leaving students, parents, and school personnel in shock, wondering what could have prevented the violence. In most school shootings, a student (current or former) takes a gun to school to shoot a specific individual, uses the firearm with at least one casualty, and then seeks to shoot others besides the intended victim (Larkin, 2009). Other kinds of school-related violence do not meet these criteria and thus are not considered school shootings.

School shootings occur in educational institutions ranging from day care facilities to colleges and universities. Although they are still relatively rare, the fear of school shootings has prompted communities to provide enhanced security, including metal detectors, police officers in the school, evacuation and lockdown drills, and zero tolerance policies regarding threats, weapons, or other behaviors deemed dangerous to the school or its students (Birkland & Lawrence, 2009). As happens on a regular basis, mass media's focus on school shootings tends to engender fear and misunderstanding about the actual nature of these events. The result, in some cases, is that even pranks and routine acting out by students move from being handled by school personnel to involvement of the criminal justice system (Altheide, 2009). In some cases, the violent behavior is categorized as terrorism.

Rampage shootings, as some have called them, have taken on a life of their own that affects not just U.S. schools but those in Europe, Argentina, and Australia. "Doing a Columbine" or copying the 1999 behavior of two students at Columbine High School in Littleton, Colorado, has become a threat used by students and others seeking to frighten school administrators and disrupt the business of education. The threat has been used in many venues, including the university with which the text's authors are affiliated. Acts such as Columbine are used for a variety of purposes, "not merely as revenge but as a means of protest for bullying, intimidation, social isolation, and public rituals of humiliation" (Larkin, 2009, p. 1309). Many perpetrators believe their behavior is a political act designed to overcome oppression.

In addition to those noted earlier, schools have responded to school shootings by identifying steps that can be taken to prevent future events or ameliorate the outcomes (Fox & Savage, 2009, pp. 1469–1474). These steps include the following:

- Develop an emergency response plan
- Create a mass notification and communication systems for emergencies
- Develop a multidisciplinary team to deal with threats and dangerous behaviors
- Educate school personnel on privacy laws governing students and others
- Enter into a memorandum of understanding with local health and law enforcement agencies
- Conduct emergency drills and training
- Instruct staff, faculty, and students about the mass notification system and what to do in an emergency

School social workers and community mental health providers are often directly involved in these emergency plans, typically serving on the multidisciplinary team, providing counseling for students and school personnel, and serving as a resource for school staff.

Determining the causes of school shootings continues to be a challenge. Media and political arguments blame the availability of guns, pop culture, particularly movies and television, violent computer games, and/or societal decay. Despite the hyping of these explanations, most of the public places responsibility on the parents and do not identify media violence or peer influence as the reason for school shootings (Birkland & Lawrence, 2009). The late 2012 killing of 26 children and staff members at Sandy Hook School in Connecticut may prove an exception as it provoked national concern over gun violence in schools. Other researchers have looked at the influence of the environment, but from a different perspective. Brown, Osterman, and Barnes (2009) compared school violence in states with what they called a *culture of honor* to states without this characteristic. Culture of honor states tend to have values that support the death penalty and behaving aggressively and using violence to defend one's family, property, or reputation. They are also more likely to support and permit violence as entertainment or sport. States most likely to fit these characteristics exist in the Southern and Western United States as opposed to Eastern or Northern states. Their findings indicate that students in the culture of honor states were significantly more likely to have brought a weapon to school in the month prior to the survey. Using data over a 20-year period, they concluded that these states had more than twice as many school shootings per capita compared to other non–culture of honor states. Because many school shootings follow a pattern in which the shooters were abused, taunted, socially ostracized, marginalized, and/or demeaned, they hypothesized that the shooters retaliated through school violence in part because they lived in cultures that sanctioned violence in defense of one's honor. The authors also noted that 97% of school shootings' perpetrators were males, and males are more likely to use violence to regain or restore their honor. Although Brown and colleagues found no basis for this conclusion, other researchers have pointed out most school shootings have taken place in rural or suburban settings and relative few (8%) in urban locations, suggesting the setting may somehow play a role (Newman, Fox, Roth, Mehta, & Harding, 2005).

Perhaps the most promising perspective for understanding the reasons for school shootings is interdisciplinary (Henry, 2009). Henry (2009) and Muschert (2008) argue that school shootings are complex events that define single explanations and must take into account individual, group, family, and community variables. Factors that have been shown to contribute to school shootings include (1) the individual, (2) community context, and (3) social/cultural contexts. Individual factors include things such as access to guns, mental illness, peer relationships, and family maltreatment. Community contextual factors include school characteristics (e.g., teaching practices, zero tolerance policies, homophobia, acceptance of violence, bad faculty–student relationship, school leadership problems, poor handling of delinquency, and community intolerance). Social and cultural factors include poor support for public schools, gender-related violence, conservative religious political climate, media violence, and a gun culture (Muschert, 2008, pp. 68–69).

Newman et al. (2005) found that 85% of school shooters suffered from psychological difficulties including depression, thoughts of suicide, mental illness, and family relationship problems. However, the authors pointed out that understanding what happened requires that we "determine how the shooter's mental state interacted with his social exclusion to foster hopelessness, despair and rage" (p. 244). This perspective is consistent with social work's perspective on understanding the person within the social environment and his or her reciprocal influence.

In a study looking at 10 school shooters, Langman (2009) categorized them into three groups: the *traumatized*, *psychotic*, and *psychopathic*. Despite the value of categories, however, the author observed, "most people who are traumatized, psychotic, and psychopathic do not commit murder" (p. 79). As a consequence, he looked more closely at those in each category to identify significant factors that might better explain the shooters' actions. The first group included those who had been *traumatized* (three student shooters). This group came from broken homes characterized by parental substance abuse and criminal behavior. Each adolescent had been physically abused and two had experienced sexual abuse outside of their home. All three had fathers whose criminal behavior included the use of guns, suggesting the potential effect of parental role modeling of criminal behavior and firearms. In addition, each of these shooters had peers who encouraged them to commit the school shooting.

The second group he identified was the *psychotic*, composed of five student shooters. Psychotic shooters suffered from schizophrenia-spectrum disorders, including both schizophrenia and schizotypal personality disorder. Each experienced paranoid or grandiose delusions or hallucinations. None came from broken homes nor had they suffered abuse. None of their parents had engaged in criminal activity with firearms; no peers seemed to have played a role in encouraging antisocial behavior. Factors that did play a role in their lives included being the youngest in their families and having higher functioning siblings with no evidence of psychosis. Thus, these shooters were markedly different from their peers in ways obvious to most adults. The result was that each shooter felt both distress and rage over being "different" from his siblings. Each shooter was male, was most engaged in substance abuse, had displayed problems early in his life, but had not been prescribed any antipsychotic medications.

Langman labeled the third group of two shooters as *psychopathic*, and neither had been abused nor suffered from psychosis. Common characteristics of this group included a lack of empathy and conscience, narcissism, and engagement in sadistic activities. These shooters were more likely to encourage others to join them than to be influenced by deviant peers. They had families with no history of firearms abuse, although they were in homes where firearms were used legally and were available. Both boys were fascinated or obsessed with guns and were able to recruit others to participate in the school shootings. Again, this finding suggests that a confluence of biology, social factors, and other causes are responsible for human behavior and that single explanations are often insufficient or simply wrong.

Some authors have identified a series of sequential steps that they believe occur in each school shooting incident (Levin & Madfis, 2009). These stages include *chronic strain* brought about by a cumulative history of frustration, maltreatment, and failure in the school setting. This stage is followed by *uncontrolled strain*, which occurs in the absence of any constraints such as positive peer relationships that protect against antisocial acts. In effect, this produces a sense of social isolation that either frees the shooter from prosocial norms or drives them into antisocial peer groups. *Acute strain* is much like the straw that broke the camel's back. It is some event, loss, or other happening that produces a sense of catastrophe in the shooter's life. In the case of school shooters, the acute strain may be a particularly egregious put down, rejection, or other loss that pushes the person over the edge. The end of a romantic relationship, rejection by peers or parents, and major academic problems (e.g., failing or expulsion) are common acute strains. An illustration of this phenomenon is the following case of Seung-Hui Cho.

Clinical Corner

Seung-Hui Cho: Notes on a School Shooter

Seung-Hui Cho was a 23-year-old Korean American male who, in April 2007, killed 33 people including himself and injured another 17 on the campus of Virginia Tech University in Blacksburg. Cho was described as a young adult who did not fit in well and was isolated from peers. As an adolescent, other students laughed at his poor English skills, absence of affect, and high level of shyness. He was said to live in his world and was generally noncommunicative (Cho & Gardner, 2007). He had been bullied and rejected by peers but had survived to his senior year. For Cho, the acute strain was impending graduation, at which point he would be forced to leave the campus and forge out on his own. While graduation always involves the unknown, in Cho's case, it meant he would be evicted from the niche he had occupied for the last few years. For Cho, this was the last straw (Levin & Madfis, 2009).

The fourth stage in school shootings is the *planning stage* during which the shooter feels there are no other options than to get even with those who he believes have wronged him. For those who have been ignored and rejected, this means a chance to show others he is a person with whom to be reckoned. Planning the means of revenge often takes time and tends not to be spontaneous. The planning stage may take a couple of days, or in the case of the Columbine students, more than a year. Prior to the shooting, Cho took the time to mail photos of himself to the news media. The photos showed Cho in the possession of weapons and looking dangerous (Levin & Madfis, 2009). In the planning stage, shooters must also assemble the firearms or other weapons they plan to use, decide how to get them to campus, and choose where to initiate their retaliation.

The final stage is the *massacre at school*. Typically the shooting occurs in areas where there are an adequate supply of potential victims and the absence of anyone who might threaten the shooter's ability to carry out the attack (Felson, 1994).

Larkin (2009, p. 1322) sums up the inherent dangers leading to school shootings: "Social structural and cultural characteristics that have led to rampage shootings, such as the toleration of predatory behaviors on the part of elite students, the lionization of winners and the punishment of losers, the male ethic of proving one's masculinity through violence, the easy availability of assault weapons to just about anyone, and the media fascination and exploitation of violence, go far beyond the communities that experienced rampage shootings. Rampage shootings can occur in almost any community."

Mallette and Chalouh (1991) and Tonso (2009) have argued that patriarchal societies are more likely to spawn the actions of school shooters and others. In their view, these societies emphasize male dominance, subjugation of women, and support aggressiveness as a means of redressing real or imagined insults. Preventing the recurrence of male-perpetrated violence requires a radical transformation of school culture, recognizing how schools contribute to the culture-bound image of male superiority, and reinforcing ways for students to develop identities that "do not rely on either violence or supremacy" (p. 1279).

It is probably impossible to identify every potential school shooter, as some simply do not appear to fit the mold. However, it is possible to recognize some of those who are at most risk. These youth appear to be experiencing some degree of difficulty, with violent tendencies that are often obvious. They have also frequently, but not always, received mental health evaluation. Peers are often aware of the problem behaviors but may not have known to share them with adults. Potential shooters have suffered humiliation while also engaging in thoughts of retribution using violence. Many experienced depression and abuse and believe that they are social outcasts. Too often, they see the remedy for these statuses and experiences lying in violence against their peers, believing that attacking their peers will raise them from the status of loser to notorious killer (Newman & Fox, 2009).

It is important to recognize that school shootings affect more than just those who directly experienced the event. While students in directly affected schools are offered counseling and other supports to help them cope with the tragedy, others may also experience stress. Fallahi and Lesik (2009) found that students from other schools not attacked experienced moderate or acute stress from closely following the event on television. Symptoms included "intrusive thoughts, sleep disturbances, distraction, stomach upset, depression, disorganization, replaying the event, and symptoms of anger" (p. 227). In general, the more closely these students followed the event, the greater their level of distress. Consequently, there may be both direct and indirect victims of school shootings. Efforts to limit access to assault weapons used in school and other shootings and other proposed restrictions on gun availability are typically met by opposition from powerful interest groups such as the National Rifle Association, a lobbying group for the gun industry.

DELINQUENCY IN ADULTHOOD (CRIMES AGAINST HUMANITY AND SOCIETY)

Some perceive delinquency as a problem of juveniles who fail to follow societal norms and graduate into adult criminals. Only a small portion of those who engaged in adolescent delinquency maintain and expand their antisocial behavior as adults. After looking at the extent to which delinquency continued into adulthood, Bersani, Nieuwbeerta, and Laub (2009) concluded that "it is difficult to predict long-term patterns of criminal offending using risk factors identified early in the life course" (p. 469). Others have suggested that some adolescent behaviors can be predicted to lead to adult criminality. For example, Hayatbakhsh, Najman, Bor, O'Callaghan, and Williams (2009) found a relationship among adolescent behaviors such as early adolescent smoking, alcohol use, aggression and delinquency, and cannabis use in young adults. They also concluded that the adolescent's social context—including maternal smoking and childhood sexual abuse—influences adult use of marijuana.

While association with deviant peers is associated with antisocial behavior in adolescents, this does not appear to be true with adults (Monahan, Steinberg, & Cauffman, 2009). As individuals enter young adulthood, the influence of peers decreases significantly. This is true even if the adult continues to spend time with antisocial peers. Those young adults, whose antisocial peers continue to be influential in their lives, tend to be emotionally and behaviorally immature. The reasons for the lessened influence of peers seem related to the individual's increased autonomy and the consequences of identity development toward the end of adolescence (Collins & Steinberg, 2006). In addition, most young adults enter into full-time work and marriage during this period, which also plays a role.

Monahan et al. (2009) found that individuals who continued their antisocial behavior into young adulthood shared several characteristics. These included deficits in psychosocial maturity and significant problems controlling aggression and impulses. Compared to their peers, they showed lower orientation to the future is associated with need for immediate gratification and weak impulse control.

Other research on the role of biology in adult criminal behavior looked at the influence of testosterone, which prior studies had linked with violent crimes committed by prisoners (Dabbs & Morris, 1990). Using a large sample of male military veterans, the authors concluded that testosterone levels were associated with antisocial behavior but that individuals of higher socioeconomic class were less likely to engage in such behaviors. This suggests that socioeconomic class may operate as a mediator allowing the individual to control problematic tendencies.

Studies looking at how environmental factors influence antisocial behavior have considered a variety of items. Religiosity, for example, has been associated with fewer antisocial behaviors, perhaps because participating in religious activities connects the individual to the larger society. However, Grasmick, Kinsey, and Cochran (1991) found that only some components of religiosity were predictive and only with regard to certain crimes.

Some individuals engage in criminal or antisocial behavior only one time in their lives while others make criminal activity a career. While the latter group may have careers lasting from 5 to 30 years, little is known about what factors affect continued criminal behavior. Piquero, Brame, and Lynam (2004) identified almost 400 serious offenders who had been incarcerated in the California Youth Authority institutions and followed them for more than 10 years. They found that youth whose families received welfare and who were incarcerated for longer periods in their teens were likely to have longer criminal careers. Early entry into the juvenile justice system seemed to predict longer criminal histories. Others whose careers in crime were shorter typically had lengthy stays in jail or prison, had their first contact with police at a later age, and had higher cognitive abilities. Apparently, lengthy incarceration has deterrent value for at least some adult criminals.

Vandiver (2006) studied 300 registered male sex offenders initially arrested for sexual offenses as teens. Most had been arrested for either sexual assault or indecent behavior with a child. She followed this group for a three- to six-year period after they reached adulthood to determine their recidivism rate. Only 13 of the 300 were arrested for a sexual offense as adults, but more than half were arrested for other offenses. Offenders initially arrested as younger adolescents were more apt to be arrested as adults. Rearrest as an adult was also more likely for those whose initial victims were females under age 12. Most offenders were related to their victims.

Scholte (1999) found that about one-third of adolescents arrested for delinquency continued this behavior into adulthood. Those more likely to recidivate had committed more serious delinquent acts as juveniles and had parents who were controlling but not supportive. Stouthamer-Loeber, Wei, Loeber, and Masten (2004) found similar results concluding that serious delinquency in late adolescence, use of hard drugs, and belonging to a gang predicted continued criminal behavior in adulthood. Adolescents less likely to recidivate had parents who used low levels of physical punishment in early adolescence. Being employed or in school during early adulthood also had a preventative effect.

One area of adult criminal behavior not yet addressed is workplace violence. The media carry regular reports of individuals engaging in violence within their place of work and sometimes in the workplace of family members. Early episodes of violence within the U.S. Postal Service gave rise to the term *going postal* as a euphemism for harming coworkers. However, most workplace violence is perpetrated by criminals with no direct connection to the workplace. Workplace violence appears to be highest in several different kinds of employment situations including (Ta et al., 2009):

- Working with unstable or violence-prone individuals as in criminal justice settings
- Mobile workplaces such as taxicabs and police cars
- Late-night operations such as fast-food and convenience stores
- Jobs involving contact with the public
- Jobs delivering goods and services or passengers
- Community-based settings
- Guarding property or possessions

There is also some evidence that characteristics of the geographical area in which a workplace is located may place a role in which employment areas are targeted. For example, Amandus, Hunter, James, and Hendricks (1995) found that high crime rate areas have a greater risk of workplace violence. Areas with high rates of poverty, lower educational levels of residents, and high unemployment rates have also been associated with workplace violence (Hendricks, Landsittel, Amandus, Malcan, & Bell, 1999; Janicak, 2004; Pridemore, 2002).

SEXUAL ABUSE

Over the past 50 years, much has been written about sexual abuse, its victims, and the perpetrators. At the same time, much of the information about perpetrators has been gleaned from incarcerated individuals with inherent limitations due to the nature of the population and settings. For example, honesty and candor can be limited by fears about confidentiality, attempts to provide socially approved responses, and selection bias. Moreover, offenders often engage in misrepresentation, denial of problems, and attempts to present themselves as normal.

Another difficulty is that most sexual abuse is never reported, meaning that a true understanding of the overall picture of abusers and survivors is compromised. Marital rape, date rape, and many cases of incest are vastly underreported, at least in part because the survivor knows the offender. Even rape by strangers is often not reported. It is estimated that only 5% of rape cases are reported to authorities (Warshaw, 1988). In addition, official statistics do not often provide an adequate estimate of actual occurrence of sexual crimes. For example, many who were initially charged with a sexual offense will plea-bargain the charge down to a lesser offense such as assault. This practice undercuts the ability to identify the number of sexual predators convicted for a given sexual offense. Since the United States lacks a centralized criminal justice record-keeping system for offenders, those who move from one jurisdiction to another may commit additional offenses but have their crime viewed as a one-time occurrence (Quackenbush, 2003).

Harkins and Dixon (2010) have reviewed sexual offending in groups, which occurs in situations such as gang rapes, fraternity rapes, and rapes during wartime. In these situations, rape and other forms of sexual assault are typically committed by multiple offenders. This may occur in the form of hazing or gang initiation, by frat parties, and by victors in military conflicts. Common variables in each of these scenarios include an emphasis on male dominance and male bonding, denigration of females, a belief in the rape myth that women "asked for it," and acceptance of coercion against women. Rapes committed during war time are often related to military goals where subjugation, infliction of terror, and punishment of the enemy is supported. This is particularly true in those cases of *ethnic cleansing*. However, as the authors note, sexual violence is visited not just upon enemies but often upon fellow military personnel. Sadler, Booth, and Doebbeling (2005) found in their study of women veterans of the Vietnam War and later conflicts that 28% reported being raped and 5% reported being gang raped.

Adult child molesters have been studied and various conclusions posited about this group. For example, Nezu, Nezu, Dudek, Peacock, and Stoll (2005) found incarcerated child molesters had deficits in all measures of social problem solving when compared to the general population. Social problem solving refers to the process individuals use to identify solutions for stressful situations in which they find themselves. Child molesters are more likely to use avoidant problem-solving styles and possess both a negative problem orientation and an impulsive/careless problem-solving style. Those with negative problem orientations believe they lack control over their environment, will not successfully resolve dilemmas, and see problems as inherently unsolvable (Nezu, 2004). As indicated by the name, impulsive/careless styles of problem solving employ hurried, impulsive, and incomplete approaches that fail to achieve their goal. Under stress, avoidance styles use procrastination and passivity, hoping others will solve the problem for them. Both impulsive and avoidance styles are dysfunctional approaches to problem solving (Nezu et al., 2005).

Some pedophiles are attracted to work in day care centers and residential care facilities where an ample supply of potential victims can be found. The extent to which these

Did You Know?

Harkins and Dixon (2010) have also looked at multiple perpetrators who sexually abused children. They point out the existence of pedophile organizations that advocate for lowering or ending age of consent laws, ending the prosecution and social stigmatization of pedophiles, and permitting adult–child sexual encounters. Those belonging to such organizations seek to normalize their deviant interest in children and engage in various cognitive distortions to justify their beliefs. Other types of multiple perpetrator organizations include child sex rings that recruit children to participate in individual and group abuse.

individuals are successful in their quests remains in question. Several investigations of sexual abuse inside day care centers have proven futile or unsubstantiated. The same cannot be said about abuse in residential care facilities. Abusers in these institutions are often charismatic, and operate in environments where poor staff training and lax supervision exist and management fails to report suspected abuse to CPS (Green, 2001; Harkins & Dixon, 2010). These characteristics are also found in clerics and other adults in mentor-like positions who engage in sexual abuse of children, a topic of frequent media attention. Many churches have been tarred because of pastors, priests, and lay leaders abused children under their care. Similar problems have occurred in sports, residential treatment centers, and other youth serving organizations.

The best evidence to date suggests that those who repeatedly engage in sexual abuse tend to choose the same victim type each time. For example, males who prey on male children are not likely to graduate to raping adult women. Same-sex child molesters have the highest risk of reoffending. The lowest risk of reoffending is for father–daughter incest in cases where there are no other victims (Quackenbush, 2003). Others have argued that so little is known about sexual offenders that it is impossible to accurately predict their future choice of victims (English, 2001).

It is important to also look at juvenile involvement in sexual offenses, an area that has had relatively little attention. It is estimated that juveniles are involved in 14% of all sexual assaults and male juveniles are involved in 20% of all rapes. They are also responsible for 30% to 50% of all child sexual assaults (Brown, Flanagan, & McLeod, 1984; Office of Juvenile Justice and Delinquency, 1999). One reason to consider this topic is the often-cited belief that sex offenders as a group tend to be persistent recidivists posing ongoing danger to society. Zimring, Piquero, and Jennings (2007) studied three birth cohorts to determine whether juvenile sex offenders continue their depredations into their adult lives. They found that only 8.5% of males with records for sexual offenses as juveniles went on to engage in adult sex offenses. This figure is not much different from other juveniles with police records. This suggests that predicting adult sexual offenses based upon sexual offenses committed as a juvenile is largely impossible and that assumptions about these juveniles evolving into adult predators are unfounded. Righthand and Welch (2004) reached the same conclusion and noted that only "a relatively small group of juveniles commit repeat sexual offenses after there has been an official response to their sexual offending" (p. 15). In contrast, Hagan, Anderson, Caldwell, and Kemper (2010) looked at a small sample (12) of juvenile sex offenders who were predicted to recidivate and found that 42% of them did so within five years of release into the community. However, they provided no information on how these predictions were made or the instruments used in the risk assessment.

We have discussed previously the topic of child sexual abuse in terms of risk factors faced by survivors. Messman-Moore and Brown (2004) found that having been sexually abused as a child was also associated with being raped as an adult. Past studies suggest sexual victimization as a child increases the likelihood of rape as an adult by up to 11 times (Fergusson, Horwood, & Lynskey, 1997). Sexual revictimization occurs in 15% to 79% of adults sexually abused as children (Roodman & Clum, 2001). Childhood emotional abuse (CEA) also appears to be a valid predictor of adult rape, perhaps because it diminishes survivors' sense of self-worth. Diminished self-worth, in turn, can lead to a lack of assertiveness in adult relationships. Coupled with being victimized as a child, survivors may conclude their only value as sexual creatures. While not always true, it is common for survivors of childhood sexual attack to have experienced other types of maltreatment. Messman-Moore and Brown (2004) concluded that childhood violence has a cumulative effect on individuals continuing into adulthood.

Community responses to sexual abuse continue to be debated. Concerns about the long-term danger of repeated offenses by sexual predators have led to many laws designed to prevent recidivism. Most states, for example, have sex registries where convicted sex offenders are listed complete with address. This is designed to serve two purposes: keeping track of the offender's location and alerting the public to their domicile. As a result, anyone with access to the Internet can look up addresses of convicted offenders by zip code. Figure 18.3, from the Utah Department of Corrections, lists those on the sex offender registry living within one mile of the author. This particular registry provides names, addresses, pictures, and the offense for which the individual was convicted. While this information is of some value, another 300 offenders on the registry have no current address on file and their location is unknown. A 2003 report indicated that California corrections officials had no locations for 33,000 sex offenders, over 40% of those who had registered at least once (Curtis, 2003).

In addition to sex offender registries, many states have adopted laws that allow for civil commitment of violent sexual predators. Unlike a prison sentence, the individual can be held until the facility determines that the person is no longer a danger. In some cases, this can be for the remainder of the offender's life. Another state policy establishes child safety zones, which typically involves specific distances from child-centric locations such as schools, day care centers, and public parks. In these states, offenders are not

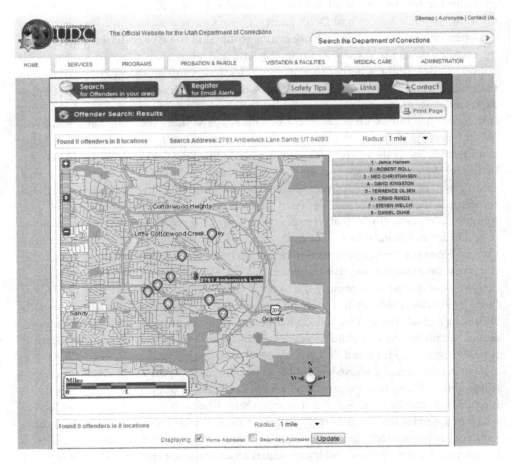

Figure 18.3
Sex Offender Search Results, Utah Department of Corrections
Source: Utah Department of Corrections (2012).

allowed to live or work within these geographical areas. In 2009, a news report indicated that 67 sex offenders were living under a bridge in Miami because this was the only location where impoverished offenders could afford to live. Allegedly, some had been left at the bridge by their probation/parole agents (Allen, 2009).

Interventions employed in sex offender treatment include cognitive behavioral therapy used within a relapse prevention model that appears to have significant success (Ikomi, Harris-Wyatt, Doucet, & Rodney, 2009). Often this model employs cognitive restructuring, learning problem-solving skills, and helping clients develop self-control skills, among others. Other methods employed with varying degrees of success or failure are "chemical castration, social skills training, aversion therapy, covert sensitization, and satiation therapy" (p. 596). Some interventions also involve anger management, empathy training, teaching coping responses, assertiveness training, communication skills, and sexuality education (Longo, 2004).

Policy Practice

Practice Behavior Example: Analyze, formulate, and advocate for policies that advance social well-being.

Critical Thinking Question: Given what you know about the recidivism of sexual predators, what is your opinion about laws that allow the state to hold a sexual offender indefinitely? Is it justified, under what circumstances, and what social work ethical issues are involved?

DOMESTIC VIOLENCE

As discussed in Chapter 17, domestic violence is a common occurrence in many cultures. Getting accurate statistics on the incidence of domestic violence is not easy. Stark (2007) argues that 14.5 million women in the United States are being abused, an extraordinarily large number. This is in contrast to the Centers for Disease Control and Prevention's (2011) estimate that 2 million women are injured by domestic violence each year and more than 2,300 women die as a result. About 25% of all women are likely to experience domestic violence during their lifetimes (Coker, Smith, McKeown, & King, 2000). Among survivors, males are the least likely to report domestic violence (Dewar, 2008). Disbelief and social prejudices about men being stronger are both explanations for this discrepancy. When men are victimized, often there are few, if any, support networks available when compared to those provided for women. A casual review of the literature from multiple countries demonstrates the near universality of domestic violence. Despite its widespread occurrence, domestic violence is not evenly distributed throughout any given population. For example, Nash (2005) found that twice as many African American women compared to White women suffer severe violence.

By definition, domestic violence is intentional physical violence by a husband, wife, or cohabitant directed toward that individual's spouse or cohabitant without consent (Martin & Law, 2006). Others have broadened the definition to include verbal, emotional, financial, and/or sexual abuse. In short, it is "an abusive exercise of power and control over others, which leaves individuals feeling scared and intimidated" (Barber, 2008, p. 35). Barber notes that some authors separate domestic violence and domestic abuse with the former limited to physical violence and the latter incorporating the other nonviolent forms of abuse. Obviously, how one defines violence plays a large role in estimates about the actual rate of domestic violence.

Domestic violence occurs in all socioeconomic strata and both women and men are victimized. However, men are most often the perpetrators in violence against women. Both straight and gay/lesbian relationships are subject to domestic violence. Regardless of which gender is the target of this violence, the outcomes are similar—diminished self-worth, fear, confusion, guilt, anger, shame, isolation, and loss of confidence (Plat-Jones, 2006).

Despite its existence for perhaps hundreds of years, domestic violence became a U.S. national priority only in the 1970s. The criminal justice system response to domestic violence came into being largely as a result of mandatory arrest laws that encouraged or required police to arrest perpetrators whether the victim wished to press charges or not. Changes in both state and federal law helped this process. In addition, treatment programs were created with a goal of working with male perpetrators.

Male perpetrators' response to battering others often involves rationalization and denial. Neighbors et al. (2010) found that violent spouses believed that their actions were normal or typical of other spouses. When asked to estimate the frequency of other men abusing their partner, their perceptions were significantly different from reality. In every type of abuse from throwing something at a partner to forcing the partner to have sex against her will, the perpetrators overestimated the percentage of other men who engaged in such abuse. In addition, abusers often deny the abuse occurred or minimize its extent (Catlett, Toews, & Walilko, 2010). Many blame the women for provoking the abuse by their actions or failure to act in a certain way. Male power and privilege become part of the narrative to justify the abuse as men use their presumed higher status to rationalize their right to strike another. In many cases, the violence is functional because it forces the spouse to do the bidding of the abuser while underscoring the man's authority and masculinity (Dobash & Dobash, 1998).

It is not uncommon for perpetrators to be court ordered into treatment programs for batterers. However, many do not finish the programs. A variety of factors appear to predict the likelihood that someone will drop out. These factors include "men who were lower income, no longer intimately involved with the women they abused, and who reported lower levels of physical violence and higher levels of hostility" (Catlett et al., 2010, p. 107).

Even among men who complete treatment programs, outcome studies have called into question their effectiveness. A meta-analysis conducted by Babcock, Green, and Robie (2004) found that most interventions were of limited value with respect to reducing battering. Similar findings have been noted by Jackson et al. (2003).

INTERVENTION OPTIONS

Efforts to prevent crime and delinquency have been ongoing for centuries. For example, early attempts to stop pickpockets involved publicly cutting off the hand of the offender. This was supposed to act both as a deterrent for other pickpockets and to prevent the offender from repeat behaviors. However, the public punishment drew crowds and offered other pickpockets multiple victims. Harsh treatment of criminals and delinquents was employed under the assumption it would result in a general and specific deterrent for future antisocial or deviant behavior. Current efforts to prevent and dealing with adult and juvenile crime and delinquency involve a mix of interventions. These range from those aimed at specific individuals considered at risk for engaging in antisocial behavior to others focused on groups of children or adults. Other methods are focused less on working with the individual in a preventative or rehabilitative way and more on creating and implementing policies that will achieve these goals. In effect, intervention options include those that prevent and remediate delinquency. We have addressed some of these efforts earlier in this chapter. In this section, we will look at other interventions that fall into either individual-focused efforts or policy-focused approaches.

Individual and Group Prevention Efforts

Some interventions are designed to prevent problems from occurring in the first place. For example, Brown (2009) discusses efforts to prevent youth with psychiatric disabilities from involvement in the juvenile justice system where they are already overrepresented. Among the efforts undertaken is the creation of a customized career plan for each individual. These career plans help link the youth to appropriate resources, as well as community-based employment. In addition, these helped produce increased self-esteem and a positive relationship between the youth and his or her community.

Faver (2010) discusses a violence prevention program for juveniles focused on treatment of animals. Her perspective is based on the connection between juveniles who engage in animal abuse and later move to interpersonal violence. The goal of such programs is to engender empathy and prosocial behavior among youth with a goal of preventing future violence. She cites research suggesting such programs produce positive outcomes that continue for months or longer when compared to children in control groups. Determining which aspects of which programs are most effective, however, requires further research.

Many delinquency prevention programs are based on the premise of disrupting the individual behavior that leads to later delinquency. For example, Loeber and Farrington (2000) review programs focused on preventing persistent disruptive behavior by children because this behavior is often associated with later serious violent juvenile offending. They point out that the beginnings of either prosocial or antisocial behavior occur in the first five years of life and noted that disruptive behavior observed as early as two to three years of age predicted child delinquency between 7 and 12 years of age. They also concluded that society appeared more interested in remediation of current delinquents than in preventing future ones.

Individual and Group Treatment Efforts

Marshall and Burton (2010) looked at existing research on current efforts to treat offenders with an emphasis on group interventions. They focused on characteristics of the therapist, client perceptions of the therapist, the quality of the client–therapist relationship, and the group treatment client. Their findings underscore the importance of these four factors, concluding that they are more responsible for positive changes in offenders than any specific theory or technique employed. This was true for both juveniles and adult offenders. Factors such as therapist empathy, support, and warmth were critically important as were the quality of the client–therapist relationship, and group cohesiveness and expressiveness. The findings are consistent with those of Norcross (2002) who found that the techniques used by the therapist accounted for only 15% of the change occurring in clients, while the therapeutic relationship accounted for 30%.

As might be expected, family variables appear to play a protective role in preventing antisocial behavior in adolescents. For example, Sen (2010) studied how the frequency of a family's dining together in the evening affected problem behavior. He found that frequent family dinners were negatively associated with running away, use of alcohol and drugs by females, and physical violence, drinking, crimes against property, and absconding in male children. This suggests the importance of parental influence on youth behavior.

Likewise, Vazsonyi and Huang (2010) found that the quality of parenting children receive even before they start school affects their development of self-control. Self-control, in turn, makes it less likely that the individual will engage in deviant social behavior. The absence of adequate self-control is a factor in both crime and delinquency.

Other studies have focused on the importance of parents and adolescents learning how to resolve conflicts in ways that prevent other problems. Multiple studies have shown that destructive styles of conflict resolution have consequences for children that include depression, aggression, anxiety, and delinquency (Branje, van Doorn,

VanderValk, & Meeus, 2009; Tucker, McHale & Crouter, 2003; Wijsbroek, Hale, Van Doorn, Raaijmakers, & Meeus, 2010).

These findings suggest one of the most important factors preventing antisocial behavior is quality parenting and this should be as much a target for support as programs designed to resocialize those who have committed delinquent acts or crimes.

We have previously mentioned the development of treatment programs aimed at men who perpetrate domestic violence. Despite the existence of many such programs across the country, their effectiveness has not been adequately demonstrated. Day, Chung, O'Leary, and Carson (2009) pointed out that while some positive outcomes have been noted (Gondolf, 2007), other reports are discouraging. At least two meta-analyses have suggested that the effectiveness of such programs ranges between 0% and 5% (Babcock et al., 2004; Feder & Wilson, 2005).

A more positive outcome involves juvenile who had engaged in delinquent and antisocial behavior that directly affected victims. Studies of four programs found juveniles who participated in victim–offender mediation were three times as likely to not reoffend as is true for other delinquency intervention programs (Nugent, Umbreit, Wiinamaki, & Paddock, 2001). These programs involve "guided face-to-face meetings between a crime victim (or victims) and the person (or persons) who victimized them" (p. 6). The meeting creates a safe environment for discussion, identification of needs, and development of a plan for the offender to redress the injury. Generally, the juvenile develops a restitution agreement that details how he or she will achieve *restorative justice* with the victim.

Policy-Focused Interventions

Besides interventions aimed at the individual, many changes in policy have been made in an attempt to reduce crime. We mentioned previously the efforts of schools to help prevent violence and combat community fears by adding metal detectors and greater police presence within the school. In addition, some schools began employing security cameras and other visible security measures (Addington, 2009). Specific steps include providing ID cards for students, locking and/or monitoring entrances during school hours, adding security fences and gates, removing locks from student lockers, random searches of lockers and backpacks, and emergency drills.

Whether these enhanced security efforts produced any demonstrable benefit has yet to be determined. Addington (2003) studied student fear levels before and after Columbine, finding a small increase in fear immediately after the event but only in 4% of the population. Changes in parental fear for their children have not been studied so it is difficult to know precisely how enhanced security affected this group. It is clear that the availability of these security measures creates an inherent perception of effectiveness but perhaps, little else. On the other hand, "use of school security measures has been associated with higher reports of student victimization and fear" (Schreck & Miller, 2003; Schreck, Miller & Gibson, 2003), as well as greater school disorder (measured as the presence of gangs, drugs, and crimes against students; Mayer & Leone, 1999). Other negative consequences include infringement on student's rights to be free of unwarranted searches and invasion of privacy and producing an unpleasant learning environment (Rosen, 2005).

Cécile and Born (2009) looked at juvenile delinquency interventions that focus on the group-based environments, such as detention facilities and special schools. These facilities are designed to both treat and protect youth. They point out that while some success has been demonstrated by such institutional efforts, there are potential and real iatrogenic effects. Citing multiple studies, the authors identify both increased delinquent behaviors and increased consumption of drugs as the result of peer contagion.

At the same time, Cécile and Born (2009) listed some of the more effective group-based interventions. These include:

- Long-term intervention programs
- Interpersonal skill training
- Individual counseling
- Behavioral programs
- Less-effective programs included vocational training and wilderness challenge programs

Boot camps appear to better demonstrate success with mild cases of delinquency than do placements in juvenile facilities. However, boot camps appear ineffective for more serious forms of delinquency. The influence of peer contagion can be reduced under some circumstances and the effectiveness of the intervention increased if:

- Adult leaders are present to mediate interactions with deviant peers
- Programs involve structured and organized group interactions supervised by adults
- Strengthening of teens relationship with families is a focus
- Increased involvement of delinquents with nondelinquent peers occurs
- Development of social skills is utilized to encourage interaction with others
- Delinquent youth develop a positive relationship with a peer counselor

Prevention and treatment programs designed to stop adult and juvenile crime include multiple approaches based on multiple understandings of why this behavior occurs. Some programs are intended to help the individual offender while others focus on the needs of the victim. Still others are based on the assumption that macro-level policy changes can reduce the incidence of antisocial and illegal behavior. Identifying the programs with the greatest degree of efficacy remains a continuing challenge for social workers and others working in this field.

Assess your analysis and evaluation of this chapter's contents by completing the Chapter Review.

Rafael Ben-Ari/Fotolia

19

Poverty and Class Influences on Human Behavior

Poverty is one of the most persistent challenges to equality and well-being in the United States and across the world. According to the National Poverty Center (2012), over 15% of Americans live in poverty, the largest percentage since 1993. While poverty rates declined in the 1960s reaching a low of about 11%, the percentage began to rise in 1980. Only older adults escaped this increase, largely due to Social Security income being adjusted annually for inflation in the 1960s.

DEFINING AND MEASURING POVERTY

Identifying the amount of income constituting poverty is the task of the U.S. Census Bureau. Its 2010 figures are shown in Table 19.1 for different groupings.

For example, two adults with no children earning below $14,602 would be considered in poverty. The threshold for what is defined as poverty is adjusted yearly based on changes in the inflation rate. In addition, a variety of noncash assistance may be available to those whose cash income is below the poverty line—supplemental nutrition assistance, Medicaid, public housing, housing subsidies, and health insurance provided by one's employer. The determination of whether someone is in poverty does not include taxes paid or earned income tax credits, but when these noncash benefits are included with cash income, the percent of people in poverty drops slightly.

As might be expected, U.S. poverty is not distributed equally across different groups. Figure 19.1 shows how the rate is different based on several factors.

Figure 19.1 demonstrates vast differences among categories of residents. For example, households headed by single women have poverty rates twice that of male-headed households. Married couples have the lowest rate, in part because the number of income earners is often double that of single-headed households. Blacks experience rates of poverty that are the highest of any cultural or ethnic group. One group not reflected in Figure 19.1 is composed of people with disabilities. Employment rates for those with any disability are about 50% of the rate for those without disabilities and the overall poverty rate for those with a disability is almost 25%, which would place them in the top portion of this graph (Stapleton, O'Day, Livermore, & Imparato, 2006). By comparison, the poverty rate for those without any disability is under 9%. In other words, people with at least one disability have a poverty rate more than twice that of those with no disability.

Homeless is an international problem. Here, a woman in Mexico lives on the street.

Another way of looking at income inequality is to compare average income in the United States for different groups. In the United States, the average income of the wealthiest 10% of the population has risen to 14 times that of the poorest 10% over the past 25 years (Blow, 2011). Put another way, the top 10% of families in this country receive roughly 50% of the total U.S. income.

Did You Know?

Today's level of discrepancy between the poorest and most affluent Americans has not been seen since 1917 (Noah, 2010).

In addition, real median household income has been trending downward since 1997 as evident in Figure 19.2.

Historically, Americans have enjoyed a steady growth in income with each generation doing better financially than the previous one. In the past, only major events such as recessions and depressions have affected this trend. However, more recently the growth in income is not equal across groups as illustrated in Figure 19.3.

Table 19.1 Poverty Guidelines in 2010 by Family Type

Family Type	Category	Income (in dollars)
Single individual	Under 65 years	11,344
	65 years and older	10,458
Single parent	One child	15,030
	Two children	17,568
Two adults	No children	14,602
	One child	17,552
	Two children	22,113
	Three children	26,023

Source: U.S. Census Bureau (2011, p. 61).

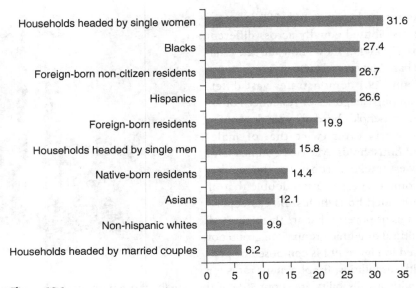

Figure 19.1
Percent of U.S. Residents Living in Poverty by Category: 2010
Source: U.S. Census Bureau (2011, Table B-2, pp. 68–73).

As is evident, in a 28-year period, the poorest Americans' incomes rose less than $20,500 while the wealthiest Americans' incomes increased more than 17 times that amount. Overall, when real family income is calculated for the 30-year period from 1979 to 2009, the bottom 20% of families experienced a drop of over 7% while the income of the top 20% increased by about 50%. This trend differs greatly from the previous 30-year period of 1947 to 1979, in which the greatest gains were made by the bottom 20%.

While it is common to think of poverty as an urban phenomenon, this is clearly not the entire story. Horton and Allen (1998) found that rural Black families were even poorer than those in urban areas. They hypothesized that this may be related to a higher number of female-headed families living in rural areas. In addition, when overall wages go up in metropolitan areas, they tend to reduce poverty in the cities, but no such improvement occurs in rural areas (Gundersen, 2006). Lichter and Johnson (2007) also found that concentrated poverty within rural minorities was still high particularly among Blacks in rural areas of the South, Native Americans dwelling on reservations in the Southwest or the Dakotas, and Hispanics living in the Rio Grande Valley and states bordering Mexico.

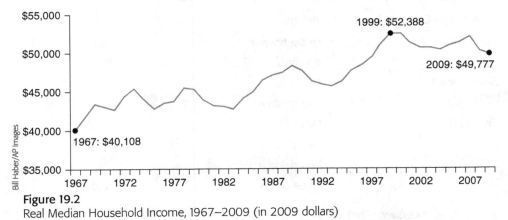

Figure 19.2
Real Median Household Income, 1967–2009 (in 2009 dollars)
Source: U.S. Census Bureau, Current Population Survey, Historical Income Tables, Table H-5. Retrieved from http://www.census.gov/hhes/www/income/data/historical/household/index.html.

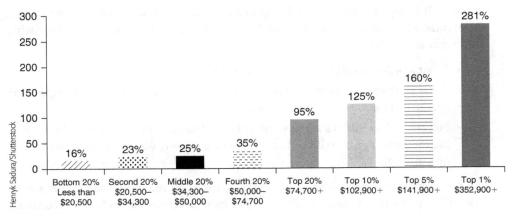

Figure 19.3

Increase in After-Tax Income by Income Group. 1979–2007 (in 2007 dollars)

Source: Congressional Budget Office (2010).

Moreover, these groups tend to live in high-poverty counties with all the disadvantages that entails. While the study's authors were able to identify some pockets of rural poverty that were being erased, they tempered their findings with an observation that declines in rural poverty may be of short duration. They conclude that "the harsh residential circumstances of rural minority children—especially the poor—jeopardize the likelihood of a successful and productive adulthood" (pp. 354–355).

Much research on poverty, including the information just provided, is based on looking at particular groups at a specific point in time and delineating those who are below the poverty line. This provides a snapshot of poverty, which is frequently used to make policy decisions. However, many researchers are beginning to look at poverty as a life course phenomenon occurring at various points in one's life. For example, 58.5% of all Americans will be classified as poor at some time during their adult lives (Pimpare, 2009). By age 75, over 90% of African Americans will have experienced poverty with the rate for Black women at 98.8% (Rank & Hirschl, 2002). The use of the life course approach better informs our view of poverty both as applied to population groups and within the context of recent history. The overall picture of economic hardship and poverty is summarized quite succinctly by Sandoval, Rank, and Hirschl (2009) as follows:

> The rise of acute poverty is consistent with the argument that the long-term economic and social policy patterns over the past 15 to 20 years have increased the likelihood of economic vulnerability, potentially leading to poverty. That is, as jobs have become more unstable and less well paying, as the social safety net has become weaker, as quality health insurance has been more scarce, and/or as levels of personal debt have skyrocketed, more Americans are at risk of falling into poverty. (p. 709)

The authors conclude their analysis by noting that "the risk of American poverty increased substantially during the 1990s in comparison with the 1970s and 1980s. As we have shown, that risk has become exceedingly high. In fact, it would appear that for most Americans, the question is no longer if, but rather when they will experience poverty. In short, poverty has become a routine and unfortunate part of the American life course" (p. 710).

POVERTY AND WELL-BEING

While many countries measure the amount and nature of the poverty within their borders, this is not necessarily the most accurate way of measuring the well-being of individuals and families. Poverty is typically measured using a specific income level, while well-being is a more complex concept. One useful definition of well-being frequently adopted is provided by McGregor (2007, p. 317) and has the following components:

- What a person has (includes all available resources)
- What a person can do with what he or she has (includes what needs and goals the person can fulfill with those resources)
- How the person thinks about what he or she has and can do (includes the meaning the person gives to his or her achievable goals and the processes used to obtain them)

One advantage of considering well-being is that it considers all the resources available to the individual or family, rather than just cash income. Another is that it considers local factors because the same amount of resources can provide vastly different lifestyles depending on location. For example, the cost of living in Decatur, Illinois, is substantially less than in Burlington, Vermont. The same is true for Fayetteville, Arkansas, versus Fresno, California. Table 19.2 shows the cost of living index for a handful of U.S. cities with 100 being the national average (Kiplinger, 2011).

Using the two Texas cities for comparison, a person with an income of $20,000 per year in Abilene would need only $17,200 to maintain the same lifestyle in Denison. Clearly, the same amount of income has different consequences depending on where a family lives. Finally, what meaning individuals give to their situation will vary. Two persons with similar resources may view their situation differently. Thus, one child growing up on public welfare may see himself or herself as poor while another in the same circumstances does not have this perception. This difference can exist despite the fact that the community may define both children as poor (Williams, 2009). Sometimes the refusal to consider oneself poor occurs because it simply does not fit the individual's sense of self. This may be because people consider the situation temporary or because they simply never even considered it applying to them (Bullock & Limbert, 2003). For some, refusing to describe or view oneself as poor is a deliberate effort to disassociate from poverty's public stigma. The importance of self-perception is one positive factor that underscores the value of well-being concept because it provides an additional dimension to our understanding of what it means to be poor.

Table 19.2   Cost of Living Index for Sample U.S. Cities (100 = national average)

City	Cost of Living Index
Abilene, TX	100
Albany, GA	92
Alexandria, VA	141
Athens, GA	100
Bakersfield, CA	98
Columbus, OH	90
Denison, TX	86
San Francisco, CA	164

Source: Kiplinger (2011).

RESOURCES

Resources for those in poverty include formal programs such as Temporary Assistance for Needy Families (TANF), Social Security, Supplemental Security Income, Unemployment Insurance Fund, supplemental nutrition assistance program, earned income tax credit, Women, Infants, and Children (WIC) programs, job training, and others designed to provide financial or similar assistance. In addition to formal resources, various organizations provide supports such as food pantries through churches, social groups, and informal mechanisms. We will explore these formal resources later as we review U.S. poverty policies.

One significant source of assistance has been help from families. This has been particularly true for African Americans who have historically relied on kin networks, or extended families, in hard times. Frequently, social workers have assumed these kin networks would be available to help with needs ranging from economic to foster care. However, recent research has called into question the continuing viability of this resource (Miller-Cribbs & Farber, 2008). Long-term family poverty, reductions in community resources, and changes in the employment sector have combined to limit how much help other family members can provide. High levels of need among multiple family members make it more difficult to address every member's concerns. Moreover, in communities with high levels of poverty, there are fewer friends to whom one can turn because most of one's circle is likewise impoverished (Cherlin, 2002). Even family resources, such as child care, are becoming insufficient to meet the needs of working parents, particularly single mothers (Iversen & Armstrong, 2006). Over time, some family members "drain the resources of the network, whereas others disproportionately are called on to give more resources than they receive" (Miller-Cribbs & Farber, 2008, p. 48). The authors suggest the importance of social workers including the kinship network in assessing client needs and resources, rather than assuming that the family may be able to help meet a client's needs.

Another critical resource for poor families is child care. Child care that is safe and affordable often makes the difference between whether a parent can afford to work out of the home. Burchinal, Nelson, Carlson, and Brooks-Gunn (2008) found that poorer communities had significantly less access to high-quality child care, rendering working either impossible or economically unfeasible.

Assess your comprehension of Defining Poverty by completing this quiz.

FAMILY AND COMMUNITY TRANSMISSION

Observers of the poor often point out that many families remain in poverty from one generation to the next. Explanations for the presence of intergenerational poverty have been suggested by many writers and public policy has often followed these explanations. Some view families as transmitting values, attitudes, and beliefs to their children that perpetuate poverty into successive generations. Others view the community as the mechanism through which people become and remain poor. Still some use a *culture of poverty* explanation that combines the influence of family and community in continuing the cycle of poverty from parents to children and beyond. In this and the following sections, we will review some of these beliefs and the evidence used to support them.

Various researchers have noted that community poverty tends to amplify or influence the impact of family poverty (Brooks-Gunn, Duncan, & Aber, 1997; McCulloch & Joshi, 2001).

Did You Know?

When community poverty is two standard deviations above the mean, it quadruples the influence of family poverty on the delinquency of youngsters (Hay, Fortson, Hollist, Altheimer, & Schaible, 2007).

In communities with high poverty levels, the expected norms may include drug use, delinquency, and family and community disorganization. Such communities have more groups holding deviant values and engaged in criminal activity. This increases the opportunity for adolescents to learn antisocial behavior. The absence of institutions and norms supporting the values of education and occupational competence can also decrease the influence of positive parental values.

Carlson (2006) studied community poverty in rural areas and its relationship to youth exposure to violence. Her results are similar to findings in urban communities, namely that higher levels of poverty were significant predictors of higher levels of exposure to violence in school and other negative delinquent and mental health outcomes. In a similar vein, Cunradi (2007) found that neighborhood poverty was a predictor of intimate partner violence, particularly for Black couples.

Growing up in a poor community may well result in adopting values and behaviors that increase the likelihood of poverty when these youngsters become adults. For example, dropping out of school and engaging in criminal behavior may appear reasonable alternatives when the community offers little or no opportunity for employment. Some have considered this a form of community transmission of poverty by which succeeding generations experience the same or greater levels of poverty as their parents.

School experiences are another area where poverty appears to play a role in how adolescents view their world. Battistich, Solomon, Kim, Watson, and Schaps (1995) found the "school experience is less pleasant and rewarding, on the whole, for students in poor than in affluent school communities" (p. 649). However, they noted schools can mitigate some negatives if they create a caring, responsive, and supportive educational community. Schools can help prevent student alienation, provide students and parents social support, and compensate for fewer community resources.

Brown, Copeland, Costello, Erkanli, and Worthman (2009) found that conditions in one's community also had a bearing on other aspects of adolescents' lives. For example, youth living in Appalachian communities where adults had lower educational attainment had lower educational goals for themselves. Students in communities with higher educational attainment appeared to have the opposite effect. The differences between the two groups were striking. Of rural males living in the poorest communities, only 16% saw a college degree as a goal in their lives compared to 44% of rural males living in more affluent communities. Again, poverty plays a role as communities with the lowest educational attainment are also those where family incomes are low.

We discussed the topic of school shootings and disorder in Chapter 18. Welsh, Stokes, and Greene (2000) studied the relationship between school disorder and the characteristics of the community immediately surrounding the school. They found community poverty indirectly affected the perceptions about and occurrence of various types of school disorders. However, not all schools were similarly affected by the immediate community. The factor serving to mediate or lessen the severity of school disorder was school climate. School climate has four dimensions: "school culture, organizational structure, social milieu and ecological environment" (p. 248). School culture is a reflection of the communication patterns, norms, roles, rewards, sanctions, and patterns of influence and accommodation used in the school. A positive example of school culture would be where students perceive they are rewarded for appropriate behavior and staff–student communication is constructive and affirmative.

Table 19.3 Comparison of Obesity and Overweight Rates by Ethnicity in Poor Communities

Ethnic Group	Percent Obese	Percent Overweight
Whites	14.37	29.11
Blacks	14.19	28.13
Hispanics	13.66	27.85
Asians	5.88	15.51
Native Americans	40	61.33

Source: Wickrama et al. (2006).

Organization structure involves administrative structure, operational patterns, rules, practices, curriculum design, and class scheduling decisions. A positive organizational structure has rules that make discipline more systematic and less arbitrary, increase relevance of curriculum to career choices, and reduce student alienation. Related factors include things such as student–teacher ratios, class size, school resources, enrollment, and quality of leadership.

School milieu includes background characteristic of students and staff including race, income, teacher experience and training, and gender. A beneficial milieu has a mix of students from different ethnicities and income levels. High percentages of male students tend to be associated with greater rates of victimization in schools.

The final dimension, ecological environment, includes factors such as condition of the physical plant, location and size of the school in the community, lighting, and number of entrances. A positive environment will have fewer unsupervised areas in the school and fewer entrances and exits. Areas of the school that cannot be adequately monitored and multiple egresses make control over the school interior more difficult (Welsh et al., 2000).

Wickrama, Wickrama, and Bryant (2006) looked at the relationship between economically disadvantaged communities and adolescent obesity. They found obesity is significantly higher in poor communities than in more well-to-do communities, independent of family poverty level. Obesity is a concern because it is associated with long-term health risks, a topic explored later in this chapter. The differences in rates by ethnicity are shown in Table 19.3.

Interestingly, a White adolescent is 48% more likely to be obese in a poor community than in a more affluent community. By comparison, Black and Hispanic adolescents are only about 4% to 5% more likely to be obese when living in poor versus affluent communities.

CULTURAL INFLUENCES

In the period 1950–1970, various writers attributed the relatively high poverty rates to a *culture of poverty* that they believed existed, particularly within poor Black families (Curran, 2003; Lewis, 1959). Despite the fact that there is little current acceptance of this theory as an explanation for poverty, policy makers continue to try to develop approaches that will reduce poverty by changing families by focusing on schools, neighborhoods, and the families themselves (Ludwig & Mayer, 2006; Rosemblatt, 2009).

Improving School Quality

The emphasis on changing families through education is based on the fact that poor children acquire less education than children from nonpoor families. This, in turn, reduces their later success in life. A portion of the cause for this situation is related to access to resources and the quality of schools available to poor and nonpoor kids. At the same time, this is not the entire explanation. Some believe that heredity and genetics play roles and that those with greater innate ability actually pursue more education and earn higher salaries than those with lower abilities. Most studies, however, have challenged this belief in genetics and demonstrate that each year of additional education equals or exceeds 10% in additional income as an adult regardless of genetic makeup (Carneiro & Heckman, 2003).

Regardless of the theories about the connection between education and income, the goals of many current state and federal programs are designed to improve the quality of schools and increase the academic achievement of students. The No Child Left Behind Act, voucher programs that permit poor children to attend private schools, and the movement toward charter schools are efforts to achieve these goals. Efforts to reduce class size, improve teacher quality, and increase teacher salaries are also undertaken with this goal in mind. However, as Rouse and Barrow (2006) point out, the success of such programs is modest. While smaller class size helps, the resources spent by affluent families on education outside of the school setting likely reduce the value of public policies aimed at improving schools to eliminate poverty. Moreover, advantaged parents are much more likely to expect their children to achieve higher levels of education beyond high school than do poor parents. Teachers also play a role in setting expectations for students, although evidence suggests a small impact (Jessim & Harber, 2005).

Likewise, the evidence of success of charter schools and the No Child Left Behind Act to improve school accountability show modest results. They also appear to be accompanied by some unintended consequences, such as teachers cheating to raise the grades of children in their classes and schools reclassifying low-performing students as learning disabled to exclude them from the school's rankings (Rouse & Barrow, 2006).

Improving Neighborhoods

The second method of dealing with the supposed intergenerational transfer of poverty focuses on neighborhoods in which poverty exists. Housing programs have been created to improve the quality of a neighborhood although, again, results are mixed. While living in a substandard neighborhood can be unpleasant, it is difficult to show this affects an adult's economic success. Studies attempting to show a relationship between where children grew up and their adult have demonstrated only a very limited influence of neighborhood. It appears that moving to less-disadvantaged neighborhoods helps reduce delinquency in girls but increases it in boys. In either case, the change of neighborhood does not improve academic achievement nor forestall dropping out of high school (Kling, Ludwig, & Katz, 2005; Sanbonmatsu, Kling, Duncan, & Brooks-Gunn, 2006). Later this chapter will discuss efforts to improve housing as an antipoverty strategy.

Improving Families

The third public policy approach to deal with intergenerational poverty attempts to change families so that their children will escape poverty in adulthood. These efforts incorporated multiple tactics that included discouraging out-of-wedlock births, encouraging mother's employment outside the home, and supporting family religious participation. These approaches are based on an assumption that poor families are inherently dysfunctional, and that by addressing the dysfunction, poverty can be reduced. This is the view often espoused by conservative commentators but as an antipoverty philosophy, it has failed to demonstrate effectiveness for a number of reasons. First, there is no evidence that church participation has any causal connection to economic well-being. That is, going to church does not automatically translate into increased income. Second, the most highly educated and economically advantaged members of society are less likely to attend church than those in poverty. For example, low-income Americans are already among the most religious members of society in terms of participating in a church of their choice and praying.

Since the U.S. Constitution forbids the government from forcing participation in any particular religion, most government efforts have been focused on supporting faith-based organizations providing social services. However, once again, there is no evidence that funding these services is any more effective than traditional governmental programs.

Social policies that encourage parents to marry also suffer from significant shortcomings. There is little or no evidence that parents' marital status improves the adult income of their children (Loh, 1996). Being raised by both parents is likely preferable to being raised by only one parent, but this too can depend on a host of other factors. There is, for instance, evidence that being raised by a stepparent may be more detrimental to a child's educational achievement than being raised by a single mother, whether divorced or never married (Boggess, 1998; McLanahan & Sandefur, 1994). While it may be safe to suggest that growing up with two married biological parents is likely to lead to more education and more income as an adult, why this occurs is much less clear. Another example may help explain this conundrum. The average household income in New Canaan, Connecticut, is $141,788. The same figure for Hidden Hill, California, is $248,355. Would you move from New Canaan to Hidden Hills expecting to increase your household income by over $100,000 per year?

Likely, you answered "no" because you can think of other things that might explain the differences between average income in the two cities. You might wonder about what industries and jobs exist in the two communities. Or, whether the cost of living is vastly different from one city to another. In short, you can see that such a cross-country move would statistically appear positive but know that other factors are likely at work producing the vast income discrepancy. While we know children growing up with both biological parents will make more money as adults, we simply don't know what causes this. We can speculate but so far have not been able to prove that encouraging parental marriage will lead to higher adult incomes for their children.

The other social policy focused on the family is one that forces or encourages parents to work rather than stay home and care for their children. This was part of the emphasis of the welfare reforms that took place in the 1990s. The hope was that having single mothers working would "increase family income, reduce reliance on welfare, and provide a role model for children's eventual work habits" (Ludwig & Mayer, 2006, p. 184). Having a single parent working also reduced government costs. At the same time, some argued that it was better for the child's development to remain at home with the mother.

Did You Know?

Roughly 91% of individuals with salaries below the U.S. mean claim a religious affiliation. In addition, African Americans are more apt to identify with a religion than is true for Whites, but are much more likely to be poor. Apparently, being pious and a church-going adult do not necessarily raise one from poverty.

Critical Thinking

Practice Behavior Example: Know about the principles of logic, scientific inquiry, and reasoned discernment.

Critical Thinking Question: What is the flaw in the logic that moving from a community with low average household income to one with high average income will result in an increase in your annual income?

Regardless of the position one takes on this topic, there is little evidence showing that children are much better or worse off as adults by having one or more working parents. In addition, studies have shown that maternal employment that occurs in the child's first year can impair a child's cognitive skills by a small amount (Ruhm, 2004). This fact alone could reduce the future income of White children by an average of 4%, suggesting that forcing the mother to work during the child's first year produces a negative impact that carries over in the child's adulthood. Other studies have shown no such negative outcomes after the child's second and third years (Ludwig & Mayer, 2006). Ludwig and Mayer conclude that "most adults who experience some economic poverty were brought up in the sort of Ozzie-and-Harriett households that many policymakers wish to make universal" (p. 188). Consequently, "while many policymakers believe that changing parental work, marriage, or religiosity can end poverty in America, based on the available evidence, that prospect does not seem likely. . . . To reduce poverty among future generations, there may be no substitute for a system of social insurance and income transfers for those children who end up poor as adults" (p. 189).

Rather than vastly improving the plight of the poor, the culture of poverty theory led to pathologizing Black family life and blaming the victim for being poor. The end result was a set of views that continue to inform conservative political positions and locate the causes of poverty in the perceived shortcomings of the poor.

Although the culture of poverty theory has little support except as a political consideration, culture differences do constitute an important factor in understanding human behavior. We know from multiple studies that culture and ethnicity play a role in poverty rates and related problems. For example, Wickrama, Noh, and Bryant (2005) found that family poverty proved more distressful for White adolescents than for Black adolescents. In addition, the degree of community poverty was more problematic for poor Blacks than for nonpoor Blacks. Among White adolescents, living in a poor community was more challenging for nonpoor than for poor families. Living in an ethnically diverse community appeared as a protective factor with respect to mental health of Black adolescents. Overall, Black adolescents experienced significantly more depressive symptoms regardless of level of poverty in the family or community. As the authors summarized (p. 276):

> The unique influence of race may be attributable to institutionalized practices in U.S. society that result in the systematic subordination and devaluation of minority groups (Spencer, 2001). It may also be attributed to the day-to-day discrimination experienced by minorities (Taylor & Turner, 2002), which may not be fully captured by traditional family and community socioeconomic indicators. Indeed, systematic subordination and devaluation of Blacks are reflected by proxies indicating that minorities have higher employment instability, lower purchasing power, lower wealth, and fewer assets than do majority Whites who have comparable levels of family income (Sampson, Squires, & Zhou, 2001). Day-to-day racial discrimination in the broader society is a powerful daily stressor that can contribute to the emotional distress of minority groups through the internalization of racist beliefs such as innate inferiority and negative self-evaluations (Harrell, Hall, & Tallaferro, 2003; Noh & Kaspar, 2003; Williams, Neighbors, & Jackson, 2003; Krieger, 2000; Noh, Beiser, Kasper, Hou, & Rummens, 1999) and subsequent development of mental health problems such as anti-self issues and nihilistic tendencies (Brown, 2003).

These observations underscore the influence of culture on perceptions about poverty. Being poor and consequently in a lower socioeconomic class carries stigma in many cultures (Williams, 2009). Like other categories—such as sexuality, gender, disability, and age—social class is negatively perceived and individuals so classified experience exclusion and maltreatment. Often this is based on a belief that being poor is the result of factors under the individual's control. Lack of effort is seen as a factor in, or the cause of, being poor. These views are in contrast to the fact that opportunities for moving up economically have decreased over the past 30 years (Williams, 2009). Combinations of structural barriers currently exist that contribute to this diminution of opportunities.

HOUSING

Housing is of significant interest within the United States as is evident from the many policies that encourage home ownership, creation of affordable housing, and provision of shelter to the homeless. An emphasis on home ownership is reflected in federal rules and programs—federally subsidized loans (e.g., FHA and VA), tax deductions for mortgage interest and property taxes, and development of highway systems allowing home construction at a distance from central cities. Some have argued that this emphasis on home ownership contributed to the collapse of the housing market and national recession of 2008–2012 by encouraging approval of loans to buyers who lacked sufficient down payments or evidence of ability to pay.

For at least the last 60 years, various city, state, and federal agencies have funded construction of housing units designed to improve the quality of housing stock. Early on, this led to building hi-rise apartment buildings for the poor based on a belief that this was a relatively cost-efficient way of providing adequate housing while simultaneously razing slum housing. Hi-rise apartment buildings for the poor soon lost their attractiveness as crime, drug use, and violence transformed many such edifices into hell holes. Subsequently, many housing experiments were destroyed, including Cabrini Green in Chicago and Pruitt Igoe in St. Louis, and often replaced by row housing and newer construction.

The failure of such projects is often the result of multiple factors, residential segregation, failure to maintain the structures, inadequate law enforcement, and the influx of gangs and drug dealers, among others. Poor neighborhoods are said to help contribute stereotypes about the residents, tend to drive out businesses and the middle class, and isolate the impoverished.

Unlike in the past, housing programs today tend to emphasize deconcentration of poverty as a means to improving both safety and well-being of urban neighborhoods (Stal & Zuveri, 2010). The goal is to integrate low-income housing with middle-class housing to increase the poor person's opportunity to succeed. This goal may be achieved through dispersing public housing units across a community and/or providing vouchers that allow the poor to relocate to more expensive areas.

These efforts are not without criticism. Some argue the goal does not consider the interests of area residents, destroys ethnic enclaves, and is undertaken to free up space for the reconstruction of city centers that will provide economic benefits to the overall community. Dispersal of the poor also reduces their power to organize to meet their needs although the political power in poverty neighborhood is frequently very weak (Wilson, 2009). Implementation of relocation efforts are often met by the Not in My Backyard (NIMBY) opposition of neighborhoods and communities afraid that an influx of the poor will drive up crime and drive down property values. Moreover, there is little evidence that moving families to new neighborhoods results in better employment, schooling opportunities, or improvement in the quality of available role models (DeLuca, 2007; Sanbonmatsu et al., 2006).

One of the federal agencies playing a major policy role in housing for low-income families is the U.S. Department of Housing and Urban Development (HUD). HUD provides rental assistance to low-income tenants residing in privately owned housing and subsidizes the construction and operation of public housing partnering with both public and private agencies and individuals. They are also responsible for setting and enforcing federal fair housing standards and laws, establishing uniform real estate settlement procedures, and operating the Federal Housing Authority, which helps individuals purchase homes by insuring loans, allowing lower down payments, and reducing closing costs.

For fine examples of services provided by Veterans Administration (VA) social workers, read Bradley Schaffer: Military Veteran Justice Outreach and the Role of a VA Social Worker.

Assess your comprehension of the Causes of Poverty by completing this quiz.

The agency also offers reverse mortgages to adults over 62 years of age and funds programs for the homeless. Other federal agencies also provide support for the homeless in addition to that provided by state, local, and private organizations. For example, the U.S. Department Health and Human Services provides grants to support services and treatment programs for the homeless, while also funding resource centers and research that provide information to consumers, government agencies, and lawmakers. The Department of Veterans Affairs provides several programs designed to assist homeless veterans to become self-sufficient and gain housing. HUD also operates several housing-related federal programs including community development block grants to local and state governments and Native American tribes, disaster housing assistance, and funding for nonprofit groups to develop rental housing for low-income adults with disabilities. They also provide assistance to areas hit hardest by foreclosures to help stabilize the neighborhoods and communities. The size and breadth of U.S. housing programs show the important of housing to survival and quality of life.

HOMELESSNESS

Most large cities in the United States and in many foreign countries have a homeless population that, by definition, lacks adequate housing. The homeless population includes individuals with severe mental illness, military veterans, families, and single individuals who have lost their home. This population includes individuals living in homeless shelters and those sleeping in cars, in parks, in abandoned buildings, and on sidewalks. Many others have no home of their own but spend periods of time staying in the homes of relatives and friends and alternating with stays in shelters. An estimated 6.8 million people have doubled up in this manner, an increase of over 50% from 2005 to 2010 (National Alliance to End Homelessness, 2012).

Counting the U.S. homeless population is a difficult task for many reasons. First, for many people being homeless is a temporary problem that will disappear when employment opportunities occur. Second, those who are living with relatives on a temporary basis are often missed in the counting. Third, many of the homeless do not stay in shelters or other locations where they can be counted. What counts of the homeless do exist are inaccurate and are likely to seriously underestimate the actual population. One of the most recent estimates is provided by the National Alliance to End Homelessness (2012) that reported about 636,000 people were homeless, a slight decrease from previous counts. However, other estimates put the picture between 600,000 and 2 million individuals.

Past studies provide some idea about the composition of the homeless as illustrated in Table 19.4 (National Coalition for the Homeless, 2009).

The length of time people remain in emergency shelters varies. Single adults typically stay for 69 days with women staying for about two weeks less than men. Families spend about 70 days in this type of facility and then often go back to living with relatives,

Table 19.4   Living Situations of Homeless Population, 2008

Category	Living on the Street	Living in Shelters	Living in Transitional Housing	Living in Permanent Supportive Housing
Single adults	94%	70%	43%	60%
Part of family	4%	29%	56%	39.5%
Unaccompanied minors	2%	1%	1%	0.5%
	100%	100%	100%	100%

Source: National Coalition for the Homeless (2009).

in cars, or under bridges. The ethnic breakdown of those in emergency shelter can be seen in Figure 19.4.

The relationship between income and homelessness is self-evident, being poor increases the likelihood of being homeless at some point in one's life. A 2012 report from the National Alliance to End Homelessness underscores the relationship by noting that the average real income of the working poor was $9,400 in 2010 and "there was not a single county in the nation where a family with an average annual income of $9400 could afford fair market rent for a one-bedroom unit" (pp. 4–5).

The odds of becoming homeless within a single year are about 1 in 12 for an individual who is living with family or friends, 1 in 13 for a released prisoner, and 1 in 11 for an adult who has aged out of foster care (National Alliance to End Homelessness, 2012). Perhaps the most encouraging news from the 2012 report is that there was an 11% decrease in the number of homeless veterans. Overall, about 21 people per 10,000 are homeless, but the rate for homeless veterans was 31 per 10,000 veterans—suggesting that this group is especially vulnerable to becoming homeless. The consequences of homelessness are

Did You Know?

About one-quarter of the homeless population suffers from mental illness and 13% have a physical disability. Around 20% are victims of domestic violence, 13% are military veterans, and 19% are employed at least part time (U.S. Conference of Mayors, 2008).

The intersection of mental illness and homelessness is well illustrated in the case by Joan Borst entitled Annie. Read the case and answer the critical thinking questions she poses.

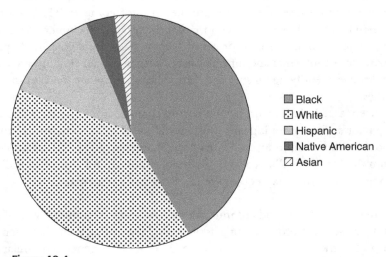

Figure 19.4
Percent of Emergency Shelter Population—2009
Source: National Coalition for the Homeless (2009).

Legend: Black, White, Hispanic, Native American, Asian

serious: The homeless are more vulnerable to being victimized, are at risk of health problems, and suffer malnourishment. The risks are even higher for those homeless who have substance abuse or mental health problems and those whose quest for income to survive involves higher levels of risk (Wenzel, Koegel, & Gelberg, 2000).

Clinical Corner

Audean

Audean was in her third stay at the Domestic Violence Shelter when she finally decided that she could no more stand it. After each incident, her partner apologized profusely, and vowed the abuse would stop, but each time it occurred again. With a broken nose and two loose teeth, she had had enough. This time he had also threatened her six-year-old daughter. As she talked with Bernice at the shelter, the latter tried to help her figure out her next steps. Without the partner's income, Audean could not make it financially on her own and was afraid of being homeless. The social worker assured Audean that there were other alternatives. She explained and helped her complete an online application for TANF. She also explained the role of Medicaid in providing some health benefits for Audean and her daughter. Finally, she accompanied Audean to the TANF office to help her cope with the anxiety she was feeling about moving out on her own. Two months later, Audean was living in a transition facility apartment owned by the shelter. The apartment was part of a remodeled motel and provided two bedrooms, kitchen, bath, and living room. Audean was becoming more comfortable there but still confided that she missed her former partner who had left town after failing to show up for a court hearing related to the abusive incident.

HEALTH CARE

Health care is a significant problem for the poor and the consequences are more serious, the longer a child lives in poverty (Malat, Oh, & Hamilton, 2005). The results of diminished health are more serious for African American children who experience poorer health compared to White children. This is likely because Black children spend more time in poverty and in higher crime rate areas. Jones (2007) studied the effects of repeated exposure to trauma of Black children between ages 9 and 11 living in areas high in both crime and poverty. She found that the experiences of these children were consistent with those contributing to the onset of complex PTSD. Fortunately, many children had high levels of Africentric support serving as a buffer to serious mental health problems. Jones defined Africentric support as a combination of spirituality and the existence of informal and formal kinship networks. Her findings are consistent with other studies identifying kinship and spirituality as resilience mechanisms in Black communities.

The absence of health insurance, exposure to environmental hazards, and risk-taking behavior such as smoking and substance abuse all play some role in the health of the poor (Collins, Pan, Johnson, Courser, & Shamblen, 2008). For example, a 2012 report from the National Alliance to End Homelessness found almost 50 million individuals (one out of every six people) are uninsured, a 4% increase over the previous year.

Dallaire et al. (2008) found communities characterized by high levels of poverty predicted depressive symptoms among adolescents, suggesting a link between poverty and one aspect of mental health. Wickrama and Bryant (2003) generated similar findings in their study of adolescent mental health as did Tracy, Zimmerman, Galea, McCauley, and Stoep (2008) with respect to children. Their conclusion was much of the depressive symptoms could be traced back to stressful events that occurred in the lives of poor families, particularly those stressors associated with breakup of the parental dyad. This research (referred to as *social causation theory*) is often used to explain the relationship between mental health problems and poverty. The theory posits the poor are more likely to develop a mental illness due to high stress levels, employment hazards, poorer quality medical care, and environmental dangers (Perry, 2005).

An alternative theory for the higher incidence of mental illness among the poor is known as *social drift*. According to this theory, for many poor people, entry into poverty is the result of mental illness. The challenges of coping with mental illness result in the person's downward drift as they become less able to work or to function at their accustomed level. Eventually, this leads to a drop in social class and a diminution in economic well-being (Thaker, Adami & Gold, 2001). The drift theory, however, does not explain the high levels of depressive symptoms in poor children because they are unlikely to have experienced this change in socioeconomic status directly. In such cases, social causation models tend to offer more explanatory value.

Other factors also play a role in why the poor lack of health care. For example, national and state policies often affect access to health care although they are ostensibly designed to deal with other areas. Housing and neighborhood policies, education policy, income-support policies, welfare policies, civil rights policies, macroeconomic policy, and employment policy all affect health care (National Poverty Center, 2009). Many other countries have recognized this pattern and are already scrutinizing different government policies to determine what impact they will have on health care for their citizens. The United States has not yet taken into account the influence of individual government policies on health care.

In the United States, being healthy is not simply a response to health care expenditures. Environmental, social, economic, behavioral, and psychological factors also play roles in whether or not one is healthy. Environmental factors include the existence of industrial by-products such as air, water, and ground pollution throughout many areas of the United States. Pollution contributes to health problems for those living near these facilities. Economic factors include reluctance on the part of state and federal governments to force companies to fully clean up the pollution they produce because doing so might produce plant closures and/or increases in the prices of the products made by the companies. Behavioral and psychological considerations include the tendency for Americans to overeat, producing an epidemic of obesity in the United States, and individual decisions to smoke, drink alcohol in access, and engage in other risky behaviors.

The United States spends more on health care than any other country in the world. Unfortunately, the outcomes are not consistent with the level of spending. For example, infant mortality in the United States has not dropped and the country now is near the bottom of developed nations in this index of health care. One reason for this disparity between the amount spent and health outcomes is that much of U.S. health care spending goes to overhead and profit among health insurance companies and related industries. Most significant medical procedures need approval from insurance carriers who employ individuals to screen and make decisions before the insurance company will agree to pay for the care. Historically, health insurance carriers

Policy Practice

Practice Behavior Example: Analyze, formulate, and advocate for policies that advance social well-being.

Critical Thinking Question: Looking at the two poverty theories mentioned earlier, the social causation theory and the social drift theory, which makes the most sense to you? What makes your chosen theory most attractive?

Policy Practice

Practice Behavior Example: Advocate for human rights and social and economic justice.

Critical Thinking Question: How would you respond to someone who states that "Social workers should focus on helping their clients and be less concerned about issues related to economics, pollution, and health care policy"?

discriminated against individuals with preexisting conditions or whose health status was considered risky. The result is that only the healthiest citizens are covered by health insurance, leaving many others vulnerable to normal and extraordinary health bills.

In addition, poor families are more likely to have children born prematurely and to experience perinatal complications (Fiscella, 2010). These increase the risk for chronic diseases when these children become adults. Likewise, low birth weight is connected to motor and cognitive development delays and lower levels of academic achievement. An indication of how important are early life experiences is what happens when poor children are adopted by affluent parents. These children experience an increase of 12 IQ points that appears related to exposure to both number of words and "sentence structure, positive parental affect, and the encouragement of exploration and curiosity" (Nisbett, 2009, p. 648). Children exposed to negative conditions such as parental depression, neglect, or abuse are likely to have this impair on their emotional development (Shonkoff, Boyce, & McEwen, 2009). Poverty has also a negative impact on children's mental health, which in turn affects their academic achievement and increases the risk to other children via acting out behavior (McLeod & Shanahan, 1996).

Poverty is clearly related to the quality and quantity of U.S. health care. This is nowhere more evident than with children. Poor families and children live in areas of communities that are themselves poor, including many inner cities. These communities often lack public resources, such as recreational facilities and services that provide low or no cost health care. Neighborhoods are devoid of economic investment and often lack the kind of political power needed to create change. These environments contribute to parental stress and child abuse as residents often lack opportunities for developing social networks that can help alleviate isolation (Wood, 2003). Crime and violence are also health risks associated with such areas.

Being poor has cognitive consequences as IQ test scores tend to be lower by a margin of 6 to 13 points. This finding has been noted in both the United States and Britain (McCulloch & Joshi, 2001; Wood, 2003). Table 19.5 shows some of the cognitive and educational risks of poverty.

Poverty has long been associated with poor and chronic health conditions (Seith & Isakson, 2011). Poor children spend more time in hospitals, are more likely to be disabled for longer periods, and have higher death rates. Access to preventive services, care for acute illnesses, and emergency care are all lower for poor children. Most of the children exposed to lead live in poor environments with unsafe levels of household lead.

Poverty is also related to birth outcomes such as low birth rate, infant mortality, and adolescent pregnancy (Wood, 2003). Among adults, poverty level is associated with high

Table 19.5   Poverty Influences on Negative Cognitive and Educational Outcomes

Negative Outcome	Poor Children Versus Nonpoor Children: Increased Likelihood of Negative Outcome
Developmental delays	1.3 times greater
Learning disability	1.4 times greater
Repeating a grade	2 times greater
Expelled or suspended	2 times greater
Dropping out of high school	2.2 times greater
Neither employed nor in school at age 24	1.9 times greater

Source: Adapted from Wood (2003).

blood pressure, heart disease, stroke, emphysema, asthma, chronic bronchitis, diabetes ulcers, liver and kidney disease, arthritis, migraines, vision problems, and loss of natural teeth compared to adults in nonpoor families (Vital and Health Statistics, 2012). Studies by Moilanen, Shaw, Dishion, Gardner, and Wilson (2010) concluded that extreme family poverty was also a factor in slower growth in children's ability to manage their behavior, thereby affecting poor children's developmental level. On an emotional level, adults in poor families were twice as likely as nonpoor families to feel hopeless, sad, nervous, and/ or worthless during the past 30 days. They also experience more than 2½ times as many days off from work due to injury or illness in a given year and are three to four times as likely to describe their overall health as fair or poor. Clearly, poverty has a inverse impact on the health and health care in the United States. Generally speaking, the greater the level of poverty, the worse the health outcomes for both adults and children.

> **Assess your comprehension of Homelessness and Healthcare by completing this quiz.**

EDUCATION

Education plays at least two roles in understanding poverty. From the standpoint of its strong association with adult income level, education is a means of both avoiding poverty and giving those who are poor a way out of poverty. Education is also a primary interest at the global level as multiple international agencies and governments emphasize the virtues of student learning and educational advancement (Tarabini, 2009). Social and economic functions of education are recognized as sufficiently important to the development of nations, particularly in the context of human capital. Education increases productivity of a country as well as spurring wholesale economic improvements. It improves living conditions and the general welfare of a country's people. Finally, it makes countries more internationally competitive.

Ironically, education does not always generate positive benefits for a specific country. For example, as the educational level of a nation increases, it also increases the amount of schooling needed in the labor market to produce higher incomes. In effect, this raises the minimum expectation for

Did You Know?

The World Bank summed up the importance of educating a nation in the following quotation:

Failure to provide basic education seriously compromises a country's efforts to reduce poverty. A large body of research points to the catalytic role of basic education for those individuals in society who are most likely to be poor. Basic education or literacy training, of adequate quality, is crucial to equipping disadvantaged individuals with the means to contribute to and benefit from economic growth. (Aoky, Bruns, & Drabble, 2002, pp. 233–234)

citizens in terms of what is required for success. In the United States, initially it was expected that a high school education was the minimum needed for successful employment. As more and more people went to college, a high school diploma was no longer sufficient and a college degree became the basic expectation. A similar process is underway across the globe (Tarabini, 2009). Moreover, as educational opportunity rises, it almost inevitably benefits some groups at the expense of others. As a result, a degree of inequality is often associated with improvements in the availability of education to a population.

The other role that education plays in poverty occurs in the classroom when teachers, unfamiliar with poverty, encounter poor children. Many new teachers from middle-class backgrounds report they simply do not understand their students (Bennett, 2008). Some struggle with the multicultural nature of the classroom while others fail to realize that their students often lack basic items frequently found in more affluent homes, such as computers and calculators. Moreover, home and neighborhood environments may preclude students completing routine homework assignments. Parents may not be able to come to parent–teacher meetings or to assist their children with homework.

For some students, afterschool activities are not possible because of either the lack of transportation home after the event or insufficient funds to participate.

Berliner (2006) provides a cogent analysis of the relationship between education and poverty in the United States. He notes first that poverty in the United States lasts longer than in other wealthy countries and poverty is clearly related to academic performance of students, especially urban minority groups. Being poor prevents the "expression of genetic talent at the lower end of the socioeconomic scale" (p. 949). By this he means that the influence of the environment greatly overshadows the ability of genetic endowment to achieve the individual's potential, the equivalent of planting high-quality grass seed in poor soil. In addition, health problems of the poor limit school achievement and reduce their life chances. The poor are more likely to have untreated ear infections and less likely to have the benefits of breast feeding that will protect them from illness in school. Poor children are also more likely to have unaddressed vision needs, asthma, and prior exposure to lead with accompanying neurological damage (Jones et al., 2009). Children born prematurely, a more common phenomenon in the poor, are also less likely to have the same level of intelligence as those born full term. This is largely a function of less brain volume and brain abnormalities (Berliner, 2006).

Family poverty levels contribute to lower academic performance and problematic behavior in the school setting. Berliner doubts that educational and school reforms will be effective in reducing poverty because too many of the variables associated with learning are outside of the school setting. He points out that the typical student spends about 1,000 hours in school but 5,000 hours out of school. Berliner is joined in this argument by Anyon (2005, p. 69) who points out that:

> Currently, relatively few poor urban students go past ninth grade: graduation rates in large comprehensive inner-city high schools are abysmally low. In fourteen such New York City schools, for example, only 10 percent to 20 percent of ninth graders

Policy Practice

Practice Behavior Example: Understand that policy affects service delivery and they actively engage in policy practice.

Critical Thinking Question: Berliner notes that poverty in the United States lasts for longer time periods than is true in other wealthy countries. What factors might explain this difference? What role might government policies play?

Clinical Corner

Rich

Rich was a social worker with the VA who helped veterans with service-connected injuries and medical needs. One day while at lunch he spotted Jose, a veteran he had worked with in the past, standing on a street corner holding up a sign that read "Will work for food." Rich parked his car nearby and walked to where Jose was standing. They began a conversation that revealed Jose had lost his job at the box factory and along with it his health insurance. He was going to be homeless in a week or so when the bank foreclosed on his home because he was unable to make the payments. In addition, Jose was experiencing a variety of flashbacks and had trouble sleeping as a result of his wartime experiences. It was clear to Rich that Jose needed immediate help if things were not to get worse. He bought Jose lunch and gave him a ride to the VA Hospital, about a mile away. There they talked for another hour as Rich arranged for a medical exam and possibly some medication to deal with the flashbacks and sleep disturbances. The hospital kept Jose overnight to treat his dehydration and low blood pressure. Rich used the time to see if there was room in the apartment building the VA leased to house veterans who were homeless or in danger of being so. He was told that a one-bedroom unit had opened up after the death of another man. Rich asked them to hold the room and later talked Jose into staying in the apartment for the time being. Over the next few weeks, Rich met regularly with Jose as they worked to find employment and get Jose back on his feet.

in 1996 graduated four years later. Despite the fact that low-income individuals desperately need a college degree to find decent employment, only 7 percent obtain a bachelors degree by age twenty-six. So, in relation to the needs of low-income students, urban districts fail their students with more egregious consequences now than in the early twentieth century.

These authors and others argue that improving the economic standing of families and children will be much more beneficial than tinkering with the educational system.

Factors related to student performance in school include access to high-quality and affordable day care. Lee and Burkam (2002) documented the educational gap between poor children and their middle-class peers and multiple studies have shown that early childhood programs are especially helpful to poor children (Lynch, 2004). Interestingly, there are other poverty-related issues that impact the educational attainment of poor children. For example, poor children tend to suffer greater losses in what they have learned during the summer compared to middle-class kids. This is likely due to the increased cultural and academic experiences available to more affluent children. While middle-class children gain in reading achievement during summers, lower-class children move in the other direction.

Other authors have studied how increased family income relates to academic achievement. Dearing, McCartney, and Taylor (2001) followed families for three years and found that when individual poor families increased in income, the academic performance of their children improved and they rated similar to those whose parents had not been poor. Not only does increased income of parents influence academic performance, it also can result in fewer emotional problems. Over a period of four years, children whose families moved out of poverty experienced a drop in psychological symptoms to the level of families who had never been poor (Costello, Compton, Keeler, & Angold 2003).

While education is clearly associated with improvements in one's life chances and higher adult socioeconomic status, it alone cannot cure poverty. What is clear is helping parents and families move out of poverty benefits both children's academic performance and behavior. It is also evident that improving the quality of education with a goal of reducing poverty is a much less-efficient method than directly dealing with impoverishment itself.

Policy Practice

Practice Behavior Example: Analyze, formulate, and advocate for policies that advance social well-being.

Critical Thinking Question: Can you summarize the reasons why education does not appear to be the answer to poverty?

BARRIERS AND BOOSTERS TO BREAKING THE CYCLE OF POVERTY

Poverty has been deemed the most severe of all threats to the well-being of families (Maluccio, Pine, & Tracy, 2002). This is evident in terms of access to health care, good and services, and other necessities. It is reflected in health care outcomes, as well as general quality of life. Efforts to end poverty have been ongoing for centuries although the responses have been very different depending on how the causes of poverty were defined. From poor houses in the distant past to antipoverty programs of the present, the challenge has been significant. In this section, we will look first at the barriers to ending poverty and then at those factors that seem to show promise.

Barriers

Determining what constitutes a barrier to moving people out of poverty can be complicated. For example, most secondary and many elementary schools in the country employ *tracking* of their students that puts students of higher academic abilities in one set of classes and students with lower ability in another set. It is often referred to as *ability grouping* (Ansalone, 2003). The rationale for tracking is that it benefits lower ability students by not putting them in the same classes with better students where their poorer skills will be more noticeable. The assumption is that such mingling of low- and high-ability students will negatively affect the self-concept of the former and simultaneously hold back academic progress of the latter. Research has shown some benefits to low-ability students when tracking is employed. Positive changes in student affective development, improved reading skills, and higher student satisfaction have been found (Mosteller, Light, & Sachs, 1996; Sternberg, 1997). Positive outcomes were also noted for high-ability students.

The downside of tracking begins with evidence that lower track enrollment is disproportionately made up of children from poor homes. Many are African American or Latino. The concern is that students in the lower track experience a loss of the opportunity to learn and that those with talent are limited in their access to knowledge. Tracking often means that poor and minority children receive an inferior education (Ansalone, 2001). Because tracking is based on presumed ability, it can both underestimate the individual student's potential and reflect racial or class bias (Ansalone, 2003). Lower track students often receive a different type and quality of education that may not provide an equal chance to learn or prepare for future employment.

Research on whether tracking improves students' academic achievement is largely inconclusive. There is some evidence that it works to the benefit of students with higher ability at the expense of other students. A primary conclusion is that tracking causes students to lose the intellectual stimulation offered in mixed classes. Whether students' self-confidence and self-esteem improve as a result of being in a lower track is debatable based on mixed findings from the United States and Great Britain (Boaler, William, & Brown, 2000; Ireson & Hallam, 1999). Student–teacher interaction appears to be less common in the lower tracks and teacher quality is lower. Teacher expectations for student success are also lower in the lower tracks and higher in the higher tracks (Entwisle, Alexander, & Olson, 1997; Kozol, 1991; Page, 1991). Ansalone (2003) concludes his analysis of tracking by looking at its overall impact on students (p. 17):

- "Cross cultural research fails to support the belief that it improves academic achievement."

- "Tracking may widen the achievement gap between advantaged and disadvantaged students, especially in homes that lack strong parental support for education."

- "Tracking and streaming often segregate students according to class and race. This separation limits learning and future career trajectories and may serve to perpetuate the cycle of poverty."

- "Tracking can create restricted learning trajectories for disadvantaged students, especially those who lack strong parental support for education. Accordingly, tracking may become an important variable in the social construction of success or failure."

While we have previously identified the value of education to escaping poverty, the ways in which schools organize and deliver that education can be a barrier or a benefit to this effort. Other barriers to eliminating poverty can include structural, economic, political, and individual factors. One example of this is the increase in poverty rates noted over the past 30 years. This increase reflects significant changes in the employment picture for millions of Americans. As manufacturing jobs in the United States declined and the country moved more into the service sector, well-paying employment opportunities disappeared. Sectors of the economy that had offered many workers the opportunity to become part of the middle-class dried up. Industries such as automotive and steel experienced dramatic drops in production as imports from other countries replaced items once made in the United States. Many companies found it cheaper to manufacture products in other countries, partly in response to trade agreements between the United States and these countries, partly as a way to avoid paying the relatively higher salaries and benefits made by American workers, and partly to escape rules designed to protect workers from injury or illness. Tax incentives helped support the outsourcing of many jobs ranging from manufacturing to call centers. At the same time, collective bargaining opportunities decreased and unions declined in membership as companies closed their doors and, too often, defaulted on their commitment to provide pensions to retired workers. Other companies chose to file bankruptcy to eliminate their debts and end contracts with their workers' unions.

Did You Know?

The factors described earlier have had a significant impact on the respective income of workers and chief executive officers (CEOs) in many industries. One way of showing the effect of all these changes is to look at average hourly wages paid to ordinary workers. From 1947 to 1972, the average hourly wage rose from $10.18 to $17.88, a gain of $7.70 or just over 75%. From 1972 to 2009, the average wage went from $17.88 to $18.63, a gain of 75 cents or about 4% (Economic Policy Institute, 2011). At the same time, the pay of corporate CEOs increased from 30 to 263 times what the average worker made (Anderson et al., 2010). This pattern of increasing poverty, a declining middle class, and a widening of the gap between the rich and poor has become evident in other countries including Australia, Germany, and England (Eardley, 1998; Leaman, 2008; Ludwig & Dietz, 2008).

While we have looked at individual barriers, often barriers interact together to produce a given outcome. For example, both family and community poverty may work together to prevent an individual from having opportunities to escape the disadvantages of being poor. Family poverty, in concert with a cultural obligation to help support others in the family, may result in a potential college student going to work after high school and foregoing an opportunity to move forward in life. Community poverty with high levels of violence and gang activity may lead an individual to join a gang whose members are the only ones making money (Hay, Fortson, Hollist, Altheimer, & Schaible, 2006).

Boosters

Boosters may be divided into two categories: those that help reduce the impact of poverty and those that are designed to eliminate poverty altogether. The effect of poverty on children can be mediated through the actions of the child's families (Attree, 2004; Gutman, McLoyd, & Tokoyawa, 2005; Jack, 2000) such as when parents socialize children into a set of values and behaviors that are similar or identical to those of the nonpoor. They can refuse to view their family as poor despite the lack of economic or other resources. Parents can set expectations for children reflecting their best aspirations in terms of education, socially acceptable behavior, and future employment. They can also model behavior that is likely to enhance, rather than detract, from the children's future success. This can include avoiding behaviors such as smoking, drinking to excess, and using drugs common to some poverty environments. Parents can also

New Orleans residents apply for disaster food stamps to help them cope with the aftermath of Hurricane Katrina.

Bill Haber/AP Images

intervene to protect their children from risks present in their immediate environments, such as gangs, opportunity for early sexual behavior, and the influence of antisocial peers. They can spend time in face-to-face interactions with their children providing social and emotional support. Dysfunctional family environments tend to increase the likelihood that children and adolescents will be affected adversely by growing up poor. The extent to which adults in the family cope with the stresses inherent to living in poverty, the more likely they are to be able to provide for the social and emotional needs of their children (Frankel & Frankel, 2006). The importance of quality parenting to the future of children in low-income households suggests that family therapy may help parents cope better with the stressors arising from poverty. We are not suggesting that clinical interventions are the answer to poverty, simply that they may prove of value to some families living in the context of inadequate resources and dysfunctional social and economic systems. Moreover, improving family stability and enhancing parental supervision skills have proven effective in keeping adolescents from engaging in delinquency, another potential benefit (Cheng, 2004).

POLICIES THAT PROMOTE AND FORESTALL POVERTY

Earlier in this chapter we listed several publicly funded programs designed to assist those grappling with poverty. The list included:

- TANF provides financial assistance mostly to single parents with dependent children using a combination of federal and state funds. (Both work requirements and time limits apply to this program.)

- Social Security (OASI) provides cash payments largely for older adults and those with disabilities (Disability Insurance [DI]) who have contributed to the program. Funds are a combination of individual and employer contributions (federal-only program).

- Supplemental Security Income (SSI) is primarily for people with disabilities and those over age 65 with few assets. Some people qualify for both Social Security and SSI. (Federal-only program although states can supplement it.)

- Unemployment Insurance is designed for those unemployed and paid for by taxes on employers (state system with federal help for economic downturns).

- Worker's Compensation provides cash and medical benefits to those suffering work-related injuries and survivors benefits in the event of their death (state-only system).

- Earned Income Tax Credit (EITC) is a federal program providing financial assistance to the working poor.

- Supplemental Nutrition Assistance Program (SNAP) (formerly Food Stamps) provides stamps for the poor useable for purchasing foods items (mostly a federal program).

- National School Lunch and School Breakfast Programs is a federal program providing free and reduced-price breakfasts and lunches for various groups of the poor.

- Children's Health Insurance Program (CHIP) provides medical coverage to children in poor families not covered by Medicaid; uses federal and state funds.

- Medicaid provides health care coverage for those below a certain income level and those over age 65 not covered by Medicare (jointly operated by federal and state government).

- Medicare provides health care coverage for those over age 65. Some people will qualify for both Medicaid and Medicare (federal only).
- Housing Subsidies provides assistance with the cost of housing for those who qualify (city, state, and federal funds).

These programs are the result of federal, state, and sometimes community policies designed to provide direct assistance to the poor. However, there are also other policies that are income related and designed to help eliminate poverty. For example, college students who qualify may receive Pell Grants designed to help them pay for higher education. Title I programs for school age children are designed to assist this group of the impoverished. Head Start programs created to help better prepare low-income preschool children for elementary school also contribute. Each program is based on the premise of building *human capital*, or the education and skills development that help individuals become successful wage earners (Aber, 2009). In addition, some states have experimented with other antipoverty efforts including New York City's use of *conditional cash transfers* (CCT). This program provides cash to parents that equal 15% to 30% of their initial income on the condition that the parents pursue actions that invest in their children. Examples include ensuring the pregnant mothers receive prenatal health care, immunizing children, and children's enrollment and attendance at school. Each educational, work, and health area has specific targets (e.g., 95% attendance, working 30 hours or more per week) that earns parents specified amounts of money. The money provided is in addition to other programs for which the parents and children might qualify, such as TANF. The idea of conditional cash transfers is new to the United States but has been used in at least 30 countries according to the World Bank (2011). Evaluations of these programs by the World Bank (2009) have found clear and positive impacts on the amount and quality/composition of food purchased by families, school enrollment of children, use of preventative health services, and reduction in poverty level. They also resulted in a decline in child labor, an intended goal.

Determining the success of this amalgam of antipoverty programs is difficult. One challenge is that the method for calculating poverty has been unchanged for over 50 years. Originally based on the cost of food needed for survival level, it no longer accurately reflects a typical household budget. When adopted, the cutoff was equal to about one-half of the median family income in the United States. Today, it represents between 25% and 33%, suggesting that it has failed to keep pace with the economy (Glennerster, 2007). Nor does it correspond to the area or region in which a person lives and where one lives does affect the cost and standard of living (Pimpare, 2009). Recognizing that the cutoff lines for poverty are relatively arbitrary, the official rates do not allow consideration for those who are barely above the official designation. Nor does it address the problems of those whose incomes are a fraction of the official level. The so-called deep poverty reached a 37-year high in 2010 (Center on Budget and Policy Priorities, 2011). Perhaps most disconcerting is whether the "poverty level" captures the reality of poverty as experienced by Americans. The life course analysis of poverty suggests it does not. Finally, as with many things, human beings tend to compare themselves with others. As a result, one might be able to accept poverty if it were not for the constant cultural reminders about what others have. Relative poverty, or what one possesses compared to others, is a reflection of this reality. As a consequence, some argue that it is a better measure of poverty than static indices.

Two common assessments are used to determine the success of antipoverty programs. One measure is the official poverty level established by the federal government and compares poverty levels across time. For example, despite the expenditure of billions of dollars, the rate of child poverty in 2009 was only 26% lower than 1969 when several antipoverty programs began (Plotnick, 2009). Whether this drop is a positive sign or an indication of failure is open to debate. Certainly, the overall poverty rate of 1980 (11%) had risen to 15% in 2011, a discouraging sign. The gap between the richest and poorest in society is greater than at any time since 1918 and real median income has been dropping for the past 12 years. After-tax income has been more or less flat since 1979 for everyone except those above the 60th percentile. On the plus side, poverty among older people has declined and various poverty programs have kept individuals and families from becoming part of those in deep poverty, below 50% of the poverty line.

A second way to measure success is to compare what the situation would be if the antipoverty programs did not exist. This calculation is based on looking at the number of families who would live below the poverty line without the existence of antipoverty programs (Ben-Shalom, Moffitt, & Scholz, 2012). One estimate suggests that antipoverty programs reduce the number of people who would otherwise be poor by about 16%. Ben-Shalom et al. pointed out that poverty rates for single-parent families and the unemployed were reduced much more in 1984 compared to 2004. This drop largely reflected expenditure reductions over the 30-year period. This drop has been more obvious for those in deep poverty to begin with. Basically, expenditures for combating poverty have been redistributed from the very poor to those who are less poor, or near poor. Funds have also been moved from targeting older adults without a disability to those with. The conclusion of Ben-Shalom et al. is that the program with highest poverty reducing impact is the OASI program. In their estimation, OASI "reduces poverty dramatically and reduces deep poverty and the poverty gap among the elderly almost to zero. The DI Program also has a major impact through its effect of reducing high deep poverty rates almost to zero among the disabled. The SSI, TANF, Food Stamp, EITC and housing assistance programs all have significant, though smaller, impacts as well. Their effects are often targeted on specific groups; for example, poverty rates among single-parent families are significantly reduced by the system" (p. 36). By contrast, the poverty rates for nondisabled families with no employed members are 80% before available programs are applied and drop only to 67% after they begin receiving benefits, a modest improvement. Since 1984, there has been a significant shift in emphasis among several antipoverty programs. These changes have moved funds away from single- and two-parent families and families with unemployed members in deep poverty and to individuals and families who have higher incomes, either above or below the poverty line. There is also a trend of expenditures toward older adults and those with disabilities. This appears to reflect a leaning toward the "worthy poor" as opposed to those considered less deserving. A similar observation can be made with respect to funding aimed at workers over those who don't work, whether unemployed men or women staying at home to raise a family. A fair conclusion from the available evidence is that the effectiveness of antipoverty programs is mixed with some clear winners and losers.

Policy Practice

Practice Behavior Example: Analyze, formulate, and advocate for policies that advance social well-being.

Critical Thinking Question: What factors might explain the movement of government antipoverty funds from the most poor to those who are less poor?

Assess your analysis and evaluation of this chapter's contents by completing the Chapter Review.

20

Mental Health and Mental Illness as Influences on Human Behavior

Sergio Stakhnyk /Shutterstock

You have been touched by mental illness, whether directly or indirectly. Statistics suggest there is a strong likelihood that you, your siblings, your parent, your child, other family members, neighbors, and friends have struggled with mental illness. In fact, roughly 26% of U.S. adults struggle with some form of mental illness during a 12-month period as can be seen in Figure 20.1.

Mental illness is a cruel condition for many reasons. Indeed, if you have ever suffered from a mental illness such as depression, anxiety, a gripping addiction, or schizophrenia you know that the term "mental illness" sounds too polite a word, too sanitized. Have you ever gone to an emergency department believing you were having a heart attack? Imagine the worry and sense of doom that must course through your mind and body given that you think you are likely to die! Well, one hospital estimated that 12% of patients who reported to the emergency department believing they were having a heart attack were actually suffering from a panic attack—a very nonlethal yet very frightening experience (Rohacek et al., 2012). Consider the implications of this finding. The fear and dread associated with a panic attack are so strong that people literally believe they are having a heart attack. Everyday language seems to have diluted the clinical meaning of panic attack. If we say "don't have a panic attack" to a friend, we likely mean to say, "it's going to be okay, don't worry." Try telling that to a friend who is having a panic attack and you will likely notice she is not comforted. In fact, even

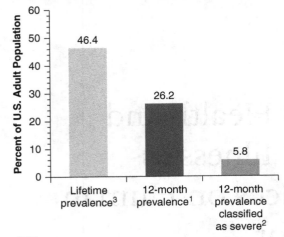

Figure 20.1
Lifetime and 12-Month Prevalence of Mental Illness in U.S. Adults.
Source: Retrieved from http://www.nimh.nih.gov/statistics/1ANYDIS_ADULT.shtml, on September 3, 2012.

after being told that they "only suffered a panic attack," roughly 40% of people who presented to the emergency department during a panic attack who believed they were suffering a heart attack returned within 12 months with the same complaint and outcome (Rohacek et al., 2012). Here, panic and fear triumph over logic.

Similarly, the term "depression" seems to have been diluted. In everyday usage we throw around "I'm depressed" to indicate when we are discouraged or if we had a bad day. However, clinical depression is so severe that it can cause people to not go to work, to not get out of bed, to not eat, or not pursue basic activities. Indeed, at its worst, depression can become so dark that people commit suicide.

MENTAL HEALTH

What is mental health? What is mental illness? Does social work care about people's mental health or mental illness? From a broad perspective, mental health and mental illness seem like straightforward concepts to understand: the functioning of our minds, emotions, and behaviors. Below, a more detailed definition is provided. With regard to the question if social work is interested in people's mental health, the clear answer is yes! Social work is very interested in human mental health as evidenced by the very first line in the National Association of Social Work's Code of Ethics (2008):

> The primary mission of the social work profession is to enhance human wellbeing and help meet the basic human needs of all people, with particular attention to the needs and empowerment of people who are vulnerable, oppressed, and living in poverty.

Assuming that "human well-being" encompasses "mental health," social work is clearly interested in promoting the mental health of all humans—in fact, promoting well-being is the primary mission of social work. Social work has many allies that strive to promote human well-being and mental health. Consider language from the World Health Organization (WHO; http://www.who.int/mediacentre/factsheets/fs220/en/, retrieved on January 4, 2012):

> Mental health is an integral and essential component of health. The WHO constitution states: "Health is a state of complete physical, mental and social well-being and not merely the absence of disease or infirmity."

An important consequence of this definition is that mental health is described as more than the absence of mental disorders or disabilities. The WHO goes on to define mental health in this way:

> Mental health is a state of well-being in which an individual realizes his or her own abilities, can cope with the normal stresses of life, can work productively and is able to make a contribution to his or her community. In this positive sense, mental health is the foundation for individual well-being and the effective functioning of a community.

Another method for understanding "mental health" is to look at definitions of mental illness. An ally in promoting mental health is the National Association for the Mentally Ill (NAMI). This organization's mission is to promote "building better lives" through the grassroots efforts designed to lower the incidence and impact of "mental illness." NAMI defines mental illness as "... *conditions that disrupt a person's thinking, feeling, mood, ability to relate to others and daily functioning*" (http://www.nami.org/template.cfm?section=about_mental_illness, retrieved on January 4, 2012) and that mental illnesses are similar to conditions such as diabetes, which are medical conditions that influence one's capacity to cope with life.

Combining the above definitions of mental health, it is clear that mental health encompasses people's social interactions, behavior, emotionality, approach to life, and general functioning. The WHO definition asserts that mental well-being is foundational for functioning at both individual and community levels.

Optimal Mental Functioning

Several allied professions have long histories of studying elements of mental health, such as psychiatry, psychology, nursing, sociology, marriage and family therapy, and social work. Historically, much of the emphasis of these professions has been to study the "absence" of mental health, that is, to study mental illness. The emphasis on "deviations" from mental health is understandable—given that professions are often called upon to help when something is "wrong." Most of us do not see a doctor to ask how to function optimally. The near singular focus on mental illness has inspired a reaction among consumers and professionals in the form of interest in topics such as "positive psychology" and "flow" that strive to promote mental health rather than emphasize its absence. This relative recent shift is hopeful because optimal mental health is good in its own right and because optimum mental functioning is incompatible with mental illness.

Positive Psychology

A mentor of *one* of the authors (BL) used to say, "Let's build protective fences at the top of the cliff rather than park our ambulances at the bottom of the cliff." This statement is consistent with a primary tenet of positive psychology: build strength and wellness with the hope that this will minimize weakness and illness (Park & Peterson, 2003). Fairly recent efforts have promoted the idea that efforts from social work and allied professions should emphasize well-being, both because wellness is desirable and because wellness and illness tend not to "co-exist" very well. Certainly, a need exists to promote well-being. One report indicates that only about 20% of Americans say they are "flourishing" (Sin & Lyubomirsky, 2009).

Positive psychology focuses on areas such as happiness, resilience, forgiveness, "flow," self-acceptance, self-determination, positive social relations, and gratitude. While these concepts may appear "lightweight" to some, research has shown that interventions focused on positive psychology consistently enhance well-being and decrease symptoms of depression (Sin & Lyubomirsky, 2009). Specifically, these authors note that if 200 individuals were randomly and equally assigned to either a positive psychology intervention or a control group, 65 of 100 in the positive psychology group would report increased well-being and decreased depression with only about 35 of 100 assigned to the control group doing better. In another study, resilience was positively associated with well-being and lower levels of depression during stressful life periods (Mak, Ng, & Wong, 2011). Further, these researchers found that certain types of thinking, namely positive views of the self, the world, and the future, were predictive of resilience. Such knowledge gives rise to the possibility that humans can be inoculated from the negative impact of stressful situations.

One researcher, Martin Seligman, has extensively studied this phenomenon of stress inoculation. Dr. Seligman is a researcher who has done remarkable amounts of research on human functioning. One of his first achievements was doing work on "learned helplessness" (Abramson, Seligman, & Teasdale, 1978). In short, learned helplessness is characterized by individuals giving up hope and becoming passive in the face of problems, clearly not an adaptive approach to problems. Learned helplessness tends to occur when people believe they cannot control outcomes and are victims to circumstance. One pivotal research study on learned helplessness randomized participants to three conditions involving the presence of a loud noise. In Phase I, one group could stop the loud, annoying noise by pushing a button four times. The second group also had a button to push, but the noise stopped regardless of participants pushing behavior—that is, effort did not result in a desired outcome. The third group received a "no noise condition" meaning that they were not exposed to noise. In Phase II, all three groups were exposed to noise that was controllable by simply moving a switch. Participants in the first and third groups—that is, the controllable-noise and "no noise" groups—were much more likely to turn off the noise relative to those in the second group who were first exposed to an uncontrollable situation. Studies like this reveal that human functioning is linked to learning from environmental stimuli and that we can learn to either promote our mental health or leave it up to chance.

Watch the video on Positive Psychology from TED. What are your reactions to the talk? What are the implications for social work?

Clinical Corner

Depression Prevention Programs? Is it possible to prevent against depression, like Fluoride to cavities?

Based on research that explained a tendency toward a form of depression, "learned helplessness," Martin Seligman and his associates developed an approach designed to inoculate students against depression . . . much like Fluoride is used to prevent cavities (Seligman, 1995). The Depression Prevention Program (DPP) targets how people respond to untoward or negative events, such as doing poorly on a test or making a social mistake. The DPP posits that people explain their experiences using three dimensions that make up our explanatory style:

- Internal/external
- Stable/unstable
- Global/specific

Table 20.1   Language That Promotes Pessimism or Optimism

	Pessimistic	Optimistic
Stability: Permanent or temporary	"I'll never get good grades."	"Well, this is just one of five tests. I still have more chances."
Personalization: Intrinsic or extrinsic	"I'm just not smart enough to do well."	"My teachers can help me learn this; so can my tutor or parents."
Pervasive: Global or specific	"I always seem to come up short."	"I took the test during a time when I was very stressed. Things will be better."

Source: Brad Lundahl, based on the work of Seligman (1995).

Using these three dimensions, people can roughly be categorized into two dimensions: pessimistic and optimistic. People who tend to be pessimistic, compared to optimistic, are less likely to pursue challenge and are more likely to give up in the face of setbacks. Further, they are more likely to experience a sense of depression or discouragement. People high on the pessimistic scale tend to explain difficult experiences or negative feedback as being (1) internal to them (they did not have the "right stuff" to succeed), (2) stable (a personality trait that is unlikely to change such as "I'm not very smart"), and (3) global (I'm not smart in a lot of areas). By contrast, a more optimistic style would explain a difficult experiences as being (1) external to them (the test was really difficult and was on material not covered in class), (2) unstable (some tests are hard, others are not that bad), and (3) specific (this one test was difficult, I can study and better prepare for others).

While some people are naturally more optimistic than others, Seligman has implemented cognitive and behavioral therapy as a method of encouraging an optimistic style. How might this work? Imagine a student is struggling with performing well on a test and has received a bad grade. Teachers and other adults could recognize pessimistic ways of thinking and promote optimistic ways of thinking. See Table 20.1, for example.

Children can be taught to use explanations that favor an optimistic approach to life through modeling, counseling techniques, and even direct educational efforts. Early results suggest that the DPP is effective (Gillham et al., 1995; Seligman et al., 2007).

Dr. Seligman's vision of positive psychology is clearly aligned with social work's mission (see Chapter 1). When he served as President of the American Psychological Association at the turn of the millennium, Dr. Seligman pushed social sciences to study and understand "positive psychology." Read the first two paragraphs of the first article of the year 2000 from Psychology's most prestigious journal *The American Psychologist*:

> Entering a new millennium, Americans face a historical choice. Left alone on the pinnacle of economic and political leadership, the United States can continue to increase its material wealth while ignoring the human needs of its people and those of the rest of the planet. Such a course is likely to lead to increasing selfishness, to alienation between the more and the less fortunate, and eventually to chaos and despair.
>
> At this juncture, the social and behavioral sciences can play an enormously important role. They can articulate a vision of the good life that is empirically sound

while being understandable and attractive. They can show what actions lead to well-being, to positive individuals, and to thriving communities. Psychology should be able to help document what kinds of families result in children who flourish, what work settings support the greatest satisfaction among workers, what policies result in the strongest civic engagement, and how people's lives can be most worth living. (Seligman & Csikszentmihalyi, 2000, p. 5)

Since this time, considerable research and model development has focused on positive psychology. Consider Figure 20.2 in which we searched the number of references to positive psychology in one database, *PsychINFO via EBSCOHOST* (accessed January 21, 2012) by time. Previous to 1980, there were only 97 such references. In the past decade, there has truly been an explosion of interest in the concepts of positive psychology.

Let's now review some major areas of focus under the positive psychology umbrella.

Resilience

The ability to respond and cope during stressful situations is known as resilience or hardiness (Eschleman et al., 2010; Mak et al., 2011). Hardiness is often characterized as a multidimensional construct with the following primary ingredients:

- *Commitment.* With regard to resilience, commitment refers to the degree to which a person is involved in specific life domains such as family, work, and friends. Commitment is synonymous with a sense of purpose and meaning. High levels of commitment to a cause are linked to strong social relations, which are positively linked to the ability to manage stress.
- *Control.* As mentioned above in the section on learned helplessness, a high sense of control is important to weather stressful situations. When people do not believe they can positively influence outcomes during stressful situations, they tend to lose confidence and hope—factors that lead to a sense of victimhood or helplessness. Confidence in one's ability to navigate stressful situations is

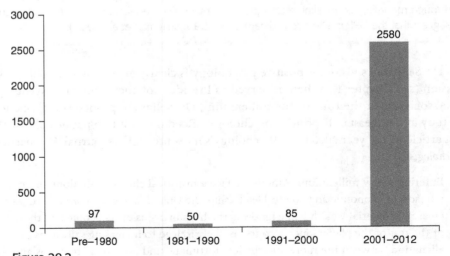

Figure 20.2
References to Positive Psychology Across Time.

Source: PsychoInfo via Ebscohost, search term "Positive Psychology" January 2012. Brad Lundahl produced

developed through practice and skill enhancement efforts. College, the military, on-the-job training, and workforce services all spend considerable time helping people develop skills that will promote confidence. Social workers can help individuals and families develop skills and confidence through counseling and pscyho-education. Health care workers, such as nurses and dieticians, can promote confidence in health-related areas through education and skill development.

- *Mental approach to challenge.* Individual difference exists in how people approach stressful or challenging situations. Some welcome challenges as enjoyable puzzles to solve. Others tend to feel threatened by challenge. Recall the sections on attachment and people's sense of security in Chapter 11. People who tend to perceive challenging situations as opportunities to learn and grow enjoy greater flexibility in their response repertoire. By contrast, people who feel highly threatened by challenges tend to become highly emotional and rigid in their response style.

- *Self-esteem.* Individuals high in hardiness and resilience tend to feel good about themselves and to believe they can succeed.

- *Social support.* When faced with stress, a key predictor of resilience is the strength of one's social network. Social networks lend both pragmatic support during stressful times as well as emotional and moral support.

- *Active coping.* High resilience is also characterized by direct, active problem solving as opposed to avoidance. Many stressors that are not dealt with tend to grow versus diminish. Consider a student who begins to have difficulty in a math class. If the student avoids what she does not understand, she is likely to fall further behind and engender more stress. Littleton and colleagues (2007) found that problem-focused coping, where one deals with stressors in a direct manner, is much more likely to lead to healthy outcomes following trauma relative to coping through avoidance.

Flow

How do you approach work? When discussing retirement, a respected mentor of one of the authors (BL) stated, "I never worked a day in my life." When asked what this meant, he said that because he thoroughly enjoyed his work, going to "work" was no different than playing. In this vein, Confucious reportedly said "Choose a job you love and you will never have to work a day in your life."

When we are fully engaged, time seems to fly.

Flow is a concept that was named by Mihaly Csikszentmihalyi (1990) who studied very talented musicians, artists, and other professionals. Flow is the mental state in which one becomes so highly absorbed in a task that time seems irrelevant. Imagine a musician or artist who becomes so completely absorbed that emotions and focus are at peak levels, providing a type of "high." Flow is only possible when motivation for the task is intrinsic, done for its own joy, and without threat of reward or punishment. Being in flow is not limited to artistic endeavors. Sports, work, writing, and exercising can become similarly absorbing.

Being in a state of flow is the opposite of boredom, an adjective often applied to endeavors such as work and education (sorry about that). Csikszentmihalyi found that people are most content when engaged in activities that have purpose and stretch them to think. That is, when people puzzle over problems that matter, they are more likely to be happy than when passively engaged in an activity such as watching television. Also helpful to developing flow is the degree of challenge a person experiences. Getting into flow is more likely if people do not feel the threat of being overwhelmed and if they can fully pay attention to the activity at hand.

Happiness

What is happiness and how can we secure it? This question, while betraying a Western bias, is central to how many people organize their thinking and behavior. Synonyms for happiness include well-being, satisfaction, positive affect, and joy. Happiness is characterized by relatively high levels of positive affect, low levels of negative affect, and global satisfaction with life (Demir & Weitekamp, 2007). The proverbial search for the elixir of happiness has long intrigued humans dating back to Socrates and beyond.

Of interest, research has actually linked happiness, subjective well-being, and life satisfaction to the "fountain of youth"; though the direction of effect is different from what mythology advances. Specifically, high levels of positive affect are linked to lower mortality (Chida & Steptoe, 2008). Of even greater interest is that positive psychological energy is connected to lower mortality and improved physical living among both "diseased" and "non-diseased" populations. That is, among those with and without a disease (such as cancer or diabetes), those with positive emotions (such as hope, optimism, and life satisfaction) tend to live longer! The power of happiness is not limited to longevity. From a market perspective, happier workers tend to enjoy higher levels of job satisfaction, which is linked to superior performance and fewer problems while at work (Bowling et al., 2010). Happiness is also linked to parenting. Rogers and White (1998) found that marital happiness had a strong, positive association with satisfaction in parenting—which in turn is linked to more desirable forms of parenting.

What factors promote happiness? Of course, the answer to this question depends on many variables. Lyubomirsky, Sheldon, and Schkade (2005) propose three primary determinants of happiness:

- *Happiness set point.* Heredity and personality traits are linked to happiness, making levels of happiness rather stable over time. Heritability is believed to be responsible for 50% of variance in happiness.

- *Intentional activities.* Humans seek to maximize happiness in direct ways. Intentional activities have been subdivided into three areas (which are sometimes targeted by psychotherapy): (a) cognitive, (b) behavioral, and (c) volitional. Intentional cognitive activities may include being grateful, pursuing spirituality, choosing to forgive, or focusing on beautiful aspects of life. Intentional behaviors may include exercise, travel, engaging in social activities, volunteering, or accomplishing a task. Intentional volition is linked to one's aspirations and achievement orientation. Developing goals and pursing them is linked to happiness, as is accomplishing activities placed on the "bucket list." Indeed, the notion of a "bucket list" involves intentionally identifying what one values and honoring oneself by attempting to fulfill ones' values. Lyubomirsky et al. (2005) estimate that 40% of happiness can be accounted for by intentional activities.

- *Life circumstances.* Contextual factors are also linked to happiness. Income, resources, gender, race, geographic local, culture, marital status, and other relatively stable life circumstances are contextual factors related to happiness. Of interest, these variables account for only about 10% of the variance—far less than the happiness set point or intentional activities.

Demir and Weitekamp (2007) propose that personality and relationship factors need to be added to Lyubomirsky's model of factors related to happiness. Research on personality types suggests that conscientiousness, openness to experience, and agreeableness are consistently linked to happiness. Relationships are also linked to happiness. Using the McGill Friendship Questionnaire, Demir and Weitekamp note six features of friendships that ultimately connect to sociability and happiness:

- Companionship: mutual participation in activities; sharing time
- Help: Both receiving and giving guidance and support
- Intimacy: open and honest self-disclosure
- Reliable alliance: possessing trust and loyalty from another
- Emotional security: Giving and receiving comfort and reassurance
- Self-validation: confidence that another person will support one's goals, success, and self

Of the six features of friendship, companionship is deemed to be one of the most important predictors of closeness and happiness (Demir & Weitekamp, 2007). Other considerations of friendship include degree of conflict (e.g., duration, frequency, intensity) and number of friends. While individuals may have many "casual" friends, a strong predictor of happiness is "close" friendships. While personality characteristics, such as openness and extroversion are linked to friendship quality and therefore happiness, note that pursuit of friendship can be intentional. That is, friendship falls into the "intentional category" of Lyubomirsky's model. The implication is that degree of friendship can be shaped through goal setting and skill building, thereby increasing the likelihood of achieving happiness.

What other factors influence happiness? In a study from the Netherlands, Koopmans, Geleijnse, Zitman, and Giltay (2010) reported that individuals who indicated having ". . . many moments of happiness" and "laugh happily often" were likely to live longer than individuals who did not endorse these two indicators of happiness. Thus, happiness is a type of "independent variable" in that it influences life mortality. However, the authors also explain that the link between happiness and mortality was partially mediated by physical activity. Happier individuals tended to exercise more. Thus, a new question arises: Which comes first, happiness or exercise? Also, it could be that individuals with many physical problems associated with poor health suffer more, thereby undermining happiness. Intuition and research have demonstrated a bidirectional relationship between happiness and physical activity—they influence each other. What about money? Does money buy happiness? Some researchers say yes, others say not so much. In support of the thesis that money buys happiness is research indicating that money can be used to solve problems, thereby decreasing stress and negative emotion (Vohs & Baumeister, 2011). Also, money may buy access to recreation and consumption that people find meaningful (Hsee, Yang, Li, & Shen 2009). By contrast, some research has shown that money can get in the way of happiness. Mogilner (2010) suggests that people who spend considerable time earning money spend less time in social relations, which is connected to happiness.

Interesting research from Europe confirms what many grandparents have told their grandchildren for generations: Do what makes you happy; don't work for money. Specifically, Garðarsdóttir, Dittmar, and Aspinall (2009) reported that individuals who had strong beliefs that money would buy them happiness tended to find an inverse link between the amount of money made and happiness. That is, if the pursuit of money is for the sake of happiness—money will likely fail to deliver happiness. It is far better to work out of a sense of curiosity and purpose, rather than to obtain money to "buy" happiness. We hope you enjoy social work!

If, as a social worker, you happen upon lots of money, the good news is that there are some suggestions on how to use it in a way that will promote happiness. Dunn, Gilbert, and Wilson (2011) suggest the following for translating money into happiness: (1) buy experiences not things, which may include trips, vacations, and time together as opposed to another television; (2) spend money on loved ones rather than on yourself. Dunn et al. (2008) found that people who spend money on others tend to be happier than when spending it on themselves. In one such study, researchers gave study participants a rather small amount of money (e.g., $20) and randomly assigned half participants to a condition where they were to spend it on themselves. The other participants were to spend the money on others. Those who spent the money on others tended to report greater happiness; (3) consider buying "many small pleasures" over large items. Other advice includes considering the happiness of others when spending money and do not become too focused on "extreme" comparison shopping which involves obsessing over features of potential purchases thereby highlighting what one does not have (Dunn et al., 2011).

Researching the link between money and happiness reveals a complex picture. It appears that money on its own, can be beneficial if it promotes autonomy, enhances ones sense of place in a social community, provides for interesting experiences, advances self-determination, and helps to avoid stress (Diener et al., 2010). However, the pursuit of money for its own sake, even with the hope that it will buy happiness, appears to be counterproductive. Well, so much for the easy adage: "Money is the root of all evil." Intentions and how one uses money can mitigate evil!

Self-Determination

Social workers value self-determination, a key concept in the positive psychology movement and a long staple of basic social work values. The National Association of Social Workers Code of Ethics states,

> Social workers respect and promote the right of clients to self-determination and assist clients in their efforts to identify and clarify their goals. Social workers may limit clients' right to self-determination when, in the social workers' professional judgment, clients' actions or potential actions pose a serious, foreseeable, and imminent risk to themselves or others. (NASW, Code of Ethics, 1.02)

Beyond legal and ethical considerations of self-determination, a group of researchers have studied self-determination as a mental health issue. Ryan and Deci (2000) have demonstrated that humans function much better and are much more content when three ingredients are in place: autonomy (read: self-determination, choice, intrinsic interest), relationships, and a sense of competence. These authors provide compelling evidence that humans are much more likely to thrive under conditions of autonomy relative to being controlled (Deci, Koestner, & Ryan 1999). High levels of autonomy are linked to an intrinsic motivation toward activities, whereas high levels of control are linked to an extrinsic motivation toward activities. Why does this matter? When intrinsically motivated, people are more likely to persist both when faced with challenge and when there is no requirement to work. How might this be of concern to social work? At a macro-level, consider some of the great advocates for social change, such as Jane Addams, Mohandas Gandhi, Saul Alinsky, Dr. Martin Luther King, and Nelson Mandela. One unifying thread for each of these leaders is that they were intrinsically motivated to effect change—and this motivation carried them through deep challenge and, at times, risk to themselves and their loved ones.

At a micro-level, intrinsic motivation will influence the degree to which people pursue a goal. Consider, for example, the impact of paying a child to engage in an activity such as school work. On average, what do you expect will happen to the motivation of groups of children who are paid to get good grades relative to those who are not paid? Deci et al. (1999) found that activities that promote an extrinsic motivation, such as paying children for getting good grades, will undermine intrinsic motivation, which then lowers the probability that children will become self-motivated learners. Ryan and Deci (2000) have demonstrated that autonomy, doing an act for its own reward, is undermined by any number of contextual controls that move the rationale for doing an activity to an outside force. When external forces are removed, motivation for the activity tends to diminish, which tends to result in less behavioral output. In the above example, if children are paid for getting good grades for a few years and then the payment disappears, expect the motivation to get good grades to also diminish.

Possibly the greatest endorsement for self-determination comes from the State of New Hampshire where the license plate motto reads "Live free or die." This sentiment says it all—self-determination is not optional. When self-determination is muzzled, a few predictable outcomes seem prominent. One outcome is that people do in fact "die," even if not physically. People feel defeated, like a doormat if not able to assert themselves. Learned helplessness, discussed earlier, is related to a sense of an inability to *self-determine*. A person living in a situation characterized by an inability to succeed may say: "If I cannot influence my future, why try at all." Another outcome of restricted self-determination is fighting to obtain self-determination, as was done in the Revolutionary War, the Women's Suffrage Movement, the Civil Rights Movement, and—more recently—the "Arab Spring," which has seen multiple countries that had lived under repressive regimens, revolt against authoritarian leaders.

Assess your comprehension of Mental Health and Mental Illness by completing this quiz.

Creativity

The movement of positive psychology has included creativity. What does creativity have to do with social work? The answer is multifaceted. On the one hand, people in a creative process experience a sort of natural high or emotional thrill (Csikszentmihalyi, 1990). Another reason is that the consumption of other people's creative artistic works is enjoyable. Whether appreciating creative architecture, enjoying a book, or admiring a painting, we value others' creativity. Indeed, the late Steve Jobs is said to have changed a vast swath of the technology through his ability to encourage creative output from the Apple Company.

Another reason social work is interested in creativity is because creativity is often about solving problems or advancement. Scientific revolutions that have brought about massive change in the world are, at their heart, creative solutions to old problems (Kuhn, 1962). Albert Einstein is reported to have said, "We can't solve problems by using the same kind of thinking we used when we created them." This statement is a clear bid to apply creativity to solve the problems we face. Of course, this applies to micro-, mezzo-, and macro-level social work. Consider examples of how gains have been made in combating poverty through the micro-loan program (http://www.cgap.org/gm/document-1.9.41443/FN59.pdf, retrieved on February 5, 2012). An organization named the Consultative Group to Assist the Poor (CGAP) brings together a number of professions and disciplines to promote financial success among groups traditionally disenfranchised from market success. In short, the microloan program attempts to get rather small amounts of money to historically poor individuals, often women, so that they can launch a business. The loan may be as small as 30 U.S. dollars to help a person buy chickens, a pottery wheel, a sewing machine, or some other resource from which they can begin to participate in the market and, therefore, be empowered. Review of these efforts shows promise in people's ability to lift themselves out of poverty with minimal help through both generating resources and building social and economic capital (Rosenberg, 2010).

Other creative efforts aimed at macro-level problems have been wildly successful. Recall that many heroes of social justice movements in the 20th century engaged creative approaches to broad reaching political problems. Mohandas Gandhi, Dr. Martin Luther King, and Saul Alinsky all engaged a creative, nonviolent approach to transforming society. Macro-level creativity also applies to policy-related issues. In the run up to the 2004 U.S. Presidential race, a relatively unknown candidate, Howard Dean, gained tremendous advantage through harnessing the power of the Internet and social media. In fact, Rice (2004) stated, "In 2003, Howard Dean transformed politics by utilizing the Internet as an integral part of his campaign" (p.2).

During the January/February months of 2012, two creative approaches to macro-level efforts were widely publicized. On January 18, 2012, websites such as Wikipedia, Google, Facebook, and others creatively opposed U.S. Legislation (H.R. 3261 and S. 968) designed to stop online piracy by shutting down for a day or relabeling their site (http://www.huffingtonpost.com/2012/01/17/wikipedia-blackout_n_1212096.html, retrieved on February 5, 2012). Regardless of your position on the subject, this creative response succeeded in temporarily stopping legislation. Another creative macro-level response to a problem came when the Susan G. Komen for the Cure of breast cancer announced it would no longer make grants available to the Planned Parenthood organization, presumably due to political pressure. Using multimedia efforts to broadcast this decision, and the resounding backlash of criticism against this decision through postings on the organization's Facebook page among other multimedia efforts, Komen reversed its position (Basset, 2012). Further, the backlash garnered considerable support for Planned Parenthood. Again, regardless of your position on Planned Parenthood or the Komen foundation, creativity was effective.

Closer to direct practice, the ankle bracelet monitoring program for individuals facing legal actions is creative in that it both reduces costs to taxpayers and importantly keeps individuals in their community so they can work and support family members. Drug court is a similar creative program that places value on overcoming addictions above punishment motives.

Hopefully, the preceding paragraphs demonstrated the importance of creativity in social work and its link to mental health. If so, what do we know about promoting or harnessing creativity? Who would be good sources of information on creativity? There is a huge global market for creativity because it sells. The marketplace strongly believes creativity gives them an edge over their competition, which boosts profits. Science, and therefore universities, is also interested in creativity because it solves problems. Let's look at a few ideas on how the creative process works. In reviewing research on creativity, Ma (2009) indicates that the creative process involves several key phases or stages that appear conceptually similar to steps in the scientific method:

1. Defining the problem, which likely comes from observing
2. Gathering information and knowledge about the problem
3. Developing possible solutions to problems
4. Developing criteria to evaluate potential solutions
5. Selecting and implementing promising solutions
6. Evaluating results

With regard to developing possible solutions to problems, several criteria are used to examine the value of creative ideas: fluency, flexibility, elaboration, quality, and originality (Ma, 2009). *Fluency* in creativity is the degree or amount to which an individual or group produces many ideas related to the problem. *Flexibility* refers to the ability to shift among ideas and solutions. *Elaboration* refers to the ability to increase both the attraction and acceptability of a solution by demonstrating increased understanding of the problem, the solution, and its implications. The *quality* of a creative output is judged largely on its ability to adequately respond to a problem, even if the problem is not entirely *original* (Ma, 2009).

Forgiveness

The last aspect of positive psychology related to mental health we discuss is forgiveness. Forgiveness is an interesting concept, ripe with preconceived notions. When you think of forgiveness, what ideas come to mind? Our guess is that spiritual, philosophical, and/or religions notions are fairly prominent, even if you do not practice any particular tradition. However, forgiveness is a broadly and deeply studied response to disappointment, insults, and offenses (see Lundahl, Taylor, Stevenson, & Roberts 2008). While positive psychology has championed forgiveness, the interest in this concept for one author came from listening to an interview with Dr. Robert Enright about his research on forgiveness (see http://www.forgiveness-institute.org). Forgiveness interventions have effectively been directed to individuals who have suffered considerable pain, such as partner infidelity, dishonesty, loss of a loved one to murder, loss of a loved one to drunk driving, child abuse, and many other interpersonal insults.

Life certainly dishes out high levels of pain. If you have worked in social work for more than a week, you have likely heard many stories in which a person has been seriously insulted and hurt. Injustice ranges up and down the micro- and macro-level scale, including individual child abuse to genocide and systematic repression. Such insults can leave people feeling depressed, discouraged, and angry. Hollywood movies and books often glorify revenge themes and "getting even"; however, getting even often does not relieve suffering. Indeed, at a macro-level attempts to "get even" clearly perpetuate further violence (e.g., Palestinian and Israeli conflict).

Forgiveness has shown itself to be an alternative to getting even, forgetting and moving on, or ignoring the offense. While certain "forgiveness programs" are based in religion, many are not (Lundahl et al., 2008). What is forgiveness and how does one apply it? To begin, it is probably best to say what forgiveness is not. According to Dr. Enright (see Enright & Fitzgibbons, 2000), forgiveness is not:

- Excusing wrongdoing
- Forgetting or ignoring wrongdoing
- Minimizing wrongdoing
- Rationalizing or excusing wrongdoing
- Dependent on justice being met
- An attempt to obtain moral high-ground over an offender
- Overlooking or skipping consequences for wrongdoing

So then, what *is* forgiveness? At a very basic level, forgiveness is a possible response to some form of offence or injustice. It is choosing to forego anger, resentment, and revenge fantasies, even when such could be considered "understandable." Thus, forgiveness is a kind of letting go of pain and negative emotion connected to an offense. Indeed, many interpersonal insults have a sort of double insult. The primary insult, such as having a child killed by a drunk driver, brings secondary pain, which can include the hurt of the loss *and* anger toward the wrongdoer, which form a "double whammy." Forgiveness is an attempt at minimizing the secondary pain.

How does one forgive and how does forgiveness work? Well, the complete answer to this is a complex subject. However, Enright and Fitzgibbons (2000) offer both a model and some steps. In general, an offended party should make a commitment to forgive. This commitment need not come from a religious or philosophical tradition, but simply awareness that the secondary pain is taxing and diminishes life quality. Indeed, secondary pain can become so intense that it drives an individual for years and possibly a lifetime (consider the character Edmond Dantes in Alexander Dumas' famous *The Count of Monte Cristo* who at the end of a long campaign of revenge wonders if it was worthwhile).

Engage, Assess Intervene, Evaluate

Practice Behavior Example: Develop a mutually agreed-upon focus of work and desired outcomes

Critical Thinking Question: How might a focus on optimal functioning, a strengths approach, versus a problem orientation influence client engagement?

The next series of steps includes efforts at gaining an appreciation for the offender. Attempts at perspective-taking are expected to build a sense of empathy for the offender which, theoretically, may humanize the offender or at least promote some form of empathy. With this as a foundation, forgiveness should be possible and may include simply stating forgiveness of the offender. This sounds simple, and it is not. However, research clearly shows that forgiveness interventions can be very successful and promote mental health (Lundahl et al., 2008). Forgiveness is a good "tool" to have in social work, as many clients with whom we work will struggle from some form of interpersonal offense.

MENTAL ILLNESS

We now turn to mental illness. Social workers dedicate considerable time to helping individuals who suffer from mental illness. In fact, a Consumer Report's article (see Seligman, 1995) indicated that 14% of all mental health psychotherapy is delivered by social workers and social workers were as effective as psychologists and psychiatrists in helping people with mental illness. The Bureau of Labor Statistics reports that, within social work as a profession, most social workers in the year 2008 were employed in some form of helping individuals with health or mental health-related issues (Bureau of Labor Statistics, 2012 http://www.bls.gov/oco/ocos060.htm, retrieved on February 8, 2012). (See Table 20.2.)

Table 20.2 shows that social work is heavily involved in helping people with mental health-related problems. Before diving into various aspects of mental illness, it's important to know that social workers attempt to "combat" mental illness by advocating for policies to support those with mental illness, as well as working directly with individuals suffering from mental illness.

Table 20.2   Most Social Workers Directly Work with Issues of Mental Health and Mental Illness

Child, family, and school social workers	292,600
Medical and public health social workers	138,700
Mental health and substance abuse social workers	137,300
Social workers, all other	73,400

Source: Bureau of Labor Statistics. Retrieved from http://www.bls.gov/oco/ocos060.htm, on February 8, 2012.

So, what is mental illness? Well, there is no simple answer. For decades, the *Diagnostic and Statistical Manual of Mental Disorders (DSM-5*; American Psychiatric Association, 2013) has been one of the leading resources on mental illnesses. Historically speaking, the *DSM* series was designed to guide policy decisions about how to help individuals suffering from mental illnesses. In the 1800s, the U.S. government sought statistical data on prevalence rates of various mental illnesses within the United States—thus the name Diagnostic (type of mental illness) and Statistical (well, statistics) of Mental Disorders. Obtaining data on the preva-

Mental illness is serious because of how it influences individuals and groups.

lence of mental illnesses allowed for the appropriation of monies to create interventions for those suffering from mental illness (unfortunately, many of the interventions were "insane asylums," which were often barbaric and inhumane).

Our understanding of mental illness has shifted dramatically over the last century and a half, resulting in a shifting landscape of what is considered a "mental illness." The first edition of the *DSM* in its present form (not simply providing prevalence rates) was published in 1952. The most recent edition was published, amidst much fanfare and controversy, in 2013. Of interest, the Director of the National Institute of Mental Health, Dr. Thomas Insel, published a blog just weeks before *DSM-5* was released to the public. The blog suggests both support and criticism of the *DSM* series and suggests separation from the *DSM* (see below).

Did You Know?

Dr. Thomas Insel, Director of NIMH

Director's Blog: Transforming Diagnosis (April 29, 2013) http://www.nimh.nih.gov/about/director/2013/transforming-diagnosis.shtml

In a few weeks, the American Psychiatric Association will release its new edition of the *Diagnostic and Statistical Manual of Mental Disorders (DSM-5)*. This volume will tweak several current diagnostic categories, from autism spectrum disorders to mood disorders. While many of these changes have been contentious, the final product involves mostly modest alterations of the previous edition, based on new insights emerging from research since 1990 when *DSM-IV* was published. Sometimes this research recommended new categories (e.g., mood dysregulation disorder) or that previous categories could be dropped (e.g., Asperger's syndrome).[1]

The goal of this new manual, as with all previous editions, is to provide a common language for describing psychopathology. While *DSM* has been described as a "Bible" for the field, it is, at best, a dictionary, creating a set of labels and defining each. The strength of each of the editions of *DSM* has been "reliability"—each edition has ensured that clinicians use the same terms in the same ways. The weakness is its lack of validity. Unlike our definitions of ischemic heart disease, lymphoma, or AIDS, the *DSM* diagnoses are based on a consensus about clusters of clinical symptoms, not any objective laboratory measure. In the rest of medicine, this would be equivalent to creating diagnostic systems based on the nature of chest pain or the quality of fever. Indeed, symptom-based diagnosis, once common in other areas of medicine, has been largely replaced in the past half century as we have understood that symptoms alone rarely indicate the best choice of treatment.

Patients with mental disorders deserve better. NIMH has launched the Research Domain Criteria (RDoC) project to transform diagnosis by incorporating genetics, imaging, cognitive science, and other levels of information to lay the foundation for a new classification system. Through a series of workshops over the past 18 months, we have tried to define several major categories for a new

(Continued)

Did You Know? (*Continued*)

nosology (see below). This approach began with several assumptions:

- A diagnostic approach based on the biology as well as the symptoms must not be constrained by the current *DSM* categories,
- Mental disorders are biological disorders involving brain circuits that implicate specific domains of cognition, emotion, or behavior,
- Each level of analysis needs to be understood across a dimension of function, and
- Mapping the cognitive, circuit, and genetic aspects of mental disorders will yield new and better targets for treatment.

It became immediately clear that we cannot design a system based on biomarkers or cognitive performance because we lack the data. In this sense, RDoC is a framework for collecting the data needed for a new nosology. But it is critical to realize that we cannot succeed if we use *DSM* categories as the "gold standard."[2] The diagnostic system has to be based on the emerging research data, not on the current symptom-based categories. Imagine deciding that EKGs were not useful because many patients with chest pain did not have EKG changes. That is what we have been doing for decades when we reject a biomarker because it does not detect a *DSM* category. We need to begin collecting the genetic, imaging, physiologic, and cognitive data to see how all the data—not just the symptoms—cluster and how these clusters relate to treatment response.

That is why NIMH will be re-orienting its research away from *DSM* categories. Going forward, we will be supporting research projects that look across current categories—or subdivide current categories—to begin to develop a better system. What does this mean for applicants? Clinical trials might study all patients in a mood clinic rather than those meeting strict major depressive disorder criteria. Studies of biomarkers for "depression" might begin by looking across many disorders with anhedonia or emotional appraisal bias or psychomotor retardation to understand the circuitry underlying these symptoms. What does this mean for patients? We are committed to new and better treatments, but we feel this

will only happen by developing a more precise diagnostic system. The best reason to develop RDoC is to seek better outcomes.

RDoC, for now, is a research framework, not a clinical tool. This is a decade-long project that is just beginning. Many NIMH researchers, already stressed by budget cuts and tough competition for research funding, will not welcome this change. Some will see RDoC as an academic exercise divorced from clinical practice. But patients and families should welcome this change as a first step towards "precision medicine," the movement that has transformed cancer diagnosis and treatment. RDoC is nothing less than a plan to transform clinical practice by bringing a new generation of research to inform how we diagnose and treat mental disorders. As two eminent psychiatric geneticists recently concluded, "At the end of the 19th century, it was logical to use a simple diagnostic approach that offered reasonable prognostic validity. At the beginning of the 21st century, we must set our sights higher."[3]

The major RDoC research domains:
Negative Valence Systems
Positive Valence Systems
Cognitive Systems
Systems for Social Processes
Arousal/Modulatory Systems

References
Mental health: On the spectrum. Adam D. Nature. 2013 Apr 25; 496(7446):416–8. doi: 10.1038/496416a. No abstract available. PMID: 23619674

Why has it taken so long for biological psychiatry to develop clinical tests and what to do about it? Kapur S, Phillips AG, Insel TR. Mol Psychiatry. 2012 Dec; 17(12):1174–9. doi: 10.1038/mp.2012.105. Epub 2012 Aug 7. PMID:22869033

The Kraepelinian dichotomy—going, going … but still not gone. Craddock N, Owen MJ. Br J Psychiatry. 2010 Feb;196(2):92–5. doi: 10.1192/bjp.bp.109.073429. PMID: 20118450

Retrieved from http://www.nimh.nih.gov/about/director/2013/transforming-diagnosis.shtml, on June 20, 2013.

Two weeks later (May 13, 2013), the same Dr. Thomas Insel co-wrote a position piece with the director of the American Psychiatric Association, Dr. Jeffrey Lieberman, discussing the relationship between the *DSM-5* and NIMH's interests. The Press Release is found on next page:

Did You Know?

DSM-5 and RDoC: Shared Interests

Press Release · May 13, 2013

Thomas R. Insel, M.D., Director, NIMH
Jeffrey A. Lieberman, M.D., President-elect, APA

NIMH and APA have a shared interest in ensuring that patients and health providers have the best available tools and information today to identify and treat mental health issues, while we continue to invest in improving and advancing mental disorder diagnostics for the future.

Today, the American Psychiatric Association's (APA) *Diagnostic and Statistical Manual of Mental Disorders (DSM)*, along with the *International Classification of Diseases (ICD)* represents the best information currently available for clinical diagnosis of mental disorders. Patients, families, and insurers can be confident that effective treatments are available and that the *DSM* is the key resource for delivering the best available care. The National Institute of Mental Health (NIMH) has not changed its position on *DSM-5*. As NIMH's Research Domain Criteria (RDoC) project website states, "The diagnostic categories represented in the *DSM-IV* and the *International Classification of Diseases-10 (ICD-10*, containing virtually identical disorder codes) remain the contemporary consensus standard for how mental disorders are diagnosed and treated."

Yet, what may be realistically feasible today for practitioners is no longer sufficient for researchers. Looking forward, laying the groundwork for a future diagnostic system that more directly reflects modern brain science will require openness to rethinking traditional categories. It is increasingly evident that mental illness will be best understood as disorders of brain structure and function that implicate specific domains of cognition, emotion, and behavior. This is the focus of the NIMH's Research Domain Criteria (RDoC) project. RDoC is an attempt to create a new kind of taxonomy for mental disorders by bringing the power of modern research approaches in genetics, neuroscience, and behavioral science to the problem of mental illness.

The evolution of diagnosis does not mean that mental disorders are any less real and serious than other illnesses. Indeed, the science of diagnosis has been evolving throughout medicine. For example, subtypes of cancers once defined by where they occurred in the body are now classified on the basis of their underlying genetic and molecular causes.

All medical disciplines advance through research progress in characterizing diseases and disorders. *DSM-5* and RDoC represent complementary, not competing, frameworks for this goal. *DSM-5*, which will be released May 18, reflects the scientific progress seen since the manual's last edition was published in 1994. RDoC is a new, comprehensive effort to redefine the research agenda for mental illness. As research findings begin to emerge from the RDoC effort, these findings may be incorporated into future *DSM* revisions and clinical practice guidelines. But this is a long-term undertaking. It will take years to fulfill the promise that this research effort represents for transforming the diagnosis and treatment of mental disorders.

By continuing to work together, our two organizations are committed to improving outcomes for people with some of the most disabling disorders in all of medicine.

The mission of the NIMH is to transform the understanding and treatment of mental illnesses through basic and clinical research, paving the way for prevention, recovery and cure. For more information, visit the NIMH website.

About the National Institutes of Health (NIH)

NIH, the nation's medical research agency, includes 27 Institutes and Centers and is a component of the U.S. Department of Health and Human Services. NIH is the primary federal agency conducting and supporting basic, clinical, and translational medical research, and is investigating the causes, treatments, and cures for both common and rare diseases. For more information about NIH and its programs, visit the NIH website.

Retrieved from http://www.nimh.nih.gov/news/science-news/2013/dsm-5-and-rdoc-shared-interests.shtml, on June 20, 2013.

Clearly, change is happening with regard to our understanding of mental illness. For the present discussion of mental illness, we review some of the main "groups" of mental illnesses advanced by *DSM-5* (APA, 2013). To begin, *DSM-5* advances approximately 22 separate "groups" of mental health difficulties. For example, the group on anxiety covers problems such as separation anxiety, phobias, social anxiety, and panic whereas the group on trauma covers problems such as reactive attachment disorder and post-traumatic stress disorder. The groups have changed considerable from *DSM-IV* to *DSM-5*. In Table 20.3 we provide a brief overview of the 22 groups with some of the conditions found within each group.

As you read through Table 20.3, you are likely to recognize many labels for mental health problems. In fact, there is a high likelihood that you have used one or more of the

Table 20.3   Overview of Mental Illness Groups

Mental Illness Groups	Specific Mental Illness Within Broad Categories
Neurodevelopmental disorders (formerly*: "Disorders usually first diagnosed in childhood")	1. Intellectual disabilities (formerly: "Mental retardation" in *DSM-IV*) 2. Specific learning disorders (such as reading, math, writing) 3. Communication disorders 4. Autism spectrum disorder (formerly: "Pervasive developmental disorders" which included: autism, Asperger's syndrome, Rhett's syndrome in *DSM-IV*) 5. Attention-deficit hyperactivity disorder (ADHD) 6. Motor disorders
Schizophrenia spectrum and psychotic disorders	1. Delusional disorders 2. Schizotypal (personality) disorder 3. Psychotic disorders 4. Catatonia
Bi-polar and related disorders (formerly, bi-polar was listed with "depressive disorders" it now claims a group of its own)	1. Bi-polar I 2. Bi-polar II 3. Cyclothymia
Depressive disorders	1. Disruptive mood dysregulation disorder (formerly close to Intermittent Explosive Disorder) 2. Major depression 3. Persistent depressive disorder (formerly "dysthymia") 4. Premenstrual dysphoric disorder
Anxiety disorders	1. Separation anxiety 2. Selective mutism 3. Phobias 4. Social anxiety 5. Panic attacks 6. Agoraphobia 7. Generalized anxiety
Obsessive-compulsive and related disorders (formerly classified with Anxiety Disorders)	1. Obsessive compulsive disorder 2. Body dysmorphic disorder 3. Hording disorder (new) 4. Conditions involving hair pulling, skin picking
Trauma- and stressor-related disorders (formerly classified with Anxiety Disorders)	1. Reactive attachment 2. Disinhibited social engagement (new) 3. Posttraumatic stress 4. Acute stress 5. Adjustment disorders
Dissociative disorders	1. Dissociative identity disorder 2. Dissociative amnesia 3. Depersonalization/derealization

Mental Illness Groups	Specific Mental Illness Within Broad Categories
Somatic symptom and related disorders	1. Somatic symptoms 2. Illness anxiety (new) 3. Conversion disorder 4. Factitious disorder
Feeding and eating disorders	1. Pica 2. Rumination 3. Anorexia 4. Bulimia 5. Binge eating (new) 6. Avoidant/Restrictive Food Intake Disorder (new)
Elimination disorders	1. Enuresis 2. Encopresis
Sleep-wake disorders (formerly "sleep disorders")	1. Insomnia 2. Hypersomnolence disorder (formerly hypersomnia) 3. Narcolepsy 4. Breathing-related sleep problems (new; many subdivisions) 5. Parasomnias (many new conditions)
Sexual dysfunctions	1. Delayed ejaculation 2. Erectile disorder 3. Female orgasmic disorder 4. Female sexual interest/arousal disorder 5. Genito-pelvic pain/penetration disorder 6. Male hypoactive sexual desire disorder 7. Premature ejaculation
Gender dysphoria	1. Gender dysphoria in children 2. Gender dysphoria in adolescents and adults
Disruptive, impulse-control, and conduct disorders (formerly some of these conditions were in a section on disorder usually first identified in early childhood)	1. Oppositional defiant disorder 2. Conduct disorder 3. Antisocial personality disorder (formerly with section on personality disorders) 4. Pyromania 5. Kleptomania
Substance-related and addictive disorders (formerly without the "addictive disorders" also terms of "addiction and abuse" in substance-related issues have been changed to "intoxication" and "withdrawal," respectively)	1. Substance-related disorders including to substances such as alcohol, cannabis, hallucinogens, inhalants, opioids, sedatives (hypnotic and/or anxiolytics), stimulants (e.g., amphetamines, cocaine), tobacco (formerly nicotine) 2. Gambling disorder (new to this section; formerly with impulse control conditions)
Neurocognitive disorders (formerly "cognitive disorders")	1. Delirium 2. Major and minor neurocognitive disorders (newly classified from other conditions such as amnesia, dementia, and behavioral disruptions) due to: Alzheimer's, frontotemporal lobar degeneration, Lewy Bodies; Vascular problems (e.g., stroke), HIV Infection, Parkinson's disease, Prion's disease, Huntington's disease, or other etiologies)

(Continued)

Mental Illness Groups	Specific Mental Illness Within Broad Categories
Personality disorders	1. Paranoid
	2. Schizoid
	3. Schizotypal
	4. Antisocial
	5. Borderline
	6. Histrionic
	7. Narcissistic
	8. Avoidant
	9. Dependent
	10. Obsessive-compulsive
Paraphilic disorders (formerly classified under "sexual dysfunctions" now in a separate group)	1. Voyeurism
	2. Exhibitionism
	3. Frotteurism
	4. Sexual masochism
	5. Sexual sadism
	6. Pedophilia
	7. Fetishism
	8. Transvestism

Source: APA's *DSM-IV* TR (2000) and *DSM-5* (2013), with some adaptation.
Note: Often times, the *DSM* will have subcategories of mental disorders that are linked to medical causes, such as "depressive disorder" due to another medical condition.
*When the word "formerly" is used it refers to what the *DSM-IV* used to state.

labels within the past 24 hours. People commonly say things such as "I'm so depressed today" or "I'm a little OCD (obsessive compulsive personality disorder)" or "I feel so bipolar today." It is important to realize that the "clinical" use of these terms is very different from common language. Indeed, the term "depression" has largely lost its meaning, just as terms such as *love, hate*, or *kill* have lost their original meaning. When a friend laughs and says "I'm going to kill you for making that remark" you know that your friend is not threatening homicide. Somehow, the term "kill" when used in everyday language has lost the emotional gravity associated with actual murder. Similarly, the everyday use of "depression" is not the same as the clinical depression that is linked to *suicide, despair*, and *mental anguish* so profound that people experience wrenching physical pain.

What then is mental illness? Is the person who says, "I'm feeling depressed" using the term incorrectly? The issue here is the degree to which a person is experiencing feelings of depression or sadness. We all feel sadness; however, some people feel sadness to such a degree that they are willing to literally kill themselves to avoid the amount of sadness they feel. When medical providers talk about mental illness they refer to experiencing an emotion or behavior that is well beyond what happens in everyday life. Remember earlier discussions of the Bell Curve or the Normal Curve at the front end of this book? Mental illness is often considered to be present when a symptom or cluster of symptoms is two standard deviations beyond the normal range. When symptoms get to roughly two standard deviations beyond the normal, the modifier "clinical" is often used. Thus, "clinical depression" connotes a situation where a person is in the 94th percentile of depressive symptoms. That is, out of 100 people, only 6 would be expected to have scores that high.

Watch the video "Fear or Phobia." What is the central message of the video in relation to "typical emotions" and "mental illness"?

Clinical Corner

To give you a sense of how mental illnesses are conceptualized, we now present some of the key considerations in diagnosing "Major Depression" based on the APA's *DSM-5*. (See *DSM-5*; APA, 2013, pp. 160–161.) Interested readers are encouraged to read the *DSM-5* for a richer description of Major Depression and other mental illnesses.

To be "eligible" for a diagnosis of Major Depression within the APA's system, four "features" or experiences must be present: symptom profile, timing and duration of symptoms, impact of symptoms, and causes of symptoms. We consider each in turn.

Symptom profile. To be eligible for a diagnosis of depression, a person must exhibit several symptoms associated with depression. To be exact, a person must exhibit at least five symptoms commonly linked to depression such as: depressed mood, loss of interest and/or pleasure in commonly enjoyed activities, irritability, change in weight not due to dieting, loss of appetite, disrupted sleep (overly tired or inability to initiate sleep), feeling restless and agitated, loss of energy and reports of fatigue, sense of worthlessness, excessive and undeserved guilt, diminished thinking ability such as poor concentration or increased indecisiveness, thoughts of death and possibly contemplation of suicide. Of these symptoms, at least one of the five symptoms must be either depressed mood or loss of interest in activities that were formerly enjoyed.

Timing and duration of symptoms. To be eligible for a diagnosis of depression, the *DSM-5* suggests that the symptoms must represent a change from "typical functioning." Thus, the timing of depression is expected to have a clear onset. Further, the symptoms (at least five) must be present for at least two contiguous weeks in adults. Thus, having a bad stretch for a few days, while unfortunate, would not reach the threshold of being depressed.

Impact of symptoms. A hallmark of all mental illnesses in the *DSM-5* series is that the symptoms produce considerable impairment in areas such as social relations (family, friends, loved ones), work, or other important life tasks or engagements. Of interest, many of the symptoms listed in the *DSM-5* for depression have language that suggests an independent observer should be able to detect the symptoms rather than simply relying on self-report giving a glimpse into the impact of the symptoms. However, the *DSM-5* does not require that the symptoms are independently observed.

Causes of symptoms. Although the *DSM-5* does not prescribe the specific mechanisms that might cause depressive symptoms (e.g., imbalance of neurotransmitters or lingering effects from a trauma), it does have a "rule out" clause. For example, a "simple diagnosis" of Major Depression would not be made if the symptoms were known to come from a source such as the side effects of a medication or drug or due to a physiological issue such as problems in the thyroid.

Note, the various mental illnesses within the *DSM-5* classification system often have different requirements for time and duration and symptom profile. Most of the mental illnesses, however, do require that the impact of the symptoms being impairing or clinically significant.

For an example, we present the case of a "depressive episode" as proposed by the American Psychiatric Association's *DSM-5* (APA, 2013).

Notice that to have a depressive episode, three conditions need to be in place represented by Categories A, B, and C. In Category A, five of the nine symptoms must be in place for the same two-week period with at least one symptom being either depression or marked loss of interest. Category B clearly states that the symptoms from Category A must cause "clinically significant distress or impairment" in how an individual functions. That is, to be considered a depressive episode, the person would need to exhibit impaired functioning in realms such as social interactions, job-related activities, family functioning, or other major life pursuits. The combination of Categories A and B clearly separates the mental illness of depression, or clinical depression, from the everyday statement of being "depressed," which likely means feeling a bit off. Category C, in this case, is mostly used to differentiate a depressive episode from other possible problems and to provide guidelines regarding diagnostic considerations.

Although not meaning to belabor the distinction between everyday language use that includes the labels given to clinical forms of mental illness, it should be noted that critiques of mental illness proper have advanced the notion that mental illness does not exist. One famous critic of diagnosable forms of mental illness was Thomas Szasz (1920–1977) a psychiatrist who advanced that mental illness is a fabrication of science, even a myth used to promote the drug and psychotherapy industry. (We authors believe Dr. Szasz argument was wrong and reckless, so you may notice a bias as your read on.) The essence of Dr. Szasz's arguments is enumerated by Wynne (2006):

1. Mental illness or mental disease is a myth because to be truly a "disease," there must be identifiable tissue pathology such as can be found in cancer. This does not exist in mental health-related areas, so mental illness does not exist.

2. The "mind" does not really exist; rather, neurons fire in the brain. Thus, there can be no disease of a mind when a mind does not really exist.

3. Because there is no mental illness or mind, any profession that claims mental illnesses exist are fraudulent.

4. People are moral agents and are, therefore, responsible for their behavior and mental illnesses cannot be blamed for uncomfortable or unwanted behavior because mental illness does not exist.

Dr. Szasz's arguments have certainly had an impact, some arguing that his thoughts have been very damaging to the acceptance of mental illness and in stigmatizing and blaming individuals who suffer from mental illness (Schoenfeld, 1976; Torrey, 2005; Wynne, 2006). Others have championed his position and continue to claim that mental illness does not really exist.

Impact of Mental Illness

At a broad level, what is the impact of mental illness? Again, there is no simple answer. Let's look at a case of clinical depression as an example.

Depression certainly influences individuals. Reviewing the symptom profile of depression indicates that those afflicted suffer immensely and by definition have a diminished ability to function in daily life activities. Ultimately, depression is one of the greatest risk factors for committing suicide which, in 2007, was the tenth leading cause of death in the United States (for more information see "A fact sheet of statistics on suicide with information on treatments and suicide prevention" published by NIMH, 2012a). Depression is also linked to higher rates of substance abuse problems, such as alcoholism, though the direction of effect is not always clear (Conner et al., 2009).

Depression also influences family members. Parents suffering from depression are more likely to engage in negative parenting behaviors such as: using harsh discipline practices; disengaging from children which may lead to neglect; and inconsistent parenting practices (Lovejoy et al., 2000; Wilson & Durbin, 2010). Harkening back to the importance of parenting, depression in parents may undermine children's ability to succeed in important developmental tasks. Depression also influences relationships. Research reveals that depression levels in one or both partners in a marriage are linked to poor problem solving and untoward communication patterns which undermine marital satisfaction (Harper & Sandberg, 2009).

Depression also influences work-related behavior. Individuals struggling with depression are much more likely to miss work and to have performance problems while at work which, not surprisingly, is associated with being unemployed (Lerner & Henke, 2008). Of course, the above findings do not reveal causality because loss of work can lead to depression and harsh workplace environments can promote stress which is linked to depression. Closer to home, consider how depression might influence performance in college. As might be expected, depression is linked to poorer performance as indicated by a lower GPA and higher expressed stress in school (Hysenbegasi et al., 2005).

Depression also has an impact on society. Considering the above data, how might depression influence society? Unemployment, underemployment, absenteeism, and lower productivity influence the economy. To the degree that parental depression negatively impacts children, this may in turn impact children's performance and engagement in school. While depression does not have a causal relationship with divorce, the strain of depression on a relationship can take a toll. Depression also influences health care. The National Institute of Mental Health reports that the estimated cost of depression in 2000 was a whopping $83 billion dollars, which included roughly $26 billion in treatment and $57 billion in productivity losses in work-related activities (NIMH, 2006; http: //www.nimh.nih.gov/health/trials/practical/stard/backgroundstudy.shtml retrieved on February 11, 2012). Further, NIMH reports that roughly 40% of all suicides are directly linked to depression and about 9.5% of the U.S. population will experience depression in any given calendar year.

The preceding discussion focused on one specific type of mental illness, depression. Of course, as was already shown in the Table 20.1, there are many forms of mental illness that range from substance abuse to learning disabilities. In Figure 20.3 notice that the total cost for serious mental illness in the United States is estimated at $300 billion dollars (Source: http://www.nimh.nih.gov/statistics/4COST_TOTAN.shtml, retrieved on May 23, 2013) with about 6% of all health care costs going to mental health-related issues.

Mental illness certainly has a tremendous impact on individuals, families, and society. As a profession, social work is committed to understanding, preventing, and treating mental illness. Social work does not stand alone in this endeavor. Other

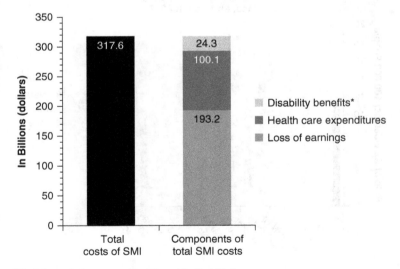

*Social security income and social security disability insurance

Figure 20.3
Annual Total Direct and Indirect Costs of Serious Mental Illness (SMI) in 2002.

Retrieved from http://www.nimh.nih.gov/statistics/4COST_TOTAN.shtml, on May 27, 2013.

Source: Insel TR. (2008 June). Assessing the economic cost of serious mental illness. *American Journal of Psychiatry, 165*(6), 663–665.

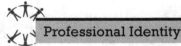

Professional Identity

Practice Behavior Example: Advocate for client access to the services of social work

Critical Thinking Question: How might social workers increase individual's comfort with seeking services for mental illness while also increasing access to such services?

Assess your comprehension of Mental Illness by completing this quiz.

disciplines such as medicine, nursing, psychology, economics, marriage and family therapy are also committed to limiting mental illness. Beyond professions, many foundations have been established to understand and treat mental illness, such as the National Alliance for the Mentally Ill (NAMI), the Nathaniel Anthony Ayers Foundation, featured in Hollywood's *The Soloist* movie, or the SAVE foundation (Suicide Awareness Voices of Education), which was established by survivors of loved ones who committed suicide. In your social work education, you will be exposed to many models of preventing and treating mental illness that include practice at micro-, mezzo-, and macro-levels.

SUICIDE

We finish this chapter talking about the somber reality of suicide that often occurs from mental illness. Suicide is a leading, preventable cause of death in the United States. Figure 20.4a and 20.4b, which follow, provide an overview of suicide by demographic variables (http://www.nimh.nih.gov/statistics/4SR07.shtml, retrieved on February 11, 2012). What do you notice? What surprises you?

The most recent statistics provided by the National Institute of Mental Health (2007) places suicide as the 7th leading cause of death for males and 15th for females. While females attempt suicide more often than males, males are more likely to actually die because they tend to use a more deadly method, firearms, as seen in Table 20.4.

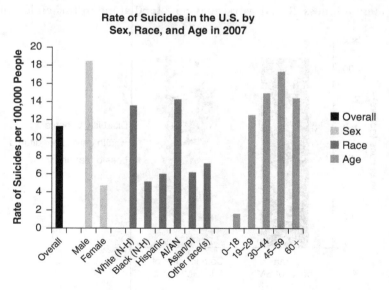

N-H = Non-Hispanic
AI/AN = American Indian/Alaska Native
PI = Pacific Islander

Figure 20.4a
Rates of Suicide by Sex, Race, and Age.

Source: Retrieved from http://www.nimh.nih.gov/statistics/4SR07.shtml, on May 27, 2013.

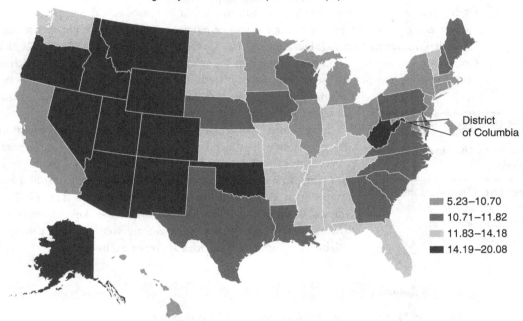

Suicide Rate 2000–2006, United States
Age-adjusted death rates per 100,000 population

District of Columbia

5.23–10.70
10.71–11.82
11.83–14.18
14.19–20.08

Note: Reports for all ages include those of unknown age.

Figure 20.4b
Suicide Rates by Geographical Region.
Source: Retrieved from http://www.nimh.nih.gov/statistics/4NAT_MAP.shtml, on October 27, 2012.

Suicide is tragic for families and loved ones, as is indicated in a study by Cerel, Jordan, and Duberstein (2008). Surviving family members are likely to experience:

- Complicated grieving, existential angst
- Guilt over what happened; self-blame
- Confusion
- Unanswered questions and attempts to understand the reasons for suicide
- Prolonged attempts to adjust and carry on with life
- Family conflict and decreased cohesion, possibly related to blame, guilt, or loss
- Financial problems
- Mental health problems
- Secrecy around the cause of death; feeling stigmatized

Table 20.4 Suicide by Males and Females (percentages)

Suicide Method	Male (%)	Female (%)
Firearms	56	30
Suffocation	24	21
Poisoning	13	40

Source: Retrieved from http://www.nimh.nih.gov/health/publications/suicide-in-the-us-statistics-and-prevention/index.shtml#factors, on February 11, 2012.

Suicide also influences social groups (including friends, community members) in a manner that is similar to how families experience loss due to suicide (Cerel et al., 2008). Of interest, a particular suicide in a community often increases suicides in peers, especially among young people, or other vulnerable parties—a phenomenon known as the "suicide contagion effect" (Hacker, Collins, Gross-Young, Almeida, & Burke, 2008). Contagion or "cluster" suicide may account for as many as 5% of all suicides, which is puzzling given the negative emotions experienced by survivors of suicide. Theories on the contagion effect include imitation efforts, glorification of the deceased, and media attention (Hacker et al., 2008).

In response to awareness that suicide does cluster, prevention efforts have been advanced. As mentioned earlier in this chapter, prevention efforts attempt to identify factors that promote a behavior, such as media exposure in this case, or forestall a behavior, such as community involvement and awareness. The Clinical Corner Box that follows summarizes key findings on how to prevent suicide contagion among young people through collaborating with how suicides are reported in the media.

Research-Based Practice

Practice Behavior Example: Use research evidence to inform practice

Critical Thinking Question: Why should the research on suicide be utilized by social workers? How might such information be employed at individual and community levels?

Clinical Corner

Aspects of News Coverage That Can Promote Suicide Contagion

Clinicians, researchers, and other health professionals at the Suicide Contagion and Its Prevention workshop convened by the Center for Disease Control focused on preventing suicides that may result from the contagion effect. (see http://www.cdc.gov/mmwr/preview/mmwrhtml/00031539.htm, retrieved on September 5, 2012) agreed that to minimize the likelihood of suicide contagion, reporting should be concise and factual. Although scientific research in this area is not complete, workshop participants believed that the likelihood of suicide contagion may be increased by the following actions:

- *Presenting simplistic explanations for suicide.* Suicide is never the result of a single factor or event, but rather results from a complex interaction of many factors and usually involves a history of psychosocial problems. Public officials and the media should carefully explain that the final precipitating event was not the only cause of a given suicide. Cataloguing the problems that could have played a causative role in a suicide is not necessary, but acknowledgment of these problems is recommended.

- *Engaging in repetitive, ongoing, or excessive reporting of suicide in the news.* Repetitive and ongoing coverage, or prominent coverage, of a suicide tends to promote and maintain a preoccupation with suicide among at-risk persons, especially among persons 15–24 years of age. This preoccupation appears to be associated with suicide contagion. Information presented to the media should include the association between such coverage and the potential for suicide contagion. Public officials and media representatives should discuss alternative approaches for coverage of newsworthy suicide stories.

- *Providing sensational coverage of suicide.* By nature, news coverage of a suicidal event tends to heighten the general public's preoccupation with suicide. This reaction is also believed to be associated with contagion and the development of suicide clusters. Public officials can help minimize sensationalism by limiting, as much as possible, morbid details in their public discussions of suicide. News media professionals should attempt to decrease the prominence of the news report and avoid the use of dramatic photographs related to the suicide (e.g., photographs of the funeral, the deceased person's bedroom, and the site of the suicide).

- *Reporting "how-to" descriptions of suicide.* Describing technical details about the method of suicide is undesirable. For example, reporting that a person died from carbon monoxide poisoning may not be harmful; however, providing details of the mechanism and procedures used to complete the suicide may facilitate imitation of the suicidal behavior by other at-risk persons.

- *Presenting suicide as a tool for accomplishing certain ends.* Suicide is usually a rare act of a troubled or depressed person. Presentation of suicide as a means of coping with personal problems (such as the break-up of a relationship or retaliation against parental discipline) may suggest suicide as a potential coping mechanism to at-risk persons. Although such factors often seem to trigger a suicidal act, other psychopathological problems are almost always involved. If suicide is presented as an effective means for accomplishing specific ends, it may be perceived by a potentially suicidal person as an attractive solution.

- *Glorifying suicide or persons who commit suicide.* News coverage is less likely to contribute to suicide contagion when reports of community expressions of grief (that is public eulogies, flying flags at half-mast, and erecting permanent public memorials) are minimized. Such actions may contribute to suicide contagion by suggesting to susceptible persons that society is honoring the suicidal behavior of the deceased person, rather than mourning the person's death.

- *Focusing on the suicide completer's positive characteristics.* Empathy for family and friends often leads to a focus on reporting the positive aspects of a suicide completer's life. For example, friends or teachers may be quoted as saying the deceased person "was a great kid" or "had a bright future," and they avoid mentioning the troubles and problems that the deceased person experienced. As a result, statements venerating the deceased person are often reported in the news. However, if the suicide completer's problems are not acknowledged in the presence of these laudatory statements, suicidal behavior may appear attractive to other at-risk persons—especially those who rarely receive positive reinforcement for desirable behaviors.

Source: Centers for Disease Control and Prevention.

Retrieved from http://www.cdc.gov/mmwr/preview/mmwrhtml/00031539.htm, on February 11, 2012.

Honorable Suicide and Assisted Suicide

Like most aspects of human behavior, suicide is complex. In some situations, suicide is considered acceptable even honorable. In war, suicide plays a role. For example, the *New York Times* reported that on December 4, 2006, U.S. Army Pfc. Ross A. McGinnis deliberately jumped on a grenade which saved four of his comrades but killed him in the process; for this act, Mr. McGinnis was posthumously awarded the Medal of Honor, our military's highest award (Bogues, 2008, June 3). Pfc McGinnis is not alone in taking such heroic actions which is a tribute to the human spirit. While having a vastly different outcome and holding more controversy, war-time suicide can inflict damage on the "enemy" as is the case with suicide bombers in modern times and the Kamikaze suicide missions flown during World War II. In such cases, suicide is viewed to have a purpose greater than a person's individual life. In U.S. culture, suicide by jumping on the grenade is honorable but taking one's life while killing non-military persons is viewed as cowardly. These divergent positions reveal the complexity of human values and impact of social and cultural forces.

Another form of deliberate dying that is controversial within the United States is assisted suicide. In short, assisted suicide or assisted dying involves the conscientious decision to take one's life when facing a terminal medical illness or irresolvable physical pain. Like many controversial actions, many terms have arisen around assisted suicide. David Muller (2011) highlights some of the controversy surrounding the terminology. Which phrase sounds either more offensive or desirable to you?

- Assisted suicide
- Physician-assisted suicide
- Rationale suicide
- Physician aid in dying
- Right to die
- Death with dignity

Notice that new language is replacing "suicide" with variations of "death" which seems to soften some of the taboos associated with taking one's life. Some of the key arguments and questions in the debate over the right to die include:

- Who can choose to die? Any rational person or only those who face terminal illness who also are rational?
- Who can perform the actual act that will end a person's life? A physician, a family member, or only the person?
- Is removing someone from life support a form of murder?
- When is ending a life murder and when is it humane?
- What role does the State have in governing the termination of life?
- If states allow for assisted suicide, must physicians participate in such actions? Alternatively, can managed care organizations block physicians from performing assistance in dying?
- Does physician-assisted suicide violate the Hippocratic Oath of "First, do not harm"?
- Is allowing assisted suicide the beginning of a slippery slope which ultimately devalues life?
- Is it moral to take life? Is it moral to prevent someone from making a decision on their own life? Does it break a religious commandment? Is this playing God?

Human Behavior

Practice Behavior Example: Critique and apply knowledge to understand person and environment

Critical Thinking Question: How do cultural and policy influences shape human ideas on life and death? How might changes in beliefs about life and death influence social work practice?

Assess your comprehension of Suicide by completing this quiz.

Assess your analysis and evaluation of this chapter's contents by completing the Chapter Review.

Currently, 37 states block the practice of physician assisted dying and two states openly allow the practice: Washington and Oregon (Severson, 2012; http://www.nytimes.com/2012/02/07/us/assisted-suicide-law-is-overturned-by-georgia-supreme-court.html?_r=1&ref=assistedsuicide). Other states are considering the issue or have legal challenges to the law. Outside of the United States, positions on the right to die vary. The Netherlands, for example, decriminalized physician-assisted suicide. As case law and policy continue to shape and shift on this issue, social workers will become involved in ancillary activities such as helping families explore this option especially because social workers deliver many mental health services to aging and medically fragile populations.

Stockbyte/Thinkstock

21

Discrimination Influences on Human Behavior

Chapter 15 previously discussed discrimination and this chapter will expand on that topic, looking at discrimination in more depth. The term *discriminate* originally suggested the ability to separate ideas, items, and individuals based on a careful analysis of facts and data. A positive term, it was an apt ability for those with strong critical thinking skills. However, the word has more recently become pejorative. Discrimination now is the act of treating another person in a prejudicial manner based solely on that person's membership in a group; a group based on ethnicity, age, gender, skin color, sexual orientation, or any other characteristic shared by its members. It is used to exclude or restrict what members of a given group are permitted to do and closes off opportunities available to nonmembers. Discrimination denies both the individual and the society of the benefits that full inclusion of group members can create. It is a component in the oppression of others. This chapter looks at discrimination based on gender, race, age, sexual orientation, ability, and religion. We recognize that these are not all of the groups facing discrimination in society; however, they appear to be the most frequently cited.

TYPICAL TYPES OF DISCRIMINATION

In general, discrimination has been separated into two categories: *de jure* and *de facto*. *De jure* discrimination exists when it is supported by law. For example, state laws against intermarriage between Blacks and Whites existed for decades in the United States. In the same

Sexism is another form of discrimination.

category are current laws that prohibit two men or two women from getting married. The recently rescinded law called "don't ask, don't tell" was used to discriminate against gay men and lesbian women in the military. As most know, much discrimination once codified in law has been eliminated through either legislative action or court decisions. Unfortunately, this has not ended discrimination.

De facto discrimination is a term used to cover other types of discrimination that are not empowered by law. In short, it means discrimination in practice. A landlord refusing to lease an apartment to a person of color is engaging in de facto discrimination even though the action is illegal. A businesswoman who subconsciously hires only women employees despite the fact that the job could easily be performed by a man is doing the same. Sometimes discrimination is much more subtle as seen in the following case.

Clinical Corner

Sand Ridge County

Sand Ridge County is a typical metropolitan county with slightly over 1 million in population served by four school districts. Some of the districts included students from both affluent and poor neighborhoods. Parents in the affluent areas of one school district (Jonesville) objected to the fact that the district often must spend its money to repair and rebuild schools in less-affluent areas of town with the greatest need. Because schools in economically depressed neighborhoods often taught children of immigrants (whose native language was not English) and had a large enrollment of children of color, this also annoyed the wealthier citizens of the district. Maintaining a claim of fairness, the affluent parents successfully instigated an effort to create two separate school districts, one rich and one poor. They argued that they were only trying to make more resources available to their children. However, the outcome was to leave the less-affluent district with more students and less income to meet the needs of their diverse student body.

SOCIAL WORK VALUES AND DISCRIMINATION

Critical Thinking

Practice Behavior Example: Use critical thinking augmented by creativity and curiosity.

Critical Thinking Question: Were affluent parents guilty of discrimination in their pursuit of a school system that would serve mostly White children from well-to-do families? Was the outcome—creation of two separate but unequal school districts—discriminatory?

The values and ethics of the social work profession are clearly opposed to discrimination. The National Association of Social Workers (NASW) Code of Ethics (2008) identifies the ethical principles undergirding social work's values, particularly the profession's commitment to social justice, and the dignity and worth of the individual. Those ethical principles, in turn, guide the ethical standards and behaviors expected of all social workers. For example, social workers are required to demonstrate commitment to their clients' well-being and maximize client self-determination. Discriminating against a client is inherently a violation of both of these expectations as it fails in its commitment to the client's well-being and reduces or eliminates opportunities for self-determination.

Social workers must also demonstrate cultural competence, particularly understanding how oppression influences the human behavior of people. The Code of Ethics also identifies a set of professional responsibilities expected of each social worker. In particular, social workers must "not practice, condone, facilitate, or collaborate with any form of discrimination on the basis of race, ethnicity, national origin, color, sex, sexual orientation, age, marital status, political belief, religion, or mental or physical disability" (NASW, 2008, pp. 22–23).

Finally, the Code of Ethics lists social workers' ethical responsibilities to society, including promoting social justice through a variety of means including social and political action. Clearly, there is no room within the profession for a social worker to engage in discrimination. To the contrary, there is an obligation to pursue actions that combat discrimination in all its forms. Social workers are committed to creating a society that is just and values every human being. This belief in equal rights and social justice is also contained in the *International Federation of Social Workers/International Association of Schools of Social Work Ethics in Social Work, Statement of Principles* (2005) and related documents such as the *Convention on the Elimination of all Forms of Discrimination Against Women* (Healy, 2007).

Ethical Practice

Practice Behavior Example: Make ethical decisions by applying standards of the NASW Code of Ethics and, as applicable, of the International Federation of Social Workers/International Association of Schools of Social Work Ethics in Social Work, Statement of Principles.

Critical Thinking Question: Are social workers who work in agencies that hire only members of a particular religion guilty of condoning discrimination based on religion? If an agency because of their religious beliefs forbids its social workers to provide all options open to a pregnant teenager, does this constitute discrimination because it fails to allow for client self-determination?

Challenges

While the profession's commitment to social justice and equality is obvious, it is not always easy to implement, especially in a cross-cultural environment. In many cultures, there is limited acceptance of some principles that undergird our professional ethics. For example, the idea that men and women are equal and should have equal opportunities clashes directly with cultures where men are considered superior to women. In some cultures, women are not permitted to engage in behaviors that we would consider common, such as driving a car, voting, and attending sporting events. Attempting to help women become more assertive in such cultures or to gain additional rights can lead to their injury or death.

Critical Thinking

Practice Behavior Example: Distinguish, appraise, and integrate multiple sources of knowledge, including research-based knowledge, and practice wisdom.

Critical Thinking Question: Which should have higher priority in a social worker's work with a family that discourages women from pursuing education—self-determination of the woman or the family's cultural norms that support traditional values but limit the freedom of individual members?

Social workers are ethically bound to practice cultural competence, or the ability to value, understand, and function within cultures different from our own. If a practice in another culture conflicts with aspects of the profession's ethical obligations, how does the social worker act? One such example is the cultural practice of female circumcision or genital mutilation. Most social workers would define this practice as a denigration of women, evidence of unequal status, and a violation of human rights. Yet, advocating for changes to this practice can run afoul of the culture's efforts to encourage, preserve, and support the family unit, as well as uphold long-held values.

Another example occurs in cultures that emphasize a person's obligation to family and society above achievement or pursuit of individual goals. Should the social worker actively work to help a daughter pursue a college degree when the family is opposed? Does not the family's opposition infringe on the daughter's self-determination? What efforts do social workers take in the face of cultures that devalue a gender or discriminate on the basis of sexual orientation? A similar question arises when practicing in a culture that expects and values the active direction of the social worker while the social worker is reluctant to impose his or her judgment on the client because of the self-determination principle. It should be obvious that social workers must employ a considerable degree of flexibility to promote social justice and combat discrimination, while simultaneously demonstrating cultural competence.

Worldviews and White Privilege

Exposure to other cultures helps inform our understanding that not everyone sees situations from the same perspective. This is important because how anyone views a particular experience reflects their own *worldviews*. For example, much of social work knowledge and practice operates from a Eurocentric perspective and ignores an African-centered worldview (Graham, 2000; Holtzhausen, 2010). An *Africentric* worldview looks at life differently because:

- It is based on the spiritual nature of human beings, which connects people and all aspects of their environment.

- It sees all things as interconnected, whether it's mind and body, material and spiritual, or person and environment. This perspective means that each person is connected in some way to every other person and that living in harmony with one's environment is the best way to experience life. You may notice that this perspective is also consistent with much of traditional Native American culture.

- An Africentric worldview is consistent with basic social work tenets, namely that the individual can be understood only within his or her context—which includes other people. This point of view reflects a belief in the commonality of human beings and a sense that what happens to the individual happens to the community, and what happens to the community affects the individual (Graham, 2000; Holtzhausen, 2010). Put another way, you are a reflection of your interactions with everything else in your life. According to this worldview, living things survive and prosper best when they are at harmony with the external world and their well-being is compromised when this is not the case.

Not all areas of social work are responsive to the concept of worldview. For example, it is possible to find theories of family intervention that still adhere to traditional views about the appropriate roles of men and women in a marriage, without regard to issues of power and inequality. Similarly, a focus on the problems of Black families has often led social workers and decision-makers to adopt policies that defined Black families as pathological or dysfunctional (Hall, Whipple, & Jackson-Elmoore, 2007; Robinson, 1995). This worldview is a form of oppression of Black families because it does not consider other frames of reference and does not recognize how cultures marginalize different groups of individuals. A common basis for this failure to consider other frames of reference is *white privilege*. White privilege "entails the set of benefits and advantages inherited by each generation of those defined as 'white' in the social process and structure of U.S. society. The actual privilege and the sense that one is entitled to them are inseparable parts of a greater whole. These white advantages can be material, symbolic, or psychological" (Feagin, 2000, p. 175). For many of us, our worldview is informed by issues of privilege, a conscious or unconscious norm of whiteness, and limitations on our ability to develop self-awareness (Jeffery, 2005). Even the best efforts to objectively view another's worldview are likely to be impacted by our own.

Other factors influencing the ability to consider the worldview of others include the power of the individual. For example, those with high power are much less likely to concern themselves with the perspective of out-groups (Bilewicz, 2009). They are much less interested in the experiences of these groups, less likely to acknowledge their own privileged status, and less accurate in reading and interpreting other's emotions (Galinsky, Magee, Inesi, & Gruenfeld, 2006).

By focusing on the ways some families deviate from the "norm," we are assuming that alternative understandings do not exist. For example, consider the following case to see how different views of the "problem" can change our understanding of a situation.

Clinical Corner

Meredith

Meredith, a divorced 35-year-old mother, leaves her five-year-old child in the care of her adolescent son while she works on weekends. The quality of care provided by the adolescent proves inadequate and the child is injured in a fall. At this point, the facts of the case are undisputed.

We can evaluate this situation as a mother who neglected her child and put the child at risk. This becomes an individual problem and is treated as such by child protective services. However, a different perspective on this scenario exists. Consider that Meredith is working two jobs to support her children, earns minimum wage, and receives no significant support from family or friends. With her salary, she cannot afford childcare, even if readily available. The lack of affordable childcare is not the mother's problem but rather a social problem caused by a society that does not adequately fund services needed to allow mothers to go to work knowing their children will be protected. The fact that the woman asked her oldest son to care for the child is evidence of (1) motivation to be employed, (2) a desire to adequately support those who are dependent upon her, and (3) an attempt to ensure at least a minimum level of care for the younger child. Rather than seeing the situation as a form of resilience and strength, we tend to focus on the pathology of a neglectful family. Clearly, the lens we use to assess this case can result in a different understanding of the problem.

The lack of exposure to alternative worldviews is not the only challenge facing social workers. Social workers often discover that they hold attitudes, biases, stereotypes, and other beliefs that clash with professional values. This discovery process optimally occurs during one's educational preparation for the field. Many students revisit and modify their opinions as they acquire greater knowledge and are challenged by teachers and field instructors. Other students simply hide their opinions and enter social work practice without truly confronting or overcoming their own dysfunctional perspectives.

Stereotyping is the practice of generalizing about characteristics supposedly shared by members of a group. It is a cognitive means of organizing other human beings into categories (Kim-Prieto, Goldstein, Ozazaki, & Kirschner, 2010). Stereotyping appears nearly universal and has been observed in many cultures (Motsaathebe, 2009; Penny & Haddock, 2007; Werhun & Penner, 2010). In some ways, stereotyping is useful because it simplifies our lives. It allows us to make some safe assumptions about the world around us. If, for example, we encounter a tiger blocking our driveway as we exit our house, we can assume that something is wrong with this picture. Tigers do not roam loose in U.S. cities because we know that their natural habitat is in India. Similarly, if we had to guess about which gender is most likely to enjoy war movies, we would think it would be men. This does not mean that no women like such movies, just that it is more likely to be true of men. Our stereotypes allow us to avoid some problems as we interact with others. For example, for a first date, few men would take their female companion to a professional wrestling match—assuming they want a second date.

Typically, we acquire our stereotypes through contact with our environment. If we hold a stereotype of Muslims, for example, we are attributing to members of that religion a set of beliefs, behaviors, characteristics, and attitudes that we have learned in the past. Too often, however, using stereotypes becomes problematic not only for us but for the stereotyped group. The existence of stereotypes can lead to *stereotype threats*. As a consequence of these threats, "individuals, fearful of confirming a negative stereotype about their group, display decreased performance on a task relevant to the negative stereotype" (Good, Woodzicka, & Singfield, 2010, p. 135). For example, a teenage girl with a life-long interest in helping people may decide not to pursue a career in social work because she's been told it is a woman's field. Not wanting to conform to this stereotype, she chooses a different major. Interestingly, if a stereotype is challenged through positive images about a group, the outcome tends to change. For example, women showed positive images about their group experienced *stereotype lift* in which they performed better on a test related to the stereotype.

Another disturbing aspect of stereotyping is the tendency for individuals to "perform down to the negative perceptions of their reference groups that are based on race, gender and age" (Anastas, 2007, p. 236). This phenomenon has been observed by Hyde and Kling (2001) who noted that people do less well on tasks that are related to the stereotype. This has been demonstrated in multiple situations including older adults being tested for memory and women tested for mathematical ability. It also shows up in the leadership aspirations of women and performance in the workplace (Bergeron, Block, & Echtenkamp, 2006). There is also evidence that "exposure to gender-stereotyped television commercials and sexist jokes has been enough to produce decreases in performance, phenomena that are ubiquitous in workplaces and in U.S. society in general" (Anastas, 2007, p. 237).

Being confined to a stereotype has the potential to affect the person's identity. Individuals in these situations may try to distance themselves from their own group as a protective strategy. It denies the individual access to protective mechanisms adopted by the group and contributes to lower self-esteem and well-being (Newman, Keough, & Lee, 2009). As noted earlier, this can have a negative effect on the individual's performance in a variety of areas.

The Resilience of Stereotypes

Stereotypes are notoriously difficult to change (Carnaghi & Yzerbty, 2007). One reason this occurs is because stereotypes are omnipresent in our daily lives. As Kim-Prieto, Goldstein, Ozazaki, and Kirschner (2010) point out "stereotypic descriptions of women, ethnic minorities, and other devalued groups abound in the popular media" (p. 535). Movies, television, and other media tend to show an overrepresentation of ethnic minorities as criminals. Commentators and political figures routinely evoke stereotypes of groups such as immigrants to stir up a situation to achieve their own ends. As might be expected, exposure to stereotypes of specific groups tends to increase negative attitudes toward this group. However, those exposed to stereotypes about a specific group also were more likely to endorse stereotypes of different groups. In other words, exposure to stereotypes toward any group is likely to engender negative attitudes toward other devalued groups. Even when exposed to evidence disconforming the stereotype, most people do not change their preexisting beliefs (Rothbart & John, 1985). Stereotypes are even resistant to change when an individual spends time working with members of an out-group (Finchilescu, 2005; Stephan & Stephan, 1985). What tends to happen is that the stereotype-holding individual simply makes an exception to the rule about the coworkers and continues to hold the same beliefs about the out-group as a whole. In fact, people engage in strenuous cognitive efforts to reconcile their divergent experiences, often by subtyping the person whose behaviors do not fit their previous stereotypes. This is achieved by viewing the member from a stereotyped group as an outlier from the norm.

Human beings tend to adopt their values and beliefs from the social groups to which they belong. If their reference group adopts beliefs that are less stereotyped, members will adjust their views accordingly and the same is true if the reference group adopts more negative stereotypes (Stangor, Sechrist, & Jost, 2001). Equally interesting, if individuals are told that they will be addressing an audience with particular views, they will tailor their positions on that view to be more in line with the intended audience (Carnaghi & Yzerbty, 2007; Galinsky, Wang, & Ku, 2008). This is a phenomenon familiar to most of us who follow political campaigns closely. As candidates seek to be seen as like their audience, they run the risk of becoming something they are not. Kurt Vonnegut (2009) is correct when he notes that "we are what we pretend to be, so we must be careful about what we pretend to be" (p. v).

Another factor that makes stereotypes so resilient is that they appear to be more or less automatic when we encounter someone from a stereotyped group (Mitchell et al., 2009). Stereotypes can be controlled, but it takes an explicit control process to achieve this goal. For example, some individuals consciously avoid making judgments about others based on group membership to avoid the dangers of stereotyping (Vorauer et al., 2000). By training ourselves to avoid stereotyped responses, we allow information learned about the other group to help us form a more accurate assessment. Moreover, resisting application of a stereotype allows us to employ a portion of the brain used for thinking rather than relying solely on those related to memory and categorization. Stewart, Latu, Kawakami, and Myers (2010) found that a technique called Situational Attribution Training was effective in reducing the automatic tendency to invoke stereotypes to explain behavior and understand others. Whether the outcomes noted in this study continue over time remains open to question, however.

Other factors also play interesting roles in stereotyping and discrimination against groups in society. For example, despite similarities between the struggles of racial and sexual minorities for civil rights, it is not uncommon to find African Americans distancing themselves from GLBT efforts to change society (Harris, 2009). In many ways, Black adult views of sexual minorities mirror those of White adults. This occurs despite the fact that hundreds of thousands of Blacks are also homosexual or bisexual. As Lorde (1999) notes, "Any attack against lesbians and gays is a Black issue, because thousands of lesbians and gay men are 'Black.' There is not a hierarchy of oppression" (p. 307).

Assess your comprehension of Social Work Values and Discrimination by completing this quiz.

SEXISM

Sexism, or discrimination against women, appears to be an almost universal pattern in most societies around the world (Werhun & Penner, 2010). This is evident in areas as diverse as health and political influence. Typically, sexism is reflected both in behaviors and attitudes that are bound to stereotypes about women. These prejudices serve to justify behavior that contributes to the diminution of individuals based on their gender. For example, an agency supervisor argues that the next social worker hired to work in the juvenile delinquency unit should be a male because the juveniles on probation are mostly male. The supervisor is assuming that a female worker will not be able to understand the male delinquent or that a male worker will be better able to develop rapport with the individual. Sexism is also reflected in past arguments that women should not be permitted to serve in military combat units because they are too emotional, or male soldiers will be endangered by having to protect their female colleagues. A recent comment by a Fox news contributor that women in the military should expect to experience rape because they are in close contact with men reflects sexual stereotypes of both men and women. This attitude assumes that men in the military are all potential rapists while women must be protected from situations involving ongoing contact with men (Media Matters, 2012).

Sexism shows up in multiple areas of American society. It explains why many women receive lower pay for doing the exact same work as men. It is also reflected in the vast disparity of women in multiple fields of endeavor from law enforcement to chemistry. Even in social work education, women experience disadvantages in pay, job responsibilities, tenure, and rank. While some of this disparity is the result of employment decisions made years ago, it is not all attributable to more men than women being hired for teaching positions in the past. As a group, women are more likely to work in undergraduate programs, more likely to hold nontenure track positions and less likely to teach in doctoral or master's programs (Sakamoto et al., 2008). The authors note that "women receive lower salaries even after controlling for numerous other job characteristics that influence salary" (p. 54).

Did You Know?

Sakamoto et al. (2008) observed that gender differences were found across most of the job characteristics used to predict salary, "indicating a pervasive problem for women in status, rank, and job duties, as well as in salary" (pp. 54–55). This salary differential was about $9,000 per year (Anastas, 2007, p. 235). Moreover, the ratio of women to men in social work education, which ranges from 58% to 65% being women, does not reflect the social work profession as a whole where 80% are women.

Similar conclusions were drawn with regard to men and women faculty in Canadian schools of social work. In addition, a 2006 study by the NASW found that the average female professional social worker earned from $3,000 to $7,000 less per year than a male colleague (p. 29).

Sex discrimination can be both obvious as has been described, or quite subtle. Benokraitis (1997) has identified nine types of sex discrimination that are subtle but still have a similar effect on those experiencing discrimination:

1. *Condescending chivalry* is the outward demonstration of courtesy and respect for women, coupled with a paternalistic attitude that "protects" women while treating them as subordinates.

2. *Supportive discouragement* involves giving women mixed messages about their intelligent, competence, or accomplishments. "Rita, you do great work, why don't you go back to college and finish that degree. I think you'd find it would really help you in your career." Coupling a compliment with a subtle dig about not having finished college is an example of supportive discouragement.

3. *Radiant devaluation* is giving a woman a backhanded compliment that infers that women are not valued highly. "Charlene, that's some of the best work I've seen from one of our administrative assistants" is an example of this. In this organization, all these assistants are female.

4. *Friendly harassment* appears to be friendly sexual behavior that embarrasses or causes discomfort to the recipient. "Ann, you look great today. How about we take the day off and hit the beach?" is such a statement said to an executive secretary by her boss.

5. *Liberated sexism* operates from the position that gender makes no difference because everyone is treated alike. It fails to consider the extra demands that are placed on women by family obligations or the physical demands of pregnancy.

6. *Benevolent exploitation* occurs when women are taught to be loyal and dutiful to their immediate bosses because this will eventually benefit the woman through advancement, fame, or compensation. The result may be a career spent in someone else's shadow with no credit for one's own contributions.

7. *Considerate domination* exists when women are asked to avoid rocking the boat, be patient and polite, and not challenge male dominance even when it is clearly inappropriate. "Marita, I'll share your concerns with Alonzo. I don't think he would appreciate a staff member directly raising this issue with him." This statement underscores the speaker's view of the woman as lower in status, insisting that she had better leave this matter to be handled by the men.

8. *Collegial exclusion* is evident when women are considered so unimportant that they are excluded from many activities. This includes professional events, social gatherings, and even physical location. An example of the latter would be the fact that male employees have offices but the staff functions in an open area like a typing pool.

9. *Subjective objectification* is the treating of women as if they were children, sex objects, or possessions.

Peel (2001) points out that heterosexism occurs every day and is grounded in the language we use, the assumptions we make, and the actions we take. She notes that these examples of micro-inequalities are for the most part, never recognized by those exhibiting the behaviors.

There are multiple reasons for disparities affecting women. They include gender stereotyping by males about the ability or competence of women that influences the opportunity to advance in their fields (Catalyst, 2005). In addition, stereotypes about gender often interact with other bias such as race, or ethnicity. Even the textbooks that students are using in high school are less likely to make reference to women's contribution to a field, and include fewer pictures of significant women. This appears to be the case in multiple disciplines including history and the sciences (Bazler & Simonis, 2006).

Sexism by its very existence diminishes both men and women. Unequal power ultimately hurts both men and women. One way that social work has attempted to recognize and deal with this inherent inequality is through *feminist* social work practice. Feminist perspectives are framed by concerns about the inherent gender bias in many existing theories that purport to understand human behavior. While many theories focus on the roles that women play in areas of society, feminist theory is interested in understanding and responding to women's needs through an egalitarian worker–client relationship. It is also particularly attentive to the different forms of oppression that women experience (Dominelli, 2002).

Interestingly, sexism can have both negative and positive justifications. Consider the person who pays a woman less based on her gender. Not only is the outcome negative (lower pay) but also the decision is likely the result of negative attitudes toward women in general. Some sexism is based on positive attitudes toward women but result in negative outcomes. For example, many who object to the idea of military women in combat are doing so through a wish to protect them from the realities of war. However,

Did You Know?

Other countries often struggle with the same issues of sexism as does the United States. For example, India is a predominantly patriarchal society in which women experience poor health at greater rates than men, receive less education than males, and are the target of violence and economic discrimination (Anand, 2009). Both structural and cultural factors perpetuate this maltreatment from one generation to another, just as occurs within the United States.

Critical Thinking

Practice Behavior Example: As a social worker, how might you handle a situation in which you discover you are paid more than others with similar experience and expertise based solely on your gender?

Assess your comprehension of Sexism by completing this quiz.

because the military system tends to reward those who have served in combat, this inhibited the ability of women to advance through the ranks and acquire the usual commendations that accompany these opportunities. Though benevolent in intent, the results are harmful to women.

RACISM

Racism is any action or attitude, conscious or unconscious, which subordinates an individual or group based on skin color or race. It is based on the belief that one's race is the major determinant of our traits and capacities and that racial difference makes one race superior to another. Racial discrimination and prejudice are other ways to define racism. Racism is a problem that appears to exist in most societies to varying degrees. Racism may be *individual*, *institutional*, or *cultural*. As you may recall, people can exhibit racism in their individual actions both intentionally or unintentionally. Even people with good intentions can engage in racist thoughts, beliefs, and behaviors. *Institutional racism* resides in the various institutions and organizations in any society. It generally includes structures, policies, and practices that oppress or subordinate people of color, while benefitting others. Finally, *cultural racism* is the overall "umbrella that influences and allows individual and institutional racism to flourish. Cultural racism is the individual and institutional expression of the superiority of one group's cultural heritage over another. The belief that one group's history, way of life, religion, arts and crafts, language, values, and traditions are superior to others makes up this particular category" (Sue, 2005, p. 104).

Most individuals think of racism as the actions of individuals, particularly those whose agendas promote hate crimes. We tend not to think of ourselves as racists but as good people. When we view the horrific acts of a few of our fellow human beings reported in the media, we are appropriately disappointed and angry at these individuals or groups. While most White individuals, for example, may hold no outright belief in the inferiority of minorities, they often believe "in the superiority of white culture and values" (Sue, 2005, p. 108). We may elect not to help someone by the side of the road who is in need for many reasons besides the color of their skin—we are in a hurry, I don't know how I could help, etc.—each reason (or excuse) provides a rationale that can cover our real discomfort. Sue (2005) raises some interesting questions about the issue of subtle racism. Why, he asks, when White men comprise about 33% of the U.S. population do they also:

- Occupy "80% of tenured positions in higher education"
- Comprise "80% of the House of Representatives"
- Make up "80% to 90% of the U.S. Senate"
- Constitute "92% of Forbes 400 executive CEO positions"
- Occupy "90% of public school superintendents" slots in the United States
- Comprise "99.9% of athletic team owners"
- Constitute "97.7% of U.S. presidents"

He suggests that this occurs because of the people we elect to office, teachers who staff our schools, business leaders who maintain existing corporate policies and practices, government employees, health care professionals, and our families and neighbors who help perpetuate the situation through the choices and decisions they make on a daily basis.

It is common to argue that these figures simply indicate that that Black Americans make bad choices in their lives that render them poorer and more likely to commit crimes than is true for Whites. Such arguments fail to recognize that all groups in society do not have the same options from which to choose.

It is not an accident that the majority of people living in neighborhoods adjacent to hazardous waste facilities are people of color, nor is it an accident that Black Americans are 79% more likely to live in neighborhoods in which industrial pollutants pause the greatest health risks (Dosomething.org, 2011). Similar concerns exist with respect to Native Americans living in areas of highly toxic pollution. Poor children of color are more likely to go to schools built with asbestos, reside in homes with peeling lead paint, and use parks that are contaminated.

Racism is evident in health care and as a recognized stressor that limits economic opportunity and impacts on social interactions. It also results in inequitable access to material, educational and social resources also with negative health implications (Adler & Rehkopf, 2008). Researchers have shown a clear relationship between the influences of stress and problems such as hypertension and heart disease. Being a victim of racism is associated with engagement in risky behaviors affecting health such as smoking and drug use (Borrell et al., 2007; Matthews et al., 2004). The lack of health care and health insurance are well-documented factors leading to poor health. Even the actions of health care providers appear to be different with respect to some ethnic/racial groups. For example, these professionals spend less time with the patient and make differential prognoses for diseases (Benkert & Peters, 2005). It is difficult to conclude from the data that anything besides racism is at work (Brondolo et al., 2009).

In many countries, racist actions are against the law, while in others there are no restrictions placed on those who would discriminate against another on the basis of the person's perceived race. The term *perceived race* is used for two reasons: First, human beings are biologically a single race and the term *race* is frequently misused to suggest that the people of the world are inherently different because of their biologic race. As we have noted earlier, the term *race* is a socially constructed concept and not grounded in biology. Second, a great deal of racism is perpetrated on the basis of an individual's perceived race. Hate crimes, for example, often harm individuals who have been mistaken as belonging to a particular race. While the victim was wrongly identified by the assailant, the intent was driven by hatred of another race and, therefore, the act falls under the rubric of racism.

Several points have been made about racism that help place it in context (Sue, 2005).

- Racism is normative in many respects and occurs as part of our everyday lives.
- The most problematic racism is that perpetrated by ordinary citizens not the actions of out and out extremist groups
- Racism does damage to both Whites and people of color
- Recognizing our own racism is a step in the right direction, but not sufficient to bring about change

Common reactions to discussions of racism tend to run from denial, "racism just isn't a problem anymore" to "whites are now the ones experiencing discriminating." Other comments include, "citing racism becomes an excuse to be used by those who

> **Did You Know?**
>
> Other evidence of racism in American society can be gleaned from government statistics. For example, Blacks make up about 14% of the U.S. population but comprise 50% of the prison population. Only 2% of American millionaires are African American.

> **Did You Know?**
>
> In Great Britain, ethnic minorities overall have twice the rate of unemployment of Whites and with some minority groups, the rates are four times as high. Australia's unemployment rate for native Australians is three times that of White people. The same is true for Native Canadians (Oracle Education Foundation, 2012).

have not worked hard enough or have their own shortcomings" and "the majority of people are not racist." Confronting racism is extremely difficult when we feel threatened by the possibility that our own actions have contributed to perpetuating racism (Sue, 2005). It is easy to become defensive and angry, especially when we are ignorant of White privilege (Smith, 2005).

While the United States has a number of laws that either restrict the opportunity or make it illegal to discriminate on the basis of race, this does not prevent racism from occurring. For example, a 30-year study of U.S. congressional campaigns—in which minority candidates were running for office—looked at what percentage of political ads involved potentially racist stereotypes (McIlwain & Stephen, 2011). The authors concluded that while the overall percentage of racist ads had declined from 44% to 30%, a surprising number of ads were still being used. For example, 21% of ads involving a White versus Black candidate used stereotypes, while White-Latino contests saw 32% of the ads using stereotypes. In the case of campaigns in which one candidate was White and the other Asian, the percentage was 33%—almost double the earlier rate.

Diversity in Practice

Practice Behavior Example: Recognize the extent to which a culture's structures and values may oppress, marginalize, alienate, or create or enhance privilege and power.

Critical Thinking Question: Is it ethical to use torture in order to force someone to divulge the location of a bomb placed in an elementary school?

Likewise, the United States has laws and policies regarding the treatment of military combatants in times of war. Despite these rules and those of the Geneva Convention of which the United States is a signatory, U.S. soldiers have murdered, tortured, and humiliated prisoners of war with relatively little consequence. One way individuals justify this treatment of others is to relegate them to subhuman status, at the same time, viewing themselves as a superior class of beings. In past conflicts, we have viewed other groups as subhuman or at least not on the same plane as the rest of us. Part of this stems from seeing ourselves as somehow exceptional when compared to others. This view contributes to the everyday racism that oppresses others.

AGEISM

Despite the fact that Americans are living longer and maintaining both their health and productivity into their later adult years, stereotypes about older adults are rampant. They are viewed as cranky, rife with physical or mental disabilities, feeble, poor in memory, senile, asexual, unmotivated, and slow in action and thought (Kane, 2007; Schuldberg, 2005). In societies where youth and beauty are emphasized and highly valued, elders compare negatively to these ideals. These stereotypes can lead to age discrimination and other negative reactions from those who come in contact with older adults. Interestingly, these attitudes are really unusual because the prejudices are expressed toward our future selves (Packer & Chasteen, 2006). Unfortunately, many social work students and practitioners as well as other professionals share some of these stereotypes (Yoon & Kolomer, 2007). An estimated 95% of MSW students never take a course on aging and relatively few select aging as their field of interest. The resistance to working with older adults tends to be highest among male and younger students (Gellis, Sherman, & Lawrance, 2003). Fortunately, experiments exposing social work students to content and cases about older adults have improved students' motivation and interest in working with this population (Gutheil, Heyman, & Chernesky, 2009).

Types of Ageism

Dennis and Thomas (2007) discuss four types of ageism identified in the literature. The first is *personal ageism* which exists when the individual's beliefs, behaviors, attitudes and ideas are biased toward older adults. This can be observed when a caretaker, family member, or professional assumes that the older adult is not sufficiently competent to make his or her own decisions. Another example occurs with physicians who dismiss the complaints of an older adult as just part of the aging process. *Institutional ageism* includes policies, rules, and other practices that discriminate against groups based solely on age. Policies that mandate a certain retirement age fall into this category. Mandatory retirement is still permitted under federal law for certain categories of employees such as state judges, firefighters, air traffic controllers, police officers, and some well paid executives (Monsees, 2002).

Intentional ageism exists when policies, rules, laws, and attitudes are deliberately undertaken with full awareness that the outcomes will be biased against older adults. This can occur when an employer views older employees as less productive and avoids hiring them. It is also evident in the media where finding the newest most attractive actor or actress often results in fewer roles for older adult thespians. Bias toward older adults can also show up in unexpected places as the following example suggests.

Clinical Corner

Gwen

Gwen, 62, was a prolific author with many published books to her credit who was considering retiring from her full-time teaching job. She mentioned this to her editor, Alice, who had just been promoted to her new position. Alice looked surprised at Gwen's retirement idea, but Gwen assured her she would still be doing her writing. Alice responded by saying, "Well, you should begin to plan to have a younger author take over writing your books. We will have to talk more about this but in the meantime see if you can find someone who could begin to write with you." Gwen was mortified that her editor appeared to be replacing her with a younger writer, especially when she had told Alice that she planned to continue to write. Slowly, she began to suspect that Alice, who was 30, saw Gwen as an old person who no longer had the same capabilities as someone younger.

After the conversation, Gwen talked with an old social work friend who reminded her that age discrimination was against the law and that she had both legal and civil rights that the editor appeared to be ignoring.

Unintentional ageism occurs without any intent on the part of the perpetrator to harm another because of age. It is likely the most common form of ageism, largely because it is consistent with multiple messages about older adults occurring in everyday life. It happens when we make assumptions about older adults, exaggerate their level of decrepitude, and make fun of them. It can sometimes be found in businesses where younger employees assume that older workers are not as knowledgeable about new technology and ideas.

Another reason for ageism is simple lack of experience. Those who have close and positive relationships with their own grandparents are more likely to have better attitudes toward older adults (Haight, Christ, & Dias, 1994) as are those who have some experience in working with this population (Snyder, Wesley, Lin, & May, 2008). Acceptance of stereotypes about older adults is a major reason why many helping professionals avoid gerontological practice (Scharlach, Damron-Rodriguez, Robinson, & Feldman, 2000). Stereotypes often creep into our everyday experiences with older adults. For example, it is easy to react negatively to the older adult ahead of us driving slower than traffic or the older individual who takes longer to make decisions. The wisdom that often accompanies older age may be responsible for both behaviors. Driving slower than traffic may help compensate for slower reaction time or demonstrate a greater degree of caution and care about the risks and responsibilities associated with driving. Taking longer to make a decision may indicate a realization that life is complicated and what initially seems easy may be much more complex. Without an understanding of this population, it is easier to accept stereotypes and find conforming evidence in our daily lives.

Stereotypes About Older Adults

Some of the stereotypes about older adults are so common that many people accept them at face value, such as:

- Older adults generally lose their eyesight until they are nearly or completely blind.
- As they age, older adults often experience a change in personality, becoming more difficult to live with.
- Most of the older population live in nursing homes or similar facilities.
- Over 75% of older adults develop Alzheimer's disease or other brain diseases.
- Both intelligence and cognitive ability decline with age.
- Interest in sex pretty much disappears by the time a person retires.
- Older adults get mentally confused and tend to forget a great deal.
- Contrast the incorrect views of older adults listed earlier with reality.
- One's eyesight will experience some changes but significant sight impairment in older adults is unusual and an indication to see an eye specialist.
- Our personality does not undergo significant change as we age. If someone is difficult to get along with in their later years, they were likely the same as young adults.
- Most older adults (95%) are in reasonable health and do not require nursing home care. Nursing home care is only needed for a small percent of seniors.
- Less than 25% of older adults develop senility associated with Alzheimer's or other brain diseases.
- If there is a decline in the intelligence of an older adult, it is unusual. Most adults maintain or enhance their intelligence as they age.
- Most older adults are capable of having a fulfilling and active sex life. This is sometimes difficult for adult children and staff in care facilities to understand or accept.
- When forgetfulness or confusion appears in an older adult, it can be caused by Alzheimer's as well as a host of temporary problems such as depression and sleeping difficulties that can be treated.

It is important for social workers not to assume that behavioral or other problem exhibited by an older adult are simply the result of aging. It is often the case that problematic behavioral symptoms are caused by other factors (Bonifas, 2006). These may include: psychiatric illness, physical health difficulties, medications, environment challenges, interpersonal relationships, and problems with various health and personal care tasks. Many an older adult has been moved to a nursing home or other care facility based on an assumption that their problems were age related. Even those in such facilities may be victims of common misconceptions. Overmedication, use of restraints, and other interventions may cause or exacerbate symptoms that could otherwise be treated with fewer negative consequences. Addressing psychosocial and environmental stressors and providing help for treatable medical conditions are often more successful.

Ageism is costly to both older adults and the rest of society (Kane, 2007). It demeans the individual by eliminating their individuality and unique characteristics. While not all stereotypes about older persons are negative, the implications are similar. At its worst, these attitudes can lead to paternalism, failure to involve clients in planning, discourage independence, and contribute to the client accepting the aging stereotypes (Kane, 2001; Kane, Lacey, & Greene, 2006).

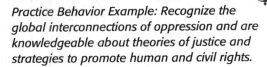

Human Rights and Justice

Practice Behavior Example: Recognize the global interconnections of oppression and are knowledgeable about theories of justice and strategies to promote human and civil rights.

Critical Thinking Question: Rudolph is 78 years old and hospitalized for what he thought was pneumonia. Neither the doctor nor Rudolph will tell him that his condition is caused by cancer and he has only about a week to live. Do you think it is ethical for a hospital social worker to support the family and doctor's decision not to tell Rudolph about his terminal state? What would you do if Rudolph asked you directly about his condition?

The actual picture of older adults is much more sanguine than the stereotypes would suggest. Older adults do not automatically suffer memory impairment and less than 20% shows either modest or more serious memory loss (National Institute on Aging, 2011; Sadock & Sadock, 2003). While perhaps 10% to 25% will experience some depression in their later years, most aging adults do not experience this mental health challenge (Centers for Disease Control and Prevention, 2112; Federal Interagency Forum on Aging Related Statistics, 2004). Assuming the worst regarding older adults underestimates their resilience and strength, both key factors that should be taken into account in any assessment.

Interestingly, ageism also is a problem for young adults (Popham, Kennison, & Bradley, 2011). The authors found a link between risk taking and ageist attitudes among undergraduates taking part in a Centers for Disease Control and Prevention study. Viewing the shortcomings or limitations of older adults as residing in the character of the individual, rather than a normal part of life, permits one to distance oneself from the aging process. By comparing their own capabilities with those of older adults, they come to see themselves as stronger, faster, smarter, and otherwise in a different realm from their elders. Few young adults ever picture themselves as aged, preferring to see their capabilities as rendering them invulnerable. This, in turn, leads to engagement in risk-taking behavior that serves to ward off fear of death and decline.

Ageism also contributes to other behaviors, such as tobacco use. Levy et al. (2009) found that people with strong negative age stereotypes were more likely to experience heart disease later in life as well as other adverse health outcomes. These outcomes may be related to lifestyle choices that involved higher risk taking including drinking, smoking, overeating, and failing to exercise.

Although it certainly continues to exist, there is some evidence that ageism in employment may be declining (Dennis & Thomas, 2007). To some extent, this may be due to the Age Discrimination in Employment Act (ADEA) enacted in 1967 and amended in subsequent years. The ADEA prohibited arbitrary age discrimination and eventually eliminated most mandatory retirements except as noted earlier. However, the number of complaints filed under this law and subsequently accepted is relatively small and other mechanisms of recourse such as going to court are expensive, lengthy, and often unsuccessful. Of all the laws against various forms of discrimination, ADEA is likely the weakest in terms of process and remedies available to someone experiencing employment discrimination.

Ageism and Sexual Minorities

There is substantial evidence that ageism combined with a large degree of homophobia is a problem for older LGBT individuals (Fredriksen-Goldsen et al., 2011). As a group, older LGBT adults experience many of the same challenges as non-LGBT people: they need health care, housing, transportation, legal assistance, and opportunities for social participation with others. Unlike most older adults, almost one-half have a disability and a third suffer from depression. Around two-thirds have been victimized three or more times because of their sexual orientation or gender identity More than one-eighth have received poor medical care or been denied healthcare altogether. Because of the discrimination many older LGBT adults have experienced in their lives, they often are reluctant to self-identify if it might open them up to further maltreatment. More than 20% fail to identify their sexual orientation or gender identity to their own physicians, which often precludes discussing critical health concerns. This further contributes to their cloak of invisibility (Fredriksen-Goldsen et al., 2011). As with many oppressed groups, this segment of the adult population is more likely to engage in behaviors that carry significant health risks, such as smoking, drinking to excess, and obesity.

Did You Know?

Accurately estimating the size of the GLBT population is always difficult because of the stigma still associated with this group. Many GLBT individuals are reluctant to divulge this information in surveys. Currently, the best estimate of the population's size is a recent Gallup Poll indicating that 3.4% of the U.S. adults self-identify as GLBT.

Source: Gates & Newport (2012).

In addition, older GLBT adults experience few of the social benefits associated with being married or partnered. This translates into a loss of social support and higher financial risk. Increased social isolation is a recognized contributor to both physical and mental health problems, diminished cognition, and premature chronic illness or death (Cacioppo & Hawkley, 2003).

As a group, older GLBT adults have a degree of resilience that comes from participation in their communities and 90% describe this part of their lives as good. Most participate in wellness and physical activities and about 40% attend religious/spiritual services, all of which are health promoting. The GLBT community often provides support and care for their members when this is not available from one's family members (Fredriksen-Goldsen et al., 2011).

For older LGBT adults, legal issues are often problematic. Partners lack the legal protections automatically awarded to spouses and they often do not qualify for programs that are designed to help non-LGBT adults. Examples include Social Security benefits, automatic inheritance rights, family leave benefits, bereavement leave, and Medicaid spenddowns. Like other oppressed groups, individual members often have "multiple identities" that increase their life risks. For example, minorities of color who are also LGBT members sometimes find themselves doubly disparaged. The same is true for older GLBT people, whose disabilities expose them to ableism, ageism, and heterosexism, a topic to be covered next.

Assess your comprehension of Racism and Ageism by completing this quiz.

HETEROSEXISM

Heterosexism is prejudice toward groups that include gay men and lesbian women, bisexual individuals and those who are transgendered. It is evident in everyday life and operates from an assumption that heterosexuality is the norm and other forms of sexuality are by definition "abnormal" or inferior. Heterosexism includes both negative attitudes toward those who are not heterosexual and discrimination in behavior. It considers nonheterosexuals as second-class citizens with respect to legal protections, social justice, and civil rights. Heterosexism produces a *sexual stigma*, defined as "the negative regard, inferior status, and relative powerlessness that society collectively accords to any nonheterosexual behavior, identity, relationship, or community. Sexual stigma is socially shared knowledge about homosexuality's devalued status in society" (Herek, 2007, pp. 906–907).

Herek (2007) points out that sexual stigma can occur in various ways with different or similar results, depending on the situation. For example, *enacted stigma* is overt as expressed in behavioral expressions that include antigay jokes, comments, ostracism, discrimination and violence aimed at sexual minorities. *Felt stigma* occurs when individuals modify their behavior to avoid instances of enacted stigma. The decision not to come out, for example, is often taken to avoid the approbation and stigmatization that accompanies outing oneself. It is a conscious decision to eliminate the opportunity for other people to demean oneself.

Internalized stigma occurs when an individual personally accepts societal definitions that define homosexuality as deviant, undesirable, or abnormal. In sexual minorities, this becomes *self-stigma* as it becomes part of his or her value system. One's self-concept also suffers when this occurs. Self-stigma has also been called internalized homophobia, internalized heterosexism, and/or internalized homonegativity. Internalized stigma can occur in heterosexuals when they allow a culture's negative evaluation of sexual minorities to shape their own beliefs, ideas, and values. In heterosexuals, internalized stigma is also known as homophobia, heterosexism, and homonegativity. Regardless of the name, the result is sexual prejudice (Herek, 2007).

Other forms of heterosexism include *over-sexualization* and *denying that sexual orientation is important* both personally and/or politically (James Madison University, 2012). In the case of over-sexualization, GLBT people are perceived as primarily sexual beings without recognizing the complexity associated with all human beings. Given this perspective, nonheterosexuals assume that all same-sex interactions are sexual or potentially so and believe that GLBT individuals will seek out sexual relationships with anyone of the same gender. This can lead to avoiding direct contact with or touching of GLBT people because it might be interpreted as a sexual come on. Over-sexualization tends to see all behaviors of GLBT individuals as sexual in nature or focus.

Denying the importance of sexual orientation is essentially the same as denying the significant of being a person of color. Attempts to be color-blind or orientation-blind are denying a major component of a person's life. At a personal level, this suggests that one's sexual orientation is irrelevant and should be ignored. "I don't care if you are a lesbian, it doesn't matter to me" is about as big a mistake as saying "I don't care if you are Hispanic" or "I don't care if you are a woman." In each comment, the speaker is pretending that differences do not matter when, in fact, they are salient aspects of all human beings. For one example of how sexual orientation differentiates individuals we only have to look at how often heterosexuals talk openly about their interest in the other sex, who they're dating, and what they did on their last date. This is a freedom that is not usually granted to most nonheterosexuals.

On a political level, heterosexism is evident when individuals, groups, and communities deny the significance of being GLBT. In most states and countries, gay and lesbian people are denied the same rights routinely available to heterosexuals—the ability to marry, participate in making health care decisions for their loved ones, and seek employment without encountering discrimination because of their sexual orientation. They also are likely to be victimized by others because of their sexual orientation or to be unwelcome in their own church. In addition, they may be prevented from adopting children and serving as foster parents. It is through the political process that these rights are granted to heterosexuals and denied to GLBT people. As has been said in terms of feminist issues, "the personal is political." Those with political power tend to see the world in their own image and construct a legal reality that reflects their understanding of normality. This often has negative consequences for those perceived as different or deviant.

Heterosexism also is reflected in beliefs about sexuality and about GLBT individuals, which include:

- Assuming that everyone is heterosexual
- Believing that homosexuality is a form of mental illness
- Believing that homosexuality can be cured through therapy
- Assuming that a young person who perceives himself or herself as gay is likely going through a phase that will change later
- Believing a heterosexual marriage will "straighten out" one's sexual orientation
- Attempting to explain a person's homosexuality as caused by parental behavior
- Thinking that GLBT people are hostile to heterosexuals
- Failing to recognize the extent to which heterosexual privilege offers multiple opportunities that are not available to nonheterosexuals

Like other forms of institutionalized discrimination, heterosexism is a "cultural ideology embodied in institutional practices that work to the disadvantage of sexual minority groups even in the absence of individual prejudice or discrimination" (Herek, 2007, p. 907).

Heterosexism has been shown to negatively affect sexual minority women and men. This is especially true when examining the experience of GLBT individuals who survived hate crimes. Consequences include increased frustration, anxiety, anger, depression, substance abuse, and posttraumatic stress disorder (Descamps et al., 2000; Herek, Gillis, & Cogan, 1999; Szymanski, 2005; Szymanski & Balsam, 2011). Even everyday workplace heterosexism such as jokes about sexual minorities and assumptions of heterosexuality can lead to "health-related problems, depression, and psychological distress, and decreased job satisfaction" (Szymanski, 2006, p. 228).

Discrimination against nonheterosexual individuals is evident in multiple societies. While much of the information in this chapter is related to heterosexism in the United States, other countries struggle with the same issues. In Chinese societies, homosexuality may be tolerated but not openly accepted (Chou, 1997). The importance of family acceptance is so strong that it has been said "only orphans can come out" (Ni, 1997, p. 201). Great Britain has struggled with this issue, first by adopting policies that essentially repressed public debate on sexual orientation and then repealing those policies in an effort to provide civil rights to GLBT people (Nixon & Givens, 2007). Countries that were once part of the Soviet Union, such as Latvia, are experiencing discrimination against sexual minorities (Waitt, 2005). Research in Australia has found multiple examples of heterosexism and homophobia toward GLBT individuals (Masser & Moffat, 2006). They concluded that "evidence suggests that discrimination against gay men in everyday life is not restricted to particularly subtle forms" (p. 132). Other Australian researchers have studied the ways in which school cultures helped control and silence nonheterosexuality by "normalizing heterosexuality as the dominant and only valid sexuality" (Ferfolja, 2007, p. 147). That this discrimination occurs in a society where it is illegal to discriminate on the basis of sexual orientation should be no surprise, given the cultural strength of many belief systems.

Interestingly, there are differences in levels of prejudice between women and men. These include (Herek & Capitanio, 1996; Parrott, Peterson, & Bakeman, 2011):

- Heterosexual women are less antagonistic and more positive in their attitudes toward sexual minorities than are heterosexual males.
- Overall, attitudes toward lesbians are more positive than those toward gay men.

- The most negative attitudes are those expressed by heterosexual men toward gay men.

- Heterosexual women tend to have more negative attitudes toward bisexuals than toward either lesbian women or gay men.

- Personal contact with sexual minority individuals tends to produce more positive attitudes compared to those without such contact. This is especially true when the heterosexual know multiple members of the sexual minority or have emotional ties GLBT individuals.

Homophobia

Homophobia or negative reactions, fears, and/or distrust of gay men and lesbian women are examples of heterosexism (Szymanski & Ikizler, 2012). As many researchers have noted, homophobic-based mistreatment of gay, lesbian, bisexual, and questioning individuals is a common occurrence (Kosciw & Diaz, 2006). It increases risk factors for these individuals in areas as diverse as academics, sexually risky behavior, substance abuse, and other psychological problems. As a form of heterosexism, homophobia not only produces a negative cultural influence that affects both personal and political worlds of GLBT people, it also can bear on one's identity. In a culture where one's sexual orientation is considered deviant, some GLBT individuals develop a degree of self-loathing and deny their own sexuality. These people are less likely to come out to others because they fear ridicule, ostracism, and hate. This is especially true for GLBT individuals in very conservative religions where being gay or lesbian is considered a sin. This can produce an internalized form of homophobia where self-hate is evident. This internal state can lead to efforts to demonize GLBT people. This has been observed in a number of public figures who took strong stands against homosexuality and were later caught participating in, soliciting, or admitting same-sex relationships. Examples include some well-known individuals whose actions made headlines (Ranker.com, 2012):

- Two television pastors
- A Washington State Representative
- An Alabama Attorney General
- Two members of the U.S. House of Representatives
- A California State Senator
- A mayor of Spokane, Washington
- A U.S. Senator
- A Florida State Representative
- An Indiana State Representative
- A chairman of the Republican National Committee.

Public figures sympathetic to the rights of GLBT people often face consequences for their positions. Religious leaders have denied communion to political figures who support gay rights and have declared that these individuals should be considered morally bankrupt. Churches across the country are divided on their positions toward GLBT people with some welcoming them and others kicking them out of the church. Some religions tolerate a gay or lesbian orientation but only if the individuals do not actively engage in sexual relationships. In other words, it is OK to be homosexual but not OK to act on your orientation.

The psychological and social consequences of homophobia and heterosexism can be great for GLBT individuals of all ages. Whether they come out or not, they may be victims of violence, ridicule, hostility, shunning, and other mistreatment that threaten their physical and mental health. Feelings of isolation and loneliness are common especially among youth who have not yet come out (Hodges & Parkes, 2005).

Heterosexism and homophobia are often observed in school venues where children and adolescents spend a large part of their waking hours. Sometimes it is subtle such as when a school system fails to create, implement, and enforce policies that deal with discrimination against GLBT individuals. Some schools create policies but provide no programs or other activities designed to discourage or eliminate discrimination on the basis of sexual orientation. The failure to anticipate such discrimination and adopt effective policies often reflects a heterosexist norm that does not even consider other orientations. Assessing the experiences of GLBT individuals should carefully include the environmental factors that facilitate or at least permit discrimination based on sexual orientation.

When schools adopt appropriate policies and programs, the incidence of victimization is less than in schools where these are absent (Goodenow, Szalacha, & Westheimer, 2006). Equally important, the schools with policies and programs are perceived by students as more welcoming, safer, and respectful toward sexual minorities than schools that have not engaged in such efforts. Schools with Gay-Straight Student Alliances (GSAs) tended to fall into the category of safer and more tolerant schools (Heck, Flentje, & Cochran, 2011; Szalacha, 2003). The advent of GSAs offer an opportunity for students to have contact with sexual minorities, an experience that appears to make heterosexual students more tolerant and less biased against homosexuals (Tee & Hegarty, 2006).

Eliminating bias toward sexual minorities is not easy, in part because heterosexism is built into the structure of societies. Changes in people's attitudes toward GLBT individuals can be facilitated by their contact and association with members of this group. Those who resist such opportunities are much less likely to change their prejudices. At the same time, it is possible to adopt policies that discourage or penalize discrimination against sexual minorities without necessarily changing the personal biases of individuals. This has been evident in a number of situations where cities, counties, and states have adopted antidiscrimination policies that cover sexual orientation. Even largely conservative populations have supported such legislation on the grounds that discrimination against anyone is unfair.

That public attitudes toward sexual minorities are changing can be seen from numerous viewpoints. In 1973, the American Psychiatric Association removed homosexuality as a disorder in the *Diagnostic and Statistical Manual of Mental Disorders (DSM)*. This was based on both existing science and changes in social norms (Drescher, 2012). The decision was endorsed by the American Psychological Association, which also encouraged mental health professionals to work for eradication of discrimination based on sexual orientation.

States that had passed sodomy laws either eliminated them or had them overturned by state courts or the U.S. Supreme Court. Sodomy laws allowed only male–female vaginal intercourse and outlawed any other sexual acts, including wife on top of husband, oral and anal sex, masturbation, sex between unmarried partners and other acts (Herek, 2007). Beginning in 2011, gay and lesbian individuals were allowed to openly serve in the military, a major change. Nine states and the District of Columbia now permit same-sex marriages, with other states considering doing so. These changes came about either through legislative action or by state courts overturning laws that were in violation of the state's constitution. In addition, some states have created legal recognition of same-sex couples short of marriage.

Currently, a group of over 90 mayors from across the United States are part of a Freedom to Marry initiative that is working in support of same-sex marriages. At the time of this writing, the group included mayors from New York, Chicago, Los Angeles, San Diego, Philadelphia, Des Moines, Milwaukee, Minneapolis, Houston, Phoenix, Washington, DC, and Boston, among many other communities. The decision by the 9th Circuit Court that overturned California's Proposition 8, which banned same-sex marriage, is being reviewed by the U.S. Supreme Court for a final decision. The changes enumerated previously suggest that attitudes about sexual minorities are changing, albeit slowly.

ABLEISM

Ableism is discrimination and/or prejudice toward people who have disabilities and it occurs very often in both the United States and in other countries. "Discrimination may be direct or indirect, legally or culturally encoded, based on scientific norms, or based on false assumptions" (Levi, 2005, p. 1). The disability may be physical, developmental, or mental. Some individuals have visible or obvious disabilities while other's disabilities may not be noticed by the casual observer. Not everyone likes the term *ableism* and other terms have been used in its place including *disability oppression, disablism,* or *handicapism*. Ableism takes the form of negative verbalization about those with disabilities, denying them physical or other access to needed resources, and refusing to hire or rent to people with disabilities. It can also be reflected in situations when able-bodied drivers park in spots reserved for those with a disability. On a larger level, ableism is reflected in policies that fail to meet the economic needs of those with disabilities. Multiple examples of the latter are reported regularly in the media where combat veterans are denied benefits and must go through a lengthy process to prove they have a disability. The same is true for civilians who seek help from the Social Security Administration because of a disability and find their claims are frequently rejected. Some ableism is borne out of ignorance and a general failure to consider that everyone is not equally able to perform a given task. Much like other "-isms," ableism operates whenever anyone assumes that being able is the norm in society. When such views occur, they are perpetuating an ableist culture that, like a heterosexual culture, must be confronted to bring about change (Cherney, 2011).

There are multiple examples of how an ableist culture influences human behavior. For example, many television advertisements are not close captioned so that people with hearing disabilities can benefit. Businesses often operate in facilities that are not accessible to those with disabilities, despite the requirements of the Americans with Disabilities Act (ADA). I visited an educational institution that had designated one specific door in a block-long building as accessible and required student with a motor disability to travel around the building to get to the one door they could open. In another university, the single toilet in the men's room was set up a box about two feet above the floor level. It was there, I was told, because the bathroom had been added after the building was built and the renovators did not want to dig into the rock foundation under the building because it was more expensive than the jerry-rigged system they came up with. Ableism also shows up in odd places. It took the better part of three years for professional golfer

Many individuals with disabilities can be accommodated in the workplace.

Keith Brofsky/Photodisc/Thinkstock

Casey Martin to receive permission to use a golf cart during PGA contests. The PGA's rules were simply considered as inviolate because they were designed to treat every player in an identical manner.

Another consequence of ableism is the lowered expectations that teachers and others have for persons with disabilities. This is especially problematic for children because lowered expectations displayed at a young age are likely to have greater influence. A disability in a particular area, such as in reading, may be generalized to other areas with the result that the person with a disability is expected to do poorly in multiple subjects. Sometimes, the assumptions of parents and teachers result in poorer outcomes for children. For example, it is common to assume that the most effective way for deaf children to survive in the world is through oral language. However, this is contrary to much research showing that learning sign language helps children achieve more in academic settings (Levi, 2005; Power, Hyde, & Leigh, 2008).

For the most part, we have removed the label "disabled" from our professional vocabulary when referring to individuals because it carries the stigma of inadequacy and/or abnormal. Labeling can have profound effects on the person who is labeled because equating having a disability with being abnormal can lead to horrific consequences. Persons with disabilities also experience hate crimes and violence that require hospitalization (Sherry, 2005, 2010). Of course, it does not take a fiendish regime or human hatred to diminish the lives of people with disabilities. In fact, those with disabilities are often abused, neglected, and otherwise maltreated by those who are charged with their care. Sullivan and Knutson (2000) reviewed school records and found maltreatment in almost a third of children with disabilities, about three times as high as other children. Sobsey, Randall, and Parilla (1997) found differences in the kind and amount of abuse experienced by children with disabilities. For example, girls with disabilities were sexually abused 62% of the time compared to 38% for boys. Girls also were more likely to be emotionally abused while boys were more likely than girls to be neglected (56% vs. 44%). Similar gender differences in sexual victimization were noted by Hughes et al. 2011).

Did You Know?

As people with disabilities age, they encounter high rates of illness and death compared to the general population (Heller & Marks, 2005). Problem areas include obesity, osteoporosis, diabetes, heart disease, high blood pressure, dental disease, thyroid disease, respiratory illness, cancer, and bowel-related challenges.

Those with disabilities may also encounter typical challenges associated with aging earlier than is true for those without a disability. This premature aging impacts families, often results in loss of employment, and marks the onset of chronic health conditions associated with aging.

Keller and Siegrist (2010) looked at the characteristics of those who held negative attitudes toward those with physical disabilities. They found that people who generally do not like other people have more negative attitudes toward individuals with physical disabilities than was true of those who had a general liking of others. This liking of people was more characteristic of individuals with high levels of self-esteem, life satisfaction, and those who are goal directed. By comparison, individuals who believe in a just world were more likely to discriminate against people with disabilities. This tendency arises from the belief that in a just world, people "get what they deserve and deserve what they get" (Keller & Siegrest, 2010, p. 391). This generally results in feeling that people are to blame for their own misfortune. The authors' findings are consistent with much of the previous research on the relationship between attitudes toward those with disabilities and the individual's psychological resources, such as self-esteem, life satisfaction, and beliefs in a just world.

Unfortunately, even laws such as the ADA cannot eradicate the beliefs and unspoken judgments that others hold toward those with disabilities (Levi, 2005; Vilchinsky, Findler, & Werner, 2010).

DISCRIMINATION AGAINST RELIGIOUS GROUPS

As with other defining characteristics, one's religion or lack thereof is often the basis for discrimination and maltreatment. Religion or the lack of it has been used as an excuse for individuals to discriminate against their neighbors, attack others who do not share one's religious persuasion, and commit genocide. It is impossible to ignore the consequences of religious discrimination as it is evident on both a national and international level. Historically, religion was a large factor in the crusades conducted by Catholic countries against Muslim nations. The Spanish Inquisition which lasted over 350 years was an attempt to produce a largely Catholic Spain and to force those with other religions to leave (Eliade, 1990). Religion was the basis for the Missouri governor's 1838 directive to exterminate any Mormon in the state and also led to their forced exodus from Illinois. As the Missouri state archivist noted, Mormons ended up in "Utah because there was no one there to shoot them" (Scianna, 2006, p. 1). In the run-up to the 2012 presidential election, the Mormon religion of the 2012 Republican candidate became an issue for some fundamentalist religious groups who viewed Mormonism as a cult. Similar concerns were raised when John F. Kennedy ran for president in 1960 because there had never been another Catholic in the White House. Even today, in some states, the religion of candidates makes a difference in whether they get elected.

On an international level, some of the disputes occurring throughout the Mideast and in other venues are based on religion. Often, religion is combined with issues of power, particularly in nations where members of a minority religion hold power over a much larger religious majority. In the second decade of the 21st century, a wholesale attack on Christians is being carried out in numerous countries. From 2003 to 2010 (Ali, 2012), terrorist attacks on Christians in Africa, the Middle East, and Asia increased over 300%. The persecution is conducted by such groups as governmental agents, rebel groups, and vigilantes. The attacks include destruction of churches and holy sites, murder, bombings, aerial bombardment, mutilation, and imprisonment. Countries where this is occurring are largely Muslim and include Nigeria, Sudan, Egypt, Iraq, Iran, Pakistan, and Indonesia. The resultant death toll is in the thousands and has been largely unreported in mainstream media.

Some authors have argued that discrimination against certain religious groups occurs within social work and the general society. In particular, the argument is made that social work oppresses Evangelical Christians (Hodge, 2002). This group is often referred to as religious conservatives because of their strict interpretation of biblical rules and laws. Hodge argues that most social workers are not as religious as the religious conservatives and that their beliefs are incongruent with those of this group. He presents data that the social work profession's values are liberal in orientation and that these differences are played out in social work education through denying admission to Evangelicals, funds to travel to religiously affiliated conferences, and practica in religiously focused agencies. He also points out that relatively few articles on the topic of Evangelicals appear in social work and social science journals. In a follow-up study, Hodge (2006) found that Evangelical Christians felt some degree of religious discrimination within social work education. This was not the case with other groups of students with a strong religious background. However, Hodge notes that without a definition of religious discrimination that was applicable to the study respondents, it is difficult to draw any additional conclusions. Hodge (2002) does point out that on many issues social workers and Evangelical Christians hold similar views, particularly toward helping the poor and the role of government in reducing income inequality. He recommends that social work continue to work to achieve a more inclusive educational environment. Hodge's conclusions and criticisms have been critiqued by other social work educators who question his premises and theoretical framework (Dessel, Shepardson, & Bolen, 2011).

Harper (2007) studied stereotyping of nonreligious people by religious students and concluded that the former may experience discrimination in certain contexts, particularly when they are in the minority or in areas where religious participation is highly valued. The nonreligious may be termed immoral, evil, sinners, and anti-Christian on the negative side while others may simply see them as independent and free spirited. The stereotype of nonreligious individuals as disregarding others and apt to challenge norms can result in a "we-they" kind of construct. As the author concludes, being nonreligious "is a potentially maligned social category to belong to" (p. 551).

Religious Discrimination and Muslims

Following the attacks of 9/11/2001, attitudes toward Muslims took a decidedly negative turn in the United States and elsewhere (Beinart, 2012). Even in places located far away from the United States, bias toward this group was evident. Ahmed (2010) found clear evidence of discrimination against Muslims in Sweden, among both students and the general public. Similar studies of Swedish life had found comparable results. The European Union countries have experienced increased hostility toward Muslims since 2001 (Human Rights First, 2008), most of it verbal as opposed to physical. In several European cities, Muslims reported being stopped by the police without reason and experiencing verbal attacks and other disrespectful treatment (Brüß, 2008). In England, there is evidence that religious discrimination is occurring in areas of employment and education (Weller, Feldman, & Purdam, 2001). In Australia, Islamophobia has resulted in mosque burning, and attacks on women wearing the traditional *hijab* (Bloul, 2008).

It is difficult to get firm numbers on the U.S. population who are Muslim. One estimate is that there are six million Muslims with the majority located in California, New York, Illinois, Indiana and Michigan. Other estimates place the number at no more than 1.4 million (Pew Research Center, 2007). There are about 2,000 mosques in the United States along with 400 Islamic schools (Khalidi, 2000). About 25% of U.S. Muslims are African American with another quarter coming from India, Pakistan, and Bangladesh. Another 27% are of Arab origin with the remainder from multiple locations in the Middle and Far East. Less than 2% are White Americans (Kahera, 2002; Zogby International, 2001). However, even these estimates as to the origin of U.S. Muslims are being challenged (PeZa, 2009). Many U.S. Muslims are doing well economically, but when taken as a group, they have a rate of poverty slightly higher than the national average (Kosmin & Mayer, 2001; Pew Research Center, 2007). The overall economic health of Muslims living in the United States, though, is much better than in several European countries.

Many Americans have distorted views and stereotypes about the Muslim religion, largely in reaction to the events of 9/11. They are likely to perceive the religion negatively and fear that mosques represent threats to their safety and culture. This has led to demonstrations and political action to stop the building of a mosque near the 9/11 Memorial and in several cities as diverse as Murfreesboro, Tennessee; Temecula, California; and Sheboygan, Wisconsin. In some cases, religious leaders have rallied to support building of a mosque while other pastors have attempted to prevent construction of any more mosques in the United States. A study of Muslim Americans between the ages of 18 and 24 found that 50% reported suffering discrimination in academic settings and in the workplace (Muslims in the American Public Square, 2004). Shammas (2009) found similar experiences in her study of over 700 community college students in California and Michigan. Livengood and Stodolska (2004) looked at a group of American Muslim students to determine what, if any, changes in their lives occurred in the year following 9/11. They found that discrimination affected the group member's leisure activities, forced them to be more vigilant about their immediate environment, change their clothing to avoid attention, travel in groups, and change their travel plans and patterns. It is clear that discrimination against Muslims is a reality in the United States and in many other countries. Moreover, this discrimination contributes to a variety of health and mental health issues experienced by Muslims (Hassouneh & Kulwicki, 2007). Muslim youth report high levels of discrimination, sometimes on a daily basis (Sirin & Fine, 2007). Interestingly, according to the authors, Muslim girls have less trouble bridging the two parts of who they are—American and Muslim, than is true for Muslim boys.

We have touched on a few areas where religious discrimination is occurring on a significant scale. However, these are not all the examples of religious discrimination by any means. Ethiopian Jews who have emigrated to Israel have faced discrimination in their new country despite their shared religion (Zegeye, 2007). A study of Muslim women seeking maternal health services in Canada found multiple examples of ignorance about their culture and religion resulting in both insensitivity and discrimination (Reitmanova & Gustafson, 2008). Several international crises involving religious discrimination have occurred in the past two decades and, in each case, have resulted in members of the international community taking action to end the crisis. For example, a combination of ethnic and religious discrimination erupted in the 1990s in Bosnia and Herzegovina, once a part of Yugoslavia. International condemnation and intervention by NATO forces forced an end to the conflict. Similar international interventions to stop religious and ethnic discrimination occurred in the Sudan, Rwanda, and Somalia as mentioned in Chapter 14. In many countries that have experienced religious strife, there is a close connection between religion and ethnicity. Religious discrimination is more likely to happen in nations which have an official state religion, where the majority belong to a single religion, or where preference is given to a particular religion (Fox, 2007). Of course, religious discrimination can occur in any culture. An example can be seen in the following box.

Clinical Corner

The following is a partial summary of a meeting of a condominium association located in a generally liberal city during the winter holiday season. The Board of Directors of a condominium association is meeting to discuss a request from one of the condo unit owners.

BOARD PRESIDENT: "Mrs. Borlex has objected to the presence of the Christmas tree in the downstairs lobby and has asked the board to remove it."

1ST MEMBER: "What is her problem?"

BOARD PRESIDENT: "I think she is Jewish and finds it offensive."

VICE PRESIDENT: "What if we also put up a menorah, would that be OK?"

2ND MEMBER: "And where will it end? Next we'll be putting up symbols for Kwanza or whatever that black thing is."

BOARD PRESIDENT: "Should we take a survey of unit owners to get a sense of their thoughts on this?"

1ST MEMBER: "I don't think we should do anything. She should have known this was a Christian building when she bought her condo. If she doesn't like it, she can buy in another building."

None of the members of the condo board would ever consider themselves as discriminating against any other religion. However, they also could never take the perspective of someone who did not automatically subscribe to their particular belief system.

As mentioned earlier in this chapter, it is not uncommon to have individuals facing multiple forms of discrimination simultaneously. One example is the African American individual who is a Muslim and can face discrimination on both counts. Another example is discrimination on the basis of gender, sexual orientation, and race that often coexist producing an additive effect on the victims' mental health (Szymanski & Owens, 2009). The authors of this study noted that the impact of any single form of discrimination may be reduced or increased depending upon the individual's most important identity, for example, as a woman or as a lesbian. In addition, there may be some moderating influences in a sexual minority's life that helps reduce the influence of a particular form of discrimination. Szymanski and Owen (2009) found that involvement in feminist activities and groups helped lessen the impact of sexism but did not affect exposure to heterosexism.

As in other "-isms," discrimination against religious minorities appears to be lessened by familiarity with the disenfranchised group. In other words, having friends and acquaintances whose religion is different from one's own tends to create a broader world view and lessens hostility to the out group (Brinkerhoff et al., 1991; Peterson, 2008). The opportunity to develop these relationships would seem to be growing as "Muslims are now the second largest religious denominational group in almost all Western countries, including Canada, Britain and the United States" (Niyozov & Pluim, 2009, p. 637). On the other hand, Rowatt et al. (2009, p. 14) found that "general religiousness appears to be linked with selective self-reported intolerance toward persons perceived to behave in a manner inconsistent with some traditional religious teachings." Their study suggests that intolerance toward other groups characterized by different religions, sexual orientations, and race is inherent in many mainstream American religions.

Factors more likely to be associated with religious discrimination include fundamentalism, which has been variously described as a mindset, a closed belief system, and right-wing authoritarianism (Kirkpatrick, 1993). Characteristics of fundamentalism include beliefs that the bible contains no errors or contradictions and is infallible. The bible is believed to contain clear definitions of what is right and wrong and moral. Finally, Christians must avoid being influenced by worldly ideas that undermine this belief system. Fundamentalism has been correlated with prejudice and discrimination against multiple minority groups in a variety of studies. Kirkpatrick found no differences between fundamentalist women and men with regard to their holding discriminatory attitudes toward religious minorities.

On a positive note, despite the challenges facing Muslims in the United States, most of the younger adults appear to be incorporating both their religious and American identities into a bicultural adaptation. They maintain involvement in social and cultural activities from both areas and have created a unified perspective on their identities. Some have created parallel identities that allow them to hold onto their identity as Muslims and as Americans. As in other areas, women were more likely to have adopted integrated identities that blended aspects of their religion and American culture. Men were more likely to have adopted parallel identities (Sirin et al., 2007). This is consistent with the adjustment patterns of other immigrant groups who maintain connections with their culture of origin while adopting the norms, values, and beliefs of their new culture. Additional research indicates that 47% of Muslim Americans with strong religious beliefs identify first as Muslims while 28% identified as American first. This is comparable to how devout U.S. Christians self-identify: 59% identified as Christian first, while 30% saw themselves as Americans first (Pew Research Center, 2007). Less devout Christians and Muslims are more likely to have higher levels of identification as Americans. Interestingly, Muslims in the United States are more likely to think of themselves as American first when compared to Muslims living in several European countries. They are also more positive about the quality of life for Muslim women living in the United States (Pew Research Center, 2007).

Discrimination is a fact for many groups throughout the world. Whether based on religion, race, sex, age, or some other difference, it is detrimental to both the victim and to the larger society. It produces or contributes to various physical and mental health problems, lowers the quality of life of those who are discriminated against, and diminishes the cultures in which it occurs. The potential contributions of different segments of a population are reduced to the detriment of the whole society.

Test your understanding and analysis of this chapter by completing the Chapter Review.

References

CHAPTER 1

Arata, C., Langhinrichsen-Rohling, J., Bowers, D., & O'Farrill-Swails, L. (2005). Single versus multi-type maltreatment: An examination of the long-term effects of child abuse. *Journal of Aggression, Maltreatment & Trauma, 11*(4), 29–52.

Barker, R. (1999). *The social work dictionary* (4th ed.). Washington, DC: NASW Press.

Copolov, D., & Crook, J. (2000). Biological markers and schizophrenia. *The Australian and New Zealand Journal of Psychiatry, 34*(Suppl.), S108–S112.

Crick, N., & Dodge, K. (1994). A review and reformulation of social information-processing mechanisms in children's social adjustment. *Psychological Bulletin, 115*(1), 74–101.

Griffin, M., & Amodeo, M. (2010). Predicting long-term outcomes for women physically abused in childhood: Contribution of abuse severity versus family environment. *Child Abuse & Neglect: The International Journal, 34*(10), 724–733.

Herrnstein, R. J., & Murray, C. (1994). *The bell curve.* New York: The Free Press.

Kim, J. (2009). Type-specific intergenerational transmission of neglectful and physically abusive parenting behaviors among young parents. *Children and Youth Services Review, 31*(7), 761–767.

Kymalainen, J. A., & Weisman de Mamani, A. G. (2008). Expressed emotion, communication deviance, and culture in families of patients with schizophrenia: A review of the literature. *Diversity and Ethnic Minority Psychology, 14*(2), 85–91. doi:10.1037/1099-9809.14.2.85

Lutz, W., Saunders, S. M., Leon, S. C., Martinovich, Z., Kosfelder, J., Schulte, D., & Tholen, S. (2006). Empirically and clinically useful decision making in psychotherapy: Differential predictions with treatment response models. *Psychological Assessment, 18*(2), 133–141. doi:10.1037/1040-3590.18.2.133

Maeda, K., Kasai, K., Watanabe, A., Henomatsu, K., Rogers, M., & Kato, N. (2006). Effect of subjective reasoning and neurocognition on medication adherence for persons with schizophrenia. *Psychiatric Services, 57*(8), 1203–1205.

Meltzer, H., Tong, C., & Luchins, D. (1984). Serum dopamine beta hydroxylase activity and lateral ventricular size in affective disorders and schizophrenia. *Biological Psychiatry, 19*(10), 1395–1402.

Milner, J. S. (2000). Social information processing and child physical abuse: Theory and research. In D. J. Hansen (Ed.), *Nebraska symposium on motivation vol. 46, 1998: Motivation and child maltreatment* (pp. 39–84). Lincoln, NE: University of Nebraska Press.

National Association of Social Worker's (NASW) *Code of ethics.* Washington, DC: Author.

Reynolds, C. (2000). Why is psychometric research on bias in mental testing so often ignored? *Psychology, Public Policy, and Law, 6*(1), 144–150.

Santrock, J. W. (2008). *Life-span development.* Boston: McGraw-Hill.

Seidenstücker, G., & Roth, W. L. (1998). Treatment decisions: Types, models and schools. *European Journal of Psychological Assessment, 14*(1), 2–13. doi:10.1027/1015-5759.14.1.2

Steele, C. M. (1997). A threat in the air: How stereotypes shape intellectual identity and performance. *American Psychologist, 52*(6), 613–629.

Steele, C. M. (2012). Conclusion: Extending and applying stereotype threat research: A brief essay. In M. Inzlicht & T. Schmader (Eds.), *Stereotype threat: Theory, process, and application* (pp. 297–303). New York: Oxford University Press.

Stith, S., Liu, T., Davies, L., Boykin, E., Alder, M., Harris, J., & Dees, J. (2009). Risk factors in child maltreatment: A meta-analytic review of the literature. *Aggression and Violent Behavior, 14*(1), 13–29.

Thompson, M., Kingree, J., & Desai, S. (2004). Gender differences in long-term health consequences of physical abuse of children: Data from a nationally representative survey. *American Journal of Public Health, 94*(4), 599–604.

U.S. Department of Health and Human Services. (2012). *Child maltreatment 2011.* Retrieved April 29, 2013, from http://www.acf.hhs.gov/sites/default/files/cb/cm11.pdf

Wilper, A. P., Woolhandler, S., Lasser, K. E., McCormick, D., Bor, D. H., & Himmelstein, D. U. (2009). Health insurance and mortality in US adults. *American Journal of Public Health, 99,* 2289–2295.

CHAPTER 2

American Psychological Association. (2009). *Resolution on appropriate affirmative responses to sexual orientation distress and change efforts.* Retrieved from http://www.apa.org/about/policy/sexual-orientation.aspx

Associated Press. (2005, July 26). U.S. stands apart from other nations on maternity leave. *USA Today.* Retrieved from http://usatoday30.usatoday.com/news/health/2005-07-26-maternity-leave_x.htm

Barker, R. (1999). *The social work dictionary* (4th ed.). Washington, DC: NASW Press.

Bell, R. (1979). Parent, child, and reciprocal influences. *American Psychologist, 34,* 821–826.

Flaherty, E. (2006). Analysis of caretaker histories in abuse: Comparing initial histories with subsequent confessions. *Child Abuse & Neglect: The International Journal, 30*(7), 789–798.

Forehand, R., & Long, N. (2010). *Parenting the strong-willed child: The clinically proven five-week program for parents of two- to six-year-olds* (3rd ed.). New York: McGraw-Hill.

Glaze, L. (2011). *Correctional populations in the United States, 2010.* Retrieved June 20, 2013, from http://www.bjs.gov/content/pub/pdf/cpus10

Jaudes, P., & Diamond, L. (1985). The handicapped child and child abuse. *Child Abuse & Neglect, 9*(3), 341–347.

King, S. (2000). Is expressed emotion cause or effect in the mothers of schizophrenic young adults? *Schizophrenia Research, 45*(1–2), 65–78.

Lundahl, B., Risser, H., & Lovejoy, M. (2006). A meta-analysis of parent training: Moderators and follow-up effects. *Clinical Psychology Review, 26*(1), 86–104.

Plöderl, M., & Fartacek, R. (2009). Childhood gender nonconformity and harassment as predictors of suicidality among gay, lesbian, bisexual, and heterosexual Austrians. *Archives of Sexual Behavior, 38*(3), 400–410.

Ray, R., Gornick, J. C., & Schmitt, J. (2009, June). *Parental leave policies in 21 countries: Assessing generosity and gender equality.* Center for Economic and Policy Research. Retrieved from http://www.cepr.net/documents/publications/parental_2008_09.pdf

Savin-Williams, R. (2006). Who's gay? Does it matter? *Current Directions in Psychological Science, 15*(1), 40–44.

Spitzer, R. L. (1981). The diagnostic status of homosexuality in DSM-III: A reformulation of issues. *The American Journal of Psychiatry, 138*(2), 210–215.

United Nations. (2003). *Forum on crime and society.* Retrieved October 19, 2012, from http://www.unodc.org/pdf/crime/forum/forum3.pdf

U.S. Census Bureau. (2012). *Income statistics.* Retrieved July 1, 2012, from http://www.census.gov/hhes/www/income/data/statistics/index.html

U.S. Department of Labor, Employment Standards Administration, Wage and Hour Division. (2009, January). *Fact sheet #28: The Family and Medical Leave Act of 1993.* Retrieved from http://www.dol.gov/esa/whd/regs/compliance/whdfs28.pdf

Vahratian, A., & Johnson, T. (2009). Maternity leave benefits in the United States: Today's economic climate underlines deficiencies. *Birth: Issues in Perinatal Care, 36,* 177–179.

Vaillant, C., & Vaillant, G. (1993). Is the U-curve of marital satisfaction an illusion? A 40-year study of marriage. *Journal of Marriage & the Family, 55*(1), 230–239.

Waldfogel, J. (2000). Reforming child protective services. *Child Welfare, 79*(1), 43–57.

Whitley, B. (1996). *Principles of research in behavioral science.* Mountain View, CA: Mayfield Publishing.

CHAPTER 3

Adams, G. (2008). *The specter of Salem: Remembering the witch trials in nineteenth-century America.* Chicago, IL: The University of Chicago Press.

Alexander, E. (2000, December 6). *Famous fried eggs: Students debate the effectiveness, accuracy of well-known anti-drug commercial.* Retrieved from http://www.cnn.com/fyi/interactive/news/brain/brain.on.drugs.html

American Iatrogenic Association. (2002a). *American Iatrogenic Association: Promoting accountability for medical professionals and institutions.* Retrieved from http://www.iatrogenic.org/

American Iatrogenic Association. (2002b). *What does the word "Iatrogenic" mean?* Retrieved from http://www.iatrogenic.org/define.html

Asch, S. (1956). Studies of independence and conformity: I. A minority of one against a unanimous majority. *Psychological Monographs: General and Applied, 70*(9), 1–70.

Bassham, G., Irwin, W., Nardone, H., & Wallace, J. (2011). *Critical thinking: A student's introduction* (4th ed.). New York: McGraw-Hill.

Belsky, J., Steinberg, L., Houts, R. M., & Halpern-Felsher, B. (2010). The development of reproductive strategy in females: Early maternal harshness? Earlier menarche? Increased sexual risk taking. *Developmental Psychology, 46*(1), 120–128. doi:10.1037/a0015549

Boysen, G. A. (2010). Integrating implicit bias into counselor education. *Counselor Education and Supervision, 49*(4), 210–227.

Bricklin, B. (1995). *The custody evaluation handbook: Research-based solutions and applications.* New York: Brunner/Mazel.

Brooke, J. (1998). Gay man dies from attack, fanning outrage and debate. *The New York Times.* Retrieved January 3, 2011, from http://query.nytimes.com/gst/fullpage.html?es=9F04E7DB173AF930A25753C1A96E958260

Chaffin, M., Hanson, R., Saunders, B., Nichols, T., Barnett, D., Zeanah, C., . . . Miller-Perrin, C. (2006). Report of the APSAC task force on attachment therapy, reactive attachment disorder, and attachment problems. *Child Maltreatment, 11*(1), 76–89. doi:10.1177/1077559505283699

Currie, C., Ahluwalia, N., Godeau, E., Nic Gabhainn, S., Due, P., & Currie, D. (2012). Is obesity at individual and national level associated with lower age at menarche? Evidence from 34 countries in the health behaviour in school-aged children study. *Journal of Adolescent Health, 50*(6), 621–626. doi:10.1016/j.jadohealth.2011.10.254

Deng, F., Tao, F., Wan, Y., Hao, J., Su, P., & Cao, Y. (2011). Early menarche and psychopathological symptoms in young Chinese women. *Journal of Women's Health, 20*(2), 207–213. doi:10.1089/jwh.2010.2102

Dewey, J. (2011). *How we think.* Eastford, CT: Martino Fine Book.

Drew, C., Hardman, M., & Hart, A. (1996). *Designing and conducting research: Inquiry in education and social science* (2nd ed.). Needham Heights, MA: Allyn & Bacon.

Freeman, D. (2008). Kenneth B. Clark and the problem of power. *Patterns of Prejudice, 42*(4/5), 413–437.

Gatti, U., Tremblay, R., & Vitaro, F. (2009). Iatrogenic effect of juvenile justice. *Journal of Child Psychology and Psychiatry, 50*(8), 991–998.

Hanson, D. (2007). *Alcohol problems and solutions: This is your brain on drugs.* Retrieved from http://www2.potsdam.edu/hansondj/controversies/1066845908.html

Helmes, E., & Gee, S. (2003). Attitudes of Australian therapists toward older clients: Educational and training imperatives. *Educational Gerontology, 29*(8), 657–670.

Hulbert, A. (2003). *Raising America: Experts, parents, and a century of advice about children.* New York: Knopf Publishing Group.

Jackson, J. (2006). Kenneth B. Clark: The complexities of activist psychology. In *Portraits of pioneers in psychology* (Vol. VI, pp. 273–286). Washington/Mahwah, DC/NJ: American Psychological Association. Retrieved from PsycINFO database

Kaplan, M. (1974). Context-induced shifts in personality trait evaluation: A comment on the evaluative halo effect and meaning change interpretations. *Psychological Bulletin, 81*(11), 891–895.

Kaplowitz, P. (2009). Treatment of central precocious puberty. *Current Opinion in Endocrinology, Diabetes, and Obesity, 16*(1), 31–36.

Kaplowitz, P., & Oberfield, S. (1999). Reexamination of the age limit for defining when puberty is precocious in girls in the United States. *Pediatrics, 104*(4), 936–941.

Koch, W. (2007). Va. 1st state to express "regret" over slavery. *USA Today.* Retrieved from http://www.usatoday.com/

Kuhn, T. (1996). *The structure of scientific revolutions* (3rd ed.). Chicago, IL: University of Chicago Press.

Lee, C. M. (2007). From clinical trials to professional training: A graduate course in evidence-based interventions for children, youth, and families. *Training in Education and Professional Psychology, 1*(3), 215–223.

Lidderdale, M. (2002). Practitioner training for counseling lesbian, gay, and bisexual clients. *Journal of Lesbian Studies, 6*(3/4), 111–120.

Marton, I., Wiener, J., Rogers, M., Moore, C., & Tannock, R. (2009). Empathy and social perspective taking in children with attention-deficit/hyperactivity disorder. *Journal of Abnormal Child Psychology, 37*(1), 107–118.

McDowell, M., Brody, D., & Hughes, J. (2007). Has age at menarche changed? Results from the national health and nutrition examination survey (NHANES) 1999-2004. *The Journal of Adolescent Health: Official Publication of the Society for Adolescent Medicine, 40*(3), 227–231.

McMillen, J., Morris, L., & Sherraden, M. (2004). Ending social work's grudge match: Problems versus strengths. *Families in Society, 85*(3), 317–325.

Mistry, R., Brown, C., Chow, K., & Collins, G. (2012). Increasing the complexity of young adolescents' beliefs about poverty and inequality: Results of an 8th grade social studies curriculum intervention. *Journal of Youth and Adolescence, 41*(6), 704–716. doi:10.1007/ s10964-011-9699-6

Monette, D., Sullivan, T., & DeJong, C. (2005). *Applied social research: A tool for the human services* (6th ed.). Belmont, CA: Brooks/Cole.

Myers, D. (2009). *Social psychology* (8th ed.). New York: McGraw-Hill.

Myers, S. (1996). An interactive model of religiosity inheritance: The importance of family context. *American Sociological Review, 61*(5), 858–866.

Nickerson, R. (1998). Confirmation bias: A ubiquitous phenomenon in many guises. *Review of General Psychology, 2*(2), 175–220.

Office of the Press Secretary. (2010). *Remarks by the president in state of the union address.* Retrieved July 24, 2012, from http:// www.whitehouse.gov/the-press-office/ remarks-president-state-union-address

Orchowski, L., Evangelista, N., & Probst, D. (2010). Enhancing supervisee reflectivity in clinical supervision: A case study illustration. *Psychotherapy: Theory, Research, Practice, Training, 47*(1), 51–67.

Overholser, J. (1995). Elements of the Socratic method: IV Disavowal of knowledge. *Psychotherapy: Theory, Research, Practice, Training, 32*(2), 283–292.

Peebles, M. J. (2012). *Beginnings: The art and science of planning psychotherapy.* Hillsdale, NJ: The Analytic Press.

Pica, M. (1998). The ambiguous nature of clinical training and its impact on the development of student clinicians. *Psychotherapy, 35*(3), 361–365.

Prochaska, J. O., & Norcross, J. C. (2010). *Systems of psychotherapy: A Transtheoretical approach.* Australia: Thompson Brooks/Cole.

Rassin, E., Eerland, A., & Kuijpers, I. (2010). Let's find the evidence: An analogue study of confirmation bias in criminal investigations. *Journal of Investigative Psychology and Offender Profiling, 7*(3), 231–246. doi:10.1002/jip.126

Scurfield, R., & Mackey, D. (2001). Racism, trauma and positive aspects of exposure to race-related experiences: Assessment and treatment implications. *Journal of Ethnic & Cultural Diversity in Social Work: Innovation in Theory, Research & Practice, 10*(1), 23–47.

Seligman, M., & Csikszentmihalyi, M. (2000). Positive psychology: An introduction. *American Psychologist, 55*(1), 5–14.

Sharkey, P. (2009). The intergenerational transmission of context. *American Journal of Sociology, 114*(4), 931–969.

Steele, C. (1997). A threat in the air: How stereotypes shape intellectual identity and performance. *American Psychologist, 52*(6), 613–629.

Steele, C. (2012). Conclusion: Extending and applying stereotype threat research: A brief essay. In M. Inzlicht & T. Schmader (Eds.), *Stereotype threat: Theory, process, and application* (pp. 297–303). New York: Oxford University Press.

Stein, J. (1964). *Fiddler on the roof.* New York: Crown.

Sternberg, R. (1997). What does it mean to be smart? *Educational Leadership, 54*(6), 20–24.

Sternberg, R., & Grigorenko, E. (1999). Myths in psychology and education regarding the gene-environment debate. *Teachers College Record, 100*(3), 536–553.

Sun, K. (2006). The legal definition of hate crime and the hate offender's distorted cognitions. *Issues in Mental Health Nursing, 27*(6), 597–604.

Watson, J. (1930). *Behaviorism* (Rev. ed.). Chicago, IL: University of Chicago Press.

Whitley, B. (1996). *Principles of research in behavioral science.* Mountain View, CA: Mayfield Publishing.

CHAPTER 4

Abbassi, V. (1998). Growth and normal puberty. *Pediatrics, 102*(2), 507.

American Academy of Pediatrics. (2001). Maternal phenylketonuria. *Pediatrics, 107*(2), 427–428.

American Psychiatric Association. (2000). *Diagnostic and statistical manual of mental disorders* (4th ed.). Washington, DC: Author.

Arias, E. (2011). United States life tables, 2007. *National Vital Statistics Reports, 59*(9). Retrieved April 8, 2013, from http://www.cdc.gov/nchs/data/nvsr/nvsr59/ nvsr59_09.pdf

Ashford, J. B., LeCroy, C. W., & Lortie, K. L. (2006). *Human behavior in the social environment: A multidimensional approach* (3rd ed.). Belmont, CA: Thomson/ Brooks Cole.

Ashworth, J., & Heyndels, B. (2007). Selection bias and peer effects in team sports: The effect of age grouping one markings of German soccer players. *Journal of Sports Economics, 8,* 355–377.

Associated Press. (2009, May 21). *Boy who fled chemo may be heading to Mexico.* Retrieved on April 29 2013, from http://www.nbcnews.com/id/30824587/ns/health-childrens_health/t/teen-who-fled-chemo-may-be-heading-mexico/#.UX60pKL2_Ig

Belsky, J., Steinberg, L., Houts, R. M., & Halpern-Felsher, B. (2010). The development of reproductive strategy in females: Early maternal harshness ➜ Earlier menarche ➜ Increased sexual risk taking. *Developmental Psychology, 46*(1), 120–128. doi:10.1037/a0015549

Bhattacharya, S., Harrild, K., Mollison, J., Wordsworth, S., Tay, C., Harrold, A., & Templeton, A. (2008). Clomifene citrate or unstimulated intrauterine insemination compared with expectant management of unexplained infertility: Pragmatic randomized controlled trial. *British Medical Journal (International Edition), 337*(7666), 387–390.

Black, R., Allen, L., Bhutta, Z., Caulfield, L., de Onis, M., Ezzati, M., & Rivera, J. (2008). Maternal and child undernutrition: Global and regional exposures and health consequences. *Lancet, 371*(9608), 243–260.

Boden, J., Fergusson, D., & Horwood, L. (2011). Age of menarche and psychosocial outcomes in a New Zealand birth cohort. *Journal of the American Academy of Child & Adolescent Psychiatry, 50*(2), 132–140. doi:10.1016/j.jaac.2010.11.007

Budge, H., Stephenson, T., & Symonds, M. (2007). Maternal nutrient restriction is not equivalent to maternal biological stress. *Current Drug Targets, 8*(8), 888–893.

Centers for Disease Control. (2012). *Epidemiological slide set on adolescents and young adults.* Retrieved from www.cdc.gov/hiv/graphics/adolesnt.htm

Chamberlain, P. (2003). *Treating chronic juvenile offenders: Advances made through the Oregon multidimensional treatment foster care model.* Washington, DC: American Psychological Association.

Chung, W. (2004). *Teratogens and their effects.* Retrieved April 4, 2013, from http://www.columbia.edu/itc/hs/medical/humandev/2004/Chpt23-Teratogens.pdf

Dishion, T. J., Andrews, D. W., & Crosby, L. (1995). Antisocial boys and their friends in early adolescence: Relationship characteristics, quality, and interactional process. *Child Development, 66*, 139–151.

Doweiko, H. E. (2009). *Concepts of chemical dependency* (7th ed.). Belmont, CA: Brooks/Cole Cengage Learning.

Feldman, J. (2007). The effect of support expectations on prenatal attachment: An evidence-based approach for intervention in an adolescent population. *Child & Adolescent Social Work Journal, 24*(3), 209–234.

The Fertility Institutes. (2012). *Sex selection and family balancing: A leading world center for 100% PGD gender selection.* Retrieved from http://www.fertility-docs.com/fertility_gender.phtml

Flaherty, E. (2006). Analysis of caretaker histories in abuse: Comparing initial histories with subsequent confessions. *Child Abuse & Neglect: The International Journal, 30*(7), 789–798.

Friedman, S., Heneghan, A., & Rosenthal, M. (2009). Characteristics of women who do not seek prenatal care and implications for prevention. *Journal of Obstetric, Gynecologic, & Neonatal Nursing: Clinical Scholarship for the Care of Women, Childbearing Families, & Newborns, 38*(2), 174–181.

Guy, S. (2009, September 1). British couples can choose baby's sex in US clinic. *BioNews.* Retrieved from http://www.bionews.org.uk/page_47648.asp

Hamilton, B. E., & Ventura, S. J. (2012, April). *Birth rates for U.S. Teenagers reach historic lows for all age and ethic groups* (HCHS Data Brief No. 89). Retrieved October 19, 2012, from http://www.cdc.gov/nchs/data/databriefs/db89.pdf

Harden, K., Cowan, P., Velasquez-Mieyer, P., & Patton, S. (2007). Effects of life style intervention and metformin on weight management and markers of metabolic syndrome in obese adolescents. *Journal of the AmericanAcademy of Nurse Practitioners, 19*(7), 368–377.

Hindin, S., & Zelinski, E. (2012). Extended practice and aerobic exercise interventions benefit untrained cognitive outcomes in older adults: A meta-analysis. *Journal of the American Geriatrics Society, 60*(1), 136–141. doi:10.1111/j.1532-5415.2011.03761.x

Hobson, W. (2009). *"Playing god" with your baby's gender?* Retrieved from http://www.examiner.com/x-15850-Charlotte-Baptist-Examiner~y2009m8d24-Playing-God-with-your-babys-gender

Hoffman, S. (2006). *By the numbers: The public costs of teen childbearing.* Washington, DC: National Campaign to Prevent Teen Pregnancy.

Horon, I., & Cheng, D. (2001). Enhanced surveillance for pregnancy-associated mortality—Maryland, 1993-1998. *Journal of the American Medical Association, 285*(11), 1455–1459.

International Human Genome Sequencing Consortium. *A brief guide to genomics fact sheet.* Retrieved April 29, 2013, from http://www.genome.gov/18016863

Jaudes, P., & Diamond, L. (1985). The handicapped child and child abuse. *Child Abuse & Neglect, 9*(3), 341–347.

Joinson, C., Heron, J., Lewis, G., Croudace, T., & Araya, R. (2011). Timing of menarche and joinson depressive symptoms in adolescent girls from a UK cohort. *The British Journal of Psychiatry, 198*(1), 17–23. doi:10.1192/bjp.bp.110.080861

Kalb, C., & Springen, K. (2004, January 26). Brave new babies. *Newsweek*, pp. 44–52.

Kaplowitz, P. (2009). Treatment of central precocious puberty. *Current Opinion in Endocrinology, Diabetes, and Obesity, 16*(1), 31–36.

Kerr, D., Leve, L., & Chamberlain, P. (2009). Pregnancy rates among juvenile justice girls in two randomized controlled trials of multidimensional treatment foster care. *Journal of Consulting and Clinical Psychology, 77*(3), 588–593.

Lanza, S. T., & Collins, L. M. (2002). Pubertal timing and the onset of substance use in females during early adolescence. *Prevention Science, 3*(1), 69–82.

Lewis, M., Phillips, G., Bowser, M., DeLuca, S., Johnson, H., & Rosen, T. (2009). Cocaine-exposed infant behavior during still-face: Risk factor analyses. *American Journal of Orthopsychiatry, 79*(1), 60–70.

Mahajan, S. D., Singh, S., Shah, P., Gupta, N., & Kochupillai, N. (2004). Effect of maternal malnutrition and anemia on endocrine regulation of fetal growth. *Endocrine Research, 30*(2), 189–203.

Malina, R., Bouchard, C., & Bar-Or, O. (2004). *Growth, maturation, and physical activity* (2nd ed.). Champaign, IL: Human Kinetics.

Mandoki, M., & Sumner, G. (1991). Klinefelter syndrome: The need for early identification and treatment. *Clinical Pediatrics, 30*, 161–164.

Marcus, S. (2009). Depression during pregnancy: Rates, risks, and consequences—Motheristupdate 2008. *Canadian Journal of Clinical Pharmacology = Journal Canadien De PharmachologieClinque, 16*(1), e15–e22.

Morgan, P., Merrell, J., Rentschler, D., & Chadderton, H. (2012). Triple whammy: Women's perceptions of midlife mothering. MCN. *The American Journal of Maternal Child Nursing, 37*(3), 156–162.

National Center for Injury Prevention and Control, Centers for Disease Control and Prevention. (2006). Retrieved from www.cdc.gov/ncipc/wisqars

National Institutes of Health. (2012). *What is DNA?* Retrieved July 26, 2012, from http://ghr.nlm.nih.gov/handbook/basics/dna

Nield, L., Cakan, N., & Kamat, D. (2007). A practical approach to precocious puberty. *Clinical Pediatrics, 46*(4), 299–306.

Perera, F. (2008). Children are likely to suffer most from our fossil fuel addiction. *Environmental Health Perspectives, 116*(8), 987–990.

Pinyerd, B., & Zipf, W. (2005). Puberty-timing is everything. *Journal of Pediatric Nursing, 20*(2), 75–82.

Ratey, J. (2002). *A user's guide to the brain: Perception, attention, and the four theaters of the brain.* New York: Vintage Books.

Robin, L., Dittus, P., Whitaker, D., Crosby, R., Ethier, K., Mezoff, J., & Pappas-Deluca, K. (2004). Behavioral interventions to reduce incidence of HIV, STD, and pregnancy among adolescents: A decade in review. *Journal of Adolescent Health, 34*(1), 3–26.

Rogol, A. D., Clark, P. A., & Roemmich, J. N. (2000). Growth and pubertal development in children and adolescents: Effects of diet and physical activity. *American Journal of Clinical Nutrition, 72*(2), 521S–528S.

Rowe, D. C. (2000). Environmental and genetic influences on pubertal development: Evolutionary life history traits. In J. L. Rodgers, D. C. Rowe, & W. B. Miller (Eds.), *Genetic influences on human fertility and sexuality: Theoretical and empirical contributions from the biological and behavioral sciences* (pp. 147–168). Boston: Kluwer Academic.

Rowe, D. C. (2002). On genetic variation in menarche and age at first sexual intercourse: A critique of the Belsky-Draper hypothesis. *Evolution and Human Behavior, 23*, 365–372.

Russell-Mayhew, S. (2007). Eating disorders and obesity as social justice issues: Implications for research and practice. *Journal for Social Action in Counseling and Psychology, 1*, 1–13.

Santrock, J. (2008). *A topical approach to life-span development* (4th ed.). New York: McGraw-Hill.

Santrock, J. (2011). *A topical approach to life-span development* (6th ed.). New York: McGraw-Hill.

Satir, V. (1967). *Conjoint family therapy.* Palo Alto, CA: Science and Behavior Books.

Schultz, K. A., & Curnow, C. (1988). Peak performance and age among super athletes: Track and field, swimming, baseball, tennis, and golf. *Journal of Gerontology, 43*(5), 113–120.

Shaffer, D., & Kipp, K. (2009). *Developmental psychology: Child and adolescence* (8th ed.). Belmont, CA: Wadsworth.

Simons, R. L., Simons, L. G., & Wallace, E. (2004). *Families, delinquency, and crime: Linking society's most basic institution to antisocial behavior.* Los Angeles: Roxbury.

Simons-Morton, B. (2004). Prospective association of peer influence, school engagement, drinking expectancies, and parent expectations with drinking initiation among sixth graders. *Addict Behavior, 29*, 299–309.

Stanton, B., Li, X., Galbraith, J., Cornick, G., Feigelman, S., Kaljee, L., & Zhou, Y. (2000). Parental underestimates of adolescent risk behavior: A randomized, controlled trial of a parental monitoring intervention. *Journal of Adolescent Health, 26*(1), 18–26.

Stattin, H., Kerr, M., & Skoog, T. (2011). Early pubertal timing and girls' problem behavior: Integrating two hypotheses. *Journal of Youth & Adolescence, 40*(10), 1271–1287.

Stein, R. S., & Morgan, D. (2003). *Handbook of cancer chemotherapy* (6th ed.). Philadelphia, PA: Lippincott Williams & Wilkins. (Table 21.2: Hodgkin's Disease: Incidence of stages and results of therapy. ISBN 0-7817-3629-3)

Stolee, P., Zaza, C., & Schuehlein, S. (2012). Evaluation of a volunteer-led in-home exercise program for home-bound older adults. *Work: Journal of Prevention, Assessment & Rehabilitation, 41*(3), 339–354.

Sturge-Apple, M. L., Daview, P. T., Winter, M. A., Cummings, E. M.,& Schermerhorn, A. (2008). Interparental conflict and children's school adjustment: The explanatory role of children's internal representations of interparental and parent-child relationships. *Developmental Psychology, 44*(6), 1678–1690.

Super, C. M. (1976). Environmental effects on motor development: The case of African infant precocity. *Developmental Medicine and Child Neurology, 18*(5), 561–567.

Sutcliffe, P., Dixon, S., Akehurst, R., Wilkinson, A., Shippam, A., White, S., & Caddy, C. (2009). Evaluation of surgical procedures for sex reassignment: A systematic review. *Journal of Plastic, Reconstructive & Aesthetic Surgery, 62*(3), 294–306.

Talge, N., Neal, C., & Glover, V. (2007). Antenatal maternal stress and long-term effects on child neurodevelopment: How and why? *Journal of Child Psychology and Psychiatry, 48*(3/4), 245–261.

Taylor, C. R., Alexander, G. R., & Hepworth, J. T. (2005). Clustering of U.S. Women receiving no prenatal care: Differences in pregnancy outcomes and implications for targeting interventions. *Maternal and Child Health Journal, 9*(2), 125–133.

Tither, J., & Ellis, B. (2008). Impact of fathers on daughters' age at menarche: A genetically and environmentally controlled sibling study. *Developmental Psychology, 44*(5), 1409–1420.

Topley, J., Windsor, D., & Williams, R. (2008). Behavioural, development and child protection outcomes following exposure to class A drugs in pregnancy. *Child: Care, Health and Development, 34*(1), 71–76.

Tremblay, L., & Frigon, J. (2005). The interaction role of obesity and pubertal timing on the psychosocial adjustment of adolescent girls: Longitudinal data. *International Journal of Obesity, 29*(10), 1204–1211.

Westling, E., Andrews, J. A., Hampson, S. E., & Peterson, M. (2008). Pubertal timing and substance use: The effects of gender, parental monitoring and deviant peers. *Journal of Adolescent Health, 42*, 555–563. doi:10.1016/j.jadohealth.2007.11.002

Yashon, R., & Cummings, M. (2011). *Human genetics and society* (2nd ed.). Belmont, CA: Brooks/Cole.

CHAPTER 5

Arroll, B., Macgillivray, S., Ogston, S., Reid, I., Sullivan, F., Williams, B., & Crombie, I. (2005). Efficacy and tolerability of tricyclic antidepressants and ssris compared with placebo for treatment of depression in primary care: A meta-analysis. *Annals of Family Medicine, 3*(5), 449–456. doi:10.1370/afm.349

Arsenio, W., & Lemerise, E. (2004). Aggression and moral development: integrating social information processing and moral domain models. *Child Development, 75*(4), 987–1002.

Atkinson, R., & Shiffrin, R. (1968). Human memory: A proposed system and its control processes. In K. W. Spence & J. Spence (Eds.), *Advances in the psychology of learning and motivation: Research and theory* (Vol. 2, pp. 1–35). New York: Academic Press.

Baars, B. J., & Gage, N. M. (2010). *Cognition, brain, and consciousness: Introduction to cognitive neuroscience* (2nd ed.). Boston, MA: Elsevier.

Bell, A., & D'Zurilla, T. (2009). Problem-solving therapy for depression: A meta-analysis. *Clinical Psychology Review, 29*(4), 348–353.

Carlson, N. R. (2009). *Physiology of Behavior* (10th ed.). Boston, MA: Allyn& Bacon.

Crick, N., & Dodge, K. (1994). A review and reformulation of social information-processing mechanisms in children' social adjustment. *Psychological Bulletin, 115*(1), 74–101.

de Zubicaray, G. (2006). Cognitive neuroimaging: Cognitive science out of the armchair. *Brain and Cognition, 60*(3), 272–281.

Donn, J., Mendoza, M., & Pritchard, J. (2008). *Pharmaceuticals lurking in U.S. Drinking water: AP probe found traces of meds in water supplies of 41 million Americans.* Retrieved from http://www.msnbc.msn.com/id/23503485

Dopke, C. A., Lundahl, B. W., Dunsterville, E., & Lovejoy, M. C. (2003). Interpretations of child compliance in individuals at high and low risk for child physical abuse. *Child Abuse & Neglect, 27*(3), 285–302.

Eliasmith, C. (2005). Moving beyond metaphors: Understanding the mind for what it is. In A. Brook & K. Atkins (Eds.), *Cognition and the brain: The philosophy and neuroscience movement* (pp. 131–159). New York: Cambridge University Press.

Foorman, B. (1994). The relevance of a connectionist model of reading for the great debate. *Educational Psychology Review, 6*(1), 25–47.

Gatchel, R., & Kishino, N. (2011). The biopsychosocial perspective of pain and emotion. In G. MacDonald & L. A. Jensen-Campbell (Eds.), *Social pain: Neuropsychological and health implications of loss and exclusion* (pp. 181–191). Washington, DC: American Psychological Association.

Kalat, J. (2009). *Biological psychology* (10th ed.). Belmont, CA: Thomson Wadsworth.

Kalueff, A. V., & Nutt, D. J. (2007). Role of GABA in anxiety and depression. *Depression and Anxiety, 24*(7), 495–517. doi:10.1002/da.20262

Kirsch, I., Deacon, B., Huedo-Medina, T., Scoboria, A., Moore, T., & Johnson, B. (2008). Initial severity and antidepressant benefits: A meta-analysis of data submitted to the food and drug administration. *PLosClinical Trials, 5*(2), 260–026. doi:10.1371/journal.pmed.0050045

Kolb, B., & Whishaw, I. (2009). *An introduction to brain and behavior* (3rd ed.). New York: Worth Publishing.

Lent, R., Azevedo, F. A., Andrade-Moraes, C. H., & Pinto, A. V. (2012). How many neurons do you have? Some dogmas of quantitative neuroscience under revision. *European Journal of Neuroscience, 35*(1), 1–9.

Li, L., Sun, M., Cao, P., Cai, C., Chai, X., Li, X., . . . Ren, Q. (2008). A visual prosethesis based on optic nerve stimulation: In vivo electrophysiological study in rabbits. *APCMBE 2008, IFMBE Proceedings, 19,* 54–57.

Liu, H., Potter, M., Woodworth, K., Yorks, D., Petty, C., Wozniak, J., & Biederman, J. (2011). Pharmacologic treatments for pediatric bipolar disorder: A review and meta-analysis. *Journal of the American Academy of Child & Adolescent Psychiatry, 50*(8), 749–762. doi:10.1016/j.jaac.2011.05.011

Logan, G. (2000). Information-processing theories. In *Encyclopedia of psychology* (Vol. 4, pp. 294–297). Washington, DC: American Psychological Association.

Lundahl, B. (2005). The impact of social expectations on parent and child behavior: Combining parenting goal perspectives with achievement goal theory. *Dissertation Abstracts International, 65*(9-B), 48–72.

Lundahl, B., & Burke, B. (2009). Does motivational interviewing work? A review of four meta-analyses for practitioners. *Journal of Clinical Psychology: In Session, 65,* 1232–1245.

Lundahl, B., Kunz, C., Brownell, C., Tollefson, D., & Burke, B. (2010). A meta-analysis of motivational interviewing: Twenty five years of research. *Research on Social Work Practice, 20*(2), 137–160.

MacLeod, A., Coates, E., & Hetherton, J. (2008). Increasing well-being through teaching goal-setting and planning skills: Results of a brief intervention. *Journal of Happiness Studies, 9*(2), 185–196.

Marks, D., Abramowitz, J., & Spielmans, G. (2012). Concerns about data reporting and interpretation in "efficacy and tolerability of the novel triple reuptake inhibitor amitifadine in the treatment of patients with major depressive disorder: A randomized, double-blind, placebo-controlled trial." *Journal of Psychiatric Research, 46*(5), 692–693. doi:10.1016/j.jpsychires.2012.02.002

Middleton, K., & Craig, C. (2012). A systematic literature review of PTSD among female veterans from 1990 to 2010. *Social Work in Mental Health, 10*(3), 233–252. doi:10.1080/15332985.2011.639929

Pratt, L. A., Brody, D. J., & Gu, Q. (2011). *Antidepressant use in persons aged 12 and over: United States, 2005 – 2008* (NCHS Data Brief No. 76). The Center for Disease Control and Prevention. Retrieved April 29, 2103, from: http://www.cdc.gov/nchs/data/databriefs/db76.pdf

Rakic, P. (2002). Progress: Neurogenesis in adult primate neocortex: An evaluation of the evidence. *Nature Reviews Neuroscience, 3*(1), 65–71.

Rosa-Alcázar, A., Sánchez-Meca, J., Gómez-Conesa, A., & Marín-Martínez, F. (2008). Psychological treatment of obsessive-compulsive disorder: A meta-analysis. *Clinical Psychology Review, 28*(8), 1310–1325.

Salloum, A., Sulkowski, M., Sirrine, E., & Storch, E. (2009). Overcoming barriers to using empirically supported therapies to treat childhood anxiety disorders in social work practice. *Child & Adolescent Social Work Journal, 26*(3), 259–273.

Snyder, P., & Nussbaum, P. (1999). *Clinical neuropsychology: Pocket handbook for assessment.* Washington, DC: American Psychological Association.

Stahl, S. (1997). *Stahl' essential psychopharmacology: Neuroscientific basis and practical applications.* New York: Cambridge University Press.

Stahl, S. (2008). *Stahl' essential psychopharmacology: Neuroscientific basis and practical applications* (3rd ed.). New York: Cambridge University Press.

Strominger, N. L., Demarest, R. J., & Laemle, L. (2012). *Noback's human nervous system: Structure and function.* New York: Springer.

Surprenantl, A., & Neath, I. (2009). The nine lives of short-term memory. In A. Thorn & M. Page (Eds.), *Interactions between short-term and long-term memory in the verbal domain* (pp. 16–43). New York: Psychology Press.

Tolman, R., Himle, J., Bybee, D., Abelson, J., Hoffman, J., & Van Etten-Lee, M. (2009). Impact of social anxiety disorder on employment among women receiving welfare benefits. *Psychiatric Services, 60*(1), 61–66.

Van Manen, T., Prins, P., & Emmelkamp, P. (2004). Reducing aggressive behavior in boys with a social cognitive group treatment: Results of a randomized, controlled trial. *Journal of the American Academy of Child & Adolescent Psychiatry, 43*(12), 14–78.

Verdellen, C., van de Griendt, J., Hartmann, A., & Murphy, T. (2011). European clinical guidelines for Tourette syndrome and other tic disorders. Part III: Behavioural and psychosocial interventions. *European Child & Adolescent Psychiatry, 20*(4), 197–207. doi:10.1007/s00787-011-0167-3

Wurtman, R., Hefti, F., & Melamed, E. (1980). Precursor control of neurotransmitters synthesis. *Pharmacological Reviews, 32*(4), 315–335.

CHAPTER 6

Acosta-Saavedra, L., Moreno, M., Rodríguez-Kessler, T., Luna, A., Arias-Salvatierra, D., Gómez, R., & Calderon-Aranda, E. (2011). Environmental exposure to lead and mercury in Mexican children: A real health problem. *Toxicology Mechanisms and Methods, 21*(9), 656–666.

Atchley, P., Hadlock, C., & Lane, S. (2012). Stuck in the 70s: The role of social norms in distracted driving. *Accident Analysis and Prevention, 48,* 279–284. doi:10.1016/j.aap.2012.01.026

Augustin, T., Glass, T., James, B., & Schwartz, B. (2008). Neighborhood psychosocial hazards and cardiovascular disease: The Baltimore Memory Study. *American Journal of Public Health, 98*(9), 1664–1670.

Baverstock, K., & Williams, D. (2006). The Chernobyl accident 20 years on: An assessment of the health consequences and the international response. *Environmental Health Perspectives, 114*(9), 1312–1317.

Benjamin, G. (2008). Reducing unhealthy behaviors: where do we start? *American Journal of Public Health, 98*(9, Suppl.1), S138

Brandt, A. (2007). *The cigarette century: The rise, fall and deadly persistence of the product that defined America.* New York: Basic Books.

Bromet, E. (2012). Mental health consequences of the Chernobyl disaster. *Journal of Radiological Protection: Official Journal of the Society for Radiological Protection, 32*(1), N71–N75.

Brugge, D., Durant, J., & Rioux, C. (2007). Near-highway pollutants in motor vehicle exhaust: A review of epidemiologic evidence of cardiac and pulmonary health risks. *Environmental Health: A Global Access Science Source, 6,* 23–12.

Buchmann, W. (1997). Adherence: A matter of self-efficacy and power. *Journal of Advanced Nursing, 26*(1), 132–137.

Carpenter, C. (2010). A meta-analysis of the effectiveness of health belief model variables in predicting behavior. *Health Communication, 25*(8), 661–669.

Centers for Disease Control and Prevention. (2011a). *Fact sheet: Health disparities in coronary heart disease and stroke.* Retrieved October 20, 2012, from http://www.cdc.gov/minorityhealth/reports/CHDIR11/FactSheets/CHDStroke.pdf

Centers for Disease Control and Prevention. (2011b). *Fact sheet: Leading causes of death.* Retrieved April 13, 2013, from http://www.cdc.gov/nchs/fastats/lcod.htm

Centers for Disease Control and Prevention. (2012). *Infant mortality statistics from the 2008 period linked birth/infant death data set.* Retrieved October 20, 2012, from http://www.cdc.gov/nchs/data/nvsr/nvsr60/nvsr60_05.pdf

Centers for Population Health and Health Disparities. (2007). *Cells to society: Overcoming health disparities.* Retrieved July 10, 2013, from http://cancercontrol.cancer.gov/populationhealthcenters/cphhd/documents/CPHHD_report.pdf

Chen, A., Huang, Z., Wan, X., Deng, W., Wu, J., Li, L., & Li, Y. (2012). Attitudes toward diabetes affect maintenance of drug-free remission in patients with newly diagnosed type 2 diabetes after short-term continuous subcutaneous insulin infusion treatment. *Diabetes Care, 35*(3), 474–481.

Cholowski, K., & Cantwell, R. (2007). Predictors of medication compliance among older heart failure patients. *International Journal of Older People Nursing, 2*(4), 250–262. doi:10.1111/j.1748-3743.2007.00082.x

Cutt, H., Giles-Corti, B., Knuiman, M., & Burke, V. (2007). Dog ownership, health and physical activity: A critical review of the literature. *Health & Place, 13*(1), 261–272.

Danielson, A. L. (2003). Emotional status and social support relations to immune status in women co-infected with HIV and HPV: Preliminary evidence for beneficial psychosocial effects of a CBSM intervention tailored for this population. *Dissertation Abstracts International, 63*(11-B), 5510.

Ellsberg, M., Jansen, H., Heise, L., Watts, C., & Garcia-Moreno, C. (2008). Intimate partner violence and women's physical and mental health in the WHO multi-country study on women's health and domestic violence: An observational study. *Lancet, 371*(9619), 1165–1172.

Felder, S., & Zhang, J. (2006). The gender longevity gap: Explaining the difference between singles and couples. *Journal of Population Economics, 19*(3), 543–557.

Fields, J. (2008). *Risky lessons: Sex education and social inequality.* New Jersey: Rutgers University Press.

Fox, J. A., & Zawitz, M. W. (2007). *Homicide trends in the U.S.: Intimate homicide, bureau of justice statistics.* Retrieved from http://bjs.ojp.usdoj.gov/content/homicide/intimates.cfm.

Fraze, J., Uhrig, J., Davis, K., Taylor, M., Lee, N., Spoeth, S., & McElroy, L. (2009). Applying core principles to the design and evaluation of the take charge. "Take the test" campaign: What worked and lessons learned. *Public Health, 123*(Suppl. 1), e23–e30.

Gehler, S., & Browne, T. (2006). *Handbook of health and social work.* New Jersey: Wiley and Sons.

Gern, J., Reardon, C., Hoffjan, S., Nicolae, D., Li, Z., Roberg, K., . . . Lemanske, R. (2004). Effects of dog ownership and genotype on immune development and atopy in infancy. *The Journal of Allergy and Clinical Immunology, 113*(2), 307–314.

Goldman, L. (2005). Child health and the environment: A review of the evidence. *Zero to Three, 26*(2), 11–19.

Grande, G., Romppel, M., & Barth, J. (2012). Association between type D personality and prognosis in patients with cardiovascular diseases: A systematic review and meta-analysis. *Annals of Behavioral Medicine, 43*(3), 299–310. doi:10.1007/s12160-011-9339-0

Grellet, L. L., & Faix, A. A. (2011). What exactly are we trying to cure when we treat someone for erectile dysfunction? *Sexologies: European Journal of Sexology and Sexual Health/ Revue Européenne De Sexologie Et De Santé Sexuelle, 20*(1), 8–11. doi:10.1016/j.sexol.2010.12.001

Haukkala, A., Konttinen, H., Laatikainen, T., Kawachi, I., & Uutela, A. (2010). Hostility, anger control, and anger expression as predictors of cardiovascular disease. *Psychosomatic Medicine, 72*(6), 556–562. Doi:10.1097/PSY.0b013e3181dbab87

Humphreys, C. (2007). A health inequalities perspective on violence against women. *Health & Social Care in the Community, 15*(2), 120–127.

Irish, L., Kobayashi, I., & Delahanty, D. (2010). Long-term physical health consequences of childhood sexual abuse: A meta-analytic review. *Journal of Pediatric Psychology, 35*(5), 450–461.

Jargin, S. (2011). Validity of thyroid cancer incidence data following the chernobyl accident. *Health Physics, 101*(6), 754–757.

Jorm, A. (2005). Social networks and health: It's time for an intervention trial. *Journal of Epidemiology and Community Health, 59*(7), 537–538.

Kalichman, S., Eaton, L., & Cherry, C. (2010). "There is no proof that HIV causes AIDS": AIDS denialism beliefs among people living with HIV/AIDS. *Journal of Behavioral Medicine, 33*(6), 432–440. doi:10.1007/s10865-010-9275-7

Karadžinska-Bislimovska, J., Minov, J., Stoleski, S., Mijakoski, D., Risteska-Kuc, S., & Milkovska, S. (2010). Environmental and occupational health risks among agricultural workers living in a rural community near petroleum refinery and motorway in Skopje region. *Arhiv Za Higijenu Rada I Toksikologiju, 61*(4), 415–424.

Knight, S., & Edwards, V. (2008). In the company of wolves: The physical, social, and psychological benefits of dog ownership. *Journal of Aging & Health, 20*(4), 437–455.

Korde, L., Zujewski, J., Kamin, L., Giordano, S., Domchek, S., Anderson, W., . . . Cardoso, F. (2010). Multidisciplinary meeting on male breast cancer: Summary and research recommendations. *Journal of Clinical Oncology, 28*(12), 2114–2122.

Lee, R., Middleton, D., Caldwell, K., Dearwent, S., Jones, S., Lewis, B., & Watters, M. (2009). A review of events that expose children to elemental mercury in the United States. *Environmental Health Perspectives, 117*(6), 871–878.

Lerner, B. (2011). Drunk driving, distracted driving, moralism, and public health. *The New England Journal of Medicine, 365*(10), 879–881. doi:10.1056/NEJMp1106640

Littrell, J. (2008). The mind-body connection: Not just a theory anymore. *Social Work in Health Care, 46,* 17–37.

Lopez, C., Antoni, M., Fekete, E., & Penedo, F. (2012). Ethnic identity and perceived stress in HIV+ minority women: The role of coping self-efficacy and social support. *International Journal of Behavioral Medicine, 19*(1), 23–28. doi:10.1007/s12529-010-9121-x

Lu, L. (1997). Social support, reciprocity, and well-being. *Journal of Social Psychology, 137*(5), 618–628.

Luker, K. (2006). *When sex goes to school: Warring views on—and sex education—since the sixties.* New York: Norton and Company.

Lundahl, B., Kunz, C., Brownell, C., Tollefson, D., & Burke, B. (2010). A meta-analysis of motivational interviewing: Twenty-five years of empirical studies. *Research Social Work Practice, 20,* 137–160.

Macy, R., Ferron, J., & Crosby, C. (2009). Partner violence and survivors' chronic health problems: Informing social work practice. *Social Work, 54*(1), 29–43.

McCarthy, B. (2002). Sexual secrets, trauma, and dysfunction. *Journal of Sex & Marital Therapy, 28*(4), 353–359.

McConnell, R., Berhane, K., Molitor, J., Gilliland, F., Kunzli, N., Thorne, P., . . . Peters, J. (2006). Dog ownership enhances symptomatic responses to air pollution in children with asthma. *Environmental Health Perspectives, 114*(12), 1910–1915.

McGarvey, E., Clavet, G., Johnson, J., Butler, A., Cook, K., & Pennino, B. (2003). Cancer screening practices and attitudes: Comparison of low-income women in three ethnic groups. *Ethnicity & Health, 8*(1), 71–82.

Meissner, K., Distel, H., & Mitzdorf, U. (2007). Evidence for placebo effects on physical but not on biochemical outcome parameters: A review of clinical trials. *BMC Medicine, 5,* 3–11.

Milhausen, R., DiClemente, R., Lang, D., Spitalnick, J., Sales, J., & Hardin, J. (2008). Frequency of sex after an intervention to decrease sexual risk-taking among African-American adolescent girls: Results of a randomized, controlled clinical trial. *Sex Education, 8*(1), 47–57. doi:10.1080/14681810701811803

Miller, L. J. (1991). Clinical strategies for the use of psychotropic drugs during pregnancy. *Psychiatric Medicine, 9*(2), 275–298.

Miller, W., & Rollnick, S. (2013). *Motivational interviewing: Helping people change* (3rd ed.). New York: Guilford Press.

National Coalition Against Domestic Violence. (2007). *Domestic violence facts.* Retrieved from http://www.ncadv.org/files/DomesticViolenceFactSheet(National).pdf

National Institutes of Health. (2007). *Two kinds of stroke.* Retrieved August 01, 2012, from http://www.nlm.nih.gov/medlineplus/magazine/issues/summer07/articles/summer07pg6.html

Neafsey, P. J., Strickler, Z., Shellman, J., & Chartier, V. (2002). An interactive technology approach to educate older adults about drug interactions arising from over-the-counter self-medication practices. *Public Health Nursing, 19*(4), 255–262.

Nimer, J., & Lundahl, B. (2007). Animal assisted therapy: A meta-analysis. *Anthrozoology, 20*(3), 225–238.

O'Donovan, A., & Hughes, B. (2008). Factors that moderate the effect of laboratory-based social support on cardiovascular reactivity to stress. *International Journal of Psychology & Psychological Therapy, 8*(1), 85–102.

Orel, N., Stelle, C., Watson, W., & Bunner, B. (2010). No one is immune: A community education partnership addressing HIV/AIDS and older adults. *Journal of Applied Gerontology, 29*(3), 352–370.

Owen, C., Nightingale, C., Rudnicka, A., Ekelund, U., McMinn, A., Sluijs, E., & Whincup, P. (2010). Family dog ownership and levels of physical activity in childhood: Findings from the child heart and health study in England. *American Journal of Public Health, 100*(9), 1669–1671.

Rollnick, S., Miller, W., & Butler, C. (2008). *Motivational interviewing in healthcare.* New York: Guilford Press.

Palermo, T., Riley, C., & Mitchell, B. (2008). Daily functioning and quality of life in children with sickle cell disease pain: Relationship with family and neighborhood socioeconomic distress. *The Journal of Pain, 9*(9), 833–840.

Peterson, J. (2011). The case for connection: Spirituality and social support for women living with HIV/AIDS. *Journal of Applied Communication Research, 39*(4), 352–369. doi:10.1080/00909882.2011.608700

Poobalan, A., Pitchforth, E., Imamura, M., Tucker, J., Philip, K., Spratt, J., . . . van Teijlingen, E. (2009). Characteristics of effective interventions in improving young people's sexual health: A review of reviews. *Sex Education, 9*(3), 319–336. doi:10.1080/14681810903059185

Price, L. H., Kao, H., Burgers, D. E., Carpenter, L. L., & Tyrka, A. R. (2012). Telomeres and early-life stress: An overview. *Biological Psychiatry, 73*(1), 15–23. doi:10.1016/j.biopsych.2012.06.025

Puhl, A., Reinhart, C., Rok, E., & Injeyan, H. (2011). An examination of the observed placebo effect associated with the treatment of low back pain—a systematic review. *Pain Research & Management, 16*(1), 45–52.

Remnick D. (1981, June 26). *Washington Post,* Friday.

Riley, G. A., & Baah-Odoom, D. (2012). Belief in a just world, generalized self-efficacy and stigma may contribute to unsafe sexual intentions via a reduced perception of vulnerability to HIV/AIDS amongst young people in Ghana. *AIDS Care, 24*(5), 642–648. doi:10.1080/09540121.2011.630348

Rosenstock, I., Strecher, V., & Becker, M. (1988). Social learning theory and the health belief model. *Health Education Quarterly, 15*(2), 175–183.

Ruppar, T. (2010). Randomized pilot study of a behavioral feedback intervention to improve medication adherence in older adults with hypertension. *Journal of Cardiovascular Nursing, 25*(6), 470–479.

Salmon, J., Timperio, A., Chu, B., & Veitch, J. (2010). Dog ownership, dog walking, and children's and parents' physical activity. *Research Quarterly for Exercise and Sport, 81*(3), 264–271.

Schwartz, C., Keyl, P., Marcum, J., & Bode, R. (2009). Helping others shows differential benefits on health and well-being for male and female teens. *Journal of Happiness Studies, 10*(4), 431–448.

Segerstrom, S. C., & Miller, G. E. (2004). Psychological stress and the human immune system: A meta-analytic study of 30 years of inquiry. *Psychological Bulletin, 130*(4), 601–630. doi:10.1037/0033-2909.130.4.601

Ship, A. (2010). The most primary of care—talking about driving and distraction. *The New England Journal of Medicine, 362*(23), 2145–2147.

Shivpuri, S., Gallo, L., Mills, P., Matthews, K., Elder, J., & Talavera, G. (2011). Trait anger, cynical hostility and inflammation in Latinas: Variations by anger type? *Brain, Behavior, & Immunity, 25*(6), 1256–1263. doi:10.1016/j.bbi.2011.04.016

Springer, K. (2009). Childhood physical abuse and midlife physical health: Testing a multi-pathway life course model. *Social Science & Medicine, 69*(1), 138–146.

Suls, J., & Bunde, J. (2005). Anger, anxiety, and depression as risk factors for cardiovascular disease: The problems and implications of overlapping affective dispositions. *Psychological Bulletin, 131*(2), 260–300.

Tanner-Smith, E., & Brown, T. (2010). Evaluating the health belief model: A critical review of studies predicting mammographic and pap screening. *Social Theory & Health, 8*(1), 95–125.

Veugelers, P., Sithole, F., Zhang, S., & Muhajarine, N. (2008). Neighborhood characteristics in relation to diet, physical activity and overweight of Canadian children. *International Journal of Pediatric Obesity, 3*(3), 152–159. doi:10.1080/17477160801970278

Wang, Y., Zhang, W., Lesch, M., Horrey, W., Chen, C., & Wu, S. (2009). Changing drivers' attitudes towards mobile phone use through participative simulation testing and feedback. *Injury Prevention, 15*(6), 384–389.

Warnecke, R., Oh, A., Breen, N., Gehlert, S., Paskett, E., Tucker, K., . . . Hiatt, R. (2008). Approaching health disparities from a population perspective: The national institutes of health centers for population health and health disparities. *American Journal of Public Health, 98*(9), 1608–1615.

Weeks, D. (2002). Sex for the mature adult: Health, self-esteem and countering ageist stereotypes. *Sexual & Relationship Therapy, 17*(3), 231–240.

Whitehead, D., Perkins-Porras, L., Strike, P., Magid, K., & Steptoe, A. (2007). Cortisol awakening response is elevated in acute coronary syndrome patients with type-d personality. *Journal of Psychosomatic Research, 62*(4), 419–425.

Wringe, A., Roura, M., Urassa, M., Busza, J., Athanas, V., & Zaba, B. (2009). Doubts, denial and divine intervention: Understanding delayed attendance and poor retention rates at a HIV treatment programme in rural Tanzania. *AIDS Care, 21*(5), 632–637.

Wu, Q., Chen, H., & Xu, X. (2012). Violence as a risk factor for postpartum depression in mothers: A meta-analysis. *Archives of Women's Mental Health, 15*(2), 107–114. doi:10.1007/s00737-011-0248-9

Young, K., Salmon, P., & Cornelissen, M. (2012). Distraction-induced driving error: An on-road examination of the errors made by distracted and undistracted drivers. *Accident Analysis and Prevention, 58*, 218–225. doi:10.1016/j.aap.2012.06.001

Zinzow, H., Grubaugh, A., Monnier, J., Suffoletta-Maierle, S., & Frueh, B. (2007). Trauma among female veterans: A critical review. *Trauma, Violence & Abuse, 8*(4), 384–400.

CHAPTER 7

Abramowitz, J., Deacon, B., & Whiteside, S. (2011). *Exposure therapy for anxiety: Principles and practice.* New York: Guilford Press.

Advisory Committee on Student Financial Assistance. (2012). *Pathways to success: Integrating learning with life and work to increase national college completion.* A report to the U.S. Congress and Secretary of Education.

Austin, E. J., Deary, I. J., Whiteman, M. C., Fowkes, F. R., Pedersen, N. L., Rabbitt, P., & McInnes, L. (2002). Relationships between ability and personality: Does intelligence contribute positively to personal and social adjustment? *Personality & Individual Differences, 32*(8), 1391–1411.

Bandura, A. (1977). *Social learning theory.* Englewood Cliffs, NJ: PrenticeHall.

Boake, C. (2002). From the Binet-Simon to the Wechsler-Bellevue: Tracing the history of intelligence testing. *Journal of Clinical and Experimental Neuropsychology, 24*(3), 383–405.

Clark, T., Smith, J., Raphael, D., Jackson, C., Denny, S., Fleming, T., & Crengle, S. (2010). Kicked out of school and suffering: The health needs of alternative education youth in New Zealand. *Youth Studies Australia, 29*(4), 10–17.

Coalition for Evidence-Based Policy. (2008). *A new bipartisan initiative for U.S. Social programs: Evidence-based reforms are key to rapid progress in education, poverty reduction, crime prevention, and other areas.* Washington, DC: Author.

Elliott, R. (1988). Tests, abilities, race, and conflict. *Intelligence, 12*(4), 333–350.

Forehand, R., & Long, N. (2010). *Parenting the strong-willed child: The clinically proven five-week program for parents of two- to six-year-olds* (3rd ed.). New York: McGraw-Hill.

Furnham, A., & Christoforou, I. (2007). Personality traits, emotional intelligence and multiple happiness. *North American Journal of Psychology, 9*(3), 439–462.

Gardner, H. (1999). *Intelligence reframed: Multiple intelligences for the 21st century.* New York: Basic Books.

Jones, P. W. (1998). Globalisation and internationalism: Democratic prospects for world education. *Comparative Education, 34,* 143–155.

Kaiser, J., Snyder, T. D., & Rogers, C. S. (1995). Adult choice of toys affects children's prosocial and anti-social behavior. *Early Child Development and Care, 111,* 181–193.

Lundahl, B., Risser, H., & Lovejoy, M. (2006). A meta-analysis of parent training: Moderators and follow-up effects. *Clinical Psychology Review, 26*(1), 86–104.

McGrew, K. S. (2005). The Cattell-Horn-Carroll theory of cognitive abilities: Past, present, and future. In D. P. Flanagan, J. L. Genshaft, & P. L. Harrison (Eds.), *Contemporary intellectual assessment: Theories, tests, and issues* (pp. 136–182). New York: Guilford.

Murdoch, S. (2007). *IQ: A smart history of a failed idea.* Hoboken, NJ: Wiley.

Nilholm, C. (1999). The zone of proximal development. A comparison of children with Down syndrome and typical children. *Journal of Intellectual and Developmental Disability, 24,* 265–279.

Peebles, M. J. (2012). *Beginnings: The art and science of planning psychotherapy.* Hillsdale, NJ: The Analytic Press.

Poehner, M. (2010). *Dynamic assessment: A Vygotskianapproach to understanding and promoting L2 development.* Berlin, CA: Springer.

Rego, A., & Pina E Cunha, M. (2009). Do the opportunities for learning and personal development lead to happiness? It depends on work-family conciliation. *Journal of Occupational Health Psychology, 14*(3), 334–348. doi:10.1037/a0014248

Reynolds, C. R., & Kamphaus, R. W. (2003). *Handbook of psychological and educational assessment of children: intelligence, aptitude, and achievement.* New York: Guilford Press.

Reynolds, C. R., & Suzuki, L. A. (2013). Bias in psychological assessment: An empirical review and recommendations. In J. R. Graham, J. A. Naglieri, & I. B. Weiner (Eds.), *Handbook of psychology. Vol 10: Assessment psychology* (2nd ed., pp. 82–113). Hoboken, NJ: John Wiley & Sons Inc.

Santrock, J. W. (2008). *Life-span development* (8th ed.). Boston, MA: McGraw-Hill.

Shaffer, D., & Kipp, K. (2009). *Developmental psychology: Child and adolescence* (8th ed.). Belmont, CA: Wadsworth.

Sjöberg, L. (2008). Emotional intelligence and life adjustment. In J. C. Cassady & M. A. Eissa (Eds.), *Emotional intelligence: Perspectives on educational & positive psychology* (pp. 169–184). New York: Peter Lang Publishing.

Sternberg, R. J. (Eds.). (2000). *Handbook of intelligence.* Cambridge: Cambridge University Press.

Vaughan, S. (1997). *The Talking Cure.* New York: Henry Holt.

Webster-Stratton, C., & Reid, M. (2010). The incredible years parents, teachers, and children training series: A multifaceted treatment approach for young children with conduct disorders. In J. Weisz & A. Kazdin (Eds.), *Evidence-based psychotherapies for children and adolescents* (2nd ed., pp. 194–210). New York: Guilford Press.

Wechsler, D. (2003). *Wechsler intelligence scale for children–fourth edition (WISC-IV).* San Antonio, TX: The Psychological Corporation.

CHAPTER 8

Allison, M. D., & Sabatelli, R. M. (1988). Differentiation and individuation as mediators of identity and intimacy in adolescence. *Journal of Adolescent Research, 3,* 1–16.

Andresen, P. A., & Telleen, S. L. (1992). The relationship between social support and maternal behaviors and attitudes: A meta-analytic review. *American Journal of Community Psychology, 20*(6), 753–774.

Berk, L. E. (2009). *Child Development* (8th ed.). Boston: Allyn& Bacon.

Bernier, A., & Meins, E. (2008). A threshold approach to understanding the origins of attachment disorganization. *Developmental Psychology, 44*(4), 969–982.

Bimmel, N., Juffer, F., van Ijzendoorn, M. H., & Bakermans-Kranenburg, M. J. (2003). Problem behavior of internationally adopted adolescents: A review and meta-analysis. *Harvard Review of Psychiatry, 11*(2), 64–77.

Borsari, B. E., & Carey., K. B. (2001). Peer influences on college drinking: A review of the research. *Journal of Substance Abuse, 13*(4), 391–424.

Bowker, J. C. W., Rubin, K. H., Burgess, K. B., Booth-LaForce, C., & Rose-Krasnor, L. (2006). Behavioral characteristics associated with stable and fluid best friendship patterns in middle childhood. *Merrill-Palmer Quarterly, 52*, 671–693.

Bowlby, J. (1969). *Attachment and Loss: Vol. 1 and 2.* New York: Basic Books.

Bowlby, J. (1989). The role of attachment in personality development and psychopathology. In S. I. Greenspan & G. H. Pollock (Eds.), *The course of life: Vol. 1. Infancy* (pp. 229–270). Madison, CT: International University Press.

Bradford, K., Barber, F. K., Olsen, J. A., Maughan, S. L., Erickson, L. D., Ward, D., & Stole, H. E. (2003). A multi-national study of interparental conflict, parenting, and adolescent functioning: South Africa, Bangladesh, China, India, Bosnia, Germany, Palestine, Columbia, and the United States. *Marriage and Family Review, 35*, 107–137.

Bronfman, E., Parsons, E., & Lyons-Ruth, K. (1999). *Atypical maternal behavior instrument for assessment and classification (AMBIANCE): Manual for coding disrupted affective communication.* Unpublished manual, Harvard University Medical School Boston.

Butterfield, O. M. (1939). *Love problems of adolescence.* New York: Columbia University.

Coie, J. D. (1990).Toward a theory of peer rejection. In S. R. Asher & J. D. Coie (Eds.), *Peer rejection in childhood* (pp. 365–401). New York: Cambridge University Press.

Cyders, M. A., Flory, K., Rainer, S., & Smith, G. T. (2008).The role of personality dispositions to risky behavior in predicting first-year college drinking. *Addiction Research Report, 104*, 193–202.

De Wolff, M., & van Ijzendoorn, M. H. (1997). Sensitivity and attachment: A meta-analysis on parental antecedents of infant attachment. *Child Development, 68*(4), 571–591.

Dishion, T. J., Ha, T., & Véronneau, M. (2012). An ecological analysis of the effects of deviant peer clustering on sexual promiscuity, problem behavior, and childbearing from early adolescence to adulthood: An enhancement of the life history framework. *Developmental Psychology, 48*(3), 703–717.

Dow, B. J., & Wood, J. (2006).*The sage handbook of gender and communication.* Thousand Oaks, CA: Sage.

Durkin, K. F., Wolfe, T. W., & Clark, G. A. (2005). College students and binge drinking: An evaluation of social learning theory. *Sociological Spectrum, 25*, 255–272.

Eisenberg, N., Cumberland, A., Guthrie, I. K., Murphy, B. C., & Shepard, S. A. (2005). Age changes in prosocial responding and moral reasoning in adolescence and early adulthood. *Journal of Research on Adolescence, 13*(3), 235–260.

Erikson, E. H. (1968). *Identity: Youth and crisis.* New York: Norton.

Fazekas, A., Senn, C. Y., & Ledgerwood, D. M. (2001). Predictors of intention to use condoms among university women: An application and extension of the theory of planned behavior. *Canadian Journal of Behavioural Science, 33*(2), 103–117.

Ferguson, C. J. (2010). A meta-analysis of normal and disordered personality across the lifespan. *Journal of Personality and Social Psychology, 98*(4), 659–667.

Ferrer-Wreder, L., Palchuk, A., Poyrazli, S., Small, M. L., &Domitrovich, C. E. (2008). Identity and adolescent adjustment. *Identity: An International Journal of Theory and Research, 8*(2), 95–105.

Fishbein, M., & Ajzen, I. (1975). *Belief, attitude, intention, and behavior: An introduction to theory and research.* Reading, MA: Addison-Wesley.

Flum, H. (1994). The evolutive style of identity formation. *Journal of Youth and Adolescence, 23*, 489–498.

Forthun, L. F., Montgomery, M. J., & Bell, N. J. (2006). Identity formation in a relational context: A person-centered analysis of troubled youth. *Identity: An International Journal of Theory and Research, 6*(2), 141–167.

Fortis, L., & Bigram, M. (1997). Risk factors exposing young children to behavior problems. *Emotional and Behavioural Difficulties, 2*(1), 3–14.

Fraley, R. C. (2002). Attachment stability from infancy to adulthood: Meta-analysis and dynamic modeling of developmental mechanisms. *Personality & Social Psychology Review, 6*(2), 123–151.

Freeman, H., & Almond, T. M. (2010). Mapping young adults' use of fathers for attachment support: Implications on romantic relationship experiences. *Early Child Development and Care, 180*(1–2), 227–248.

Gallo, L. C., Trowel, W. M., Matthews, K. A., & Kuller, L. W. (2003). Marital status and quality in middle-aged women: Associations with levels and trajectories of cardiovascular risk factors. *Health Psychology, 22,* 453–463.

Gilligan, C., & Attanucci, J. (1988). Two moral orientations: Gender differences and similarities. *Merrill Palmer Quarterly, 34,* 223–238.

Goldsmith, H. H., &Alansky, J. A. (1987). Maternal and infant temperamental predictors of attachment: A meta-analytic review. *Journal of Consulting and Clinical Psychology, 55*(6), 805–816.

Gove, W. R., Style, C. B., & Hughes, M. (1990). The effect of marriage on the sell-being of adults: A theoretical analysis. *Journal of Health and Social Behavior, 24,* 122–131.

Grant, K. E., Compas, B. E., Thurm, A. E., McMahon, S. D., Gipson, P. Y., Campbell, A. J., & Westerholm, R. I. (2006). Stressors and child and adolescent psychopathology: Evidence of moderating and mediating effects. *Clinical Psychology Review, 26,* 257–283.

Guerin, B. (2001). Individuals as social relationships: 18 ways that acting alone can be thought of as social behavior. *Review of General Psychology, 5*(4), 406–428.

Guerra, N. G., & Slaby, R. G. (1990). Cognitive mediators of aggression in offenders: II. Intervention. *Developmental Psychology, 26,* 269–277.

Haller, C. J., & Courvoisier, D. S. (2010). Personality and thinking style in different creative domains. *Psychology of Aesthetics, Creativity, and the Arts, 4*(3), 149–160.

Hannon, K. (2011, October 25). Boomer women flunk mentoring: New Linkedin survey. *Forbes.* Retrieved from http://www.forbes.com/sites/kerryhannon/2011/10/25/boomer-women-flunk-mentoring-new-linkedin-survey/

Heimlich, J. E., & Ardoin, N. M. (2008). Understanding behavior to understand behavior change: A literature review. *Environmental Education Research, 14*(3), 215–237.

Helson, R., Jones, C., & Kwan, V. S. Y. (2002). Personality change over 40 years of adulthood: Hierarchical linear modeling analysis of two longitudinal samples. *Journal of Personality and Social Psychology, 83*(3), 752–766.

Horn, S. S. (2003). Adolescents' reasoning about exclusion from social groups. *Developmental Psychology, 39*(1), 71–84.

Howard, C. L. (1997).The mother-daughter attachment, self-esteem, and disordered eating. *Dissertation Abstracts International: Section B: The Sciences & Engineering, 58*(6-B), 3317.

Ichiyama, M. A., & Kruse, M. I. (1998). The social contexts of binge drinking among private university freshman. *Journal of Alcohol and Drug Education, 44*(1), 18–33.

Jaffee, S., & Hyde, J. S. (2000). Gender differences in moral orientation: A meta-analysis. *Psychological Bulletin, 126,* 703–726.

Javdani, S., Sadeh, N., & Verona, E. (2011). Suicidality as a function of impulsivity, callous-unemotional traits, and depressive symptoms in youth. *Journal of Abnormal Psychology, 120*(2), 400–413.

Johnston, L. D., O'Malley, P. M., & Bachman, J. G. (2002). *National survey results on drug use from the monitoring the future study, 1975–2000.* Bethesda, MD: National Institute on Drug Abuse.

Kazdin, A. E. (1987). Treatment of antisocial behavior in children: Current status and future directions. *Psychological Bulletin, 102*(2), 187–203.

Kohlberg, L. (1984). *Essays on moral development. Vol. II. The psychology of moral development.* San Francisco: Harper and Row.

Kuebli, J., Butler, S., & Fivush, R. (1995). Mother–child talk about past emotions: Relations of maternal language and child gender over time. *Cognition and Emotion, 9,* 265–283.

La Greca, A. M., & Prinstein, M. J. (1999). Peer group. In W. K. Silverman & T. H. Ollendick (Eds.), *Developmental issues in the clinical treatment of children* (pp. 171–198). Needham Heights, MA: Allyn& Bacon.

Lahey, B. B., McBurnett, K., Raine, A., Stouthamer-Loeber, M., & Loeber, R. (2002, July 30). *Neurohormonal correlates of conduct problems among male adolescents in a psychological stress paradigm.* Unpublished paper presented at the developmental origins of aggressive behavior Conference, McGill University, Montreal.

Li, A. (2008).*The impact of divorce on children's behavior problems.* Retrieved July 14, 2012, from http://www.contemporaryfamilies.org/children-parenting/behavior.html

Lou, E., Lalonde, R. N., & Wilson, C. (2011). Examining a multidimensional framework of racial identity across different biracial groups. *Asian American Journal of Psychology, 2*(2), 79–90.

Mackey, E. R., & La Greca, A. M. (2008). Does this make me look fat? Peer crowd and peer contributions to adolescent girls' weight control behaviors. *Journal of Youth and Adolescence, 37,* 1097–1110.

Madigan, S., Moran, G., Schuengel, C., Pederson, D. R., & Otten, R. (2007). Unresolved maternal attachment representations, disrupted maternal behavior and disorganized attachment in infancy: Links to toddler behavior problems. *Journal of Child Psychology and Psychiatry, 48*(10), 1042–1050.

McBurnett, K., Lahey, B. B., Frick, P. J., & Risch, C. (1991). Anxiety, inhibition, and conduct disorder in children: II. Relation to salivary cortisol. *Journal of the American Academy of Child and Adolescent Psychiatry, 30,* 192–196.

McCarthy, A. M. (1998). Paternal characteristics associated with disturbed father-daughter attachment and superation among women with eating disorder symptoms. *Dissertation Abstracts International: Section B: The Sciences &Enginering, 59*(4-B), 1861.

McCrae, R. R., Costa, P. T., Jr., Lima, M. P., Simoes, A., Ostendorf, F., Angleitner, A., et al. (1999). Age differences in personality across the adult lifespan: Parallels in five cultures. *Developmental Psychology, 35,* 466–477.

Murray, J., Farrington, D. P., & Sekol, I. (2012). Children's antisocial behavior, mental health, drug use, and educational performance after parental incarceration: A systematic review and meta-analysis. *Psychological Bulletin, 138*(2), 175–210.

Murray-Close, D., Crick, N. R., & Galotti, K. M. (2006). Children's moral reasoning regarding physical and relational aggression. *Social Development, 15*(3), 345–372.

Newcomb, A. F., Bukowski, W. M., & Pattee, L. (1993). Children's peer relations: A metaanalytic review of popular, rejected, neglected, controversial, and average sociometric status. *Psychological Bulletin, 113*(1), 99–128.

NICHD Early Child Care Research Network. (2006). Infant-mother attachment classifications: Risk and protection in relation to changing maternal caregiving quality. *Developmental Psychology, 42,* 38–58.

Noe, R. A. (1988). Women and mentoring: A review and research agenda. *Academy of Management Review, 13,* 65–78.

Nucci, L. P. (1996). Morality and the personal sphere of action. In E. Reed, E. Turiel, & T. Brown (Eds.), *Values and knowledge* (pp. 41–60). Hillsdale, NJ: Erlbaum.

Papini, D. R., Micka, J. C., & Barnett, J. K. (1989). Perceptions of intrapsychic and extrapsychic functioning as bases of adolescent ego identity statuses. *Journal of Adolescent Research, 4,* 462–482.

Patterson, G. R., Reid, J. B., &Dishion, T. J. (1992).*Antisocial boys.* Eugene, Oregon: Castalia.

Piotrowski, C. C. (2011). Patterns of adjustment among siblings exposed to intimate partner violence. *Journal of Family Psychology, 25*(1), 19–28.

Power, T. G., & Shanks, J. A. (1989). Parents as socializers: Maternal and paternal views. *Journal of Youth and Adolescence, 18,* 203–220.

Ramirez, J. M. (2002). Hormones and aggression in childhood and adolescence. *Aggression and Violent Behavior, 8,* 621–644.

Ranson, K. E., & Urichuk, L. J. (2008). The effect of parent-child attachment relationships on child biopsychosocial outcomes: A review. *Early Child Development and Care, 178*(2), 129–152.

Rice, K. G. (1990). Attachment in adolescence: A narrative and meta-analytic review. *Journal of Youth and Adolescence, 19*(5), 511–538.

Rohrer, L. M., Cicchetti, D., Rogosch, F. A., Toth, S. L., & Maughan, A. (2011). Effects of maternal negativity and of early and recent recurrent depressive disorder on children's false belief understanding. *Developmental Psychology, 47*(1), 170–181.

Rose, C. D. (1999). Peer cluster theory and adolescent alcohol use: An explanation of alcohol use and a comparative analysis between two causal models. *Journal of Drug Education 29,* 205–215.

Santrock, J. W. (2008). *Life-span development.* Boston: McGraw-Hill.

Schechtman, Z., & Gilat, I. (2005).The effectiveness of counseling groups in reducing stress of parents of children with learning disabilities. *Group Dynamics: Theory, Research, and Practice, 9*(4), 275–286.

Schwartz, D., Gorman, A. H., Nakamoto, J., & McKay, T. (2006). Popularity, social acceptance, and aggression in adolescent peer groups: Links with academic performance and school attendance. *Developmental Psychology, 42*(6), 1116–1127.

Scott-Sheldon, L. A. J., Terry, D. L., Carey, K. B., Garey, L., & Carey, M. P. (2012, March 19). Efficacy of expectancy challenge interventions to reduce college student drinking: A meta-analytic review. *Psychology of Addictive Behaviors.* doi:10.1037/a0027565.

Shih, M., & Sanchez, D. T. (2005). Perspectives and research on the positive and negative implications of having multiple racial identities. *Psychological Bulletin, 131*(4), 569–591.

Specht, J., Egloff, B., & Schmukle, S. C. (2011). Stability and change of personality across the life course: The impact of age and major life events on mean-level and rank-order stability of the Big Five. *Journal of Personality and Social Psychology, 101*(4), 862–882.

Sturge-Apple, M. L., Daview, P. T., Winter, M. A., Cummings, E. M., & Schermerhorn, A. (2008).

Interparental conflict and children's school adjustment: The explanatory role of children's internal representations of interparental and parent-child relationships. *Developmental Psychology, 44*(6), 1678–1690.

Susman, E. J., Worrall, B. K., Murowchick, E., Frobose, C. A., & Schwab, J. E. (1996). Experience and neuroendocrine parameters of development: Aggressive behavior and competencies. In D. M. Stoff & R. B. Cairns (Eds.), *Aggression and violence. Genetic, neurobiological, and biological perspectives* (pp. 267–290). Mahwah, NJ: Lawrence Erlbaum Associates.

van Goozen, S. H. M., Fairchild, G., Snoek, H., & Harold, G. T. (2007). The evidence for a neurobiological model of childhood antisocial behavior. *Psychological Bulletin, 133*(1), 149–182.

van Goozen, S. H.M., Matthys, W., Cohen-Kettenis, P. T., Thijssen, J. H., & van Engeland, H. (1998). Adrenal androgens and aggression in conduct disorder prepubertal boys and normal controls. *Biological Psychiatry, 43*(2), 156–158.

Wentzel, K. R., Barry, C. M., & Caldwell, K. A. (2004). Friendships in middle school: Influences on motivation and school adjustment. *Journal of Educational Psychology, 96,* 195–203.

White, F. A., Charles, M. A., & Nelson, J. K. (2008). The role of persuasive arguments in changing affirmative action attitudes and expressed behavior in higher education. *Journal of Applied Psychology, 93*(6), 1271–1286.

Williams-Nickelson, C. (2009). Mentoring women graduate students: A model for professional psychology. *Professional Psychology: Research and Practice, 40*(3), 284–291.

Wilson, D. K., & Evans, A. E. (2003). Health promotion in children and adolescents: An integration of psychosocial and environmental approaches. In M. Roberts (Ed.), *Handbook of pediatric psychology,* (3rd ed., pp. 69–83). New York: Guildford Press.

Wu, K. D., & Clark, L. A. (2003). Relations between personality traits and self-reports of daily behavior. *Journal of Research in Personality, 37,* 231–256.

CHAPTER 9

Abramowitz, J., Deacon, B., & Whiteside, S. (2011). *Exposure therapy for anxiety: Principles and practice.* New York: Guilford Press.

Akhtari, M. (2011). Reassessment of the weather effect: Stock prices and wall street weather. *Undergraduate Economic Review, 7*(1). Article19.

Arcelus, J., Mitchell, A., Wales, J., & Nielsen, S. (2011). Mortality rates in patients with anorexia nervosa and other eating disorders: A meta-analysis of 36 studies. *Archives of General Psychiatry, 68*(7), 724–731.

Bariola, E., Gullone, E., & Hughes, E. (2011). Child and adolescent emotion regulation: The role of parental emotion regulation and expression. *Clinical Child and Family Psychology Review, 14*(2), 198–212.

Barrett, L. F., & Wager, T. D. (2006). The structure of emotion: Evidence from neuroimaging studies. *Current Directions in Psychological Science, 15*(2), 79–83.

Blum, D. (2002). *Love at Goon Park: Harry Harlow and the Science of Affection.* Cambridge, MA: Perseus Publishing.

Brooks-Gunn, J. (2010). The neighborhoods where young children grow up. In S. L. Kagan & K. Tarrant (Eds.), *Transitions in the early years: Creating connections across early childhood systems* (pp. 211–225). Baltimore, MD: Brookes Publishing.

Brooks-Gunn, J., Duncan, G., & Aber, J. L. (Eds.). (1997). *Neighborhood poverty: Context and consequences for development.* New York: Russell Sage Foundation.

Brown, L. A., Forman, E. M., Herbert, J. D., Hoffman, K. L., Yuen, E. K., & Goetter, E. M. (2011). A randomized controlled trial of acceptance-based behavior therapy and cognitive therapy for test anxiety: A pilot study. *Behavior Modification, 35*(1), 31–53. doi:10.1177/0145445510390930

Clark, L., Dombrovski, A. Y., Siegle, G., Butters, M., Shollenberger, L., Sahakian, B., & Szanto, K. (2011). Impairment in risk-sensitive decision-making in older suicide attempters with depression. *Psychology and Aging, 26*(2), 321–330.

Cohen, M., Ben-Zur, H., & Rosenfeld, M. (2008). Sense of coherence, coping strategies, and test anxiety as predictors of test performance among college students. *International Journal of Stress Management, 15*(3), 289–303.

Ekman, P. (1992). An argument for basic emotions. *Cognition & Emotion, 6*(3–4), 169–200.

ElHage, W., Powell, J. F., & Surguladze, S. A. (2009). Vulnerability to depression: what is the role of stress genes in gene× environment interaction? *Psychological Medicine, 39*(9), 1407–1411.

Emde, R., & Plomin, R. (1992). Temperament, emotion, and cognition at fourteen months: The MacArthur longitudinal twin study. *Child Development, 63*(6), 1437–1455. doi:10.1111/1467-8624.ep9308195012

Goldsmith, H. H., & Alansky, J. A. (1987). Maternal and infant temperamental predictors of attachment: A meta-analytic review. *Journal of Consulting and Clinical Psychology, 55*(6), 805–816.

Goleman, D. (1995). *Emotional intelligence.* New York: Bantam Books.

Harris, M., & Skyles, A. (2011). Kinship care for African American children: Disproportionate and disadvantageous. In J. E. B. Myers (Ed.), *Child maltreatment: A collection of readings.* Thousand Oaks, CA: Sage.

Hayes, S. C., Strosahl, K. D., & Wilson, K. G. (2003). *Acceptance and commitment therapy: An experiential approach to behavior change.* New York: Guilford Press.

Healey, D., Flory, J., Miller, C., & Halperin, J. (2011). Maternal positive parenting style is associated with better functioning in hyperactive/inattentive preschool children. *Infant and Child Development, 20*(2), 148–161. doi:10.1002/icd.682

Hendriks, M. C., & Vingerhoets, A. J. (2006). Social messages of crying faces: Their influence on anticipated person perception, emotions and behavioural responses. *Cognition and Emotion, 20*(6), 878–886.

Hepworth, D. H., Rooney, R. H., Rooney, G. D., Strom-Gottfried, K., & Larsen, J. A. (2010). *Direct social work practice: Theory and skills* (8th ed.). Pacific Grove, CA: Brooks/Cole.

Izard, C. (2011). Forms and functions of emotions: Matters of emotion–cognition interactions. *Emotion Review, 3*(4), 371–378. doi:10.1177/1754073911410737

James, W. (1884). What is an emotion? *Mind, 9*, 188–205.

Johnson-Laird, P. N., & Oatley, K. (1989). The language of emotions: An analysis of a semantic field. *Cognition and Emotion, 3*(2), 81–123.

Keize, K., Lindenberg, S., & Steg, L. (2008). The spreading of disorder. *Science, 322*(5908), 1681–1685.

Kiff, C., Lengua, L., & Bush, N. (2011). Temperament variation in sensitivity to parenting: Predicting changes in depression and anxiety. *Journal of Abnormal Child Psychology, 39*(8), 1199–1212. doi:10.1007/s10802-011-9539-x

Koole, S. (2009). The psychology of emotion regulation: An integrative review. *Cognition and Emotion, 23*(1), 4–41.

Kruger, D. (2008). Verifying the operational definition of neighborhood for the psychosocial impact of structural deterioration. *Journal of Community Psychology, 36*(1), 53–60.

Kwag, K., Jang, Y., Rhew, S., & Chiriboga, D. (2011). Neighborhood effects on physical and mental health: A study of Korean American older adults. *Asian American Journal of Psychology, 2*(2), 91–100.

Lau, G., Moulds, M., & Richardson, R. (2009). Ostracism: How much it hurts depends on how you remember it. *Emotion, 9*(3), 430–434.

Lavigne, J., LeBailly, S., Gouze, K., Cicchetti, C., Jessup, B., Arend, R., . . . Binns, H. (2008). Predictor and moderator effects in the treatment of oppositional defiant disorder in pediatric primary care. *Journal of Pediatric Psychology, 33*(5), 462–472.

Lazarus, R. (1991). Progress on a cognitive-motivational-relational theory of emotion. *American Psychologist, 46*(8), 819–834.

Lee, L., Lee, D., & Woo, J. (2010). The psychosocial effect of Tai Chi on nursing home residents. *Journal of Clinical Nursing, 19*(7–8), 927–938.

Livingstone, A. G., Spears, R., Manstead, A., Bruder, M., & Shepherd, L. (2011). We feel, therefore we are: Emotion as a basis for self-categorization and social action. *Emotion, 11*(4), 754–767.

Maslow, A. (1943). A theory of human motivation. *Psychological Review, 50*(4), 370–396. doi:10.1037/h0054346

Mason, M. J. (2010). Mental health, school problems, and social networks: Modeling urban adolescent substance use. *The Journal of Primary Prevention, 31*(5–6), 321–331.

McMahon, C., Barnett, B., Kowalenko, N., Tennant, C., & Don, N. (2001). Postnatal depression, anxiety and unsettled infant behavior. *Australian and New Zealand Journal of Psychiatry, 35*(5), 581–588.

Mehall, K., Spinrad, T., Eisenberg, N., & Gaertner, B. (2009). Examining the relations of infant temperament and couples' marital satisfaction to mother and father involvement: A longitudinal study. *Fathering, 7*(1), 23–48.

Mendelson, T., Turner, A., & Tandon, S. (2010). Violence exposure and depressive symptoms among adolescents and young adults disconnected from school and work. *Journal of Community Psychology, 38*(5), 607–621.

Moretti, L., & diPellegrino, G. (2010). Disgust selectively modulates reciprocal fairness in economic interactions. *Emotion, 10*(2), 169–180.

Neighbors, B., Clark, D., Donovan, J., & Brody, G. (2000). Difficult temperament, parental relationships, and adolescent alcohol use disorder symptoms. *Journal of Child & Adolescent Substance Abuse, 10*(1), 69–86.

Paranjape, A., & Kaslow, N. (2010). Family violence exposure and health outcomes among older African American women: Does spirituality and social support play a protective role? *Journal of Women's Health, 19*(10), 1899–1904.

Parrott, W. (2001). Implications of dysfunctional emotions for understanding how emotions function. *Review of General Psychology, 5*(3), 180–186.

Pérez-Edgar, K., Bar-Haim, Y., McDermott, J., Chronis-Tuscano, A., Pine, D. S., & Fox, N. A. (2010). Attention biases to threat and behavioral inhibition in early childhood shape adolescent social withdrawal. *Emotion, 10*(3), 349–357.

Plomin, R., Reiss, D., Hetherington, E., & Howe, G. (1994). Nature and nurture: Genetic contributions to measures of the family environment. *Developmental Psychology, 30*(1), 32–43.

Plunkett, S., Abarca-Mortensen, S., Behnke, A., & Sands, T. (2007). Neighborhood structural qualities, adolescents' perceptions of neighborhoods, and Latino youth development. *Hispanic Journal of Behavioral Sciences, 29*(1), 19–34.

Plutchik, R. (2005). The nature of emotions. In P. W. Sherman & J. Alcock (Eds.), *Exploring animal behavior: Readings from American Scientist* (4th ed., pp. 85–91). Sunderland, MA: SinauerAssociates.

Rivaux, S. L., James, J., Wittenstrom, K., Baumann, D., Sheets, J., Henry, J., & Jeffries, V. (2008). The intersection of race, poverty, and risk: Understanding the decision to provide services to clients and to remove children. *Child Welfare, 87*(2), 151–168.

Russell, J. A. (2003). Core affect and the psychological construction of emotion. *Psychological Review, 110*(1), 145–172.

Saleebey, D. (2012). *Strengths perspective in social work practice* (6th ed.). Boston: Pearson.

Sanders, C., Field, T., Diego, M., & Kaplan, M. (2000). The relationship of internet use to depression and social isolation among adolescents. *Adolescence, 35*(138), 237–242.

Seligman, M., & Csikszentmihalyi, M. (2000). Positive psychology: An introduction. *American Psychologist, 55*(1), 5–14.

Sheeber, L., & Johnson, J. (1994). Evaluation of a temperament-focused, parent-training program. *Journal of Clinical Child Psychology, 23*(3), 249–259.

Svensson, T., Müssener, U., & Alexanderson, K. (2006). Pride, empowerment, and return to work: On the significance of promoting positive social emotions among sickness absentees. *Work: Journal of Prevention, Assessment & Rehabilitation, 27*(1), 57–65.

Tani, C., Chavez, E., & Deffenbacher, J. (2001). Peer isolation and drug use among White non-Hispanic and Mexican American adolescents. *Adolescence, 36*(141), 127–139.

Thomas, A., & Chess, S. (1991). Temperament in adolescence and its functional significance. In R. M. Lerner, A. C. Petersen, & J. Brooks-Gunn (Eds.), *Encyclopedia of adolescence* (Vol. 2). New York: Garland.

Wickrama, K. S., & Noh, S. (2010). The long arm of community: The influence of childhood community contexts across the early life course. *Journal of Youth and Adolescence, 39*(8), 894–910.

Winningham, R. G., & Pike, N. L. (2007). A cognitive intervention to enhance institutionalized older adults' social support networks and decrease loneliness. *Aging & Mental Health, 11*(6), 716–721.

Yen, I., Yelin, E., Katz, P., Eisner, M., & Blanc, P. (2006). Perceived neighborhood problems and quality of life, physical functioning, and depressive symptoms among adults with asthma. *American Journal of Public Health, 96*(5), 873–879.

Young, A. S., Klap, R., Shoai, R., & Wells, K. (2008). Persistent depression and anxiety in the United States: Prevalence and quality of care. *Psychiatric Services, 59*(12), 1391–1398.

CHAPTER 10

Adair, L., & Gordon-Larsen, P. (2001). Maturational timing and overweight prevalence in U.S. adolescent females. *American Journal of Public Health, 91*, 642–644.

Agnew, C. R., Hoffman, A. M., Lehmiller, J. J., & Duncan, N. T. (2007). From the interpersonal to the international: Understanding commitment to the "war on terror". *Personality and Social Psychology Bulletin, 33*, 1559–1571.

Alan Guttmacher Institute (AGI). (2002). *Sexual and reproductive health: Women and men. 2002.* New York: Author. Retrieved from http://www.guttmacher.org/pubs/fb_10-02.html

American Association of University Women. (2001). *Hostile hallways: Bullying, teasing, and sexual harassment in school.* New York: Harris/Scholastic Research.

American Psychological Association. (2007). *Report of the APA task force on the sexualization of girls.* Washington, DC: Author.

Auyeung, B., Baron-Cohen, S., Ashwin, E., Knickmeyer, R., Taylor, K., Hackette, G., & Hines, M. (2009). Fetal testosterone predicts sexually differentiated childhood behavior in girls and in boys. *Psychological Science, 20*(2), 144–148.

Baron-Cohen, S. (2002). The extreme male brain theory of autism. *Trends in Cognitive Science, 6*, 248–254.

Barron, L. G., & Hebl, M. (2013). The force of law: The effects of sexual orientation antidiscrimination legislation on interpersonal discrimination in employment. *Psychology, Public Policy, and Law, 19*(2), 191–205. doi:10.1037/a0028350

Basson, R., Berman, J., Burnett, A., Degrogatis, L., Ferguson, D., Foucroy, J., . . . Whipple, B. (2000). Report of the international consensus development conference on female sexual dysfunction: Definitions and classifications. *Journal of Urology, 163,* 888–893.

Baucom, B. R., Saxbe, D. E., Ramos, M. C., Spies, L. A., Iturralde, E., Duman, S., & Margolin, G. (2012). Correlates and characteristics of adolescents' encoded emotional arousal during family conflict. *Emotion, 12*(6), 1281–1291. doi:10.1037/a0028872

Baumeister, R. F. (2000). Gender differences in erotic plasticity: The female sex drive as socially flexible and responsive. *Psychological Bulletin, 126,* 347–374.

Baumle, A. K. (2010). Border identities: Intersections of ethnicity and sexual orientation in the U.S.-Mexico borderland. *Social Science Research, 39,* 231–245.

Berk, L. E. (2009). *Child development* (8th ed.). Boston: Allyn & Bacon.

Binik, Y. M. (2010). The DSM diagnostic criteria for dyspareunia. *Archives of Sexual Behavior, 39*(2), 292–303.

Bishop, H. N., Caraway, C., & Stader, D. L. (2010). A case for legal protection for sexual minority educators. *The Clearing House, 83,* 84–88.

Bogaert, A. F. (2010). Physical development and sexual orientation in men and women: An analysis of NATSAL-2000. *Archives of Sexual Behavior, 39,* 110–116.

Bornstein, M. H. (2002). *Handbook of parenting: Practical issues in parenting* (2nd ed., Vol. 5). Mahwah, NJ: Lawrence Erlbaum Associates, Inc.

Bostwick, W. B., Boyd, C. J., Hughes, T. L., & McCabe, S. E. (2010). Sexual orientation and the prevalence of mood and anxiety disorders in the United States. *American Journal of Public Health, 100*(3), 468–475.

Bowie, B. H. (2007). Relational aggression, gender, and the developmental process. *Journal of Child and Adolescent Psychiatric Nursing, 20*(2), 107–115.

Brownmiller, S. (1975). *Against our will: Men, women, and rape.* New York: Simon & Schuster.

Burns, J. M. (1978). *Leadership.* New York: Harper & Row.

Buzzell, T. (2005). Demographic characteristics of persons using pornography in three technological contexts. *Sexuality & Culture, 9*(1), 28–48.

Cahill, L. (2006). Why sex matters for neuroscience. *National Review of Neuroscience, 7,* 477–484.

Carver, P. R., Egan, S. K., & Perry, D. G. (2004). Children who question their heterosexuality. *Developmental Psychology, 40,* 43–53.

Centers for Disease Control and Prevention (CDC). 2004. *Surveillance Summaries: Morbidity and Mortality Weekly Report, Vol. 53. Surveillance Summary no. 2: Youth Risk Behavior Surveillance.*

Centers for Disease Control/National Center for Health Statistics (CDC/NCHS). (2009). *National survey of family growth, 2006-2008.* Washington, DC: Author.

Cheung, F. M., & Halpern, D. F. (2010). Women at the top: Powerful leaders define success as work + family in a culture of gender. *American Psychologist, 65*(3), 182–193.

Cleveland, M. J., Feinberg, M. E., & Jones, D. E. (2012). Predicting alcohol use across adolescence: Relative strength of individual, family, peer, and contextual risk and protective factors. *Psychology of Addictive Behaviors, 26*(4), 703–713. doi:10.1037/a0027583

Coall, C., & Chisholm, J. S. (2003). Evolutionary perspectives on pregnancy: Maternal age at menarche and infant birth weight. *Social Science & Medicine, 57*(10), 1771–1781.

Cohen, R. Z., Seeman, M. V., Gotowiec, A., & Kopala, L. (1999). Earlier puberty as a predictor of later onset of schizophrenia in women. *American Journal of Psychiatry, 156*(7), 1059–1064.

Cohen-Kettenis, P. T., & Pfäfflin, F. (2010). The DSM diagnostic criteria for gender identity disorder in adolescents and adults. *Archives of Sexual Behavior, 39,* 499–513.

Coker, T. R., Austin, S. B., & Schuster, M. A. (2010). The health and health care of lesbian, gay, and bisexual youth. *Annual Review of Public Health, 31,* 457–477.

Compian, L. J., Gowen, L. K., & Hayward, C. (2009). The interactive effects of puberty and peer victimization on weight concerns and depression symptoms among early adolescent girls. *Journal of Early Adolescence, 29*(3), 357–375.

Conley, C. S., & Rudolph, K. D. (2009). The emerging sex difference in adolescent depression: Interacting contributions of puberty and peer stress. *Development and Psychopathology, 21,* 593–620.

Cooper, A., Scherer, C., Boies, S., & Gordon, B. (1999). Sexuality on the internet: From sexual exploration to pathological expression. *Professional Psychology: Research and Practice, 30*(2), 154–164.

Corliss, H. L., Grella, C. E., Mays, V. M., & Cochran, S. D. (2006). Drug use, drug severity, and help-seeking behaviors of lesbian and bisexual women. *Journal of Women's Health, 15*(5), 556–568.

Corliss, H. L., Rosario, M., Wypij, D., Wylie, S. A., Frazier, A. L., & Austin, S. B. (2010). Sexual orientation and drug use in a longitudinal cohort study of U.S. adolescents. *Addictive Behaviors, 35*(5), 517–521.

Coyne, S. M., & Archer, J. (2005). The relationship between indirect and physical aggression on television and in real life. *Social Development, 14*(2), 324–338.

Davis, C. M., Blank, J., Hung-Yu, L., & Bonillas, C. (1996). Characteristics of vibrator use among women. *Journal of Sex Research, 33*(4), 313–320.

Den Hond, E., Roels, H. A., Hoppenbrouwers, K., Nawrot, T., Thijs, L., Vandermeulen, C., . . . Staessen, J. A. (2002). Sexual maturation in relation to polychlorinated aromatic hydrocarbons: Sharpe and skakkebaek's hypothesis revisited. *Environmental Health Perspectives, 110*(8), 771–776.

Dodge, K. A. (1991). Emotion and social information processing. In J. Garber & K. A. Dodge (Eds.), *The development of emotion regulation and dysregulation* (pp. 159–181). Cambridge: Cambridge University Press.

Dunn, J., Brown, J., Slomkowski, C., Tesla, C., & Youngblade, L. (1991). Young children's understanding of other people's feelings and beliefs: Individual differences and their antecedents. *Child Development, 62,* 1352–1366.

Dunn, K. M., Croft, P. R., & Hackett, G. I. (1999). Association of sexual problems with social, psychological and physical problems in men and women: A cross sectional population survey. *Journal of Epidemiology and Community Health, 53,* 144–148.

Eagly, A. H., & Carli, L. L. (2007). Women and the labyrinth of leadership. *Harvard Business Review, 85*(9), 63–71.

Eagly, A. H., & Crowley, M. (1986). Gender and helping behavior: A meta-analytic review of the social psychological literature. *Psychological Bulletin, 100*(3), 283–308.

Eagly, A. H., & Johannesen-Schmidt, M. C. (2003). Transformational, transactional, and laissez-faire leadership styles: A meta-analysis comparing women and men. *Psychological Bulletin, 129*(4), 569–591.

Eagly, A. H., Makhijani, M. G., & Klonsky, B. G. (1992). Gender and the evaluation of leaders: A meta-analysis. *Psychological Bulletin, 111*(1), 3–22.

Eisenberg, N., Cumberland, A., & Spinrad, T. L. (1998). Parental socialization of emotion. *Psychological Inquiry, 9*(4), 241–273.

Elias, C. F. (2012). Leptin action in pubertal development: Recent advances and unanswered questions. *Trends in Endocrinology & Metabolism, 23*(1), 9–15.

Ellis, B. J., & Essex, M. J. (2007). Family environments, adrenarche, and sexual maturation: A longitudinal test of a life history model. *Child Development, 78,* 1799–1817.

Estrem, T. L. (2005). Relational and physical aggression among pre-schoolers: The effect of language skills and gender. *Early Education and Development, 16*(2), 207–231.

Feldhaus-Dahir, M. (2009). The physiology and causes of female sexual arousal disorder: Part I. *Urologic Nursing, 29*(6), 440–443.

Flynn, K., & Fitzgibbon, M. (1996). Body image ideals of low-income African American mothers and their preadolescent daughters. *Journal of Youth and Adolescence, 25*(5), 615–631.

Forbes, E. E., & Dahl, R. E. (2010). Pubertal development and behavior: Hormonal activation of social and motivational tendencies. *Brain and Cognition, 72,* 66–72.

Frodi, A., Macaulay, J., & Thome, P. R. (1977). Are women always less aggressive then men? A review of the experimental literature. *Psychological Bulletin, 84*(4), 634–660.

Fugl-Meyer, A. R., & Fugl-Meyer, K. S. (1999). Sexual disabilities, problems and satisfaction in 18-74 year old Swedes. *Scandinavian Journal of Sexology, 2,* 79–97.

Garcia, J., MacKillop, J., Aller, E. L., Merriwether, A. M., Wilson, D. S., & Lum, J. K. (2010). Associations between dopamine d4 receptor gene variation with both infidelity and sexual promiscuity. *PLoS ONE, 5*(11), E14162. doi:10.1371/journal.pone.0014162.

Gardner, M., & Steinberg, L. (2012). Peer influence on risk taking, risk preference, and risk decision making in adolescence and adulthood: An experimental study: Correction to Gardner and Steinberg (2005). *Developmental Psychology, 48*(2), 589.

Geary, D. C. (2002). Sexual selection and sex differences in social cognition. In A. V. McGillicuddy & R. DeLisi (Eds.), *Biology, Society, and Behavior: The Development of Sex Differences in Cognition.* Greenwich, CT: Ablex.

Golombok, S., & Hines, M. (2002). Sex differences in social behavior. In P. K. Smith & C. H. Hart (Eds.), *Blackwell handbook of childhood social development* (pp. 117–136). Oxford, England: Blackwell.

Graber, J. A., Lewinsohn, P. M., Seeley, J. R., & Brooks-Gunn, J. (1997). Is psychopathology associated with the timing of pubertal development? *Journal of the American Academy of Child and Adolescent Psychiatry, 36*, 1768–1776.

Graham, C. A. (2010). The DSM diagnostic criteria for female sexual arousal disorder. *Archives of Sexual Behavior, 39*, 240–255.

Hall, G. C., & Barongan, C. (1997). Prevention of sexual aggression: Sociocultural risk and protective factors. *American Psychologist, 52*, 5–14.

Halpern, C. T. (2003). Biological influences on adolescent romantic and sexual behavior. In P. Florsheim (Ed.), *Adolescent romantic relations and sexual behavior: Theory, research, and practical implications* (pp. 57–84). Mahwah, NJ: Lawrence Erlbaum Associates.

Harter, S. (2006). The self. In N. Eisenberg (Ed.), *Handbook of child psychology: Vol. 3. Social, emotional, and personality development* (6th ed., pp. 505–570). Hoboken, NJ: Wiley.

Hayatbakhsh, M. R., Najman, J. M., McGee, T. R., Bor, W., & O'Callaghan, M. J. (2008). Early pubertal maturation in the prediction of early adult substance use: A prospective study. *Addiction Research Report, 104*, 59–66.

Haynie, D. L., & Piquero, A. R. (2006). Pubertal development and physical victimization in adolescence. *Journal of Research in Crime and Delinquency, 43*(1), 3–35.

Herman-Giddens, M. E., Slora, E. J., Wasserman, R. C., Bourdony, C. J., Bhapkar, M. V., Koch, G. G., & Hasemeier, C. M. (1997). Secondary sexual characteristics and menses in young girls seen in office practice: A study from the pediatric research in office settings network. *Pediatrics, 99*, 505–512.

Hombeck, G. N., & Hill, J. P. (1991). Conflictive engagement, positive affect, and menarche in families with seventh-grade girls. *Child Development, 62*(5), 1030–1048.

Isler, A., Tas, F., Beytut, D., & Conk, Z. (2009). Sexuality in adolescents with intellectual disabilities. *Sex and Disability, 27*, 27–34.

Jackson, T., & Chen, H. (2011). Risk factors for disordered eating during early and middle adolescence: Prospective evidence from mainland Chinese boys and girls. *Journal of Abnormal Psychology, 120*(2), 454–464.

Jaffee, S. R. (2002). Pathways to adversity in young adulthood among early childbearers. *Journal of Family Psychology, 16*, 38–49.

Jean, R. T., Bondy, J. L., Wilkinson, A. V., & Forman, M. R. (2009). Pubertal development in Mexican American girls: The family's perspective. *Qualitative Health Research, 19*(9), 1210–1222.

Jena, A., Goldman, D. P., Kamdar, A., Lakdawalla, D. N., & Lu, Y. (2010). Sexually transmitted diseases among users of erectile dysfunction drugs: Analysis of claims data. *Annals of Internal Medicine, 153*, 1–7.

Johnson, R. D. (2003). Homosexuality: Nature or nurture. *AllPsych Journal.* Retrieved from http://allpsych.com/journal/homosexuality.html

Kim, K. H., Bursac, Z., DiLillo, V., White, D. B., & West, D. S. (2009). Stress, race, and body weight. *Health Psychology, 28*(1), 131–135.

Knickmeyer, R., Baron-Cohen, S., Raggatt, P., Taylor, K., & Hackett, G. (2006). Fetal testosterone and empathy. *Hormones and Behavior, 49*, 282–292.

Kontula, O., & Haavio-Mannila, E. (2009). The impact of aging on human sexual activity and sexual desire. *The Journal of Sex Research, 46*(1), 46–56.

Kumanyika, S. K., Whitt-Glover, M. C., Gary, T. L., Prewitt, T. E., Odoms-Young, A. M., Banks-Wallace, J., . . . Samuel-Hodge, C. D. (2007). Expanding the obesity research paradigm to reach African American communities. *Preventing Chronic Disease, 4*(4). Retrieved October 16, 2013, from http://www.cdc.gov/pcd/issues/2007/oct/07_0067.htm

Lasser, J., Ryser, G., & Price, L. (2010). Development of a lesbian, gay, bisexual visibility management scale. *Journal of Homosexuality, 57*, 415–428.

Lau, R. R., Quadrel, M. J., & Hartman, K. A. (1990). Development and change of young adults' preventive health beliefs and behavior: Influence of parents and peers. *Journal of Health and Social Behavior, 31*, 240–259.

Laumann, E., Gagnon, J. H., Michael, R. T., & Michaels, S. (1994). *The social organization of sexuality: Sexual practices in the United States.* Chicago: University of Chicago Press.

Laumann, E. O., Paik, A., & Rosen, R. C. (1999). Sexual dysfunction in the United States: Prevalence and predictors. *Journal of the American Medical Association, 281*, 537–544.

Laurent, S. M., & Simons, A. D. (2009). Sexual dysfunction in depression and anxiety: Conceptualizing sexual dysfunction as part of an internalizing dimension. *Clinical Psychology Review, 29*, 573–585.

Lawrence, C. M., & Thelen, M. H. (1995). Body image, dieting, and self-concept: Their relation in African American and Caucasian children. *Journal of Clinical Child Psychology, 24*, 41–48.

Lear, D. (1995). Sexual communication in the age of AIDS: The construction of risk and trust among young adults. *Social Science and Medicine, 41*(9), 1311–1323.

Lee, J. (2009). Bodies at menarche: Stories of shame, concealment, and sexual maturation. *Sex Roles, 60,* 615–627.

Lehmiller, J. J. (2010). Differences in relationship investments between gay and heterosexual men. *Personal Relationships, 17,* 81–96.

Lindberg, S. M., Grabe, S., & Hyde, J. S. (2007). Gender, pubertal development, and peer sexual harassment predict objectified body consciousness in early adolescence. *Journal of Research on Adolescence, 17,* 723–742.

Maniglio, R. (2009). The impact of child sexual abuse on health: A systematic review of reviews. *Clinical Psychology Review, 29,* 647–657.

McAndrew, S., & Warne, T. (2010). Coming out to talk about suicide: Gay men and suicidality. *International Journal of Mental Health Nursing, 19,* 92–101.

McMasters, L., Connolly, J., Pepler, D., & Craig, W. (2002). Peer to peer sexual harassment in early adolescence: A developmental perspective. *Development and Psychopathology, 14,* 91–105.

Meier, A. M. (2007). Adolescent first sex and subsequent mental health. *American Journal of Sociology, 112*(6), 1811–1847.

Mernissi, F. (1987). *Beyond the veil: Male-female dynamics in modern muslim society.* Bloomington, IN: Indiana University Press.

Meyer, I. H. (2003). Prejudice, social stress and mental health in lesbian, gay, and bisexual populations: Conceptual issues and research evidence. *Psychological Bulletin, 129,* 674–697.

Mitchell, K. J., Becker-Blease, K. A., & Finkelhor, D. (2005). Inventory of problematic internet experiences encountered in clinical practice. *Professional Psychology: Research and Practice, 36*(5), 498–509.

Moore, T. M., & Stuart, G. L. (2004). Effects of masculine gender role stress on men's cognitive, affective, physiological, and aggressive responses to intimate conflict situations. *Psychology of Men & Masculinity, 5,* 132–142.

Mosher, W. D., Chandra, A., & Jones, J. (2005). *Sexual behavior and selected health measures: Men and women 15–44 years of age, United States, 2002* (Advance data from vital and health statistics No 362). Hyattsville, MD: National Center for Health Statistics.

Muehlenhard, C. L., & McCoy, M. L. (1991). Double standard/double bind: The sexual double standard

and women's communication about sex. *Psychology of Women Quarterly, 15,* 447–461.

Murnen, S. K., Wright, C., & Kaluzny, G. (2002). If "boys will be boys," then girls will be victims? A meta-analytic review of the research that relates masculine ideology to sexual aggression. *Sex Roles, 46*(11/12), 359–375.

Murray-Close, D., Crick, N. R., & Galotti, K. M. (2006). Children's moral reasoning regarding physical and relational aggression. *Social Development, 15*(3), 345–372.

National Dissemination Center for Children with Disabilities. (2011). *NICHCY disability fact sheet #8: Intellectual disabilities* Retrieved August 9, 2012, from http://nichcy.org/disability/specific/intellectual.

National School Climate Survey: LGBT youth face pervasive, but decreasing levels of harassment. (2012). Retrieved from http://www.glsen.org/cgi-bin/iowa/all/news/record/2897.html

National Survey of Sexual Health and Behavior (NSSHB). (2010). Findings from the national survey of sexual health and behavior, centre for sexual health promotion, Indiana University. *Journal of Sexual Medicine, 7*(Suppl. 5), 243–373.

Neufang, S., Specht, K., Hausmann, M., Güntürkün, O., Herpertz-Dahlmann, B., Fink, G. R., & Konrad, K. (2009). Sex differences and the impact of steroid hormones on the developing human brain. *Cerebral Cortex, 19,* 464–473.

O'Neil, J. M. (2008). Summarizing 25 years of research on men's gender role conflict using the gender role conflict scale: New research paradigms and clinical implications. *The Counseling Psychologist, 36,* 358–445.

Olvera, N., Suminski, R., & Power, T. G. (2005). Intergenerational perceptions of body image in hispanics: Role of BMI, gender, and acculturation. *Obesity Research, 13*(11), 1970–1979.

Ozer, E. M., Macdonald, T., & Irwin, C. E. J. (2002). Adolescent health care in the United States: Implications and projections for the new millennium. In J. T. Mortimer & R. W. Larson (Eds.), *Changing adolescent experience: Societal trends and the transition to adulthood.* Cambridge: Cambridge University Press.

Peper, J. S., Brouwer, R. M., Schnack, H. G., van Baal, G. C., van Leeuwen, M., van den Berg, S. M., . . . Hulshoff Pol, H. E. (2009). Sex steroids and brain structure in pubertal boys and girls. *Psychoneuroendocrinology, 34,* 332–342.

Petersen, J. L., & Hyde, J. S. (2009). A longitudinal investigation of peer sexual harassment victimization in adolescence. *Journal of Adolescence, 32,* 1173–1188.

Ponseti, J., Siebner, H. R., Kloppel, S., Wolff, S., Granert, O., Jansen, O., . . . Bosinski, H. A. (2007). Homosexual women have less grey matter in perirhinal cortex than heterosexual women. *PLoS ONE, 2*(8), E762.

Pratt, C. A., & Pratt, C. B. (1996). Nutritional advertisements in consumer magazines: Health implications for African Americans. *Journal of Black Studies, 26*(4), 504–523.

Quinlan, R. J. (2003). Father absence, parental care, and female reproductive development. *Evolution and Human Behavior, 24,* 376–390.

Rahman, Q., Cockburn, A., & Govier, E. (2007, January 6). A comparative analysis of functional cerebral asymmetry in lesbian women, heterosexual women, and heterosexual men. *Archives of Sexual Behavior, 37*(4), 566–571. doi:10.1007/ s10508-006-9137-0

Ramagopalan, S. V., Valdar, W., Criscuoli, M., DeLuca, G. C., Dyment, D. A., Orton, S. M., . . . Sadovnick, A. D. (2009). Age of puberty and risk of multiple sclerosis: A population based study. *European Journal of Neurology, 16,* 342–347.

Reardon, L. E., Leen-Feldner, E. W., & Hayward, C. (2009). A critical review of the empirical literature on the relation between anxiety and puberty. *Clinical Psychology Review, 29,* 1–23.

Richards, M. H., Viegas-Miller, B., O'Donnell, P. C., Wasserman, M. S., & Colder, C. (2004). Parental monitoring mediates the effects of age and sex on problem behaviors among African American urban young adolescents. *Journal of Youth and Adolescence, 33*(3), 221–233.

Roberts, D. F., Henriksen, L., & Foehr, U. G. (2004). Adolescents and media. In R. M. Learner & L. Steinberg (Eds.), *Handbook of adolescent psychology* (pp. 487–521). Hobokoken, NJ: Wiley & Sons.

Romeo, R. D., Richardson, H. N., & Sisk, C. L. (2002). Puberty and the maturation of the male brain and sexual behavior: Recasting a behavioral potential. *Neuroscience and Biobehavioral Reviews, 26,* 381–391.

Sanchez-Hucles, J. V., & Davis, D. D. (2010). Women and women of color in leadership. *American Psychologist, 65*(3), 171–181.

Santrock, J. W. (2008). *Life-span development.* Boston: McGraw-Hill.

Savic, I., & Lindstrom, P. (2008). *PET and MRI Show differences in cerebral asymmetry and functional connectivity between homo- and heterosexual subjects.* Retrieved October 18, 2013, from http://www.pnas.org/content/ early/2008/06/13/0801566105

Savin-Williams, R. (2001). Suicide attempts among sexual-minority youths: Population and measurement issues. *Journal of Consulting and Clinical Psychology, 69*(6), 983–991.

Savin-Williams, R., & Diamond, L. M. (2004). Sex. In R. M. Lerner & L. Steinberg (Eds.), *Handbook of adolescent development* (2nd ed., pp. 189–231). Hoboken, NJ: Wiley.

Savin-Williams, R., & Ream, G. (2003). Suicide attempts among sexual-minority male youth. *Journal of Clinical Child and Adolescent Psychology, 32,* 509–522.

Schubert, C. M., Chumlea, W. C., Kulin, H. E., Lee, P. A., Himes, J. H., & Sun, S. S. (2005). Concordant and discordant sexual maturation among U.S. children in relation to body weight and BMI. *Journal of Adolescent Health, 37,* 356–362.

Servin, A., Bohlin, G., & Berlin, D. (1999). Sex differences in 1-, 3-, and 5-year-olds' toy-choice in a structured play-session. *Scandinavian Journal of Psychology, 40,* 43–48.

Shaywitz, B. A., Shaywitz, S. E., Pugh, K. R., Constable, R. T., Skudlarski, P., Fulbright, R. K., . . . Gore, J. C. (1995). Sex differences in the functional organization of the brain for language. *Nature, 373*(6515), 607–609.

Shirtcliff, E. A., Dahl, R. E., & Pollak, S. D. (2009). Pubertal development: Correspondence between hormonal and physical development. *Child Development, 80*(2), 327–337.

Steinberg, L., Albert, D., Cauffman, E., Banich, M., Graham, S., & Woolard, J. (2008). Age differences in sensation seeking and impulsivity as indexed by behavior and self-report: Evidence for a dual systems model. *Developmental Psychology, 44*(6), 1764–1778.

Sun, S. S., Schubert, C. M., Liang, R., Roche, A. F., Kulin, H. E., Lee, P. A., . . . Chumlea, W. C. (2005). Is sexual maturity occurring earlier among U.S. children? *Journal of Adolescent Health, 37*(5), 345–355.

Susman, E. J., Houts, R. M., Steinberg, L., Belsky, J., Cauffman, E., DeHart, G., . . . Eunice Kennedy Shriver NICHD Early Child Care Research Network. (2010). Longitudinal development of secondary sexual characteristics in girls and boys between ages 9 ½ and 15 ½ years. *Archives of Pediatric Adolescent Medicine, 164*(2), 166–173.

Talpade, M. (2004). Nutritional differences as a function of early sexual maturation among African American girls. *North American Journal of Psychology, 6*(3), 383–392.

Talpade, M. (2010). Project HEALTH: Stages of secondary sexual characteristics and nutrition related correlates. *North American Journal of Psychology, 12*(1), 15–30.

Tamres, L. K., Janicki, D., & Helgeson, V. S. (2002). Sex differences in coping behavior: A meta-analytic review and an examination of relative coping. *Personality and Social Psychology Review, 6*(1), 2–30.

Thigpen, J. W. (2009). Early sexual behavior in a sample of low-income, African American children. *Journal of Sex Research, 46*(1), 67–79.

Tolman, D. L., & Diamond, L. M. (2001). Desegregating sexuality research: Cultural and biological perspectives on gender and desire. *Annual Review of Sex Research, 12*, 33–74.

Treynor, W., Gonzalez, R., & Nolen-Hoeksema, S. (2003). Rumination reconsidered: A psychometric analysis. *Cognitive Therapy and Research, 27*, 247–259.

Udry, J. R., & Billy, J. O. (1987). Initiation of coitus in early adolescence. *American Sociological Review, 52*, 841–855.

U.S. Census Bureau. (2005). *National Epidemiological Survey on Alcohol and Related Conditions, Wave 2, 2004-2005*. Washington, DC: Author.

Vander Zanden, J. W., Crandell, T. L., & Crandell, C. H. (2007). *Human development* (8th ed.). Boston: McGraw-Hill.

Verschuren, J. E. A., Enzlin, P., Dijkstra, P. U., Geertzen, J. H. B., & Dekker, R. (2010). Chronic disease and sexuality: A generic conceptual framework. *Journal of Sex Research, 47*(2–3), 153–170.

Whitehead, A. L. (2010). Sacred rites and civil rights: Religion's effect on attitudes toward same-sex unions and the perceived cause of homosexuality. *Social Science Quarterly, 91*(1), 63–78.

Wood, W., & Eagly, A. H. (2002). A cross-cultural analysis of the behavior of women and men: Implications for the origins of sex differences. *Psychological Bulletin, 128*(5), 699–727.

Worthington, R. L., & Reynolds, A. L. (2009). Within-group differences in sexual orientation and identity. *Journal of Counseling Psychology, 56*(1), 44–55.

Wronka, I., & Pawlinska-Chmara, R. (2005). Menarcheal age and socio-economic factors in Poland. *Annals of Human Biology, 32*, 630–638.

Xie, B., Chou, C. P., Spruit-Metz, D., Lie, C., Xia, J., Gong, J., . . . Johnson, C. A. (2005). Effects of perceived peer isolation and social support availability on the relationship between body mass index and depression symptoms. *International Journal of Obesity, 29*, 1137–1143.

Zahn-Waxler, C., & Polanichka, N. (2004). All things interpersonal: Socialization and female aggression. In M. Puttallaz & K. Bierman (Eds.), *Aggression, antisocial behavior, and violence among girls: A developmental perspective* (pp. 48–68). New York: Guilford Press.

Zakhari, R. (2009). Female sexual dysfunction: A primary care perspective. *Journal of the American Academy of Nurse Practitioners, 21*, 498–505.

CHAPTER 11

Abidin, R. R. (1992). The determinants of parenting behavior. *Journal of Clinical Child Psychology, 21*, 407–412.

Ainsworth, M. S. (1989). Attachments beyond infancy. *American Psychologist, 44*(4), 709.

Bank, L., Forgatch, M. S., Patterson, G. R., & Fetrow, R. A. (1993). Parenting practices of single mothers: Mediators of negative contextual factors. *Journal of Marriage and Family, 55*, 371–384.

Barber, B. K. (1996). Parental psychological control: Revisiting a neglected construct. *Child Development, 67*, 3296–3319.

Barth, J. M., & Parke, R. D. (1993). Parent-child relationship influences on children's transition to school. *Merrill-Palmer Quarterly, 39*, 173–195.

Bell, R. Q., & Chapman, M. (1986). Child effects in studies using experimental or brief longitudinal approaches to socialization. *Developmental Psychology, 22*, 595–603.

Belsky, J. (1984). The determinants of parenting: A process model. *Child Development, 55*, 83–96.

Belsky, J. (1993). Etiology of child maltreatment: A developmental-ecological analysis. *Psychological Bulletin, 114*(3), 413–434. doi:10.1037/0033-2909.114.3.413

Benzies, K., Trute, B., Worthington, C., Reddon, J., Keown, L., & Moore, M. (2011). Assessing psychological well-being in mothers of children with disability: Evaluation of the parenting morale index and family impact of childhood disability scale. *Journal of Pediatric Psychology, 36*(5), 506–516. doi:10.1093/jpepsy/jsq081

Betancourt, T., Borisova, I., de la Soudière, M., & Williamson, J. (2011). Sierra Leone's child soldiers: War exposures and mental health problems by gender. *Journal of Adolescent Health, 49*(1), 21–28.

Bretherton, I., & Munholland, K. A. (2008). Internal working models in attachment relationships: Elaborating a central construct in attachment theory.

In J. Cassidy & P. R. Shaver (Eds.), *Handbook of attachment* (pp. 102–127). New York: Guilford Press.

Bugental, D. B., Blue, J., & Cruzcosa, M. (1989). Perceived control over caregiving outcomes: Implications for child abuse. *Developmental Psychology, 25,* 532–539.

Bugental, D. B., Blue, J., & Lewis, J. (1990). Caregiver beliefs and dysphoric affect directed to difficult children. *Developmental Psychology, 26,* 631–638.

Burton, L., Henninger, D., Hafetz, J., & Cofer, J. (2009). Aggression, gender-typical childhood play, and a prenatal hormonal index. *Social Behavior and Personality, 37*(1), 105–116

Campbell, S. B. (1997). Behavior problems in preschool children: Developmental and family issues. In T. H. Ollendick & R. J. Prinz (Eds.), *Advances in clinical child psychology* (Vol. 19, pp. 1–26). New York: Plenum Press.

Cassidy, J., & Shaver, P. (Eds.). (2008). *Handbook of attachment: Theory, research, and clinical applications.* New York: Guilford Press.

Chamberlain, P., & Patterson, G. R. (1995). Discipline and child compliance in parenting. In M. H. Bornstein (Ed.), *Handbook of parenting, Vol. 4: Applied and practical parenting* (pp. 205–225). Hillsdale, NJ: Lawrence Erlbaum.

Chao, R. (2001). Extending research on the consequences of parenting style for Chinese Americans and European Americans. *Child Development, 72,* 1832–1843.

Cherney, I., & Dempsey, J. (2010). Young children's classification, stereotyping and play behaviour for gender neutral and ambiguous toys. *Educational Psychology, 30*(6), 651–669.

Clark, D., Thatcher, D., & Martin, C. (2010). Child abuse and other traumatic experiences, alcohol use disorders, and health problems in adolescence and young adulthood. *Journal of Pediatric Psychology, 35*(5), 499–510.

Cooper, H., Lindsay, J. J., & Nye, B. (2000). Homework in the home: How student, family, and parenting-style differences relate to the homework process. *Contemporary Educational Psychology, 25,* 464–487.

Crnic, K., & Acevedo, M. (1995). Everyday stresses and parenting. In M. H. Bornstein (Ed.), *Handbook of parenting: Applied and practical parenting* (Vol. 4, pp. 277–297). Mahwah, NJ: Lawrence Erlbaum.

Crockenberg, S., Jackson, S., & Langrock, A. M. (1996). Autonomy and goal attainment: Parenting, gender, and children's social competence. In

M. Killen (Ed.), *Children's autonomy, social competence, and interactions with adults and other children: Exploring connections and consequences* (pp. 41–56). San Francisco: Jossey-Bass.

Darling, N. (1999, March). *Parenting style and its correlates. ERIC DIGEST.* Champaign: ERIC Clearinghouse on Elementary and Early Childhood Education, University of Illinois (EDO-PS-99-3).

Darling, N., & Steinberg, L. (1993). Parenting style as context: An integrative model. *Psychological Bulletin, 113,* 487–496.

Deater-Deckard, K., & Dodge, K. A. (1997). Externalizing behavior problems and discipline revisited: Nonlinear effects and variation by culture, context, and gender. *Psychological Inquiry, 8,* 161–175.

DeWalt, D., & Hink, A. (2009). Health literacy and child health outcomes: A systematic review of the literature. *Pediatrics, 124*(5, Suppl. 3), S265–S274.

Dix, T. (1991). The affective organization of parenting: Adaptive and maladaptive processes. *Psychological Bulletin, 100,* 3–25.

Dix, T. (1992). Parenting on behalf of the child: Empathic goals in the regulation of responsive parenting. In I. E. Sigel, A. V. McGillicuddy-DeLisi, & J. J. Goodnow (Eds.), *Parental belief system* (pp. 319–346). Hillsdale, NJ: Lawrence Erlbaum Associates.

Dix, T., & Grusec, J. E. (1985). Parent attribution processes in the socialization of children. In I. Sigel (Ed.), *Parental belief systems* (pp. 201–234). Hillsdale, NJ: Lawrence Erlbaum.

Dix, T., & Lochman, J. (1990). Social cognition and negative reactions to children: A comparison of mothers of aggressive and nonaggressive boys. *Journal of Social and Clinical Psychology, 9,* 418–438.

Dyer, S., & Moneta, G. (2006). Frequency of parallel, associative, and co-operative play in British children of different socioeconomic status. *Social Behavior and Personality, 34*(5), 587–592.

Farley, T., Meriwether, R., Baker, E., Rice, J., & Webber, L. (2008). Where do the children play? The influence of playground equipment on physical activity of children in free play. *Journal of Physical Activity & Health, 5*(2), 319–331.

Fonagy, P., Gergely, G., Jurist, E., & Target, M. (2005). *Affect regulation, mentalization, and the development of the self.* New York: Other Press.

Frick, P. J., Lahey, B. B., Loeber, R., Tannenbaum, L., Van Horn, Y., Christ, M. A. G., . . . Hanson, K. (1993). Oppositional defiant disorder and conduct disorder: A meta-analytic review of factor analyses and cross-validation in a clinical sample. *Child Psychology Review, 13,* 319–340.

Friedrich, W. N., Tyler, J. D., & Clark, J. A. (1985). Personality and psychophysiological variables in abusive, neglectful, and low-income mothers. *The Journal of Nervous and Mental Disease, 173,* 449–460.

Geller, J., & Johnston, C. (1995). Predictors of mothers' responses to child noncompliance: Attributions and attitudes. *Journal of Clinical Child Psychology, 24,* 272–278.

Gershoff, E. T. (2002). Corporal punishment by parents and associated child behaviors and experiences: A meta-analytic and theoretical review. *Psychological Bulletin, 128*(4), 539.

George, C., & Solomon, J. (2008). The caregiving system: A behavioral systems approach to parenting. In J. Cassidy & P. R. Shaver (Eds.), *Handbook of attachment: Theory, research, and clinical applications* (2nd ed., pp. 833–856). New York: Guilford.

Ginsburg, G. S., & Bronstein, P. (1993). Family factors related to children's intrinsic/extrinsic motivational orientation and academic performance. *Child Development, 64,* 1461–1474.

Glasgow, K. L., Dornbusch, S. M., Troyer, L., Steinberg, L., & Ritter, P. L. (1997). Parenting styles, adolescents' attributions, and educational outcomes in nine heterogeneous high schools. *Child Development, 68,* 507–529.

Goodman, A., Joyce, R., & Smith, J. (2011). The long shadow cast by childhood physical and mental problems on adult life. *PNAS Proceedings of the National Academy of Sciences of the United States of America, 108*(15), 6032–6037.

Grolnick, W. S., Deci, E. L., & Ryan, R. R. (1997). Internalization within the family: The self-Determination theory perspective. In J. E. Grusec & L. Kuczynski (Eds.), *Parenting and children's internalization of values* (pp. 135–161). New York: John Wiley & Sons.

Grolnick, W. S., Kurowski, C. O., & Gurland, S. T. (1999). Family processes and the development of children's self-regulation. *Educational Psychologist, 34,* 3–14.

Grolnick, W. S., & Ryan, R. M. (1989). Parent styles associated with children's self-regulation and competence in school. *Journal of Educational Psychology, 81,* 143–154.

Grusec, J. E., & Goodnow, J. J. (1994). Impact of parental discipline methods on the child's internalization of values: A reconceptualization of current points of view. *Developmental Psychology, 30,* 4–19.

Grusec, J. E., Goodnow, J. J., & Kuczynski, L. (2000). New directions in analyses of parenting contributions to children's acquisition of values. *Child Development, 71,* 205–211.

Gutman, L. M., & Eccles, J. S. (1999). Financial strain, parenting behaviors, and adolescents' achievement: Testing model equivalence between African American and European American single- and two-parent families. *Child Development, 70,* 1464–1476.

Harkness, S., Zylicz, P., Super, C., Welles-Nyström, B., Bermúdez, M., Bonichini, S., & Mavridis, C. (2011). Children's activities and their meanings for parents: A mixed-methods study in six Western cultures. *Journal of Family Psychology, 25*(6), 799–813.

Hartley, S., Barker, E., Seltzer, M., Floyd, F., Greenberg, J., Orsmond, G., & Bolt, D. (2010). The relative risk and timing of divorce in families of children with an autism spectrum disorder. *Journal of Family Psychology, 24*(4), 449–457. doi:10.1037/a0019847

Hastings, P. D., & Grusec, J. E. (1998). Parenting goals as organizers of responses to parent-child disagreement. *Developmental Psychology, 34,* 465–479.

Hedegaard, M. (2009). Children's development from a cultural-historical approach: Children's activity in everyday local settings as foundation for their development. *Mind, Culture, and Activity, 16*(1), 64–81.

Hess, R. D., Halloway, S. D., Dickson, W. P., & Price, G. G. (1984). Maternal variables as redictors of children's school readiness and later achievement in vocabulary and mathematics in sixth grade. *Child Development, 55,* 1902–1912.

Holzman, L. (2008). *Vygotsky at work and play.* Routledge: Taylor & Francis.

Houck, C., Nugent, N., Lescano, C., Peters, A., & Brown, L. (2010). Sexual abuse and sexual risk behavior: Beyond the impact of psychiatric problems. *Journal of Pediatric Psychology, 35*(5), 473–483.

Human Rights Watch. (1996). *The small hands of slavery: Bonded child labor in India.* Retrieved October, 10, 2011, from http://www.hrw.org/reports/1996/India3.htm

Human Rights Watch. (2008). *Facts about child soldiers.* Retrieved October 9, 2011, from http://www.hrw.org/news/2008/12/03/facts-about-child-soldiers

Huntsinger, C. S., Jose, P. E., & Larson, L. (1998). Do parent practices to encourage academic competence influence the social adjustment of young European American and Chinese American children. *Developmental Psychology, 34,* 747–756.

Irish, L., Kobayashi, I., & Delahanty, D. (2010). Long-term physical health consequences of childhood sexual abuse: A meta-analytic review. *Journal of Pediatric Psychology, 35*(5), 450–461.

Kempe, C., Silverman, F., Steele, B., Droegemuller, W., & Silver, H. (1984). Landmark article July 7, 1962: The battered-child syndrome. *Journal of the American Medical Association, 251*(24), 3288–3294.

Knutson, J., Taber, S., Murray, A., Valles, N., & Koeppl, G. (2010). The role of care neglect and supervisory neglect in childhood obesity in a disadvantaged sample. *Journal of Pediatric Psychology, 35*(5), 523–532.

Kochanska, G. (1995). Children's temperament, mothers' discipline, and security of attachment: Multiple pathways to emerging internalization. *Child Development, 66*, 597–615.

Kochanska, G. (1997). Mutually responsive orientation between mothers and their young children: Implications of early socialization. *Child Development, 68*, 94–112.

Kochanska, G., Aksan, N., & Koenig, A. L. (1995). A longitudinal study of the roots of preschoolers' conscience: Committed compliance and emerging internalization. *Child Development, 66*, 1752–1769.

Kochanska, G., Kuczynski, L., & Maguire, M. (1989). Impact of diagnosed depression and self-reported mood on mothers' control strategies: A longitudinal study. *Journal of Abnormal Child Psychology, 17*, 493–511.

Kuczynski, L., & Kochanska, G. (1995). Function and content of maternal demands: Developmental significance of early demands for competent action. *Child Development, 66*, 616–628.

Kuczynski, L., Marshall, S., & Schell, K. (1997). Value socialization in a bidirectional context. In J. E. Grusec & L. Kuczynski (Eds.), *Parenting and children's internalization of values* (pp. 23–52). New York: John Wiley & Sons.

Lamborn, S., Mounts, N., Steinberg, L., & Dornbusch, S. M. (1991). Patterns of competence and adjustment from authoritative, authoritarian, indulgent, and neglectful families. *Child Development, 62*, 1049–1065.

Lanier, P., Jonson-Reid, M., Stahlschmidt, M., Drake, B., & Constantino, J. (2010). Child maltreatment and pediatric health outcomes: A longitudinal study of low-income children. *Journal of Pediatric Psychology, 35*(5), 511–522.

Leung, K., Lau, S., & Lam, W.-L. (1998). Parenting styles and academic achievement: A cross-cultural study. *Merrill-Palmer Quarterly, 44*, 157–172.

Lindsay, E. W., Mize, J., & Pettit, G. S. (1997). Differential play patterns of mothers and fathers of sons and daughters: Implications for children's gender role development. *Sex Roles, 37*, 643–661.

Lovejoy, M., Graczyk, P., O'Hare, E., & Neuman, G. (2000). Maternal depression and parenting behavior: A meta-analytic review. *Clinical Psychology Review, 20*(5), 561–592.

Lytton, H. (1990). Child and parent effects in boys' conduct disorder: A reinterpretation. *Developmental Psychology, 26*(5), 683–697. doi:10.1037/0012-1649.26.5.683

Lundahl, B. W., Bettmann, J., Hurtado, M., & Goldsmith, D. (2013). Different histories, different stories: Using a narrative tool to assess children's internal worlds. *Infant and Child Development: Child & Adolescent Social Work Journal*, doi:10.1007/s10560-013-0312-6

Maccoby, E. E. (1992). The role of parents in the socialization of children: An historical overview. *Developmental Psychology, 28*, 1006–1017.

Maccoby, E. E. (2002). Parenting effects: Issues and controversies. In J. G. Borkowski, S. L. Ramey, & M. Bristol-Power (Eds.), *Parenting and the child's world: Influences on academic, intellectual, and social-emotional development* (pp. 35–46). Mahwah, NJ: Lawrence Erlbaum.

Maccoby, E. E., & Martin, J. A. (1983). Socialization in the context of the family: Parent-child interaction. In E. M. Hetherington (Ed.), *Handbook of child psychology* (Vol. 4, pp. 1–101). New York: Wiley.

MacMillan, H. (2010). Commentary: Child maltreatment and physical health: A call to action. *Journal of Pediatric Psychology, 35*(5), 533–535.

Mann, B. J., & MacKenzie, E. P. (1996). Pathways among marital functioning, parental behaviors, and child behavior problems in school-age boys. *Journal of Clinical Child Psychology, 25*, 183–191.

Mason, D. A., & Frick, P. J. (1994). The heritability of antisocial behavior: A meta-analysis of twin and adoption studies. *Journal of Psychopathology and Behavioral Assessment, 16*, 301–323.

Miller, S. A. (1995). Parents' attributions for their children's behavior. *Child Development, 66*, 1557–1584.

Noll, J., & Shenk, C. (2010). Introduction to the special issue: The physical health consequences of childhood maltreatment—implications for public health. *Journal of Pediatric Psychology, 35*(5), 447–449.

Oswald, S., Heil, K., & Goldbeck, L. (2010). History of maltreatment and mental health problems in foster children: A review of the literature. *Journal of Pediatric Psychology, 35*(5), 462–472.

Parpal, M., & Maccoby, E. M. (1985). Maternal responsiveness and subsequent child compliance. *Child Development, 56,* 1326–1334.

Parten, M. (1933). Leadership among preschool children. *The Journal of Abnormal and Social Psychology, 27*(4), 430–440.

Patterson, G. R. (1986). Performance models for antisocial boys. *American Psychologist, 41,* 432–444.

Patterson, G. R. (1993). Orderly change in a stable world: The antisocial trait as a chimera. *Journal of Consulting and Clinical Psychology, 61*(6), 911–919. doi:10.1037/0022-006X.61.6.911

Patterson, G. R., Reid, J. B., & Dishion, T. J. (1992). *Antisocial boys.* Eugene, Oregon: Castalia.

Paxton, R., Jones, L., Rosoff, P., Bonner, M., Ater, J., & Demark-Wahnefried, W. (2010). Associations between leisure-time physical activity and health-related quality of life among adolescent and adult survivors of childhood cancers. *Psycho-Oncology, 19*(9), 997–1003.

Pinderhughes, E. E., Dodge, K. A., Bates, J. E., Pettit, G. S., & Zelli, A. (2000). Discipline responses influences of parents' socioeconomic status, ethnicity, beliefs about parenting, stress, and cognitive-emotional processes. *Journal of Family Psychology, 14,* 380–400.

Pomerantz, E. M., & Eaton, M. M. (2001). Maternal intrusive support in the academic context: Transactional socialization processes. *Developmental Psychology, 37,* 174–186.

Ritchie, K. L., & Holden, G. W. (1998). Parenting stress in low income battered and community women: Effects on parenting behavior. *Early Education & development, 9,* 97–112.

Roose, R., & Bouverne-De Bie, M. (2007). Do children have rights or do their rights have to be realised? The United Nations convention on the rights of the child as a frame of reference for pedagogical action. *Journal of Philosophy of Education, 41*(3), 431–443.

Rubin, K. H., & Mills, R. S. L. (1992). Parents' thoughts about children's socially adaptive and maladaptive behaviors: Stability, change, and individual. In I. E. Sigel, A. V. McGillicuddy-DeLisi, & J. J. Goodnow (Eds.), *Parental belief systems: The psychological consequences for children* (pp. 41–70). Hillsdale, NJ: Lawrence Erlbaum.

Rutter, M., Maughan, B., Meyer, J., Pickles, A., Silberg, J., Simonoff, E., & Taylor, E. (1996). Heterogeneity of antisocial behavior: Causes, continuities, and consequences. In R. A. Dienstbier & D. W. Osgood (Eds.), *Motivation and delinquency: Volume 44 of the Nebraska symposium on motivation* (pp. 45–119). Nebraska: The University of Nebraska Press.

Shaw, D. S., Keenan, K., & Vondra, J. I. (1994). Developmental precursors of externalizing behavior: Ages 1 to 3. *Developmental Psychology, 30,* 355–364.

Shaw, D. S., Winslow, E. B., Owens, E. B., Vondra, J. I., Cohn, J. F., & Bel l, R. Q. (1998). The development of early externalizing problems among children from low-income families: A transformational perspective. *Journal of Abnormal Child Psychology, 26,* 95–107.

Sofronoff, K., Jahnel, D., & Sanders, M. (2011). Stepping stones triple p seminars for parents of a child with a disability: A randomized controlled trial. *Research in Developmental Disabilities, 32*(6), 2253–2262. doi:10.1016/j.ridd.2011.07.046

Steinberg, L., Elmen, J., & Mounts, N. S. (1989). Authoritative parenting, psychosocial maturity, and academic success among adolescents. *Child Development, 60,* 1424–1436.

Steinberg, L., Lamborn, S. D., Darling, N., Mounts, N. S., & Dornbusch, S. M. (1994). Over-time changes in adjustment and competence among adolescents from authoritative, authoritarian, indulgent, and neglectful families. *Child Development, 65,* 754–770.

Steinberg, L., Lamborn, S. D., Dornbusch, S. M., & Darling, N. (1992). Impact of parenting practices on adolescent achievement: Authoritative parenting, school involvement, and encouragement to succeed. *Child Development, 63,* 1266–1281.

Stormshak, E. A., Bierman, K. L., McMahon, R. J., Lenguna, L. J., & CPPRG (2000). Parenting practices and child disruptive behavior problems in early elementary school. *Clinical Child Psychology, 29,* 17–29.

Sutton, S. E., Cowen, E. L., Crean, H. F., & Wyman, P. A. (1999). Pathways to aggression in young, highly stressed urban children. *Child Study Journal, 29,* 49–67.

Tewksbury, R., & Vito, G. (1994). Improving the educational skills of jail inmates: Preliminary program findings. *Federal Probation, 58*(2), 55–59.

Topitzes, J., Mersky, J., & Reynolds, A. (2010). Child maltreatment and adult cigarette smoking: A long-term developmental model. *Journal of Pediatric Psychology, 35*(5), 484–498.

Vacca, J. S. (2008). Crime can be prevented if schools teach juvenile offenders to read. *Children and Youth Services Review, 30*(9), 1055–1062.

Vinayak, S., & Sekhon, P. (2012). Parenting of children with learning disabilities and their siblings. *Journal of the Indian Academy of Applied Psychology, 38*(1), 84–92.

Wahler, R. G. (1997). On the origins of children's compliance and opposition: Family context, reinforcement, and rules. *Journal of Child and Family Studies, 6,* 191–208.

Wahler, R. G., Castellani, M. E., Smith, G. D., & Keathley, E. A. (1996). Solitary behavior and friendly social activity: Differential gateways for conduct problem versus normal child-mother dyads. *Journal of Clinical Child Psychology, 25,* 238–245.

Wakschlag, L. S., & Hans, S. L. (1999). Relation of maternal responsiveness during infancy to the development of behavior problems in high-risk youths. *Developmental Psychopathology, 35,* 569–579.

Wallin, D. J. (2007). *Attachment in psychotherapy.* New York: Guilford Press.

Westerman, M. A. (1990). Coordination of maternal directives with preschoolers' behavior in compliance-problem and healthy dyads. *Developmental Psychology, 26,* 621–630.

Williams, G. (1983). Child protection: A journey into history. *Journal of Clinical Child Psychology, 12*(3), 236–243.

Xu, Y. (2010). Children's social play sequence: Parten's classic theory revisited. *Early Child Development and Care, 180*(4), 489–498.

CHAPTER 12

Abma, J. C., Martinez, G. M., Mosher, W. D., & Dawson, B. S. (2004). Teenagers in the United States: Sexual activity, contraceptive use, and childbearing, 2002. *Vital Health Stat, 23*(24), 1–48. Hyattsville, MD: National Center for Health Statistics.

Allen, J., Porter, M., McFarland, F., Marsh, P., & McElhaney, K. (2005). The two faces of adolescents' success with peers: Adolescent popularity, social adaptation, and deviant behavior. *Child Development, 76,* 757–760.

American Psychiatric Association. (2000). *Diagnostic and statistical manual of mental disorders* (4th ed., text rev.). Washington, DC: Author.

Apte, U. M., Karmarkar, U. S., & Nath, H. (2008). Information services in the U.S. Economy: Value, jobs, and management implications. *California Management Review, 50*(3), 12–30.

Aud, S., Hussar, W., Planty, M., Snyder, T., Bianco, K., Fox, M., . . . Drake, L. (2010). *The Condition of Education 2010* (NCES 2010-028). Washington, DC: National Center for Education Statistics, Institute of Education Sciences, U.S. Department of Education.

Black, S. E., & Lynch, L. (2003). What's driving the new economy: The benefits of workplace innovation. *The Economic Journal, 114,* 97–116.

Boostup.org. (2012). *National dropout rates.* Retrieved July 31, 2012, from boostup.org/en/facts/statistics

Buchmann, C., & DiPrete, T. A. (2006). The growing female advantage in college completion: The role of family background and academic achievement. *American Sociological Review, 71,* 515–541.

Buchmann, C., DiPrete, T. A., & McDaniel, A. (2008). Gender inequalities in education. *Annual Review of Sociology, 34,* 319–337.

Bureau of Labor Statistics. (2010). *Back to college.* Retrieved from http://www.bls.gov/spotlight/2010/college/

Bureau of Labor Statistics. (2012). *Fastest growing occupations.* Retrieved from http://www.bls.gov/emp/ep_table_103.htm

Burwell, R., & Shirk, S. (2007). Subtypes of rumination in adolescence: Associations among brooding, reflection, depressive symptoms, and coping. *Journal of Clinical Child and Adolescent Psychology, 36,* 56–65.

Carver, K. P., Joyner, K., & Udry, R. (2003). National estimates of adolescent romantic relationships. In P. Florscheim (Ed.), *Adolescent romantic relations and sexual behavior* (pp. 23–56). Mahwah, NJ: Lawrence Erlbaum Associates.

Centers for Disease Control.(2012). *Epidemiological slide set on adolescents and young adults.* Retrieved from www.cdc.gov/hiv/graphics/adolesnt.htm

Centers for Disease Control and Prevention (CDC). (2004). Surveillance Summary no. 2: Youth Risk Behavior Surveillance. *Surveillance Summaries: Morbidity and Mortality Weekly Report, Vol. 53* (SS-2).

Centers for Disease Control and Prevention (CDC). (2011). *Attention-deficit/hyperactivity disorder (ADHD).* Retrieved from http://www.cdc.gov/ncbddd/adhd/data.html

Centers for Disease Control/National Center for Health Statistics (CDC/NCHS). (2009). *National survey of family growth, 2006–2008.* Washington, DC: Author.

Child Trends. (2011). *High school dropout rates.* Retrieved from http://www.childtrendsdatabank.org/?=node/162

Council on Competitiveness. (2008). *Thrive. The skills imperative.* Washington, DC: Author.

De Bellis, M. D. (2001). Developmental traumatology: The psychobiological development of maltreatment children and its implications for research, treatment and policy. *Development and Psychopathology, 13,* 537–561.

DiPrete, T. A., & Jennings, J. L. (2009). *Social/behavioral skill and the gender gap in early educational achievement.* Retrieved from http://www.ssc.wisc.edu/soc/faculty/docs/diprete/gender_social02232009.pdf

Eccles, J., & Roeser, R. W. (2003). Schools as developmental contexts. In G. Adams & M. Berzonsky (Eds.), *Blackwell handbook of adolescence* (pp. 129–148). Malden, MA: Blackwell.

Ennett, S., Tobler, N., Ringwalt, C., & Flewelling, R. (1994). How effective is drug abuse resistance education? A meta-analysis of project DARE outcome evaluations. *American Journal of Public Health, 84,* 1394–1400.

Entwisle, D. R., Alexander, K. L., & Olson, L. S. (1997). *Children, schools, and inequality.* Boulder, Colo: Westview Press.

Erikson, E. H. (1972). *Childhood and society.* Harmondsworth, Middlesex: Penguin Books.

Fallon, P., Katzman, M., & Wooley, S. C. (Eds.). (1996). *Feminist perspectives on eating disorders.* New York: Guilford Press.

Farrington, D. P., & Ttofi, M. M. (2009 December). School-based programs to reduce bullying and victimization. *Campbell Systematic Reviews, 6.*

Ferrer-Wreder, L., Palchuk, A., Poyrazli, S., Small, M. L., & Domitrovich, C. E. (2008). Identity and adolescent adjustment. *Identity: An International Journal of Theory and Research, 8(2),* 95–105.

Flum, H. (1994). The evolutive style of identity formation. *Journal of Youth and Adolescence, 23,* 489–498.

Forthun, L. F., Montgomery, M. J., & Bell, N. J. (2006). Identity formation in a relational context: A person-centered analysis of troubled youth. *Identity: An International Journal of Theory and Research, 6(2),* 141–167.

Francis, D. R. (2012). *Why do women outnumber men in college?* Cambridge, MA: National Bureau of Economic Research. Retrieved July 31, 2012, from http://www.nber.org/digest/jan07/w12139.html

Garbarino, J. (1999). *Lost boys: Why our sons turn violent and how we can save them.* New York: Free Press.

Gilligan, C. (1982). *In a different voice: Psychological theory and women's development.* Cambridge, MA: Harvard University Press.

Giordano, P. C., Longmore, M. A., & Manning, W. D. (2006). Gender and the meanings of adolescent romantic relationships: A focus on boys. *American Sociological Review, 71(2),* 260–287.

Grigg, W. S., Lauko, M. A., & Brockway, D. M. (2006). *The nation's report card: Science 2005* (NCES 2006–466). Washington, DC: National Center for Education Statistics, Institute of Education Sciences, U.S. Department of Education.

Harris, M. B., & Allgood, J. G. (2009). Adolescent pregnancy prevention: Choosing an effective program that fits. *Children and Youth Services Review, 31(12),* 1314–1320.

Heller, N. R. (2009). Eating disorders and treatment planning. In A. R. Roberts (Ed.), *Social workers' desk reference* (pp. 531–537). New York: Oxford University Press.

Henshaw, S. K. (2003). *U.S. teenage pregnancy statistics with comparative statistics for women aged 20–24.* New York: The Alan Guttmacher Institute. Data based on reports from National Center for Health Statistics (NCHS), AGI, CDC, and the Bureau of the Census.

Hick, K. M., & Katzman, D. K. (1999). Self-assessment of sexual maturation in adolescent females with anorexia nervosa. *Journal of Adolescent Health, 24,* 206–211.

Hoyle, R. H., Fejfar, M. C., & Miller, J. D. (2000). Personality and sexual risk-taking: A quantitative review. *Journal of Personality, 68,* 1203–1231.

Hunter College School of Social Work. (2007). *Preparation for adulthood supervising for success.* New York: Author.

Kaiser Family Foundation and Seventeen. (2001). *SexSmarts: Sexual Health Care and Counsel, 2001.* Washington, DC: Author.

Kaiser Family Foundation/ABC Television. (1998). *Sex in the 90s: 1998 National Survey of Americans on Sex and Sexual Health.*

Kaltiala-Heino, R., Marttunen, M., Rantanen, P., & Rimpela, M. (2003). Early puberty is associated with mental health problems in middle adolescence. *Social Science and Medicine, 57,* 1055–1064.

Kanof, M. E. (2003). *Youth illicit drug use prevention: DARE long-term evaluations and federal efforts to identify effective programs.* Washington, DC: General Accounting Office.

Kaye, W., Gendall, K., & Strober, M. (1998). Serotonin neuronal function and SSRI treatment in anorexia and bulimia nervosa. *Biological Psychiatry, 44,* 825–838.

Kirisci, L., Vanyukov, M., & Tarter, R. (2005). Detection of youth at high risk for substance use disorder: A longitudinal study. *Psychology of Addictive Behaviors, 19,* 243–252.

Klimstra, T. A., Hale, W. W., Raaijmakers, Q. A. W., Branje, S. J. T., & Meeus, W. H. J. (2010). Identity formation in adolescence: Change or stability? *Journal of Youth and Adolescence, 39,* 150–162.

Kost, K., Henshaw, S., & Carlin, L. (2010). *U.S. teenage pregnancies, births and abortions: National and state trends and trends by race and ethnicity.* Retrieved from http://www.guttmacher.org/pubs/USTPtrends.pdf

Kozol, J. (2005). *The shame of the nation.* New York: Crown.

Lee, J., Grigg, W. S. & Dion, G. (2007).*The nation's report card: Mathematics 2007* (NCES 2007–494). Washington, DC: National Center for Education Statistics, Institute of Education Sciences, U.S. Department of Education.

Levine, S. B., & Coupey, S. M. (2003). Adolescent substance use, sexual behavior, and metropolitan status: Is "urban" a risk factor? *Journal of Adolescent Health, 32,* 350–355.

LoGerfo, L., Nichols, A., & Chaplin, D. (2006). *Gender gaps in math and reading gains during elementary and high school by race and ethnicity.* Washington, DC: Urban Institute.

Markey, C. N., Markey, P. M., & Tinsley, B. J. (2003). Personality, puberty, and preadolescent girls' risky behaviors: Examining the predictive value of the five-factor model of personality. *Journal of Research in Personality, 37,* 405–419.

Meeus, W., Iedema, J., Heisen, M., & Vollebergh, W. (1999). Patterns of adolescent identity development: Review of literature and longitudinal analysis. *Developmental Review, 19,* 419–461.

Meredith, J. P. (2010). Combating cyberbullying: Emphasizing education over criminalization. *Federal Communications Law Journal, 63,* Article 13.

Moilanen, K. L., Crockett, L. J., Raffaelli, M., & Jones, B. L. (2010). Trajectories of sexual risk from mid-adolescence to early adulthood. *Journal of Research on Adolescence, 20,* S114–S139.

Moore, K., Miller, B., Sugland, B., Morrison, D., Glei, D., & Blumenthal, C. M. (2009). *Beginning too soon: Adolescent sexual behavior, pregnancy, and parenthood.* Retrieved from http://aspe.hhs.gov/hsp/cyp/xsteesex.htm

Mosher, W. D., & Jones, J. (2010). Use of contraception in the United States: 1982–2008. *Vital and Health Statistics, 29*(23).

National Runaway Switchboard. (2010). *NRS call statistics, 2010.* Retrieved March 14, 2010, from http://www.nrscrisisline.org/media/call_stats.html.

New York Administration for Children's Services (NYACS). (2006). *Preparing youth for adulthood.* New York: Author.

Nixon, K., Tutty, L., Downe, P., Gorkoff, K., & Ursel, J. (2002). The everyday occurrence: Violence in the lives of girls exploited through prostitution. *Violence against Women [Special Issue on Prostitution], 8*(9), 1016–1043.

Oakes, J. (1990). Opportunities, achievement and choice: Women and minority students in science and mathematics. In C. B. Casden (Ed.), *Review of educational research* (16th ed., pp. 153–222). Washington, DC: American Educational Research Association.

Ogbu, J. U. (2003). *Black American students in an affluent suburb: A study of academic disengagement.* New Jersey: Lawrence Erlbaum.

Orfield, G., Losen, D., Wald, J., & Swanson, C. (2004). *Losing our future: How minority youth are being left behind by the graduation rate crisis.* Cambridge, MA: The Civil Rights Project at Harvard University.

Organization for Economic Cooperation and Development. (2004). *Problem solving for tomorrow's world.* Paris: Author.

Partnership for 21st Century Skills. (2008). *21st century skills, education & competitiveness.* Tuscon, AZ: Author.

Patrick, H., Mantzzicopoulos, P., & Samarapungayan, A. (2009). Motivation for learning science in kindergarten: Is there a gender gap and does integrated inquiry and literacy instruction make a difference? *Journal of Research in Science Teaching, 46*(2), 166–191.

Pergamit, M. (2010). *On the lifetime prevalence of running away from home.* Washington, DC: The Urban Institute.

Reis, O., & Youniss, J. (2004). Patterns in identity change and development in relationships with mothers and friends. *Journal of Adolescent Research, 19,* 31–44.

Reynolds, M. D., Tarter, R. K., Kirillova, L., Brown, S., Clark, D. B., & Gavaler, J. (2007). Testosterone levels and sexual maturation predict substance disorders in adolescent boys: A prospective study. *Biological Psychiatry, 61*(11), 1223–1227.

Rice, K. G. (1990). Attachment in adolescence: A narrative and meta-analytic review. *Journal of Youth and Adolescence, 19*(5), 511–538.

Rigby, K. (2002). *New perspectives on bullying.* London, Jessica: Kingsley Publishers.

Rosenbaum, J. E. (2008). Reborn a Virgin: The validity of adolescent self-report of risk behaviors and the efficacy of abstinence pledges as a marker of subsequent sexual activity. *Dissertation Abstracts International, 69*(4).

Salahu-Din, D., Persky, H., & Miller, J. (2008). *The nation's report card: Writing 2007* (NCES 2008–468). Washington, DC: National Center for Education

Statistics, Institute of Education Sciences, U.S. Department of Education.

Santrock, J. W. (2008). *Life-span development*. Boston: McGraw-Hill.

Sloboda, Z., Stephens, R. C., Grey, S. S., Teasdale, B., Hawthorne, R. D., Williams, J., & Marquette, J. F. (2009). The adolescent substance abuse prevention study: A randomized field trial of a universal substance abuse prevention program. *Drug and Alcohol Dependence, 102*(1–3), 1–10.

Stage, S. A., & Quiroz, D. R. (1997). A meta-analysis of interventions to decrease disruptive classroom behavior in public education settings. *School Psychology Review, 26*(3), 333–368.

Tapia, J. (1998). The schooling of Puerto Ricans: Philadelphia's most impoverished community. *Anthropology and Education Quarterly, 29*(3), 297–323.

Thernstrom, S., & Thernstrom, A. (2003). *No excuses: Closing the racial gap in learning*. New York: Simon and Schuster.

Tozer, S., Senese, G., & Viloas, P. (2006). *School and society: Historical and contemporary perspectives*. New York: McGraw-Hill.

Trenholm, C., Devaney, B., Fortson, K., Quay, L., Wheeler, J., & Clark, M. (2007). *Impacts of four title V, section 510 abstinence education programs*. Princeton, NJ: Mathematica Policy Research, Inc.

UNICEF. (2011). *Life skills*. Retrieved from http://www.unicef.org/lifeskills/index_whichskills.html

Vander Zanden, J. W., Crandell, T. L., & Crandell, C. H. (2007). *Human development* (8th ed.). Boston: McGraw-Hill.

Veltman, M., & Browne, K. (2001). Three decades of child maltreatment research: Implications for the school years. *Trauma, violence and Abuse, 2*(3), 215–239.

Volz, A. R., & Kerig, P. K. (2010). Relational dynamics associated with adolescent dating violence: The roles of rejection sensitivity and relational insecurity. *Journal of Aggression, Maltreatment, and Trauma, 19*(6), 587–602.

Waterman, A. S. (1982). Identity development from adolescence to adulthood: An extension of theory and a review of research. *Developmental Psychology, 18*, 342–358.

Wentzel, K. R., Barry, C. M., & Caldwell, K. A. (2004). Friendships in middle school: Influences on motivation and school adjustment. *Journal of Educational Psychology, 96*, 195–203.

Wigfield, A., Byrnes, J. B., & Eccles, J. S. (2006). Adolescent development. In P. A. Alexander & P. Winne (Eds.), *Handbook of educational psychology* (2nd ed., pp. 87–113). Mahwah, NJ: Erlbaum.

Wilson, H. W., & Widom, C. S. (2010). The role of youth problem behaviors in the path from child abuse and neglect to prostitution: A prospective examination. *Journal of Research on Adolescence, 20*(1), 210–236.

Yoder, K., Whitbeck, L., & Hoyt, D. (2001). Event history analysis of antecedents to running away from home and being on the street. *American Behavioral Scientist, 45*, 61–65.

CHAPTER 13

AARP American Association of Retired Persons. (2003). *These four walls... Americans 45+ talk about home and community*. Washington, DC: Author.

Abrums, M. (2000). Death and meaning in a storefront church. *Public Health Nursing, 17*(2), 132–142.

Ahn, S., & Fedewa, A. (2011). A meta-analysis of the relationship between children's physical activity and mental health. *Journal of Pediatric Psychology, 36*(4), 385–397.

Alley, D. E., Soldo, B. J., Pagán, J. A., McCabe, J., deBlois, M., Field, S. H., . . . Cannuscio, C. C. (2009). Material resources and population health: Disadvantages in health care, housing, and food among adults over 50 years of age. *American Journal of Public Health, 99*, S693–S701.

Amato, P. R. (2000). The consequences of divorce for adults and children. *Journal of Marriage and the Family, 62*, 1269–1287.

Apatira, L., Boyd, E. A., Malvar, G., Evans, L. R., Luce, J. M., Lo, B., & White, D., B. (2008). Hope, truth, and preparing for death: Perspectives of surrogate decision makers. *Annals of Internal Medicine, 149*(12), 861–868.

Apovian, C. M. (2010). The causes, prevalence, and treatment of obesity revisited in 2009: What have we learned so far. *American Journal of Clinical Nutrition, 91*, 277–279.

Baker, L., & Gringart, E. (2009). Body image and self-esteem in older adulthood. *Aging and Society, 29*, 977–995.

Banister, E. M. (2000). Women's midlife confusion: "Why am i feeling this way?" *Issues in Mental Health Nursing, 21*, 745–764.

Banks, J., Breeze, E., Lessof, C., & Nazroo, J. (2006). *Retirement, health and relationships of the older population in England. The 2004 English longitudinal study of ageing (Wave 2)*. London: IFS.

Battaglia, D. M., Richard, F. D., Datteri, D. L., & Lord, C. G. (1998). Breaking up is (relatively) easy to do: A script for the dissolution of close relationships. *Journal of Social and Personal Relationships, 15,* 829–845.

Becker, D. (2006). Therapy for the middle-aged: The relevance of existential issues. *American Journal of Psychotherapy, 60*(1), 87–99.

Ben-Zur, H., & Michael, K. (2009). Social comparisons and well-being following widowhood and divorce. *Death Studies, 33,* 220–238.

Birditt, K. S., Miller, L. M., Fingerman, K. L., & Lefkowitz, E. S. (2009). Tensions in the parent and adult child relationship: Links to solidarity and ambivalence. *Psychology and Aging, 24,* 287–295.

Blazer, D. G. (2010). The origins of late-life depression. *Psychiatric Annals, 40*(1), 13–18.

Blazer, D. G., & Hybels, C. F. (2005). Origins of depression in later life. *Psychological Medicine, 35,* 1241–1252.

Boerner, K., Wang, S., & Cimarolli, V. R. (2006). The impact of functional loss: Nature and implications of life changes. *Journal of Loss and Trauma, 11,* 265–287.

Boul, L. A. (2003). Men's health and middle age. *Sexualities, Evolution & Gender, 5*(1), 5–22.

Bowling, A. (2009). Predictors of mortality among a national sample of elderly widowed people: Analysis of 28-year mortality rates. *Age and Aging, 38,* 527–530.

Braam, A., Beekman, A., Deeg, D., Smith, J., & van Tilburg, W. (1997). Religiosity as a protective or prognostic factor of depression in later life: Results from the community survey in the Netherlands. *Acta Psychiatra Scandinavica, 96,* 199–205.

Brown, B. B., Feiring, C., & Furman, W. (1999). Missing the love boat: Why researchers have shied away from adolescent romance. In W. Furman, B. B. Brown, & C. Feiring (Eds.), *The development of romantic relationships in adolescence* (pp. 1–18). New York: Cambridge University Press.

Brown, J. P., Gallicchio, L., Flaws, J. A., & Tracy, J. K. (2009). Relations among menopausal symptoms, sleep disturbance and depressive symptoms in midlife. *Maturitas, 62,* 184–189.

Brownson, R. C., Baker, E. A., Housemann, R. A., Brennan, L. K., & Bacak, S. J. (2001). Environmental and policy determinants of physical activity in the United States. *American Journal of Public Health, 91*(12), 1995–1200.

Brunell, A. B., Kernis, M. H., Goldman, B. M., Heppner Davis, P., Cascio, E. V., & Webster, G. D. (2010). Dispositional authenticity and romantic relationship functioning. *Personality and Individual Differences.* doi:10.1016/j.paid.2010.02.018

Buckley, T., McKinley, S., Tofler, G., & Bartrop, R. (2010). Cardiovascular risk in early bereavement: A literature review and proposed mechanisms. *International Journal of Nursing Studies, 47*(2), 229–238.

Bureau of Labor Statistics. (2011). *America's young adults at 23: School enrollment, training, and employment transitions between ages 22 and 23 summary.* Retrieved from http://www.bls.gov/news.release/nlsyth.nr0.htm

Butterworth, P., Gill, S., Rodgers, B., Anstey, K., Villamil, E., & Melzer, D. (2006). Retirement and mental health: Analysis of the Australian national survey of mental health and well-being. *Social Science Medicine, 62,* 1179–1191.

California State Parks. (2005). *The health and social benefits of recreation.* Sacramento: Author.

Cappeliez, P., & O'Rourke, N. (2002). Personality traits and existential concerns as predictors of the functions of reminiscence in older adults. *Journal of Gerontology: Psychological Sciences, 57B*(2), 116–123.

Carpenter, L. M., Nathanson, C. A., & Kim, Y. J. (2009). Physical women, emotional men: Gender and sexual satisfaction in midlife. *Archives of Sexual Behavior, 38,* 87–107.

Carr, D, & Boerner, K. (2009). Do spousal discrepancies in marital quality assessments affect psychological adjustment to widowhood? *Journal of Marriage and Family, 71,* 495–509.

Centers for Disease Control and Prevention. (2007, December). United States Life Tables. *National vital statistics reports, 56*(9). Hyattsville, MD: National Center for Health Statistics.

Centers for Disease Control and Prevention. (2010). *Obesity and overweight. fastStats.* Retrieved from http://www.cdc.gov/nchs/fastats/overwt.htm

Centers for Disease Control and Prevention, National Center for Injury Prevention and Control. (2005). *Web-based Injury Statistics Query and Reporting System (WISQARS)* [online]. Retrieved from www.cdc.gov/ncipc/wisqars

Chew, K. K., Earle, C. M., Stuckey, B. G. A., Jamrozik, K., & Keogh, E. J. (2000). Erectile dysfunction in general medical practice: Prevalence and clinical correlates. *International Journal of Impotence Research, 12,* 1–5.

Christakis, N. A., & Iwashyna, T. I. (2003). The health impact of health care on families: A matched cohort study of hospice use by decedents and mortality outcomes in surviving, widowed spouses. *Social Science & Medicine, 57,* 465–475.

Christopher, F. S., & Sprecher, S. (2000). Sexuality in marriage, dating, and other relationships: A decade review. *Journal of Marriage and the Family, 62,* 999–1017.

Cohen, J. A., Mannarino, A. P., & Knudsen, K. (2004). Treating childhood traumatic grief: A pilot study. *Journal of the American Academy of Child and Adolescent Psychiatry, 43,* 1225–1233.

Cui, M., Fincham, F. D., & Durtschi, J. A. (2010). The effect of parental divorce on young adults' romantic relationship dissolution: What makes a difference? *Personal Relationships.* doi:10.1111/j.1475-6811.2010.01306.x

Degges-White, S. (2001). Midlife transitions in women: Cultural and individual factors. *Adultspan Journal, 3*(1), 4–11.

Dinero, R. E., Conger, R. D., Shaver, P. R., Widaman, K. F., & Larsen-Rife, D. (2011). Influence of family of origin and adult romantic partners on romantic attachment security. *Journal of Couple and Family Psychology, 22*(3), 622–632.

Donnelly, P., & Coakley, J. (n.d.). *The role of recreation in promoting social inclusion.* Kanata, ON: Canadian Council on Social Development. Retrieved March 27, 2011, from. http://www.ccsd.ca/subsites/inclusion/bp/pd.html

Duntley, J. D., & Buss, D. M. (2002, June). *Stalking as a strategy of human mating.* Paper presented to the Annual Meeting of the Human Behavior and Evolution Society, Rutgers University, NJ.

Dupre, M. E., Beck, A. N., & Meadows, S. O. (2009). Marital trajectories and mortality among US adults. *American Journal of Epidemiology, 170*(5), 546–555.

Earle, J. R., Smith, M. H., Harris, C. T., & Longino, C. F. (1998). Women, marital status, and symptoms of depression in a midlife national sample. *Journal of Women and Aging, 10,* 41–57.

Ekeland, E., Heian, F., & Hagen, K. B. (2005). Can exercise improve self esteem in children and young people? A systematic review of randomized controlled trials. *British Journal of Sports Medicine, 39,* 792–798.

Elwert, F., & Christakis, N. A. (2008). The effects of widowhood on mortality by the causes of death of both spouses. *American Journal of Public Health, 98*(11), 2092–2098.

Erikson, E. H. (1972). *Childhood and society.* Harmondsworth, Middlesex: Penguin Books.

Fight Crime: Invest in Kids, California (FCIK). (2001). *California's after-school choice: Juvenile crime of safe learning time.* Retrieved from http://www.fightcrime.org/ca

Fingerman, K. L., Hay, E. L., Kamp Dush, C. M., Cichy, K. E., & Hosterman, S. (2007). Parents' and offsprings perceptions of change and continuity when parents experience the transition to old age. *Advances in Life Course Research, 12,* 275–306.

Fontaine, K. R. (2000). Physical activity improves mental health. *The Physician and Sport Medicine, 28*(10), 83–84.

Fors, S., Lennartsson, C., & Lundberg, O. (2009). Childhood living conditions, socioeconomic position in adulthood, and cognition in later life: Exploring the associations. *Journal of Gerontology: Social Science, 64B*(6), 750–757.

Fraley, R. C. (2010). *A brief overview of adult attachment theory and research.* Retrieved from http://internal.psychology.illinois.edu/~rcfraley/attachment.htm

Frazier, P. A., Byer, A. L., Fischer, A. R., Wright, D. M., & DeBord, K. A. (1996). Adult attachment style and partner choice: Correlational and experimental findings. *Personal Relationships, 3,* 117–137.

Freund, A. M., & Ritter, J. O. (2009). Midlife crisis: A debate. *Gerontology, 55,* 582–591.

Geda, Y. E., Roberts, R. O., Knopman, D. S., Christianson, T. J. H., Pankratz, V. S., Ivnik, R. J., . . . Rocca, W. A. (2010). Physical exercise, aging, and mild cognitive impairment: A population-based study. *Archives of Neurology, 67*(1), 80–86.

Gillen, M., & Kim, H. (2009). Older women and poverty transition. *Journal of Applied Gerontology, 28*(3), 320–341.

Gough, H. G., & Bradley, P. (1996). *California psychological inventory manual.* Palo Alto, CA: Consulting Psychologists Press.

Greenfield, E. A., & Marks, N. F. (2006). Linked lives: Adult children's problems and their parents' psychological and relational well-being. *Journal of Marriage and Family, 68,* 442–454.

Groese, R. (2002). VIP mission: Strengthening safety and security. *California Parks & Recreation Magazine, 58*(1), 42–44.

Haavio-Mannila, E., & Kontula, O. (1997). Correlates of increased sexual satisfaction. *Archives of Sexual Behavior, 26,* 399–419.

Haennel, R. G., & Lemire, F. (2002). Physical activity to prevent cardiovascular disease. How much is enough? *Canadian Family Physician, 48,* 65–71.

Hare, A. L., Miga, E. M., & Allen, J. P. (2009). Intergenerational transmission of aggression in romantic relationships: The moderating role of attachment security. *Journal of Family Psychology, 23*(6), 808–818.

Harvard Medical School. (2005). Living wills and health care proxies. *Harvard Health Letter, 30*(8), 1–3.

Hay, E. L., Fingerman, K. L., & Lefkowitz, E. S. (2008). The worries adult children and their parents experience for one another. *International Journal of Aging and Human Development, 67*, 101–127.

Hazan, C., & Shaver, P. (1987). Romantic love conceptualized as an attachment process. *Journal of Personality and Social Psychology, 52*, 511–524.

Hebert, R. S., Schulz, R., Copeland, V. C., & Arnold, R. M. (2009). Preparing family caregivers for death and bereavement: Insights from caregivers of terminally ill patients. *Journal of Pain Symptom Management, 37*(1), 3–12.

Helson, R., Jones, C., & Kwan, V. S. Y. (2002). Personality change over 40 years of adulthood: Hierarchical linear modeling analysis of two longitudinal samples. *Journal of Personality and Social Psychology, 83*(3), 752–766.

Helson, R., & Soto, C. J. (2005). Up and down in middle age: Monotonic and nonmonotonic changes in roles, status, and personality. *Journal of Personality and Social Psychology, 89*(2), 194–204.

Hinrichsen, G. A. (2009). Interpersonal psychotherapy: A treatment for late-life depression. *Psychiatric Annals, 39*(9), 838–843.

Holland, J. M., Schutte, K. K., Brennan, P. L., & Moos, R. H. (2010). The structure of late-life depressive symptoms across a 20-year span: A taxometric investigation. *Psychology and Aging, 25*(1), 142–156.

Howard, D. L., Sloane, P. D., Zimmerman, S., Eckert, K., Walsh, J. F., Buie, V. C., . . . Koch, G. G. (2002). Distribution of African Americans in residential care/assisted living and nursing homes: More evidence of racial disparity? *American Journal of Public Health, 92*(8), 1272–1277.

Howarth, R. A. (2011). Concepts and controversies in grief and loss. *Journal of Mental Health Counseling, 33*(1), 4–10.

Huckaby, R. W. (2008). Choosing a career. *eJournal USA.* Retrieved March 26, 2011, from http://www.America.gov/publications/ejournalusa/1208.html

InfoPlease. (2011). *Young adults living at home 1960-2005.* Retrieved March 25, 2011, from http://www.info-please.com/ipa/A0922218.html

Institute of Medicine. (1998). *Approaching death: Providing care at the end of life.* Washington, DC: Author.

Jacobs, H. S. (2000). The male menopause: Does it exist? Against: Problems of senescence in men are not analogous to female menopause. *British Medical Journal, 302*, 858–861.

Jaques, E. (1965). Death and the mid-life crisis. *International Journal of Psychoanalysis, 46*, 502–514.

Johnson, J. G., First, M. B., Block, S. D., Vanderwerker, L. C., Bambauer, K., Zhang, B., & Prigerson, H. G. (2009). Stigmatization and receptivity to mental health services among recently bereaved adults. *Death Studies, 33*, 691–711.

Johnston, S. G., & Thomas, A. M. (1996). Divorce versus, intact parental marriage and perceived risk and dyadic trust in present heterosexual relationships. *Psychological Reports, 79*, 387–390.

Jonasson, J. M., Hauksdottir, A., Valdirsmarsdottir, U., Furst, C. J., Onelöv, E., & Steineck, G. (2009). Unrelieved symptoms of female cancer patients during their last months of life and long-term psychological morbidity in their widowers: A nationwide population-based study. *European Journal of Cancer, 45*, 1839–1845.

Jung, C. G. (1971). *The portable Jung.* New York: Viking.

Karney, B. R., Beckett, M. K., Collins, R. L., & Shaw, R. (2007). *Adolescent romantic relationships as precursors of healthy adult marriages: A review of theory, research, and programs.* Santa Monica, CA: Rand Corporation.

Kearns-Bodkin, J. N., & Leonard, K. E. (2008). Relationship functioning among adult children of alcoholics. *Journal of Studies in Alcohol and Drugs, 69*(6), 941–950.

Keeley, T. J. H., & Fox, K. R. (2009). The impact of physical activity and fitness on academic achievement and cognitive performance in children. *International Review of Sport and Exercise Psychology, 2*(2), 198–214.

Keyes, C. L. M., & Ryff, C. D. (1999). Psychological well-being at midlife. In S. L. Willis & J. D. Reid (Eds.), *Life in the middle: Psychological and social development in middle age* (pp. 161–181). San Diego, CA: Academic Press.

Kotter-Gruhn, D., Kleinspehn-Ammerlahn, A., Gerstorf, D., & Smith, J. (2009). Self-perceptions of aging predict mortality and change with approaching death: 16-year longitudinal results from the Berlin Aging Study. *Psychology and Aging, 24*(3), 654–667.

Kraaij, V., Arensman, E., & Spinhoven, P. (2002). Negative life events and depression in elderly persons: A meta-analysis. *Journal of Gerontology. Series B: Psychological Sciences and Social Sciences, 57*(1), 87–94.

Krause, N. (2007). Stressors arising in highly valued roles and change in feeling close to god over time.

The International Journal for the Psychology of Religion, 17(1), 17–36.

Kubler-Ross, E. (1969). *On death and dying*. New York: Touchstone.

Kurpius, S. E., Nicpon, M. F., & Maresh, S. E. (2001). Mood, marriage, and menopause. *Journal of Counseling Psychology, 48*(1), 77–84.

Ladin, K., Daniels, N., & Kawachi, I. (2009). Exploring the relationship between absolute and relative position and late-life depression: Evidence from 10 European countries. *The Gerontologist, 50*(1), 48–59.

Lampinen, P., Heikkinen, R. L., Kauppinen, M., & Heikkinen, E. (2006). Activity as a predictor of mental well-being among older adults. *Aging and Mental Health, 10*, 454–466.

Langer, N. (2009). Late life love and intimacy. *Educational Gerontology, 35*, 752–764.

Larun, L., Nordheim, L. V., Ekeland, E., Hagen, K. B., & Heian, F. (2006). Exercise in prevention and treatment of anxiety and depression among children and young people. *Cochrane Database of Systematic Reviews, 2006*(3), CD004691. doi:10.1002/14651858. CD004691.pub2

Lock, M. (1991). Contested meanings of the menopause. *The Lancet, 337*, 1270–1272.

Mahatmya, D., & Lohman, B. (2011). Predictors of late adolescent delinquency: The protective role of after-school activities in low-income families. *Children and Youth Services Review, 33*(7), 1309–1317.

Manor, O., & Eisenbach, Z. (2003). Mortality after spousal loss: Are there socio-demographic differences? *Social Science and Medicine, 56*(2), 405–413.

Marcus-Newhall, A., Thompson, S., & Thomas, C. (2001). Examining a gender subtype: Menopausal women. *Journal of Applied Social Psychology, 31*, 698–719.

McFadden, J. R., & Swan, K. T. R. (2012). Women during midlife: Is it transition or crisis? *Family and Consumer Sciences Research Journal, 40*(3), 313–325.

McNamara, P. (2009). Workplace surfing hounds have new hero. *Network World, 26*(14), 34–34.

MedlinePlus. (2012). *Exercise and immunity*. Retrieved from http://www.nlm.nih.gov/medlineplus/ency/article/007165.htm

Merrick, E. L., Horgan, C. M., Hodgkin, D., Garnick, D. W., Houghton, S. F., & Panas, L. (2008). Unhealthy drinking patterns in older adults: Prevalence and associated characteristics. *Journal of the American Geriatrics Society, 58*, 214–223.

Mills, D. (2011). *A look at menopause across cultures. Women to women*. Retrieved from http://www.

womentowomen.com/menopause/menopause-acrosscultures.aspx

Montine, T. J., & Larson, E. B. (2010). Late-life dementias. *Journal of the American Medical Association, 302*(23), 2593–2594.

Mooney, L., Stanten, M., & Yeager, S. (2002). Cut your sick days [Electronic Version]. *Prevention, 54*(2), 66–69. Retrieved March 28, 2011, from EBSCOhost database

Moos, R. H., Schutte, K. K., Brennan, P. L., & Moos, B. S. (2009). Older adults' alcohol consumption and late-life drinking problems: a 20-year perspective. *Addiction, 104*, 1293–1302.

National Association of Home Builders (NAHB). (2005). *The National Older Adult Housing Survey*. Retrieved from http://www.toolbase.org/PDF/CaseStudies/NOAHSecondaryAnalysis.pdf

National Institute on Aging. (2010). *Alzheimer's disease fact sheet*. Silver Springs, MD: Author.

Nuttman-Shwartz, O. (2007). Is there life after work? *International Journal of Aging and Human Development, 64*, 129–147.

O'Rourke, N. (2004). Psychological resilience and the well-being of widowed women. *Ageing International, 29*(3), 267–280.

Ogilvie, D. M., & Rose, K. M. (1995). Self-with-other representations and a taxonomy of motives: Two approaches to studying persons. *Journal of Personality, 63*, 643–679.

Olofsson, A. S., & Collins, A. (2000). Psychosocial factors, attitude to menopause and symptoms in Swedish perimenoppausal women. *Climacteric, 3*(1), 33–42.

Osborne, J. W. (2009). Commentary on retirement, identity, and Erikson's developmental stage model. *Canadian Journal on Aging, 28*(4), 295–301.

Perillous, C., & Buss, D. M. (2008). Breaking up romantic relationships: Costs experienced and coping strategies. *Evolutionary Psychology, 6*(1), 164–181.

Phillips, L., Scott, C., Henry, J., Mowat, D., & Bell, S. (2010). Emotion perception in Alzheimer's disease and mood disorder in old age. *Psychology and Aging, 25*(1), 38–47.

Pillemer, K., & Suitor, J. J. (2002). Explaining mothers ambivalence toward their adult children. *Journal of Marriage and Family, 64*, 602–613.

Plante, T. G., Cage, C., Clements, S., & Stover, A. (2006). Psychological benefits of exercise paired with virtual reality: Outdoor exercise energizes while indoor virtual exercise relaxes. *International Journal of Stress Management, 13*, 108–117.

Rapp, E. (2004). *Childhood experiences and adult relationships*. SexualHealth.com. Retrieved March 19, 2010, from http://www.sexualhealth.com/article/read/love-relationships/healing-from-sexual-abuse/279/

Richardson, C. R., Faulkner, G., McDevitt, J., Skirinar, G. S., Hutchinson, D. S., & Piette, J. D. (2005). Integrating Physical Activity into Mental Health Services for Persons with Serious Mental Illness. *Psychiatric Services, 56*(3), 324–331.

Roisman, G. I., Clausell, E., Holland, A., Fortuna, K., & Elieff, C. (2008). Adult romantic relationships as contexts of human development: A multi-method comparison of same-sex couples with opposite-sex dating, engaged, and married dyads. *Developmental Psychology, 44*(1), 91–101.

Saisan, J., Smith, M., & Segal, J. (2010). *Relationship help*. Retrieved March 17, 2011, from http://www.helpguide.org/mental/improve_relationships.htm

Salary.com. (2012). *Wasting time at work 2012*. Retrieved from http://www.salary.com/wasting-time-at-work-2012/slide/2/

Santrock, J. W. (2008). *Life-span development*. Boston: McGraw-Hill.

Schwingel, A., Niti, M., Tang, C., & Ng, P. N. (2009). Continued work employment and volunteerism and mental well-being of older adults: Singapore longitudinal ageing studies. *Age and Ageing, 38,* 531–537.

Segal, J., Jaffee, J., & Barston, S. (2010). *Attachment and adult relationships*. Retrieved March 17, 2011, from http://www.helpguide.org/mental/eqa_attachment_bond.htm

Sevak, P., Weir, D., & Willis, R. (2004). The economic consequences of a husband's death: Evidence from the HRS and AHEAD. *Social Security Bulletin, 65*(3), 31–44.

Shaw, B. A., Liang, J., & Krause, N. (2010). Age and race differences in the trajectories of self-esteem. *Psychology and Aging, 25*(1), 84–94.

Siegler, I. C., & Costa, P. T., Jr. (1999, August). *Personality continuity and change in midlife men and women*. Symposium presented at the 107th Annual Convention of the American Psychological Association, Boston, MA.

Simpson, J. A., Rholes, W. S., & Phillips, D. (1996). Conflict in close relationships: An attachment perspective. *Journal of Personality and Social Psychology, 71,* 899–914.

Slattery, M. L. (2004). Physical activity and colorectal cancer. *Sports Medicine, 34*(4), 239–252.

Smith, K. P., & Christakis, N. A. (2009). Association between widowhood and risk of diagnosis with a sexually transmitted infection in older adults. *American Journal of Public Health, 99*(11), 2055–2062.

Smith, T. P., Kennedy, S. L., & Fleshner, M. (2004). Influence of age and physical activity on the primary in vivo antibody and T cell-mediated responses in men. *Journal of Applied Physiology, 97,* 491–498.

Stewart, A. J., & Ostrove, J. M. (1998). Women's personality in middle age. *American Psychologist, 53*(11), 1185–1194.

Tarrant, M. (1996). Attending to past outdoor recreation experiences: Symptom reporting and changes in affect. *Journal of Leisure Research, 28*(1), 1–17.

U.S. Department of Health and Human Services. (2002). *Trends in residential long-term care: Use of nursing homes and assisted living and characteristics of facilities and residents*. Washington, DC: Author.

Umberton, D. (2006). Parents, adult children, and immortality. *Contexts, 5*(4), 48–53.

Vig, E. K., & Pearlman, R. A. (2003). Quality of life while dying: A qualitative study of terminally ill older men. *Journal of the American Geriatrics Society, 51*(11), 1595–1601.

Walker, E. M., & Steffens, D. C. (2010). Understanding depression and cognitive impairment in the elderly. *Psychiatric Annals, 40*(1), 29–40.

Wallerstein, J. S., & Lewis, J. M. (2004). The unexpected legacy of divorce: Report of a 25-year study. *Psychoanalytic Psychology, 21,* 353–370.

Wannamethee, S. G., Shaper, A. G., & Alberta, K. G. M. M. (2000). Physical activity, metabolic factors, and the incidence of coronary heart disease and type 2 diabetes [Electronic version]. *Archives of Internal Medicine, 160*(14), 2108–2116.

Watson, J. (2000). Men's health: Some conclusions. In J. Watson (Ed.). *Male bodies: health, culture, and identity*. Buckingham: Open University Press.

Welk, G., & Blair, S. (2000). Physical activity protects against the health risks of obesity. *President's Council on Physical Fitness & Sport Research Digest, 3*(12).

Westerlund, H., Kivimäki, M., Singh-Manoux, A., Melchior, M., Ferrie, J. E., Jokela, M., Leineweber, C., Goldberg, M., Zins, M., & Vahtera, J. (2009). Self-rated health before and after retirement in France: a cohort study. *Lancet, 374,* 1889–1896.

Wethington, E. (2000). Expecting stress: Americans and the "midlife crisis." *Motivation and Emotion, 24*(2), 85–103.

Wethington, E., Kessler, R. C., & Pixley, J. E. (2004). Psychological turning points and the "midlife crisis." In O. G. Brim, C. D. Ryff, & R. C. Kessler (Eds.), *How healthy are we? A national study of well-being at midlife.* Chicago: University of Chicago Press.

Whitton, S. W., Waldinger, R. J., Schulz, M. S., Allen, J. P., Crowell, J. A., & Hauser, S. T. (2008). Prospective associations from family-of-origin interactions to adult marital interactions and relationship adjustment. *Journal of Family Psychology, 22,* 274–286.

Widom, C. S., Marmostein, N. R., & White, H. R. (2006). Childhood victimization and illicit drug use in middle adulthood. *Psychology of Addictive Behaviors, 20,* 394–403.

Wilson, H. W., & Widom, C. S. (2010). The role of youth problem behaviors in the path from child abuse and neglect to prostitution: A prospective examination. *Journal of Research on Adolescence, 20*(1), 210–236.

Winneke, A. H., Godde, B., Reuter, E., Vieluf, S., & Voelcker-Rehage, C. (2012). The association between physical activity and attentional control in younger and older middle-aged adults: An ERP study. *Gero-Psych: The Journal of Gerontopsychology and Geriatric Psychiatry, 25*(4), 207–221.

Zayas, V., Mischel, W., Shoda, Y., & Aber, J. L. (2010). Roots of adult attachment: Maternal caregiving at 18 months predicts adult peer and partner attachment. *Social Psychological and Personality Science,* Prepublished November 15, 2010, doi:10.1177/1948550610389822

CHAPTER 14

Acevedo, B. P., & Aron, A. (2009). Does a long-term relationship kill romantic love? *Review of General Psychology, 13*(1), 59–65.

Alegre, A. (2011). Parenting styles and children's emotional intelligence: What do we know? *The Family Journal: Counseling and Therapy for Couples and Families, 19*(1), 56–62.

Allen, K. R., & Demo, D. H. (1995). The families of lesbians and gay men: A new frontier fin family research. *Journal of Marriage and Family, 57,* 111–127.

Amato, P. R. (2000). The consequences of divorce for adults and children. *Journal of Marriage and the Family, 62,* 1269–1287.

Anderson, E. R., & Greene, S. M. (2005). Transitions in parental repartnering after divorce. *Journal of Divorce and Remarriage, 43*(3/4), 47–62.

Anderson, E. R., Greene, S. M., Walker, L., Malerba, C. A., Forgatch, M. S., & DeGarmo, D. S. (2004). Ready to take a chance again: Transitions into dating among divorcing parents. *Journal of Divorce & Remarriage, 40,* 61–75.

Arbuckle, N., & de Vries, B. (1995). The long term effects of late life spousal and parental bereavement on personal functioning. *The Gerontologist, 35,* 637–647.

Attar-Schwartz, S., Tan, J., & Buchanan, A. (2009). Adolescents' perspectives on relationships with grandparents: The contribution adolescent, grandparent, and parent-grandparent relationship variables. *Children and Youth Services Review, 31*(9), 1057–1066.

Baldwin, A. L., Baldwin, C. P., & Cole, R. E. (1990). Stress-resistant families and stress-resistant children. In J. Rolf, A. S. Masten, D. Cicchetti, K. H. Neuchterlein, & S. Weintraub (Eds.), *Risk and protective factors in the development of psychopathology* (pp. 257–280). New York: Cambridge University Press.

Bandura, A. (1977). *Social Learning Theory.* Englewood Cliffs, NJ: Prentice Hall.

Baxter, L. A., Braithwaite, D. O., & Nicholson, J. (1999). Turning points in the development of blended family relationships. *Journal of Social and Personal Relationships, 16*(3), 291–313.

Bernard, J. (1982). *The future of marriage.* New Haven, CT: Yale University Press.

Bernstein, A. C. (2000). Remarriage: Redesigning couplehood. In P. Papp (Ed.), *Couples on the fault line: New directors for therapists* (pp. 284–311). New York: Guilford Press.

Bowen, M. (1978). *Family therapy in clinical practice.* New York: Jason Aronson.

Bowser, B. P., Word, C. O., Stanton, M. D., & Coleman, S. B. (2003). Death in the family and HIV risk-taking among intravenous drug users. *Family Process, 42*(2), 291–304.

Braithwaite, D. O., Olson, L. N., Golish, T. D., Soukup, C., & Turman, P. (2001). "Becoming a family": Developmental processes represented in blended family discourse. *Journal of Applied Communication Research, 29*(3), 221–247.

Bramlett, M. D., & Mosher, W. D. (2002). Cohabitation, marriage, divorce, and remarriage in the United States. National Center for Health Statistics. *Vital Health and Statistics, 23*(22).

Brien, M. J., Lillard, L. A., & Waite, L. J. (1999). Interrelated family-building behaviors: Cohabitation, marriage, and nonmarital conception. *Demography, 36*, 535–551.

Brown, J. D. (2008). Foster parents' perceptions of factors needed for successful foster placements. *Journal of Child and Family Studies, 17*, 538–554.

Brown, S. L. (2000). Union transitions among cohabitors: The signifance of relationship assessments and expectations. *Journal of Marriage and the Family, 62*, 833–846.

Brown, S. L., & Booth, A. (1996). Cohabitation versus marriage: A comparison of relationship quality. *Journal of Marriage and the Family, 58*, 668–678.

Buehler, C., Cox, M. E., & Cuddeback, G. (2003). Foster parents' perceptions of factors that promote or inhibit successful fostering. *Qualitative Social Work: Research and Practice, 2*, 61–83.

Calzada, E. J., Huang, K.-Y., Anicama, C., Fernandez, Y., & Brotman, L. M. (2012, June 11). Test of a cultural framework of parenting with Latino families of young children.

Cano, A., & Vivian, D. (2003). Are life stressors associated with marital violence? *Journal of Family Psychology, 17*(3), 302–314.

Carson, D.K., Gertz, L.M., Donaldson, M.A., & Wonderlich, S. A. (1991). Intrafamilial sexual abuse: family-of-origin and family-of-procreation characteristics of female adult victims. *Journal of Psychology, 125*(5), 579–597.

Carter, B., & McGoldrick, M. (2005). *The expanded family life cycle* (3rd ed.). Boston: Allyn & Bacon.

Centers for Disease Control and Prevention. (2001). *First marriage dissolution, divorce, and remarriage: United States*. Hyattsville, MD: Author.

Centers for Disease Control and Prevention. (2002). *Cohabitation, marriage, divorce, and remarriage in the United States*. Retrieved from http://www.cdc.gov/nchs/pressroom/02news/div_mar_cohab.htm

Cerel, J., & Roberts, T. A. (2005). Suicidal behavior in the family and adolescent risk behavior. *Journal of Adolescent Health, 36*, 352–416.

Cerel, J., Jordan, J., & Duberstein, P. (2008). The impact of suicide on the family. *Crisis: The Journal of Crisis Intervention and Suicide Prevention, 29*(1), 38–44.

Chan, R. W., Raboy, B., & Patterson, C. J. (1998). Psychosocial adjustment among children conceived via donor insemination by lesbian and heterosexual mothers. *Child Development, 69*, 443–457.

Charlton, R., Sheahan, K., Smith, G., & Campbell, I, (2001). Spousal bereavement – implications for health. *Family Practice, 18*, 614–618.

Chipungu, S. S., & Bent-Goodley, T. B. (2004). Meeting the challenges of contemporary foster care. *The Future of Children, 14*, 75–93.

Coall, D. A.., Meier, M., Hertwig, R., Wänke, M., & Höpflinger, F. (2009). Grandparental investment: The influence of reproductive timing and family size. *American Journal of Human Biology, 21*, 455–463.

Cobb, N. P., Larson, J. H., & Watson, W. L. (2003). Development of the attitudes about romance and mate selection scale. *Family Relations, 52*, 222–231.

Cole, S. A. (2005). Foster caregiver motivation and infant attachment: How do reasons for fostering affect relationships? *Child and Adolescent Social Work Journal, 22*, 441–457.

Coplan, R. J., Hastings, P. D., Lagace, Seguin, D. G., & Moulton, C. E. (2002). Authoritative and authoritarian mothers' parental goals, attributions and emotions across different childrearing contexts. *Parenting: Science and Practice, 2*, 1–26.

Crum, W. (2010). Foster parent parenting characteristics that lead to increased placement stability or disruption. *Children and Youth Services Review, 32*, 185–190.

Cunningham, M., & Thornton, A. (2005). The influence of union transitions on White adults attitudes toward cohabitation. *Journal of Marriage and Family, 67*, 710–720.

De Vries, B., & Johnson, C. L. (2002). The death of a friend in later life. *Advances in Life Course Research: New Frontiers in Socialization, 7*, 299–324.

Delsol, C., & Margolin, G. (2004). The role of family-of-origin violence in men's marital violence perpetration. *Clinical Psychology Review, 24*, 99–122.

Dennerstein, L., Dudley, E., & Guthrie, J. (2002). Empty nest or revolving door? A prospective study of women's quality of life in midlife during the phase of children leaving and re-entering the home. *Psychological Medicine, 32*, 545–550.

Denuwelaere, M., & Bracke, P. (2007). Support and conflict in the foster family and children's well-being: A comparison between foster and birth children. *Family Relations, 56*, 67–79.

Domenech Rodríguez, M. M., Donovick, M. R., & Crowley, S. L. (2009). Parenting styles in a cultural context: Observations of "protective parenting" in first-generation Latinos. *Family Process, 48*, 195–210.

Dudley, J. R., & Stone, G. (2001). *Fathering at risk*. New York: Springer.

Dupuis, S. B. (2007). Examining remarriage: A look at issues affecting remarried couples and implications toward therapeutic techniques. *Journal of Divorce & Remarriage, 48*(1/2), 91–103.

Dush, C. M. K., Cohan, C. L., & Amato, P. R. (2003). The relationship between cohabitation and marital quality and stability: Change across cohorts? *Journal of Marriage and Family, 65,* 539–549.

Dutton, D. G. (2003). The *abusive personality: Violence and control in intimate relationships.* New York: Guilford Press.

Edwards, O. W. (2009). Empirical investigation of the psychosocial functioning of children raised by grandparents. *Journal of Applied School Psychology, 25,* 128–145.

Erickson, M. J. (1998). Re-visioning the family life cycle theory and paradigm in marriage and family therapy. *The American Journal of Family Therapy, 26,* 341–356.

Faber, A. J. (2004). Examining remarried couples through a Bowenian family systems lens. *Journal of Divorce & Remarriage, 40*(3/4), 121–133.

Fite, P. J., Stoppelbeing, L., & Greening, L. (2009). Predicting readmission fto a child psychiatric inpatient unit: The impact of parenting styles. *Journal of Child and Family Studies, 18,* 621–629.

Garcia Coll, C. T., & Pachter, L. (2002). Ethnic and minority parenting. In M. H. Bornstein (Ed.), *Handbook of parenting* (pp. 189–209). Mahwah, NJ: Erlbaum.

Gilligan, C. (1982). *In a different voice: Psychological theory and women's development.* Cambridge, MA: Harvard University Press.

Ginsburg, K. R., Durbin, D. R., García-España, J. F., Kalicka, E. A., & Winston, F. K. (2009). The Association Between Parenting Style and Teen Driving Safety-related Behaviors and Attitudes. *Pediatrics, 124*(4), 1040–1051.

Glass, J. C. Jr., & Huneycutt, T. L. (2002). Grandparents parenting grandchildren: Extent of situation, issues involved and educational implications. *Educational Gerontology, 28*(2), 193–161.

Glenn, N., & Marquardt, E. (2001). *Hooking up, hanging out, and hoping for Mr. Right: College women on dating and mating today.* New York: Institute for American Values.

Goldenberg, H., & Goldenberg, I. (2008). Family Therapy. Belmont, CA: Brooks/Cole.

Golish, T. D. (2003). Stepfamily communication strengths: Understanding the ties that bind. *Human Communication Research, 29*(1), 41–80.

Golombok, S., Perry, B., Burston, A., Murray, C., Mooney-Sommers, J, Stevens, M., & Golding, J. (2003). Children with lesbian parents: A community study. *Developmental Psychology, 38,* 20–33.

Gottman, J. S. (1994). What *predicts divorce?* Hillsdale, NJ: Erlbaum.

Green, J. B. (2003). *Introduction to family theory & therapy.* Pacific Grove, CA: Brooks/Cole.

Greening, L., Stoppelbein, L., & Luebbe, A. (2010). The moderating effects of parenting styles on African-American and Caucasian children's suicidal behavior. *Journal of Youth and Adolescence, 39,* 357–369.

Harris, G. T., Hilton, N. Z., Rice, M. E., & Eke, A. W. (2007). Children killed by genetic parents versus stepparents. *Evolution and Human Behavior, 28,* 85–95.

Heller, S. S., Smyke, A. T., & Boris, N. W. (2002). Very young foster children and foster families: Clinical challenges and interventions. *Infant Mental Health Journal, 23*(5), 555–575.

Hiedemann, B., Suhomlinova, O., & O'Rand. (1998). Economic independence, economic status, and empty nest in midlife marital disruption. *Journal of Marriage and the Family, 60,* 219–231.

Howell, M. J., & Pugliesi, K. L. (1988). Husbands who harm: Predicting spousal violence by men. *Journal of Family Violence, 3,* 272–279.

Huston, T. L., Caughlin, J. P., Houts, R. M., Smith, S. E., & George, L. J. (2001). The connubial crucible: Newlywed years as predictors of marital delight, distress, and divorce. *Journal of Personality and Social Psychology, 80,* 237–252.

Julian, T. W., McKenry, P. C., Gavazzi, S. M., & Law, J. C. (1999). Test of family of origin structural models of male verbal and physical aggression. *Journal of Family Issues, 20*(3), 397–423.

Kapinus, C. A., & Johnson, M. P. (2003). The utility of family life cycle as a theoretical and empirical tool. *Journal of Family Issues, 24*(2), 155–184.

Katz-Wise, S. L., Priess, H. A., & Hyde, J. S. (2010). Gender-role attitudes and behavior across the transition to parenthood. *Developmental Psychology, 46*(1), 18–28.

Kaufman, G., & Elder, G. H. (2003). Grandparenting and age identity. *Journal of Aging Studies, 17,* 269–282.

Kelly, J. B. (2003). Parents with enduring child disputes: Multiple pathways to enduring disputes. *Journal of Family Studies, 9*(1), 37–50.

Kerr, M., & Bowen, M. (1987). *Family Evaluation: An Approach Based on Bowen* Theory. New York: W. W. Norton.

Kirton, D., Beecham, J., & Ogilvie, K. (2006). Adoption by foster carers: A profile of interest and outcomes. *Child and Family Social Work, 11*, 139–146.

Lambert, S. (2005). Gay and lesbian families: What we know and where to go from here. *The Family Journal: Counseling and Therapy for Couples and Families, 13*(1), 43–51.

Landau, J. (2009). Straightening out (the politics of) same-sex parenting: Representing gay families in U.S. print new stories and photographs. *Critical Studies in Media Communication, 26*(1), 80–100.

Larson, J. H. (1992). You're my one and only: Premarital counseling for unrealistic beliefs about mate selection. *American Journal of Family Therapy, 20*, 242–253.

Larson, J. H., & Holman, T. B. (1994). Premarital predictors of marital quality and stability. *Family Relations, 43*, 228–237.

Larson, J. H., Peterson, D. J., Heath, V. A., & Birch, P. (2000). The relationship between perceived dysfunctional family-of-origin rules and intimacy in young adult dating relationships. *Journal of Sex & Marital Therapy, 26*, 161–175.

Levant, R., & Pollack, W., (Eds.) (1995). *A new psychology of men*. New York: Basic.

Levant, R. F., Hall, R. J., Williams, C. M., & Hasan, N. T. (2009). Gender differences in Alexithymia. *Psychology of Men & Masculinity, 19*(3), 190–203.

Li, J. H., & Wojtkiewicz, R. A. (1994). Childhood family structure and entry into first marriage. *The Sociological Quarterly, 35*(2), 247–268.

Linares, L. O., Montalto, D., Li, M., & Oza, V. S. (2006a). A promising parenting intervention in foster care. *Journal of Consulting and Clinical Psychology, 74*, 32–41.

Lincoln, K. D., Taylor, R. J., & Jackson, J. S. (2008). Romantic relationships among unmarried African Americans and Caribbean Blacks: Findings from the National Survey of American Life. *Family Relationships, 57*, 254–266.

Lohan, J. A. (2002). Family functioning and family typology after an adolescent or young adult's sudden violent death. *Journal of Family Nursing, 8*, 49.

Manning, W. D., Longmore, M. A., & Giordano, P. C. (2005). Adolescents' involvement in nonromantic sexual activity. *Social Science Research, 34*, 384–407.

Manning, W. D. (1993). Marriage and cohabitation following premarital conception. *Journal of Marriage and the Family, 55*, 839–850.

Manning, W. D., & Lamb, K. A. (2003). Adolescent well-being in cohabiting, married, and single-parent families. *Journal of Marriage and Family, 65*, 876–893.

Manning, W. D., & Landale, N. S. (1996). Racial and ethnic differences in the role of cohabitation in premarital childbearing. *Journal of Marriage and the Family, 58*, 63–77.

Mason, J., May, V., & Clarke, L. (2007). Ambivalence and the paradoxes of grandparenting. *The Sociological Review, 55*(4), 687–706.

McNiel, D. E., Hatcher, C., & Reubin, R. (1988). Family survivors of suicide and accidental death: consequences for widows. *Suicide & Life Threat Behavior, 18*(2), 137–148.

Miles , D. R., & Carey, G. (1997). Genetic and environmental architecture of human aggression. *Journal of Personality and Social Psychology, 72*, 207–217.

Mitchell, B. A., & Lovegreen, L. D. (2009). *The empty nest syndrome in midlife families. Journal of Family Issues, 30*(12), 1651–1670.

Morrill, M. I., Hines, D. A., Mahmood, S., & Cordova, J. V. (2010). Pathways between marriage and parenting for wives and husbands: The role of coparenting. *Family Process, 49*(1), 59–73.

Moss, M., Lesher, L., & Moss, S. (1986–1987). Impact of the death of an adult child on elderly parents: Some observations. *Omega, 17*, 209–218.

Moss, S., & Moss, M. (1989). The impact of the death of an elderly sibling. *American Behavioral Scientist, 33*, 94–106.

Mueller, M. M., Wilhelm, B., & Elder, G. H. (2002). Variations in grandparenting. *Research on Aging, 24*(3), 360–388.

Niehuis, S., Skogrand, L., & Huston, T. L. (2006). When marriages die: Premarital and early marriage precursors to divorce. *The Forum for Family and Consumer Issues, 11*(1), 1–9. Retrieved from http://ncsu.edu/ffci/publications/2006/v11-n1-2006-june/fa-1-marriages-die.php

O'Rand, A. M., & Krecker, M. L. (1990). Concepts of the life cycle: Their history, meanings, and uses in the social sciences. *Annual Review of Sociology, 16*, 241–262.

Orme, J. G., Buehler, C., McSurdy, M., Rhodes, K. W., Cox, M. E., & Patterson, D. A. (2004). Parental and familial characteristics of family foster care applicants. *Children and Youth Services Review, 26*, 307–329.

Oswald, R. F. (2002). Resilience within the family networks of lesbians and gay men: Intentionality and redefinition. *Journal of Marriage and Family, 64*(2), 374–383.

Peel, E., & Harding, R. (2004). Divorcing romance, rights and radicalism: Beyond pro and anti in the lesbian and gay marriage debate. *Feminism & Psychology, 14*(4), 588–599.

Perlman, S. B., Camras, L. A., & Pelphrey, K. A. (2008). Physiology and functioning: Parent vagal tone, emotion socialization, and children's emotion knowledge. *Journal of Experimental Child Psychology, 100*(4), 308–315.

Pinsof, W. M. (2002). Introduction to the special issue on marriage in the 20th century in western civilization: Trends, research, therapy, and perspectives. *Family Process, 41*, 133–134.

Portie, T., & Hill, N. R. (2005). Blended families: A critical review of the current research. *The Family Journal: Counseling and Therapy for Couples and Families, 13*(4), 445–451.

Radziszewska, B., Richardson, J. L., Dent, C. W., & Flay, B. R. (1996). Parenting style and Adolescent Depressive symptoms, Smoking, and Academic Achievement: Ethnic, Gender, and SES Differences. *Journal of Behavioral Medicine, 19*(3), 289–305.

Raley, R. K., Crissey, S., & Muller, C. (2007). Of sex and romance: Late adolescent relationships and young adult union formation. *Journal of Marriage and Family, 69*, 1210–1226.

Rao, K., & DeMaris, A., (1995). Coital frequency among married and cohabiting couples in the United States. *Journal of Biosocial Science, 27*, 135–150.

Rice, J. K. (1994). Reconsidering research on divorce, family life cycle, and the meaning of family. *Psychology of Women Quarterly, 18*, 559–584.

Robitaille, C., & Saint-Jacques, M. (2009). Social stigma and the situation of young people in lesbian and gay stepfamilies. *Journal of Homosexuality, 56*, 421–442.

Rodriguez, C. M. (2010). Parent-child aggression: Association with child abuse potential and parenting styles. *Violence and Victims, 25*(6), 728–741.

Rossiter, A. (1991). Initiator status and separation adjustment. *Journal of Divorce and Remarriage, 15*, 141–155.

Rothrauff, T. C., Cooney, T. M., & An, J. S. (2009). Remembered parenting styles and adjustments in middle and late adulthood. *Journal of Gerontology: Social Sciences, 64B*(1), 137–146.

Sakraida, T. J. (2005). Divorce transition differences of midlife women. *Issues in Mental Health Nursing, 26*, 225–249.

Sakraida, T. J. (2008). Stress and coping of midlife women in divorce transition. *Western Journal of Nursing Research, 30*(7), 869–887.

Schmidt, P. J., Murphy, J. H., Haq, N., Rubinow, D. R., & Danaceau, M. A. (2004). Stressful life events, personal losses, and perimenopause-related depression. *Archives of Women's Mental Health, 7*(1), 19–26.

Schoen, R., Landale, N. S., & Daniels, K. (2007). Family transitions in young adulthood. *Demography, 44*, 807–820.

Schofield, G., & Beek, M. (2005). Providing a secure base: Parenting children in long-term foster family care. *Attachment & Human Development, 7*(1), 3–25.

Shaw , B. A. , Krause, N. , Chatters, L. M. , Connell, C. M. , & Ingersoll-Dayton, B. (2004). Emotional support from parents early in life, aging, and health. *Psychology and Aging, 19*, 4–12.

Sichel, M., & Cervini, A. L. (ND). The ties that bind, the ties that strangle. *Psyber Square*. Retrieved April 21, 2011, from http://www.psybersquare.com/family/bind.html.

Sigle-Rushton, W., & McLanahan, S. (2002). The Living Arrangements of New Unmarried Mothers." *Demography, 39*(3), 415–433.

Simons, L. G., & Conger, R. D. (2007). Linking mother-father differences in parenting to a typology of family parenting styles and adolescent outcomes. *Journal of Family Issues, 28*(2), 212–241.

Sinclair, I., & Wilson, K. (2003). Matches and mismatches: The contribution of carers and children to the success of foster placements. *British Journal of Social Work, 33*, 871–884.

Spivey, C. (2010). Desperation or desire? The role of risk aversion in marriage. *Economic Inquiry, 48*(2), 499–516.

Stallman, H. M., & Sanders, M. R. (2007). Family transitions triple p: The theoretical basis and development of a program for parents going through divorce. *Journal of Divorce and Remarriage, 47*(3/4), 133–153.

Steinhauer, J. (1995, April 10). Big benefits in marriage, studies say. *New York Times*, p. A10.

Taft, C. T., Pless, A. P., Stalans, L. J., Koenen, K.'C., King, L. A., & King, D. W. (2005). Risk factors for partner violence among a national sample of combat veterans. *Journal of Consulting and Clinical Psychology, 73*(1), 151–159.

Taylor, Z. E., Larsen-Rife, D., Conger, R. D., Widaman, K. F., & Cutrona, C. E. (2010). Life stress, maternal optimism, and adolescent competence in single mother, African American families. *Journal of Family Psychology, 24*(4), 468–477.

Topham, G. L., Hubbs-Tait, L., Rutledge, J. M., Page, M. C., Kennedy, T. S., Shriver, L. H., & Harrist, A. H. (2011). Parenting styles, parental response to child emotion, and family emotional expressiveness are related to child emotional eating. *Appetite, 56*, 261–264.

Trokan, J. (1998). Stages of the marital and family life cycle: Marital miracles. *Pastoral Psychology, 46*(4), 281–295.

U. S. Census Bureau. Current Population Survey. March and Annual Social and Economic Supplements: 1970-2003.

U.S. Census Bureau. (2004). *America's Families and Living Arrangements: 2003*. Washington, DC: Author.

U.S. Census Bureau. (2007). *Custodial Mothers and Fathers and Their Child Support*. Retrieved August 9, 2012, from http://www.census.gov/prod/2009pubs/p60-237.pdf

U.S. Census Bureau. (2007). *2006 American Community Survey*. Retrieved from http://www.census.gov/acs/www/Products/users_guide/index.htm

U.S. Census Bureau. (2008). *Living Arrangements of Children: 2004*. Washington, DC: Author.

U.S. Census Bureau. (2009a). *2009 Population Estimates*. Washington, DC: Author

U.S. Census Bureau. (2009b). *American Community Survey 2009*. Washington, DC: Author.

U.S. Census Bureau. (2010). *Facts for Features: Grandparents Day 2010*. Washington, DC: Author.

U.S. Census Bureau. (2011). *Same-Sex Couple Households*. Retrieved from http://www.census.gov/prod/2011pubs/acsbr10-03.pdf

U.S. Census Bureau. (2012). *Households and Families: 2010*. Retrieved August 9, 2012, from http://www.census.gov/prod/cen2010/briefs/c2010br-14.pdf

U.S. Department of Health and Human Services. (2008). *The AFCARS Report: Preliminary FY 2006 Estimates as of January 2008*. Retrieved from

VanDenBerghe, E. (2000). The enduring, happy marriage: Findings and implications from research. In D. C. Dollahite (Ed.), *Strengthening our families* (pp. 18–20). Salt Lake City: Deseret Book Company.

Varner, F., & Mandara, J. (2009). Marital transitions and changes in African American mothers' depressive symptoms: The buffering role of financial resources. *Journal of Family Psychology, 23*(6), 839–847.

Wade, T. J., Veldhuizen, S., & Cairney, J. (2011). Prevalence of psychiatric disorder in lone fathers and mothers: Examining the intersection of gender and family structure on mental health. *Canadian Journal of Psychiatry, 56*(9), 567–573.

Waite, L. J., & Gallagher, M. (2000), *The case for marriage*. New York: Broadway Books.

Weigel, D. J., Bennett, K. K., & Ballard-Reisch, D. S. (2003). Family influences on commitment: Examining the family of origin correlates of relationship commitment attitudes. *Personal Relationships, 10*, 453–474.

Weigel, D. J., Bennett, K. K., & Ballard-Reisch, D. S. (2006). Influence strategies in marriage: Self and partner links between equity, strategy use, and marital satisfaction and commitment. *The Journal of Family Communication, 6*, 77–95.

Wildmon-White, M. L., & Young, J. S. (2002). Family-of-origin characteristics among women married to sexually addicted men. *Sexual Addiction & Compulsivity, 9*, 263–273.

Williams, B. R., Sawyer Baker, P., Allman, R. M., Roseman, J. M. (2007). Bereavement among African American and White older adults. *Journal of Aging Health, 19*, 313–333.

Wolfinger, N. H. (2001). The effects of family structure of origin on offspring cohabitation duration. *Sociological Inquiry, 71*(3), 293–313.

Xie, Y., Raymo, J. M., Goyette, K., & Thornton, A. (2003). Economic potential and entry into marriage and cohabitation. *Demography, 40*, 351–367.

Yu, J. J., & Gamble, W. C. (2008). Pathways of influence: Marital relationships and their association in parenting styles and sibling relationship quality. *Journal of Child and Family Studies, 17*, 757–778.

Zinn, A. (2009). Foster family characteristics, kinship, and permanence. *Social Service Review*, (June), 185–219.

CHAPTER 15

Alford, K. A. (2003). Cultural themes in rites of passage: Voices of young African American males. *Journal of African American Studies, 7*(1), 3–26.

Althaus, F. A. (1997). Female circumcision: Rite of passage or violation of rights? *International Family Planning Perspectives, 23*(3), 130–133. doi:10.1363/2313097

American Academy of Pediatrics. (2009). Media violence. *Pediatrics, 124*(5), 1495–1503.

American Public Health Association. (2011). *Eliminating health disparities*. Retrieved from http://www.apha.org/advocacy/priorities/issues/disparities/

Amodio, D. M., Devine, P. G., & Harmon-Jones, E. (2008). Individual differences in the regulation of intergroup bias: The role of conflict monitoring and neural signals for control. *Journal of Personality and Social Psychology, 94*(1), 60–74. doi:10.1037/0022-3514.94.1.60

Anand, M. (2009). Gender in social work education and practice in India. *Social Work Education, 28*(1), 95–105.

Bandura, A. (2002). Social cognitive theory of mass communication. In J. Bryant & D. Zillmann (Eds.), *Media effects: Advances in theory and research* (pp. 121–153). London: Erlbaum.

Banks-Wallace, J., & Parks, L. (2004). It's all sacred: African American women's perspectives on spirituality. *Issues in Mental Health Nursing, 25*(1), 25–45.

Barg, F. K., & Gullatte, M. M. (2001). Cancer support groups: Meeting the needs of African Americans with cancer. *Seminars in Oncology Nursing, 17*(3), 171–178.

Bell, B. (2003). The rites of passage and outdoor education: Critical concerns for effective programming. *Journal of Experiential Education, 26*(1), 41–50.

Bennett, D. H. (1990). *The party of fear: From* nativist movements to the new right in American history. New York: Vintage Books.

Bialystok, E., & Viswanathan, M. (2009). Components of executive control with advantages for bilingual children in two cultures. *Cognition, 112*, 494–500.

Bierman, A. (2006). Does religion buffer the effects of discrimination on mental health: Differing effects by race. *Journal for the Scientific Study of Religion, 45*(4), 551–565.

Bizumic, B., & Duckitt, J. (2008). My group is not worthy of me: Narcissism and ethnocentrism. *Political Psychology, 29*(3), 437–453.

Bloul, R. A. D. (2008). Anti-discrimination laws, islamophobia, and ethnicization of muslim identies in Europe and Australia. *Journal of Muslim Minority Affairs, 28*(1), 7–35.

Brondolo, E., Gallo, L. C., & Myers, H. F. (2009). Race, racism, and health: Disparities, mechanisms and interventions. *Journal of Behavioral Medicine, 32*, 1–8.

Brookfield, S. (1986). Media power and the development of media literacy: An adult educational interpretation. *Harvard Educational Review, 56*, 151–170.

Brown, S., & Souto-Manning, M. (2008). "Culture is the way they live here": Young latinas and parents navigate linguistic and cultural borderlands in U.S. Schools. *Journal of Latinos and Education, 7*(1), 25–42.

Byrd, D. (2010). *California's new majority*. Berkeley, CA: The Greenlining Institute.

CDC/NCHS Centers for Disease Control/National Center for Health Statistics. (2009). *National survey of family growth, 2006-2008*. Washington, DC: Author.

Chao, G. T., & Willaby, H. W. (2007). International employment discrimination and implicit social cognition: New directions for theory and research. *Applied Psychology: An International Review, 56*(4), 678–688.

Child Rights Portal. (2012). *The convention on* the rights of the child. Retrieved August 14, 2012, from http://childrensrightsportal.org/convention/signatory-states/

Chouikha, L. (2007). Satellite television in the maghreb: Plural reception and interference of identities. *History and Anthropology, 18*(3), 367–377.

Collins, F. S., Green, E. D., Guttmacher, A. E., & Guyer, M. S. (2003). A vision for the future of genomics research: A blueprint for the genomic era. *Nature, 422*, 835–847.

Crabb, P. B. (2005). The material culture of suicidal fantasies. *Journal of Psychology, 139*(3), 211–220.

Crawford, J. (2004). *Educating English learners: Language diversity in the classroom*. Los Angeles: Bilingual Educational Services, Inc.

Daniels, R. (1991). *Coming to America: A history of immigration and ethnicity in American life*. New York: HarperPerennial.

Darity, W. (2005). Interrogating unstable boundaries: An introduction. *The Review of Black Political Economy, 33*(2), 69–72.

DeBraganza, N., & Hausenblas, H. A. (2010). Media exposure of the ideal physique on women's body dissatisfaction and mood. *Journal of Black Studies, 40*(4), 700–716.

Debrix, F. (2001). Cyberterror and media-induced fears: The production of emergency culture. *Strategies, 14*(1), 149–168.

Dedert, E. A., Studts, J. L., Weissbecker, I., Salmon, P. G., Banis, P. L., & Sephton, S. E. (2004). Religiosity may help preserve the cortisol rhythm in women with stress-related illness. *International Journal of Psychiatry in Medicine, 34*(1), 61–77.

Devine, P. G., Plant, E. A., Amodio, D. M., Harmon-Jones, E., & Vance, S. L. (2002). The regulation of explicit and implicit race bias: The role of motivations to respond without prejudice. *Journal of Personality and Social Psychology, 82*, 835–848.

Dicker, S. J. (2006). Dominican Americans in Washington heights, New York: Language and culture in a transnational community. *International Journal of Bilingual Education and Bilingualism, 9*(6), 713–727.

Dohnt, H., & Tiggemann, M. (2005). Peer influences on body image and dieting awareness in young girls. *British Journal of Developmental Psychology, 23*, 103–116.

Dohnt, H., & Tiggemann, M. (2006). The contribution of peer and media influences to the development of body satisfaction and self-esteem in young girls: A prospective study. *Developmental Psychology, 42*(5), 929–936.

Draper, J. B., & Hicks, J. (1996). Foreign language enrollments in public secondary schools. *Foreign Language Annals, 29*(3), 303–306.

Dubiner, D. (2010). The impact of incipient trilinguality on the socio-affective development of jewish elementary school children in Israel. *Journal of Multilingual and Multicultural Development, 31*(1), 1–12.

Durkheim, E. (1897/1951). *Le suicide* (J. A. Spaulding & G. Simpson, Trans.). London: Routledge.

Eriksen, K. P., & Kress, V. E. (2005). *Beyond the DSM story: Ethical quandaries, challenges and best practices.* Thousand Oaks, CA: Sage.

Erikson, E. H. (1968). *Identity: Youth and crisis.* New York: Norton.

Fox, J. (2007). Religious discrimination: A world survey. *Journal of International Affairs, 61*(1), 47–67.

Fox, J., & Flores, D. (2009). Religions, constitutions, and the state: A cross-national study. *Journal of Politics, 71*(4), 1499–1513.

Freeman, B. C. (2010). Through a Western lens. *The International Communication Gazette, 72*(3), 269–285.

Fu, K., Chan, Y., & Yip, P. S. F. (2009). Testing a theoretical model based on social cognitive theory for media influences on suicidal ideation: Results from a panel study. *Media Psychology, 12*, 26–49.

Gillum, R. F., & Dupree, N. (2006). Religiousness, health, and health behavior in public-use data of the national center for health statistics. *Journal of Religion and Health, 46*(1), 155–165.

Groce, N., Mawar, N., & Macnamara, M. (2006). Inclusion of AIDS educational messages in rites of passage ceremonies: Reaching young people in tribal communities. *Culture, Health & Sexuality, 8*(4), 303–315.

Harper, M. (2007). The stereotyping of nonreligious people by religious students: Contents and subtypes. *Journal for the Scientific Study of Religion, 46*(4), 539–552.

Harvey, A. R., & Hill, R. B. (2004). Africentric youth and family rites of passage program: Promoting resilience among at-risk African American youths. *Social Work, 49*(1), 65–74.

Hays, D. G., Prosek, E. A., & McLeod, A. L. (2010). Assessment & diagnosis: A mixed methodological analysis of the role of culture in the clinical decision-making process. *Journal of Counseling and Development, 88*, 114–121.

HealthReform.Gov. (2011). *Health disparities: A case for closing the gap.* Retrieved from http://www.healthreform.gov/reports/healthdisparities/

Herring, C., Keith, V. M., & Horton, H. D. (Eds.). (2004). *Skin deep: How race and complexion matter in the "color-blind" era.* Chicago and Urbana-Champaign: IRRPP and University of Illinois Press.

Hill, P. (1992). *Coming of age: African American males rites-of-passage.* Chicago: African American Images.

Hodge, D. R. (2005). Spiritual lifemaps: A client-centered pictorial instrument for spiritual assessment, planning, and intervention. *Social Work, 50*(1), 78–87.

Houts, S., & Kassab, C. (1997). Rotter's social learning theory and fear of crime: Differences by race and ethnicity. *Social Science Quarterly, 78*(1), 122–136.

Huston, T. L., Caughlin, J. P., Houts, R. M., Smith, S. E., & George, L. J. (2001). The connubial crucible: Newlywed years as predictors of marital delight, distress, and divorce. *Journal of Personality and Social Psychology, 80*, 237–252.

Jackson, L. (2010). Images of islam in US media and their educational implications. *Educational Studies, 46*, 3–24.

Jasinskaja-Lahti, I., Liebkind, K., & Solheim, E. (2009). To identify or not to identify? National disidentification as an alternative reaction to perceived ethnic discrimination. *Applied Psychology, 58*(1), 105–128.

Johnson, F., & Wardle, J. (2005). Dietary restraint, body dissatisfaction, and psychological distress: A prospective analysis. *Journal of Abnormal Psychology, 114*, 119–125.

Keith, V. M., Lincoln, K. D., Taylor, R. J., & Jackson, J. S. (2010). Discriminatory experiences and depressive symptoms among African American women: Do skin tone and mastery matter? *Sex Roles, 62*, 48–59.

Kivel, B. D., & Johnson, C. W. (2009). Consuming media, making men: Using collective memory work to understand leisure and the construction of masculinity. *Journal of Leisure Research, 41*(1), 109–133.

Lazar, M. M. (2006). Discover the power of femininity: Analyzing global power feminity in local advertising. *Feminist Media Studies, 6*(4), 505–517.

Lee, S. (2005). *A theoretical model of national image processing and international public relations.* Paper presented at the annual meeting of the International Communication Association, New York City.

Leonard, K. M., Van Scotter, J. R., & Pakdil, F. (2009). Culture and communication: Cultural variations and media effectiveness. *Administration & Society, 41*(7), 850–877.

Lewis, L. M. (2008). Spiritual assessment in African-Americans: A review of measures of spirituality used in health research. *Journal of Religion and Health, 47,* 458–475.

Luna, D., Ringberg, T., & Peracchio, L. A. (2008). One individual, two identities: Frame switching among biculturals. *Journal of Consumer Research, 35,* 279–293.

Markstrom, C. A., & Ibora, A. (2003). Adolescent identity formation and rites of passage: The Navajo Kinaald ceremony for girls. *Journal of Research on Adolescence, 13*(4), 399–425.

Martinez, J. S., Smith, T. B., & Barlow, S. H. (2007). Spiritual interventions in psychotherapy: Evaluations by highly religious clients. *Journal of Clinical Psychology, 63*(10), 943–960.

Massey, D. S. (1995). The new immigration and ethnicity in the United States. *Population and Development Review, 2*(3), 256–276.

McLuhan, M. (1960). Classroom without walls. In E. Carpenter & M. McLuhan (Eds.), *Explorations in communication.* Toronto: Beacon Press.

Meyerstein, I. (2004). A Jewish spiritual perspective on psychopathology and psychotherapy: A clinician's view. *Journal of Religion and Health, 43*(4), 329–341.

Meyrowitz, J. (2008). Power, pleasure, patterns: Intersecting narratives of media influence. *Journal of Communication, 58,* 641–663.

Mohseni, M., & Lindstrom, M. (2008). Ethnic differences in anticipated discrimination, generalised trust in other people and self-rated health: A population-based study in Sweden. *Ethnicity & Health, 13*(5), 417–434.

Morling, B., & Lamoreaux, M. (2008). Measuring culture outside the head: A meta-analysis of individualism—collectivism in cultural products. *Personality and Social Psychology Review, 12*(3), 199–221.

National Cancer Institute. (2008). *Cancer health disparities.* Retrieved June 19, 2011, from http://www.cancer.gov/cancertopics/factsheet/disparities/cancer-health-disparities

National Education Association. (2007). The benefits of second language study. *Regarding World Language Education: NEA Research,* 1–12.

National Women's Health Information Center. (2009). *Female Genital Cutting.* Washington, DC: Author. Retrieved June 8, 2011, from http://www.womenshealth.gov/faq/female-genital-cutting.cfm#c

Newsweek. (2005). *Newsweek/beliefnet poll results.* Retrieved June 6, 2011, from http://www.beliefnet.

com/News/2005/08/Newsweekbeliefnet-Poll-Results.aspx#spiritrel

Nielsenwire. (2011). *Nielsen estimates number of U.S. Television homes to be 114.7 million.* Retrieved from http://blog.nielsen.com/nielsenwire/media_entertainment/nielsen-estimates-number-of-u-s-television-homes-to-be-114-7-million/

Nieto, D. (2009). A brief history of bilingual education in the United States. *Perspectives on Urban Education,* 61–72.

Omer, I. (2005). How ethnicity influences residential distributions: An agent-based simulation. *Environmental and Planning B: Planning and Design, 32,* 657–672.

Oyserman, D. (2006). High power, low power and equality: Culture beyond individualism and collectivism. *Journal of Consumer Psychology, 16*(4), 352–356.

Paniagua, F. A. (2005). *Assessing and treating culturally diverse clients: A practical guide* (3rd ed.). Thousand Oaks, CA: Sage.

Piedmont, R. L., & Leach, M. M. (2002). Cross-cultural generalizability of the spiritual transcendence scale in India. *American Behavioral Scientist, 45*(12), 1888–1901.

Pratt, J. A., Hauser, K., Urgray, Z., & Patterson, O. (2007). Looking at human-computer interface design: Effects of ethnicity in computer agents. *Interacting with Computers, 19,* 512–523.

Prazak, M. (2007). Introducing alternative rites of passage. *African Today, 53*(4), 19–40.

Raden, D. (2003). Ingroup bias, classic ethnocentrism, and non-ethnocentrism among American whites. *Political Psychology, 24*(4), 803–828.

Rethinking Schools. (2003). Bilingual education is a human and civil right. *Rethinking Schools, 17*(2). Retrieved August 16, 2011, from http://www.rethinkingschools.org/archive/17_02/Bili172.shtml

Rhodes, N. C., & Pufahl, I. (2009). *Foreign language teaching in U.S. Schools: Results of a national survey.* Washington, DC: Center for Applied Linguistics.

Rostosky, S. S., Wilcox, B. L., Wright, M. L. C., & Randall, B. A. (2004). The impact of religiosity on adolescent sexual behavior: A review of the evidence. *Journal of Adolescent Research, 19*(6), 677–697.

Singelis, T. M., & Brown, W. J. (1995). Culture, self, and collectivist communication linking culture to individual behavior. *Human Communication Research, 21*(3), 354–389.

Spiers, A., & Walker, G. J. (2009). The effects of ethnicity and leisure satisfaction on happiness, peacefulness, and quality of life. *Leisure Sciences, 31,* 84–99.

Stack, S. (2003). Media coverage as a risk factor in suicide. *Journal of Epidemiology and Community Health, 57,* 238–240.

Stack, S. (2005). Suicide in the media: A quantitative review of studies based on non-fictional stories. *Suicide and Life-Threatening Behavior, 35,* 121–133.

Stevenson, H., Lee, S. Y., & Mu, X. (2000). Successful achievement in mathematics: China and the United States. In C. E. M. Van Lieshout & P. G. Heymans (Eds.), *Developing talent across the life span* (pp. 167–183). Philadelphia: Psychology Press.

Tamis-LeMonda, C. S., Way, N., Hughes, D., Yoshikawa, H., Kalman, R., & Niwa, E. Y. (2008). Parents' goals for children: The dynamic co-existence of individualism and collectivism in cultures and individuals. *Social Development, 17,* 183–209.

Tran, A. (2008). Vietnamese language education in the United States. *Language, Culture, and Curriculum, 21*(3), 256–267.

Triandis, H. C. (2002). Individualism-collectivism and personality. *Journal of Personality, 69*(6), 907–924.

Tsai, C. L. (2009). Media systems and their effects on women's sport participation in Taiwan. *Sport, Education and Society, 14*(1), 37–53.

Tsai, M., Chang, Y., Lien, P., & Wong, Y. (2011). Survey on eating disorders related thoughts, behaviors and dietary intake in female junior high school students in Taiwan. *Asia Pacific Journal of Clinical Nutrition, 20*(2), 196–205.

Center for Advanced Research on Language Acquisition. (2010). *What is Culture? Minneapolis: University of Minnesota.* Retrieved from http://www.carla.umn.edu/culture/definitions.html

U.S. Department of Health and Human Services. (2004). *National healthcare disparities report, 2003.* Retrieved from http://www.ahrq.gov/qual/nhdr03/nhdr03.htm

Van Gennep, A. (1960). *The rites of passage.* Chicago: University of Chicago Press.

Van Hook, M., Hugen, B., & Aguilar, M. (Eds.). (2001). *Spirituality within religious traditions in social work practice.* Pacific Grove, CA: Brooks/Cole.

Welles, E. (2004). Foreign language enrollments in United States institutions of higher learning, fall 2002. *ADFL Bulletin, 35*(2&3), 7–26.

Williams, D. R., Neighbors, H. W., & Jackson, J. S. (2003). Racial/ethnic discrimination and health: Findings from community studies. *American Journal of Public Health, 93*(2), 200–208.

Wooten, D. B. (1995). One-of-a-kind in a full house: Some consequences of ethnic and gender distinctiveness. *Journal of Consumer Psychology, 4*(3), 205–224.

World Health Organization. (2012). *Female genital mutilation.* Retrieved from http://www.who.int/mediacentre/factsheets/fs241/en/

Wright, V. (2003). A phenomenological exploration of spirituality among African American women recovering from substance abuse. *Archives of Psychiatric Nursing, 18*(4), 173–185.

Zha, P., Walczyk, J. J., Griffith-Ross, D. A., Tobacyk, J., & Walczyk, D. F. (2006). The impact of culture and individualism-collectivism on the creative potential and achievement of American and Chinese students. *Creativity Research Journal, 18,* 355–366.

CHAPTER 16

Abdulahad, R., Delanley, R., & Brownlee, K. (2009). Valuing interdependence: An examination of Iraqi Canadian acculturation. *International Social Work, 52*(6), 757–771.

Adoption and Safe Families Act. (1997). U.S. Public Law 105–89, Section 103

Akhtar, S. (1999). *Immigration & identity: Turmoil, treatment & transformation.* Northvale, NJ: Jason Aronson.

Akhtar, S., & Choi, L. W. (2004). When evening falls: The immigrant's encounter with middle and old age. *American Journal of Psychoanalysis, 64*(2), 183–191.

Araújo, Z. (1996). Portuguese families. In M. McGoldrick, J. Giordano, & N. Garcia-Preto (Eds.), *Ethnicity and family therapy* (3rd ed., pp. 629–640). New York: Guilford.

Ayón, C. (2009). Shorter time-lines, yet higher hurdles: Mexican families' access to child welfare mandated services. *Children and Youth Services Review, 31*(6), 609–616.

Berry, J. W. (1996). Acculturation and psychological adaptation. In K. Bade (Ed.), *Migration, ethnizitÃ¤t, konflikt, systemfragen und fallstudien* (pp. 171–186). Osnabruck: Rasch.

Bhagwati, J. N. (2000). *The wind of the hundred days: How washington mismanaged globalization.* Cambridge, MA: MIT Press.

Bhattacharya, G. (2008). The Indian diaspora in transnational context: Social relations and cultural identities of immigrants to New York city. *Journal of Intercultural Studies, 29*(1), 65–80.

Bloemraad, I. (2005). The limits of de Tocqueville: How government facilitates organizational capacity in newcomer communities. *Journal of Ethnic and Migration Studies, 31*(5), 865–887.

Bloom, D. E., & Canning, D., & Fink, G. (2010). Implications of population ageing for economic growth. *Oxford Review of Economic Policy, 26*(4), 583–612,

Breslau, J., Borges, G., Hagar, Y., Tancredi, D., & Gilman, S. (2009). Immigration to the USA and risk for mood and anxiety disorders: Variation by origin and age at immigration. *Psychological Medicine, 39*, 1117–1127.

Brookings Institution. (2010). *Ten economic facts about immigration.* Retrieved from http://www.brookings.edu/~/media/research/files/reports/2010/9/immigration%20greenstone%20looney/09_immigration

Brüß, J. (2005). Proud but isolated? Effects of in-group favouritism and acculturation preferences on inter-ethnic attitudes and contact between German, Turkish and Resettler adolescents. *Journal of Ethnic and Migration Studies, 31*(1), 3–27.

Bui, H. N. (2009). Parent-child conflicts, school troubles, and differences in delinquency across immigration generations. *Crime & Delinquency, 55*(3), 412–441.

Butcher, K. F., & Piehl, A. M. (1997). *Recent immigrants: Unexpected implications for crime and incarceration (working paper no. 6067).* Cambridge, MA: National Bureau of Economic Research.

Capitman, J. (2002). Defining diversity: A primer and a review. *Generations, 26*(3), 8–14.

Capps, R., & Fortuny, K. (2006). *Immigration and child and family policy. Paper 3.* Washington, DC: Urban Institute and Child Trends.

Capps, R., Passel, J. S., Periz-Lopez, D., & Fix, M. (2003). *The new neighbors: A users's guide to data on immigrants in U.S. Communities.* Washington, DC: Urban Institute.

Carnegie Corporation of New York. (2010). *A place to call home: What immigrants say now about life in America.* New York: Author.

Castles, S. (2000). *Ethnicity and globalization: From migrant worker to transnational citizen.* London: Sage.

Center for American Progress. (2010). *The costs of mass deportation.* Retrieved from http://www.americanprogress.org/issues/2010/03/deportation_cost.html

Center for an Urban Future. (2007). *A world of opportunity.* Retrieved from www.nycfuture.org

Center for Immigration Studies. (2012). *Poverty and income.* Retrieved from http://www.cis.org/articles/2001/Mexico/poverty.html

Centers for Disease Control and Prevention. (2010). *HIV/AIDS surveillance report, 2009.* Atlanta, GA: U.S. Department of Health and Human Services.

Centers for Disease Control and Prevention. (2012). *Guidelines for mental health screenings during the domestic medical examination for newly arrived refugees.* Retrieved from http://www.cdc.gov/immigrantrefugeehealth/guidelines/domestic/mental-health-screening-guidelines.html

Chahine, Z., & van Straaten, J. (2005). Serving immigrant families and children in new york city's child welfare system. *Child Welfare, 84*(5), 713–723.

Choi, J., & Thomas, M. (2009). Predictive factors of acculturation attitudes and social suppor among Asian immigrants in the USA. *International Journal of Social Welfare, 18*, 76–84.

Cleaveland, C. (2010). We are not criminals: Social work advocacy and unauthorized migrants. *Social Work, 55*(1), 74–81.

Congressional Budget Office. (2007). *The impact of unauthorized immigrants on the budgets of state and local governments.* Washington, DC: Author.

Cornfield, D. B., & Arzubiaga, A. (2004). Immigrants and education in the U.S. Interior: Integrating and segmenting tendencies in Nashville, Tennessee. *Peabody Journal of Education, 79*(2), 157–179.

Cubberly, E. P. (1909). *Changing conceptions of education.* Boston: Houghton.

Davies, I. (2009). Latino immigration and social change in the United States: Toward an ethical immigration policy. *Journal of Business Ethics, 88*, 377–391.

De Silva, E. C. (2006). A united front on immigration. *NASWNews.* Retrieved from http://www.socialworkers.org/pubs/news/2006/02/desilva.asp

De Zoysa, R. (2006). Immigration: Europe and the USA–common cause or American exceptionalism. *Contemporary Politics, 12*(3–4), 261–285.

Decker, M. R., Raj, A., & Silverman, J. G. (2007). Sexual violence against adolescent girls: Influences of immigration and acculturation. *Violence Against Women, 13*(5), 498–513.

Devetak, R. (2004). In fear of refugees: The politics of border protection in Australia. *International Journal of Human Rights, 8*(1), 101–109.

Dumka, L. E., Roosa, M. W., & Jackson, K. M. (1997). Risk, conflict, mothers' parenting and children's adjustment in low-income, Mexican immigrant, and Mexican American families. *Journal of Marriage and the Family, 59*, 309–323.

Dundon, T., Gonzalez-Perez, M., & McDonough, T. (2007). Bitten by the celtic tiger: Immigrant workers and industrial relations in the new globalized Ireland. *Economic and Industrial Democracy, 28*(4), 501–522.

Elrick, T., & Ciobanu, O. (2009). Migration networks and policy impacts: Insights from Romanian-Spanish migration. *Global Networks, 9*(1), 100–116.

Fetzer, J. S. (2000). Economic self-interest or cultural marginality? Anti-immigration sentiment and nativist political movements in France, Germany, and the USA. *Journal of Ethnic and Migration Studies, 26*(1), 5–23.

Forbes. (2007). *Out of china.* Retrieved from http://www.forbes.com/2007/05/21/outsourcing-entrepreneurs-immigrants-oped-cx_mc_0522entrepreneurs.html

Furman, R., Negi, N. J., Iwamoto, D. K., Rowan, D., Shukraft, A., & Graff, J. (2009). Social work practice with latinos: Key issues for social workers. *Social Work, 54*(2), 167–174.

Furman, R., Sanchez, T. W., Langer, C. L., & Negi, N. J. (2007). A qualitative study of immigration policy and practice dilemmas for social work students. *Journal of Social Work Education, 43*(1), 133–146.

Gaertner, S. L., & Dovidio, J. (2000). *Reducing intergroup bias.* Hove, England: Psychology Press.

Hadley, C., & Patil, C. (2009). Perceived discrimination among three groups of refugees resettled in the USA: Associations with language, time in the USA, and continent of origin. *Journal of Immigrant Minority Health, 11*, 505–512.

Hancock, T. U. (2005). Cultural competence in the assessment of poor Mexican families in the rural southeastern United States. *Child Welfare, 84*(5), 689–711.

Henry, H. M., Stiles, W. B., Biran, M. W., Mosher, J. K., Brinegar, M. G., & Banerjee, P. (2009). Immigrants' continuing bonds with their native culture: Assimilation analysis of three interviews. *Transcultural Psychiatry, 46*(2), 257–284.

Hou, F., & Beiser, M. (2006). Learning the language of a new country: A ten-year study of English acquisition by South-East Asian refugees in Canada. *International Migration, 44*, 135–165.

Hovey, J. (2001). Accullturative stress, depression, and suicidal ideation among Central American immigrants. *Suicide and Life-Threatening Behavior, 30*, 327–338.

Jackson, J. S., & Knight, K. M. (2006). Race and self-regulatory behaviors: The role of stress response and hpa axis in physical and mental health disparities. In L. L. Carstensen & K. W. Schaie (Eds.), *Social structure, aging and self-regulation in the elderly* (pp. 189–207). New York: Springer.

Jasinskaja-Lahti, I., Liebkind, K., & Solheim, E. (2001). Perceived discrimination and psychological adjustment among Russian-speaking immigrant adolescents in Finland. *International Journal of Psychology, 36*, 174–185.

Jasso, G., Massey, D., Rosenzweig, M. R., & Smith, J. (2000). The new immigrant survey pilot. *Demography, 37*(1), 127–138.

Kalmijn, M. (1999). Father involvement in child rearing and the perceived stability of marriage. *Journal of Marriage and the Family, 69*, 409–421.

Kibria, N. (1993). *Family tightrope: The changing lives of Vietnamese Americans.* Princeton, NJ: Princeton University Press.

Lai, D. W., & Chau, S. B. Y. (2007). Predictors of health service barriers for older Chinese immigrants in Canada. *Health and Social Work, 32*(1), 57–65.

Lazarus, R., & Folkman, S. (1984). *Stress, appraisal, and coping.* New York: Springer.

Lee, C. M. (2007). From clinical trials to professional training: A graduate course in evidence-based interventions for children, youth, and families. *Training in Education and Professional Psychology, 1*(3), 215–223.

Lim, T. C. (2009). Will South Korea follow the German experience? Democracy, the migratory process, and the prospects for permanent immigration in Korea. *Korean Studies, 32*, 28–55.

Liu, L. L., Lau, A. S., Chen, A. C., Dinh, K. T., & Kim, S. Y. (2009). The influence of material acculturation, neighborhood disadvantage, and parenting on Chinese American adolescents' conduct problems: Testing the segmented assimilation hypothesis. *Journal of Youth and Adolescence, 38*, 691–702.

Ma, A. X., Griffin, M. T. Q., Capitulo, K. L., & Fitzpatrick, J. J. (2010). Demands of immigration among Chinese immigrant nurses. *International Journal of Nursing Practice, 16*(5), 443–453.

Madianos, M. G., Gonidakis, F., Ploubidis, D., Papadopoulou, E., & Rogakou, E. (2008). Measuring acculturation and symptoms of depression of foreign immigrants in the athens area. *International Journal of Social Psychiatry, 54*(4), 338–349.

Mana, A., Orr, E., & Mana, Y. (2009). An integrated acculturation model of immigrants' social identity. *Journal of Social Psychology, 149*(4), 450–473.

Martinez-Brawley, E., & Gualda, E. (2009). Portraying immigrants to the public: Mexican workers in the

USA and African workers in Spain. *International Social Work, 52*(3), 299–312.

Miller, M. J. (2002). The world on the move: Current trends in international migration. *Global Dialogue, 4*(4), 1–11.

Morgan, E., & Sampsel, D. D. (1994). Diversity among seniors. A toledo, OH hospital assesses the healthcare needs of elderly African Americans and hispanics. *Health Progress, 75*(10), 38–40.

Morland, L., Duncan, J., Hoebing, J., Kirschke, J., & Schmidt, L. (2005). Bridging refugee youth and children's services: A case study of cross-service training. *Child Welfare, 84*(5), 791–812.

Morrison, M., & James, S. (2009). Portuguese immigrant families: The impact of acculturation. *Family Process, 48*(1), 151–166.

Moses, J. W., & Letnes, B. (2004). The economic costs to international labor restrictions: Revisiting the empirical discussion. *World Development, 32*(10), 1609–1626.

Moya, J. C. (2005). Immigrants and associations: A global and historical perspective. *Journal of Ethnic and Migration Studies, 31*(5), 833–864.

Murray, A. J. (2001). Loss as a universal concept: A review of the literature to identify common aspects of loss in diverse situations. *Journal of Loss and Trauma, 6*(3), 219–242.

National Intelligence Council. (2001). The US national intelligence council on growing global migration. *Population and Development Review, 27*(4), 817–819.

Nelson, L., & Hiemstra, N. (2008). Latino immigrants and renegotiation of place and belonging in small town America. *Social and Cultural Geography, 9*(3), 319–342.

Padilla, Y. C. (1997). Immigrant policy: Issues for social work practice. *Social Work, 42*(6), 595–606.

Peña, J. B., Wyman, P. A., Brown, C. H., Matthieu, M. M., Olivares, T. E., Hartel, D., & Zayas, L. H. (2009). Immigration generation status and its association with suicide attempts, substance use, and depressive symptoms among Latino adolescents in the USA. *Prevention Science, 9*, 299–310.

Pew Hispanic Center. (2009). *Statistical portrait of the foreign-born population in the United States, 2009.* Retrieved from http://pewhispanic.org/factsheets/factsheet.php?actsheetID=69

Pew Research Center. (2011). *Unauthorized immigrant populations: National and state trends, 2010.* Retrieved from http://www.pewhispanic.org/2011/02/01/v-workers/

Pine, B. A., & Drachman, D. (2005). Effective child welfare practice with immigrant and refugee children and their families. *Child Welfare, 84*(5), 537–562.

Police Foundation. (2009). *The role of local police.* Retrieved from http://policefoundation.org/indexStriking.html

Ponizovsky, A. M., Radomislensky, I., & Grinshpoon, A. (2009). Psychological distress and its demographic associations in an immigrant population: Findings from the Israeli national health survey. *Australian and New Zealand Journal of Psychiatry, 43*, 68–75.

Portes, A., & Rumbaut, R. (1996). *Immigrant American: A portrait* (2nd ed.). Berkeley: University of California Press.

Portes, A., & Rumbaut, R. G. (2006). *Immigrant America: A portrait.* Berkeley: The California University Press.

Portes, A., & Sensenbrenner, J. (1998). Embreddedness and immigration: Notes on the social determinants of economic action. In M. Brinton & V. Nee (Eds.), *The new institutionalism in sociology* (pp. 127–150). New York: Russell Sage Foundation.

Ramirez, M., Perez, M., Valdez, G., & Hall, B. (2009). Assessing the long-term effects of an experimental bilingual-multicultural programme: Implications for drop-out prevention, multicultural development and immigration policy. *International Journal of Bilingual Education and Bilingualism, 12*(1), 47–59.

Ratha, D., Mohapatra, S., & Silwa, A. (2010). Outlook for remittance flows 2010-11: Remittance flows to developing countries remained resilient in 2009, expected to recover during 2010-11. In *Migration and development brief 12.* Washington, DC: World Bank.

Relinger, R. (2010). *NAFTA and U.S. corn subsidies: Explaining the displacement of Mexico's corn farmers. Prospect: Journal of international affairs at UCSD.* Retrieved from http://prospectjournal.ucsd.edu/index.php/2010/04/nafta-and-u-s-corn-subsidies-explaining-the-displacement-of-mexicos-corn-farmers/

Reyneri, E. (2003). *Illegal immigration and the underground economy.* Paper presented to the challenges of immigration and integration in the European union and Australia conference, February 18–20, University of Sydney.

Reynolds, R. (2009). Igbo professional migratory orders, hometown associations and ethnicity in the USA. *Global Networks, 9*(2), 209–226.

Rhodes, S. D., Hergenrather, K. C., Griffith, D. M., Yee, L. J., Zometa, C. S., Montano, J., & Vissman, A. T. (2009). Sexual and alcohol risk behaviors of immigrant

Latino men in the South-Eastern USA. *Culture, Health & Sexuality, 11*(1), 17–34.

Rouse, R. (1995). Questions of identity: Personhood and collectivity in transnational migration to the United States. *Critique of Anthropology, 15*(4), 351–380.

Sakamoto, I. (2007). A critical examination of immigrant acculturation: Toward an anti-oppressive social work model with immigrant adults in a pluralistic society. *British Journal of Social Work, 37,* 515–535.

Schwarzbaum, S. E. (2004). Low-income latinos and dropout: Strategies to prevent dropout. *Journal of Multicultural Counseling and Development, 32,* 296–306.

Shariff, F. (2008). Straddling the cultural divide: Second-generation South Asian identity and the namesake. *Changing English, 15*(4), 457–466.

Siedentop, L. (2001). *Democracy in Europe.* New York: Columbia University Press.

Simon, J. (1999). *The economic consequences of immigration* (2nd ed.). Ann Arbor: University of Michigan Press.

Slonim-Nevo, V., Mirsky, J., Rubinstein, L., & Nauck, B. (2009). The impact of familial and environmental factors on the adjustment of immigrants. *Journal of Family Issues, 30*(1), 92–123.

Smith, B. D., & Donovan, S. E. F. (2003). Child welfare practices in organizational and institutional contexts. *Social Service Review, 77,* 541–563.

Substance Abuse and Mental Health Services Administration. (2010). *Mental health, United States, 2010.* Rockville, MD: Author.

Teitelbaum, M. S., & Weiner, M. (1995). *Threatened peoples, threatened borders: World migration and U.S. Policy.* New York: W.W. Norton.

Thomas, K. J. A. (2010). Household context, generational status, and English proficiency among the children of African immigrants in the United States. *International Migration Review, 44*(1), 142–172.

Torsch, V. L., & Ma, G. X. (2000). Cross-cultural comparison of health perceptions, concerns, and coping strategies among Asian and pacific islander American elders. *Qualitative Health Research, 10,* 471–489.

Tsai, D. T., & Lopez, R. A. (1997). The use of social supports by elderly Chinese immigrants. *Journal of Gerontological Social Work, 29*(1), 77–94.

U.S. Department of Health and Human Services. (2011). *Child welfare information gateway.* Retrieved from http://www.childwelfare.gov/systemwide/laws_policies/state/index.cfm?vent=stateStatutes.processSearch

U.S. Department of State. (2008). Department of State's Refugee Processing Center; Arrivals by origin: Office of Refugee Resettlement, U.S. Administration for Children and Families.

United Nations Population Division. (2000). Replacement migration: Is it a solution to declining and aging populations? *ESA/p/WP, 160,* March 21.

United Nations Population Division. (2001). *World population prospects: The 2000 revision volume III.* Retrieved from http://www.un.org/esa/population/publications/wpp2000/wpp2000_volume3.htm

United Nations Population Division. (2002). *International migration report 2002.* New York: United Nations.

United Nations Population Division. (2011). *International migration in a globalizing world: The role of youth.* New York: United Nations.

United Nations. (2009). *World population aging 2009.* New York: Author.

Van Tubergen, F., & Kalmijn, M. (2009). A dynamic approach to the determinants of immigrants' language proficiency: The United States, 1980-2000. *International Migration Review, 43*(3), 519–543.

Vanguard News Network website: http://www.vanguard-newsnetwork.com/. (c) 2010 Alex Linder. A. Linder, POB 101, Kirksville MO 63501.

Vega, W. A. (2001). Profile of crime, violence, and drug use among Mexican immigrants. In *Perspectives on crime and justice: 1999-2000 lecture series* (Vol. 4, pp. 51–67). Rockville, MD: National Institute of Justice.

Wall Street Journal Classroom Edition. (2005). *The underground economy.* Retrieved from http://wsjclassroom.com/archive/05apr/econ_underground.htm

Walsh, F. (2006). *Strengthening family resilience* (2nd ed.). New York: Guilford. *What is the minimum wage in Mexico?* Retrieved from http://www.maquilareference.com/index.php/doing-business-in-Mexico/115-what-is-the-minimum-wage-in-Mexico

Whitehead, T. (1997). Urban low-income African American men, HIV/AIDS and gender identity. *Medical Anthropology Quarterly, 11*(4), 411–447.

Wise, R. D., & Covarrubias, H. M. (2008). Capitalist restructuring, development and labour migration: The Mexico-US case. *Third World Quarterly, 29*(7), 1359–1374.

Yaglom, M. (1993). Role of psycho-cultural factors in the adjustment of soviet Jewish refugees: Applying

Kleinian theory of mourning. *Journal of Contemporary Psychotherapy, 23*(2), 135–145.

Youdelman, M. K. (2008). The medical tongue: U.S. Laws and policies on language access. *Health Affairs, 27*(2), 424–433.

Zhou, M., & Bankston, C. L., III. (1998). *Growing up American: How Vietnamese children adapt to life in the United States.* New York: Russell Sage.

CHAPTER 17

Aarons, G. A., Monn, A., Hazen, A., Connelly, C. Leslie, L. , Landsverk, J. A., et al. (2008). Substance involvement among youths in Child Welfare: The role of common and unique risk factors. *American Journal of Orthopsychiatry, 78,* 340–349.

Ahern, J., Galea, S., Resnick, H., & Vlahov, D. (2004). Television images and probable posttraumatic stress disorder after September 11: the role of background characteristics, event exposures, and prevalent panic. *Journal of Nervous and Mental Disease, 192 (3),* 217–226.

Allen-Collinson, J. (2009). A marked man: Female-perpetrated intimate partner abuse. *International Journal of Men's Health, 8*(1), 22–40.

American Academy of Pediatrics. (2000). Developmental issues for young children in foster care. *Pediatrics, 106*(5), 1145–1151.

American Psychiatric Association. (2000). *Diagnostic and statistical manual of mental disorders.* (4th ed., text rev.). Washington, DC: Author.

Astin, M. C. (1997). Traumatic therapy: How helping rape victims affects me as a therapist. *Women & Therapy, 20*(1), 101–109.

Bartholet, E. (2009). The racial disproportionality movement in child welfare: False facts and dangerous directions. *Arizona Law Review, 51,* 871–932.

Bartoi, M. G., & Kinder, B. N. (1998). Effects of child and adult sexual abuse on adult sexuality. *Journal of Sex and Marital Therapy, 24,* 75–90.

Beeble, M. L., Bybee, D., & Sullivan, C. M. (2009). Main, mediating and moderating effects of social support on the well-being of survivors of intimate partner violence across two years. *Journal of Consulting and Clinical Psychology, 77*(4), 718–729.

Benbenishty. R., Osmo, R., & Gold, N. (2003). Rationales provided for risk assessments and for recommended interventions in child protection: a comparison between Canadian and Israeli professionals. *British Journal of Social Work, 33,* 137–155.

Blome, W. W. (1997). What happens to foster kids: Educational experiences of a random sample of foster care youth and a matched group of non-foster care youth. *Child and Adolescent Social Work Journal, 14*(1), 41–53.

Boscarino, J. A., Figley, C. R., & Adams, R. E. (2004). Compassion fatigue following september terrorist attacks; of secondary trauma among New York city social workers. *International Journal of Emergency Mental Health, 6*(2), 57–66.

Bostock, J., Plumpton, M., & Pratt, R. (2009). Domestic violence against women: Understanding social processes and women's experiences. *Journal of Community and Applied Social Psychology, 19,* 95–110.

Brohl, K. (2004). *The New Miracle Workers: Overcoming contemporary challenges in child welfare work.* Washington, DC: CWLA Press.

Brown, N. (2007). Stories from outside the frame: Intimate partner abuse in sexual-minority women's relationships with transsexual men. *Feminism and Psychology, 17*(3), 373–393.

Browne, K., & Herbert, M. (1997). *Preventing family violence.* Chichester, England: Wiley.

Buddie, A. M., & Miller, A. G. (2001). Beyond rape myths: A more complex view of perceptions of rape victims. *Sex Roles, 45*(3/4), 139–160.

Buehler, C., Orme, J. G., Post, J., & Patterson, D. (2000). The long-term correlates of family foster care. *Children and Youth Services Review, 22*(8), 595–625.

Bureau of Justice Statistics (2012). Intimate Partner Violence in the U.S.: Victim characteristic. Retrieved from http://bjs.ojp.usdoj.gov/content/pub/pdf/ipvus.pdf

Burley, M., & Hapern, M. (2001). *Educational attainment of foster youth: Achievement and graduation outcomes for children in state care.* Washington, DC: Washington State Institute for Public Policy, Document #01-11-3901.

Campbell, R. (1998). The community response to rape: Victims experiences with the legal, medical, and mental health systems. *American Journal of Community Psychology, 26*(3), 355–379.

Campbell, R. (2005). What really happened? A validation study of rape survivors' help-seeking experiences with legal and medical systems. *Violence and Victims, 20*(1), 55–68.

CAPTA: Child Abuse Protection and Treatment Act. CAPTA Reauthorization Act of 2010 (P.L. 111-320, 12/20/10).

Carlson, B. E. (2000). Children exposed to intimate partner violence: Research findings and implications for intervention. *Trauma, Violence, and Abuse, 1*(4), 321–340.

Chan, Y., & Yeung, J. W. (2009). Children living with violence within the family and its sequel: A meta-analysis from 1995-2006. *Aggression and Violent Behavior, 14*, 313–322.

Child Welfare Information Gateway. (2009). *Domestic violence and the child welfare system*. Retrieved from http://www.childwelfare.gov/pubs/factsheets/domesticviolence.cfm

Child Welfare Information Gateway. (2011). *Worker turnover*. Retrieved from http://www.childwelfare.gov/management/workforce/retention/turnover.cfm

Child Welfare Information Gateway. (2012). *Major Federal Legislation Concerned with Child Protection, Child Welfare, and Adoption*. Retrieved from https://www.childwelfare.gov/pubs/otherpubs/majorfedlegis.cfm

Choice, P., D'Andrade, A., Gunther, K., Downes, D., Schaldach, J., Dsiszar, C., & Austin, M. (2001). *Education for foster children: Removing barriers to academic success*. Berkeley, CA: Bay Area Social Services Consortium, Center for Social Services Research, University of California at Berkeley, School of Social Welfare.

Clancy, S. A., & McNally, R. J. (2005/2006). Who needs repression? Normal memory processes can explain "forgetting" of childhood sexual abuse. *Scientific Review of Mental Health Practice, 4*, 66–73.

Clemmons, J. C., Walsh, K., DiLillo, D., & Messman-Moore, T. L. (2007). Unique and combined contributions of multiple child abuse types and abuse severity to adult trauma symptomatology. *Child Maltreatment, 12*(2), 172–181.

Cohen, P., Brown, J., & Smailes, E. (2001). Child abuse and neglect and the developmental of mental disorders in the general population. *Development and Psychopathology, 13*, 981–999.

Cohn, I. (2006). Armies of the young: child soldiers in war and terrorism. *American Anthropologist, 108*, 431–432.

Condly, S. J. (2006). Resilience in children: A review of literature with implications for education. *Urban Education, 41*(3), 211–236.

Conger, D., & Rebeck, A. (2001). *How children's foster care experiences affect their education*. New York: New York City Administration for Children's Services and Vera Institute of Justice.

Conoscenti, L. M., & McNally, R. J. (2005). Health complaints in acknowledged and unacknowledged rape victims. *Journal of Anxiety Disorders, 20*, 372–379.

Cook, R. J. (1994). Are we helping foster care youth prepare for their future. *Child and Youth Services Review, 16*(3), 213–229.

Corby, B. (1997). Risk assessment in child protection work. In H. Kemshall & J. Pritchard, (Eds.). *Good Practice in Risk Assessment and Risk Management* (pp. 13–30). London: Jessica Kingsley Publishers.

Creamer, M., Burgess, P., Buckingham, W., & Pattison, P. (1990). A community based mental health response to a multiple shooting. *Australian Psychologist, 26*(2), 99–102.

Davies, M., Rogers, P., & Whitelegg, L. (2009). Effects of victim gender, victim sexual orientation, victim response and respondent gender on judgements of blame in a hypothetical adolescent rape. *Legal and Criminological Psychology, 14*, 331–338.

Davis, R. E. (2002). The strongest women: Exploration of the inner resources of abused women. *Qualitative Health Research, 12*, 1248–1263.

DeGue, S., & Widom, C. S. (2009). Does out-of-home placement mediate the relationship between child maltreatment and adult criminality. *Child Maltreatment, 14*(4), 344–355.

Drake, B., Jolley, J. M., Lanier, P., Fluke, J., Barth, R., & Jonson-Reid, M. (2011). Racial bias in child protection? A comparison of competing explanations using national data. *Pediatrics, 127*(3), 471–478.

Dunlap, E., Golub, A., & Johnson, B. D. (2003). Girls sexual development in the inner city: From compelled childhood sexual contact to sex=for-things exchanges. *Journal of Child Sexual Abuse, 12*(2), 73–96.

Edmond, T., Auslander, W., Elze, D. E., McMillen, C., & Thompson, R. (2002). Differences between sexually abused and non-sexually abused adolescent girls in foster care. *Journal of Child Sexual Abuse, 11*(4), 73–99.

Eggertsen, L. (2008). Primary factors related to multiple placements for children in out-of-home care. *Child Welfare, 87*(6), 71–90.

Elliott, D. M., Mok, D. S., & Briere, J. (2004). Adult sexual assault: Prevalence, symptomatology, and sex differences in the general population. *Journal of Trauma & Stress, 17*, 203–211.

Enander, V. (2010). A fool to keep staying: Battered women labeling themselves stupid as an expression of gendered shame. *Violence Against Women, 16*(1), 5–31.

English, D. J., Edleson, J. L., & Herrick, M. E. (2005). Domestic violence in one state's child protective caseload: A study of differential case dispositions and outcomes. *Children and Youth Services Review, 27,* 1183–1201.

Evans, L. D. (2001). Interactional models of learning disabilities: Evidence from students entering foster care. *Psychology in the Schools, 36*(4), 381–390.

Fantuzzo, J., & Perlman, S. (2007). The unique impact of out-of-home placement and the mediating effects of child maltreatment and homelessness on early school success. *Children and Youth Services Review, 29,* 941–960.

Field, C. A., & Caetano, R. (2004). Ethnic differences in intimate partner violence in the U.S. general population: The role of alcohol use and socioeconomic status. *Trauma, Violence, & Abuse, 5,* 303–317.

Figley, C. R. (Ed.) (1995). *Compassion fatigue: Coping with secondary traumatic stress disorder in those who treat the traumatized.* New York: Brunner/Mazel.

Figley C. R. (Ed.). (1997). *Burnout in families: The systematic costs of caring.* New York: CRC Press.

Figley, C. R., & Klever, R. J. (1995). Beyond the victim: Secondary traumatic stress. In R. J. Kleber, C. R. Figley, & B. P. R. Gersons (Eds.). *Beyond Trauma: Cultural and Societal Dynamics* (pp. 75–98). New York: Plenum Press.

Fitzroy, L. (2001). Violent women: questions for feminist theory, practice and policy. *Critical Social Policy, 21*(1), 7–34.

Foster, H., & Brooks-Gunn, J. (2009). Toward a stress process model of children's exposure to physical family and community violence. *Clinical Child and Family Psychological Review, 12,* 71–94.

Frederick, J., & Goddard, C. (2008). Living on an island: consequences of childhood abuse, attachment disruption and adversity in later life. *Child and Family Social Work, 13,* 300–310.

Fremouw, W. J., Westrup, D., & Pennypacker, B. A. (1997). Stalking on campus: The prevalence and strategies for coping with stalking. *Journal of Forensic Science, 42,* 666–669.

Friend, C., Shlonsky, A., & Lambert, L. (2008). From evolving discourses to new practice approaches in domestic violence and child protective services. *Children and Youth Service Review, 30,* 689–698.

Garmezy, N. (1991). Resilience in children's adaptation to negative life events and stressed environments. *Pediatric Annals, 20,* 459–466.

Glick, P., Diebold, J., Bailey-Werner, B., & Zhu, L. (1997). The two faces of Adam: Ambivalent sexism and polarized attitudes toward women. *Personality and Social Psychology Bulletin, 23,* 1323–1334.

Goodman, L. A., & Epstein, D. (2007). *Listening to Battered Women: A Survivor-Centered Approach to Advocacy, Mental Health, and Justice.* Washingnton, DC: American Psychological Association.

Hahm, H. C., Lee, Y. I., Ozonoff, A., & Van Wert, J. J. (2010). The impact of multiple types of child maltreatment on subsequent risk behaviors among women during the transition from adolescence to young adulthood. *Journal of Youth & Adolescence, 39,* 528–540.

Hall, K. (2005). *A new view of understanding and treating the sexual repercussions of child sexual abuse.* Paper presented at Women and the New Sexual Politics: Profits vs. Pleasures, July, Montreal, Canada.

Harrison, C. A., & Kinner, S. A. (1998). Correlates of psychological distress following armed robbery. *Journal of Traumatic Stress, 11*(4), 787–798.

Hetzel, M. D., & McCanne, T. R. (2005). The roles of peritraumatic dissociation, child physical abuse, and child sexual abuse in the development of posttraumatic stress disorder and adult victimization. *Child Abuse and Neglect, 29,* 915–930.

Higgins, D. J., & McCabe, M. P. (2000). Multi-type maltreatment and the long-term adjustment of adults. *Child Abuse Review, 9,* 6–18.

Hochman, G., Hochman, A., & Miller, J. (2004). *Foster care: Voices from the inside.* Washington, DC: The Pew Commission on Children in Foster Care.

Hoge, C. W., Castro, C. A., Messer, S. C., McGurk, D. Cotting, D. I., & Koffman, R. L. (2004). Combat duty in Iraq and Afghanistan, mental health problems, and barriers to care. *New England Journal of Medicine, 351,* 13–22.

Hohman, M., Oliver, R., & Wright, W. (2004). Methamphetamine abuse and manufacture: The child welfare response. *Social Work, 49*(3), 373–381.

Hoven, C. W., Duarte, C. S., Lucas, C. P., Wu, P., Mandell, D. J., Goodwin, R. D., et al. (2005). Psychopathology among New York City public school children 6 months after September 11. *Archives of General Psychiatry, 62,* 545–552.

Howe, D. (2005). *Child abuse and neglect: Attachment, development and intervention.* Basingstoke, England: Palgrave Macmillan.

Institute for the Advancement of Social Work Research. (2005). *Factors influencing retention of Child Welfare Staff: A systematic review of research.* Washington, DC: Author.

Ireland, T. O., & Smith, C. A. (2009). Living in partner-violent families: Developmental links to antisocial behavior and relationship violence. *Journal of Youth and Adolescence, 38*, 323–339.

Jonson-Reid, M., & Barth, R. P. (2003). Probation foster care as an outcome for children exiting child welfare foster care. *Social Work, 48*(3), 348–361.

Kaniasty, K., & Norris, F. H. (1992). Social support and victims of crime: Matching event, support and outcome. *American Journal of Community Psychology, 20*(2), 211–241.

Keane, F. E., Young, S. M., Boyle, H. M., & Curry, K. M. (1995). Prior sexual assault reported by male attenders at a department of genitourinary medicine. *International Journal of STD and AIDS, 6*, 95–100.

King, S. (2000). Is expressed emotion cause or effect in the mothers of schizophrenic young adults? *Schizophrenia Research, 45*(1–2), 65–78.

Knickmeyer, N., Levitt, H., & Horne, S. G. (2010). Putting on Sunday best: The silencing of battered women within Christian faith communities. *Feminism & Psychology, 20*(1), 94–113.

Kortnenkamp, K., & Ehrle, J. (2001). *The well being of children involved with the child welfare system: A national overview.* Washington, DC: The Urban Institute.

Koss, M. P., Goodman, L. A., Browne, A., Fitzgerald, L. F., Keita, G. P., & Russo, N. F. (1994). No safe haven: *Male violence against women at home, at work, and in the community.* Washington, DC: American Psychological Association.

Krane, J., & Davies, L. (2000). Mothering and child protection practice: Rethinking risk assessment. *Child and Family Social Work, 5*, 35–45.

Kroll, B. (2004). Living with an elephant: Growing up with parental substance misuse. *Child and Family Social Work, 9*, 129–140.

Lachman, P., & Bernard, C. (2006). Moving from blame to quality: How to respond to failures in child protective services. *Child Abuse and Neglect, 30*, 963–968.

Leeners, B., Richter-Appelt, H., Imthurn, B., & Rath, W. (2006). Influence of childhood sexual abuse on pregnancy, delivery, and the early postpartum period in adult women. *Journal of Psychomatic Research, 61*, 139–151.

Leisey, M., Kupstas, P. K., & Cooper, A. (2009). Domestic violence in the second half of life. *Journal of Elder Abuse & Neglect, 21*, 141–155.

Lemmon, J. (2006). The effects of maltreatment recurrence and child welfare services on dimensions of delinquency. *Criminal Justice Review, 31*, 5–32.

Lindsey, D., & Schwartz, I. M. (2004). Advances in child welfare: Innovations in child protection, adoptions and foster care. *Children and Youth Services Review, 26*(11), 999–1113.

Litz, B. T. (2006). *A brief primer on the mental health impact of the wars in Afghanistan and Iraq. National Center for PTSD.* Retrieved from www.ptsd.ne.gov/pdfs/impact-of-the-wars-in-afghanistan-iraq.pdf

Litz, B. T., Stein, N., Delaney, E., Lebowitz, L., Nash, W. P., Silva, C., et al. (2009). Moral injury and moral repair in war veterans: a preliminary model and intervention strategy. *Clinical Psychology Review, 29*(8), 695–706.

Lu, Y. E., Landsverk, J., Ellis-MacLeod, E., Newton, R., Ganger, W., & Johnson, I. (2004). Race, ethnicity and case outcomes in child protective services. *Children and Youth Services Review, 26*(5), 447–461.

Mackey, T. F., Hacker, S. S., Weissfelt, L. A., Ambrose, N. C., Fisher, M. G., & Zobel, D. L.(1991). Comparative effects of sexual assault on sexual functioning of child sexual abuse survivors and others. *Issues in Mental Health Nursing, 12*, 89–112.

Martsolf, D. S., & Draucker, C. B. (2008). The legacy of childhood sexual abuse and family adversity. *Journal of Nursing Scholarship, 40*(4), 333–340.

McCauley, J. L., Amstadter, A. B., Danielson, C. K., & Ruggiero, K. J. (2009). Mental health and rape history in relation to non-medical use of prescription drugs in a national sample of women. *Addictive Behaviors, 34*, 641–648.

McDaniel, M. (2005). In the eye of the beholder: The role of reporters in bringing families to the attention of child protective services. *Children and Youth Services Review, 28*, 306–324.

McLean, I. A., Balding, V., & White, C. (2005). Further aspects of male-on-male rape and sexual assault in greater Manchester. *Medicine, Science and the Law, 45*, 225–232.

McMullin, D., Wirth, R. G., & White, J. W. (2007). The impact of sexual victimization on personality: A longitudinal study of gendered attributes. *Sex Roles, 56*(7/8), 403–414.

Mech, E., Ludy-Dobson, C., & Hulsemann, F. (1994). Life skills knowledge: A survey of foster adolescents in three placement setting. Special Issue: Preparing foster care youth for adulthood. *Children and Youth Services Review, 16*(3–4), 181–200.

Medrano, M. A., Hatch, J. P., Zule, W. A., & Desmond, D. P. (2003). Childhood trauma and adult prostitution behavior in a multiethnic heterosexual drug-using population. *American Journal of Drug and Alcohol Abuse, 29*(2), 463–486.

Messman, T. L., & Long, P. J. (1996). Child sexual abuse and its relationship to revictimization in adult women: A review. *Clinical Psychology Review, 16,* 397–420.

Messman-Moore, T. L., & Brown, A. L. (2004). Child maltreatment and perceived family environment as risk factors for adult rape: Is child sexual abuse the most salient experience? *Child Abuse and Neglect, 28,* 1019–1034.

Migliaccio, T. A. (2002). Abused husbands: A narrative analysis. *Journal of Family Issues, 23*(1), 26–52.

Miller, L. (2004). Psychotherapeutic interventions for survivors of terrorism. *American Journal of Psychotherapy, 58*(1), 1–16.

Miller, O. A., & Ward, K. J. (2008). Emerging strategies for reducing disproportionality and disparate outcomes in child welfare: The results of a national breakthrough series collaborative. *Child Welfare, 87*(2), 211–240.

Miller, W. R., Williams, A. M., & Berstein, M. H. (1982). The effects of rape on marital adjustment. *American Journal of Family Therapy, 18,* 51–58.

Munro, E. (2005). What tools do we need to improve identification of child abuse? *Child Abuse Review, 14,* 374–388.

Nadelson, C. C., Notman, M. T., Zackson, H. Z., & Gornick, J. (1982). A follow-up study of rape victims. *American Journal of Psychiatry, 139,* 1266–1270.

Nam, Y., Meezan, W., & Danziger, S. K. (2006). Welfare recipients' involvement with child protective services after welfare reform. *Child Abuse and Neglect, 30,* 1181–1199.

National Institute on Mental Health. (2011). Post-Traumatic Stress Disorder (PTSD Retrieved November 17, 2011, from http://www.nimh.nih.gov/health/publications/post-traumatic-stress-disorder-ptsd/what-is-post-traumatic-stress-disorder-or-ptsd.shtml

New, A. S., Fan, J., Murrough, J. W., Liu, X., Liebman, R. E., Guise, K. G., et al. (2009). A functional magnetic resonance imaging study of deliberate emotion regulation in resilience and posttraumatic stress disorder. *Biological Psychiatry, 66,* 656–664.

Nissly, J. A., Mor Barak, M. E., & Levin, A. (2005). Stress, social support, and workers' intentions to leave their jobs in public child welfare. *Administration in Social Work, 29,* 79–100.

Norris, F. H., Friedman, M. J., Watson, P. J., Byrne, C. M., Diaz, E., & Kaniasty, K. (2002). 60,000 disaster victims speak: Part I. An empirical review of the empirical literature, 1981–2001. *Psychiatry, 65,* 207–239. New York: Norton.

Osofsky, J. D. (2003). Prevalence of children's exposure to domestic violence and child maltreatment: Implications for prevention and intervention. *Clinical Child and Family Psychology Review, 6*(3), 161–170.

Øverlien, C. (2010). Children exposed to domestic violence. *Journal of Social Work, 10*(1), 80–97.

Ozer, E. J. (2005). The impact of violence on urbgan adolescents: Longitudinal effects of perceived school connectedness and family support. *Journal of Adolescent Research, 20,* 167–192.

Palarea, R. E., Zona, M. A., Lane, J. C., & Langhin-richsen-Rohling, J. (1999). Breaking up is hard to do: Unwanted pursuit behaviors following the dissolution of a romantic relationship. *Violence and Victims, 15,* 73–90.

Paranjape A., Sprauve-Holmes N. E., Gaughan J., & Kaslow, N. J. (2009). Lifetime exposure to family violence: implications for the health status of older African American women. *Journal of Women's Health, 18*(2), 171–175.

Park, J. M., Metraux, S., & Culhane, D. P. (2005). Childhood out-of-home placement and dynamics of public shelter utilization among young homeless adults. *Child and Youth Services Review, 27,* 533–546.

Parrish, T., Dubois, J., Delano, C., Dixon, Webster, D., Berrick, J. D., et al. (2001). *Education of foster group home children, whose responsibility is it?* Sacramento, CA: California Department of Education.

Pecora, P. J., Kessler, R. C., O'Brien, K., White, C. R., Williams, J., Hiripi, E., English, D., White, J., & Herrick, M. A. (2006). Educational and employment outcomes of adults formerly placed in foster care: Results from the Northwest Foster Care Alumni Study. *Children and Youth Services Review, 28*(12), 1459–1481.

Penzerro, R. M., & Lein, L. (1995). Buring their bridges: Disordered attachment and foster care discharge. *Child Welfare, 74*(2), 351–366.

Perry, R. W., & Lindell, M. K. (2003). Understanding citizen response to disasters with implications for terrorism. *Journal of Contingencies and Crisis Management, 11,* 49–60.

Purcell, R., Path, M., & Mullen, P. E. (2001). A study of women who stalk. *American Journal of Psychiatry, 158,* 2056–2069.

Purcell, R., Path, M., & Mullen, P. E. (2005). Associations between stalking victimization and psychiatric morbidity in a random community sample. *British Journal of Psychiatry, 187,* 416–420.

Renzetti, C. M., & Miley, C. H. (Eds.) (1996). *Violence in gay and lesbian domestic partnerships.* New York: Haworth Press.

Rodriguez, N., Ryan, S. W., Kemp, H. V., & Foy, D. W. (1997). Posttraumatic stress disorder in adult female survivors of childhood sexual abuse: A comparison study. *Journal of Consulting and Clinical Psychology, 65*(1), 53–59.

Schechter, L. R. (2008). From 9/11 to Hurricane Katrina: Helping others and oneself cope following disasters. *Traumatology, 14*(4), 38–47.

Shariat, S., Mallonee, S., Kruger, E., Farmer, K., and North, C., (1999). A prospective study of long-term health outcomes among Oklahoma City bombing survivors. *Journal of Oklahoma State Medical Association, 98,* 178–186.

Shen, A. C. (2009). Long-term effects of interparental violence and child physical maltreatment experiences on PTSD and behavior problems: A national survey of Taiwanese college students. *Child Abuse & Neglect, 33,* 148–160.

Shore, N., Kelly, E. S., Le Prohn, N. S., & Keller, T. (2002). Foster parent and teacher assessments of youth in kinship and non-kinship foster care placements: Are behaviors perceived differently across settings? *Children and Youth Services Review, 24*(1/2), 109–134.

Silver, J., DiLorenzo, P., Zukoski, M., Ross, P. E., Amster, B. J., & Schlegel, D. (1999). Starting young: Improving the health and developmental outcomes of infants and toddlers in the child welfare system. *Child Welfare, 78,* 148–165.

Smithgall, C., Gladden, R. M., Howard, E., George, R., & Courtney, M. (2004). *Educational Experiences of Children in Out-Of-Home Care.* Chicago: Chapin Hall Center for Children.

Southerland, D., Casanueva, C. E., & Ringeisen, H. (2009). Young adult outcomes and mental health problems among transition age youth investigated for maltreatment during adolescence. *Children and Youth Services Review, 31*(9), 947–956.

Stalcup, A. (2000, April). *Methamphetamine use and treatment.* Paper presented at the California Asssociation of Alcohol and Drug Educators, San Diego.

Stamm, S. (2009). Intimate partner violence in the military: Securing our country, starting with the home. *Family Court Review, 47*(2), 321–339.

Stark, E. (2006). Commentary on Johnson's "Conflict and Control: Gender Symmetry and Asymmetry in Domestic Violence." *Violence Against Women, 12*(11), 1019–1025.

Stone, S. (2007). Child maltreatment, out-of-home placement and academic vulnerability: A fifteen-year review of evidence and future directions. *Children and Youth Services Review, 29,* 139–161.

Testa, M. F., Cohen, L., & Smith, G. (2003). *Illinois subsidized guardianship waiver demonstration: Final evaluation report.* Chicago: Illinois Department of Children and Family Services February.

Tewksbury, R. (2007). Effects of sexual assault on men: Physical, mental and sexual consequences. *International Journal of Men's Health, 6*(1), 22–35.

Trotter, J. L., & Allen, N. E. (2009). The good, the bad, and the ugly: Domestic survivors' experiences with their informal social networks. *American Journal of Community Psychology, 43,* 221–231.

Turchik, J. A. (2012). Sexual victimization among male college students: Assault severity, sexual functioning, and health risk behaviors. *Psychology of Men & Masculinity, 13*(3), 243–255.

Tyson, J. (2007). Compassion fatigue in the treatment of combat-related trauma during wartime. *Clinical Social Work Journal, 35,* 183–192.

U.S. Children's Bureau. (2012). *Trends in Foster Care and Adoption.* Washington, DC: Author. Retrieved from http://www.acf.hhs.gov/sites/default/files/cb/trends_fostercare_adoption.pdf

U.S. Department of Health and Human Services. (2011). *Child Welfare Information Gateway.* Retrieved from http://www.childwelfare.gov/systemwide/laws_policies/state/index.cfm?event=stateStatutes.processSearch

U.S. Department of Justice (2002). *Rape and sexual assault: Reporting to police and medical attention, 1992-2000.* Washington, DC: Author.

U.S. Department of Veterans Affairs. (2012). *Suicide Data Report, 2012.* Retrieved from http://www.va.gov/opa/docs/Suicide-Data-Report-2012-final.pdf

Unrau, Y. A., Font, S. A., & Rawls, G. (2012). Readiness for college engagement among students who have aged out of foster care. *Children & Youth Services Review, 34*(1), 76–83.

Vlahov, D., Galea, S., Ahern, J., Rudenstine, S., Resnick, H., Kilpatrick, D., et al. (2006). Alcohol drinking problems among New York City residents after the September 11 terrorist attacks. *Substance Use and Misuse, 41*(9), 1295–1311.

Waldfogel, J. (2000). Reforming child protective services. *Child Welfare, 79*(1), 43–57.

Walker, J., Archer, J., & Davies, M. (2005). Effects of rape on men: A descriptive analysis. *Archives of Sexual Behavior, 34,* 69–80.

Walser, R. D., & Kern, J. M. (1996). Relationships among childhood sexual abuse, sex guilt, and sexual behavior in adult clinical samples. *The Journal of Sex Research, 33,* 321–326.

Wareham, J., Boots, D. P., & Chavez, J. M. (2009). A test of social learning and intergenerational transmission among batterers. *Journal of Criminal Justice, 37,* 163–173.

Wasco, S. M., & Campbell, R. (2002). Emotional reactions of rape victim advocates: A multiple case study of anger and fear. *Psychology of Women Quarterly, 26,* 120–130.

Washington, P. A. (1999). Second assault of male survivors of sexual violence. *Journal of Interpersonal Violence, 14,* 713–730.

Webb, M. B., & Harden, B. J. (2003). Beyond child protection: Promoting mental health for children and families in the child welfare system. *Journal of Emotional and Behavioral Disorders, 11*(1), 49–58.

White, C. R., Gallegos, A. H., O'Brien, K., Weisberg, S., Pecora, P. J., & Medina, R. (2011). The Relationship Between Homelessness and Mental Health Among Alumni of Foster Care: Results From the Casey Young Adult Survey. *Journal of Public Child Welfare, 4,* 369–389.

Wilson, H.W., &Widom, C.S. (2009). A prospective examination of the path from child abuse and neglect to illicit drug use in middle adulthood: The potential mediating role of four risk factors. *Journal of Youth and Adolescence, 38,* 340–354.

Widom, C. S. (1991). The role of placement experiences in mediating the criminal consequences of early childhood victimization. *American Journal of Orthopsychiatry, 61*(2), 195–209.

Wigman, S. A. (2009). Male victims of former-intimate stalking: A selected review. *International Journal of Men's Health, 8*(2), 101–115.

Williams, B. R., Sawyer Baker, P., Allman, R. M., & Roseman, J. M. (2007). Bereavement among African American and White older adults *Journal of Aging Health, 19,* 313–333.

Wisconsin Department of Children and Families. (2010). *Child Abuse and Neglect Program, Child Protective Services, Structure of CPS.* Retrieved from http://dcf.wisconsin.gov/children/cps/progserv/structure.HTM

Wisnivesky, J. P., Teitelbaum, S. L., Todd, A. C., Boffetta, P., Crane, M., Crowley, L., et al. (2011). Persistence of multiple illnesses in World Trade Center rescue and recovery workers: A cohort study. *Lancet, 378*(9794), 888–897.

Wolf, K. A., & Foshee, V. A. (2003). Family violence, anger expression styles, and adolescent dating violence. *Journal of Family Violence, 18*(6), 309–316.

World Health Organization. (2010). *Child Maltreatment Fact Sheet.* Retrieved from http://www.who.int/mediacentre/factsheets/fs150/en/. Geneva, Switzerland: Author.

Wright, W. (2000, May). *Medical concerns when children are exposed to meth and its precursors.* Paper presented at the Drug Endangered Children's Conference, Sacramento, CA.

Wulczyn, F., Kogan, J., & Harden, B. J. (2003). Placement stability and movement trajectories. *Social Service Review, 77*(2), 212–236.

Wyatt, G., Guthrie, D., & Notgrass, C. M. (1992). Differential effects of women's child sexual abuse and subsequent sexual victimization. *Journal of Consulting and Clinical Psychology, 60,* 167–173.

Zinzow, H., Ruggiero, K., Resnick, H., Hanson, R., Smith, D., Saunders, B., et al. (2009). Prevalence and mental health correlates of witnessed parental and community violence in a national sample of adolescents. *Journal of Child Psychology & Psychiatry, 50*(4), 441–450.

Zoellner, L. A., Goodwin, M. L., & Foa, E. B. (2000). PTSD severity and health perceptions in female victims of sexual assault. *Journal of Traumatic Stress, 13,* 635–649.

CHAPTER 18

Addington, L. A. (2003). Students' fear after Columbine: Findings from a randomized experiment. *Journal of Quantitative Criminology, 19,* 367–387.

Addington, L. A. (2009). Cops and Cameras: Public school security as a policy response to Columbine. *American Behavioral Scientist, 52*(10), 1426–1446.

Agnew, R. (2006). *Pressured into Crime: An Overview of General Strain Theory.* Los Angeles: Roxbury.

Alaggia, R., Lambert, E., & Regehr, C. (2009). Where is the justice? Parental experiences of the Canadian justice system in cases of child sexual abuse. *Family Court Review, 47*(4), 634–649.

Allen, G. (2009). *Sex offenders forced to live under Miami Bridge.* National Public Radio. Retrieved from http://www.npr.org/templates/story/story.php?storyId=104150499

Altheide, D. L. (2009). The Columbine shootings and the discourse of fear. *American Behavioral Scientist, 52*(10), 1354–1370.

Amandus, H. E., Hunter, R. D., James, E., & Hendricks, S. (1995). Reevaluation of the effectiveness of environmental designs to reduce robbery risk in Florida convenience stores. *Journal of Occupational and Environmental Medicine, 37*(6), 711–717.

Anderson, E. (1999). *Code of the street: Decency, violence, and the moral life of the inner city.* New York: Norton.

Asendorpf, J. B., Denissen, J. J. A., & van Aken, M. A. G. (2008). Inhibited and aggressive preschool children at 23 years of age: Personality transitions into adulthood. *Developmental Psychology, 44*(4), 997–1011.

Ashworth, A. J. (1994). Justifying the grounds of mitigation. *Criminal Justice Ethics, 13*(1), 5–10.

Avenevoli, S., & Merikangas, K. R. (2003). Familial influences on adolescent smoking. *Addiction, 98*(Suppl. 1), 1–20.

Babcock, J. C., Green, C. E., & Robie, C. (2004). Does baterers' treatment work? A meta-analytic review of domestic violence treatment. *Clinical Psychology Review, 23*, 1023–1053.

Barber, C. F. (2008). Domestic violence against men. *Nursing Standard, 22*(51), 35–39.

Baron, S. W., (2003). Self-control, social consequences, and criminal behavior: Street youth and the general theory of crime. *Journal of Research in Crime & Delinquency, 40*(4), 403–425.

Beaver, K. M., Ratchford, M., & Ferguson, C. J. (2009). Evidence of genetic and environmental effects on the development of low self-control. *Criminal Justice and Behavior, 36*(11), 1158–1172.

Bender, K. (2010). Why do some maltreated youth become juvenile offenders? A call for further investigation and adaptation of youth services. *Children and Youth Services Review, 32*, 466–473.

Bergen, H. A., Martin, G., Richardson, A. S., Allison, S., & Roeger, L. (2004). Sexual abuse, antisocial behavior and substance use: Gender differences in young community adolescents. *Australian and New Zealand Journal of Psychiatry, 38*, 34–41.

Bersani, B., Nieuwbeerta, P., & Laub, J. H. (2009). Predicting trajectories of offending over the life course: Findings from a Dutch Conviction Cohort. *Journal of Research in Crime and Delinquency, 46*, 468–494.

Betancourt, B., Dolmage, K., Johnson, C., Leach, T. Menchaca, J., Montero, D., & Wood, T. (2006). Social

workers' roles in the criminal justice system. *International Social Work, 49*(5), 615–627.

Birkland, T. A., & Lawrence, R. G. (2009). Media framing and policy change after Columbine. *American Behavioral Scientist, 52*(10), 1405–1425.

Boislard-P., M.-A., Poulin, F., Kiesner, J., & Dishion, T. J. (2009). A longitudinal examination of risky sexual behaviors among Canadian and Italian adolescents: Considering individual, parental, and friend characteristics. *International Journal of Behavioral Development, 33*, 265–276.

Bowie, B. H. (2010). Understanding the gender differences in pathways to social deviancy: Relational aggression and emotion regulation. *Archives of Psychiatric Nursing, 24*(1), 27–37.

Branje, S. J. T., van Doorn, M., VanderValk, I., & Meeus, W. H. J. (2009). Parent–adolescent conflict, conflict resolution, and adolescent adjustment. *Journal of Applied Developmental Psychology, 30*, 195–204.

Brezina, T., Tekin, E., & Topalli, V. (2009). *Might not be a tomorrow: A multi-methods approach to anticipated early death & youth.* Cambridge, MA: National Bureau of Economic Research.

Brown, F., Flanagan, T., & McLeod, M. (Eds.). (1984). *Sourcebook of criminal justice statistics.* Washington, DC: Bureau of Justice Statistics.

Brown, K. (2009). Connecting youth and communities: Customized career planning for youth with psychiatric disabilities. *Journal of Sociology and Social Welfare, 36*(4), 93–110.

Brown, R. P., Osterman, L. L., & Barnes, C. D. (2009). School violence and the culture of honor. *Psychological Science, 20*(11), 1400–1405.

Ccile, M, & Born, M. (2009). Intervention in juvenile delinquency: Danger of iatrogenic effects. *Children and Youth Services Review, 31*, 1217–1221.

Caspi, A. (2000). The child is father of the man: Personality continuities from childhood to adulthood. *Journal of Personality and Social Psychology, 78*, 158–172.

Catlett, B. S., Toews, M. L., & Walilko, V. (2010). Men's gendered constructions of intimate partner violence as predictors of court-mandated batterer treatment drop out. *American Journal of Community Psychology, 45*, 107–123.

CDC (Centers for Disease Control and Prevention). (2011). *Attention-Deficit/Hyperactivity Disorder (ADHD).* Retrieved from http://www.cdc.gov/ncbddd/adhd/data.html

Chabrol, H., Rodgers, R. F., Sobolewski, G., & van Leeuwen, N. (2010). Cannabis use and delinquent behaviors in a non-clinical sample of adolescents. *Addictive Behaviors, 35*, 263–265.

Chassin, L., Dmietrieva, J., Modecki, K., Steinberg, L., Cauffman, E., Knight, G., Piquero, A., & Losoya, S.. (2010). Does adolescent alcohol and marijuana use predict suppressed growth in psychosocial maturity among male juvenile offenders?. *Psychology of Addictive Behaviors 24*(1), 48–60.

Chilenski, S. M., & Greenberg, M. T. (2009). The importance of the community context in the epidemiology of early adolescent substance use and delinquency in a rural sample. *American Journal of Community Psychology, 44*, 287–301.

Cho, D., & Gardner, A. (2007, April 21). An isolated boy in a world of strangers. *The Washington Post*, p. A1.

Coker, A., Smith, P. H., McKeown, R., & King, M. J. (2000). Frequency and correlates of intimate partner violence by type: Physical, sexual, and psychological battering. *American Journal of Public Health, 90*(4), 553–559.

Collins, W. A., & Steinberg, L. (2006). Adolescent development in interpersonal context. In N. Eisenberg (Vol. Ed.) & W. Damon and R. Lerner (Series Eds.), *Handbook of child psychology: Vol. 3. Social, emotional, and personality development* (6th ed., pp. 1003–1067). New York: Wiley.

Corff, Y. L., & Toupin, J. (2009). Comparing persistent juvenile delinquency and normative peers with the Five-Factor Model of Personality. *Journal of Research in Personality, 43*, 1105–1108.

Crick, N. R., & Grotpeter, J. K. (1995). Relational aggression, gender, and social psychological adjustment. *Child Development, 66*, 710–722.

Crooks, C. V., Scott, K. L., Wolfe, D. A., Chiodo, D., & Killip, S. (2007). Understanding the link between childhood maltreatment and violent delinquency: What do schools have to add? *Child Maltreatment, 12*, 269–280.

Curtis, K. (2003, February 6). *California loses track of more than 30,000 sex offenders.* Retrieved from AP Online.

Dabs, J. M., & Morris, R. (1990). Testosterone, social class, and antisocial behavior in a sample of 4,462 men. *Psychological Science, 1*(3), 209–211.

Day, A., Chung, D., O'Leary, P., & Carson, E. (2009). Programs for men who perpetrate domestic violence: An examination of the issues underlying the effectiveness of intervention programs. *Journal of Family Violence, 24*, 203–212.

Dellaire, D. H. (2007). Children with incarcerated mothers: Developmental outcomes, special challenges and recommendations. *Journal of Applied Developmental Psychology, 28*, 15–24.

Dembo, R., Schmeidler, J., & Childs, K. (2007). Correlates of male and female juvenile offender abuse experiences. *Journal of Child Sexual Abuse, 16*(3), 75–94.

Dewar, D. (2008). Plight of male victims of domestic violence. Retrieved August 18, 2008, from www.dewar4research.org/DOCS/PlightofmaleVictimsSummaryMay08.pdf

Dishion, T. J. (2000). Cross-setting consistency in early adolescent psychopathology: Deviant friendships and problem behavior sequelae. *Journal of Personality, 68*(6), 1109–1126.

Dishion, T. J., Andrews, D. W., & Crosby, L. (1995). Antisocial boys and their friends in early adolescence: Relationship characteristics, quality, and interactional process. *Child Development, 66*, 139–151.

Dishion, T. J., & Patterson, G. R. (1999). Model-building in developmental psychopathology: A pragmatic approach to understanding and intervention. *Journal of Clinical Child Psychology, 28*, 502–512.

Dobash, R. E., & Dobash, R. P. (1998). Violent men in violent contexts. In R. E. Dobash & R. P. Dobash (Eds.), *Rethinking Violence Against Women* (pp. 141–168). Thousand Oaks, CA: Sage.

Plat-Jones, Du. (2006). Domestic violence: The role of health professionals. *Nursing Standard, 21*(14–16), 44–48.

Duckett, P., & Schinkel, M. (2008). Community psychology and injustice in the criminal justice system. *Journal of Community and Applied Social Psychology, 18*, 518–526.

English, K. (2001, Spring). *A different look at who reoffends.* Paper presented to Illinois Association for the Treatment of Sexual Abusers Meeting, Chicago, IL.

Estell, D. B., Cairns, R. B., Farmer, T. W., & Cairns, B. D. (2002). Aggression in inner-city early elementary classrooms: Individual and peer group configurations. *Merrill-Palmer Quarterly, 48*, 52–76.

Fallahi, C. R., & Lesik, S. A. (2009). The effects of vicarious exposure to the recent massacre at Virginia Tech. *Psychological Trauma: Theory, Research, Practice, and Policy, 1*(3), 220–230.

Faver, C. A. (2010) School-based humane education as a strategy to prevent violence: Review and recommendations. *Children and Youth Services Review, 32*, 365–370.

Feder, L., & Wilson, D. B. (2005). A meta-analytic view of court mandated batterer intervention programs: can courts affect abuser's behaviour? *Journal of Experimental Criminology, 1* 239–262.

Federal Bureau of Investigation. (2008). *The MS-13 Threat.* Retrieved from http://www.fbi.gov/news/stories/2008/january/ms13_011408

Federal Bureau of Investigation. (2012). *2011 National Gang Threat Assessment – Emerging Trends 2011.* Retrieved from http://www.fbi.gov/stats-services/publications/2011-national-gang-threat-assessment

Federal Bureau of Investigation. (2012). *Gangs.* Retrieved from http://www.fbi.gov/about-us/investigate/vc_majorthefts/gangs/gangs

Felson, M. (1994). *Crime and everyday life: Insight and implications for society.* Thousands Oaks, CA: Pine Forge.

Ferguson, C. J. (2010). Genetic contributions to antisocial personality and behavior (APB): A meta-analytic review from an evolutionary perspective. *Journal of Social Psychology, 150*(2) 160–180. *Retrieved from http://www.tamiu.edu/%7Ecferguson/evmeta.pdf*

Fergusson, D. M., Horwood, L. J., & Lynskey, M. T. (1997). Childhood sexual abuse, adolescent sexual behaviors and sexual revictimization. *Child Abuse and Neglect, 21*(8), 789–802.

Fox, J. A., & Savage, J. (2009). Mass murder goes to college: An examination of changes on college campus following Virginia Tech. *American Behavioral Scientist, 52*(10), 1465–1485.

French, D. C., & Dishion, T. J. (2003). Predictors of early initiation of sexual intercourse among high risk adolescents. *Journal of Early Adolescence, 23*, 295–315.

Glaze, L. E., & Palla, S. (2005). Probation and parole in the United States, 2004. *Bureau of Justice Statistics Bulletin*, NCJ 210676, 1–10.

Glaze, L. E., & Maruschak, L. M. (2008). *Parents in prison and their minor children (NCJ 222984).* Washington, DC: Bureau of Justice Statistics.

Gondolf, E. W. (2007). Theoretical and research support for the Duluth model: a reply to Dutton and Corvo. *Aggression and Violent Behavior, 12*, 644–657.

Grasmick, H. G., Kinsey, K., & Cochran, J. K. (1991). Denomination, religiosity and compliance with the law: A study of adults. *Journal for the Scientific Study of Religion, 30*(1), 99–107.

Green, L. (2001). Analyzing the sexual abuse of children by workers in residential care homes: Characteristics, dynamics and contributory factors. *Journal of Sexual Aggression, 7*, 5–25.

Hagan, M. P., Anderson, D. L., Caldwell, M. S., & Kemper, T. S. (2010). Five-year accuracy of assessments of high risk for sexual recidivism of adolescents. *International Journal of Offender Therapy and Comparative Criminology, 54*(1), 61–70.

Hagner, D., Malloy, J. M., Mazzone, M. W., & Cormier, G. M. (2008). Youth with disabilities in the criminal justice system: Considerations for transition and rehabilitation planning. *Journal of Emotional and Behavioral Disorders, 16*(4), 240–247.

Harkin, L., & Dixon, L. (2010). Sexual offending in groups: An evaluation. *Aggression and Violent Behavior, 15*, 87–99.

Hayatbakhsh, M. R., Najman, J. M., Bor, W., O'Callaghan, M. J., & Williams, G. M. (2009). Multiple Risk Factor Model Predicting Cannabis Use and Use Disorders: A Longitudinal Study. *The American Journal of Drug and Alcohol Abuse, 35*(6), 399–407.

Hendricks, S. A., Landsittel, D. P., Amandus, E. E., Malcan, J., & Bell, J. (1999). A matched case-control study of convenience store robbery risk factors. *Journal of Occupational and Environmental Medicine, 41*(11), 995–1004.

Henry, S. (2009). School violence beyond Columbine. *American Behavioral Scientist, 52*(9), 1246–1265.

Howell, J. C. (1998). Promising programs for youth gang violence prevention and intervention. In R. Loeber & D. P. Farrington (Eds.) *Serious and Violent Juvenile Offender*, pp. 284–312.; Thousand Oaks, CA: Sage.

Ikomi, P. A., Harris-Wyatt, G., Doucet, G., & Rodney, H. E. (2009). Treatment of juveniles who sexually offend in a Southwestern state. *Journal of Child Sexual Abuse, 18*, 594–610.

Jackson, S., Feder, L., Forde, D. R., Davis, R. C., Maxwell, C. D., & Taylor, B. G. (2003). *Batter intervention programs: Where do we go from here?* (NCJ 195079). Washington, DC: U.S. Department of Justice, National Institute of Justice.

Janicak, C. A. (2004). "Regional Variations in the Rates for Fatal Occupational Assaults: 1997-2000." Reprinted in Fatal Workplace Injuries in 2002: A Collection of Data and Analysis, United States Department of Labor, Bureau of Labor Statistics (September 2004), 46–52.

Jennings, W. G., Maldonado-Molina, M. M., Piquero, A. R., & Canino, G. (2010). Parental Suicidality as a risk factor for delinquency among Hispanic Youth. *Journal of Youth Adolescence, 39*, 315–325.

Keenan. K., Coyne, C., & Lahey, B. B. (2008). Should relational aggression be included in The DSM-IV nosology for disruptive behavior disorders? *Journal of the American Academy of Child and Adolescent Psychiatry*, 47, 86–93.

Kirisci, L., Mezzich, A., Aytaclar, S., Reynolds, M., & Tarter, R. (2009). Prospective study of the association between neurobehavior disinhibition and peer environment on illegal drug use in boys and girls. *The American Journal of Drug and Alcohol Abuse*, 35, 145–150.

Lane, J., & Meeker, J. W. (2000). Subcultural diversity and the fear of crime and gangs. *Crime and Delinquency*, 46(4), 497–521.

Lane, J., & Meeker, J. W. (2003). Fear of gang crime: A look at three theoretical models. *Law and Society Review*, 37(2), 425–456.

Langman, P. (2009). Rampage school shooters: A typology. *Aggression and Violent Behavior*, 14, 79–86.

Larkin, R. W. (2009). The Columbine legacy: Rampage shootings as political acts. *American Behavioral Scientist*, 52(9), 1309–1326.

Laux, J. M., Dupuy, P. J., Moe, J. L., Cox, J. A., Lambert, E., Ventura, L. A., et al. (2008). The substance abuse counseling needs of women in the criminal justice system: A needs assessment approach. *Journal of Addictions & Offender Counseling*, 29, 36–48.

Levin, J., & Madfis, E. (2009). Mass murder at school and cumulative strain. *American Behavioral Scientist*, 52(9), 1227–1245.

Loeber, R., & Farrington, D. P. (2000). Young children who commit crime: epidemiology, developmental origins, risk factors, early interventions, and policy implications. *Development and Psychopathology*, 12, 737–762.

Longo, R. E. (2004). An integrated experiential approach to treating young people who sexually abuse. *Journal of Child Sexual Abuse*, 13(3/4), 193–213.

Mallette, L., & Chalouh, M. (1991). *The Montreal Massacre*. Charlottetown, Prince Edward Esland, Canada: Gynergy Press.

Malouff, J. M., Thorsteinsson, E. B., & Schutte, N. S. (2005). The relationship between the Five-Factor Model of Personality and symptoms of clinical disorders: A meta-analysis. *Journal of Psychopathology and Behavioral Assessment*, 27, 101–114.

Marshall, W. L., & Burton, D. L. (2010). The importance of group process in offender treatment. *Aggression and Violent Behavior*, 15, 141–149.

Martin, E., & Law, J. (Eds.) (2006). *A Dictionary of Law*. London: Oxford University Press.

Mason, D. A., & Frick, P. J. (1994). The heritability of antisocial behavior: A meta-analysis of twin and adoption studies. *Journal of Psychopathology and Behavioral Assessment*, 16, 301–323.

Mayer, M. J., & Leone, P. E. (1999). A structural analysis of school violence and disruption: Implications for creating safer schools. *Education and Treatment of Children*, 22, 333–356.

Messman-Moore, T. L., & Brown, A. L. (2004). Child maltreatment and perceived family environment as risk factors for adult rape: Is child sexual abuse the most salient experience? *Child Abuse and Neglect*, 28, 1019–1034.

Miles, D. R., & Carey, G. (1997). Genetic and environmental architecture of human aggression. *Journal of Personality and Social Psychology*, 72, 207–217.

Monahan, K. C., Steinberg, L., & Cauffman, E. (2009). Affiliation with antisocial peers, susceptibility to peer influence, and antisocial behavior during the transition to adulthood. *Developmental Psychology*, 45(6), 1520–1530.

Muschert, G. W. (2008). Research in school shootings. *Social and Personality Compass*, 2(3), 60–80.

NASH, S. T. (2005). Through Black eyes: African American Women's constructions of their experiences with intimate male partner violence. *Violence Against Women*, 11, 1420–1440.

National Center for Educational Statistics. (2012). *Indicators of School Crime and Safety: 2011*. Retrieved from http://nces.ed.gov/programs/crimeindicators/crimeindicators2011/tables/table_08_1.asp

Natsuaki, M. N., Ge, X., Reiss, D., & Neiderhiser, J. M. (2009). Aggressive behavior between siblings and the development of externalizing problems: Evidence from a genetically sensitive study. *Developmental Psychology*, 45(4), 1009–1018.

Neighbors, C., Walker, D., Mbilinyi, L., O'Rourke, A., Edleson, J. L., Zegree, J., & Roffman, R. A. (2010). Normative misperceptions of abuse among perpetrators of intimate partner violence. *Violence Against Women*, 16(4), 370–386.

Newman, K., & Fox, C. (2009). Repeat tragedy: Rampage shootings in American high school and college settings, 2002-2008. *American Behavioral Scientist*, 52(9), 1286–1308.

Newman, K. S., Fox, D., Roth, W., Mehta, J., & Harding, D. (2005). *Rampage: The Social Roots of School Shootings*. New York: Basic Books.

Nezu, A. M. (2004). Problem solving and behavior therapy revisited. *Behavior Therapy, 35*, 1–33.

Nezu, C M., Nezu, A.,M., Dudek, J. A., Peacock, M., & Stoll, J. (2005). Social problem-solving correlates of sexual deviancy among child molesters, *Journal of Sexual Aggression 11*, 27–36.

Norcross, J. C. (2002). *Psychotherapy Relationships That Work*. New York: Oxford University Press.

Nugent, W. R., Umbreit, M. S., Wiinamaki, L., & Paddock, J. (2001). Participation in victim-offender mediation and reoffense: Successful replications?*Research on Social Work Practice, 11*(1), 5–23.

Office of Juvenile Justice and Delinquency. (1999, September 30). *OJJDP statistical briefing Book*. Retrieved from http://www.ojjdp.ncjrs.org/ojstatbb/qa136.html.

Overbeek, G., Vollebergh, M., Meeus, W., Engels, R. and Luijpers, E. (2001). Course, Co-Occurrence, and Longitudinal Associations of Emotional Disturbance and Delinquency from Adolescence to Young Adulthood: A Six- Year Three-Wave Study. *Journal of Youth and Adolescence 30*(4): 401–26.

Parker, R. N., Luther, K., & Murphy, L. (2007). Availability, gang violence, and alcohol policy: Gaining support for alcohol regulation via harm reduction strategies. *Contemporary Drug Problems, 34*, 611–633.

Phillips, S. D., & Dettlaff, A. J. (2009). More than parents in prison: The broader overlap between the criminal justice and child welfare systems. *Journal of Public Child Welfare, 3*, 3–22.

Phillips, S. D., Burns, B. J., Wagner, H. R., & Barth, R. P. (2004). Parental arrest and children in child welfare services agencies. *American Journal of Orthopsychiatry, 2*, 174–186.

Phillips, S. D., Dettlaff, A. J., & Baldwin, M. J. (2010). An exploratory study of the range of implications of families' criminal justice system involvement in child welfare cases. *Children and Youth Services Review, 32*, 544–550.

Phillips, S. D., Erkanli, A., Costello, E. J., & Angold, A. (2007). Differences among children whose mothers have a history of arrest. *Women & Criminal Justice, 17*(2/3), 45–63.

Phillips, S. D., Leathers, S. J., & Erkanli, A. (2009). Children of probationers in the child welfare system and their families. *Journal of Child and Family Studies, 18*, 183–191.

Piquero, A. R., Brame, R., Lynam &, D. (2004). Studying criminal career length through early adulthood among serious offenders. *Crime and Delinquency, 50*(3), 412–435.

Poehlmann, J. (2005). Children's family environments and intellectual outcomes during maternal incarceration. *Journal of Marriage and Family, 67*, 1275–1285.

Pridemore, W. A. (2002). What we know about social structure and homicide: A review of the theoretical and empirical literature. *Violence and Victims, 17*(2), 127–156.

Quackenbush, R. E. (2003). The role of theory in the assessment of sex offenders. *Journal of Child Sexual Abuse, 12*(3/4), 77–102.

Rhee, S. H., & Waldman, I. D. (2002). Genetic and environmental influences on antisocial behavior: A meta-analysis of twin and adoption studies. *Psychological Bulletin, 128*, 490–529.

Righthand, S., & Welch, C. (2004). Characteristics of youth who sexually offend. *Journal of Child Sexual Abuse, 13*(3/4), 15–32.

Roodman, A. A., & Clum, G. A. (2001). Revictimization rates and method variance: A meta-analysis. *Clinical Psychology Review, 21*(2), 183–204.

Rosen, J. (2005). *The naked crowd: Reclaiming security and freedom in an anxious age*. New York: Random House.

Sadler, A. G., Booth, B. M., & Doebbeling, B. N. (2005). Gant and multiple rapes during military service: Health consequences and health care. *Women's Health, 60*, 33–41.

Scholte, E. M. (1999). Factors predicting continued violence into young adulthood. *Journal of Adolescence, 22*, 3–20.

Schreck, C. J., & Miller, J. M.(2003). Sources of fear of crime at school. *Journal of School Violence, 2*, 57–79.

Schreck, C. J., Miller, J. M., & Gibson, C. L. (2003). Trouble in the school yard: A study of the risk factors of victimization at school. *Crime & Delinquency, 49*, 460–484.

Sen, B. (2010). The relationship between frequency of family dinner and adolescent problem behaviors after adjusting for other family characteristics. *Journal of Adolescence, 33*, 187–196.

Short, J. F. (1990). *Delinquency and Society*. Englewood Cliffs, NJ: Prentice Hall.

Sigfusdottir, I. D., Gudjonsson, G. H., & Sigurdsson, J. F. (2010). Bullying and delinquency: The mediating role of anger. *Personality and Individual Difference, 48*, 391–396.

Simons, R. L., Simons, L. G., & Wallace, E. (2004). *Families, Delinquency, and Crime: Linking Society's Most Basic Institution to Antisocial Behavior*. Los Angeles: Roxbury.

Slomkowski, C., Rende, R., Novak, S., Richardson, E., & Niaura, R. (2005). Sibling effects on smoking in adolescence: Evidence for social influence from a genetically-informative design. *Addiction, 100,* 430–448.

Snyder, C. S., Wesley, S. C., Lin, M. B., & May, J. D. (2008). Bridging the gap: Gerontology and Social Work Education. *Gerontology & Geriatrics Education, 28*(4), 1–21.

Snyder, J., Schrepferman, L., Oeser, J., Patterson, G. R., Stoolmiller, M., Johnson, K., & Snyder, A. (2005). Deviancy training and association with deviant peers in young children: Occurrence and contribution to early-onset conduct problems. *Development and Psychopathology, 17,* 397–413.

Spergel, I. A., & Grossman, S. F. (1997). The Little Village Project: A community approach to the gang problem. *Social Work, 42*(5), 456–470.

Spergel, I. A., (1990). Youth gangs: Continuity and change. In M. Tonry & N. Morris, (Eds.). *Crime and Justice: A Review of Research, Vol. 12.* Chicago: University of Chicago Press.

Stark, E. (2007). *Coercive Control: How Men Entrap Women in Personal Life.* New York: Oxford University Press.

Stouthamer-Loeber, M., Wei, E. Loeber, R., & Masten, A. S. (2004). Desistance from persistent serious delinquency in the transition to adulthood. *Development and Psychopathology, 16,* 897–918.

Sullivan, T. N., Farrell, A. D., & Kliewer, W. (2006). Peer victimization in early adolescence: Association between physical and relational victimization and drug use, aggression, and delinquent behaviors among urban middle school students. *Development and Psychopathology, 18,* 119–137.

Ta, M. L., Marshall, S. W., Kaufman, J. S., Loomis, D., Casteel, C., & Land, K. C. (2009). Area-Based Socioeconomic Characteristics of Industries at High Risk for Violence in the Workplace. *American Journal of Community Psychology, 44* (3–4), 249–260.

Tonso, K. L. (2009). Violent masculinities as tropes for school shooters. *American Behavioral Scientist, 52*(9), 1266–1285.

Tremblay, R. E. (2000). The development of aggressive behavior during childhood: What have we learned in the past century? *International Journal of Behavioral Developments, 24,* 129–141.

Tucker, C. J., McHale, S. M., & Crouter, A. C. (2003). Conflict resolution: Links with adolescents' family relationships and individual well-being. *Journal of Family Issues, 24,* 715–736.

Utah Department of Corrections: http://corrections.utah.gov/programs/sex_offender_unit.html. Contact information: http://corrections.utah.gov/mail/mailform.html.

Vandiver, D. M. (2006). A prospective analysis of juvenile male sex offenders. *Journal of Interpersonal Violence, 21*(5), 673–688.

Vazsonyi, A. T., & Huang, L. (2010). Where self-control comes from: On the development of self-control and its relationship to deviance over time. *Developmental Psychology, 46*(1), 245–257.

Warshaw, R. (1988). *I never called it rape: The Ms. report on recognizing, fighting, and surviving date and acquaintance rape.* New York: Sarah Lazin.

Wijsbroek, S. A. M., Hale, III, W. W., Van Doorn, M. D., Raaijmakers, A. W., & Meeus, W. H. J. (2010). Is the resolution style 'exiting statements' related to adolescent problem behavior? *Journal of Applied Developmental Psychology, 31,* 60–69.

Wright, J. P., & Beaver, K. M. (2005). Do parents matter in creating self-control in their children? A genetically informed test of Gottfredson and Hirschi's theory of low self-control. *Criminology, 43,* 1169–1202.

Zahn-Waxler, C., Park, J.-H., Essex, M., Slattery, M., & Cole, P. M. (2005). Relational and overt aggression in disruptive adolescents: Prediction from early social representations and links with concurrent problems. *Early Education and Development, 16,* 259–282.

Zhang, L., Messner, S. F., Lu, Z., & Deng, X. (1997). Gang crime and its punishment in China. *Journal of Criminal Justice, 25*(4), 289–302.

Zimring, F. E., Piquero, A. R., & Jennings, W. G. (2007). Sexual delinquency in Racine: Does early sex offending predict later sex offending in youth and young adulthood. *Criminology and Public Policy, 6*(3), 507–534.

CHAPTER 19

Aber, L. (2009). Experiments in 21st century antipoverty policy. *Public Policy Research,* 57–63.

Ansalone, G. (2001). Schooling, tracking and inequality. *Journal of Children and Poverty, 7*(1), 33–47.

Ansalone, G. (2003). Poverty, tracking, and the social construction of failure: International perspectives on tracking. *Journal of Children and Poverty, 9*(1), 3–20.

Anyon, J. (2005). What "counts" as educational policy? Notes toward a new paradigm. *Harvard Educational Review, 75*(1), 65–88.

Aoky, A., Bruns, B., & Drabble, M. (2002). Education. In J. Klugman (Ed.), *A sourcebook for poverty reduction strategies, vol. II: Macroeconomic and sectoral approaches* (pp. 233–273). Washington, DC: World Bank.

Attree, P. (2004). Growing up in disadvantage: A systematic review of the qualitative evidence. *Child Care, Health and Development, 30*(6), 679–689.

Battistich, V., Solomon, D., Kim, D., Watson, M., & Schaps, E. (1995). Schools as communities, poverty levels of student populations, and students attitudes, motives, and performance: A multilevel analysis. *American Education Research Journal, 32*(3), 627–658.

Bennett, M. M. (2008). Understanding the students we teach: Poverty in the classroom. *The Clearing House,* pp. 251–256.

Ben-Shalom, Y., Moffit, R., & Scholz, J. K. (2012). An assessment of the effectiveness of anti-poverty programs in the United States. In P. M. Jefferson (Ed.), *The Oxford handbook of the economics of poverty.* New York: Oxford University Press.

Berliner, D. C. (2006). Our impoverished view of educational research. *Teachers College Record, 108*(6), 949–995.

Blow, C. M. (2011). Inconvenient income inequality. *New York Times.* Retrieved December 12, 2011, from http://www.nytimes.com/2011/12/17/opinion/blow-inconvenient-income-inequality.html

Boaler, J., William, D., & Brown, M. (2000). Students' experiences of ability grouping–disaffection, polarization and construction of failure. *British Educational Research Journal, 26*(5), 631–648.

Boggess, S. (1998). Family structure, economic status, and educational attainment. *Journal of Population Economics, 1*(2), 205–222.

Brooks-Gunn, J., Duncan, G., & Aber, J. L. (1997). *Neighborhood poverty: Context and consequences for development.* New York: Russell Sage Foundation.

Brown, R., Copeland, W. E., Costello, E. J., Erkanli, A., & Worthman, C. M. (2009). Family and community influences on educational outcomes among appalachian youth. *Journal of Community Psychology, 37*(7), 795–808.

Brown, N. T. (2003). Critical race theory speaks to the sociology of mental health: Mental health problems produced by racial stratification. *Journal of Health and Social Behavior, 44,* 292–301.

Bullock, H. E., & Limbert, W. M. (2003). Scaling the socioeconomic ladder: Low ES women's perspectives of class status and opportunity. *Journal of Social Issues, 5,* 693–709.

Burchinal, M., Nelson, L., Carlson, M., & Brooks-Gunn, J. (2008). Neighborhood characteristics and child care type and quality. *Early Education and Development, 19*(5), 702–725.

Carlson, K. T. (2006). Poverty and youth violence exposure: Experiences in rural communities. *Children and Schools, 28*(2), 87–96.

Carneiro, P., & Heckman, J. J. (2003). Human capital policy. In B. M. Friedman (Ed.), *Inequality in America: What role for human capital policies?* (pp. 148–149). Cambridge, MA: MIT Press.

Center on Budget and Policy Priorities. (2011). *Poverty rate second-highest in 45 years; record numbers lack health insurance, lived in deep poverty.* Retrieved from http://www.cbpp.org/cms/index.cfm?a=view&id=3580

Cheng, T. (2004). Impact of family stability on children's delinquency: An implication for family preservation. *Journal of Family Social Work, 8*(1), 47–60.

Cherlin, A. (2002). *Public and private families.* New York: McGraw-Hill.

Collins, D., Pan, Z. F., Johnson, K., Courser, M., & Shamblen, S. (2008). Individual and contextual predictors of inhalant use among 8th graders: A multilevel analysis. *Journal of Drug Education, 38*(3), 193–210.

Congressional Budget Office. (2010). *Average federal taxes by income group: Average after-tax household income.* Retrieved from http://www.cbo.gov/publication/43302

Costello, E. J., Compton, S. N., Keeler, G., & Angold, A. (2003). Relationships between poverty and psychopathology: A natural experiment. *Journal of the American Medical Association, 290,* 2023–2029.

Cunradi, C. (2007). Drinking level, neighborhood social disorder, and mutual intimate partner violence. *Alcoholism: Clinical and Experimental Research, 31*(6), 1012–1019.

Curran, L. (2003). The culture of race, class, and poverty: The emergence of a cultural discourse in early cold war social work (1946–1963). *Journal of Sociology and Social Welfare, 30*(3), 15–38.

Dallaire, D. H., Cole, D. A., Smith, T. M., Ciesla, J. A., LaGrange, B., Jacquez, F. M., et al. (2008). Predicting children's depressive symptoms from community and individual risk factors. *Journal of Youth and Adolescence, 37*(7), 830–846.

Dearing, E., McCartney, K., & Taylor, B. A. (2001). Change in family income-to-needs matters more for children with less. *Child Development, 72*(6), 1779–1793.

DeLuca, S. (2007). All over the map: Explaining educational outcomes in the moving to opportunity program. *Education next, 7*(4), 29–36.

Eardley, T. (1998). Low pay and family poverty: Tracing the links. *Family Matters, 51*, 29–32.

Entwisle, D. R., Alexander, K. L., & Olson, L. S. (1997). *Children, schools, and inequality*. Boulder, Colo: Westview Press.

Fiscella, K. (2010). Breaking the cycle of poverty and poor health: Pediatricians can make a difference. *Acta Paediatrica, 99*, 648–650.

Frankel, H., & Frankel, S. (2006). Family therapy, family practice, and child and family poverty: Historical perspectives and recent developments. *Journal of Family Social Work, 10*(4), 43–80.

Glennerster, H. (2007). United States poverty studies and poverty measurement: The past twenty-five years. *Social Service Review, 76*(1), 83–107.

Gundersen, C. (2006). Are the effects of the macroeconomy and social policies on poverty different in nonmetro areas in the United States? *Rural Sociology, 71*(4), 545–572.

Gutman, L. M., McLoyd, V. C., & Tokoyawa, T. (2005). Financial strain, neighborhood stress, parenting behaviors and adolescent adjustment in urban African American families. *Journal of Research on Adolescence, 15*(4), 425–449.

Harrell, J. P., Hall, S., & Tallaferro, J. (2003). Physiological responses to racism and discrimination: An assessment of the evidence. *American Journal of Public Health, 93*, 243–248.

Hay, C., Fortson, E. N., Hollist, D. R., Altheimer, I., & Schaible, L. M. (2006). The impact of community disadvantage on the relationship between the family and juvenile crime. *Journal of Research in Crime and Delinquency, 43*(4), 326–356.

Hay, C., Fortson, E. N., Hollist, D. R., Altheimer, I., & Schaible, L. M. (2007). Compounded risk: The implications for delinquency of coming from a poor family that lives in a poor community. *Journal of Youth and Adolescence, 36*(5), 593–605.

Horton, H. D., & Allen, B. L. (1998). Race, family structure and rural poverty: An assessment of population and structural change. *Journal of Comparative Family Studies, 29*(2), 397–406.

Ireson, J., & Hallam, S. (1999). Raising standards: Is ability grouping the answer? *Oxford Review of Education, 25*(3), 344–360.

Iversen, R. R., & Armstrong, A. L. (2006). *Jobs aren't enough: Toward a new economic mobility for low-income families*. Philadelphia: Temple University.

Jack, G. (2000). Ecological influences on parenting and child development. *British Journal of Social Work, 30*(6), 703–720.

Jessim, L., & Harber, K. D. (2005). Teacher expectations and self-fulfilling prophecies: Knowns and unknowns, resolved and unresolved controversies. *Personality and Social Psychology Review, 9*(2), 131–155.

Jones, J. M. (2007). Exposure to chronic community violence: Resilience in African American children. *Journal of Black Psychology, 33*(2), 125–149.

Jones, R. L., Homa, D. M., Meyer, P. A., Brody, D. J., Caldwell, K. L., Pirkle, J. L., et al. (2009). Trends in blood lead levels and blood lead testing among US children aged 1 to 5 years, 1988-2004. *Pediatrics, 123*(3), 376–385.

Kiplinger. (2011). *How does your city stack up?* Retrieved February 3, 2012, from http://www.kiplinger.com/tools/bestcities_sort/

Kling, J. R., Ludwig, J., & Katz, L. F. (2005). Neighborhood effects on crime for female and male youth: Evidence from a randomized housing voucher experiment. *Quarterly Journal of Economics, 120*(1), 87–130.

Kozol, J. (1991). *Savage inequalities*. New York: Harper Perennial.

Krieger, N. (2000). Discrimination and health. In L. F. Berkman & I. Kawachi (Eds.), *Social epidemiology* (pp. 36–75). New York: Oxford University Press.

Leaman, J. (2008). Managing poverty: Great Britain in comparative perspective. *Journal of Contemporary European Studies, 16*(1), 41–56.

Lee, V. E., & Burkam, D. T. (2002). *Inequality at the starting gate*. Washington, DC: Economic.

Lewis, O. (1959). *Five families: Mexican case studies in the culture of poverty*. New York: Basic Books.

Lichter, D. T., & Johnson, K. M. (2007). The changing spatial concentration of America's rural poor population. *Rural Sociology, 72*(3), 331–358.

Loh, E. S. (1996). Changes in family structure, attained schooling and adult poverty status. *Social Science Quarterly, 77*(1), 145–158.

Ludwig, C., & Dietz, B. (2008). There's not a single book there, no PC, no internet: Increasing poverty in German and a lack of political answers. *Journal of Contemporary European Studies, 16*(1), 25–39.

Ludwig, J., & Mayer, S. (2006). Culture and the intergenerational transmission of poverty: The prevention paradox. *The Future of Children, 16*(2), 175–195.

Lynch, R. G. (2004). *Exceptional returns: Economic, fiscal, and social benefits of investment in early childhood development*. Washington, DC: Economic Policy Institute.

Malat, J., Oh, H. J., & Hamilton, M. A. (2005). Poverty experience, race, and child health. *Public Health Reports, 120,* 442–447.

Maluccio, A. N., Pine, B. A., & Tracy, E. M. (2002). *Social work practice with families and children.* New York: Columbia University Press.

McCulloch, A., & Joshi, H. E. (2001). Neighbourhood and family influences on the cognitive ability of children in the British national child development study. *Social Science and Medicine, 53,* 579–591.

McGregor, J. A. (2007). Researching wellbeing: From concepts to metholodogy. In I. Gough & J. A. McGregor (Eds.), *Wellbeing in developing countries* (pp. 337–358). Cambridge: Cambridge University Press.

McLanahan, S., & Sandefur, G. (1994). *Growing up with a single parent: What hurts, what helps?* Boston: Harvard University Press.

McLeod, J. D., & Shanahan, M. J. (1996). Trajectories of poverty and children's mental health. *Journal of Health and Social Behavior, 37,* 207–220.

Miller-Cribbs, J. E., & Farber, N. B. (2008). Kin networks and poverty among African Americans: Past and present. *Social Work, 53*(1), 43–51.

Moilanen, K. L., Shaw, D. S., Dishion, T. J., Gardner, F., & Wilson, M. N. (2010). Predictors of longitudinal growth in inhibitory control in early childhood. *Social Development, 19,* 326–347.

Mosteller, F., Light, R., & Sachs, J. (1996). Sustained inquiry in education. *Harvard Educational Review, 66*(4), 797–842.

National Alliance to End Homelessness. (2012). *The state of homelessness in America 2012.* Washington, DC: Author.

National Coalition for the Homeless. (2009). *How many people experience homelessness?* Retrieved from http://www.nationalhomeless.org/factsheets/How_Many.html

National Poverty Center. (2012). *Poverty in the United States.* Ann Arbor, MI: University of Michigan. Retrieved January 27, 2012, from http://www.npc.umich.edu/poverty/

National Poverty Center. (2009). *The health effects of social and economic policy: The promise and challenge for research and policy* [Policy Brief #20]. Retrieved January 1, 2012, from http://npc.umich.edu/publications/policy_briefs/brief20/index.php.

Nisbett, R. E. (2009). *Intelligence and how to get it: Why schools and cultures count.* New York: W. W. Norton Company.

Noah, T. (2010). The United States of inequality. *Slate.* Retrieved February 2, 2012, from http://www.slate.com/articles/news_and_politics/the_great_divergence/features/2010/the_united_states_of_inequality/introducing_the_great_divergence.html

Noh, S., & Kaspar, V. (2003). Perceived discrimination and distress: Moderating effects of coping, acculturation, and ethnic support. *American Journal of Public Health, 93,* 232–238.

Noh, S., Beiser, M., Kasper, V., Hou, F., & Rummens, J. (1999). Discrimination and emotional well-being: Perceived racial discrimination, depression, and coping: A study of southeast Asian refugees in Canada. *Journal of Health and Social Behavior, 40,* 193–207.

Page, R. (1991). *Lower track classrooms.* New York: Teachers College.

Perry, M. (2005). The relationship between social class and mental disorder. *The Journal of Primary Prevention, 17*(1), 17–30.

Pimpare, S. (2009). The failures of American poverty measures. *Journal of Sociology and Social Welfare, 36*(1), 103–122.

Plotnick, R. D. (2009). Measuring poverty and assessing the role of income transfers in contemporary antipoverty policy: Comments on Besharov and call. *The Policy Studies Journal, 37*(4), 633–644.

Rank, M. R., & Hirschl, T. A. (2002). Welfare use as a life course event: Toward a new understanding of the U.S. Safety net. *Social Work, 47*(3), 237–248.

Rosemblatt, K. A. (2009). Other Americas: Transnationalism, scholarship, and the culture of poverty in Mexico and the United States. *Hispanic American Historical Review, 89*(4), 603–641.

Rouse, C. E., & Barrow, L. (2006). U.S. Elementary and secondary schools: Equalizing opportunity or replicating the status quo? *The Future of Children, 16*(2), 99–123.

Ruhm, C. J. (2004). Parental employment and child cognitive development. *Journal of Human Resources, 39*(1), 155-192.

Sampson, R. J., Squires, G. D., & Zhou, M. (2001). *How neighborhoods matter: The value of investing at the local level.* Washington, DC: American Sociological Association.

Sanbonmatsu, L., Kling, J. R., Duncan, G. J., & Brooks-Gunn, J. (2006). Neighborhoods and academic achievement: Results from the moving to opportunity experiment. *Journal of Human Resources, 41*(4), 649–691.

Sandoval, D. A., Rank, M. R., & Hirschl, T. A. (2009). The increasing risk of poverty across the American life course. *Demography, 46*(4), 717–713.

Seith, D., & Isakson, E. (2011). *Who are America's poor children? Examining health disparities among children in the United States.* New York: National Center for Children in Poverty.

Shonkoff, J. P., Boyce, W. T., & McEwen, B. S. (2009). Neuroscience, molecular biology, and the childhood roots of health disparities: Building a new framework for health promotion and disease prevention. *Journal of the American Medical Association, 301,* 2252–2259.

Spencer, M. B. (2001). Resiliency and frailty factors associated with the contextual experiences of low resource urban African male youth and families. In A. Booth & A. C. Crouter (Eds.), *Does it take a village? Community effects on children, adolescents, and families* (pp. 51–77). Hillsdale, NJ: Lawrence Erlbaum Associates.

Stal, G. Y., & Zuveri, D. M. (2010). Ending the cycle of poverty through socio-economic integration: A comparison of moving to opportunity (MTO) in the United States and the bijlmermeer revival project in the Netherlands. *Cities, 27,* 3–12.

Stapleton, D., O'Day, B., Livermore, G., & Imparato, A. (2006). Dismantling the poverty trap: Disability policy for the twenty-first century. *The Milbank Quarterly, 84*(4), 701–732.

Sternberg, R. (1997). What does it mean to be smart? *Educational Leadership, 54*(6), 20–24.

Tarabini, A. (2009). Education and poverty in the global development agenda: Emergence, evolution and consolidation. *International Journal of Educational Development, 30,* 204–212.

Taylor, J., & Turner, P. J. (2002). Perceived discrimination, social stress, and depression in the transition to adulthood: Racial contrasts. *Social Psychology Quarterly, 65,* 213–325.

Thaker, G., Adami, H., & Gold, J. (2001). Functional deterioration in individuals with schizophrenia spectrum personality symptoms. *Journal of Personality Disorders, 15*(3), 229–234.

Tracy, M., Zimmerman, F. J., Galea, S., McCauley, E., & Stoep, A. V. (2008). What explains the relation between family poverty and childhood depressive symptoms? *Journal of Psychiatric Research, 42,* 1163–1175.

U.S. Census Bureau. (2011). *Income, poverty and health insurance coverage in the United States: 2010.* Retrieved from http://www.census.gov/newsroom/releases/archives/income_wealth/cb11-157.html

U.S. Conference of Mayors. (2008). *2008 Status report on hunger & homelessness.* Retrieved from http://usmayors.org/pressreleases/documents/hungerhomelessnessreport_121208.pdf

Vital and Health Statistics. (2012). *Summary health statistics for U.S. adults: National health interview survey, 2010.* Hyattsville, MD: U.S. Department of Health and Human Services.

Welsh, W. N., Stokes, R., & Greene, J. R. (2000). A macro-level model of school disorder. *Journal of Research in Crime and Delinquency, 37*(3), 243–283.

Wenzel, S. L., Koegel, P., & Gelberg, L. (2000). Antecedents of physical and sexual victimization among homeless women: A comparison to homeless men. *American Journal of Community Psychology, 28*(3), 367–390.

Wickrama, K. A., Wickrama, K. A. S., & Bryant, C. (2006). Community influence on adolescent obesity: Race/ethnic differences. *Journal of Youth and Adolescence, 35*(4), 647–657.

Wickrama, K. A. S., & Bryant, C. M. (2003). Community context of social resources and adolescent mental health. *Journal of Marriage and Family, 65,* 850–866.

Wickrama, K. A. S., Noh, S., & Bryant, C. M. (2005). Racial differences in adolescent distress: Differential effects of the family and community for blacks and whites. *Journal of Community Psychology, 33*(3), 261–282.

Williams, D. R., Neighbors, H. W., & Jackson, J. S. (2003). Racial/ethnic discrimination and health: Findings from community studies. *American Journal of Public Health, 93*(2), 200–208.

Williams, W. R. (2009). Struggling with poverty: Implications for theory and policy of increasing research on class-based stigma. *Analyses of Social Issues and Public Policy, 9*(1), 37–56.

Wilson, W. J. (2009). *More than just race. Being black and poor in the inner city.* New York: W.W. Norton.

Wood, D. (2003).). Effect of child and family poverty on child health in the United States. *Pediatrics, 112*(3), 707–711.

World Bank. (2009). *Conditional cash transfers: A world bank policy research report.* Washington, DC: Author.

World Bank. (2011). *Conditional cash transfers.* Retrieved from http://web.worldbank.org/WBSITE/EXTERNAL/TOPICS/EXTSOCIALPROTECTION/EXTSAFETYNETSANDTRANSFERS/0,contentMDK:20615138~menuPK:282766~pagePK:148956~piPK:216618~theSitePK:282761,00.html

CHAPTER 20

Abramson, L., Seligman, M., & Teasdale, J. (1978). Learned helplessness in humans: Critique and reformulation. *Journal of Abnormal Psychology, 87*(1), 49–74.

American Psychiatric Association. (2000). *Diagnostic and statistical manual of mental disorders* (TR, 4th ed.). Washington, DC: Author.

American Psychiatric Association. (2013). *Diagnostic and statistical manual of mental disorders* (5th ed.). Washington, DC: Author.

Basset, L. (2012). Susan g. Komen reverses planned parenthood decision, does not promise to renew grants. *The Huffington Post*. Retrieved February 5, 2012, from http://www.huffingtonpost.com/2012/02/03/susan-g-komen-planned-parenthood_n_1252651.html?ef=mostpopular

Bureau of Labor Statistics. Retrieved from http://www.bls.gov/oco/ocos060.htm, on February 8, 2012.

Bogues, A. (2008). Medal of honor is awarded to soldier who saved others. *The New York Times*. Retrieved September 5, 2012, from http://www.nytimes.com/2008/06/03/washington/03medal.html

Bowling, N., Eschleman, K., & Wang, Q. (2010). A meta-analytic examination of the relationship between job satisfaction and subjective well-being. *Journal of Occupational and Organizational Psychology, 83*(4), 915–934.

Cerel, J., Jordan, J., & Duberstein, P. (2008). The impact of suicide on the family. *Crisis: The Journal of Crisis Intervention and Suicide Prevention, 29*(1), 38–44.

Chida, Y., & Steptoe, A. (2008). Positive psychological well-being and mortality: A quantitative review of prospective observational studies. *Psychosomatic Medicine, 70*(7), 741–756.

Conner, K., Pinquart, M., & Gamble, S. (2009). Meta-analysis of depression and substance use among individuals with alcohol use disorders. *Journal of Substance Abuse Treatment, 37*(2), 127–137.

Csikszentmihalyi, M. (1990). *Flow: The psychology of optimal experience*. New York: Harper and Row.

Deci, E., Koestner, R., & Ryan, R. (1999). A meta-analytic review of experiments examining the effects of extrinsic rewards on intrinsic motivation. *Psychological Bulletin, 125*(6), 627–668.

Demir, M., & Weitekamp, L. (2007). I am so happy because today I found my friend: Friendship and personality as predictors of happiness. *Journal of Happiness Studies, 8*(2), 181–211.

Diener, E., Ng, W., Harter, J., & Arora, R. (2010). Wealth and happiness across the world: Material prosperity predicts life evaluation, whereas psychosocial prosperity predicts positive feeling. *Journal of Personality and Social Psychology, 99*(1), 52–61.

Dunn, E., Gilbert, D., & Wilson, T. (2011). If money doesn't make you happy, then you probably aren't spending it right. *Journal of Consumer Psychology (Elsevier Science), 21*(2), 115–125.

Enright, R. D., & Fitzgibbons, R. P. (2000). *Helping clients forgive: An empirical guide for resolving anger and restoring hope*. Washington, DC: American Psychological Association.

Eschleman, K., Bowling, N., & Alarcon, G. (2010). A meta-analytic examination of hardiness. *International Journal of Stress Management, 17*(4), 277–307.

Gardarsdattir, R., Dittmar, H., & Aspinall, C. (2009). It's not the money, it's the quest for a happier self: The role of happiness and success motives in the link between financial goals and subjective well-being. *Journal of Social and Clinical Psychology, 28*(9), 1100–1127.

Gillham, J. E., Reivich, K. J., Jaycox, L. H., & Seligman, M. P. (1995). Prevention of depressive symptoms in schoolchildren: Two-year follow-up. *Psychological Science, 6*(6), 343–351. doi:10.1111/j.1467-9280.1995.tb00524.x

Hacker, K., Collins, J., Gross-Young, L., Almeida, S., & Burke, N. (2008). Coping with youth suicide and overdose: One community's efforts to investigate, intervene, and prevent suicide contagion. *Crisis: The Journal of Crisis Intervention and Suicide Prevention, 29*(2), 86–95.

Harper, J., & Sandberg, J. (2009). Depression and communication processes in later life marriages. *Aging & Mental Health, 13*(4), 546–556.

Hsee, C., Yang, Y., Li, N., & Shen, L. (2009). Wealth, warmth, and well-being: Whether happiness is relative or absolute depends on whether it is about money, acquisition, or consumption. *Journal of Marketing Research, 46*(3), 396–409.

Hysenbegasi, A., Hass, S., & Rowland, C. (2005). The impact of depression on the academic productivity of university students. *Journal of Mental Health Policy and Economics, 8*(3), 145–151.

Insel, T. R. (2008). Assessing the economic costs of serious mental illness. *American Journal of Psychiatry, 165*(6), 663–665. doi:10.1176/appi.ajp.2008.08030366

Koopmans, T. A., Geleijnse, J. M., Zitman, F. G., & Giltay, E. J. (2010). Effects of happiness on all-cause mortality during 15 years of follow-up: The Arnhem elderly study. *Journal of Happiness Studies, 11*(1), 113–124.

Kuhn, T. (1962). *The structure of scientific revolutions.* Chicago: University of Chicago Press.

Lerner, D., & Henke, R. (2008). What does research tell us about depression, job performance, and work productivity? *Journal of Occupational and Environmental Medicine, 50*(4), 401–410.

Lovejoy, M., Graczyk, P., O'Hare, E., & Neuman, G. (2000). Maternal depression and parenting behavior: A meta-analytic review. *Clinical Psychology Review, 20*(5), 561–592.

Lundahl, B. W., Taylor, M. J., Stevenson, R., & Roberts, K. D. (2008). Process-based forgiveness interventions: A meta-analytic review. *Research on Social Work Practice, 18*(5), 465–478.

Lyubomirsky, S., Sheldon, K., & Schkade, D. (2005). Pursuing happiness: The architecture of sustainable change. *Review of General Psychology, 9*(2), 111–131.

Ma, H. (2009). The effect size of variables associated with creativity: A meta-analysis. *Creativity Research Journal, 21*(1), 30–42.

Mak, W. W., Ng, I. S., & Wong, C. C. (2011). Resilience: Enhancing well-being through the positive cognitive triad. *Journal of Counseling Psychology, 58*(4), 610–617.

Mogilner, C. (2010). The pursuit of happiness: Time, money, and social connection. *Psychological Science, 21*(9), 1348–1354.

Muller, D. (2011). Attention to language in a request for physician aid in dying. *American Journal of Hospice & Palliative Medicine, 28*(1), 63–64. doi:10.1177/1049909110381080

National Association of Social Work's. (2008). *Code of ethics.* Retrieved May 20, 2013, from https://www.socialworkers.org/pubs/code/default.asp

National Institute of Mental Health. (2002). *Annual total direct and indirect costs of serious mental illness.* Retrieved May 21, 2013, from http://www.nimh.nih.gov/statistics/4COST_TOTAN.shtml

National Institute of Mental Health. (2006). *Questions and answers about the NIMH sequenced treatment alternatives to relieve depression (STAR*d) study – background.* Retrieved February 11, 2012, from http://www.nimh.nih.gov/trials/practical/stard/backgroundstudy.shtml

National Institute of Mental Health. (2012a). *Any disorders among adults.* Retrieved May 21, 2013, from http://www.nimh.nih.gov/statistics/1ANYDIS_ADULT.shtml

National Institute of Mental Health. (2012b). *A fact sheet of statistics on suicide with information on treatments and suicide prevention.* Retrieved May 21, 2013, from http://www.nimh.nih.gov/health/publications/suicide-in-the-us-statistics-and-prevention/index.shtml

Park, N., & Peterson, C. (2003). Early intervention from the perspective of positive psychology. *Prevention & Treatment, 6*(1).

Rice, A. (2004). *Campaigns online: The profound impact of the internet, blogs, and e-technologies in presidential political campaigning. Campaigns online.org. Project of the center for the study of American government at john Hopkins University.* Retrieved from http://www.campaignsonline.org/reports/online.pdf

Rogers, S., & White, L. (1998). Satisfaction with parenting: The role of marital happiness, family structure, and parents' gender. *Journal of Marriage & the Family, 60*(2), 293–308.

Rosenberg, R. (2010). *Does microcredit really help poor people?* Focus Note 59. Retrieved from http://www.cgap.org/gm/document-1.9.41443/fn59.pdf

Rohacek, M., Bertolotti, A., Grazmaller, N., Simmen, U., Marty, H., Zimmermann, H., et al. (2012). The challenge of triaging chest pain patients: The bernese university hospital experience. *Emergency Medicine International.*

Ryan, R., & Deci, E. (2000). Self-determination theory and the facilitation of intrinsic motivation, social development, and well-being. *American Psychologist, 55*(1), 68–78.

Schoenfeld, C. (1976). An analysis of the views of Thomas S. Szasz. *Journal of Psychiatry & Law, 4*(2), 245–263.

Seligman, M. E., Schulman, P., & Tryon, A. M. (2007). Group prevention of depression and anxiety symptoms. *Behaviour Research and Therapy, 45*(6), 1111–1126.

Seligman, M. E. (1995). The effectiveness of psychotherapy: The consumer reports study. *American Psychologist, 50*(12), 965–974.

Seligman, M., & Csikszentmihalyi, M. (2000). Positive psychology: An introduction. *American Psychologist, 55*(1), 5–14.

Sin, N., & Lyubomirsky, S. (2009). Enhancing well-being and alleviating depressive symptoms with positive psychology interventions: A practice-friendly meta-analysis. *Journal of Clinical Psychology, 65*(5), 467–487.

Torrey, E. (2005). Psychiatric fraud and force: A reply to Szasz. *Journal of Humanistic Psychology, 45*(3), 397–402.

Vohs, K., & Baumeister, R. (2011). What's the use of happiness? It can't buy you money. *Journal of Consumer Psychology, 21*(2), 139–141.

Wilson, S., & Durbin, C. (2010). Effects of paternal depression on fathers' parenting behaviors: A meta-analytic review. *Clinical Psychology Review, 30*(2), 167–180.

Wynne, L. (2006). Dr. Szasz's gauntlet: A critical review of the work of American psychiatry's most vocal gadfly. *Ethical Human Psychology and Psychiatry, 8*(2), 111–122.

CHAPTER 21

Adler, N. E., & Rehkopf, D. H. (2008). U.S. Disparities in health: Descriptions, causes, and mechanisms. *Annual Review of Public Health, 29*, 235–252.

Ahmed, A. M. (2010). Muslim discrimination: Evidence from two lost-letter experiments. *Journal of Applied Social Psychology, 40*(4), 888–898.

Ali, A. H. (2012). The rise of christophobia. *Newsweek*, pp. 26–35.

Anand, M. (2009). Gender in social work education and practice in India. *Social Work Education, 28*(1), 95–105.

Anastas, J. W. (2007). Theorizing (in)equity for women in social work. *Affilia: Journal of Women and Social Work, 22*(3), 235–239.

Bazler, J. A., & Simonis, D. A. (2006). Are high school chemistry textbooks gender fair? *Journal of Research in Science Teaching, 28*, 353–362.

Beinart, P. (2012). *New American foundation.* http://www.newamerica.net/publications/articles/2012/a_quiet_campaign_of_violence_against_american_muslims_70656

Benkert, R., & Peters, R. M. (2005). African-American women's coping with health care prejudice. *Western Journal of Nursing Research, 27*, 863–889.

Benokraitis, N. V. (Eds.). (1997). *Subtle sexism: Current practice and prospects for change.* Thousand Oaks, CA: Sage.

Bergeron, D. M., Block, C. J., & Echtenkamp, B. A. (2006). Disabling the able: Stereotype and women's work performance. *Human Performance, 19*, 133–158.

Bilewicz, M. (2009). Perspective taking and intergroup helping intentions: The moderating role of power relations. *Journal of Applied Social Psychology, 32*(12), 2279–2786.

Bloul, R. A. D. (2008). Anti-discrimination laws, islamophobia, and ethnicization of muslim identies in Europe and Australia. *Journal of Muslim Minority Affairs, 28*(1), 7–35.

Borrell, L. N., Jacobs, D. R., Jr., Williams, D. R., Pletcher, M. J., Houston, T. K., & Kiefe, C. I. (2007). Self-reported racial discrimination and substance use in the coronary artery risk development in adults study. *American Journal of Epidemiology, 166*, 1068–1079.

Bonifas, R. P. (2006). *Mental health needs of persons residing in skilled nursing facilities.* CSWE Gero-Ed Center. Alexandria, VA: Council on Social Work Education.

Brinkerhoff, M. B., Grandin, E., Hexham, I., & Pue, C. (1991). The perception of mormons by rural Canadian youth. *Journal for the Scientific Study of Religion, 30*(4), 479–486.

Brondolo, E., ver Halen, N. B., Pencille, M., Beatty, D., & Contrada, R. J. (2009). Coping with racism: A selective review of the literature and a theoretical and methodological critique. *Journal of Behavioral Medicine, 32*, 64–88.

Brüß, J. (2008). Experiences of discrimination reported by Turkish, Moroccan and Bangladeshi Muslims in three European cities. *Journal of Ethnic and Migration Studies, 34*(6), 875–894.

Cacioppo, J. T., & Hawkley, L. C. (2003). Social isolation and health, with an emphasis on underlying mechanisms. *Perspectives in Biological Medicine, 46*(3 Suppl.), 39–52

Carnaghi, A., & Yzerbyt, V. (2007). Subtyping and social consensus: The role of the audience in the maintenance of stereotypic beliefs. *European Journal of Social Psychology, 37*, 902–922.

Catalyst. (2005). *Women "take care," men "take charge." stereotyping of U.S. Business leaders exposed.* New York: Author.

Centers for Disease Control and Prevention. (2012). *Healthy aging.* Retrieved August 30, 2012, from http://www.cdc.gov/aging/mentalhealth/depression.htm

Cherney, J. L. (2011). The rhetoric of ableism. *Disability Studies Quarterly, 31*(3). Retrieved February 3, 2012, from dsq-sds.org/article/view/1665/1606

Chou, W. (1997). *Post-colonial tongzhi.* Hong Kong: Hong Kong Queer Press.

Dennis, H., & Thomas, K. (2007). Ageism in the workplace. *Generations, 31*(1), 84–89.

Descamps, M. J., Rothblum, E., Bradford, J., & Ryan, C. (2000). Mental health impact of child sexual abuse, rape, intimate partner violence, and hate crimes in the national lesbian health care survey. *Journal of Gay and Lesbian Social Services, 11*, 27–55.

Dessel, A., Bolen, R., & Shepardson, C. (2011). Can religious expression and sexual orientation affirmation coexist in social work? A critique of hodge's theoretical, theological, and conceptual frameworks. *Journal of Social Work Education, 47*(2), 213–234.

Dominelli, L. (2002). *Feminist social work: Theory and practice.* New York: Palgrave.

Dosomething.org. (2011). *11 Facts about environmental racism.* Retrieved from http://www.dosomething.org/tipsandtools/11-facts-about-environmental-racism

Drescher, J. (2012). The removal of homosexuality from the DSM: Its impact on today's marriage equality debate. *Journal of Gay & Lesbian Mental Health, 16*(2), 124–135.

Eliade, M. (1990). *The encyclopedia of religion.* New York: MacMillan.

Feagin, J. R. (2000). *Racist America: Roots, current realities, and future reparations.* New York: Routledge.

Federal Interagency Forum on Aging Related Statistics. (2004). *Older Americans 2004: Key indicators of well-being.* Washington, DC: US Government Printing Office.

Ferfolja, T. (2007). Schooling cultures: Institutionalizing heteronormativity and heterosexism. *International Journal of Inclusive Education, 11*(2), 147–162.

Finchilescu, G. (2005). Meta-stereotypes may hinder inter-racial contact. *South African Journal of Psychology, 35*(3), 460–472.

Fox, J. (2007). Religious discrimination: A world survey. *Journal of International Affairs, 61*(1), 47–67.

Fredriksen-Goldsen, K. I., Kim, H. J., Emlet, C. A., Muraco, A., Erosheva, E. A., Hoy-Ellis, C. P., Goldsen, J., & Petry, H. (2011). *The aging and health report: Disparities and resilience among lesbian, gay, bisexual, and transgender older adults.* Seattle: Institute for Multigenerational Health.

Galinsky, A. D., Magee, J. C., Inesi, M. E., & Gruenfeld, D. H. (2006). Power and perspectives not taken. *Psychological Science, 17*, 1068–1074.

Galinsky, A. D., Wang, C. S., & Ku, G. (2008). Perspective-takers behave more stereotypically. *Journal of Personality and Social Psychology, 95*(2), 404–419.

Gates, G. J., & Newport, F. (2012). *Gallup special report: The U.S. Adult LGBT population.* Los Angeles: The Williams.

Gellis, Z. D., Sherman, S., & Lawrance, F. (2003). First year graduate social work students: Knowledge of and attitude toward older adults. *Educational Gerontology, 29*, 1–16.

Good, J. J., Woodzicka, J. A., & Wingfield, L. C. (2010). The effects of gender stereotypic and counter-stereotypic textbook images on science performance. *The Journal of Social Psychology, 150*(2), 132–147.

Goodenow, C., Szalacha, L., & Westheimer, K. (2006). School support groups, other school factors, and the safety of sexual minority adolescents. *Psychology in the Schools, 43*(5), 573–589.

Graham, M. (2000). Honouring social work principles—exploring the connections between anti-racist social work and African-centred worldviews. *Social Work Education, 19*(5), 423–436.

Gutheil, I. A., Heyman, J. C., & Chernesky, R. H. (2009). Graduate social work students' interest in working with older adults. *Social Work Education, 28*(1), 54–64.

Haight, B. K., Christ, M. A., & Dias, J. K. (1994). Does nursing education promote ageism? *Journal of Advanced Nursing, 20*, 382–390.

Hall, R. E., Whipple, E. E., & Jackson-Elmoore, C. (2007). Blaming the victim' vis-a-vis child-focused Western law: Implications of evidence-based policy-making for the rescue of black families. *Policy Studies, 29*(1), 51–69.

Harper, M. (2007). The stereotyping of nonreligious people by religious students: Contents and subtypes. *Journal for the Scientific Study of Religion, 46*(4), 539–552.

Harris, A. C. (2009). Marginalization by the marginalized: Race, homophobia, heterosexism, and "the problem of the 21st century." *Journal of Gay and Lesbian Social Services, 21*, 430–448.

Hassouneh, D. M., & Kulwicki, A. (2007). Mental health, discrimination, and trauma in Arab muslim women living in the U.S.: A pilot study. *Mental Health, Religion & Culture, 10*(3), 257–262.

Healy, L. (2007). Universalism and cultural relativism in social work ethics. *International Social Work, 50*(1), 11–26.

Heck, N. C., Flentje, A., & Cochran, B. N. (2011). Offsetting risks: High school gay-straight alliances and lesbian, gay, bisexual, and transgender (LGBT) youth. *School Psychology Quarterly, 26*(2), 161–174.

Heller, T., & Marks, B. (2005). Aging. In G. Albrecht, J. Bickenbach, D. T. Mitchell, W. O. Schalick, & S. L. Snyder (Eds.), *Encyclopedia of disability, in three parts* (pp. 68–78). Thousand Oaks, CA: Sage.

Herek, G. M., & Capitanio, J. P. (1996). "Some of my best friends": Intergroup contact, concealable stigma, and heterosexuals' attitudes toward gay men and lesbians. *Personality and Social Psychology Bulletin, 22,* 412–424.

Herek, G. M., Gillis, J. R., & Cogan, J. C. (1999). Psychological sequelae of hate crime victimization among lesbian, gay, and bisexual adults. *Journal of Consulting and Clinical Psychology, 67,* 945–951.

Herek, G. M. (2007). Confronting sexual stigma and prejudice: Theory and practice. *Journal of Social Issues, 63*(4), 905–925.

Hodge, D. R. (2002). Does social work oppress evangelical christians? A "new class" analysis of society and social work. *Social Work, 47*(4), 401–414.

Hodge, D. R. (2006). Moving toward a more inclusive educational environment? A multi-sample exploration of religious discrimination as seen through the eyes of students from various faith traditions. *Journal of Social Work Education, 42*(2), 249–267.

Hodges, N., & Parkes, N. (2005). Tackling homophobia and heterosexism. *Learning Disability Practice, 8*(3), 10–16.

Holtzhausen, L. (2010). When values collide: Finding common ground for social work education in the United Arab Emirates. *International Social Work, 54*(2), 191–208.

Hughes, R. B., Lund, E. M., Gabrielli, J., Powers, L. E., & Curry, M. A. (2011). Prevalence of interpersonal violence against community-living adults with disabilities: A literature review. *Rehabilitation Psychology, 56*(4), 302–319.

Human Rights First. (2008). *Violence against Muslims.* Retrieved from http://www.humanrightsfirst.org/our-work/fighting-discrimination/2008-hate-crime-survey/2008-hate-crime-survey-muslims/

Hyde, J. S., & Kling, K. C. (2001). Women, motivation, and achievement. *Psychology of Women Quarterly, 25,* 364–378.

James Madison University. (2012). *Fact and information sheet about heterosexism.* Retrieved from www.jmu.edu/safezone/wm_library/Heterosexism%20Fact%20Sheet.pdf

Jeffery, D. (2005). What good is anti-racist social work if you can't master it? Exploring a paradox in anti-racist social work education. *Race, Ethnicity and Education, 8*(4), 409–425.

Kahera, A. I. (2002). Urban enclaves, muslim identity and the urban mosque in America. *Journal of Muslim Minority Affairs, 22*(2), 369–380.

Kane, M. N. (2001). Legal guardianship and other alternatives in the care of elders with Alzheimer's disease.

American Journal of Alzheimer' Disease and Other Dementias, 16, 89–96.

Kane, M. N., Lacey, D., & Green, D. (2006). Correlates of perceptions of elders' suffering from depression. *Advances in Social Work, 7*(1), 49–64.

Kane, M. N. (2007). Social work and criminal justice students' perceptions of elders. *Journal of Social Service Research, 34*(1), 13–26.

Keller, C., & Siegrist, M. (2010). Psychological resources and attitudes toward people with physical disabilities. *Journal of Applied Social Psychology, 40*(2), 389–401.

Khalidi, O. (2000). Mosque. In W. C. Roof (Ed.), *Contemporary American religion.* New York: Macmillan.

Kim-Prieto, C., Goldstein, L. A., Ozazaki, S., & Kirschner, B. (2010). Effect of exposure to an American Indian mascot on the tendency to stereotype a different minority group. *Journal of Applied Social Psychology, 40*(3), 534–553.

Kirkpatrick, L. A. (1993). Fundamentalist, christian orthodoxy, and intrinsic religious orientation as predictors of discriminatory attitudes. *Journal for the Scientific Study of Religion, 32*(3), 256–268.

Kosciw, J. G., & Diaz, E. M. (2006). *The 2005 national school climate survey: The experiences of lesbian, gay, bisexual and transgender youth in our nation's schools.* New York: GLSEN.

Kosmin, B., & Mayer, E. (2001). *American religious identification survey 2001.* New York: City University of New York.

Levi, S. J. (2005). Ableism. In G. Albrecht, J. Bickenbach, D. T. Mitchell, W. O. Schalick, & S. L. Snyder (Eds.), *Encyclopedia of disability, in three parts* (pp. 1–2). Thousand Oaks, CA: Sage.

Levin, J., & Madfis, E. (2009). Mass murder at school and cumulative strain. *American Behavioral Scientist, 52*(9), 1227–1245.

Levy, B. R., Zonderman, A. B., Slade, M. D., & Ferrucci, L. (2009). Age Stereotypes Held Earlier in Life Predict Cardiovascular Events in Later Life. *Psychological Science, 20,* 296–298. Livengood, J. S., & Stodolska, M. (2004). The effects of discrimination and constraints negotiation on leisure behavior of American muslims in the post-september 11 America. *Journal of Leisure Research, 36*(2), 183–208.

Lorde, A. (1999). There is no hierarchy of oppressions. In E. Brandt (Ed.), *Dangerous liaisons: Blacks, gays, and the struggle for equality* (pp. 306–307). New York: New Press.

Livengood, J.S., & Stodolska, M. (2004). The effects of discrimination and constraints negotiation on leisure behavior of American Muslims in the post-September 11 America. *Journal of Leisure Research, 36*(2), 183–208.

Masser, B., & Moffat, K. B. (2006). With friends like these. . .the role of prejudice and situational norms on discriminatory helping behavior. *Journal of Homosexuality, 51*(2), 121–138.

Matthews, K. A., Katholi, C. R., McCreath, H., Whooley, M. A., Williams, D. R., & Zhu, S. (2004). Blood pressure reactivity to psychological stress predicts hypertension in the CARDIA study. *Circulation, 110,* 74–78.

McIlwain, C. D., & Caliendo, S. M. (2011). *How candidates invoke race in U.S. Political campaigns.* Philadelphia: Temple.

Media Matters for America. (2012). *Fox's liz trotta on sexual assault in military: "what did they expect? These people are in close contact.* Retrieved February 16, 2012, from http://mediamatters.org/blog/201202120002

Mitchell, J. P., Ames, D. L., Jenkins, A. C., & Banaji, M. R. (2009). Neural correlates of stereotype application. *Journal of Cognitive Neuroscience, 21*(3), 594–604.

Monsees, C. V. (2002). Ageism. In *Encyclopedia of aging.* Farmington Hills, MI: Gale. Retrieved March 04, 2012, from http://www.encyclopedia.com/doc/1G2-3402200022.html

Motsaathebe, G. (2009). Gendered roles, images and behavioural patterns in the soap opera generations. *Journal of African Media Studies, 1*(3), 429–448.

Muslims in the American Public Square. (2004). Retrieved February 28, 2011 from www.themosqueinmorgantown.com...ProjectMAPSAmericanMuslimPoll-1.pdf.

National Association of Social Workers (NASW). (2008). *Code of ethics.* Washington, DC: Author.

NASW Center for Workforce Studies. (2006, March). Perspectives on social work practice (Supplement to the National Study of Licensed Social Workers). Washington, DC: National Association of Social Workers. Retrieved February 20, 2012, from http://workforce.socialworkers.org/studies/supplemental/supplement_ch5.pdf.

National Institute on Aging. (2011). *Growing older in America: The health and retirement study.* Retrieved from http://www.nia.nih.gov/health/publication/growing-older-America-health-and-retirement-study/chapter-1-health

Newman, M. L., Keough, K. A., & Lee, R. M. (2009). Group identification and college adjustment: The

experience of encountering a novel stereotype. *The Journal of Social Psychology, 149*(6), 694–708.

Ni, C. (1997). Queer politics' symposium. In J. H. Chuen-juei' (Ed.), *Visionary essays in sexuality/gender studies: Proceedings of the first international conference on sexuality education, sexology, gender studies and lesbigay studies.* Taipei: Yuanzun.

Nixon, D., & Givens, N. (2007). An epitaph to section 28? Telling tales out of school about changes and challenges to discourses of sexuality. *International Journal of Qualitative Studies in Education, 20*(4), 449–471.

Niyozov, S., & Pluim, G. (2009). Teachers' perspectives on the education of Muslim students: A missing voice in Muslim education research. *Curriculum Inquiry, 39*(5), 637–677.

Oracle Education Foundation. (2012). *Racism around the world.*

Packer, D. J., & Chasteen, A. L. (2006). Looking to the future: How possible aged selves influence prejudice toward older adults. *Social Cognition, 24,* 218–247.

Parrott, D. J., Peterson, J. L., & Bakeman, R. (2011). Determinants of aggression toward sexual minorities in a community sample. *Psychology of Violence, 1*(1), 41–52.

Peaz, A. (2009). American muslims' civil liberties and the challenge to effectively avert xenophobia. *The Muslim World, 99,* 202–220.

Peel, E. (2001). Mundane heterosexism: Understanding incidents of the everyday. *Women's Studies International Forum, 24*(5), 541–554.

Penny, H., & Haddock, G. (2007). Children's stereotypes of overweight children. *British Journal of Developmental Psychology, 25,* 409–4418.

Peterson, J. W. (2008). Teaching world religion in the public schools. *Encounter, 21*(4), 40–42.

PEW Research Center. (2007). *Muslim-Americans: Middle class and mostly mainstream.* Retrieved from pewresearch.org/assets/pdf/muslim-Americans.pdf

Popham, L. E., Kennison, S. M., & Bradley, K. I. (2011). Ageism and risk-taking in young adults: Evidence for a link between death anxiety and ageism. *Death Studies, 35,* 751–763.

Power, D., Hyde, M., & Leigh, G. (2008). Learning English from signed English: An impossible task? *American Annals of the Deaf, 153*(1), 37–47.

Ranker.com. (2012). *Top 10 anti-gay activists caught being gay.* Retrieved from http://www.ranker.com/list/top-10-anti-gay-activists-caught-being-gay/joanne?age=2

Reitmanova, S., & Gustafson, D. L. (2008). "They can't understand it": Maternity health and care needs of immigrant muslim women in St. John's, newfoundland. *Journal of Maternal and Child Health, 12*, 101–111.

Robinson, L. (1995). *Psychology for social workers, black perspectives.* London: Routledge.

Rothbart, M., & John, O. P. (1985). Social categorization and behavioral episodes: A cognitive analysis of the effects of intergroup contact. *Journal of Social Issues, 41*, 81–104.

Rowatt, W. C., LaBouff, J., Johnson, M., Froese, P., & Tsang, J. (2009). Associations among religiousness, social attitudes, and prejudice in a national random sample of American adults. *Psychology of Religion and Spirituality, 1*(1), 14–24.

Sadock, B. J., & Sadock, V. A. (2003). *Kaplan & sadock's synopsis of psychiatry* (9th ed.). Philadelphia, PA: Lippincott Williams & Wilkins.

Sakamoto, I., Anastas, J. W., McPhail, B. A., & Colarossi, L. G. (2008). Status of women in social work education. *Journal of Social Work Education, 44*(1), 37–62.

Scharlach, A., Damron-Rodriguez, J., Robinson, B., & Feldman, R. (2000). Educating social workers for an aging society: A vision for the 21st century. *Journal of Social Work Education, 36*(3), 521–538.

Schuldberg, J. (2005). It is easy to make judgments if it's not familiar: The use of simulation kits to develop self-awareness and reduce ageism. *Journal of Social Work Education, 41*(3), 441–455.

Scianna, A. (2006, October 15). Missouri's mormon past. *The Missourian.* Retrieved February 22, 2012, from http://www.rickross.com/reference/mormon/mormon342.html

Shammas, D. S. (2009). Post-9/11 Arab and muslim American community college students: Ethno-religious enclaves and perceived discrimination. *Community College Journal of Research and Practice, 33*, 283–308.

Sherry, M. (2005). Abuse and hate crimes. In G. Albrecht, J. Bickenbach, D. T. Mitchell, W. O. Schalick, & S. L. Snyder (Eds.), *Encyclopedia of disability, in three parts* (pp. 5–9). Thousand Oaks, CA: Sage.

Sherry, M. (2010). *Disability hate crimes: Does anyone really hate disabled people?* Surrey, England: Ashgate.

Sirin, S. R., & Fine, M. (2007). Hyphenated selves: Muslim American youth negotiating identities on the fault lines of global conflict. *Applied Development Science, 11*(3), 151–163.

Sirin, S. R., Bikmen, N., Mir, M., Fine, M., Zaal, M., & Katsiaficas, D. (2007). Exploring dual identification among muslim-American emerging adults: A mixed methods study. *Journal of Adolescence, 31*, 259–279.

Smith, D. (2005). These house-negroes still think we're cursed. *Cultural Studies, 19*(4), 439–454.

Snyder, C. S., Wesley, S. C., Lin, M. B., & May, J. D. (2008). Bridging the gap: Gerontology and social work education. *Gerontology & Geriatrics Education, 28*(4), 1–21.

Sobsey, D., Randall, W., & Parrila, R. K. (1997). Gender differences in abused children with and without disabilities. *Child Abuse and Neglect, 21*(8), 707–720.

Stangor, C., Sechrist, G. B., & Jost, J. T. (2001). Changing racial beliefs by providing social consensus. *Personality and Social Psychology Bulletin, 27*, 486–496.

Stephan, W. G., & Stephan, C. W. (1985). Intergroup anxiety. *Journal of Social Issues, 41*, 157–175.

Stewart, T. L., Latu, I. M., Kawakami, K., & Myers, A. C. (2010). Consider the situation: Reducing automatic stereotyping through situational attribution training. *Journal of Experimental Social Psychology, 46*, 221–225.

Sue, D. W. (2005). Racism and the conspiracy of silence: Presidential address. *The Counseling Psychologist, 33*(1), 100–114.

Sullivan, P. M., & Knutson, J. F. (2000). Maltreatment and disabilities: A population-based epidemiological study. *Child Abuse and Neglect, 24*(10), 1257–1273.

Szalacha, L. A. (2003). Safer sexual diversity climates: Lessons learned from an evaluation of massachusetts safe schools program for gay and lesbian students. *American Journal of Education, 110*, 58–88.

Szymanski, D. M. (2005). Heterosexism and sexism as correlates of psychological distress in lesbians. *Journal of Counseling & Development, 83*, 355–360.

Szymanski, D.M. (2006). Does internalized heterosexism moderate the link between heterosexist events and lesbians' psychological distress? *Sex Roles, 54*(3/4), 227–234.

Szymanski, D. M., & Balsam, K. F. (2011). Insidious trauma: Examining the relationship between heterosexism and lesbians' PTSD symptoms. *Traumatology, 17*(2), 4–13.

Szymanski, D. M., & Ikizler, A. S. (2012). Internalized heterosexism as a mediator in the relationship between gender role conflict, heterosexist discrimination, and depression. *Psychology of Men & Masculinity.*

Szymanski, D. M., & Owens, G. P. (2009). Group-level coping as a moderator between heterosexism and sexism and psychological distress in sexual minority women. *Psychology of Women Quarterly, 33,* 195–205.

Tee, N., & Hegarty, P. (2006). Predicting opposition to the civil rights of transpersons in the united Kingdom. *Journal of Community & Applied Social Psychology, 16,* 70–80.

Vilchinsky, N., Findler, L., & Werner, S. (2010). Attitudes toward people with disabilities: The perspective of attachment theory. *Rehabilitation Psychology, 55*(3), 298–306.

Vonnegut, K. (2009). *Mother night.* New York: Random House.

Vorauer, J. D., Hunter, A. J., Main, K. J., & Roy, S. A. (2000). Meta-stereotype activation: Evidence from indirect measures for specific evaluative concerns experienced by members of dominant groups in intergroup interaction. *Journal of Personality and Social Psychology, 78,* 690–707.

Waitt, G. (2005). Sexual citizenship in Latvia: Geographies of the Latvian closet. *Social and Cultural Geography, 6*(2), 161–181.

Weller, P., Feldman, A., & Purdam, K. (2001). *Religious discrimination in England and Wales.* London: Home Office.

Werhun, C. D., & Penner, A. J. (2010). The effects of stereotyping and implicit theory on benevolent prejudice toward aboriginal Canadians. *Journal of Applied Social Psychology, 40*(4), 899–916.

Yoon, E., & Kolomer, S. R. (2007). Refining the measure and dimensions of social values of older people (SVOP). *Educational Gerontology, 33,* 649–663.

Zegeye, A. (2007). The religious experience of Ethiopian Jews in Israel. *Religion and Theology, 14,* 347–394.

Zogby International. (2001). *Survey commissioned by the American Muslim Council quoted in US Department of State, Fact Sheet: Islam in the United States.* Washington, DC: Office of International Information Programs.

Index

Note: Locators "*f*" and "*t*" denote figures and tables in the text